KEY TO MAPS

THE WORLD
MAPS 2 – 5

1   SYMBOLS LEGEND

2–3   THE WORLD Political 1:80M
4–5   THE WORLD Physical 1:80M

EUROPE
MAPS 6 - 45

6-7   EUROPE Political *Global View*
8-9   EUROPE 1:16M
10-11   BRITISH ISLES 1:4M
12-13   ENGLAND AND WALES 1:2M
14   SCOTLAND 1:2M
15   IRELAND 1:2M
16   THE LOW COUNTRIES 1:2M
17   FRANCE 1:5M
18-19   NORTHERN FRANCE 1:2½M
20-21   SOUTHERN FRANCE 1:2½M
22-23   MEDITERRANEAN LANDS 1:10M
24   IBERIAN PENINSULA 1:5M
25   EASTERN SPAIN 1:2½M
26-27   WESTERN SPAIN AND PORTUGAL 1:2½M
28-29   ITALY AND THE BALKANS 1:5¼M
30-31   NORTHERN ITALY AND NORTHERN BALKANS 1:2½M
32-33   SOUTHERN ITALY 1:2½M
34-35   GREECE AND ALBANIA 1:2½M
36-37   CENTRAL EUROPE 1:5M
38-39   GERMANY AND SWITZERLAND 1:2½M
40-41   SCANDINAVIA AND BALTIC LANDS 1:5M
         Iceland 1:5M
42-43   SOUTHERN SCANDINAVIA 1:2½M
44-45   RUSSIAN FEDERATION, WEST & UKRAINE 1:10M

By reference to this Key to Maps, and its continuation on the back endpaper, the most suitable map of a required area can be found.

The map pages of the core World Atlas section are keyed according to their continental subsections and scale category. There are three scale categories, as indicated below. All scales are quoted as representative ratios expressed in millions (as denoted by the abbreviation M).

 Large scale: between 1:1M and 2½M

 Medium scale: between 1:2½M and 1:7½M

 Small scale: smaller than 1:7½M

ASIA
MAPS 46 - 67

46-47   ASIA Political *Global View*
48-49   ASIA AND INDIAN OCEAN 1:45M
50-51   NORTH ASIA 1:20M
52-53   EAST ASIA 1:16M
54-55   EAST CHINA 1:7½M
56   INDO-CHINA 1:10M
57   JAPAN 1:7½M Central Honshū 1:2½M
58-59   SOUTHEAST ASIA 1:15M Java 1:7½M
60-61   SOUTH ASIA 1:14M
62-63   NORTHERN INDIA, PAKISTAN AND BANGLADESH 1:7½M
64-65   SOUTHWEST ASIA 1:9M
66   THE LEVANT 1:3½M
67   THE HOLY LAND 1:1M

AFRICA
MAPS 68 — 81

68-69   AFRICA Political *Global View*
70   AFRICA 1:37M
71   THE HORN OF AFRICA 1:15M
72-73   NILE VALLEY 1:10M
74-75   NORTHWEST AFRICA 1:10M
76-77   WEST AFRICA 1:10M
78-79   CENTRAL AND EAST AFRICA 1:10M
80-81   SOUTHERN AFRICA AND MADAGASCAR 1:10M

Continued on Back Endpaper

COLLINS
ATLAS OF THE
WORLD

COLLINS

Atlas
OF THE
WORLD

HarperCollins*Publishers*

Collins Atlas of the World

Collins
An Imprint of HarperCollins*Publishers*
77-85 Fulham Palace Road, Hammersmith, London W6 8JB

First published 1983 by William Collins Sons & Co Ltd
Reprinted 1983, 1985, 1986, 1987
2nd Edition 1988
Reprinted 1989, 1990
3rd Edition 1991
4th Edition 1993
Revised 1994, 1995

Printed in Hong Kong

ISBN 0 00 448227 1

HH8213

Photograph credits

XII-XIII David Parker/Science Photo Library; Peter Menzell/Science Photo Library; Professor Stewart Lowther/Science
Photo Library

XX-XXI David Campione/Science Photo Library; Dr L. Wright

XXII-XXIII Dr Morley Read/Science Photo Library

XXVI-XXVII D. R. Austen/Telegraph Colour Library; Martin Bond/Science Photo Library

XXVIII-XXIX Marcelo Brodsky/Science Photo Library

XXX-XXXI Simon Fraser/Science Photo Library

XXXII-XXXIII Oxfam; Jeremy Hartley/Oxfam; Hugh Goyder/Oxfam; Malcolm McClean/Oxfam

XXXIV-XXXV Bibliothèque Nationale, Paris; National Maritime Museum, London; Österreichische Nationalbibliothek,
Vienna; New York Public Library, New York; British Library, London

XXXVI-XXXVII Sefton Photo Library

XXXVIII-XXXIX USGS; The Times Atlas and Encyclopaedia of the Sea

XL © Nicholson, produced from the Bartholomew London Digital Database

The Publishers would like to thank the following:

Dr J. Allen, Dr B. Alloway, Professor B. Atkinson, Dr R. Hall and Dr L. Wright
from Queen Mary and Westfield College, University of London

H. A. G. Lewis OBE

Illustrations: Contour Publishing and Swanston Graphics

FOREWORD

MAPS, as essential aids in the understanding of the world around us, would appear to have been made ever since man first moved about the Earth. To begin with they were relatively primitive plans of very limited areas, carved in wood or painted on rock, bark or skins. Later, the highly organized peoples of the ancient civilizations, in conducting their everyday life, made many functional maps on such materials as clay tablets, papyrus and eventually paper.

However, the first attempt to map the whole of the known world, as opposed to producing local plans of small areas, is attributed to the famous Greek cosmographer, Ptolemy (AD 87-150). The many maps of the classical world that accompanied his celebrated manuscript Geographia – itself to be regarded as the standard geographical reference work for many centuries – represent the forerunner of the atlas as we know it today.

ATLASES, in the modern sense of systematic collections of maps of uniform size, were born, much later still, in the Netherlands of the 16th century, during the world's great age of exploration. Indeed, it was the eminent Flemish cartographer Mercator (1512-1594) who first used the word Atlas: taking the name of the ancient Greek mythological titan who symbolically supported the world on his shoulders.

Since the time of these early atlases our knowledge of the world has been greatly increased through continued exploration and scientific discovery. Today, the fast developing space age technology allows man to survey our planet, and beyond, in the most precise detail. The resulting mass of geographical and astronomical data is such that the non-specialist atlas user could easily be overwhelmed. This current information explosion, combined with a new awareness of our world brought about by the views of our planet from space, improved communications, greater opportunity for leisure and travel, and increased media exposure, we believe, calls for a new type of atlas that presents to the general reader, not only an up-to-date collection of well-documented maps, but also an illuminating and readily accessible record of the latest findings and essential facts about our world.

COLLINS ATLAS OF THE WORLD is published with the explicit aim of meeting this need for a convenient and moderately priced reference atlas, that places at our fingertips an accurate, authoritative, comprehensive and clearly presented picture of the world as it is known today. To achieve this objective, Collins, building on its traditions and experience of over one hundred years' innovative atlas publishing, assembled a talented team of geographers, cartographers, designers, editors and writers. Working to a carefully devised plan, this team has brought together in a single volume a complete set of maps, a compendium of contemporary geographical data, and an informative and in-depth geographical encyclopaedia.

As a result of the detailed process of research, compilation and design, together with the latest cartographic techniques, which have gone into the production of Collins Atlas of the World, we believe that our readers will have the best and most up-to-date atlas available in its class. In terms of cartographic presentation, geographical knowledge and visual elegance, the publication of Collins Atlas of the World represents a major step forward, which we hope will contribute to a better awareness and understanding of our fascinating and fast changing world as we approach the 21st century.

CONTENTS

V   Foreword
VI-VII   Contents
VIII-IX   Guide to the Atlas

GEOGRAPHICAL ENCYCLOPAEDIA

X-XI   Earth Structure
XII-XIII   Earthquakes and Volcanoes
XIV-XV   Oceans
XVI-XVII   Atmosphere
XVIII-XIX   Climate
XX-XXI   Landscapes
XXII-XXIII   Natural Vegetation
XXIV-XXV   Population
XXVI-XXVII   Food
XXVIII-XXIX   Minerals and Energy
XXX-XXXI   Environmental Problems
XXXII-XXXIII   Pollution
XXXIV-XXXV   History of Maps
XXXVI-XXXVII   The Key to Maps
XXXVIII-XL   The Use of Maps

WORLD ATLAS

1   Symbols Legend

THE WORLD

2-3   The World *Political*
4-5   The World *Physical*

EUROPE

6-7   Europe *Political*
8-9   Europe
10-11   British Isles
12-13   England and Wales
14   Scotland
15   Ireland
16   The Low Countries
17   France
18-19   Northern France
20-21   Southern France
22-23   Mediterranean Lands
24   Iberian Peninsula
25   Eastern Spain
26-27   Western Spain and Portugal
28-29   Italy and the Balkans
30-31   Northern Italy and Northern Balkans
32-33   Southern Italy
34-35   Greece and Albania
36-37   Central Europe
38-39   Germany and Switzerland
40-41   Scandinavia and Baltic Lands
42-43   Southern Scandinavia
44-45   Russian Federation, West and Ukraine

ASIA

46-47   Asia *Political*
48-49   Asia and Indian Ocean
50-51   North Asia
52-53   East Asia
54-55   East China
56   Indo-China
57   Japan
58-59   Southeast Asia
60-61   South Asia
62-63   Northern India, Pakistan and Bangladesh
64-65   Southwest Asia
66   The Levant
67   The Holy Land

AFRICA

68-69   Africa *Political*
70   Africa
71   The Horn of Africa
72-73   Nile Valley
74-75   Northwest Africa
76-77   West Africa
78-79   Central and East Africa
80-81   Southern Africa and Madagascar

OCEANIA

82-83   Oceania *Political*
84-85   Pacific Ocean
86   New Zealand
87   Australia
88-89   Western Australia
90-91   Eastern Australia
92-93   Southeast Australia

NORTH AMERICA

94-95   North America *Political*
96-97   North America
98-99   Canada and Alaska
100-101   Western Canada
102-103   Eastern Canada
104-105   South Central Canada
106-107   United States
108-109   Western United States
110-111   Central United States
112-113   Eastern United States
114-115   Northeastern United States
116-117   Central America and the Caribbean

SOUTH AMERICA

118-119   South America *Political*
120-121   South America
122-123   South America – North
124-125   South America – South
126   South America – East
127   Atlantic Ocean
128   Polar Regions

GEOGRAPHICAL DATA

WORLD

130   World Physical Data
131   World Political Data
132-134   Nations of the World

GLOSSARY OF GEOGRAPHICAL TERMS

136   Introduction and Language Abbreviations
136-138   Alphabetical Glossary

WORLD INDEX

140   Introduction and Abbreviations
141-224   Alphabetical Index

GUIDE TO THE ATLAS

COLLINS ATLAS OF THE WORLD consists of three self-
contained but interrelated sections. First, in the
GEOGRAPHICAL ENCYCLOPAEDIA there is a complete and
informative guide to contemporary geographical issues. Next,
the WORLD ATLAS section, comprising 128 pages of maps,
using the most modern cartographic techniques and up-to-date
sources. Finally, a detailed compendium of GEOGRAPHICAL
DATA.

GEOGRAPHICAL ENCYCLOPAEDIA

This illustrated section covers essential topics such as the structure of the Earth, earthquakes and volcanoes, atmosphere and climate, vegetation, population, food, minerals, energy and environmental problems. There is a special feature on the history of cartography and the use of maps.

WORLD ATLAS

The main section of 128 pages of maps has been carefully planned and designed to meet the contemporary needs of the atlas user. Full recognition has been given to the many different purposes that currently call for map reference.

Map coverage extends to every part of the world in a balanced scheme that avoids any individual country or regional bias. Map areas are chosen to reflect the social, economic, cultural or historical importance of a particular region. Each double spread or single page map has been planned deliberately to cover an entire physical or political unit. Generous map overlaps are included to maintain continuity. Following two world maps, giving separate coverage of the main political and physical features, each of the continents is treated systematically in a subsection of its own. Apart from being listed in the contents, full coverage of all regional maps of each continent is also clearly depicted in the Key to Maps to be found on the front and back endpapers. Also at the beginning of each continental subsection, alongside a special Global View political map, all map coverage, country by country, is identified in an additional handy page index. Finally, as a further aid to the reader in locating the required area, a postage stamp key map is incorporated into the title margin of each map page.

Map projections have been chosen to reflect the different requirements of particular areas. No map can be absolutely true on account of the impossibility of representing a spheroid accurately on a flat surface without some distortion in either area, distance, direction or shape. In a general world atlas it is the equal area property that is most important to retain for comparative map studies and feature size evaluation and this principle has been followed wherever possible in this map section. As a special feature of this atlas, the Global View projections used for each continental political map have been specially devised to allow for a realistic area comparison between the land areas of each continent.

Map scales, as expressions of the relationship which the distance between any two points of the map bears to the corresponding distance on the ground, are in the context of this atlas grouped into three distinct categories.

Large scales, of between 1:1 000 000 (1 centimetre to 10 kilometres or 1 inch to 16 miles) and 1:2 500 000 (1 centimetre to 25 kilometres or 1 inch to 40 miles), are used to cover particularly densely populated areas of Western Europe, United States, Canada and Japan, as well as a special detailed map of the Holy Land.

Medium scales, of between 1:2 500 000 and 1:7 500 000 are used for maps of parts of Europe, North America, Australasia, India, China, etc.

Small scales, those of less than 1:7 500 00 (e.g. 1:10 000 000, 1:15 000 000, 1:25 000 000 etc.) are selected for maps of the complete world, continents, oceans, polar regions and many of the larger countries.

The actual scale at which a particular area is mapped therefore reflects its shape, size and density of detail, and as a basic principle the more detail required to be shown of an area, the greater its scale. However, throughout this atlas, map scales have been limited in number, as far as possible, in order to facilitate comparison between maps.

Map measurements give preference to the metric system which is now used in nearly every country throughout the world. All spot heights and ocean depths are shown in metres and the relief and submarine layer delineation is based on metric contour levels. However, all linear scalebar and height reference column figures are given metric and imperial equivalents to facilitate conversion of measurements for the non-metric reader.

Map symbols used are fully explained in the legend to be found on the first page of the World Atlas section. Careful study and frequent reference to this legend will aid in the reader's ability to extract maximum information.

Topography is shown by the combined means of precise spot heights, contouring, layer tinting and three-dimensional hill shading. Similar techniques are also used to depict the sea bed on the World Physical map and those of the oceans and polar regions.

Hydrographic features such as coastlines, rivers, lakes, swamps and canals are clearly differentiated.

Communications are particularly well represented with the contemporary importance of airports and road networks duly emphasized.

International boundaries and national capitals are fully documented and internal administrative divisions are shown with the maximum detail that the scale will allow. Boundary delineation reflects the 'de facto' rather than the 'de jure' political interpretation and where relevant an undefined or disputed boundary is distinguished. However there is no intended implication that the publishers necessarily endorse or accept the status of any political entity recorded on the maps.

Settlements are shown by a series of graded town stamps from major cities to tiny villages.

Other features, such as notable ancient monuments, oases, national parks, oil and gas fields, are selectively included on particular maps that merit their identification.

Lettering styles used in the maps have been chosen with great care to ensure maximum legibility and clear distinction of named feature categories. The size and weight of the various typefaces reflect the relative importance of the features. Town names are graded to correspond with the appropriate town stamp.

Map place names have been selected in accordance with maintaining legibility at a given scale and at the same time striking an appropriate balance between natural and man-made features worthy of note. Name forms have been standardized according to the widely accepted principle, now well established in international reference atlases, of including place names and geographical terms in the local language of the country in question. In the case of non-Roman scripts (e.g. Arabic), transliteration and transcription have either been based on the rules recommended by the Permanent Committee on Geographical Names and the United States Board of Geographical Names, or as in the case of the adopted Pinyin transcription of Chinese names, a system officially proposed by the country concerned. The diacritical signs used in each language or transliteration have been retained on all the maps and throughout the index. However the english language reader's requirements have also been recognised in that the names of all countries, oceans, major seas and land features as well as familiar alternative name versions of important towns are presented in English.

Map sources used in the compilation of this atlas were many and varied, but always of the latest available information. At each stage of their preparation the maps were submitted to a thorough process of research and continual revision to ensure that on publication all data would be as accurate as practicable. A well-documented data bank was created to ensure consistency and validity of all information represented on the maps.

GEOGRAPHICAL DATA

This detailed data section forms an appropriate complement to the preceding maps and illustrated texts. There are three parts, each providing a different type of geographical information.

World Facts and Figures Drawn from the latest available official sources, these tables present an easy reference profile of significant world physical, political and demographic as well as national data.

Glossary of Geographical Terms This explains most of the foreign language and geographical terms which are to be found incorporated in the place names on the maps and the index.

World Index This concluding part of the atlas lists in alphabetical order all individual place names to be found on the maps, which total about 40,000. Each entry in the index is referenced to the appropriate map page number, the country or region in which the name is located and the position of the name on the map, given by its co-ordinates of latitude and longitude. A full explanation of how to use the index is to be found on page 140.

EARTH STRUCTURE

The major three-fold division of the solid Earth into an inner core, a mantle and an outer crust is based largely on the physical properties of these layers as revealed by the passage of seismic waves generated by both earthquakes and man-made explosions.

THE Earth's crust is a thin shell covering the whole surface of the planet, but only accounts for 0.2% of the total mass of the Earth. There is a fundamental difference between the crust of the continents and that beneath the ocean basins. The oceanic crust is very thin (average 7km), and is composed of relatively dense material. By contrast, the continental crust is thicker and less dense. The crust as a whole is split into a number of distinct plates, which float on the chemically distinct and denser second layer, the mantle. The boundary between the crust and the underlying mantle is known as the Mohorovičić Discontinuity (Moho). At the centre of the Earth lies the core itself, which forms 33% of the planet's mass, and is divided into two zones: the outer layer, thought to be liquid, probably metallic iron with sulphur, silicon, oxygen, potassium or hydrogen; and the inner core, which evidence suggests consists of nickel-iron alloy.

The measurement by a world-wide network of seismographic stations of the vibrational waves generated by earthquakes has provided a relatively accurate picture of where the boundaries between the layers of the Earth lie. The velocity of seismic waves depends on the composition and physical state of the transmitting medium. At the point where the physical or chemical properties of the Earth change, the velocity and path of the waves are changed, too.

The outer layer, the crust in conjuction with that part of the upper mantle immediately below, is in a constant state of movement. Plate tectonics is the name given to the study of the processes which produce faults, joints or folds or cause magma (hot molten rock) to rise to the surface in response to forces deep within the Earth. At the mid-ocean ridges, new crust is created by the rise of magma. This intrusion of new material forces the plates apart. Where two plates meet, pushing from different directions, one plate is forced under the other. Where plates slide past each other, along fault lines, crust is neither created or destroyed.

By studying the way in which new crust has been formed in the ocean beds, a fairly authoritative account can be given of the way the continents have drifted over the past 200 million years. Only a very incomplete picture can be inferred of the preceding 400 million years, and only a sketchy picture before that.

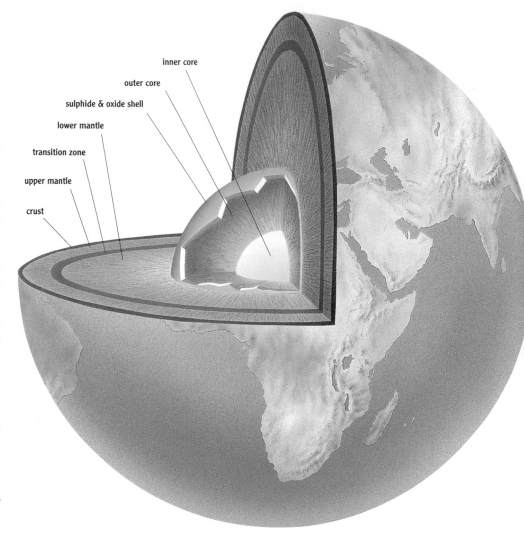

inner core
outer core
sulphide & oxide shell
lower mantle
transition zone
upper mantle
crust

(above) *A section through the Earth's crust. Internally, the Earth is divided into three main areas: crust, mantle and core. The mantle is divided into two parts separated by a transition zone. The core, likewise, is divided into two parts. The solid inner core is surrounded by a liquid outer layer.*

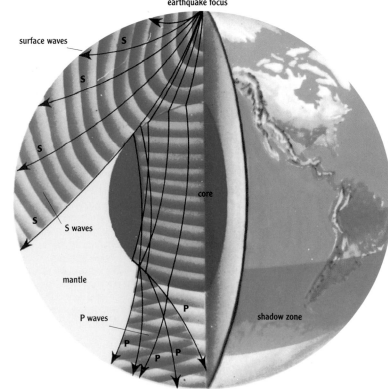

earthquake focus
surface waves
S
S
S
S
S waves
core
mantle
P waves
P
P
P
P
shadow zone

(right) *In an earthquake, the shock generates vibrations, or seismic waves, which radiate from the focus. Surface waves cause most motion at ground level. The body waves, both primary (P) and secondary (S), reveal by the way they travel, the internal layers of the Earth.*

50 million years ago

100 million years ago

150 million years ago

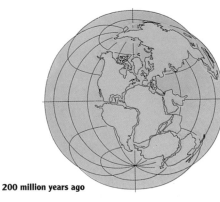

200 million years ago

(left) *From around 200 million years ago, when the Earth's landmasses formed one giant super-continent known as Pangaea, the continents have drifted, divided and collided to produce the present disposition of land and sea.*

(right) *Plate tectonic cycle from continental rifting to continental collision. (1) Rifting following old faults. (2) Continental break-up with the formation of new oceanic crust. Transform faults follow continental fractures. (3) A large Atlantic-type ocean has now formed on the site of the former continent. A mountain belt is formed where the subduction zone dips beneath the continent. (4) Where continental collision occurs a Himalayan-type mountain belt is formed.*

(right) *Faults occur when the Earth's surface breaks. When tension stretches the crust, normal faulting occurs and the rocks on one side of the fault-plane override those on the other. A horst is a block of the crust thrust up between faults; the reverse is a graben or rift valley.*

(below) *Particular features are associated with different types of mineral deposits: continental rifts with tin and fluorine, mid-ocean ridges with marine metallic sulphides, island arcs and cordilleran-type mountains with a variety of metallic deposits.*

Plate Tectonic Cycle

EARTHQUAKES AND VOLCANOES

Violent earthquakes and spectacular volcanic eruptions, the most destructive natural events, are controlled by processes occurring deep below the Earth's surface. Although we understand broadly why and where they happen, we are still some way from being able to predict the exact time and place of the next catastrophic event.

MAJOR zones of seismic and volcanic activity follow the boundaries of the tectonic plates into which the Earth's rigid surface layers are divided (see map right). Where these are moving apart from each other (in the deep oceans), the lithosphere is relatively thin and pliant, earthquakes are shallow and weak, and volcanic lava flows out of long fissures, solidifying to make new ocean floor (see diagram bottom right). If the flow of lava is copious and sustained, a giant shield volcano may build up on the ocean floor and project above the surface as a island. Hawaii is part of a chain of shield volcanoes that have grown over a sustained source of lava, called a hot spot, which is unrelated to plate boundaries and has remained active while the Pacific ocean plate has moved slowly over it.

The most powerful earthquakes and most violent volcanic eruptions occur at boundaries where two plates are in collision. When a thick continental plate meets a thin oceanic plate then the latter is overridden by the former, a process known as subduction. The oceanic plate remains rigid to depths of a few hundred kilometres, causing earthquakes along an inclined surface (referred to as the Wadati-Benioff zone). The frictional heat developed along this zone encourages local partial melting of the rocks; the rather sticky lava ascends slowly to the surface, where highly explosive eruptions send vast clouds of ash and larger fragments into the atmosphere. While the lightest particles may reach the stratosphere and be carried all round the world, most of the material falls back to earth where, in combination with intermittent flows of lava, a massive stratovolcano builds up. Some volcanic eruptions produce searingly hot dense clouds of gas and ash (known as *nuées ardentes*) that descend from the crater at very high speeds, hugging the ground and destroying everything in their path.

Where the colliding plates are both oceanic, subduction of one of the plates results in a similar descending zone of violent earthquakes, and the accompanying volcanic activity builds up an arc of islands on the overriding plate. However, if both plates carry thick continental crust, subduction is no longer possible and volcanic activity ceases, but, as in the Himalayas, the compressive forces continue to generate powerful earthquakes along the collision zone.

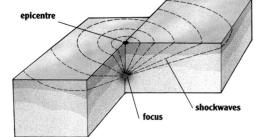

(left) *The San Andreas Fault in California marks the boundary between the Pacific plate and the American plate.*
(top right) *Mauna Loa on the Island of Hawaii, a shield volcano.*
(centre right) *Mount St. Helens, a stratovolcano, in the Cascade Range. The violent eruption of 18 May* 1980 killed 57 people.
(below) *The place at which an earthquake originates within the Earth's crust is known as the focus, while the point on the surface directly above is called the epicentre. The strain energy released by the earthquake spreads out in all directions as shock waves from the focus.*

Earthquakes, Volcanoes and Plate Tectonics

Subduction Zone

Collision Zone

Spreading Ridge and direction

Gibbs Fracture Zone

Boundary Uncertain

High Magnitude Earthquake (over 7.8 Richter scale)

Lesser Magnitude Earthquake

1954 Catastrophic Earthquakes (over 1000 dead)

Active Volcano

EURASIAN PLATE

Gibbs

Faraday

Oceanographer

Atlantis
Kane

Vema
Doldrums

Romanche

Chain
Ascension

St Helena

Rio Grande

Walfisch-Gough

Falkland-Agulhas

ARABIAN PLATE

AFRICAN PLATE

SOUTH AMERICAN PLATE

INDO-AUSTRALIAN PLATE

Rodriguez

Malagasy

Amsterdam

1976 1940 1977 1915 1963 1976 1988 1908 1983 1974 1905 1970 1966 1962 1975 1968 1978 1954 1960 1972 1935 1988 1950 1982 1967

trench

continental crust

folded mountains

molten magma at the subduction zone works its way up to the surface

mid-ocean ridge

volcano forming over hotspot

oceanic crust

trench   island Arc

OCEANS

Covering some 70% of the Earth's surface, oceans have long been vital for navigation, and they are becoming increasingly important for their resources of food, minerals and energy, and also as a final depository for waste. They affect our daily weather and influence long-term changes of climate, but their relative inaccessibility means our knowledge of them is fragmentary.

THE dramatic topography of the ocean floors has been fully revealed only within the last 40 years (see map below right). Its most striking feature, the world's longest mountain chain, is the system of mid-oceanic ridges that extends from the Arctic southwards through the Atlantic, then passes eastwards through the Indian Ocean and northwards into the Pacific. It marks the boundary where adjacent tectonic plates are moving apart from each other as new ocean floor is created from solidifying lava flows. This junction is typically marked by a deep rift valley along the crest of the ridge, and the rugged topography of the ridge flanks is dissected by the cliff-like features of innumerable fracture zones.

Away from the ridges, the level of topography of the deep ocean floors, or abyssal plains, is disturbed by extinct submarine volcanoes.

Some project above sea level as isolated islands, while others, whose tops have been planed off by the erosive power of the waves, may provide a foundation for coral atolls. In the Pacific Ocean, they often occur in long chains where a deep source of lava, or hot spot, has remained active while the Pacific plate has moved slowly over it. The Hawaiian-Emperor chain formed over a period of 75 million years, the sharp bend west of Midway Island signifying a change in the direction of plate movement about 45 million years ago. Elsewhere, sustained volcanic activity combined with plate motion has produced linear features, such as the Walvis Ridge in the eastern South Atlantic. Iceland has formed on the North Atlantic ridge over an unusually active and relatively immobile source of lava.

Deep narrow trenches are a feature of the margins of the Pacific Ocean. The margins of other oceans, especially the North Atlantic, are characterized by wide continental shelves; geologically these are part of the continents, not the oceans, and their width has varied over time in response to changing sea levels. Significant fragments of largely submerged continental lithosphere have been identified in the deep oceans; for example, the Faeroe-Rockall Plateau in the North Atlantic.

The surface waters of the oceans are driven by the prevailing wind systems in the large-scale circulatory patterns, or gyres, which are broadly symmetrical north and south of the equator (see map below). Along the western boundaries of the major ocean basins, intense warm currents, such as the Gulf Stream, travel polewards; these are counterbalanced by less intense cool currents flowing towards the equator along the eastern margins. Close to the equator an eastwards flowing countercurrent separates the circulations of the two hemispheres. The pattern of currents in the northern Indian Ocean reverses seasonally with the monsoon. In the North Atlantic and Pacific Oceans, weaker anticlockwise circulations complement the main gyres, while in the Southern Ocean the vigorous Antarctic Circumpolar current is unimpeded by the presence of any land masses.

SOUTH PACIFIC OCEAN

A — rise · basin · ridge · trench · basin · seamount chain · ridge · fracture zone · abyssal plain — A

(above and right) *The relative proportions of the topographic features in the three ocean basins relate to their tectonic geological histories. An extensive mid-oceanic ridge dominates the relatively narrow Atlantic; its margins are tectonically passive with wide continental shelves. The much larger Pacific Ocean, in contrast, has a less extensive ridge system, with active trenches around most of its margins and generally narrow continental shelves. Like the Pacific, the Indian Ocean is dominated by deep ocean floor and has poorly developed continental margins, but it shares with the Atlantic its relative lack of island arcs and trenches.*

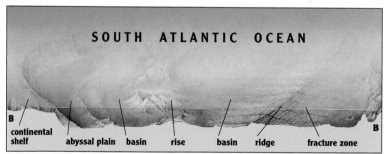

SOUTH ATLANTIC OCEAN

B — continental shelf · abyssal plain · basin · rise · basin · ridge · fracture zone — B

INDIAN OCEAN

C — trench · basin · plateau · mid-ocean ridge · ridge · basin — C

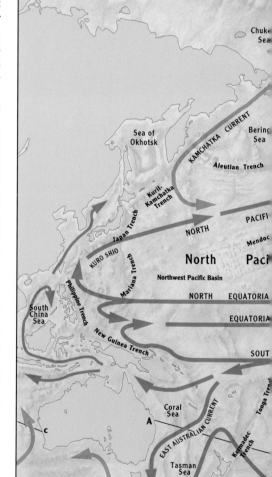

East Siberian Sea · Arcti· · Chuk· Sea · Sea of Okhotsk · Bering Sea · KAMCHATKA CURRENT · Aleutian Trench · Kuril-Kamchatka Trench · Japan Trench · PACIFI· · NORTH · Mendoc· · KURO SHIO · Mariana Trench · North · Paci· · Philippine Trench · Northwest Pacific Basin · NORTH · EQUATORIA· · South China Sea · EQUATORIA· · New Guinea Trench · SOUT· · Coral Sea · A · Tonga Trench · EAST AUSTRALIAN CURRENT · Kermadec Trench · Tasman Sea · Macquarie Ridge Complex · WEST · WIND

XIV

Features of the Ocean Basins

The proportions of the major oceanic features represented in pie charts.

- Continental margins
- Ridges, rises and fracture zones
- Deep ocean floor
- Island arcs and trenches

PACIFIC

ATLANTIC

INDIAN

Average Ocean Depths

metres

3000

3500

4000

PACIFIC   INDIAN   ATLANTIC   WORLD

Land Area Drained

million sq. metres

69

19

13

101

PACIFIC   INDIAN   ATLANTIC   WORLD (Total)

0

Greenland Sea

Beaufort Sea

Barents Sea

WEST GREENLAND CURRENT

EAST GREENLAND CURRENT

Hudson Bay

LABRADOR CURRENT

IRMINGER CURRENT

Labrador Sea

NORTH ATLANTIC DRIFT

NORWEGIAN CURRENT

Faeroe-Rockall Plateau

North Sea

Baltic Sea

ALASKA CURRENT

Ocean

CALIFORNIAN CURRENT

GULF STREAM

North Atlantic Ocean

CANARIES CURRENT

Black Sea

Mediterranean Sea

Red Sea

Clarion Fracture Zone

Sargasso Sea

Gulf of Mexico

Caribbean Sea

Arabian Sea

Bay of Bengal

WEST & NORTH EAST MONSOON DRIFT (SUMMER)

Carlsberg Ridge

Java Trench

COUNTER CURRENT

EQUATORIAL CURRENT

Mid-Atlantic Ridge

GUINEA CURRENT

SOUTH EQUATORIAL CURRENT

B

C

Central Indian Ridge

Central Pacific Basin

Chile Basin

BRAZIL CURRENT

BENGUELA CURRENT

INDIAN COUNTER CURRENT

C

South Pacific Ocean

Rise

Pacific

Peru-Chile Trench

CURRENT

South Atlantic Ocean

Mid-Atlantic Ridge

Walvis Ridge

MOZAMBIQUE CURRENT

Indian Ocean

Southeast Indian Ridge

thwestern Pacific Basin

East

PERU

FALKLAND CURRENT

A   B

Atlantic Ridge

AGULHAS CUR.

Southwest Indian Ridge

DRIFT

CAPE HORN CURRENT

WEST WIND DRIFT

Southern Ocean

XV

ATMOSPHERE

The atmosphere is a mixture of gases with constant proportions up to a height of 80km. The main constituents are: nitrogen (78%); oxygen (21%); and argon; (less than 1%). Other minor constituents include carbon dioxide, ozone and water vapour. All three have important effects on the energy budget of the atmosphere.

OZONE, lying largely in the stratosphere, absorbs ultraviolet solar radiation which would otherwise damage lifeforms. A reduction in ozone, the ozone hole, is therefore cause for concern. Carbon dioxide, being an effective absorber of terrestrial long-wave radiation, is an important 'greenhouse' gas. If it increases, it may lead to an increase in temperature – global warming. Water vapour is also an important greenhouse gas and varies in quantity from 1-4% by volume.

As air is compressible, its lower layers are much more dense than those above. Half of the total mass of air is found below 5km, with the average surface pressure being 1013.25 millibars.

The atmosphere receives heat from the sun by solar radiation, and loses heat by terrestrial radiation. In general the input and output balance and the Earth's climate changes relatively little. Nevertheless, such changes as do occur create the glacial and inter-glacial periods such as experienced in the past million years. The mean temperature structure of the atmosphere reveals five layers: troposphere; stratosphere; mesosphere; thermosphere and exosphere. About 80% of the atmosphere lies in the troposphere, where all weather occurs.

The input and output of radiation vary in different ways with latitude. There is a net input between latitudes 38°, and a net output in other latitudes. This inequality leads to pressure gradients that drive the winds. In turn, these broadly transfer heat down the thermal gradient produced by the radiation distribution. Such a transfer could be achieved by a single large cell comprising air rising at low latitudes, moving polewards at high levels, sinking over the poles, and returning equatorwards at low levels. The rotation of the earth prevents such an occurrence, leading instead to two regimes: the Hadley cell in the tropics; and the Rossby waves in the extra-tropics. The former is associated with the Trade Winds, the latter with the Westerlies. Within these large wind regimes, frontal cyclones, hurricanes and anticyclones form in preferred locations, and within these systems, smaller circulations (for example, sea breezes) and individual clouds bring our day-to-day weather.

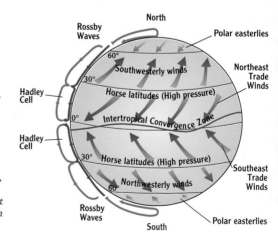

(left) Over three-quarters of the atmosphere is nitrogen. Water vapour, carbon dioxide (greenhouse gases) and ozone are very small in quantity but critical in their effects on the planetary energy balance.

(right) The atmospheric circulation is three-dimensional, and comprises two main regimes: vertical over-turning in the Hadley cell, and waves in the Rossby regime. These are manifest as the Trade Winds (which meet in the Inter-Tropical Convergence Zone) and the Westerlies.

Exosphere

500km

Aurora

Thermosphere

Aurora

2200°C

1500°C

740°C

-90°C

80km

Mesosphere

Meteors

50km

Stratosphere

10°C

Ozone Layer

18km

-55°C

Troposphere

15°C

CLIMATE

The climate of an area is represented by the statistical description of its weather conditions during a specified time. Weather consists of short-term atmospheric variations, most particularly temperature, humidity, precipitation, cloudiness and wind. Earth's climate results from the general circulation of its atmosphere, which produces different regimes of atmospheric variables in different parts of the globe. This allows us to identify different climatic types.

THE mean conditions so frequently used to describe climate result from transfers and transformations of energy, water and momentum between the atmosphere and the Earth. The main source of energy is the Sun, which radiates energy at a virtually constant rate. The Earth's daily rotation and annual precession around the Sun mean that more solar radiation is received near the surface in lower than in higher latitudes. As the Earth's long-wave radiation out to space is distributed more evenly with latitude, the net radiation (input minus output) is positive between latitudes 38 degrees and negative in other latitudes. This energy imbalance leads to pressure gradients that drive the general circulation, which in turn transports heat polewards and upwards. These transports mean that climatic gradients of temperature are smaller than they would be in the absence of the transports.

Nevertheless, it is clear that surface temperatures in January (map top right) range from about -40°C to +40°C, the lowest values being in the continental areas of the northern hemisphere. Land areas gain and lose heat far more rapidly than water areas. As the Sun is in the southern hemisphere in January, the hottest areas are in the Australian desert and parts of South America. In July (map centre right) the desert stretching from the west coast of North Africa to Iran has the highest temperatures. The more maritime southern hemisphere does not reveal very low land temperatures in its winter season, with the notable exception of Antarctica.

The annual precipitation distribution (map below right) also reflects the general circulation. The large amounts in the tropics result from the frequent occurrence of deep cloud systems capable of producing heavy downpours. In the sub-tropics, subsiding air leads to the classic, hot deserts such as the Sahara and Central Australia. Further polewards eastward-moving cyclones produce wet west-coast regimes such as in the UK. In the continental interiors precipitation amounts are less. Further polewards again, precipitation amounts are low, but the water remains on the surface as ice, which gives the impression of a high precipitation area.

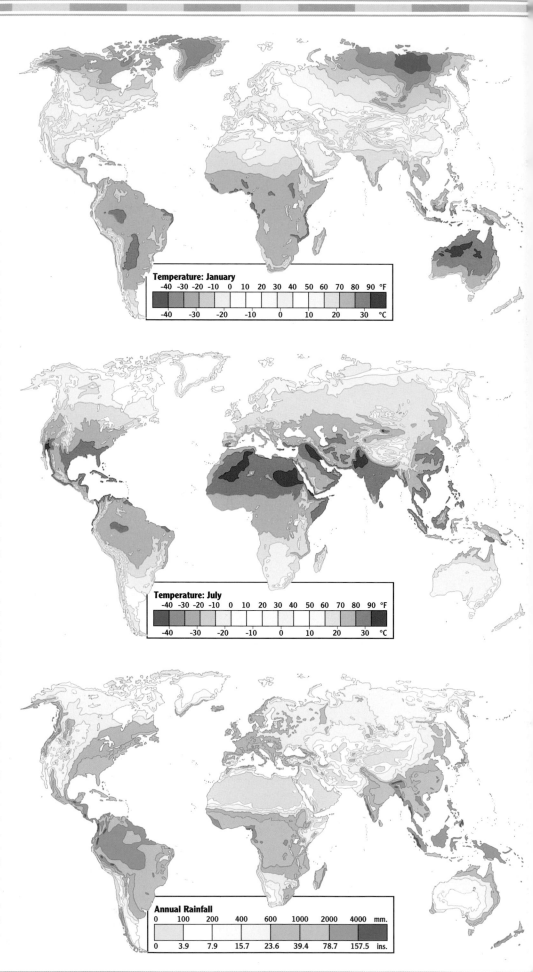

Temperature: January

| °F | -40 | -30 | -20 | -10 | 0 | 10 | 20 | 30 | 40 | 50 | 60 | 70 | 80 | 90 |
| °C | -40 | | -30 | | -20 | | -10 | | 0 | | 10 | | 20 | | 30 | |

Temperature: July

| °F | -40 | -30 | -20 | -10 | 0 | 10 | 20 | 30 | 40 | 50 | 60 | 70 | 80 | 90 |
| °C | -40 | | -30 | | -20 | | -10 | | 0 | | 10 | | 20 | | 30 | |

Annual Rainfall

| mm. | 0 | 100 | 200 | 400 | 600 | 1000 | 2000 | 4000 |
| ins. | 0 | 3.9 | 7.9 | 15.7 | 23.6 | 39.4 | 78.7 | 157.5 |

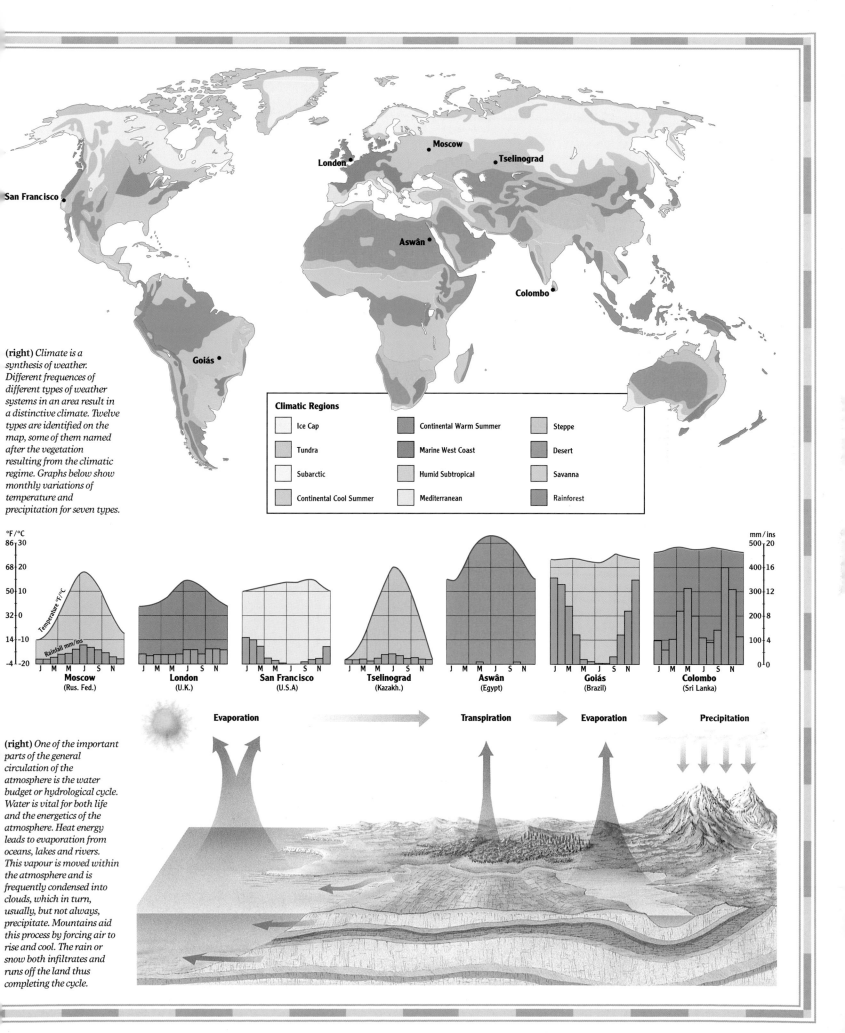

(right) *Climate is a synthesis of weather. Different frequences of different types of weather systems in an area result in a distinctive climate. Twelve types are identified on the map, some of them named after the vegetation resulting from the climatic regime. Graphs below show monthly variations of temperature and precipitation for seven types.*

Moscow

London

Tselinograd

San Francisco

Aswân

Colombo

Goiás

Climatic Regions

Ice Cap	Continental Warm Summer	Steppe
Tundra	Marine West Coast	Desert
Subarctic	Humid Subtropical	Savanna
Continental Cool Summer	Mediterranean	Rainforest

°F/°C
86 30
68 20
50 10
32 0
14 -10
-4 -20

Temperature °F/°C

Rainfall mm/ins

mm/ins
500 20
400 16
300 12
200 8
100 4
0 0

J M M J S N

Moscow
(Rus. Fed.)

London
(U.K.)

San Francisco
(U.S.A)

Tselinograd
(Kazakh.)

Aswân
(Egypt)

Goiás
(Brazil)

Colombo
(Sri Lanka)

Evaporation

Transpiration

Evaporation

Precipitation

(right) *One of the important parts of the general circulation of the atmosphere is the water budget or hydrological cycle. Water is vital for both life and the energetics of the atmosphere. Heat energy leads to evaporation from oceans, lakes and rivers. This vapour is moved within the atmosphere and is frequently condensed into clouds, which in turn, usually, but not always, precipitate. Mountains aid this process by forcing air to rise and cool. The rain or snow both infiltrates and runs off the land thus completing the cycle.*

LANDSCAPES

The shape of the Earth's surface has been produced through a combination of internal and external forces. The former tend to produce the major landforms of structural origin, notably the great mountain ranges and oceanic rises (underwater mountains) but also volcanic cones, lava fields and faulted (crevassed) landscapes. The externally driven forces of running water, ice, waves and wind produce a greater variety of features, though on a smaller scale. To both of these must be added the landforms produced by weathering processes, notably the erosional and depositional features of limestone (karst) areas.

JUST a few areas of the Earth's surface appear to have been exposed to the external processes continually for tens and even hundreds of millions of years. The area around the Macdonnell Range in Central Australia is one such example. However, most of the landforms we see today are geologically quite young. Most date in large part from the Quaternary Era, which began 2 million years ago, and many have been created in the past 25,000 years as the ice sheets in the northern hemisphere began their final retreat, and the sea level started to rise from its low point.

Our planet's surface today is probably more dynamic and varied than at almost any time in its history. Tertiary (occurring from 65 million years ago) and Quaternary mountain building coupled with the effects of the Ice Age have combined to produce great relief and an intricately varied land surface. This contrasts with the extensive plains and more uniform climate that seem to have been the norm through most of geological time.

The ever-changing nature of the land surface is illustrated by the occurrence of landslip seas and the huge amounts of sediments that are moved annually by the world's rivers and by coastal waves and currents. Sometimes erosion and deposition are so rapid that the surface form can be seen to be changing. More often the full extent of the changes going on can only be determined by careful field measurements. The development of instruments and techniques to record these data has been a major advance over the past few years.

(right) *Stalactites are icicle-like growths of calcium carbonate formed by moisture percolating through calcareous substance, usually the roof of a limestone cave. The mineral is deposited from solution and over time increases in length and width.*

(far right) *Landslips usually require a trigger action. In this case it was a small earthquake but, more often, it is a heavy rainstorm. The basic movement is initially in the form of a fall, slide or flow, but as movement proceeds, clear distinction disappears.*

1 *Solution in limestone areas produces karst landforms: swallow holes, polje and caves. There is often little surface drainage.*

2 *Fluvial (stream) action creates distinctive river patterns, meanders, oxbow lakes, gorges, flood plains and river terraces. In rivers with shingle beds, braiding occurs.*

3 *Glacial erosion in mountain areas may create cirques (deep semicircular basins) and glacial troughs which may later become lakes.*

4 *Deltas form where large river sediment loads enter the sea (or lake), where wave and current action is weak. The classic delta shape (e.g. the Nile) is just one of the many forms.*

Desert landforms include both windblown and deposits (seif dunes, archans) and eroded areas littered with stones or bare rock.

6 Glaciers help create pyramidal peaks and sharp ridges (aretes). They also carry rock debris (moraine).

7 Landslides occur on steep slopes and under favourable geological conditions, notably on clays and especially in areas of heavy rainfall.

8 Hard-rock coasts have steep cliffs and often offshore rocks and natural arches. The slope of the cliff is variable and depends on the interaction between geology, climate and the energy of the waves at the base.

9 U-shaped valleys may result from glacial erosion. Beyond the ice limit fluvio-glacial deposition and erosion occurs, often creating terraces.

10 Soft-rock coasts are characterized by deposition. Beaches abound. Spits may dominate river mouths, and salt marsh accumulates in sheltered localities.

NATURAL VEGETATION

Our natural vegetation has evolved in conjunction with the other elements of the environment to produce clear-cut patterns. Climate is an especially important control, but many other factors are influential. Vegetation is a resource for human-kind, and as such has been subject to modification and destruction at an ever-increasing rate.

THE natural vegetation has increased in diversity and complexity over the past 400 million years. Trees are the dominant plant form. Gymnosperms (conifers) evolved first, but have been out-stripped by the angiosperms (flowering plants) and now only dominate in harsher, often cooler, environments. Exceptions include the famous redwood forests on the Pacific coast of North America, and the Podocarp forests of New Zealand.

Most plants require warmth, moisture and sunlight for growth, and a soil to act as an anchor and provide nutrients. Equatorial regions provide the optimum conditions for growth, and support the greatest diversity of tree species. A 10 x 1000m sample area of vegetation through the Amazon forest might contain over 150 species. A similar area in an ancient woodland in Britain might reveal only 15-20 tree types. Species diversity is even lower in northern coniferous forests.

Plants are adapted to the prevailing climate. In equatorial regions there are few limits to growth, and trees are tall, rarely deciduous, and often large leaved. In the absence of strong winds, pollination is mainly by insects, bats and birds. Brightly coloured, highly scented flowers are characteristic. Competition for light is important, and many plants (lianes) scramble and climb up existing trunks or grow directly on the branches (epiphytes).

In drier areas, conservation of moisture is necessary. Leaf loss, small leaves, sunken stomata (similar to skin pores), and aromatic oils within leaves are some of the many survival strategies adopted. Eventually moisture availability is insufficient to support trees, which are replaced by scrub and grass communities.

The impact of human action has been more dramatic and speedy than the gradual evolution of the pattern of natural vegetation over the past 2 million years. The effects have been especially marked in the last 50 years on both forests and rangelands. The speed and scale of tropical forest destruction for timber, settlements, shifting agriculture and large-scale ranching have raised fears about soil erosion and climatic change both locally and globally. Destruction of rangeland vegetation through fire, over-grazing and ploughing has prompted fears of desertification. One resolution is to establish conservation areas but their successful implementation is very difficult.

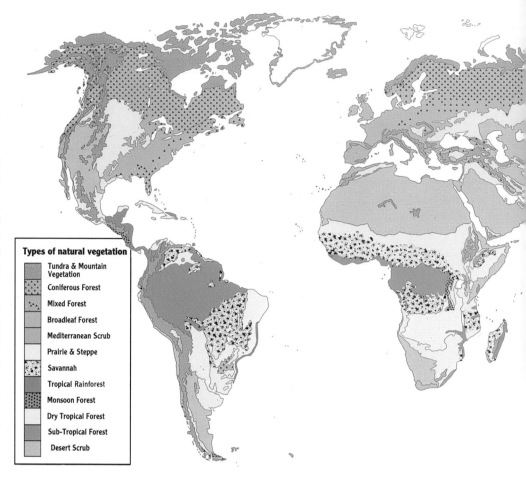

Types of natural vegetation

- Tundra & Mountain Vegetation
- Coniferous Forest
- Mixed Forest
- Broadleaf Forest
- Mediterranean Scrub
- Prairie & Steppe
- Savannah
- Tropical Rainforest
- Monsoon Forest
- Dry Tropical Forest
- Sub-Tropical Forest
- Desert Scrub

The Amazon rainforest is the largest area of natural tropical forest remaining, but it too, is now being exploited by human activities, particularly since a road network has been pushed through the area. Much of the forest is being burnt to provide pasture land or land for peasant farms, or is cleared for the timber industry. Mineral extraction and oil exploration (right) are other causes of deforestation. It is expected that forest destruction will cause climatic changes to Amazonia, and there may also be globally felt effects.

Deforestation and economic development in Brazilian Amazonia

- Tropical rainforest
- Vegetation other than rainforest dominant
- Deforestation: over 50% of rainforest lost
- Extent of Amazonia
- Major road
- under construction
- Major development project

Shrinking Forests

1950 — Rest of the earth
Tropical forest — Temperate and coniferous forest

1975

2000

In 1950 the forests of the temperate and tropical areas covered about 40% of the Earth's land surface. European forests had almost been depleted. Since 1950 there has been a dramatic increase in forest destruction. By 1975 forests occupied 30% of the land surface; by 1985 this had declined towards 20%. Destruction is taking place in both temperate and tropical areas although most publicity has focused on the tropical rain forests.

(left and right) The distribution of the major world vegetation groups is determined, ultimately, by climatic considerations coupled with evolutionary developments in the plants themselves. However, dispersal limitations makes vegetation vulnerable to external changes such as the lateral shifting of the continents through plate tectonics, and major climatic changes induced by ice advances and retreats. These factors help explain inter-continental variations. At the local level, variations in soil conditions and topography account for small-scale changes within the overall vegetation type. Human interference has not only stripped large areas of the natural vegetation, but elsewhere has initiated changes that range from the subtle to the profound.

Distance from sun, composition of atmosphere, speed of rotation.

Latitude → Climate ← Altitude

World vegetation groups ← Evolution

Plate tectonics → Intercontinental variation ← Geological history

Topography → Local variation ← Soil conditions

Natural disasters → ← Human interference

Succession — Physical isolation

(left) Vertical changes in climate are vastly more concentrated than latitudinal changes. Mount Everest is about 8km tall. Its top is a windswept snow and ice desert. Eight kilometres lower, tropical forest flourishes in the moist, warm climate. Other mountain ranges, the Pyrenees, the Alps, the Andes and the Southern Alps, for example, all show a similar pattern. The topmost area may be permanently snow covered (1). Below this will be a zone of alpine vegetation (2), low growing herbs and shrubs, often adept at surviving in clefts and crevices. Lower down is the treeline (3), arguably the most striking vegetation boundary there is, which marks the beginning of the forest zone (4). The highest part of this tree covered landscape is often a cloud forest or Krumholtz zone with gnarled, moss-festooned trees. Conifers typically occur at these higher levels (5) but in the Southern Hemisphere Southern Beech forests are encountered. Ideally a zone of temperate deciduous woodland then occurs (6) before the more heat-loving vegetation is met with at the base of the mountain (7).

POPULATION

The growth of world population is among the most important features of this century, and has sparked debate about its economic, social and environmental implications. Growth may not cease until numbers reach over 12 billion, more than double present figures. The most rapidly growing populations are in poorer regions, and the pressures on resources are enormous.

WORLD population reached 5.5 billion in mid-1992, and is projected to grow to 6.2 billion by the year 2000. Numbers have increased rapidly in the second half of the 20th century, with growth rates reaching 2.1% per annum in the 1960s. The present growth rate is 1.7% per annum (an extra 93 million people each year), and is projected to decline to about 1.0% per annum by 2025 when population is projected to be 8.5 billion.

The exceptional nature of this growth is apparent when placed in the context of world population history. In the past, population growth was exceedingly slow, with birth and death rates generally in balance. Growth rates began to increase around the beginning of the 18th century, and the first thousand million was reached in the early 19th century. In 1900 the world total was less than 1.7 billion.

The major impetus behind growth has been the lowering of mortality and improvements in life expectancy. These have been especially important in the period after the Second World War for the populations of the less developed regions of the world. Meanwhile, declines in birth rates have been much less rapid; parts of Africa have even seen increases in fertility. The result has been explosive rates of growth, particularly in the less developed world, where between 1950 and 1990 the population increased by 143% compared with 45% elsewhere.

Today, growth is most rapid in Africa, parts of Asia and Latin America. Growth is projected to remain high in Africa well into the next century, so that by 2025 Africa will account for 35% of world population growth (20% in 1990) and make up 19% of total world population (12% in 1990). Kenya has one of the highest rates of growth of any country, and population here is expected to increase 13 times from the 1950 total.

How rapidly world population growth decelerates depends on the speed with which birth rates are reduced in those countries where they are still high. Fertility reduction depends on many factors, including the education levels and status of women. For many poor people, children remain their greatest security. The success of government efforts to lower birth rates will depend to a great extent on how successfully they also improve economic and social conditions for their people.

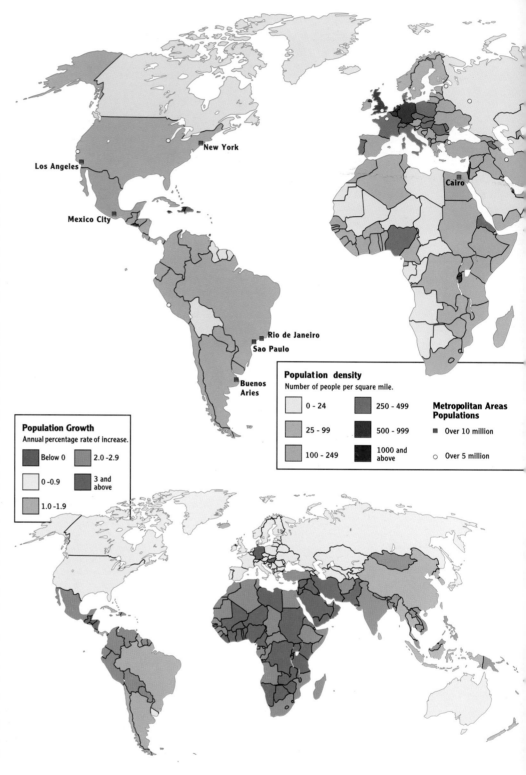

Population density
Number of people per square mile.

0 - 24	250 - 499
25 - 99	500 - 999
100 - 249	1000 and above

Metropolitan Areas Populations
- Over 10 million
- Over 5 million

Population Growth
Annual percentage rate of increase.

Below 0	2.0 -2.9
0 -0.9	3 and above
1.0 -1.9	

(above) *World population growth rates show a clear north-south division with dramatic growth gradients evident where the less developed world impinges on the more developed world. This is particularly evident in the countries surrounding the Mediterranean Sea where some of the faster growing populations of the world in north Africa are adjacent to the slowest growing in Europe.*
(above right) *World population grew at a steady rate until the 18th century when the rate of growth accelerated dramatically.*
(right) *Demographic transition model showing the four broad stages of development as undeveloped societies with high birth and death rates and low rates of growth progress through periods of rapidly growing population before reaching stage 4 where birth and death rates are very low and growth rates stable or even declining.*

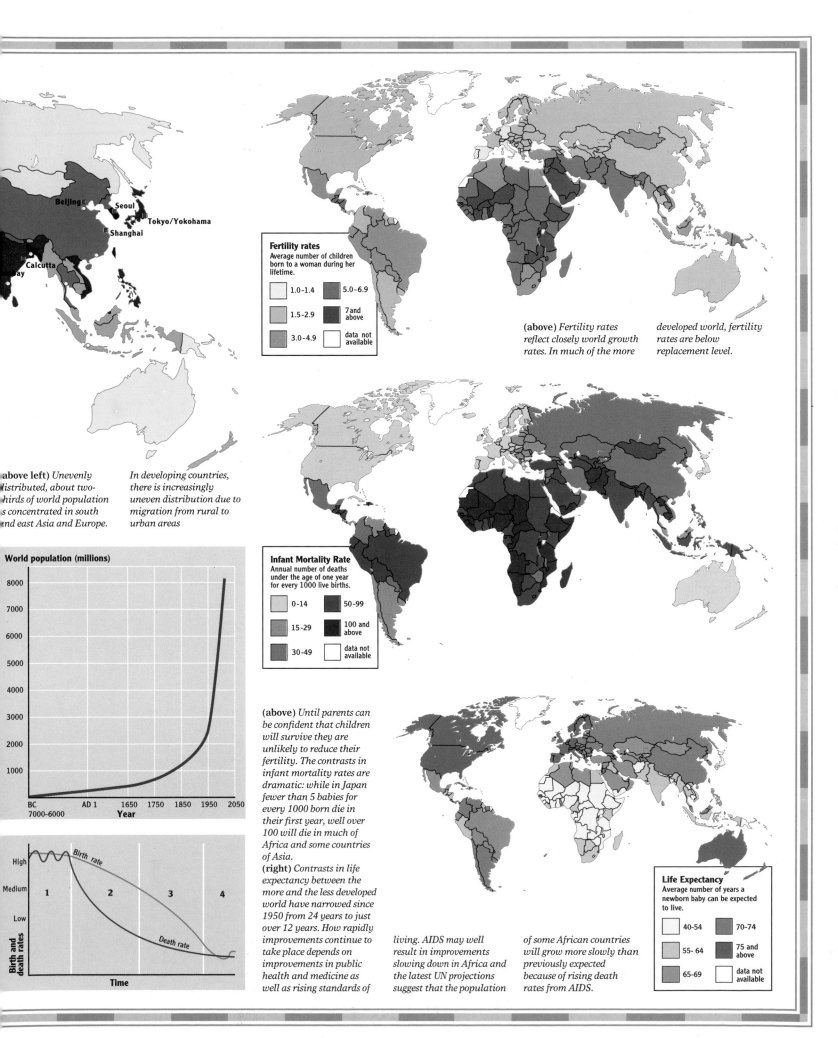

Fertility rates
Average number of children born to a woman during her lifetime.

1.0-1.4	5.0-6.9
1.5-2.9	7 and above
3.0-4.9	data not available

(above) *Fertility rates reflect closely world growth rates. In much of the more* *developed world, fertility rates are below replacement level.*

Infant Mortality Rate
Annual number of deaths under the age of one year for every 1000 live births.

0-14	50-99
15-29	100 and above
30-49	data not available

Life Expectancy
Average number of years a newborn baby can be expected to live.

40-54	70-74
55-64	75 and above
65-69	data not available

World population (millions)

(x-axis: BC 7000-6000, AD 1, 1650, 1750, 1850, 1950, 2050 — Year)
(y-axis: 1000 to 8000)

Birth and death rates

(Birth rate, Death rate; High, Medium, Low; phases 1, 2, 3, 4; Time)

(above left) *Unevenly distributed, about two-thirds of world population is concentrated in south and east Asia and Europe.*

In developing countries, there is increasingly uneven distribution due to migration from rural to urban areas

(Beijing, Seoul, Tokyo/Yokohama, Shanghai, Calcutta, Bombay)

(above) *Until parents can be confident that children will survive they are unlikely to reduce their fertility. The contrasts in infant mortality rates are dramatic: while in Japan fewer than 5 babies for every 1000 born die in their first year, well over 100 will die in much of Africa and some countries of Asia.*

(right) *Contrasts in life expectancy between the more and the less developed world have narrowed since 1950 from 24 years to just over 12 years. How rapidly improvements continue to take place depends on improvements in public health and medicine as well as rising standards of living. AIDS may well result in improvements slowing down in Africa and the latest UN projections suggest that the population of some African countries will grow more slowly than previously expected because of rising death rates from AIDS.*

FOOD

Enough food is produced in the world to satisfy the basic needs of all its 5.5 billion inhabitants, yet malnutrition and famine are commonplace. While food production has increased steadily in nearly all countries over the last 50 years, the UN nevertheless estimates that under-nourishment still afflicts one person out of every five.

ABOUT one third of the world's land area is too cold, dry or mountainous for food production. Of the rest, about 10% is under intensive cultivation and 25% used for extensive grazing, with some of the remaining land, mostly semi-arid or forested, potentially available for agricultural use (see map right). The most productive regions of the oceans are nearly all located in relatively shallow waters.

Since 1950, world food production has been increasing at an annual rate of between 2 and 3%. Today the more developed countries produce half the world's food with less than 10% of its agricultural workforce through the intense application of chemicals and widespread use of machinery, giving very high yields per hectare of land. In many developing countries, especially in Africa, farming is labour intensive and yields are low; over much of the Far East and Latin America, on the other hand, the development of high-yielding varieties of cereals, together with increased use of irrigation, fertilizers and pesticides (often referred to as the green revolution), has achieved much greater yields.

The sea is an important source of food for many coastal and island peoples, particularly in the Far East, but opportunities for further expansion of the marine harvest appear limited. Food production in many developing countries has generally kept pace with population growth, and a few, such as Thailand, have become net exporters of food. Most countries in Africa, on the other hand, have experienced a decline in food availability as their population has grown faster than the food supply; technological innovations there have often been in respect of high-value crops intended for export (so-called cash crops), rather than staple foods such as cereals.

Over much of Africa, together with parts of Asia and Latin America, average daily food consumption is below optimum levels both in quantity, or energy content, as well as quality, or nutritional make-up. In contrast, a similar proportion of the population in nearly all developed countries suffers from over-nutrition, with its attendant problems of obesity and dietary-related diseases. This inequality is apparent not only in the average daily intake of food energy (see diagram top right), but more especially in the proportion of the diet derived from animal sources (see map bottom right).

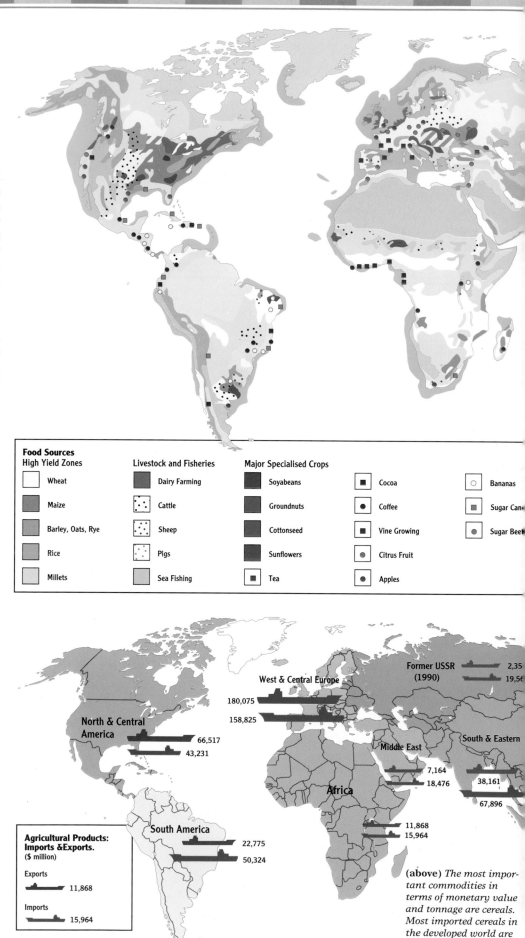

Food Sources

High Yield Zones
- Wheat
- Maize
- Barley, Oats, Rye
- Rice
- Millets

Livestock and Fisheries
- Dairy Farming
- Cattle
- Sheep
- Pigs
- Sea Fishing

Major Specialised Crops
- Soyabeans
- Groundnuts
- Cottonseed
- Sunflowers
- Tea
- Cocoa
- Coffee
- Vine Growing
- Citrus Fruit
- Apples
- Bananas
- Sugar Cane
- Sugar Beet

Agricultural Products: Imports & Exports. ($ million)

Exports — 11,868
Imports — 15,964

Former USSR (1990) — 2,35 / 19,56
West & Central Europe — 180,075 / 158,825
North & Central America — 66,517 / 43,231
Middle East — 7,164 / 18,476
South & Eastern — 38,161 / 67,896
Africa — 11,868 / 15,964
South America — 22,775 / 50,324

(above) The most important commodities in terms of monetary value and tonnage are cereals. Most imported cereals in the developed world are fed to livestock.

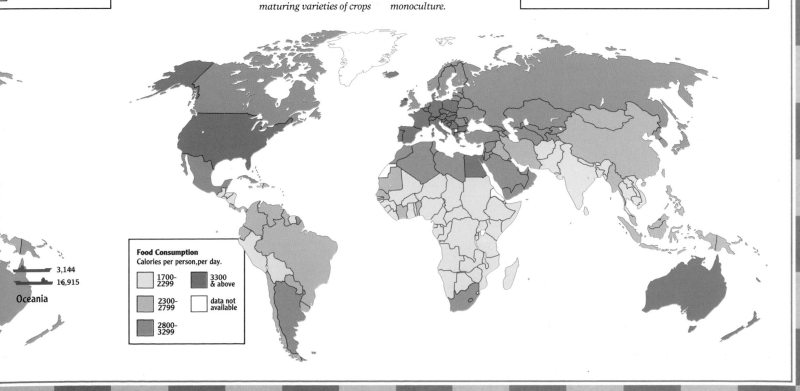

Low Yield Zones

	Tundra, Ice-cap
	Forest
	Mountain
	Extensive Grassland
	Desert, Semi-desert

The green revolution has brought dramatic increases in food production from high-yielding varieties of cereals requiring the application of chemicals to supply essential nutrients and to protect from pests and diseases.
(top) In SE Asia highly controllable irrigation techniques applied to early maturing varieties of crops allow two or three harvests each year.
(above) In temperate regions productivity has been further increased through extensive mechanization; over much of Europe this has resulted in the amalgamation of small fields, which now resemble the great expanses of North American monoculture.

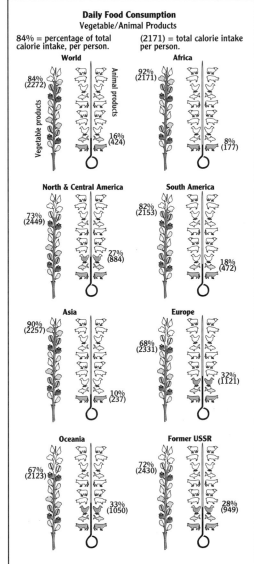

Daily Food Consumption
Vegetable/Animal Products

84% = percentage of total calorie intake, per person.

(2171) = total calorie intake per person.

World
84% (2272) Vegetable products
16% (424) Animal products

Africa
92% (2171)
8% (177)

North & Central America
73% (2449)
27% (884)

South America
82% (2153)
18% (472)

Asia
90% (2257)
10% (237)

Europe
68% (2331)
32% (1121)

Oceania
67% (2123)
33% (1050)

Former USSR
72% (2430)
28% (949)

3,144
16,915

Oceania

Food Consumption
Calories per person, per day.

	1700-2299
	2300-2799
	2800-3299
	3300 & above
	data not available

MINERALS AND ENERGY

Life for most people in the world today is sustained by the consumption of both minerals and energy, often in quite considerable quantities. Knowledge of their location and availability is therefore of great importance, and in many cases the search for new or alternative sources has very high priority.

WHILE metal-yielding minerals are widely distributed in the Earth's crust, it is usually only where they have been concentrated into an ore body that exploitation is possible. The quantity of ore that can be extracted at sufficient profit is known as the reserve of that mineral; its size will change in response to variations in demand and technological advances, as well as to findings of new deposits.

Although no metal is destroyed by use, the proportion that can be recycled seldom exceeds 50%, so there is a continuing need for new sources of supply or the introduction of substitutes. While metals such as aluminium and iron are widely distributed and relatively plentiful, the supply of others, such as copper, has only been maintained with recourse to increasingly less concentrated ore deposits. A few important metals are intrinsically rare and deposits are limited to very few countries; for example, metals of the platinum group occur mainly in South Africa. The economy of many developing countries is largely dependent upon the export of one particular metal (Guinea and Jamaica rely extensively on their reserves of aluminium).

Compared with metals, non-metalliferous minerals (those that do not yield or contain metals) generally have lower intrinsic value but a wider distribution; they are, however, rarely capable of being recycled. The most important sources of energy, fossil hydrocarbon fuels, are totally consumed by use. Whereas coal and lignite are widely distributed and relatively abundant, reserves of gas and oil are more localized. World dependence on oil and gas has increased dramatically since 1945, and supplies are predicted to approach exhaustion during the next century. Nuclear and hydro-power each account for about 20% of world electricity supply, but the uranium fuel on which the former depends has few rich deposits and is non-renewable. Hydro-power, however, constitutes an inexhaustible resource in principle, though most of its potential contribution resides in developing countries.

The amount of energy obtained from fuel-wood is estimated to be comparable with that supplied by nuclear and hydro-power. It is the dominant fuel in much of Africa and parts of Latin America and southeast Asia. Although it is a renewable resource, many developing countries are already experiencing an acute shortage of this source of energy.

World Energy Consumption

- North America
- Latin America
- Western Europe
- Eastern Europe plus former USSR (1990)
- Middle East
- Africa
- Asia and Australia

Colours also refer to World Energy Reserves.

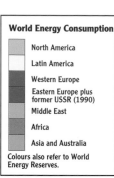

World

(above) *The industrialized world's high standard of living requires the consumption of huge quantities of energy.*

Oil

(left) *Because it supplies essential fuels for transport, and despite political uncertainties, oil remains the world's most important source of energy.*

(right) *Widely available, coal is a significant source of energy, and is especially prominent in the (former) communist states and in many developing countries.*

Coal

Natural Gas

(left) *Consumption of natural gas has doubled over the last 20 years, and is now the principal energy source for many industrialized countries.*

Renewable sources are making an increasing contribution to world energy needs. One of the most promising is wind power (see diagram and photograph below), which already supplies some 2% of electricity demand in both California and Denmark and also has a realistic potential contribution of up to 20% in many countries. The cost of solar cells is still falling, encouraging an expansion of applications mainly within tropical latitudes. In favoured locations electricity from the sea (from both tidal energy and wave power), and geothermal heat can be significant. As valuable replacements for fossil hydrocarbons, similar fuels can be derived from organic material (biomass) of many kinds, including crops such as sugar cane or timber which is grown specifically for the purpose, as well as agricultural or domestic wastes.

European Wind Energy Resources
The potential for wind energy development based upon mean speeds greater than 5m/s.

United Kingdom

Republic of Ireland

Italy
France
Germany

Greece
Spain
Netherlands
Portugal
Denmark
Belgium

Sites of main energy sources.

- oil
- gas
- coal
- lignite
- hydro-electric
- uranium

1800 10 20 30 40 50 60 70
Year

Economic Minerals   World yield and known reserves of each mineral.

	Rare Metals			Ferro-alloy Metals		Iron Fe
Nb	Niobium		Cr	Chromium		
Ta	Tantalum		Co	Cobalt		
U	Uranium		Mn	Manganese		
			Mo	Molybdenum		**Precious Metals**
	Light Metals		Ni	Nickel		Gold Au
Al	Aluminium		W	Tungsten		Platinum Pt
Ti	Titanium		V	Vanadium		Silver Ag

Base Metals
Sb Antimony
Cu Copper
Pb Lead
Hg Mercury
Sn Tin
Zn Zinc

Chemical and Fertiliser Minerals
B   Borax
F   Fluorite
K   Potash
P   Phosphate (rock)
S   Sulphur
Ap Apatite

Other Industrial Minerals
Cly China Clay
Mgs Magnesite
MI   Mica
Tc   Talc
Asb Asbestos

Diamonds

Importance of Sites
over 5%
over 1%

(above) *Amongst metal-liferous minerals, iron is unusual in that it has widespread rich-deposits; many, like lead and zinc, though widely distributed are much less common and have reserves of less than 50 years. A few are intrinsically rare and their production is dominated by very few countries.*
(left) *Coal is relatively evenly distributed. In contrast, some 95% of proven reserves of oil are located in just 20 countries. Reserves of natural gas are dominated by the former USSR and the Middle East. Uranium reserves are concentrated in North America, Africa and Australia.*

World Energy Reserves

Oil

Gas

Coal

(left) *At present rates of consumption, known reserves of oil will last rather less, and gas reserves rather more, than 50 years; however, as recently as 1979 the equivalent estimate for oil was about 25 years. Supplies of coal are sufficient for at least 300 years.*

Growth in World Primary Energy Demand.
Nuclear
Hydro-Electric
Natural Gas
Oil
Coal and Lignite
Wood

12,000
11,000
10,000
9000
8000
7000
6000
5000
4000
3000
2000
1000
0

Million tonnes oil equivalent

90   **1900**   10   20   30   40   50   60   70   80   90

ENVIRONMENTAL PROBLEMS

People have always suffered from the results of too little or too much water but, as world population has grown and people have been obliged to live in more marginal areas, so pressure on the environment has intensified. As a result droughts, floods and other related problems are increasing in severity and frequency.

Dᴿᴼᵁᴳᴴᵀˢ are a natural part of climatic variability, but in temperate latitudes such as Britain they are seldom long-lived or give rise to more than local inconvenience. Nearer to the equator, where rainfall is both seasonal and highly variable from year to year, drought is much more likely to occur, and it is quite common for unusually dry (or wet) years to follow each other in sequence. Much of Africa experiences low rainfall regimes of this type.

Gradual erosion of the land surface by wind and water is an ongoing natural process, but removal of vegetation cover and short-sighted farming practices can result in accelerated loss of topsoil. Preventative measures involve direct protection from the erosive effects of wind and water (using windbreaks or terracing, for example) and modifying cultivation practices to maximize the extent and persistence of vegetation cover.

Floods are the most frequent natural disasters and cause the most damage in terms of loss of life and livelihood. River floods, which occur when the volume of water exceeds the capacity of the channel, are the most common , but incursions by the sea can be equally disastrous. Low lying coasts and the flood plains of large rivers are most at risk, regions which typically support dense populations and intensive agricultural activity. The risk of flooding is often further increased by human activities such as urbanization and deforestation. Although considerable protection to life and property is provided by engineering works, regulation of land use together with warning systems is usually more cost effective.

The borders of desert regions are slowly changing all the time, but human activity can greatly accelerate their advance. The semi-arid margins of subtropical deserts are at risk where rising numbers of poor people struggle to survive. The sparse vegetation cover is rapidly lost through increased collection of fuelwood and grazing of more livestock, and the soil is impoverished through expansion of cultivated land and reductions in the fallow period. Erosion and drought hasten the degradation of the land. An important additional factor in regions where irrigation is common is an excessive concentration of salts in the soil, resulting from high evaporation rates coupled with insufficient drainage.

Drought
Dry Climate Regions based on Köppen classification.

steppe regions

desert regions

1986
✳ major droughts since 1965

Rainfall, Sahel 1941-1989.

Wetter than average   Drier than average

TIBET

Forest clearance increases run-off.

Ganges

Brahmaputra

River levels rise due to heavy rain and melting snow.

• Dhaka

Rivers wash away dams and bridges.

BANGLADESH

Silt settles in channels causing rivers to burst their banks.

The Ganges discharges more water in August and September than the total for the rest of the year.

Flooding

Country suffering severe flooding.

1985. Floods resulting in over 300 deaths and/or 40,000 homeless and/or extensive damage (1980-1991).

Major river prone to flooding.

U.S.A. 1980, 1981, 1982, 1983, 1984, 1986.

Peru 1982, 1983, 1986.

Brazil 1985.

Benin 1985.

Nepal 1980

India 1981, 1982, 1983, 1985, 1986.

Somalia 1981.

Japan 1982, 1983.

Korea 1984.

China 1981, 1982, 1983

Bangladesh 1991.

Indonesia 1986.

(left) *Accompanying the map, which shows the main desert and steppe regions of the world, are the sites of major droughts in recent years.*
(below left) *A run of dry years in the Sahel region has had very severe consequences for the local population.*
(below) *Millet breaks through the parched earth in Sudan.*

(right) *Desertification, or the spread of deserts, threatens over a third of the world's cultivated land*
(below right) *Soil degradation can be halted, and even sometimes reversed, through preventative measures.*
(below) *Loss of vegetation is a critical factor in desertification.*

Desertification

- existing desert
- moderate desertification
- severe desertification
- very severe desertification

Preventative Measures

1 Reforestation
2 Plant barriers along gullies
3 Terrace steep land
4 Cultivate along contours
5 Control surface water
6 Plant windbreaks
7 Stabilise sand dunes
8 Interplant crops
9 Plant leguminous crops, allow fallow periods
10 Grow drought resistant crops

Types of Soil Degradation

Water erosion 56%
Physical degradation 4%
Wind erosion 28%
Chemical degradation 12%

Sources of Soil Degradation

Over exploitation 7%
Deforestation 30%
Overgrazing 35%
Agricultural activities 28%
Industrialization 1%

(left) *Countries suffering disastrous floods are often those least able to cope with the effects.*
(above left) *Flooding, although part of the natural cycle in Bangladesh, has increased in severity in recent years.*
(above) *Flooding causes more damage than any other environmental hazard.*

(right) *Each year some 75 million tonnes of topsoil are lost around the world, causing harvests to fail and blocking rivers and reservoirs.*
(above right) *Poor land management is one of the fundamental causes of soil erosion.*
(above) *The dramatic effects of gully erosion in Somalia.*

Soil Erosion

- severe erosion
- very severe erosion
- erosion by water
- erosion by wind

POLLUTION

Over the last two centuries, advances in science and technology and a rising standard of living have led to increasing volumes of waste materials, which are beginning to have a world-wide impact on the environment.

IT is easy to suppose that the atmosphere has an unlimited capacity for our waste products. Its local capacity is often exceeded in large cities, however, and while the demise of the open coal fire has eliminated dense smogs from cities such as London, other cities, where high traffic densities coincide with intense sunlight, (Los Angeles, Mexico City and Tokyo, for example), increasingly suffer from smogs of a different kind. Increasing road traffic is one reason for a steadily rising consumption of fossil fuels; when burnt these produce carbon dioxide which will in time lead to a significant warming of the climate.

Most fossil fuels, particularly coal, contain sulphur as an impurity. When burnt, both sulphur dioxide and oxides of nitrogen are produced, which may escape into the atmosphere and give rise to acid rain and snowfall. In susceptible regions this has the effect of killing fish and other aquatic life, as well as forest trees.

Chlorofluorocarbons, or CFCs, are a group of highly inert, non-toxic, volatile chemicals with widespread applications as aerosol propellants, refrigerants, foam-blowing agents and industrial solvents. Their extreme stability in the lower atmosphere means they disperse over the globe and only decompose when exposed to ultra-violet sunlight high in the stratosphere. Chlorine atoms are set free and act to decrease the concentration of the protective ozone layer. Although losses have been detected in northern latitudes, at present they are most severe above the Antarctic.

Four million tonnes of waste are produced every day. While household and municipal waste is adequately dealt with via recycling, reclamation, incineration, composting, landfilling or, less desirably, dumping at sea, about a quarter is industrial waste for which there is no safe disposal method other than total isolation from the environment.

The accidental discharge of toxic industrial effluent into rivers and lakes results in the large-scale loss of fish stocks. More widespread is an increase of nutrient levels from agricultural drainage or sewage effluent, which initiates an explosive growth of aquatic plants, followed by depressed levels of oxygen when they die and decompose; this, too, leads to the death of fish. Pollutants released into lakes and rivers find their way to the sea, where sewage contaminated beaches pose less of an environmental threat than does oil, large quantities of which are discharged every day.

Air Pollution
CO2 Emissions from Industrial Processes and Road Transport
(emissions in tonnes per annum)

0.00–0.99	10.00 and above
1.00–4.99	data not available
5.00–9.99	

124 — total of metropolitan area pollution (tonnes).
78 — % attributable to road transport

Although there is no general agreement that acid rain is the sole cause of dieback in forest trees, the extent of the problem is quite well known. Most affected are North West and Central Europe, especially Germany, together with North East USA and Eastern Canada; there are early signs of damage in many other industrializing countries including Brazil, China, India, Venezuela and Zambia.

Acid Rain Damage to the Major Forests of Europe

	Forest (Km²)	Damage (Km²)	Percentage
Austria	375,400	9,600	24.2
Finland	194,000	67,900	35.0
France	150,750	2,796	1.85
Germany	102,230	41,740	40.8
Norway	83,330	4,100	4.9
Poland	86,770	22,730	26.2
Sweden	265,000	10,600	4.0

(top) CO₂ is the most important of the greenhouse gases. The industrialized countries are responsible for 75% of global emissions.

(below) Nearly half of oil pollution in the marine environment derives from land based sources; the rest from shipping activities.

(right) Water pollution tends to be most severe where there is a high concentration of people and industrial activities.

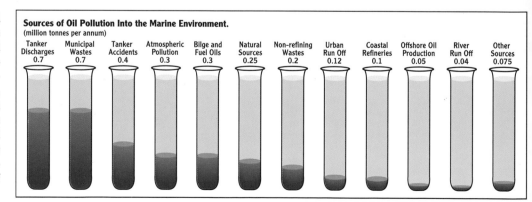

Sources of Oil Pollution Into the Marine Environment.
(million tonnes per annum)

Tanker Discharges	Municipal Wastes	Tanker Accidents	Atmospheric Pollution	Bilge and Fuel Oils	Natural Sources	Non-refining Wastes	Urban Run Off	Coastal Refineries	Offshore Oil Production	River Run Off	Other Sources
0.7	0.7	0.4	0.3	0.3	0.25	0.2	0.12	0.1	0.05	0.04	0.075

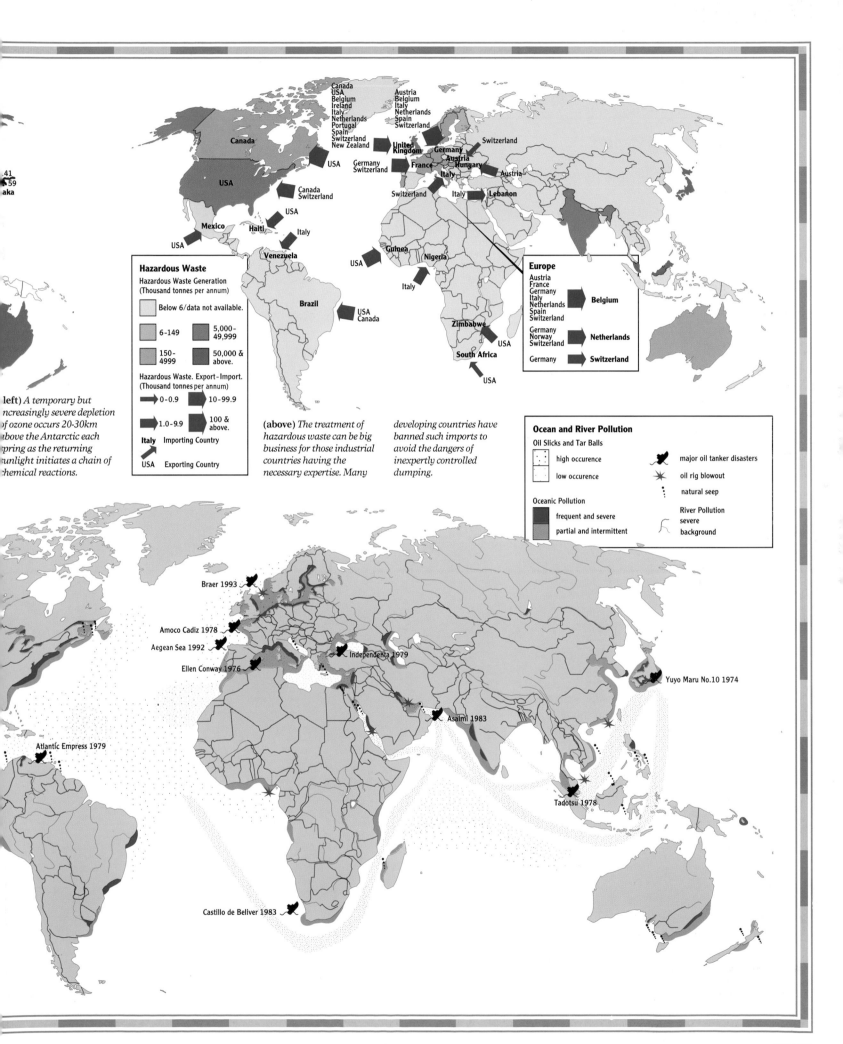

Hazardous Waste

Hazardous Waste Generation
(Thousand tonnes per annum)

Below 6/data not available.

6-149

150-4999

5,000-49,999

50,000 & above.

Hazardous Waste. Export-Import.
(Thousand tonnes per annum)

0-0.9

1.0-9.9

10-99.9

100 & above.

Italy — Importing Country

USA — Exporting Country

(left) A temporary but increasingly severe depletion of ozone occurs 20-30km above the Antarctic each spring as the returning sunlight initiates a chain of chemical reactions.

(above) The treatment of hazardous waste can be big business for those industrial countries having the necessary expertise. Many developing countries have banned such imports to avoid the dangers of inexpertly controlled dumping.

Europe

Austria
France
Germany
Italy
Netherlands
Spain
Switzerland — **Belgium**

Germany
Norway
Switzerland — **Netherlands**

Germany — **Switzerland**

Ocean and River Pollution

Oil Slicks and Tar Balls

high occurence

low occurence

major oil tanker disasters

oil rig blowout

natural seep

Oceanic Pollution

frequent and severe

partial and intermittent

River Pollution
severe
background

Braer 1993

Amoco Cadiz 1978

Aegean Sea 1992

Ellen Conway 1976

Independenta 1979

Yuyo Maru No.10 1974

Asaimi 1983

Atlantic Empress 1979

Tadotsu 1978

Castillo de Beliver 1983

HISTORY OF MAPS

Maps were drawn long before words were written, which was some time before 3200 BC. In the third millennium BC, maps were given an orientation. Finally, land-division in Mesopotamia, Egypt and China brought into use the concept of scale and the accurate spatial relationship required in the true map.

GEOGRAPHY developed in Greece from the 7th century BC, leading to the first world maps. The world was known to be a sphere from the 4th century BC. Eratosthenes, in the 3rd century BC, measured the circumference as 252,000 stades.(The Greek stade had many values. It was the length of the short foot-race , 125 double paces). In the following century, Hipparchus devised our system of 360 degrees, with 60 minutes of 60 seconds. Claud Ptolemy (c AD 150) wrote his *Geography* based on the work of a Phoenician predecessor, Marinus of Tyre, the culmination of Greek geography. By Ptolemy's reckoning, the world's circumference was only 180,000 stades. The Romans abandoned Greek concepts of mapping in favour of road maps and itineraries.

With the eclipse of Rome, the ancient world's geographical knowledge was lost to the West, and passed into the hands of Arab geographers. It was painfully rediscovered only in the late Middle Ages. New types of ocean-going ships, the compass, and, from the mid-13th century, a new type of chart, known as the portolan, revolutionized navigation.

The introduction into Europe of paper and the invention of printing led to widespread dissemination of the rediscovered maps of Ptolemy in the Age of Discovery. The supposedly small size of Ptolemy's world misled Columbus and others into believing China could be reached across the western ocean.

The theodolite, invented in 1570, the plane-table 20 years later and the telescope another 20 years on, followed by the invention of triangulation in 1617, established foundations of modern surveying and mapping. Satellites now provide the ultimate precision in surveying.

(above) *This map of 2500 BC in cuneiform script, on a clay tablet, is the earliest known map with true orientation. It contains the words north, west and east. A private estate is shown near a river with mountains on either side, east and west.*
(above right) *Chinese cartography developed in isolation from the rest of the world. This map drawn on silk in the 2nd century BC is typical of the period. After the invention of paper, maps were widely distributed in China.*
(below) *A reconstruction of a map by Hecataeus of Miletus in c 500 BC. (It shows the world known to the Greeks at the time).*

(bottom left) *Muslim geographers made only a small contribution to cartography. Their main interests were astronomy, mathematics and the calculation of distances and the size of the Earth.*
(bottom centre) *Portolans were made from the mid-13th century by which time the magnetic compass was in widespread use. Coastlines were accurately drawn on sheepskin. One or two central wind-roses were joined by lines of various colours to 16 peripheral roses. All the lines were, therefore, compass bearings but their use is not known. Portolans continued to be made up to the end of the 16th century.*

(above left) *A 10th century Anglo-Saxon map reflects Roman cartography, a decline from Greek cartography of the 2nd century.*

(below left) *In about AD 150, Claud Ptolemy of Alexandria described how to make maps and gave the latitude and longitude of 8000 places. His world map showed seven climatic zones (climes). He made the length of the Mediterranean 62° instead of 42°. This error, and others, were not finally corrected until 1700. Translated into Latin in 1405, Ptolemy dominated European geography for most of three centuries.*

(above) *Delisle's map of 1700 marked a turning point. He restored the Mediterranean to its true length. Lower California became once more a* peninsula. *It had been shown as an island.*

(below) *In Tasman's map of New Holland (Australia), New Guinea is connected to Queensland. From the time of the Greeks Terra Australis had been an imaginary southern continent which proved to be the lands we now call Australia and Antarctica.*

(bottom) *This satellite map of Las Vegas and environs was prepared from Landsat imagery. The map is in false colour. Crops and grass are bright red; trees a duller red. The yellow patch at the eastern edge is red rock. This map is best used together with a normal map, preferably one of the same scale.*

THE KEY TO MAPS

A map is a representation of the whole Earth or some part of it. It, therefore, reduces the Earth to a size convenient for a given purpose. In order to relate the map to the real world a knowledge of that reduction in size (the scale) is required as well as a means of defining orientation and position relative to other places on the surface of the Earth.

MAP scale defines the relationship of distances on the ground to corresponding distances on the Earth. It can be expressed as 1 cm represents 50 km or as a representative fraction 1:5,000,000. The content of a map depends on the map scale. Orientation determines the way directions are defined. It ought to mean finding the direction of east, but the Pole Star and the magnetic compass have led to the north supplanting the east as the primary reference. It is customary to put north at the top of a map, but that has not always been the case. Muslim geographers placed south at the top and at various times, and in various places, east or west have been put there. The direction of north should be indicated when north is not at the top of a map.

Our system of geographical co-ordinates (latitude and longitude) dates back to the 2nd century BC. It is based on 360° in a circle with degrees sub-divided into minutes, seconds and fractions of a second. Co-ordinates can be given to any desired degree of accuracy e.g. 48°40'51" N, 35°51'35" E (latitude is normally given first).

Because such coordinates are unwieldy, rectangular grids are used. A simple system of letters and numerals will show that a point lies within the quadrangle A3, for example. A kilometric grid is a system of squares formed by lines spaced at 1 km or 10 km intervals. In grid references the eastings co-ordinate is given before the northings co-ordinate, the reverse of latitude and longitude.

Map projection is the means by which the graticule (the lines of latitude and longitude) are transferred from the round Earth to flat paper. That transfer cannot be made without introducing distortion. Each map projection is designed to meet certain limited criteria only. In no projection can all distances and all bearings be preserved as true.

Spot heights and contour lines show the elevation of the land with respect to mean sea-level. Contour lines join points with the same elevation. Hypsometric (layer) tints indicate the major character of the relief. Hill-shading simulates the shadows cast by an imaginary sun placed in the north-west so that the shadows falling to the south and east reveal the varying slopes of the terrain. Tonal relief produces an effect similar to the combination of hill-shading and hypsometric tints.

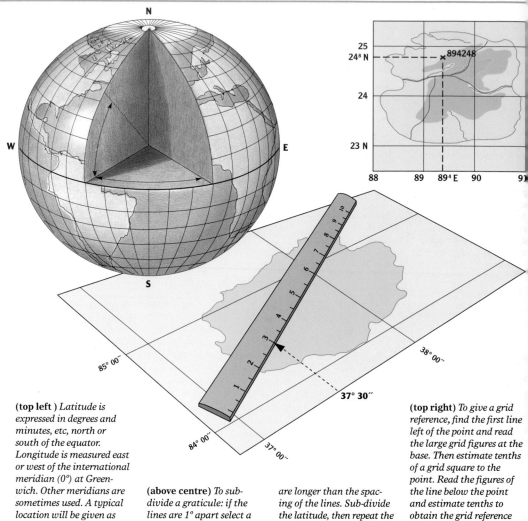

(top left) *Latitude is expressed in degrees and minutes, etc, north or south of the equator. Longitude is measured east or west of the international meridian (0°) at Greenwich. Other meridians are sometimes used. A typical location will be given as 33°18'N, 70°31'W.*

(above centre) *To sub-divide a graticule: if the lines are 1° apart select a scale on which 60 divisions are longer than the spacing of the lines. Sub-divide the latitude, then repeat the operation for the longitude.*

(top right) *To give a grid reference, find the first line left of the point and read the large grid figures at the base. Then estimate tenths of a grid square to the point. Read the figures of the line below the point and estimate tenths to obtain the grid reference 894248.*

(right) *Map projection is the means by which the lines of latitude and longitude on the globe are transferred to a flat sheet of paper. This is conveniently performed by way of an encircling cylinder or by a cone or plane which rests on the globe. The projection can be made to preserve scale at any point or areas or else distances and bearings from a selected point. No single projection can preserve any two of these three properties - conformality, equal-area, equidistance. Scale errors may be reduced by making the cylinder, cone or plane intersect the globe. The projection is then said to be secant conic, etc. The darker the colour on the map examples shown, the greater the level of distortion*

(below) *Polar Azimuthal projection allows comparison of the various projections. Parallels are equally spaced in the equidistant projection. They become more widely spaced as they near the equator in the stereographic and gnomonic, and more closely spaced in the equal-area and orthographic.*

tangent cylinder

cylindrical projection

tangent cone

conic projection

tangent plane

azimuthal projection

secant cone

conic projection

Field Sketch

Hill Drawing

Hachures

Hachured Map

Contours

Contours with layer tints

Contours with layer tints and hill shading

Tonal Relief

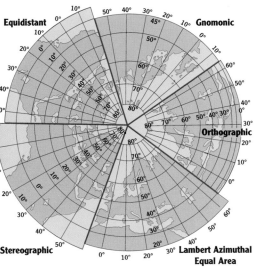

Equidistant

Gnomonic

Orthographic

Stereographic

Lambert Azimuthal Equal Area

(left) *Scale is the relationship of distances on a map compared to the corresponding distances on the surface of the Earth. Scale is indicated either by a 'bar scale' showing the length of kilometres, miles or nautical miles as represented on the map. Scale is also expressed as a 'representative fraction' e.g. 1/25,000 which means 1 cm on the map represents 250m on the ground (1 mm represents 25 m). A map at 1/6,000,000 is, compared with a map at 1/25,000 a small-scale map, the larger the number in the denominator, the smaller the scale. A degree of latitude is approximately equal to 111 km (about 69 miles or 60 nautical miles). Each meridian is therefore a kind of barscale which can be used to measure distances on a map or chart. Navigators in ships and aircraft make use of meridians in this way to plot distances.*

(right) *Relief representation. From the earliest times mountains have been shown on maps. For many centuries they were drawn in profile as seen from one direction, usually the south. Later viewed from above they were drawn as so-called 'hairy caterpillars'. By the end of the 18th century hachures were employed to give an accurate representation of slopes but they gave no indication of the elevation above sea-level. Spot heights provide such information for selected points. Contour lines also show elevations above sea-level. They replaced hachures from the mid-19th century onwards. Adding hypsometric (layer) tints aided the reading of relief. Hill-shading brings out the form of the land. A realistic depiction is obtained when contours, hypsometric tints and hill shading are used together on a map.*

THE USE OF MAPS

The scale and content of a map are determined by the purpose for which it was designed. Thematic maps are a valuable aid in the presentation of complex statistical data. Computers aid their production and increase their scope. Modern databases offer access to map data in digital form to an ever-widening range of users as well as providing new types of maps and related products.

MORE than 1000 years ago the Greeks distinguished geography from chorography. Geography was concerned with the whole world and chorography with only a local area. The word chorography has passed from our vocabulary but the word topography (to do with places) is used in its place. A topographic map contains details of the land surface appropriate for its scale. It is usually part of a map series whose sheets cover all or part of a country. It is typically the standard map of a national map series. Cadastral maps are maps of very large scale which serve the purposes of land ownership, valuation and taxation.

Scale is the dominant factor in determining the contents of maps. A compromise has to be made between what is desired and what can be achieved in the quantity of information included. Choice of scale and type of map is critical in the use of maps. Small scale maps are used for general planning but the need for larger scales becomes evident when more detailed information is needed of a specific area.

The English language, unlike other languages, makes a distinction between a chart and a map. In its original use, the word chart implied a nautical chart but aviators took over the word for their own navigational charts. Nautical charts pay little attention to the land. Aeronautical charts require much less topographical information than maps used on the ground. Elevations are in feet to conform with aircraft instrumentation. Originally aeronautical charts were of the same size as land maps but increases in the speed of aircraft necessitated a change in size. Many charts are four times their previous size to reduce the number handled by the navigator. Both at sea and in the air the nautical mile (1852m) is used for measuring distance.

Maps play an important part in recording and disseminating statistical information. Those maps which are specifically designed for a particular topic are known as thematic maps (maps with a theme). They range from simple diagrams to complex forms of the conventional map. Numerous special symbols have been invented in the presentation of statistics. Among the commonest terms are isopleths (lines of equal area), choropleths

(above) A topographic map at 1:100 000 scale has a wide range of uses, including study of terrain, land use, environmental planning, transportation and hydrological studies. Road widths and individual buildings are exaggerated. Other map detail is displaced.
(above right) A topographic map at a scale of 1:24 000 contains much more detail and has less exaggeration in the size of features than the map at 1:100 000. One mm represents 24m and more than 16 maps
are required to cover the same area of ground as a map at 1:100 000 scale.
(right) In a cadastral map at 1:1000 scale, map detail is drawn to scale without generalization. Maps of this type are used for recording land ownership, taxation and urban planning. Unless such maps are contoured, they are of limited use in engineering works.
(below) Isopleths, or isorithms, are lines which join points of the same numerical value. The maps use isopleths to show heat flow from the interior of the Earth.

(top right) Nautical charts show depths of water by soundings and bathymetric contours. Attention is paid to under-sea features, rocks, wrecks and other hazards and to lights, beacons and aids to navigation, including magnetic variation. The Mercator projection is used for sea charts.
(right) Relief, including man-made vertical obstructions, is of great importance in aeronautical charts. Navigation aids, aerodromes and other air information are shown at the expense of map detail not essential to air use. Elevations are in feet.
(top far right) Maps which show relief, like the one on the right, must, of necessity, be highly coloured and this
makes political information difficult to extract when it is included in the same map. For this reason a separate political map, like the one on the left, is required.
(centre right) Choropleth (measure per area) maps show statistical data by use of line patterns, or colour, applied to areas. Choropleth maps can be used to show density of population by country, state or province using data from a census.
(below right) Dot maps belong to the family of distribution maps. In a population map the dot represents a certain number of people. On the example shown, the density of dots gives an immediate impression of the distribution of world population.

(areas of equal measure) and isorithms (lines of equal number).

Dots, circles, squares, cubes and spheres, as well as an untold number of pictorial symbols, graphs and bar charts are among the items used for thematic maps.

Cartograms are widely used in conveying statistical information. As its name implies, a cartogram is neither a true map nor a diagram. Roman road maps were an early type of cartogram. Road distances were given, but true road alignments were ignored. Determining relative areas of countries by visual comparison on a map is extremely difficult. The areas can be readily compared when they are converted to rectangular form in a cartogram. Some ingenuity is required in arranging the rectangular figures to preserve their geographical position in relation to other countries similarly portrayed.

A popular form of symbol is the pie-chart or pie-graph. It can be used like any other circular symbol, the value of the quantity being in proportion to the area of the circle. Giving the pie-graph thickness can add another set of values.

The computer processing of economic and other types of statistical data led to a requirement for systems capable of handling geographic information by computer. Geographic information systems (GIS) were developed as a tool for handling vast amounts of geographical information and associated data to supply an infinite range of outputs which include graphs, diagrams, cartograms, tabular summaries and maps. Applying the same computer techniques to the production of the ordinary topographic map was not feasible until computers of sufficient power and capacity were available at low cost. A major obstacle was the unavoidable requirement for a very large database whose creation demanded a colossal amount of time and manpower. The benefits which flow from its creation are undeniable. Maps can be designed, produced and stored without going through the conventional processes of manual drafting and printing. Maps held in the computer can be displayed on a screen or can be transmitted from computer to computer. An infinite variety of data can be superimposed. The output can be a map or part of a map or a combination of parts of several maps extracted from the individual source maps which are stored in the database. Perspective views can be generated and construction and engineering problems solved on the computer screen. Such is the ultimate goal in the management of geographic information. That does not mean the end of the paper map. On the contrary, it promises a future in which an endless variety of paper maps can be produced to suit any purpose.

(far left) *A cartogram showing countries by area. In cartograms geographic shape is lost but the rectangular outline which replaces it allows areas to be readily compared. Economic and other statistical data are conveniently presented in this way.*
(below right) *Pie-charts or pie-graphs are used to present statistical data. When used on a map, the diameter of the circle can be made proportion-* *ate to the quantity involved.*
(below left) *Map data stored in a database can be viewed on a graphics screen in whole, or in part, in a range of scales. Any element can be selected for display. Information can be superimposed. Aerial photography or satellite imagery can be combined with the map data. Output can be in plotted form or as digital data.*

WORLD ATLAS

SYMBOLS

Relief

	Land contour
▲ 8848	Spot height (metres)
⋈	Pass
	Permanent ice cap

Feet	Relief	Metres
16404		5000
9843		3000
6562		2000
3281		1000
1640		500
656		200
0	Sea Level	
Land Dep. 656		200
13123		4000
22966		7000

Hydrography

	Submarine contour
▼11034	Ocean depth (metres)
(217)	Lake level
	Reef
	River
	Intermittent river
	Falls
	Dam
	Gorge
	Canal
	Lake/Reservoir
	Intermittent lake
	Marsh/Swamp

Communications

	Main railway (Tunnel)
⊕	Main airport
- - - -	Track

Road representation varies with the scale category.

═══	Principal road	} 1 : 1M-1 : 2½M
───	Other main road	

───	Principal road	} 1 : 2½M-1 : 7½M
───	Other main road	

───	Principal road	1 : 7½M or smaller

Administration

	International boundary
- - -	Undefined/Disputed international boundary
....	Cease-fire line
-·-·-	Internal division : First order
-··-··-	Internal division : Second order
▨ ◉ ▣ ◎ ▢ ▪	National capitals

Settlement

Each settlement is given a town stamp according to its relative importance and scale category.

	1:1M-1:2½M	1:2½M-1:7½M	1:7½M or smaller
▨	Major City	Major City	Major City
◉	City	City	City
◎	Large Town	Large Town	Large Town
⊙	Town	Town	Town
○	Small Town	Small Town	–
•	Village	–	–
	Urban area (1:1M-1:2½M only)		

The size of type used for each settlement is graded to correspond with the appropriate town stamp.

Other features

	Ancient monument
◡	Oasis
	National Park
▲	Oil field
Δ	Gas field
-·-·-	Oil/Gas pipeline

Lettering

Various styles of lettering are used-each one representing a different type of feature.

ALPS	Physical feature	KENYA	Country name
Red Sea	Hydrographic feature	IOWA	Internal division
Paris	Settlement name	*(Fr.)*	Territorial administration

THE WORLD : Political

ARCTIC OCEAN

GREENLAND
(Den.)

Godthåb

Reykjavík ICELAND

Faroe Is.
(Den.)

U.S.A.
ALASKA

Arctic Circle

CANADA

Edmonton

Vancouver •Winnipeg

Seattle

Ottawa Montreal

Chicago Detroit •Toronto• Boston

UNITED STATES Pittsburgh New York

San Francisco •St. Louis Philadelphia

OF AMERICA Washington

Los Angeles

Dallas

Houston

Miami

Monterrey Nassau

BAHAMAS

Guadalajara Havana CUBA

Mexico
City

JAMAICA HAITI DOMINICAN
REP.

PUERTO
RICO

BELIZE S.K. ANTIGUA

Belmopan DOMINICA

Guatemala City Honduras Kingston ST. LUCIA

GUAT B.A.

EL SALVADOR Tegucigalpa S.V. GR

Managua NICARAGUA Caracas TRINIDAD

COSTA San José Panama & TOBAGO

RICA PANAMA City VENEZUELA

Bogotá Georgetown

Paramaribo

COLOMBIA Cayenne

GUIANA(Fr.)

Quito SURINAM

ECUADOR

PERU

BRAZIL Recife

Lima

La Paz Brasília

BOLIVIA

Sucre Belo Horizonte

PARAGUAY Rio de Janeiro

Asunción São Paulo

CHILE

ARGENTINA

URUGUAY

Santiago Buenos Montevideo

Aires

NORTH

ATLANTIC

OCEAN

Bermuda
(U.K.)

UNITED DEN
KINGDOM

REP. OF Dublin Ams
IRELAND

London

Brussels

Paris Be

FRANC

PORTUGAL

Azores Lisbon SPAIN Madrid

(Port.)

Rabat Algiers

MOROCCO M

Canary Is. ALGERI

(Sp.)

MAURITANIA MALI

Nouakchott

CAPE VERDE Dakar Bamako BURKINA Niar

SENEGAL Ouagadou

GAMBIA GUINEA N

Bissau Conakry COTE Abu

G.B. Freetown D'IVOIRE GHAN TOGO

SIERRA LEONE Yamoussoukro Mala

Monrovia IVORY Accra Lomé

LIBERIA COAST Porto-Novo

S.

Li

Ascension I.
(U.K.)

St. Helena
(U.K.)

SOUTH

ATLANTIC

Tristan da Cunha (U.K.)

Gough I. (U.K.)

OCEAN

PACIFIC

OCEAN

KIRIBATI

Marquesas Is.
(Fr.)

Samoa
(U.S.A.)

Cook Is. Tahiti

(N.Z.) Society Is.

(Fr.)

Tuamotu Archipelago

Pitcairn Is.
(U.K.)

Easter I.
(Chile)

Galapagos Is.
(Ec.)

Equator

Tropic of Cancer

Tropic of Capricorn

Hawaiian Is.
(U.S.A.)

Falkland Is.
(U.K.)

South Georgia
(U.K.)

Chilean Claim Argentinian Claim

Antarctic Circle

BRITISH ANTARCTIC TERRITORY NORWEG

Anta

A.: ANDORRA
ALB.: ALBANIA
AR.: ARMENIA
AUS.: AUSTRIA
AZ.: AZERBAIJAN
B.: BELGIUM
B.-H.: BOSNIA-HERZEGOVINA
BA.: BARBADOS
BANGLA.: BANGLADESH
BULG.: BULGARIA
C.: CROATIA
CAMB.: CAMBODIA
C.R.: CZECH REPUBLIC
E.: ESTONIA
EQ.G.: EQUATORIAL GUINEA
G.: GEORGIA
G.B.: GUINEA BISSAU
GERM.: GERMANY
GR.: GRENADA
GUAT: GUATEMALA
H.: HUNGARY
KYRG.: KYRGYZSTAN
L.: LUXEMBOURG
LA.: LATVIA
LEB.: LEBANON
LI.: LIECHTENSTEIN
LIT.: LITHUANIA
M.: MONACO
MA.: MALTA
MAC.: MACEDONIA
MOL.: MOLDOVA
NETH.: NETHERLANDS
R.F.: RUSSIAN FEDERATION

S.: SWITZERLAND
SA.: SLOVAKIA
S.K.: ST. KITTS-NEVIS
SL.: SLOVENIA
S.M.: SAN MARINO
S.T.: SÃO TOME & PRINCIPE
S.V.: ST. VINCENT AND THE GRENADINES
T.: TURKEY (in Europe)
TAJ.: TAJIKISTAN
U.A.E.: UNITED ARAB EMIRATES
UZBEK.: UZBEKISTAN
V.C.: VATICAN CITY
YUGO.: YUGOSLAVIA

ARCTIC OCEAN

Spitsbergen
(Nor.)

Arctic Circle

FINLAND
Helsinki
Tallinn
St. Petersburg
Riga
stholm
enhagen
clin
Minsk
Moscow
Warsaw
BELARUS
POLAND
Kiev
UKRAINE
Bratislava
Budapest
ROMANIA
Kharkov
B.-H. Belgrade
BULG.
Bucharest
Sofia
Black Sea
GREECE
Athens
Ankara
TURKEY
CYPRUS
LEB.
SYRIA
Damascus
ean Sea
ISRAEL
Jerusalem
JORDAN
Amman
IRAQ
Baghdad
Cairo
EGYPT
KUWAIT
SAUDI
Riyadh
QATAR
ARABIA
BAHRAIN
IBYA
CHAD
SUDAN
Khartoum
N'Djamena
ENTRAL AFRICAN
REPUBLIC
ngui
ERIT-
REA
Sana
YEMEN
Asmara
DJIBOUTI
ETHIOPIA
Addis Ababa
SOMALI REPUBLIC
ZAIRE
UGANDA
KENYA
Kampala
Nairobi
RWANDA
Kigali
Brazzaville
BURUNDI
Bujumbura
TANZANIA
Dodoma
Kinshasa
Dar es Salaam
unde
Luanda
NGOLA
MALAWI
ZAMBIA
Lilongwe
Lusaka
Harare
ZIM-
BABWE
MOZAMBIQUE
dhoek
BOTSWANA
MIBIA
Gaborone
Pretoria
Maputo
Johannesburg
WAZILAND
REP.
Mbabane
OF
LESOTHO
Maseru
SOUTH AFRICA
Town

Yekaterinburg
Nizhniy
Novgorod
Omsk
Novosibirsk
Samara

RUSSIAN FEDERATION

KAZAKHSTAN

Ulan Bator

MONGOLIA

Harbin

Shenyang

N.KOREA
Pyongyang
Beijing
(Peking)
Tientsin
Dalian
S.KOREA
Seoul

JAPAN
Tokyo

Osaka

Caspian Sea
Tbilisi
AZ.
Baku
Yerevan
TURKMENISTAN
Ashkhabad
UZBEK.
Tashkent
Alma Ata
Bishkek
KYRG.
TAJ.
Dushanbe
Tehrān

IRAN

AFGHAN-
ISTAN
Kabul

JAMMU &
KASHMIR
Islamabad

PAKISTAN
Lahore

Delhi

Muscat
OMAN

CHINA

Lanchow

Sian

Chengdu

Chungking

Kunming

Wuhan

Nanking

Shanghai

Canton

Taipei

TAIWAN

Kathmandu
NEPAL
BHUTAN

INDIA
Calcutta
BANGLA
Dacca

Bombay

Madras

SRI
LANKA
Colombo

MALDIVES

Hanoi

HONG KONG (U.K.)

Rangoon

MYANMAR
(BURMA)

THAILAND
Bangkok

Vientiane

CAMB.
Phnom
Penh

Ho Chi
Minh City

PACIFIC

Manila
PHILIPPINES

Bonin Is.
(Japan)

Aleutian Islands
(U.S.A.)

International Date Line

Tropic of Cancer

Northern Mariana
Islands
(U.S.A.)

FED. STATES OF MICRONESIA

MARSHALL ISLANDS

PALAU
(BELAU)

Caroline
Islands

OCEAN

MALAYSIA
BRUNEI

Kuala Lumpur
SINGAPORE

INDONESIA

SEYCHELLES

INDIAN

Jakarta

OCEAN

COMOROS

Cocos Is.
(Aus.)

Christmas I.
(Aus.)

MADAGASCAR
Antananarivo

MAURITIUS

PAPUA
NEW
GUINEA

Port
Moresby

NAURU

Equator

KIRIBATI

SOLOMON
ISLANDS

TUVALU

Wallis Is.
(Fr.)
W.
SAMOA

VANUATU

New
Caledonia
(Fr.)

FIJI

TONGA

Tropic of Capricorn

AUSTRALIA

Brisbane

Perth

Adelaide

Sydney
Canberra

Melbourne

Auckland

NEW
ZEALAND
Wellington

Prince Edward Is.
(R.S.A.)

Kerguelen Is.
(Fr.)

SOUTHERN

OCEAN

Note: Under the Antarctic
Treaty of 1959 all territorial
claims in the region were held in
abeyance in the interest of
international cooperation for scientific
purposes. The treaty binds the 12 original,
and all subsequent signatory states to use the
region solely for peaceful purposes and scientific
research. A concensus is being sought with regard
to mineral rights and exploitation before the Treaty
expires.

Antarctic Circle

PENDENCY

AUSTRALIAN ANTARCTIC TERRITORY

TERRE ADÉLIE (Fr.)

AUSTRALIAN ANTARCTIC
TERRITORY

ROSS
DEPENDENCY
(N.Z.)

tica

Equatorial Scale 1:80 000 000

| 0 | 500 | 1000 | 1500 | 2000 | 2500 Miles |

| 0 | 1000 | 2000 | 3000 | 4000 Kms. |

Flat Polar Equal Area Projection

© Collins

THE WORLD : Physical

ARCTIC OCEAN

Queen Elizabeth Islands
Ellesmere Island
Greenland
Beaufort Sea
Banks I.
Victoria Island
Baffin Bay
Baffin Island
Norwe...
Davis Strait
Denmark Strait
Arctic Circle
Iceland
Sea
Brooks Range
Yukon
Alaska Range
5194
Mt. McKinley
Gulf of Alaska
Aleutian Is.
Mackenzie
Gt. Bear Lake
Gt. Slave Lake
Peace
Hudson Bay
Canadian Shield
K. Farvel
Uummannarsuaq
(C. Farewell)
British Isles
Nor...
Se...
Coast Mts.
Vancouver I.
Columbia
Cascade Range
NORTH AMERICA
Saskatchewan
Nelson
L. Winnipeg
Great Lakes
St. Lawrence
Newfoundland
Basin
N.E. Atlantic Basin
Seine
Loire
Mt. Bla...
Great Basin
Rocky Mts.
Great Plains
Missouri
Arkansas
Ohio
Mississippi
Appalachian Mts
C. Sable
Bermuda
North
Western
Atlantic
MID ATLANTIC RIDGE
Atlas Mts.
Colorado
Sierra Madre Occidental
Rio Grande
Tropic of Cancer
C. San Lucas
Hawaiian Islands
Gulf of Mexico
Bahama Is.
Cuba
Puerto Rico Trench
8528
A T L A N T I C
North
Islas Canarias
Saha...
A F...
P O L Y N E S I A
PACIFIC
Kiritimati (Christmas I.)
Line Islands
Equator
Sierra Madre Oriental
Guatemala Trench
Caribbean Sea
Lesser Antilles
Cape Verde Is.
Cape Verde Basin
O C E A N
Senegal
Fouta Djalon
Su...
Gulf of Guinea
Is. Galapagos
Orinoco
Llanos
Negro
Guiana Highlands
Amazonas (Amazon)
SOUTH
Madeira
Tapajós
Cabo de São Roque
Ascension
Brazilian Basin
St. Helena
Îles Marquises (Marquesas Is.)
Pacific Ridge
Îles Tuamotu
Selvas
São Francisco
Îles de la Société (Society Is.)
Cook Is.
Tropic of Capricorn
Peru Basin
AMERICA
Andes
Planalto Brasil
South Eastern Atlan...
MID ATLANTIC RIDGE
Walvis Ridge
East Pacific Ridge
Isla de Pascua (Easter I.)
Peru-Chile Trench
8066
Paraguay
P. Paraná
Bromley Plateau
Tristan da Cunha
Aconcagua 6960
Pampas
Argentine Basin
Gough I.
South Western Pacific Basin
Patagonia
Falkland Is.
Atlantic - Antarcti...
Pacific-Antarctic Ridge
C. de Hornos (C. Horn)
Tierra del Fuego
Scotia Sea
South Georgia
Antarctic Circle
Pacific - Antarctic Basin
South Shetland Is.
Atlantic...
Amundsen Sea
Bellingshausen Sea
Antarctic Peninsula
Weddell Sea
A N T A R...

Relief

Feet		Metres
16 404		5000
9 843		3000
6 562		2000
3 281		1000
1 640		500
656		200
0		Sea Level
Land Dep.		
656		200
13 123		4000
22 966		7000

ARCTIC OCEAN

bergen
Zemlya
Frantsa Iosifa
Novaya
Zemlya
Severnaya
Zemlya
Novosibirskiye
Ostrova

Barents Sea
Karskoye More
More
Laptevykh
Vostochno
Sibirskoye More

Nordkapp
(N. Cape)

inavia
Baltic
Shield
Zapadno
Siberia
Bering Sea
Aleutian
Basin

Uralskiy Khr.
(Ural Mts.)
Ob
Yenisey
Sev. Dvina
Sibirskaya
ASIA
Sea of
Okhotsk
Poluostrov
Kamchatka
Aleutian Trench
7822

tic
North
European
Plain
Irtysh
Ob
Ravnina
(W. Siberian Plain)
Altai
Lena
Amur
Sakhalin
Hokkaidō
10542

ROPE
Drina
Don
Volga
Aral
Sea
(Aralskoye
More)
Oz. Balkhash
Oz. Baykal
Gobi
Dongbei
Pingyuan
(Manchurian
Plain)
Kuril Trench
Sea of
Japan
40°

Danube
Stara
Planina
Black Sea
Caucasus
Caspian Sea
Syr Darya
Tian Shan
Tarim
Pendi
Huang He
Huabei
Pingyuan
(N China Plain)
Yellow
Sea
Honshū
Japan Trench
10500

ranean Sea
Dicle (Tigris)
Zagros Mts.
Kunlun Shan
Qing Zang Gaoyuan
(Tibetan Plateau)
Kyūshū

Amu Darya
Hindu Kush
Chang Jiang
Kūh-e
Al Furāt (Euphrates)
The Gulf
Indus
Himalaya
8848
Mt. Everest
Yungui
Gaoyuan
East
China
Sea
Tropic of Cancer
20°

Tibesti
Red Sea
Arabia
Thar
Desert
Brahmaputra
Ganga (Ganges)
Salween
Taiwan
PACIFIC

L. Chad
n
Gulf of Aden
Arabian
Sea
Deccan
Bay of
Bengal
Andaman Is.
South
China
Sea
Mariana Trench

ICA
Ethiopian
Highlands
Arabian
Basin
Sri
Lanka
Nicobar Is.
Philippines
11034
M
I
C
R
O
N
Marshall
Is.

Ubangi
Zaïre
Basin
Somali
Basin
Carlsberg
Maldive
Maldive Ridge
Philippine Trench
10497
Caroline Is.
E
S
I
A
Equator
0°

Kasai
Lake
Victoria
5895
Kilimanjaro
Seychelles
INDIAN
Mid-
Sumatera
(Sumatra)
Borneo
Sulawesi
(Celebes)
Puncak Jaya
5030
New Guinea
Solomon Is.
Gilbert Is.

Bié
Plateau
Rift Valley
L. Malawi
Zambezi
Tanganika
OCEAN
MID-
Ridge
West
Indian
Jawa
(Java)
Christmas I.
Timor
Timor
Sea
Arafura Sea
A
U
S
T
R
A
L
A
S
I
A
Coral Sea
Vanuatu
North Fiji
Basin
Samoa
Is.
Fiji
Is.

Limpopo
Madagascar
Mozambique Channel
Mauritius
Réunion
Australian
Basin
Cocos Is.
Great
Sandy Desert
Great
Artesian
Basin
Nouvelle Calédonie
(New Caledonia)
Tropic of Capricorn
South Fiji
Basin
10882
Tonga Is.
Tonga Trench
20°

Kalahari
Desert
Vaal
Drakensberg
Orange
Natal Basin
Mauritius
Basin
Basin
INDIAN
Australia
L. Eyre
Great Dividing Range
Tasman
Sea

C. of Good Hope
Cape
Rise
Kerguelen
Basin
Île Amsterdam
RIDGE
C. Leeuwin
Great
Australian
Bight
South Australian
Basin
Murray
Darling
Chatham
Is.
40°

Agulhas
Basin
Prince Edward-
Crozet Ridge
Tasmania
New
Zealand

Prince Edward Is.
Îles Crozet
Îles de Kerguelen
SOUTHERN OCEAN

ge
Heard I.
Indian - Antarctic Ridge

dian - Antarctic Basin
Eastern Indian - Antarctic Basin
60°

Antarctic Circle

Ross
Sea

Equatorial Scale 1:80 000 000

| 0 | 500 | 1000 | 1500 | 2000 | 2500 Miles |

| 0 | 1000 | 2000 | 3000 | 4000 Kms. |

Flat Polar Equal Area Projection

80°

CTICA

20° 40° 60° 80° 100° 120° 140° 160° 180°

© Collins ◇ Longman Atlases Cbi

5

ARCTIC OCEAN

North America

NORTH ATLANTIC OCEAN

Spitsbergen (Nor.)

Barents Sea

Novaya Zemlya (Rus. Fed.)

Denmark Strait

Arctic Circle

ICELAND

Reykjavik

Faeroes (Den.)

NORWAY

SWEDEN

FINLAND

Helsinki

St. Petersburg (Leningrad)

RUSSIAN FEDERATION

Bergen

Oslo Stockholm

Tallinn ESTONIA

Nizhniy Novgorod

Moscow

North Sea

Gothenburg

Riga LATVIA

Samara

REP. OF IRE.

Dublin UNITED KINGDOM

Århus DENMARK

Copenhagen

LITHUANIA

Vilnius

Birmingham

Hamburg Berlin

POLAND

Minsk

Kharkov

London

NETH. Amsterdam

Warsaw

BELARUS (BELORUSSIA)

Kiev

Bay of Biscay

Brussels LUX.

Bonn Leipzig GERMANY

Łódź

Prague CZ.R. Brno

UKRAINE

Paris

Zürich

Vienna Bratislava SLOVAKIA

Azores (Port.)

FRANCE

Bern SW. L. AUSTRIA HUNGARY Budapest

MOLDOVA Kishinev

Lyon

Ljubljana M. SLOV. Milan Zagreb CRO. B.-H.

Odessa

Oporto

AN.

ITALY S.M.

Belgrade ROMANIA Bucharest

Black Sea

Caspian Sea

Lisbon

Madrid

SPAIN

Barcelona

Corsica (Fr.)

Rome V.C.

Sarajevo Y.U.G.

Skopje MAC. Sofia BULGARIA

Istanbul

PORTUGAL

Tirana ALB. Salonika

T.

Madeira (Port.)

Balearic Is. (Sp.)

Sardinia (It.)

GREECE Athens

Canary Islands (Sp.)

Tropic of Cancer

Sicily MALTA

Mediterranean Sea

Crete

20°

10°

Africa

South America

SOUTH ATLANTIC OCEAN

Equator

10°

20° Tropic of Capricorn

30°

ALB.: ALBANIA
AN.: ANDORRA
B.: BELGIUM
B.-H.: BOSNIA-
        HERZEGOVINA
CRO.: CROATIA
CZ.R.: CZECH REPUBLIC
L.: LIECHTENSTEIN
LUX.: LUXEMBOURG
M.: MONACO
MAC.: MACEDONIA
NETH. NETHERLANDS
REP. OF IRE.: REPUBLIC OF IRELAND
SLOV.: SLOVENIA
S.M.: SAN MARINO
SW.: SWITZERLAND
T.: TURKEY (in Europe)
V.C.: VATICAN CITY

EUROPE

COUNTRY	PAGE
ALBANIA	34
ANDORRA	20
AUSTRIA	36; 39; 30-31
BELARUS (BELORUSSIA)	37; 44
BELGIUM	16
BOSNIA-HERZEGOVINA	31
BULGARIA	23; 24
CROATIA	31
CZECH REPUBLIC	36-37; 38-39
DENMARK	42-43
ESTONIA	44
FINLAND	44; 40-41
FRANCE	17; 18-19; 20-21
GERMANY	38-39
GREECE	34-35
HUNGARY	36-37; 31
ICELAND	40
IRELAND, REPUBLIC OF	15
ITALY	28-29; 30-31; 32-33
LATVIA	44; 41
LIECHTENSTEIN	39
LITHUANIA	44; 41
LUXEMBOURG	16
MACEDONIA	34
MALTA	28
MOLDOVA (MOLDAVIA)	37
MONACO	21
NETHERLANDS	16
NORWAY	40-41; 42-43
POLAND	36-37
PORTUGAL	26-27
ROMANIA	37
RUSSIAN FEDERATION (IN EUROPE)	44-45; 8-9
SAN MARINO	30
SLOVENIA	31
SLOVAKIA	36-37
SPAIN	24; 25; 26-27
SWEDEN	40-41; 42-43
SWITZERLAND	39
UKRAINE	44-45; 37
UNITED KINGDOM	10-11; 12-13; 14-15
YUGOSLAVIA	28-29; 30-31; 34

EUROPE

OCEAN
40'N
45°
50°
55°
60°
65°
70°
75°
80°

Kolskiy
Poluostrov
Beloye More (White Sea)
Narvan Mar
Narodnaya
1894
Ural'skiy
Zapadno-
Sibirskaya
Ravnina
(West Siberian Plain)
Surgut
Ob
Novosibirsk
Novokuznetsk

Murmansk
Kandalaksha
Pechora
Telpos Iz
1617
Ob
Barnaul

Mezen
Berezovo

rovsk
Onega
Arkhangel'sk
Glotova
Ukhta
Troitsko-Pechorsk
Tobol'sk
Tara
Barabinsk
Slavgorod

RUSSIAN
Syktyvkar
FEDERATION
Tyumen'
Omsk
Pavlodar

ozhskoye
Ozero
Petrozavodsk
Sev. Dvina
Vychegda
Kotlas
Murashi
Kamskoye
Vdkhr.
Krasnokamsk
Nizhniy Tagil
Asbest
Pervoural'sk
Serov
Ishim
Petropavlovsk
Kokshetau
Karkaralinsk
Semipalatinsk

kt-Peterburg
(Leningrad)
Vologda
Cherepovets
Rybinskoye
Vdkhr.
Vyatka
Perm
Yekaterinburg
(Sverdlovsk)
Kyshtym
Chelyabinsk
Kopeysk
Kurgan
Kustanay
Makinsk
Atbasar
Akmola
Karaganda

orod
Rybinsk
Kostroma
Kineshma
Yoshkar Ola
Izhevsk
Sarapul
Nizhnekamskoye
Vdkhr.
Zlatoust
Troitsk
Balkhash

Valdayskaya
Vozvyshennost
Vyshniy-
Volochek
Yaroslavl
Ivanovo
Kovrov
Nizhniy
Novgorod
(Gor'kiy)
Cheboksary
Kazan
Kama
Ufa
Magnitogorsk
Sterlitamak
Oz.
Tengiz
Mointy
Ozero
Balkhash

Velikiye-Luki
Tver
Volga
Vladimir
Dzerzhinsk
Gorkovskoye
Vdkhr.
Kuybyshevskoye
Vdkhr.
Simbirsk
Tol'yatti
Orsk
KAZAKHSTAN
Step
Stepp
45°

Moskva
(Moscow)
Flektrostal
Oka
Saransk
Penza
Samara
(Kuybyshev)
Orenburg
Ural
Turgay
Karsakpay
Kirgiziya
Kzyl Orda
Kzyl
Kargan

Vitebsk
Serpukhov
Kolomna
Ryazan
Syzran
Privolzhskaya
Vozvyshennost
Aktyubinsk
Oktyab'sk
Irgiz
Irgiz
Aralsk (Kirgiz
Steppe)

Mogilev
Smolensk
Kaluga
Tula
Novomoskovsk
Tambov
Balashov
Saratov
Ural'sk
Makat
Novokazalinsk
Syr Darya

RUS-
SIA)
Bobruysk
Sredne
Russkaya
Bryansk
Orel
Yelets
Lipetsk
Pokrovsk
Volgogradskoye
Vdkhr.
Caspian Depression
(Prikaspiyskaya
Nizmennost')
Aral
Sea
(Aral'skoye More)
Kzyl
Shymkent
Chirchik
Tashkent
(Toshkent)

Gomel
Chernigov
Kursk
Belgorod
Don
Volgograd
Atyrau
Peski Kyzylkum
Aralsk

Kiyev
(Kiev)
Sumy
Vozvyshennost
Kharkov
Sev. Donets
Tsimlyanskoye
Vdkhr.
Volga
Astrakhan
Ustyurt
Plateau
UZBEKISTAN
Samarkand

NE
Vinnitsa
Poltava
Dnepr (Dnieper)
Dnepropetrovsk
Gorlovka
Lugansk
Shakhty
Novocherkassk
Pov.
Mangyshlak
Zaliv
Kara-
Bogaz
Gol
Tashauz
Amu
Bukhara
Darya

Yuzhnyy
Bug
Kremenchug
Kirovograd
Dneprodzerzhinsk
Zaporozhye
Donetsk
Makeyevka
Rostov
Aktau
Navoi
Peski

DOVA
Krivoy Rog
Nikolayev
Melitopol
Taganrog
Kuma
Peski
Karakumy
Chardzhou
Darya

Kishinev
Odessa
Kherson
Sea of
Azov
(Azovskoye More)
Krasnodar
Stavropol
Armavir
Pyatigorsk
Makhachkala
TURKMENISTAN

Balti
Simferopol
Krym
(Crimea)
Kerch
CASPIAN
Ashkhabad

DOVA
Yalta
Novorossiysk
Tuapse
Sochi
Caucasus
Kavkaz
Groznyy
Vladikavkaz
Derbent
SEA
(-28)
Baku
Krasnovodsk

Sevastopol'
Elbrus
5633
Kazbek
5043
Sukhumi
Mashhad

BLACK SEA
2211
Batumi
Kutaisi
GEORGIA
Tbilisi
Gyandzha
995
Bojnurd
Herat

Varna
Sinop
Leninakan
Oz.
Sevan
AZERBAIJAN
Ozel Owzan
AFGHAN-
ISTAN

Burgas
Samsun
Trabzon
ARMENIA
Ardabil
Rasht
Emamshahr

Istanbul
Bog.
Kastamonu
Kuzey Anadolu Dağları
Erzurum
Yerevan
Ağrı Dağı
5165
Tabriz
Reshteh-ye Kūhhā-ye Alborz
(Elburz Mts)
Dara[5601]
Gorgan
Damavand
Dasht-e Kavir

Marmara
Denizi
Uskudar
Zonguldak
Sivas
Van
Gölü
Daryacheh-ye
Orumiyeh
(L. Urmia)
Tehran
IRAN
Dasht-e Lut

Bursa
Ankara
Kizil
Kayseri
TURKEY
Malatya
Diyarbakir
Qom
Kashan
Dasht-e Lut

Eskisehir
20°
Tuz
Gölü
Al Mawsil
Irbil
Hamadan
3356
Esfahan
(Isfahan)
Kerman

Izmir
Konya
Toros Dağları
Adana
Iskenderun
Gaziantep
Kirkuk
Kūhhā-ye
Zagros
(Zagros Mts)
Yazd

Aydin
Antalya
Mersin
Al-Lādhiqiyah
SYRIA
Nahr al Furāt
(Euphrates)
Ar Ramādi
IRAQ
Kermanshah
4548
Shiraz

Rhodes
SEA
CYPRUS
Levkosia
(Nicosia)
LEBANON
Tarabulus
Hamāh
Hims
Baghdad
Dijlah (Tigris)
Ahwaz

Scale 1:16 000 000
0   100   200   300   400   500 Miles
0 100 200 300 400 500 600 700 800 Kms
Conic Projection

© Collins o Longman Atlases Cb

9

BRITISH ISLES

ENGLAND AND WALES

Scale 1:2 000 000

Lambert Conformal Conic Projection

50 Miles
80 Kms.

Relief									
Metres	1000	500	200	100	Sea Level	20	50	100	200
Feet	3281	1640	656	328	0	66	164	328	656

NORTH SEA

IRISH SEA

NORTHERN IRELAND

12

SCOTLAND

IRELAND

THE LOW COUNTRIES

Scale 1:2 000 000

0 10 20 30 40 50 60 Miles

0 20 40 60 80 Kms.

Conic Projection

Relief

Feet	Metres
16 404	5000
9843	3000
6562	2000
3281	1000
1640	500
656	200
0	Sea Level
Land Dep.	
656	200
13 123	4000
22 966	7000

NORTH SEA

NETHERLANDS

BELGIUM

GERMANY

FRANCE

LUXEMBOURG

Waddeneilanden

Waddenzee

IJsselmeer

NOORD HOLLAND

ZUID HOLLAND

FLEVOLAND

Amsterdam

's Gravenhage (The Hague)

Rotterdam

Utrecht

GELDERLAND

OVERIJSSEL

DRENTHE

FRIESLAND

GRONINGEN

NIEDERSACHSEN

UTRECHT

NOORD BRABANT

LIMBURG

ZEELAND

Eindhoven

Antwerpen (Antwerp)

Bruxelles Brussel (Brussels)

VLAANDEREN

WEST VLAANDEREN

OOST VLAANDEREN

BRABANT

HAINAUT

NAMUR

LIÈGE

LIMBURG

Brugge

Gent

Liège

Namur

Charleroi

Maastricht

Aachen

Düsseldorf

Köln (Cologne)

Bonn

Dortmund

Essen

Duisburg

NORDRHEIN-WESTFALEN

RHEINLAND-PFALZ

SAARLAND

Trier

Luxembourg

ARDENNE

Ardennes

Eifel

Hunsrück

PICARDIE

CHAMPAGNE

ARTOIS

NORD

Lille

© Collins · Longman Atlases Cbiii

FRANCE

NORTHERN FRANCE

UNITED KINGDOM

Bude Bay, Holsworthy, North Tawton, Tiverton, Ilminster, Yeovil, Sturminster, Southampton, Eastleigh, WEST SUSSEX, Haywards Heath, EAST SUSSEX, Battle, Rye, Dungeness

Boscastle, Bude, Okehampton, Crewkerne, Chard, Axminster, DORSET, Blandford Forum, New Forest, Fareham, Havant, Chichester, South Downs, Borges Hill, Lewes, Hailsham

Pt. Isaac Bay, Bodmin Moor, DEVON, Crediton, Honiton, Dorchester, Poole, Lyndhurst, Portsmouth, Hove, Brighton, Bexhill, Hastings, Eastbourne

Padstow, Launceston, Dartmoor Forest, Tavistock, Chudleigh, Lyme Regis, Bournemouth, Ryde, Bognor Regis, Worthing, Beachy Head

Newquay, CORNWALL, Bodmin, Newton Abbot, Dawlish, Teignmouth, Sidmouth, Weymouth, Swanage, ISLE OF WIGHT, Ventnor, Selsey Bill

Perranporth, St. Austell, Liskeard, Looe, Torquay, Berry Hd., Brixham, Lyme Bay, Abbotsbury, The Needles, Newport, Sandown, St. Catherine's Point

St. Ives, Redruth, Truro, Fowey, Polperro, Dartmouth, Kingsbridge, Bill of Portland, Durlston Hd.

Penzance, Camborne, Helston, Dodman Pt., Rame Hd., Salcombe, Start Pt.

Lands End, Mount's Bay, Falmouth, Lizard Pt.

English Channel

CHANNEL ISLANDS

Alderney, Guernsey, St. Martin, St. Peter Port, Sark, Jersey, St. Helier, St. Mary

Cap de La Hague, St. Pierre-Église, Pointe de Barfleur, Barfleur, Cap d'Antifer, Étretat, Fécamp, St. Valéry, Dieppe, Le Tréport

Beaumont, Équeurdreville, Octeville, Cherbourg, Quettehou, Valognes, Baie de la Seine, Le Havre, Honfleur, Rouen, SEINE-MARITIME

Délette, Les Pieux, Briquebec, Sainte Mère-Église, Carentan, Isigny, Port-en-Bessin, Arromanches, Deauville, Trouville, Le Grand-Quevilly, Pont-Audemer

Barneville, La Haye-du-Puits, Bayeux, Douvres, Ouistreham, Villers-sur-Mer, Pont-l'Évêque, Cormeilles, Bourg-Achard, HAUTE-NORMANDIE

Coutances, Périers, Bessay, Caen, Troarn, Lisieux, Louviers, Le Roger, EURE, Évreux, Conches, Brionne

Regnéville, St. Lô, Villers-Bocage, Thury-Harcourt, Mézidon, Livarot, Breteuil-sur-Iton, Nonancourt

Granville, Bréhal, Villedieu, Condé-sur-Noireau, Falaise, Trun, Vimoutiers, L'Aigle, Verneuil

Sartilly, Brécey, MANCHE, Vire, Flers, Collines de Normandie, Argentan, Sées, La Ferté-Vidame

Avranches, Mortain, Domfront, La Ferté-Macé, Les Avaloirs, Mortagne, Tourouvre

Pontorson, St. Hilaire-du-Harcouët, ORNE, Écouché, Carrouges, Pré-en-Pail, Mamers, Bellême

Dol-de-Bretagne, Dinan, Combourg, Antrain, Fougères, Mayenne, Villaines, La Ferté-Bernard, La Loupe

Golfe de St. Malo, St. Malo, Cancale, Dinard, Pleurtuit, Matignon

Perros-Guirec, Sillon de Talbert, Roscoff, Lannion, Tréguier, Paimpol, Plouha, Étables, Pléneuf, Lamballe, Jugon, Broons, Quesnon, Mayenne

Plouescat, St. Pol-de-Léon, Morlaix, Guingamp, Quintin, Moncontour, Montfort-sur-Meu, Montauban, Vitré, Laval

Île d'Ouessant (Ushant), St. Renan, Landivisiau, Callac, Corlay, Loudéac, Ménéac, Montfort, Rennes, Argentré, MAYENNE, Argentré, SARTHE, Le Mans

Brest, Sizun, Monts d'Arrée, Carhaix, Plouguenast, Josselin, ILLE-ET-VILAINE, Janzé, La Guerche-de-Bretagne, Meslay-du-Maine, Sablé-sur-Sarthe, Château-du-Loir

FINISTÈRE, Montagne Noire, Brest-Nantes Canal, Gourin, Pontivy, Guichen, Maure-de-Bretagne, Bain-de-Bretagne, Craon, Château-Gontier, La Flèche, La Suze

Le Conquet, Pointe de Camaret-sur-Mer, Sainte-Mathieu, Crozon, Châteaulin, Huelgoat, Guémené-sur-Scorff, Ploërmel, Malestroit, Grand-Fougeray, Nozay, Candé, Le Lion-d'Angers, Segré, Bougon, Baugé

Iroise, Douarnenez, Pont-Croix, Quimper, Rosporden, Le Faouët, Baud, Blavet, Oust, Pouancé, Châteauneuf-sur-Sarthe

Pointe du Raz, Audierne, Pont-l'Abbé, Concarneau, Quimperlé, Hennebont, Vannes, MORBIHAN, Questembert, Redon, Derval, Châteaubriant, Ancenis

St. Guénolé, Pointe de Penmarc'h, Guilvinec, Îles de Glénans, Île de Groix, Lorient, Port Louis, Belz, Auray, Elven, Vilaine, Moisdon, Blain

Pointe de Penmarc'h, Quiberon, Carnac, Sarzeau, La Roche-Bernard, Pontchâteau, Savenay, LOIRE-ATLANTIQUE, PAYS DE LA LOIRE, Angers, Trélazé

ATLANTIC OCEAN

Belle Île, Le Palais, Guérande, St. Nazaire, Paimbœuf, La Baule, Le Croisic, Nantes, Rezé, Vertou, Vallet, Beaupréau, Chemillé, MAINE-ET-LOIRE, Gennes, Saumur

Île de Noirmoutier, Noirmoutier-en-l'Île, Pornic, Bourgneuf-en-Retz, Lac de Grand Lieu, Le Pellerin, Machecoul, Montaigu, Les Herbiers, Montreuil-Bellay, Cholet, Vihiers, Thouars, Loudun

Île d'Yeu, St. Jean-de-Monts, Challans, Beauvoir, VENDÉE, Les Essarts, La Châtaigneraie, Hauteurs de Gâtine, Parthenay, Airvault, Lencloître, Châtellerault

St. Gilles-Croix-de-Vie, La Mothe-Achard, La Roche-sur-Yon, La Châtaigneraie, Chantonnay, Pouzauges, Thénezay, Neuville-de-Poitou, Vivonne, Chauvigny

Les Sables-d'Olonne, Talmont, Champdeniers, Sainte Hermine, Fontenay-le-Comte, Maillezais, VIENNE, Poitiers, Montmorillon

Luçon, Chaillé-les-Marais, Marais, DEUX-SÈVRES, St. Maixent, Lusignan, Gençay, Lussac-les-Châteaux

Pertuis Breton, Île de Ré, Ars-en-Ré, Niort, Melle, Couhé, L'Isle Jourdain

La Rochelle, La Jarrie, Surgères, Beauvoir-sur-Niort, Aulnay, Ruffec, Confolens, HAUTE-VIENNE

Île d'Oléron, St. Pierre d'Oléron, Rochefort, St. Jean-d'Angély, Aigre, St. Claude, St. Junien, Plateau de Limousin

Le Château d'Oléron, Marennes, Tonnay-Boutonne, CHARENTE-MARITIME, Saintes, Cognac, Jarnac, La Rochefoucauld, St. Mathieu, du Limousin

La Tremblade, Savinou, Matha, Rouillac, Châbanais, Rochechouart

Pointe de la Coubre, Royan, CHARENTE, Châteauneuf-sur-Charente, Angoulême, Montbron, Nontron

Pointe de Grave, Le Verdun, Soulac-sur-Mer, Archiac, St. Ciers, Blaye

Relief

Feet		Metres
16404		5000
9843		3000
6562		2000
3281		1000
1640		500
656		200
0		Sea Level

Land Dep.		
656		200
13123		4000
22966		7000

Scale 1:2 500 000

0   25   50   75   100 Miles

0   50   100   150 Kms.

Conic Equidistant Projection

© Collins

19

SOUTHERN FRANCE

Le Creusot
Givry
Montceau-les-Mines
Chalon-sur-Saône
SAÔNE-ET-LOIRE
St. Bonnet-de-Joux
Charolles
Cluny
Mâcon
Monts du Beaujolais
Villefranche
Trévoux
OPHONE
Monts du Lyonnais
Givors
Rive-de-Gier
LYON
Villeurbanne
Bron
Vienne
St. Jean-de-Bournay
ISÈRE
Firminy
St. Chamond
CALPES
Grenoble
Fontaine
St. Martin d'Hères
St. Marcellin
Romans
Villard-de-Lans
RDÈCHE
Valence
DRÔME
Crest
Die
DAUPHINE
HAUTES-ALPES
Gap
PROVENCE
Montélimar
Orange
Carpentras
VAUCLUSE
Avignon
ALPES DE HAUTE-PROVENCE
Digne
ALPES MARITIMES
Sisteron
Forcalquier
Manosque
Aix-en-Provence
BOUCHES-DU-RHÔNE
Arles
Salon
Martigues
Marseille
St. Louis
La Ciotat
Aubagne
Toulon
La Seyne
Hyères
Cap Sicié
Îles d'Hyères

Lausanne
Annecy
HAUTE-SAVOIE
Genève (Geneva)
Thonon
Bourg
AIN
Bellegarde
SWITZERLAND
Alpes Pennines
Matterhorn
Mont Blanc
SAVOIE
Massif de la Vanoise
Chambéry
Albertville
Massif du
Les Écrins
Pelvoux
Briançon
Mont Pelat
ALPES
VAR
Fréjus
St. Raphaël
Sainte Maxime
St. Tropez
Cap Camarat
Cavalaire-sur-Mer
Côte d'Azur
Grasse
Cannes
Antibes
Nice
MONACO
Menton
Bordighera
Ventimiglia
San Remo
Imperia
Riviera di Ponente

ITALY
VALLE D'AOSTA
Gran Paradiso
PIEMONTE
Torino
Chieri
Moncalieri
Pinerolo
Carmagnola
Cuneo
Mondovì
Biella
Novara
Vercelli
Vigevano
Chivasso
Asti
Alessandria
Voghera
Tortona
Novi Ligure
Savona
Finale Ligure
Albenga
Alassio
Genova (Genoa)
Rapallo
Chiavari
Santa Margherita Ligure
Sestri Levante
La Spezia
Lerici
Riviera di Levante
Golfo di Genova
(G. of Genoa)

SWITZERLAND
Como
Lago di Como
Lecco
Lugano
Lago Maggiore
Varese
Verbania
LOMBARDIA
Bergamo
Monza
Milano
Treviglio
Crema
Lodi
Pavia
Piacenza
Cremona
Mantova
Brescia
Verona
Desenzano del Garda
EMILIA-ROMAGNA
Parma
Reggio
Correggio
Sassuolo
Monte Cusna 2120

La Spezia
Massa
Carrara
Forte dei Marmi
Viareggio
Lucca
Pisa
TOSCANA
Livorno (Leghorn)
Rosignano Marittimo
Cecina
San Vincenzo
Piombino
Portoferraio
Elba 1019
Pianosa
Capraia
Cap Corse

LIGURIAN
SEA

Lion
Lions)

Corse
(Corsica)
(Fr.)

CORSE
HAUTE CORSE
L'Île Rousse
Calvi
St. Florent
Bastia
Belgodère
Monte Cinto 2710
Piana
Cap Rosso
Ajaccio
Capo di Feno
Capo di Muro
Golfe de Valinco
Punta di Senetosa
CORSE-DU-SUD
Sartène
Bonifacio
Strait of Bonifacio
Porto-Vecchio
Sainte-Lucia
Aléria

Montecristo

Relief
Feet		Metres
16404		5000
9843		3000
6562		2000
3281		1000
1640		500
656		200
0		Sea Level

Land Dep.
656		200
13123		4000
22966		7000

Scale 1: 2 500 000

0   25   50   75   100 Miles
0   50   100   150 Kms.

Conic Equidistant Projection

© Collins.

MEDITERRANEAN LANDS

POLAND
Gniezno · Koło 20° · Lowicz · Siedlce · Pinsk · Polesye · BELARUS · Chernigov · Konotop · Pavlovsk · Log
Leszno · Warta · Kalisz · Krosno · Radom · Brest · (Pripet Marshes) (BELORUSSIA) · Yelsk · Nezhin · Seym · Bakhmach · Rossosh · Kantemirovka · Hovlya
Wrocław · Piotrkow · Lublin · Kovel · Sarny · Rakitnoye · Sluch · Kiyev · Brovary · Piryatin · Priluki · Sula · Belgorod · Kalach-na-Donu · Don
Częstochowa · Kielce · Trybunalski · Lutsk · Rovno · Novograd · Zhitomir · Fastov · (Kiev) · Pereyaslav · Lubny · Sumy · Akhtyrka · Chertkovo · Tsimlyanskoye Vdkhr. · 48°
Opole · Chorzów · Tarnobrzeg · Brody · Volynskiy · Berdichev · Belaya · Tserkov · Vasilkov · Kremenchugskoye · Poltava · Krasnograd · Slavyansk · Artemovsk · Kamensk-Shakhtinskiy · Tsimlyansk
Katowice · Kraków · Jasło · Przemyśl · Ternopol · Khmelnitskiy · Vinnitsa · Dnepr · Cherkassy · Kremenchug · Dnieper · Novomoskovsk · Pavlograd · Makeyvka · Shakhty · Don · Kotelnikovo · Sal
SLOVAKIA · Uzhgorod · Ivano-Frankovsk · Kolomyya · Kamenets · Podolskiy · Mogilev · Uman · Kirovograd · Dneprodzerzhinsk · Dnepropetrovsk · Stakhanov · Lugansk · Novoshakhtinsk
Bratislava · Košice · Mukachevo · Chernovtsy · Podolskiy · Bug · Pervomaysk · Zheltyye · Kremenchug · Znamenka · Dolinskaya · Zaporozhye · Donetsk · Krivoy Rog · RUS. FED.
Miskolc · Nyíregyháza · Satu Mare · Carei · Suceava · Botoșani · Iași · Orgeyev · Balta · Voznesensk · Nikopol · Berdyansk · Mariupol · Rostov
HUNGARY · Budapest · Karcag · Oradea · Cluj-Napoca · Dej · 2102 · Roman · MOLDOVA · Kishinev · Tiraspol · Nikolayev · Kherson · Melitopol · Taganrog · Taganrogskiy Zaliv · Yeysk · Salsk
Szeged · Békéscsaba · Mureș · Bacău · MOLDAVIA · Bendery · Belgorod · Krym · Krasnoperekopsk · Dzhankoy · Sea of · Azov · Pavlovskaya · Tikhoretsk
ROMANIA · Sfîntu-Gheorghe · Focșani · Galați · Brăila · Izmail · Dnestrovskiy · Odessa · (Crimea) · (Azovskoye More) · Kerch · Kushchevskaya · Stavropolskaya
YUGOSLAVIA · Timișoara · Pitești · București · Buzău · Ploiești · Sulina · Delta Dunării · Yevpatoriya · Simferopol · Feodosiya · Kavkaz · Krymsk · Krasnodar · Nevinnomyssk
Belgrade · Craiova · Caracal · Giurgiu · Silistra · (Mouths of the Danube) · Sevastopol · Yalta · Novorossiysk · Tuapse · Cherkessk
BULGARIA · Dunav · Ruse · Razgrad · Dobrich · Varna · BLACK SEA · Sochi · GEO.
BOSNIA-HERZEGOVINA · Niš · Pleven · Veliko · Turnovo · Burgas · 2211 · Sukhumi · Caucasus
Sofiya · Plovdiv · Stara · Zagora · Yambol · Sliven · Inebolu · Sinop · Kizil · Samsun · Giresun · Trabzon · Rize
MACEDONIA · Skopje · Plovdiv · Khaskovo · Edirne · Lüleburgaz · Istanbul Boğ. · Zonguldak · Ereğli · Kastamonu · Merzifon · Anadolu Dağları · Gümüşhane · Bayburt
ALBANIA · Tirane · Bitola · Xánthi · Komotiní · Tekirdağ · İstanbul · (Bosporus) · Bolu · Çankırı · Çorum · Niksar · Kelkit · Erzincan · Tercan
Thessaloniki · Samothráki · Gökçeada · Marmara · Denizi · Bursa · İnegöl · Eskişehir · Ankara · Kırşehir · Kayseri · Sivas · TURKEY · Malatya · Diyarbakır
GREECE · Límnos · Balıkesir · Anadolu · (Anatolia) · Aksaray · Ürgüp · Erciyes Dağı · Elâzığ · Bingöl
Aegean · Lésvos · Manisa · İzmir · Uşak · Afyon · Konya · Toros Dağları · Adana · Gaziantep · Halab
Athína · (Athens) · Sámos · Denizli · Burdur · Antalya · Mersin · Silifke · SYRIA
MEDITERRANEAN SEA · Ródhos · (Rhodes) · CYPRUS · Lefkosia · (Nicosia) · Ammókhostos · (Famagusta) · Tarabulus · (Tripoli) · Dimashq · (Damascus)
Kríti · (Crete) · Néa Páfos · (Paphos) · Lemesós · (Limassol) · LEBANON · Bayrút
ISRAEL · Tel Aviv-Yafo · Yerushalayim · GAZA · JORDAN · Amman
Al Iskandariyah · (Alexandria) · Būr Sa'īd · (Port Said) · Al 'Arish · Be'er Sheva
LIBYA · Banghāzī · (Benghazi) · Marsá Matrúh · As Sallum · EGYPT · Al Qāhirah · (Cairo) · Suways · (Suez) · Sīnā' · (Sinai) · Elat · Al 'Aqabah
Khalīj Surt · (Gulf of Sidra) · Barqah · (Cyrenaica) · Qattara Depression · Fayyūm

IBERIAN PENINSULA

Scale 1:5 000 000

Conic Projection

© Collins ⬥ Longman Atlases Cbi

B A Y   O F   B I S C A Y

A T L A N T I C   O C E A N

M E D I T E R R A N E A N   S E A

PYRENEES

FRANCE

ANDORRA

ESPAÑA / SPAIN

PORTUGAL

MOROCCO

ALGERIA

Islas Baleares (Spain)

Mallorca (Majorca)

Menorca (Minorca)

Ibiza (Iviza)

Formentera

Madrid

Barcelona

Valencia

Sevilla

Lisboa (Lisbon)

Porto (Oporto)

Bilbao

Zaragoza

Málaga

Granada

Murcia

Alicante

Cartagena

Córdoba

Valladolid

Salamanca

Cáceres

Badajoz

Huelva

Cádiz

Almería

Pamplona

San Sebastián

Santander

Gijón

Oviedo

La Coruña

Vigo

Santiago de Compostela

León

Palencia

Burgos

Logroño

Vitoria

Lérida

Gerona

Tarragona

Castellón

Sagunto

Alcoy

Elche

Elda

Lorca

Jaén

Linares

Úbeda

Antequera

Ronda

Ceuta (Sp.)

Gibraltar (U.K.)

Tánger (Tangier)

Tétouan (Tetuan)

Oran

Alger (Algiers)

CASTILLA LA MANCHA

CASTILLA Y LEÓN

EXTREMADURA

ANDALUCÍA

GALICIA

ARAGÓN

NAVARRA

LA RIOJA

PAÍS VASCO

ASTURIAS

CANTABRIA

Golfo de Valencia

Golfo de Cádiz

Cabo de Creus

Strait of Gibraltar

Delta del Ebro

Sierra Nevada

Cordillera Cantábrica

Sierra Morena

Serranía de Cuenca

Montes de Toledo

Tajo (Tagus)

Duero

Guadiana

Guadalquivir

Ebro

EASTERN SPAIN

MEDITERRANEAN

SEA

Menorca
(Minorca)

Mallorca
(Majorca)

Islas Baleares
(Balearic Islands)

Ibiza
(Iviza)

Formentera

Feet	Relief	Metres
16404		5000
9843		3000
6562		2000
3281		1000
1640		500
656		200
0		Sea Level
Land Dep.		
656		200
13123		4000
22966		7000

Scale 1 : 2 500 000

0   25   50   75   100 Miles

0   50   100   150 Kms.

Conic Equidistant Projection

© Collins

WESTERN SPAIN AND PORTUGAL

MEDITERRANEAN SEA

ATLANTIC OCEAN

Golfo de Cádiz

Relief
Feet	Metres
16404	5000
9843	3000
6562	2000
3281	1000
1640	500
656	200
0	Sea Level
	Land Dep.
656	0
13123	200
22966	7000

Scale 1:2 500 000

Conic Equidistant Projection

100 Miles
150 Kms

© Collins

ITALY AND THE BALKANS

LIGURIAN
SEA

Golfo di Genova
(G. of Genoa)

Riviera di Ponente

Riviera di Levante

Feet	Relief	Metres
16404		5000
9843		3000
6562		2000
3281		1000
1640		500
656		200
0		Sea Level
Land Dep.		
656		200
13123		4000
22966		7000

Corse
(Corsica)
(Fr.)

CORSE

HAUTE
CORSE

CORSE
DU SUD

Scale 1 : 2 500 000

| 0 | 25 | 50 | 75 | 100 Miles |

| 0 | 50 | 100 | 150 Kms |

Conic Equidistant Projection

SOUTHERN ITALY

MOLISE

Vasto
Termoli
Lago di Lesina
Rodi Garganico
Vieste
Sannicandro
Monte Calvo
1056
Testa del Gargano
Monte Sant'Angelo
San Severo
San Giovanni Rotondo
Manfredonia

Lucera

Foggia
Golfo di Manfredonia

Campobasso

Margherita di Savoia
Barletta
Trani
Bisceglie
Molfetta

Andria
Corato
Bari
Bitonto
Mola di Bari

Minervino Murge
Ruvo

Monopoli
Castellana Grotte

Cerignola

Venosa
Altamura
Noci
Alberobello
Fasano

Gioia del Colle
Martina Franca
Ostuni

Potenza
Matera
Ceglie
Mottola
San Vito dei Normanni

Brindisi
Mesagne

BASILICATA
Taranto
Francavilla
PUGLIA
Squinzano
Trepuzzi
Lecce

METAPONTUM
Pulsano
Sava
Manduria
Copertino
Galatina
Nardò
Otranto

Golfo di Taranto

Gallipoli
Casarano
Santa Cesarea Terme
Tricase

Golfo di Policastro
Monte Pollino
2248
Capo Spulico
Trebisacce
Alessano
Gagliano del Capo
Capo Santa Maria di Leuca

ADRIATIC SEA

Strait of Otranto

Ulcinj
Pelleg i Drinit
Shëngjin
TIRANË DURRËS
Kep-i-Rodonit
Bishti i Pallës
Tiranë
Durrës
Kavajë
Rrogozhinë
ELBASAN BERAT
Fier
Seman
Berat
Kuçovë
Vlorë
Kep-i-Gjuhëzës
VLORË
DHËRMI
Himare
Sarandë
BUTHROTUM

Kérkira (Corfu)
Kérkira
Othonoi
Liapádhes
Levkímmi

CALABRIA

Cosenza
Lago di Cecita
Rossano
Corigliano
Cariati
Punta Alice
Cirò Marina
Strongoli

Crotone
Capo Colonna

Catanzaro
Capo Rizzuto
Isola di Capo Rizzuto

2340

Nicastro
Golfo di Sant'Eufemie
Golfo di Squillace
Squillace
Soverato

Pizzo
Vibo Valentia
Tropea
Capo Vaticano
Serra San Bruno
Guardavalle
Punta Stilo

Isole Eolie
Stromboli
926

Isola Filicudi
Isola Salina
Isola Panarea
962
Isola Lipari
Lipari
Isola Vulcano

Rosarno
Gioia Tauro
Palmi
Bagnara
400

Cittanova
Polistena
Marina di Gioiosa Ionica
Rocella
Siderno
Locri
Bovalino Marina

Milazzo
Golfo di Patti
Messina
Barcellona
Montalto
1955

Reggio
Brancaleone Marina

Sant'Agata di Militello
Nebrodi
Monti
1847

Melito di Porto Salvo
Capo Spartivento
Stretto di Messina

Mt. Etna
3340
Riposto
Giarre
Acireale

Nicosia
Adrano
Belpasso
Paternò

Enna
Catania
Golfo di Catania

Lentini
Augusta
Golfo di Augusta

Monte Lauro
986
Siracusa (Syracuse)

Comiso
Modica
Golfo di Noto
Capo Passero

IONIAN SEA

SEA

Relief
Feet | Metres
16404 | 5000
9843 | 3000
6562 | 2000
3281 | 1000
1640 | 500
656 | 200
0 | Sea Level
Land Dep.
656 | 200
13123 | 4000
22966 | 7000

Scale 1:2 500 000

0   25   50   75   100 Miles
0   50   100   150 Kms
Conic Equidistant Projection

© Collins

33

GREECE AND ALBANIA

IONIAN SEA

SEA

© Collins

Relief

Feet	Metres
16404	5000
9843	3000
6562	2000
3281	1000
1640	500
656	200
	Sea Level
	Land Dep.
656	200
13123	4000
22966	7000

Scale 1:2 500 000

Conic Equidistant Projection

0   25   50   75   100   150 Kms.

0   25   50   75   100 Miles

CENTRAL EUROPE

GERMANY AND SWITZERLAND

39

SCANDINAVIA AND BALTIC LANDS

Scale 1:5 000 000
Conic Projection

Relief

Metres		Feet
5000		16404
3000		9843
2000		6562
1000		3281
500		1640
200		656
Sea Level		Land Dep. 656
200		
4000		13123
7000		22966

ICELAND
on the same scale

© Collins

FAROE IS.
(Denmark)
on the same scale

ATLANTIC OCEAN

SOUTHERN SCANDINAVIA

NORTH

SEA

Relief

Feet		Metres
16 404		5000
9843		3000
6562		2000
3281		1000
1640		500
656		200
0		Sea Level
Land Dep.		
656		200
13 123		4000
22 966		7000

Scale 1 : 2 500 000

0	25	50	75	100 Miles
0	50	100	150 Kms.	

Conic Equidistant Projection

© Collins

45

North America

ARCTIC OCEAN

International Date Line   Bering Strait

Europe

RUSSIAN FEDERATION

Sea of
Okhotsk

Black Sea

Yekaterinburg

Omsk

Novosibirsk

KAZAKHSTAN

Sakhalin 50°

Aral
Sea

Ankara
GEORG.
Yerevan
ARM.
AZER.
Tbilisi
Baku

UZBEKISTAN

Sapporo

Harbin

MONGOLIA

Ulan Bator

Sea of
Japan

TURKEY
Nicosia
CYPRUS
LEB.
SYRIA
Beirut
Damascus
JOR.
Amman
Jerusalem
IS.

Caspian Sea

TURKMENISTAN

Tashkent

Bishkek

Alma
Ata

KYRGYZSTAN

Changchun

Shenyang
Anshan

Fushun

N. KOREA
Pyŏngyang

Sapporo

Honshū

JAPAN

Yokohama
Osaka
Shik

IRAQ
Baghdad

Ashkhabad

IRAN
Tehrān

Dushanbe

TAJIKISTAN

Beijing
(Peking)

Seoul

S. KOREA

Kitakyūshū

Taegu
Pusan

Kyūsh

SAUDI

Red Sea

Kuwait

Riyadh
Manama
BAH.
QAT.
Doha
U.A.E.

OMAN

AFGHANISTAN
Kabul

Islamābād

PAKISTAN

Lahore

JAMMU
AND
KASHMIR

Tsingtao

Taiyuan

Tsinan

Lanchow

Sian

CHINA

Nanking

Chengchow

Wuhan

Shanghai

East
China
Sea

ARABIA

Muscat

Karachi

Delhi

NEPAL
Kathmandu
BHU.
Thimbu

Chengdu

Chungking

Kunming

Canton

Taipei

TAIWAN

Saṇa
YEMEN

Socotra
(Yemen)

Arabian
Sea

Ahmadābād

Kānpur

BANGLA.
Dacca

HONG
KONG
(U.K.)

Bombay

Hyderabad

INDIA

Calcutta

MYANMAR
(BURMA)

Hanoi

Hainan

South
China
Sea

Luzon

PHILIPPIN

Bangalore

Madras

Bay of
Bengal

Rangoon
(Yangon)

THAILAND

Vientiane

LAOS

VIETNAM

Manila

Mindanao

Andaman
Islands
(Ind.)

Bangkok

CAMBODIA

Phnom
Penh

Ho Chi
Minh

20°

Africa

SRI
LANKA

Colombo

MALDIVES

Nicobar
Islands
(Ind.)

Kuala
Lumpur

MALAYSIA

Brunei
BANDAR SERI
BEGAWAN

Bandar Seri
Begawan

Borneo

Sulawesi

INDONE

Singapore
SINGAPORE

Sumatra

90° Equator

INDIAN

Jakarta
Java
Surabaya

Bandung

Timor Sea

10°

OCEAN

20°

Tropic of Capricorn

30°

40°

Kerguelen
(Fr.)

50°

ASIA

COUNTRY	PAGE
AFGHANISTAN	48; 60
ARMENIA	45
AZERBAIJAN	45
BAHRAIN	65
BANGLADESH	63
BHUTAN	63
BRUNEI	58
CAMBODIA	56
CHINA	52-53; 54-55
CYPRUS	66
GEORGIA	45
HONG KONG	55
INDIA	60-61; 62-63
INDONESIA	58-59
IRAN	65
IRAQ	64-65
ISRAEL	66; 67
JAPAN	57
JORDAN	64; 66; 67
KAZAKHSTAN	50; 52
KUWAIT	65
KYRGYZSTAN	50
LAOS	56
LEBANON	66
MACAU	55
MALAYSIA	58
MALDIVES	60
MONGOLIA	52-53; 54
MYANMAR (BURMA)	56
NEPAL	63
NORTH KOREA	53
OMAN	60
PAKISTAN	60; 62
PHILIPPINES	58-59
QATAR	65
RUSSIAN FEDERATION (IN ASIA)	50-51
SAUDI ARABIA	71;64-65
SINGAPORE	58
SOUTH KOREA	53
SRI LANKA	61
SYRIA	64; 66; 67
TAIWAN	55
TAJIKISTAN	50
THAILAND	56
TURKEY	64
TURKMENISTAN	50;65
UNITED ARAB EMIRATES	65
UZBEKISTAN	50
VIETNAM	56
YEMEN	71

ASIA AND INDIAN OCEAN

INDONESIA

Moluccas
(Seram)
Seram
Buru
Laut
Banda
Flores
Sumba
Celebes
Kupang

AUSTRALIA

Melville I.
Darwin
Derby
Port Hedland
Wyndham
Macdonnell Res.
Alice Springs
Port Augusta
Adelaide
Port Lincoln
Kangaroo I.
Bass Strait
Tasmania

Borneo
Kuching
Kalimantan
Balikpapan
Ujung Pandang
Banjarmasin
Semarang Surabaya
Malang
Jakarta
Bandung
Palembang
Jambi
Singapore
Kuala Lumpur
Malacca
Sumatera
Medan
Kep. Mentawai
Padang
Tanjungkarang
Jawa (Java)
Laut Jawa (Java)
Laut Jawa

Timor Sea

Kalgoorlie
Nullarbor Plain
Great Australian Bight
Geraldton Meckatharra
Perth
Albany

Java Trench
7450
Java
Christmas I.
(Aus.)
6459
Cocos Is.
(Aus.)
1787

West Australian Basin

Mid-Indian Basin

INDIAN OCEAN

MID-INDIAN RIDGE

West

5243

2352

Ninety-East Ridge

South-East Indian Ridge
S.E. Indian Basin
6857
1011
2719

SOUTHERN OCEAN

Indian-Antarctic Ridge
5465

Eastern Indian-Antarctic Basin

Antarctica

Antarctic Circle

South Australian Basin

S.W. Australian Ridge

Scale 1 : 45 000 000

Lambert Azimuthal Equal Area Projection

1200 Miles
2000 Kms.

I. Amsterdam (Fr.)
I. St. Paul (Fr.)

Kerguelen-Gaussberg Ridge
188

Heard I.
(Aus.)
Is. de Kerguelen
(Fr.)

Kerguelen Basin
5605
5441

Atlantic-Indian-Antarctic Basin

SEYCHELLES
Mascarene Ridge
Basin
Chagos Archipelago
(U.K.)

Maldive Ridge

Madingley Rise
Mascarene Ridge

Nazareth Trough
Rodrigues
Ridge
16

MAURITIUS
Mascarene Is.
Réunion (Fr.)
Mauritius Basin
6400
2152

South-West Indian Ridge

Prince Edward Is.
Is. Crozet (Fr.)
Prince Edward-Crozet Ridge
Prince Edward Is.
(R.S.A.)

Tromelin
Mascarene Basin

Antananarivo
(Tananarive)

MADAGASCAR

Mahajanga
Bassas da India
Europa

COMOROS

Mozambique Channel

Tropic of Capricorn

1503

Natal Basin

Cape Rise

Agulhas Basin
5716

Durban

© Collins ◇ Longman Atlases

NORTH
ASIA

NORWAY

SWEDEN

FINLAND

DENMARK

GERMANY

POLAND

CZECH

SLOVAKIA

HUNGARY

ROMANIA

UKRAINE

BELARUS

LITHUANIA

LATVIA

ESTONIA

Stockholm

Sankt-Peterburg

Moskva

Gulf of Bothnia

G. of Finland

BALTIC SEA

BARENTS SEA

ARCTIC OCEAN

Zemlya Frantsa Iosifa
(Franz Josef Land)

Novaya Zemlya

KARSKOYE MORE

Beloye More
(White Sea)

Vorkuta

R U S S I A N

Zapadno-
Sibirskaya
Ravnina
(West Siberian
Plain)

Nizhniy Novgorod (Gorky)

Kazan

Perm

Izhevsk

Yekaterinburg

Chelyabinsk

Omsk

Novosibirsk

Novokuznetsk

Barnaul

Ufa

Samara

Tol'yatti

Saratov

Volgograd

Rostov

Donetsk

Dnepropetrovsk

Zaporozh'ye

Kharkov

Kiyev

Odessa

Kriviy Rog

Mariupol

BLACK SEA

TURKEY

GEORGIA

ARMENIA

AZERBAIJAN

Tbilisi

Yerevan

Baku (Baky)

CASPIAN SEA

Caspian Depression
(Prikaspiyskaya Nizmennost')

Astrakhan

Vladikavkaz

Grozny

IRAN

IRAQ

Tehrān

Mashhad

Esfahān

AFGHANISTAN

TURKMENISTAN

Ashkhabad

Peski Karakumy

UZBEKISTAN

Tashkent

Samarkand

Dushanbe

TAJIKISTAN

KYRGYZSTAN

Bishkek

Almaty

K A Z A K H S T A N

Aral Sea
(Aral'skoye More)

Kzyl Orda

Syr Darya

Peski Kyzyl Kum

Ustyurt Plateau

Orenburg

Karaganda

Semipalatinsk

Ozero Balkhash

Ozero Zaysan

XINJIANG UYGUR ZIZHIQU
(SINKIANG)

Tarim He

Scale 1 : 20 000 000

0 100 200 300 400 500 Miles

0   200   400   600   800 Kms.

Conic Projection

© Collins ◇ Longman Atlases CDi

50

EAST ASIA

BAY OF BENGAL

EAST CHINA

INDO-CHINA

JAPAN

CHINA
RUSSIAN FEDERATION

Rebun jima
Rishiri tō
Wakkanai
Sea of Okhotsk

Teshio
Tetyukhe
Pristan
Olga

Kunashir
Nemuro kaikyo
Rus.Fed.admin./
claimed by Japan

Ussuriysk
Uryu ko
Nayoro
Abashiri wan
Kitami
Shibecha

Wangqing
Artem
Rumoi
Fukagawa
Asahikawa
Asahi dake
Kushharo ko
Nemuro

Vladivostok
Suchang
Kamui misaki
Ishikari
HOKKAIDO
Urahoro

Jingpo Hu
Yanji
Hunchun
Pinzolcau
Nakhodka
Sudzuke
Otaru
Sapporo
Shikotsu ko
Yubari
Obihiro
Kushiro

Hoeryong
Songbong
Aoji
Najin
Zaliv Petra Velikogo
Valentin
Setana
Noboribetsu
Tomakomai
HOKKAIDO

Ch'ōngjin
Nanam
Uchiura wan
Muroran
Urakawa
Erimo misaki

NORTH KOREA
Kimch'aek
Tanch'ōn
Okushiri tō
Kameda
Hakodate
Shiriya saki
PACIFIC

Ô shima
Matsumae
Tsugaru-kaikyo
Mutsu
OCEAN

SEA OF JAPAN
Mutsu wan
Aomori
Misawa

Hirosaki
Towada ko
Hachinohe

Ôdate
Mi saki

Noshiro
Morioka
Miyako

SOUTH KOREA
Samch'ōk
Ullŭng do
Oga
Akita
Tazawa ko
Kamaishi
Ôfunato

Honjo
Hanamaki
Mizusawa

Tobi shima
Chokai zan
Sakata
TOHOKU
Ishinomaki

P'ohang
Kamp'o
Awa shima
Tsuruoka
Yamagata
Ojika Hantô

Hajiki saki
Nanyo
Sendai

Ulsan
Sado
Ryōtsu
Shiroishi
Fukushima

Hekura jima
Niigata
Aizuwakamatsu
Kōriyama
Iwaki

Wajima
Suzu misaki
Nagaoka
Shirakawa
Hitachi

Nanao
Takaoka
Toyama
Nagano
Utsunomiya
Mito

Oki guntō
Himi
Joetsu
KANTÔ
Ashikaga
Nakaminato

Kanazawa
Maebashi
Kiryū
Gyōda

Komatsu
Yatsuo
Takayama
Kumagaya
Tsuchiura

Fukui
Matsumoto
Ôtake san
Niiza
Kawaguchi
Funabashi

Matsue
Tottori
CHÛBU
Mino
Kōfu
TÔKYÔ
Kawasaki
Tsuchiura

Izumo
Yonago
Maizuru
Gifu
Yokohama
Yokosuka

Masuda
Tsuyama
KINKI
Kyōto
Nagoya
Okazaki
Odawara
Numazu

Hagi
Okayama
Amagasaki
Yokkaichi
Toyohashi
Shizuoka

Hiroshima
Kurashiki
Kyōto
Ôsaka
Matsusaka
Hamamatsu

Yamaguchi
Iwakuni
Fukuyama
Kôbe
Sakai
Ise

Kitakyūshū
Ube
Takamatsu
Himeji nada
Higashiōsaka
Nii shima

Iki shima
Suō nada
Tokuyama
Takamatsu
Yoshino
Kôzu shima

Fukuoka
Matsuyama
Ilyo nada
Tokushima
Kii sanchi
Miyake jima

Saga
Bepu
Ôita
SHIKOKU
Anan
Mikura jima

Sasebo
Ômuta
Kurume
Kôchi
Ôwase
Shingū

Nagasaki
Kuju san
SHIKOKU
Uwajima
Sukumo
Mugi
Shiono zaki
Mikura jima

Kumamoto
Yatsushiro
Nobeoka
Ashizuri zaki
Tosa wan

Shimo jima
Kyūshū sanchi
KYÛSHÛ
Minamata
Miyazaki
Miyakonojō

Koshikijima retto
Sendai
Kanoya

Kagoshima
Ibusuki
Kagoshima wan
Ôsumi kaikyo

Kuchinoerabu jima
Yaku shima
Taneĝa shima

Kuchino shima

Relief

Feet	Metres
16 404	5000
9843	3000
6562	2000
3281	1000
1640	500
656	200
0	Sea Level
Land Dep.	
656	200
13 123	4000
22 966	7000

Scale 1:7 500 000

0 50 100 150 Miles
0 50 100 150 200 Kms.
Conic Projection

© Collins ◦ Longman Atlases Cbii

(Inset map - Scale 1:2 500 000)

Tsuchiura
Kasukabe
Ryūgasaki

Kumagaya
Higashimatsuyama
Kazo
Mizukaidō
Kanto heiya

Chichibu
SAITAMA
Kawagoe
Sayama
Omiya
Kasukabe

Kantō sanchi
Higashimurayama
Niiza
Urawa
Matsudo
Ichikawa
Narita

Ina
Komagane
Enzan
Yamanashi
Kodaira
Tachikawa
Funabashi

Komaga take
Nirasaka
Ôtsuki
Kōfu
Hachiōji
Fuchū
TÔKYÔ
Chiba

GIFU
NAGANO
Shirane san
Sagamihara
Chōfu
Machida
Kawasaki
CHIBA

Nakatsugawa
Iida
YAMANASHI
KANAGAWA
Atsugi
Yamato
Yokohama
Ichihara

Gifu
Seki
Mino-kamo
Fuji-yoshida
Hiratsuka
Kamakura
Yokosuka

Ôgaki
Kani
Toki
Mizunami
Gotemba
Odawara
Chigasaki
Fujisawa
Zushi
Katsuura

Ichinomiya
Kōnan
Tajimi
Fujinomiya
Misima
Miura
Bōsō hantô

Inazawa
Komaki
Seto
YAMANASHI
Fuji san
Numazu
Atami
Uraga-suido
Tateyama

Kasugai
Nagoya
SHIZUOKA
Shimizu
Nojima-zaki

Yōkaichi
Toyota
AICHI
Fuji
Shimizu
Sagami-nada

Kyōto
Kusatsu
Ôbu
Anjo
Okazaki
Shinshiro
Fujieda
Shizuoka

Takarazuka
SHIGA
Kariya
Handa
Toyokawa
Shimada
Yaizu
Izu hantô

Itami
Ibaraki
Suita
Yokkaichi
Suzuka
Gamagōri
Tenryū
Hamakita
Ô shima

Nishinomiya
Hirakata
Neyagawa
Nara
Tokoname
Toyohashi
Hamamatsu
Fukuroi
Shimoda

Kôbe
Akashi
Amagasaki
Ôsaka
Daitō
Gamagōri
Iwata
Sagara
Omae-zaki
Irō-zaki

Miki
Sakai
Yao
Matsubara
MIE
Atsumi-wan
Yūto

Itami
Habikino
NARA
Tsu
Matsusaka
Irago-suido

Izumi-ōtsu
Kawachi nagano
Gojō
Hisai
Ise
Shima-hantô
Enshū-nada

Kishiwada
Izumi-sano
Sennan
Hashimoto
Yoshino
Toba
Shima

Wakayama
Kino
Ago

Scale 1:2 500 000

0 20 40 60 Miles
0 20 40 60 80 Kms.
Conic Projection

57

SOUTHEAST ASIA

TAIWAN
(FORMOSA)

Batan Is.

Luzon Strait

Babuyan Is.

C. Engaño

Aparri

Taichung
Shanchung
nian
nan
ngtung

Taguegarao

LUZON

Pulag
2929

Fernando

Baguio
gunan

San Carlos

Bayombong

Cabanatuan

Iba

Quezon City
Manila

San Pablo   Daet

Lucena   Naga   *Catanduanes*

Burias   Legazpi   *Virac*

Mindoro   Bulan   Sorsogon

Looc   *Masbate*   Catarman   *Samar*

Sablayan   Roxas   Calbayog   Oras

Pandan   *Panay*   *Visayan*   Catbalogan   Guiuan
                      Sea
Iloilo   Cadiz   Tacloban
Pototon   *Cebu*   *Leyte*
Negros   Bohol   Dinagat
Bacolod   Cebu   Surigao   *Siargao*
Tanjay   Taghilaran   *Cape Johnson*
Dumaguete   *Bohol*   *Depth 10497*

Dipolog   *Mindanao*   Butuan
Liloy   *Sea*   Cagayan de Oro   San Juan
Ozamiz   Iligan   Tagum   **MINDANAO**
Pagadian   **Davao**
Zamboanga   Cotabato   Mati
Moro   Datu Maita
Basilan   *Basilan*   *Gulf*   Lebak   General   *Dawo G.*
Jolo   *Jolo*   Piang   Santos
Sulu
Arch.
wi

L E B E S   Tahuna   *Kep.*
                 Talaud
S E A   Siau   Bulu
              Sangihe   *Kep.*
                         Sangihe

Manado   *Morotai*
Paleleh   Kema   Tobelo
Buol   Kuandang   Tondano   Belang   Akelamo
2207   Gorontalo   Ternate   Jailolo
Tomini   1970   Soasiu   Weda   **Halmahera**
Poso   *Kep. Togian*   Wosi   Labuha
mini   Peleng   Bacan

Tokala   *Kep.*   Obi
2639   Peleng   *Sula*   *Misoöl*
Tolli   *Teluk*   Banggai   **Misoöl**
         Tolo   *Kep. Sula*   **LAUT SERAM**
                               (CERAM SEA)

kombola   Manui   Wamsasi   Namlea   Buru   Wahai
3027   Mekongga   Kendari   **Buru**   Binaiya   **Seram**
2790   Wowoni   Ambon   3055   (Ceram)
luk   Kolaka   **M A L U K U**   Tum
one   Raha   Kabaena   Muna   Buton   *Kep.*   *Banda*
      Baubau   *Tukangbesi*   *Besar*
Selayar   *S I A*   **L A U T   B A N D A**   Nila
                      (BANDA SEA)

F L O R E S   Labao   Wasiri   Teun   Damar
(ORES SEA)   Kalabahi   **Alor**   Romang   Tepa   Yamdena
ra   Maumere   *Alor*   Tutuala   *Kep. Babar*
lands)   **NUSA**   Atapupu   **TIMOR**   Vikeke
ngu   **TENGGARA**   **TIMUR**   Nikiniki
       TIMUR   2495
Endeh   *Timor*
ngapu   *Laut Sawu*
         (Savu Sea)   Kupang
Sawu   *Roti*

Tanjung   *Tanjung*   *Bawean*
1281 *Cina*   *Tua*
Selat Sunda   Anyer Lor   Serang   **JAKARTA**
6° Cina   Tanjung   Pandeglang   **Jakarta**   Krawang   Pamanukan
        Tua   Labuan   Cikampek   Indramayu
Malingping   Rangkasbitung   Jatinegara
Tanjung   2211   Bogor   Purwakarta   Cirebon   Tegal   Pekalongan   Muria   Kudus   Kragan   Tuban   *Madura*   Ketapang
Cangkuang   Sukabumi   **Bandung**   Cianjur   Cledug   Pemalang   Kendal   1602   Pati   Kembang   Blora   Cepu   Lamongan   Bangkalan   *Kangean*
Pelabuanratu   *JAWA BARAT*   Garut   Ciamis   Purwokerto   Slamet   Ambarawa   **Semarang**   Demak   Purwodadi   Ngawi   Bojonegoro   Gresik   Pamekasan   Ambunten
        Jampang   2608   Tasikmalaya   Kroya   Purworejo   3428   Salatiga   Sragen   *JAWA*   Jombang   *Madura*   Sumenep
        Kulon   Pangandaran   Cilacap   Kebumen   Magelang   Surakarta   Jambang   Mojokerto   **Surabaya**   Pamekasan
                    Cijulang   Purworejo   YOGYAKARTA   Yogyakarta   Wonosari   Pacitan   Madiun   Kediri   3339   Pasuruan   Probolinggo   Situbondo   *Laut Bali*
                                                         Wonogiri   Ponorogo   Trenggalek   Blitar   **Malang**   Semeru   Bondowoso   (Bali Sea)
                                                                              Tulungagung   3676   Jember   Banyuwangi   Singaraja   Tejakula
                                                                                         JAWA   *TIMUR*   3342   **BALI** 3142
                                                                                                                      Negara   *Bali*   Klungkung
                                                                                                                      J A W A   (J A V A)   Denpasar

Scale 1:7 500 000

0   50   100   150 Miles
0   50   100   150   200 Kms
Mercator Projection

P A C I F I C

Nero Deep
9637

Challenger Depth
11034

Yap   **FEDERATED STATES OF MICRONESIA**   Gaferut

Faraulep   Pigailoe

Sorol   *Ifalik*   Lamotrek

O C E A N   PALAU   Koror
               (BELAU)   *Eauripik*   *I s l a n d s*

Sonsorol   C a r o l i n e

Merir

Tobi   *Helen Reef*   *Kep.*   *Equator*
                        Mapia

Kep.
Schouten
Korim
Waigeo   Wakre   Biak   Manus
Sorong   Kweka   Manokwari   Biak   Lorengau
Selat Dampier   Klamono   Arfak   Korim   Bosnik   **Admiralty Is**
Gebe   2939   Warkapi   Mokmer
Lenmalu   Inanwatan   Waslan   Sarmi   Ansudu   *Bismarck*
Kokas   *Teluk Berau*   Serui   Yapen   Jayapura   *Sea*
Babo   *Teluk*   Wewak
Fakfak   Weri   *Cenderawasih*   Vanimo   Dagua
        Wasior   Peg. Gunung   Aitape   Maprik
Kaimana   1340   *Taritatu*   Angoram   Karkar I.
        Karufa   **IRIAN**   Sepik
        Adi   *Pegunungan*   Madang
Wanapiri   *Sudirman*   *Mapke*   Bogia
Kokenau   Puncak   Peg. Jayawijaya   **PAPUA NEW**   Bohu
        Jaya   5030   Mt. Wilhelm   Goroka
        Mindiptana   3055   4694   Lae   Finschhafen
N E W   G U I N E A   **JAYA**   Pk Mandala   Wabag   Huon Pen.
        Tanahmerah   4760   Wau   Morobe
Dobo   *Kep.*   Kepi   Digul   **GUINEA**   Kikori   Balimo
Kep.   *Kai*   Wokam   Mapi   Lake   Kundiawa   Manau
Aru   Kobroor   Murray   Kikori   3990   Popondetta
Trangan   Rebi   Pulau Yos   *Aramia*   Kerema
        Sudarsa   Kimaan   *Fly*   **Gulf of**
        (Kolepom)   Merauke   Sebidiro   Daru   **Papua**
Kep.   Tanjung   Mapi   Port Moresby   Kila Kila
Leti   Vals   Mulgrave I.
Selaru   **A R A F U R A   S E A**   Banks I.
                                        Torres Str.
                                        Thursday I.   C. York   *C o r a l*
                                        Prince of Wales I.   *S e a*

Relief

Feet	Metres
16 404	5000
9843	3000
6562	2000
3281	1000
1640	500
656	200
0	Sea Level
Land Dep.	200
656	
13 123	4000
22 966	7000

SOUTH ASIA

XINJIANG UYGUR

Kunlun Shan
Margai Caka
Qing Zang Gaoyuan
(Tibetan Plateau)

QINGHAI

GANSU

SHANXI

Chengdu
SICHUAN
Chongqing
(Chungking)

XIZANG ZIZHIQU
(TIBET)

C H I N A

Kunming

GUIZHOU
Guiyang

H I M A L A Y A

Lhasa

Mt. Everest

NEPAL

BHUTAN

Kathmandu

ARUNACHAL PRADESH

Lucknow
Kānpur
UTTAR PRADESH

ASSAM
MEGHALAYA
Shillong

NAGALAND
MANIPUR

VIETNAM
Hanoi

Allāhābād
Vārānasi
(Benares)
Patna
BIHĀR

BANGLADESH
Dhaka
(Dacca)

MIZORAM

MYANMAR
(BURMA)
Mandalay

LAOS

Jabalpur
MADHYA PRADESH

Dhānbād
Rānchī
Jamshedpur
W. BENGAL
Calcutta
Howrah

Chittagong

Nāgpur

ORISSA

Bhubaneswar
Puri

THAILAND

Chiang Mai

Yangon
(Rangoon)

Irrawaddy Delta

Moulmein
(Mawlamyine)

CAMBODIA

Bangkok
(Krung Thep)

Phnom Penh

B A Y   O F

Vishākhapatnam

B E N G A L

Vijayawāda

A N D H R A
PRADESH

ANDAMAN SEA

Gulf of
Martaban

GULF
OF
THAILAND

Madras

Andaman
Islands
(India)

Isthmus
of Kra

THAILAND

Pondicherry

Little
Andaman

Nicobar
Islands
(India)

Ko Phuket

Relief

Feet		Metres
16 404		5000
9843		3000
6562		2000
3281		1000
1640		500
656		200
0	Sea Level	
Land Dep.		
656		200
13123		4000
22 966		7000

Ten Degree Channel

Car Nicobar

Katchall
Little Nicobar
Gt Nicobar

Songkhla

SRI LANKA

Colombo

Scale 1:14 000 000

0	100	200	300	400	500 Miles
0	200	400	600	800 Kms.	

Conic Projection

INDONESIA

MALAYSIA
George Town
(Penang)

Kuala Lumpur

NORTHERN INDIA, PAKISTAN AND BANGLADESH

ARABIAN

Relief	
Feet	Metres
16404	5000
9843	3000
6562	2000
3281	1000
1640	500
656	200
0	Sea Level
Land Dep.	
656	200
13123	4000
22966	7000

SEA

Scale 1:7 500 000

0   50   100   150 Miles

0   50 100   200 Kms.

Conic Projection

BAY
OF
BENGAL

© Collins

63

SOUTHWEST ASIA

CASPIAN

SEA

AZERBAIJAN

ARMENIA

AZE.

TURKMENISTAN

PESKI KARAKUMY

(Black Sand Desert)

UZBEKISTAN

KAZA.

Baku
(Baky)

Sumgait

Ashkhabad

Mashhad

Herāt

AFGHANISTAN

Tabrīz

Orūmīyeh
L. Urmia

Tehrān

Qom

DASHT-E KAVĪR
(Salt Desert)

Esfahān

DASHT-E LŪT
(Barren Desert)

I   R   A   N

Baghdād

IRAQ

Hamadān

Arāk

Khorramābād

KŪH HĀ-YE ZĀGROS (Mts)

Shīrāz

PERSEPOLIS

Kermān

Zāhedān

PAKISTAN

Ahvāz

Abādān

KUWAIT

Al Kuwayt
(Kuwait)

Bandar-e ʿAbbās

Ar Riyād
(Riyadh)

THE

GULF

BAHRAIN

Al Manāmah

QATAR

Ad Dawhah (Doha)

Abū Zaby
(Abu Dhabi)

Dubayy
(Dubai)

Ash Shāriqah

UNITED ARAB EMIRATES

Str. of Hormuz

GULF OF OMAN

Masqaṭ
(Muscat)

OMAN

ARABIAN

SEA

Tropic of Cancer

© Collins • Longman Atlases Cbi

Feet	Relief	Metres
16 404		5000
9843		3000
6562		2000
3281		1000
1640		500
656		200
0	Sea Level	
Land Dep.		
656		200
13 123		4000
22 966		7000

THE LEVANT

Relief

Feet	Metres
16 404	5000
9843	3000
6562	2000
3281	1000
1640	500
656	200
0	Sea Level

Land Dep.
656	200
13123	4000
22966	7000

Scale 1:3 500 000

0   20   40   60   80   100 Miles
0   50   100   150 Kms.
Polyconic Projection

M E D I T E R R A N E A N

S E A

CYPRUS

Kólpos
Mórfou

Kólpos
Ammókhostou

Akr. Apostólou
Andréa

Rizokárpason

Leonárison

Trikómon

Morfou   Lévkosía
(Nicosia)

Ammókhostos
(Famagusta)

Akr. Akámas

Akr. Pidálion

Polís

Tróödos
Ólimbos 1952

Pano
Plátres

Néa Páfos
(Paphos)

Koúklia

Akrotíri

Lárnax
(Larnaca)

Lemesós
(Limassol)

Akr. Gátas

Al Iskandarïyah
(Alexandria)

Al Burj
Buhayrat
al Burullus

Baltim

Rashid

Dumyât

Kafr al Battïkh

Bûr Saïd
(Port Said)

Sabkhat
al Bardawïl

Al 'Arïsh

Rummânah

Bï'r
Lahfân

E G Y P T

Shibh Jazïrat Sïnâ'

(Sinai Peninsula)

Gulf of Aqaba

S A U D I

A R A B I A

AL LÄdhiqïyah
(Latakia)

Jablah

Bäniyäs

Masyäf

Hamäh

Tarfüs

S Y R I A

LEBANON

Bayrüt
(Beirut)

Dimashq
(Damascus)

Golan Heights

Tel Aviv-Yafo

ISRAEL

GAZA

Be'er Sheva

JORDAN

Ammän

West
Bank

Yerushalayim
(Jerusalem)

Dead
Sea

PETRA

HaNegev
(Negev)

RED SEA

© Collins · Longman Atlases Cbil

Relief

Feet		Metres
16 404		5000
9843		3000
6562		2000
3281		1000
1640		500
656		200
0	Sea Level	
Land Dep.		
656		200
13123		4000
22966		7000

Scale 1:1 000 000

0   10   20   30 Miles
0 10 20 30 40 50 Kms.
Conic Projection

© Collins

North America

Arctic Circle

Europe

NORTH

ATLANTIC

OCEAN

Mediterranean Sea

Algiers

Tunis

TUNISIA

Tripoli

Alexandria

Giza

Cairo

Rabat

Casablanca

MOROCCO

Madeira
(Port.)

Canary
Is.(Sp.)

Tropic of Cancer

Western Sahara

ALGERIA

LIBYA

EGYPT

Red Sea

MAURITANIA

Nouakchott

NIGER

CHAD

Khartoum

ERITREA

Asmara

Gulf of Aden

CAPE
VERDE

Dakar

SENEGAL

GAMBIA

Banjul

Bissau

G.B.

Conakry

Freetown

S.L.

Monrovia

LIBERIA

Bamako

M A L I

BURKINA

Ouagadougou

GUINEA

CÔTE
D'IVOIRE
(IVORY COAST)

Yamoussoukro

GHANA

Accra

Niamey

NIGERIA

TOGO

BENIN

Lomé

Abidjan

Porto-
Novo

Ibadan

Abuja

Lagos

Ndjamena

SUDAN

CENTRAL
AFRICAN REPUBLIC

DJIBOUTI

Djibouti

Addis Ababa

ETHIOPIA

SOMALI REPUBLIC

Mogadishu

CAMEROON

Malabo

Yaoundé

Bangui

Gulf of Guinea

SÃO TOMÉ
AND
PRINCIPE

EQUATORIAL
GUINEA

Príncipe

São
Tomé

Libreville

GABON

CONGO

Brazzaville

Kinshasa

ANGOLA

Kananga

ZAÏRE

UGANDA

Kampala

Kigali

RW.

BUR.

Bujumbura

KENYA

Nairobi

TANZANIA

Dodoma

Dar es Salaam

SEYCHE

SOUTH

Luanda

Equator

ANGOLA

Lusaka

ZAMBIA

MAL.

Lilongwe

COMOROS

Mozambique Channel

MADAGASCAR

Antananarivo

MAU

South
America

ATLANTIC

Harare

ZIMBABWE

MOZAMBIQUE

NAMIBIA

BOTSWANA

Tropic of Capricorn

Windhoek

Gaborone

Pretoria

Johannesburg

Soweto

Maputo

Mbabane

SW.

Maseru

LES.

Durban

REPUBLIC
OF
SOUTH AFRICA

OCEAN

Cape Town

Antarctic Circle

Antarctica

BUR. : BURUNDI
G.B. : GUINEA BISSAU
LES. : LESOTHO
MAL. : MALAWI
RW. : RWANDA
S.L. : SIERRA LEONE
SW. : SWAZILAND

© Collins

AFRICA

COUNTRY	PAGE
ALGERIA	74-75
ANGOLA	78
BENIN	76-77
BOTSWANA	80
BURKINA	76-77
BURUNDI	79
CAMEROON	77
CAPE VERDE	68
CENTRAL AFRICAN REPUBLIC	70; 73; 77
CHAD	70; 72-73; 77
COMOROS	79
CONGO	78
CÔTE D'IVOIRE (IVORY COAST)	76
DJIBOUTI	73
EGYPT	72
EQUATORIAL GUINEA	78
ERITREA	71; 72-73
ETHIOPIA	71; 72-73
GABON	78
GAMBIA	76
GHANA	76
GUINEA	76
GUINEA BISSAU	76
KENYA	79
LESOTHO	80
LIBERIA	76
LIBYA	70; 72; 75
MADAGASCAR	81
MALAŴI	79
MALI	70; 74; 76-77
MAURITANIA	70; 74; 76
MAURITIUS	68
MOROCCO	74
MOZAMBIQUE	70; 79; 81
NAMIBIA	80
NIGER	76-77
NIGERIA	77
RWANDA	79
SÃO TOMÉ AND PRÍNCIPE	70; 77
SENEGAL	76
SEYCHELLES	68
SIERRA LEONE	76
SOMALI REPUBLIC	71
SOUTH AFRICA, REPUBLIC OF	80-81
SUDAN	72-73
SWAZILAND	80-81
TANZANIA	79
TOGO	76-77
TUNISIA	75
UGANDA	79
ZAÏRE	70; 73; 78-79
ZAMBIA	78-79
ZIMBABWE	80-81

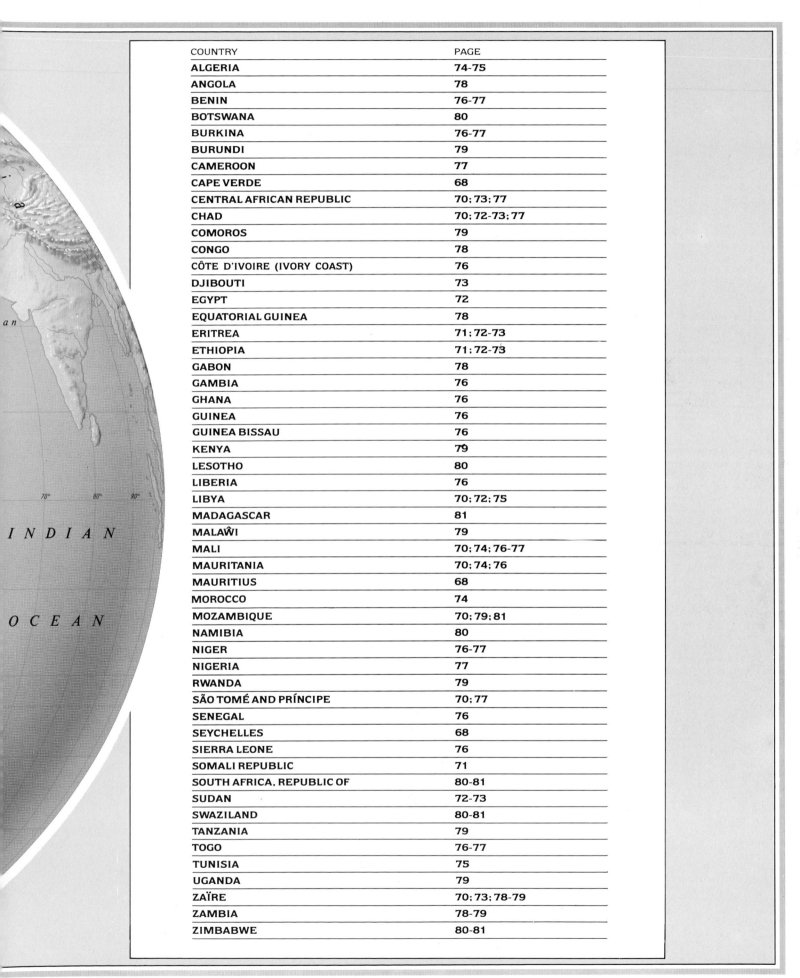

a n

I N D I A N

O C E A N

70° 80° 90°

AFRICA

Relief

Feet		Metres
16 404		5000
9 843		3000
6 562		2000
3 281		1000
1 640		500
656		200
0		Sea Level
Land Dep.		
656		200
13 123		4000
22 966		7000

Scale 1:37 000 000

0   200   400   600   800   1000 Miles

0   400   800   1200   1600 Kms.

Lambert Azimuthal Equal Area Projection

© Collins ◇ Longman Atlases Cbi

Mediterranean Sea

ISRAEL
JORDAN
EGYPT
SUDAN
SAUDI ARABIA
IRAQ
KUWAIT
BAHRAIN
QATAR
UNITED ARAB EMIRATES
OMAN
IRAN
YEMEN
ETHIOPIA
DJIBOUTI
SOMALI REPUBLIC
KENYA
UGANDA
TANZANIA
ZAIRE
ERITREA

An Nafūd (Great Sandy Desert)

Ar Rub' al Khālī

Nubian Desert

Red Sea

Gulf of Oman

Gulf of Aden

Indian Ocean

Lake Victoria

Al Qāhirah (Cairo)
Al Khartūm (Khartoum)
Ar Riyāḍ (Riyadh)
Al Kuwayt (Kuwait)
Makkah (Mecca)
Jiddah (Jedda)
Al Madīnah (Medina)
Ṣan'ā' (Sana)
Ādīs Ābeba (Addis Ababa)
Muqdisho (Mogadishu)
Nairobi

Suquṭrá (Socotra) (Yemen)

Relief		
Feet		Metres
16404		5000
9843		3000
6562		2000
3281		1000
1640		500
656		200
0		Sea Level
Land Dep.		
656		200
13123		4000
22966		7000

Scale 1:15 000 000

0   100   200   300 Miles

0 100 200 300 400 500 Kms

Lambert Zenithal Equal Area Projection

© Collins

NILE VALLEY

NORTHWEST AFRICA

Scale 1:10 000 000

Lambert Zenithal Equal Area Projection

Feet	Metres
16 404	5000
9843	3000
6562	2000
3281	1000
1640	500
656	200
0	Sea Level
Land Dep.	
656	200
13123	4000
22966	7000
	Metres

ATLANTIC

OCEAN

Arquipélago da Madeira (Madeira Is.) (Port.) Funchal   Porto Santo   Madeira

Islas Canarias (Sp.) (Canary Is.)   Lanzarote   Arrecife
La Palma   Tenerife   Santa Cruz de Tenerife   Fuerteventura
Gomera   Las Palmas de Gran Canaria   Gran Canaria   C. Juby
Hierro

Tropic of Cancer

SPAIN   Jerez de la Frontera   Sierra Nevada   Almería
Golfo de Cádiz   Cádiz   **Málaga**   C. de Gata
Algeciras   Gibraltar (U.K.)
Strait of Gibraltar   Ceuta (Sp.)   Melilla (Sp.)   Beni Saf   **Oran**
Tanger (Tangier)   Tétouan (Tetuan)   Nador   Nedroma   Mostaga
Asilah   Chechaouene   Al-Hoceima   Sidi bel Abbès
Larache   Ksar-el-Kebir   Ouezzane   Taza   Oujda   Tlemcen
Kenitra   Sidi Kacem   **Fès**   Jerada   Hauts Plat
Rabat   Salé   Meknes   Sefrou   Mecheria
Mohammedia   Khemisset   Azrou   Tendrara   Ain Sefra
Casablanca   Berrechid   Khouribga   Oued Zem   Kenifra   Bou Arfa   MOROCCO
El Jadida   Settat   Moyen Atlas   Boudenib   Atl
Sidi Smaïl   El-Kelâa-des-Srarhna   Er Rachidia   Abadla
Safi   Beni Mellal   Erfoud   Igli
    Oum er Rbia   M'goun   Rissani   Hamada du Guir   Beni Abbès
Essaouira   Marrakech   Aït-Burir   Béchar
    J. Aoulime   Toubkal   Jbel Sarho   Oued Namous
Tamanar   Taroudannt   Ouarzazate   Grand E
C. Rhir   Tamri   Tazenakht   Tabelbala
Agadir   Oued Sous   Tagounit   Sbaa
    Jbel Bani   Hamada du Drâa   Hamada Tounassine
Tiznit   Tafraout   ALG
Sidi Ifni   Bou-Izakarn   Oued Drâa
Goulimime   Tarhjicht   El Eglab
Tiglit   Oued Drâa   Reggane
Tarfaya   Hamada   Tindouf   Sebkha de Tindouf
El Aaiún (Laâyoune)   Mahbés   Bordj Flye Ste. Marie   Sebkha Azzel Matti
Lemsid   Saguia el Hamra
Cabo Bojador   Bu Craa   Semara   Ain ben Tili   Chenachane   Aoule
    Bir Mogrein   I-n-Bel
Western   Guelta Zemmur   Tourassine   TIRIS ZEMMOUR   Chegga
    Sebjet Agsumal   Sebkhet Oumm ed Droûs Telli   Oued el-Ma   El Eglab
Dakhla   Sahara   El Mreiti   Poste Weygand
    Sebkhet Oumm ed Droûs Guebli   Erg Chech
    Terhazza   Ouallen
    Fdérik   Zouîrât   Bir Zreigat   Tni Haïa   Tanezrou
Uad Atui   915   Kediet Ijill   Aguêraktem   Taoudenni   Poste Maurice Cortier (Bidon Cinq)
Tichla   El Khnâchîch
Nouadhibou   Choum   A D R   Bîr Ounâne   Erg i-n-Sâkâne
C. Blanc   Passe de Ouararda   A R   S A   El Ouassi   Tessalit
DAKHLET   Ouarane   El Djouf   Tessalit
NOUAD-   Ouadane   TOMBOUCTOU   Kidal
HIBOU   Atar   El Mreyyé   In Ta
INCHIRI   MAURITANIA   Mabrouk   M A L
Akjoujt   Araouane
C. Timiris   Bouraga   Aguelhok
Sebkha de Ndrhamcha   HODH   Anefis i-n-Da
Nouakchott   Tidjikdja   ECH   GA
    Tichît   CHARGUI   Bamba   Tombouctou (Timbuktu)
Trarza   TAGANT   Azaouâd   L. Faguibine   Bourem
    Boutilimit   420   Tagant   Gourma-Rharous   Tondibi
Mederdra   Moudjéria   HODH EL   Goundam   Diré   Niger   Gao
    Aleg   Boumdeit   GHARBI   Oualâta   Gossi   Ansongo
Rosso   BRAKNA   Tamchaket   Ayoûn el 'Atroûs   L. Faguibine   Doro   Ouasso
Dagana   Bogué   Kiffa   Néma   Niafounké   Gossi   Fafa
Podor   ASSABA   Niout   Goundam   Hombori   Labbezanga
St. Louis   Mbagne   Kaédi   Timbédra   MOPTI
L. de Guiers   Pouté   GUID   Kankossa   KOUMBISALEH
Louga   Dahra   Linguère   Matam   IMAKA   Yélimané   Nioro   Nara   Douentza
Tivaouane   Namari   Bakel   Nioro
Dakar   Thiès   SENEGAL   KAYES   BAMAKO   SÉGOU
Diourbel   © Collins

74

WEST AFRICA

Western
Sahara

TIRIS ZEMMOUR

Nouadhibou

DAKHLET
NOUAD-
HIBOU   INCHIRI

C. Blanc

C. Timiris

MAURITANIA

TOMBOUCTOU

Nouakchott

TRARZA

TAGANT

Tidjikdja   TAGANT   Tichît

HODH ECH
CHARGUI

Rosso
Mederdra

BRAKNA

HODH EL
GHARBI

KOUMBISALEH

MALI

St. Louis

SENEGAL

KAYES

BAMAKO

MOPTI

SEGOU

SAHEL

BURKINA

Dakar

C. Vert

Thiès

Banjul

GAMBIA

Bamako

M   A   L   I

NORD
OUAHIGOUYA
CENTRE
NORD

VOLTA-
NOIRE

CENTRE

GUINEA

BISSAU

GUINEA

SIKASSO

HAUTS BASSINS

CENTRE
OUEST

SUD
OUEST

UPPER
WEST

Conakry

SIERRA
LEONE

Freetown

CÔTE D'IVOIRE

(IVORY COAST)

NORTHERN

G H A N A

BRONG-AHAFO

ASHANTI

LIBERIA

Monrovia

EASTERN

WESTERN

CENTRAL

Accra

ATLANTIC

OCEAN

C. Palmas   Harper

Relief

Feet	Metres
16 404	5000
9843	3000
6562	2000
3281	1000
1640	500
656	200
	Sea Level
Land Dep. 0	
656	200
13123	4000
22 966	7000

Scale 1:10 000 000

| 0 | 100 | 200 | 300 Miles |

| 0 | 100 | 200 | 300 | 400 Kms. |

Lambert Azimuthal Equal Area Projection

© Collins ◇ Longman Atlases Cbi

ALGERIA

Ahaggar

Tit ▲2918
Abalessa Tamanrasset
Silet Amsel

Oued Tamanrasset

597 ▲
Adrar des Ifōras

In Tasik

In Abbaggarit

Anou
Ti-n Ehaoua
Admer

Ti *Tassili oua-n Ahaggar*

Sidaouet

Aïr (Azbine)

Iferouâne ▲1796

1994 ▲ Mt. Gréboun

A H A G G A R

Plateau du Djado

Djado

Plateau du Tchigaï

Ténéré du Tafássasset

Séguédine

A G A D E Z

Aney

Bilma

Zouar

T i b e s t i

Bardai
Tarso Ouri ▲3150 Ouri
Bettê ▲2286
Aozou
▲3205
▲3325
Tarso Ahon
Emi Koussi ▲3415
Gouro

BORKOU-ENNEDI-TIBESTI

LIBYA

Tropic of Cancer

Toummo

15°

20°

Grand Erg de Bilma

Aïn Galakka

Largeau

Enneri Yao

Koro
Toro

N I G E R

Teguidda
I-n-Tessoum
Agadez

I-n-Gall

DIFFA

B o d é l é

Tillabéri
Ouallam

Ménaka

Filingué

Tahoua
Illéla

Tamaské

Tanout

Gangara

Tegouma

508

ZINDER

Gouré

Boultoum

Nguigmi

Bosso
(281)

Nokou
Zigey

Mao

Moussoro

Ati

Bahr el Ghazal

Batha

KANEM

C H A D

BATHA

Lac Fitri
Yao

Batha

Massakory

TAHOUA

NIAMEY
Gothèye
Niamey
Loga

Dosso
Say

BOSSO

Borou

Matankari
Birni N'Konni
Gada

Madaoua

MARADI
Maradi
Tessaoua
Zinder

Geidam
Kantché
Matameye

Nguru
Gashua

Diffa

Zari

Plain of Bornu

Marte

Anala

CHARI-BAGUIRMI
N'Djamena

GUERA

Abou Deia

Melfi

Mongo

Bokoro

Massenya

Massaqam

Matsena

Gueskérou

Titiwa

Dikwa

Kousséri

Chari

Maïduguri

Bama

Mora

Gelengdeng
Bongor

Yagoua

Kaélé

MOYEN

B. Salamat

CHARI

Sarh

Kyabé

Miltou

TANDJILÉ

Léré
Pala
Laï

Koumra

Doba

Bahr Aouk

BAMINGUI-
BANGORAN

Gwadabawa
Binji
Wurno
Sabon Birni

Isa

Kaura Namoda

Argungu
Sokoto
Talata Mafara
Gummi

Moriki
KATSINA
Katsina
Daura
Kazaure

Yashi

Hadejia

Gumel
Hadejia

Gamawa

Azare

Potiskum

Damaturu

Masba

Lantewa

Gubio

YOBE

Gana

Komadugu

Yajua

Massba

Gonni

Mubi

Marl
1295

Maroua
Mindif

Gombi

Garko

Yan

Numan

Léré

TANDJILÉ

Ergig

Bousso

Gore
Maroua

Batangafo

NANA

OUHAM

Bossangoa

Bouca

Kouki

NANA

Bocaranga

OUHAM
PENDE

Bozoum

CENTRAL
AFRICAN
REPUBLIC

NANA-
GRÉBIZI

Kaga
Bandoro

Sibut

Bambari

Niger

KEBBI

SOKOTO
Sokoto
Birnin
Kebbi

Zamfara
Anka
Chafe

Gusau

Funtua

Malumfashi

Paki

KANO

Jamaari

Kari

Gongola

Gongola

BORNO
Buni
Chibuk

Nafada

ADAMAWA

Jimeta
Yola

Song

Lab

Jalingo

Ganye

Poli

Tcholliré

Moundou
LOGONE
ORIENTAL

Gounou

Moïssala

Kélo

Doba

Ouham

Maïkona
Bétaré Oya

Baboua

Babua

KADÉ

Berbérati

Boda

Bangui

Zongo

Ouadda

M'Baiki

Libenge

Karimama
Goya
Kamba

Dakingari
Koko
Zuru

Birnin
Gwari

Zaria
KADUNA

Anchau

Foggo

Jamaari

Bauchi
BAUCHI
Bara

Ako

Gombe

ZAÏRE

Banikoara
Kandi

Gogonou
Gamia

Nikki
Ndali

Babana
New Bussa

Auna

Kontagora

Tegina

Minna

Lame
Jos
Bukuru

Pindiga

Pankshin

1595

Wamba

NIGER

Kaduna

Kajuru

Gwagwada

Jos Plateau

BENIN

Birni

Chamba

Parakou

Okuta
Bode
Sadu

Shaki

Jebba

Lafiagi
Bida

Pategi

Kaiama

Bokani

Kontagora

Tegina

Baro

FED. CAP.
TER.

Abuja

PLATEAU

Keffi

Nasarawa

Lafia

Doma

Umaisha

Gassol

Gassol

Ibi

Wukari

Beli

1500

Tigane

Ngaoundéré

Dibi

Tibati

Kontcha

Benoué

Dyerem

Massif de l'Adamaoua

1600

Babokoum

Padua

MAMBÉRÉ

Bétaré Oya

Batouri

Gamboula

Bocaranga

Carnot

Bossembélé

Ft. de Possel

Mboko

OMBELLA

MBAÉRÉ

SANGHA

Nola

Lobaye

Lipeité

Lopi

Kaga

Batangafo

Savalou
Zoumé
Cové
Pobè

Ogbomosho
 Offa
Ila

OYO
Iwo
Oshogbo
Ilesha

Iseyin

Ede
Ibadan

KWARA

Ilorin

Iloro

Akure

Ikerre

ONDO

Owo

Oka

KOGI

Idah

Ankpa

Dekina

Makurdi

BENUE

Otukpo

Gboko

Obudu

Takum

Donga

Riti

Gassol

TARABA

Katsina Ala

Mayo-Daga

Banyo

Dumbo

Wum

Bamenda

Mamfé

Foumban

Yoko

Nanga
Eboko

Belabo

Bertoua

Doumé

Minta

Ayos

Diang

Garoua Boulaï

Bertoua

Batouri

Doumé

Yokaduma

Doumé

Ndélélé

Lomié

Dja

Souflay

Impfondo

CONGO

Abeokuta
Ijebu Ode

Shagamu

Mushin
LAGOS
Lagos

Badagri

Porto-Novo
Cotonou

Aného

Saketé

OSUN

Ife
Ondo

EDO

Benin City

ANAMBRA

Onitsha

ABIA

Umuahia

IMO
Owerri

Aba

AKWA-IBOM
Uyo

RIVERS

Port Harcourt

Bonny

Buguma
Nembe

Brass

Warri
Sapele

DELTA

Bomadi

Yenagoa

Buruta

Niger Delta

3261

Bight of Benin

Gulf

of

Guinea

Enugu
ENUGU

Nkalagu

Abakaliki

Ikom

Ogoja

Ugep

Calabar

Oron
Eket

Mamfé

CAMEROON

Kumba

Mt. Cameroun ▲4070
Buea
Limbe

Douala

Malabo

Bioco

EQUATORIAL

GUINEA

Edea

Nyong

Yaoundé

Mbalmayo

Zoétélé

Ebolowa

Sangmélima

Ambam

Bitam

Campo

Kribi

Sanaga

Eséka

Akonolinga

Okola

Ayos

Bight of Bonny

SÃO TOMÉ
& PRÍNCIPE *Príncipe*

Bata

GABON

Ndjolé

Lambaréné

Lomié

Moloundou

Ubangi

ZAÏRE

Bomboma

Gandou

77

CENTRAL AND EAST AFRICA

Relief

Feet		Metres
16404		5000
9843		3000
6562		2000
3281		1000
1640		500
656		200
0		Sea Level
Land Dep.		
656		200
13123		4000
22966		7000

Scale 1:10 000 000

Lambert Azimuthal Equal Area Projection

SOMALI
REP

NORTH

EASTERN

Muqdisho
(Mogadishu)

Marka

Baraawe

Equator

KENYA

UGANDA

Kampala

Nairobi

COAST

RIFT

VALLEY

NYANZA

CENTRAL

Mombasa

RWANDA

KAGERA

Lake Victoria

MARA

ARUSHA

Pemba I.

Zanzibar I.

Zanzibar

BURUNDI

MWANZA

SHINYANGA

KIGOMA

TANZANIA

TABORA

DODOMA

DAR ES SALAAM

Dar es Salaam

INDIAN

OCEAN

RUKWA

MBEYA

IRINGA

MOROGORO

PWANI

Mafia I.

NORTHERN

MTWARA

Mtwara

LUAPULA

RUVUMA

Cabo Delgado

CABO

DELGADO

Grande Comore
(Njazidja)

Moroni

Mohéli
(Mwali)

Anjouan
(Nzwani)

COMOROS

Île Mayotte
(Fr.)

COPPERBELT

NIASSA

Nampula

NAMPULA

ZAMBIA

EASTERN

MALAWI

TETE

ZAMBEZIA

Mozambique Channel

Lusaka

ZIMBABWE

Harare

SOFALA

MANICA

MOZAMBIQUE

Juan de Nova

MADAGASCAR

© Collins ● Longman Atlases Cbi

SOUTHERN AFRICA AND MADAGASCAR

WESTERN

Metangula
Nkhotakota
Kasungu
Maniamba
Chipata
Bua
Mponela
Dowa
Mchinji
Salima
Ulongwe
Ncheu
Dedza
Balaka
Mozambique

NIASSA
Lichinga
Guerra
Marrupa
Nungo
Balama
Namapa
Marru

CABO
DELGADO
Ancuabe
Pemba
Mecufi
Lurio
Chaonde
Simuco
Memba
Nacala
Mossuril

NAMPULA
Nampula
Meconta
Moçambique
Mogincual
Namaponda
Angoche
Gilé
Moma

ZAMBEZIA

Mozambique Channel

MOZAMBIQUE

SOFALA

Beira
Nova Sofala

INHAMBANE

GAZA

MAPUTO

INDIAN

OCEAN

Tj. Bobaomby
Antsiranana

Nosy Be
Ambilobe
Andoany
Vohimarina
Anorotsangana
Ambanja
Massif de
Tsaratanana
Sambava
Analalava
Antsohihy
Antalaha
Befandriana
Maroantsetra
Mahajanga
Port Bergé
Mampikony
Mandritsara
Mitsinjo
Marovoay
Mananara
Tj. Masoala
Soalala
Ambato-Boeni
Maevatanana
Tsaratanana
Soanierana Ivongo
Tanjona
Vilanandro
Besalampy
Nosy
Boraha
Moningori
Ambodifototra
Fenoarivo
Atsinanana
Kandreho
Andriba
Juan de Nova
Tambohorano
Morafenobe
Maintirano
Antsalova
Tsiroanomandidy
Arivonimamo
Miarinarivo
Soavinandriana
Miandrivazo
Belo-sur-Tsiribihina
Betsiboka
Ankazobe
Anjozorobe
Fihaonana
Antananarivo
(Tananarive)
Ambatolampy
Faratsiho
Antsirabe
Ambatondrazaka
L. Alaotra
Toamasina
Anivorano
Vohibinany
Andevoranto
Moramanga
Vatomandry
Mahanoro
Marolambo
Mandoto
Betafo
Antsirabe
Fandriana
Morondava
Malaimbandy
Mahabo
Ambatofinandrahana
Ambohimahasoa
Ambositra
Ambohimanga du Sud
Nosy-Varika
Mananjary
Mandabe
Manja
Massif du Makay
Matsiatra
Fianarantsoa
Ihosy
Ikalamavony
Hanadiana
Fort Carnot
Manakara
Morombe
Tanjona
Ankaboa
Befandriana
Beroroha
Ankazoabo
Ivohibe
Ankaramena
Ambalavao
Vondrozo
Vohipeno
Farafangana
Manombo
Ihosy
Ranohira
Manakara
Toliara
Tongobory
Onilahy
Iakora
Betroka
Vangaindrano
Benenitra
Midongy-Sud
Betioky
Bekily
Tsivory
Manantenina
Ampanihy
Tranoroa
Menarandra
Behara
Tj. Masoala

Tropic of Capricorn

Androka
Tsihombe
Ambovombe
Tôlanaro

Tj. Vohimena

Relief

Feet		Metres
16 404		5000
9 843		3000
6 562		2000
3 281		1000
1 640		500
656		200
0		Sea Level
Land Dep.		200
656		4000
13 123		7000
22 966		

Scale 1:10 000 000

| 0 | 100 | 200 | 300 Miles |

| 0 | 100 | 200 | 300 | 400 | 500 Kms. |

Lambert Azimuthal Equal Area Projection

N O R T H

Tropic of Cancer

P A C I F I C

Hawaiian
Islands
(U.S.A.)

A S I a

Northern Mariana
Islands
(U.S.A.)

MARSHALL
ISLANDS

O C E A N

Guam (U.S.A.)

M I C R O N E

Philippine
Sea

FED. STATES OF MICRONESIA

S I A

Caroline   Islands

Equator

PALAU
(BELAU)

NAURU

Gilbert
Is.

M E L A N E

Pheonix
Islands   KIRIBÃTI

New
Ireland

S I A

PAPUA
NEW
GUINEA

Bougainville

New Britain

SOLOMON
ISLANDS

Santa Cruz
Is.

TUVALU

Tokelau
Is.

N
E
S
I
A

Guadalcanal

WESTERN
SAMOA
Apia
(U.S.A.)

Cook

Port
Moresby

Espiritu
Santo
Malekula

VANUATU

(France) Wallis
Is.

Vanua
Levu

(N.Z.)

Islands

Society
Islands

Papeete
Tahiti

Tuamotu Archip

Arafura Sea

Vila

FIJI   Suva

TONGA

Alofi
Niue
(N.Z.)

Avarua

P O L Y

Timor
Sea

Coral
Sea

New
Caledonia
(France)
Nouméa

Loyalty Is.

Nuku'alofa

Tropic of Capricorn

(France)

S O U T

INDIAN

Brisbane

A U S T R A L I A

Sydney
Canberra

N
E
S
I
A

Adelaide

Melbourne

Auckland

North
Island

NEW

P A C I F I

OCEAN

Perth

Tasmania   Hobart

Tasman
Sea

South
Island

Wellington

ZEALAND

Christchurch

Chatham
Is.

O C E A N

Dunedin

Stewart I.

International Date Line

SOUTHERN

OCEAN

Antarctic Circle

A n t a r c t i c a

© Collins

82

OCEANIA

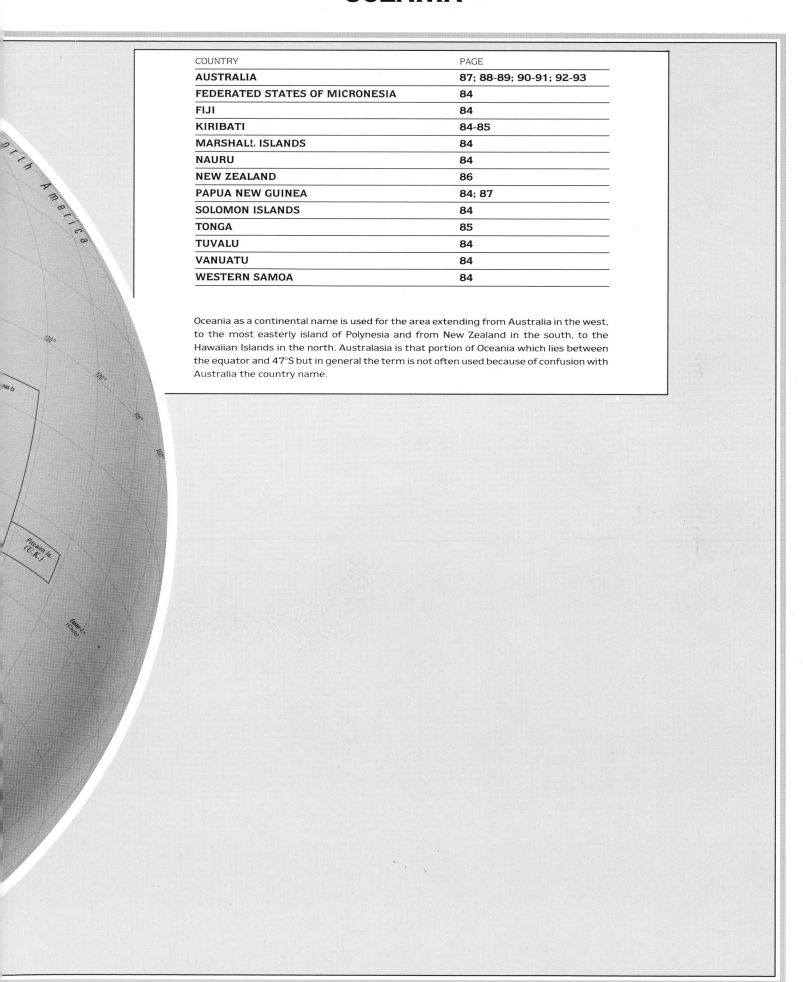

COUNTRY	PAGE
AUSTRALIA	87; 88-89; 90-91; 92-93
FEDERATED STATES OF MICRONESIA	84
FIJI	84
KIRIBATI	84-85
MARSHALL ISLANDS	84
NAURU	84
NEW ZEALAND	86
PAPUA NEW GUINEA	84; 87
SOLOMON ISLANDS	84
TONGA	85
TUVALU	84
VANUATU	84
WESTERN SAMOA	84

Oceania as a continental name is used for the area extending from Australia in the west, to the most easterly island of Polynesia and from New Zealand in the south, to the Hawaiian Islands in the north. Australasia is that portion of Oceania which lies between the equator and 47°S but in general the term is not often used because of confusion with Australia the country name.

PACIFIC OCEAN

SAMOA ISLANDS
Scale 1:7 500 000

Falealupo Aopo Fagamalo
Salailua Puapua
Savai'i Balelologa
Matautu Apia Upolu
Salani Tiavea
WESTERN Samoa
SAMOA (U.S.A.)
Manua Is.
Pago Pago Ofu Olosega
Tutuila C. Matatula Tau
Steps Pt.

FIJI
Undu C.
Gt. Sea Reef Vanua Levu
Lambasa Mbutha
Mbua Taveuni
Yathata
Lautoka Koro
Nandi Viti Ngau Koro
Singatoka Levu Sea
Suva
Kandavu Passage Lau
Kandavu Group
Scale 1:15 000 000

RAROTONGA
(N.Z.)
Avatiu
Pokoinu Avarua
438 Matavera
Arorangi Te 663 Ngatangiia
Manga
Muri
Titikaveka
Scale 1:500 000

NIUE
(N.Z.)
Hikutavake Mutalau
Toi
Makefu Tuapa Lakepa
Alofi Alofi Motutapu Liku
Bay
Avatele 68
Avatele Bay Avatele Hakupu
Tepa Pt. Vaiea
Scale 1:1 000 000

GUAM
(U.S.A.)
Ritidian Pt.
Philippine Pati Pt.
Sea Mt. Santa Rosa 262
Agana Catalina Pt.
Orote Yona
Pen. Talofofo
Merizo Mafolos
Inarajan
Scale 1:2 000 000

VANUATU AND NEW CALEDONIA
Banks Is.
C. Cumberland
Espiritu C. Quiros
Santo I. Maewo
1890 Oba
Luganville Pentecost I.
Malekula Ambrim
Epi Shepherd
Islands
Emae Tongoa
Vila Efate
VANUATU
Eromanga
Tana
Lenakel Aneityum

Récifs
d'Entrecasteaux
Grand Passage
Grand
Récif
de
Cook
Koumac Île Îles Loyauté
Ile Lifou (Loyalty Is.)
1628 Ile Uvéa
Vao Kone
Bourail Île Maré
Nouvelle
Calédonie
(New Caledonia) Yaté
(Fr.) Nouméa
Île des Pins
Scale 1:15 000 000

© Collins

Sea of Okhotsk
BERING SEA
Aleutian Basin
Komandorskiye
Ostrova
Amur Sakhalin Poluostrov Kamchatka
8100
7429
Aleutian Islands
Aleutian Trench

Vladivostok Sapporo
Kurilskiye Ostrova
NORTH Kuril Trench
Beijing Pyongyang KOREA 10542
(Peking) Hokkaido
Xi'an Qingdao SOUTH Sea of
(Sian) (Seoul) KOREA Japan
CHINA Kobe Tokyo JAPAN
Chengdu Nanjing Osaka
Chongqing (Nanking) Shikoku
(Chungking) Wuhan Shanghai Kyushu
Nanchang East China
Sea
Guangzhou Taipei
(Canton) Nansei Shoto
Nanning TAIWAN Okinawa
HONG KONG Nansei Shoto Okinawa Trench
(U.K.)
Hainan
Beibu South China
Wan Sea

1962 1634
Midway Is.
(U.S.A.)
Marcus I.
(Jap.) Lisianski Laysan Hawaiian
Islands
(U.S.A.)

NORTH PACIFIC OCEAN

Bonin Is. 10500
(Jap.) 6148 Wake I. 1477 Johnston I.
Volcano Is. (U.S.A.) 1440 (U.S.A.)
(Jap.)
PHILIPPINE Northern Mariana
7559 SEA Islands
Luzon (U.S.A.)
Quezon Guam (U.S.A.) MARSHALL International Date Line
City Enewetak Bikini ISLANDS
Manila 11034 Yap
PHILIPPINES Mariana Trench Caroline Namonuito Chuuk Ralik Chain
Philippine Woleai Pohnpei Majuro Kingman
Ho Chí Minh Trench PALAU Eauripik Chuuk Pingelap Ralik Chain Palmyra
(Saigon) Palawan 10497 (BELAU) Caroline Ebon Jaluit (U.S.A.)
West East
Caroline Basin Caroline Islands
Sulu Caroline Basin
Sea FED. STATES OF MICRONESIA Butaritari
BRUNEI Mindanao Halmahera Admiralty Is. Tarawa Gilbert
Sulu Manus NAURU Banaba Is. Kingsmill
Archipelago Kep. Sula (Ocean I.) Group
Celebes Sea Puncak Jaya Bismarck New Nanumea
5520 4630 PAPUA Sea Ireland Bougainville TUVALU Nui Vaitupu Phoenix Abariringa
Sulawesi Seram NEW New Funafuti Islands Rawaki
INDONESIA (Celebes) Buru GUINEA Britain SOLOMON Nukumanu Nukunono KIRIBATI Orona
Laut 7440 Port ISLANDS Malaita Nukufetau
Jakarta Maluku Kep. Moresby Guadalcanal Tokelau Is. (N.Z.)
Java Surabaya Laut Aru Santa Cruz Atafu Swains
(Jawa) Banda Kep. Is. Fakaofo (U.S.A.) Danger Is.
Flores Tanimbar Nassau I.
Timor Arafura WESTERN
Sumba Sea Torres Strait Coral Sea SAMOA
Java Trench Thursday I. Basin 4716 Espíritu Savai'i Apia
7450 6218 Gulf of Santo Upolu Manua Is. (U.S.A.)
Darwin Carpentaria Malekula North Tutuila
Timor Cairns New Hebrides Basin VANUATU FIJI Vanua Levu Alofi
Sea Great VANUATU Vila Fiji Viti Suva Niue
Wyndham Barrier Iles Chesterfield Levu Lau TONGA (N.Z.)
Broome Reef (Fr.) Tana Loyauté Group
Nouvelle (Loyalty I. Ridge 5303 Nuku'alofa
Tennant Calédonie Is.) Noumea South Haʻapai 10882
Creek (New Caledonia) Fiji Group (N.Z.) Tonga Trench
(Fr.) Norfolk Basin
AUSTRALIA Norfolk I. Kermadec
Geraldton Brisbane Lord Howe (Aus.) Is.
Middleton Rise Raoul
Reef Lord Howe I. Ridge I. (N.Z.) 10047
Newcastle Ball's Pyramid Three Kings Is. Kermadec
Perth Port Sydney TASMAN Auckland Trench
Kalgoorlie Augusta Canberra 126 NEW
Great Murray SEA ZEALAND
Australian Adelaide North Island
Bight Melbourne King I. Flinders I. Furneaux Wellington
Albany South Australian Group Chatham Rise Chatham Is.
Basin Tasmania Christchurch
Hobart South Island Dunedin
Bruny I. Bluff Stewart I. Bounty Is.
Tasmania Ridge The Snares New Zealand Antipodes Is.
Auckland Is. 6098
Plateau
SOUTHERN OCEAN Campbell I.

Macquarie I.
(Aus.)

Indian-Antarctic Ridge
Eastern Indian- Macquarie-Balleny Ridge Balleny Is.
Antarctic Basin (N.Z.)

INDIAN OCEAN

NEW ZEALAND

Relief

Feet	Metres
16 404	5000
9843	3000
6562	2000
3281	1000
1640	500
656	200
0	Sea Level

Land Dep.

656	200
13123	4000
22 966	7000

North Cape
Ninety Mile Beach
Doubtless Bay
Mangonui
Kaitaia
C. Brett
Rawene
Paihia
Bay of Islands
Kaikohe
Hikurangi
NORTHLAND
Whangarei
Dargaville
Waipu
Bream Bay
Gt. Barrier I.
Warkworth
Hauraki Gulf
Helensville
Kaipara Harbour
Coromandel
Takapuna
Coromandel Peninsula
Auckland
Manukau
Whitianga
AUCKLAND
Pukekohe
Manukau Harbour
Waiuku
Waikato
Huntly
Waihi
Mayor I.
Morrinsville
Bay of Plenty
Hamilton
Tauranga
Matakana
Cambridge
Te Kaha
Hicks Bay
WAIKATO
Matamata
Te Araroa
East Cape
Kawhia
Tokoroa
Rotorua
Opotiki
Tikitiki
Te Kuiti
Rotorua
Matawai
Hikurangi 1754
Benneydale
BAY OF PLENTY
Murupara
GISBORNE
Waipiro
Mokau
Lake Taupo
Taupo
Kaimanawa Mts
Huiarau Ra.
Tolaga Bay
North Taranaki Bight
Waitara
Turangi
Ngauruhoe 2291
Gisborne
New Plymouth
Inglewood
Ruapehu 2797
Kaimai
Waikokopu
Mt. Taranaki (Mt. Egmont)
Stratford
Ngaruroro
Mahia Peninsula
TARANAKI
Ruahine Mts
HAWKES BAY
Opunake
Normanby
Wairoa
Hawke Bay
Hawera
MANAWATU
Bay View
Napier
Patea
Mangaweka
Hastings
Wanganui
WANGANUI
Waipawa
Marton
Waipukurau
Bulls
Feilding
Dannevirke
Palmerston North
Woodville
112
Foxton
Kapiti I.
Levin
WELLINGTON
Paraparaumu
Porirua
Masterton
Upper Hutt
Carterton
Lower Hutt
Wellington
Cook Strait
C. Palliser

NORTH ISLAND
2297

TASMAN SEA

Cape Farewell
Collingwood
Golden Bay
D'Urville I.
Takaka
Tasman Mts
Tasman Bay
Karamea Bight
Motueka
Nelson
Picton
Karamea
Richmond
Havelock
Blenheim
Seddon
Granity
Tapawera
Wairau
NELSON
Westport
Murchison
MARLBOROUGH
Cape Campbell
Cape Foulwind
Buller
Inangahua
Kaikoura Ra.
Reefton
Mt. Travers 2338
Clarence
Kaikoura
Greymouth
Grey
Ahaura
Hanmer Springs
Kumara
Brunner
Lewis Pass
Waiau
Hokitika
Otira
Waiau
Ross
Arthur's Pass
Cheviot
Whataroa
Waipara
Pegasus Bay
Okarito
Springfield
Rangiora
Fox Glacier
Waimakariri
Kaiapoi
SOUTHERN ALPS
Rakaia
Christchurch
Mt. Cook (Mt. Aoraki) 3754
Lincoln
Cascade Pt.
Ukuru
L. Pukaki
Darfield
Banks Peninsula
L. Tekapo
Ashburton
Akaroa
Mt. Aspiring 3027
Leeston
Milford Sound
Homer Tunnel
Wanaka
L. Wanaka
Fairlie
Geraldine
Arrowtown
L. Hawea
Omarama
Timaru
Queenstown
Dunstan Mts
Kurow
Canterbury Bight
L. Wakatipu
Cromwell
Omarama
Waitaki
Waimate
Te Anau
Garvie Mts
Clyde
Naseby
Pukeuri
L. Te Anau
Alexandra
Ranfurly
Oamaru
OTAGO
Roxburgh
L. Manapouri
Mossburn
Palmerston
Resolution I.
Lumsden
SOUTHLAND
Lawrence
Waikouaiti
Cameron Mts
Nightcaps
Tapanui
Port Chalmers
Otago Peninsula
Ohai
Winton
Gore
Clinton
Mataura
Dunedin
Puysegur Pt.
Tuatapere
Edendale
Balclutha
Riverton
Invercargill
Owaka
Foveaux Strait
Bluff
Ruapuke I.
Stewart I.
Halfmoon Bay
Southwest Cape

SOUTH ISLAND
4870

PACIFIC OCEAN

Scale 1:6 000 000

| 0 | 50 | 100 | 150 Miles |

| 0 | 50 | 100 | 150 | 200 Kms. |

Conic Projection

AUSTRALIA

Scale 1:20 000 000

| 0 | 100 | 200 | 300 | 400 | 500 Miles |

| 0 | 200 | 400 | 600 | 800 Kms. |

Lambert Azimuthal Equal Area Projection

© Collins ◇ Longman Atlases Cbi

WESTERN AUSTRALIA

SOUTH
AUSTRALIA

Great Victoria Desert

Nullarbor Plain

Great Australian Bight

Spencer Gulf

Eyre Pen.

Warrina
Cooker Pedy
Tarcoola
L. Gairdner
Gawler Ranges
Cowell
Kimba
Cleve
Kyancutta
Elliston
Port Lincoln
Coffin I.
Kangaroo I.

Kingoonya
Wynbring
Ooldea
Penong
Ceduna
Streaky Bay
Anxious B.
Flinders I.

Maralinga
Fowler's B.
Nuyts Archipelago
C. Adieu
Colona
Head of Bight

Hughes
Nurina
Cocklebiddy
Balladonia

INDIA
OCEAN

Geraldton
Northampton
Dongara
Eneabba
Mullewa
Mongers L.
Paynes Find
L. Moore
Wubin
Kalannie
Wongan Hills
Moora
Coorow
Gingin
Perth
Fremantle
Kwinana
Pinjarra
Mandurah
Bunbury
Busselton
C. Naturaliste
Geographe B.
C. Leeuwin
Augusta
Pemberton
Denmark
Albany
King George Sd.

Leverton
Malcolm
Leonora
Menzies
Kalgoorlie
Coolgardie
Widgiemooltha
Norseman
L. Lefroy
L. Cowan
L. Dundas
Kumarl
Esperance
Archipelago of the Recherche
Israelite Bay
Zanthus
Rawlinna

Scale 1:10 000 000
Lambert Zenithal Equal Area Projection

INDIAN OCEAN

Pt. Dover
Pt. Culver
Rawlinna
Kitchener
Naretha
Cook
Balladonia
Zanthus
Russell Range Mt. Ragged
Israelite Bay
Pt. Malcolm
C. Pasley
C. Arid
Sandy
Middle I.
South East Is.
Pollock Reef
Termination I.
Archipelago of the Recherche

L. Roe
Yindarlgooda
Kanowna
Boulder
Kambalda
Coolgardie
Widgiemooltha
Norseman
L. Lefroy
Salmon Gums
Kumarl
L. Dundas
L. Cowan
Karonie
Coonana

Esperance
Gibson
Hopetoun

Ora Banda
Broad Arrow
Kalgoorlie
Centenary
Bullabulling
Barker L.
L. Johnston
L. Cowan
L. Hope
Brazier Ra.
Ravensthorpe
Phillips R.

Koolyanobbing
Southern Cross
L. Deborah
Seabrook
Bullfinch
Marvel Loch
Yellowdine
Bodallin
Moorine
Burracoppin
Mukinbudin
Bonnie Rock
Bencubbin
Wialki
Koorda
Kulja
Burakin

Geraldton
Northampton
Dongara
Eneabba
Mullewa

Cumberland
Watheroo
Moora
Dandaragan
Lancelin
Gingin
Yanchep
Perth
Rottnest I.
Fremantle
Kwinana
Rockingham
Peel Inlet
Mandurah
Pinjarra

Bunbury
Brunswick
Harvey
Collie
Boyanup
Busselton
C. Naturaliste
Dunsborough
Geographe Bay
C. Leschenault
Margaret River
Hamelin Bay
Augusta
C. Leeuwin
Flinders Bay

INDIAN OCEAN

Scale 1:5 000 000
Lambert Zenithal Equal Area Projection

© Collins

89

EASTERN AUSTRALIA

SOUTHEAST AUSTRALIA

Asia

Europ

ARCTIC
OCEAN

Ellesmere I.

G R E E N L A N D
(KALAALLIT NUNAAT)
(Denmark)

Denmark
Strait

Arctic Circle

Bering Strait

ALASKA

U.S.A.

Anchorage

Parry Islands

Baffin
Bay

Baffin Island

Godthåb/
Nuuk

Victoria
Island

Hudson
Bay

International Date Line

C A N A D A

Edmonton

Newfoundland

50°

Vancouver

Seattle

Winnipeg

Québec

Montreal
Ottawa

Portland

U N I T E D   S T A T E S

Toronto
Hamilton

Boston

Milwaukee

Detroit
Cleveland

Buffalo
Paterson
Newark

New York

40°

Chicago

Pittsburgh

Baltimore

Philadelphia

N O R T H

San Francisco

O F

Denver

Indianapolis

Cincinnati

Washington

San Jose

Kansas City

St. Louis

Honolulu

A M E R I C A

Bermuda
(U.K.)

P A C I F I C

Hawaiian
Islands
(U.S.A.)

Los Angeles
San Bernardino

San Diego

30°

Atlanta

Tijuana

Dallas

I. de
Guadalupe
(Mex.)

Ciudad
Juárez

Houston

New Orleans

O C E A N

Tropic of Cancer

Miami

BAHAMAS

170°

M E X I C O

20°

Monterrey

Gulf of
Mexico

Havana

CUBA

Santiago
de Cuba

PUERTO
RICO
San
Juan

ST. K

AN

160°

León

Guadalajara

JAMAICA

HAITI DOM
REP.
Port-
au-
Prince

Santo
Domingo

DOMINIC

Guadeloupe

Martiniq

ST. LU

Kingston

Is. de
Revilla Gigedo
(Mex.)

Mexico
City

Caribbean   Sea

ST. V. AND
ST. V. AND G
GRENAD

150°

Belmopan

BELIZE

Guatemala GUA.
City

HONDURAS

(Neth.)

140°

San Salvador

EL
SAL.

Tegucigalpa

NICARAGUA

130° Equator

Managua

COSTA RICA

Panama
City

San José

PANAMA

10°

S O U T H

So

120°

110°

90°

Am

100°

P A C I F I C

10°

20°

Tropic of Capricorn

30°

O C E A N

NORTH AMERICA

COUNTRY	PAGE
ANTIGUA	**117**
BAHAMAS	**117**
BARBADOS	**117**
BELIZE	**117**
CANADA	**98-99; 100-101; 102-103; 104-105**
COSTA RICA	**117**
CUBA	**117**
DOMINICA	**117**
DOMINICAN REPUBLIC	**117**
EL SALVADOR	**116-117**
GREENLAND	**96; 99**
GRENADA	**117**
GUATEMALA	**116-117**
HAITI	**117**
HONDURAS	**117**
JAMAICA	**117**
MEXICO	**116-117**
NICARAGUA	**117**
PANAMA	**117**
PUERTO RICO	**117**
ST. KITTS — NEVIS	**117**
ST. LUCIA	**117**
ST. VINCENT AND THE GRENADINES	**117**
UNITED STATES	**106-107; 108-109; 110-111; 112-113; 114-115**

NORTH AMERICA

OCEAN

ATLANTIC

Tropic of Cancer

6339 ▼

BAHAMAS

Grand Bahama I.
Gt. Abaco I.

Nassau

Caicos Is. (U.K.)

Gt. Inagua I.

Washington
Newport News
Norfolk
Richmond
VIRGINIA
Greensboro
Charlotte
NORTH CAROLINA
Columbia
SOUTH
CAROLINA
Charleston
Savannah
Jacksonville
Daytona
Beach
Orlando
West
Palm
Beach
Miami
Fort Lauderdale

Wilmington
C. Hatteras
C. Lookout
C. Fear
Florence
Augusta
Macon
Albany
Tallahassee

Tampa
St. Petersburg

C. Canaveral

C. Sable

Key West
Straits of Florida
Key West of Florida

La Habana
(Havana)

Pinar del Rio
Guane

Yucatan Channel

Cienfuegos
Sancti
Spiritus

Santa Clara
Camaguey
Holguin
Santiago
de Cuba
Guantánamo

Cuba

JAMAICA
Montego
Bay
Kingston

7680 ▼

HAITI
Cap-Haïtien
PRINCE
DOMINICAN
REPUBLIC
Santo
Domingo
Hispaniola
Les Cayes

Greater Antilles

Pta. Gallinas

VENEZUELA
Maracaibo
Cristóbal
Santa Marta
Barranquilla
Cartagena
G. del Darién

COLOMBIA

Cúcuta
Bucaramanga
Medellín
Central
Manizales
Armenia
Bogotá
Cali
Pasto

Cordillera

Buenaventura

Tumaco
Esmeraldas
C. San Francisco
Equator
Manta

Quito
ECUADOR
Chimborazo
6272
Guayaquil
G. de
Guayaquil
Machala
Sullana
Piura
Punta Negra
Chiclayo

ANDES

PERU

Marañón

Cajamarca
Trujillo

Caribbean Sea

Puerto
Cabezas
Bluefields

COSTA
RICA
San José
Limón

PANAMA
Colón
Panamá
G. de
Panamá

C. Gracias à Dios

Gulf of
Honduras
BELIZE
Belize
Belmopan
GUATEMALA
Guatemala
San Salvador
EL SALVADOR

HONDURAS
San Pedro
Sula
Tegucigalpa

NICARAGUA
Managua
L. de
Nicaragua
Rivas

6662 ▼

Mérida
Campeche
Bahía de Campeche
(Campeche Bay)

Chetumal

Yucatan
Pen.

Villahermosa
Coatzacoalcos
Tapachula

Veracruz
Minatitlán

Gulf of
Mexico

Tropic of Cancer

Memphis
TENNESSEE
Nashville
Knoxville
Chattanooga
Atlanta
GEORGIA
Columbus
Montgomery
ALABAMA
Birmingham
Meridian
MISSISSIPPI
Jackson
Mobile
Pensacola

Huntsville

St. Louis
MISSOURI
Springfield
Cairo
KENTUCKY
Louisville
Indianapolis
Cincinnati
OHIO
Columbus

New Orleans
Baton Rouge

Shreveport
ARKANSAS
Little
Rock
Ozark
Plateau

5203 ▼

Tuxpan
Poza Rica
Tampico
Ciudad Madero

Mérida

Oaxaca
Puebla
Cd. de México
(Mexico City)
Popocatépetl
5452
Acapulco

Salina Cruz

Tampico

Matamoros
Brownsville
Corpus Christi
Laredo
Nuevo
Laredo
Reynosa
Monterrey
Saltillo

Dallas
Fort Worth
Waco
Austin
Houston
San
Antonio
Galveston
Beaumont
Port
Arthur
Alexandria
Lafayette

Tulsa
OKLAHOMA
Oklahoma City
Wichita Falls
Abilene

Texarkana

Red R.

TEXAS

Edwards
Plateau

Rio Grande

El Paso
Ciudad
Juárez

Chihuahua
Ciudad
Delicias
Camargo
Jiménez
Gómez
Palacio
Torreón
Durango

San Luis
Potosí
Aguascalientes
León
Guadalajara
Guanajuato
Querétaro
Morelia

Manzanillo

Mazatlán

Culiacán
Los Mochis
Ciudad
Obregón
Guaymas
Hermosillo

Sierra Madre Occidental
Sierra Madre Oriental
MEXICO

M E X I C O

PACIFIC

OCEAN

Golfo de California (Gulf of California)

La Paz
C. San Lucas

Baja California (Lower California)

I. de Guadalupe (Mex.)

Is. de
Revilla Gigedo (Mex.)
I. Socorro

Clipperton
(Fr.)

Is. Galapagos
(Ecuador)

Pueblo
Denver
COLORADO
Colorado Springs
Mt. Elbert
4399
Sangre de Cristo
San
Juan Mts.
Santa Fe
Truchas
3994
NEW MEXICO
Albuquerque
Gallup
Roswell
Carlsbad

Alpine

Wichita
KANSAS
Dodge City
Garden City
Liberal

Amarillo
Lubbock

ARIZONA
Phoenix
Tucson
Nogales
Mexicali
Tijuana
Ensenada

San Diego
Los Angeles
Long Beach
Santa Monica
Pt. Conception
Bakersfield
Death Valley

Mt. Whitney

Mesa

Flagstaff

Nuevo
Casas Grandes

Tropic of Cancer

Equator

Relief
Feet   Metres
16404   5000
9843   3000
6562   2000
3281   1000
1640   500
656   200
        Sea Level
0
656   Land Dep. 656
        13123   4000
        22966   7000

Scale 1:25 000 000

Lambert Azimuthal Equal Area Projection

© Collins • Longman Atlases Cbi

1000 Miles
1500 Kms.
1000
800
600
500
400
200
0
0

CANADA AND ALASKA

GREENLAND (KALAALLIT NUNAAT) (Denmark)

Kong Christian den IX Land

Kong Frederik den VI Kyst

Mt Forel ▲3360

Arctic Circle

K. Gustav Holm

Køge Bugt

K. Møsting

Ammassalik/ Tasiilaq

Nuuk

BAFFIN Bay

Axel Heiberg I.

Nares Strait

K. Parry (Kangaarsussuaq)

Thule/ Qaanaaq

Coburg I.

C. Parker

Ellesmere Island

Jones Sd.

Devon Island

Cornwallis I.

Resolute

Lancaster Sound

Somerset Island

Prince of Wales Island

Boothia Peninsula

Prince Regent Inlet

Brodeur Peninsula

Arctic Bay

Borden Peninsula

Bylot I.

Pond Inlet

C. Adair

C. Hewett

Upernavik

2136

Nunavik

Disko

Godhavn/ Qeqertarsuaq

Christianshåb/ Qasigiannguit

Umanak/ Uummannaq

Liverpool Bay

Home Bay

Clyde

Baffin Island

Penny Highland ▲2591

Padloping Island

C. Dyer

Cape Dyer

Sondrestromfjord/ Kangerlussuaq

Holsteinsborg/ Sisimiut

Sukkertoppen/ Maniitsoq

Godthåb/ Nuuk

Igloolik Island

Hall Lake

Foxe Basin

Cumberland Pen.

Pangnirtung

Cumberland Sound

C. Mercy

Hoare Bay

Frederikshåb/ Paamiut

Frobisher Bay/ Iqaluit

Hall Pen.

Frobisher Bay

Melville Peninsula

Prince Charles Island

Nettilling L.

Amadjuak L.

Resolution Island

Lake Harbour

Frederikshåb

Paamiut

Fiskenaesset/ Qeqertarsuatsiaat

Ivigtut Ivittut

Julianehåb/ Qaqortoq

K. Farvel/ Uummannarsuaq (C. Farewell)

Boothia Peninsula 572

King William I.

Gjoa Haven

Adelaide Pen.

Taloyoak

Pelly Bay

Repulse Bay

Cape Dorchester

Foxe Peninsula

Cape Dorset

Hudson Strait

Akpatok I.

C. Chidley

Labrador Sea

ATLANTIC OCEAN

Garry L.

Wager Bay

Baker Lake

Chesterfield Inlet

Coral Harbour

Southampton Island

Coats I.

Mansel I.

Fisher Strait

Salluit

Kangiqsujuaq

Quaqtaq

Kangirsuk

Ungava Bay

Kangiqsualujjuaq

Hebron

Nutak

Nain

C. Harrison

Indian Harbour

Rankin Inlet

Whale Cove

Tavani

Eskimo Point

Padlei

KEEWATIN

Péninsule D'Ungava

L. Payne

Arnaud

Anautau

L. aux Feuilles

Kuujjuaq (Fort Chimo)

Koksoak

George

La Baleine

Hopedale

C. Harrison

Makkovik

Rigolet

Cartwright

257

Hudson Bay

Inukjuak (Fort Harrison)

Minto

L. à l'Eau-Claire

L. Bienville

Schefferville

Petitsikapau L.

Labrador City

Wabush L.

 Shmallwood Resr.

West River

Churchill

North West River

Battle Harbour

C. Bauld

St. Anthony

Nueltin L.

Churchill

C. Churchill

Port Nelson

York Factory

C. Tatnam

Winisk

C. Henrietta Maria

King George Is.

Belcher Is.

Kuujjuarapik

La Grande Résr. 2

La Grande Résr. 3

Chisasibi (Fort George)

1128 ▲

Eastmain

Résr. Caniapiscau

NEWFOUNDLAND

Labrador

QUÉBEC

Gagnon

Sept-Îles

Mingan

Natashquan

St. Augustin

Blanc Sablon

Str. of Belle Isle

Corner Brook

Grand Falls

Buchans

Gander

Bonavista

Carbonear

St. John's

Newfoundland

Harbour Grace

Placentia

Trepassey

C. Race

Île d'Anticosti

P. de l'Est

Gaspé

C. de Gaspé

Péninsule de Gaspé

Gulf of St. Lawrence

Îles de la Madeleine

Cape Breton

PR. EDWARD I.

Charlottetown

St. Pierre and Miquelon (Fr.)

Sydney

Port Hawkesbury

Mulgrave

Sable I.

Seal

Churchill

Nelson

Southern Indian L.

Thompson

Howse L.

MANITOBA

Gods L.

L. Sachigo

Severn

Winisk

Big Trout L.

Sandy L.

Winisk Lake

Attawapiskat

Akimiski I.

James Bay

Fort Albany

Moosonee

Waskaganish (Fort Rupert)

Nemiscau

Eastmain

ONTARIO

Nottaway

Harricana

Mistassini

L. Mistassini

Broadback

Rupert

Nova L.

The Pas

Norway House

Grand Rapids

L. Winnipeg

Hodgson

Riverton

Victoria Beach

Red Lake

L. St. Joseph

Pickle Crow

Nakina

Hearst

Cochrane

Kapuskasing

Smooth Rock

Amos

Val d'Or

Noranda

Rouyn

Senneterre

L. Kipawa

QUÉBEC

Réservoir Gouin

Roberval

St-Maurice

Chibougamau

L. Matagami

Matagami

Abitibi

L. Abitibi

Chicoutimi Jonquière

Tadoussac

Baie-Comeau

Betsiamites

Hauterive

Forestville

Port Cartier

Baie-Trinité

Rimouski

Matane

Rivière-du-Loup

Mont-Joli

Campbellton

Bathurst

Chatham

NEW BRUNSWICK

Moncton

Amherst

NOVA SCOTIA

Truro

Dartmouth

Halifax

Bridgewater

Liverpool

Shelburne

C. Sable

Yarmouth

Bay of Fundy

Saint John

Fredericton

Edmundston

Lac-St-Jean

Saguenay

Tadoussac

St. Lawrence

Lévis

Québec

Thetford Mines

Trois-Rivières

Shawinigan

Joliette

Sorel

St-Hyacinthe

Sherbrooke

Granby

St-Jean

Montreal

Ottawa-Hull

Hull

Cornwall

Brockville

Kingston

Bangor

Portland

Montpelier

Manchester

Lawrence

Worcester

Boston

Providence

New Haven

Hartford

Long Island

NEW YORK

Albany

Syracuse

Utica

Rochester

Scranton

Winnipeg

St Boniface

Portage la Prairie

Morden

Emerson

Kenora

L. of the Woods

Ignace

Dryden

Fort Frances

Sioux Lookout

L. Nipigon

Nipigon

Thunder Bay

Steep Rock

Atikokan

L. Superior

Sault Sainte Marie

Michipicoten

Franz

Longlac

Geraldton

Terrace Bay

Marathon

White River

Wawa

Sudbury

Copper Cliff

North Bay

Pembroke

Perth

Ottawa

Brockville

Kingston

Trans Canada Highway

Red Lake

Bemidji

Virginia

Hibbing

Duluth

Ironwood

Iron River

Marquette

Manistique

Cliff

Georgian Bay

Parry Sound

Midland

Huntsville

Owen Sound

Barrie

Collingwood

Orillia

Peterborough

Oshawa

L. Ontario

Toronto

Hamilton

St. Catharines

Niagara Falls

Buffalo

L. Erie

Rochester

Utica

Syracuse

Ithaca

Williamsport

Harrisburg

Reading

Paterson

Newark

New York

Long Island

New Jersey

Trenton

Philadelphia

Baltimore

MINNESOTA

Minneapolis

St. Cloud

St. Paul

Mankato

Austin

Winona

WISCONSIN

Green Bay

Sheboygan

Milwaukee

Madison

Rhinelander

Merrill

Wausau

Traverse City

Cadillac

L. Michigan

MICHIGAN

Grand Rapids

Bay City

Saginaw

Flint

Lansing

Kalamazoo

Detroit

Windsor

London

Sarnia

Kitchener

Brantford

St. Thomas

DAKOTA

Aberdeen

Sioux Falls

Mitchell

IOWA

Sioux City

Waterloo

Cedar Rapids

Mason City

NEBRASKA

ILLINOIS

Chicago

Gary

INDIANA

Fort Wayne

Lima

Toledo

OHIO

Cleveland

Youngstown

PENNSYLVANIA

Pittsburgh

MARYLAND

UNITED STATES OF AMERICA

Red River

Fargo

Valley City

Grand Forks

Bismarck

Grafton

Rugby

NORTH DAKOTA

Leech L.

Bemidji

Superior

Marquette

Cheboygan

Davis Strait

NORTHWEST TERRITORIES

KEEWATIN

CANADA

© Collins ◇ Longman Atlases Cbi

WESTERN CANADA

Relief

Feet	Metres
16 404	5000
9843	3000
6562	2000
3281	1000
1640	500
656	200
0	Sea Level

Land Dep.

656	200
13 123	4000
22 966	7000

Scale 1:7 500 000

0   50   100   150   200 Miles

0   100   200   300 Kms.

Conic Equidistant Projection

© Collins

Walmsley L.

McLeod B.

ristie B.

owdrift)

TERRITORIES

Artillery L.

Mary Frances L.

Whitefish L. Nicholson

Dubawnt L.

Tulemalu L.

Yathkyed L.

Kaminak

Whale Cove
Tavani

Howard L.

Beaverhill L.

Kamilukuak Lake

Angikuni L.

North Henik L.

Padlei

Barlow L.

363

KEEWATIN

Kazan

South Henik L.

Eskimo Point

Maguse River

HUDSON

odge

Hjalmar L.

341

Penylan L.

Firedrake L.

Tatinnai L.

Th-anne

Edehon L.

257

Noman L.

Doran L.

Alcantara L.

Snowbird L.

Ennadai

Ennadai L.

BAY

Thekulthili L.

Thoa L.

Dubawnt L.

Kasba L.

(266) Nueltin L.

Hill Island L.

Abitau L.

533

Wholdaia L.

Scott L.

Selwyn L.

Nejanilini L.

Caribou

Leland Lakes

Tazin L.

Fond du Lac

Phelps L.

N. Seal

Seal

Churchill
C.Churchill

49

Uranium City
Eldorado

Goldfields

Black Lake

Stony Rapids

(213)

Wollaston L.

(396)

L. Brochet

Tadoule L.

S. Knife

N. Knife

Churchill

Cromarty

C. Tatnam

Lake Athabasca

Old Fort

Pasfield L.

Waterbury Lake

Cree L.

Brochet

S. Seal L.

Big Sand L.

361

Northern Indian L.

M'Clintock

Owl

Port Nelson

York Factory

Machichi

Kettle

Black Duck

Fort Severn

Pipestone Cree

654

(478)

Reindeer Lake

Goldsand

Wells L.

Southern Indian Lake

Gauer L.

Silcox

Nelson

Hayes

Kaskattama

Niskibi

Beaver

Firebag

ackay

Highrock L.

Sandy Lake

Wheeler

Wathaman L.

Lynn Lake

Granville L.

Baldock L.

Bird

Gods

196

Severn

Shagamu

Murray

Clearwater

Frobisher L.

Hickson L.

Royal L.

Russell L.

Split L.

Ilford

High Hill L.

Stupart

Fawn

Winisk

Christina

Peter Pond L.

Churchill L.

Otter L.

Sisipuk L.

Highrock L.

Thompson

Thicket Portage

Arnot

Hayes

Sachigo

Shibogama

Buffalo Narrows

Pinehouse L.

LAC LA RONGE PROV. PARK

Stanley Mission

Churchill

Pikwitonei

Stipiwesk L.

Bearskin Lake

Canoe L.

L. la Plonge

La Ronge

Kississing L.

Sherridon

Cross L.

Molson L.

Bolton L.

Gods Lake

Red Sucker

Big Trout L.

SASKATCHEWAN

Primrose L.

Beauval

Doré L.

L. la Ronge

Flin Flon

MANITOBA

Wekusko L.

Norway House

Bigstone Lake

Stevenson L.

Island Lake

Sachigo L.

Big Beaver House

Wunnummin Winisk L.

Cold L.

Cold Lake

Thunder Hills

Montreal L.

Amisk Lake

Kiskitto L.

ville

Grand Centre

PRINCE ALBERT NAT. PARK

Montreal Lake

Cumberland Lake

Cormorant

Gunisao L.

Gunisao L.

Cobham L.

Opasquia

Sandy Lake

N. Caribou L.

Meadow Lake

Waskesiu L.

Candle L.

The Pas

Cedar Lake

Grand Rapids

Poplar R.

333

Miminiska L.

Frenchman Butte

Delaronde L.

Squaw Rapids

Westray

Lake Winnipegosis

(217)

Berens River

Little Grand Rapids

Pipestone

Miminiska L.

Lloydminster

Witchekan L.

Smeaton

Tobin L.

Pasquia Hills

Hudson Bay

Mafeking

Easterville

Berens

Pikangikum

Birch L.

Cat Lake

Pickle Crow

Vermilion

Medstead

Shell L.

Prince Albert

Carrot R.

Porcupine Hills

Swan L.

Chitek

St. Martin

Little Berens

Trout L.

Fawcett L.

St. Joseph

Albany

Wainwright

North Battleford

515

Basin

Lenore L.

823

Gypsumville

L. St. Martin

Red Lake

Savant Lake

Macklin

Battleford

Rosthern

Tisdale

Reserve

Assiniboine

Swan R.

Pine River

Ashern

Hodgson

Bissett

Goldpines

Lac Seul

Sesekanaga L.

Unity

Wilkie

Dana

Humboldt

Watson

Ketchington

Canora

Roblin

Dauphin

Rorketon

Riverton

Victoria Beach

Winnipeg R.

Sioux Lookout

Minnitaki L.

Sturgeon L.

914

Biggar

Asquith

Saskatoon

Plunkett

Big Quill Lake

Little Quill Lake

Kamsack

Yorkton

RIDING MTN. NAT. PARK

Dauphin L.

Alonsa

Eriksdale

Gimli

WHITESHELL PROV. PARK

Minaki

Kenora

Dryden

Paguchi L.

Salvador

Kerrobert

Harris

Kenaston

Nokomis

Leross

Wynyard

Melville

Rosseau

Gladstone

Amaranth

Neepawa

Ashern

Selkirk

Beausejour

Vermilion Bay

Ignace

English River

Hemaruka

Kirriemuir

Hanley

Watrous

Whitesand R.

Foam Lake

Riding Mountain

Minnedosa

Portage la Prairie

Winnipeg

St. Boniface

(321)

White Otter L.

Marmion L.

L. des Mille Lacs

Oyen

Alsask

Elrose

Strongfield

Last Mountain Lake

Southey

Qu'Appelle

(248)

Birtle

Neepawa

Birds

Carman

Steinbach

Lac du Bonnet

Steep Rock

Rainy Lake

Acadia Valley

Buffalo

Beechy

Diefenbaker L.

Broadview

Binscarth

Beulah

Elkhorn

Brandon

Fort Frances

QUETICO PROVINCIAL PARK

Fox Valley

Cabri

Main Centre

Parkbeg

Moose Jaw

Regina

Qu'Appelle

Head

Mossbank

Broadview

Niden

Souris

Tiger Hills

Morden

Winkler

Roseau

Middleboro

Warroad

Interlake

Grand L.

Medicine Hat

Great Sand Hills

Gull Lake

Swift Current

Corinne

Fillmore

Elgin

Boissevain

Killarney

Rainy River

Fort Frances

International Falls

Big Falls

Lake of the Woods

Schuler

Maple Creek

Ponteix

Assiniboia

Parry

Amulet

Weyburn

832

Carlyle

South

Deloraine

Cartwright

Roseau

Greenbush

Littlefork

Northome

Virginia

Ely

Lake Superior

Bow Island

Cypress Hills

Consul

Climax

Kincaid

Radville

Midale

Souris

Estevan

UNITED STATES OF AMERICA

Cavalier

Karlstad

Thief River Falls

Argyle

Upper Red L.

Big Falls

Grand Marais

Foremost

Shaunavon

Val Marie

Wood Mtn.

Whitetail

Fortuna

Noonan

Flaxton

Westhope

Bottineau

Rolla

Langdon

Egeland

Bella

Roseau

Cavalier

Langdon

Greenbush

Warren

Thief River Falls

Newfolden

Blackduck

Chisholm

Hibbing

Two Harbors

Gildford

Chinook

Harlem

Milk R.

Poplar R.

Scobey

Plentywood

Wildrose

Medicine Lake

Kenmare

Powers Lake

Rugby

Devils L.

Lakota

Grand Forks

East Grand Forks

Crookston

Lower Red L.

Bemidji

Grand Rapids

Bass Lake

Cloquet

Ashland

Chester

Havre

Dodson

Malta

Hinsdale

Glasgow

Poplar

Stanley

Ray

Williston

Minot

Granville

Towner

Drake

New Rockford

Sheyenne

Carrington

Harvey

Casselton

Twin Valley

Walker

Mahnomen

Leech L.

Detroit Lakes

Hill City

Bass L.

Aitkin

Mille Lacs L.

Spooner

Webster

Mississippi

Moose L.

Solon Springs

Superior

Duluth

Fort Benton

Loma

Fort Peck Dam

Wolf Point

Missouri

Sidney

Watford City

Fairview

Garrison Resr. (L. Sakakawea)

Washburn

Hazen

Anamoose

Hannaford

Valley City

Jamestown

Moorhead

Fargo

MINNESOTA

Brainerd

Great Falls

Winifred

Circle

Savage

Killdeer

Beulah

Wilton

Tuttle

Medina

Enderlin

Wahpeton

Fergus Falls

EASTERN CANADA

SOUTH CENTRAL CANADA

UNITED STATES

WESTERN UNITED STATES

CENTRAL UNITED STATES

ATLANTIC

OCEAN

BAHAMAS

New Providence Island

Nassau

Eleuthera I.

Cat I.

Great Abaco I.

Little Bahama Bank

Grand Bahama I.

Freeport

Northwest Providence Ch.

Great Bahama Bank

Andros

Nicholls Town

▼5462

▼866

Relief

	Feet	Metres
	16 404	5000
	9843	3000
	6562	2000
	3281	1000
	1640	500
	656	200
	Sea Level	
	0	Land Dep.
	656	200
	13123	4000
	22 966	7000

Scale 1:7 500 000

Conic Equidistant Projection

0   50   100   150   200 Miles
0   100   200   300 Kms.

VIRGINIA

Richmond
Chesapeake
Norfolk
Virginia Beach
Hampton
Newport News
Portsmouth
Suffolk
Petersburg
Roanoke
Lynchburg
Danville

Chincoteague
C. Hatteras
C. Lookout
C. Fear
Elizabeth City
Albemarle Sound
Pamlico Sound
Raleigh Bay
Onslow Bay

NORTH CAROLINA

Raleigh
Greensboro
Winston-Salem
Durham
Charlotte
Gastonia
Wilmington
Fayetteville
Goldsboro
Greenville
Jacksonville
Rocky Mount
Asheville
Hickory
Kingston
Wilson
New Bern
Morehead City
Southport
Myrtle Beach
Georgetown

SOUTH CAROLINA

Columbia
Charleston
Florence
Spartanburg
Greenville
Rock Hill
Anderson
C. Romain
Mt. Pleasant
Sumter
Orangeburg
Aiken
Beaufort
Hilton Head I.

GEORGIA

Atlanta
Savannah
Augusta
Macon
Athens
Columbus
Albany
Brunswick
Valdosta
Waycross
Dublin
Rome
Marietta
Ossabaw I.
Sapelo I.
Cumberland I.

KENTUCKY

TENNESSEE

Nashville
Chattanooga
Knoxville
Johnson City
Kingsport
SMOKY MT. NAT. PARK
Mt. Mitchell

ALABAMA

Birmingham
Montgomery
Tuscaloosa
Decatur
Gadsden
Florence
Huntsville
Selma
Dothan
Pensacola
Panama City

FLORIDA

Jacksonville
Tallahassee
Orlando
Tampa
St. Petersburg
Clearwater
Bradenton
Sarasota
Lakeland
Gainesville
Ocala
Daytona Beach
Melbourne
Fort Pierce
West Palm Beach
Boca Raton
Pompano Beach
Fort Lauderdale
Hollywood
Miami Beach
Miami
Homestead
Fort Myers
Naples
Key West
Key Largo
Ormond Beach
New Smyrna Beach
Cocoa Beach
C. Canaveral
Titusville
Vero Beach
Sebastian
Jupiter
Palm Beach
Stuart
Okeechobee
L. Okeechobee
EVERGLADES NAT. PARK
Big Cypress Swamp
C. Romano
C. Sable
Florida Keys
Florida Bay
St. Augustine
Marineland
Jacksonville Beach
Fernandina Beach
Amelia City
Crystal River
Tarpon Springs
Dunedin
Venice
Englewood
Captiva
Pine I.
Florida
Straits of Florida

© Collins

113

NORTHEASTERN UNITED STATES

ADIRONDACK PARK

Mexico Bay

VERMONT

NEW HAMPSHIRE

MAINE

Adirondack Mts.

Syracuse

Utica

Rome

Oneida Lake

Albany

MASSACHUSETTS

Boston

Massachusetts Bay

Cape Cod

Cape Cod Bay

Springfield

Providence

RHODE ISLAND

Hartford

CONNECTICUT

Scranton

Wilkes-Barre

NEW JERSEY

New York

Newark

Long Island

Long Island Sound

Martha's Vineyard

Nantucket Island

Block I.

Allentown

Reading

Trenton

Philadelphia

Camden

Wilmington

DELAWARE

Atlantic City

ATLANTIC

OCEAN

Delaware Bay

Chesapeake Bay

DELMARVA PENINSULA

Relief		
Feet		Metres
16404		5000
9843		3000
6562		2000
3281		1000
1640		500
656		200
0		Sea Level
Land Dep.		
656		200
13123		4000
22966		7000

Scale 1:2 500 000

0 10 20 30 40 50 Miles

0 20 40 60 80 Kms.

Conic Equidistant Projection

© Collins

115

CENTRAL AMERICA AND THE CARIBBEAN

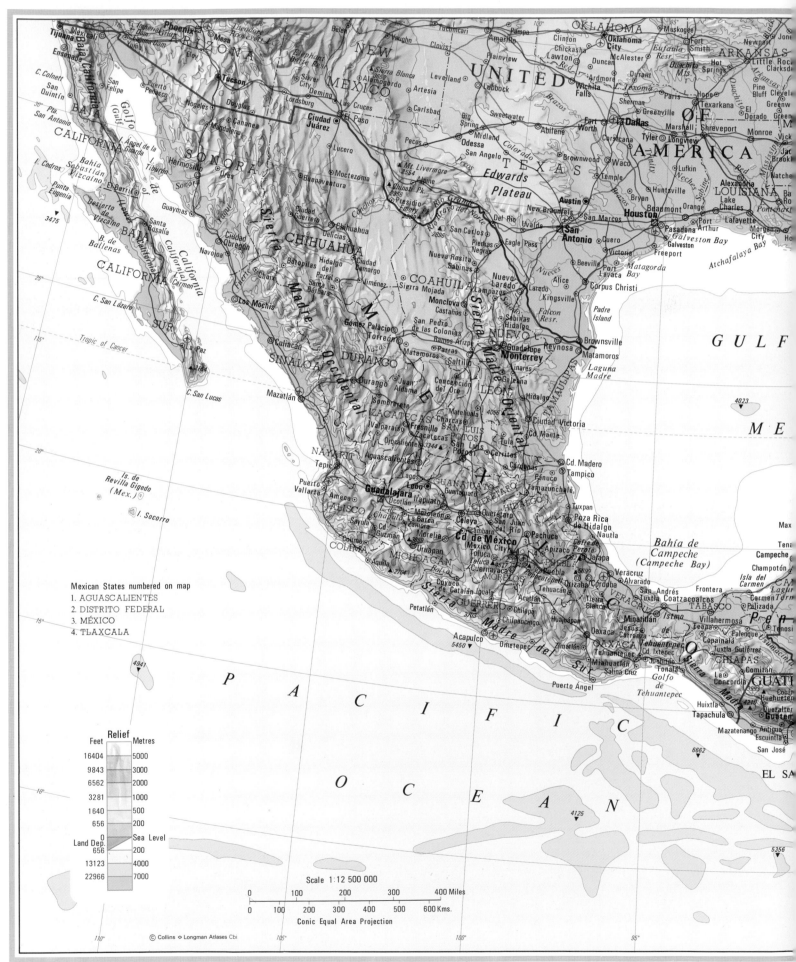

Mexican States numbered on map
1. AGUASCALIENTES
2. DISTRITO FEDERAL
3. MÉXICO
4. TLAXCALA

Relief
Feet		Metres
16404		5000
9843		3000
6562		2000
3281		1000
1640		500
656		200
0		Sea Level
Land Dep.		
656		200
13123		4000
22966		7000

Scale 1:12 500 000

0   100   200   300   400 Miles

0   100   200   300   400   500   600 Kms.
Conic Equal Area Projection

© Collins ○ Longman Atlases Cbi

TENNESSEE
Columbia
Asheville
NORTH
Fayetteville
New Bern
C. Lookout
phis
Pickwick L.
Chattanooga
Cleveland
Charlotte
Greenville
SOUTH
Spartanburg
CAROLINA
Wilmington
Corinth
Huntsville
Gadsden
Rome
Anderson
Columbia
Florence
C. Fear
pelo
(Tenn.)
Güntersville
CAROLINA
Georgetown
TATES
Birmingham
Bessemer
Atlanta
Griffin
Augusta
C. Romain
columbus
Tuscaloosa
Phenix
City
GEORGIA
Orangeburg
Charleston
IPPI
ALABAMA
Columbus
Macon
Ogeechee
Savannah
el
Montgomery
Greenville
Albany
Altamaha
Savannah
eridian
Mobile
Pensacola
Andalusia
Dothan
Waycross
Brunswick
Tombigbee
Chattahoochee
Flint
Suwannee
Okefenokee
Swamp
Gulfport
Panama
City
Tallahassee
Madison
Lake
City
Jacksonville
ans
Chandeleur
Is
C. San Blas
Apalachee
Bay
Gainesville
St. Augustine
Mississippi
Delta
866
Ocala
Daytona Beach
OF
Sanford
Cape Canaveral
Orlando
Clearwater
Lakeland
Fort Pierce
St. Petersburg
Tampa
Bradenton
Lake
Okeechobee
West Palm
Beach
Tampa B.
Sarasota
Freeport
Grand
Bahama I.
Great
Abaco I.
Fort Myers
Fort
Lauderdale
C. Romano
The Everglades
Miami
New
Providence
Eleuthera I.
Rock Sound
Nicolls
Town
Nassau
Cat I.
C. Sable
Andros
Town
San
Salvador
Key West
Florida Keys
Andros
Rolleville
Rum Cay
of Florida
Gt.
Exuma
Long I.
Samana Cay

ATLANTIC

OCEAN

1137

OF

CO

Straits
Cárdenas
Matanzas
Archp. de Sabana
Archp. de Camaguey
La Habana
(Havana)
Sagua
la Grande
Caibarién
Crooked I.
Plana Cays
Mayaguana I.
Acklin's I.
Turks and Caicos Is.
(U.K.)
Little
Inagua
Caicos Is.
Turks Is.
Marianao
Güines
Santa Clara
Morón
Pinar del Río
Golfo de
Batabanó
Cienfuegos
Sancti
Spíritus
Ciego de Avila
Nuevitas
Great
Inagua
Guane
Nueva
Gerona
Archp. de los
Canarreos
Trinidad
CUBA
Camagüey
Holguín
Banes
Matthew
Town
Île de
la Tortue
Puerto Plata
Puerto Rico Trench
8528
Isla de Pinos
Jardines de la
Reina
Victoria de
las Tunas
Bayamo
S. Luis
Baracoa
Port-de-Paix
San Francisco
de Macorís
Samaná
San Juan
Manzanillo
S. Maestra
Guantánamo
Gonaïves
Santiago
La Vega
DOMINICAN
REP.
4647
Little
Cayman
Cayman Brac
Tuquino
1971
C. Cruz
Santiago
de Cuba
G. de la Gonâve
Cap Haitien
St. Marc
Azua
S. Cristóbal
S. Pedro
Mayagüez
Mona
Grand Cayman
Georgetown
Cayman Is.
(U.K.)
Île de la
Gonâve
HAITI
2414
Jérémie
Port-au-
Prince
2680
Santo
Domingo
La Romana
Saona
Ponce
PUERTO
RICO
(U.S.A.)
Montego Bay
St. Ann's Bay
Port
Antonio
Les
Cayes
Hispaniola
Antilles
Black River
May Pen
Kingston
JAMAICA
4297

C A R I B B E A N   S E A

BELIZE
Gulf of Honduras
Is
de la Bahía
C. Camarón
Laguna de
Carataska
Netherlands
Antilles
Punta
Gorda
Turneffe Is.
Dangriga
Pto.
Barrios
Pto. Cortés
Balfate
Trujillo
C. Gracias á Dios
Aruba
(Neth.)
Curaçao (Neth.)
Bonaire
Tela
La Ceiba
Pta. Gallinas
Pen. de la
Guajira
Willemstad
mopan
Belize
Sta.
Yoro
Mosquitia
Golfo de
Venezuela
Pen. de
Paraguaná
Punto Fijo
La Vela
Coro
Tucacas
HONDURAS
Juticalpa
Patuca
Pto. Cabezas
Pta. de
Castilletes
Uribia
La
Concepción
Puerto
Cabello
S. Pedro
Sula
Danlí
Ocotal
I. de
Providencia
(Col.)
Ríohacha
Maracaibo
Labinas
Barquisimeto
Valencia
Tegucigalpa
2400
Prinzapolca
Santa
Marta
Sa. Nevada de
Sta. Marta
5775
Ciudad Ojeda
Barquisimeto
Comayagua
NICARAGUA
Río Grande
I. de
San Andrés
(Col.)
Barranquilla
Sabana larga
San Carlos
del Zulia
Valera
Trujillo
Cartagena
Turbaco
Calamar
L. de
Maracaibo
Machiques
Chinandega
León
Lago de
Managua
Rama
Bluefields
Carmen
Valledupar
Barinas
Managua
Granada
L. de
Nicaragua
San Carlos
S. Juan del Norte
Magangué
Ocaña
Mérida
VENEZUELA
Jinotepe
Rivas
Sincelejo
Ríonegro
Cúcuta
Apure
C. Sta. Elena
San
Carmen
Montería
S. Jorge
Mompós
COSTA
RICA
Liberia
Pen. de
Nicoya
Puntarenas
San
José
Irazú
Limón
Laguna de Chiriquí
Golfo de
los Mosquitos
Colón
Gatun
Lake
San Miguelito
Golfo del
Darién
Magdalena
Endrenados
Puerto
Bucaramanga
San Cristóbal
COLOMBIA
Arauca
Meta
C. Blanco
Chirripó
3432
4920
Panamá City
Balboa
Puerto Rey
Turbo
G. de Urabá
Encontrados
Puerto de
Nutrias
Golfito
3477
Penonomé
Archp. de
las Perlas
El Real
PANAMA
de Panamá
Pto. Armuelles
David
Santiago
Pen. de
Azuero
Golfo de
San Miguel
Jurado
Ríosucio
Yanamal
San
Socorro
5493
Pamplona
Bucaramanga

Puerto
Rico
Trench
Anegada
Virgin Is.(U.K.)
Anguilla (U.K.)
St. Barthélemy
(Fr.)
BARBUDA
San Juan
Bayamón
Tortola
Virgin
Gorda
St. Martin
(Fr.-Neth.)
ANTIGUA
St. John's
Leeward Islands
Arecibo
Virgin
Is.
St. Thomas
St. Croix
Sint Maarten
(Neth.)
Saba (Neth.)
Sint Eustatius (Neth.)
ST. KITTS
NEVIS
Montserrat
(U.K.)
1484
Marie-Galante
Mayagüez
Ponce
Caguas
Vieques
PUERTO
RICO
(U.S.A.)
Guadeloupe
(Fr.)
Basse-Terre
Roseau
DOMINICA
Lesser
Antilles
Martinique
(Fr.)
Fort-de-France
15
Castries
ST. LUCIA
Windward Islands
BARBADOS
Bridgetown
ST.
VINCENT
AND THE
GRENADINES
St. Kingstown
St. George's
GRENADA
Lesser Antilles
TOBAGO
5630
Bonaire
Los
Roques
La
Orchila
La Blanquilla
Isla de
Margarita
Porlamar
Dragon's Mouth
Pto. La Cruz
Port of Spain
San Fernando
TRINIDAD
La Tortuga
Pen. de Araya
Carúpano
Cumaná
G. of
Paria
Serpent's
Mouth
Barcelona
Maturín
Delta
del
Orinoco
Same Scale
La Guaira

Tropic of Cancer

North America

NORTH
ATLANTIC
OCEAN

Tropic of Cancer

40°
30°
20°

Caribbean Sea

Barranquilla

Maracaibo •Caracas
VENEZUELA

TRINIDAD
AND TOBAGO

Medellín
•Bogotá

Georgetown
Paramaribo
•Cayenne
GUIANA
(Fr.)

Cali
COLOMBIA

GUYANA

SURINAM

10°

Quito
ECUADOR

•Belém

40°

Guayaquil•

30° Equator

Galapagos
Is. (Ec.)

90°

B R A Z I L

Fortaleza

100°

P
E
R
U

•Recife

110°

Lima

10°

La Paz
BOLIVIA

120°

•Salvador

•Brasília

130°

•Sucre

Belo
Horizonte

PARAGUAY

Rio de
Janeiro

São Paulo

20°

S O U T H

Asunción

Curitiba

•Santo André

140°

San Félix (Chile)
San Ambrosio

A
R
G
E
N
T
I
N
A

Tropic of Capricorn

S

Córdoba

Pôrto
Alegre

A
T
L
A

Islas
Juan
Fernández

Valparaíso
Santiago

Rosario

URUGUAY

30°

(Chile)

C
H
I
L
E

Buenos
Aires
La Plata

Montevideo

O C E

P A C I F I C

40°

Falkland
Is. (U.K.)

O C E A N

50°

Tierra del
Fuego

South
Georgia
(U.K.)

60°

Antarctic Circle

70°

International Date Line

Antarctica

© Collins

118

SOUTH AMERICA

COUNTRY	PAGE
ARGENTINA	124-125
BOLIVIA	124
BRAZIL	120-121; 122-123; 126
CHILE	124-125
COLOMBIA	122
ECUADOR	122
GUIANA (Fr.)	123
GUYANA	122-123
PARAGUAY	124
PERU	120; 122; 124
SURINAM	123
TRINIDAD AND TOBAGO	122
URUGUAY	126
VENEZUELA	122

South America as a continental name is used for the land area extending south from the Isthmus of Panama to Cape Horn and lying between 34°W and 82°W. Latin America is a term widely used to cover those parts of the Americas where Spanish, or Portuguese as in Brazil, are the adopted national languages, and thus refers to an area that includes all of South America, Central America, Mexico and the Caribbean, except for the few English, French and Dutch speaking countries and dependencies.

SOUTH AMERICA

© Collins ◇ Longman Atlases Cbi

Relief

Feet		Metres
16 404		5000
9843		3000
6562		2000
3281		500
1640		500
656		200
0		Sea Level
Land Dep.		
656		200
13 123		4000

Scale 1:12 500 000

0	100	200	300	400	500 Miles
0	100	200 300	400 500	600 700	800 Kms.

Lambert Azimuthal Equal Area Projection

etown
New Amsterdam
Paramaribo
Nieuw
Nickerie
Albina   St. Laurent
du Maroni
Afobaka
Cayenne
W. J. Van
Blommestein Meer
Kaw   C. Orange
SURINAM   GUIANA
(Fr.)
Camopi   St. Georges
Tumuc Humac Mts.
Meriruma   Amapá
C. Norte
A M A P Á   Serra do Navio   Araguari
Pto. Grande
Macapá   Estuario do
Rio Amazonas
Mazagão   Ilha
Caviana   (Amazon Delta)
Chaves
I. Grande
do Gurupá   I. de Marajó
Salinópolis
Bragança
Capanema
Obidos   Prainha   Gurupá   Muaná   Icoraci   Viseu
Farò   Monte   Amazonas   Pôrto de Moz   Belém
LITIGATED   Alegre   (Amazon)   Abaetetuba   Turiaçu   Cururupu
AREA   Juruti   Santarém   Cametá   Acará   Guimarães
Parintins   Belterra   Baião   São Luís
Maués   Altamira   Xingu   Capim   Viana   Rosário   Tutóia
Tapajós   Anapu   Jacunda   Gurupi   Itapecuru   Parnaíba   Camocim
Mirim   Granja
Itaituba   Iriri   P A R A   Tucuruí   Turiaçu   Caroatá   Piracuruca   Antônio Bezerra
Represa de   Sobral   Fortaleza
Tucuruí   Grajaú   Bacabal   Codó   União   Parangaba
Bacabal   Marabá   Pedreiras   LITIGATED   Ipu   Baturité
Itacajuna   Barra do   Caxias   AREA   C E A R Á   Aracati
Imperatriz   Corda   Teresina   Campo   Crateús
Tocantinópolis   Meárim   Colinas   Maior   Mossoró
M A R A N H Ã O   Poti   Senador   Macau
Pôrto Franco   Amarante   Pompeu   Iguatu   Açu
Carolina   Loreto   Floriano   Oeiras   RIO GRANDE   Natal
Conceição   Riachão   Represa da Boa   Picos   DO NORTE
do Araguaia   Piacá   Esperança   Uruçui   Sousa   Caicó
Sta.   P I A U Í   Itaim   Cajázeiras   Pombal   João
Araguacema   Filomena   São João   Paulistana   Crato   Patos   Pessoa
do Piauí   Serra Talhada   Juàzeiro   PARAÍBA   Campina Grande
Pedro   do Norte   Salgueiro   Itabaiana   Goiana
Afonso   Gurgueia   PERNAMBUCO   Pesqueira   Caruaru   Olinda
Palmas   Chapada   Remanso   Petrolina   Arcoverde   Belo   Recife
Pto. Nacional   das   Parnaguá   Juàzeiro   Paulo Afonso   Garanhuns   Jardim   Palmares
Balsas   Maracebeiras   884   Represa   Palmeira   Barreiros
Sta. Isabel   T O C A N T I N S   de Sobradinho   dos Índios   Viçosa   Rio Largo
do Morro   Parnã   Senhor do Bonfim   ALAGOAS   Maceió
Peixe   Bacra   Xique Xique   Quebradas   Arapiraca
Paranã   Barreiras   Jacobina   Itapicuru   Propriá   Penedo
M A T O   G R O S S O   Campos   B A H I A   Serrinha   SERGIPE
Belos   Ibotirama   Feira de   Pedrinhas   Aracaju
Planalto   do   Santana   Estância
Diamantino   915   Posse   Carinhanha   Alagoinhas   Santo Amaro
Aruanã   Uruaçu   P l a n a l t o   Brumado   Maragogipe   Salvador
M a t o   G r o s s o   1006   Niquelândia   B r a s i l   Jequié   Nazaré   Valença
G O I Á S   (Brazilian Highlands)   Januária   Vitória da   Ipiaú
Cuiabá   Aragarças   Goiás   DIST. FED.   Formosa   Conquista   Ibicaraí   Ilhéus
ceres   Brasília   Monte Azul   Itabuna
Rondonópolis   Anápolis   M I N A S   G E R A I S   Itapetinga
Alto Araguaia   Luziânia   Salto da
Goiânia   Divisa   Canavieiras

SOUTH AMERICA — SOUTH

PACIFIC

OCEAN

SOUTH   ATLANTIC   OCEAN

CHILE

ARGENTINA

URUGUAY

BRAZIL

BUENOS AIRES

Montevideo
Buenos Aires
Rosario
Santiago
Valparaíso
Mar del Plata
Bahía Blanca
Comodoro Rivadavia
Río Gallegos

Falkland Is.
(U.K.)
(Islas Malvinas)
Stanley
East Falkland
West Falkland
Falkland Sound

TIERRA DEL FUEGO
Ushuaia
Cabo de Hornos
(Cape Horn)

Golfo San Matías
Golfo San Jorge
Península Valdés

Estrecho de Magallanes

Río de la Plata (R. Plate)

Scale 1 : 12 500 000

Lambert Azimuthal Equal Area Projection

© Collins ◊ Longman Atlases C6i-65°

Scale 1 : 7 500 000

© Collins

Relief

Feet	Metres
16404	5000
9843	3000
6562	2000
3281	1000
1640	500
656	200
	Sea Level
Land Dep.	0
656	200
13123	4000
22966	7000

0 100 200 300 400 Miles

0 200 400 600 Kms.

0 40 80 120 Kms.
0 40 80 Miles

Guaporé · Vilhena · Juruena · Utiarita · *Planalto do Mato Grosso* · Ranuro de Juruena · *Serra dos Parecís* · Diamantino · ▲915 · TOCANTINS · Parana · Ibotirama · *Planalto* · Paranacu · *BAHIA* · *Brasil*

Mato Grosso · MATO GROSSO · Cuiabá · Cáceres · Manso (Morres) · Araguaia · Campos Belos · Barreiras · *Brazilian Highlands* · Vitória da Conquista · Itabuna · Ibicaraí · Ipiaí

San Javier · San Ignacio · San Matías · Afuarças · Goiás · Aruanã · Niquelândia · 1606 · ▲1500 · Brumado · Itapetinga · Pardo

SANTA CRUZ · San José de Chiquitos · Roboré · DISTRIT FEDERAL · Formosa · Januária · Monte Azul · Montes Claros · *Jequitinhonha*

Montero · BOLIVIA · Santa Cruz · *Bañados de Izozog (Izozog Marshes)* · Acapolis · Brasília · Corumbá · Coxim · Daús · GOIÁS · ▲4010 · Goiânia · Luziânia · Paracatu · Salto da Divisa

Villa Montes · Pto. Esperança · Bahía Negra · MATO GROSSO · Rio Verde · Barragem de São Simão · *Verde* · Corumbá · Araguari · Patos de Minas · Teófilo Otoni · Diamantina · ▲2033 · Curvelo · Governador Valadares

Mariscal Estigarribia · Pto. Murtinho · Bela Vista · DO · Aquidauana · Campo Grande · Três Lagoas · Ituiutaba · Uberlândia · Uberaba · Araxá · MINAS · Bom Despacho · Sete Lagoas · GERAIS · Belo Horizonte · Almorés · Colatina · Doce

Pto. Sastre · Pto. Casado · Pto. Pinasco · Represa Pôrto Primavera · Pres. Epitácio · SUL · *Invinhema* · São José de Rio Preto · Catanduva · Ribeirão Prêto · Guaxupé · Passos · Varginha · Divinópolis · Nova Lima · Itabira · Conselheiro Lafaiete · ESPÍRITO · Vila Velha · SANT · Vitória

Pedro Juan Caballero · Concepción · Dourados · Ponta Porã · *Represa Ilha Grande* · Adamantina · Lins · Araçatuba · Marília · SÃO · Bauru · São Carlos · Limeira · Rio Claro · Pocos de Caldas · Lavras · Cachoeiro de Itapemirim · Itanhaém

PARAGUAY · San Pedro · Ivaí · Maringá · Londrina · PARANÁ · Pres. Prudente · Assis · Tupã · Jaú · Botucatu · Piracicaba · Campinas · Jundiaí · Guaratinguetá · Itajubá · Volta Redonda · Juiz de Fora · Campos

Asunción · Paraguarí · Villarrica · Represa Itaipu · Guaíra · Apucarana · Araraquara · Sorocaba · São Paulo · Sto. André · Taubaté · São José dos Campos · Petrópolis · Niterói · Rio de Janeiro · C. Frio

Clorinda · Formosa · Foz do Iguaçu · Saltos do Iguaçu (Iguassu Falls) · Guarapuava · Ponta Grossa · Curitiba · Paranaguá

FORMOSA · Residencia Roque Sáenz Peña · Villa Angela · Pilar · Abaí · Yegros · União da Vitória · Rio Negro · Joinville · São Francisco do Sol

SANTIAGO · Campo Gallo · DEL · CHACO · ESTERO · Resistencia · Corrientes · Posadas · MISIONES · Oberá · São Miguel d'Oeste · SANTA · Blumenau · Itajaí · CATARINA · Florianópolis

Quimilí · Añatuya · Barranqueras · Empedrado · Apóstoles · S. Ignacio · Encarnación · Santa Rosa · Erechim · Lajes · Laguna · Tubarão · Criciúma

ARGENTINA · Pinto · Reconquista · Vera · Goya · CORRIENTES · Bella Vista · Santo Tomé · Santo Ângelo · Ijuí · Cruz Alta · Passo Fundo · Caxias do Sul · São Leopoldo · Novo Hamburgo · Canoas

Ojo de Agua · Tostado · Saladito · Mercedes · Paso de Los Libres · Uruguaiana · RIO GRANDE · Santa Maria · São Gabriel · Cachoeira do Sul · Pôrto Alegre

SANTA · San Cristóbal · La Paz · Curuzú Cuatiá · Alegrete · Quaraí · DO · Rosario do Sul · Canguçu · Pelotas

Mar Chiquita · Rafaela · Esperanza · ENTRE · Salto · Artigas · Santana do Livramento · Rivera · SUL · Bagé · *Lagoa dos Patos*

San Francisco · Santa Fé · Paraná · Villaguay · Concordia · Paysandú · Tacuarembó · Melo · Rio Grande

CORDOBA · Oliva · Galvez · RIOS · Diamante · Victoria · Nogoyá · Concepción del Uruguay · Paso de los Toros · Jaguarão · L. Mirim

Bell Ville · Villa María · Cañada de Gómez · San Lorenzo · Rosario · Gualeguay · URUGUAY · Durazno · Treinta y Tres · Sta. Vitória do Palmar · L. Mangueira

General Pico · Casilda · Villa Constitución · San Nicolás · Fray Bentos · Mercedes · Trinidad · Florida · Minas · Rocha

LA · Venado Tuerto · Pergamino · Zárate · Campana · Dolores · Carmelo · San José de Mayo · Las Piedras

Rufino · Junín · Chacabuco · Mercedes · Buenos Aires · Canelones · Montevideo · *Río de la Plata (R. Plate)*

Lincoln · Chivilcoy · Bragado · Lomas de Zamora · Avellaneda · Ensenada · La Plata · Maldonado

Nueve de Julio · BUENOS · Chascomús · *Bahía Samborombón* · Punta Norte

PAMPA · Trenque Lauquen · AIRES · Las Flores · Dolores · Maipú · General Madariaga

Catriló · Pehuajó · Olavarría · Azul · Ayacucho · Tandil · Balcarce · Loberia · Quequén

Santa Rosa · Carhué · Juárez · Coronel Pringles · Mar del Plata · Tres Arroyos · Necochea

Coronel Suárez · Puán · ▲1243 · Tornquist · Punta Alta · *Bahía Blanca*

Bahía Blanca · Colorado

Relief

Feet	Metres
16 404	5000
9843	3000
6562	2000
3281	1000
1640	500
656	200
0	Sea Level
Land Dep.	
656	200
13123	4000

Scale 1:12 500 000

0 · 100 · 200 · 300 · 400 Miles

0 · 100 · 200 · 300 · 400 · 500 · 600 Kms.

Lambert Azimuthal Equal Area Projection

Scale 1:7 500 000

0 · 40 · 80 Miles

0 · 40 · 80 · 120 Kms.

© Collins ○ Longman Atlases Cbi

BERMUDA (U.K.)
Scale 1:1 000 000
St. George's I. · St. George
Ireland I. · St. David's I.
Castle Harbour
Somerset I. · Great Sound · Hamilton · Flatts Village

CANARY ISLANDS (Spain)
Scale 1:10 000 000
Lanzarote
Arrecife
La Palma · Santa Cruz · Fuerteventura
Los Llanos de Aridane · Tenerife de Tenerife · Tuineje
Gomera · La Orotava · 3718 · Arucas
Hierro · Las Palmas de Gran Canaria
Maspalomas · Gran Canaria
Islas Canarias (Canary Isles) · Western Sahara

MADEIRA ISLANDS
Scale 1:4 000 000 (Portugal)
Porto Santo
Porto Moniz · Santana · Madeira
Paúl do Mar · 1862 · Sta. Cruz
Funchal
Arquipélago da Madeira (Madeira Is.) · Deserta Grande

ASCENSION (U.K.)
Scale 1:1 000 000
Georgetown · The Peak 859 · S.E. Head
Portland Pt.

ST. HELENA (U.K.)
Scale 1:1 000 000
Flagstaff B.
Jamestown · Longwood
Diana's Peak 823 · Gill Pt.
S.W. Pt. · Sandy B.

TRISTAN DA CUNHA (U.K.)
Scale 1:1 000 000
Settlement of Edinburgh · 2180
Tristan da Cunha
Inaccessible I.
Nightingale I.

Scale 1:60 000 000
0 500 1000 1500 2000 2500 Kms.
0 500 1000 1500 Miles
Zenithal Equal-Area Projection
© Collins

127

POLAR REGIONS

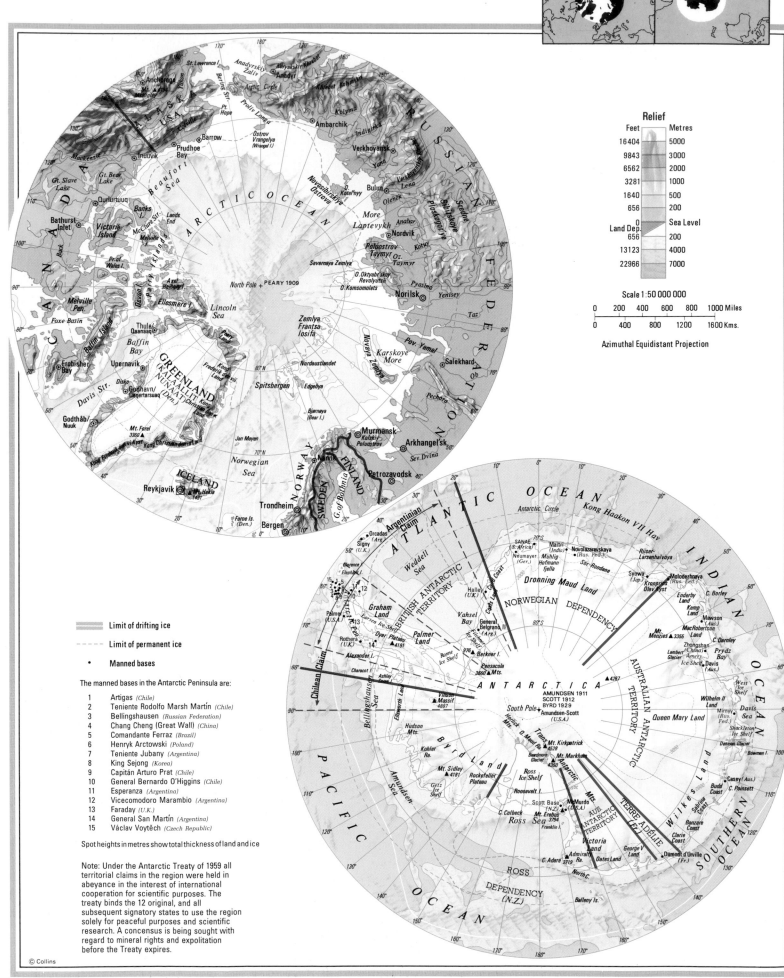

Relief

Feet		Metres
16404		5000
9843		3000
6562		2000
3281		1000
1640		500
656		200
0		Sea Level
Land Dep.		
656		200
13123		4000
22966		7000

Scale 1:50 000 000

0	200	400	600	800	1000 Miles
0	400	800	1200	1600 Kms.

Azimuthal Equidistant Projection

≡≡≡ Limit of drifting ice

- - - Limit of permanent ice

• Manned bases

The manned bases in the Antarctic Peninsula are:

1. Artigas *(Chile)*
2. Teniente Rodolfo Marsh Martín *(Chile)*
3. Bellingshausen *(Russian Federation)*
4. Chang Cheng (Great Wall) *(China)*
5. Comandante Ferraz *(Brazil)*
6. Henryk Arctowski *(Poland)*
7. Teniente Jubany *(Argentina)*
8. King Sejong *(Korea)*
9. Capitán Arturo Prat *(Chile)*
10. General Bernardo O'Higgins *(Chile)*
11. Esperanza *(Argentina)*
12. Vicecomodoro Marambio *(Argentina)*
13. Faraday *(U.K.)*
14. General San Martín *(Argentina)*
15. Václav Voytěch *(Czech Republic)*

Spot heights in metres show total thickness of land and ice

Note: Under the Antarctic Treaty of 1959 all territorial claims in the region were held in abeyance in the interest of international cooperation for scientific purposes. The treaty binds the 12 original, and all subsequent signatory states to use the region solely for peaceful purposes and scientific research. A concensus is being sought with regard to mineral rights and expolitation before the Treaty expires.

© Collins

WORLD PHYSICAL DATA

GEOGRAPHICAL DATA
Part 1

WORLD
FACTS
AND
FIGURES

WORLD PHYSICAL DATA

Earth's Dimensions

Superficial area	196 936 679 miles^2	510 066 000 km^2
Land surface	57 268 725 miles^2	148 326 000 km^2
Water surface	139 667 953 miles^2	361 740 000 km^2
Equatorial circumference	24 902 miles	40 075 km
Meridional circumference	24 859 miles	40 007 km
Volume	259 902x10^6 miles^3	1 083 230x10^6 km^3
Mass	5.882x10^{21} tons	5.976x10^{21} tonnes

The Continents

Asia	16 837 065 miles^2	43 608 000 km^2
Africa	11 720 077 miles^2	30 355 000 km^2
North America	9 787 258 miles^2	25 349 000 km^2
South America	6 799 613 miles^2	17 611 000 km^2
Antarctica	5 150 000 miles^2	13 338 500 km^2
Europe	4 053 281 miles^2	10 498 000 km^2
Oceania	3 300 000 miles^2	8 547 000 km^2

Oceans and Sea Areas

Pacific Ocean	63 854 826 miles^2	165 384 000 km^2
Atlantic Ocean	31 744 015 miles^2	82 217 000 km^2
Indian Ocean	28 371 042 miles^2	73 481 000 km^2
Arctic Ocean	5 427 027 miles^2	14 056 000 km^2
Mediterranean Sea	967 181 miles^2	2 505 000 km^2
South China Sea	894 980 miles^2	2 318 000 km^2
Bering Sea	876 061 miles^2	2 269 000 km^2
Caribbean Sea	750 193 miles^2	1 943 000 km^2
Gulf of Mexico	596 138 miles^2	1 544 000 km^2
Okhotskoye More	589 961 miles^2	1 528 000 km^2
East China Sea	481 853 miles^2	1 248 000 km^2
Hudson Bay	476 061 miles^2	1 233 000 km^2
Sea of Japan	389 189 miles^2	1 008 000 km^2
North Sea	222 007 miles^2	575 000 km^2
Black Sea	177 992 miles^2	461 000 km^2

Island Areas

Greenland; Arctic / Atlantic Ocean	839 998 miles^2	2 175 597 km^2
New Guinea; Indonesia / P. N. G.	312 166 miles^2	808 510 km^2
Borneo; Malaysia / Indonesia / Brunei	292 297 miles^2	757 050 km^2
Madagascar; Indian Ocean	229 413 miles^2	594 180 km^2
Sumatera (Sumatra) ; Indonesia	202 355 miles^2	524 100 km^2
Baffin Island; Canada	183 810 miles^2	476 068 km^2
Honshū; Japan	88 978 miles^2	230 455 km^2
Great Britain; United Kingdom	88 751 miles^2	229 867 km^2
Ellesmere Island; Canada	82 118 miles^2	212 688 km^2
Victoria Island; Canada	81 930 miles^2	212 199 km^2
Sulawesi (Celebes) ; Indonesia	72 988 miles^2	189 040 km^2
South Island; New Zealand	58 093 miles^2	150 461 km^2
Jawa (Java) ; Indonesia	51 754 miles^2	134 045 km^2
North Island; New Zealand	44 281 miles^2	114 688 km^2
Cuba; Caribbean Sea	44 218 miles^2	114 525 km^2

River Lengths

An Nīl (Nile) ; Africa	4160 miles	6695 km
Amazonas (Amazon) ; South America	4048 miles	6516 km
Chang Jiang (Yangtze) ; Asia	3964 miles	6380 km
Mississippi - Missouri; North America	3740 miles	6020 km
Ob-Irtysh; Asia	3461 miles	5570 km
Huang He (Hwang Ho) ; Asia	3395 miles	5464 km
Zaïre; Africa	2900 miles	4667 km
Mekong; Asia	2749 miles	4425 km
Amur; Asia	2744 miles	4416 km
Lena; Asia	2734 miles	4400 km
Mackenzie; North America	2640 miles	4250 km
Yenisey; Asia	2541 miles	4090 km
Niger; Africa	2504 miles	4030 km
Murray - Darling; Oceania	2330 miles	3750 km
Volga; Europe	2291 miles	3688 km

Mountain Heights (Selected)

Everest; Nepal / China	29 028 feet	8848 m
K2; Jammu & Kashmir / China	28 251 feet	8611 m
Kāngchenjunga; Nepal / India	28 208 feet	8598 m
Dhaulāgiri; Nepal	26 811 feet	8172 m
Annapurna; Nepal	26 502 feet	8078 m
Aconcagua; Argentina	22 834 feet	6960 m
Ojos del Salado; Argentina / Chile	22 664 feet	6908 m
McKinley; Alaska, U.S.A.	20 321 feet	6194 m
Logan; Canada	19 551 feet	5959 m
Kilimanjaro; Tanzania	19 340 feet	5895 m
Elbrus; Russian Federation	18 480 feet	5633 m
Kirinyaga; Kenya	17 060 feet	5200 m
Vinson Massif; Antarctica	16 863 feet	5140 m
Puncak Jaya; Indonesia	16 502 feet	5030 m
Blanc; France / Italy	15 774 feet	4808 m

Lake and Inland Sea Areas

Some areas are subject to seasonal variations.

Caspian Sea; Central Asia	143 550 miles^2	371 795 km^2
Lake Superior; U.S.A. / Canada	32 150 miles^2	83 270 km^2
Lake Victoria; East Africa	26 828 miles^2	69 485 km^2
Lake Huron; U.S.A. / Canada	23 436 miles^2	60 700 km^2
Lake Michigan; U.S.A.	22 400 miles^2	58 016 km^2
Aral Sea; Central Asia	14 092 miles^2	36 500 km^2
Lake Tanganyika; East Africa	12 700 miles^2	32 893 km^2
Great Bear Lake; Canada	12 274 miles^2	31 792 km^2
Ozero Baikal (Lake Baykal) ; Rus. Fed.	11 779 miles^2	30 510 km^2
Great Slave Lake; Canada	11 169 miles^2	28 930 km^2
Lake Erie; U.S.A. / Canada	9910 miles^2	25 667 km^2
Lake Winnipeg; Canada	9464 miles^2	24 514 km^2
Lake Malaŵi; Malaŵi / Mozambique	8683 miles^2	22 490 km^2
Lake Ontario; U.S.A. / Canada	7540 miles^2	19 529 km^2
Ladozhskoye Ozero (Lake Ladoga) ; Rus. Fed.	7100 miles^2	18 390 km^2

Volcanoes (Selected)

	Last Eruption	Height	Height
Cameroun; Cameroon	1922	13 353 feet	4070 m
Cotopaxi; Ecuador	1975	19 347 feet	5897 m
Elbrus; Russian Federation	extinct	18 510 feet	5642 m
Erebus; Antarctica	1979	12 447 feet	3794 m
Etna; Sicilia, Italy	1983	10 958 feet	3340 m
Fuji san (Fujiyama) ; Japan	extinct	12 388 feet	3776 m
Hekla; Iceland	1981	4891 feet	1491 m
Kilimanjaro; Tanzania	extinct	19 340 feet	5895 m
Mauna Loa; Hawaii	1978	13 684 feet	4171 m
Ngauruhoe; New Zealand	1975	7516 feet	2291 m
Popocatépetl; Mexico	1920	17 887 feet	5452 m
St. Helens; U.S.A.	1981	9675 feet	2949 m
Stromboli; Italy	1975	3038 feet	926 m
Tristan da Cunha; Atlantic Ocean	1962	7086 feet	2160 m
Vesuvio (Vesuvius) ; Italy	1944	4189 feet	1277 m

WORLD POLITICAL DATA

National Areas

Russian Federation; Asia / Europe	6 593 822 miles²	17 078 000 km²
Canada; North America	3 831 036 miles²	9 922 385 km²
China; Asia	3 698 455 miles²	9 579 000 km²
United States; North America	3 615 108 miles²	9 363 130 km²
Brazil; South America	3 286 472 miles²	8 511 965 km²
Australia; Oceania	2 966 138 miles²	7 682 300 km²
India; Asia	1 222 714 miles²	3 166 830 km²
Argentina; South America	1 072 515 miles²	2 777 815 km²
Sudan; Africa	967 496 miles²	2 505 815 km²
Saudi Arabia; Asia	926 988 miles²	2 400 900 km²
Algeria; Africa	919 592 miles²	2 381 745 km²
Zaïre; Africa	905 563 miles²	2 345 410 km²
Greenland; North America	840 000 miles²	2 175 600 km²
Mexico; North America	761 600 miles²	1 972 545 km²
Indonesia; Asia	741 098 miles²	1 919 445 km²
Libya; Africa	679 359 miles²	1 759 540 km²
Iran; Asia	636 293 miles²	1 648 000 km²
Mongolia; Asia	604 247 miles²	1 565 000 km²
Peru; South America	496 222 miles²	1 285 215 km²
Chad; Africa	495 752 miles²	1 284 000 km²

National Populations

China; Asia	1 139 060 000
India; Asia	843 931 000
United States; North America	249 975 000
Indonesia; Asia	179 300 000
Brazil; South America	150 368 000
Russian Federation; Asia / Europe	148 263 000
Japan; Asia	123 537 000
Bangladesh; Asia	115 594 000
Pakistan; Asia	112 049 000
Nigeria; Africa	88 500 000
Mexico; North America	86 154 000
Germany; Europe	79 479 000
Vietnam; Asia	66 200 000
Philippines; Asia	61 480 000
Italy; Europe	57 662 000
United Kingdom; Europe	57 411 000
Thailand; Asia	57 196 000
France; Europe	56 440 000
Turkey; Asia / Europe	56 098 000
Iran; Asia	54 608 000

World Cities

Ciudad de México (Mexico City) ; Mexico	20 200 000
Tōkyō; Japan	18 100 000
São Paulo; Brazil	17 400 000
New York; United States	16 200 000
Shanghai; China	13 400 000
Chicago; United States	11 900 000
Calcutta; India	11 800 000
Buenos Aires; Argentina	11 500 000
Bombay; India	11 200 000
Sŏul (Seoul) ; South Korea	11 000 000
Beijing (Peking) ; China	10 800 000
Rio de Janeiro; Brazil	10 700 000
Tianjin; China	9 400 000
Jakarta; Indonesia	9 300 000
Al Qāhirah (Cairo) ; Egypt	9 000 000

Major International Organisations

United Nations - by December 1994 the United Nations had 184 members. Independent states not represented are Kiribati, Nauru, Switzerland, Taiwan, Tonga and Tuvalu. The membership of Yugoslavia (Serbia and Montenegro) was suspended.

Commonwealth

Antigua	Australia	Bahamas	Bangladesh
Barbados	Belize	Botswana	Brunei
Canada	Cyprus	Dominica	Fiji
Gambia	Ghana	Grenada	Guyana
India	Jamaica	Kenya	Kiribati
Lesotho	Malaŵi	Malaysia	Maldives
Malta	Mauritius	Namibia	Nauru
New Zealand	Nigeria	Pakistan	Papua New Guinea
St. Kitts & Nevis	St. Lucia	St. Vincent	Seychelles
Sierra Leone	Singapore	Solomon Islands	South Africa
Sri Lanka	Swaziland	Tanzania	Tonga
Trinidad & Tobago	Tuvalu	Uganda	United Kingdom
Vanuatu	Western Samoa	Zambia	Zimbabwe

OAU - Organisation of African Unity

Algeria	Angola	Benin	Botswana
Burkina	Burundi	Cameroon	Cape Verde
Central African Rep.	Chad	Comoros	Congo
Côte d'Ivoire	Djibouti	Egypt	Equatorial Guinea
Eritrea	Ethiopia	Gabon	Gambia
Ghana	Guinea	Guinea Bissau	Kenya
Lesotho	Liberia	Libya	Madagascar
Malaŵi	Mali	Mauritania	Mauritius
Mozambique	Namibia	Niger	Nigeria
Rwanda	São Tomé & Príncipe	Senegal	Seychelles
Sierra Leone	Somali Rep.	South Africa	Sudan
Swaziland	Tanzania	Togo	Tunisia
Uganda	Western Sahara	Zaïre	Zambia
Zimbabwe			

OAS - Organisation of American States

Antigua	Argentina	Bahamas	Barbados
Belize	Bolivia	Brazil	Canada
Chile	Colombia	Costa Rica	Dominica
Dominican Rep.	Ecuador	El Salvador	Grenada
Guatemala	Guyana	Haiti	Honduras
Jamaica	Mexico	Nicaragua	Panama
Paraguay	Peru	St. Kitts & Nevis	St. Lucia
St. Vincent	Surinam	Trinidad & Tobago	United States
Venezuela			

EU - European Union

Austria	Belgium	Denmark	Finland
France	Germany	Greece	Ireland
Italy	Luxembourg	Netherlands	Portugal
Spain	Sweden	United Kingdom	

EFTA - European Free Trade Association

Iceland	Norway	Switzerland

ASEAN - Association of Southeast Asian Nations

Brunei	Indonesia	Malaysia	Philippines
Singapore	Thailand		

ECOWAS - Economic Community of West African States

Benin	Burkina	Cape Verde	Côte d'Ivoire
Gambia	Ghana	Guinea	Guinea Bissau
Liberia	Mali	Mauritania	Niger
Nigeria	Senegal	Sierra Leone	Togo

CARICOM - Caribbean Community and Common Market

Antigua	Bahamas	Barbados	Belize
Dominica	Grenada	Guyana	Jamaica
Montserrat	St. Kitts & Nevis	St. Lucia	St. Vincent
Trinidad & Tobago			

NATIONS OF THE WORLD

COUNTRY	AREA		POPULATION			FORM OF GOVERNMENT	CAPITAL CITY	MAIN LANGUAGES	CURRENCY
	miles²	km²	total	density per mile²	km²				
AFGHANISTAN	251,824	652,225	16,120,000	64	25	republic	Kābol	Pushtu,Dari	afghani
ALBANIA	11,100	28,750	3,250,000	293	113	republic	Tiranë	Albanian	lek
ALGERIA	919,593	2,381,745	25,012,000	27	11	republic	Alger (Algiers)	Arabic	dinar
ANDORRA	180	465	52,000	290	112	principality	Andorra	Catalan	French franc,Spanish peseta
ANGOLA	481,351	1,246,700	10,020,000	21	8	republic	Luanda	Portuguese	kwanza
ANTIGUA & BARBUDA	171	442	77,000	451	174	constitutional monarchy	St John's	English	East Caribbean dollar
ARGENTINA	1,072,515	2,777,815	32,322,000	30	12	federal republic	Buenos Aires	Spanish	austral
ARMENIA	11,506	29,800	3,324,000	289	112	republic	Yerevan	Armenian,Russian	rouble
AUSTRALIA	2,966,139	7,682,300	17,086,000	6	2	monarchy (federal)	Canberra	English	dollar
AUSTRIA	32,376	83,855	7,712,000	238	92	federal republic	Wien (Vienna)	German	schilling
AZERBAIJAN	33,436	86,600	7,153,000	214	83	republic	Baku	Azerbaijani,Russian	rouble
BAHAMAS	5353	13,865	253,000	47	18	constitutional monarchy	Nassau	English	dollar
BAHRAIN	255	661	503,000	1971	761	emirate	Al Manāmah	Arabic	dinar
BANGLADESH	55,598	144,000	115,594,000	2079	803	republic	Dhaka	Bengali	taka
BARBADOS	166	430	255,000	1536	593	constitutional monarchy	Bridgetown	English	dollar
BELARUS (BELORUSSIA)	80,309	208,000	10,278,000	128	49	republic	Minsk	Belorussian	rouble
BELGIUM	11,784	30,520	9,845,000	835	323	constitutional monarchy	Bruxelles (Brussels) Brussel	French,Dutch, German	franc
BELIZE	8867	22,965	188,000	21	8	constitutional monarchy	Belmopan	English	dollar
BENIN	43,483	112,620	4,736,000	109	42	republic	Porto-Novo	French	CFA franc
BHUTAN	18,000	46,620	1,517,000	84	33	constitutional monarchy	Thimbu	Dzongkha	Indian rupee,ngultrum
BOLIVIA	424,160	1,098,575	7,400,000	17	7	republic	La Paz / Sucre	Spanish,Aymara	boliviano
BOSNIA-HERZEGOVINA	19,741	51,130	4,200,000	213	82	republic	Sarajevo	Serbo-Croat	dinar
BOTSWANA	231,804	600,372	1,291,000	6	2	republic	Gaborone	English,Tswana	pula
BRAZIL	3,286,473	8,511,965	150,368,000	46	18	federal republic	Brasília	Portuguese	cruzeiro
BRUNEI	2226	5,765	266,000	120	46	sultanate	Bandar Seri Begawan	Malay	dollar
BULGARIA	42,822	110,910	8,980,000	210	81	people's republic	Sofiya (Sofia)	Bulgarian	lev
BURKINA	105,869	274,200	9,001,000	85	33	republic	Ouagadougou	French	CFA franc
BURUNDI	10,747	27,834	5,458,000	508	196	republic	Bujumbura	French,Kirundi	franc
CAMBODIA	69,884	181,000	8,246,000	118	46	republic	Phnom Penh	Cambodian,Khmer	riel
CAMEROON	183,591	475,500	11,834,000	64	25	republic	Yaoundé	French,English	CFA franc
CANADA	3,831,037	9,922,385	26,603,000	7	3	monarchy (federal)	Ottawa	English,French	dollar
CAPE VERDE	1558	4,035	370,000	237	92	republic	Praia	Portuguese,Creole	escudo
CENTRAL AFRICAN REPUBLIC	241,303	624,975	3,039,000	13	5	republic	Bangui	French,Sango	CFA franc
CHAD	495,753	1,284,000	5,679,000	11	4	republic	N'Djamena	French,Arabic	CFA franc
CHILE	290,203	751,625	13,173,000	45	18	republic	Santiago	Spanish	peso
CHINA	3,698,456	9,579,000	1,139,060,000	308	119	people's republic	Beijing (Peking)	Mandarin	yuan
COLOMBIA	439,736	1,138,915	32,987,000	75	29	republic	Bogotá	Spanish	peso
COMOROS	718	1,860	551,000	767	296	federal republic	Moroni	Comoran,Arabic,French	CFA franc
CONGO	132,046	342,000	2,271,000	17	7	republic	Brazzaville	French	CFA franc
COSTA RICA	19,653	50,900	2,994,000	152	59	republic	San José	Spanish	colon
CÔTE D'IVOIRE (IVORY COAST)	124,504	322,465	11,998,000	96	37	republic	Yamoussoukro	French	CFA franc
CROATIA	21,830	56,540	4,600,000	211	81	republic	Zagreb	Serbo-Croat	Dinar
CUBA	44,218	114,525	10,609,000	240	93	people's republic	La Habana (Havana)	Spanish	peso
CYPRUS	3571	9,250	702,000	197	76	republic	Levkosía (Nicosia)	Greek	pound
CZECH REPUBLIC	30,448	78,864	10,300,000	340	131	federal republic	Praha (Prague)	Czech	koruna
DENMARK	16,631	43,075	5,140,000	309	119	constitutional monarchy	København (Copenhagen)	Danish	krone
DJIBOUTI	8880	23,000	409,000	46	18	republic	Djibouti	French,Somali,Afar	franc
DOMINICA	290	751	83,000	286	111	republic	Roseau	English,French	East Caribbean dollar
DOMINICAN REPUBLIC	18,703	48,440	7,170,000	383	148	republic	Santo Domingo	Spanish	peso
ECUADOR	178,176	461,475	10,782,000	61	23	republic	Quito	Spanish	sucre
EGYPT	386,197	1,000,250	53,153,000	138	53	republic	Al Qāhirah (Cairo)	Arabic	pound
EL SALVADOR	8261	21,395	5,252,000	636	245	republic	San Salvador	Spanish	colón
EQUATORIAL GUINEA	10,830	28,050	348,000	32	12	republic	Malabo	Spanish	CFA franc
ERITREA	36,169	93,679	3,500,000	96	37	republic	Āsmera (Asmara)	Tigrinya, Arabic, English	Ethiopian birr
ESTONIA	17,413	45,100	1,583,000	91	35	republic	Tallinn	Estonian,Russian	kroon
ETHIOPIA	471,776	1,221,900	50,974,000	108	42	people's republic	Ādīs Ābeba (Addis Ababa)	Amharic	birr
FEDERATED STATES OF MICRONESIA	271	702	99,000	365	141	federal republic	Palikir on Pohnpei	English,Kosrean,Yapese, Pohnpeian,Trukese	US dollar
FIJI	7077	18,330	765,000	108	42	republic	Suva	English,Fiji,Hindustani	dollar
FINLAND	130,127	337,030	4,986,000	38	15	republic	Helsinki	Finnish,Swedish	markka
FRANCE	210,025	543,965	56,440,000	269	104	republic	Paris	French	franc
GABON	103,346	267,665	1,172,000	11	4	republic	Libreville	French	CFA franc
GAMBIA	4127	10,690	861,000	209	81	republic	Banjul	English	dalasi
GEORGIA	26,911	69,700	5,464,000	203	78	republic	Tbilisi	Georgian,Russian	rouble
GERMANY	138,173	357,868	79,479,000	575	222	federal republic	Berlin,Bonn	German	mark
GHANA	92,010	238,305	15,028,000	163	63	military regime	Accra	English	cedi

COUNTRY	AREA miles²	AREA km²	POPULATION total	POPULATION density per mile²	POPULATION density per km²	FORM OF GOVERNMENT	CAPITAL CITY	MAIN LANGUAGES	CURRENCY
GREECE	50,959	131,985	10,123,000	199	77	republic	Athinai (Athens)	Greek	drachma
GRENADA	133	345	85,000	638	246	constitutional monarchy	St George's	English	East Caribbean dollar
GUATEMALA	42,042	108,890	9,197,000	219	84	republic	Guatemala	Spanish	quetzal
GUINEA	98,400	254,855	5,756,000	58	23	military regime	Conakry	French	franc
GUINEA-BISSAU	13,948	36,125	965,000	69	27	republic	Bissau	Portuguese	peso
GUYANA	83,000	214,970	796,000	10	4	republic	Georgetown	English	dollar
HAITI	10,714	27,750	6,486,000	605	234	republic	Port-au-Prince	French, Creole	gourde
HONDURAS	43,276	112,085	5,105,000	118	46	republic	Tegucigalpa	Spanish	lempira
HUNGARY	35,919	93,030	10,553,000	294	113	republic	Budapest	Magyar	forint
ICELAND	39,699	102,820	255,000	6	2	republic	Reykjavík	Icelandic	króna
INDIA	1,222,714	3,166,830	843,931,000	676	266	republic	New Delhi	Hindi, English	rupee
INDONESIA	741,098	1,919,445	179,300,000	242	93	republic	Jakarta	Bahasa Indonesia	rupiah
IRAN	636,293	1,648,000	54,608,000	86	33	Islamic republic	Tehrān	Persian	rial
IRAQ	169,284	438,445	18,920,000	112	43	republic	Baghdād	Arabic, Kurdish	dinar
IRELAND, REPUBLIC OF	26,600	68,895	3,503,000	132	51	republic	Dublin	English, Irish	punt
ISRAEL	8019	20,770	4,659,000	581	224	republic	Yerushalayim (Jerusalem)	Hebrew	shekel
ITALY	116,311	301,245	57,662,000	496	191	republic	Roma (Rome)	Italian	lira
JAMAICA	4411	11,425	2,420,000	549	212	constitutional monarchy	Kingston	English	dollar
JAPAN	142,741	369,700	123,537,000	865	334	monarchy	Tōkyō	Japanese	yen
JORDAN	37,066	96,000	4,010,000	108	42	monarchy	Ammān	Arabic	dinar
KAZAKHSTAN	1,049,151	2,717,300	16,742,000	16	6	republic	Almaty	Kazakh, Russian	rouble
KENYA	224,959	582,645	24,032,000	107	41	republic	Nairobi	Kiswahili, English	shilling
KIRIBATI	264	684	66,000	250	96	republic	Bairiki on Tarawa Atoll	English, Gilbertese, I-Kiribati	Australian dollar
KUWAIT	9375	24,280	2,143,000	229	88	emirate	Al Kuwayt (Kuwait)	Arabic	dinar
KYRGYZSTAN (KIRGHIZIA)	76,641	198,500	4,394,000	57	22	republic	Bishkek	Kirghiz, Russian	rouble
LAOS	91,400	236,725	4,139,000	45	17	people's republic	Vientiane (Viangchan)	Lao	new kip
LATVIA	24,595	63,700	2,686,000	109	42	republic	Rīga	Latvian, Russian	Latvian rouble
LEBANON	4015	10,400	2,701,000	673	260	republic	Bayrūt (Beirut)	Arabic	pound
LESOTHO	11,716	30,345	1,774,000	151	58	monarchy	Maseru	English, Sesotho	maluti
LIBERIA	43,000	111,370	2,607,000	61	23	republic	Monrovia	English	dollar
LIBYA	679,359	1,759,540	4,545,000	7	3	socialist state	Tarābulus (Tripoli)	Arabic	dinar
LIECHTENSTEIN	62	160	29,000	469	181	constitutional monarchy	Vaduz	German	Swiss franc
LITHUANIA	25,174	65,200	3,731,000	148	57	republic	Vilnius	Lithuanian	rouble, Litas prop.
LUXEMBOURG	998	2,585	381,000	382	147	constitutional monarchy	Luxembourg	Letzeburgish, French, German	franc
MACEDONIA	9,928	25,713	2,034,000	204	79	republic	Skopje	Macedonian	denar
MADAGASCAR	229,413	594,180	11,197,000	49	19	republic	Antananarivo	Malagasy, French	Malagasy franc
MALAŴI	36,324	94,080	8,289,000	228	88	republic	Lilongwe	English, Chichewa	Kwacha
MALAYSIA	128,558	332,965	17,861,000	139	54	constitutional monarchy	Kuala Lumpur	Bahasa Malay	ringgit
MALDIVES	115	298	215,000	1869	721	republic	Malé	Divehi	rufiyaa
MALI	478,819	1,240,140	8,156,000	17	7	republic	Bamako	French, Bambara	CFA franc
MALTA	122	316	354,000	2901	1120	republic	Valletta	Maltese, English	pound
MARSHALL ISLANDS	70	181	40,000	572	221	republic	Dalap-Uliga-Darrit	Marshallese, English	US dollar
MAURITANIA	397,954	1,030,700	2,025,000	5	2	republic	Nouakchott	Arabic, French	ouguiya
MAURITIUS	720	1,865	1,075,000	1493	576	constitutional monarchy	Port Louis	English, Creole	rupee
MEXICO	761,600	1,972,545	86,154,000	113	44	federal republic	Ciudad de México (Mexico City)	Spanish	peso
MOLDOVA (MOLDAVIA)	13,012	33,700	4,368,000	336	130	republic	Kishinev	Romanian, Russian	rouble
MONACO	1	2	29,000	29,000	14500	constitutional monarchy	Monaco	French	French franc
MONGOLIA	604,247	1,565,000	2,190,000	4	1	republic	Ulaanbaatar (Ulan Bator)	Khalka Mongol	tugrik
MOROCCO	172,413	446,550	25,061,000	145	56	monarchy	Rabat	Arabic	dirham
MOZAMBIQUE	302,994	784,755	15,656,000	52	20	republic	Maputo	Portuguese	metical
MYANMAR (BURMA)	261,788	678,030	41,675,000	159	61	military regime	Yangon (Rangoon)	Burmese	kyat
NAMIBIA	318,261	824,295	1,781,000	6	2	republic	Windhoek	Afrikaans, English	Namibian dollar
NAURU	8	21	10,000	1233	476	republic	Yaren	Nauruan, English	Australian dollar
NEPAL	54,600	141,415	18,916,000	346	134	monarchy	Kathmandu	Nepali	rupee
NETHERLANDS	15,892	41,160	14,935,000	940	363	constitutional monarchy	Amsterdam	Dutch	guilder
NEW ZEALAND	102,375	265,150	3,346,000	33	13	constitutional monarchy	Wellington	English, Maori	dollar
NICARAGUA	57,143	148,000	3,871,000	68	26	republic	Managua	Spanish	córdoba
NIGER	458,073	1,186,410	7,732,000	17	7	republic	Niamey	French	CFA Franc
NIGERIA	356,699	923,850	88,500,000	248	96	federal republic	Abuja	English	naira
NORTH KOREA	47,224	122,310	21,773,000	461	178	people's republic	Pyŏngyang	Korean	won
NORWAY	125,056	323,895	4,242,000	34	13	constitutional monarchy	Oslo	Norwegian	krone
OMAN	105,000	271,950	1,502,000	14	6	sultanate	Masqaṭ (Muscat)	Arabic	rial
PAKISTAN	310,402	803,940	112,049,000	361	139	federal Islamic republic	Islāmābād	Urdu, Punjabi, English	rupee
PANAMA	30,315	78,515	2,418,000	80	31	republic	Panamá City	Spanish	balboa

NATIONS OF THE WORLD

COUNTRY	AREA		POPULATION			FORM OF GOVERNMENT	CAPITAL CITY	MAIN LANGUAGES	CURRENCY
	miles²	km²	total	density per mile²	km²				
PAPUA NEW GUINEA	178,703	462,840	3,699,000	21	8	constitutional monarchy	Port Moresby	English,Pidgin,Motu	kina
PARAGUAY	157,046	406,750	4,277,000	27	11	republic	Asunción	Spanish,Guaraní	guaraní
PERU	496,222	1,285,215	21,550,000	43	17	republic	Lima	Spanish,Quechua	sol
PHILIPPINES	115,830	300,000	61,480,000	531	205	republic	Manila	Pilipino,English	peso
POLAND	120,728	312,685	38,180,000	316	122	republic	Warszawa (Warsaw)	Polish	zloty
PORTUGAL	34,340	88,940	10,525,000	306	118	republic	Lisboa (Lisbon)	Portuguese	escudo
QATAR	4415	11,435	486,000	110	43	emirate	Ad Dawḥah (Doha)	Arabic	riyal
ROMANIA	91,699	237,500	23,200,000	253	98	republic	Bucureşti (Bucharest)	Romanian	leu
RUSSIAN FEDERATION	6,593,822	17,078,000	148,263,000	22	9	republic	Moskva (Moscow)	Russian	rouble
RWANDA	10,166	26,330	7,181,000	706	273	republic	Kigali	Kinyarwanda,French	franc
ST KITTS-NEVIS	101	261	44,000	437	169	constitutional monarchy	Basseterre	English	East Caribbean dollar
ST LUCIA	238	616	151,000	635	245	constitutional monarchy	Castries	English,French	East Caribbean dollar
ST VINCENT & THE GRENADINES	150	389	116,000	772	298	constitutional monarchy	Kingstown	English	East Caribbean dollar
SAN MARINO	24	61	24,000	1019	393	republic	San Marino	Italian	Italian lira
SÃO TOMÉ & PRÍNCIPE	372	964	121,000	325	126	republic	São Tomé	Portuguese,Creole	dobra
SAUDI ARABIA	926,988	2,400,900	14,870,000	16	6	monarchy	Ar Riyāḍ (Riyadh)	Arabic	riyal
SENEGAL	75,954	196,720	7,327,000	96	37	republic	Dakar	French	CFA franc
SEYCHELLES	156	404	67,000	430	166	republic	Victoria	English,French,Creole	rupee
SIERRA LEONE	27,925	72,325	4,151,000	149	57	republic	Freetown	English	leone
SINGAPORE	238	616	3,003,000	12,626	4875	republic	Singapore	Bahasa Malay,English, Chinese,Tamil	dollar
SLOVAKIA	18,933	49,035	5,300,000	278	108	republic	Bratislava	Slovak	koruna
SLOVENIA	7819	20,250	1,900,000	243	94	republic	Ljubljana	Slovene	dinar
SOLOMON ISLANDS	11,502	29,790	321,000	28	11	constitutional monarchy	Honiara	English	dollar
SOMALI REPUBLIC	243,243	630,000	7,497,000	31	12	republic	Muqdisho (Mogadishu)	Arabic,Somali,Italian, English	shilling
SOUTH AFRICA,REPUBLIC OF	457,461	1,184,825	35,282,000	77	30	republic	Cape Town (Kaapstad) / Pretoria	Afrikaans,English	rand
SOUTH KOREA	38,010	98,445	42,793,000	1126	435	republic	Sŏul (Seoul)	Korean	won
SPAIN	194,934	504,880	38,959,000	200	77	constitutional monarchy	Madrid	Spanish	peseta
SRI LANKA	25,332	65,610	16,993,000	671	259	republic	Colombo	Sinhala,Tamil	Rupee
SUDAN	967,496	2,505,815	25,204,000	26	10	military regime	Al Kharṭūm (Khartoum)	Arabic	pound
SURINAM	53,251	163,820	422,000	7	3	republic	Paramaribo	Dutch,English	guilder
SWAZILAND	6705	17,365	768,000	115	44	monarchy	Mbabane	English,Siswati	lilangeni
SWEDEN	173,664	449,790	8,559,000	49	19	constitutional monarchy	Stockholm	Swedish	krona
SWITZERLAND	15,940	41,285	6,712,000	421	163	federal republic	Bern (Berne)	German,French,Italian, Romansh	franc
SYRIA	71,691	185,680	12,116,000	169	65	republic	Dimashq (Damascus)	Arabic	pound
TAIWAN	13,896	35,990	20,300,000	1461	564	republic	Taipei	Mandarin	dollar
TAJIKISTAN	55,251	143,100	5,303,000	96	37	republic	Dushanbe	Tajik,Russian	rouble
TANZANIA	362,842	939,760	25,635,000	71	27	republic	Dodoma	Kiswahili,English	shilling
THAILAND	198,456	514,000	57,196,000	288	111	monarchy	Bangkok (Krung Thep)	Thai	baht
TOGO	21,925	56,785	3,531,000	161	62	republic	Lomé	French	CFA franc
TONGA	270	699	95,000	352	136	constitutional monarchy	Nuku'alofa	English,Tongan	pa'anga
TRINIDAD AND TOBAGO	1981	5,130	1,227,000	619	239	republic	Port of Spain	English	dollar
TUNISIA	63,378	164,150	8,180,000	129	50	republic	Tunis	Arabic	dinar
TURKEY	300,946	779,450	56,098,000	186	72	republic	Ankara	Turkish	lira
TURKMENISTAN	188,456	488,100	3,670,000	19	8	republic	Ashkhabad	Turkmenian	rouble
TUVALU	10	25	10,000	1036	400	constitutional monarchy	Funafuti	English,Tuvaluan	Australian dollar
UGANDA	91,344	236,580	18,795,000	206	79	republic	Kampala	Kiswahili,English	shilling
UKRAINE	233,089	603,700	51,857,000	222	86	republic	Kiev	Ukrainian,Russian	rouble
UNITED ARAB EMIRATES	29,015	75,150	1,589,000	55	21	federation of emirates	Abū Ẓaby (Abu Dhabi)	Arabic	dirham
UNITED KINGDOM	94,500	244,755	57,411,000	608	235	constitutional monarchy	London	English	pound
UNITED STATES OF AMERICA	3,615,108	9,363,130	249,975,000	69	27	federal republic	Washington	English	dollar
URUGUAY	72,172	186,925	3,096,000	43	17	republic	Montevideo	Spanish	peso
UZBEKISTAN	172,741	447,400	20,531,000	119	46	republic	Tashkent	Uzbek,Russian	rouble
VANUATU	5701	14,765	147,000	26	10	republic	Vila	English,French,Bislama	vatu
VATICAN CITY	0.5	1	1000	2000	1000	ecclesiastical state	Vatican City	Italian	lira
VENEZUELA	352,141	912,045	19,735,000	56	22	federal republic	Caracas	Spanish	bolívar
VIETNAM	127,245	329,565	66,200,000	520	201	people's socialist republic	Hanoi	Vietnamese	dong
WESTERN SAMOA	1097	2,840	164,000	150	58	constitutional monarchy	Apia	Samoan,English	tala
YEMEN	203,850	527,969	11,282,000	55	21	republic	San'a	Arabic	rial,dinar
YUGOSLAVIA	49,376	127,885	10,000,000	203	78	federal republic	Beograd (Belgrade)	Serbo-Croat, Macedonian,Albanian	dinar
ZAÏRE	905,564	2,345,410	35,562,000	39	15	republic	Kinshasa	French,Lingala	zaïre
ZAMBIA	290,585	752,615	7,818,000	27	10	republic	Lusaka	English	kwacha
ZIMBABWE	150,699	390,310	9,369,000	62	24	republic	Harare	English	dollar

GEOGRAPHICAL DATA
Part 2

GLOSSARY
OF
GEOGRAPHICAL
TERMS

GLOSSARY

Introduction to Glossary

The Glossary of Geographical Terms lists in alphabetical order a selection of foreign language names and geographical terms, inclusive of any abbreviations, which are found in the names on the maps and in the index. The terms occur either as separate words (e.g. côte which means coast) or as parts of compound words (e.g. - oog in Langeoog which means island). A term preceded by a hyphen usually appears as an ending of a name on the map (e.g. -vesi in Puulavesi; -holm in Bornholm). Each term is followed by its language which is identified by abbreviations in brackets. A complete list of the language abbreviations used in the glossary is found below.

Language Abbreviations

Afr.	Afrikaans	Fin.	Finnish	Man.	Manchurian
Alb.	Albanian	Fr.	French	Mon.	Mongolian
Ar.	Arabic	Gae.	Gaelic	Nor.	Norwegian
Ba.	Baluchi	Ger.	German	Per.	Persian
Ber.	Berber	Gr.	Greek	Pol.	Polish
Blg.	Bulgarian	Heb.	Hebrew	Port.	Portugese
Bur.	Burmese	Hin.	Hindi	Rom.	Romanian
Cat.	Catalan	I.-C.	Indo-Chinese	Rus.	Russian
Cbd.	Cambodian	Ice.	Icelandic	S.-C.	Serbo-Croat
Ch.	Chinese	It.	Italian	Sp.	Spanish
Cz.	Czech	Jap.	Japanese	Swe.	Swedish
Dan.	Danish	Kor.	Korean	Th.	Thai (Siamese)
Dut.	Dutch	Lao.	Laotian	Tur.	Turkish
Est.	Estonian	Lat.	Latvian	Ur.	Urdu
Eth.	Ethiopian	Ma.	Malagasy	Viet.	Vietnamese
Fae.	Faeroese	Mal.	Malay		

Glossary of Geographical Terms

A

āb *(Per.)*	water
ada *(Tur.)*	island
adrar *(Ber., Ar.)*	mountain region
ákra, akrotírion *(Gr.)*	cape
alb *(Rom.)*	white
alin *(Man., Mon.)*	mountain range
alpes *(Fr.)*	alps
alpi *(It.)*	alps
alt/a/o *(It., Sp., Port.)*	high
-an *(Swe.)*	river
ao *(Ch., Th.)*	bay, gulf
arquipélago *(Port.)*	archipelago
-ås, -åsen *(Swe.)*	hills

B

bāb *(Ar.)*	gate
backe *(Swe.)*	hill
bādiya/t *(Ar.)*	desert
baelt *(Dan.)*	strait
b., bahía *(Sp.)*	bay
baḥr *(Ar.)*	great river/lake
baía *(Port.)*	bay
b., baie *(Fr.)*	bay
ban *(Hin., Ur.)*	forest
ban *(I.-C.)*	village
bañados *(Sp.)*	marshes
bandao *(Ch.)*	peninsula
bassin *(Fr.)*	basin
baṭha *(Ar.)*	plain
beloyy *(Rus.)*	white
ben, beinn *(Gae.)*	mountain
bereg *(Rus.)*	shore

berg/en *(Ger., Swe.)*	mountain/s
biq'at *(Heb.)*	valley
birkat *(Ar.)*	lake
bog., bogazi *(Tur.)*	strait
bois *(Fr.)*	woods
bol., bol'shaya *(Rus.)*	big
bory *(Pol.)*	forest
bredning *(Dan.)*	bay
brú *(Ice.)*	bridge
bucht *(Ger.)*	bay
bugt *(Dan.)*	bay
buḥayrat *(Ar.)*	lake
bukt/en *(Nor., Swe.)*	bay
burnu *(Tur.)*	cape
busen *(Ger.)*	bay
büyük *(Tur.)*	big

C

c., cabo *(Sp., Port.)*	cape
campo *(Sp.)*	field
c., cap *(Fr.)*	cape
capo *(It.)*	cape
causse *(Fr.)*	upland
cerro *(Sp.)*	mountain
chaco *(Sp.)*	jungle region
chaîne *(Fr.)*	chain
chapada *(Port.)*	hills
chott *(Ar.)*	salt lake
cime *(Fr.)*	summit
co *(Ch.)*	lake
co *(Viet.)*	mountain
col *(Fr.)*	pass

colline/s *(Fr.)*	hill/s
con *(Viet.)*	islands
cordillera *(Sp.)*	mountain range
costa *(Sp.)*	coast
côte *(Fr.)*	coast

D

d., daği, dağlari *(Tur.)*	mountain, mountain range
dake *(Jap.)*	peak
dal/en *(Nor., Swe.)*	valley
danau *(Mal.)*	lake
daqq *(Per.)*	salt flat
darya *(Rus.)*	river
daryācheh *(Per.)*	lake
dasht *(Per.)*	desert
denizi *(Tur.)*	sea
desierto *(Sp.)*	desert
détroit *(Fr.)*	strait
dhiórix *(Gr.)*	canal
dian *(Ch.)*	lake
-dijk *(Dut.)*	dyke
ding *(Ch.)*	mountain
do *(Kor.)*	island

E

eiland/en *(Afr., Dut.)*	island/s
embalse *(Sp.)*	reservoir
'emeq *(Heb.)*	valley
erg *(Ar.)*	sand desert
estrecho *(Sp.)*	strait
estuario *(Sp.)*	estuary

étang *(Fr.)*	pond	i., is., isla/s *(Sp.)*	island/s	lule *(Swe.)*	eastern
		isola/e *(It.)*	island/s		
F		istmo *(Sp.)*	isthmus	**M**	
		iztochni *(Blg.)*	eastern		
feng *(Ch.)*	peak			maa *(Est., Fin.)*	land
firth *(Gae.)*	strait	**J**		mae *(Th.)*	river
fjället *(Swe.)*	mountain			mar/e *(It., Port., Sp.)*	sea
fjell *(Nor.)*	mountain	j., jabal *(Ar., Per.)*	mountain	marsch *(Ger.)*	marsh
fj., fjorden *(Dan., Nor., Swe.)*	fjord	jarvi *(Fin.)*	lake	meer *(Afr., Dut.)*	lake, sea
fjördhur *(Fae., Ice.)*	fjord	jaure *(Swe.)*	lake	mer *(Fr.)*	sea
flói *(Ice.)*	bay	jawb *(Ar.)*	basin, waterhole	mifraẓ *(Heb.)*	bay
fonn *(Nor.)*	glacier	jazā'ir *(Ar.)*	island	misaki *(Jap.)*	cape
		jezero *(S.-C., Cz.)*	lake	mont *(Fr.)*	mountain
G		jezioro *(Pol.)*	lake	montagne *(Fr.)*	mountain
		jiang *(Ch.)*	river	mont/e/i *(It., Port., Sp.)*	mountain/s
gau *(Ger.)*	district	jima *(Jap.)*	island	moor *(Ger.)*	swamp, moor
gave *(Fr.)*	torrent	jökulen *(Nor.)*	glacier	more *(Rus.)*	sea
gebirge *(Ger.)*	mountains	jökull *(Ice.)*	glacier	mörön *(Mon.)*	river
ghubbat *(Ar.)*	bay	jūras līcis *(Lat.)*	gulf, bay	mui *(Viet.)*	point
gji *(Alb.)*	bay			mull *(Gae.)*	headland
gobi *(Mon.)*	desert	**K**		munkhafaḍ *(Ar.)*	depression
gol *(Mon.)*	river			munti/i *(Rom.)*	mountain/s
g., golfe *(Fr.)*	gulf	kaikyō *(Jap.)*	strait	m., mys *(Rus.)*	cape
g., golfo *(Sp., It.)*	gulf	kaise *(Swe.)*	mountain range		
gölö *(Tur.)*	lake	kamm *(Ger.)*	ridge	**N**	
golyam *(Blg.)*	great	k., kanal *(Ger., Pol., Rus., S.-C., Swe.)*	canal		
g., gora/y *(Rus.)*	mountain/s	kap *(Ger.)*	cape	nada *(Jap.)*	sea, bay
gorje *(S.C.)*	mountain range	kapp *(Nor.)*	cape	nafūd *(Ar.)*	sandy desert
gross *(Ger.)*	great	kep *(Alb.)*	cape	najd *(Ar.)*	pass
guba *(Rus.)*	bay	kep., kepulauan *(Mal.)*	archipelago	nam *(I.-C., Kor.)*	southern
guntō *(Jap.)*	island group	khalīj *(Ar., Per.)*	gulf, bay	nes *(Ice., Nor.)*	promontory
guoyuan *(Ch.)*	plateau	khazzān *(Ar.)*	dam	ness *(Gae.)*	promontory
gura *(Rom.)*	mouth	khr., khrebet *(Rus.)*	mountain range	nevada *(Sp.)*	snow-capped mountains
		kladenets *(Blg.)*	well	ngoc *(Viet)*	mountain
H		klong *(Th.)*	canal, creek	nísoi *(Gr.)*	islands
		ko *(Jap.)*	lake, bay	nizh., nizhne, nizhniy *(Rus.)*	lower
hai *(Ch.)*	sea	ko *(Th.)*	island	nizmennost' *(Rus.)*	depression
haixia *(Ch.)*	strait	-kogen *(Jap.)*	plateau	nord *(Dan., Fr., Ger., Nor., Swe.)*	northern
ḥajar *(Ar.)*	mountain range	koh *(Per.)*	mountains	nur *(Ch.)*	lake, salt lake
halvö *(Dan.)*	peninsula	kílpos *(Gr.)*	gulf	nusa *(mal.)*	island
halvöya *(Nor.)*	peninsula	kör., körfezi *(Tur.)*	gulf, bay	nuur *(Mon.)*	lake
hāmūn *(Per.)*	plain	kou *(Ch.)*	estuary		
hantō *(Jap.)*	peninsula	kryazh *(Rus.)*	ridge	**O**	
har *(Heb.)*	mountain range	kūh/ha *(Per.)*	mountain/s		
hauteurs *(Fr.)*	hills	kul *(Rus.)*	lake	occidental *(Sp.)*	western
hav *(Dan., Nor., Swe.)*	sea	kuppe *(Ger.)*	hilltop	odde *(Dan., Nor.)*	headland
hawr *(Ar.)*	lake	kyst *(Dan.)*	coast	ojo/s *(Sp.)*	spring/s
hāyk' *(Eth.)*	lake			oki *(Jap.)*	bay
he *(Ch.)*	river	**L**		-oog *(Ger.)*	island
heiya *(Jap.)*	plain			óros, óri *(Gr.)*	mountain, mountains
hoch *(Ger.)*	high	lac *(Fr.)*	lake	oriental/e *(Sp.)*	eastern
hohe *(Ger.)*	height	lacul *(Rom.)*	lake	ort *(Ger.)*	settlement
höj *(Dan.)*	high, height	l., lago *(It. Sp.)*	lake	o., os., ostrov/a *(Rus.)*	island/s
-holm *(Dan.)*	island	lagoa *(Port.)*	lagoon	ost *(Ger.)*	east
holt *(Nor.)*	wood	laguna *(Sp.)*	lagoon, lake	oued *(Ar.)*	dry river bed
hory *(Cz.)*	mountain	laut *(Mal.)*	north, sea	öy, öya *(Nor.)*	island
hu *(Ch.)*	lake	liedao *(Ch.)*	islands	oz., ozero *(Rus.)*	lake
-huk *(Swe.)*	cape	liehtao *(Ch.)*	islands		
		l., límni *(Gr.)*	lake	**P**	
I		ling *(Ch.)*	mountain range		
		llanos *(Sp.)*	plains	pampa/s *(Sp.)*	plain/s
Î., Îs., Île/s *(Fr.)*	island/s	l., loch *(Gae.)*	lake	parbat *(Ur.)*	mountain
ilha/s *(Port.)*	island/s	lora *(Ba.)*	stream	passo *(It.)*	pass
insel/n *(Ger.)*	island/s	l., lough *(Gae.)*	lake	peg., pegunungan *(Mal.)*	mountain range

GLOSSARY

pélagos (Gr.) — sea
pelleg (Alb.) — bay
peña (Sp.) — cliff
pendi (Ch.) — depression
péninsule (Fr.) — peninsula
pertuis (Fr.) — strait
peski (Rus.) — sand
phanom (I.-C., Th.) — mountain
phou (Lao.) — mountain
phu (Th.) — mountain
pic (Fr.) — peak
pico (Sp.) — peak
pik (Rus.) — peak
pingyuan (Ch.) — plain
plaine (Fr.) — plain
plana (Sp.) — plain
planalto (Port.) — plateau
pl., planina (Blg., S.-C.) — mountain range
plato (Afr., Blg., Rus.) — plateau
platosu (Tur.) — plateau
platte (Ger.) — plateau, plain
playa (Sp.) — beach
ploskogor'ye (Rus.) — plateau
pohorie (Cz.) — mountain range
pointe (Fr.) — promontory
pojezierze (Pol.) — lakeland
poleseye (Rus.) — area of marsh
polje (S.-C.) — plain, basin
pov., poluostrov (Rus.) — peninsula
porthmós (Gr.) — strait
porţi (Rom.) — entrance
portillo (Sp.) — gap
prliv (Rus.) — strait
puig (Cat.) — peak
pulau (Mal.) — island
pta., punta (It., Sp.) — point
puy (Fr.) — peak

Q

qā' (Ar.) — salt flat
qanāt (Ar., Per.) — canal
qolleh (Per.) — mountain
qu (Ch.) — canal, stream
qūr (Ar.) — buttes, ridge

R

ramlat (Ar.) — dunes
rann (Hin.) — swampy region
ras, ra's, rās (Per., Ar.) — cape
ravnina (Rus.) — plain
reprêsa (Port.) — reservoir
reshteh (Per.) — mountain range
retto (Jap.) — island group
ria, ría (Port., Sp.) — mouth of river
rijeka (S.-C.) — river
r., rio, río (Port., Sp.) — river
riviera (It.) — coast, river
r., riviàre (Fr.) — river
rocca (It.) — rock
rücken (Ger.) — ridge
rūd (Per.) — river

S

sable/s (Fr.) — sand/s
sadd (Ar.) — dam
sāgar (Hin., Ur.) — lake
şaḥrā (Ar.) — desert
şa'īd (Ar.) — highland
saki (Jap.) — cape
salar (Sp.) — salt flat
salina/s (Sp.) — salt marsh
sammyaku (Jap.) — mountain range
san (Jap., Kor.) — mountain
-sanchi (Jap.) — mountains
see (Ger.) — lake
seenplatte (Ger.) — lakeland
selat (Mal.) — strait
selatan (Mal.) — southern
selkä (Fin.) — ridge
selseleh (Per.) — mountain range
selva (Sp.) — forest
serra (Port.) — mountain range
serranía (Sp.) — ridge
sev., severo, severnyy (Rus.) — north
sha'īb (Ar.) — ravine, wadi
shamo (Ch.) — desert
shan (Ch.) — mountain
shankou (Ch.) — mountain pass
shaṭṭ (Ar.) — large river
shibh jazīrat (Ar.) — peninsula
shima (Jap.) — island
shotō (Jap.) — island group
shui (Ch.) — river
sa., sierra (Sp.) — mountain range
-sjon (Swe.) — lake
skog (Nor., Swe.) — forest
skov (Dan.) — forest
slieve (Gae.) — mountain
sor (Rus.) — salt flat
sör (Nor.) — southern
spitze (Ger.) — peak
sredne (Rus.) — central
step (Rus.) — steppe
stora (Fae.) — large
strath (Gae.) — valley
stretto (It.) — strait
suidō (Jap.) — strait
īummān (Ar.) — escarpment
sund (Dan., Ger., Ice., Nor., Swe.) — sound
svart (Nor., Swe.) — black

T

take (Jap.) — peak
tall (Ar.) — mountain
tanjona (Ma.) — cape
tanjung (Mal.) — cape
tau (Rus.) — mountain
teluk (Mal.) — bay
testa (It.) — head
thale (Th.) — lagoon, sea
tierra (Sp.) — land, territory
tind (Nor.) — sharp peak
tō (Jap.) — island, eastern
tônlé (Cbd.) — lake

träsk (Swe.) — marsh
tunturi (Fin.) — treeless mountain

U

'urūq (Ar.) — dunes
utara (Mal.) — northern
uul (mon., Rus.) — mountain range

V

väïn (Est.) — strait
val (Fr., It.) — valley
vand (Dan.) — water
vatn (Ice., Nor.) — lake
vatnet (Nor.) — lake
vatten (Swe.) — lake
veld (Afr.) — field
veliki (S.-C.) — large
verkh., verkhne, verkhniy (Rus.) — upper
-vesi (Fin.) — lake
vest, vester (Dan., Nor.) — west
vidda (Nor.) — plateau
-viken (Nor., Swe.) — gulf, bay
vdkhr., vodokhranilishche (Rus.) — reservoir
volcán (Sp.) — volcano
vostochno, vostochnyy (Rus.) — eastern
vozvyshennost (Rus.) — uplands
vrata (Blg.) — gate
vrh (S.-C.) — peak

W

wāhāt (Ar.) — oasis
wald (Ger.) — forest
wan (Ch., Jap.) — bay

Y

yam (Heb.) — sea
yama (Jap.) — mountain
yanchi (Ch.) — salt lake
yarimadasi (Tur.) — peninsula
yazovir (Blg.) — dam
yoma (Bur.) — mountain range
yumco (Ch.) — lake
yunhe (Ch.) — canal
yuzhnyy (Rus.) — south

Z

zaki (Jap.) — cape, peninsula
zaliv (Rus.) — bay
zan (Jap.) — mountain range
zangbo (Ch.) — stream, river
zapadno, zapadnyy (Rus.) — western
zatoka (Pol.) — bay
zemlya (Rus.) — land
zhou (Ch.) — island
zuid (Dut.) — south

GEOGRAPHICAL DATA
Part 3

WORLD INDEX

WORLD INDEX

Introduction to World Index

The index includes an alphabetical list of all names appearing on the maps in the World Atlas section. Each entry indicates the country or region of the world in which the name is located. This is followed by a page reference and finally the name's location on the map, given by latitude and longitude co-ordinates. Most features are indexed to the largest scale map on which they appear, however when the name applies to countries or other extensive features it is generally indexed to the map on which it appears in its entirety. Areal features are generally indexed using co-ordinates which indicate the centre of the feature. The latitude and longitude indicated for a point feature gives the location of the point on the map. In the case of rivers the mouth or confluence is always taken as the point of reference.

Names in the index are generally in the local language and where a conventional English version exists, this is cross referenced to the entry in the local language. Names of features which extend across the boundaries of more than one country are usually named in English if no single official name exists. Names in languages not written in the Roman alphabet have been transliterated using the official system of the country if one exists, e.g. Pinyin system for China, otherwise the systems recognised by the United States Board on Geographical Names have been used.

Names abbreviated on the maps are given in full in the Index. Abbreviations are used for both geographical terms and administrative names in the Index. All abbreviations used in the Index are listed below.

Moldavia (Moldova) is now referred to by its local form Moldova in the first instance with the English form (Moldavia) as an alternative. This change is reflected on the maps of this atlas but not in the index.

Abbreviations of Geographical Terms

b., B.	bay, Bay	f.	physical feature e.g. valley, plain, geographic district or region	mts., Mts.	mountains, Mountains
c., C.	cape, Cape			pen., Pen.	peninsula, Peninsula
d.	internal division e.g county, region, state			Pt.	Point
		g., G.	gulf, Gulf	r.	river
des.	desert	i., I., is., Is.	island, Island, islands, Islands	resr., Resr.	reservoir, Reservoir
est.	estuary	I., L.	lake, Lake	Sd.	Sound
		mtn., Mtn.	mountain, Mountain	str., Str.	strait, Strait

Abbreviations of Country / Administrative Names

Afghan.	Afghanistan	Man.	Manitoba	Raj.	Rājasthān
A.H. Prov.	Alpes de Haut Provence	Mass.	Massachusetts	Rep. of Ire.	Republic of Ireland
Ala.	Alabama	Md.	Maryland	Rhein.-Pfalz	Rheinland-Pfalz
Alas.	Alaska	Mich.	Michigan	R.I.	Rhode Island
Alta.	Alberta	Minn.	Minnesota	R.S.A.	Republic of South Africa
Ariz.	Arizona	Miss.	Mississippi	Russian Fed.	Russian Federation
Ark.	Arkansas	Mo.	Missouri	S.A.	South Australia
Baja Calif.	Baja California	Mont.	Montana	Sask.	Saskatchewan
Baja Calif. Sur	Baja California Sur	M.-Pyr.	Midi-Pyrénées	S.C.	South Carolina
Bangla.	Bangladesh	N.B.	New Brunswick	Sch.-Hol.	Schleswig-Holstein
B.C.	British Columbia	N.C.	North Carolina	S. Dak.	South Dakota
Bos.-Her.	Bosnia-Herzegovina	N. Dak.	North Dakota	S. Korea	South Korea
B.-Würt	Baden-Württemberg	Nebr.	Nebraska	S. Mar.	Seine Maritime
Calif.	California	Neth.	Netherlands	Sogn og Fj.	Sogn og Fjordane
C.A.R.	Central African Republic	Nev.	Nevada	Somali Rep.	Somali Republic
Char. Mar.	Charente Maritime	Nfld.	Newfoundland	Switz.	Switzerland
Colo.	Colorado	N.H.	New Hampshire	Tas.	Tasmania
Conn.	Connecticut	N. Ireland	Northern Ireland	Tenn.	Tennessee
C.P.	Cape Province	N.J.	New Jersey	Tex.	Texas
D.C.	District of Columbia	N. Korea	North Korea	T.G.	Tarn-et-Garonne
Del.	Delaware	N. Mex	New Mexico	Trans.	Transvaal
Dom. Rep.	Dominican Republic	Nschn.	Niedersachsen	U.A.E.	United Arab Emirates
Equat. Guinea	Equatorial Guinea	N.S.W.	New South Wales	U.K.	United Kingdom
Eth.	Ethiopia	N. Trönd.	North Tröndelag	U.S.A.	United States of America
Fla.	Florida	N.T.	Northern Territory	Uttar P.	Uttar Pradesh
Ga.	Georgia	N.-Westfalen	Nordrhein-Westfalen	Va.	Virginia
Guang. Zhuang	Guangxi Zhuangzu	N.W.T.	Northwest Territories	Vic.	Victoria
H.-Gar.	Haute Garonne	N.Y.	New York State	Vt.	Vermont
Himachal P.	Himachal Pradesh	O.F.S.	Orange Free State	W.A.	Western Australia
H. Zaïre	Haut Zaïre	Okla.	Oklahoma	Wash.	Washington
Ill.	Illinois	Ont.	Ontario	W. Bengal	West Bengal
Ind.	Indiana	Oreg.	Oregon	Wisc.	Wisconsin
Kans.	Kansas	P.E.I.	Prince Edward Island	W. Sahara	Western Sahara
K. Occidental	Kasai Occidental	Penn.	Pennsylvania	W. Va.	West Virginia
K. Oriental	Kasai Oriental	Phil.	Philippines	Wyo.	Wyoming
Ky.	Kentucky	P.N.G.	Papua New Guinea	Xin. Uygur	Xinjiang Uygur Zizhiqu
La.	Louisiana	Poit.-Char.	Poitou-Charente	Yugo.	Yugoslavia
Liech.	Liechtenstein	Pyr. Or.	Pyrénées Orientales		
Lux.	Luxembourg	Qld.	Queensland		
Madhya P.	Madhya Pradesh	Que.	Québec		

A

Aa *r.* France **19** 51.01N 2.06E
Aachen Germany **38** 50.47N 6.05E
Aalen Germany **39** 48.50N 10.05E
A 'ãli an Nïl *d.* Sudan **73** 9.35N 31.05E
Aalsmeer Neth. **16** 52.17N 4.46E
Aalst Belgium **16** 50.57N 4.03E
Äänekoski Finland **40** 62.36N 25.44E
Aarau Switz. **39** 47.23N 8.03E
Aarburg Switz. **39** 47.19N 7.54E
Aardenburg Neth. **16** 51.16N 3.26E
Aare *r.* Switz. **39** 47.37N 8.13E
Aargau *d.* Switz. **39** 47.25N 8.10E
Aarschot Belgium **16** 50.59N 4.50E
Aba China **61** 32.55N 101.42E
Aba Nigeria **77** 5.06N 7.21E
Aba Zaïre **73** 3.52N 30.14E
Abã as Su'ûd Saudi Arabia **71** 17.28N 44.06E
Abadab, Jabal *mtn.* Sudan **72** 18.53N 35.59E
Ãbãdãn Iran **65** 30.21N 48.15E
Abadan, Jazïreh-ye *i.* Iran **65** 30.10N 48.30E
Ãbãdeh Iran **65** 31.10N 52.40E
Abadla Algeria **74** 31.01N 2.44W
Abaetetuba Brazil **123** 1.45S 48.54W
Abagnar Qi China **54** 43.58N 116.02E
Abag Qi China **54** 43.53N 114.33E
Abaí Paraguay **124** 26.01S 55.57W
Abajo Peak *mtn.* U.S.A. **108** 37.51N 109.28W
Abakaliki Nigeria **77** 6.17N 8.04E
Abakan Russian Fed. **51** 53.43N 91.25E
Abalessa Algeria **75** 22.54N 4.50E
Abancay Peru **124** 13.35S 72.55W
Abariringa *i.* Kiribati **84** 2.50S 171.40W
Ãbãr Murrãt *wells* Sudan **72** 21.03N 32.55E
'Abasãn Egypt **67** 31.19N 34.21E
Abashiri wan *b.* Japan **57** 44.02N 144.17E
Abasolo Mexico **111** 25.18N 104.40W
Abau P.N.G. **90** 10.10S 148.40E
Abay Kazakhstan **50** 49.40N 72.47E
Abãy *r.* Ethiopia *see* Azraq, Al Bahr al *r.* Sudan **72**
Ãbaya Hãyk' Ethiopia **73** 6.20N 37.55E
Abba C.A.R. **77** 5.20N 15.11E
Abbadia San Salvatore Italy **30** 42.53N 11.41E
Abbasanta Italy **32** 40.08N 8.50E
Abbekãs Sweden **43** 55.24N 13.36E
Abbeville France **19** 50.06N 1.50E
Abbeville La. U.S.A. **113** 29.58N 92.08W
Abbeville S.C. U.S.A. **113** 34.10N 82.23W
Abbiategrasso Italy **30** 45.24N 8.54E
Abbotsbury U.K. **13** 50.40N 2.36W
Abbotsford Canada **105** 45.27N 72.55W
Abbottãbãd Pakistan **62** 34.09N 73.13E
'Abd al Kûrï *i.* Yemen **71** 12.12N 52.13E
Abdëra *site* Greece **34** 40.59N 24.58E
Abdulino Russian Fed. **44** 53.42N 53.40E
Abéché Chad **72** 13.49N 20.49E
Abéjar Spain **26** 41.48N 2.47W
Ãbeltï Ethiopia **73** 8.10N 37.37E
Abengourou Côte d'Ivoire **76** 6.42N 3.27W
Abenójar Spain **26** 38.53N 4.21W
Ãbenrã Denmark **42** 55.02N 9.26E
Abensberg Germany **39** 48.49N 11.51E
Abeokuta Nigeria **77** 7.10N 3.26E
Aberayron U.K. **13** 52.15N 4.16W
Abercrombie *r.* Australia **93** 33.50S 149.10E
Aberdare U.K. **13** 51.43N 3.27W
Aberdare Range *mts.* Kenya **79** 0.20S 36.40E
Aberdeen Australia **93** 32.10S 150.54E
Aberdeen R.S.A. **80** 32.28S 24.03E
Aberdeen U.K. **14** 57.08N 2.07W
Aberdeen Md. U.S.A. **115** 39.30N 76.14W
Aberdeen Miss. U.S.A. **113** 33.49N 88.33W
Aberdeen Ohio U.S.A. **112** 38.39N 83.46W
Aberdeen S. Dak. U.S.A. **110** 45.28N 98.29W
Aberdeen Wash. U.S.A. **108** 46.59N 123.50W
Aberdovey U.K. **13** 52.33N 4.03W
Aberfeldy U.K. **14** 56.37N 3.54W
Abergavenny U.K. **13** 51.49N 3.01W
Abersoch U.K. **12** 52.50N 4.31W
Aberystwyth U.K. **13** 52.25N 4.06W
Abetone Italy **30** 44.08N 10.40E
Abez Russian Fed. **44** 66.33N 61.51E
Abhã Saudi Arabia **72** 18.13N 42.30E
Abhar Iran **65** 36.09N 49.13E
Ãbhë bid Hãyk' *l.* Ethiopia **73** 11.06N 41.50E
Abia *d.* Nigeria **77** 5.45N 7.40E
Abidjan Côte d'Ivoire **76** 5.19N 4.01W
Abilene Kans. U.S.A. **110** 38.55N 97.13W
Abilene Tex. U.S.A. **111** 32.27N 99.44W
Abingdon U.K. **13** 51.40N 1.17W
Abisko Sweden **40** 68.20N 18.51E
Abitau *r.* Canada **101** 59.53N 109.03W
Abitibi *r.* Canada **102** 51.03N 80.55W
Abitibi, L. Canada **102** 48.42N 79.45W
Ãbïy Ãdï Ethiopia **73** 13.38N 39.00E
Abnûb Egypt **64** 27.16N 31.09E
Ãbo *see* Turku Finland **41**
Abohar India **62** 30.08N 74.12E
Abomey Benin **77** 7.14N 2.00E
Abong Mbang Cameroon **77** 3.59N 13.12E
Abou Deïa Chad **77** 11.20N 19.20E
Aboyne U.K. **14** 57.05N 2.48W
Abrantes Portugal **27** 39.28N 8.12W
'Abrï Sudan **72** 20.48N 30.20E
Abring Jammu & Kashmir **62** 33.42N 76.35E
Abrud Romania **37** 46.17N 23.04E
Abruzzi *d.* Italy **31** 42.35N 13.38E
Abruzzo, Parco Nazionale d' *Nat. Park* Italy **31** 41.45N 13.45E
Absaroka Range *mts.* U.S.A. **108** 44.45N 109.50W
Absecon U.S.A. **115** 39.26N 74.30W
Abtenau Austria **39** 47.33N 13.21E
Abû 'Arïsh Saudi Arabia **71** 16.58N 42.50E

Abû Bahr *f.* Saudi Arabia **71** 21.30N 48.15E
Abû Ballãs *hill* Egypt **72** 24.26N 27.39E
Abu Dhabi *see* Abû Zaby U.A.E. **65**
Abû Dharbah Egypt **66** 28.29N 33.20E
Abû Dulayq Sudan **72** 15.54N 33.49E
Abû Hamad Sudan **72** 19.32N 33.19E
Abû Harãz Sudan **72** 19.04N 32.07E
Abuja Nigeria **77** 9.12N 7.11E
Abû Jãbirah Sudan **73** 11.04N 26.51E
Abû Kabïr Egypt **66** 30.44N 31.40E
Abû Kamãl Syria **64** 34.27N 40.55E
Abû Madd, Ra's *c.* Saudi Arabia **64** 24.50N 37.07E
Abunã Brazil **122** 9.41S 65.20W
Abû Qashsh Jordan **67** 31.57N 35.11E
Abû Qurqãs Egypt **66** 27.56N 30.50E
Abu Road *town* India **62** 24.29N 72.47E
Abû Shajarah, Ra's *c.* Sudan **72** 21.04N 37.14E
Abû Shanab Sudan **73** 10.47N 29.32E
Abû Sultãn Egypt **66** 30.25N 32.19E
Abû Sunbul Egypt **64** 22.18N 31.40E
Abû Tabarï *well* Sudan **72** 17.35N 28.31E
Abû Tarafah Jordan **66** 30.00N 35.56E
Abû Tïj Egypt **64** 27.06N 31.17E
Abuya Mexico **109** 24.16N 107.01W
Abuyê Mêda *mtn.* Ethiopia **73** 10.28N 39.44E
Abû Zabad Sudan **73** 12.21N 29.15E
Abû Zaby U.A.E. **65** 24.27N 54.23E
Abû Zanïmah Egypt **66** 29.03N 33.06E
Abwong Sudan **73** 9.07N 32.12E
Ãby Sweden **43** 58.40N 16.11E
Abyaq Sudan **72** 13.46N 26.28E
Abyaq, Al Bahr al *r.* Sudan **72** 15.38N 32.31E
Abyãr ash Shuwayrïf *wells* Libya **75** 29.59N 14.16E
Ãbybro Denmark **42** 57.09N 9.45E
Abyei Sudan **73** 9.36N 28.26E
Acacio Mexico **111** 24.50N 102.44W
Acadia Valley *town* Canada **101** 51.08N 110.13W
Acámbaro Mexico **116** 20.01N 101.42W
Acapulco Mexico **116** 16.51N 99.56W
Acará Brazil **123** 1.57S 48.11W
Acarigua Venezuela **122** 9.35N 69.12W
Acatlán Mexico **116** 18.12N 98.02W
Accra Ghana **76** 5.33N 0.15W
Accrington U.K. **12** 53.46N 2.22W
Aceh *d.* Indonesia **58** 4.00N 97.30E
Acerra Italy **33** 40.57N 14.22E
Acevedo Argentina **125** 33.46S 60.27W
Achacachi Bolivia **124** 16.03S 68.43W
Achalpur India **63** 21.16N 77.31E
Acheng China **55** 45.32N 126.59E
Achern Germany **39** 48.37N 8.04E
Achill I. Rep. of Ire. **15** 53.57N 10.00W
Ãchïn Afghan. **62** 34.08N 70.42E
Achinsk Russian Fed. **50** 56.10N 90.10E
Achray Canada **105** 45.52N 77.45W
Acklin's I. Bahamas **117** 22.30N 74.10W
Aconcagua *mtn.* Argentina **124** 32.39S 70.00W
Açores, Arquipélago dos *is.* Atlantic Oc. **127** 38.30N 28.00W
A Coruña *see* La Coruña Spain **26**
Acquapendente Italy **30** 42.44N 11.52E
Acqui Italy **30** 44.41N 8.28E
Acraman, L. Australia **92** 32.02S 135.26E
Acre *d.* Brazil **122** 8.50S 71.30W
Acri Italy **33** 39.29N 16.23E
Acton Canada **104** 43.37N 80.02W
Acton Vale Canada **105** 45.39N 72.34W
Açu Brazil **123** 5.35S 36.57W
Acuña Argentina **125** 29.54S 57.57W
Ada U.S.A. **111** 34.46N 96.41W
Ada Yugo. **31** 45.48N 20.08E
Ãdaba Ethiopia **73** 7.07N 39.20E
Adair, Bahía de *b.* Mexico **109** 31.30N 113.50W
Adair, C. Canada **99** 71.24N 71.13W
Adaja *r.* Spain **26** 41.32N 4.52W
Adam Oman **71** 22.23N 57.32E
Adamantina Brazil **126** 21.42S 51.04W
Adamaoua, Massif de l' *mts.* Cameroon/Nigeria **77** 7.05N 12.00E
Adamawa *d.* Nigeria **77** 9.55N 12.30E
Adamello *mtn.* Italy **30** 46.09N 10.30E
Adaminaby Australia **93** 36.04S 148.42E
Adams Mass. U.S.A. **115** 42.37N 73.07W
Adams, Mt. U.S.A. **108** 46.13N 121.28W
'Adan Yemen **71** 12.50N 45.00E
Adana Turkey **64** 37.00N 35.19E
Adanero Spain **26** 40.56N 4.36W
Adapazari Turkey **64** 40.45N 30.23E
Adarama Sudan **72** 17.05N 34.54E
Adare, C. Antarctica **128** 71.30S 171.00E
Adavale Australia **90** 25.55S 144.36E
Adda *r.* Italy **30** 45.08N 9.53E
Ad Dab'ah Egypt **64** 31.02N 28.26E
Ad Dabbah Sudan **72** 18.03N 30.57E
Ad Dafïnah Saudi Arabia **64** 23.18N 41.58E
Ad Dãmir Sudan **72** 17.35N 33.58E
Ad Dammãm Saudi Arabia **65** 26.23N 50.08E
Ad Darb Saudi Arabia **72** 17.44N 42.15E
Ad Dawãdïmï Saudi Arabia **65** 24.29N 44.23E
Ad Dawhah Qatar **65** 25.15N 51.34E
Ad Diffah *f.* Africa **64** 30.45N 26.00E
Ad Dikãkah *f.* Saudi Arabia **71** 19.25N 51.30E
Ad Dilam Saudi Arabia **65** 23.59N 47.10E
Ad Dimãs Syria **66** 33.35N 36.05E
Addis Ababa *see* Ãdïs Ãbeba Ethiopia **73**
Addison U.S.A. **114** 42.06N 77.14W
Ad Dïwãnïyah Iraq **65** 31.59N 44.57E
Ad Du'ayn Sudan **73** 11.26N 26.09E
Ad Duwaym Sudan **72** 14.00N 32.19E
Adel U.S.A. **113** 31.07N 83.27W
Adelaide Australia **92** 34.56S 138.36E
Adelaide Pen. Canada **99** 68.09N 97.45W

Adelaide River *town* Australia **88** 13.14S 131.06E
Adelong Australia **93** 35.21S 148.04E
Aden *see* 'Adan Yemen **71**
Adena U.S.A. **114** 40.13N 80.53W
Adendorp R.S.A. **80** 32.18S 24.31E
Aden, G. of Indian Oc. **71** 13.00N 50.00E
Adi *i.* Indonesia **59** 4.10S 133.10E
Ãdï Da'iro Ethiopia **72** 14.27N 38.16E
Adieu, C. Australia **89** 31.59S 132.09E
Ãdïgala Ethiopia **73** 10.25N 42.17E
Adige *r.* Italy **30** 45.10N 12.20E
Ãdïgrat Ethiopia **72** 14.18N 39.31E
Ãdï K'eyih Eritrea **72** 14.49N 39.23E
Ãdïlãbãd India **63** 19.40N 78.32E
Adilang Uganda **79** 2.44N 33.28E
Adin U.S.A. **108** 41.12N 120.57W
Adirondack Mts. U.S.A. **115** 44.00N 74.00W
Adirondack Park U.S.A. **115** 43.28N 74.23W
Ãdïs Ãbeba Ethiopia **73** 9.03N 38.42E
Ãdï Ugrï Eritrea **72** 14.55N 38.53E
Adiyaman Turkey **64** 37.46N 38.15E
Adjud Romania **37** 46.04N 27.11E
Admer *well* Algeria **75** 20.23N 5.27E
Admiralty G. Australia **88** 14.20S 125.50E
Admiralty I. U.S.A. **100** 57.50N 134.30W
Admiralty Is. P.N.G. **59** 2.30S 147.20E
Admiralty Range *mts.* Antarctica **128** 72.00S 164.00E
Adolphustown Canada **105** 44.04N 77.00W
Adour *r.* France **20** 43.32N 1.32W
Adra Spain **27** 36.44N 3.01W
Adrano Italy **33** 37.40N 14.50E
Adrar *d.* Mauritania **74** 21.00N 10.00W
Adrar des Iforas *mts.* Mali/Algeria **75** 20.00N 2.30E
Adraskan Afghan. **62** 33.39N 62.16E
Adria Italy **30** 45.03N 12.03E
Adrian Mich. U.S.A. **104** 41.54N 84.02W
Adrian Mo. U.S.A. **110** 38.24N 94.21W
Adrian Tex. U.S.A. **111** 35.16N 102.40W
Adrian W.Va. U.S.A. **114** 38.54N 80.17W
Adriatic Sea Med. Sea **31** 43.30N 14.30E
Ãdwa Ethiopia **72** 14.12N 38.56E
Adzhen Ethiopia **72** 14.12N 38.56E
Adzopé Côte d'Ivoire **76** 6.07N 3.49W
Adzva *r.* Russian Fed. **44** 66.30N 59.30E
Aegean Sea Med. Sea **34** 37.00N 25.00E
Aerö *i.* Denmark **42** 54.53N 10.20E
Aëtos Greece **35** 37.15N 21.50E
Afándou Greece **35** 36.18N 28.12E
Ãfdem Ethiopia **73** 9.26N 41.02E
Afghanistan Asia **62** 32.45N 65.00E
'Afïf Saudi Arabia **64** 23.53N 42.59E
Afikpo Nigeria **77** 5.53N 7.55E
Afjord Norway **40** 63.57N 10.12E
Aflou Algeria **75** 34.07N 2.06E
Afmadow Somali Rep. **79** 0.27N 42.05E
Afobaka Surinam **123** 5.00N 55.05W
Afognak I. U.S.A. **98** 58.15N 152.30W
Afonso Cláudio Brazil **126** 20.05S 41.06W
Africa **70**
Afsluitdijk *f.* Neth. **16** 53.04N 5.11E
'Afula Israel **67** 32.36N 35.17E
Afyon Turkey **64** 38.46N 30.32E
Agadez Niger **77** 17.00N 7.56E
Agadez *d.* Niger **77** 19.25N 11.00E
Agadir Morocco **74** 30.26N 9.36W
Agalak Sudan **73** 11.01N 32.42E
Agana Guam **84** 13.28N 144.45E
Agano *r.* Japan **57** 37.58N 139.02E
Agapa Russian Fed. **51** 71.29N 86.16E
Agar India **62** 23.42N 76.01E
Ãgaro Ethiopia **73** 7.50N 36.40E
Agartala India **63** 23.49N 91.16E
Agaru Sudan **73** 10.59N 34.44E
Agboville Côte d'Ivoire **76** 5.55N 4.15W
Agde France **20** 43.19N 3.28E
Agde, Cap d' *c.* France **20** 43.16N 3.30E
Agen France **20** 44.12N 0.37E
Ageo Japan **57** 35.58N 139.36E
Agger *r.* Germany **16** 50.45N 7.06E
Aghada Rep. of Ire. **15** 51.50N 8.13W
Agia Greece **33** 37.39N 14.32E
Agira Italy **33** 37.39N 14.32E
Agly *r.* France **20** 42.47N 3.02E
Agnew Australia **89** 28.01S 120.30E
Agnone Italy **31** 41.48N 14.22E
Ago Japan **57** 34.17N 136.48E
Agordo Italy **30** 46.17N 12.02E
Agout *r.* France **20** 43.47N 1.41E
Ãgra India **63** 27.11N 78.01E
Agra *r.* Spain **24** 42.12N 1.43W
Agraciada Uruguay **125** 33.48S 58.15W
Ãgreda Spain **25** 41.51N 1.56W
Ãgri *r.* Italy **33** 40.13N 16.44E
Ãgri Turkey **64** 39.44N 43.04E
Agri Bavnehöj *hill* Denmark **42** 56.14N 10.33E
Ãgri Dagi *mtn.* Turkey **65** 39.45N 44.15E
Agrigento Italy **32** 37.18N 13.35E
Agrínion Greece **35** 38.37N 21.24E
Ãgropoli Italy **33** 40.21N 15.00E
Agryz Russian Fed. **44** 56.30N 53.00E
Agsumal, Sebjet *f.* W. Sahara **74** 24.21N 12.52W
Agua Caliente, Cerro *mtn.* Mexico **109** 26.27N 106.12W
Aguanish Canada **103** 50.16N 62.10W
Aguanus *r.* Canada **103** 50.12N 62.10W
Agua Prieta Mexico **109** 31.18N 109.34W
Aguas *r.* Spain **27** 37.09N 1.49W
Aguas Blancas Chile **124** 24.13S 69.50W
Aguascalientes Mexico **116** 21.51N 102.18W
Aguascalientes *d.* Mexico **116** 22.00N 102.00W
Aguasvivas *r.* Spain **25** 41.20N 0.25W
Agudos Brazil **126** 22.27S 49.03W
Ãgueda Portugal **26** 40.34N 8.27W
Ãgueda *r.* Spain **26** 41.02N 6.56W
Aguelhok Mali **74** 19.28N 0.52E
Aguema *r.* Angola **78** 12.03S 21.52E
Aguêraktem *well* Mali **74** 23.07N 6.12W

Aguilar Spain **27** 37.31N 4.39W
Aguilar de Campóo Spain **26** 42.47N 4.15W
Aguilas Spain **25** 37.24N 1.35W
Aguit China **54** 41.42N 113.20E
Ãgula'i Ethiopia **72** 13.42N 39.35E
Agulhas Basin *f.* Indian Oc. **49** 45.00S 28.00E
Agulhas, C. R.S.A. **80** 34.50S 20.00E
Agulhas Negras *mtn.* Brazil **126** 22.20S 44.43W
Agung, Gunung *mtn.* Indonesia **59** 8.20S 115.28E
'Agur Israel **67** 31.41N 34.54E
Ahaggar *f.* Algeria **75** 23.36N 5.50E
Ahar Iran **65** 38.25N 47.07E
Ahaura New Zealand **86** 42.21S 171.33E
Ahaus Germany **16** 52.04N 7.01E
Ahirli Turkey **35** 38.37N 26.31E
Ahklun Mts. U.S.A. **98** 59.15N 161.00W
Ahlen Germany **38** 51.46N 7.53E
Ahlenmoor *f.* Germany **38** 53.40N 8.45E
Ahmadãbãd India **62** 23.02N 72.37E
Ahmadï Iran **65** 27.56N 56.42E
Ahmadnagar India **62** 19.05N 74.44E
Ahmadpur East Pakistan **62** 29.09N 71.16E
Ahmadpur Siãl Pakistan **62** 30.41N 71.46E
Ahmad Wãl Pakistan **62** 29.25N 65.56E
Ahmar Mts. Ethiopia **73** 9.15N 41.00E
Ahmic Harbour Canada **104** 45.39N 79.42W
Ahmic L. Canada **104** 45.37N 79.42W
Ahoada Nigeria **77** 5.06N 6.39E
Ahr *r.* Germany **16** 50.34N 7.16E
Ahram Iran **65** 28.52N 51.16E
Ahraura India **63** 25.01N 83.01E
Ahsã', Wãhat al *oasis* Saudi Arabia **65** 25.37N 49.40E
Ãhtãri Finland **40** 62.34N 24.06E
Ahun France **20** 46.05N 2.05E
Ãhus Sweden **43** 55.55N 14.17E
Ahvãz Iran **65** 31.17N 48.44E
Ahvenanmaa *d.* Finland **41** 60.15N 20.00E
Ahvenanmaa *is.* Finland **41** 60.15N 20.00E
Aichach Germany **39** 48.28N 11.08E
Aichi *d.* Japan **57** 35.02N 137.15E
Aigle Switz. **39** 46.19N 6.58E
Aigre France **20** 45.54N 0.01E
Aigueperse France **20** 46.01N 3.12E
Aigues *r.* France **21** 44.07N 4.43E
Aigues-Mortes France **21** 43.34N 4.11E
Aiguilles France **21** 44.47N 6.52E
Aigurande France **19** 46.26N 1.50E
Aiken U.S.A. **113** 33.34N 81.44W
Aileron Australia **90** 22.38S 133.20E
Ailette *r.* France **19** 49.35N 3.09E
Ailsa Craig *i.* U.K. **14** 55.15N 5.07W
Aim Russian Fed. **51** 58.50N 134.15E
Aimorés Brazil **126** 19.30S 41.04W
Ain *d.* France **21** 46.05N 5.20E
Ain *r.* France **21** 45.48N 5.10E
Aïna *r.* Gabon **78** 0.38N 12.47E
Ainaži Estonia **41** 57.52N 24.21E
Aïn Beïda Algeria **75** 35.50N 7.27E
Aïn ben Tili Mauritania **74** 26.00N 9.32W
Aïn Draham Tunisia **32** 36.47N 8.42E
Aïn Galakka Chad **75** 18.04N 18.24E
Aïn Sefra Algeria **74** 32.45N 0.35W
Aïr *mts.* Niger **77** 18.30N 8.30E
Aird I. Canada **104** 46.08N 82.25W
Airdrie U.K. **14** 55.52N 3.59W
Aire France **20** 43.42N 0.16E
Aire *r.* France **19** 49.19N 4.49E
Aire *r.* U.K. **12** 53.42N 0.54W
Airolo Switz. **39** 46.32N 8.37E
Airvault France **18** 46.50N 0.08W
Aisch *r.* Germany **39** 49.46N 11.01E
Aisne *d.* France **19** 49.30N 3.30E
Aisne *r.* France **19** 49.26N 2.50E
Aitana *mtn.* Spain **25** 38.40N 0.16W
Aitape P.N.G. **59** 3.10S 142.17E
Aitkin U.S.A. **110** 46.32N 93.43W
Aitolikón Greece **35** 38.27N 21.22E
Aït Ourir Morocco **74** 31.38N 7.42W
Aitutaki Atoll Cook Is. **85** 18.52S 159.46W
Aiud Romania **37** 46.19N 23.44E
Aix-en-Provence France **21** 43.32N 5.26E
Aix-les-Bains France **21** 45.42N 5.55E
Aíyina Greece **35** 37.44N 23.27E
Aíyina *i.* Greece **35** 37.46N 23.26E
Aíyínion Greece **34** 40.30N 22.33E
Aíyion Greece **35** 38.15N 22.05E
Aizpute Latvia **41** 56.43N 21.38E
Aizuwakamatsu Japan **57** 37.30N 139.58E
Ajaccio France **21** 41.55N 8.44E
Ajanta Range *mts.* India **62** 20.15N 75.30E
Ajax Canada **104** 43.51N 79.02W
Ajdãbïyã Libya **72** 30.46N 20.14E
Ajdovščina Slovenia **31** 45.53N 13.53E
Ajibar Ethiopia **73** 10.41N 38.37E
'Ajlûn Jordan **67** 32.20N 35.45E
'Ajmah, Jabal al *f.* Egypt **66** 29.12N 33.58E
'Ajmãn U.A.E. **65** 25.23N 55.26E
Ajmer India **62** 26.27N 74.38E
Ajnãla India **62** 31.51N 74.47E
Ajo U.S.A. **109** 32.22N 112.52W
Ajo, Cabo de *c.* Spain **26** 43.31N 3.35W
Akaishi sammyaku *mts.* Japan **57** 35.20N 138.10E
Akámas, Akrotírion *c.* Cyprus **66** 35.06N 32.17E
Akaroa New Zealand **86** 43.50S 172.59E
'Akasha East Sudan **72** 21.05N 30.43E
Akashi Japan **57** 34.38N 134.59E
Akbarpur India **63** 26.25N 82.33E
Akbulak Russian Fed. **45** 51.00N 55.40E
Akelamo Indonesia **59** 1.35N 129.40E
Akershus *d.* Norway **42** 60.10N 11.25E
Aketi Zaïre **78** 2.46N 23.51E
Akhaltsikhe Georgia **64** 41.37N 42.59E
Akharnaí Greece **35** 38.05N 23.44E
Akhdar, Al Jabal al *mts.* Libya **72** 32.30N 21.30E
Akhdar, Al Jabal al *mts.* Oman **65** 23.10N 57.25E
Akhdar, Wãdï *r.* Egypt **66** 28.42N 33.41E
Akhdar, Wãdï al *r.* Saudi Arabia **66** 28.30N 36.48E
Akhelóós Greece **29** 38.20N 21.04E

Akhelóös *r.* Greece 35 38.36N 21.14E
Akhisar Turkey 29 38.54N 27.49E
Akhladhókambos Greece 35 37.31N 22.35E
Akhmîm Egypt 64 26.34N 31.44E
Akhtyrka Ukraine 45 50.19N 34.54E
Akimiski I. Canada 102 53.00N 81.20W
Åkirkeby Denmark 43 55.04N 14.56E
Akita Japan 57 39.44N 140.05E
Akjoujt Mauritania 74 19.44N 14.26W
Akkajaure *l.* Sweden 40 67.40N 17.30E
'Akko Israel 67 32.55N 35.05E
Akkol Kazakhstan 52 45.04N 75.39E
Akkoy Turkey 35 37.29N 27.15E
Aklavik Canada 98 68.12N 135.00W
Akmola Kazakhstan 9 51.10N 71.28E
Ako Nigeria 77 10.19N 10.48E
Åkobo *r.* Ethiopia 73 8.30N 33.15E
Akola India 62 20.44N 77.00E
Åk'ordat Eritrea 72 15.35N 37.55E
Akot India 62 21.11N 77.04E
Åkrafjorden *est.* Norway 42 59.46N 6.06E
Akranes Iceland 40 64.19N 22.05W
Åkrehamn Norway 42 59.16N 5.11E
Akrítas, Ákra *c.* Greece 35 36.43N 21.54E
Akron Colo. U.S.A. 110 40.10N 103.13W
Akron Ohio U.S.A. 114 41.05N 81.31W
Akrotírí Cyprus 66 34.36N 32.57E
Aksaray Turkey 64 38.22N 34.02E
Aksarka Russian Fed. 50 66.31N 67.50E
Aksay China 52 39.28N 94.15E
Aksay Kazakhstan 45 51.24N 52.11E
Akşehir Turkey 64 38.22N 31.24E
Aksu China 52 42.10N 80.00E
Åksum Ethiopia 72 14.08N 38.48E
Aktag *mtn.* China 52 36.45N 84.40E
Aktau Kazakhstan 45 43.37N 51.11E
Aktogay Kazakhstan 52 46.59N 79.42E
Aktyubinsk Kazakhstan 45 50.16N 57.13E
Akûbû Sudan 73 7.47N 33.01E
Akûbû *r. see* Åkobo *r.* Sudan 73
Akula Zaïre 78 2.22N 20.11E
Akure Nigeria 77 7.14N 5.08E
Akureyri Iceland 40 65.41N 18.04W
Akuse Ghana 76 6.04N 0.12E
Akwa-Ibom *d.* Nigeria 77 4.45N 7.50E
Akyab *see* Sittwe Myanmar 56
Akyel Ethiopia 73 12.30N 37.04E
Ål Norway 41 60.38N 8.34E
Alabama *d.* U.S.A. 113 32.50N 87.00W
Alabama *r.* U.S.A. 111 31.08N 87.57W
Al 'Abbāsīyah Sudan 73 14.27N 33.31E
Alaçati Turkey 35 38.16N 26.23E
Älädägh, Küh-e *mts.* Iran 65 37.15N 57.30E
Alagoas *d.* Brazil 123 9.30S 37.00W
Alagoinhas Brazil 123 12.09S 38.21W
Alagón Spain 24 41.46N 1.12W
Alakol, Ozero *l.* Kazakhstan 52 46.00N 81.40E
Alakurtti Russian Fed. 44 67.00N 30.23E
Al'Ål Syria 67 32.48N 35.44E
Al 'Alamayn Egypt 64 30.49N 28.57E
Al 'Amārah Iraq 65 31.52N 47.50E
Al Åmirîyah Egypt 66 31.01N 29.48E
Alamogordo U.S.A. 109 32.54N 105.57W
Alamosa U.S.A. 108 37.28N 105.52W
Alamos, Rio de los *r.* Mexico 111 27.53N 101.12W
Åland *is. see* Ahvenanmaa *is.* Finland 41
Ålands Hav *sea* Finland 43 59.50N 19.25E
Alanreed U.S.A. 111 35.14N 100.45W
Alanson U.S.A. 104 45.27N 84.47W
Alanya Turkey 64 36.32N 32.02E
Alaotra, Lac *l.* Madagascar 81 17.30S 48.30E
Alapayevsk Russian Fed. 44 57.55N 61.42E
Alappuzha *see* Alleppey India 60
Al 'Aqabah Jordan 66 29.32N 35.00E
Al 'Aramah *f.* Saudi Arabia 65 25.30N 46.30E
Al 'Arîsh Egypt 66 31.08N 33.48E
Alaşehir Turkey 64 38.22N 28.29E
Al 'Asimah *d.* Jordan 67 31.45N 36.05E
Alaska *d.* U.S.A. 98 65.00N 153.00W
Alaska, G. of U.S.A. 98 58.45N 145.00W
Alaska Pen. U.S.A. 98 56.00N 160.00W
Alaska Range *mts.* U.S.A. 98 62.10N 152.00W
Alassio Italy 30 44.00N 8.10E
Al 'Atîqah Lebanon 66 33.42N 35.27E
Alatri Italy 30 41.43N 13.21E
Al 'Atrun Sudan 72 18.11N 26.36E
Alatyr Russian Fed. 44 54.51N 46.35E
Alausí Ecuador 122 2.00S 78.50W
Álava *d.* Spain 26 42.55N 2.50W
Alavus Finland 40 62.35N 23.37E
Alawoona Australia 92 34.44S 140.33E
Al 'Ayn *wells* Sudan 72 16.36N 29.19E
Alayor Spain 25 39.56N 4.08E
Al 'Ayyāt Egypt 66 29.37N 31.15E
Alazani *r.* Georgia 65 41.06N 46.40E
Alba Italy 30 44.42N 8.02E
Albacete Spain 25 38.59N 1.51W
Albacete *d.* Spain 25 39.05N 1.45W
Al Bad' Saudi Arabia 66 28.29N 35.02E
Al Badārî Egypt 64 26.59N 31.25E
Alba de Tormes Spain 26 40.49N 5.31W
Ålbaek Denmark 42 57.36N 10.25E
Al Bahnasā Egypt 66 28.32N 30.39E
Al Baḩr al Aḩmar *d.* Sudan 72 19.30N 35.30E
Al Baḩr al Mayyit *see* Dead Sea Jordan 67
Albaida Spain 25 38.51N 0.31W
Alba-Iulia Romania 37 46.04N 23.33E
Al Balqā' *d.* Jordan 67 32.00N 35.40E
Alban France 20 43.54N 2.28E
Albania Europe 34 41.00N 20.00E
Albano Laziale Italy 30 41.44N 12.39E
Albany *r.* Canada 102 52.10N 82.00W
Albany Australia 89 34.57S 117.54E
Albany Ga. U.S.A. 113 31.37N 84.10W
Albany Ky. U.S.A. 113 36.42N 85.08W

Albany Minn. U.S.A. 110 45.38N 94.34W
Albany N.Y. U.S.A. 115 42.39N 73.45W
Albany Ohio U.S.A. 114 39.14N 82.12W
Albany Oreg. U.S.A. 108 44.38N 123.06W
Al Bāriḩah Jordan 67 32.34N 35.50E
Albarracín Spain 25 40.25N 1.26W
Albarracín, Sierra de *mts.* Spain 25 40.30N 1.40W
Al Başrah Iraq 65 30.33N 47.50E
Al Bāṭinah *f.* Oman 65 24.25N 56.50E
Albatross B. Australia 90 12.45S 141.43E
Al Batrûn Lebanon 66 34.16N 35.40E
Al Bawîṭî Egypt 64 28.21N 25.52E
Al Bayāḍ *f.* Saudi Arabia 71 22.00N 47.00E
Al Baydā' Libya 75 32.46N 21.43E
Albegna *r.* Italy 30 42.30N 11.11E
Albemarle Sd. U.S.A. 107 36.10N 76.00W
Albens France 21 45.47N 5.57E
Alberche *r.* Spain 27 39.58N 4.46W
Alberga Australia 91 27.12S 135.28E
Alberga *r.* Australia 91 27.12S 135.28E
Albergaria-a-Velha Portugal 26 40.42N 8.29W
Alberique Spain 25 39.07N 0.31W
Albermarle U.S.A. 113 35.21N 80.12W
Albermarle Sd. U.S.A. 113 36.03N 76.12W
Albert Australia 93 32.21S 147.33E
Albert France 19 50.00N 2.39E
Alberta *d.* Canada 100 54.00N 115.00W
Alberti Argentina 125 35.01S 60.16W
Albertirsa Hungary 37 47.15N 19.38E
Albert Kanaal *canal* Belgium 16 51.00N 5.15E
Albert, L. Australia 92 35.38S 139.17E
Albert, L. Uganda/Zaïre 79 1.45N 31.00E
Albert Lea U.S.A. 110 43.39N 93.22W
Albert Nile *r.* Uganda 79 3.30N 32.00E
Alberton Canada 103 46.49N 64.04W
Albertville France 21 45.41N 6.23E
Albi France 20 43.56N 2.08E
Al Bidia Chad 73 10.33N 20.13E
Albin U.S.A. 108 41.26N 104.08W
Albina Surinam 123 5.30N 54.03W
Albino Italy 30 45.46N 9.47E
Albion Mich. U.S.A. 112 42.14N 84.45W
Albion Mont. U.S.A. 108 45.11N 104.15W
Albion Nebr. U.S.A. 110 41.42N 98.00W
Albion N.Y. U.S.A. 114 43.15N 78.12W
Albion Penn. U.S.A. 114 41.53N 80.22W
Al Bi'r Saudi Arabia 66 28.52N 36.15E
Al Bîrah Jordan 67 31.54N 35.13E
Albocácer Spain 25 40.21N 0.02E
Albo, Monte *mtn.* Italy 32 40.29N 9.33E
Alborán, Isla de *i.* Spain 27 35.58N 3.02W
Ålborg Denmark 42 57.03N 9.56E
Ålborg Bugt *b.* Denmark 42 56.45N 10.30E
Alborz, Reshteh-ye Kūhhā-ye *mts.* Iran 65 36.00N 52.30E
Albufeira Portugal 27 37.05N 8.15W
Al Buḩayrāt *d.* Sudan 73 6.50N 29.40E
Albuñol Spain 27 36.47N 3.12W
Albuquerque U.S.A. 109 35.05N 106.40W
Al Buraymî U.A.E. 65 24.15N 55.45E
Alburg U.S.A. 105 44.59N 73.18W
Al Burj Egypt 66 31.35N 30.59E
Alburquerque Spain 27 39.13N 7.00W
Albury Australia 93 36.03S 146.53E
Al Butanah *f.* Sudan 72 14.50N 34.30E
Al Buwayḍah Jordan 67 32.21N 36.03E
Alby Sweden 40 62.30N 15.25E
Alcácer do Sal Portugal 27 38.22N 8.30W
Alcains Portugal 27 39.55N 7.27W
Alcalá de Chisvert Spain 25 40.19N 0.13E
Alcalá de Guadaira Spain 27 37.20N 5.50W
Alcalá de Henares Spain 26 40.29N 3.22W
Alcalá la Real Spain 27 37.28N 3.56W
Alcamo Italy 32 37.59N 12.58E
Alcanadre *r.* Spain 25 41.37N 0.12W
Alcanar Spain 25 40.33N 0.29E
Alcañices Spain 26 41.42N 6.21W
Alcañiz Spain 25 41.03N 0.08W
Alcántara Spain 27 39.43N 6.53W
Alcántara, Embalse de *resr.* Spain 27 39.45N 6.25W
Alcantara L. Canada 101 60.57N 108.09W
Alcantarilla Spain 25 37.58N 1.13W
Alcaraz Spain 26 38.40N 2.29W
Alcaraz, Sierra de *mts.* Spain 27 38.40N 2.30W
Alcarrache *r.* Portugal 27 38.16N 7.24W
Alcaudete Spain 27 37.36N 4.05W
Alcázar de San Juan Spain 27 39.24N 3.12W
Alcira Spain 25 39.09N 0.26W
Alcobaça Portugal 27 39.33N 8.59W
Alcobendas Spain 26 40.32N 3.38W
Alcolea del Pinar Spain 26 41.02N 2.28W
Alconchel Portugal 27 38.31N 7.04W
Alcova U.S.A. 108 42.35N 106.34W
Alcoy Spain 25 38.42N 0.28W
Alcubierre Spain 25 41.48N 0.27W
Alcubierre, Sierra de *mts.* Spain 25 41.45N 0.21W
Alcudia Spain 25 39.52N 3.07E
Alcudia, Bahía de *b.* Spain 25 39.48N 3.13E
Alcudia, Sierra de la *mts.* Spain 28 39.34N 4.30W
Aldabra *is.* Seychelles 70 9.00S 46.30E
Aldan Russian Fed. 51 58.44N 125.22E
Aldan *r.* Russian Fed. 51 63.30N 130.00E
Aldeburgh U.K. 13 52.09N 1.35E
Aldeia Nova de Santo Bento Portugal 27 37.55N 7.25W
Alder Creek *town* U.S.A. 115 43.27N 75.17W
Alderney *i.* Channel Is. Europe 13 49.42N 2.11W
Aldershot U.K. 13 51.15N 0.47W
Alderson Canada 101 50.20N 111.25W
Aldridge U.K. 13 52.36N 1.55W
Aledo U.S.A. 110 41.12N 90.45W
Aleg Mauritania 74 17.03N 13.55W
Alegre Brazil 126 20.46S 41.30W
Alegrete Brazil 125 29.46S 55.46W
Aleksandrov Gay Russian Fed. 45 50.08N 48.34E

Aleksandrovsk Sakhalinskiy Russian Fed. 51 50.55N 142.12E
Aleksinac Yugo. 34 43.31N 21.42E
Alembe Gabon 78 0.03N 10.57E
Além Paraíba Brazil 126 21.49S 42.36W
Alençon France 18 48.26N 0.05E
Alenuihaha Channel Hawaiian Is. 85 20.26N 156.00W
Aleppo *see* Halab Syria 64
Aléria France 21 42.05N 9.30E
Alès France 21 44.08N 4.05E
Alessandria Italy 30 44.54N 8.37E
Alessano Italy 33 39.53N 18.20E
Ålestrup Denmark 42 56.42N 9.31E
Ålesund Norway 40 62.28N 6.11E
Aleutian Basin Bering Sea 84 57.00N 179.00E
Aleutian Is. U.S.A. 48 57.00N 180.00
Aleutian Range *mts.* U.S.A. 98 58.00N 156.00W
Aleutian Trench Pacific Oc. 84 50.00N 176.00W
Alexander *r.* Israel 67 32.24N 34.52E
Alexander U.S.A. 110 47.42.54N 78.16W
Alexander Archipelago *is.* U.S.A. 100 56.30N 134.30W
Alexander Bay *town* R.S.A. 80 28.36S 16.26E
Alexander I. Antarctica 128 72.00S 70.00W
Alexandra Australia 93 37.12S 145.14E
Alexandra New Zealand 86 45.14S 169.26E
Alexandria B.C. Canada 100 52.35N 122.27W
Alexandria Ont. Canada 105 45.19N 74.38W
Alexandria *see* Al Iskandarîyah Egypt 66
Alexandria Romania 34 43.58N 25.20E
Alexandria R.S.A. 80 33.39S 26.24E
Alexandria La. U.S.A. 111 31.18N 92.27W
Alexandria Minn. U.S.A. 110 45.53N 95.22W
Alexandria Va. U.S.A. 114 38.48N 77.03W
Alexandria Bay *town* U.S.A. 105 44.20N 75.55W
Alexandrina, L. Australia 92 35.26S 139.10E
Alexandroúpolis Greece 34 40.50N 25.52E
Alexis *r.* Canada 103 52.32N 56.08W
Alexis Creek *town* Canada 100 52.05N 123.20W
Aleysk Russian Fed. 50 52.32N 82.45E
Alfambra Spain 25 40.33N 1.02W
Al Fant Egypt 66 28.46N 30.53E
Alfaro Spain 25 42.11N 1.45W
Alfarràs Spain 25 41.49N 0.35E
Al Fāshir Sudan 73 13.38N 25.21E
Al Fashn Egypt 66 28.49N 30.54E
Al Fāw Iraq 65 29.57N 48.30E
Al Fayyûm Egypt 66 29.19N 30.50E
Alfeld Germany 38 51.59N 9.50E
Alfenas Brazil 126 21.28S 45.48W
Al Fifi Sudan 73 10.03N 25.01E
Alfiós *r.* Greece 35 37.40N 21.33E
Alfonsine Italy 30 44.30N 12.03E
Alford U.K. 14 57.14N 2.42W
Alfred U.S.A. 114 42.15N 77.47W
Al Fujayrah U.A.E. 65 25.10N 56.20E
Alga Kazakhstan 50 49.49N 57.16E
Ålgård Norway 42 58.46N 5.51E
Al Gebir Sudan 73 13.33N 29.49E
Algeciras Spain 27 36.08N 5.30W
Algemesí Spain 25 39.11N 0.26W
Algena Eritrea 72 16.20N 38.34E
Alger Algeria 75 36.50N 3.00E
Alger U.S.A. 104 44.08N 84.08W
Algeria Africa 74 28.00N 2.00E
Al Ghawr *f.* Jordan 67 32.00N 35.30E
Al Ghayl Saudi Arabia 65 22.36N 46.19E
Alghero Italy 32 40.34N 8.19E
Al Ghurdaqah Egypt 64 27.14N 33.50E
Algiers *see* Alger Algeria 75
Alginet Spain 25 39.16N 0.28W
Algoa B. R.S.A. 80 33.50S 26.00E
Algodor *r.* Spain 27 39.55N 3.53W
Algoma U.S.A. 104 46.10N 82.50W
Algoma Mills Canada 104 46.11N 82.50W
Algoma Uplands Canada 104 47.00N 83.35W
Algona U.S.A. 110 43.04N 94.14W
Algonquin Park *town* Canada 104 45.34N 78.36W
Algonquin Prov. Park Canada 104 45.27N 78.26W
Algonquin Upland Canada 104 45.40N 78.47W
Algorta Uruguay 125 32.25S 57.23W
Al Ḩajar al Gharbî *mts.* Oman 65 24.00N 56.30E
Al Ḩajar ash Sharqî *mts.* Oman 65 22.45N 58.45E
Alhama Spain 25 37.51N 1.25W
Alhama de Granada Spain 27 37.00N 3.59W
Al Ḩamar Saudi Arabia 65 22.26N 46.12E
Alhambra U.S.A. 109 34.06N 118.08W
Al Ḩamîdîyah Syria 66 34.43N 35.56E
Al Ḩanākîyah Saudi Arabia 64 24.53N 40.30E
Al Ḩarāk Syria 67 32.44N 36.18E
Al Ḩarîq Saudi Arabia 65 23.37N 46.31E
Al Ḩarrah Syria 67 33.33N 36.00E
Al Ḩarûj al Aswad *hills* Libya 75 27.00N 17.10E
Al Ḩasakah Syria 64 36.29N 40.45E
Alhaurín el Grande Spain 27 36.38N 4.41W
Al Ḩawāmidîyah Egypt 66 29.54N 31.15E
Al Ḩayz Egypt 66 28.02N 28.39E
Al Ḩijāz *f.* Saudi Arabia 64 26.00N 37.30E
Al Ḩillah Iraq 65 32.28N 44.29E
Al Ḩillah Saudi Arabia 65 23.30N 46.51E
Al Ḩirmil Lebanon 66 34.25N 36.23E
Al Ḩişn Jordan 67 32.29N 35.53E
Al-Hoceima Morocco 74 35.15N 3.55W
Al Ḩudaydah Yemen 72 14.50N 42.58E
Al Ḩufûf Saudi Arabia 65 25.20N 49.34E
Al Ḩumrah *des.* Libya 75 22.45N 55.10E
Al Ḩusaynîyah Egypt 66 30.52N 31.55E
Al Ḩuwaymî Yemen 71 14.05N 47.44E
Aliābād, Kūh-e *mtn.* Iran 65 34.09N 50.48E
Aliaga Spain 25 40.40N 0.42W
Aliákmon *r.* Greece 34 40.30N 22.36E
Aliákmona, Limni *resr.* Greece 34 40.15N 22.00E
Alicante Spain 25 38.23N 0.29W
Alicante *d.* Spain 25 38.30N 0.40W
Alice Canada 105 45.16N 77.19W
Alice R.S.A. 80 32.47S 26.49E
Alice U.S.A. 111 27.45N 98.04W

Alice Arm Canada 100 55.29N 129.31W
Alice, Punta *c.* Italy 33 39.24N 17.10E
Alice Springs *town* Australia 90 23.42S 133.52E
Alicudi, Isola *i.* Italy 33 38.33N 14.21E
Al Ifranj Jordan 67 31.11N 35.41E
Aligarh India 63 27.53N 78.05E
Aligûdarz Iran 65 33.25N 49.38E
'Alîjûq, Kūh-e *mtn.* Iran 65 31.27N 51.43E
Alima *r.* Congo 78 1.36S 16.35E
Alindao C.A.R. 73 5.02N 21.13E
Alingsås Sweden 43 57.56N 12.31E
Alîpur Pakistan 62 29.23N 70.55E
Alîpur Duār India 63 26.29N 89.44E
Alîpur Janûbi Pakistan 62 30.13N 71.18E
Aliquippa U.S.A. 114 40.37N 80.15W
Al 'Irq Libya 75 29.05N 15.48E
Ali Sabieh Djibouti 73 11.09N 42.42E
Aliseda Spain 27 39.26N 6.41W
Al Iskandarîyah Egypt 66 31.13N 29.55E
Al Ismā'îlîyah Egypt 66 30.36N 32.15E
Alistráti Greece 35 38.24N 24.02E
Alivérion Greece 35 38.24N 24.02E
Al Jabal al Akhḍar *d.* Libya 75 32.00N 21.30E
Al Jafr Jordan 66 30.16N 36.11E
Al Jāfûrah *des.* Saudi Arabia 65 24.40N 50.20E
Al Jaghbūb Libya 72 29.45N 24.31E
Al Jahrah Kuwait 65 29.20N 47.41E
Al Jaladah *f.* Saudi Arabia 71 18.30N 46.25E
Al Janûb *d.* Lebanon 67 33.10N 35.22E
Al Jawārah Oman 60 18.55N 57.17E
Al Jawb *f.* Saudi Arabia 65 23.00N 50.00E
Al Jawf Saudi Arabia 64 29.49N 39.52E
Al Jawsh Libya 75 32.00N 11.40E
Al Jazîrah *f.* Iraq 64 35.00N 41.00E
Al Jazîrah *d.* Sudan 72 14.35N 33.30E
Al Jazîrah *f.* Sudan 72 14.25N 33.00E
Al Jibāb Syria 67 33.06N 36.15E
Al Jîzah Egypt 66 30.01N 31.12E
Al Jîzah Jordan 67 31.42N 35.57E
Al Jubayl Saudi Arabia 65 27.59N 49.40E
Al Judayyidah Jordan 67 31.15N 35.49E
Al Junaynah Sudan 73 13.27N 22.27E
Aljustrel Portugal 27 37.52N 8.10W
Al Karabah Sudan 72 18.33N 33.42E
Al Karak Jordan 67 31.11N 35.42E
Al Karak *d.* Jordan 67 31.10N 36.00E
Al Kawah Sudan 73 13.44N 32.30E
Al Khābûr *r.* Syria 64 35.07N 40.30E
Al Khābûrah Oman 65 23.58N 57.10E
Al Khalîl Jordan 67 31.32N 35.06E
Al Khalîl *d.* Jordan 67 31.29N 35.10E
Al Khamāsîn Saudi Arabia 71 20.29N 44.49E
Al Khandaq Sudan 72 18.36N 30.34E
Al Khānkah Egypt 66 30.13N 31.21E
Al Khārijah Egypt 64 25.26N 30.33E
Al Kharṭûm Sudan 72 15.33N 32.35E
Al Kharṭûm *d.* Sudan 72 15.45N 32.30E
Al Kharṭûm Baḩrî Sudan 72 15.39N 32.34E
Al Khasfah *well* Oman 71 19.45N 54.19E
Al Khawr Qatar 65 25.41N 51.32E
Al Khirbah as Samrā' Jordan 67 32.11N 36.10E
Al Khubar Saudi Arabia 65 26.18N 50.06E
Al Khufayfîyah Saudi Arabia 65 24.55N 44.42E
Al Khums Libya 75 32.39N 14.16E
Al Khums *d.* Libya 75 31.00N 14.00E
Al Khunn Saudi Arabia 65 23.18N 49.15E
Al Khushnîyah Syria 67 33.00N 35.48E
Al Kidn *des.* Saudi Arabia 65 22.20N 54.20E
Al Kiswah Syria 66 33.21N 36.14E
Alkmaar Neth. 16 52.37N 4.44E
Al Kufrah Libya 72 24.14N 23.15E
Al Kuntillah Egypt 66 30.00N 34.41E
Al Kût Iraq 65 32.30N 45.51E
Al Kuwayt Kuwait 65 29.20N 48.00E
Al Labwah Lebanon 66 34.11N 36.21E
'Allal al Lādhiqîyah Syria 66 35.31N 35.47E
Al Lagowa Sudan 73 11.24N 29.08E
Allāhābād India 63 25.27N 81.51E
Allakaket U.S.A. 98 66.30N 152.45W
'Allān *r.* Syria 67 32.45N 35.57E
Allanche France 20 45.14N 2.56E
'Allāqî, Wādî al *r.* Egypt 64 22.55N 33.02E
Allariz Spain 26 42.11N 7.48W
Allauch France 21 43.20N 5.29E
Ålleberg *hill* Sweden 43 58.08N 13.36E
Allegany U.S.A. 114 42.06N 78.30W
Allegany State Park U.S.A. 114 42.04N 78.44W
Allegheny *r.* U.S.A. 114 42.00N 78.56W
Allegheny Mts. U.S.A. 114 38.30N 80.00W
Allegheny Resr. U.S.A. 114 42.00N 78.50W
Allenby Bridge *see* Jisr al Ḩusayn Jordan 67
Allenford Canada 104 44.32N 81.10W
Allen, Lough Rep. of Ire. 15 54.07N 8.04W
Allentown U.S.A. 115 40.37N 75.30W
Alleppey India 60 9.30N 76.22E
Aller *r.* Germany 38 52.57N 9.11E
Allevard France 21 45.24N 6.04E
Allgäu *f.* Germany 38 47.40N 10.15E
Allgäuer Alpen *mts.* Germany 38 47.26N 10.15E
Alliance Nebr. U.S.A. 110 42.06N 102.52W
Alliance Ohio U.S.A. 114 40.55N 81.06W
Allier *d.* France 20 46.25N 3.00E
Allier *r.* France 20 46.58N 3.30E
Allinge Denmark 43 55.16N 14.49E
Al Lisān *pen.* Jordan 67 31.17N 35.28E
Alliston Canada 104 44.09N 79.52W
Al Liṭānî *r.* Lebanon 66 33.22N 35.14E
Al Lîth Saudi Arabia 72 20.09N 40.16E
Al Liwā' *f.* U.A.E. 71 23.00N 54.00E
Alloa U.K. 14 56.07N 3.49W
Allos France 21 44.14N 6.38E
Al Luḩayyah Yemen 72 15.43N 42.42E
Alluitsup-Paa *see* Sydprøven Greenland 99
Alma Canada 103 48.32N 71.40W
Alma Ga. U.S.A. 113 31.33N 82.29W

Alma Mich. U.S.A. **112** 43.23N 84.40W
Al Ma'ānīyah well Iraq **64** 30.44N 43.00E
Almada Portugal **27** 38.41N 9.09W
Almadén Spain **26** 38.46N 4.50W
Almadén de la Plata Spain **27** 37.52N 6.04W
Al Madīnah Saudi Arabia **64** 24.30N 39.35E
Al Madīnah al Fikrīyah Egypt **66** 27.56N 30.49E
Al Madwar Jordan **67** 32.17N 36.00E
Al Mafraq Jordan **67** 32.21N 36.12E
Al Maghrah well Egypt **64** 30.14N 28.56E
Almagor Israel **67** 32.55N 35.36E
Almagro Spain **26** 38.53N 3.43W
Al Maḥallah al Kubrá Egypt **66** 30.59N 31.12E
Al Maḥārīq Egypt **64** 25.37N 30.39E
Alma Hill U.S.A. **114** 42.03N 78.01W
Al Maḥmūdīyah Egypt **66** 31.10N 30.30E
Al Majma'ah Saudi Arabia **65** 25.52N 45.25E
Al Manāmah Bahrain **65** 26.12N 50.36E
Almanor U.S.A. **108** 40.15N 121.08W
Almansa Spain **25** 38.52N 1.05W
Al Manshāh Egypt **64** 26.28N 31.48E
Almansor r. Portugal **27** 38.56N 8.54W
Al Manṣūrah Egypt **66** 31.03N 31.23E
Almanza Spain **26** 42.39N 5.02W
Al Manzil Jordan **66** 31.03N 36.01E
Almanzora r. Spain **24** 37.16N 1.49W
Almanzor, Pico de mtn. Spain **26** 40.15N 5.18W
Almar r. Spain **26** 40.54N 5.29W
Al Marj Libya **72** 32.30N 20.50E
Al Maṭarīyah Egypt **66** 31.12N 32.02E
Al Matnah Sudan **72** 13.47N 35.03E
Almaty see Alma-Ata Kazakhstan **52**
Almaty Kazakhstan **52** 43.19N 76.55E
Al Mawṣil Iraq **64** 36.21N 43.08E
Al Mayādīn Syria **64** 35.01N 40.28E
Almazán Spain **26** 41.29N 2.32W
Almazora Spain **25** 39.57N 0.03W
Al Mazra'ah Jordan **67** 31.16N 35.31E
Almeida Portugal **26** 40.43N 6.54W
Almeirim Portugal **27** 39.12N 8.38W
Almelo Neth. **16** 52.21N 6.40E
Almenara, Sierra de mts. Spain **25** 37.30N 1.40E
Almenar de Soria Spain **25** 41.41N 2.12W
Almendra, Embalse de resr. Spain **26** 41.15N 6.10W
Almendralejo Spain **27** 38.41N 6.24W
Almería Spain **27** 36.50N 2.27W
Almería d. Spain **27** 37.05N 2.30W
Almería, Golfo di g. Spain **27** 36.45N 2.30W
Älmhult Sweden **43** 56.33N 14.08E
Al Midhnab Saudi Arabia **65** 25.52N 44.15E
Al Miḥrāḍ des. Saudi Arabia **65** 20.00N 52.30E
Al Minyā Egypt **66** 28.06N 30.45E
Almiropótamos Greece **35** 38.16N 24.11E
Almirós Greece **35** 39.11N 22.46E
Almiroú, Kólpos g. Greece **35** 35.23N 24.20E
Al Mismīyah Syria **66** 33.08N 36.24E
Almodôvar Portugal **27** 37.31N 8.36W
Almodóvar del Campo Spain **26** 38.43N 4.10W
Almont U.S.A. **114** 42.55N 83.03W
Almonte Canada **105** 45.14N 76.12W
Almonte r. Spain **27** 39.42N 6.20W
Almora India **63** 29.37N 79.40E
Al Mudawwarah Jordan **66** 29.20N 36.00E
Almudébar Spain **25** 42.03N 0.35W
Al Muglad Sudan **73** 11.02N 27.44E
Al Muharraq Bahrain **65** 26.31N 50.38E
Al Mukallā Yemen **71** 14.34N 49.09E
Al Mukhā Yemen **73** 13.19N 43.15E
Almuñécar Spain **27** 36.43N 3.41W
Al Muwaqqar site Jordan **67** 31.39N 36.06E
Al Muwayh Saudi Arabia **64** 22.41N 41.37E
Alnwick U.K. **12** 55.25N 1.41W
Alofi Niue **84** 19.03S 169.55W
Alofi B. Niue **84** 19.02S 169.55W
Alónnisos Greece **35** 39.08N 23.50E
Alónnisos i. Greece **35** 39.08N 23.50E
Alonsa Canada **101** 50.50N 99.00W
Alor i. Indonesia **59** 8.20S 124.30E
Álora Spain **27** 36.48N 4.42W
Alor Setar Malaysia **58** 6.06N 100.23E
Alosno Spain **27** 37.33N 7.07W
Alozero Russian Fed. **44** 65.02N 31.10E
Alpena U.S.A. **104** 45.04N 83.26W
Alpes-de-Haute-Provence d. France **21** 44.08N 6.10E
Alpes Maritimes d. France **21** 44.00N 7.10E
Alpes Maritimes mts. France **17** 44.07N 7.08E
Alpes Pennines mts. Switz. **39** 46.08N 7.34E
Alpha Australia **90** 23.39S 146.38E
Alphen Neth. **16** 52.08N 4.40E
Alpiarça Portugal **27** 39.15N 8.35W
Alpine U.S.A. **111** 30.22N 103.40W
Alps mts. Europe **17** 46.00N 7.30E
Al Qaḍārif Sudan **72** 14.02N 35.24E
Al Qaḍīmah Saudi Arabia **72** 22.21N 39.09E
Al Qaffā' des. U.A.E. **65** 23.30N 53.30E
Al Qāhirah Egypt **66** 30.03N 31.15E
Al Qā'īyah Saudi Arabia **64** 24.18N 43.30E
Al Qā'īyah well Saudi Arabia **65** 26.27N 45.35E
Al Qalibah Saudi Arabia **64** 28.24N 37.42E
Al Qanāṭir al Khayrīyah Egypt **66** 30.12N 31.08E
Al Qanṭarah Egypt **66** 30.52N 32.20E
Al Qaryatayn Syria **64** 34.13N 37.13E
Al Qaşabāt Libya **75** 32.35N 14.03E
Al Qaşr Egypt **64** 25.43N 28.54E
Al Qaşr Jordan **67** 31.19N 35.45E
Al Qaşşāşin Egypt **66** 30.34N 31.56E
Al Qaţīf Saudi Arabia **65** 26.31N 50.00E
Al Qaṭrānah Jordan **67** 31.15N 36.03E
Al Qaṭrūn Libya **75** 24.56N 14.38E
Al Qayşūmah Saudi Arabia **65** 28.20N 46.07E
Al Qiṣfah Jordan **67** 32.38N 35.52E
Al Quds d. Jordan **67** 31.46N 35.25E
Al Qunayṭirah Syria **67** 33.08N 35.49E
Al Qunayṭirah d. Syria **67** 33.07N 35.50E
Al Qunfudhah Saudi Arabia **72** 19.08N 41.05E
Al Qurnah Iraq **65** 31.00N 47.26E

Al Quşaymah Egypt **66** 30.40N 34.22E
Al Quşayr Egypt **64** 26.06N 34.17E
Al Qūşīyah Egypt **64** 27.26N 30.49E
Alroy Downs town Australia **90** 19.18S 136.04E
Als i. Denmark **42** 54.59N 9.55E
Alsace d. France **19** 48.25N 7.40E
Alsask Canada **101** 51.23N 109.59W
Alsasua Spain **25** 42.54N 2.10W
Ålsborg d. Sweden **41** 58.00N 12.20E
Alsek Ranges mts. Canada **100** 59.21N 137.05W
Alsfeld Germany **38** 50.45N 9.16E
Alsten i. Norway **40** 65.55N 12.35E
Alsterbro Sweden **43** 56.57N 15.55E
Alston U.K. **14** 54.48N 2.26W
Alta Norway **40** 70.00N 23.15E
Alta r. Norway **40** 69.50N 23.30E
Altafjorden est. Norway **40** 70.10N 23.00E
Alta Gracia Argentina **124** 31.40S 64.26W
Altagracia de Orituco Venezuela **122** 9.54N 66.24W
Altai mts. Mongolia **52** 46.30N 93.30E
Altamaha r. U.S.A. **113** 31.19N 81.17W
Altamira Brazil **123** 3.12S 52.12W
Altamont N.Y. U.S.A. **115** 42.42N 74.02W
Altamont Oreg. U.S.A. **108** 42.12N 121.44W
Altamura Italy **33** 40.50N 16.33E
Altar, Desierto de des. Mexico **109** 31.50N 114.15W
Altavista U.S.A. **113** 37.07N 79.18W
Altay China **52** 47.48N 88.07E
Altay Mongolia **52** 46.20N 97.00E
Altdorf Switz. **39** 46.53N 8.39E
Altea Spain **25** 38.38N 0.02W
Altenburg Germany **38** 50.59N 12.27E
Altenkirchen Germany **16** 50.41N 7.40E
Altentreptow Germany **38** 53.42N 13.14E
Alter do Chão Portugal **27** 39.12N 7.40W
Althofen Austria **31** 46.54N 14.27E
Altiplanicie Mexicana mts. Mexico **111** 29.00N 105.00W
Altkirch France **19** 47.37N 7.15E
Altmar U.S.A. **115** 43.31N 76.00W
Altmark f. Germany **38** 52.45N 11.15E
Altmühl r. Germany **39** 48.55N 11.52E
Altnaharra U.K. **14** 58.16N 4.26W
Alto Araguaia Brazil **123** 17.19S 53.10W
Alto Molocue Mozambique **79** 15.38S 37.42E
Altomünster Germany **39** 48.28N 11.58E
Alton Canada **104** 43.52N 80.04W
Alton U.K. **13** 51.08N 0.59W
Alton U.S.A. **110** 38.55N 90.10W
Altona Germany **38** 53.32N 9.56E
Altoona U.S.A. **114** 40.30N 78.24W
Altötting Germany **39** 48.13N 12.40E
Altsasu see Alsasua Spain **25**
Altun Shan mts. China **52** 38.10N 87.50E
Altus U.S.A. **111** 34.38N 99.20W
Al Ubayyiḍ Sudan **73** 13.11N 30.13E
Al Uḍayyah Sudan **73** 12.03N 28.17E
Aluk Sudan **73** 8.26N 27.32E
Al 'Ulá Saudi Arabia **64** 26.39N 37.58E
Alunda Sweden **43** 60.04N 18.05E
Al 'Uqaylah Libya **75** 30.16N 19.12E
Al Uqṣur Egypt **64** 25.41N 32.24E
Al Urdunn r. Asia **67** 31.47N 35.31E
Al 'Uwaynah well Saudi Arabia **65** 26.46N 48.13E
Al 'Uwaynāt Libya **75** 25.48N 10.33E
Al 'Uyūn Saudi Arabia **65** 26.32N 43.41E
Alva U.S.A. **111** 36.48N 98.40W
Alvalázere Portugal **27** 39.49N 8.23W
Älvängen Sweden **43** 57.58N 12.07E
Alvarado Mexico **116** 18.49N 95.46W
Älvdalen Sweden **41** 61.14N 14.02E
Alverca Portugal **27** 38.54N 9.02W
Alvesta Sweden **43** 56.54N 14.33E
Älvho Sweden **41** 61.30N 14.46E
Alvinston Canada **104** 42.49N 81.52W
Alvito Portugal **27** 38.15N 8.00W
Alvito, Barragem do resr. Portugal **27** 38.20N 7.50W
Älvkarleby Sweden **41** 60.34N 17.27E
Älvsborg d. Sweden **43** 57.50N 12.50E
Älvsbyn Sweden **40** 65.39N 20.59E
Al Wajh Saudi Arabia **64** 26.16N 36.28E
Al Wakrah Qatar **65** 25.09N 51.36E
Alwar India **62** 27.34N 76.36E
Al Wazz Sudan **72** 15.01N 30.10E
Al Yamāmah Saudi Arabia **65** 24.11N 47.21E
Al Yāmūn Jordan **67** 32.29N 35.14E
Alyaty Azerbaijan **65** 39.59N 49.20E
Alytus Lithuania **37** 54.24N 24.03E
Alzada U.S.A. **108** 45.01N 104.26W
Alzette r. Lux. **16** 49.52N 6.07E
Alzey Germany **39** 49.40N 8.07E
Amadeus, L. Australia **88** 24.50S 130.45E
Amadi Sudan **73** 5.31N 30.20E
Amadjuak Canada **99** 64.00N 72.50W
Amadjuak L. Canada **99** 65.00N 71.00W
Amagasaki Japan **57** 34.43N 135.25E
Amager i. Denmark **43** 55.37N 12.37E
Åmål Sweden **43** 59.03N 12.42E
Amalfi Italy **33** 40.38N 14.36E
Amaliás Greece **35** 37.49N 21.23E
Amalner India **62** 21.03N 75.04E
Amami ō shima i. Japan **53** 28.20N 129.30E
Amamula Zaïre **79** 0.17S 27.49E
Amanã, L. Brazil **122** 2.35S 64.40W
Amānganj India **63** 24.26N 80.02E
Amantea Italy **33** 39.08N 16.05E
Amapá Brazil **123** 2.00N 50.50W
Amapá d. Brazil **123** 2.00N 52.00W
Amarante Brazil **123** 6.14S 42.51W
Amaranth Canada **101** 50.36N 98.43W
Amareleja Portugal **27** 38.12N 7.14W
Amares Portugal **26** 41.38N 8.21W
Amarillo U.S.A. **111** 35.13N 101.49W
Amar Jadīd Sudan **72** 14.28N 25.14E
Amarkantak India **63** 22.40N 81.45E

Amaro, Monte mtn. Italy **31** 42.05N 14.05E
Amasya Turkey **64** 40.37N 35.50E
Amatrice Italy **30** 42.38N 13.17E
Amazon r. see Amazonas r. Brazil **123**
Amazonas d. Brazil **122** 4.50S 64.00W
Amazonas r. Brazil **123** 2.00S 52.00W
Amazonas, Estuario do Rio f. Brazil **123** 0.00 50.30W
Amazon Delta see Amazonas, Estuario do Rio f. Brazil **123**
Amazya Israel **67** 31.32N 34.55E
Amb Pakistan **62** 34.19N 72.51E
Ambāla India **62** 30.23N 76.46E
Ambalavao Madagascar **81** 21.50S 46.56E
Ambam Cameroon **77** 2.25N 11.16E
Ambarawa Indonesia **59** 7.12S 110.30E
Ambarchik Russian Fed. **51** 69.39N 162.27E
Ambarnāth India **62** 19.11N 73.10E
Ambarnyy Russian Fed. **44** 65.59N 33.53E
Ambato Ecuador **122** 1.18S 78.36W
Ambato-Boeni Madagascar **81** 16.28S 46.43E
Ambatofinandrahana Madagascar **81** 20.33S 46.48E
Ambatolampy Madagascar **81** 19.23S 47.25E
Ambatondrazaka Madagascar **81** 17.50S 48.25E
Ámbelos, Ákra c. Greece **34** 39.56N 23.55E
Amberg Germany **38** 49.27N 11.52E
Ambergris Cay i. Belize **117** 18.00N 87.58W
Ambérieu-en-Bugey France **21** 45.57N 5.21E
Amberley Canada **104** 44.02N 81.44W
Ambert France **20** 45.33N 3.45E
Ambidédi Mali **76** 14.35N 11.47W
Ambikāpur India **63** 23.07N 83.12E
Ambilobe Madagascar **81** 13.12S 49.04E
Amble U.K. **12** 55.20N 1.34W
Ambleside U.K. **12** 54.26N 2.58W
Ambodifototra Madagascar **81** 16.59S 49.52E
Ambohidratrimo Madagascar **81** 18.50S 47.26E
Ambohimahasoa Madagascar **81** 21.07S 47.13E
Ambohimanga du Sud Madagascar **81** 20.52S 47.36E
Amboise France **18** 47.25N 0.59E
Ambon Indonesia **59** 4.50S 128.10E
Ambositra Madagascar **81** 20.31S 47.15E
Ambovombe Madagascar **81** 25.11S 46.05E
Amboy U.S.A. **109** 34.33N 115.44W
Ambridge U.S.A. **114** 40.36N 80.14W
Ambrières France **18** 48.24N 0.38W
Ambrim i. Vanuatu **84** 16.15S 168.10E
Ambriz Angola **78** 7.54S 13.12E
Ambunten Indonesia **59** 6.55S 113.45E
Am Dam Chad **73** 12.46N 20.29E
Amderma Russian Fed. **50** 69.44N 61.35E
Amdo China **63** 32.22N 91.07E
Ameca Mexico **116** 20.33N 104.02W
Ameland i. Neth. **16** 53.28N 5.48E
Amelia Italy **30** 42.33N 12.25E
Amelia City U.S.A. **113** 30.37N 81.27W
Americana Brazil **126** 22.44S 47.19W
American Falls Resr. U.S.A. **108** 43.00N 113.00W
American Fork U.S.A. **108** 40.23N 111.48W
Americus U.S.A. **113** 32.04N 84.14W
Amersfoort Neth. **16** 52.10N 5.23E
Amery Australia **89** 31.09S 117.05E
Amery Ice Shelf Antarctica **128** 70.00S 70.00E
Amesbury U.S.A. **115** 42.51N 70.56W
Ameson Canada **102** 49.50N 84.35W
Ametinho Angola **78** 17.20S 17.20E
Amfíklia Greece **35** 38.38N 22.35E
Amfilokhia Greece **35** 38.51N 21.10E
Ámfissa Greece **35** 38.32N 22.22E
Amga Russian Fed. **51** 60.51N 131.59E
Amga r. Russian Fed. **51** 62.40N 135.20E
Am Géréda Chad **73** 12.52N 21.10E
Amgu Russian Fed. **54** 45.48N 137.36E
Amguid Algeria **75** 26.26N 5.22E
Amgun r. Russian Fed. **51** 53.10N 139.47E
Amhara Plateau f. Ethiopia **73** 11.00N 38.00E
Amherst Canada **103** 45.49N 64.14W
Amherst Mass. U.S.A. **115** 42.23N 72.31W
Amherstburg Canada **104** 42.06N 83.06W
Amherst I. Canada **105** 44.06N 76.45W
Amiata mtn. Italy **30** 42.53N 11.37E
Amiens France **19** 49.54N 2.18E
Amíndaion Greece **34** 40.42N 21.42E
Amīr Chāh well Pakistan **62** 29.13N 62.28E
Amisk L. Canada **101** 54.35N 102.13W
Amistad Resr. U.S.A. **111** 29.34N 101.15W
Amite U.S.A. **111** 30.44N 90.33W
Amla India **63** 21.56N 78.07E
Amlekhganj Nepal **63** 27.17N 85.00E
Åmli Norway **42** 58.47N 8.30E
Amlwch U.K. **12** 53.24N 4.21W
'Ammān Jordan **67** 31.57N 35.56E
Ammanford U.K. **13** 51.48N 4.00W
Ammassalik Greenland **99** 65.40N 38.00W
Åmmeberg Sweden **43** 58.52N 15.00E
Ammersee l. Germany **39** 48.00N 11.08E
'Ammi'ad Israel **67** 32.55N 35.32E
Ammókhostos Cyprus **66** 35.07N 33.57E
Ammókhostou, Kólpos b. Cyprus **66** 35.12N 34.05E
Amo r. India **63** 25.58N 89.36E
Åmol Iran **65** 36.26N 52.24E
Amorgós i. Greece **35** 36.49N 25.54E
Amorgós town Greece **35** 36.49N 25.54E
Amory U.S.A. **111** 33.59N 88.29W
Amos Canada **102** 48.35N 78.07W
Åmot Buskerud Norway **42** 59.54N 9.54E
Åmot Telemark Norway **42** 59.35N 8.00E
Amoy see Xiamen China **55**
Ampala Honduras **117** 13.16N 87.39W
Ampanihy Madagascar **81** 24.42S 44.45E
Amparo Brazil **126** 22.44S 46.44W
Amper r. Germany **39** 48.10N 11.50E
Ampezzo Italy **30** 46.25N 12.48E
Amposta Spain **25** 40.43N 0.35E
'Amqa Israel **67** 32.58N 35.10E
Amqui Canada **103** 48.28N 67.26W
Amrāvati India **63** 20.56N 77.45E
Amreli India **62** 21.37N 71.14E
Amritsar India **62** 31.38N 74.53E

Amroha India **63** 28.55N 78.28E
Amrum i. Germany **38** 54.39N 8.21E
Am Saterna Chad **73** 12.26N 21.25E
Amsel Algeria **75** 22.37N 5.26E
Amstelveen Neth. **16** 52.18N 4.51E
Amsterdam Neth. **16** 52.22N 4.54E
Amsterdam N.Y. U.S.A. **115** 42.57N 74.11W
Amsterdam Ohio U.S.A. **114** 40.28N 80.55W
Amsterdam, Île i. Indian Oc. **49** 37.52S 77.32E
Am Timan Chad **73** 11.02N 20.17E
Amu Darya r. Uzbekistan **9** 43.50N 59.00E
Amulet Canada **101** 49.40N 104.45W
Amundsen G. Canada **98** 70.30N 122.00W
Amundsen Sea Antarctica **128** 72.00S 120.00W
Amuntai Indonesia **58** 2.24S 115.14E
Amur r. Russian Fed. **51** 53.17N 140.00E
Amurrio Spain **26** 43.04N 3.00W
'Amūr, Wādī r. Sudan **72** 18.56N 33.34E
Amurzet Russian Fed. **53** 47.50N 131.05E
Amvrakikós Kólpos b. Greece **35** 39.00N 21.00E
Anabar r. Russian Fed. **51** 72.40N 113.30E
Anabranch r. Australia **92** 34.08S 141.46E
'Anabtā Jordan **67** 32.19N 35.07E
Anaco Venezuela **122** 9.27N 64.28W
Anaconda U.S.A. **108** 46.08N 112.57W
Anadarko U.S.A. **111** 35.04N 98.15W
Anadolu f. Turkey **64** 38.00N 35.00E
Anadyr Russian Fed. **51** 64.40N 177.32E
Anadyr r. Russian Fed. **51** 65.00N 176.00E
Anadyrskiy Zaliv g. Russian Fed. **51** 64.30N 177.50W
Anáfi i. Greece **35** 36.21N 25.50E
Anagni Italy **30** 41.44N 13.09E
Anaheim U.S.A. **109** 33.51N 117.57W
Analalava Madagascar **81** 14.38S 47.45E
Anambas, Kepulauan is. Indonesia **58** 3.00N 106.10E
Anambra d. Nigeria **77** 6.20N 7.25E
Anamoose U.S.A. **110** 47.53N 100.15W
Anamur Turkey **64** 36.06N 32.49E
Anan Japan **57** 33.55N 134.39E
Ānand India **62** 22.34N 72.56E
Anandpur India **63** 21.16N 86.13E
Anantapur India **60** 14.41N 77.36E
Anantnāg Jammu & Kashmir **62** 33.44N 75.09E
Anápolis Brazil **126** 16.19S 48.58W
Anapú r. Brazil **123** 1.53S 50.53W
Anār Iran **65** 30.54N 55.18E
Anārak Iran **65** 33.20N 53.42E
Anār Darreh Afghan. **62** 32.46N 61.39E
Anatolia f. see Anadolu f. Turkey **64**
Anatone U.S.A. **108** 46.08N 117.09W
Añatuya Argentina **124** 28.26S 62.48W
Ancenis France **18** 47.22N 1.11W
Anchau Nigeria **77** 11.00N 8.23E
Anchorage U.S.A. **98** 61.10N 150.00W
Anchuras Spain **27** 39.29N 4.50W
Ancien Goubéré C.A.R. **73** 5.51N 26.46E
Ancohuma mtn. Bolivia **124** 16.05S 68.36W
Ancón Peru **122** 11.50S 77.10W
Ancona Italy **31** 43.38N 13.30E
Ancuabe Mozambique **79** 13.00S 39.50E
Ancud Chile **125** 41.05S 73.50W
Ancy-le-Franc France **19** 47.46N 4.10E
Anda China **53** 46.25N 125.20E
Andalsnes Norway **40** 62.33N 7.43E
Andalucía d. Spain **27** 37.30N 4.30W
Andalusia U.S.A. **113** 31.20N 86.30W
Andaman Is. India **56** 12.00N 92.45E
Andaman Sea Indian Oc. **56** 10.00N 95.00E
Andamooka Australia **92** 30.27S 137.12E
Andanga Russian Fed. **44** 59.11N 45.44E
Andara Namibia **80** 18.04S 21.26E
Andelot France **19** 48.15N 5.18E
Andenes Norway **40** 69.18N 16.10E
Andenne Belgium **16** 50.29N 5.06E
Anderlecht Belgium **16** 50.51N 4.18E
Andermatt Switz. **39** 46.38N 8.36E
Andernach Germany **39** 50.26N 7.24E
Anderson r. Canada **98** 69.45N 129.00W
Anderson Ind. U.S.A. **112** 40.05N 85.41W
Anderson S.C. U.S.A. **113** 34.30N 82.39W
Anderstorp Sweden **43** 57.17N 13.38E
Andes mts. S. America **125** 32.40S 70.00W
Andevoranto Madagascar **81** 18.57S 49.06E
Andfjorden est. Norway **40** 68.55N 16.00E
Andhra Pradesh d. India **61** 17.00N 79.00E
Andikíthira i. Greece **29** 35.52N 23.18E
Andímilos i. Greece **35** 36.49N 27.04E
Andíparos i. Greece **35** 37.00N 25.03E
Andirrion Greece **35** 38.20N 21.46E
Andissa Greece **35** 39.15N 26.00E
Andizhan Uzbekistan **52** 40.48N 72.23E
Andoany Madagascar **81** 13.25S 48.16E
Andong S. Korea **53** 36.37N 128.44E
Andorra town Andorra **20** 42.30N 1.31E
Andorra Europe **20** 42.30N 1.32E
Andover U.K. **13** 51.13N 1.29W
Andover N.J. U.S.A. **115** 40.59N 74.45W
Andover N.Y. U.S.A. **114** 42.09N 77.48W
Andover Ohio U.S.A. **114** 41.36N 80.34W
Andøy i. Norway **40** 69.05N 15.40E
Andradá Brazil **78** 7.41S 21.22E
Andrews N.C. U.S.A. **113** 35.13N 83.49W
Andrews Tex. U.S.A. **111** 32.19N 102.33W
Andrews Pt. U.S.A. **115** 42.42N 70.44W
Andreyevo-Ivanovka Ukraine **37** 47.28N 30.29E
Andria Italy **33** 41.13N 16.18E
Andriba Madagascar **81** 17.36S 46.55E
Andrijevica Yugo. **34** 42.45N 19.48E
Andrítsaina Greece **35** 37.29N 21.52E
Androka Madagascar **81** 25.02S 44.05E
Ándros Greece **35** 37.50N 24.57E
Ándros i. Greece **35** 37.45N 24.42E
Andros I. Bahamas **113** 24.25N 78.00W
Andros Town Bahamas **117** 24.43N 77.47W
Andrushevka Ukraine **37** 50.00N 28.59E
Andújar Spain **26** 38.03N 4.04W
Andulo Angola **78** 11.28S 16.43E

Anduze France 20 44.03N 3.59E
Aneby Sweden 43 57.50N 14.48E
Anefis I-n-Darane Mali 76 17.57N 0.35E
Anegada i. B.V.Is. 117 18.46N 64.24W
Aného Togo 77 6.17N 1.40E
Aneityum i. Vanuatu 84 20.12S 169.45E
Añelo Argentina 125 38.20S 68.45W
Aneto, Pico de mtn. Spain 25 42.38N 0.40E
Aney Niger 77 19.24N 12.56E
Angara r. Russian Fed. 51 58.00N 93.00E
Angarsk Russian Fed. 51 52.31N 103.55E
Angaston Australia 91 34.30S 139.03E
Angathonísi i. Greece 35 37.28N 27.00E
Angatuba Brazil 126 23.27S 48.25W
Ånge Sweden 40 62.31N 15.40E
Ángel de la Guarda, Isla i. Mexico 109 29.20N 113.25W
Angel Falls f. Venezuela 122 5.55N 62.30W
Ängelholm Sweden 43 56.15N 12.51E
Angelica U.S.A. 114 42.18N 78.01W
Angels Camp U.S.A. 108 38.04N 120.32W
Ångereb r. Ethiopia 73 13.45N 36.40E
Ångerman r. Sweden 40 63.00N 17.43E
Angermünde Germany 38 53.01N 14.00E
Angers France 18 47.28N 0.33W
Angerville France 19 48.19N 2.00E
Ångesån r. Sweden 40 66.22N 22.58E
Angikuni L. Canada 101 62.00N 100.00W
Anglesey i. U.K. 12 53.16N 4.25W
Angleton U.S.A. 111 29.10N 95.26W
Anglin r. France 18 46.42N 0.50E
Ango Zaïre 73 4.02N 25.52E
Angoche Mozambique 81 16.10S 39.57E
Angol Chile 125 37.48S 72.43W
Angola Africa 78 11.00S 18.00E
Angola Ind. U.S.A. 112 41.38N 85.01W
Angola N.Y. U.S.A. 114 42.38N 79.02W
Angoram P.N.G. 59 4.04S 144.04E
Angoulême France 20 45.39N 0.09E
Angra dos Reis Brazil 126 22.59S 44.17W
Ang Thong Thailand 56 14.35N 100.25E
Angul India 63 20.51N 85.06E
Angumu Zaïre 79 0.10S 27.38E
Anhalt f. Germany 38 52.07N 11.15E
Anholt i. Denmark 42 56.42N 11.34E
Anholt Germany 16 51.51N 6.26E
Anh Son Vietnam 56 18.54N 105.18E
Anhua China 55 28.24N 111.13E
Anhui d. China 55 32.00N 117.00E
Aniak U.S.A. 98 61.32N 159.40W
Anie, Pic d' mtn. France 20 42.57N 0.43W
Animas U.S.A. 109 31.57N 108.48W
Anin Myanmar 56 15.40N 97.46E
Anina Romania 37 45.05N 21.51E
Anivorano Madagascar 81 18.44S 48.58E
Anjad India 62 22.02N 75.03E
Anjangaon India 62 21.10N 77.18E
Anjär India 62 23.08N 70.01E
'Anjarah Jordan 67 32.18N 35.45E
Anjō Japan 57 34.57N 137.05E
Anjouan i. Comoros 79 12.25S 44.28E
Anjozorobe Madagascar 81 18.24S 47.52E
Anju N. Korea 53 39.36N 125.42E
Anka Nigeria 77 12.06N 5.56E
Ankang China 54 32.38N 109.12E
Ankara Turkey 64 39.55N 32.50E
Ankaramena Madagascar 81 21.57S 46.39E
Ankarsrum Sweden 43 57.42N 16.19E
Ankazoabo Madagascar 81 22.18S 44.31E
Ankazobe Madagascar 81 18.21S 47.07E
Anklam Germany 38 53.51N 13.41E
Anklesvar India 62 21.38N 72.59E
Änkober Ethiopia 73 9.30N 39.44E
Ankpa Nigeria 77 7.26N 7.38E
Anlong China 55 25.06N 105.31E
Anlu China 55 31.15N 113.40E
Anna U.S.A. 111 37.28N 89.15W
Annaba Algeria 75 36.55N 7.47E
Annaberg-Buchholz Germany 38 50.35N 13.00E
An Nabk Syria 66 34.02N 36.43E
Anna Creek town Australia 92 28.50S 136.07E
An Nafūd des. Saudi Arabia 64 28.40N 41.30E
An Najaf Iraq 65 31.59N 44.19E
An Nakhl Egypt 66 29.55N 33.45E
An Nakhl Syria 67 33.01N 36.07E
Annam Highlands see Annamitique, Chaîne mts. Laos/Vietnam 56
Annamitique, Chaîne mts. Laos/Vietnam 56 17.00N 106.00E
Annan U.K. 14 54.59N 3.16W
Annan r. U.K. 14 54.58N 3.16W
Annandale f. U.K. 14 55.12N 3.25W
Anna Plains Australia 88 19.18S 121.34E
Annapolis U.S.A. 115 38.59N 76.30W
Annapurna mtn. Nepal 63 28.34N 83.50E
An Naqirah well Saudi Arabia 65 27.53N 48.15E
An Nāqūrah Lebanon 67 33.07N 35.08E
Ann Arbor U.S.A. 104 42.18N 83.45W
An Nāşiriyah Iraq 65 31.04N 46.16E
An Nawfaliyah Libya 75 30.47N 17.50E
Annecy France 21 45.54N 6.07E
Annemasse France 21 46.12N 6.15E
An Nil d. Sudan 72 18.30N 33.10E
An Nil al Abyad d. Sudan 73 13.10N 32.00E
An Nil al Azraq d. Sudan 73 13.00N 34.00E
Anniston U.S.A. 113 33.38N 85.50W
Annobón i. Equat. Guinea 127 1.25S 5.36E
Annonay France 21 45.14N 4.40E
Annuello Australia 92 34.52S 142.54E
An Nuhūd Sudan 72 12.42N 28.26E
Anoka U.S.A. 110 45.11N 93.20W
Anorotsangana Madagascar 81 13.56S 47.55E
Anou Ti-n Elhaoua well Algeria 75 20.02N 2.55E
Anpu China 55 21.27N 110.01E
Anqing China 55 30.40N 117.03E
Ansager Denmark 42 55.42N 8.45E

Ansbach Germany 39 49.17N 10.34E
Anshan China 54 41.06N 122.58E
Anshun China 55 26.11N 105.50E
Anson B. Australia 88 13.10S 130.00E
Ansongo Mali 76 15.40N 0.30E
Ansonia U.S.A. 115 41.20N 73.05W
Anstruther U.K. 14 56.14N 2.42W
Ansudu Indonesia 59 2.11S 139.22E
Antakya Turkey 64 36.12N 36.10E
Antalaha Madagascar 81 14.53S 50.16E
Antalya Turkey 64 36.53N 30.42E
Antalya Körfezi g. Turkey 64 36.38N 31.00E
Antananarivo Madagascar 81 18.55S 47.31E
Antarctica 128
Antarctic Pen. Antarctica 121 65.00S 64.00W
Antas Brazil 123 10.20S 38.20W
Antela, Laguna de i. Spain 26 42.07N 7.41W
Antequera Spain 27 37.01N 4.33W
Anthony U.S.A. 111 37.09N 89.02W
Antibes France 21 43.35N 7.07E
Anticosti, Île d' i. Canada 103 49.20N 63.00W
Anticosti Prov. Park Canada 103 49.20N 63.00W
Antifer, Cap d' c. France 18 49.41N 0.10E
Antigo U.S.A. 110 45.09N 89.09W
Antigua Guatemala 116 14.33N 90.42W
Antigua i. Leeward Is. 117 17.09N 61.49W
Anti-Lebanon mts. see Sharqī, Al Jabal ash mts. Lebanon 66
Antipodes Is. Pacific Oc. 84 49.42S 178.50E
Antlers U.S.A. 111 34.14N 95.47W
Antofagasta Chile 124 23.39S 70.24W
Antônio Bezerra Brazil 123 3.44S 38.35W
Antônio Carlos Brazil 126 21.18S 43.48W
Antonito U.S.A. 108 37.05N 106.00W
Antrain France 18 48.27N 1.29W
Antrim U.K. 15 54.43N 6.14W
Antrim d. U.K. 15 54.58N 6.20W
Antrim, Mts. of U.K. 15 55.00N 6.10W
Antrodoco Italy 32 42.25N 13.05E
Antsalova Madagascar 81 18.40S 44.37E
Antsirabé Madagascar 81 19.51S 47.02E
Antsiranana Madagascar 81 12.16S 49.17E
Antsohihy Madagascar 81 14.52S 47.59E
Anttis Sweden 40 67.16N 22.52E
Antwerp see Antwerpen Belgium 16
Antwerp U.S.A. 115 44.12N 75.37W
Antwerpen Belgium 16 51.13N 4.25E
Antwerpen d. Belgium 16 51.16N 4.45E
Anūpgarh India 62 29.11N 73.12E
Anvik U.S.A. 98 62.38N 160.20W
Anxi Fujian China 55 25.03N 118.13E
Anxi Gansu China 52 40.32N 95.57E
Anxious B. Australia 92 33.25S 134.35E
Anyama Côte d'Ivoire 76 5.30N 4.03W
Anyang China 54 36.05N 114.20E
Anyer Lor Indonesia 59 6.02S 105.57E
Anyi China 55 28.50N 115.32E
Anyuan China 55 25.09N 115.21E
Anyue China 55 30.09N 105.18E
Anzhero-Sudzhensk Russian Fed. 50 56.10N 86.10E
Anzio Italy 32 41.27N 12.37E
Ao Ban Don b. Thailand 56 9.00N 99.20E
Aohan Qi China 54 42.23N 119.59E
Aoíz Spain 25 42.47N 1.22W
Aoji N. Korea 57 42.31N 130.23E
Aomori Japan 57 40.50N 140.43E
Aóös r. Greece 34 40.37N 19.20E
Aopo W. Samoa 84 13.29S 172.30W
Aoraki, Mt. see Cook, Mt. New Zealand 86
Aosta Italy 30 45.44N 7.20E
Aoulef Algeria 74 26.58N 1.05E
Aoulime, Jbel mtn. Morocco 74 30.48N 8.50W
Aozou Chad 77 21.49N 17.25E
Apache U.S.A. 111 34.54N 98.22W
Apalachee B. U.S.A. 113 30.00N 84.13W
Apalachicola U.S.A. 113 29.43N 85.01W
Apalachicola r. U.S.A. 113 29.44N 84.59W
Apaporis r. Colombia 122 1.45S 69.20W
Aparri Phil. 59 18.22N 121.40E
Apatin Yugo. 31 45.40N 18.59E
Apatity Russian Fed. 44 67.32N 33.21E
Apeldoorn Neth. 16 52.13N 5.57E
Api mtn. Nepal 63 30.01N 80.56E
Apia W. Samoa 84 13.48S 171.45W
Apizaco Mexico 116 19.25N 98.09W
Apoka Uganda 73 3.42N 33.38E
Apolakkiá Greece 35 36.04N 27.48E
Apollo Bay town Australia 92 38.45S 143.40E
Apostle Is. U.S.A. 110 46.50N 90.30W
Apóstoles Argentina 124 27.55S 55.45W
Apostólou Andréa, Akrotírion c. Cyprus 66 35.40N 34.35E
Apoteri Guyana 122 4.02N 58.32W
Appalachian Mts. U.S.A. 114 41.00N 77.00W
Appennino mts. Italy 30 44.33N 9.55E
Appennino Abruzzese mts. Italy 30 42.10N 13.25E
Appennino Ligure mts. Italy 30 44.30N 9.00E
Appennino Lucano mts. Italy 33 40.30N 15.50E
Appennino Tosco-Emiliano mts. Italy 30 44.05N 11.00E
Appennino Umbro-Marchigiano mts. Italy 30 43.05N 13.00E
Appenzell Switz. 39 47.20N 9.25E
Appenzell d. Switz. 39 47.00N 8.05E
Appiano Italy 30 46.28N 11.15E
Appingedam Neth. 16 53.18N 6.52E
Appleby U.K. 12 54.35N 2.29W
Appleton U.S.A. 110 44.16N 88.25W
Apsheronsk Russian Fed. 45 44.26N 39.45E
Apsheronskiy Poluostrov pen. Azerbaijan 65 40.28N 50.00E
Apsley Australia 92 36.58S 141.08E
Apsley Canada 104 44.45N 78.06W
Apt France 21 43.53N 5.24E
Apucarana Brazil 126 23.34S 51.28W
Apure r. Venezuela 122 7.40N 66.30W
Apurímac r. Peru 122 10.43S 73.55W

Aqaba, G. of Asia 66 28.45N 34.45E
Aqabat al Hijāziyah Jordan 66 29.40N 35.55E
'Aqdā Iran 65 32.25N 33.38E
'Aqīq Sudan 72 18.14N 38.12E
Aqqikkol Hu i. China 52 35.44N 81.34E
'Aqrabā Syria 67 33.28N 36.20E
'Aqrabah Jordan 67 32.08N 35.21E
Aquidauana Brazil 124 20.27S 55.45W
Aquila Mexico 116 18.30N 103.50W
Aquitaine d. France 20 44.40N 0.00
'Ara Israel 67 32.30N 35.05E
Arabādād Iran 65 33.02N 57.41E
'Arabah, Wādī r. Egypt 66 29.07N 32.40E
'Arab, Bahr al r. Sudan 73 9.12N 29.28E
Arabian Basin f. Indian Oc. 48 12.00N 65.00E
Arabian Sea Asia 60 16.00N 65.00E
'Arab, Wādī al Jordan 67 32.35N 35.35E
Araç Turkey 64 41.14N 33.20E
Aracaju Brazil 123 10.54S 37.07W
Aracanguy, Montañas de mts. Paraguay 124 24.00S 55.50W
Aracati Brazil 123 4.32S 37.45W
Araçatuba Brazil 126 21.12S 50.24W
Aracena Spain 27 37.53N 6.33W
Aracena, Sierra de mts. Spain 27 37.50N 7.00W
'Arad Israel 67 31.15N 35.13E
Arad Romania 37 46.12N 21.19E
Arada Chad 75 15.01N 20.40E
Arafura Sea Austa. 90 9.00S 133.00E
Aragarças Brazil 123 15.55S 52.12W
Aragats mtn. Armenia 65 40.32N 44.11E
Aragón d. Spain 25 41.30N 0.30W
Aragón r. Spain 25 42.13N 1.44W
Aragona Italy 32 37.24N 13.37E
Araguacema Brazil 123 8.50S 49.34W
Araguaia r. Brazil 123 5.20S 48.30W
Araguari Brazil 126 18.38S 48.13W
Araguari r. Brazil 123 1.15N 50.05W
Arak Algeria 75 25.18N 3.45E
Āräk Iran 65 34.06N 49.44E
Araka Sudan 73 4.16N 30.21E
Arakan d. Myanmar 56 19.00N 94.15E
Arakan Yoma mts. Myanmar 56 19.30N 94.30E
Arákhova Greece 35 38.28N 22.35E
Arakhthos r. Greece 35 39.01N 21.03E
Aral Sea Asia 9 45.00N 60.00E
Aralskoye More sea see Aral Sea Asia 9
Aralsk Kazakhstan 9 46.56N 61.43E
Aralsor, Ozero l. Kazakhstan 45 49.00N 48.40E
Aramac Australia 90 22.59S 145.14E
Arāmbāgh India 63 22.53N 87.47E
Aramia r. P.N.G. 59 8.00S 143.20E
Arana, Sierra mts. Spain 27 37.20N 3.30W
Aranda de Duero Spain 26 41.41N 3.41W
Aran I. Rep. of Ire. 15 55.00N 8.32W
Aran Is. Rep. of Ire. 15 53.07N 9.38W
Aranjuez Spain 27 40.02N 3.36W
Aranos Namibia 80 24.09S 19.09E
Aransas Pass town U.S.A. 111 27.54N 97.09W
Araouane Mali 76 18.53N 3.31W
Arapahoe U.S.A. 110 40.18N 99.54W
Arapey Uruguay 125 30.58S 57.30W
Arapey Grande r. Uruguay 125 30.55S 57.49W
Arapiraca Brazil 123 9.45S 36.40W
Arapkir Turkey 64 39.03N 38.29E
Araquil r. Spain 25 42.48N 1.45W
Araraquara Brazil 126 21.46S 48.08W
Araras Brazil 126 22.20S 47.23W
Ararat Australia 92 37.20S 143.00E
Ararat mtn. see Ağri Daği mtn. Turkey 65
'Ar'ar, Wādī r. Iraq 64 32.00N 42.30E
Aras r. Asia 65 40.00N 48.28E
Arauca Colombia 122 7.04N 70.41W
Arauca r. Venezuela 122 7.05N 70.45W
Araure Venezuela 122 9.36N 69.15W
Arävalli Range mts. India 62 25.00N 73.45E
Araviana r. Spain 25 41.41N 2.07W
Araviana r. Spain 26 41.35N 2.25W
Araxá Brazil 126 19.37S 46.50W
Araxes r. Iran see Araks r. Azerbaijan 65
Arba r. Spain 25 41.52N 1.18W
Ārba Minch' Ethiopia 73 6.02N 37.40E
Arbatax Italy 32 39.57N 9.42E
Arboga Sweden 43 59.24N 15.50E
Arbois France 20 43.31N 1.25E
Arbon Switz. 39 47.31N 9.26E
Arborea Italy 32 39.47N 8.34E
Arborg Canada 101 50.55N 97.15W
Arbroath U.K. 14 56.34N 2.35W
Arc r. France 21 45.34N 6.12E
Arcachon France 20 44.37N 1.12W
Arcachon, Bassin d' b. France 20 44.40N 1.10W
Arcade U.S.A. 114 42.32N 78.25W
Arcadia Fla. U.S.A. 113 27.12N 81.52W
Arcadia Wisc. U.S.A. 110 44.15N 91.30W
Arcata U.S.A. 108 40.52N 124.05W
Arce Italy 32 41.35N 13.34E
Arcevia Italy 30 43.30N 12.56E
Archbald U.S.A. 115 41.30N 75.32W
Archer r. Australia 90 13.28S 141.41E
Archers Post Kenya 79 0.42N 37.40E
Archiac France 20 45.31N 0.18W
Archidona Spain 27 37.05N 4.23W
Arcidosso Italy 30 42.52N 11.33E
Arcis-sur-Aube France 19 48.32N 4.08E
Arckaringa r. Australia 92 27.56S 134.45E
Arco Italy 30 45.55N 10.53E
Arco U.S.A. 108 43.38N 113.18W
Arco de Baúlhe Portugal 26 41.29N 7.58W
Arcoona Australia 92 31.06S 137.19E
Arcos Brazil 126 20.12S 45.30W
Arcos Spain 27 36.45N 5.48W
Arcoverde Brazil 123 8.23S 37.00W
Arctic Bay town Canada 99 73.05N 85.20W
Arctic Ocean 128
Arctic Red r. Canada 98 67.26N 133.48W
Arctic Red River town Canada 98 67.27N 133.46W
Arda r. Greece 34 41.39N 26.29E

Ardabīl Iran 65 38.15N 48.18E
Ardahan Turkey 64 41.08N 42.41E
Årdalstangen Norway 41 61.14N 7.43E
Ardara France 19 46.17N 5.08E
Ardara Rep. of Ire. 15 51.58N 7.43W
Arç aş Şawwān r. Jordan 66 30.45N 37.15E
Ardbeg Canada 104 45.38N 80.05W
Ardèche d. France 21 44.40N 4.20E
Ardèche r. France 21 44.16N 4.39E
Ardee Rep. of Ire. 11 53.51N 6.33W
Ardennes mts. Belgium 16 50.10N 5.30E
Ardennes d. France 19 49.40N 4.40E
Ardennes, Canal des France 19 49.26N 4.02E
Ardestān Iran 65 33.22N 52.25E
Ardfert Rep. of Ire. 15 52.20N 9.48W
Ardila r. Portugal 27 38.09N 7.28W
Ardino Bulgaria 34 41.35N 25.08E
Ardlethan Australia 93 34.20S 146.53E
Ardmore Rep. of Ire. 15 51.58N 7.43W
Ardmore Okla. U.S.A. 111 34.10N 97.08W
Ardmore Penn. U.S.A. 115 40.01N 75.18W
Ardnamurchan, Pt. of U.K. 14 56.44N 6.14W
Ardrossan Australia 92 34.25S 137.55E
Ardrossan U.K. 14 55.38N 4.49W
Ards Pen. U.K. 15 54.30N 5.30W
Åre Sweden 40 63.25N 13.05E
Arecibo Puerto Rico 117 18.29N 66.44W
Areia Branca Brazil 123 4.56S 37.07W
Arena, Pt. U.S.A. 106 38.58N 123.44W
Arena, Punta c. Mexico 109 23.32N 109.30W
Arenas de San Pedro Spain 26 40.12N 5.05W
Arendal Norway 42 58.27N 8.48E
Arendsee Germany 38 52.53N 11.30E
Arenys de Mar Spain 25 41.35N 2.33E
Areópolis Greece 35 36.40N 22.22E
Arequipa Peru 122 16.25S 71.32W
Arès France 20 44.46N 1.08W
Arévalo Spain 26 41.04N 4.43W
Arezzo Italy 30 43.25N 11.53E
Arfak mtn. Indonesia 59 1.30S 133.50E
Arfará Greece 35 37.10N 23.03E
Arga r. Spain 25 42.18N 1.47W
Argalastí Greece 35 39.13N 23.13E
Argamasilla de Alba Spain 27 39.07N 3.06W
Arganda Spain 26 40.18N 3.26W
Argelès-Gazost France 20 43.01N 0.06W
Argelès-sur-Mer France 20 42.33N 3.01E
Argens r. France 21 43.24N 6.44E
Argenta Italy 30 44.37N 11.50E
Argentan France 18 48.45N 0.01W
Argentat France 20 45.06N 1.56E
Argentera Italy 30 44.24N 6.57E
Argentera mtn. Italy 30 44.10N 7.18E
Argenteuil France 19 48.57N 2.15E
Argentia Canada 103 47.18N 53.59W
Argentina S. America 125 36.00S 63.00W
Argentine Basin f. Atlantic Oc. 127 40.00S 40.00W
Argentino, L. Argentina 125 50.15S 72.25W
Argenton France 19 46.35N 1.31E
Argenton-Château France 18 47.00N 0.27W
Argentré France 18 48.05N 0.39W
Argentré du Plessis France 18 48.03N 1.08W
Argeş r. Romania 29 44.13N 26.22E
Arghandāb r. Afghan. 62 31.27N 64.23E
Argolikós Kólpos g. Greece 35 37.33N 22.45E
Argonne d. France 19 49.30N 5.00E
Árgos Greece 35 37.38N 22.43E
Argos Orestikón Greece 34 40.27N 21.26E
Arguello, Pt. U.S.A. 109 34.35N 120.39W
Argun r. Russian Fed. 53 53.30N 121.48E
Argungu Nigeria 77 12.45N 4.35E
Argyle U.S.A. 110 48.20N 96.49W
Ar Horqin Qi China 54 43.45N 120.00E
Århus Denmark 42 56.09N 10.13E
Ariah Park town Australia 93 34.20S 147.10E
Ariana Tunisia 32 36.52N 10.12E
Ariano Italy 33 41.09N 15.05E
Ariano nel Polesine Italy 30 44.56N 12.07E
Arica Chile 124 18.29S 70.20W
Arica Colombia 122 2.07S 71.46W
Arid, C. Australia 89 33.58S 123.05E
Aridhaía Greece 34 40.58N 22.03E
Ariège d. France 20 43.00N 1.30E
Ariège r. France 20 43.31N 1.25E
Ariesş r. Romania 37 46.26N 23.59E
Ārifwāla Pakistan 62 30.17N 73.04E
Arīhā Al Karak Jordan 67 31.25N 35.47E
Arīhā Al Quds Jordan 67 31.51N 35.27E
Arima Trinidad 122 10.38N 61.17W
Arinos r. Brazil 123 10.20S 57.35W
Aripuanã Brazil 122 9.10S 60.38W
Aripuanã r. Brazil 122 5.05S 60.30W
Ariquemes Brazil 122 9.56S 63.04W
Aris Namibia 80 22.48S 17.10E
Arisaig U.K. 14 56.55N 5.51W
'Arish, Wādī r. Egypt 66 31.09N 33.49E
Aristazabal I. Canada 100 52.40N 129.10W
Arivonimamo Madagascar 81 19.01S 47.15E
Ariza Spain 25 41.19N 2.03W
Arizgoiti Spain 26 43.11N 2.57W
Arizona d. U.S.A. 106 34.00N 112.00W
Årjäng Sweden 43 59.23N 12.08E
Arjeplog Sweden 40 66.00N 17.58E
Arjona Colombia 122 10.14N 75.22W
Arjona Spain 27 37.56N 4.03W
Arkadelphia U.S.A. 111 34.07N 93.04W
Arkaig, Loch U.K. 14 56.58N 5.08W
Arkansas d. U.S.A. 111 34.20N 92.00W
Arkansas r. U.S.A. 111 33.48N 91.04W
Arkansas City U.S.A. 111 37.04N 97.02W
Arkhángelos Greece 35 36.13N 28.07E
Arkhangel'sk Russian Fed. 44 64.32N 41.10E
Árki i. Greece 29 37.22N 26.45E
Arklow Rep. of Ire. 15 52.47N 6.10W
Arkösund Sweden 43 58.30N 16.56E
Arkport U.S.A. 114 42.24N 77.42W
Arkville U.S.A. 115 42.09N 74.37W

Arlanc France 20 45.25N 3.44E
Arlanza r. Spain 26 42.06N 4.09W
Arlanzón Spain 26 42.03N 4.17W
Arlberg Pass Austria 36 47.00N 10.05E
Arles France 21 43.40N 4.38E
Arlington Colo. U.S.A. 108 38.20N 103.19W
Arlington Oreg. U.S.A. 108 45.16N 120.13W
Arlington Tex. U.S.A. 111 32.44N 97.07W
Arlington Va. U.S.A. 114 38.52N 77.05W
Arlington Heights town U.S.A. 110 42.06N 88.00W
Arlon Belgium 16 49.41N 5.49E
Armada U.S.A. 114 42.51N 82.53W
Armadale Australia 89 32.10S 115.57E
Armagh U.K. 15 54.21N 6.41W
Armagh d. U.K. 15 54.16N 6.35W
Armançon r. France 19 47.57N 3.30E
Armavir Russian Fed. 45 44.59N 41.10E
Armenia Colombia 122 4.32N 75.40W
Armenia Europe 65 40.00N 45.00E
Armeniş Romania 37 45.12N 22.19E
Armenistís i. Greece 35 37.36N 26.08E
Armentières France 19 50.41N 2.53E
Armidale Australia 93 30.32S 151.40E
Armori India 63 20.28N 79.59E
Armstrong Canada 100 50.25N 119.10W
Armstrong U.S.A. 111 26.55N 97.47W
Ärmür India 63 18.48N 78.17E
Arnaía Greece 34 40.29N 23.35E
Arnaud r. Canada 99 60.00N 69.45W
Arnay-le-Duc France 19 47.08N 4.29E
Arnedo Spain 26 42.13N 2.06W
Årnes Norway 42 60.09N 11.28E
Arnett U.S.A. 111 36.08N 99.46W
Arnhem Neth. 16 52.00N 5.55E
Arnhem B. Australia 90 12.20S 136.12E
Arnhem, C. Australia 90 12.10S 137.00E
Arnhem Land f. Australia 90 13.10S 134.30E
Árnissa Greece 34 40.47N 21.49E
Arno r. Italy 30 43.41N 10.17E
Arno Bay town Australia 92 33.54S 136.34E
Arnon r. France 19 47.12N 2.03E
Arnot Canada 101 55.46N 96.41W
Årnotfors Sweden 43 59.46N 12.22E
Arnprior Canada 105 45.26N 76.21W
Arnsberg Germany 38 51.24N 8.03E
Arnstadt Germany 38 50.50N 10.57E
Arolsen Germany 38 51.23N 9.01E
Aroma Sudan 72 15.49N 36.08E
Aron r. France 19 47.15N 2.02E
Arona Italy 30 45.46N 8.34E
Arorangi Rarotonga Cook Is. 84 21.13S 159.49W
Arosa Switz. 39 46.47N 9.41E
Arosa, Ría de est. Spain 26 42.28N 8.57W
Arpajon France 19 48.35N 2.15E
Arpino Italy 32 41.40N 13.35E
Arra Côte d'Ivoire 76 6.42N 3.57W
Ar Rabbah Jordan 67 31.16N 35.44E
Ar Rafid Syria 67 32.57N 35.53E
Arrah India 63 25.34N 84.40E
Ar Rahad Sudan 73 12.43N 30.39E
Ar Ramādī Iraq 64 33.27N 43.19E
Ar Ramthā Jordan 67 32.34N 36.00E
Arran i. U.K. 14 55.35N 5.14W
Ar Rank Sudan 73 11.45N 32.48E
Ar Raqqah Syria 64 35.57N 39.03E
Arras France 19 50.17N 2.47E
Ar Rass Saudi Arabia 64 25.54N 43.30E
Ar Rastān Syria 66 34.55N 36.44E
Arrats r. France 20 44.06N 0.52E
Arrecife Canary Is. 74 28.57N 13.32W
Arrecifes Argentina 125 34.05S 60.05W
Arrée, Monts d' mts. France 18 48.26N 3.55W
Arrey U.S.A. 109 32.51N 107.19W
Ar Riyāḍ Saudi Arabia 65 24.39N 46.44E
Arrochar U.K. 14 56.12N 4.44W
Arromanches France 18 49.20N 0.38W
Arronches Portugal 27 39.07N 7.17W
Arros r. France 20 43.40N 0.02W
Arroux r. France 19 46.29N 3.58E
Arrow, Lough Rep. of Ire. 15 54.03N 8.20W
Arrowsmith, Pt. Australia 90 13.18S 136.24E
Arrowtown New Zealand 86 44.56S 168.50E
Arroyo de la Luz Spain 27 39.29N 6.35W
Arroyo Feliciano r. Argentina 125 31.06S 59.53W
Arroyo Villimanca r. Argentina 125 35.36S 59.05W
Ar Ru'at Sudan 73 12.21N 32.17E
Ar Rub' al Khālī des. Saudi Arabia 60 20.20N 52.30E
Ar Rumaythah Iraq 65 31.32N 45.12E
Ar Rummān Jordan 67 32.10N 35.50E
Ar Ruşayriş Sudan 73 11.51N 34.23E
Ar Ruţbah Iraq 64 33.40N 39.59E
Ar Ruwaydah Saudi Arabia 65 23.46N 44.46E
Års Denmark 42 56.48N 9.32E
Ars-en-Ré France 20 46.12N 1.31W
Ārsī d. Ethiopia 73 7.50N 39.50E
Ársos Cyprus 66 34.50N 32.46E
Árta Greece 35 39.09N 20.59E
Artá Spain 25 39.42N 3.21E
Artemón Greece 35 36.59N 24.43E
Artemovsk Ukraine 45 48.35N 38.00E
Artenay France 19 48.05N 1.53E
Artesia U.S.A. 109 32.51N 104.24W
Arthabaska Canada 105 46.02N 71.55W
Arthal Jammu & Kashmir 62 33.16N 76.11E
Arthington Liberia 76 6.35N 10.45W
Arthur Canada 104 43.50N 80.32W
Arthur's Pass New Zealand 86 42.50S 171.45E
Artigas Uruguay 125 30.25S 56.28W
Artillery L. Canada 101 63.09N 107.52W
Artois f. France 16 50.16N 2.50E
Artux China 52 39.40N 75.49E
Artvin Turkey 64 41.12N 41.48E
Arua Uganda 79 3.02N 30.56E
Aruaddin Eritrea 72 16.16N 38.46E
Aruanã Brazil 123 14.54S 51.05W
Aruba i. South America 117 12.30N 70.00W
Arucas Canary Is. 127 28.08N 15.32W

Aru, Kepulauan is. Indonesia 59 6.00S 134.30E
Arun r. U.K. 11 50.48N 0.32W
Arunachal Pradesh d. India 61 28.40N 94.60E
Arundel Canada 105 45.58N 74.37W
Arusha Tanzania 79 3.21S 36.40E
Arusha d. Tanzania 79 4.00S 37.00E
Aruwimi r. Zaïre 78 1.20N 23.36E
Arvada Colo. U.S.A. 108 39.50N 105.05W
Arvada Wyo. U.S.A. 108 44.39N 105.05W
Arvagh Rep. of Ire. 15 53.56N 7.35W
Arve r. France 21 46.12N 6.08E
Arvi India 63 20.59N 78.14E
Arvidsjaur Sweden 40 65.35N 19.07E
Arvika Sweden 43 59.39N 12.35E
Arzachena Italy 32 41.05N 9.22E
Arzamas Russian Fed. 44 55.24N 43.48E
Arzgir Russian Fed. 45 45.24N 44.04E
Arzignano Italy 30 45.31N 11.20E
Arzúa Spain 26 42.56N 8.09W
Ås Norway 42 59.40N 10.48E
Asaba Nigeria 77 6.12N 6.44E
Asadābād Afghan. 62 34.52N 71.09E
Asahi dake mtn. Japan 57 43.42N 142.54E
Asahikawa Japan 57 43.46N 142.23E
Asansol India 63 23.41N 86.59E
Åsarna Sweden 40 62.40N 14.20E
Asarum Sweden 43 56.12N 14.50E
Āsayita Ethiopia 73 11.33N 41.30E
Asbest Russian Fed. 9 57.05N 61.30E
Asbestos Canada 105 45.46N 71.57W
Asbury Park U.S.A. 115 40.13N 74.01W
Ascension i. Atlantic Oc. 127 7.57S 14.22W
Aschaffenburg Germany 39 49.59N 9.09E
Aschendorf Germany 38 53.04N 7.22E
Aschersleben Germany 38 51.45N 11.27E
Asciano Italy 30 43.14N 11.33E
Ascoli Piceno Italy 31 42.51N 13.34E
Ascoli Satriano Italy 33 41.12N 15.34E
Ascona Switz. 39 46.09N 8.46E
Åseb Eritrea 73 13.01N 42.47E
Åseda Sweden 43 57.10N 15.20E
Asedjrad Algeria 75 24.42N 1.40E
Åsela Ethiopia 73 7.58N 39.08E
Åsele Sweden 40 64.10N 17.20E
Åsenbruk Sweden 43 58.48N 12.25E
Asenovgrad Bulgaria 34 42.01N 24.51E
Åseral Norway 42 58.37N 7.25E
Asfeld France 19 49.27N 4.05E
Asha Nigeria 77 7.07N 3.43E
Ashanti d. Ghana 76 6.30N 1.30W
Ashaway U.S.A. 115 41.25N 71.47W
Ashbourne Rep. of Ire. 15 53.31N 6.25W
Ashburn U.S.A. 113 31.42N 83.41W
Ashburton r. Australia 88 21.15S 115.00E
Ashburton New Zealand 86 43.54S 171.46E
Ashby de la Zouch U.K. 13 52.45N 1.29W
Ashcroft Canada 100 50.40N 121.20W
Ashdod Israel 67 31.48N 34.38E
Asheboro U.S.A. 113 35.42N 79.50W
Ashern Canada 101 51.11N 98.21W
Asheville U.S.A. 113 35.35N 82.35W
Ashewat Pakistan 62 31.22N 68.32E
Ash Flat town U.S.A. 111 36.12N 91.38W
Ashford Australia 93 29.19S 151.07E
Ashford Kent U.K. 13 51.08N 0.53E
Ash Fork U.S.A. 109 35.13N 112.29W
Ashghabat see Ashkhabad Turkmenistan 65
Ashikaga Japan 57 36.21N 139.26E
Ashington U.K. 12 55.11N 1.34W
Ashiya Japan 57 34.43N 135.17E
Ashizuri zaki c. Japan 57 32.45N 133.05E
Ashkhabad Turkmenistan 65 37.58N 58.24E
Ashland Ky. U.S.A. 114 38.29N 82.39W
Ashland N.H. U.S.A. 105 43.42N 71.38W
Ashland Ohio U.S.A. 114 40.52N 82.19W
Ashland Oreg. U.S.A. 108 42.12N 122.42W
Ashland Wisc. U.S.A. 110 46.35N 90.53W
Ashley Australia 93 29.19S 149.52E
Ashley U.S.A. 110 38.20N 89.10W
Ashley Snow I. Antarctica 128 72.30S 77.00W
Ashmün Egypt 66 30.18N 30.59E
Ashoknagar India 63 24.34N 77.43E
Ashqelon Israel 67 31.40N 34.35E
Ash Shabb well Egypt 72 22.19N 29.46E
Ash Shāghür Jordan 67 31.50N 35.39E
Ash Shajarah Jordan 67 32.39N 35.56E
Ash Shallūfah Egypt 66 30.07N 32.34E
Ash Shāmah des. Saudi Arabia 64 31.20N 38.00E
Ash Shamāliyah d. Sudan 72 19.30N 29.50E
Ash Shāmiyah des. Iraq 65 30.30N 45.30E
Ash Shāriqah U.A.E. 65 25.20N 55.26E
Ash Sharmah Saudi Arabia 66 28.01N 35.14E
Ash Shawbak Jordan 66 30.34N 35.35E
Ash Shaykh Faḍl Egypt 66 28.29N 30.50E
Ash Shaykh 'Ibādah Egypt 66 27.48N 30.52E
Ash Shaykh Miskīn Syria 67 32.49N 36.09E
Ash Shiḥr Yemen 71 14.45N 49.36E
Ash Shu'aybah Egypt 66 30.30N 47.40E
Ash Shu'aybah Saudi Arabia 64 27.53N 42.43E
Ash Shumlül Saudi Arabia 65 26.29N 47.20E
Ashta India 62 23.01N 76.43E
Ashtabula U.S.A. 114 41.52N 80.48W
Ashton R.S.A. 80 33.49S 20.04E
Ashton U.S.A. 108 44.04N 111.27W
'Āsi r. Lebanon 66 34.37N 36.30E
Asiago Italy 32 45.52N 11.30E
Asilah Morocco 74 35.32N 6.00W
Asinara i. Italy 32 41.05N 8.18E
Asinara, Golfo dell' g. Italy 32 41.00N 8.30E
'Asīr f. Saudi Arabia 71 19.00N 42.00E
Aska India 63 19.36N 84.39E
Askeaton Rep. of Ire. 15 52.36N 9.00W
Asker Norway 42 59.50N 10.26E
Askersund Sweden 43 58.53N 14.54E
Askim Norway 42 59.35N 11.10E
Askvoll Norway 41 61.21N 5.04E
Asmara see Åsmera Eritrea 72
Åsmera Eritrea 72 15.20N 38.58E

Asnaes Denmark 42 55.49N 11.31E
Åsnen I. Sweden 43 56.38N 14.42E
Asola Italy 32 45.13N 10.24E
Åsosa Ethiopia 73 10.03N 34.32E
Asoteriba, Jabal mtn. Sudan 72 21.51N 36.30E
Aspe Spain 25 38.21N 0.46W
Aspe, Gave d' r. France 20 43.15N 0.29W
Aspen U.S.A. 108 39.11N 106.49W
Aspermont U.S.A. 111 33.08N 100.14W
Aspiring, Mt. New Zealand 86 44.20S 168.45E
Aspres-sur-Buëch France 21 44.31N 5.45E
Asquith Canada 101 52.08N 107.13W
Assaba d. Mauritania 74 16.40N 11.40W
As Sadd al 'Ālī dam Egypt 72 23.59N 32.54E
Aş Şaff Egypt 66 29.34N 31.17E
As Saffānīyah Saudi Arabia 65 28.00N 48.48E
Aş Şa'īd f. Egypt 66 25.30N 32.00E
Aş Şāliḥīyah Egypt 66 30.47N 31.59E
As Sallüm Egypt 64 31.31N 25.09E
As Salt Jordan 67 32.03N 35.44E
As Salwa Saudi Arabia 65 24.44N 50.50E
As Sāmirah r. Egypt 72 32.15N 35.15E
As Samū' Jordan 67 31.24N 35.04E
As Sanām f. Saudi Arabia 71 22.00N 51.10E
Aş Şanamayn Syria 67 33.05N 36.10E
Aş Şarafand Lebanon 66 33.27N 35.18E
Aş Şarīḥ Jordan 67 32.30N 35.54E
As Saririyah Egypt 66 28.20N 30.45E
Assebroek Belgium 16 51.11N 3.16E
Assen Neth. 16 53.00N 6.34E
Assens Denmark 42 55.16N 9.55E
As Simākīyah Jordan 67 31.18N 35.48E
As Sinbillāwayn Egypt 66 30.53N 31.27E
Assiniboia Canada 101 49.38N 105.59W
Assiniboine r. Canada 101 49.53N 97.08W
Assinica Prov. Park Canada 102 50.24N 75.00W
Assis Brazil 126 22.37S 50.25W
Assisi Italy 30 43.04N 12.37E
As Sudd Sudan 73 7.50N 30.00E
Aş Şufayyah Sudan 73 15.30N 34.42E
As Sukhnah Jordan 67 32.08N 36.04E
As Sulaymānīyah Iraq 65 35.32N 45.27E
As Sulaymānīyah Saudi Arabia 65 24.10N 47.20E
As Sulayyil Saudi Arabia 71 20.27N 45.34E
As Sulţān Libya 75 31.07N 17.09E
As Sumayh Sudan 73 9.49N 27.39E
Aş Şummān f. Saudi Arabia 65 27.00N 47.00E
As Süq Saudi Arabia 72 21.55N 42.02E
As Suwaydā' Syria 66 32.43N 36.33E
As Suways Egypt 66 29.59N 32.33E
Astaffort France 20 44.04N 0.40E
Astakós Greece 35 38.32N 21.05E
Asti Italy 30 44.54N 8.13E
Astillero Spain 26 43.24N 3.49W
Astipálaia Greece 35 36.32N 26.22E
Astipálaia i. Greece 35 36.35N 26.25E
Astorga Spain 26 42.27N 6.03W
Astoria U.S.A. 108 46.11N 123.50W
Åstorp Sweden 43 56.08N 12.57E
Astrakhan Russian Fed. 45 46.22N 48.00E
Åsträsk Sweden 40 64.38N 20.00E
Astudillo Spain 26 42.12N 4.18W
Asturias d. Spain 26 43.20N 6.10W
Asturias d. Spain 26 43.20N 6.10W
Asunción Paraguay 126 25.15S 57.40W
Åsunden I. Sweden 43 57.58N 15.50E
'Āşūr, Tall mtn. Jordan 67 31.59N 35.17E
Aswān Egypt 64 24.05N 32.56E
Aswan High Dam see As Sadd al 'Ālī Egypt 64
Asyūţ Egypt 64 27.14N 31.07E
Atacama Desert see Atacama, Desierto des. S. America 124
Atacama, Desierto des. S. America 124 20.00S 69.00W
Atacama, Salar de f. Chile 124 23.30S 68.46W
Atafu Pacific Oc. 84 8.40S 172.40W
Atakpamé Togo 77 7.34N 1.14E
Ataléndi Greece 35 38.39N 22.58E
Atami Japan 57 35.05N 139.04E
Atapupu Indonesia 59 9.00S 124.51E
Atar Mauritania 74 20.32N 13.08W
Atara Russian Fed. 51 63.10N 129.10E
'Aţārüt Jordan 67 31.52N 35.13E
'Aţbarah Sudan 72 17.42N 33.59E
'Aţbarah r. Sudan 72 17.40N 33.58E
Atbasar Kazakhstan 9 51.49N 68.18E
Atchafalaya B. U.S.A. 111 29.25N 91.20W
Atchison U.S.A. 110 39.34N 95.07W
Ateca Spain 25 41.20N 1.47W
Aterno r. Italy 31 42.11N 13.51E
Ath Belgium 16 50.38N 3.45E
Athabasca Canada 100 54.45N 113.20W
Athabasca r. Canada 101 58.40N 110.50W
Athabasca, L. Canada 101 59.07N 110.00W
Athea Rep. of Ire. 15 52.28N 9.19W
Athenry Rep. of Ire. 15 53.18N 8.45W
Athens see Athínai Greece 35
Athens Ga. U.S.A. 113 33.57N 83.24W
Athens Ohio U.S.A. 114 39.20N 82.06W
Athens Penn. U.S.A. 115 41.57N 76.31W
Athens Tenn. U.S.A. 113 35.27N 84.38W
Athens Tex. U.S.A. 111 32.12N 95.51W
Atherley Canada 104 44.36N 79.22W
Atherton Australia 90 17.15S 145.29E
Athínai Greece 35 38.00N 23.44E
Athlone Rep. of Ire. 15 53.26N 7.57W
Athol U.S.A. 115 42.36N 72.14W
Atholl, Forest of U.K. 14 56.50N 3.55W
Áthos mtn. Greece 34 40.09N 24.19E
Ath Thamad Jordan 67 31.10N 35.43E
Ath Thaniyah Jordan 67 31.10N 35.43E
Ati Chad 77 13.11N 18.20E

Atico Peru 122 16.12S 73.37W
Atienza Spain 26 41.12N 2.52W
Atikonak L. Canada 103 52.40N 64.30W
Atimaono Tahiti 85 17.46S 149.28W
Atkarsk Russian Fed. 45 51.55N 45.00E
Atkinson U.S.A. 113 34.33N 78.12W
Atlanta Ga. U.S.A. 113 33.45N 84.23W
Atlanta Mich. U.S.A. 104 45.00N 84.09W
Atlanta Tex. U.S.A. 111 33.07N 94.09W
Atlantic Iowa U.S.A. 110 41.24N 95.01W
Atlantic-Antarctic Ridge f. Atlantic Oc. 127 53.00S 0.00
Atlantic City U.S.A. 115 39.22N 74.26W
Atlantic-Indian-Antarctic Basin f. Atl.Oc./Ind.Oc. 49 59.00S 40.00E
Atlantic Ocean 127
Atlas Mts. Africa 22 33.00N 2.00W
Atlas Saharien mts. Algeria 75 34.00N 2.00E
Atlin Canada 100 59.26N 133.45W
Atlin L. Canada 100 59.26N 133.45W
'Atlit Israel 67 32.41N 34.56E
'Atlit site Israel 67 32.42N 34.56E
Atmore U.S.A. 111 31.02N 87.29W
Atnarko Canada 100 52.25N 126.00W
Atnosen Norway 41 61.44N 10.49E
Atoka U.S.A. 111 34.23N 96.08W
Atouat mtn. Laos 56 16.03N 107.17E
Atouguia Portugal 27 39.20N 9.20W
Åtrå Norway 42 59.59N 8.45E
Atrak r. Iran see Atrek r. Asia 65
Åtran r. Sweden 43 56.53N 12.30E
Atrato r. Colombia 122 6.15N 76.58W
Atrauli India 63 28.02N 78.17E
Atrek r. Asia 65 37.23N 54.00E
Atsugi Japan 57 35.27N 139.22E
Atsumi-hantō pen. Japan 57 34.40N 137.20E
Atsumi-wan b. Japan 57 34.45N 137.10E
Aţ Ţafilah Jordan 66 30.52N 35.36E
Aţ Ţā'if Saudi Arabia 72 21.15N 40.21E
At Tall Syria 66 33.36N 36.18E
Attapu Laos 56 14.51N 106.56E
Attar, Oued el wadi Algeria 75 33.23N 5.12E
Attaviros mtn. Greece 35 36.12N 27.52E
Attawapiskat r. Canada 102 53.00N 82.30W
Attawapiskat L. Canada 102 52.20N 88.00W
Aţ Ţayrīyah Egypt 66 30.39N 30.46E
Aţ Ţayyibah Jordan 67 31.57N 35.18E
Attendorn Germany 38 51.07N 7.54E
Attersee I. Austria 39 47.55N 13.33E
Attica N.Y. U.S.A. 114 42.52N 78.17W
Attica Ohio U.S.A. 114 41.04N 82.53W
Attigny France 19 49.29N 4.35E
Attikamagen L. Canada 103 55.00N 66.38W
'Attil Jordan 67 32.22N 35.04E
Attleboro U.S.A. 115 41.56N 71.17W
Attleborough U.K. 13 52.31N 1.01E
Attnang Austria 39 48.01N 13.43E
Aţ Ţubayq mts. Saudi Arabia 64 29.30N 37.15E
Aţ Ţunayb Jordan 67 31.48N 35.56E
Aţ Ţür Egypt 66 28.14N 33.36E
Aţ Ţür Jordan 67 31.47N 35.15E
At Tuwayrifah well Saudi Arabia 71 21.30N 49.35E
Atucha Argentina 125 33.58S 59.17W
Atuel r. Argentina 125 36.15S 66.55W
Atui I. Cook Is. 85 20.00S 158.07W
Atui, Uad wadi Mauritania 74 20.03N 15.35W
Atuona Îs. Marquises 85 9.48S 139.02W
Åtvidaberg Sweden 43 58.12N 16.00E
Atwater U.S.A. 108 37.21N 120.36W
Atwood U.S.A. 110 39.48N 101.03W
Atyrau Kazakhstan 45 47.08N 51.59E
Aubagne France 21 43.17N 5.34E
Aube d. France 19 48.15N 4.05E
Aube r. France 19 48.34N 3.43E
Aubenton France 19 49.50N 4.12E
Auberive France 19 47.47N 5.03E
Aubigny-sur-Nère France 19 47.29N 2.26E
Aubin France 20 44.32N 2.14E
Aubinadong r. Canada 104 46.51N 83.22W
Aubrac, Monts d' mts. France 20 44.40N 3.00E
Auburn Ala. U.S.A. 113 32.38N 85.38W
Auburn Calif. U.S.A. 108 38.54N 121.04W
Auburn Ind. U.S.A. 112 41.22N 85.02W
Auburn Maine U.S.A. 112 44.06N 70.14W
Auburn N.Y. U.S.A. 115 42.56N 76.34W
Auburn Wash. U.S.A. 108 47.18N 122.13W
Aubusson France 20 45.57N 2.11E
Auce Latvia 41 56.28N 22.53E
Auch France 20 43.40N 0.35E
Auchi Nigeria 77 7.05N 6.16E
Auchterarder U.K. 14 56.18N 3.43W
Auckland New Zealand 86 36.55S 174.45E
Auckland d. New Zealand 86 36.45S 174.45E
Auckland Is. Pacific Oc. 84 50.35S 166.00E
Aude d. France 20 43.05N 2.30E
Aude r. France 20 43.13N 3.14E
Auden Canada 102 50.17N 87.54W
Audenge France 20 44.41N 1.31W
Audierne France 18 48.01N 4.32W
Audincourt France 19 47.29N 6.50E
Audo Range mts. Ethiopia 73 6.30N 41.30E
Audubon U.S.A. 110 41.43N 94.55W
Aue Germany 38 50.35N 12.42E
Augathella Australia 90 25.48S 146.35E
Augrabies Falls f. R.S.A. 80 28.33S 20.27E
Au Gres U.S.A. 104 44.03N 83.42W
Augsburg Germany 39 48.23N 10.53E
Augusta Australia 89 34.19S 115.09E
Augusta Italy 33 37.13N 15.13E
Augusta Ga. U.S.A. 113 33.29N 82.00W
Augusta Ill. U.S.A. 110 40.14N 90.56W
Augusta Kans. U.S.A. 111 37.41N 96.58W
Augusta Maine U.S.A. 112 44.19N 69.47W
Augusta, Golfo di g. Italy 33 37.10N 15.20E
Augustín Codazzi Colombia 122 10.01N 73.10W
Augustów Poland 37 53.51N 22.59E
Augustus, Mt. Australia 88 24.20S 116.49E
Aulis site Greece 35 38.27N 23.35E

Aulla Italy 30 44.12N 9.58E
Aulnay France 20 46.01N 0.21W
Aulne r. France 18 48.17N 4.16W
Aulnoye-Aymeries France 19 50.12N 3.50E
Ault France 18 50.06N 1.27E
Ault U.S.A. 108 40.35N 104.44W
Aumale France 19 49.46N 1.45E
Aumont-Aubrac France 20 44.43N 3.17E
Auna Nigeria 77 10.11N 4.46E
Auneau France 19 48.27N 1.46E
Auning Denmark 42 56.26N 10.23E
Aura Finland 41 60.36N 22.34E
Auraiya India 63 26.28N 79.31E
Aurangābād Bihār India 63 24.45N 84.22E
Aurangābād Mahār India 62 19.53N 75.20E
Auray France 18 47.40N 2.59W
Aurdal Norway 41 60.56N 9.24E
Aure Norway 40 63.16N 8.34E
Aurich Germany 38 53.28N 7.29E
Aurillac France 20 44.56N 2.26E
Aurora Canada 104 44.00N 79.28W
Aurora Colo. U.S.A. 108 39.44N 104.52W
Aurora Ill. U.S.A. 110 41.45N 88.20W
Aurora Mo. U.S.A. 111 36.58N 93.43W
Aursunden l. Norway 40 62.37N 11.40E
Aurukun Australia 90 13.20S 141.42E
Aus Namibia 80 26.41S 16.14E
Au Sable r. U.S.A. 104 44.25N 83.20W
Au Sable Forks U.S.A. 105 44.27N 73.41W
Aust-Agder d. Norway 42 58.50N 7.50E
Austin Minn. U.S.A. 110 43.40N 92.59W
Austin Nev. U.S.A. 108 39.30N 117.04W
Austin Penn. U.S.A. 114 41.38N 78.05W
Austin Tex. U.S.A. 111 30.16N 97.45W
Austin, L. Australia 88 27.40S 118.00E
Austral Downs town Australia 90 20.28S 137.55E
Australia Austa. 87
Australian Alps mts. Australia 91 36.30S 148.30E
Australian Antarctic Territory Antarctica 128 73.00S 90.00E
Australian Capital Territory d. Australia 93 35.30S 149.00E
Austral Ridge Pacific Oc. 85 24.00S 148.00W
Austria Europe 39 47.20N 12.30E
Austvågøy i. Norway 40 68.20N 14.40E
Authie r. France 19 50.21N 1.38E
Autun France 19 46.57N 4.18E
Auvergne d. France 20 45.25N 2.30E
Auvézère r. France 20 45.12N 0.51E
Aux Barques, Pointe c. U.S.A. 104 44.04N 82.58W
Auxerre France 19 47.48N 3.34E
Auxi-le-Château France 19 50.14N 2.07E
Auxonne France 19 47.12N 5.23E
Aux Sables r. Canada 104 46.13N 82.04W
Auzances France 20 46.02N 2.30E
Ava Myanmar 56 21.49N 95.57E
Avaldsnes Norway 42 59.21N 5.16E
Avallon France 19 47.29N 3.54E
Avaloirs, Les hills France 18 48.28N 0.07W
Avalon U.S.A. 115 39.06N 74.43W
Avalon Pen. Canada 103 47.00N 53.15W
Avanos Turkey 64 38.44N 34.51E
Avaré Brazil 126 23.06S 48.57W
Avarua Rarotonga Cook Is. 84 21.12S 159.46W
Ávas Greece 34 40.57N 25.56E
Avatele Niue 84 19.06S 169.54W
Avatele B. Niue 84 19.05S 169.56W
Avatiu Rarotonga Cook Is. 84 21.12S 159.47W
Ave r. Portugal 26 41.20N 8.45W
Aveiro Portugal 26 40.38N 8.39W
Aveiro d. Portugal 26 40.50N 8.35W
Aveiro, Ria de est. Portugal 26 40.38N 8.44W
Avellaneda Argentina 125 34.40S 58.20W
Avellino Italy 33 40.54N 14.47E
Aversa Italy 33 40.58N 14.12E
Avery U.S.A. 108 47.15N 115.49W
Avesnes France 19 50.07N 3.56E
Avesta Sweden 43 60.09N 16.12E
Aveyron d. France 20 44.15N 2.40E
Aveyron r. France 20 44.05N 1.16E
Avezzano Italy 31 42.02N 13.25E
Aviemore U.K. 14 57.12N 3.50W
Avigliano Italy 33 40.44N 15.44E
Avignon France 21 43.57N 4.49E
Ávila Spain 26 40.39N 4.42W
Ávila d. Spain 26 40.35N 5.00W
Ávila, Sierra de mts. Spain 26 40.35N 5.00W
Avilés Spain 26 43.33N 5.55W
Avis U.S.A. 114 41.11N 77.19W
Aviz Portugal 27 39.03N 7.53W
Avium Denmark 42 56.16N 8.48E
Avoca r. Australia 92 35.56S 143.44E
Avoca Vic. Australia 92 37.04S 143.29E
Avola Canada 100 51.45N 119.19W
Avola Italy 33 36.54N 15.09E
Avon r. Australia 89 31.40S 116.07E
Avon d. U.K. 13 51.35N 2.40W
Avon r.Avon U.K. 13 51.59N 2.10W
Avon r. Dorset U.K. 13 50.43N 1.45W
Avon r. Glos. U.K. 13 52.00N 2.10W
Avon U.S.A. 114 42.55N 77.45W
Avon Downs town Australia 90 20.05S 137.30E
Avonmouth U.K. 13 51.30N 2.42W
Avon Park town U.S.A. 113 27.36N 81.30W
Avranches France 18 48.41N 1.22W
Avre r. France 19 49.53N 2.20E
Awal Edo Ethiopia 73 4.14N 40.39E
Awara Ethiopia 73 5.30N 40.00E
Āwarē Ethiopia 71 8.15N 44.10E
'Awartā Jordan 67 32.10N 35.17E
Awasa Hāyk' l. Ethiopia 73 7.05N 38.25E
Āwash r. Ethiopia 73 11.45N 41.05E
Awa shima i. Japan 57 38.30N 139.20E
Awaso Ghana 76 6.20N 2.22W
Awat China 52 40.38N 80.22E
Awbārī Libya 75 26.35N 12.46E
Awbārī d. Libya 75 25.10N 12.45E
Awbārī, Şaḩrā' des. Libya 75 27.30N 11.30E

Awdah, Hawr al l. Iraq 65 31.36N 46.53E
Awe, Loch U.K. 14 56.18N 5.24W
'Awjā', Wādī al Jordan 67 31.56N 35.31E
Axarfjördhur est. Iceland 40 66.10N 16.30W
Axat France 20 42.48N 2.14E
Axel Heiberg I. Canada 99 79.30N 90.00W
Axim Ghana 76 4.53N 2.14W
Axiós r. Greece 34 40.35N 22.50E
Ax-les-Thermes France 20 42.43N 1.50E
Axminster U.K. 13 50.47N 3.01W
Ayabaca Peru 122 4.40S 79.53W
Ayachi, Ari n' mtn. Morocco 74 32.29N 4.57W
Ayacucho Argentina 125 37.10S 58.30W
Ayacucho Peru 122 13.10S 74.15W
Ayaguz Kazakhstan 52 47.59N 80.27E
Ayamonte Spain 27 37.13N 7.24W
Ayan Russian Fed. 51 56.29N 138.00E
'Aybāl, Jabal mtn. Jordan 67 32.14N 35.16E
Aydin Turkey 64 37.52N 27.50E
Ayelu mtn. Ethiopia 73 10.04N 40.46E
Ayer U.S.A. 115 42.34N 71.35W
Ayers Cliff town Canada 105 45.10N 72.03W
Ayers Rock see Uluru Australia 90
Ayiá Greece 34 39.43N 22.45E
Ayiá Ánna Greece 35 38.52N 23.24E
Ayiá Marína Greece 35 37.11N 26.46E
Ayiá Paraskeví Greece 35 39.14N 26.16E
Áyion Óros f. Greece 34 40.15N 24.15E
Áyios Andréas Greece 35 37.21N 22.45E
Áyios Evstrátios l. Greece 34 39.34N 24.58E
Áyios Kírikos Greece 35 37.37N 26.14E
Áyios Matthaíos Greece 34 39.30N 19.47E
Áyios Nikólaos Greece 35 35.11N 25.42E
Aylássos Greece 35 39.05N 26.23E
Aylen L. Canada 105 45.37N 77.52W
Aylesbury U.K. 13 51.48N 0.49W
Aylmer Ont. Canada 104 42.47N 80.58W
Aylmer Que. Canada 105 45.23N 75.51W
Aylmer L. Canada 98 64.05N 108.30W
Aylmer, L. Que. Canada 105 45.50N 71.22W
Aylsham U.K. 12 52.48N 1.16E
'Ayn Dāllah well Egypt 64 27.19N 27.20E
'Ayn, Wādī al r. Oman 65 22.18N 55.35E
Ayod Sudan 73 8.07N 31.26E
Ayom Sudan 73 7.52N 28.23E
Ayon, Ostrov i. Russian Fed. 51 70.00N 169.00E
Ayora Spain 25 39.04N 1.03W
Ayos Cameroon 77 3.55N 12.30E
'Ayoûn el' Atroûs Mauritania 74 16.40N 9.37W
Ayr Australia 90 19.35S 147.24E
Ayr Canada 104 43.17N 80.27W
Ayr U.K. 14 55.28N 4.37W
Ayr r. U.K. 14 55.28N 4.38W
Ayre, Pt. of I.o.M. Europe 12 54.25N 4.22W
Ayrolle, Etang de L' l. France 20 43.05N 3.03E
Aysha Ethiopia 73 10.46N 42.37E
Ayutthaya Thailand 56 14.20N 100.40E
Ayvacik Turkey 34 39.36N 26.23E
Ayvalik Turkey 29 39.19N 26.42E
Azalia Spain 25 41.17N 0.29W
Azambuja Portugal 27 39.04N 8.52W
Azamgarh India 63 26.04N 83.11E
Azao mtn. Algeria 75 25.12N 8.08E
Azaouâd des. Mali 76 18.00N 3.00W
Azaouak, Vallée de l' f. Mali 77 16.00N 3.40E
Azare Nigeria 77 11.40N 10.08E
Azay-le-Rideau France 18 47.16N 0.28E
Azbine mts. see Aïr mts. Niger 77
Azerbaijan Asia 65 40.10N 47.50E
Azogues Ecuador 122 2.35S 78.00W
Azopolye Russian Fed. 44 65.15N 45.18E
Azor Israel 67 32.01N 34.48E
Azores is. see Açores, Arquipélago dos is. Atlantic Oc. 127
Azoum r. Chad 73 10.53N 20.15E
Azov, Sea of Ukraine/Russian Fed. 45 46.00N 36.30E
Azovskoye More sea see Azov, Sea of Ukraine/Russian Fed. 45
Azpeitia Spain 26 43.11N 2.16W
Azraq, Al Baḥr al r. Sudan 72 15.38N 32.31E
Azrou Morocco 74 33.27N 5.14W
Aztec U.S.A. 109 32.48N 113.26W
Azua Dom. Rep. 117 18.29N 70.44W
Azuaga Spain 26 38.16N 5.41W
Azuer r. Spain 27 39.08N 3.36W
Azuero, Península de pen. Panama 117 7.30N 80.30W
Azul Argentina 125 36.46S 59.50W
'Azūm, Wādī r. Sudan see Azoum r. Chad 73
Azurduy Bolivia 124 19.59S 64.29W
Az Zāb al Kabīr r. Iraq 65 35.37N 43.20E
Az Zāb aş Şaghīr r. Iraq 65 35.15N 43.27E
Az Zabdānī Syria 66 33.43N 36.05E
Az Zāhirīyah Jordan 67 31.25N 34.58E
Az Zahrān Saudi Arabia 65 26.18N 50.08E
Az Zaqāziq Egypt 66 30.36N 31.30E
Az Zarqā' Jordan 67 32.05N 36.06E
Az Zarqā' r. Jordan 67 32.08N 35.32E
Az Zāwiyah d. Libya 75 32.40N 12.10E
Azzel Matti, Sebkha f. Algeria 74 26.00N 0.55E
Az Zilfi Saudi Arabia 65 26.15N 44.50E
Az Zrārīyah Lebanon 66 33.21N 35.20E

B

Baan Baa Australia 93 30.28S 149.58E

Baardheere Somali Rep. 79 2.18N 42.18E
Baargaal Somali Rep. 71 11.18N 51.07E
Baarle-Hertog Neth. 16 51.26N 4.56E
Baba Burnu c. Turkey 34 39.29N 26.02E
Babadag Romania 37 44.54N 28.43E
Babahoyo Ecuador 122 1.53S 79.31W
Babai Gaxun China 54 40.30N 104.43E
Babakin Australia 89 32.11S 117.58E
Babana Nigeria 77 10.26N 3.51E
Babanūsah Sudan 73 11.20N 27.48E
Babar, Kepulauan is. Indonesia 59 8.00S 129.30E
Babayevo Russian Fed. 44 59.24N 35.50E
B'abdā Lebanon 66 33.50N 35.31E
Babia Gora mtn. Slovakia/Poland 37 49.38N 19.38E
Babina India 63 25.15N 78.28E
Babina Greda Croatia 31 45.07N 18.33E
Babine L. Canada 100 54.48N 126.00W
Babo Indonesia 59 2.33S 133.25E
Bābol Iran 65 36.32N 52.42E
Baboua C.A.R. 77 5.49N 14.51E
Babuyan Channel Phil. 55 18.40N 121.30E
Babuyan Is. Phil. 59 19.20N 121.30E
Babylon ruins Iraq 65 32.33N 44.25E
Babylon U.S.A. 115 40.42N 73.20W
Bacabal Maranhão Brazil 123 4.15S 44.45W
Bacabal Para Brazil 123 5.20S 56.45W
Bacău Romania 37 46.32N 26.59E
Baccarat France 19 48.27N 6.45E
Bacchus Marsh town Australia 92 37.41S 144.27E
Bacharach Germany 39 50.04N 7.46E
Bacheli India 61 18.40N 81.16E
Bachelina Russian Fed. 50 57.45N 67.20E
Back r. Canada 99 66.37N 96.00W
Bačka Palanka Yugo. 31 45.15N 19.24E
Bačka Topola Yugo. 31 45.49N 19.38E
Backbone Mtn. U.S.A. 114 39.18N 79.25W
Bäckefors Sweden 43 58.48N 12.10E
Bački Petrovac Yugo. 31 45.22N 19.35E
Backnang Germany 39 48.56N 9.25E
Backstairs Passage str. Australia 92 35.42S 138.05E
Bac Lieu Vietnam 56 9.16N 105.45E
Bac Ninh Vietnam 56 21.10N 106.04E
Bacolod Phil. 59 10.38N 122.58E
Bac Phan f. Vietnam 56 22.00N 105.00E
Bac Quang Vietnam 55 22.30N 104.52E
Bácsalmás Hungary 31 46.08N 19.20E
Bács-Kiskun d. Hungary 31 46.30N 19.20E
Badagara India 60 11.36N 75.35E
Badajós, Lago l. Brazil 122 3.15S 62.47W
Badajoz Spain 27 38.53N 6.58W
Badajoz d. Spain 27 38.40N 6.10W
Badal Khān Goth Pakistan 62 26.31N 67.06E
Badalona Spain 25 41.27N 2.15E
Badanah Saudi Arabia 64 30.59N 41.02E
Bad Ausee Austria 39 47.36N 13.47E
Bad Axe U.S.A. 112 43.49N 82.59W
Bad Bergzabern Germany 39 49.07N 8.00E
Bad Blankenburg Germany 38 50.41N 11.16E
Bad Bramstedt Germany 38 53.55N 9.53E
Baddo r. Pakistan 62 28.15N 65.00E
Bad Doberan Germany 38 54.06N 11.53E
Bad Dürrenberg Germany 38 51.18N 12.04E
Badeggi Nigeria 77 9.04N 6.09E
Bad Ems Germany 39 50.20N 7.43E
Baden Austria 36 48.01N 16.14E
Baden Eritrea 72 17.00N 38.00E
Baden Switz. 39 47.29N 8.18E
Baden-Baden Germany 39 48.46N 8.14E
Badenweiler Germany 39 47.48N 7.40E
Baden-Württemberg d. Germany 39 48.15N 9.00E
Bad Freienwalde Germany 38 52.47N 14.01E
Badgastein Austria 39 47.07N 13.08E
Bad Godesberg Germany 38 50.41N 7.09E
Bad Hall Austria 39 48.02N 14.13E
Bad Harzburg Germany 38 51.53N 10.33E
Bad Hersfeld Germany 38 50.52N 9.42E
Bad Homburg Germany 39 50.13N 8.37E
Bad Honnef Germany 38 50.39N 7.13E
Badīn Pakistan 62 24.39N 68.50E
Bad Ischl Austria 39 47.43N 13.37E
Badiyah Oman 71 22.27N 58.48E
Bādiyat ash Shām des. Asia 64 32.00N 39.00E
Bad Kissingen Germany 39 50.12N 10.04E
Bad Kreuznach Germany 39 49.52N 7.51E
Bad Langensalza Germany 38 51.07N 10.40E
Bad Lauterberg Germany 38 51.38N 10.28E
Bad Mergentheim Germany 39 49.30N 9.46E
Bad Münstereifel Germany 38 50.33N 6.46E
Bad Nauheim Germany 39 50.22N 8.44E
Badnera India 63 20.52N 77.44E
Bad Neuenahr-Ahrweiler Germany 38 50.33N 7.08E
Bad Neustadt an der Saale Germany 39 50.19N 10.13E
Bad Oeynhausen Germany 38 52.12N 8.48E
Bad Oldesloe Germany 38 53.48N 10.22E
Badong China 55 31.02N 110.20E
Bad Orb Germany 39 50.14N 9.20E
Badou Togo 76 7.37N 0.37E
Badoumbé Mali 76 13.42N 10.09W
Bad Pyrmont Germany 38 51.59N 9.15E
Bad Ragaz Switz. 39 47.00N 9.30E
Bad Reichenhall Germany 39 47.43N 12.52E
Badrīnāth India 63 30.44N 79.29E
Bad Salzuflen Germany 38 52.05N 8.44E
Bad Salzungen Germany 38 50.48N 10.13E
Bad Sankt Leonhard im Lavanttal Austria 31 46.58N 14.48E
Bad Schwartau Germany 38 53.55N 10.40E
Bad Segeberg Germany 38 53.56N 10.17E
Bad Sülze Germany 38 54.06N 12.38E
Bad Tölz Germany 39 47.46N 11.34E
Badu I. Australia 90 10.07S 142.08E
Bad Waldsee Germany 39 47.55N 9.45E
Bad Wildungen Germany 38 51.07N 9.07E
Bad Wörishofen Germany 39 48.00N 10.36E
Baena Spain 27 37.37N 4.19W

Baerami Australia 93 32.23S 150.30E
Baeza Spain 27 37.59N 3.28W
Bafa Gölü l. Turkey 35 37.30N 27.29E
Bafang Cameroon 77 5.11N 10.12E
Bafatá Guinea Bissau 76 12.09N 14.38W
Baffin d. Canada 99 66.00N 72.00W
Baffin B. Canada 99 74.00N 70.00W
Baffin I. Canada 99 68.50N 70.00W
Bafia Cameroon 77 4.39N 11.14E
Bafing r. Mali 76 14.48N 12.10W
Bafoulabé Mali 76 13.49N 10.50W
Bāfq Iran 65 31.35N 55.21E
Bafra Turkey 64 41.34N 35.56E
Bafut Cameroon 77 6.06N 10.02E
Bafwasende Zaïre 79 1.09N 27.12E
Bagaha India 63 27.06N 84.05E
Bagamoyo Tanzania 79 6.26S 38.55E
Bağarasi Turkey 35 37.42N 27.33E
Bagasra India 62 21.29N 70.57E
Bagawi Sudan 73 12.19N 34.21E
Bagbele Zaïre 73 4.21N 29.17E
Bagdarin Russian Fed. 51 54.28N 113.38E
Bagé Brazil 126 31.22S 54.06W
Baggy Pt. U.K. 13 51.08N 4.15W
Baghdād Iraq 65 33.20N 44.26E
Bāgherhāt Bangla. 63 22.40N 89.48E
Bagheria Italy 32 38.05N 13.30E
Baghlān Afghan. 60 36.11N 68.44E
Baghrān Khowleh Afghan. 62 33.01N 64.58E
Bagnara Italy 33 38.18N 15.49E
Bagnères-de-Bigorre France 20 43.04N 0.09E
Bagnères-de-Luchon France 20 42.47N 0.36E
Bagni di Lucca Italy 30 44.01N 10.35E
Bagnols-sur-Cèze France 21 44.10N 4.37E
Bago see Pegu Myanmar 56
Bagodar India 63 24.05N 85.52E
Bagoé r. Mali 76 12.34N 6.30W
Bagolino Italy 30 45.49N 10.28E
Bagrationovsk Russian Fed. 37 54.26N 20.38E
Baguio Phil. 59 16.25N 120.37E
Bäh India 63 26.53N 78.36E
Bahamas C. America 113 24.15N 76.00W
Bahāwalnagar Pakistan 62 29.59N 73.16E
Bahāwalpur Pakistan 62 29.24N 71.41E
Baheri India 63 28.47N 79.30E
Bahi Tanzania 79 5.59S 35.15E
Bahía d. Brazil 123 12.30S 42.30W
Bahía Blanca Argentina 126 38.45S 62.15W
Bahía de Caráquez Ecuador 122 0.40S 80.25W
Bahía, Islas de la is. Honduras 117 16.10N 86.30W
Bahía Kino Mexico 109 28.50N 111.55W
Bahía Laura Argentina 125 48.18S 66.30W
Bahía Negra Paraguay 126 20.15S 58.12W
Bahir Dar Ethiopia 73 11.35N 37.28E
Bahraich India 63 27.35N 81.36E
Bahrain Asia 65 26.00N 50.35E
Baḩr al Ghazāl d. Sudan 73 8.00N 26.30E
Baḩr al Jabal r. Sudan 70 9.30N 18.10E
Bahrām Chāh Afghan. 62 29.26N 64.03E
Bahr Aouk r. C.A.R. 77 8.50N 18.50E
Bahr el Ghazal r. Chad 77 12.26N 15.25E
Bahr Salamat r. Chad 77 9.30N 18.10E
Bāhū Kalāt Iran 65 25.42N 61.28E
Baia-Mare Romania 37 47.40N 23.35E
Baião Brazil 123 2.41S 49.41W
Baia Sprie Romania 37 47.40N 23.42E
Baïbokoum Chad 77 7.46N 15.43E
Baicheng China 54 45.40N 122.52E
Baie Comeau Canada 103 49.13N 68.10W
Baie des Ha! Ha! town Canada 103 50.56N 58.58W
Baiersbronn Germany 39 48.30N 8.22E
Baies, Lac des l. Canada 105 47.18N 77.40W
Baie St. Paul town Canada 103 47.27N 70.30W
Baigneux-les-Juifs France 19 47.36N 4.38E
Baihar India 63 22.06N 80.33E
Baijnāth India 63 29.55N 79.37E
Baikunthapur India 63 23.15N 82.33E
Bailén Spain 27 38.05N 3.46W
Băileşti Romania 37 44.02N 23.21E
Bailleul France 19 50.44N 2.44E
Bailundo Angola 78 12.13S 15.46E
Baimuru P.N.G. 59 7.30S 144.49E
Bainang China 63 29.10N 89.15E
Bainbridge Ga. U.S.A. 113 30.54N 84.33W
Bainbridge N.Y. U.S.A. 115 42.18N 75.29W
Bain-de-Bretagne France 18 47.50N 1.41W
Baing Indonesia 88 10.15S 120.34E
Baingoin China 63 31.45N 89.50E
Bains-les-Bains France 19 48.00N 6.16E
Bāïr Jordan 66 30.46N 36.41E
Baird Mts. U.S.A. 98 67.35N 161.30W
Bairin Zuoqi China 54 43.59N 119.11E
Bairnsdale Australia 93 37.51S 147.38E
Bā'ir, Wādī r. Jordan 66 31.10N 36.55E
Bais France 18 48.15N 0.22W
Baïse r. France 20 44.07N 0.17E
Baisha China 55 19.13N 109.26E
Baiyang Dian l. China 54 38.55N 116.00E
Baiyin China 54 36.40N 104.15E
Baja Hungary 31 46.11N 18.57E
Baja California d. Mexico 109 29.45N 115.30W
Baja California pen. Mexico 109 28.40N 114.40W
Baja California Sur d. Mexico 109 26.00N 113.00W
Bajánsenye Hungary 31 46.48N 16.22E
Bajina Bašta Yugo. 31 43.58N 19.34E
Bajmok Yugo. 31 45.58N 19.25E
Bakal Russian Fed. 44 54.58N 58.45E
Bakali r. Zaïre 78 3.58S 17.10E
Bakel Senegal 76 14.54N 12.26W
Baker Calif. U.S.A. 109 35.16N 116.04W
Baker Mont. U.S.A. 108 46.22N 104.17W
Baker Oreg. U.S.A. 108 44.47N 117.50W
Baker I. U.S.A. 100 55.20N 133.36W
Baker Lake town Canada 99 64.20N 96.10W
Baker, Mt. U.S.A. 108 48.47N 121.49W
Bakersfield Calif. U.S.A. 109 35.23N 119.01W
Bakersfield Vt. U.S.A. 105 44.48N 72.42W
Bā Kêv Cambodia 56 13.42N 107.12E

Bākhtarān Iran 65 34.19N 47.04E
Bako Côte d'Ivoire 76 9.08N 7.40W
Bako Ethiopia 73 5.50N 36.40E
Bakony mts. Hungary 31 47.00N 17.50E
Bakouma C.A.R. 73 5.42N 22.47E
Baku Azerbaijan 65 40.22N 49.53E
Baky see Baku Azerbaijan 65
Bala Canada 104 45.01N 79.37W
Bal'ā Jordan 67 32.20N 35.07E
Bala Senegal 76 14.01N 13.08W
Bala U.K. 12 52.54N 3.36W
Balabac i. Phil. 58 7.57N 117.01E
Balabac Str. Malaysia/Phil. 58 7.30N 117.00E
Ba'labakk Lebanon 66 34.00N 36.12E
Bālāghāt India 63 21.48N 80.11E
Bālāghāt Range mts. India 62 19.00N 76.30E
Balaguer Spain 24 41.50N 0.50E
Balaka Malaŵi 79 15.00S 34.56E
Balaka Zaïre 78 4.51S 19.57E
Balaklava Australia 92 34.08S 138.24E
Balaklava Ukraine 45 44.31N 33.35E
Balakovo Russian Fed. 44 52.04N 47.46E
Bal'amā Jordan 67 32.14N 36.05E
Balama Mozambique 79 13.19S 38.35E
Bālā Morghāb Afghan. 65 35.34N 63.20E
Balāngīr India 63 20.43N 83.29E
Balaquer Spain 25 41.47N 0.49E
Balarāmpur India 63 23.07N 86.13E
Balashov Russian Fed. 45 51.30N 43.10E
Balasore India 63 21.30N 86.56E
Balassagyarmat Hungary 37 48.05N 19.18E
Balāt Egypt 64 25.33N 29.16E
Balazote Spain 26 38.53N 2.08W
Balboa Panama 117 8.37N 79.33W
Balbriggan Rep. of Ire. 15 53.36N 6.12W
Balcad Somali Rep. 71 2.22N 45.25E
Balcarce Argentina 125 37.52S 58.15W
Balchik Bulgaria 37 43.24N 28.10E
Balclutha New Zealand 86 46.16S 169.46E
Bald Eagle Mtn. U.S.A. 114 41.00N 77.45W
Baldock L. Canada 101 56.33N 97.57W
Baldwin Fla. U.S.A. 113 30.18N 81.59W
Baldwin Mich. U.S.A. 112 43.54N 85.50W
Baldwin Penn. U.S.A. 114 40.23N 79.58W
Baldwinsville U.S.A. 115 43.09N 76.20W
Baldy Mt. Canada 100 51.28N 120.02W
Balē Ethiopia 73 6.30N 40.45E
Bâle see Basel Switz. 39
Baleanoona Australia 92 30.33S 139.22E
Baleares d. Spain 25 39.00N 2.10E
Baleares, Islas is. Spain 25 39.20N 2.00E
Balearic Is. see Baleares, Islas is. Spain 25
Baleine, Grande rivière de la r. Canada 102 55.20N 77.40W
Baleine, Petite rivière de la r. Canada 102 56.00N 76.45W
Balfate Honduras 117 15.48N 86.25W
Balfour Downs town Australia 88 22.57S 120.46E
Balfouriyya Israel 67 32.38N 35.18E
Bali India 62 25.50N 74.05E
Bali d. Indonesia 59 8.45S 114.56E
Bali i. Indonesia 59 8.20S 115.07E
Balıkesir Turkey 29 39.38N 27.51E
Balīkh r. Syria 64 35.58N 39.05E
Balikpapan Indonesia 58 1.15S 116.50E
Bali, Laut sea Indonesia 59 7.30S 115.15E
Balingen Germany 39 48.16N 8.51E
Bali Sea see Bali, Laut Indonesia 59
Bali, Selat str. Indonesia 59 8.21S 114.30E
Balkan Mts. see Stara Planina mts. Bulgaria 34
Balkhash Kazakhstan 52 46.51N 75.00E
Balkhash, Ozero l. Kazakhstan 9 46.40N 75.00E
Ballachulish U.K. 14 56.40N 5.08W
Balladonia Australia 89 32.27S 123.51E
Ballālpur India 63 19.50N 79.22E
Ballandean Australia 93 28.39S 151.50E
Ballantrae U.K. 14 55.06N 5.01W
Ballarat Australia 92 37.36S 143.58E
Ballard, L. Australia 89 29.27S 120.55E
Ballater U.K. 14 57.03N 3.03W
Ballenas, Bahía de b. Mexico 109 26.45N 113.25W
Ballenas, Canal de str. Mexico 109 29.10N 113.30W
Balleny Is. Antarctica 128 66.30S 163.00E
Balleroy France 18 49.11N 0.50W
Ballia India 63 25.45N 84.10E
Ballina Australia 93 28.50S 153.37E
Ballina Rep. of Ire. 15 54.08N 9.10W
Ballinasloe Rep. of Ire. 15 53.20N 8.15W
Ballingeary Rep. of Ire. 15 51.50N 9.15W
Ballinger U.S.A. 111 31.44N 99.57W
Ball's Pyramid i. Pacific Oc. 84 31.45S 159.15E
Ballybay Rep. of Ire. 15 54.08N 6.56W
Ballycastle U.K. 15 55.12N 6.15W
Ballyclare U.K. 15 54.45N 6.00W
Ballyconnell Rep. of Ire. 15 54.06N 7.37W
Ballydehob Rep. of Ire. 15 51.34N 9.28W
Ballydonegan Rep. of Ire. 15 51.38N 10.04W
Ballygar Rep. of Ire. 15 53.32N 8.20W
Ballygawley U.K. 15 54.28N 7.03W
Ballykelly U.K. 15 55.03N 7.00W
Ballymena U.K. 15 54.52N 6.17W
Ballymoney U.K. 15 55.04N 6.31W
Ballyquintin Pt. U.K. 15 54.40N 5.30W
Ballyragget Rep. of Ire. 15 52.47N 7.21W
Ballyshannon Rep. of Ire. 15 54.30N 8.11W
Ballyvaughan Rep. of Ire. 15 53.06N 9.09W
Ballyvourney Rep. of Ire. 15 51.57N 9.10W
Balmoral Australia 92 37.17S 141.50E
Balochistān d. Pakistan 62 28.30N 65.00E
Balombo Angola 78 12.20S 14.45E
Balonne r. Australia 93 28.30S 148.20E
Bālotra India 62 25.50N 72.14E
Balrāmpur India 63 27.26N 82.11E
Balranald Australia 92 34.37S 143.37E
Balş Romania 37 44.21N 24.06E
Balsam L. Canada 104 44.35N 78.50W
Balsas r. Brazil 123 9.00S 48.10W

Balsas r. Mexico 116 18.10N 102.05W
Bålsta Sweden 43 59.35N 17.30E
Balta Ukraine 37 47.58N 29.39E
Baltanás Spain 26 41.56N 4.15W
Baltasar Brum Uruguay 125 30.44S 57.19W
Baltic Sea Europe 41 57.00N 20.00E
Balţīm Egypt 66 31.34N 31.05E
Baltimore Canada 104 44.03N 78.08W
Baltimore Md. U.S.A. 115 39.17N 76.37W
Baltimore Ohio U.S.A. 114 39.51N 82.36W
Baltiysk Russian Fed. 41 54.39N 19.55E
Baluchistan f. Pakistan 60 28.00N 66.00E
Balumbah Australia 92 33.16S 136.14E
Bālurghāt India 63 25.13N 88.46E
Balygychan Russian Fed. 51 63.55N 154.12E
Balykshi Kazakhstan 45 47.04N 51.55E
Bām Iran 65 29.07N 58.20E
Bama Nigeria 77 11.35N 13.40E
Bamaga Australia 90 10.52S 142.23E
Bamako Mali 76 12.40N 7.59W
Bamako d. Mali 76 12.40N 7.55W
Bamba Kenya 79 3.33S 39.32E
Bamba Mali 76 17.05N 1.23W
Bamba Zaïre 78 5.45S 18.23E
Bambari C.A.R. 73 5.45N 20.40E
Bamberg Germany 39 49.53N 10.53E
Bambesa Zaïre 78 3.27N 25.43E
Bambesi Ethiopia 73 9.45N 34.40E
Bambili Zaïre 78 3.34N 26.07E
Bambio C.A.R. 77 3.55N 16.57E
Bambuí Brazil 126 20.01S 45.59W
Bam Co l. China 63 31.30N 91.10E
Bamenda Cameroon 77 5.55N 10.09E
Bāmīān Afghan. 62 34.50N 67.50E
Bamingui C.A.R. 73 7.34N 20.11E
Bamingui Bangoran d. C.A.R. 73 8.30N 20.30E
Bampton Devon U.K. 13 51.00N 3.29W
Bampūr Iran 65 27.13N 60.29E
Bampūr r. Iran 65 27.18N 59.02E
Bāmra Hills India 63 21.20N 84.30E
Banaba i. Kiribati 84 0.52S 169.35E
Banagher Rep. of Ire. 15 53.12N 8.00W
Banalia Zaïre 78 1.33N 25.23E
Banamba Mali 76 13.29N 7.22W
Banana Zaïre 78 5.55S 12.27E
Bananal, Ilha do f. Brazil 123 11.30S 50.15W
Baña, Punta de la c. Spain 25 40.34N 0.38E
Ban Aranyaprathet Thailand 56 13.43N 102.31E
Banās r. India 62 25.54N 76.45E
Banās, Ra's c. Egypt 64 23.54N 35.48E
Ban Ban Laos 56 19.38N 103.34E
Banbridge U.K. 15 54.21N 6.17W
Ban Bua Chum Thailand 56 15.15N 101.15E
Banbury U.K. 13 52.04N 1.21W
Banchory U.K. 14 57.03N 2.30W
Bancroft Canada 105 45.03N 77.51W
Band Afghan. 62 33.17N 68.39E
Banda Gabon 78 3.47S 11.04E
Banda Madhya P. India 63 24.03N 78.57E
Bānda Uttar P. India 63 25.29N 80.20E
Banda Aceh Indonesia 58 5.35N 95.20E
Banda Besar i. Indonesia 59 4.30S 129.55E
Bānda Dāūd Shāh Pakistan 62 33.16N 71.11E
Bandak l. Norway 42 59.24N 8.15E
Banda, Laut sea Indonesia 59 5.00S 128.00E
Bandama r. Côte d'Ivoire 76 5.10N 4.59W
Bandar 'Abbās Iran 65 27.10N 56.15E
Bandar Beheshtī Iran 65 25.17N 60.41E
Bandar-e Anzalī Iran 65 37.26N 49.29E
Bandar-e Deylam Iran 65 30.05N 50.11E
Bandar-e Khomeynī Iran 65 30.26N 49.03E
Bandar-e Lengeh Iran 65 26.34N 54.53E
Bandar-e Rīg Iran 65 29.30N 50.40E
Bandar-e Torkeman Iran 65 36.55N 54.05E
Bandar Seri Begawan Brunei 58 4.56N 114.58E
Banda Sea see Banda, Laut sea Indonesia 59
Bandawe Malaŵi 79 11.57S 34.11E
Bande Spain 26 42.02N 7.58W
Bandeira mtn. Brazil 126 20.25S 41.45W
Bāndhi Pakistan 62 26.36N 68.18E
Bandiagara Mali 76 14.12N 3.29W
Bāndikūl India 62 27.03N 76.34E
Bandīpur Nepal 63 27.56N 84.25E
Bandipura Jammu & Kashmir 62 34.25N 74.39E
Bandirma Turkey 29 40.22N 28.00E
Bandon Rep. of Ire. 15 51.45N 8.45W
Bandon r. Rep. of Ire. 15 51.43N 8.38W
Bandundu Zaïre 78 3.20S 17.24E
Bandundu d. Zaïre 78 4.00S 18.30E
Bandung Indonesia 59 6.57S 107.34E
Banes Cuba 117 20.59N 75.24W
Banff Canada 100 51.10N 115.34W
Banff U.K. 14 57.40N 2.31W
Banff Nat. Park Canada 100 51.30N 116.15W
Banfora Burkina 76 10.36N 4.45W
Bangalore India 60 12.58N 77.35E
Bangassou C.A.R. 73 4.50N 23.07E
Banggai, Kepulauan is. Indonesia 59 1.30S 123.10E
Banggi i. Malaysia 58 7.17N 117.12E
Banggong Co l. China 63 33.45N 79.15E
Banghāzi Libya 75 32.07N 20.05E
Banghāzi d. Libya 75 25.40N 21.00E
Bangil Indonesia 59 7.34S 112.47E
Bangka i. Indonesia 58 2.20S 106.10E
Bangkalan Indonesia 59 7.05S 112.44E
Bangkog Co l. China 63 31.45N 89.30E
Bangkok Thailand 56 13.44N 100.30E
Bangladesh Asia 63 24.30N 90.00E
Bangor Down U.K. 15 54.40N 5.41W
Bangor Gwynedd U.K. 12 53.13N 4.08W
Bangor Maine U.S.A. 112 44.49N 68.47W
Bangor Penn. U.S.A. 115 40.52N 75.13W
Bang Saphan Thailand 56 11.14N 99.31E
Bangui C.A.R. 77 4.23N 18.37E
Bangui Phil. 58 18.33N 120.45E
Banguru Zaïre 79 0.30N 27.10E
Bangweulu, L. Zambia 79 11.15S 29.45E

Banhã Egypt 66 30.28N 31.11E
Ban Hat Yai Thailand 56 7.10N 100.28E
Ban Houayxay Laos 56 20.21N 100.32E
Bani r. Mali 76 14.30N 4.15W
Bani, Jbel mtn. Morocco 74 30.00N 8.00W
Banikoara Benin 77 11.21N 2.25E
Banī Mazār Egypt 66 28.29N 30.48E
Banīnah Libya 75 32.05N 20.16E
Banī Na'īm Jordan 67 31.31N 35.10E
Banī Suwayf Egypt 66 29.05N 31.05E
Banī Walīd Libya 75 31.46N 13.59E
Bāniyās Syria 66 35.09N 35.58E
Bāniyās Syria 67 33.15N 35.41E
Banja Luka Bosnia-Herzegovina 31 44.46N 17.11E
Banjarmasin Indonesia 58 3.22S 114.36E
Banjul Gambia 76 13.28N 16.39W
Bānka India 63 24.53N 86.55E
Banka Banka Australia 90 18.48S 134.01E
Ban Kan Vietnam 56 22.08N 105.49E
Ban Kantang Thailand 56 7.25N 99.35E
Bankasse Mali 76 14.01N 3.29W
Bankeryd Sweden 43 57.51N 14.07E
Banks I. B.C. Canada 100 53.25N 130.10W
Banks I. N.W.T. Canada 98 73.00N 122.00W
Banks Is. Vanuatu 84 13.50S 167.30E
Banks Pen. New Zealand 86 43.45S 173.10E
Banks Str. Australia 91 40.37S 148.07E
Bānkura India 63 23.15N 87.04E
Ban-m'drack Vietnam 56 12.45N 108.50E
Bann r. U.K. 15 55.10N 6.46W
Banon France 21 44.02N 5.38E
Baños de Cerrato Spain 26 41.55N 4.28W
Ban Pak Phraek Thailand 56 8.13N 100.13E
Bānsda India 62 20.45N 73.22E
Banská Bystrica Slovakia 37 48.44N 19.07E
Bansko Bulgaria 34 41.52N 23.28E
Bānswāra India 62 23.33N 74.27E
Bantaeng Indonesia 59 5.32S 119.58E
Banté Benin 77 8.26N 1.54E
Bantry Rep. of Ire. 15 51.41N 9.27W
Bantry B. Rep. of Ire. 15 51.40N 9.40W
Bāntva India 62 21.29N 70.05E
Banyak, Kepulauan is. Indonesia 58 2.15N 97.10E
Banyo Cameroon 77 6.47N 11.50E
Banyoles Spain 25 42.07N 2.46E
Banyuwangi Indonesia 59 8.12S 114.22E
Banzare Coast f. Antarctica 128 66.30S 125.00E
Baode China 54 39.00N 111.05E
Baoding China 54 38.50N 115.26E
Bao Ha Vietnam 55 22.10N 104.22E
Baoji China 54 34.20N 107.17E
Baoqing China 55 28.43N 109.37E
Bao-Loc Vietnam 56 11.30N 107.54E
Baoshan China 61 25.07N 99.08E
Baotou China 54 40.35N 109.59E
Baoulé r. Mali 76 13.47N 10.45W
Bāp India 62 27.23N 72.21E
Bapaume France 19 50.06N 2.51E
Bāqa el Gharbiyya Israel 67 32.25N 35.03E
Baqên China 63 31.56N 94.00E
Ba'qūbah Iraq 65 33.45N 44.38E
Bar Ukraine 37 49.05N 27.40E
Bar Yugo. 34 42.05N 19.05E
Bara Nigeria 77 10.24N 10.43E
Baraawe Somali Rep. 79 1.02N 44.02E
Barabinsk Russian Fed. 9 55.20N 78.18E
Baraboo U.S.A. 110 43.28N 89.50W
Baracaldo Spain 26 43.18N 2.59W
Baracoa Cuba 117 20.23N 74.31W
Baradero Argentina 125 33.50S 59.30W
Baradine Australia 93 30.56S 149.05E
Baradine r. Australia 93 30.17S 148.27E
Baragoi Kenya 73 1.47N 36.47E
Bārah Sudan 73 13.42N 30.22E
Barahona Dom. Rep. 117 18.13N 71.07W
Baraka Zaïre 79 4.09S 29.05E
Barakaldo see Baracaldo Spain 26
Barakī Barak Afghan. 62 33.56N 68.55E
Bārākot India 63 21.33N 85.01E
Bārāmūla Jammu & Kashmir 62 34.12N 74.21E
Bārān India 62 25.06N 76.31E
Baranagar India 63 22.38N 88.22E
Baranoa Colombia 122 10.50N 74.55W
Baranof I. U.S.A. 100 57.00N 135.00W
Baranovichi Belarus 37 53.09N 26.00E
Baranya d. Hungary 31 45.55N 18.20E
Baratta Australia 92 32.01S 139.10E
Barbacena Brazil 126 21.13S 43.47W
Barbadillo del Mercado Spain 26 42.02N 3.21W
Barbados Lesser Antilles 117 13.20N 59.40W
Barbar Sudan 72 18.01N 33.59E
Barbastro Spain 25 42.02N 0.05E
Barbate r. Spain 27 36.11N 5.55W
Barbate de Franco Spain 27 36.12N 5.55W
Barberton R.S.A. 80 25.46S 31.02E
Barberton U.S.A. 114 41.01N 81.36W
Barbezieux France 20 45.28N 0.09W
Barbil India 63 22.06N 85.20E
Barbuda i. Leeward Is. 117 17.41N 61.48W
Barcaldine Australia 90 23.31S 145.15E
Barcarrota Spain 27 38.31N 6.51W
Barcellona Italy 33 38.09N 15.13E
Barcelona Spain 25 41.23N 2.11E
Barcelona Venezuela 122 10.08N 64.43W
Barcelos Brazil 122 0.59S 62.58W
Barcelos Portugal 26 41.32N 8.37W
Barcoo r. Australia 90 25.30S 142.50E
Barcs Hungary 31 45.58N 17.28E
Bardai Chad 77 21.21N 16.56E
Bardejov Slovakia 37 49.18N 21.16E
Bardi Italy 30 44.38N 9.44E
Bardīa Nepal 63 28.18N 81.23E

Bardīyah Libya 72 31.46N 25.06E
Bardoli India 62 21.07N 73.07E
Bardonecchia Italy 30 45.05N 6.42E
Bardsey i. U.K. 12 52.45N 4.48W
Bardu Norway 40 68.54N 18.20E
Bardufoss Norway 40 69.00N 18.30E
Bareilly India 63 28.21N 79.25E
Barellan Australia 93 34.17S 146.34E
Barengapāra India 63 25.14N 90.14E
Barentsovo More see Barents Sea Arctic Oc. 44
Barents Sea Arctic Oc. 44 73.00N 40.00E
Barentu Eritrea 72 15.04N 37.37E
Barfleur France 18 49.40N 1.15W
Barfleur, Pointe de c. France 18 49.42N 1.16W
Barga China 63 30.51N 81.20E
Bargarh India 63 21.20N 83.37E
Bargas Spain 27 39.56N 4.02W
Barge Ethiopia 73 6.15N 37.00E
Barge Italy 30 44.43N 7.20E
Barghanak Afghan. 62 33.56N 62.26E
Barguzin Russian Fed. 51 53.40N 109.35E
Barham Australia 92 35.37S 144.10E
Barharwa India 63 24.52N 87.47E
Barhi India 63 24.18N 85.25E
Bāri Madhya P. India 63 23.03N 78.05E
Bāri Rāj. India 63 26.39N 77.36E
Bari Italy 33 41.07N 16.52E
Baricho Kenya 79 3.07S 39.47E
Barika Algeria 75 35.25N 5.19E
Barīm i. Yemen 71 12.40N 43.24E
Barinas Venezuela 122 8.36N 70.15W
Baripāda India 63 21.56N 86.43E
Bariri Brazil 126 22.04S 48.41W
Bârîs Egypt 64 24.40N 30.36E
Bari Sādri India 62 24.25N 74.28E
Barisāl Bangla. 63 22.42N 90.22E
Barisan, Pegunungan mts. Indonesia 58 3.30S 102.30E
Barito r. Indonesia 58 3.35S 114.35E
Barjac France 21 44.18N 4.21E
Barjols France 21 43.33N 6.00E
Barjūj, Wādī Libya 75 26.03N 12.50E
Barker U.S.A. 114 43.20N 78.33W
Barker L. Australia 89 31.45S 120.05E
Bārkhān Pakistan 62 29.54N 69.31E
Barking U.K. 13 51.32N 0.05E
Bark L. Canada 104 46.54N 82.28W
Barkley Sd. Canada 100 48.53N 125.20W
Barkly East R.S.A. 80 30.58S 27.33E
Barkly Tableland f. Australia 90 19.00S 136.40E
Barkly West R.S.A. 80 28.32S 24.29E
Bar-le-Duc France 19 48.47N 5.10E
Barlee, L. Australia 89 29.30S 119.30E
Barlee Range mts. Australia 88 23.40S 116.00E
Barletta Italy 33 41.19N 16.17E
Barlow L. Canada 101 62.00N 103.00W
Barmedman Australia 93 34.08S 147.25E
Barmer India 62 25.45N 71.23E
Barmera Australia 92 34.15S 140.31E
Barm Fīrūz, Kūh-e mtn. Iran 65 30.21N 52.00E
Barmouth U.K. 12 52.44N 4.03W
Barnagar India 62 23.03N 75.22E
Barnāla India 62 30.22N 75.33E
Barnard Castle town U.K. 12 54.33N 1.55W
Barnato Australia 93 31.38S 144.59E
Barnaul Russian Fed. 9 53.21N 83.15E
Barnegat U.S.A. 115 39.52N 74.07W
Barnegat B. U.S.A. 115 39.52N 74.06W
Barnesboro U.S.A. 114 40.40N 78.50W
Barnesville U.S.A. 114 39.59N 81.11W
Barnet U.K. 13 51.39N 0.11W
Barneveld Neth. 16 52.10N 5.39E
Barneville France 18 49.23N 1.45W
Barneys L. Australia 92 33.16S 144.13E
Barnsley U.K. 12 53.33N 1.29W
Barnstable U.S.A. 115 41.42N 70.18W
Barnstaple U.K. 13 51.05N 4.03W
Baro r. Ethiopia 73 8.26N 33.13E
Baro Nigeria 77 8.37N 6.19E
Barpeta India 63 26.19N 91.00E
Barqah f. Libya 72 31.00N 23.00E
Barquisimeto Venezuela 122 10.03N 69.18W
Barra Brazil 123 11.06S 43.15W
Barra i. U.K. 14 56.59N 7.28W
Barraba Australia 93 30.24S 152.36E
Barra do Corda Brazil 123 5.30S 45.15W
Barra do Piraí Brazil 126 22.28S 43.49W
Barrafranca Italy 33 37.23N 14.13E
Barragem Agua Vermelha resr. Brazil 126 19.50S 50.00W
Barragem de São Simão resr. Brazil 126 18.35S 50.00W
Barra Head U.K. 10 56.47N 7.36W
Barra Mansa Brazil 126 22.35S 44.12W
Barranca Peru 122 4.50S 76.40W
Barrancabermeja Colombia 122 7.06N 73.54W
Barrancas Venezuela 122 8.45N 62.13W
Barranco do Velho Portugal 27 37.14N 7.56W
Barrancos Portugal 27 38.08N 6.59W
Barranqueras Argentina 126 27.30S 58.55W
Barranquilla Colombia 122 11.10N 74.50W
Barra, Sd. of U.K. 14 57.04N 7.20W
Barraute Canada 102 48.26N 77.39W
Barrax Spain 27 39.03N 2.12W
Barre U.S.A. 105 44.12N 72.30W
Barreiras Brazil 123 12.09S 44.58W
Barreiro Portugal 27 38.40N 9.04W
Barreiros Brazil 123 8.49S 35.12W
Barrême France 21 43.57N 6.22E
Barretos Brazil 126 20.37S 48.38W
Barrhead Canada 100 54.10N 114.24W
Barrhead U.K. 14 55.47N 4.24W
Barrie Canada 104 44.24N 79.40W
Barrie I. Canada 104 45.55N 82.40W
Barrier Range mts. Australia 92 31.25S 141.25E
Barrington Tops mts. Australia 93 32.30S 151.28E
Barringun Australia 93 29.01S 145.43E

Barron U.S.A. 108 48.44N 120.43W
Barrow r. Rep. of Ire. 15 52.17N 7.00W
Barrow U.S.A. 98 71.16N 156.50W
Barrow Creek town Australia 90 21.32S 133.53E
Barrow I. Australia 88 21.40S 115.27E
Barrow-in-Furness U.K. 12 54.08N 3.15W
Barrow, Pt. U.S.A. 96 71.22N 156.30W
Barrow Range mts. Australia 88 26.04S 127.28E
Barry U.K. 13 51.23N 3.19W
Barry's Bay town Canada 105 45.30N 77.41W
Barryville U.S.A. 115 41.29N 74.55W
Barsinghausen Germany 38 52.18N 9.27E
Barstow U.S.A. 109 34.54N 117.01W
Bar-sur-Aube France 19 48.14N 4.43E
Bar-sur-Seine France 19 48.07N 4.22E
Barth Germany 38 54.22N 12.43E
Bartica Guyana 122 6.24N 58.38W
Bartin Turkey 64 41.37N 32.20E
Bartle Frere, Mt. Australia 90 17.23S 145.49E
Bartlesville U.S.A. 111 36.45N 95.59W
Bartlett L. Canada 100 63.05N 118.20W
Bartolomeu Dias Mozambique 81 21.10S 35.09E
Barton U.S.A. 105 44.45N 72.11W
Barton-upon-Humber U.K. 12 53.41N 0.27W
Bartoszyce Poland 37 54.16N 20.49E
Bartow U.S.A. 113 27.54N 81.51W
Bäruni India 63 25.29N 85.59E
Barwäh India 62 22.16N 76.03E
Barwäni India 62 22.02N 74.54E
Barwa Sägar India 63 25.23N 78.44E
Barwon r. Australia 93 30.00S 148.05E
Barysh Russian Fed. 44 53.40N 47.09E
Basäl Pakistan 62 33.33N 72.15E
Basankusu Zaïre 73 1.12N 19.50E
Basavilbaso Argentina 125 32.20S 58.52W
Basel Switz. 39 47.33N 7.35E
Basella Spain 25 42.01N 1.18E
Baselland d. Switz. 39 47.30N 7.50E
Basento Italy 33 40.21N 16.50E
Bashi Channel Taiwan/Phil. 55 21.30N 121.00E
Basilan Phil. 59 6.40N 121.59E
Basilan i. Phil. 59 6.40N 122.10E
Basildon U.K. 13 51.34N 0.25E
Basilicata d. Italy 33 40.30N 16.10E
Basin U.S.A. 108 44.23N 108.02W
Basingstoke U.K. 13 51.15N 1.05W
Basin L. Canada 101 52.38N 105.18W
Baška Croatia 31 44.58N 14.46E
Baskatong, Résr. Canada 105 46.48N 75.50W
Basmat India 62 19.19N 77.10E
Bäsoda India 63 23.51N 77.56E
Basoko Zaïre 73 1.20N 23.30E
Basongo Zaïre 73 4.23S 20.28E
Bas-Rhin d. France 19 48.35N 7.40E
Bassano Canada 100 50.48N 112.20W
Bassano Italy 30 45.46N 11.44E
Bassari Togo 76 9.12N 0.18E
Bassein Myanmar 56 16.46N 94.45E
Basse-Kotto d. C.A.R. 73 5.00N 21.30E
Basse Normandie d. France 18 49.00N 0.00
Basse Santa Su Gambia 76 13.23N 14.15W
Basse-Terre Guadeloupe 117 16.00N 61.43W
Bassett U.S.A. 110 42.35N 99.32W
Basse-Yutz France 19 49.21N 6.11E
Bass Is. U.S.A. 114 41.42N 82.49W
Bass Str. Australia 91 39.45S 146.00E
Bassum Germany 38 52.51N 8.43E
Båstad Sweden 43 56.26N 12.51E
Bastak Iran 65 27.15N 54.26E
Bastelica France 21 42.00N 9.02E
Basti India 63 26.48N 82.43E
Bastia France 21 42.42N 9.27E
Bastogne Belgium 16 50.00N 5.43E
Bastrop U.S.A. 111 32.47N 91.55W
Basyün Egypt 66 30.57N 30.49E
Bas Zaïre d. Zaïre 78 5.15S 14.00E
Bata Equat. Guinea 78 1.51N 9.49E
Batabanó, Golfo de g. Cuba 117 23.15N 82.30W
Batak Bulgaria 34 41.57N 24.12E
Batak, Yazovir l. Bulgaria 34 42.00N 24.11E
Batäla India 62 31.48N 75.13E
Batalha Portugal 27 39.39N 8.50W
Batang China 61 30.02N 99.01E
Batangafo C.A.R. 77 7.27N 18.11E
Batangas Phil. 59 13.46N 121.01E
Batan Is. Phil. 59 20.50N 121.55E
Bátaszék Hungary 31 46.12N 18.44E
Batatais Brazil 126 20.54S 47.37W
Batavia U.S.A. 114 43.00N 78.11W
Bataysk Russian Fed. 45 47.09N 39.46E
Batchawana Canada 104 46.54N 84.34W
Batchawana r. Canada 104 46.55N 84.32W
Batchawana I. Canada 104 46.45N 84.14W
Batchawana Mtn. Canada 104 47.04N 84.24W
Batchelor Australia 90 13.04S 131.01E
Bätdâmbâng Cambodia 56 13.06N 103.12E
Batemans Bay town Australia 93 35.55S 150.09E
Batesville Ark. U.S.A. 111 35.46N 91.39W
Batesville Miss. U.S.A. 111 34.18N 90.00W
Bath N.B. Canada 103 46.31N 67.37W
Bath Ont. Canada 105 44.11N 76.47W
Bath U.K. 13 51.22N 2.22W
Bath Maine U.S.A. 113 43.55N 69.49W
Bath N.Y. U.S.A. 114 42.20N 77.19W
Batha d. Chad 77 14.31N 18.30E
Batha r. Chad 77 12.47N 17.34E
Batḥā, Wädi al r. Oman 65 20.01N 59.39E
Bathgate U.K. 14 55.44N 3.38W
Bathurst Australia 93 33.27S 149.35E
Bathurst Canada 103 47.36N 65.39W
Bathurst R.S.A. 80 33.30S 26.48E
Bathurst, C. Canada 98 70.30N 128.00W
Bathurst I. Australia 88 11.45S 130.15E
Bathurst I. Canada 99 76.00N 100.00W
Bathurst Inlet town Canada 98 66.48N 108.00W
Batibla C.A.R. 73 5.56N 21.09E
Batié Burkina 76 9.42N 2.53W
Batina Croatia 31 45.51N 18.51E

Batir Jordan 67 31.16N 35.42E
Batiscan r. Canada 105 46.31N 72.15W
Batley U.K. 12 53.43N 1.38W
Batlow Australia 93 35.32S 148.10E
Batman Turkey 64 37.52N 41.07E
Batna Algeria 75 35.35N 6.11E
Baton Rouge U.S.A. 111 30.23N 91.11W
Batopilas Mexico 109 27.00N 107.45W
Batouri Cameroon 77 4.26N 14.27E
Bat Shelomo Israel 67 32.36N 35.00E
Batson U.S.A. 111 30.15N 94.37W
Batticaloa Sri Lanka 61 7.43N 81.42E
Battle r. Canada 101 52.43N 108.15W
Battle U.K. 13 50.55N 0.30E
Battle Creek town U.S.A. 112 42.20N 85.11W
Battleford Canada 101 52.43N 108.15W
Battle Harbour Canada 103 52.17N 55.35W
Batu mtn. Ethiopia 71 6.55N 39.46E
Batu, Kepulauan is. Indonesia 58 0.30S 98.20E
Batumi Georgia 64 41.37N 41.36E
Batu Pahat Malaysia 58 1.50N 102.48E
Baturaja Indonesia 58 4.10S 104.10E
Baturité Brazil 123 4.20S 38.53W
Bat Yam Israel 67 32.01N 34.45E
Baubau Indonesia 59 5.30S 122.37E
Bauchi Nigeria 77 10.16N 9.50E
Bauchi d. Nigeria 77 10.40N 10.00E
Baud France 18 47.52N 3.01W
Baudh India 63 20.50N 84.19E
Baugé France 18 47.33N 0.06W
Bauld, C. Canada 103 51.38N 55.25W
Baume-les-Dames France 19 47.21N 6.22E
Baunei Italy 32 40.02N 9.40E
Bauru Brazil 126 22.19S 49.07W
Baús Brazil 126 18.19S 53.10W
Bauska Latvia 41 56.24N 24.14E
Bautzen Germany 38 51.11N 14.26E
Bavay France 16 50.18N 3.48E
Båven l. Sweden 43 59.01N 16.56E
Bawean i. Indonesia 59 5.50S 112.39E
Bawku Ghana 76 11.05N 0.13W
Bayamo Cuba 117 20.23N 76.39W
Bayamón Puerto Rico 117 18.24N 66.10W
Bayäna India 62 26.54N 77.17E
Bäyan, Band-e mts. Afghan. 62 34.20N 65.00E
Bayan Har Shan mts. China 54 34.00N 97.20E
Bayan Nur China 54 38.14N 103.56E
Bayard U.S.A. 114 39.16N 79.22W
Bayburt Turkey 64 40.15N 40.16E
Bay City Mich. U.S.A. 104 43.36N 83.53W
Bay City Tex. U.S.A. 111 28.59N 95.58W
Baydaratskaya Guba b. Russian Fed. 50 70.00N 66.00E
Baydhabo Somali Rep. 79 3.08N 43.34E
Bayerische Alpen mts. Germany 39 47.38N 11.30E
Bayerischer Wald mts. Germany 39 49.00N 12.50E
Bayern d. Germany 38 49.06N 11.30E
Bayeux France 18 49.17N 0.42W
Bayfield Canada 104 43.33N 81.41W
Bayfield U.S.A. 110 46.49N 90.49W
Baykal, Ozero l. Russian Fed. 52 53.30N 100.00E
Baykit Russian Fed. 51 61.45N 96.22E
Baykonyr Kazakhstan 50 47.50N 66.03E
Bayo Spain 26 43.05N 8.58W
Bay of Plenty d. New Zealand 86 38.00S 177.10E
Bayombong Phil. 59 16.27N 121.10E
Bayon France 19 48.29N 6.19E
Bayona Spain 26 42.07N 8.51W
Bayonne France 20 43.29N 1.29W
Bayovar Peru 122 5.50S 81.03W
Bay Port U.S.A. 104 43.51N 83.23W
Bayramic Greece 34 39.48N 26.37E
Bayreuth Germany 38 49.57N 11.35E
Bayrischzell Germany 39 47.40N 12.00E
Bayrüt Lebanon 66 33.52N 35.30E
Bay Shore U.S.A. 115 40.44N 73.15W
Bays, L. of Canada 104 45.15N 79.04W
Baysville Canada 104 45.09N 79.10W
Baytä al Fawqä Jordan 67 32.09N 35.17E
Bayt Awlä Jordan 67 31.36N 35.02E
Bayt Ḥänün Egypt 67 31.32N 34.32E
Baytik Shan mts. China 52 45.15N 90.50E
Bayt Immar Jordan 67 31.37N 35.06E
Bayt Jälä Jordan 67 31.43N 35.11E
Bayt Lähiyah Egypt 67 31.33N 34.30E
Bayt Laḥm Jordan 67 31.43N 35.12E
Baytown U.S.A. 111 29.44N 94.58W
Bayt Rïmä Jordan 67 32.02N 35.06E
Baytünïyä Jordan 67 31.53N 35.10E
Bay View New Zealand 86 39.26S 176.52E
Bay Village U.S.A. 114 41.29N 81.55W
Baza Spain 27 37.29N 2.46W
Bazaliya Ukraine 37 49.42N 26.29E
Bazaruto, Ilha do i. Mozambique 81 21.40S 35.28E
Bazas France 20 44.26N 0.13W
Baza, Sierra de mts. Spain 27 37.20N 2.45W
Bazdär Pakistan 62 26.21N 65.03E
Bazhong China 55 31.51N 106.42E
Baziège France 20 43.27N 1.37E
Bazmän Iran 65 27.48N 60.12E
Bazmän, Küh-e mtn. Iran 65 28.06N 60.00E
Beach U.S.A. 110 46.55N 103.52W
Beachburg Canada 105 45.43N 76.53W
Beach Haven U.S.A. 115 39.34N 74.14W
Beachport Australia 92 37.29S 140.01E
Beachwood U.S.A. 115 39.56N 74.12W
Beachy Head U.K. 13 50.43N 0.15E
Beacon U.S.A. 115 41.30N 73.58W
Beagle Bay town Australia 88 16.58S 122.40E
Bealanana Madagascar 81 14.33S 48.44E
Bear Brook State Park U.S.A. 115 43.05N 71.26W
Beardstown U.S.A. 110 40.01N 90.26W
Bear I. see Bjørnøya i. Arctic Oc. 128
Bear Island town Canada 104 46.59N 80.05W
Bear L. U.S.A. 108 42.00N 111.20W
Bearskin Lake town Canada 102 53.58N 91.02W
Beas r. India 62 31.10N 75.00E
Beasain Spain 26 43.03N 2.11W

Beas de Segura Spain 26 38.15N 2.53W
Beatrice U.S.A. 110 40.16N 96.44W
Beatrice, C. Australia 90 14.15S 136.59E
Beatton r. Canada 100 56.15N 120.45W
Beatton River town Canada 100 57.26N 121.20W
Beatty U.S.A. 108 36.54N 116.46W
Beattyville Canada 102 48.53N 77.10W
Beaucaire France 21 43.48N 4.38E
Beauce f. France 19 48.22N 1.50E
Beauchêne Canada 104 46.39N 78.55W
Beaudesert Australia 93 27.58S 153.01E
Beaufort Australia 92 37.28S 143.28E
Beaufort U.S.A. 113 32.26N 80.40W
Beaufort Sea N. America 98 72.00N 141.00W
Beaufort West R.S.A. 80 32.20S 22.34E
Beaugency France 19 47.47N 1.38E
Beauharnois Canada 105 45.19N 73.52W
Beaujolais, Monts du mts. France 21 46.00N 4.30E
Beaulieu r. Canada 100 62.03N 113.11W
Beauly U.K. 14 57.29N 4.29W
Beauly r. U.K. 14 57.29N 4.25W
Beaumaris U.K. 12 53.16N 4.07W
Beaumetz-lès-Loges France 19 50.14N 2.39E
Beaumont Belgium 16 50.14N 4.16E
Beaumont France 18 49.40N 1.51W
Beaumont France 18 44.45N 0.47E
Beaumont Miss. U.S.A. 111 31.11N 88.55W
Beaumont Tex. U.S.A. 111 30.05N 94.06W
Beaumont-le-Roger France 18 49.05N 0.47E
Beaumont-sur-Sarthe France 18 48.13N 0.08E
Beaune France 19 47.02N 4.50E
Beaune-la-Rolande France 19 48.04N 2.26E
Beaupréau France 18 47.12N 1.00W
Beaurepaire France 21 45.20N 5.03E
Beauséjour Canada 101 50.04N 96.33W
Beauvais France 19 49.26N 2.05E
Beauval Canada 101 55.09N 107.35W
Beauville France 20 44.17N 0.52E
Beauvoir France 18 46.55N 2.02W
Beauvoir-sur-Niort France 18 46.11N 0.28W
Beaver r. N.W.T. Canada 100 59.43N 124.16W
Beaver r. Ont. Canada 102 55.55N 87.50W
Beaver Alaska U.S.A. 98 66.22N 147.24W
Beaver Okla. U.S.A. 111 36.49N 100.31W
Beaver Penn. U.S.A. 114 40.42N 80.18W
Beaver r. U.S.A. 114 40.40N 80.18W
Beaver Dam town U.S.A. 110 43.28N 88.50W
Beaver Falls town U.S.A. 114 40.46N 80.19W
Beaverhill L. Alta. Canada 100 53.27N 112.32W
Beaverhill L. N.W.T. Canada 101 63.02N 104.22W
Beaver I. U.S.A. 112 45.42N 85.28W
Beaverton Canada 104 44.26N 79.09W
Beaverton U.S.A. 104 43.53N 84.29W
Beäwar India 62 26.06N 74.19E
Bebedouro Brazil 126 20.54S 48.31W
Bebington U.K. 12 53.23N 3.01W
Bécancour Canada 105 46.20N 72.26W
Beccles U.K. 13 52.27N 1.33E
Bečej Yugo. 31 45.37N 20.03E
Béchar Algeria 74 31.37N 2.13W
Bechater Tunisia 32 37.18N 9.45E
Bechet Romania 34 43.46N 23.58E
Beckley U.S.A. 113 37.46N 81.12W
Beckum Germany 38 51.45N 8.02E
Beclean Romania 37 47.11N 24.10E
Bédarieux France 20 43.37N 3.09E
Bedésa Ethiopia 73 8.50N 40.45E
Bedford Canada 105 45.07N 72.59W
Bedford U.K. 13 52.08N 0.29W
Bedford U.S.A. 114 40.01N 78.30W
Bedford, C. Australia 90 15.14S 145.21E
Bedford Levels f. U.K. 12 52.35N 0.08W
Bedfordshire d. U.K. 13 52.04N 0.28W
Bedi India 62 22.30N 70.02E
Bedlington U.K. 12 55.08N 1.34W
Bedourie Australia 90 24.21S 139.28E
Beech Grove U.S.A. 112 39.42N 86.06W
Beechworth Australia 93 36.23S 146.42E
Beenleigh Australia 93 27.43S 153.09E
Be'eri Israel 67 31.25N 34.29E
Be'er Menuha Israel 66 30.19N 35.08E
Be'erotayim Israel 67 32.19N 34.59E
Be'er Sheva' Israel 67 31.15N 34.47E
Be'er Sheva', Nahal wadi Israel 67 31.11N 34.35E
Beerta Neth. 16 53.12N 7.07E
Be'er Toviyya Israel 67 31.44N 34.44E
Beeskow Germany 38 52.10N 14.14E
Beeston U.K. 12 52.55N 1.11W
Beeville U.S.A. 111 28.24N 97.45W
Befale Zaïre 78 0.27N 21.01E
Befandriana Madagascar 81 15.16S 48.32E
Befandriana Madagascar 81 22.06S 43.54E
Bega Australia 93 36.41S 149.50E
Begamganj India 63 23.36N 78.20E
Bègles France 20 44.47N 0.34W
Begna r. Norway 42 60.10N 10.18E
Begur, Cap de c. Spain 25 41.57N 3.14E
Begusarai India 63 25.25N 86.08E
Behara Madagascar 81 25.00S 46.25E
Behbehän Iran 65 30.35N 50.17E
Bel'an China 53 48.17N 126.33E
Beihai China 55 21.29N 109.09E
Bei Jiang r. China 55 23.19N 112.51E
Beijing China 54 39.55N 116.25E
Beijing d. China 54 40.00N 116.30E
Beijing Shi d. China 53 40.15N 116.30E
Beilen Neth. 16 52.51N 6.31E
Beinn Dearg mtn. U.K. 14 57.47N 4.55W
Beipa'a P.N.G. 90 8.30S 146.35E
Beipiao China 54 41.47N 120.40E
Beira Mozambique 81 19.49S 34.52E
Beirut see Bayrüt Lebanon 66
Beitang China 54 39.06N 117.43E
Beitbridge Zimbabwe 80 22.10S 30.01E
Beit Jann Israel 67 32.58N 35.23E
Beiuș Romania 37 46.40N 22.21E
Beja Portugal 27 38.01N 7.52W
Beja d. Portugal 27 37.50N 7.55W

Béja Tunisia 32 36.44N 9.11E
Bejaïa Algeria 75 36.45N 5.05E
Béjar Spain 26 40.23N 5.46W
Bejestän Iran 65 34.32N 58.08E
Bejhi r. Pakistan 62 29.47N 67.58E
Bejoording Australia 89 31.22S 116.30E
Békés Hungary 37 46.46N 21.08E
Békéscsaba Hungary 37 46.41N 21.06E
Bekily Madagascar 81 24.13S 45.19E
Bela India 63 25.56N 81.59E
Bela Pakistan 62 26.14N 66.19E
Bélabo Cameroon 77 5.00N 13.20E
Bela Crkva Yugo. 37 44.54N 21.26E
Bel Air U.S.A. 115 39.32N 76.21W
Belalcázar Spain 26 38.34N 5.10W
Belampalli India 63 19.02N 79.30E
Belang Indonesia 59 0.58N 124.56E
Bela Palanka Yugo. 34 43.13N 22.17E
Belarus Europe 37 53.30N 28.00E
Belau see Palau is. Pacific Oc. 59
Bela Vista Brazil 124 22.05S 56.22W
Bela Vista Mozambique 81 26.20S 32.41E
Belaya r. Russian Fed. 50 55.40N 52.30E
Belaya Glina Russian Fed. 45 46.04N 40.54E
Belaya Tserkov Ukraine 37 49.40N 30.10E
Belcher Is. Canada 102 56.00N 79.00W
Belchite Spain 25 41.18N 0.45W
Belda India 63 22.05N 87.21E
Belebey Russian Fed. 44 54.05N 54.07E
Beled Weyne Somali Rep. 71 4.47N 45.12E
Belém Brazil 123 1.27S 48.29W
Belem Mozambique 81 14.11S 35.59E
Belén Uruguay 125 30.47S 57.47W
Belen U.S.A. 109 34.40N 106.46W
Belén, Cuchilla de mts. Uruguay 125 30.49S 56.28W
Belene Bulgaria 34 43.39N 25.07E
Beles r. Ethiopia 71 11.10N 35.10E
Belev Russian Fed. 44 53.50N 36.08E
Belfast U.K. 15 54.36N 5.57W
Belfast Maine U.S.A. 112 44.27N 69.01W
Belfast N.Y. U.S.A. 114 42.21N 78.07W
Belfast Lough U.K. 15 54.42N 5.45W
Belfield U.S.A. 110 46.53N 103.12W
Belfort France 17 47.38N 6.52E
Belfry U.S.A. 108 45.09N 109.01W
Belgaum India 60 15.54N 74.36E
Belgium Europe 16 51.00N 4.30E
Belgodere France 21 42.35N 9.01E
Belgorod Russian Fed. 23 50.38N 36.36E
Belgorod-Dnestrovskiy Ukraine 37 46.10N 30.19E
Belgrade see Beograd Yugo. 37
Beli Nigeria 77 7.53N 10.59E
Beli Drim r. Yugo. 34 42.25N 20.34E
Beli Manastir Croatia 31 45.46N 18.36E
Belin France 20 44.30N 0.47W
Belington U.S.A. 114 39.01N 79.56W
Belitung i. Indonesia 58 3.00S 108.00E
Belize Belize 117 17.29N 88.20W
Belize C. America 117 17.00N 88.30W
Belka Australia 89 31.45S 118.09E
Bellac France 20 46.07N 1.02E
Bella Coola Canada 100 52.25N 126.40W
Bellagio Italy 30 45.59N 9.15E
Bellaire Ohio U.S.A. 114 40.02N 80.45W
Bellaire Tex. U.S.A. 111 29.44N 95.03W
Bellaria Italy 30 44.09N 12.28E
Bellary India 60 15.11N 76.54E
Bellata Australia 93 29.55S 149.50E
Bella Unión Uruguay 125 30.15S 57.35W
Bella Vista Corrientes Argentina 124 28.30S 59.00W
Bella Vista Tucuman Argentina 124 27.02S 65.19W
Bellbrook Australia 93 30.48S 152.30E
Belle U.S.A. 114 38.14N 81.32W
Belledonne, Chaîne de mts. France 21 45.18N 6.08E
Bellefontaine U.S.A. 112 40.22N 83.45W
Bellefonte U.S.A. 114 40.55N 77.46W
Belle Fourche r. U.S.A. 110 44.26N 102.19W
Bellegarde France 21 46.06N 5.49E
Belle Glade U.S.A. 113 26.41N 80.41W
Belle Île France 17 47.20N 3.10W
Belle Île r. France 18 47.20N 3.10W
Belle Isle Canada 103 51.55N 55.20W
Belle Isle, Str. of Canada 103 51.35N 56.30W
Bellême France 18 48.22N 0.34E
Belleoram Canada 103 47.32N 55.28W
Belleterre Canada 102 47.25N 78.41W
Belleville Canada 105 44.10N 77.23W
Belleville Kans. U.S.A. 110 39.49N 97.38W
Belleville-sur-Saône France 21 46.06N 4.45E
Bellevue Canada 104 46.42N 84.09W
Bellevue Canada 100 49.35N 114.22W
Bellevue Idaho U.S.A. 108 43.28N 114.16W
Bellevue Ohio U.S.A. 114 41.17N 82.50W
Bellevue Penn. U.S.A. 114 40.30N 80.03W
Bellevue Wash. U.S.A. 108 47.37N 122.12W
Bell Ewart Canada 104 44.16N 79.33W
Belley France 21 45.46N 5.41E
Belle Yella Liberia 76 7.24N 10.09W
Bellingen Australia 93 30.28S 152.43E
Bellingham U.K. 12 55.09N 2.15W
Bellingham U.S.A. 108 48.46N 122.29W
Bellingshausen Sea Antarctica 128 70.00S 88.00W
Bellinzona Switz. 39 46.11N 9.02E
Bello Colombia 122 6.20N 75.41W
Bellows Falls town U.S.A. 115 43.08N 72.27W
Bellpat Pakistan 62 28.59N 68.00E
Belluno Italy 30 46.09N 12.13E
Bell Ville Argentina 124 32.35S 62.41W
Bellville U.S.A. 114 40.37N 82.31W
Bellwood U.S.A. 114 40.36N 78.20W
Belmar U.S.A. 115 40.11N 74.01W
Bélmez Spain 26 38.16N 5.12W
Belmond U.S.A. 110 42.51N 93.37W
Belmont Australia 93 33.02S 151.40E
Belmont U.S.A. 114 42.13N 78.02W
Belmonte Portugal 26 40.21N 7.21W
Belmonte Cuenca Spain 27 39.34N 2.42W

Belmonte Oviedo Spain **26** 43.16N 6.13W
Belmopan Belize **117** 17.25N 88.46W
Belmullet Rep. of Ire. **15** 54.14N 10.00W
Belogradchik Bulgaria **34** 43.37N 22.40E
Belo Horizonte Brazil **126** 19.45S 43.54W
Beloit Kans. U.S.A. **110** 39.28N 98.06W
Beloit Wisc. U.S.A. **110** 42.31N 89.02W
Belo Jardim Brazil **123** 8.22S 36.22W
Belokorovichi Ukraine **37** 51.04N 28.00E
Belomorsk Russian Fed. **44** 64.34N 34.45E
Belonia India **63** 23.15N 91.27E
Belorado Spain **26** 42.25N 3.11W
Beloretsk Russian Fed. **44** 53.59N 58.20E
Belorussia see Belarus Europe **37**
Beloye More sea Russian Fed. **44** 65.30N 38.00E
Beloye Ozero l. Russian Fed. **44** 60.12N 37.45E
Belozersk Russian Fed. **44** 60.00N 37.49E
Belpasso Italy **33** 37.35N 14.59E
Belper U.K. **12** 53.02N 1.29W
Belpre U.S.A. **114** 39.17N 81.34W
Beltana Australia **92** 30.40S 138.27E
Belterra Brazil **123** 2.38S 54.57W
Belton Australia **92** 32.12S 138.45E
Belton U.S.A. **111** 31.04N 97.28W
Beltsy Moldova **37** 47.45N 27.59E
Belukha, Gora mtn. Russian Fed. **52** 49.48N 86.40E
Belvedere Marittimo Italy **33** 39.37N 15.52E
Belvès France **20** 44.47N 1.00E
Belvidere U.S.A. **110** 40.49N 75.05W
Belvís de la Jara Spain **27** 39.45N 4.57W
Belyando r. Australia **90** 21.38S 146.50E
Belyayevka Ukraine **37** 46.30N 30.12E
Belynichi Belarus **37** 54.00N 29.42E
Belyy, Ostrov Russian Fed. **50** 73.10N 70.45E
Belyy Yar Russian Fed. **50** 58.28N 85.03E
Belz France **18** 47.41N 3.10W
Belzec Poland **37** 50.24N 23.26E
Belzig Germany **38** 52.08N 12.35E
Bemaraha, Plateau du mts. Madagascar **81** 20.00S 45.15E
Bemarivo r. Madagascar **81** 15.27S 47.40E
Bembézar Spain **26** 37.45N 5.13W
Bemidji U.S.A. **110** 47.29N 94.53W
Benaberre Spain **25** 42.07N 0.29E
Bena Dibele Zaïre **78** 4.07S 22.50E
Benagerie Australia **92** 31.30S 140.21E
Benalla Australia **93** 36.35S 145.58E
Benamejí Spain **27** 37.16N 4.32W
Ben 'Ammi Israel **67** 33.00N 35.07E
Benanee Australia **92** 34.32S 142.56E
Benares see Vārānasi India **63**
Benavente Spain **26** 42.01N 5.41W
Benbecula i. U.K. **14** 57.26N 7.18W
Bencha China **54** 32.31N 120.53E
Ben Cruachan mtn. U.K. **14** 56.26N 5.18W
Bencubbin Australia **89** 30.48S 117.52E
Bend U.S.A. **108** 44.03N 121.19W
Bende Nigeria **77** 5.34N 7.37E
Bendemeer Australia **93** 30.52S 151.10E
Bender Beyla Somali Rep. **71** 9.30N 50.30E
Bendery Moldova **37** 46.50N 29.29E
Bendigo Australia **92** 36.48S 144.21E
Bendoc Australia **93** 37.10S 148.55E
Bendorf Germany **39** 50.25N 7.34E
Bene Berāq Israel **67** 32.06N 34.51E
Bénéna Mali **76** 13.09N 4.17W
Benenitra Madagascar **81** 23.27S 45.05E
Benešov Czech Republic **36** 49.45N 14.22E
Bénestroff France **19** 48.55N 6.45E
Benevento Italy **33** 41.08N 14.45E
Benfeld France **19** 48.22N 7.36E
Bengal, B. of Indian Oc. **63** 20.00N 90.00E
Bengal Plateau f. Indian Oc. **48** 15.00N 89.00E
Bengbu China **54** 32.53N 117.26E
Benghazi see Banghāzī Libya **75**
Bengkulu Indonesia **58** 3.46S 102.16E
Bengo d. Angola **78** 9.00S 13.40E
Bengtsfors Sweden **43** 59.02N 12.13E
Benguela Angola **78** 12.34S 13.24E
Benguela d. Angola **78** 12.45S 14.00E
Ben Hope mtn. U.K. **14** 58.24N 4.36W
Beni r. Bolivia **124** 10.23S 65.24W
Beni Zaïre **79** 0.29N 29.27E
Beni Abbes Algeria **74** 30.08N 2.10W
Benicarló Spain **25** 40.25N 0.26E
Benidorm Spain **25** 38.33N 0.08W
Beni-Mellal Morocco **74** 32.22N 6.29W
Benin Africa **77** 9.00N 2.30E
Benin, Bight of Africa **77** 5.30N 3.00E
Benin City Nigeria **77** 6.19N 5.41E
Benisa Spain **25** 38.43N 0.03E
Beni Saf Algeria **74** 35.19N 1.23W
Benjamin Constant Brazil **122** 4.22S 70.02W
Benkelman U.S.A. **110** 40.03N 101.32W
Benkovac Croatia **31** 44.02N 15.37E
Ben Lawers mtn. U.K. **14** 56.33N 4.14W
Ben Lomond mtn. U.K. **14** 56.12N 4.38W
Ben Macdhui mtn. U.K. **14** 57.04N 3.40W
Ben More mtn. Central U.K. **14** 56.23N 4.31W
Ben More mtn. Strath. U.K. **14** 56.26N 6.02W
Ben More Assynt mtn. U.K. **14** 58.07N 4.52W
Bennett Canada **100** 59.49N 135.01W
Bennett, L. Australia **90** 22.50S 131.10E
Bennettsville U.S.A. **113** 34.36N 79.40W
Ben Nevis mtn. U.K. **14** 56.48N 5.00W
Benneydale New Zealand **86** 38.31S 175.21E
Bennington N.H. U.S.A. **115** 43.01N 71.56W
Bennington Vt. U.S.A. **115** 42.53N 73.12W
Benny Canada **104** 46.47N 81.37W
Benoni R.S.A. **80** 26.12S 28.18E
Bénoué r. Cameroon see Benue r. Nigeria **77**
Bensheim Germany **39** 49.41N 8.37E
Benson Ariz. U.S.A. **109** 31.58N 110.18W
Benson Minn. U.S.A. **110** 45.19N 95.36W
Bentiaba Angola **78** 14.18S 12.26E
Bentinck I. Australia **90** 17.04S 139.30E
Bentiu Sudan **73** 9.14N 29.50E

Bentley U.S.A. **104** 43.57N 84.08W
Bentleyville U.S.A. **114** 40.07N 80.01W
Benton U.S.A. **110** 38.01N 88.54W
Benton Harbor U.S.A. **112** 42.07N 86.27W
Benue d. Nigeria **77** 7.20N 8.00E
Benue r. Nigeria **77** 7.52N 6.45E
Ben Wyvis mtn. U.K. **14** 57.40N 4.35W
Benxi China **54** 41.21N 123.47E
Beograd Yugo. **37** 44.49N 20.28E
Beohāri India **63** 24.03N 81.23E
Beowawe U.S.A. **108** 40.35N 116.29W
Beppu Japan **57** 33.18N 131.30E
Berat Albania **34** 40.43N 19.59E
Berau, Teluk b. Indonesia **59** 2.20S 133.00E
Berbera Somali Rep. **71** 10.28N 45.02E
Berbérati C.A.R. **77** 4.19N 15.51E
Berbería, Cabo c. Spain **25** 38.38N 1.23E
Berceto Italy **33** 44.31N 9.59E
Berchem Belgium **16** 50.48N 3.32E
Berchtesgaden Germany **39** 47.38N 13.01E
Berck France **19** 50.24N 1.36E
Bercu France **19** 50.31N 3.17E
Berdichev Ukraine **37** 49.54N 28.39E
Berdsk Russian Fed. **50** 54.51N 82.51E
Berdyansk Ukraine **45** 46.45N 36.47E
Berea U.S.A. **114** 41.22N 81.52W
Beregovo Ukraine **37** 48.12N 22.39E
Bereko Tanzania **79** 4.27S 35.43E
Berens r. Canada **101** 52.21N 97.02W
Berens River town Canada **101** 52.22N 97.02W
Beresford Australia **92** 29.14S 136.40E
Berettyóújfalu Hungary **37** 47.14N 21.32E
Berevo Madagascar **81** 19.44S 44.58E
Bereza Belarus **37** 52.32N 25.00E
Berezhany Ukraine **37** 49.27N 24.56E
Berezina r. Belarus **37** 54.10N 28.10E
Berezna Ukraine **37** 51.34N 31.46E
Berezniki Russian Fed. **44** 59.26N 56.49E
Berezno Ukraine **37** 51.00N 26.41E
Berezovka Ukraine **37** 47.12N 30.56E
Berezovo Russian Fed. **9** 63.58N 65.00E
Berga Spain **25** 42.06N 1.51E
Berga Sweden **43** 57.14N 16.03E
Bergama Turkey **29** 39.08N 27.10E
Bergamo Italy **30** 45.41N 9.43E
Bergen Germany **38** 54.26N 13.27E
Bergen Nschn. Germany **38** 52.48N 9.58E
Bergen Neth. **16** 52.40N 4.41E
Bergen Norway **42** 60.23N 5.20E
Bergen U.S.A. **114** 43.05N 77.57W
Bergen op Zoom Neth. **16** 51.30N 4.17E
Bergerac France **20** 44.51N 0.29E
Bergheim Germany **38** 50.55N 6.38E
Berghem Neth. **16** 51.46N 5.32E
Bergisch Gladbach Germany **38** 50.59N 7.07E
Bergkamen Germany **38** 51.38N 7.38E
Bergkvara Sweden **43** 56.23N 16.05E
Bergland U.S.A. **112** 46.36N 89.33W
Bergoo U.S.A. **114** 38.29N 80.18W
Bergslagen f. Sweden **43** 59.55N 15.00E
Bergues France **19** 50.58N 2.26E
Bergum Neth. **16** 53.14N 5.59E
Berhampore India **63** 24.06N 88.15E
Berhampur India **63** 19.19N 84.47E
Bering Sea N. America/Asia **98** 65.00N 170.00W
Bering Str. Russian Fed./U.S.A. **98** 65.00N 170.00W
Berislav Ukraine **45** 46.51N 33.26E
Berja Spain **27** 36.51N 2.57W
Berkåk Norway **42** 62.48N 10.03E
Berkel r. Neth. **16** 52.10N 6.12E
Berkeley U.S.A. **108** 37.57N 122.18W
Berkeley Springs town U.S.A. **114** 39.38N 78.14W
Berkner I. Antarctica **128** 79.30S 50.00W
Berkovitsa Bulgaria **34** 43.16N 23.08E
Berkshire d. U.K. **13** 51.25N 1.03W
Berkshire Downs hills U.K. **13** 51.32N 1.36W
Berkshire Hills mts. U.S.A. **115** 42.20N 73.10W
Berland r. Canada **100** 54.00N 116.50W
Berlanga de Duero Spain **26** 41.28N 2.51W
Berlin Germany **38** 52.31N 13.24E
Berlin d. Germany **38** 52.30N 13.20E
Berlin Md. U.S.A. **115** 38.20N 75.13W
Berlin N.H. U.S.A. **112** 44.29N 71.10W
Berlin Penn. U.S.A. **114** 39.55N 78.57W
Berlin L. U.S.A. **114** 41.00N 81.00W
Bermagui Australia **93** 36.28S 150.03E
Bermeja, Sierra mts. Spain **27** 36.30N 5.10W
Bermejo r. San Juan Argentina **124** 31.40S 67.15W
Bermejo r. Tucumán Argentina **124** 26.47S 58.30W
Bermeo Spain **26** 43.26N 2.43W
Bermillo de Sayago Spain **26** 41.22N 6.06W
Bermo India **63** 23.47N 85.57E
Bermuda Atlantic Oc. **127** 32.18N 64.45W
Bermuda Rise f. Atlantic Oc. **127** 34.00N 60.00W
Bern Switz. **39** 46.57N 7.26E
Bern d. Switz. **39** 46.55N 7.50E
Bernalda Italy **33** 40.24N 16.41E
Bernard L. Canada **104** 45.44N 79.24W
Bernau Germany **38** 52.40N 13.35E
Bernay France **18** 49.06N 0.36E
Bernburg Germany **38** 51.48N 11.44E
Berne see Bern Switz. **39**
Berner Alpen mts. Switz. **39** 46.30N 7.37E
Bernier I. Australia **88** 24.51S 113.09E
Bernina mtn. Italy/Switz. **30** 46.21N 9.51E
Bernkastel Germany **39** 49.55N 7.04E
Bernsdorf Germany **38** 51.22N 14.04E
Beror Hayil Israel **67** 31.33N 34.38E
Beroroha Madagascar **81** 21.41S 45.10E
Beroun Czech Republic **38** 49.58N 14.04E
Berounka r. Czech Republic **39** 50.00N 14.24E
Berovo Macedonia **34** 41.42N 22.51E
Berrechid Morocco **74** 33.17N 7.35W
Berre, Étang de b. France **21** 43.28N 5.11E
Berri Australia **92** 34.17S 140.36E
Berridale Australia **93** 36.21S 148.51E
Berrigan Australia **93** 35.41S 145.48E
Berry Head U.K. **13** 50.24N 3.28W

Berryville Ark. U.S.A. **111** 36.22N 93.34W
Berryville Va. U.S.A. **114** 39.09N 77.59W
Bersenbrück Germany **38** 52.33N 7.56E
Bershad Ukraine **37** 48.20N 29.30E
Berté, Lac l. Canada **103** 50.47N 68.30W
Berthierville Canada **105** 46.05N 73.10W
Bertinoro Italy **30** 44.09N 12.08E
Bertoua Cameroon **77** 4.34N 13.42E
Bertraghboy B. Rep. of Ire. **15** 53.23N 9.52W
Berwick Maine U.S.A. **115** 43.16N 70.51W
Berwick Penn. U.S.A. **115** 41.03N 76.15W
Berwick-upon-Tweed U.K. **12** 55.46N 2.00W
Besalampy Madagascar **81** 16.45S 44.30E
Besançon France **19** 47.15N 6.02E
Besor, Nahal wadi Egypt **67** 31.28N 34.22E
Bessarabia f. Moldova **37** 46.30N 28.40E
Bessemer U.S.A. **113** 33.22N 87.00W
Betafo Madagascar **81** 19.50S 46.51E
Bet Alpha Israel **67** 32.31N 35.26E
Betanzos Spain **26** 43.17N 8.12W
Betanzos, Ría de est. Spain **26** 43.23N 8.15W
Bétaré Oya Cameroon **77** 5.34N 14.09E
Bet Dagan Israel **67** 32.00N 34.50E
Bete Hor Ethiopia **73** 11.40N 39.00E
Bétera Spain **25** 39.35N 0.27W
Bet Guvrin site Israel **67** 31.36N 34.54E
Bet Ha'Emeq Israel **67** 32.58N 35.09E
Bethal R.S.A. **80** 26.26S 29.27E
Bet Hananya Israel **67** 32.32N 34.54E
Bethany Canada **104** 44.11N 78.34W
Bethany Beach town U.S.A. **115** 38.33N 75.00W
Bet HaShitta Israel **67** 32.33N 35.26E
Bethel Alas. U.S.A. **98** 60.48N 161.46W
Bethel Penn. U.S.A. **115** 40.28N 76.18W
Bethesda U.S.A. **114** 38.59N 77.06W
Bethlehem see Bayt Laḥm Jordan **67**
Bethlehem R.S.A. **80** 28.13S 28.18E
Bethlehem N.H. U.S.A. **105** 44.17N 71.42W
Bethlehem Penn. U.S.A. **115** 40.37N 75.25W
Béthune France **19** 50.32N 2.38E
Béthune r. France **18** 49.53N 1.09E
Betim Brazil **126** 19.55S 44.07W
Betioky Madagascar **81** 23.42S 44.22E
Bet Oren Israel **67** 32.44N 35.00E
Bet Qama Israel **67** 31.27N 34.46E
Bet Qeshet Israel **67** 32.43N 35.24E
Betroka Madagascar **81** 23.16S 46.06E
Bet She'an Israel **67** 32.30N 35.30E
Bet Shemesh Israel **67** 31.45N 35.00E
Betsiamites Canada **103** 48.56N 68.40W
Betsiboka r. Madagascar **81** 16.03S 46.36E
Bette mtn. Libya **75** 22.00N 19.12E
Bettiah India **63** 26.48N 84.30E
Bettles U.S.A. **98** 66.53N 151.51W
Betül India **63** 21.55N 77.54E
Betwa r. India **63** 25.55N 80.12E
Betws-y-Coed U.K. **11** 53.05N 3.48W
Betzdorf Germany **16** 50.48N 7.54E
Beulah Australia **92** 35.59S 142.26E
Beulah Canada **101** 50.16N 101.02W
Beulah U.S.A. **114** 48.16N 101.47W
Beuvron r. France **19** 47.29N 3.31E
Bevensen Germany **38** 53.05N 10.34E
Beverley Australia **89** 32.06S 116.56E
Beverley U.K. **12** 53.52N 0.26W
Beverly Mass. U.S.A. **115** 42.33N 70.53W
Beverly Ohio U.S.A. **114** 39.34N 118.26W
Beverly W.Va. U.S.A. **114** 38.51N 79.53W
Beverungen Germany **38** 51.39N 9.22E
Beverwijk Neth. **16** 52.29N 4.40E
Bewcastle Fells hills U.K. **12** 55.05N 2.50W
Bewdley Canada **104** 44.05N 78.19W
Bexhill U.K. **13** 50.51N 0.29E
Bexley U.K. **13** 51.26N 0.10E
Beyla Guinea **76** 8.42N 8.39W
Beyneu Kazakhstan **45** 45.16N 55.04E
Beypazari Turkey **64** 40.10N 31.56E
Beyşehir Gölü l. Turkey **64** 37.47N 31.30E
Bezau Austria **39** 47.23N 9.54E
Bezet Israel **67** 33.05N 35.08E
Bezhanovo Bulgaria **34** 43.13N 24.26E
Bezhetsk Russian Fed. **44** 57.49N 36.40E
Bezhitsa Russian Fed. **44** 53.19N 34.17E
Béziers France **20** 43.21N 3.15E
Bhadohi India **63** 25.25N 82.34E
Bhādra r. India **63** 29.07N 75.10E
Bhadrakh India **63** 21.04N 86.30E
Bhāg Pakistan **62** 29.02N 67.49E
Bhāgalpur India **63** 25.15N 87.00E
Bhaï Pheru Pakistan **62** 31.12N 73.57E
Bhairoṅghāti India **63** 31.01N 78.53E
Bhaisa U.S.A. India **63** 19.06N 77.58E
Bhakkar Pakistan **62** 31.38N 71.04E
Bhaktapur Nepal **63** 27.42N 85.27E
Bhalwāl Pakistan **62** 32.16N 72.54E
Bhamo Myanmar **56** 24.10N 97.30E
Bhandāra India **63** 21.10N 79.39E
Bhānvad India **62** 21.56N 69.47E
Bharānīpātna India **63** 19.54N 83.10E
Bharatpur India **63** 27.13N 77.29E
Bharthana India **63** 26.45N 79.14E
Bhātāpāra India **63** 21.44N 81.56E
Bhatewar India **62** 24.40N 74.05E
Bhātiāpāra Ghāt Bangla. **63** 23.12N 89.42E
Bhatinda India **62** 30.13N 74.56E
Bhatkal India **60** 13.58N 74.34E
Bhātpāra India **63** 22.52N 88.24E
Bhaunagar India **62** 21.46N 72.09E
Bhavānipatna India **63** 19.54N 83.10E
Bhawāni Mandi India **62** 24.25N 75.50E
Bhera Pakistan **62** 32.29N 72.55E
Bhikangaon India **62** 21.52N 75.57E
Bhilai India **63** 21.13N 81.26E
Bhīlwāra India **62** 25.21N 74.38E
Bhima r. India **60** 16.30N 77.10E
Bhind India **63** 26.34N 78.48E
Bhīnmāl India **62** 25.00N 72.15E

Bhiwandi India **62** 19.18N 73.04E
Bhiwāni India **62** 28.47N 76.08E
Bhognīpur India **63** 26.12N 79.48E
Bhojpur Nepal **63** 27.11N 87.02E
Bhokardan India **62** 20.16N 75.46E
Bhopāl India **63** 23.16N 77.24E
Bhor India **60** 18.12N 73.53E
Bhuban India **63** 20.53N 85.50E
Bhubaneswar India **63** 20.15N 85.50E
Bhuj India **62** 23.16N 69.40E
Bhusāwal India **62** 21.03N 75.46E
Bhutan Asia **63** 27.15N 91.00E
Biābānak Afghan. **62** 32.11N 64.11E
Biak Indonesia **59** 1.10S 136.05E
Biak i. Indonesia **59** 0.55S 136.00E
Biała Podlaska Poland **37** 52.02N 23.06E
Białogard Poland **36** 54.00N 16.00E
Białystok Poland **37** 53.09N 23.10E
Biankouma Côte d'Ivoire **76** 7.51N 7.34W
Biaora India **62** 23.55N 76.54E
Bia, Phou mtn. Laos **56** 18.59N 103.11E
Biarritz France **20** 43.29N 1.34W
Biasca Switz. **39** 46.22N 8.58E
Bibā Egypt **66** 28.56N 30.59E
Bibala Angola **78** 14.46S 13.21E
Biberach Germany **39** 48.20N 9.30E
Bibey r. Spain **26** 42.24N 7.13W
Bic Canada **103** 48.22N 68.42W
Bicas Brazil **126** 21.44S 43.04W
Bicester U.K. **13** 51.53N 1.09W
Bickle Knob mtn. U.S.A. **114** 38.56N 79.44W
Bida Nigeria **77** 9.06N 5.59E
Bidar India **60** 17.54N 77.33E
Biddeford U.S.A. **115** 43.30N 70.26W
Biddiyā Jordan **67** 32.07N 35.05E
Biddū Jordan **67** 31.50N 35.09E
Bideford U.K. **13** 51.01N 4.13W
Bidon Cinq see Poste Maurice Cortier Algeria **74**
Bi Doup mtn. Vietnam **56** 12.05N 108.40E
Bidwell U.S.A. **114** 38.55N 82.18W
Bié d. Angola **78** 13.00S 17.30E
Biedenkopf Germany **38** 50.55N 8.32E
Biel Switz. **39** 47.10N 7.12E
Bielefeld Germany **38** 52.01N 8.31E
Bielersee l. Switz. **39** 47.05N 7.10E
Biella Italy **30** 45.34N 8.03E
Bielsko-Biała Poland **37** 49.49N 19.02E
Bielsk Podlaski Poland **37** 52.47N 23.12E
Bien Hoa Vietnam **56** 10.58N 106.50E
Bienville, Lac l. Canada **103** 55.05N 72.40W
Bié Plateau f. Angola **78** 13.00S 16.00E
Bietigheim Germany **39** 48.58N 9.07E
Biferno r. Italy **33** 41.59N 15.02E
Big Bald Mtn. Canada **103** 47.12N 66.25W
Big Bear Lake town U.S.A. **109** 34.15N 116.53W
Big Beaver House town Canada **102** 52.59N 89.50W
Big Belt Mts. U.S.A. **108** 46.40N 111.25W
Big Bend Nat. Park U.S.A. **111** 29.12N 103.12W
Bigbury B. U.K. **13** 50.15N 3.56W
Big Cypress Swamp f. U.S.A. **113** 26.10N 81.38W
Big Falls town U.S.A. **110** 48.12N 93.48W
Biggar Canada **101** 52.04N 107.59W
Biggar U.K. **14** 55.38N 3.31W
Big Hickory U.S.A. **115** 41.43N 74.22W
Bighorn r. U.S.A. **108** 46.09N 107.28W
Bighorn L. U.S.A. **108** 45.06N 108.08W
Bighorn Mts. U.S.A. **108** 44.00N 107.30W
Bight, Head of b. Australia **91** 31.29S 131.16E
Big Moose U.S.A. **105** 43.49N 74.57W
Bignasco Switz. **39** 46.20N 8.36E
Bignona Senegal **76** 12.48N 16.18W
Big Pine U.S.A. **108** 37.10N 118.17W
Big Piney U.S.A. **108** 42.32N 110.07W
Big Quill L. Canada **101** 51.55N 104.22W
Big Run U.S.A. **114** 40.58N 78.53W
Big Salmon Canada **98** 61.53N 134.55W
Big Salmon r. Canada **100** 61.52N 134.56W
Big Sand L. Canada **101** 57.45N 99.42W
Big Sandy U.S.A. **108** 48.11N 110.07W
Big Smoky Valley f. U.S.A. **108** 38.30N 117.15W
Big Snowy Mtn. U.S.A. **108** 46.50N 109.30W
Big Spring town U.S.A. **111** 32.15N 101.28W
Big Stone Gap town U.S.A. **113** 36.52N 82.46W
Bigstone L. Canada **101** 53.42N 95.44W
Big Stone L. U.S.A. **110** 45.25N 96.40W
Big Sur U.S.A. **109** 36.15N 121.48W
Big Timber U.S.A. **108** 45.50N 109.57W
Big Trout L. Canada **102** 53.40N 90.00W
Bihać Bosnia-Herzegovina **31** 44.49N 15.52E
Bihar India **63** 25.11N 85.31E
Bihar d. India **63** 24.30N 86.00E
Biharamulo Tanzania **79** 2.34S 31.20E
Bihor mtn. Romania **37** 46.26N 22.43E
Bihu China **55** 28.21N 119.47E
Bijagós, Arquipélago dos is. Guinea Bissau **76** 11.30N 16.00W
Bijainagar India **62** 25.56N 74.38E
Bijaipura India **63** 24.46N 77.48E
Bijāpur India **60** 16.52N 75.47E
Bijāpur India **63** 18.48N 80.49E
Bijār Iran **65** 35.52N 47.39E
Bijāwar India **63** 24.38N 79.30E
Bijbān Chāh Pakistan **62** 26.54N 64.42E
Bijeljina Bosnia-Herzegovina **31** 44.45N 19.13E
Bijelo Polje Yugo. **31** 43.02N 19.44E
Bijeypur India **62** 26.03N 77.22E
Bijie China **55** 27.28N 105.20E
Bijnor India **63** 29.22N 78.08E
Bikaner India **62** 28.01N 73.22E
Bikin Russian Fed. **53** 46.52N 134.15E
Bikini i. Pacific Oc. **84** 11.35N 165.23E
Bikoro Zaïre **78** 0.45S 18.09E
Bilāra India **62** 26.10N 73.42E
Bilāspur Himachal P. India **62** 31.19N 76.45E
Bilāspur Madhya P. India **63** 22.05N 82.09E
Bilauktaung Range mts. Thailand **56** 13.00N 99.15E
Bilbao Spain **26** 43.15N 2.58W
Bilbays Egypt **66** 30.25N 31.34E

Bilbilis Spain 25 41.25N 1.39W
Bilbo see Bilbao Spain 26
Bileća Bosnia-Herzegovina 31 42.53N 18.26E
Bilecik Turkey 64 40.10N 29.59E
Bilgräm India 63 27.11N 80.02E
Bili r. Zaïre 73 4.09N 22.29E
Bilibino Russian Fed. 51 68.02N 166.15E
Bilimora India 62 20.45N 72.57E
Bílina Czech Republic 38 50.35N 13.45E
Billabong Creek r. Australia 92 35.04S 144.06E
Bill Baileys Bank f. Atlantic Oc. 10 60.45N 10.30W
Billengen f. Sweden 43 58.20N 13.43E
Billingham U.K. 12 54.36N 1.18W
Billings U.S.A. 108 45.47N 108.27W
Billingsfors Sweden 43 58.59N 12.15E
Bill of Portland c. U.K. 13 50.32N 2.28W
Billom France 20 45.44N 3.21E
Bilma Niger 75 18.41N 12.56E
Biloela Australia 90 24.24S 150.30E
Biloxi U.S.A. 111 30.24N 88.53W
Bilqās Qism Awwal Egypt 66 31.14N 31.22E
Biltine Chad 75 14.32N 20.55E
Biltine d. Chad 75 15.00N 21.00E
Bilto Norway 40 69.26N 21.35E
Bima r. Zaïre 78 3.24N 25.10E
Bimberi, Mt. Australia 93 35.40S 148.47E
Bimbo C.A.R. 78 4.15N 18.33E
Bimidji U.S.A. 96 47.29N 94.53W
Bina-Etāwa India 63 24.11N 78.11E
Binaiya mtn. Indonesia 59 3.10S 129.30E
Binālūd, Kūh-e mts. Iran 65 36.15N 59.00E
Binbee Australia 90 20.20S 147.55E
Binche Belgium 16 50.25N 4.10E
Bindki India 63 26.02N 80.36E
Bindura Zimbabwe 81 17.18S 31.20E
Binéfar Spain 25 41.51N 0.18E
Binga Zimbabwe 80 17.38S 27.19E
Binga, Mt. Zimbabwe 81 19.47S 33.03E
Bingara Australia 93 29.51S 150.38E
Bingen Germany 39 49.58N 7.55E
Bingerville Côte d'Ivoire 76 5.20N 3.53W
Bingham U.K. 12 52.57N 0.57W
Bingham U.S.A. 112 45.03N 69.53W
Binghamton U.S.A. 115 42.08N 75.54W
Bingkor Malaysia 58 5.26N 116.15E
Bingöl Turkey 23 38.54N 40.29E
Binhai China 54 34.00N 119.55E
Binh Dinh Vietnam 56 13.53N 109.07E
Binjai Indonesia 58 3.37N 98.25E
Binji Nigeria 77 13.12N 4.55E
Binnaway Australia 93 31.32S 149.23E
Binscarth Canada 101 50.37N 101.16W
Bintan i. Indonesia 58 1.10N 104.30E
Bint Jubayl Lebanon 67 33.07N 35.26E
Bintulu Malaysia 58 3.12N 113.01E
Bin Xian China 54 35.02N 108.04E
Binyamina Israel 67 32.31N 34.57E
Binyang China 55 23.12N 108.48E
Binzert Tunisia 32 37.17N 9.52E
Bioco Equat. Guinea 77 3.25N 8.45E
Biograd Croatia 31 43.56N 15.27E
Biq'at Bet Netofa f. Israel 67 32.49N 35.19E
Bīr India 62 18.59N 75.46E
Bi'r Abū 'Uwayqīlah well Egypt 66 30.50N 34.07E
Bi'r ad Dakhal well Egypt 66 28.40N 32.24E
Birāk Libya 75 27.32N 14.17E
Birak Sulaymān site Jordan 67 31.41N 35.10E
Bi'r al Ḥarash well Egypt 75 25.30N 22.06E
Bi'r al Jidy well Egypt 66 30.13N 33.03E
Bi'r al Jufayr well Egypt 66 30.49N 32.40E
Bi'r al 'Udayd well Egypt 66 28.59N 34.05E
Birao C.A.R. 73 10.17N 22.47E
Bi'r aş Şafrā' well Egypt 66 28.46N 34.20E
Bi'r ath Thamadah well Egypt 66 30.10N 33.28E
Birātnagar Nepal 63 26.18N 87.17E
Bi'r Buerāt well Egypt 66 28.59N 32.10E
Bi'r Bukhayt well Egypt 66 29.13N 32.17E
Bîrca Romania 34 43.59N 23.36E
Birch r. Canada 100 58.30N 112.15W
Birchip Australia 92 35.59S 142.59E
Birch L. N.W.T. Canada 100 62.04N 116.33W
Birch L. Ont. Canada 102 51.24N 92.20W
Birch Mts. Canada 100 57.30N 112.30W
Bird Canada 101 56.30N 94.13W
Birdsboro U.S.A. 115 40.16N 75.48W
Birdsville Australia 90 25.54S 139.22E
Birecik Turkey 64 37.03N 37.59E
Bīrganj Nepal 63 27.01N 84.54E
Birhan mtn. Ethiopia 73 11.00N 37.50E
Bi'r Ḥasanah well Egypt 66 30.29N 33.47E
Bi'r Hooker well Egypt 66 30.23N 30.20E
Bīrjand Iran 65 32.54N 59.10E
Bi'r Jifjafah well Egypt 66 30.28N 33.11E
Birkeland Norway 42 58.20N 8.14E
Birkenfeld B.-Würt. Germany 39 48.52N 8.38E
Birkenfeld Rhein.-Pfalz Germany 39 49.39N 7.10E
Birkenhead U.K. 12 53.24N 3.01W
Birkeröd Denmark 43 55.50N 12.26E
Birksgate Range mts. Australia 88 27.10S 129.45E
Bi'r Kusaybah well Egypt 66 22.41N 29.55E
Birk, Wādī r. Saudi Arabia 65 24.08N 47.35E
Bîrlad Romania 37 46.14N 27.40E
Bi'r Lahfān well Egypt 66 31.01N 33.52E
Birmingham U.K. 13 52.30N 1.55W
Birmingham Ala. U.S.A. 113 33.30N 86.55W
Birmingham Mich. U.S.A. 104 42.33N 83.15W
Birmitrapur India 63 22.24N 84.46E
Bir Mogrein Mauritania 74 25.14N 11.35W
Birni Benin 77 9.59N 1.34E
Birnin Gwari Nigeria 77 11.02N 6.47E
Birnin Kebbi Nigeria 77 12.30N 4.11E
Birni N'Konni Niger 77 13.49N 5.19E
Birobidzhan Russian Fed. 53 48.49N 132.54E
Bīr Ounâne well Mali 74 21.02N 3.18W
Birr Rep. of Ire. 15 53.06N 7.56W
Bir, Ras c. Djibouti 71 11.59N 43.25E
Birrie r. Australia 93 29.43S 146.37E

Birsilpur India 62 28.11N 72.15E
Birsk Russian Fed. 44 55.28N 55.31E
Bi'r Tābah well Egypt 66 29.30N 34.53E
Bi'r Ṭarfāwī well Egypt 72 22.55N 28.53E
Birtle Canada 101 50.32N 101.02W
Bi'r Umm Sa'īd well Egypt 66 29.40N 33.34E
Bi'r Umm 'Umayyid well Egypt 66 27.53N 32.30E
Bi'r Ya'qūb well Jordan 67 32.13N 35.17E
Biržai Lithuania 44 56.10N 24.48E
Bi'r Zalṭan well Libya 75 28.27N 19.46E
Bir Zreigat Mauritania 74 22.27N 8.53W
Bisaccia Italy 33 41.01N 15.22E
Bisalpur India 63 28.18N 79.48E
Bisbee U.S.A. 109 31.27N 109.55W
Blanca, Bahía b. Argentina 125 39.20S 62.00W
Biscarosse France 20 44.24N 1.10W
Biscarosse, Étang de b. France 20 44.20N 1.10W
Biscay, B. of France 20 44.00N 4.00W
Bisceglie Italy 33 41.14N 16.31E
Bischheim France 19 48.37N 7.45E
Bischofswerda Germany 38 51.07N 14.10E
Biscotasi L. Canada 104 47.19N 82.07W
Biscotasing Canada 104 47.18N 82.08W
Bīsha Eritrea 72 15.28N 37.34E
Bishkek Kyrgyzstan 52 42.53N 74.46E
Bishnupur India 63 23.05N 87.19E
Bishop Calif. U.S.A. 108 37.22N 118.24W
Bishop Tex. U.S.A. 111 27.35N 97.48W
Bishop Auckland U.K. 12 54.40N 1.40W
Bishop's Stortford U.K. 13 51.53N 0.09E
Bisina, L. Uganda 79 1.38S 34.08E
Biskra Algeria 75 34.48N 5.40E
Bismarck U.S.A. 110 46.48N 100.47W
Bismarck Range mts. P.N.G. 59 6.00S 145.00E
Bismarck Sea Pacific Oc. 59 4.00S 146.30E
Bison U.S.A. 110 45.31N 102.28W
Bīsotūn Iran 65 34.22N 47.29E
Bispgården Sweden 40 63.02N 16.40E
Bissau Guinea Bissau 76 11.52N 15.39W
Bissett Canada 101 51.02N 95.40W
Bissikrima Guinea 76 10.50N 10.58W
Bistcho L. Canada 100 59.45N 118.50W
Bistreţ Romania 34 43.54N 23.23E
Bistriţa Romania 37 47.08N 24.30E
Bistriţa r. Romania 37 46.30N 26.54E
Biswān India 63 27.30N 81.00E
Bitam Gabon 78 2.05N 11.30E
Bitburg Germany 39 49.58N 6.31E
Bitche France 19 49.03N 7.26E
Bitéa, Ouadi wadi Chad 73 13.11N 20.10E
Bitlis Turkey 64 38.23N 42.04E
Bitola Macedonia 34 41.01N 21.20E
Bitonto Italy 33 41.06N 16.42E
Bitter Creek town U.S.A. 108 41.31N 109.27W
Bitterfeld Germany 38 51.37N 12.20E
Bitterfontein R.S.A. 80 31.02S 18.14E
Bitterroot Range mts. U.S.A. 108 47.06N 115.10W
Bitti Italy 32 40.29N 9.23E
Biu Nigeria 77 10.36N 12.11E
Biumba Rwanda 79 1.38S 30.02E
Biwa ko i. Japan 57 35.10N 136.00E
Biyalā Egypt 66 31.11N 31.13E
Biysk Russian Fed. 9 52.35N 85.16E
Bizerte see Binzert Tunisia 32
Bizerte d. Tunisia 32 37.07N 9.45E
Bizerte, Lac de l. Tunisia 32 37.12N 9.52E
Bjärnum Sweden 43 56.17N 13.42E
Bjelasica mts. Yugo. 31 42.50N 19.40E
Bjelovar Croatia 31 45.54N 16.51E
Bjerringbro Denmark 42 56.23N 9.40E
Björkelangen Norway 42 59.53N 11.34E
Bjorli Norway 41 62.16N 8.13E
Björna Sweden 40 63.32N 18.36E
Björnafjorden est. Norway 42 60.06N 5.22E
Bjørnøya i. Arctic Oc. 128 74.30N 19.00E
Bjuv Sweden 43 56.05N 12.54E
Blace Yugo. 34 43.18N 21.17E
Black r. Canada 104 44.20N 79.20W
Black r. Ark. U.S.A. 111 35.38N 91.19W
Black r. Mich. U.S.A. 104 43.00N 82.25W
Black r. Mich. U.S.A. 104 45.39N 84.29W
Black r. N.Y. U.S.A. 105 44.01N 75.59W
Black r. Ohio U.S.A. 114 41.28N 82.11W
Black r. see Dà r. Vietnam 56
Blackall Australia 90 24.25S 145.28E
Blackburn U.K. 12 53.44N 2.30W
Black Diamond Canada 100 50.45N 114.14W
Black Duck r. Canada 101 56.51N 89.02W
Blackduck U.S.A. 110 47.44N 94.33W
Blackfoot U.S.A. 108 43.11N 112.20W
Black Hills U.S.A. 110 44.00N 104.00W
Black L. Canada 101 59.10N 105.20W
Black L. Mich. U.S.A. 104 45.28N 84.15W
Black L. N.Y. U.S.A. 105 44.31N 75.35W
Black Lake town Canada 101 59.10N 105.20W
Black Mtn. U.K. 13 51.52N 3.50W
Black Mts. U.K. 13 51.52N 3.10W
Blackpool U.K. 12 53.48N 3.03W
Black River town Jamaica 117 18.02N 77.52W
Black River town Mich. U.S.A. 104 44.47N 83.19W
Black River town N.Y. U.S.A. 105 44.01N 75.48W
Black Rock town U.S.A. 108 38.41N 112.59W
Black Rock Desert U.S.A. 108 41.10N 119.00W
Black Sand Desert see Karakumy, Peski Turkmenistan 65
Black Sea Europe 37 44.00N 30.00E
Blacksod B. Rep. of Ire. 15 54.04N 10.00W
Blackstone U.S.A. 113 37.05N 78.02W
Black Sugarloaf Mt. Australia 93 31.24S 151.34E
Blackville Australia 93 31.34S 150.10E
Blackville U.S.A. 113 33.22N 81.17W
Black Volta r. Ghana 76 8.14N 2.11W
Blackwater Australia 90 23.34S 148.53E
Blackwater r. Waterford Rep. of Ire. 15 51.58N 7.52W
Blackwater r. U.K. 11 54.31N 6.36W
Blackwell U.S.A. 111 36.48N 97.17W
Blackwood r. Australia 89 34.15S 115.10E
Blaenau Ffestiniog U.K. 12 53.00N 3.57W
Blagaj Bosnia-Herzegovina 31 43.15N 17.50E

Blagoevgrad Bulgaria 34 42.02N 23.05E
Blagoveshchensk Russian Fed. 53 50.19N 127.30E
Blain France 18 47.29N 1.46W
Blain U.S.A. 114 40.20N 77.31W
Blair U.S.A. 110 41.33N 96.08W
Blair Athol Australia 90 22.42S 147.33E
Blair Atholl U.K. 14 56.46N 3.51W
Blairgowrie U.K. 14 56.36N 3.21W
Blairmore Canada 100 49.40N 114.25W
Blairsville Ga. U.S.A. 113 34.52N 83.52W
Blairsville Penn. U.S.A. 114 40.26N 79.16W
Blakely U.S.A. 113 31.22N 84.58W
Blakeslee U.S.A. 115 41.06N 75.36W
Blanca, Sierra mtn. U.S.A. 109 33.23N 105.48W
Blanc, Cap c. Mauritania 76 20.44N 17.05W
Blanc, Cap c. Tunisia 32 37.20N 9.50E
Blanchard U.S.A. 108 48.01N 116.59W
Blanche, L. Australia 92 29.15S 139.40E
Blanc, Mont mtn. France 21 45.50N 6.52E
Blanco, C. Argentina 125 47.12S 65.20W
Blanco, C. Costa Rica 117 9.36N 85.06W
Blanco, C. U.S.A. 108 42.50N 124.34W
Bland r. Australia 93 33.42S 147.30E
Blandburg U.S.A. 114 40.41N 78.25W
Blandford Forum U.K. 13 50.52N 2.10W
Blanes Spain 25 41.41N 2.48E
Blangy-sur-Bresle France 19 49.56N 1.38E
Blankenberge Belgium 16 51.18N 3.08E
Blankenburg Germany 38 51.48N 10.58E
Blanquefort France 20 44.53N 0.39W
Blansko Czech Republic 36 49.22N 16.39E
Blantyre Malawi 79 15.46S 35.00E
Blarney Rep. of Ire. 15 51.56N 8.34W
Blatná Czech Republic 38 49.26N 13.53E
Blatnica Bulgaria 37 43.42N 28.31E
Blaubeuren Germany 39 48.24N 9.47E
Blaufelden Germany 39 49.18N 9.58E
Blavet r. France 18 47.43N 3.18W
Blaye France 20 45.08N 0.39W
Blayney Australia 93 33.32S 149.19E
Bled Slovenia 31 46.22N 14.06E
Blednaya, Gora mtn. Russian Fed. 50 76.23N 65.08E
Bleiburg Austria 31 46.35N 14.48E
Blekinge d. Sweden 43 56.20N 15.15E
Blekinge f. Sweden 43 56.20N 15.20E
Blenheim Canada 104 42.20N 82.00W
Blenheim New Zealand 86 41.32S 173.58E
Bléone r. France 21 44.03N 6.00E
Bléré France 18 47.20N 1.00E
Blerick Neth. 16 51.22N 6.08E
Bletchley U.K. 13 51.59N 0.45W
Bletterans France 19 46.45N 5.27E
Bleu, Lac l. Canada 104 46.35N 78.20W
Blida Algeria 75 36.30N 2.50E
Blidö i. Sweden 43 59.37N 18.54E
Bligh Entrance Australia 90 9.18S 144.10E
Blind River town Canada 104 46.10N 82.58W
Blinman Australia 92 31.05S 138.11E
Blitar Indonesia 59 8.06S 112.12E
Blitta Togo 77 8.23N 1.06E
Block I. U.S.A. 115 41.11N 71.35W
Bloemfontein R.S.A. 80 29.07S 26.14E
Bloemhof R.S.A. 80 27.37S 25.34E
Blois France 18 47.35N 1.20E
Blönduós Iceland 40 65.39N 20.18W
Bloody Foreland c. Rep. of Ire. 15 55.09N 8.17W
Bloomfield Canada 105 43.59N 77.14W
Bloomfield Iowa U.S.A. 110 40.45N 92.25W
Bloomfield Nebr. U.S.A. 110 42.36N 97.39W
Bloomfield N.J. U.S.A. 115 40.48N 74.12W
Bloomingdale U.S.A. 105 44.25N 74.06W
Bloomington Ill. U.S.A. 110 40.29N 89.00W
Bloomington Ind. U.S.A. 112 39.10N 86.31W
Bloomington Minn. U.S.A. 110 44.50N 93.17W
Bloomsburg U.S.A. 115 41.00N 76.27W
Blora Indonesia 59 6.55S 111.29E
Blossburg U.S.A. 114 41.41N 77.04W
Blovice Czech Republic 38 49.35N 13.33E
Bludenz Austria 39 47.09N 9.49E
Blueberry r. Canada 100 56.45N 120.49W
Bluefield U.S.A. 113 37.14N 81.17W
Bluefields Nicaragua 117 12.00N 83.49W
Blue Hills of Couteau Canada 103 47.59N 57.43W
Bluemont U.S.A. 114 39.06N 77.51W
Blue Mountain Lake town U.S.A. 105 43.53N 74.26W
Blue Mts. Australia 93 33.16S 150.19E
Blue Mts. U.S.A. 108 45.30N 118.15W
Blue Mud B. Australia 90 13.26S 135.56E
Blue Nile r. see Azraq, Al Baḥr al r. Sudan 72
Bluenose L. Canada 98 68.30N 119.35W
Blue River town Canada 100 52.05N 119.09W
Blue Stack Mts. Rep. of Ire. 15 54.44N 8.09W
Bluff New Zealand 86 46.38S 168.21E
Bluff U.S.A. 108 37.17N 109.33W
Bluff, C. Canada 103 52.48N 55.53W
Bluff Knoll mtn. Australia 89 34.25S 118.15E
Blumberg Germany 39 47.50N 8.31E
Blumenau Brazil 126 26.55S 49.07W
Blunt U.S.A. 110 44.31N 99.59W
Blyth r. Australia 90 12.12S 135.30E
Blyth Northum. U.K. 12 55.07N 1.29W
Blythe U.S.A. 109 33.37N 114.36W
Blytheville U.S.A. 111 35.56N 89.55W
Bø Nordland Norway 40 68.38N 14.35E
Bø Telemark Norway 42 59.25N 9.04E
Bo Sierra Leone 76 7.58N 11.45W
Boa Esperança Brazil 126 21.03S 45.37W
Boa Esperança, Reprêsa da resr. Brazil 123 6.45S 44.15W
Bo'al Henan China 54 35.10N 113.04E
Boane Mozambique 81 26.02S 32.19E
Boa Vista Brazil 122 2.51N 60.43W
Bobadah Australia 93 32.18S 146.42E
Bobadilla Spain 27 37.02N 4.44W
Bobbili India 61 18.34N 83.22E
Bobbio Italy 30 44.46N 9.23E

Blagoevgrad Bulgaria 34 42.02N 23.05E
Bobcaygeon Canada 104 44.33N 78.33W
Böblingen Germany 39 48.41N 9.01E
Bobo-Dioulasso Burkina 76 11.11N 4.18W
Bobonong Botswana 80 21.59S 28.29E
Bobr Belarus 37 54.19N 29.18E
Bóbr r. Poland 36 52.04N 15.04E
Bobruysk Belarus 37 53.08N 29.10E
Bôca do Acre Brazil 122 8.45S 67.23W
Bocaranga C.A.R. 77 7.01N 15.35E
Boca Raton U.S.A. 113 26.22N 80.05W
Bochnia Poland 37 49.58N 20.26E
Bocholt Germany 38 51.50N 6.36E
Bochum Germany 38 51.28N 7.13E
Bochum R.S.A. 80 23.12S 29.12E
Bockum-Hövel Germany 38 51.42N 7.46E
Bocognano France 21 42.05N 9.03E
Boconó Venezuela 122 9.17N 70.17W
Boda C.A.R. 77 4.19N 17.26E
Böda Sweden 43 57.15N 17.03E
Boda Glasbruk Sweden 43 56.44N 15.40E
Bodalla Australia 93 36.05S 150.03E
Bodallin Australia 89 31.22S 118.52E
Bodélé f. Chad 77 16.50N 17.10E
Boden Sweden 40 65.50N 21.42E
Bodensee l. Europe 39 47.35N 9.25E
Bode Sadu Nigeria 77 8.57N 4.49E
Bodfish U.S.A. 109 35.36N 118.30W
Bodmin U.K. 13 50.28N 4.44W
Bodmin Moor U.K. 13 50.53N 4.35W
Bodø Canada 101 52.11N 110.04W
Bodø Norway 40 67.18N 14.26E
Bodrum Turkey 35 37.02N 27.26E
Boembé Congo 78 2.59S 15.34E
Boende Zaïre 78 0.15S 20.49E
Boën-sur-Lignon France 20 45.44N 3.59E
Boeo, Capo c. Italy 32 37.48N 12.26E
Boffa Guinea 76 10.12N 14.02W
Bofors Sweden 43 59.20N 14.32E
Bogale Myanmar 56 16.17N 95.24E
Bogalusa U.S.A. 111 30.47N 89.52W
Bogan r. Australia 93 30.00S 146.20E
Bogan Gate town Australia 93 33.08S 147.50E
Bogata U.S.A. 111 33.28N 95.13W
Bogcang Zangbo r. China 63 31.56N 87.25E
Bogen Germany 39 48.55N 12.43E
Bogenfels Namibia 80 27.26S 15.22E
Bogense Denmark 42 55.34N 10.06E
Boggabilla Australia 93 28.36S 150.21E
Boggabri Australia 93 30.42S 150.02E
Boggeragh Mts. Rep. of Ire. 15 52.03N 8.53W
Bogia P.N.G. 59 4.16S 145.00E
Bognes Norway 40 68.15N 16.00E
Bognor Regis U.K. 13 50.47N 0.40W
Bog of Allen f. Rep. of Ire. 15 53.17N 7.00W
Bogol Manyo Ethiopia 73 4.32N 41.32E
Bogong, Mt. Australia 93 36.45S 147.21E
Bogor Indonesia 58 6.34S 106.45E
Bogotá Colombia 122 4.38N 74.05W
Bogra Bangla. 63 24.51N 89.22E
Bogué Mauritania 74 16.35N 14.16W
Boguslav Ukraine 37 49.32N 30.52E
Bo Hai b. China 54 38.30N 119.30E
Bohain France 19 49.59N 3.27E
Bohai Wan b. China 54 38.30N 117.55E
Bohemian Forest see Böhmerwald mts. Germany 39
Bohinjska Bistrica Slovenia 31 46.17N 13.57E
Böhmerwald mts. Germany 39 49.12N 12.55E
Bohol i. Phil. 59 9.45N 124.10E
Bohuslän f. Sweden 42 58.15N 11.50E
Boiaçu Brazil 122 0.27S 61.46W
Boiano Italy 33 41.29N 14.29E
Boigu i. Australia 90 9.16S 142.12E
Boing Sudan 73 9.58N 33.44E
Boiro Spain 26 42.39N 8.54W
Bois Blanc I. U.S.A. 104 45.45N 84.28W
Bois du Roi mtn. France 19 47.00N 4.02E
Boise U.S.A. 108 43.37N 116.13W
Boise City U.S.A. 111 36.44N 102.31W
Bois-Guillaume France 19 49.28N 1.08E
Bois, Lac des l. Canada 98 66.40N 125.15W
Boissevain Canada 101 49.15N 100.00W
Boizenburg Germany 38 53.22N 10.43E
Bojador, Cabo c. W. Sahara 74 26.08N 14.30W
Bojana r. Albania 31 41.50N 19.25E
Bojeador, C. Phil. 55 18.30N 120.36E
Bojnūrd Iran 65 37.28N 57.20E
Bojonegoro Indonesia 59 7.06S 111.50E
Bokani Nigeria 77 9.27N 5.13E
Boké Guinea 76 10.57N 14.13W
Bokhara r. Australia 93 29.55S 146.42E
Boknafjorden est. Norway 42 59.10N 5.35E
Bokoro Chad 77 12.17N 17.04E
Bokote Zaïre 78 0.05S 20.08E
Bokpyin Myanmar 56 11.16N 98.46E
Bokungu Zaïre 78 0.44S 22.28E
Bol Chad 77 13.27N 14.40E
Bol Croatia 31 43.16N 16.40E
Bolac Lake town Australia 92 37.42S 142.50E
Bolafa Zaïre 78 1.23N 22.06E
Bolama Guinea Bissau 76 11.35N 15.30W
Bolan r. Pakistan 62 29.05N 67.45E
Bolanda, Jabal mtn. Sudan 73 7.44N 25.28E
Bolaños de Calatrava Spain 26 38.54N 3.40W
Bolan Pass Pakistan 62 29.45N 67.35E
Bolbec France 18 49.34N 0.29E
Bole China 52 44.55N 82.04E
Bolesławiec Poland 36 51.16N 15.34E
Bolgatanga Ghana 76 10.42N 0.52W
Bolgrad Ukraine 37 45.42N 28.40E
Bolia Zaïre 78 1.36S 18.23E
Bolívar Argentina 125 36.14S 61.07W
Bolívar N.Y. U.S.A. 114 42.04N 78.10W
Bolívar Tenn. U.S.A. 111 35.16N 88.59W
Bolivia S. America 124 17.00S 65.00W
Bollène France 21 44.17N 4.45E
Bollnäs Sweden 41 61.21N 16.25E
Bollon Australia 93 28.02S 147.28E

Bollstabruk Sweden 40 62.59N 17.42E
Bollullos par del Condado Spain 27 37.20N 6.32W
Bolmen l. Sweden 43 56.55N 13.40E
Bolobo Zaïre 78 2.10S 16.17E
Bologna Italy 30 44.29N 11.20E
Bologoye Russian Fed. 44 57.58N 34.00E
Bolomba Zaïre 78 0.30N 19.13E
Bolombo Zaïre 78 3.59S 21.22E
Bolondo Equat. Guinea 78 1.40N 9.38E
Bolongongo Angola 78 8.28S 15.16E
Bolovens, Plateau des f. Laos 56 15.10N 106.30E
Bolsena Italy 30 42.39N 11.59E
Bolsena, Lago di l. Italy 30 42.36N 11.56E
Bolshaya Glushitsa Russian Fed. 44 52.28N 50.30E
Bolshaya Pyssa Russian Fed. 44 64.11N 48.44E
Bolsherechye Russian Fed. 50 56.07N 74.40E
Bol'shevik, Ostrov i. Russian Fed. 51 78.30N 102.00E
Bolshezemelskaya Tundra f. Russian Fed. 44 67.00N 56.10E
Bolshoy Atlym Russian Fed. 50 62.17N 66.30E
Bol'shoy Balkhan, Khrebet mts. Turkmenistan 65 39.38N 54.30E
Bol'shoy Irgiz r. Russian Fed. 44 52.00N 47.20E
Bol'shoy Lyakhovskiy, Ostrov i. Russian Fed. 51 73.30N 142.00E
Bol'shoy Onguren Russian Fed. 51 53.40N 107.40E
Bolshoy Uzen r. Kazakhstan 45 49.00N 49.40E
Bolsover U.K. 12 53.14N 1.18W
Boltaña Spain 25 42.27N 0.04E
Bolton U.K. 12 53.35N 2.26W
Bolton L. Canada 100 61.16N 95.47W
Bolu Turkey 64 40.45N 31.38E
Bolus Head Rep. of Ire. 15 51.47N 10.20W
Bolvadin Turkey 64 38.43N 31.02E
Boly Hungary 31 45.58N 18.32E
Bolzano Italy 30 46.31N 11.22E
Boma Zaïre 78 5.50S 13.03E
Bomaderry Australia 93 34.21S 150.34E
Bomadi Nigeria 77 5.13N 6.01E
Bombala Australia 93 36.55S 149.16E
Bombarral Portugal 27 39.16N 9.09W
Bombay India 62 18.58N 72.50E
Bombo Uganda 79 0.35N 32.32E
Bomboma Zaïre 78 2.25N 18.54E
Bom Despacho Brazil 126 19.46S 45.15W
Bomi China 52 29.50N 95.45E
Bomi Hills Liberia 76 7.01N 10.38W
Bömitz Germany 38 53.08N 11.13E
Bömlafjorden est. Norway 42 59.39N 5.20E
Bömlo i. Norway 42 59.46N 5.12E
Bomokandi r. Zaïre 79 3.37N 26.09E
Bomongo Zaïre 78 1.30N 18.21E
Bomu r. Zaïre see Mbomou r. C.A.R. 73
Bonaigarh India 63 21.50N 84.57E
Bonaire i. Neth. Antilles 122 12.15N 68.27W
Bonanza U.S.A. 108 40.01N 109.11W
Bonaparte r. Canada 100 50.46N 121.17W
Bonaparte Archipelago is. Australia 88 14.17S 125.18E
Bonar-Bridge town U.K. 14 57.53N 4.21W
Bonarcado Italy 32 40.04N 8.38E
Bonavista Canada 103 48.39N 53.07W
Bonavista Canada 103 48.45N 53.20W
Bonavista, C. Canada 103 48.42N 53.05W
Bon Bon Australia 92 30.26S 135.28E
Bon, Cap c. Tunisia 32 37.05N 11.03E
Bondeno Italy 30 44.53N 11.25E
Bondo Equateur Zaïre 78 1.22S 23.53E
Bondo Haut Zaïre Zaïre 78 3.47N 23.45E
Bondoukou Côte d'Ivoire 76 8.03N 2.15W
Bondowoso Indonesia 59 7.54S 113.50E
Bo'ness U.K. 14 56.01N 3.36W
Bone, Teluk b. Indonesia 59 4.00S 120.50E
Bonfield Canada 104 46.14N 79.10W
Bonga Ethiopia 73 7.17N 36.15E
Bongaigaon India 63 26.28N 90.34E
Bongak Sudan 73 7.27N 33.14E
Bongandanga Zaïre 78 1.28N 21.03E
Bongor Chad 77 10.18N 15.22E
Bongos, Massif des mts. C.A.R. 73 8.20N 21.35E
Bongouanou Côte d'Ivoire 76 6.44N 4.10W
Bonham U.S.A. 111 33.35N 96.11W
Bonifacio France 21 41.23N 9.10E
Bonifacio, Str. of Italy 32 41.20N 9.15E
Bonin Is. Japan 84 27.00N 142.10E
Bonn Germany 38 50.44N 7.05E
Bonnechere Canada 105 45.39N 77.35W
Bonnechère r. Canada 105 45.31N 76.33W
Bonners Ferry U.S.A. 108 48.41N 116.18W
Bonnétable France 18 48.11N 0.26E
Bonneval France 18 48.11N 1.24E
Bonneville France 21 46.05N 6.25E
Bonneville Salt Flats f. U.S.A. 108 40.45N 113.52W
Bonney, L. Australia 92 37.47S 140.23E
Bonnie Rock town Australia 89 30.32S 118.21E
Bonny Nigeria 77 4.25N 7.10E
Bonny, Bight of Africa 77 2.58N 7.00E
Bonnyville Canada 101 54.16N 110.44W
Bonorva Italy 32 40.25N 8.45E
Bonshaw Australia 93 29.08S 150.53E
Bontang Indonesia 58 0.05N 117.31E
Bonthe Sierra Leone 76 7.32N 12.30W
Bonyhád Hungary 31 46.19N 18.32E
Bonython Range mts. Australia 88 23.51S 129.00E
Bookaloo Australia 92 31.56S 137.21E
Boola Guinea 76 8.22N 8.41W
Booleroo Centre Australia 92 32.53S 138.21E
Booligal Australia 93 33.54S 144.54E
Boom Belgium 16 51.07N 4.21E
Boomi Australia 93 28.44S 149.36E
Boomrivier R.S.A. 80 29.34S 20.26E
Boone U.S.A. 110 42.04N 93.53W
Booneville U.S.A. 111 34.39N 88.34W
Boonsboro U.S.A. 114 39.30N 77.39W
Boonville Ind. U.S.A. 114 38.03N 87.16W
Boonville N.Y. U.S.A. 115 43.29N 75.20W
Boonville Mo. U.S.A. 110 38.58N 92.44W
Boorabbin Australia 89 31.14S 120.21E
Boorama Somali Rep. 71 9.58N 43.07E
Boorindal Australia 93 30.23S 146.11E

Booroorban Australia 93 34.56S 144.46E
Boorowa Australia 93 34.26S 148.48E
Boort Australia 92 36.08S 143.46E
Boosaaso Somali Rep. 71 11.13N 49.08E
Boothia, G. of Canada 99 70.00N 90.00W
Boothia Pen. Canada 99 70.30N 95.00W
Bootra Australia 92 30.00S 143.00E
Booué Gabon 78 0.00 11.58E
Bopeechee Australia 92 29.36S 137.23E
Bophuthatswana Africa 80 27.00S 23.30E
Boppard Germany 39 50.14N 7.35E
Boquilla, Presa de la l. Mexico 109 27.30N 105.30W
Bor Czech Republic 38 49.43N 12.47E
Bor Sudan 73 6.12N 31.33E
Bor Yugo. 29 44.05N 22.07E
Bora Bora i. Is. de la Société 85 16.30S 151.45W
Borah Peak mtn. U.S.A. 108 44.08N 113.38W
Borås Sweden 43 57.43N 12.55E
Boräzjän Iran 65 29.14N 51.12E
Borba Brazil 122 4.24S 59.35W
Borba Portugal 27 38.48N 7.27W
Borda Cape town Australia 92 35.45S 136.34E
Bordeaux France 20 44.50N 0.34W
Borden Australia 89 34.05S 118.16E
Borden I. Canada 98 78.30N 111.00W
Borden Pen. Canada 99 73.00N 83.00W
Borders d. U.K. 14 55.30N 2.53W
Bordertown Australia 92 36.18S 140.49E
Bordesholm Germany 38 54.11N 10.01E
Bordheyri Iceland 40 65.12N 21.06W
Bordighera Italy 30 43.46N 7.39E
Bordj Bou Arreridj Algeria 75 36.04N 4.46E
Bordj Flye Sainte Marie Algeria 74 27.17N 2.59W
Bordj Omar Driss Algeria 75 28.09N 6.49E
Bordö i. Faroe Is. 40 62.10N 7.13W
Bore Ethiopia 73 4.40N 37.40E
Boreda Ethiopia 73 6.32N 37.48E
Borensberg Sweden 43 58.34N 15.17E
Borgå Finland 41 60.24N 25.40E
Borga Sweden 40 64.49N 15.05E
Börgefjell mtn. Norway 40 65.20N 13.45E
Börgefjell Nat. Park Norway 40 65.00N 13.58E
Borger Neth. 16 52.57N 6.46E
Borger U.S.A. 111 35.39N 101.24W
Borgholm Sweden 43 56.53N 16.39E
Borghorst Germany 16 52.08N 7.27E
Borgo Italy 30 46.03N 11.27E
Borgomanero Italy 30 45.42N 8.28E
Borgo San Dalmazzo Italy 30 44.20N 7.30E
Borgo San Lorenzo Italy 30 43.57N 11.23E
Borgosesia Italy 30 45.43N 8.16E
Borgo Val di Taro Italy 30 44.29N 9.46E
Borgund Norway 41 61.03N 7.49E
Borislav Ukraine 37 49.18N 23.28E
Borisoglebsk Russian Fed. 45 51.23N 42.02E
Borisov Belarus 37 54.09N 28.30E
Borispol Ukraine 37 50.21N 30.59E
Borja Peru 122 4.20S 77.40W
Borja Spain 25 41.50N 1.32W
Borken Germany 38 51.51N 6.51E
Borkou-Ennedi-Tibesti d. Chad 75 18.15N 20.00E
Borkum Germany 38 53.35N 6.40E
Borkum i. Germany 38 53.35N 6.41E
Borlänge Sweden 41 60.29N 15.25E
Borley, C. Antarctica 128 66.15S 55.00E
Bormes-les-Mimosas France 21 43.09N 6.20E
Bormio Italy 30 46.28N 10.22E
Borna Germany 38 51.07N 12.30E
Borndiep g. Neth. 16 53.28N 5.35E
Borneo i. Asia 58 1.00N 114.00E
Bornheim Germany 38 50.46N 6.59E
Bornholm i. Denmark 43 55.10N 15.00E
Borno d. Nigeria 77 11.20N 12.40E
Bornos, Embalse de resr. Spain 27 36.50N 5.42W
Bornu, Plain of f. Nigeria 77 12.30N 13.00E
Boro r. Sudan 73 8.52N 26.11E
Borodyanka Ukraine 37 50.38N 29.59E
Boromo Burkina 76 11.43N 2.53W
Borotou Côte d'Ivoire 76 8.46N 7.30W
Boroughbridge U.K. 12 54.06N 1.23W
Borovan Bulgaria 34 43.27N 23.45E
Borovichi Russian Fed. 44 58.22N 34.00E
Borraan Somali Rep. 71 10.10N 48.48E
Borrby Sweden 43 55.27N 14.10E
Borrika Australia 92 35.00S 140.05E
Borroloola Australia 90 16.04S 136.17E
Borşa Romania 37 46.56N 23.40E
Borşa Romania 37 47.39N 24.40E
Borsad India 62 22.25N 72.54E
Borth U.K. 13 52.29N 4.03W
Bort-les-Orgues France 20 45.24N 2.30E
Borüjerd Iran 65 33.54N 48.47E
Bory Tucholskie f. Poland 37 53.45N 17.30E
Borzna Ukraine 45 51.15N 32.25E
Borzya Russian Fed. 51 50.24N 116.35E
Bosa Italy 32 40.18N 8.30E
Bosanska Dubica Bosnia-Herzegovina 31 45.11N 16.49E
Bosanska Gradiška Croatia 31 45.09N 17.15E
Bosanska Krupa Bosnia-Herzegovina 31 44.53N 16.10E
Bosanski Novi Bosnia-Herzegovina 31 45.03N 16.23E
Bosanski Petrovac Bosnia-Herzegovina 31 44.33N 16.22E
Bosanski Šamac Bosnia-Herzegovina 31 45.03N 18.28E
Bosansko Grahovo Bosnia-Herzegovina 31 44.11N 16.22E
Boscastle U.K. 13 50.42N 4.42W
Bose China 53 23.58N 106.32E
Boshan China 54 36.29N 117.50E
Boshof R.S.A. 80 28.33S 25.12E
Bosilegrad Yugo. 34 42.29N 22.28E
Bosna r. Bosnia-Herzegovina 31 45.04N 18.29E
Bosnia-Herzegovina Europe 31 44.20N 18.00E
Bosnik Indonesia 59 1.09S 136.14E
Bosobolo Zaïre 73 4.11N 19.54E

Bösö-hantö pen. Japan 57 35.08N 140.00E
Bosporus str. see Istanbul Boğazi str. Turkey 29
Bossangoa C.A.R. 77 6.27N 17.21E
Bossembélé C.A.R. 77 5.10N 17.44E
Bossier City U.S.A. 111 32.31N 93.43W
Bosso Niger 77 13.43N 13.19E
Bostän Pakistan 62 30.26N 67.02E
Bosten Hu l. China 52 42.00N 87.00E
Boston U.K. 12 52.59N 0.02W
Boston U.S.A. 115 42.21N 71.04W
Bosut r. Croatia/Yugo 31 44.57N 19.22E
Boswell U.S.A. 114 40.10N 79.02W
Botād India 62 22.10N 71.40E
Botany B. Australia 93 34.04S 151.08E
Botev mtn. Bulgaria 34 42.43N 24.55E
Botevgrad Bulgaria 34 42.54N 23.47E
Bothnia, G. of Europe 40 63.30N 20.30E
Bothwell Canada 104 42.38N 81.52W
Boticas Portugal 26 41.41N 7.40W
Botletle r. Botswana 80 21.06S 24.47E
Botoşani Romania 37 47.44N 26.41E
Botou Burkina 77 12.47N 2.02E
Botrange mtn. Belgium 16 50.30N 6.04E
Botro Côte d'Ivoire 76 7.51N 5.19W
Botswana Africa 80 22.00S 24.15E
Bottrop Germany 38 51.31N 6.55E
Botucatu Brazil 126 22.52S 48.30W
Bouaflé Côte d'Ivoire 76 7.01N 5.47W
Bouaké Côte d'Ivoire 76 7.42N 5.00W
Bouar C.A.R. 77 5.58N 15.35E
Bou Arfa Morocco 74 32.30N 1.59W
Bouaye France 18 47.09N 1.42W
Bouca C.A.R. 77 6.30N 18.21E
Bouches-du-Rhône d. France 21 43.30N 5.00E
Bouchette Canada 105 46.11N 75.59W
Bouchoir France 19 49.45N 2.41E
Boudenib Morocco 74 31.57N 4.38W
Boufarik Algeria 75 36.36N 2.54E
Bougainville i. Pacific Oc. 84 6.00S 155.00E
Bougouni Mali 76 11.25N 7.28W
Bouillon Belgium 16 49.48N 5.03E
Bouïra Algeria 75 36.23N 3.54E
Bou-Izakarn Morocco 74 29.09N 9.44W
Boulay-Moselle France 19 49.11N 6.30E
Boulder Australia 89 30.55S 121.32E
Boulder U.S.A. 110 40.01N 105.17W
Boulder City U.S.A. 109 35.59N 114.50W
Boulia Australia 90 22.54S 139.54E
Boulogne France 19 50.43N 1.37E
Boulogne r. France 18 46.50N 1.25W
Boulogne-Billancourt France 19 48.50N 2.15E
Boulogne-sur-Gesse France 20 43.18N 0.39E
Boultoum Niger 77 14.45N 10.25E
Bouma r. Cameroon 77 2.00N 15.10E
Boumdeit Mauritania 74 17.26N 9.50W
Boumo Chad 77 9.01N 16.24E
Bouna Côte d'Ivoire 76 9.19N 2.53W
Boundary Peak mtn. U.S.A. 108 37.51N 118.21W
Boundiali Côte d'Ivoire 76 9.30N 6.31W
Bountiful U.S.A. 108 40.53N 111.53W
Bounty Is. Pacific Oc. 86 48.00S 178.30E
Bouraga well Mali 76 19.00N 3.36W
Bourail N. Cal. 84 21.34S 165.30E
Bourbon-Lancy France 19 46.38N 3.46E
Bourbonne-les-Bains France 19 47.57N 5.45E
Bourem Mali 76 16.59N 0.20W
Bourg France 21 46.12N 5.13E
Bourganeuf France 20 45.57N 1.46E
Bourges France 19 47.05N 2.24E
Bourget Canada 105 45.26N 75.09W
Bourget, Lac du l. France 21 45.44N 5.52E
Bourg Madame France 20 42.26N 1.55E
Bourgneuf-en-Retz France 18 47.02N 1.57W
Bourgogne d. France 19 47.10N 4.20E
Bourgogne, Canal de France 19 47.58N 3.30E
Bourgoin France 21 45.36N 5.17E
Bourg-St. Andéol France 21 44.22N 4.39E
Bourg-St. Maurice France 21 45.37N 6.46E
Bourgueil France 18 47.17N 0.10E
Bourke Australia 93 30.09S 145.59E
Bournemouth U.K. 13 50.43N 1.53W
Bou Saâda Algeria 75 35.12N 4.11E
Bou Salem Tunisia 32 36.36N 8.59E
Boussac France 20 46.21N 2.13E
Bousso Chad 77 10.32N 16.45E
Bouteldja Algeria 32 36.47N 8.13E
Boutilimit Mauritania 74 17.33N 14.42W
Boutonne r. France 20 45.54N 0.50W
Bouvard, C. Australia 89 32.40S 115.34E
Bouvetöya i. Atlantic Oc. 127 54.26S 3.24E
Bovalino Marino Italy 33 38.09N 16.11E
Bovec Slovenia 31 46.20N 13.33E
Bovill U.S.A. 108 46.51N 116.24W
Bovril Argentina 125 31.22S 59.25W
Bow r. Canada 100 51.10N 115.00W
Bowelling Australia 89 33.25S 116.27E
Bowen Australia 93 37.11S 148.34E
Bowen, Mt. Australia 93 37.11S 148.34E
Bowie Ariz. U.S.A. 109 32.19N 109.29W
Bowie Tex. U.S.A. 111 33.34N 97.51W
Bow Island town Canada 101 49.52N 111.22W
Bowling Green U.S.A. 113 37.00N 86.29W
Bowling Green, C. Australia 90 19.19S 146.25E
Bowman U.S.A. 110 46.11N 103.24W
Bowman I. Antarctica 128 65.00S 104.00E
Bowmanville Canada 104 43.55N 78.41W
Bowral Australia 93 34.30S 150.24E
Bowser Australia 93 36.19S 146.23E
Boxholm Sweden 43 58.12N 15.03E
Bo Xian China 54 33.50N 115.46E
Boxing China 54 37.08N 118.05E
Box Tank Australia 92 32.13S 142.17E
Boxtel Neth. 16 51.36N 5.20E
Boyabat Turkey 64 41.27N 34.45E
Boyang China 55 29.00N 116.40E
Boyanup Australia 89 33.29S 115.40E
Boyarka Ukraine 37 50.20N 30.26E
Boyd r. Australia 93 29.51S 152.25E

Boykétté C.A.R. 73 5.28N 20.50E
Boyle Rep. of Ire. 15 53.58N 8.19W
Boyne r. Rep. of Ire. 15 53.43N 6.17W
Boyoma Falls f. Zaïre 78 0.18N 25.32E
Boyup Brook Australia 89 33.50S 116.22E
Bozburun Turkey 35 36.43N 28.08E
Bozcaada Turkey 34 39.49N 26.03E
Bozca Ada i. Turkey 34 39.49N 26.03E
Bozel France 21 45.27N 6.39E
Bozeman U.S.A. 108 45.41N 111.02W
Bozen see Bolzano Italy 30
Bozoum C.A.R. 77 6.16N 16.22E
Bra Italy 30 44.42N 7.51E
Braås Sweden 43 57.04N 15.03E
Brabant d. Belgium 16 50.47N 4.30E
Brač i. Croatia 29 43.20N 16.38E
Bracadale, Loch U.K. 14 57.22N 6.30W
Bracciano Italy 32 42.06N 12.10E
Bracciano, Lago di l. Italy 30 42.07N 12.14E
Bracebridge Canada 104 45.02N 79.19W
Bracieux France 19 47.33N 1.33E
Bräcke Sweden 40 62.44N 15.30E
Brački Kanal str. Croatia 31 43.24N 16.40E
Brad Romania 29 46.06N 22.48E
Bradano r. Italy 33 40.23N 16.51E
Bradenton U.S.A. 113 27.29N 82.33W
Bradford Canada 104 44.07N 79.34W
Bradford U.K. 12 53.47N 1.45W
Bradford N.H. U.S.A. 115 43.17N 71.59W
Bradford Penn. U.S.A. 114 41.58N 78.39W
Bradford Vt. U.S.A. 105 43.59N 72.09W
Bradley U.S.A. 111 33.06N 93.39W
Bradworthy U.K. 13 50.54N 4.22W
Brady U.S.A. 111 31.08N 99.20W
Braemar U.K. 14 57.01N 3.24W
Braga Portugal 26 41.33N 8.26W
Braga d. Portugal 26 41.30N 8.05W
Bragado Argentina 125 35.10S 60.30W
Bragança Brazil 123 1.03S 46.46W
Bragança Portugal 26 41.49N 6.45W
Bragança d. Portugal 26 41.30N 6.50W
Bragança Paulista Brazil 126 22.59S 46.32W
Bragin Belarus 37 51.49N 30.16E
Brähmanbäria Bangla. 63 23.59N 91.07E
Brähmani r. India 63 20.39N 86.46E
Brahmaputra r. Asia 63 23.50N 89.45E
Braidwood Australia 93 35.27S 149.50E
Bräila Romania 37 45.18N 27.58E
Brainerd U.S.A. 107 46.20N 94.10W
Braintree U.K. 13 51.53N 0.32E
Brake Germany 38 53.19N 8.28E
Brakna d. Mauritania 74 17.00N 13.20W
Brälanda Sweden 43 58.34N 12.22E
Bramfield Australia 92 33.37S 134.59E
Bramming Denmark 42 55.28N 8.42E
Brampton Canada 104 43.41N 79.46W
Brampton U.K. 12 54.56N 2.43W
Bramsche Germany 38 52.24N 7.58E
Brancaleone Marina Italy 33 37.58N 16.06E
Branco r. Brazil 122 1.00S 62.00W
Brandberg mtn. Namibia 80 21.08S 14.35E
Brande Denmark 42 55.57N 9.07E
Brandenburg Germany 38 52.24N 12.32E
Brandenburg d. Germany 38 52.15N 13.10E
Brandenburg f. Germany 38 52.40N 13.00E
Brandfort R.S.A. 80 28.41S 26.27E
Brandon Canada 101 49.50N 99.57W
Brandon U.S.A. 105 43.48N 73.05W
Brandon Mtn. Rep. of Ire. 15 52.14N 10.15W
Brandon Pt. Rep. of Ire. 15 52.17N 10.11W
Braniewo Poland 37 54.24N 19.50E
Bransby Australia 92 28.40S 142.00E
Branson U.S.A. 111 36.39N 93.13W
Brantas r. Indonesia 59 7.13S 112.45E
Brantford Canada 104 43.08N 80.16W
Brantôme France 20 45.22N 0.39E
Bras d'Or L. Canada 103 45.52N 60.50W
Brasher Falls U.S.A. 105 44.48N 74.48W
Brasiléia Brazil 122 11.00S 68.44W
Brasília Brazil 123 15.45S 47.57W
Brasil, Planalto mts. Brazil 123 17.02S 50.00W
Braşov Romania 37 45.40N 25.35E
Brass Nigeria 77 4.20N 6.15E
Brasschaat Belgium 16 51.18N 4.28E
Bratislava Slovakia 37 48.10N 17.10E
Bratsk Russian Fed. 51 56.20N 101.15E
Bratsk Vodokhranilishche resr. Russian Fed. 51 54.40N 103.00E
Bratslav Ukraine 37 48.49N 28.51E
Brattleboro U.S.A. 115 42.51N 72.34W
Braunau Austria 39 48.15N 13.02E
Braunschweig Germany 38 52.16N 10.31E
Braunton U.K. 13 51.06N 4.09W
Bräviken b. Sweden 43 58.38N 16.32E
Bravo del Norte, Rio r. Mexico see Rio Grande r. Mexico/U.S.A. 111
Brawley U.S.A. 109 32.59N 115.31W
Bray France 19 48.25N 3.14E
Bray Rep. of Ire. 15 53.12N 6.07W
Bray Head Kerry Rep. of Ire. 15 51.53N 10.26W
Brazeau r. Canada 100 52.55N 115.15W
Brazil S. America 120 10.00S 52.00W
Brazilian Basin f. Atlantic Oc. 127 15.00S 25.00W
Brazilian Highlands see Brasil, Planalto mts. Brazil 123
Brazos r. U.S.A. 111 28.53N 95.23W
Brazzaville Congo 78 4.14S 15.10E
Brčko Bosnia-Herzegovina 31 44.53N 18.48E
Brda r. Poland 37 53.07N 18.08E
Breadalbane f. U.K. 14 56.30N 4.20W
Bream B. New Zealand 86 36.00S 174.30E
Brebes Indonesia 59 6.54S 109.00E
Brécey France 18 48.44N 1.10W
Brechin U.K. 14 56.44N 2.40W
Breckenridge Mich. U.S.A. 104 43.24N 84.29W
Breckenridge Tex. U.S.A. 111 32.45N 98.54W
Breckland f. U.K. 13 52.28N 0.40E
Břeclav Czech Republic 36 48.46N 16.53E

Brecon U.K. 13 51.57N 3.23W
Brecon Beacons mts. U.K. 13 51.53N 3.27W
Breda Neth. 16 51.35N 4.46E
Bredasdorp R.S.A. 80 34.31S 20.03E
Bredbo Australia 93 35.57S 149.10E
Bredstedt Germany 38 54.37N 8.59E
Breezewood U.S.A. 114 40.01N 78.15W
Bregalnica r. Macedonia 34 41.50N 22.20E
Bregenz Austria 39 47.30N 9.46E
Bregovo Bulgaria 29 44.08N 22.39E
Bréhal France 18 48.54N 1.31W
Breidhafjördhur est. Iceland 40 65.15N 23.00W
Breim Norway 41 61.44N 6.25E
Breisach Germany 39 48.01N 7.40E
Brekstad Norway 40 63.42N 9.40E
Bremangerland i. Norway 41 61.51N 5.02E
Bremen Germany 38 53.05N 8.49E
Bremen d. Germany 38 53.08N 8.46E
Bremen U.S.A. 114 39.42N 82.26W
Bremer Bay town Australia 89 34.21S 119.20E
Bremerhaven Germany 38 53.33N 8.34E
Bremer Range mts. Australia 89 32.40S 120.55E
Bremerton U.S.A. 108 47.34N 122.38W
Bremervörde Germany 38 53.29N 9.08E
Brenes Spain 27 37.33N 5.52W
Brenham U.S.A. 111 30.10N 96.24W
Brenner Pass Austria/Italy 39 47.00N 11.30E
Breno Italy 30 45.57N 10.18E
Brent Canada 104 46.02N 78.29E
Brenta r. Italy 30 45.11N 12.18E
Brentwood U.K. 13 51.38N 0.18E
Brescia Italy 30 45.33N 10.15E
Breskens Neth. 16 51.24N 3.34E
Bresle r. France 19 50.04N 1.22E
Bressanone Italy 30 46.43N 11.39E
Bressay i. U.K. 14 60.08N 1.05W
Bresse, Plaine de f. France 19 46.20N 5.10E
Bressuire France 18 46.51N 0.30W
Brest Belarus 37 52.08N 23.40E
Brest Bulgaria 34 43.38N 24.35E
Brest France 18 48.24N 4.29W
Brestanica Slovenia 31 45.59N 15.29E
Brest-Nantes Canal France 18 48.13N 3.26W
Bretagne d. France 18 48.15N 2.30W
Breteuil France 19 49.38N 2.18E
Breteuil-sur-Iton France 18 48.50N 0.55E
Breton, Pertuis str. France 20 46.25N 1.20W
Breton Sd. U.S.A. 111 29.30N 89.30W
Brett, C. New Zealand 86 35.15S 174.20E
Bretten Germany 39 49.02N 8.42E
Breuil-Cervinia Italy 30 45.56N 7.38E
Brevik Norway 42 59.04N 9.42E
Brewarrina Australia 93 29.57S 147.54E
Brewer U.S.A. 112 44.48N 68.46W
Brewster N.Y. U.S.A. 115 41.24N 73.37W
Brewster Ohio U.S.A. 114 40.43N 81.36W
Brewster, Kap c. Greenland 96 70.00N 25.00W
Brewton U.S.A. 113 31.07N 87.04W
Brežice Slovenia 31 45.54N 15.36E
Březnice Czech Republic 38 49.33N 13.57E
Breznik Bulgaria 34 42.44N 22.50E
Brezovo Bulgaria 34 42.20N 25.06E
Bria C.A.R. 73 6.32N 21.59E
Briançon France 21 44.54N 6.39E
Briare France 19 47.38N 2.44E
Bribbaree Australia 93 34.07S 147.51E
Brichany Moldova 37 48.20N 27.01E
Bricquebec France 18 49.28N 1.38W
Bride I.o.M. Europe 12 54.23N 4.24W
Bridge r. Canada 100 50.50N 122.40W
Bridgen Canada 104 42.47N 82.16W
Bridgend U.K. 13 51.30N 3.35W
Bridgeport Calif. U.S.A. 108 38.10N 119.13W
Bridgeport Conn. U.S.A. 115 41.11N 73.11W
Bridgeport Nebr. U.S.A. 110 41.40N 103.06W
Bridgeport Tex. U.S.A. 111 33.13N 97.45W
Bridgeport W.Va. U.S.A. 114 39.17N 80.15W
Bridger U.S.A. 108 45.18N 108.55W
Bridgeton U.S.A. 115 39.26N 75.14W
Bridgetown Australia 89 33.57S 116.08E
Bridgetown Barbados 117 13.06N 59.37W
Bridgetown Canada 103 44.51N 65.18W
Bridgetown Rep. of Ire. 15 52.14N 6.33W
Bridgeville U.S.A. 115 38.45N 75.36W
Bridgewater Canada 103 44.23N 64.31W
Bridgewater U.S.A. 114 38.18N 78.59W
Bridgewater, C. Australia 92 38.25S 141.28E
Bridgnorth U.K. 13 52.33N 2.25W
Bridgwater U.K. 13 51.08N 3.00W
Bridlington U.K. 12 54.06N 0.11W
Brie f. France 19 48.40N 3.20E
Briec France 18 48.06N 4.00W
Brienne-le-Château France 19 48.24N 4.32E
Brienz Switz. 19 46.46N 8.03E
Briey France 19 49.15N 5.56E
Brig Switz. 19 46.19N 8.00E
Brigantine U.S.A. 115 39.24N 74.22W
Brigg U.K. 12 53.33N 0.30W
Briggsdale U.S.A. 110 40.38N 104.20W
Brigham City U.S.A. 108 41.31N 112.01W
Bright Australia 93 36.42S 146.58E
Brighton Canada 105 44.02N 77.44W
Brighton U.K. 13 50.50N 0.09W
Brighton Colo. U.S.A. 108 39.59N 104.49W
Brighton Fla. U.S.A. 113 27.13N 81.06W
Brighton Mich. U.S.A. 104 42.32N 83.47W
Brignoles France 21 43.24N 6.04E
Brihuega Spain 26 40.48N 2.52W
Brikama Gambia 76 13.15N 16.39W
Brilon Germany 38 51.24N 8.34E
Brindisi Italy 33 40.38N 17.56E
Brinje Croatia 31 45.00N 15.08E
Brinkley U.S.A. 111 34.53N 91.12W
Brinkworth Australia 92 33.42S 138.24E
Brionne France 18 49.12N 0.43E
Brioude France 20 45.18N 3.23E
Briouze France 18 48.42N 0.22W
Brisbane Australia 93 27.30S 153.00E

Brisighella Italy 30 44.13N 11.46E
Bristol U.K. 13 51.26N 2.35W
Bristol Conn. U.S.A. 115 41.41N 72.57W
Bristol N.H. U.S.A. 115 43.36N 71.45W
Bristol Penn. U.S.A. 115 40.06N 74.52W
Bristol R.I. U.S.A. 115 41.40N 71.16W
Bristol S.Dak. U.S.A. 110 45.21N 97.45W
Bristol Tenn. U.S.A. 113 36.33N 82.11W
Bristol Vt. U.S.A. 105 44.08N 73.05W
Bristol B. U.S.A. 98 58.00N 158.50W
Bristol Channel U.K. 13 51.17N 3.20W
British Antarctic Territory Antarctica 128 70.00S 50.00W
British Columbia d. Canada 100 55.00N 125.00W
British Mts. Canada 98 69.00N 140.20W
British Virgin Is. C. America 117 18.30N 64.30W
Britstown R.S.A. 80 30.34S 23.30E
Britt Canada 104 45.46N 80.35W
Britton U.S.A. 110 45.48N 97.45W
Brive France 20 45.10N 1.32E
Briviesca Spain 26 42.33N 3.19W
Brixham U.K. 13 50.24N 3.31W
Brno Czech Republic 36 49.11N 16.39E
Broach India 62 21.42N 72.58E
Broad Arrow Australia 89 30.32S 121.20E
Broad B. U.K. 14 58.15N 6.15W
Broadback r. Canada 102 51.20N 78.50W
Broadford Australia 93 37.16S 145.03E
Broadmere Australia 90 25.30S 149.30E
Broad Sd. Australia 90 22.20S 149.50E
Broadsound Range mts. Australia 90 22.30S 149.30E
Broadus U.S.A. 108 45.27N 105.25W
Broadview Canada 101 50.20N 102.30W
Broadway U.K. 13 52.02N 1.51W
Brochet Canada 101 57.53N 101.40W
Brochet, L. Canada 101 58.36N 101.35W
Brocken mtn. Germany 38 51.50N 10.50E
Brockport U.S.A. 114 43.13N 77.56W
Brockton U.S.A. 115 42.05N 71.01W
Brockville Canada 105 44.35N 75.41W
Brockway Mont. U.S.A. 108 47.15N 105.45W
Brockway Penn. U.S.A. 114 41.15N 78.47W
Brocton U.S.A. 114 42.23N 79.27W
Brod Croatia 31 45.10N 18.01E
Brod Macedonia 34 41.30N 21.17E
Brodeur Pen. Canada 99 73.00N 88.00W
Brodick U.K. 14 55.34N 5.09W
Brodnica Poland 37 53.16N 19.23E
Brody Ukraine 37 50.05N 25.08E
Broglie France 18 49.01N 0.32E
Broke Inlet Australia 89 34.55S 116.25E
Broken Arrow U.S.A. 111 36.03N 95.48W
Broken B. Australia 93 33.34S 151.18E
Broken Bow U.S.A. 110 41.24N 99.38W
Broken Hill town Australia 92 31.57S 141.30E
Bromley U.K. 13 51.24N 0.02E
Bromley Plateau f. Atlantic Oc. 127 30.00S 34.00W
Bromölla Sweden 43 56.04N 14.28E
Bromsgrove U.K. 11 52.20N 2.03W
Bron France 21 45.44N 4.55E
Brønderslev Denmark 42 57.16N 9.58E
Brong-Ahafo d. Ghana 76 7.45N 1.30W
Brønnøysund Norway 40 65.30N 12.10E
Bronte Canada 104 43.23N 79.43W
Bronte Italy 33 37.48N 14.50E
Brooke's Point town Phil. 58 8.50N 117.52E
Brookfield U.S.A. 110 39.47N 93.04W
Brookhaven U.S.A. 111 31.35N 90.26W
Brookings Oreg. U.S.A. 108 42.03N 124.17W
Brookings S.Dak. U.S.A. 110 44.19N 96.48W
Brooklin Canada 104 43.57N 78.57W
Brooklyn U.S.A. 104 42.06N 84.15W
Brooklyn Center U.S.A. 110 45.05N 93.20W
Brooks Canada 98 50.35N 111.53W
Brooks B. Canada 100 50.15N 127.55W
Brooks Range mts. U.S.A. 98 68.50N 152.00W
Brooksville U.S.A. 113 28.34N 82.24W
Brookton Australia 89 32.22S 117.01E
Brookville U.S.A. 114 41.09N 79.05W
Broome Australia 88 17.58S 122.15E
Broomehill town Australia 89 33.50S 117.35E
Broome, Mt. Australia 88 17.21S 125.23E
Broons France 18 48.19N 2.16W
Brora U.K. 14 58.01N 3.52W
Brora r. U.K. 14 58.00N 3.51W
Brörup Denmark 42 55.29N 9.01E
Brosna r. Rep. of Ire. 15 53.13N 7.58W
Brossac France 20 45.20N 0.03W
Brothers U.S.A. 108 43.49N 120.36W
Broto Spain 26 42.36N 0.06W
Brou France 18 48.13N 1.11E
Brough England U.K. 12 54.32N 2.19W
Brough Scotland U.K. 14 60.29N 1.12W
Broughton r. Australia 92 33.21S 137.46E
Broughton in Furness U.K. 12 54.17N 3.12W
Brouwershaven Neth. 16 51.44N 3.53E
Brovary Ukraine 37 50.30N 30.45E
Brovst Denmark 42 57.06N 9.32E
Brown City U.S.A. 114 43.13N 82.59W
Brownfield U.S.A. 111 33.11N 102.16W
Browning U.S.A. 108 48.34N 113.01W
Brownsburg Canada 105 45.41N 74.25W
Brownsville Penn. U.S.A. 114 40.01N 79.53W
Brownsville Tenn. U.S.A. 111 35.36N 89.15W
Brownsville Tex. U.S.A. 111 25.54N 97.30W
Brownville U.S.A. 105 44.01N 75.59W
Brownwood U.S.A. 111 31.43N 98.59W
Brozas Spain 27 39.37N 6.46W
Bruay-en-Artois France 19 50.29N 2.33E
Bruce Mines Canada 104 46.18N 83.48W
Bruce Pen. Canada 104 45.00N 81.20W
Bruce Rock town Australia 89 31.52S 118.09E
Bruche r. France 19 48.31N 7.41E
Bruchsal Germany 39 49.07N 8.35E
Bruck Austria 39 47.17N 12.49E
Brückenau Germany 39 50.18N 9.47E

Bruges see Brugge Belgium 16
Brugg Switz. 19 47.29N 8.12E
Brugge Belgium 16 51.13N 3.14E
Brühl Germany 38 50.48N 6.54E
Brûlé, Lac l. Que. Canada 103 52.17N 63.52W
Brûlé, Lac l. Que. Canada 103 46.57N 77.13W
Brumadinho Brazil 126 20.09S 44.11W
Brumado Brazil 123 14.13S 41.40W
Brumath France 19 48.44N 7.43E
Brunei Asia 58 4.56N 114.58E
Brünen Germany 38 51.43N 6.39E
Brunflo Sweden 40 63.04N 14.50E
Brunico Italy 30 46.48N 11.56E
Brunkeberg Norway 42 59.26N 8.29E
Brunner New Zealand 86 42.28S 171.12E
Brunsbüttel Germany 38 53.54N 9.05E
Brunssum Neth. 16 50.57N 5.59E
Brunswick Ga. U.S.A. 113 31.09N 81.30W
Brunswick Maine U.S.A. 112 43.55N 69.58W
Brunswick Md. U.S.A. 114 39.18N 77.37W
Brunswick B. Australia 88 15.05S 125.00E
Brunswick Junction Australia 89 33.15S 115.45E
Bruny I. Australia 91 43.15S 147.16E
Brushton U.S.A. 105 44.51N 74.30W
Brusilovka Kazakhstan 45 50.39N 54.59E
Brussel see Bruxelles Belgium 16
Brussels see Bruxelles Belgium 16
Bruthen Australia 93 37.44S 147.49E
Bruton U.K. 13 51.06N 2.28W
Bruxelles Belgium 16 50.50N 4.23E
Bruyères France 19 48.12N 6.43E
Bryagovo Bulgaria 34 41.58N 25.08E
Bryan Ohio U.S.A. 112 41.30N 84.34W
Bryan Tex. U.S.A. 111 30.40N 96.22W
Bryan, Mt. Australia 92 33.26S 138.27E
Bryansk Russian Fed. 44 53.15N 34.09E
Bryne Norway 42 58.44N 5.39E
Bryson U.S.A. 105 45.40N 76.36W
Bryson City U.S.A. 113 35.26N 83.27W
Bryson, Lac l. Canada 105 46.27N 77.00W
Brzeg Poland 37 50.52N 17.27E
Bsharrī Lebanon 66 34.15N 36.00E
Bua r. Malawi 79 12.42S 34.15E
Bua Yai Thailand 56 15.34N 102.24E
Bu'ayrāt al Ḥasūn Libya 75 31.24N 15.44E
Buba Guinea Bissau 76 11.36N 14.55W
Bübiyān, Jazīrat i. Kuwait 71 29.45N 48.15E
Bubye r. Zimbabwe 80 22.18S 31.00E
Bucak Turkey 64 37.28N 30.36E
Bucaramanga Colombia 122 7.08N 73.10W
Buccino Italy 33 40.37N 15.23E
Buchach Ukraine 37 49.09N 25.20E
Buchan r. Australia 93 37.28N 30.36W
Buchanan Liberia 76 5.57N 10.02W
Buchanan, L. Australia 90 21.28S 145.52E
Buchanan L. U.S.A. 111 30.48N 98.25W
Buchan Ness c. U.K. 14 57.28N 1.47W
Buchans Canada 103 48.49N 56.52W
Bucharest see Bucureşti Romania 37
Buchen Germany 39 49.32N 9.17E
Buchloe Germany 39 48.02N 10.44E
Bucholz Germany 38 53.20N 9.52E
Buchs Switz. 39 47.10N 9.28E
Buchy France 18 49.35N 1.22E
Buckambool Mt. Australia 93 31.55S 145.40E
Bückeburg Germany 38 52.16N 9.02E
Buckeye Lake U.S.A. 114 39.56N 82.29W
Buckhannon U.S.A. 114 38.59N 80.14W
Buckhaven and Methil U.K. 12 56.11N 3.03W
Buckhorn Canada 104 44.33N 78.20W
Buckhorn L. Canada 104 44.28N 78.23W
Buckie U.K. 14 57.40N 2.58W
Buckingham Canada 105 45.35N 75.25W
Buckingham U.K. 13 52.00N 0.59W
Buckingham B. Australia 90 12.10S 135.46E
Buckinghamshire d. U.K. 13 51.50N 0.48W
Buckland Tableland f. Australia 90 25.00S 148.00E
Buckleboo Australia 92 32.55S 136.12E
Buckley U.S.A. 110 40.35N 88.04W
Bucklin U.S.A. 111 37.33N 99.38W
Buco Zau Angola 78 4.46S 12.34E
Bucquoy France 19 50.08N 2.42E
Bu Craa W. Sahara 74 26.21N 12.57W
Bucureşti Romania 37 44.25N 26.06E
Bucyrus U.S.A. 114 40.48N 82.58W
Bud Norway 40 62.54N 6.56E
Budapest Hungary 37 47.30N 19.03E
Budaun India 63 28.03N 79.07E
Budda Australia 92 31.12S 144.16E
Buddh Gaya India 63 24.42N 84.59E
Buddusò Italy 32 40.35N 9.16E
Bude U.K. 13 50.49N 4.33W
Bude B. U.K. 13 50.50N 4.40W
Budennovsk Russian Fed. 45 44.50N 44.10E
Büdingen Germany 39 50.17N 9.07E
Budjala Zaïre 78 2.38N 19.48E
Buea Cameroon 77 4.09N 9.13E
Buenaventura Colombia 122 3.54N 77.02W
Buenaventura Mexico 109 29.51N 107.29W
Buena Vista U.S.A. 113 37.44N 79.22W
Buendia, Embalse de resr. Spain 26 40.25N 2.43W
Buenos Aires Argentina 125 34.40S 58.25W
Buenos Aires d. Argentina 125 36.30S 59.00W
Buenos Aires, L. Argentina/Chile 125 46.35S 72.00W
Buffalo Canada 101 50.49N 110.42W
Buffalo r. Canada 100 60.55N 115.00W
Buffalo Mo. U.S.A. 111 37.39N 93.06W
Buffalo N.Y. U.S.A. 114 42.54N 78.53W
Buffalo Okla. U.S.A. 111 36.50N 99.38W
Buffalo S.Dak. U.S.A. 110 45.35N 103.33W
Buffalo W.Va. U.S.A. 114 38.39N 81.57W
Buffalo Wyo. U.S.A. 108 44.21N 106.42W
Buffalo Head Hills Canada 100 57.25N 115.55W
Buffalo L. Canada 100 60.10N 115.30W
Buffalo Narrows town Canada 101 55.51N 108.30W
Bug r. Poland 37 52.29N 21.11E
Buga Colombia 122 3.53N 76.17W

Bugaldie Australia 93 31.02S 149.08E
Bugeat France 20 45.35N 1.59E
Bugembe Uganda 79 0.26N 33.16E
Bugene Tanzania 79 1.34S 31.07E
Buggs Island L. U.S.A. 113 36.35N 78.28W
Bugojno Bosnia-Herzegovina 31 44.03N 17.27E
Bugrino Russian Fed. 44 68.45N 49.15E
Bugt China 53 48.45N 121.58E
Buguma Russian Fed. 44 54.32N 52.46E
Buguma Nigeria 77 4.43N 6.53E
Buguruslan Russian Fed. 44 53.36N 52.30E
Buhera Zimbabwe 81 19.21S 31.25E
Bühl Germany 39 48.42N 8.08E
Buhuşi Romania 37 46.43N 26.41E
Builth Wells U.K. 13 52.09N 3.24W
Buinsk Russian Fed. 44 54.58N 48.15E
Bu'in-Sofiā Iran 65 35.51N 46.02E
Buitenpost Neth. 16 53.15N 6.09E
Bujalance Spain 27 37.54N 4.22W
Bujaraloz Spain 25 41.30N 0.09W
Buje Croatia 31 45.24N 13.40E
Buji P.N.G. 90 9.07S 142.26E
Bujumbura Burundi 79 3.22S 29.21E
Bukama Zaïre 78 9.16S 25.52E
Bukavu Zaïre 79 2.30S 28.49E
Bukene Tanzania 79 4.13S 32.52E
Bukhara Uzbekistan 65 39.47N 64.26E
Buki Ukraine 37 49.02N 30.29E
Bukima Tanzania 79 1.48S 33.25E
Bukittinggi Indonesia 58 0.18S 100.20E
Bukoba Tanzania 79 1.20S 31.49E
Bukovica f. Croatia 31 44.10N 15.40E
Bukrale Ethiopia 73 4.30N 42.03E
Bukuru Nigeria 77 9.48N 8.52E
Bula Indonesia 59 3.07S 130.27E
Bülach Switz. 39 47.31N 8.32E
Bulahdelah Australia 93 32.25S 152.13E
Bulan Phil. 59 12.40N 123.53E
Bulandshahr India 63 28.24N 77.51E
Bulawayo Zimbabwe 80 20.10S 28.43E
Bulbjerg hill Denmark 42 57.09N 9.02E
Buldāna India 62 20.32N 76.11E
Buldern Germany 16 51.52N 7.21E
Bulgan Mongolia 52 48.34N 103.12E
Bulgaria Europe 34 42.35N 25.30E
Būl, Kūh-e mtn. Iran 65 30.48N 52.45E
Bullabulling Australia 89 31.05S 120.52E
Bullaque r. Spain 27 38.59N 4.17W
Bullara Australia 88 22.40S 114.03E
Bullas Spain 25 38.03N 1.40W
Bullaxaar Somali Rep. 71 10.23N 44.27E
Bulle Switz. 39 46.37N 7.04E
Buller r. New Zealand 86 41.45S 171.35E
Buller, Mt. Australia 93 37.11S 146.26E
Bullfinch Australia 89 30.59S 119.06E
Bulli Australia 93 34.20S 150.55E
Bull Mts. U.S.A. 108 46.05N 109.00W
Bulloo r. Australia 92 28.43S 142.27E
Bulloo Downs town Australia 92 28.30S 142.45E
Bull Run Mtn. U.S.A. 114 38.52N 77.53W
Bull Shoals L. U.S.A. 113 36.30S 92.50W
Bululo P.N.G. 59 7.13S 146.35E
Bulsār India 62 20.38N 72.56E
Bultfontein R.S.A. 80 28.17S 26.09E
Bulu Indonesia 59 4.34N 126.45E
Bulu, Gunung mtn. Indonesia 58 3.00N 116.00E
Bulun Russian Fed. 51 70.50N 127.20E
Bulunde Tanzania 79 4.19S 32.57E
Bumba Bandundu Zaïre 78 6.55S 19.16E
Bumba Equateur Zaïre 78 2.15N 22.32E
Bumbuli Zaïre 78 3.25S 20.30E
Buna Kenya 79 2.49N 39.27E
Buna P.N.G. 90 8.40S 148.25E
Bunbury Australia 89 33.20S 115.34E
Buncrana Rep. of Ire. 15 55.08N 7.27W
Bundaberg Australia 90 24.50S 152.21E
Bundaleer Australia 88 28.39S 146.31E
Bundarra Australia 93 30.11S 151.04E
Bünde Nschn. Germany 38 52.12N 8.35E
Bunde Nschn. Germany 38 53.11N 7.16E
Bundella Australia 93 31.35S 149.59E
Bündi India 62 25.27N 75.39E
Bundoran Rep. of Ire. 15 54.28N 8.17W
Bündu India 63 23.11N 85.35E
Bungay U.K. 13 52.27N 1.26E
Bungo Angola 78 7.26S 15.23E
Bungo suidō str. Japan 57 32.52N 132.30E
Bungu Tanzania 79 7.37S 39.07E
Buni Nigeria 77 11.20N 11.59E
Bunia Zaïre 79 1.30N 30.10E
Buninyong Australia 92 37.41S 143.58E
Bunker Hill town U.S.A. 114 39.22N 78.04W
Bunkie U.S.A. 111 30.57N 92.11W
Buñol Spain 25 39.25N 0.47W
Bunyala Kenya 71 0.07N 34.00E
Bunyan Australia 93 36.11S 149.09E
Buol Indonesia 59 1.12N 121.28E
Buqayq Saudi Arabia 65 25.55N 49.40E
Bura Coast Kenya 79 1.09S 39.55E
Bura Coast Kenya 79 1.06S 39.58E
Burakin Australia 89 30.30S 117.08E
Burang China 63 30.16N 81.13E
Buras U.S.A. 111 29.21N 89.32W
Buraydah Saudi Arabia 65 26.18N 43.58E
Burbach Germany 38 50.45N 8.05E
Burcher Australia 93 33.32S 147.18E
Burco Somali Rep. 71 9.30N 45.30E
Burdur Turkey 23 37.44N 30.17E
Burdwān India 63 23.15N 87.51E
Bure Ethiopia 73 10.40N 37.04E
Büren Germany 38 51.33N 8.33E
Burford Canada 104 43.06N 80.26W
Burg Germany 38 52.26N 11.12E
Burg Sachsen-Anhalt Germany 38 52.16N 11.51E
Burgas Bulgaria 29 42.30N 27.29E
Burgas d. Bulgaria 34 42.30N 26.25E
Burgdorf Switz. 39 47.04N 7.37E
Burgenland d. Austria 36 47.30N 16.20E

Burgeo Canada 103 47.36N 57.34W
Burgess Hill U.K. 13 50.57N 0.07W
Burghausen Germany 39 48.09N 12.49E
Burglengenfeld Germany 39 49.13N 12.03E
Burgos Spain 26 42.21N 3.42W
Burgos d. Spain 26 42.25N 3.40W
Burgstädt Germany 38 50.55N 12.49E
Burgsteinfurt Germany 38 52.08N 7.20E
Burgsvik Sweden 43 57.03N 18.16E
Burhānpur India 62 21.18N 76.14E
Buri Brazil 126 23.46S 48.39W
Burias i. Phil. 59 12.50N 123.10E
Burica, Punta c. Panama 117 8.05N 82.50W
Burin Pen. Canada 103 47.00N 55.40W
Buriram Thailand 56 14.59N 103.08E
Burjasot Spain 25 39.31N 0.25W
Burkburnett U.S.A. 111 34.06N 98.34W
Burke r. Australia 90 23.12S 139.33E
Burketown Australia 90 17.44S 139.22E
Burkina Africa 76 12.30N 2.00W
Burk's Falls Canada 104 45.37N 79.25W
Burleigh Falls Canada 104 44.34N 78.11W
Burley U.S.A. 108 42.32N 113.48W
Burlington Canada 104 43.19N 79.47W
Burlington Iowa U.S.A. 110 40.49N 91.14W
Burlington Kans. U.S.A. 110 38.12N 95.45W
Burlington N.C. U.S.A. 113 36.05N 79.27W
Burlington N.J. U.S.A. 115 40.04N 74.49W
Burlington Vt. U.S.A. 104 44.29N 73.13W
Burlington Wisc. U.S.A. 110 42.41N 88.17W
Burma see Myanmar Asia 56
Burngup Australia 89 33.00S 118.39E
Burnham-on-Crouch U.K. 13 51.37N 0.50E
Burnham-on-Sea U.K. 13 51.15N 3.00W
Burnie Australia 91 41.03S 145.55E
Burnley U.K. 12 53.47N 2.15W
Burns Oreg. U.S.A. 108 43.35N 119.03W
Burns Wyo. U.S.A. 108 41.11N 104.21W
Burnside r. Canada 98 66.51N 108.04W
Burns Lake town Canada 100 54.20N 125.45W
Burnsville U.S.A. 114 38.51N 80.40W
Buronga Australia 92 34.08S 142.11E
Burqā Jordan 67 32.18N 35.12E
Burqin Jordan 67 32.27N 35.16E
Burra Australia 92 33.40S 138.57E
Burracoppin Australia 89 31.22S 118.30E
Burragorang, L. Australia 93 33.58S 150.27E
Burrel Albania 34 41.36N 20.01E
Burren Junction Australia 93 30.08S 148.59E
Burrewarra Pt. Australia 93 35.56S 150.12E
Burriana Spain 25 39.53N 0.05W
Burrinjuck Australia 93 35.01S 148.33E
Burrinjuck Resr. Australia 93 35.00S 148.40E
Burro, Serranías del mts. Mexico 111 29.20N 102.00W
Burry Port U.K. 13 51.41N 4.17W
Bursa Turkey 29 40.11N 29.04E
Būr Safājah Egypt 64 26.44N 33.56E
Būr Sa'īd Egypt 66 31.17N 32.18E
Būr Sūdān Sudan 72 19.39N 37.01E
Burta Australia 92 32.30S 141.05E
Būr Tawfiq Egypt 66 29.57N 32.34E
Burt L. U.S.A. 104 45.27N 84.40W
Burton upon Trent U.K. 12 52.58N 1.39W
Burtundy Australia 92 33.45S 142.22E
Buru i. Indonesia 59 3.30S 126.30E
Burullus, Buḥayrat al l. Egypt 66 31.30N 30.45E
Burundi Africa 79 3.00S 30.00E
Bururi Burundi 79 3.58S 29.35E
Burutu Nigeria 77 5.20N 5.31E
Burwash Canada 104 46.19N 80.48W
Bury G.M. U.K. 12 53.36N 2.19W
Bury St. Edmunds U.K. 13 52.15N 0.42E
Burzil Jammu & Kashmir 62 34.52N 75.07E
Burzil Pass Jammu & Kashmir 62 34.54N 75.06E
Busalla Italy 30 44.34N 8.57E
Busambra, Rocca mtn. Italy 32 37.51N 13.24E
Busca Italy 30 44.31N 7.29E
Būsh Egypt 66 29.09N 31.07E
Būshehr Iran 65 28.57N 50.52E
Bushkill U.S.A. 115 41.06N 75.00W
Bushmanland f. R.S.A. 80 29.25S 19.40E
Busi Ethiopia 71 5.30N 44.30E
Busigny France 19 50.02N 3.28E
Businga Zaïre 78 3.16N 20.55E
Busira r. Zaïre 78 0.05N 18.18E
Buskerud Norway 41 60.20N 9.00E
Buskerud d. Norway 42 60.07N 9.45E
Buṣrá al Ḥarīrī Syria 67 32.50N 36.20E
Buṣrá ash Shām Syria 66 32.30N 36.29E
Busselton Australia 89 33.43S 115.15E
Bussum Neth. 16 52.17N 5.10E
Bustard Head c. Australia 90 24.02S 151.48E
Busto Arsizio Italy 30 45.37N 8.51E
Busu Djanoa Zaïre 78 1.42N 21.23E
Büsum Germany 38 54.08N 8.51E
Buta Zaïre 78 2.50N 24.50E
Butan Bulgaria 34 43.39N 23.45E
Butari Rwanda 79 2.38S 29.43E
Butaritari i. Kiribati 84 3.07N 172.48E
Buṭayḥah Syria 67 32.56N 35.53E
Bute i. U.K. 14 55.51N 5.07W
Bute Australia 92 33.24S 138.01E
Butedale Canada 100 53.12N 128.45W
Butera Italy 33 37.11N 14.11E
Bute, Sd. of U.K. 14 55.44N 5.10W
Buthroton site Albania 34 39.46N 20.00E
Butiaba Uganda 79 1.48N 31.15E
Butler Mo. U.S.A. 111 38.16N 94.20W
Butler N.J. U.S.A. 115 41.00N 74.21W
Butler Penn. U.S.A. 114 40.52N 79.54W
Butman U.S.A. 104 44.09N 84.34W
Buton i. Indonesia 59 5.00S 122.50E
Butte Mont. U.S.A. 108 46.00N 112.32W
Butte Nebr. U.S.A. 110 42.58N 98.51W
Butterworth Malaysia 58 5.24N 100.22E
Buttevant Rep. of Ire. 15 52.14N 8.41W
Butt of Lewis c. U.K. 14 58.31N 6.15W
Butty Head Australia 89 33.52S 121.35E

Butuan Phil. 59 8.56N 125.31E
Butwal Nepal 63 27.42N 83.28E
Butzbach Germany 39 50.26N 8.40E
Butzow Germany 38 53.50N 11.59E
Buuhoodle Somali Rep. 71 8.16N 46.24E
Buulo Berde Somali Rep. 71 3.52N 45.40E
Buur Gaabo Somali Rep. 73 1.10S 41.50E
Buur Hakaba Somali Rep. 79 2.43N 44.10E
Buxtehude Germany 38 53.28N 9.41E
Buxton U.K. 12 53.16N 1.54W
Buxy France 19 46.43N 4.41E
Buy Russian Fed. 44 58.23N 41.27E
Buyaga Russian Fed. 51 59.42N 126.59E
Buynaksk Russian Fed. 45 42.48N 47.07E
Büyük Turkey 34 41.02N 26.35E
Büyük Menderes r. Turkey 35 37.28N 27.10E
Buzachi, Poluostrov pen. Kazakhstan 45 45.00N 51.55E
Buzançais France 18 46.53N 1.25E
Buzancy France 19 49.25N 4.57E
Buzău Romania 37 45.10N 26.49E
Buzău r. Romania 37 45.24N 27.48E
Buzaymah Libya 75 24.55N 22.02E
Buzi r. Mozambique 81 19.52S 34.00E
Buzuluk Russian Fed. 44 52.49N 52.19E
Buzzards B. U.S.A. 115 41.33N 70.47W
Bwasiaia P.N.G. 90 10.06S 150.48E
Byala Bulgaria 34 43.28N 25.44E
Byala Slatina Bulgaria 34 43.26N 23.55E
Byam Martin I. Canada 98 75.15N 104.00W
Bydgoszcz Poland 37 53.16N 17.33E
Byemoor Canada 100 52.00N 112.17W
Byesville U.S.A. 114 39.58N 81.32W
Bygland Norway 42 58.50N 7.49E
Byglandsfjord town Norway 42 58.51N 7.48E
Byglandsfjorden l. Norway 42 58.48N 7.50E
Byhalia U.S.A. 111 34.52N 89.41W
Bykhov Belarus 37 53.30N 30.15E
Bykle Norway 42 59.21N 7.20E
Bylot I. Canada 99 73.00N 78.30W
Byng Inlet Canada 104 45.46N 80.33W
Byrd, Lac l. Canada 105 47.01N 76.56W
Byrd Land f. Antarctica 128 79.30S 125.00W
Byrock Australia 93 30.40S 146.25E
Byron Bay town Australia 93 28.43S 153.34E
Byron, C. Australia 93 28.37S 153.40E
Byrranga, Gory mts. Russian Fed. 51 74.50N 101.00E
Byske Sweden 40 64.57N 21.12E
Byske r. Sweden 40 64.57N 21.13E
Byten Belarus 37 52.50N 25.28E
Bytom Poland 37 50.22N 18.54E
Byxelkrok Sweden 43 57.20N 17.00E
Bzipi Georgia 45 43.15N 40.24E

C

Ca r. Vietnam 55 18.47N 105.40E
Caballería, Cabo de c. Spain 25 40.05N 4.05E
Caballos Mesteños, Llano de los f. Mexico 111 28.15N 104.00W
Cabanatuan Phil. 59 15.30N 120.58E
Cabeza del Buey Spain 26 38.43N 5.13W
Cabimas Venezuela 122 10.26N 71.27W
Cabinda Angola 78 5.34S 12.12E
Cabinet Mts. U.S.A. 108 48.08N 115.46W
Cabo Delgado d. Mozambique 79 12.30S 39.00E
Cabo Frio town Brazil 126 22.51S 42.03W
Cabonga, Résr. Canada 105 47.20N 76.35W
Cabool U.S.A. 111 37.07N 92.06W
Caboolture Australia 91 27.05S 152.57E
Cabo Pantoja Peru 122 1.00S 75.10W
Cabot Head c. Canada 104 45.14N 81.17W
Cabot, Mt. U.S.A. 105 44.31N 71.24W
Cabot Str. Canada 103 47.20N 59.30W
Cabra Spain 27 37.28N 4.27W
Cabras Italy 32 39.56N 8.32E
Cabrera i. Spain 25 39.09N 2.56E
Cabrera r. Spain 26 42.25N 6.49W
Cabrera, Sierra mts. Spain 26 42.10N 6.45W
Cabri Canada 101 50.37N 108.28W
Cabriel r. Spain 25 39.14N 1.03W
Cabruta Venezuela 122 7.40N 66.16W
Čačak Yugo. 34 43.53N 20.21E
Caçapava Brazil 126 23.05S 45.40W
Caccamo Italy 32 37.56N 13.40E
Caccia, Capo c. Italy 32 40.34N 8.09E
Cáceres Brazil 123 16.05S 57.40W
Cáceres Spain 27 39.29N 6.22W
Cáceres d. Spain 27 39.40N 6.20W
Cacharí Argentina 125 36.23S 59.29W
Cache Bay town Canada 104 46.23N 80.00W
Cachimo r. Zaïre 78 7.02S 21.13E
Cachoeira Brazil 123 12.35S 38.59W
Cachoeira do Sul Brazil 126 30.03S 52.52W
Cachoeiro de Itapemirim Brazil 126 20.51S 41.07W
Cacín r. Spain 27 37.13N 4.00W
Cacine Guinea 76 11.08N 14.57W
Cacolo Angola 78 10.09S 19.15E
Caconda Angola 78 13.46S 15.06E
Cacongo Angola 78 5.11S 12.10E
Cacuso Angola 78 9.26S 15.43E
Cadaqués Spain 25 42.17N 3.17E
Čadca Slovakia 37 49.26N 18.48E
Cader Idris mtn. U.K. 13 52.40N 3.55W
Cadibarrawirracanna, L. Australia 92 28.52S 135.27E

Cadillac France 20 44.38N 0.19W
Cadillac U.S.A. 112 44.15N 85.23W
Cadí, Sierra del mts. Spain 25 42.17N 1.42E
Cadiz Phil. 59 10.57N 123.18E
Cádiz Spain 27 36.32N 6.18W
Cádiz d. Spain 27 36.40N 5.50W
Cadiz U.S.A. 114 40.16N 81.00W
Cádiz, Golfo de g. Spain 27 37.00N 7.00W
Cadomin Canada 100 53.02N 117.20W
Cadoux Australia 89 30.47S 117.05E
Caen France 18 49.11N 0.21W
Caernarfon U.K. 12 53.08N 4.17W
Caernarfon B. U.K. 12 53.05N 4.25W
Caerphilly U.K. 13 51.34N 3.13W
Caesarea see Horbat Qesari Israel 67
Caeté Brazil 126 19.54S 43.37W
Cafima Angola 78 16.34S 16.30E
Cafu Angola 78 16.16S 15.14E
Cagayan de Oro Phil. 59 8.29N 124.40E
Cagli Italy 33 43.33N 12.39E
Cagliari Italy 32 39.13N 9.06E
Cagliari, Golfo di g. Italy 32 39.05N 9.10E
Cagnes France 21 43.40N 7.09E
Caguán r. Colombia 122 0.08S 74.18W
Caguas Puerto Rico 117 18.08N 66.00W
Cahama Angola 78 16.16S 14.23E
Caha Mts. Rep. of Ire. 15 51.44N 9.45W
Cahelli Jordan 67 30 44.43N 8.17E
Caherciveen Rep. of Ire. 15 51.51N 10.14W
Cahir Rep. of Ire. 15 52.23N 7.56W
Cahora Bassa Dam Mozambique 79 15.36S 32.41E
Cahore Pt. Rep. of Ire. 15 52.34N 6.12W
Cahors France 20 44.27N 1.26E
Cahuapanas Peru 122 5.15S 77.00W
Caia r. Portugal 27 38.50N 7.05W
Caianda Angola 78 11.02S 23.29E
Caibarién Cuba 117 22.31N 79.28W
Caicó Brazil 123 6.25S 37.04W
Caicos Is. C. America 117 21.30N 72.00W
Caicos Is. Turks & Caicos Is. 117 21.30N 72.00W
Caird Coast f. Antarctica 128 75.00S 20.00W
Cairngorms mts. U.K. 14 57.04N 3.30W
Cairns Australia 90 16.51S 145.43E
Cairo see Al Qāhirah Egypt 66
Cairo Ill. U.S.A. 111 37.01N 89.09W
Cairo N.Y. U.S.A. 115 42.18N 74.00W
Cairo W.Va. U.S.A. 114 39.13N 81.09W
Cairo Montenotte Italy 30 44.24N 8.16E
Caiundo Angola 78 15.43S 17.30E
Caiwarro Australia 93 28.38S 144.45E
Caizhai China 54 37.20N 118.10E
Caizi Hu l. China 55 30.50N 117.00E
Cajamarca Peru 122 7.09S 78.32W
Cajarc France 20 44.29N 1.50E
Cajàzeiras Brazil 123 6.52S 38.31W
Čajniče Bosnia-Herzegovina 31 43.33N 19.04E
Cajuru Brazil 126 21.15S 47.18W
Čakovec Croatia 31 46.23N 16.26E
Calabar Nigeria 77 4.56N 8.22E
Calabogie Canada 105 45.18N 76.43W
Calabozo Venezuela 122 8.58N 67.28W
Calabria d. Italy 33 39.25N 16.30E
Calacuccia France 21 42.20N 9.03E
Cala, Embalse de resr. Spain 27 37.45N 6.05W
Calafat Romania 34 43.58N 22.59E
Calafate Argentina 125 50.20S 72.16W
Calahorra Spain 26 42.18N 1.59W
Calais France 19 50.57N 1.50E
Calais U.S.A. 113 45.11N 67.16W
Calama Brazil 122 8.03S 62.53W
Calama Chile 121 22.30S 68.55W
Calamar Colombia 122 10.15N 74.55W
Calamian Group is. Phil. 59 12.00N 120.05E
Cala Millor Spain 25 39.35N 3.22E
Calamocha Spain 25 40.55N 1.18W
Calañas Spain 27 37.39N 6.53W
Calanda Spain 25 40.56N 0.14W
Calangianus Italy 32 40.56N 9.12E
Calapan Phil. 59 13.23N 121.10E
Călăraşi Romania 37 44.11N 27.21E
Calatafimi Italy 32 37.55N 12.52E
Calatayud Spain 25 41.21N 1.38W
Calatrava Equat. Guinea 78 1.09N 9.24E
Calau Germany 38 51.45N 13.56E
Calayan i. Phil. 59 19.20N 121.25E
Calbayog Phil. 59 12.04N 124.58E
Calbe Germany 38 51.54N 11.46E
Calcutta India 63 22.32N 88.22E
Caldaro Italy 30 46.25N 11.14E
Caldas Colombia 122 6.05N 75.36W
Caldas da Rainha Portugal 27 39.24N 9.08W
Caldas de Reyes Spain 26 42.36N 8.38W
Caldeirão, Serra do mts. Portugal 27 37.25N 8.10W
Caldera Chile 124 27.04S 70.50W
Caldwell Idaho U.S.A. 108 43.40N 116.41W
Caldwell Ohio U.S.A. 114 39.45N 81.31W
Caledon r. R.S.A. 80 30.27S 26.12E
Caledon B. Australia 90 12.58S 136.52E
Caledonia Canada 104 43.04N 79.56W
Caledonia U.S.A. 114 42.58N 77.51W
Caledonia Hills Canada 103 45.40N 65.00W
Calella Spain 25 41.37N 2.40E
Calexico Mexico 109 32.40N 115.30W
Calf of Man i. I.o.M. Europe 12 54.03N 4.49W
Calgary Canada 100 51.00N 114.10W
Cali Colombia 122 3.24N 76.30W
Calicut India 60 11.15N 74.45E
Caliente U.S.A. 108 37.37N 114.31W
California d. U.S.A. 108 37.29N 119.58W
California, G. of see California, Golfo de g. Mexico 116
California, Golfo de g. Mexico 109 28.00N 112.00W
Calingasta Argentina 124 31.19S 69.30W
Calingiri Australia 89 31.07S 116.27E
Calitri Italy 33 40.54N 15.27E
Callabonna Creek r. Australia 92 29.37S 140.08E
Callabonna, L. Australia 92 29.47S 140.07E
Callac France 18 48.24N 3.26W
Callander Canada 104 46.13N 79.23W
Callander U.K. 14 56.15N 4.13W

Callao Peru 124 12.05S 77.08W
Callicoon U.S.A. 115 41.46N 75.03W
Callosa de Ensarriá Spain 25 38.39N 0.07W
Callosa de Segura Spain 25 38.08N 0.52W
Caloocan Phil. 59 14.38N 120.58E
Caloundra Australia 91 26.47S 153.08E
Caltagirone Italy 33 37.14N 14.31E
Caltanissetta Italy 33 37.29N 14.04E
Caluire-et-Cuire France 21 45.48N 4.51E
Calulo Angola 78 10.05S 14.56E
Calumbo Angola 78 9.08S 13.24E
Calumet Canada 105 45.39N 74.41W
Calundau Angola 78 12.06S 20.55E
Caluula Somali Rep. 71 11.58N 50.48E
Calvados d. France 18 49.10N 0.30W
Calvert I. Canada 100 51.30N 128.00W
Calverton U.S.A. 114 39.03N 76.56W
Calvi France 21 42.34N 8.45E
Calvinia R.S.A. 80 31.29S 19.44E
Calvo, Monte mtn. Italy 33 41.44N 15.46E
Calw Germany 39 48.43N 8.44E
Cam r. U.K. 13 52.34N 0.21E
Camabatela Angola 78 8.20S 15.29E
Camacupa Angola 78 12.01S 17.22E
Camagüey Cuba 117 21.25N 77.55W
Camagüey, Archipiélago de Cuba 117 22.30N 78.00W
Camaiore Italy 30 43.56N 10.18E
Camarat, Cap c. France 21 43.12N 6.41E
Camarès France 20 43.49N 2.53E
Camaret-sur-Mer France 18 48.16N 4.37W
Camargue d. France 21 43.20N 4.38E
Camariñas Spain 26 43.08N 9.12W
Camarón, C. Honduras 117 15.59N 85.00W
Camaronero, Laguna l. Mexico 109 23.00N 106.07W
Camarones Argentina 125 44.45S 65.40W
Camas Spain 27 37.24N 6.01W
Camas U.S.A. 108 45.35N 122.24W
Cambados Spain 26 42.30N 8.48W
Cambay India 62 22.18N 72.37E
Camberg Germany 39 50.18N 8.16E
Camberley U.K. 13 51.21N 0.45W
Cambodia Asia 56 12.45N 105.00E
Camborne U.K. 13 50.12N 5.19W
Cambrai Australia 92 34.39S 139.17E
Cambrai France 19 50.10N 3.14E
Cambria U.S.A. 109 35.34N 121.05W
Cambrian Mts. U.K. 13 52.33N 3.33W
Cambridge Canada 104 43.22N 80.19W
Cambridge New Zealand 86 37.53S 175.29E
Cambridge U.K. 13 52.13N 0.08E
Cambridge Idaho U.S.A. 108 44.34N 116.41W
Cambridge Mass. U.S.A. 115 42.22N 71.06W
Cambridge Md. U.S.A. 115 38.34N 76.04W
Cambridge Minn. U.S.A. 110 45.31N 93.14W
Cambridge N.Y. U.S.A. 115 43.02N 73.23W
Cambridge Ohio U.S.A. 114 40.02N 81.35W
Cambridge Bay town Canada 98 69.09N 105.00W
Cambridgeshire d. U.K. 13 52.15N 0.05E
Cambridge Springs town U.S.A. 114 41.48N 80.04W
Cambrils de Mer Spain 25 41.04N 1.03E
Cambundi-Catembo Angola 78 10.09S 17.35E
Camden U.K. 13 51.33N 0.10W
Camden Ark. U.S.A. 111 33.35N 92.50W
Camden N.J. U.S.A. 115 39.57N 75.07W
Camden N.Y. U.S.A. 115 43.20N 75.45W
Camden S.C. U.S.A. 113 34.16N 80.36W
Cameia Nat. Park Angola 78 12.00S 21.30E
Camelford U.K. 13 50.37N 4.41W
Camerino Italy 30 43.08N 13.04E
Cameron Canada 104 44.27N 78.46W
Cameron Ariz. U.S.A. 109 35.51N 111.25W
Cameron La. U.S.A. 111 29.48N 93.19W
Cameron Mo. U.S.A. 110 39.44N 94.14W
Cameron Tex. U.S.A. 111 30.51N 96.59W
Cameron W.Va. U.S.A. 114 39.50N 80.34W
Cameron Hills Canada 100 59.48N 118.00W
Cameron Mts. New Zealand 86 45.50S 167.00E
Cameroon Africa 77 6.00N 12.30E
Camerota Italy 33 40.00N 15.23E
Cameroun, Mont mtn. Cameroon 77 4.20N 9.05E
Cametá Brazil 123 2.12S 49.30W
Caminha Portugal 26 41.52N 8.50W
Camiri Bolivia 124 20.03S 63.31W
Camocim Brazil 123 2.55S 40.50W
Camooweal Australia 90 19.55S 138.07E
Camopi Guiana 123 3.12N 52.15W
Campagna Italy 33 40.40N 15.08E
Campana Argentina 125 34 38S 58.57W
Campana, Isla i. Chile 125 48.25S 75.20W
Campanario Spain 26 38.52N 5.36W
Campania d. Italy 33 40.50N 14.50E
Campbell U.S.A. 114 41.05N 80.36W
Campbell, C. New Zealand 86 41.45S 174.15E
Campbellford Canada 105 44.18N 77.48W
Campbell I. Pacific Oc. 84 52.30S 169.02E
Campbellpore Pakistan 62 33.46N 72.22E
Campbell River town Canada 100 50.05N 125.20W
Campbells Bay town Canada 105 45.44N 76.36W
Campbellsville U.S.A. 113 37.20N 85.21W
Campbellton Canada 103 48.00N 66.40W
Campbell Town Australia 91 41.55S 147.30E
Campbelltown Australia 93 34.04S 150.49E
Campbeltown U.K. 14 55.25N 5.36W
Camp Borden Canada 104 44.18N 79.52W
Campeche Mexico 116 19.50N 90.30W
Campeche d. Mexico 116 19.00N 90.00W
Campeche B. see Campeche, Bahía de b. Mexico 116
Campeche, Bahía de b. Mexico 116 19.30N 94.00W
Camperdown Australia 92 38.15S 143.14E
Cam Pha Vietnam 56 21.07N 107.19E
Campiglia Marittima Italy 30 43.03N 10.37E
Campillo de Llerena Spain 26 38.30N 5.50W
Campillos Spain 27 37.03N 4.51W
Campina Grande Brazil 123 7.15S 35.50W
Campinas Brazil 126 22.54S 47.06W
Campo Cameroon 77 2.22N 9.50E
Campo r. Cameroon 78 2.21N 9.51E

Campo U.S.A. **111** 37.06N 102.35W
Campobasso Italy **33** 41.34N 14.39E
Campobello di Mazara Italy **32** 37.38N 12.45E
Campo Belo Brazil **126** 20.52S 45.16W
Campo de Criptana Spain **27** 39.24N 3.07W
Campo Gallo Argentina **124** 26.35S 62.50W
Campo Grande Brazil **124** 20.24S 54.35W
Campo Maior Brazil **123** 4.50S 42.12W
Campo Maior Portugal **27** 39.01N 7.04W
Campos Brazil **126** 21.45S 41.18W
Campos Belos Brazil **123** 13.09S 47.03W
Campos do Jordão Brazil **126** 23.28S 46.10W
Campo Tures Italy **30** 46.55N 11.57E
Campton U.S.A. **105** 43.53N 71.38W
Camp Wood U.S.A. **111** 29.40N 100.01W
Cam Ranh Vietnam **56** 11.54N 109.14E
Camrose Canada **100** 53.00N 112.50W
Canaan Conn. U.S.A. **115** 42.02N 73.20W
Canaan Vt. U.S.A. **105** 45.00N 71.32W
Canada N. America **98** 60.00N 105.00W
Cañada de Gómez Argentina **124** 32.49S 61.25W
Canadian U.S.A. **111** 35.55N 100.23W
Canadian r. U.S.A. **111** 35.27N 95.03W
Canadian Shield f. Canada **96** 50.00N 82.00W
Canajoharie U.S.A. **115** 42.56N 74.38W
Çanakkale Turkey **34** 40.09N 26.24E
Çanakkale Boğazi str. Turkey **34** 40.15N 26.25E
Canal du Midi France **17** 43.18N 2.00E
Canal Fulton U.S.A. **114** 40.54N 81.36W
Canandaigua U.S.A. **114** 42.54N 77.17W
Canandaigua L. U.S.A. **114** 42.49N 77.16W
Cananea Mexico **109** 30.57N 110.18W
Canarias, Islas is. Atlantic Oc. **74** 28.00N 15.00W
Canary Is. see Canarias, Islas is. Atlantic Oc. **74**
Canaseraga U.S.A. **114** 42.45N 77.50W
Canastota U.S.A. **115** 43.10N 75.45W
Canastra, Serra da mts. Brazil **126** 20.05S 46.30W
Canaveral, C. U.S.A. **113** 28.27N 80.32W
Cañaveras Spain **26** 40.22N 2.24W
Canavieiras Brazil **123** 15.44S 38.58W
Canbelego Australia **93** 31.33S 146.19E
Canberra Australia **93** 35.18S 149.08E
Canby Calif. U.S.A. **108** 41.27N 120.52W
Canby Minn. U.S.A. **110** 44.43N 96.16W
Cancale France **18** 48.41N 1.51W
Canche r. France **19** 50.31N 1.39E
Cancon France **20** 44.32N 0.38E
Candás Spain **26** 43.35N 5.46W
Candé France **18** 47.34N 1.02W
Candeias Brazil **126** 20.44S 45.18W
Candelaro r. Italy **33** 41.34N 15.53E
Candeleda Spain **27** 40.09N 5.14W
Candle L. Canada **101** 53.50N 105.18W
Candlewood, L. U.S.A. **115** 41.32N 73.27W
Candor U.S.A. **115** 42.14N 76.21W
Canelles, Embalse de resr. Spain **25** 42.10N 0.30E
Canelli Italy **30** 44.43N 8.17E
Canelones Uruguay **125** 34.32S 56.17W
Cañete Peru **122** 13.06S 76.30W
Cañete Spain **25** 40.03N 1.35W
Canfield Canada **104** 42.59N 79.43W
Canfranc Spain **25** 42.43N 0.31W
Cangamba Angola **78** 13.40S 19.50E
Cangas Spain **26** 42.16N 8.47W
Cangas de Narcea Spain **26** 43.11N 6.33W
Cangas de Onís Spain **26** 43.21N 5.07W
Cangkuang, Tanjung c. Indonesia **59** 6.45S 105.15E
Cangombe Angola **78** 14.27S 20.00E
Canguçu Brazil **124** 31.24S 52.41W
Cangwu China **55** 23.27N 111.17E
Cangzhou China **54** 38.15N 116.58E
Caniapiscau r. Canada **103** 57.40N 69.30W
Caniapiscau, Rèsr. Canada **103** 54.10N 69.55W
Canicattì Italy **32** 37.21N 13.51E
Canigou, Pic du mtn. France **20** 42.30N 2.27E
Canisteo U.S.A. **114** 42.07N 77.08W
Canisteo r. U.S.A. **105** 42.07N 77.08W
Canjáyar Spain **27** 37.00N 2.44W
Çankiri Turkey **64** 40.35N 33.37E
Canna i. U.K. **14** 57.03N 6.30W
Cannes France **21** 43.33N 7.01E
Cannich U.K. **14** 57.20N 4.45W
Cannington Canada **104** 44.21N 79.02W
Cannock U.K. **13** 52.42N 2.02W
Cann River town Australia **93** 37.35S 149.06E
Canóas Brazil **126** 29.55S 51.10W
Canoe L. Canada **101** 55.11N 108.15W
Canojoharie U.S.A. **105** 42.56N 74.38W
Canonba Australia **93** 31.19S 147.22E
Canon City U.S.A. **108** 38.27N 105.14W
Canonsburg U.S.A. **114** 40.16N 80.11W
Canopus Australia **92** 33.30S 140.57E
Canora Canada **101** 51.37N 102.26W
Canosa Italy **33** 41.13N 16.04E
Canossa site Italy **30** 44.35N 10.27E
Canowindra Australia **93** 33.34S 148.30E
Canso Canada **103** 45.20N 61.00W
Cantabria d. Spain **26** 43.15N 4.00W
Cantabria, Sierra de mts. Spain **26** 42.35N 2.30W
Cantábrica, Cordillera mts. Spain **26** 43.00N 5.00W
Cantagalo Brazil **126** 21.59S 42.22W
Cantal d. France **20** 45.05N 2.45E
Cantalejo Spain **26** 41.15N 3.55W
Cantanhede Portugal **26** 40.21N 8.36W
Cantaura Venezuela **122** 9.22N 64.24W
Canterbury d. New Zealand **86** 43.30S 172.00E
Canterbury U.K. **13** 51.17N 1.05E
Canterbury Bight New Zealand **86** 44.15S 172.00E
Can Tho Vietnam **56** 10.03N 105.40E
Canton see Guangzhou China **55**
Canton Miss. U.S.A. **111** 32.37N 90.02W
Canton N.C. U.S.A. **113** 35.33N 82.51W
Canton N.Y. U.S.A. **105** 44.36N 75.10W
Canton Ohio U.S.A. **114** 40.48N 81.22W
Canton Okla. U.S.A. **111** 36.03N 98.35W
Canton Penn. U.S.A. **114** 41.39N 76.51W
Cantù Italy **30** 45.44N 9.08E
Cantua Creek town U.S.A. **109** 36.30N 120.19W

Cantung Canada **100** 62.00N 128.09W
Cañuelas Argentina **125** 35.03S 58.44W
Canumã r. Brazil **122** 3.55S 59.10W
Canutama Brazil **122** 6.32S 64.20W
Canutillo Mexico **109** 26.21N 105.25W
Cany-Barville France **18** 49.47N 0.38E
Canyon Tex. U.S.A. **111** 34.59N 101.55W
Canyon Wyo. U.S.A. **108** 44.43N 110.32W
Cao Bang Vietnam **55** 22.37N 106.18E
Caombo Angola **78** 8.45S 16.50E
Caorle Italy **30** 45.36N 12.53E
Capac U.S.A. **114** 43.01N 82.56W
Capanema Brazil **123** 1.08S 47.07W
Cap-Chat Canada **103** 48.56N 66.53W
Cap de la Madeleine Canada **105** 46.22N 72.31W
Cape Barren I. Australia **91** 40.25S 148.15E
Cape Basin f. Atlantic Oc. **127** 38.00S 10.00E
Cape Breton Highlands Canada **103** 46.45N 60.45W
Cape Breton I. Canada **103** 46.00N 60.30W
Cape Coast town Ghana **76** 5.10N 1.13W
Cape Cod B. U.S.A. **115** 41.52N 70.22W
Cape Crawford town Australia **90** 16.38S 135.43E
Cape Croker town Canada **104** 44.55N 81.01W
Cape Dyer town Canada **99** 66.30N 61.20W
Cape Girardeau U.S.A. **111** 37.19N 89.32W
Cape Johnson Depth Pacific Oc. **59** 10.20N 127.20E
Capellen Lux. **16** 49.39N 5.59E
Capelongo Angola **78** 14.55S 15.03E
Cape May town U.S.A. **115** 38.56N 74.55W
Cape Rise f. Indian Oc. **49** 38.00S 27.00E
Capernaum see Kefar Nahum Israel **67**
Cape Town R.S.A. **80** 33.55S 18.27E
Cape Verde Atlantic Oc. **127** 16.00N 24.00W
Cape Verde Basin f. Atlantic Oc. **127** 15.00N 35.00W
Cape Vincent town U.S.A. **105** 44.08N 76.20W
Cape York Pen. Australia **90** 12.40S 142.20E
Cap-Haïtien town Haiti **117** 19.47N 72.17W
Capim r. Brazil **123** 1.40S 47.47W
Capljina Bosnia-Herzegovina **31** 43.07N 17.42E
Capon Bridge U.S.A. **114** 39.21N 78.23W
Capoompeta, Mt. Australia **93** 29.22S 151.59E
Cappoquin Rep. of Ire. **15** 52.09N 7.52W
Capraia i. Italy **30** 43.03N 9.50E
Caprarola Italy **30** 42.19N 12.14E
Capreol Canada **104** 46.43N 80.56W
Caprera i. Italy **32** 41.12N 9.28E
Capri i. Italy **33** 40.33N 14.13E
Caprivi Strip f. Namibia **80** 17.50S 23.10E
Captains Flat Australia **93** 35.34S 149.28E
Captieux France **20** 44.18N 0.16W
Captiva U.S.A. **113** 26.31N 82.12W
Capua Italy **33** 41.06N 14.12E
Caqueta r. Colombia **122** 1.20S 70.50W
Caracal Romania **37** 44.08N 24.18E
Caracas Venezuela **122** 10.35N 66.56W
Caragabal Australia **93** 33.49S 147.46E
Caraguatatuba Brazil **126** 23.39S 45.26W
Carandaí Brazil **126** 20.55S 43.46W
Carangola Brazil **126** 20.44S 42.03W
Caransebeş Romania **37** 45.25N 22.13E
Caratasca, Laguna de b. Honduras **117** 15.10N 84.00W
Caratinga Brazil **126** 19.50S 42.06W
Caravaca Spain **25** 38.06N 1.51W
Caravaggio Italy **30** 45.30N 9.38E
Caravelí Peru **122** 15.45S 73.25W
Carballino Spain **26** 42.26N 8.04W
Carballo Spain **26** 43.13N 8.41W
Carbenyabba Creek r. Australia **92** 29.02S 143.28E
Carberry Canada **101** 49.52N 99.20W
Carbonara, Capo c. Italy **32** 39.06N 9.31E
Carbon-Blanc France **20** 44.53N 0.31W
Carbondale III. U.S.A. **111** 37.44N 89.13W
Carbondale Penn. U.S.A. **115** 41.35N 75.30W
Carbonear Canada **103** 47.45N 53.14W
Carboneras de Guadazaon Spain **25** 39.53N 1.48W
Carbonia Italy **32** 39.11N 8.32E
Carbonin Italy **30** 46.37N 12.13E
Carcajou Canada **100** 57.47N 117.06W
Carcans, Étang de b. France **20** 45.08N 1.08W
Carcassonne France **20** 43.13N 2.21E
Carcastillo Spain **25** 42.23N 1.26W
Carcross Canada **100** 60.13N 134.45W
Cárdenas Cuba **117** 23.02N 81.12W
Cárdenas Mexico **116** 22.00N 99.40W
Cardenete Spain **25** 39.46N 1.41W
Cardiff Canada **104** 44.59N 78.01W
Cardiff U.K. **13** 51.28N 3.11W
Cardigan U.K. **13** 52.06N 4.41W
Cardigan B. U.K. **13** 52.30N 4.30W
Cardigan State Park U.S.A. **105** 43.38N 71.54W
Cardinal Canada **105** 44.47N 75.23W
Cardington U.S.A. **114** 40.30N 82.53W
Cardona Spain **25** 41.56N 1.40E
Cardona Uruguay **125** 33.53S 57.23W
Cardoner r. Spain **25** 41.41N 1.51E
Cardwell Australia **90** 18.21S 146.04E
Carei Romania **37** 47.42N 22.28E
Carentan France **18** 49.18N 1.14W
Cares r. Spain **26** 43.22N 4.31W
Carey U.S.A. **108** 43.18N 113.56W
Carey, L. Australia **89** 29.05S 122.15E
Carey L. Canada **101** 62.12N 102.55W
Carhaix France **18** 48.17N 3.35W
Carhué Argentina **125** 37.11S 62.45W
Cariati Italy **33** 39.30N 16.56E
Caribbean Sea C. America **117** 15.00N 75.00W
Cariboo Mts. Canada **100** 53.00N 121.00W
Caribou r.Man. Canada **101** 59.20N 94.44W
Caribou r.N.W.T. Canada **100** 61.27N 125.45W
Caribou U.S.A. **112** 46.52N 68.01W
Caribou Is. Canada **100** 61.55N 113.15W
Caribou Mts. Canada **100** 59.12N 115.40W
Carignan Canada **105** 47.18N 72.47W
Carignan France **19** 49.38N 5.10E
Carinda Australia **93** 30.29S 147.45E
Cariñena Spain **25** 41.20N 1.13W

Carinhanha Brazil **123** 14.18S 43.47W
Carini Italy **32** 38.08N 13.11E
Caritianas Brazil **122** 9.25S 63.06W
Carlentini Italy **33** 37.16N 15.02E
Carlet Spain **25** 39.14N 0.31W
Carleton Place Canada **105** 45.08N 76.09W
Carlingford Rep. of Ire. **15** 54.03N 6.12W
Carlingford Lough Rep. of Ire. **15** 54.03N 6.09W
Carlinville U.S.A. **111** 39.17N 89.52W
Carlisle U.K. **12** 54.54N 2.55W
Carlisle U.S.A. **114** 40.12N 77.12W
Carloforte Italy **32** 39.08N 8.18E
Carlos Reyles Uruguay **125** 33.03S 56.29W
Carlow Rep. of Ire. **15** 52.50N 6.46W
Carlow d. Rep. of Ire. **15** 52.43N 6.50W
Carlsbad Calif. U.S.A. **109** 33.10N 117.21W
Carlsbad N.Mex. U.S.A. **109** 32.25N 104.14W
Carlsberg Ridge f. Indian Oc. **49** 4.00N 65.00E
Carlyle Canada **101** 49.38N 102.16W
Carmacks Canada **98** 62.04N 136.21W
Carmagnola Italy **30** 44.51N 7.43E
Carman Canada **101** 49.32N 98.00W
Carmarthen U.K. **13** 51.52N 4.20W
Carmarthen B. U.K. **13** 52.30N 4.30W
Carmaux France **20** 44.03N 2.09E
Carmel U.S.A. **115** 41.26N 73.41W
Carmel Head U.K. **12** 53.24N 4.35W
Carmel, Mt. see Karmel, Har mtn. Israel **67**
Carmelo Uruguay **125** 34.00S 58.17W
Carmen Colombia **122** 9.46N 75.06W
Carmen Mexico **116** 18.38N 91.50W
Carmen Uruguay **125** 33.15S 56.01W
Carmen de Areco Argentina **125** 34.20S 59.50W
Carmen de Patagones Argentina **125** 40.48S 63.00W
Carmen, Isla i. Mexico **109** 25.55N 111.10W
Carmen, Isla del i. Mexico **116** 18.35N 91.40W
Carmi U.S.A. **110** 38.05N 88.11W
Carmichael U.S.A. **108** 38.38N 121.19W
Carmila Australia **90** 21.55S 149.25E
Carmo Brazil **126** 21.56S 42.37W
Carmody, L. Australia **89** 32.27S 119.20E
Carmona Spain **27** 37.28N 5.38W
Carnac France **18** 47.35N 3.05W
Carnarvon Australia **88** 24.53S 113.40E
Carnarvon Canada **104** 45.03N 78.40W
Carnarvon R.S.A. **80** 30.58S 22.07E
Carndonagh Rep. of Ire. **15** 55.15N 7.15W
Carnegie Australia **88** 25.43S 122.59E
Carnegie, L. Australia **88** 26.15S 123.00E
Carnew Rep. of Ire. **15** 52.43N 6.31W
Carniche, Alpi mts. Italy/Austria **30** 46.35N 13.00E
Car Nicobar i. India **56** 9.11N 92.45E
Carnot C.A.R. **77** 4.59N 15.56E
Carnot, C. Australia **92** 34.57S 135.38E
Carnoustie U.K. **14** 56.30N 2.44W
Carnsore Pt. Rep. of Ire. **15** 52.10N 6.21W
Caro U.S.A. **114** 43.29N 83.24W
Carolina Brazil **123** 7.20S 47.25W
Carolina Puerto Rico **117** 18.23N 65.57W
Carolina R.S.A. **80** 26.04S 30.07E
Caroline I. Kiribati **85** 10.00S 150.30W
Caroline Is. Pacific Oc. **59** 7.50N 145.00E
Caroline-Solomon Ridge Pacific Oc. **84** 8.00N 150.00E
Caroní r. Venezuela **122** 8.20N 62.42W
Carora Venezuela **122** 10.12N 70.07W
Carp Canada **105** 45.21N 76.02W
Carpathians mts. Europe **37** 48.45N 23.45E
Carpatii Meridionali mts. Romania **37** 45.35N 24.40E
Carpentaria, G. of Australia **90** 14.00S 139.00E
Carpenter Ridge f. Indian Oc. **49** 3.00N 90.00E
Carpentras France **21** 44.03N 5.03E
Carpi Italy **30** 44.47N 10.53E
Carpio Spain **26** 41.13N 5.07W
Carquefou France **18** 47.18N 1.30W
Carra, Lough Rep. of Ire. **15** 53.41N 9.15W
Carrara Italy **30** 44.05N 10.06E
Carrathool Australia **93** 34.25S 145.24E
Carrauntoohil mtn. Rep. of Ire. **15** 52.00N 9.45W
Carrickfergus U.K. **15** 54.43N 5.49W
Carrickmacross Rep. of Ire. **15** 53.58N 6.43W
Carrick-on-Shannon Rep. of Ire. **15** 53.57N 8.06W
Carrick-on-Suir Rep. of Ire. **15** 52.21N 7.26W
Carrieton Australia **92** 32.28S 138.34E
Carrington U.S.A. **110** 47.27N 99.08W
Carrión r. Spain **26** 41.53N 4.32W
Carrión de los Condes Spain **26** 42.20N 4.36W
Carrizo U.S.A. **111** 34.32N 105.53W
Carrizo Springs town U.S.A. **111** 28.31N 99.52W
Carrizozo U.S.A. **109** 33.38N 105.53W
Carroll U.S.A. **110** 42.04N 94.52W
Carrollton Mich. U.S.A. **104** 43.27N 83.54W
Carrollton Mo. U.S.A. **110** 39.22N 93.30W
Carrollton Ohio U.S.A. **114** 40.34N 81.05W
Carrot r. Canada **101** 53.50N 101.17W
Carrowmore Lough Rep. of Ire. **15** 54.11N 9.47W
Carrum Australia **93** 38.05S 145.08E
Çarşamba Turkey **64** 41.13N 36.43E
Çarşamba r. Turkey **64** 37.52N 31.48E
Carson U.S.A. **110** 46.25N 101.34W
Carson City U.S.A. **108** 39.10N 119.46W
Carstairs U.K. **14** 55.42N 3.41W
Cartagena Colombia **122** 10.24N 75.33W
Cartagena Spain **25** 37.36N 0.59W
Cartago Colombia **122** 4.45N 75.55W
Cartago Costa Rica **117** 9.50N 83.52W
Cartaxo Portugal **27** 39.09N 8.47W
Cartaya Spain **27** 37.17N 7.09W
Carter U.S.A. **108** 41.27N 110.25W
Carteret France **18** 49.22N 1.48W
Cartersville U.S.A. **113** 34.09N 84.49W
Carterton New Zealand **86** 41.01S 175.31E
Carthage Tunisia **32** 36.51N 10.21E
Carthage site Tunisia **32** 36.52N 10.20E
Carthage Mo. U.S.A. **111** 37.11N 94.19W
Carthage N.Y. U.S.A. **105** 43.59N 75.37W
Carthage S.Dak. U.S.A. **110** 44.10N 97.43W
Carthage Tex. U.S.A. **111** 32.09N 94.20W

Cartier Canada **104** 46.43N 81.34W
Cartwright Canada **103** 53.50N 56.45W
Caruarú Brazil **123** 8.15S 35.55W
Carúpano Venezuela **122** 10.39N 63.14W
Caruthersville U.S.A. **111** 36.11N 89.39W
Carvin France **19** 50.29N 2.58E
Carvoeiro Brazil **122** 1.24S 61.59W
Carvoeiro, Cabo c. Portugal **27** 39.21N 9.24W
Caryapundy Swamp Australia **92** 29.00S 142.36E
Casablanca Morocco **74** 33.39N 7.35W
Casa Branca Brazil **126** 21.45S 47.06W
Casacalenda Italy **31** 41.44N 14.51E
Casa Grande U.S.A. **109** 32.53N 111.45W
Casalbordino Italy **31** 42.09N 14.35E
Casale Italy **30** 45.08N 8.27E
Casarano Italy **33** 40.00N 18.10E
Casar de Cáceres Spain **27** 39.34N 6.25W
Casas Ibáñez Spain **25** 39.17N 1.28W
Casasimarro Spain **25** 39.22N 2.02W
Casavieja Spain **26** 40.17N 4.46W
Cascade Idaho U.S.A. **108** 44.31N 116.02W
Cascade Mont. U.S.A. **108** 47.16N 111.42W
Cascade Pt. New Zealand **86** 44.01S 168.22E
Cascade Range mts. U.S.A. **108** 46.15N 121.00W
Cascina Italy **30** 43.41N 10.33E
Caserta Italy **33** 41.04N 14.20E
Caseville U.S.A. **104** 43.56N 83.16W
Cashel Tipperary Rep. of Ire. **15** 52.31N 7.54W
Casilda Argentina **125** 33.03S 61.10W
Casimiro de Abreu Brazil **126** 22.28S 42.12W
Casino Australia **93** 28.50S 153.02E
Casma Peru **122** 9.30S 78.20W
Casoli Italy **31** 42.07N 14.18E
Caspe Spain **25** 41.14N 0.02W
Casper U.S.A. **108** 42.51N 106.19W
Caspian Depression f. Russian Fed./Kazakhstan **45** 47.00N 48.00E
Caspian Sea Europe/Asia **45** 42.00N 51.00E
Cass r. U.S.A. **114** 43.23N 83.59W
Cassai r. Angola **78** 10.38S 22.15E
Cassano allo Ionio Italy **33** 39.47N 16.20E
Cass City U.S.A. **114** 43.36N 83.10W
Casselman Canada **105** 45.19N 75.05W
Casselton U.S.A. **110** 46.54N 97.13W
Cassiar Canada **100** 59.16N 129.40W
Cassiar Mts. Canada **100** 59.00N 129.00W
Cassilis Australia **93** 32.01S 149.59E
Cassino Italy **32** 41.30N 13.49E
Cass Lake town U.S.A. **110** 47.22N 94.35W
Casslar Mts. Canada **96** 59.30N 130.30W
Castanheira de Pêra Portugal **27** 40.00N 8.13W
Castaños Mexico **111** 26.48N 101.26W
Castelbuono Italy **33** 37.56N 14.06E
Castel del Piano Italy **30** 42.53N 11.32E
Castelfiorentino Italy **30** 43.36N 10.58E
Castelfranco Veneto Italy **30** 45.40N 11.55E
Casteljaloux France **20** 44.19N 0.05E
Castellammare Italy **33** 40.42N 14.29E
Castellammare del Golfo Italy **32** 38.01N 12.53E
Castellammare, Golfo di g. Italy **32** 38.10N 12.55E
Castellana Grotte Italy **33** 40.53N 17.11E
Castellaneta Italy **33** 40.37N 16.57E
Castell' Arquato Italy **30** 44.51N 9.52E
Castelli Argentina **125** 36.07S 57.50W
Castellón Spain **25** 39.59N 0.02W
Castellón d. Spain **25** 40.00N 0.00
Castellote Spain **25** 40.48N 0.19W
Castelmassa Italy **30** 45.01N 11.18E
Castelmoron-sur-Lot France **20** 44.24N 0.30E
Castelnaudary France **20** 43.19N 1.57E
Castelnau-Montratier France **20** 44.16N 1.21E
Castelnovo ne'Monti Italy **30** 44.26N 10.24E
Castelnuovo di Garfagnana Italy **30** 44.06N 10.24E
Castelo Brazil **126** 20.33S 41.14W
Castelo Branco Portugal **27** 39.49N 7.30W
Castelo Branco d. Portugal **27** 40.00N 7.30W
Castel San Giovanni Italy **30** 45.04N 9.26E
Castelsardo Italy **32** 40.55N 8.42E
Castelsarrasin France **20** 44.02N 1.06E
Casteltermini Italy **32** 37.32N 13.39E
Castelvetrano Italy **32** 37.41N 12.47E
Casterton Australia **92** 37.35S 141.25E
Castets France **20** 43.53N 1.09W
Castiglion Fiorentino Italy **30** 43.20N 11.55E
Castile U.S.A. **114** 42.38N 78.03W
Castilla Peru **122** 5.16S 80.36W
Castilla la Mancha d. Spain **27** 39.50N 3.00W
Castilla y León d. Spain **26** 41.20N 4.30W
Castilletes Colombia **122** 11.55N 71.20W
Castillon-la-Bataille France **20** 44.51N 0.03W
Castlebar Rep. of Ire. **15** 53.52N 9.19W
Castlebar r. U.K. **15** 53.52N 9.19W
Castleblaney Rep. of Ire. **15** 54.08N 6.46W
Castle Douglas U.K. **14** 54.56N 3.56W
Castleford U.K. **12** 53.43N 1.21W
Castlegar Canada **100** 49.20N 117.40W
Castlegate U.S.A. **108** 39.44N 110.52W
Castle Harbour b. Bermuda **127** 32.20N 64.40W
Castleisland Rep. of Ire. **15** 52.13N 9.28W
Castlemaine Australia **92** 37.05S 144.19E
Castlerea Rep. of Ire. **15** 53.45N 8.30W
Castlereagh r. Australia **93** 30.12S 147.32E
Castle Rock town Colo. U.S.A. **108** 39.22N 104.51W
Castle Rock town Wash. U.S.A. **108** 46.17N 122.54W
Castleton on Hudson U.S.A. **115** 42.32N 73.45W
Castletown I.o.M. Europe **12** 54.04N 4.38W
Castletownshend Rep. of Ire. **15** 51.32N 9.12W
Castres France **20** 43.36N 2.15E
Castries St. Lucia **117** 14.01N 60.59W
Castro Chile **125** 42.30S 73.46W
Castro Daire Portugal **26** 40.54N 7.56W
Castro del Río Spain **27** 37.41N 4.28W
Castrojeriz Spain **26** 42.17N 4.08W
Castro Marim Portugal **27** 37.13N 7.26W
Castronuño Spain **26** 41.23N 5.16W
Castropol Spain **26** 43.32N 7.02W
Castro Urdiales Spain **26** 43.23N 3.13W
Castro Verde Portugal **27** 37.42N 8.05W
Castrovillari Italy **33** 39.49N 16.13E

Castuera Spain 26 38.43N 5.33W
Casula Mozambique 79 15.26S 33.32E
Cataguases Brazil 126 21.23S 42.39W
Çatalca Turkey 29 41.09N 28.29E
Catalina Pt. Guam 84 13.31N 144.55E
Cataluña d. Spain 25 41.30N 1.00E
Catamarca Argentina 124 28.30S 65.45W
Catamarca d. Argentina 124 27.45S 67.00W
Catanduanes i. Phil. 59 13.45N 124.20E
Catanduva Brazil 126 21.03S 49.00W
Catania Italy 33 37.30N 15.06E
Catania, Golfo di g. Italy 33 37.25N 15.15E
Catanzaro Italy 33 38.54N 16.36E
Catarman Phil. 59 12.28N 124.50E
Catarroja Spain 25 39.24N 0.24W
Catbalogan Phil. 59 11.46N 124.55E
Catete Angola 78 9.09S 13.40E
Cathcart Australia 93 36.49S 149.25E
Cathcart R.S.A. 80 32.17S 27.08E
Cat I. Bahamas 113 24.33N 75.36W
Cat L. Canada 102 51.40N 91.50W
Catoche, C. Mexico 117 21.38N 87.08W
Catonsville U.S.A. 114 39.16N 76.44W
Catriló Argentina 125 36.23S 63.24W
Catskill U.S.A. 115 42.13N 73.52W
Catskill Mts. U.S.A. 115 42.10N 74.30W
Catskill Park U.S.A. 115 42.10N 74.10W
Cattaraugus U.S.A. 114 42.20N 78.52W
Catterick U.K. 12 54.23N 1.38W
Cattolica Italy 30 43.58N 12.44E
Catuane Mozambique 81 26.49S 32.17E
Catus France 20 44.34N 1.20E
Cauca r. Colombia 122 8.57N 74.30W
Caucasus mts. Europe 45 43.00N 44.00E
Caudry France 19 50.07N 3.25E
Caulonia Italy 33 38.23N 16.25E
Caungula Angola 78 8.26S 18.35E
Cauquenes Chile 125 35.58S 72.21W
Caura r. Venezuela 122 7.38N 64.53W
Caussade France 20 44.10N 1.32E
Causse du Larzac f. France 20 44.00N 3.15E
Causse Méjean f. France 20 44.15N 3.30E
Cava Italy 33 40.42N 14.42E
Cávado r. Portugal 26 41.32N 8.48W
Cavaillon France 21 43.50N 5.02E
Cavalaire-sur-Mer France 21 43.10N 6.32E
Cavalese Italy 30 46.17N 11.27E
Cavalier U.S.A. 110 48.48N 97.37W
Cavally r. Côte d'Ivoire 76 4.20N 7.39W
Cavan Rep. of Ire. 15 54.00N 7.22W
Cavan d. Rep. of Ire. 15 53.58N 7.10W
Cavarzere Italy 30 45.08N 12.05E
Caviana, Ilha i. Brazil 123 0.20N 50.00W
Cavtat Croatia 31 42.35N 18.13E
Cawndilla L. Australia 92 32.30S 142.18E
Caxambu Brazil 126 21.59S 44.54W
Caxias Brazil 123 4.53S 43.20W
Caxias do Sul Brazil 126 29.14S 51.10W
Caxito Angola 78 8.32S 13.38E
Cayambe Ecuador 122 0.03N 78.08W
Cayenne Guiana 123 4.55N 52.18W
Caylus France 20 44.14N 1.46E
Cayman Brac i. Cayman Is. 117 19.44N 79.48W
Cayman Is. C. America 117 19.00N 81.00W
Cayman Trough Carib. Sea 127 18.00N 8.00W
Cayuga Canada 104 42.56N 79.51W
Cayuga L. U.S.A. 115 42.45N 76.44W
Cazalla de la Sierra Spain 27 37.56N 5.45W
Cazaux, Étang de b. France 20 44.30N 1.10W
Cazenovia U.S.A. 115 42.56N 75.51W
Čazma Croatia 31 45.45N 16.37E
Cazombo Angola 78 11.54S 22.56E
Cazorla Spain 27 37.55S 3.00W
Cea r. Spain 26 42.00N 5.36W
Ceara d. Brazil 123 4.50S 39.00W
Ceba Canada 101 53.07N 102.14W
Ceballos Mexico 111 26.32N 104.09W
Cebollera, Sierra de mts. Spain 26 41.55N 2.30W
Cebreros Spain 26 40.27N 4.28W
Cebu Phil. 59 10.17N 123.56E
Cebu i. Phil. 59 10.15N 123.45E
Ceccano Italy 32 41.34N 13.20E
Cecina Italy 30 43.19N 10.31E
Cecita, Lago di l. Italy 33 39.24N 16.30E
Cedar City U.S.A. 108 37.41N 113.04W
Cedar Falls town U.S.A. 110 42.32N 92.27W
Cedar Grove U.S.A. 114 38.13N 81.26W
Cedar Key U.S.A. 113 29.08N 83.03W
Cedar L. Man. Canada 101 53.20N 100.00W
Cedar L. Ont. Canada 104 46.02N 78.30W
Cedar Rapids town U.S.A. 110 41.59N 91.40W
Cedarville U.S.A. 115 39.20N 75.12W
Cedeira Spain 26 43.39N 8.03W
Cedillo, Embalse de resr. Spain/Portugal 27 39.40N 7.25W
Cedrino r. Italy 32 40.23N 9.44E
Cedrón r. Spain 27 39.57N 3.51W
Cedros, Isla i. Mexico 109 28.10N 115.15W
Ceduna Australia 92 32.07S 133.42E
Ceel Afweyne Somali Rep. 71 9.55N 47.14E
Ceel Buur Somali Rep. 71 4.40N 46.40E
Ceel Dhaab Somali Rep. 71 8.58N 46.38E
Ceel Dheere Somali Rep. 71 3.55N 47.10E
Ceel Xamurre Somali Rep. 71 7.11N 48.55E
Ceepeecee Canada 100 49.52N 126.42W
Ceerigaabo Somali Rep. 71 10.40N 47.20E
Cefalù Italy 33 38.02N 14.01E
Cega r. Spain 26 41.33N 4.46W
Cegléd Hungary 37 47.10N 19.48E
Ceglie Italy 33 40.39N 17.31E
Cela Angola 78 11.26S 15.05E
Celanova Spain 26 42.09N 7.58W
Celaya Mexico 116 20.32N 100.48W
Celebes i. see Sulawesi i. Indonesia 59

Celebes Sea Indonesia 59 3.00N 122.00E
Celina U.S.A. 112 40.34N 84.35W
Celje Slovenia 31 46.14N 15.16E
Celle Germany 38 52.37N 10.05E
Celorico da Beira Portugal 26 40.38N 7.23W
Cemaes Head U.K. 13 52.08N 4.42W
Cenderawasih, Teluk b. Indonesia 59 2.20S 135.50E
Ceno r. Italy 30 44.41N 10.05E
Centerburg U.S.A. 114 40.18N 82.42W
Center Cross U.S.A. 113 37.48N 76.48W
Centerville Iowa U.S.A. 110 40.43N 92.52W
Centerville S.Dak. U.S.A. 110 43.07N 96.58W
Centerville Tenn. U.S.A. 113 35.45N 87.29W
Cento Italy 30 44.43N 11.17E
Central d. Botswana 80 21.45S 26.15E
Central d. Ghana 76 5.30N 1.10W
Central d. Kenya 79 0.30S 37.00E
Central d. U.K. 14 56.10N 4.20W
Central d. Zambia 80 14.30S 29.30E
Central African Republic Africa 70 7.00N 20.00E
Central Brāhui Range mts. Pakistan 62 29.15N 67.15E
Central City Ky. U.S.A. 113 37.17N 87.08W
Central City Nebr. U.S.A. 110 41.07N 98.00W
Central, Cordillera mts. Bolivia 124 18.30S 65.00W
Central, Cordillera mts. Colombia 120 6.00N 75.00W
Central I. Kenya 79 3.30N 36.02E
Centralia Ill. U.S.A. 110 38.32N 89.08W
Centralia Wash. U.S.A. 108 46.43N 122.58W
Central Makrān Range mts. Pakistan 62 26.30N 65.00E
Central Siberian Plateau see Sredne Sibirskoye Ploskogor'ye Russian Fed. 51
Central Square U.S.A. 115 43.17N 76.09W
Centre d. Burkina 76 11.50N 1.10W
Centre d. France 19 47.40N 1.45E
Centre, Canal du France 19 46.27N 4.07E
Centre Est d. Burkina 76 11.20N 0.10W
Centre Nord d. Burkina 76 13.30N 1.00W
Centre Ouest d. Burkina 76 12.00N 2.20W
Centreville Ala. U.S.A. 113 32.57N 87.08W
Centreville Md. U.S.A. 115 39.03N 76.04W
Century Fla. U.S.A. 113 30.59N 87.18W
Century W.Va. U.S.A. 114 39.06N 80.11W
Cepu Indonesia 59 7.07S 111.35E
Ceram i. see Seram i. Indonesia 59
Ceram Sea see Seram, Laut sea Pacific Oc. 59
Cère r. France 20 44.55N 1.53E
Ceres U.S.A. 108 37.35N 120.57W
Ceresole Reale Italy 30 45.26N 7.15E
Céret France 20 42.29N 2.45E
Cereté Colombia 122 8.54N 75.51W
Cerignola Italy 33 41.16N 15.54E
Cérilly France 20 46.37N 2.49E
Cerisiers France 19 48.08N 3.29E
Cerknica Slovenia 31 45.48N 14.22E
Cernavodă Romania 37 44.20N 28.02E
Cernay France 19 47.49N 7.10E
Cerralvo, Isla i. Mexico 109 24.17N 109.52W
Cërrik Albania 34 41.02N 19.57E
Cerritos Mexico 116 22.26N 100.17W
Cerro de Pasco Peru 122 10.43S 76.15W
Cervaro r. Italy 33 41.30N 15.52E
Cervati, Monte mtn. Italy 33 40.17N 15.29E
Cervera Lérida Spain 25 41.40N 1.17E
Cervera Logroño Spain 26 42.01N 1.57W
Cervera de Pisuerga Spain 26 42.52N 4.30W
Cervia Italy 30 44.15N 12.22E
Cervialto, Monte mtn. Italy 33 40.47N 15.08E
Cervignano del Friuli Italy 30 45.49N 13.20E
Cervione France 21 42.20N 9.31E
Cervo Spain 26 43.40N 7.25W
Cesena Italy 30 44.08N 12.15E
Cesenatico Italy 30 44.12N 12.24E
Cēsis Latvia 44 57.18N 25.18E
Česká Kamenice Czech Republic 38 50.47N 14.26E
Česká Lípa Czech Republic 38 50.42N 14.32E
České Budějovice Czech Republic 36 49.00N 14.30E
Český Krumlov Czech Republic 39 48.49N 14.19E
Çeşme Turkey 35 38.18N 26.19E
Cessnock Australia 93 32.51S 151.21E
Cetinje Yugo. 31 42.23N 18.55E
Ceuta Spain 27 35.53N 5.19W
Ceva Italy 30 44.23N 8.01E
Cévennes mts. France 21 44.00N 3.30E
Ceyhan Turkey 64 37.02N 35.48E
Ceyhan r. Turkey 64 36.54N 34.58E
Cèze r. France 21 44.06N 4.42E
Chabanais France 20 45.52N 0.43E
Chablis France 19 47.49N 3.48E
Chacabuco Argentina 125 34.38S 60.29W
Chachani mtn. Peru 122 16.12S 71.32W
Cháchro Pakistan 62 25.07N 70.15E
Chachapoyas Peru 122 6.13S 77.54W
Chaco d. Argentina 124 26.30S 60.00W
Chad Africa 70 16.00N 18.00E
Chad, L. Africa 77 13.30N 14.00E
Chadron U.S.A. 110 42.50N 103.02W
Chafe Nigeria 77 11.56N 6.56E
Chāgai Pakistan 62 29.18N 64.42E
Chāgai Hills Pakistan 62 29.10N 63.35E
Chagda Russian Fed. 51 58.44N 130.38E
'Chaghchārān Afghan. 62 34.32N 65.15E
Chagny France 19 46.55N 4.45E
Chagos Archipelago is. Indian Oc. 49 7.00S 72.00E
Chagrin Falls town U.S.A. 114 41.26N 81.24W
Cha'gyūngoinba China 63 31.10N 90.42E
Chāhār Borjak Afghan. 62 30.17N 62.03E
Chāh Sandan well Pakistan 62 28.59N 63.27E
Chaibāsā India 63 22.34N 85.49E
Chaillé-les-Marais France 18 46.24N 1.01W
Chainat Thailand 56 15.11N 100.10E
Chaiyaphum Thailand 56 15.46N 101.57E
Chajarí Argentina 125 30.45S 57.59W
Chākāi India 63 24.34N 86.24E
Chākdaha India 63 23.05N 88.31E
Chake Chake Tanzania 79 5.13S 39.46E
Chakhānsūr Afghan. 62 31.10N 62.04E
Chakradharpur India 63 22.42N 85.38E

Chakwāl Pakistan 62 32.56N 72.52E
Chala Peru 122 15.48S 74.20W
Chalais France 20 45.16N 0.02E
Chalhuanca Peru 122 14.20S 73.10W
Chālisgaon India 62 20.28N 75.01E
Chalk River town Canada 105 46.01N 77.27W
Challans France 18 46.51N 1.53W
Challenger Depth Pacific Oc. 59 11.19N 142.15E
Challis U.S.A. 108 44.30N 114.14W
Chalonnes-sur-Loire France 18 47.21N 0.46W
Châlons-sur-Marne France 19 48.57N 4.22E
Chalon-sur-Saône France 19 46.47N 4.51E
Chalosse f. France 20 43.45N 0.30W
Châlus France 20 45.39N 0.59E
Cham Germany 39 49.13N 12.41E
Chama U.S.A. 108 36.54N 106.35W
Chama Zambia 79 11.09S 33.10E
Chaman Pakistan 62 30.55N 66.27E
Chamba India 62 32.34N 76.08E
Chambal r. India 63 26.29N 79.15E
Chamberlain U.S.A. 110 43.49N 99.20W
Chambersburg U.S.A. 114 39.56N 77.39W
Chambéry France 21 45.34N 5.56E
Chambeshi Zambia 79 10.57S 31.04E
Chambeshi r. Zambia 79 11.15S 30.37E
Chambley-Bussières France 19 49.03N 5.54E
Chambly Canada 105 45.27N 73.17W
Chambly France 19 49.10N 2.15E
Chambon-sur-Voueize France 20 46.11N 2.25E
Chamburi Kalāt Pakistan 62 26.09N 64.43E
Cha Messengue Angola 78 11.04S 18.56E
Chamical Argentina 124 30.22S 66.19W
Ch'amo Hāyk' i. Ethiopia 73 5.49N 37.35E
Chamoli India 63 30.24N 79.21E
Chamonix France 21 45.55N 6.52E
Chāmpa India 63 22.03N 82.39E
Champagne France 100 60.47N 136.29W
Champagne-Ardenne d. France 19 49.00N 4.30E
Champagnole France 19 46.45N 5.55E
Champaign U.S.A. 112 40.07N 88.14W
Champdeniers France 18 46.29N 0.24W
Champdoré, Lac l. Canada 103 55.55N 65.50W
Champeix France 20 45.36N 3.08E
Champéry Switz. 39 46.10N 6.52E
Champlain Canada 105 46.27N 72.21W
Champlain U.S.A. 105 44.59N 73.27W
Champlain, L. U.S.A. 105 44.45N 73.15W
Champlitte-et-le-Prélot France 19 47.37N 5.31E
Champotón Mexico 117 19.21N 90.43W
Chamusca Portugal 27 39.21N 8.29W
Chañaral Chile 124 26.21S 70.37W
Chānasma India 62 23.43N 72.07E
Chandausi India 63 28.27N 78.46E
Chandeleur Is. U.S.A. 111 29.48N 88.51W
Chandigarh India 62 30.44N 76.47E
Chandigarh d. India 62 30.45N 76.45E
Chāndil India 63 22.58N 86.03E
Chandler Canada 105 48.21N 64.41W
Chandler U.S.A. 111 35.42N 96.53W
Chāndor Hills India 62 20.30N 74.00E
Chandos L. Canada 105 44.49N 78.00W
Chāndpur Bangla. 61 22.08N 91.55E
Chāndpur Bangla. 63 23.13N 90.39E
Chāndpur India 63 29.09N 78.16E
Chandrapur India 63 19.57N 79.18E
Chāndvad India 62 20.20N 74.15E
Chānf Iran 65 26.40N 60.31E
Changchun China 53 43.51N 125.15E
Changde China 55 29.00N 111.35E
Changfeng China 55 32.27N 117.09E
Changhua Jiang r. China 55 19.20N 108.38E
Chang Jiang r. China 55 31.40N 121.15E
Changjin N. Korea 53 40.21N 127.20E
Chang, Ko i. Thailand 56 12.04N 102.23E
Changle China 54 36.42N 118.49E
Changli China 54 39.43N 119.08E
Changling China 54 44.16N 123.58E
Changning China 55 26.24N 112.24E
Changping China 54 40.12N 116.12E
Changsha China 55 28.09N 112.59E
Changshan China 55 28.57N 118.31E
Changshan Qundao is. China 54 39.20N 123.00E
Changshou China 55 29.50N 107.02E
Changshu China 55 31.48N 120.52E
Changting China 55 25.59N 116.20E
Changyi China 54 36.51N 119.23E
Changzhi China 54 36.09N 113.00E
Changzhou China 55 31.46N 119.58E
Channel Is. Europe 13 49.20N 2.13W
Channel Is. U.S.A. 109 34.00N 120.00W
Channel-Port-aux-Basques town Canada 103 47.35N 59.11W
Channing Mich. U.S.A. 112 46.08N 88.06W
Channing Tex. U.S.A. 111 35.41N 102.20W
Chantada Spain 26 42.37N 7.46W
Chanthaburi Thailand 56 12.35N 102.05E
Chantilly France 19 49.12N 2.28E
Chanute U.S.A. 111 37.41N 95.27W
Chao'an China 55 23.40N 116.32E
Chao Hu l. China 55 31.35N 117.30E
Chaonde Mozambique 81 13.43S 40.31E
Chao Phraya r. Thailand 56 13.34N 100.35E
Chao Xian China 55 31.36N 117.52E
Chaoyang Guangdong China 55 23.25N 116.31E
Chaoyang Liaoning China 54 41.35N 120.20E
Chapada das Mangabeiras mts. Brazil 123 10.00S 46.30W
Chapada Diamantina Brazil 126 13.30S 42.30W
Chapala, Lago de l. Mexico 116 20.00N 103.00W
Chapayevo Kazakhstan 45 50.12N 51.09E
Chapayevsk Russian Fed. 44 52.58N 49.44E
Chapeau de Paille Canada 105 47.10N 73.30W
Chapelle-d'Angillon France 19 47.22N 2.26E

Chapicuy Uruguay 125 31.39S 57.54W
Chapleau Canada 102 47.50N 83.24W
Chāpra India 63 25.46N 84.45E
Chaqui Bolivia 124 19.36S 65.32W
Characot I. Antarctica 128 70.00S 75.00W
Charay Mexico 109 26.01N 108.50W
Charcas Mexico 116 23.08N 101.07W
Chard U.K. 13 50.52N 2.59W
Chardon U.S.A. 114 41.35N 81.12W
Charduār India 63 26.52N 92.46E
Chardzhou Turkmenistan 65 39.09N 63.34E
Charente r. France 20 45.40N 0.10E
Charente r. France 20 45.57N 1.05W
Charente-Maritime d. France 20 45.30N 0.45W
Charenton-du-Cher France 19 46.44N 2.38E
Chari r. Chad 77 13.00N 14.30E
Chari-Baguirmi d. Chad 77 12.20N 15.30E
Chārīkār Afghan. 62 35.01N 69.11E
Charing U.K. 13 51.12N 0.49E
Chariton U.S.A. 110 41.01N 93.19W
Charleroi Belgium 16 50.25N 4.27E
Charlesbourg Canada 105 46.51N 71.16W
Charles City U.S.A. 110 43.04N 92.40W
Charles Pt. Australia 88 12.23S 130.37E
Charleston Miss. U.S.A. 111 34.00N 90.04W
Charleston S.C. U.S.A. 113 32.48N 79.58W
Charleston W.Va. U.S.A. 114 38.21N 81.38W
Charlestown Rep. of Ire. 15 53.57N 8.48W
Charlestown Ind. U.S.A. 112 38.28N 85.40W
Charlestown N.H. U.S.A. 115 43.14N 72.26W
Charles Town W.Va. U.S.A. 114 39.17N 77.52W
Charlesville Zaïre 78 5.27S 20.58E
Charleville Australia 90 26.25S 146.13E
Charleville-Mézières France 19 49.46N 4.43E
Charlieu France 21 46.10N 4.10E
Charlotte N.C. U.S.A. 113 35.03N 80.50W
Charlotte Va. U.S.A. 113 37.03N 78.44W
Charlottenberg Sweden 43 59.53N 12.17E
Charlottesville U.S.A. 113 38.02N 78.29W
Charlottetown Canada 103 46.14N 63.08W
Charlton Australia 92 36.18S 143.27E
Charlton I. Canada 102 52.00N 79.30W
Charly-sur-Marne France 19 48.58N 3.17E
Charmes France 19 48.22N 6.17E
Charny Canada 105 46.43N 71.16W
Charolles France 19 46.26N 4.17E
Charroux France 18 46.09N 0.24E
Chārsadda Pakistan 62 34.09N 71.44E
Charters Towers Australia 90 20.05S 146.16E
Chartres France 18 48.27N 1.30E
Chascomús Argentina 125 35.35S 58.00W
Chase City U.S.A. 113 36.59N 78.30W
Châteaubriant France 18 47.43N 1.23W
Château-Chinon France 19 47.04N 3.56E
Château d'Oex Switz. 39 46.28N 7.08E
Château-du-Loir France 18 47.42N 0.25E
Châteaudun France 18 48.05N 1.20E
Chateaugay U.S.A. 105 44.56N 74.05W
Château Gontier France 18 47.50N 0.42W
Châteauguay, Lac l. Canada 103 56.27N 70.05W
Château Landon France 19 48.09N 2.42E
Château-la-Vallière France 18 47.33N 0.19E
Châteaulin France 18 48.12N 4.05W
Châteaumeillant France 19 46.34N 2.12E
Châteauneuf-de-Randon France 20 44.39N 3.40E
Châteauneuf-en-Thymerais France 18 48.35N 1.15E
Châteauneuf-sur-Charente France 20 45.36N 0.03W
Châteauneuf-sur-Loire France 19 47.52N 2.14E
Châteauneuf-sur-Sarthe France 18 47.41N 0.30W
Château-Porcien France 19 49.32N 4.15E
Château Renault France 18 47.35N 0.55E
Châteauroux France 19 46.49N 1.42E
Château-Salins France 19 48.49N 6.30E
Château-Thierry France 19 49.03N 3.24E
Châtelet Belgium 16 50.24N 4.32E
Châtellerault France 18 46.49N 0.33E
Châtel-sur-Moselle France 19 48.18N 6.24E
Châtelus-Malvaleix France 20 46.18N 2.01E
Chatham N.B. Canada 103 47.02N 65.28W
Chatham Ont. Canada 104 42.24N 82.11W
Chatham U.K. 13 51.23N 0.32E
Chatham Alas. U.S.A. 100 57.30N 135.00W
Chatham Mass. U.S.A. 115 41.41N 69.58W
Chatham N.Y. U.S.A. 115 42.22N 73.36W
Chatham Is. Pacific Oc. 84 44.00S 176.35W
Chatham Rise Pacific Oc. 84 43.30S 178.00W
Chatham Str. U.S.A. 100 57.30N 134.45W
Châtillon Italy 30 45.45N 7.37E
Châtillon-Coligny France 19 47.50N 2.51E
Châtillon-en-Bazois France 19 47.03N 3.49E
Châtillon-sur-Chalaronne France 21 46.07N 4.58E
Châtillon-sur-Indre France 18 46.59N 1.11E
Châtillon-sur-Seine France 19 47.51N 4.33E
Chatra India 63 24.13N 84.52E
Chatrapur India 63 19.21N 84.59E
Chatsworth Canada 104 44.27N 80.54W
Chattahoochee U.S.A. 113 30.42N 84.51W
Chattahoochee r. U.S.A. 113 30.52N 84.57W
Chattanooga U.S.A. 113 35.02N 85.18W
Chatteris U.K. 13 52.27N 0.03E
Chaudes-Aigues France 20 44.51N 3.00E
Chauk Myanmar 56 20.52N 94.50E
Chaulnes France 19 49.49N 2.48E
Chaumont France 19 48.07N 5.08E
Chaumont-en-Vexin France 19 49.16N 1.53E
Chaungwabyin Myanmar 56 13.41N 98.22E
Chauny France 19 49.37N 3.13E
Chaupāran India 63 24.23N 85.15E
Chau Phu Vietnam 56 10.42N 105.03E
Chaussin France 19 46.58N 5.25E
Chausy Belarus 37 53.49N 30.57E
Chautauqua L. U.S.A. 114 42.12N 79.27W
Chauvigny France 18 46.34N 0.39E
Chavanges France 19 48.31N 4.34E
Chaves Brazil 123 0.10S 49.55W
Chaves Portugal 26 41.44N 7.28W
Chavuma Zambia 78 13.04S 22.43E

Chawang Thailand 56 8.25N 99.32E
Cheat r. U.S.A. 114 39.06N 79.33W
Cheat Mtn. U.S.A. 114 38.43N 79.51W
Cheb Czech Republic 39 50.01N 12.25E
Cheboksary Russian Fed. 44 56.08N 47.12E
Cheboygan U.S.A. 104 45.39N 84.29W
Chebsara Russian Fed. 44 59.14N 38.59E
Chebula Angola 78 12.27S 23.49E
Chechaouene Morocco 74 35.10N 5.16W
Chech, Erg des. Mali/Algeria 74 24.30N 2.30W
Chechersk Belarus 37 52.54N 30.54E
Checiny Poland 37 50.48N 20.28E
Cheduba I. Myanmar 56 18.50N 93.35E
Chef-Boutonne France 18 46.07N 0.04W
Chegdomyn Russian Fed. 51 51.09N 133.01E
Chegga well Mauritania 74 25.30N 5.46W
Chegutu Zimbabwe 80 18.09S 30.07E
Chehalis U.S.A. 108 46.40N 122.58W
Cheil, Ras el c. Somali Rep. 71 7.45N 49.48E
Cheiron, Cime du mtn. France 21 43.49N 6.58E
Cheju S. Korea 53 33.31N 126.29E
Cheju do i. S. Korea 53 33.20N 126.30E
Cheleken Turkmenistan 65 39.26N 53.11E
Chelforó Argentina 125 39.04S 66.33W
Chelif, Oued r. Algeria 75 36.15N 2.05E
Chelkar Kazakhstan 50 47.48N 59.39E
Chelles France 19 48.53N 2.36E
Chelm Poland 37 51.10N 23.28E
Chelmer r. U.K. 11 51.43N 0.40E
Chelmsford Canada 104 46.35N 81.12W
Chelmsford U.K. 13 51.44N 0.28E
Chelmza Poland 37 53.12N 18.37E
Chelsea Canada 105 45.29N 75.48W
Chelsea Mich. U.S.A. 104 42.19N 84.01W
Chelsea Vt. U.S.A. 105 43.59N 72.27W
Cheltenham U.K. 13 51.53N 2.07W
Chelva Spain 25 39.45N 1.00W
Chelyabinsk Russian Fed. 9 55.12N 61.25E
Chelyuskin, Mys c. Russian Fed. 51 77.20N 106.00E
Chemainus Canada 100 48.55N 123.48W
Chemba Mozambique 79 17.11S 34.53E
Chemillé France 18 47.13N 0.44W
Chemnitz Germany 38 50.50N 12.55E
Chemult U.S.A. 108 43.13N 121.47W
Chenâb r. Pakistan 62 29.23N 71.02E
Chenachane Algeria 74 26.00N 4.15W
Chenango r. U.S.A. 115 42.05N 75.55W
Chénéville Canada 105 45.53N 75.03W
Cheney U.S.A. 108 47.29N 117.34W
Chengchow see Zhengzhou China 54
Chengde China 54 41.00N 117.52E
Chengdu China 55 30.41N 104.05E
Chenggu China 55 33.10N 107.22E
Chenghai China 55 23.31N 116.43E
Chengkou China 55 31.58N 108.48E
Chengmai China 55 19.44N 109.59E
Chên, Gora mtn. Russian Fed. 51 65.30N 141.20E
Cheng Xian China 54 33.42N 105.36E
Chenoa U.S.A. 110 40.44N 88.43W
Chen Xian China 55 25.45N 113.00E
Chepelare Bulgaria 34 41.44N 24.41E
Chepén Peru 122 7.15S 79.20W
Chepstow U.K. 13 51.38N 2.40W
Cher d. France 17 47.05N 2.30E
Cher r. France 18 47.21N 0.29E
Cherbourg France 18 49.39N 1.39W
Cherdyn Russian Fed. 44 60.25N 55.22E
Chereiato Ethiopia 73 6.00N 38.10E
Cheremkhovo Russian Fed. 51 53.08N 103.01E
Cherepovets Russian Fed. 44 59.05N 37.55E
Chergui, Chott ech f. Algeria 75 34.21N 0.30E
Cherikov Belarus 37 53.35N 31.23E
Cherkassy Ukraine 45 49.27N 32.04E
Cherkessk Russian Fed. 45 44.14N 42.05E
Cherkovitsa Bulgaria 34 43.41N 24.49E
Cherlak Russian Fed. 50 54.10N 74.52E
Chernigov Ukraine 37 51.30N 31.18E
Chernikovsk Russian Fed. 44 54.50N 56.06E
Chernobyl Ukraine 37 51.17N 30.15E
Chernovtsy Ukraine 37 48.19N 25.52E
Chernyakhov Ukraine 37 50.30N 28.38E
Chernyakhovsk Russian Fed. 41 54.38N 21.49E
Cherokee Iowa U.S.A. 110 42.45N 95.33W
Cherokee Okla. U.S.A. 111 36.45N 98.21W
Cherquenco Chile 125 38.41S 72.00W
Cherrapunji India 63 25.18N 91.42E
Cherry Creek r. U.S.A. 110 44.36N 101.30W
Cherry Creek town Nev. U.S.A. 108 39.54N 113.53W
Cherry Creek town S.Dak. U.S.A. 110 44.36N 101.26W
Cherry Valley town U.S.A. 115 42.48N 74.45W
Cherskogo, Khrebet mts. Russian Fed. 51 65.50N 143.00E
Chertkovo Russian Fed. 45 49.22N 40.12E
Chertsey U.K. 13 51.23N 0.27W
Cherven-Bryag Bulgaria 34 43.17N 24.07E
Chervonograd Ukraine 37 50.25N 24.10E
Cherwell r. U.K. 13 51.44N 1.15W
Chesaning U.S.A. 104 43.11N 84.07W
Chesapeake Ohio U.S.A. 114 38.26N 82.28W
Chesapeake Va. U.S.A. 113 36.43N 76.15W
Chesapeake W.Va. U.S.A. 114 38.12N 81.33W
Chesapeake B. U.S.A. 115 38.40N 76.25W
Chesapeake Beach town U.S.A. 115 38.41N 76.32W
Chesham U.K. 13 51.43N 0.38W
Cheshire d. U.K. 12 53.14N 2.30W
Chêshskaya Guba g. Russian Fed. 44 67.20N 46.30E
Chesht-e Sharif Afghan. 62 34.21N 63.44E
Chesil Beach f. U.K. 13 50.37N 2.33W
Chesley Canada 104 44.17N 81.05W
Chester U.K. 12 53.12N 2.53W
Chester Mont. U.S.A. 108 48.31N 110.58W
Chester Penn. U.S.A. 115 39.51N 75.21W
Chester Vt. U.S.A. 115 43.16N 72.36W
Chesterfield U.K. 12 53.14N 1.26W
Chesterfield, Îles is. N. Cal. 84 20.00S 159.00E
Chesterfield Inlet town Canada 99 63.00N 91.00W
Chestertown Md. U.S.A. 115 39.13N 76.04W
Chestertown N.Y. U.S.A. 115 43.38N 73.49W

Chesterville Canada 105 45.06N 75.14W
Chestnut Ridge mtn. U.S.A. 114 40.09N 79.24W
Chesuncook L. U.S.A. 112 46.00N 69.20W
Chéticamp Canada 103 46.38N 61.01W
Chetumal Mexico 117 18.30N 88.17W
Chetumal B. Mexico 117 18.30N 88.00W
Chetwynd Canada 100 55.45N 121.45W
Cheviot New Zealand 86 42.49S 173.16E
Cheviot U.S.A. 114 39.10N 84.32W
Ch'ew Bahir l. Ethiopia 73 4.40N 36.50E
Cheyenne Okla. U.S.A. 111 35.37N 99.40W
Cheyenne r. U.S.A. 110 44.40N 101.15W
Cheyenne Wyo. U.S.A. 108 41.08N 104.49W
Cheyne B. Australia 89 34.35S 118.50E
Chhabra India 62 24.40N 76.50E
Chhātak Bangla. 63 25.02N 91.40E
Chhatarpur Bihār India 63 24.23N 84.11E
Chhatarpur Madhya P. India 62 24.54N 79.36E
Chhattïsgarh f. India 63 21.00N 82.00E
Chhindwâra India 63 22.04N 78.56E
Chhota-Chhindwāra India 63 23.03N 79.29E
Chhota Udepur India 62 22.19N 74.01E
Chiali Taiwan 55 23.10N 120.11E
Chiang Mai Thailand 56 18.48N 98.59E
Chiapas d. Mexico 116 16.30N 93.00W
Chiaramonte Gulfi Italy 33 37.01N 14.43E
Chiaravalle Centrale Italy 33 38.41N 16.25E
Chiari Italy 30 45.32N 9.56E
Chiavari Italy 30 44.19N 9.19E
Chiavenna Italy 30 46.19N 9.24E
Chiba Japan 57 35.36N 140.07E
Chiba d. Japan 57 35.10N 140.00E
Chibemba Angola 80 15.43S 14.07E
Chibia Angola 78 15.10S 13.32E
Chibougamau Canada 102 49.56N 74.24W
Chibougamau Lac l. Canada 102 49.50N 74.20W
Chibougamau Prov. Park Canada 103 49.25N 73.50W
Chibuk Nigeria 77 10.52N 12.50E
Chibuto Mozambique 81 24.41S 33.32E
Chicago U.S.A. 110 41.50N 87.45W
Chichagof I. U.S.A. 100 57.55N 135.45W
Chicheng China 54 40.52N 115.50E
Chichester U.K. 13 50.50N 0.47W
Chichibu Japan 57 35.59N 139.05E
Chickasha U.S.A. 111 35.02N 97.58W
Chiclana Spain 27 36.25N 6.08W
Chiclayo Peru 122 6.47S 79.47W
Chico r. Chubut Argentina 125 43.45S 66.10W
Chico r. Santa Cruz Argentina 125 50.03S 68.35W
Chico U.S.A. 108 39.44N 121.50W
Chicomo Mozambique 81 24.33S 34.11E
Chicopee U.S.A. 115 42.10N 72.36W
Chicora U.S.A. 114 40.57N 79.45W
Chicoutimi-Jonquière Canada 103 48.26N 71.06W
Chicualacuala Mozambique 81 22.06S 31.42E
Chidambaram India 61 11.24N 79.42E
Chidembo Angola 78 14.34S 19.17E
Chidenguele Mozambique 81 24.54S 34.13E
Chidley, C. Canada 99 60.30N 65.00W
Chiemsee l. Germany 39 47.54N 12.29E
Chieri Italy 30 45.01N 7.49E
Chieti Italy 31 42.21N 14.10E
Chifeng China 54 42.17N 118.56E
Chigasaki Japan 57 35.19N 139.24E
Chignecto B. Canada 103 45.35N 64.45W
Chiguana Bolivia 124 21.05S 67.58W
Chigubo Mozambique 81 22.38S 33.18E
Chigu Co l. China 63 28.40N 91.50E
Chihuahua Mexico 109 28.38N 106.05W
Chihuahua d. Mexico 109 28.40N 106.00W
Chili Kazakhstan 50 44.10N 66.37E
Chikhli India 62 20.21N 76.15E
Chikumbi Zambia 79 15.14S 28.21E
Chikwawa Malaŵi 79 16.00S 34.54E
Chili r. Iran 65 25.12N 61.30E
Chilanga Zambia 79 15.33S 28.17E
Chilapa Mexico 116 17.38N 99.11W
Chilcoot U.S.A. 108 39.49N 120.08W
Childers Australia 90 25.14S 152.17E
Childress U.S.A. 111 34.25N 100.13W
Chile S. America 124 33.20S 71.00W
Chile Basin Pacific Oc. 85 34.20S 80.00W
Chile Chico Chile 125 46.33S 71.44W
Chilka L. India 63 19.46N 85.20E
Chilko L. Canada 98 51.20N 124.05W
Chillagoe Australia 90 17.09S 144.32E
Chillán Chile 125 36.36S 72.07W
Chillicothe Mo. U.S.A. 110 39.48N 93.33W
Chillicothe Ohio U.S.A. 112 39.20N 82.59W
Chilliwack Canada 100 49.10N 122.00W
Chiloé, Isla de i. Chile 125 43.00S 73.00W
Chilonga Zambia 79 12.02S 31.17E
Chilpancingo Mexico 116 17.33N 99.30W
Chiltern Australia 93 36.11S 146.36E
Chiltern Hills U.K. 13 51.40N 0.53W
Chilton U.S.A. 110 44.04N 88.10W
Chilumba Malaŵi 79 10.25S 34.18E
Chilwa, L. Malaŵi 79 15.15S 35.45E
Chimakela Angola 78 11.12S 16.58E
Chimanimani Zimbabwe 81 19.48S 32.52E
Chimay Belgium 16 50.03N 4.20E
Chimbas Argentina 124 31.28S 68.30W
Chimborazo mtn. Ecuador 122 1.29S 78.52W
Chimbote Peru 122 9.04S 78.34W
Chimishliya Moldova 37 46.30N 28.50E
Chimoio Mozambique 81 19.04S 33.29E
Chin d. Myanmar 56 23.00N 93.30E
China Asia 52 33.00N 103.00E
China Lake town U.S.A. 109 35.46N 117.39W
Chinandega Nicaragua 117 12.35N 87.10W
Chinati Peak U.S.A. 109 29.57N 104.29W
Chincha Alta Peru 122 13.25S 76.07W
Chinchaga r. Canada 100 58.50N 118.20W
Chinchilla Australia 91 26.44S 150.39E
Chinchón Spain 27 40.08N 3.25W
Chinchoua Gabon 78 0.00 9.48E

Chincilla de Monte Aragón Spain 25 38.55N 1.45W
Chincoteague U.S.A. 113 37.55N 75.23W
Chinde Mozambique 81 18.37S 36.24E
Chindio Mozambique 79 17.46S 35.23E
Chindwin r. Myanmar 56 21.30N 95.12E
Chinga Mozambique 79 15.14S 38.40E
Chingleput India 61 12.42N 79.59E
Chingola Zambia 79 12.29S 27.53E
Chingombe Zambia 79 14.25S 29.56E
Chingshui Taiwan 55 24.15N 120.35E
Chin Hills Myanmar 56 22.30N 93.30E
Chinhoyi Zimbabwe 80 17.22S 30.10E
Chini India 63 31.32N 78.15E
Chiniot Pakistan 62 31.43N 72.59E
Chinjan Pakistan 62 30.34N 67.58E
Chinkapook Australia 92 35.11S 142.57E
Chinko r. C.A.R. 73 4.50N 23.53E
Chinle U.S.A. 109 36.09N 109.33W
Chinon France 18 47.10N 0.15E
Chinook U.S.A. 108 48.35N 109.14W
Chino Valley town U.S.A. 109 34.45N 112.27W
Chinsali Zambia 79 10.33S 32.05E
Chintheche Malaŵi 79 11.50S 34.13E
Chiny Belgium 16 49.45N 5.20E
Chióco Mozambique 79 16.27S 32.49E
Chioggia Italy 30 45.13N 12.17E
Chipata Zambia 79 13.37S 32.40E
Chipera Mozambique 79 15.20S 32.35E
Chipie r. Canada 102 51.25N 83.20W
Chipinge Zimbabwe 81 20.12S 32.38E
Chippenham U.K. 13 51.27N 2.07W
Chippewa r. U.S.A. 110 44.25N 92.10W
Chippewa Falls town U.S.A. 110 44.56N 91.24W
Chipping Norton U.K. 13 51.56N 1.32W
Chiquian Peru 122 10.10S 77.00W
Chiquinquirá Colombia 122 5.37N 73.50W
Chir r. Russian Fed. 45 48.34N 42.53E
Chirâwa India 62 28.15N 75.38E
Chirchik Uzbekistan 51 41.28N 69.31E
Chiredzi Zimbabwe 81 21.03S 31.39E
Chiredzi r. Zimbabwe 81 21.10S 31.50E
Chiricahua Peak mtn. U.S.A. 109 31.52N 109.20W
Chiriquí mtn. Panama 117 8.49N 82.38W
Chiriquí, Laguna de b. Panama 117 9.00N 82.00W
Chiromo Malaŵi 79 16.28S 35.10E
Chirpan Bulgaria 34 42.10N 25.19E
Chirripó mtn. Costa Rica 117 9.31N 83.30W
Chirundu Zimbabwe 80 16.04S 28.51E
Chisamba Zambia 80 14.58S 28.23E
Chisasibi Canada 102 53.50N 79.00W
Chishan Taiwan 55 22.53N 120.29E
Chisholm U.S.A. 110 47.29N 92.53W
Chisholm Mills Canada 100 54.55N 114.09W
Chishtïan Mandi Pakistan 62 29.48N 72.52E
Chishui China 55 28.29N 105.38E
Chişinău see Kishinev Moldova 37
Chisone r. Italy 30 44.49N 7.25E
Chistopol Russian Fed. 44 55.25N 50.38E
Chita Russian Fed. 53 52.03N 113.35E
Chitek L. Canada 101 52.25N 99.20W
Chitembo Angola 78 13.33S 16.47E
Chitipa Malaŵi 79 9.41S 33.19E
Chitorgarh India 62 24.53N 74.38E
Chitrakūt Dham India 63 25.11N 80.52E
Chitré Panama 97 7.58N 80.26W
Chittagong Bangla. 63 22.20N 91.50E
Chittenango U.S.A. 115 43.03N 75.52W
Chittoor India 61 13.13N 79.06E
Chiumbe r. Zaïre 78 6.37S 21.04E
Chiume Angola 78 15.08S 21.11E
Chiusi Italy 30 43.01N 11.57E
Chiuta, L. Malaŵi/Mozambique 79 14.45S 35.50E
Chiva Spain 25 39.28N 0.43W
Chivasso Italy 30 45.11N 7.53E
Chivhu Zimbabwe 80 19.01S 30.53E
Chivilcoy Argentina 125 34.52S 60.02W
Chiwanda Tanzania 79 11.21S 34.55E
Chobe d. Botswana 80 18.30S 25.15E
Chobe r. Namibia/Botswana 80 17.48S 25.12E
Chobe Swamp f. Namibia 80 18.20S 23.40E
Chocolate Mts. U.S.A. 109 33.20N 115.15W
Chocope Peru 122 7.47S 79.12W
Choele-Choel Argentina 125 39.15S 65.30W
Chōfu Japan 57 35.39N 139.33E
Chohtan India 62 25.29N 71.04E
Choix Mexico 109 26.43N 108.17W
Chojnice Poland 37 53.42N 17.32E
Chokai zan mtn. Japan 57 39.08N 140.04E
Ch'ok'ē Mts. Ethiopia 73 11.00N 37.30E
Cholet France 18 47.04N 0.53W
Cholon Vietnam 56 10.40N 106.30E
Choluteca Honduras 117 13.16N 87.11W
Choma Zambia 79 16.51S 27.04E
Chomu India 62 27.10N 75.44E
Chomutov Czech Republic 39 50.28N 13.26E
Chon Buri Thailand 56 13.20N 101.02E
Chone Ecuador 122 0.44S 80.04W
Chong'an China 55 27.46N 118.01E
Ch'ŏngjin N. Korea 53 41.55N 129.50E
Ch'ŏngju S. Korea 53 36.39N 127.31E
Chŏng Kal Cambodia 56 13.57N 103.35E
Chongming i. China 55 31.36N 121.33E
Chongqing China 55 29.31N 106.35E
Chongren China 55 27.44N 116.02E
Chŏnju S. Korea 53 35.50N 127.05E
Chonos, Archipelago de los is. Chile 125 45.00S 74.00W
Cho Oyu mtn. China/Nepal 63 28.06N 86.40E
Chopda India 62 21.15N 75.18E
Choptank r. U.S.A. 115 38.38N 76.13W
Chorges France 21 44.33N 6.17E
Chorley U.K. 12 53.39N 2.39W
Chorokh r. Georgia 65 41.36N 41.35E
Chorzów Poland 37 50.19N 18.56E
Chosica Peru 122 11.55S 76.38W
Chos Malal Argentina 125 37.20S 70.15W

Choszczno Poland 36 53.10N 15.26E
Choteau U.S.A. 108 47.49N 112.11W
Chotila India 62 22.25N 71.11E
Choum Mauritania 74 21.10N 13.00W
Chowchilla U.S.A. 108 37.07N 120.16W
Christchurch New Zealand 86 43.33S 172.40E
Christchurch U.K. 13 50.44N 1.47W
Christian I. Canada 104 44.50N 80.13W
Christian Sd. U.S.A. 100 55.56N 134.40W
Christiansfeld Denmark 42 55.21N 9.29E
Christianshâb Greenland 99 68.50N 51.00W
Christie B. Canada 101 62.32N 111.10W
Christina r. Canada 101 56.40N 111.03W
Christmas Creek town Australia 88 18.55S 125.56E
Christmas I. Indian Oc. 58 10.30S 105.40E
Christmas I. see Kiritimati i. Kiribati 85
Chrudim Czech Republic 36 49.57N 15.48E
Chu r. Kazakhstan 52 42.30N 76.10E
Chuādānga Bangla. 63 23.38N 88.51E
Chubbuck U.S.A. 109 34.22N 115.20W
Chūbu d. Japan 57 35.25N 137.40E
Chubut d. Argentina 125 44.00S 68.00W
Chubut r. Argentina 125 43.18S 65.06W
Chu Chua Canada 100 51.22N 120.10W
Chudleigh U.K. 13 50.35N 3.36W
Chudnov Ukraine 37 50.05N 28.01E
Chudovo Russian Fed. 44 59.10N 31.41E
Chūgoku d. Japan 57 35.00N 133.00E
Chūgoku sanchi mts. Japan 57 35.30N 133.00E
Chugwater U.S.A. 108 41.46N 104.49W
Chuiquimula Guatemala 117 15.52N 89.50W
Chukai Malaysia 58 4.16N 103.24E
Chukchi Sea Arctic Oc. 96 69.30N 172.00W
Chukotskiy Poluostrov pen. Russian Fed. 51 66.00N 174.30W
Chukudukraal Botswana 80 22.30S 23.22E
Chula Vista U.S.A. 109 32.39N 117.05W
Chulman Russian Fed. 51 56.54N 124.55E
Chulucanas Peru 122 5.08S 80.00W
Chulym Russian Fed. 50 55.09N 80.59E
Chum Russian Fed. 44 67.05N 63.15E
Chumbicha Argentina 124 28.50S 66.18W
Chumikan Russian Fed. 51 54.40N 135.15E
Chumphon Thailand 56 10.34N 99.15E
Chuna r. Russian Fed. 51 58.00N 94.00E
Ch'unch'ŏn S. Korea 53 37.53N 127.45E
Chungking see Chongqing China 55
Chunya Tanzania 79 8.31S 33.28E
Chuquicamata Chile 124 22.20S 68.56W
Chuquisaca d. Bolivia 124 21.00S 64.00W
Chur Switz. 39 46.51N 9.32E
Churchill Canada 101 58.46N 94.10W
Churchill r. Man. Canada 101 58.47N 94.12W
Churchill r. Nfld. Canada 103 53.20N 60.11W
Churchill, C. Canada 101 58.46N 93.12W
Churchill L. Canada 101 55.55N 108.20W
Churchill Peak mtn. Canada 100 58.10N 125.10W
Church Stretton U.K. 13 52.32N 2.49W
Churia Range mts. Nepal 63 28.40N 81.30E
Churu India 62 28.18N 74.57E
Chusovoy Russian Fed. 44 58.18N 57.50E
Chu Xian China 54 32.25N 118.15E
Chuxiong China 61 25.03N 101.33E
Chu Yang Sin mtn. Vietnam 56 12.25N 108.25E
Ciamis Indonesia 59 7.20S 108.21E
Cianjur Indonesia 59 6.50S 107.09E
Cibatu Indonesia 59 7.10S 107.59E
Cičarija mts. Slovenia/Croatia 31 45.30N 14.00E
Cidacos r. Spain 25 42.21N 1.38W
Ciego de Avila Cuba 117 21.51N 78.47W
Ciempozuelos Spain 26 40.10N 3.37W
Ciénaga Colombia 122 11.11N 74.15W
Cienfuegos Cuba 117 22.10N 80.27W
Cíes, Islas is. Spain 26 42.13N 8.54W
Cieszyn Poland 37 49.45N 18.38E
Cieza Spain 25 38.14N 1.25W
Cifuentes Spain 26 40.47N 2.37W
Cigüela r. Spain 27 39.08N 3.44W
Cijara, Embalse de resr. Spain 27 39.18N 4.52W
Cijulang Indonesia 59 7.44S 108.30E
Cikampek Indonesia 59 6.21S 107.25E
Cilacap Indonesia 59 7.44S 109.00E
Ciledug Indonesia 59 6.56S 108.43E
Cili China 55 29.24N 111.04E
Cilleruelo de Bezana Spain 26 43.00N 3.51W
Cimanuk r. Indonesia 59 6.20S 108.12E
Cimarron U.S.A. 111 37.48N 100.21W
Cimarron r. U.S.A. 111 36.10N 96.17W
Cimone, Monte mtn. Italy 30 44.12N 10.42E
Cîmpina Romania 29 45.08N 25.44E
Cîmpulung Romania 29 45.16N 25.03E
Cinca r. Spain 25 41.26N 0.21E
Cincar mtn. Bosnia-Herzegovina 31 43.54N 17.04E
Cincinnati U.S.A. 112 39.10N 84.30W
Ciney Belgium 16 50.17N 5.06E
Cingoli Italy 30 43.22N 13.13E
Cinto, Monte mtn. France 21 42.23N 8.56E
Cipolletti Argentina 125 38.56S 67.59W
Circeo, Parco Nazionale del Nat. Park Italy 32 41.17N 13.05E
Circle U.S.A. 108 47.25N 105.35W
Circleville Ohio U.S.A. 112 39.36N 82.57W
Circleville Utah U.S.A. 108 38.10N 112.16W
Cirebon Indonesia 59 6.46S 108.33E
Cirencester U.K. 13 51.43N 1.59W
Cirey-sur-Vezouse France 19 48.35N 6.57E
Cirié Italy 30 45.14N 7.36E
Cirò Marina Italy 33 39.22N 17.08E
Cisco U.S.A. 111 32.23N 98.59W
Ciskei Africa 80 32.45S 27.00E
Cisterna di Latina Italy 32 41.35N 12.49E
Cistierna Spain 26 42.48N 5.07W
Citlaltepeti mtn. Mexico 97 19.00N 97.18W
Citra U.S.A. 113 29.24N 82.06W
Cittadella Italy 30 45.39N 11.47E
Città di Castello Italy 30 43.27N 12.14E
Cittanova Italy 33 38.21N 16.05E

Ciudad Acuña Mexico 111 29.18N 100.55W
Ciudad Allende Mexico 111 28.20N 100.51W
Ciudad Bolívar Venezuela 122 8.06N 63.36W
Ciudad Camargo Mexico 109 27.40N 105.10W
Ciudad Delicias Mexico 97 28.13N 105.28W
Ciudad de México Mexico 116 19.25N 99.10W
Ciudadela Spain 25 40.00N 3.50E
Ciudad Guayana Venezuela 122 8.22N 62.40W
Ciudad Guerrero Mexico 116 28.33N 107.28W
Ciudad Guzmán Mexico 116 19.41N 103.29W
Ciudad Ixtepec Mexico 116 16.32N 95.10W
Ciudad Jiménez Mexico 109 27.08N 104.55W
Ciudad Juárez Mexico 109 31.44N 106.29W
Ciudad Lerdo Mexico 111 25.32N 103.32W
Ciudad Madero Mexico 116 22.19N 97.50W
Ciudad Mante Mexico 116 22.44N 98.57W
Ciudad Melchor Múzquiz Mexico 111 27.53N 101.31W
Ciudad Mier Mexico 111 26.26N 99.09W
Ciudad Obregón Mexico 109 27.29N 109.56W
Ciudad Ojeda Venezuela 122 10.05N 71.17W
Ciudad Piar Venezuela 122 7.27N 63.19W
Ciudad Real Spain 26 38.59N 3.56W
Ciudad Real d. Spain 27 38.50N 4.00W
Ciudad Rodrigo Spain 26 40.36N 6.32W
Ciudad Victoria Mexico 116 23.43N 99.10W
Ciurana r. Spain 25 41.08N 0.39E
Civita Castellana Italy 30 42.17N 12.25E
Civitanova Italy 31 43.18N 13.44E
Civitavecchia Italy 30 42.06N 11.48E
Civray France 18 46.09N 0.18E
Çivril Turkey 64 38.18N 29.43E
Ci Xian China 54 36.22N 114.23E
Cizre Turkey 64 37.21N 42.11E
Clackline Australia 89 31.43S 116.31E
Clacton on Sea U.K. 13 51.47N 1.10E
Clain r. France 18 46.47N 0.32E
Claire, L. Canada 100 58.30N 112.00W
Clairton U.S.A. 114 40.18N 79.53W
Clairvaux-les-Lacs France 19 46.34N 5.45E
Claise r. France 18 46.54N 0.45E
Clamecy France 19 47.27N 3.31E
Clanton U.S.A. 113 32.50N 86.38W
Clapperton I. Canada 104 46.02N 82.13W
Clara Rep. of Ire. 15 53.21N 7.37W
Clare N.S.W. Australia 92 33.27S 143.55E
Clare S.A. Australia 92 33.50S 138.38E
Clare d. Rep. of Ire. 15 52.52N 8.55W
Clare r. Rep. of Ire. 15 53.19N 9.04W
Clare U.S.A. 112 43.49N 84.47W
Clare I. Rep. of Ire. 15 53.48N 10.00W
Claremont U.S.A. 115 43.23N 72.20W
Claremore U.S.A. 111 36.19N 95.36W
Claremorris Rep. of Ire. 15 53.44N 9.00W
Clarence r. Australia 93 29.25S 153.02E
Clarence r. New Zealand 86 42.10S 173.55E
Clarence U.S.A. 114 41.03N 77.56W
Clarence I. Antarctica 128 61.30S 53.50W
Clarence Str. Australia 88 12.00S 131.00E
Clarence Str. U.S.A. 100 55.40N 132.10W
Clarendon U.S.A. 111 34.56N 100.53W
Clarendon L. Canada 105 44.52N 76.53W
Claresholm Canada 100 50.00N 113.45W
Clarie Coast f. Antarctica 128 67.00S 133.00E
Clarinda U.S.A. 110 40.44N 95.02W
Clarington Ohio U.S.A. 114 39.47N 80.53W
Clarington Penn. U.S.A. 114 41.20N 79.07W
Clarion U.S.A. 114 41.13N 79.24W
Clarion r. U.S.A. 114 41.07N 79.41W
Clarke I. Australia 91 40.30S 148.10E
Clark Fork r. U.S.A. 108 48.09N 116.15W
Clark, L. U.S.A. 98 60.15N 154.15W
Clark, Pt. c. Canada 104 44.04N 81.45W
Clarksburg U.S.A. 114 39.17N 80.21W
Clarksdale U.S.A. 111 34.12N 90.34W
Clarks Summit U.S.A. 115 41.30N 75.42W
Clarkston U.S.A. 108 46.26N 117.02W
Clarksville Ark. U.S.A. 111 35.28N 93.28W
Clarksville Tenn. U.S.A. 113 36.31N 87.21W
Clarksville Tex. U.S.A. 111 33.37N 95.03W
Clary France 19 50.05N 3.24E
Clausthal-Zellerfeld Germany 38 51.48N 10.20E
Clay U.S.A. 114 38.28N 81.05W
Clayoquot Sd. Canada 100 49.11N 126.08W
Claysburg U.S.A. 114 40.18N 78.27W
Claysville U.S.A. 114 40.07N 80.25W
Clayton r. Australia 92 29.06S 137.59E
Clayton Idaho U.S.A. 108 44.16N 114.25W
Clayton N.J. U.S.A. 115 39.39N 75.06W
Clayton N.Mex. U.S.A. 111 36.27N 103.11W
Clayton N.Y. U.S.A. 105 44.14N 76.05W
Clear, C. Rep. of Ire. 15 51.25N 9.32W
Clearfield Penn. U.S.A. 114 41.02N 78.27W
Clearfield Utah U.S.A. 108 41.07N 112.01W
Clear I. Rep. of Ire. 15 51.26N 9.30W
Clear L. U.S.A. 108 39.02N 122.50W
Clear Lake town Iowa U.S.A. 110 43.08N 92.23W
Clear Lake town S.Dak. U.S.A. 110 44.45N 96.41W
Clear Spring U.S.A. 114 39.39N 77.55W
Clearwater Canada 100 51.38N 120.02W
Clearwater r. Canada 101 56.40N 109.30W
Clearwater U.S.A. 113 27.57N 82.48W
Clearwater Mts. U.S.A. 108 46.00N 115.30W
Cle Elum U.S.A. 108 47.12N 120.56W
Cleethorpes U.K. 12 53.33N 0.02W
Clefmont France 19 48.06N 5.31E
Clelles France 21 44.50N 5.37E
Clendenin U.S.A. 114 38.30N 81.21W
Clermont Australia 90 22.49S 147.39E
Clermont France 19 49.23N 2.24E
Clermont-en-Argonne France 19 49.05N 5.05E
Clermont-Ferrand France 20 45.47N 3.05E
Clervaux Lux. 16 50.04N 6.01E
Cles Italy 30 46.22N 11.02E
Cleve Australia 92 33.37S 136.32E
Clevedon U.K. 13 51.26N 2.52W
Cleveland U.K. 12 54.37N 1.08W
Cleveland Miss. U.S.A. 111 33.45N 90.50W
Cleveland Ohio U.S.A. 114 41.30N 81.41W

Cleveland Tenn. U.S.A. 113 35.10N 84.51W
Cleveland Tex. U.S.A. 111 30.21N 95.05W
Cleveland, C. Australia 90 19.11S 147.01E
Cleveland Heights town U.S.A. 114 41.30N 81.34W
Cleveland Hills U.K. 12 54.25N 1.10W
Cleveleys U.K. 12 53.52N 3.01W
Clew B. Rep. of Ire. 15 53.50N 9.47W
Clifden Rep. of Ire. 15 53.29N 10.02W
Clifford Canada 104 43.58N 80.58W
Clifford U.S.A. 114 43.19N 83.11W
Cliffy Head Australia 89 34.58S 116.24E
Clifton Ariz. U.S.A. 109 33.03N 109.18W
Clifton N.J. U.S.A. 115 40.53N 74.08W
Clifton Tex. U.S.A. 111 31.47N 97.35W
Clifton Forge U.S.A. 113 37.49N 79.49W
Climax Canada 101 49.13N 108.23W
Clint U.S.A. 109 31.35N 106.14W
Clinton B.C. Canada 100 51.05N 121.35W
Clinton Ont. Canada 104 43.37N 81.32W
Clinton New Zealand 86 46.13S 169.23E
Clinton Ark. U.S.A. 111 35.36N 92.38W
Clinton Conn. U.S.A. 115 41.17N 72.32W
Clinton Ill. U.S.A. 110 40.10N 88.59W
Clinton Iowa U.S.A. 110 41.51N 90.12W
Clinton Mass. U.S.A. 115 42.25N 71.41W
Clinton Mich. U.S.A. 104 42.04N 83.58W
Clinton Mo. U.S.A. 110 38.22N 93.46W
Clinton N.C. U.S.A. 113 35.00N 78.20W
Clinton N.J. U.S.A. 115 40.38N 74.55W
Clinton Okla. U.S.A. 111 35.31N 98.59W
Clintwood U.S.A. 113 37.09N 82.30W
Clio U.S.A. 104 43.11N 83.44W
Clipperton I. Pacific Oc. 85 10.17N 109.13W
Clisham mtn. U.K. 14 57.58N 6.50W
Clisson France 18 47.05N 1.17W
Clive L. Canada 100 54.13N 118.54W
Cliza Bolivia 124 17.36S 65.56W
Cloghan Offaly Rep. of Ire. 15 53.13N 7.54W
Clogher Head Kerry Rep. of Ire. 15 52.09N 10.28W
Clonakilty Rep. of Ire. 15 51.37N 8.54W
Cloncurry Australia 90 20.42S 140.30E
Clones Rep. of Ire. 15 52.21N 7.44W
Clonmel Rep. of Ire. 15 52.21N 7.44W
Clonroche Rep. of Ire. 15 52.27N 6.45W
Cloppenburg Germany 38 52.50N 8.02E
Cloquet U.S.A. 110 46.43N 92.28W
Clorinda Argentina 124 25.20S 57.40W
Cloud Peak mtn. U.S.A. 108 44.25N 107.10W
Cloughton U.K. 12 54.20N 0.27W
Cloverdale U.S.A. 108 38.48N 123.01W
Clovis Calif. U.S.A. 108 36.49N 119.42W
Clovis N.Mex. U.S.A. 111 34.24N 103.12W
Clowne U.K. 12 53.18N 1.16W
Cluj-Napoca Romania 37 46.47N 23.37E
Clunes France 21 46.04N 6.34E
Clunes Australia 92 37.16S 143.47E
Cluny France 19 46.26N 4.39E
Cluses France 21 46.04N 6.36E
Clusone Italy 30 45.53N 9.57E
Clutha r. New Zealand 86 46.18S 169.05E
Clwyd d. U.K. 12 53.07N 3.20W
Clwyd r. U.K. 12 53.19N 3.30W
Clyde Canada 99 70.30N 68.30W
Clyde New Zealand 86 45.11S 169.19E
Clyde r. U.K. 14 55.56N 4.53W
Clyde N.Y. U.S.A. 114 43.05N 76.52W
Clyde Ohio U.S.A. 114 41.18N 82.59W
Clydebank U.K. 14 55.53N 4.23W
Clyde Forks Canada 105 45.07N 76.41W
Clymer U.S.A. 114 40.40N 79.01W
Côa r. Portugal 26 41.05N 7.05W
Coachella U.S.A. 109 33.41N 116.10W
Coahuila d. Mexico 111 27.40N 102.00W
Coal r. Canada 100 59.39N 126.57W
Coalgate U.S.A. 111 34.32N 96.13W
Coal Grove U.S.A. 114 38.30N 82.39W
Coalinga U.S.A. 109 36.09N 120.21W
Coalport U.S.A. 114 40.45N 78.32W
Coalville U.K. 13 52.43N 1.21W
Coast d. Kenya 79 3.00S 39.30E
Coast Mts. Canada 100 55.00N 129.00W
Coast Range mts. U.S.A. 108 42.40N 123.30W
Coatbridge U.K. 14 55.52N 4.02W
Coatesville U.S.A. 115 39.59N 75.49W
Coaticook Canada 105 45.08N 71.48W
Coats I. Canada 99 62.30N 83.00W
Coats Land f. Antarctica 128 77.00S 25.00W
Coatzacoalcos Mexico 116 18.10N 94.25W
Cobán Guatemala 116 15.28N 90.20W
Cobar Australia 93 31.32S 145.51E
Cobargo Australia 93 36.24S 149.52E
Cobden Australia 92 38.21S 143.07E
Cobden Canada 105 45.38N 76.53W
Cobh Rep. of Ire. 15 51.50N 8.18W
Cobham L. Australia 92 30.09S 142.05E
Cobija Bolivia 124 11.02S 68.44W
Cobleskill U.S.A. 115 42.41N 74.29W
Cobourg Canada 104 43.58N 78.10W
Cobourg Pen. Australia 90 11.20S 132.15E
Cobram Australia 93 35.56S 145.40E
Cobre U.S.A. 108 41.07N 114.25W
Cobue Mozambique 79 12.10S 34.50E
Coburg Germany 39 50.15N 10.58E
Coburg I. Canada 99 76.00N 79.25W
Cocentaina Spain 25 38.45N 0.26W
Cochabamba Bolivia 124 17.24S 66.09W
Cochabamba d. Bolivia 124 17.30S 65.40W
Cochem Germany 39 50.11N 7.09E
Cochin India 60 9.56N 76.15E
Cochise U.S.A. 109 32.06N 109.56W
Cochran U.S.A. 113 32.22N 83.21W
Cochrane Alta. Canada 100 51.11N 114.30W
Cochrane Ont. Canada 102 49.00N 81.00W
Cochrane Chile 125 47.20S 72.30W
Cockaleechie Australia 92 34.07S 135.53E
Cockburn Australia 92 32.05S 141.00E
Cockburn I. Canada 104 45.55N 83.24W
Cockburn Island town Canada 104 45.58N 83.22W

Cockburnspath U.K. 14 55.56N 2.22W
Cockeysville U.S.A. 115 39.29N 76.39W
Cocklebiddy Australia 89 32.02S 126.05E
Cocksackie U.S.A. 115 42.21N 73.48W
Coco r. Honduras 117 14.58N 83.15W
Cocoa U.S.A. 113 28.21N 80.46W
Cocoa Beach U.S.A. 113 28.19N 80.36W
Cocobeach Gabon 78 0.59N 9.36E
Coco, Isla del i. Pacific Oc. 85 5.32N 87.04W
Cocoparra Range mts. Australia 93 34.00S 146.00E
Cocos Is. Indian Oc. 4 10.00S 96.00E
Codǎeşti Romania 37 46.52N 27.46E
Codajás Brazil 122 3.55S 62.00W
Cod, C. U.S.A. 115 41.42N 70.15W
Codigoro Italy 30 44.49N 12.08E
Codó Brazil 123 4.28S 43.51W
Codogno Italy 30 45.09N 9.42E
Codroipo Italy 30 45.58N 12.59E
Cody U.S.A. 108 44.32N 109.03W
Coen Australia 90 13.56S 143.12E
Coesfeld Germany 38 51.56N 7.10E
Coeur d'Alene U.S.A. 106 47.40N 116.46W
Coevorden Neth. 16 52.39N 6.45E
Coffeyville U.S.A. 111 37.02N 95.37W
Coffin B. Australia 92 34.27S 135.19E
Coffin Bay Pen. Australia 92 34.30S 135.14E
Coff's Harbour Australia 93 30.19S 153.05E
Cofre de Perote mtn. Mexico 116 19.30N 97.10W
Cofrentes Spain 25 39.14N 1.04W
Coghinas r. Italy 32 40.55N 8.48E
Coghinas, Lago di r. Italy 32 40.43N 9.05E
Cognac France 20 45.42N 0.20W
Cogolludo Spain 26 40.57N 3.05W
Cohocton U.S.A. 114 42.09N 77.05W
Cohoes U.S.A. 115 42.46N 73.42W
Cohuna Australia 92 35.45S 144.15E
Coiba, Isla de i. Panama 117 7.23N 81.45W
Coihaique Chile 125 45.35S 72.08W
Coimbatore India 60 11.00N 76.57E
Coimbra Brazil 126 19.55S 57.47W
Coimbra Portugal 26 40.12N 8.25W
Coimbra d. Portugal 26 40.10N 8.20W
Coín Spain 27 36.40N 4.45W
Cojimies Ecuador 122 0.20N 80.00W
Cokeville U.S.A. 108 42.05N 110.57W
Colac Australia 92 38.22S 143.38E
Colares Portugal 27 38.48N 9.27W
Colatina Brazil 126 19.35S 40.37W
Colbeck, C. Antarctica 128 77.20S 159.00W
Colborne Canada 105 44.00N 77.53W
Colby U.S.A. 110 39.24N 101.03W
Colchester U.K. 13 51.54N 0.55E
Colchester U.S.A. 115 41.34N 72.20W
Cold L. Canada 101 54.33N 110.05W
Cold Lake town Canada 101 54.27N 110.10W
Coldstream U.K. 14 55.39N 2.15W
Coldwater Canada 104 44.44N 79.39W
Coldwater U.S.A. 112 41.57N 85.01W
Coldwell Canada 102 48.45N 86.30W
Coleambally Australia 93 34.48S 145.53E
Colebrook U.S.A. 105 44.54N 71.30W
Coleman r. Australia 90 15.06S 141.38E
Coleman Tex. U.S.A. 111 31.50N 99.26W
Coleman Wisc. U.S.A. 110 45.04N 88.02W
Colenso R.S.A. 80 28.43S 29.49E
Coleraine Australia 92 37.36S 141.42E
Coleraine U.K. 15 55.08N 6.40W
Colesberg R.S.A. 80 30.43S 25.05E
Colfax U.S.A. 111 31.31N 92.42W
Colgong India 63 25.16N 87.13E
Colico Italy 30 46.08N 9.22E
Colima Mexico 116 19.14N 103.41W
Colima d. Mexico 116 19.05N 104.00W
Colinas Brazil 123 6.02S 44.14W
Coll i. U.K. 14 56.38N 6.34W
Collarenebri Australia 93 29.33S 148.36E
College U.S.A. 98 64.54N 147.55W
College Park town Ga. U.S.A. 113 33.39N 84.28W
College Park town Md. U.S.A. 114 39.00N 76.55W
College Station U.S.A. 111 30.37N 96.21W
Collerina Australia 93 29.22S 146.32E
Collesalvetti Italy 30 43.35N 10.28E
Collie N.S.W. Australia 93 31.41S 148.22E
Collie W.A. Australia 89 33.21S 116.09E
Collie Cardiff Australia 89 33.27S 116.09E
Collier B. Australia 88 16.10S 124.15E
Collingwood U.S.A. 115 39.55N 75.04W
Collingwood Canada 104 44.29N 80.13W
Collingwood New Zealand 86 40.41S 172.41E
Collingwood B. P.N.G. 90 9.20S 149.30E
Collinsville Australia 90 20.34S 147.51E
Collinsville U.S.A. 115 41.49N 72.55W
Collin Top mtn. U.K. 15 54.58N 6.08W
Collon Rep. of Ire. 15 53.47N 6.30W
Collooney Rep. of Ire. 15 54.11N 8.29W
Colmar France 19 48.32N 5.54E
Colmars France 21 44.11N 6.38E
Colmenar Spain 27 36.54N 4.20W
Colmenar de Oreja Spain 27 40.06N 3.23W
Colmenar Viejo Spain 26 40.40N 3.46W
Colne r. Essex U.K. 13 51.50N 0.59E
Colnett, Cabo c. Mexico 109 31.00N 116.20W
Colo r. Australia 93 33.26S 150.53E
Cologne see Köln Germany 38
Colombey-les-Belles France 19 48.32N 5.54E
Colombia S. America 122 4.00N 72.30W
Colombian Basin f. Carib. Sea 127 14.00N 76.00W
Colombo Sri Lanka 61 6.55N 79.52E
Colón Argentina 125 32.15S 58.10W
Colón Panama 122 9.21N 79.54W
Colona Australia 91 31.38S 132.05E
Colonelganj India 63 27.08N 81.42E
Colonia del Sacramento Uruguay 125 34.28S 57.51W
Colonia Las Heras Argentina 125 46.33S 68.57W
Colonia Lavalleja Uruguay 125 31.06S 57.01W
Colonna, Capo c. Italy 33 39.02N 17.11E
Colonsay i. U.K. 14 56.04N 6.13W
Colorado r. Argentina 125 39.50S 62.02W

Colorado d. U.S.A. 108 39.07N 105.27W
Colorado r. Ariz. U.S.A. 109 31.45N 114.40W
Colorado r. Tex. U.S.A. 111 28.36N 95.58W
Colorado City U.S.A. 111 32.24N 100.52W
Colorado Plateau f. U.S.A. 109 36.30N 108.00W
Colorado Springs town U.S.A. 108 38.50N 104.49W
Colton N.Y. U.S.A. 105 44.33N 74.56W
Colton S.Dak. U.S.A. 110 43.47N 96.56W
Columbia La. U.S.A. 111 32.06N 92.05W
Columbia Miss. U.S.A. 111 31.15N 89.56W
Columbia Mo. U.S.A. 110 38.57N 92.20W
Columbia r. U.S.A. 108 46.15N 124.05W
Columbia S.C. U.S.A. 113 34.00N 81.00W
Columbia Tenn. U.S.A. 113 35.37N 87.02W
Columbia Basin f. U.S.A. 108 46.55N 117.36W
Columbia, District of U.S.A. 114 39.13N 76.52W
Columbia Falls town U.S.A. 108 48.23N 114.11W
Columbia, Mt. Canada 100 52.08N 117.20W
Columbiana U.S.A. 114 40.53N 80.42W
Columbia Plateau f. U.S.A. 108 44.00N 117.30W
Columbia, Sierra mts. Mexico 109 29.30N 114.50W
Columbretes, Islas is. Spain 25 39.52N 0.40E
Columbus Ga. U.S.A. 113 32.28N 84.59W
Columbus Ind. U.S.A. 112 39.12N 85.57W
Columbus Miss. U.S.A. 111 33.30N 88.26W
Columbus Mont. U.S.A. 108 45.38N 109.15W
Columbus Nebr. U.S.A. 110 41.25N 97.22W
Columbus N.Mex. U.S.A. 109 31.50N 107.38W
Columbus Ohio U.S.A. 114 39.57N 83.00W
Columbus Tex. U.S.A. 111 29.42N 96.33W
Colville r. U.S.A. 98 70.06N 151.30W
Colville U.S.A. 108 48.33N 117.54W
Colwyn Bay town U.K. 12 53.18N 3.43W
Comacchio Italy 30 44.42N 12.11E
Comacchio, Valli di b. Italy 30 44.38N 12.06E
Comai China 63 28.28N 91.33E
Comanche U.S.A. 111 34.22N 97.58W
Comayagua Honduras 117 14.30N 87.39W
Combeaufontaine France 19 47.43N 5.53E
Comber Canada 104 42.14N 82.33W
Combermere Canada 105 45.22N 77.37W
Comblain-au-Pont Belgium 16 50.29N 5.32E
Combles France 19 50.01N 2.52E
Combourg France 18 48.25N 1.45W
Comboyne Australia 93 31.35S 152.27E
Combronde France 20 45.59N 3.05E
Comeragh Mts. Rep. of Ire. 15 52.17N 7.34W
Comilla Bangla. 63 23.28N 91.10E
Comino, Capo c. Italy 32 40.31N 9.50E
Comiso Italy 33 36.56N 14.37E
Comitán Mexico 116 16.15N 92.08W
Commentry France 20 46.17N 2.44E
Commerce U.S.A. 111 33.15N 95.54W
Commercy France 19 48.45N 5.35E
Comminges f. France 20 43.15N 0.45E
Commonwealth Territory d. Australia 93 35.00S 151.00E
Como Italy 30 45.48N 9.04E
Comodoro Rivadavia Argentina 125 45.50S 67.30W
Como, Lago di l. Italy 30 46.00N 9.20E
Comorin, C. India 48 8.04N 77.35E
Comoros Africa 79 12.15S 44.00E
Compiègne France 19 49.25N 2.50E
Cona China 63 27.59N 91.59E
Co Nag l. China 63 32.00N 91.15E
Conakry Guinea 76 9.30N 13.43W
Concarneau France 18 47.53N 3.55W
Conceição Mozambique 81 18.45S 36.10E
Conceição do Araguaia Brazil 123 8.15S 49.17W
Concepción Argentina 124 27.20S 65.36W
Concepción Chile 125 36.50S 73.03W
Concepción r. Mexico 109 30.32N 112.59W
Concepción Paraguay 124 23.22S 57.26W
Concepción del Oro Mexico 111 24.38N 101.25W
Concepción del Uruguay Argentina 125 32.30S 58.14W
Conception B. Namibia 80 23.53S 14.28E
Conception, Pt. U.S.A. 109 34.27N 120.27W
Conches France 18 48.58N 0.58E
Conchillas Uruguay 125 34.15S 58.04W
Conchos r. Mexico 109 29.32N 104.25W
Concord Mass. U.S.A. 115 42.27N 71.21W
Concord N.C. U.S.A. 113 35.25N 80.34W
Concord N.H. U.S.A. 115 43.12N 71.32W
Concordia Argentina 125 31.24S 58.02W
Concórdia Brazil 122 4.35S 66.35W
Concordia Mexico 109 23.17N 106.04W
Concordia U.S.A. 110 39.34N 97.39W
Condé France 18 48.51N 0.33W
Condé-sur-l'Escaut France 19 50.27N 3.36E
Condobolin Australia 93 33.03S 147.11E
Condom France 20 43.58N 0.22E
Conegliano Italy 30 45.53N 12.18E
Conemaugh River Resr. U.S.A. 114 40.28N 79.17W
Confluence U.S.A. 114 39.49N 79.21W
Confolens France 20 46.01N 0.41E
Conghua China 55 23.33N 113.34E
Congleton U.K. 12 53.10N 2.12W
Congo Africa 78 1.00S 16.00E
Congo r. see Zaïre r. Zaïre 78
Congo Basin f. Zaïre 70 1.00N 21.00E
Congonhas Brazil 126 20.30S 43.53W
Coningsby U.K. 12 53.07N 0.09W
Coniston Canada 104 46.29N 80.51W
Coniston U.K. 12 54.22N 3.06W
Conkouati Congo 78 4.00S 11.16E
Connah's Quay town U.K. 12 53.13N 3.03W
Conneaut U.S.A. 114 41.57N 80.34W
Conneaut Lake town U.S.A. 114 41.36N 80.19W
Conneautville U.S.A. 114 41.36N 80.18W
Connecticut d. U.S.A. 115 41.45N 72.45W
Connecticut r. U.S.A. 115 41.17N 72.21W
Connellsville U.S.A. 114 40.01N 79.35W
Connemara f. Rep. of Ire. 15 53.32N 9.56W
Conner, Mt. Australia 90 25.35S 131.49E
Conn, Lough Rep. of Ire. 15 54.01N 9.15W
Conodoguinet r. U.S.A. 114 40.17N 76.55W
Conon r. U.K. 14 57.33N 4.33W
Conrad U.S.A. 108 48.10N 111.57W

Conroe U.S.A. 111 30.19N 95.27W
Consecon Canada 105 44.00N 77.31W
Conselheiro Lafaiete Brazil 126 20.40S 43.48W
Consett U.K. 12 54.52N 1.50W
Con Son is. Vietnam 56 8.45N 106.38E
Constance, L. see Bodensee Europe 39
Constanţa Romania 29 44.10N 28.31E
Constantia U.S.A. 115 43.15N 76.00W
Constantina Spain 27 37.52N 5.37W
Constantine Algeria 75 36.22N 6.38E
Constância Portugal 27 39.28N 8.20W
Constitución Chile 125 35.20S 72.25W
Constitución Uruguay 125 31.05S 57.50W
Consuegra Spain 27 39.28N 3.36W
Consul Canada 101 49.21N 109.30W
Contact U.S.A. 108 41.48N 114.46W
Contai India 63 21.47N 87.45E
Contamana Peru 122 7.19S 75.00W
Contas r. Brazil 123 14.15S 39.00W
Contreras, Embalse de resr. Spain 25 39.32N 1.30W
Contres France 18 47.25N 1.26E
Contwoyto L. Canada 98 65.42N 110.50W
Conty France 19 49.44N 2.09E
Conversano Italy 33 40.58N 17.08E
Conway Ark. U.S.A. 111 35.05N 92.26W
Conway N.H. U.S.A. 112 43.59N 71.07W
Conway S.C. U.S.A. 113 33.51N 79.04W
Conway, L. Australia 92 28.17S 135.35E
Conwy r. U.K. 11 53.17N 3.49W
Coober Pedy Australia 92 29.01S 134.43E
Cooch Behār India 63 26.19N 89.26E
Cook, C. Canada 98 50.08N 127.55W
Cooke, Mt. Australia 89 32.26S 116.18E
Cookeville U.S.A. 113 36.10N 85.30W
Cookhouse R.S.A. 80 32.44S 25.47E
Cook Inlet U.S.A. 98 60.30N 152.00W
Cook Is. Pacific Oc. 84 15.00S 160.00W
Cook, Mt. New Zealand 86 43.45S 170.12E
Cookshire Canada 105 45.25N 71.38W
Cookstown Canada 104 44.11N 79.42W
Cookstown U.K. 15 54.39N 6.46W
Cook Str. New Zealand 86 41.15S 174.30E
Cooktown Australia 90 15.29S 145.15E
Coolabah Australia 93 31.02S 146.45E
Coolah Australia 93 31.48S 149.45E
Coolamara Australia 93 31.59S 143.42E
Coolamon Australia 93 34.48S 147.12E
Coolangatta Australia 93 28.10S 153.26E
Coolgardie Australia 89 31.01S 121.12E
Coolidge U.S.A. 109 32.59N 111.31W
Coolville U.S.A. 114 39.13N 81.49W
Cooma Australia 93 36.15S 149.07E
Coombah Australia 92 32.58S 141.39E
Coomberdale Australia 89 30.29S 116.03E
Coonabarabran Australia 93 31.16S 149.18E
Coonalpyn Australia 92 35.41S 139.52E
Coonamble Australia 93 30.55S 148.26E
Coonana Australia 89 31.01S 123.05E
Coonawarra Australia 92 37.16S 140.50E
Coondambo Australia 92 31.07S 135.20E
Cooper Creek r. Australia 92 28.33S 137.46E
Cooperstown U.S.A. 115 42.42N 74.56W
Coorow Australia 89 29.53S 116.01E
Coos Bay town U.S.A. 108 43.22N 124.13W
Cootamundra Australia 93 34.41S 148.03E
Cootehill Rep. of Ire. 15 54.05N 7.05W
Copainalá Mexico 116 17.05N 93.12W
Copán ruins Honduras 117 14.52N 89.10W
Cope U.S.A. 108 39.40N 102.51W
Copenhagen see København Denmark 43
Copertino Italy 33 40.16N 18.03E
Copiapó Chile 124 27.22S 70.20W
Copparo Italy 30 44.54N 11.49E
Copperbelt d. Zambia 80 13.00S 28.00E
Copper Belt f. Zambia 79 12.40S 28.00E
Copper Center U.S.A. 98 61.58N 145.19W
Copper Cliff town Canada 104 46.28N 81.04W
Copper Harbor U.S.A. 112 47.28N 87.54W
Coppermine r. Canada 98 67.54N 115.10W
Coppermine town Canada 98 67.49N 15.12W
Copper Mountain town Canada 100 49.20N 120.30W
Copper Queen Zimbabwe 80 17.31S 29.20E
Copperton R.S.A. 80 30.00S 22.15E
Copp L. Canada 100 60.14N 114.40W
Coqên China 63 31.13N 85.12E
Coquet r. U.K. 12 55.21N 1.35W
Coquille U.S.A. 108 43.11N 124.11W
Coquimbo Chile 124 29.58S 71.21W
Corabia Romania 34 43.48N 24.30E
Coracora Peru 122 15.02S 73.48W
Coraki Australia 93 23.00S 153.17E
Coral Bay town Australia 88 23.02S 113.48E
Coral Harbour town Canada 99 64.10N 83.15W
Coral Sea Pacific Oc. 90 14.30S 149.30E
Coral Sea Basin Pacific Oc. 84 14.00S 152.00E
Corangamite, L. Australia 92 38.10S 143.25E
Corato Italy 33 41.09N 16.25E
Corbeil Canada 104 46.17N 79.18W
Corbeil France 19 48.36N 2.29E
Corbeny France 19 49.28N 3.49E
Corbières mts. France 20 42.55N 2.38E
Corbigny France 19 47.15N 3.40E
Corbin U.S.A. 113 36.58N 84.06W
Corby U.K. 13 52.29N 0.41W
Corcubión Spain 26 42.57N 9.11W
Cordes France 20 44.04N 1.56E
Córdoba Argentina 124 31.25S 64.10W
Córdoba d. Argentina 124 30.30S 64.30W
Córdoba Mexico 116 18.55N 96.55W
Córdoba Spain 27 37.53N 4.46W
Córdoba d. Spain 27 38.10N 4.50W
Córdoba, Sierras de mts. Argentina 124 30.30S 64.40W
Cordova U.S.A. 98 60.33N 139.44W
Corentyne r. Guyana 123 5.10N 57.20W
Corfield Australia 90 21.43S 143.22E
Corfu i. see Kérkira i. Greece 34
Coria Spain 27 39.59N 6.32W

Coria del Río Spain 27 37.16N 6.03W
Coricudgy, Mt. Australia 93 32.51S 150.25E
Corigliano Italy 33 39.36N 16.31E
Corindi Australia 93 30.00S 153.21E
Corinne Canada 101 50.04N 104.40W
Corinth Miss. U.S.A. 111 34.56N 88.31W
Corinth N.Y. U.S.A. 115 43.15N 73.49W
Corinth, G. of see Korinthiakos Kólpos g. Greece 35
Corinto Nicaragua 117 12.29N 87.14W
Cork Rep. of Ire. 15 51.54N 8.28W
Cork d. Rep. of Ire. 15 52.00N 8.40W
Cork Harbour est. Rep. of Ire. 15 51.50N 8.17W
Corlay France 18 48.19N 3.03W
Corleone Italy 32 37.49N 13.18E
Corleto Italy 33 40.23N 16.03E
Cormeilles France 18 49.15N 0.23E
Cormons Italy 31 45.58N 13.28E
Cormorant Canada 101 54.14N 100.35W
Corner Brook town Canada 103 48.57N 57.57W
Corner Inlet b. Australia 93 38.43S 146.20E
Corning Ark. U.S.A. 111 36.24N 90.35W
Corning N.Y. U.S.A. 114 42.09N 77.04W
Corning Ohio U.S.A. 114 39.36N 82.05W
Corno, Monte mtn. Italy 31 42.28N 13.34E
Cornwall Canada 105 45.02N 74.44W
Cornwall d. U.K. 13 50.26N 4.40W
Cornwallis I. Canada 99 75.00N 95.00W
Coro Venezuela 122 11.27N 69.41W
Coroatá Brazil 123 4.08S 44.08W
Coroico Bolivia 124 16.10S 67.44W
Coromandel New Zealand 86 36.46S 175.30E
Coromandel Pen. New Zealand 86 36.45S 175.30E
Corona U.S.A. 109 34.15N 105.36W
Coronation G. Canada 98 68.00N 112.00W
Coronation I. U.S.A. 100 55.52N 134.20W
Coronda Argentina 125 31.55S 60.55W
Coronel Chile 125 37.01S 73.08W
Coronel Brandsen Argentina 125 35.10S 58.15W
Coronel Pringles Argentina 125 37.56S 61.25W
Coronel Suárez Argentina 125 37.30S 61.52W
Coropuna mtn. Peru 122 15.31S 72.45W
Corowa Australia 93 36.00S 146.20E
Corozal Belize 117 18.23N 88.23W
Corpus Christi U.S.A. 111 27.48N 97.24W
Corral de Almaguer Spain 27 39.46N 3.11W
Correggio Italy 30 44.46N 10.47E
Correntes, Cabo das c. Mozambique 81 24.11S 35.35E
Corrèze d. France 20 45.20N 1.50E
Corrib, Lough Rep. of Ire. 15 53.26N 9.14W
Corrientes Argentina 124 27.30S 58.48W
Corrientes d. Argentina 124 28.00S 57.00W
Corrientes, Cabo c. Colombia 122 5.30N 77.34W
Corrigan U.S.A. 111 31.00N 94.50W
Corrigin Australia 89 32.21S 117.52E
Corry U.S.A. 114 41.56N 79.39W
Corryong Australia 93 36.11S 147.58E
Corse i. France 21 42.00N 9.00E
Corse i. France 21 42.00N 9.10E
Corse, Cap c. France 21 43.00N 9.25E
Corse-du-Sud d. France 21 41.45N 9.00E
Corsham U.K. 13 51.25N 2.11W
Corsica i. see Corse i. France 21
Corsicana U.S.A. 111 32.06N 96.28W
Corte France 21 42.18N 9.08E
Cortegana Spain 27 37.55N 6.49W
Cortez Colo. U.S.A. 108 37.21N 108.35W
Cortez Nev. U.S.A. 108 40.09N 116.38W
Cortina Italy 30 46.32N 12.08E
Cortland N.Y. U.S.A. 115 42.36N 76.11W
Cortland Ohio U.S.A. 114 41.20N 80.44W
Cortona Italy 30 43.16N 11.59E
Coruche Portugal 27 38.58N 8.31W
Çoruh Nehri r. Turkey see Chorokh r. Georgia 64
Çorum Turkey 64 40.31N 34.57E
Corumbá Brazil 124 19.00S 57.27W
Corumbá r. Brazil 126 18.15S 48.55W
Corunna U.S.A. 104 42.59N 84.07W
Corvallis U.S.A. 108 44.34N 123.16W
Corwen U.K. 12 52.59N 3.23W
Cosenza Italy 33 39.17N 16.15E
Coshocton U.S.A. 114 40.16N 81.51W
Cosne France 19 47.24N 2.55E
Coso Junction U.S.A. 109 36.03N 117.58W
Cosson r. France 19 47.30N 1.15E
Costa Blanca f. Spain 25 38.30N 0.05E
Costa Brava f. Spain 25 41.55N 3.15E
Costa del Sol f. Spain 27 36.30N 4.30W
Costa Mesa U.S.A. 109 33.39N 117.55W
Costa Rica C. America 117 10.00N 84.00W
Costeşti Romania 29 44.40N 24.53E
Coswig Sachsen Germany 38 51.07N 13.34E
Coswig Sachsen-Anhalt Germany 38 51.53N 12.26E
Cotabato Phil. 59 7.14N 124.15E
Cotagaita Bolivia 124 20.50S 65.41W
Côte d'Azur f. France 21 43.30N 7.00E
Côte d'Ivoire Africa 76 8.00N 5.30W
Côte-d'Or d. France 19 47.30N 4.50E
Côte d'Or f. France 19 47.10N 4.50E
Côtes d'Armor d. France 18 48.26N 2.40W
Cotonou Benin 77 6.24N 2.31E
Cotopaxi mtn. Ecuador 122 0.40S 78.28W
Cotswold Hills U.K. 13 51.50N 2.00W
Cottage Grove U.S.A. 108 43.48N 123.03W
Cottbus Germany 38 51.45N 14.19E
Cottennes, Alpes mts. France 21 44.45N 7.00E
Cottonvale Australia 93 28.32S 151.57E
Cottonwood U.S.A. 109 34.45N 112.01W
Cotulla U.S.A. 111 28.26N 99.14W
Coubre, Pointe de la c. France 20 45.41N 1.13W
Coucy France 19 49.31N 3.19E
Coudersport U.S.A. 114 41.46N 78.01W
Couer d'Alene U.S.A. 108 47.41N 117.00W
Couesnon r. France 18 48.37N 1.31W
Couhé France 18 46.18N 0.11E
Coulagh B. Rep. of Ire. 15 51.42N 10.00W
Coulee City U.S.A. 108 47.37N 119.17W
Coulommiers France 19 48.49N 3.05E

Coulon r. France 21 43.51N 5.00E
Coulonge r. Canada 105 45.51N 76.45W
Council U.S.A. 98 64.55N 163.44W
Council Bluffs U.S.A. 110 41.16N 95.52W
Coupar Angus U.K. 14 56.33N 3.17W
Courçon France 20 46.15N 0.49W
Courland Lagoon Russian Fed./Lithuania 41 55.00N 21.00E
Courpière France 20 45.45N 3.33E
Courson-les-Carrières France 19 47.36N 3.30E
Courtalain France 18 48.05N 1.09E
Courtenay Canada 100 49.41N 125.00W
Courtrai see Kortrijk Belgium 16
Coutances France 18 49.03N 1.26W
Coutras France 20 45.02N 0.08W
Couvin Belgium 16 50.03N 4.30E
Cové Benin 77 7.16N 2.20E
Cove City U.S.A. 113 35.11N 77.20W
Cove I. Canada 104 45.17N 81.44W
Coventry U.K. 13 52.25N 1.31W
Covilhã Portugal 26 40.17N 7.30W
Covington Ga. U.S.A. 113 33.35N 83.52W
Covington Ky. U.S.A. 112 39.04N 84.30W
Covington Okla. U.S.A. 111 36.18N 97.35W
Covington Tenn. U.S.A. 111 35.34N 89.38W
Covington Va. U.S.A. 113 37.48N 80.01W
Cowal, L. Australia 93 33.36S 147.22E
Cowan Canada 101 52.05N 100.45W
Cowan, L. Australia 89 32.00S 122.00E
Cowansville Canada 105 45.12N 72.45W
Cowcowing Lakes Australia 89 31.01S 117.18E
Cowdenbeath U.K. 14 56.07N 3.21W
Cowell Australia 92 33.41S 136.55E
Cowen U.S.A. 114 38.25N 80.34W
Cowes Australia 93 38.27S 145.15E
Cowes U.K. 13 50.45N 1.18W
Cowra Australia 93 33.50S 148.45E
Cox r. Australia 90 15.19S 135.25E
Coxim Brazil 124 18.28S 54.37W
Coxsackie U.S.A. 105 42.21N 73.48W
Cox's Bāzār Bangla. 63 21.26N 91.59E
Coyuca de Catalán Mexico 116 18.20N 100.39W
Cozad U.S.A. 110 40.52N 99.59W
Cozes France 20 45.35N 0.50W
Cozumel, Isla de I. Mexico 117 20.30N 87.00W
Cradock Australia 92 31.59S 138.34E
Cradock R.S.A. 80 32.10S 25.35E
Craig Alas. U.S.A. 100 55.29N 133.09W
Craig Colo. U.S.A. 108 40.31N 107.33W
Craigavon U.K. 15 54.28N 6.25W
Craignure U.K. 14 56.28N 5.42W
Craigsville U.S.A. 114 38.05N 79.23W
Crail U.K. 14 56.16N 2.38W
Crailsheim Germany 39 49.08N 10.04E
Craiova Romania 29 44.18N 23.46E
Cranberry L. U.S.A. 105 44.10N 74.50W
Cranbourne Australia 93 38.07S 145.19E
Cranbrook Australia 89 34.15S 117.32E
Cranbrook Canada 100 49.31N 115.46W
Crane U.S.A. 108 43.25N 118.34W
Cranston U.S.A. 115 41.47N 71.26W
Craon France 18 47.51N 0.57W
Craonne France 19 49.26N 3.47E
Craponne France 21 43.40N 4.39E
Craponne, Canal de France 21 43.40N 4.39E
Crater L. U.S.A. 108 42.56N 122.06W
Crateús Brazil 123 5.10S 40.39W
Crati r. Italy 33 39.41N 16.30E
Crato Amazonas Brazil 122 7.25S 63.00W
Crato Ceará Brazil 123 7.10S 39.25W
Craughwell Rep. of Ire. 15 53.14N 8.44W
Crawford U.S.A. 110 42.41N 103.25W
Crawfordsville U.S.A. 112 40.03N 86.54W
Crawfordville U.S.A. 113 30.12N 84.21W
Crawley U.K. 13 51.07N 0.10W
Crazy Mts. U.S.A. 108 46.08N 110.20W
Crécy France 19 50.15N 1.53E
Crécy-sur-Serre France 19 49.42N 3.37E
Cree r. Canada 101 59.00N 105.47W
Creede U.S.A. 108 37.51N 106.56W
Cree L. Canada 101 57.30N 106.30W
Creemore Canada 104 44.19N 80.06W
Creil France 19 49.16N 2.29E
Crema Italy 30 45.22N 9.41E
Cremona Italy 30 45.07N 10.02E
Crépy France 19 49.36N 3.31E
Crépy-en-Valois France 19 49.14N 2.54E
Cres i. Croatia 31 44.50N 14.25E
Cres town Croatia 31 44.58N 14.25E
Cresaptown U.S.A. 114 39.36N 78.50W
Crescent U.S.A. 108 43.29N 121.41W
Crescent City U.S.A. 108 41.45N 124.12W
Crescent Head Australia 93 31.10S 152.59E
Crespo Argentina 125 32.02S 60.20W
Cresson U.S.A. 114 40.28N 78.35W
Cressy Australia 92 38.02S 143.38E
Crest France 21 44.44N 5.02E
Crestline U.S.A. 114 40.47N 82.44W
Creston Canada 100 49.10N 116.31W
Creston Iowa U.S.A. 110 41.04N 94.22W
Creston Ohio U.S.A. 114 40.59N 81.54W
Creston Oriental de la Sierra Madre mts. Mexico 109 28.40N 107.50W
Crestview U.S.A. 113 30.44N 86.34W
Creswick Australia 92 37.25S 143.54E
Crete i. see Kríti i. Greece 35
Crete U.S.A. 110 40.38N 96.58W
Crete, Sea of see Kritikón Pélagos sea Greece 35
Crétéville Tunisia 32 36.40N 10.20E
Creus, Cabo de c. Spain 25 42.19N 3.19E
Creuse d. France 20 46.05N 2.00E
Creuse r. France 17 47.00N 0.35E
Creussen Germany 38 49.51N 11.37E
Crevillente Spain 25 38.15N 0.48W
Crewe U.S.A. 113 37.10N 78.07W
Crewe U.K. 12 53.06N 2.28W
Crianlarich U.K. 14 56.23N 4.37W
Criccieth U.K. 12 52.55N 4.15W

Criciúma Brazil 126 28.40S 49.23W
Crieff U.K. 14 56.23N 3.52W
Crikvenica Croatia 31 45.11N 14.42E
Crillon, Mt. U.S.A. 100 58.39N 137.14W
Crimea pen. see Krym pen. Ukraine 45
Crimmitschau Germany 38 50.49N 12.23E
Crinan U.K. 14 56.06N 5.34W
Cristóbal Colón mtn. Colombia 122 10.53N 73.48W
Crişu Alb r. Romania 37 46.42N 21.17E
Crivitz Germany 38 53.35N 11.38E
Crna r. Macedonia 34 41.35N 21.59E
Crna Gora d. Yugo. 31 42.55N 19.00E
Crnoljeva Planina mts. Yugo. 34 42.20N 21.00E
Črnomelj Slovenia 31 45.34N 15.11E
Croaghnameal mtn. Rep. of Ire. 15 54.40N 7.57W
Croatia Europe 31 45.35N 16.10E
Crockett U.S.A. 111 31.19N 95.28W
Crocodile r. Trans. R.S.A. 80 24.11S 26.48E
Croghan U.S.A. 105 43.54N 75.24W
Croker I. Australia 90 11.12S 132.32E
Cromarty Canada 101 58.03N 94.09W
Cromarty U.K. 14 57.40N 4.02W
Cromarty Firth est. U.K. 14 57.41N 4.10W
Cromer U.K. 12 52.56N 1.18E
Cromwell New Zealand 86 45.03S 169.14E
Crooked I. Bahamas 117 22.45N 74.00W
Crookhaven Rep. of Ire. 15 51.29N 9.45W
Crookston U.S.A. 110 47.47N 96.37W
Crooksville U.S.A. 114 39.46N 82.06W
Crookwell Australia 93 34.27S 149.28E
Croom Rep. of Ire. 15 52.31N 8.43W
Croppa Creek town Australia 93 29.08S 150.20E
Crosby I.o.M. Europe 12 54.11N 4.34W
Crosby U.S.A. 111 31.17N 91.04W
Cross City U.S.A. 113 29.39N 83.09W
Crossett U.S.A. 111 33.08N 91.58W
Cross Fell mtn. U.K. 12 54.43N 2.28W
Cross L. Canada 101 54.45N 97.30W
Cross River d. Nigeria 77 5.45N 8.25E
Crossroads U.S.A. 111 33.30N 103.21W
Cross Sd. U.S.A. 100 58.10N 136.30W
Crossville U.S.A. 113 35.57N 85.02W
Croswell U.S.A. 114 43.16N 82.37W
Crotone Italy 33 39.05N 17.07E
Crow r. Canada 100 59.41N 124.20W
Crow Agency U.S.A. 108 45.36N 107.27W
Crowell U.S.A. 111 33.59N 99.43W
Crowl Creek r. Australia 93 31.58S 144.53E
Crown Point town U.S.A. 105 43.57N 73.25W
Crowsnest Pass Canada 100 49.40N 114.40W
Croyde U.K. 13 51.07N 4.13W
Croydon Australia 90 18.12S 142.14E
Croydon U.K. 13 51.23N 0.06W
Crozet, Îles is. Indian Oc. 49 46.00S 52.00E
Crozon France 18 48.15N 4.29W
Crucero U.S.A. 109 35.03N 116.10W
Cruger U.S.A. 111 33.14N 90.14W
Cruz Alta Brazil 126 28.38S 53.38W
Cruz, Cabo c. Cuba 117 19.52N 77.44W
Cruz del Eje Argentina 124 30.44S 64.49W
Cruzeiro Brazil 126 22.33S 44.59W
Cruzeiro do Sul Brazil 122 7.40S 72.39W
Crvenka Yugo. 31 45.39N 19.28E
Crystal U.S.A. 110 45.00N 93.25W
Crystal Brook town Australia 92 33.21S 138.13E
Crystal City U.S.A. 111 28.41N 99.50W
Crystal River town U.S.A. 113 28.54N 82.36W
Csongrád Hungary 31 46.43N 20.09E
Csongrád d. Hungary 31 46.25N 20.10E
Csorna Hungary 37 47.37N 17.16E
Csurgó Hungary 31 46.16N 17.06E
Cuamba Mozambique 79 14.48S 36.32E
Cuando r. Angola 80 18.30S 23.32E
Cuando-Cubango d. Angola 80 16.00S 20.00E
Cuangar Angola 78 17.34S 18.39E
Cuango r. see Kwango r. Zaïre 78
Cuanza r. Angola 78 9.20S 13.09E
Cuanza Norte d. Angola 78 8.45S 15.00E
Cuanza Sul d. Angola 78 11.00S 15.00E
Cua Rao Vietnam 56 19.16N 104.27E
Cuaró Uruguay 125 30.37S 56.54W
Cuaró r. Uruguay 125 30.15S 57.01W
Cuauhtémoc Mexico 109 28.25N 106.52W
Cuba C. America 117 22.00N 79.00W
Cuba Portugal 27 38.10N 7.53W
Cuba U.S.A. 109 36.01N 107.04W
Cuballing Australia 89 32.50S 117.07E
Cubango r. see Okavango r. Angola 78
Cubia r. Angola 78 16.00S 21.46E
Cubo Mozambique 81 23.48S 33.55E
Cuchi r. Angola 80 15.23S 17.12E
Cuckfield U.K. 13 51.00N 0.08W
Cucuí Brazil 122 1.12N 66.50W
Cúcuta Colombia 122 7.55N 72.31W
Cudahy U.S.A. 110 42.57N 87.52W
Cuddalore India 61 11.43N 79.46E
Cue Australia 88 27.25S 117.54E
Cuéllar Spain 26 41.25N 4.19W
Cuenca Ecuador 122 2.54S 79.00W
Cuenca Spain 25 40.04N 2.08W
Cuenca d. Spain 25 40.00N 2.30W
Cuenca, Serranía de mts. Spain 25 40.00N 1.45W
Cuernavaca Mexico 116 18.57N 99.15W
Cuero U.S.A. 111 29.06N 97.18W
Cuers France 21 43.14N 6.04E
Cuervo U.S.A. 109 35.02N 104.24W
Cuevas del Almanzora Spain 27 37.19N 1.52W
Cuglieri Italy 32 40.11N 8.34E
Cuiabá Brazil 123 15.32S 56.05W
Cuiabá r. Brazil 124 18.00S 57.25W
Cuidado, Punta c. I. de Pascua 85 27.08S 109.19W
Cuillin Hills U.K. 14 57.12N 6.13W
Cuiseaux France 19 46.30N 5.24E
Cuito r. Angola 78 18.01S 20.50E
Cuito Cuanavale Angola 80 15.11S 19.11E
Culbertson U.S.A. 108 48.09N 104.31W
Culcairn Australia 93 35.40S 147.03E

Culebra, Sierra de la *mts.* Spain 26 41.55N 6.30W
Culemborg Neth. 16 51.57N 5.14E
Culgoa *r.* Australia 93 29.56S 146.20E
Culiacán Mexico 109 24.48N 107.24W
Culiacán *r.* Mexico 109 24.30N 107.31W
Cúllar de Baza Spain 27 37.35N 2.34W
Cullen U.K. 14 57.41N 2.50W
Cullera Spain 25 39.10N 0.15W
Cullin Sd. U.K. 14 57.03N 6.13W
Culloden Moor U.K. 14 57.29N 3.55W
Culpeper U.S.A. 114 38.28N 77.53W
Culuene *r.* Brazil 123 12.56S 52.51W
Culver, Pt. Australia 89 32.52S 124.41E
Cuma Angola 78 12.52S 15.05E
Cumali Turkey 35 36.42N 27.28E
Cumaná Venezuela 122 10.29N 64.12W
Cumberland Ky. U.S.A. 113 36.58N 82.59W
Cumberland Md. U.S.A. 114 39.39N 78.46W
Cumberland *r.* U.S.A. 113 37.09N 88.25W
Cumberland Va. U.S.A. 113 37.31N 78.16W
Cumberland Wisc. U.S.A. 110 45.32N 92.01W
Cumberland, C. Vanuatu 84 14.39S 166.37E
Cumberland I. U.S.A. 113 30.51N 81.27W
Cumberland L. Canada 101 54.02N 102.17W
Cumberland, L. U.S.A. 113 36.45N 84.51W
Cumberland Pen. Canada 99 66.50N 64.00W
Cumberland Plateau *f.* U.S.A. 113 36.00N 85.00W
Cumberland Sd. Canada 99 65.00N 65.30W
Cumbernauld U.K. 14 55.57N 4.00W
Cumbria *d.* U.K. 12 54.30N 3.00W
Cumbrian Mts. U.K. 12 54.32N 3.05W
Cuminá *r.* Brazil 123 1.30S 56.00W
Cummins Australia 92 34.16S 135.44E
Cumnock Australia 93 32.56S 148.46E
Cumnock U.K. 14 55.27N 4.15W
Cunderlin Australia 89 31.39S 117.15E
Cunene *d.* Angola 78 16.00S 16.00E
Cunene *r.* Angola 78 17.15S 11.50E
Cuneo Italy 30 44.23N 7.32E
Cungena Australia 92 32.33S 134.40E
Cunlhat France 20 45.38N 3.35E
Cunnamulla Australia 93 28.04S 145.40E
Cuokkaraš'ša *mtn.* Norway 40 69.57N 24.32E
Cuorgnè Italy 30 45.23N 7.39E
Cupar U.K. 14 56.19N 3.01W
Cupica, Golfo de *g.* Colombia 122 6.35N 77.25W
Cuprija Yugo. 34 43.56N 21.23E
Curaçao *i.* Neth. Antilles 122 12.15N 69.00W
Curacautín Chile 125 38.26S 71.53W
Curaco *r.* Argentina 125 38.45S 65.01W
Curanilahue Chile 125 37.28S 73.21W
Curaray *r.* Peru 122 2.20S 74.05W
Curban Australia 93 31.33S 148.36E
Curdlawidny L. Australia 92 30.16S 136.20E
Curepipe Mauritius 79 20.19S 57.31E
Curiapo Venezuela 122 8.33N 61.05W
Curicó Chile 125 34.59S 71.14W
Curitiba Brazil 126 25.24S 49.16W
Curlewis Australia 93 31.08S 150.16E
Currane, Lough Rep. of Ire. 15 51.50N 10.07W
Currant U.S.A. 108 38.44N 115.30W
Curranyalpa Australia 93 30.57S 144.33E
Currie Australia 91 39.56S 143.52E
Currie U.S.A. 108 40.17N 114.44W
Curtin Australia 89 30.50S 122.05E
Curtis Spain 26 43.07N 8.03W
Curtis U.S.A. 110 40.38N 100.31W
Curtis I. Australia 90 23.38S 151.09E
Curuá *r.* Brazil 123 5.23S 54.22W
Čurug Yugo. 31 45.29N 20.04E
Cururupu Brazil 123 1.50S 44.52W
Curuzú Cuatiá Argentina 125 29.50S 58.05W
Curvelo Brazil 126 18.45S 44.27W
Curwensville U.S.A. 114 40.58N 78.32W
Cushendall U.K. 15 55.06N 6.05W
Cushing U.S.A. 111 35.59N 96.46W
Cusna, Monte *mtn.* Italy 30 44.17N 10.23E
Cut Bank U.S.A. 108 48.38N 112.20W
Cutro Italy 33 39.02N 16.59E
Cuttaburra Creek *r.* Australia 93 29.18S 145.00E
Cuttack India 63 20.30N 85.50E
Cuxhaven Germany 38 53.52N 8.42E
Cuyahoga Falls *town* U.S.A. 114 41.08N 81.29W
Cuyuni *r.* Guyana 122 6.24N 58.38W
Cuzco Peru 122 13.32S 71.57W
Cuzna *r.* Spain 26 38.04N 4.41W
Cwmbran U.K. 13 51.39N 3.01W
Cyclades *is.* see Kikládhes *is.* Greece 35
Cynthiana U.S.A. 112 38.22N 84.18W
Cypress Hills Canada 101 49.40N 109.30W
Cyprus Asia 66 35.00N 33.00E
Cyrenaica *f.* see Barqah *f.* Libya 72
Czech Republic Europe 36 49.30N 15.00E
Czeremcha Poland 37 52.32N 23.15E
Czersk Poland 37 53.48N 18.00E
Częstochowa Poland 37 50.49N 19.07E

D

Dà *r.* Vietnam 56 21.20N 105.24E
Da'an China 54 45.30N 124.18E
Dab'ah Jordan 67 31.36N 36.04E
Dabakala Côte d'Ivoire 76 8.19N 4.24W
Daba Shan *mts.* China 55 32.00N 109.00E

Dabat Ethiopia 73 12.58N 37.48E
Dabbāgh, Jabal *mtn.* Saudi Arabia 66 27.51N 35.43E
Dabhoi India 62 22.11N 73.26E
Dabie Shan. *mts.* China 55 31.15N 115.20E
Dabola Guinea 76 10.48N 11.02W
Dabra India 63 25.54N 78.20E
Dabu Jiangxi China 55 26.47N 116.04E
Dacca see Dhāka Bangla. 63
Dachau Germany 39 48.15N 11.26E
Dacre Canada 105 45.22N 76.59W
Dadanawa Guyana 122 2.30N 59.30W
Dade City U.S.A. 113 28.23N 82.11W
Dādhar India 62 29.28N 67.39E
Dādra & Nagar Haveli *d.* India 62 20.05N 73.00E
Dādu Pakistan 62 26.44N 67.47E
Dadu He *r.* China 52 28.47N 104.40E
Daet Phil. 59 14.07N 122.58E
Dagali Norway 41 60.25N 8.27E
Dagana Senegal 76 16.28N 15.35W
Daga Post Sudan 73 9.12N 33.58E
Dagash Sudan 72 19.22N 33.24E
Dagu China 54 38.58N 117.40E
Dagua P.N.G. 59 3.25S 143.20E
Daguan China 52 27.44N 103.53E
Dagupan Phil. 59 16.02N 120.21E
Daguragu Australia 88 17.33S 130.30E
Dagzê China 63 29.45N 105.45E
Dagzê Co *l.* China 63 31.45N 87.50E
Dahan-e Qowmghī Afghan. 62 34.28N 66.31E
Da Hinggan Ling *mts.* China 53 50.00N 122.10E
Dahlak Archipelago *is.* Ethiopia 72 15.45N 40.30E
Dahlak Kebir I. Ethiopia 72 15.38N 40.11E
Dahlem Germany 39 50.23N 6.33E
Dahlgren U.S.A. 114 38.20N 77.03W
Dahme Germany 38 51.52N 13.25E
Dahra Senegal 76 15.21N 15.29W
Dahujiang China 55 26.06N 114.58E
Dahūk Iraq 64 36.52N 43.00E
Dahyah, 'Urūq *f.* Yemen 71 18.45N 51.15E
Dahy, Nafūd ad *f.* Saudi Arabia 71 22.00N 45.25E
Dai Hai *l.* China 54 40.31N 112.43E
Dā'īl Syria 67 32.45N 36.08E
Dailekh Nepal 63 28.50N 81.43E
Daimiel Spain 27 39.04N 3.37W
Daitō Japan 57 34.42N 135.38E
Daiyun Shan *mtn.* China 55 25.41N 118.11E
Dājal Pakistan 62 29.33N 70.23E
Dajarra Australia 90 21.42S 139.31E
Dajing China 55 28.25N 121.10E
Dakar Senegal 76 14.38N 17.27W
Dakhal, Wādī ad *r.* Egypt 66 28.49N 32.45E
Dākhilah, Al Wāḥāt ad *oasis* Egypt 64 25.30N 28.10E
Dakhla W. Sahara 74 23.43N 15.57W
Dakhlet Nouadhibou *d.* Mauritania 74 20.30N 16.00W
Dakhovskaya Russian Fed. 23 44.13N 40.13E
Dakingari Nigeria 77 11.40N 4.06E
Dakota City U.S.A. 110 42.25N 96.25W
Dakovica Yugo. 34 42.22N 20.26E
Dakovo Croatia 31 45.19N 18.25E
Dal *r.* Sweden 41 60.38N 17.27E
Dala Congo 78 1.40N 16.89E
Dalaba Guinea 76 10.47N 12.12W
Dalai Nur *l.* China 54 43.27N 116.25E
Dalandzadgad Mongolia 52 43.30N 104.18E
Dalane *f.* Norway 42 58.35N 6.20E
Da Lat Vietnam 56 11.56N 108.25E
Dālbandin Pakistan 62 28.53N 64.25E
Dalbeattie U.K. 14 54.55N 3.49W
Dalbosjön *b.* Sweden 43 58.45N 12.48E
Dalby Australia 91 27.11S 151.12E
Dalby Sweden 43 55.40N 13.20E
Dale Hordaland Norway 41 60.35N 5.49E
Dale Sogn og Fj. Norway 41 61.22N 5.24E
Dalen Norway 42 59.27N 8.00E
Dalhart U.S.A. 111 36.04N 102.31W
Dalhousie Canada 103 48.04N 66.23W
Dalhousie Jammu & Kashmir 62 32.32N 75.59E
Dali China 52 25.42N 100.11E
Dali China 52 25.33N 100.09E
Dalian China 54 38.49N 121.48E
Dalías Spain 27 36.49N 2.52W
Dāliyat el Karmel Israel 67 32.42N 35.03E
Dalj Croatia 31 45.29N 18.59E
Dalkeith U.K. 14 55.54N 3.04W
Dallas Oreg. U.S.A. 108 44.55N 123.19W
Dallas Tex. U.S.A. 111 32.47N 96.48W
Dallastown U.S.A. 115 39.54N 76.39W
Dall I. U.S.A. 100 55.00N 133.00W
Dalli Rajhāra India 63 20.35N 81.04E
Dalmacija *f.* Croatia 31 43.33N 16.40E
Dalmally U.K. 14 56.25N 4.58W
Dalmas, Lac *l.* Canada 103 53.27N 71.50W
Dalmellington U.K. 14 55.19N 4.24W
Dalnerechensk Russian Fed. 53 45.55N 133.45E
Daloa Côte d'Ivoire 76 6.56N 6.28W
Dalou Shan *mts.* China 55 28.25N 107.15E
Dalqū Sudan 72 20.07N 30.35E
Dalrymple, Mt. Australia 90 21.02S 148.38E
Dalsingh Sarai India 63 25.40N 85.50E
Dalsland *f.* Sweden 43 59.00N 12.10E
Dalton Canada 102 48.10N 84.00W
Dalton U.S.A. 113 34.46N 84.59W
Daltonganj India 63 24.02N 84.04E
Dalupiri *i.* Phil. 55 19.05N 121.13E
Dalvík Iceland 40 65.58N 18.28W
Dalwhinnie U.K. 14 56.56N 4.15W
Daly *r.* Australia 88 13.20S 130.19E
Daly City U.S.A. 108 37.42N 122.29W
Daly Waters *town* Australia 90 16.15S 133.22E
Damān India 62 20.25N 72.51E
Damān *d.* India 62 20.10N 73.00E
Damanhūr Egypt 66 31.03N 30.28E
Damar *i.* Indonesia 59 7.10S 128.30E
Damascus see Dimashq Syria 64
Damaturu Nigeria 77 11.49N 11.50E
Damāvand, Qolleh-ye *mtn.* Iran 65 35.47N 52.04E
Damā, Wādī *r.* Saudi Arabia 64 27.04N 35.48E
Damba Angola 78 6.44S 15.17E

Damen *i.* China 55 27.58N 121.05E
Dāmghān Iran 65 36.09N 54.22E
Damiaoshan China 55 24.43N 109.15E
Daming Shan *mts.* China 55 23.23N 108.30E
Dāmiyā Jordan 67 32.06N 35.33E
Dammartin-en-Goële France 19 49.03N 2.41E
Dāmodar *r.* India 63 22.17N 88.05E
Damoh India 63 23.50N 79.27E
Damongo Ghana 76 9.06N 1.48W
Dampier Australia 88 20.40S 116.42E
Dampier Land Australia 88 17.20S 123.00E
Dampier, Selat *str.* Pacific Oc. 59 0.30S 130.50E
Damqawt Yemen 71 16.34N 52.50E
Damxung China 63 30.32N 91.06E
Dan Israel 67 33.14N 35.39E
Dana Canada 101 52.18N 105.42W
Danané Côte d'Ivoire 76 7.21N 8.10W
Da Nang Vietnam 56 16.04N 108.13E
Dānāpur India 63 25.38N 85.03E
Danba China 52 30.57N 101.55E
Danbury Conn. U.S.A. 115 41.23N 73.27W
Danbury N.H. U.S.A. 115 43.32N 71.54W
Dand Afghan. 62 31.37N 65.41E
Dandaragan Australia 89 30.40S 115.42E
Dande *r.* Angola 78 8.30S 13.23E
Dandeldhura Nepal 63 29.17N 80.36E
Dandenong Australia 93 37.59S 145.14E
Dandong China 54 40.10N 124.25E
Danger Is. Cook Is. 84 10.53S 165.49W
Dangila Ethiopia 73 11.18N 36.54E
Dangqên China 63 31.41N 91.51E
Dangriga Belize 117 16.58N 88.13W
Dangshan China 54 34.25N 116.24E
Dangyang China 55 30.52N 111.40E
Daniel U.S.A. 108 42.52N 110.04W
Daniel's Harbour Canada 103 50.14N 57.35W
Danielson U.S.A. 115 41.48N 71.53W
Danilov Russian Fed. 44 58.10N 40.12E
Daning China 54 36.32N 110.47E
Danisa Hills Kenya 79 3.10N 39.37E
Danja Nigeria 77 11.29N 7.30E
Danjiangkou shuiku *resr.* China 54 32.42N 111.20E
Danlí Honduras 117 14.02N 86.30W
Dannenberg Germany 38 53.06N 11.05E
Dannevirke New Zealand 86 40.12S 176.08E
Dannhauser R.S.A. 80 28.00S 30.03E
Dansville U.S.A. 114 42.34N 77.42W
Dantewāra India 63 18.54N 81.21E
Danube *r.* Europe 31 45.20N 29.40E
Danube, Mouths of the *see* Dunării, Delta *f.* Romania 37
Danvers U.S.A. 115 42.34N 70.56W
Danville Canada 105 45.47N 72.01W
Danville Ill. U.S.A. 110 40.09N 87.37W
Danville Ky. U.S.A. 113 37.40N 84.49W
Danville Penn. U.S.A. 115 40.57N 76.37W
Danville Va. U.S.A. 113 36.34N 79.25W
Danville Vt. U.S.A. 105 44.25N 72.09W
Dan Xian China 55 19.30N 109.35E
Dāo *r.* Portugal 26 40.20N 8.11W
Daordeng China 54 46.47N 119.05E
Daosa India 62 26.53N 76.20E
Daoukro Côte d'Ivoire 76 7.10N 3.58W
Daoulas France 18 48.21N 4.15W
Dao Xian China 55 25.32N 111.35E
Daozhen China 55 28.46N 107.45E
Dapango Togo 76 10.51N 0.15E
Dapingfang China 54 41.25N 120.07E
Da Qaidam China 52 37.44N 95.08E
Daqinggou China 54 41.22N 114.13E
Daqing Shan *mts.* China 54 41.00N 111.00E
Daqqāq Sudan 73 12.56N 26.58E
Daqq-e Patargān *f.* Iran 65 33.30N 60.40E
Dar'ā Syria 67 32.37N 36.06E
Dar'ā *d.* Syria 67 32.50N 36.10E
Dārāb Iran 65 28.45N 54.34E
Dārāban Pakistan 62 31.44N 70.20E
Darabani Romania 37 48.11N 26.35E
Darakht-e Yahyá Afghan. 62 31.50N 68.08E
Dārān Iran 65 33.00N 50.27E
Darband, Kūh-e *mtn.* Iran 65 31.33N 57.08E
Darbhanga India 63 26.10N 86.00E
Darby Mont. U.S.A. 108 46.01N 114.11W
Darby Penn. U.S.A. 115 39.54N 75.15W
D'Arcy Canada 100 50.33N 122.32W
Darda Croatia 31 45.37N 18.41E
Dardanelles *see* Çanakkale Boğazi *str.* Turkey 34
Dar es Salaam Tanzania 79 6.51S 39.18E
Dar es Salaam *d.* Tanzania 79 6.45S 39.10E
Darfield New Zealand 86 43.29S 172.07E
Dargan Ata Turkmenistan 50 40.30N 62.10E
Dargaville New Zealand 86 35.57S 173.53E
Dargo Australia 93 37.30S 147.16E
Darhan Mongolia 52 49.34N 106.23E
Darie Hills Somali Rep. 71 8.15N 47.25E
Darien U.S.A. 115 41.05N 73.28W
Darién, Golfo del *g.* Colombia 122 9.20N 77.30W
Darjeeling see Dārjiling India 63
Dārjiling India 63 27.02N 88.16E
Darkan Australia 89 33.19S 116.42E
Darke Peak *mtn.* Australia 92 33.28S 136.12E
Darling *r.* Australia 92 34.05S 141.57E
Darling Downs *f.* Australia 91 28.00S 149.45E
Darling Range *mts.* Australia 89 32.00S 116.30E
Darlington U.K. 12 54.33N 1.33W
Darlington Point *town* Australia 93 34.36S 146.01E
Darłowe Poland 36 54.26N 16.23E
Darmstadt Germany 39 49.53N 8.40E
Darnah Libya 72 31.30N 23.30E
Darnah *d.* Libya 72 31.30N 22.00E
Darnétal France 18 49.27N 1.09E
Darney France 19 48.05N 6.03E
Darnick Australia 92 32.55S 143.39E
Darnley, C. Antarctica 128 68.00S 69.00E
Daroca Spain 25 41.07N 1.25W
Darreh Gaz Iran 65 37.22N 59.08E
Dar Rounga *f.* C.A.R. 73 9.25N 21.30E

Darsser Ort *c.* Germany 38 54.29N 12.31E
Dartmoor Australia 92 37.58S 141.19E
Dartmoor Forest *hills* U.K. 13 50.33N 3.55W
Dartmouth Canada 103 44.40N 63.34W
Dartmouth U.K. 13 50.21N 3.35W
Dartmouth Resr. Australia 93 36.36S 147.38E
Dartry Mts. Rep. of Ire. 15 54.23N 8.25W
Dartuch, Cabo *c.* Spain 25 39.56N 3.48E
Daru P.N.G. 90 9.04S 143.12E
Daruvar Croatia 31 45.36N 17.13E
Darvaza Turkmenistan 50 40.12N 58.24E
Darvel, Teluk *b.* Malaysia 58 4.40N 118.30E
Darwen U.K. 12 53.42N 2.29W
Dārwha India 63 20.19N 77.46E
Darwin Australia 90 12.23S 130.44E
Daryācheh-ye Bakhtegān *l.* Iran 65 29.20N 54.05E
Daryācheh-ye Namak *l.* Iran 65 34.45N 51.36E
Daryācheh-ye Orūmīyeh *l.* Iran 65 37.40N 45.28E
Daryācheh-ye Sīstān *f.* Iran 65 31.00N 61.15E
Darya Khān Pakistan 62 31.48N 71.06E
Daryāpur India 62 20.56N 77.20E
Dasāda India 62 23.19N 71.50E
Dasht *r.* Pakistan 62 25.10N 61.40E
Dashte-e Mārgow *des.* Afghan. 65 30.45N 63.00E
Dasht-e Kavīr *des.* Iran 65 34.40N 55.00E
Dasht-e Lūt *des.* Iran 65 31.30N 58.00E
Dashui Nur *l.* China 54 42.45N 116.47E
Daspalla India 63 20.21N 84.51E
Dassa-Zoumé Benin 77 7.50N 2.13E
Dassow Germany 38 53.50N 10.59E
Dastgardān Iran 65 34.19N 56.51E
Dastjerd Iran 65 34.19N 50.15E
Datça Turkey 35 36.46N 27.40E
Datia India 63 25.40N 78.28E
Datong China 54 40.10N 113.15E
Datteln Germany 38 51.40N 7.23E
Datu Piang Phil. 59 7.02N 124.30E
Datu, Tanjung *c.* Malaysia 58 2.00N 109.30E
Daua *r.* Kenya *see* Dawa *r.* Ethiopia 73
Dāud Khel Pakistan 62 32.53N 71.34E
Daudnagar India 63 25.02N 84.24E
Daugavpils Latvia 44 55.52N 26.31E
Daun Germany 39 50.11N 6.50E
Dauphin Canada 101 51.09N 100.03W
Dauphiné, Alpes du *mts.* France 21 44.35N 5.45E
Dauphin L. Canada 101 51.17N 99.48W
Daura Nigeria 77 13.05N 8.18E
Dāvangere India 60 14.30N 75.52E
Davao Phil. 59 7.05N 125.38E
Davao G. Phil. 59 6.30N 126.00E
Daveluyville Canada 105 46.12N 72.08W
Davenport U.S.A. 110 41.32N 90.36W
Daventry U.K. 13 52.16N 1.10W
Davenyns, L. Canada 105 47.05N 73.45W
David Panama 117 8.26N 82.26W
David-Gorodok Belarus 37 52.04N 27.10E
Davis U.S.A. 108 38.33N 121.44W
Davis Creek *town* U.S.A. 108 41.44N 120.24W
Davison U.S.A. 104 43.02N 83.31W
Davis Sea Antarctica 128 66.00S 90.00E
Davis Str. N. America 99 66.00N 58.00W
Davlekanovo Russian Fed. 44 54.12N 55.00E
Davos Switz. 39 46.48N 9.50E
Davutlar Turkey 35 37.43N 27.17E
Dawa China 54 40.58N 122.00E
Dawa *r.* Ethiopia 73 4.11N 42.06E
Dawaxung China 63 31.26N 85.06E
Dawei *see* Tavoy Myanmar 56
Dawei *see* Tavoy Myanmar 56
Dawlish U.K. 13 50.34N 3.28W
Dawna Range *mts.* Myanmar 56 17.00N 98.00E
Dawson Canada 98 64.04N 139.24W
Dawson U.S.A. 113 31.47N 84.27W
Dawson Creek *town* Canada 100 55.45N 120.15W
Dawson Range *f.* Canada 98 62.40N 139.00W
Dawu China 52 31.00N 101.09E
Dax France 20 43.43N 1.03W
Daxian China 55 31.10N 107.28E
Daxing China 54 39.44N 116.20E
Daylesford Australia 92 37.22S 144.12E
Dayman *r.* Uruguay 125 31.25S 58.00W
Dayong Hunan China 55 29.06N 110.24E
Dayr Abū Sa'īd Jordan 67 32.30N 35.41E
Dayr al Balaḥ Egypt 67 31.25N 34.21E
Dayr al Ghuşūn Jordan 67 32.21N 35.05E
Dayr az Zawr Syria 64 35.20N 40.08E
Dayr Dibwān Jordan 67 31.55N 35.16E
Dayr Sharaf Jordan 67 32.15N 35.11E
Dayton N.Y. U.S.A. 114 42.25N 78.58W
Dayton Ohio U.S.A. 112 39.45N 84.10W
Dayton Penn. U.S.A. 114 40.53N 79.16W
Dayton Tenn. U.S.A. 113 35.30N 85.01W
Dayton Wash. U.S.A. 108 46.19N 117.59W
Daytona Beach *town* U.S.A. 113 29.11N 81.01W
Dayu China 55 25.24N 114.22E
Da Yunhe *canal* China 54 39.10N 117.12E
Dazhu China 55 30.50N 107.12E
De Aar R.S.A. 80 30.39S 24.01E
Dead Sea Jordan 67 31.25N 35.30E
Deal U.K. 13 51.13N 1.25E
De'an China 55 29.20N 115.46E
Deán Funes Argentina 124 30.25S 64.20W
Dean Lake *town* Canada 104 46.13N 83.09W
Dearborn U.S.A. 104 42.18N 83.10W
Dease *r.* Canada 100 59.54N 128.30W
Dease Arm *b.* Canada 98 66.52N 119.37W
Dease L. Canada 100 58.05N 130.04W
Death Valley *f.* U.S.A. 109 36.30N 117.00W
Death Valley *town* U.S.A. 108 36.18N 116.25W
Death Valley Nat. Monument U.S.A. 108 36.30N 117.00W
Deauville France 18 49.22N 0.04E
Debar Macedonia 34 41.31N 20.30E
Debica Poland 37 50.04N 21.24E
Deblin Poland 37 51.35N 21.50E
Deborah, L. Australia 89 30.45S 119.07E
Debre Birhan Ethiopia 73 9.40N 39.33E
Debrecen Hungary 37 47.30N 21.37E

Debre Tabor to Djelfa

Debre Tabor Ethiopia 73 11.50N 38.05E
Dečani Yugo. 34 42.30N 20.10E
Decatur Ala. U.S.A. 113 34.36N 87.00W
Decatur Ga. U.S.A. 113 33.45N 84.17W
Decatur Ill. U.S.A. 110 39.51N 89.32W
Decatur Ind. U.S.A. 112 40.50N 84.57W
Decazeville France 20 44.34N 2.15E
Deccan f. India 60 18.30N 77.30E
Decelles, Lac l. Canada 102 47.40N 78.10W
Dechu India 62 26.47N 72.20E
Decimomannu Italy 32 39.19N 8.58E
Děčín Czech Republic 38 50.48N 14.13E
Decize France 19 46.50N 3.27E
Deckerville U.S.A. 114 43.32N 82.44W
De Cocksdorp Neth. 16 53.12N 4.52E
Decorah U.S.A. 110 43.18N 91.48W
Decs Hungary 31 46.17N 18.46E
Deda Romania 37 46.57N 24.53E
Dédi Côte d'Ivoire 76 8.34N 3.33W
Dediäpada India 62 21.35N 73.40E
Dedza Malaŵi 79 14.20S 34.24E
Dee r. D. and G. U.K. 14 54.50N 4.05W
Dee r. Grampian U.K. 14 57.07N 2.04W
Dee r. Wales U.K. 12 53.13N 3.05W
Deep B. Canada 100 61.15N 116.35W
Deep Creek L. U.S.A. 114 39.30N 79.19W
Deep River town Canada 105 46.06N 77.30W
Deep River town U.S.A. 115 41.23N 72.26W
Deepwater Australia 93 29.26S 151.51E
Deep Well Australia 90 24.25S 134.05E
Deerfield r. U.S.A. 115 42.35N 72.35W
Deer Lake town Canada 103 49.11N 57.35W
Deer Lodge U.S.A. 108 46.24N 112.44W
Deesa India 62 24.15N 72.10E
Deeth U.S.A. 108 41.04N 115.18W
Deex Nugaaleed r. Somali Rep. 71 7.58N 49.52E
Defiance U.S.A. 112 41.17N 84.21W
De Funiak Springs town U.S.A. 113 30.41N 86.08W
Deganya Bet Israel 67 32.42N 35.35E
Degeberga Sweden 43 55.50N 14.05E
Degerby Finland 43 60.02N 20.23E
Degerfors Sweden 43 59.14N 14.26E
Degerhamn Sweden 43 56.21N 16.24E
Deggendorf Germany 39 48.51N 12.59E
De Grey r. Australia 88 20.12S 119.11E
Deh Bid Iran 65 30.38N 53.12E
Dehej India 62 21.42N 72.35E
Dehibat Tunisia 75 32.01N 10.42E
Dehra Dūn India 63 30.19N 78.02E
Dehri India 63 24.52N 84.11E
Deh Shū Afghan. 62 30.28N 63.25E
Dehua China 55 25.30N 118.14E
Deinze Belgium 16 50.59N 3.32E
Dej Romania 37 47.08N 23.55E
Deje Sweden 43 59.36N 13.28E
Dejiang China 55 28.19N 108.05E
Dek'emhäre Eritrea 72 15.05N 39.02E
Dekese Zaïre 78 3.25S 21.24E
Dekina Nigeria 77 7.43N 7.04E
De Land U.S.A. 113 29.02N 81.18W
Delano U.S.A. 109 35.41N 119.15W
Delārām Afghan. 62 32.11N 63.25E
Delaronde L. Canada 101 54.05N 107.05W
Delaware d. U.S.A. 115 39.10N 75.30W
Delaware r. U.S.A. 115 39.20N 75.25W
Delaware town U.S.A. 112 40.18N 83.06W
Delaware B. U.S.A. 115 39.05N 75.15W
Delaware, East Branch r. U.S.A. 115 41.55N 75.17W
Delaware Water Gap town U.S.A. 115 40.59N 75.09W
Delaware Water Gap Nat. Recreation Area U.S.A. 115 41.07N 75.06W
Delaware, West Branch r. U.S.A. 115 41.56N 75.17W
Delčevo Macedonia 34 41.58N 22.46E
Delegate Australia 93 37.03S 148.58E
Delémont Switz. 39 47.22N 7.21E
Delfinópolis Brazil 126 20.21S 46.51W
Delft Neth. 16 52.01N 4.23E
Delfzijl Neth. 16 53.20N 6.56E
Delgado, C. Mozambique 79 10.45S 40.38E
Delhi Canada 104 42.51N 80.30W
Delhi India 62 28.40N 77.13E
Delhi d. India 62 28.37N 77.10E
Delhi U.S.A. 115 42.17N 74.55W
Delicias Mexico 109 28.13N 105.28W
Délimbé C.A.R. 73 9.53N 22.37E
Delingha China 52 37.16N 97.12E
Delitzsch Germany 38 51.31N 12.20E
Dell City U.S.A. 109 31.56N 105.12W
Delle France 19 47.30N 7.00E
Delmar U.S.A. 115 38.27N 75.34W
Delmarva Pen. U.S.A. 115 38.48N 75.47W
Delmenhorst Germany 38 53.03N 8.38E
Delnice Croatia 31 45.24N 14.48E
De Long Mts. U.S.A. 98 68.20N 162.00W
Delphos U.S.A. 112 40.50N 84.21W
Del Rio U.S.A. 111 29.22N 100.54W
Delta d. Nigeria 77 5.30N 6.00E
Delta Colo. U.S.A. 108 38.44N 108.04W
Delta Utah U.S.A. 108 39.21N 112.35W
Delungra Australia 93 29.38S 150.50E
Delvinë Albania 34 39.57N 20.06E
Demak Indonesia 59 6.53S 110.40E
Demanda, Sierra de la mts. Spain 26 42.10N 3.00W
Demba Zaïre 78 5.28S 22.14E
Dembī Ethiopia 73 8.05N 36.27E
Dembia C.A.R. 73 5.07N 24.25E
Dembī Dolo Ethiopia 73 8.30N 34.48E
Demer r. Belgium 16 50.59N 4.42E
Deming U.S.A. 109 32.16N 107.45W
Demmin Germany 36 53.54N 13.02E
Demmitt Canada 100 55.20N 119.50W
Demonte Italy 30 44.19N 7.17E
Demopolis U.S.A. 111 32.31N 87.50W
Demotte U.S.A. 112 41.07N 87.14W
Dêmqog China 63 32.43N 79.29E
Denain France 19 50.20N 3.23E
Denakil f. Ethiopia 73 13.00N 41.00E
Denbigh Canada 105 45.08N 77.16W

Denbigh U.K. 12 53.11N 3.25W
Den Burg Neth. 16 53.03N 4.47E
Dendermonde Belgium 16 51.01N 4.07E
Dendre r. Belgium 16 51.01N 4.07E
Dengkou China 54 40.18N 106.59E
Deng Xian China 54 32.44N 112.00E
Denham Australia 34 41.44N 24.24E
Denham Range mts. Australia 90 21.55S 147.46E
Den Helder Neth. 16 52.58N 4.46E
Denia Spain 25 38.51N 0.07E
Deniliquin Australia 93 35.33S 144.58E
Denison Iowa U.S.A. 110 42.01N 95.21W
Denison Tex. U.S.A. 111 33.45N 96.33W
Denizli Turkey 64 37.46N 29.05E
Denman Australia 93 32.23S 150.42E
Denmark Australia 89 34.54S 117.25E
Denmark Europe 42 56.05N 10.00E
Denmark Str. Greenland/Iceland 96 65.00N 30.00W
Dennison U.S.A. 114 40.24N 81.19W
Den Oever Neth. 16 52.56N 5.01E
Denpasar Indonesia 59 8.40S 115.14E
Denton Mont. U.S.A. 108 47.19N 109.57W
Denton Tex. U.S.A. 111 33.13N 97.08W
D'Entrecasteaux, Pt. Australia 89 34.50S 116.00E
D'Entrecasteaux Is. P.N.G. 90 9.30S 150.40E
D'Entrecasteaux, Recifs reef N. Cal. 84 18.00S 163.10E
Denver U.S.A. 108 39.43N 105.01W
Denys r. Canada 102 55.05N 77.22W
Denzlingen Germany 39 48.04N 7.52E
Deo r. Cameroon 77 8.33N 12.45E
Deogarh Madhya P. India 63 24.33N 78.15E
Deogarh mtn. India 63 23.32N 82.16E
Deogarh Orissa India 63 21.32N 84.44E
Deogarh Räj. India 62 25.32N 73.54E
Deogarh Hills India 63 23.45N 82.30E
Deoghar India 63 24.29N 86.42E
Deolāli India 62 19.57N 73.50E
Deoli India 62 25.45N 75.23E
Deori India 63 23.08N 78.41E
Deoria India 63 26.31N 83.47E
Deori Khās India 63 23.24N 79.01E
Deosil India 63 23.42N 82.15E
De Peel f. Belgium 16 51.30N 5.50E
Depew U.S.A. 114 42.54N 78.42W
Deposit U.S.A. 115 42.04N 75.25W
Depot Harbour town Canada 104 45.19N 80.06W
Dêqên China 52 28.45N 98.58E
De Queen U.S.A. 111 34.02N 94.21W
De Quincy U.S.A. 111 30.27N 93.26W
Dera Bugti Pakistan 62 29.02N 69.09E
Dera Ghāzi Khān Pakistan 62 30.03N 70.38E
Dera Ismāīl Khān Pakistan 62 31.50N 70.54E
Derazhnya Ukraine 37 49.18N 27.28E
Derbent Russian Fed. 65 42.03N 48.18E
Derby Tas. Australia 91 41.08S 147.47E
Derby W.A. Australia 88 17.19S 123.38E
Derby U.K. 12 52.55N 1.28W
Derby Conn. U.S.A. 115 41.19N 73.05W
Derby N.Y. U.S.A. 114 42.41N 78.58W
Derby Center U.S.A. 105 44.58N 72.09W
Derbyshire d. U.K. 12 52.55N 1.28W
Derg, Lough Donegal Rep. of Ire. 15 54.37N 7.55W
Derg, Lough Tipperary Rep. of Ire. 15 52.57N 8.18W
De Ridder U.S.A. 111 30.51N 93.17W
Dernieres, Isles is. U.S.A. 111 29.02N 90.47W
Déroute, Passage de la str. France/U.K. 13 49.10N 1.45W
Derry U.S.A. 115 42.53N 71.19W
Derrynasaggart Mts. Rep. of Ire. 15 51.58N 9.15W
Derryveagh Mts. Rep. of Ire. 15 55.00N 8.07W
Derudeb Sudan 72 17.32N 36.06E
De Ruyter U.S.A. 115 42.46N 75.53W
Derval France 18 47.40N 1.40W
Derveni Greece 35 38.08N 22.25E
Derventa Bosnia-Herzegovina 31 44.58N 17.55E
Derwent r. Cumbria U.K. 12 54.38N 3.34W
Derwent r. Derbys. U.K. 11 52.52N 1.19W
Derwent r. N. Yorks. U.K. 12 53.44N 0.57W
Desaguadero r. Bolivia 124 18.24S 67.05W
Desappointement, Îles du is. Pacific Oc. 85 14.02S 141.24W
Desaulniers Canada 104 46.34N 80.08W
Descanso Mexico 109 32.14N 116.58W
Descartes France 18 46.58N 0.42E
Deschaillons Canada 105 46.32N 72.07W
Deschutes r. U.S.A. 108 45.38N 120.54W
Desē Ethiopia 73 11.05N 39.41E
Deseado Argentina 125 47.39S 65.20W
Deseado r. Argentina 125 47.45S 65.50W
Desenzano del Garda Italy 30 45.28N 10.32E
Deseronto Canada 105 44.12N 77.03W
Deserta Grande is. Madeira Is. 127 32.32N 16.30W
Desert Center U.S.A. 109 33.44N 115.25W
Desfiladero de Despeñaperros Spain 26 38.24N 3.30W
Deshnoke India 62 27.48N 73.21E
Des Moines Iowa U.S.A. 110 41.35N 93.37W
Des Moines r. U.S.A. 110 40.22N 91.26W
Des Moines N.Mex. U.S.A. 108 36.46N 103.50W
Desna r. Ukraine 37 50.32N 30.37E
De Soto U.S.A. 111 38.08N 90.33W
Dessau Germany 38 51.50N 12.14E
Dessvres France 19 50.40N 1.50E
Dete Zimbabwe 80 18.39S 26.49E
Detlor Canada 105 45.02N 77.45W
Detmold Germany 38 51.56N 8.52E
De Tour Village U.S.A. 104 46.00N 83.56W
Detroit U.S.A. 114 42.20N 83.03W
Detroit Lakes town U.S.A. 110 46.49N 95.51W
Deûlgaon Rāja India 62 20.01N 76.02E
Deurne Belgium 16 51.13N 4.26E
Deurne Neth. 16 51.29N 5.44E
Deutsche Bucht b. Germany 38 54.10N 8.00E
Deutschlandsberg Austria 31 46.49N 15.13E
Deux Rivières town Canada 104 46.15N 78.19W
Deux-Sevres d. France 18 46.30N 0.20W
Deva Romania 37 45.54N 22.55E

Deventer Neth. 16 52.15N 6.10E
Deveron r. U.K. 14 57.40N 2.30W
Devès, Monts du mts. France 20 45.00N 3.45E
Devīkot India 62 26.42N 71.12E
Devil's Bridge U.K. 13 52.23N 3.50W
Devils Lake town U.S.A. 110 48.07N 98.59W
Devin Bulgaria 34 41.44N 24.24E
Devizes U.K. 13 51.21N 2.00W
Devoll r. Albania 34 40.57N 20.15E
Devon d. U.K. 13 50.50N 3.40W
Devon I. Canada 99 75.00N 86.00W
Devonport Australia 91 41.09S 146.16E
Devrez r. Turkey 64 41.07N 34.25E
Dewās India 62 22.58N 76.04E
De Witt U.S.A. 111 34.18N 91.20W
Dewsbury U.K. 12 53.42N 1.38W
Dexter Mich. U.S.A. 104 42.20N 83.53W
Dexter Mo. U.S.A. 111 36.48N 89.57W
Dexter N.Y. U.S.A. 105 44.01N 76.03W
Deyang China 55 31.08N 104.18E
Dey-Dey L. Australia 91 29.12S 131.02E
Dez r. Iran 65 31.38N 48.54E
Dezadeash L. Canada 100 60.28N 136.58W
Dezfūl Iran 65 32.24N 48.27E
Dezhneva, Mys c. Russian Fed. 48 66.05N 169.40W
Dezhou China 54 37.23N 116.16E
Dezh Shāhpūr Iran 65 35.31N 46.10E
Dháfni Greece 35 37.48N 22.01E
Dhahab Egypt 66 28.30N 34.31E
Dhahran see Az Zahrān Saudi Arabia 65
Dhākā Bangla. 63 23.43N 90.25E
Dhamār Yemen 71 14.33N 44.24E
Dhamtari India 63 20.41N 81.34E
Dhānbād India 63 23.48N 86.22E
Dhandhuka India 62 22.22N 71.59E
Dhangarhi Nepal 63 28.41N 80.38E
Dhankuta Nepal 63 26.59N 87.21E
Dhār India 62 22.36N 75.18E
Dharampur India 62 20.32N 73.11E
Dharān Bāzār Nepal 63 26.49N 87.17E
Dharangaon India 62 21.01N 75.16E
Dhāri India 62 21.20N 71.01E
Dharmābād India 63 18.54N 77.51E
Dharmjaygarh India 63 22.28N 83.13E
Dharmshāla India 62 32.13N 76.19E
Dhārni India 62 21.33N 76.53E
Dhaulāgiri mtn. Nepal 63 28.42N 83.31E
Dhebar L. India 62 24.16N 74.00E
Dhenkānāl India 63 20.40N 85.36E
Dhenoúsa i. Greece 35 37.08N 25.48E
Dhèrmiu site Albania 34 40.08N 19.42E
Dheskáti Greece 34 39.55N 21.49E
Dhestina Greece 35 38.25N 22.31E
Dhíavolítsion Greece 35 37.18N 21.58E
Dhíbān Jordan 67 31.30N 35.47E
Dhidhimótikhon Greece 34 41.22N 26.29E
Dhíinsoor Somali Rep. 71 2.28N 43.00E
Dhíkti mtn. Greece 35 35.08N 25.22E
Dhílos i. Greece 35 37.26N 25.16E
Dhimitsána Greece 35 37.37N 22.03E
Dhodhekánisos is. Greece 35 36.35N 27.10E
Dhodhóni site Greece 34 39.34N 20.47E
Dholiana Greece 34 39.54N 20.32E
Dholka India 62 22.43N 72.28E
Dholpur India 63 26.42N 77.54E
Dhomokós Greece 35 39.10N 22.18E
Dhorāji India 62 21.44N 70.27E
Dhoxáton Greece 34 41.05N 24.14E
Dhrāngadhra India 62 22.59N 71.28E
Dhrol India 62 22.34N 70.25E
Dhubri India 63 26.02N 89.58E
Dhule India 62 20.54N 74.47E
Dhulian India 63 24.41N 87.58E
Dhuudo Somali Rep. 71 9.20N 50.14E
Día i. Greece 35 35.26N 25.13E
Dialakoro Mali 76 12.18N 7.54W
Diamante Argentina 125 32.05S 60.35W
Diamantina r. Australia 90 26.45S 139.10E
Diamantina Brazil 126 18.17S 43.37W
Diamantina, Chapada hills Brazil 123 13.00S 42.30W
Diamantino Brazil 126 14.25S 56.29W
Diamond Harbour India 63 22.12N 88.12E
Dianalund Denmark 42 55.32N 11.30E
Diana's Peak mtn. St. Helena 127 15.58S 5.42W
Dianbai China 55 21.30N 111.01E
Diane Bank is. Australia 90 15.50S 149.48E
Dianjiang China 55 30.14N 107.27E
Diapaga Burkina 77 12.04N 1.48E
Dibai India 63 28.13N 78.15E
Dibaya Zaïre 78 6.31S 22.57E
Dibi Cameroon 77 7.09N 13.43E
Dibrugarh India 61 27.29N 94.56E
Dibs Syria 64 34.57N 40.23E
Dickinson U.S.A. 110 46.53N 102.47W
Dicle r. Turkey see Dijlah r. Asia 64
Didcot U.K. 13 51.36N 1.14W
Didiéni Mali 76 14.05N 7.50W
Didwāna India 62 27.24N 74.34E
Didyma site Turkey 35 37.25N 27.16E
Die France 21 44.45N 5.22E
Dieburg Germany 38 49.54N 8.50E
Diefenbaker, L. Canada 101 51.00N 106.55W
Diekirch Lux. 16 49.52N 6.10E
Diélette France 18 49.33N 1.52W
Diéma Mali 76 14.32N 9.03W
Diemen Neth. 16 52.22N 4.58E
Diemuchuoke Jammu & Kashmir 63 32.42N 79.29E
Dien Bien Phu Vietnam 56 21.23N 103.02E
Diepholz Germany 38 52.35N 8.21E
Dieppe France 18 49.56N 1.05E
Dierdorf Germany 38 50.33N 7.39E
Dieren Neth. 16 52.03N 6.06E
Dierks U.S.A. 111 34.07N 94.01W
Diesdorf Germany 38 52.45N 10.52E
Diest Belgium 16 50.59N 5.03E
Dieulefit France 21 44.31N 5.04E
Dieuze France 19 48.49N 6.43E
Diez Germany 39 50.22N 8.01E

Dif Kenya 73 1.04N 40.57E
Diffa Niger 77 13.19N 12.35E
Diffa d. Niger 77 16.00N 13.00E
Dig India 62 27.20N 77.25E
Digby Canada 103 44.30N 65.47W
Dighton U.S.A. 110 38.29N 100.28W
Digne France 21 44.06N 6.14E
Digoin France 19 46.29N 3.59E
Digras India 63 20.07N 77.43E
Digri Pakistan 62 25.10N 69.07E
Digul r. Indonesia 59 7.10S 139.08E
Dijlah r. Asia 65 31.00N 47.27E
Dijle r. Belgium 16 51.02N 4.25E
Dijon France 19 47.19N 5.01E
Dikhil Djibouti 73 11.06N 42.22E
Dikili Turkey 29 39.05N 26.52E
Dikirnis Egypt 66 31.05N 31.35E
Dikodougou Côte d'Ivoire 76 9.00N 5.45W
Diksmuide Belgium 16 51.01N 2.52E
Dikwa Nigeria 77 12.01N 13.55E
Dili Indonesia 59 8.35S 125.35E
Dillenburg Germany 38 50.44N 8.17E
Dilley U.S.A. 111 28.40N 99.10W
Dilling Sudan 73 12.03N 29.39E
Dillingen Germany 39 48.34N 10.29E
Dillingham U.S.A. 98 59.02N 158.29W
Dillon U.S.A. 108 45.13N 112.38W
Dillsburg U.S.A. 114 40.07N 77.02W
Dilolo Zaïre 78 10.39S 22.20E
Dimashq Syria 66 33.30N 36.19E
Dimbelenge Zaïre 78 5.32S 23.04E
Dimbokro Côte d'Ivoire 76 6.43N 4.46W
Dimboola Australia 92 36.27S 142.02E
Dîmboviţa r. Romania 37 44.13N 26.22E
Dimitrovgrad Bulgaria 34 42.05N 25.35E
Dimitrovo see Pernik Bulgaria 34
Dimona Israel 67 31.04N 35.01E
Dinagat i. Phil. 59 10.15N 125.30E
Dinājpur Bangla. 63 25.38N 88.38E
Dinan France 18 48.27N 2.02W
Dinant Belgium 16 50.16N 4.55E
Dinar Turkey 64 38.05N 30.09E
Dinara Planina mts. Europe 31 43.40N 17.00E
Dinard France 18 48.38N 2.04W
Dinaric Alps mts. see Dinara Planina mts. Europe 31
Dīnār, Kūh-e mtn. Iran 65 30.45N 51.39E
Dindar r. Sudan 72 14.06N 33.40E
Dindar Nat. Park Sudan 73 12.00N 35.00E
Dindigul India 60 10.23N 78.00E
Dindori India 63 22.57N 81.05E
Dinga Pakistan 62 25.26N 67.10E
Dingbian China 54 37.36N 107.38E
Dinggyê China 63 28.18N 88.06E
Dingle Rep. of Ire. 15 52.09N 10.17W
Dingle B. Rep. of Ire. 15 52.05N 10.12W
Dingmans Ferry town U.S.A. 115 41.14N 74.53W
Dingolfing Germany 39 48.38N 12.31E
Dinguiraye Guinea 76 11.19N 10.49W
Dingwall U.K. 14 57.35N 4.26W
Dingxi China 54 35.33N 104.32E
Ding Xian China 54 38.30N 115.00E
Dingxing China 54 39.17N 115.46E
Dinkelsbühl Germany 39 49.04N 10.19E
Dinokwe Botswana 80 23.24S 26.40E
Dinuba U.S.A. 109 36.32N 119.23W
Diö Sweden 43 56.38N 14.33E
Diodār India 62 24.06N 71.47E
Dioíla Mali 76 12.30N 6.49W
Diourbel Senegal 76 14.30N 16.10W
Diplo Pakistan 62 24.28N 69.35E
Dipolog Phil. 59 8.34N 123.28E
Dirdal Norway 42 58.47N 6.14E
Diré Mali 76 16.16N 3.24W
Direction, C. Australia 90 12.51S 143.32E
Dirē Dawa Ethiopia 73 9.35N 41.50E
Dirico Angola 78 17.58S 20.40E
Dirj Libya 75 30.09N 10.26E
Dirk Hartog I. Australia 88 25.50S 113.00E
Dirranbandi Australia 93 28.35S 148.10E
Disappointment, L. Australia 88 23.30S 122.55E
Disaster B. Australia 93 37.20S 149.58E
Discovery Canada 89 63.10N 113.58W
Discovery B. Australia 92 38.12S 141.07E
Disentis Switz. 39 46.43N 8.51E
Disko i. Greenland 99 69.45N 53.00W
Disneyland Paris France 19 48.50N 2.50E
Diss U.K. 13 52.23N 1.06E
District of Columbia d. U.S.A. 114 38.55N 77.00W
Distrito Federal d. Brazil 123 15.45S 47.50W
Distrito Federal d. Mexico 116 19.20N 99.10W
Disūq Egypt 66 31.09N 30.39E
Dithmarschen f. Germany 38 54.10N 9.15E
Diu India 62 20.42N 70.59E
Diu d. India 62 20.45N 70.59E
Diver Canada 104 46.42N 79.30W
Dives r. France 18 49.19N 0.05W
Divinópolis Brazil 126 20.08S 44.55W
Divnoye Russian Fed. 45 45.55N 43.21E
Divo Côte d'Ivoire 76 5.48N 5.15W
Divriği Turkey 64 39.23N 38.06E
Diwāl Qol Afghan. 62 34.19N 67.54E
Dixcove Ghana 76 4.49N 1.57W
Dixie U.S.A. 108 45.34N 115.28W
Dix Milles, Lac l. Canada 105 46.46N 77.45W
Dixon Ill. U.S.A. 110 41.50N 89.29W
Dixon N.Mex. U.S.A. 109 36.12N 105.33W
Dixon Entrance str. U.S.A./Canada 100 54.25N 132.30W
Diyālā r. Iraq 65 33.13N 44.33E
Diyarbakir Turkey 64 37.55N 40.14E
Dja r. Cameroon 78 1.38N 16.03E
Djabéta Gabon 78 0.45N 14.00E
Djado Niger 77 21.00N 12.20E
Djado, Plateau du f. Niger 77 22.00N 12.30E
Djambala Congo 78 2.33S 14.38E
Djanet Algeria 75 24.34N 9.29E
Djebel Abiod Tunisia 32 36.58N 9.05E
Djelfa Algeria 75 34.40N 3.15E

Djema C.A.R. **73** 6.03N 25.19E
Djénne Mali **76** 13.55N 4.31W
Djerba, Île de *i.* Tunisia **75** 33.48N 10.54E
Djerid, Chott *f.* Tunisia **75** 33.42N 8.26E
Djibo Burkina **76** 14.09N 1.38W
Djibouti Africa **73** 12.00N 42.50E
Djibouti *town* Djibouti **73** 11.35N 43.11E
Djilbabo Plain *f.* Ethiopia **73** 4.00N 39.10E
Djolu Zaïre **78** 0.35N 22.28E
Djouah *r.* Gabon **78** 1.16N 13.12E
Djougou Benin **77** 9.40N 1.47E
Djugu Zaïre **79** 1.55N 30.31E
Djúpivogur Iceland **40** 64.41N 14.16W
Djurö *i.* Sweden **43** 58.52N 13.28E
Dmitriya Lapteva, Proliv *str.* Russian Fed. **51** 73.00N 142.00E
Dnepr *r.* Ukraine *see* Dnieper *r.* Europe **37**
Dneprodzerzhinsk Ukraine **45** 48.30N 34.37E
Dnepropetrovsk Ukraine **45** 48.29N 35.00E
Dneprovskaya Nizmennost *f.* Belarus **37** 52.30N 29.45E
Dneprovsko-Bugskiy Kanal Belarus **37** 52.03N 25.35E
Dnestr *r.* Ukraine *see* Dniester *r.* Europe **37**
Dnieper *r.* Europe **37** 50.00N 31.00E
Dniester *r.* Europe **37** 46.21N 30.20E
Dno Russian Fed. **44** 57.50N 30.00E
Doba Chad **77** 8.40N 16.50E
Dobane C.A.R. **73** 6.24N 24.42E
Dobbiaco Italy **30** 46.44N 12.14E
Dobele Latvia **41** 56.37N 23.16E
Döbeln Germany **38** 51.07N 13.07E
Dobo Indonesia **59** 5.46S 134.13E
Doboj Bosnia-Herzegovina **31** 44.44N 18.06E
Dobra *r.* Croatia **31** 45.33N 15.31E
Dobrich Bulgaria **29** 43.34N 27.52E
Dobrodzień Poland **37** 50.44N 18.27E
Dobruja *f.* Romania **37** 44.30N 28.15E
Dobrush Belarus **37** 52.24N 31.19E
Dobryanka Russian Fed. **44** 58.30N 56.26E
Dobzha China **63** 28.28N 88.13E
Doce *r.* Brazil **126** 19.32S 39.57W
Docking U.K. **12** 52.55N 0.39E
Doda Jammu & Kashmir **62** 33.08N 75.34E
Doda, Lac *l.* Canada **102** 49.24N 75.14W
Dodecanese *is. see* Dhodhekánisos *is.* Greece **35**
Dodge City U.S.A. **111** 37.45N 100.01W
Dodman Pt. U.K. **13** 50.13N 4.49W
Dodoma Tanzania **79** 6.10S 35.40E
Dodoma *d.* Tanzania **79** 6.00S 36.00E
Dodson U.S.A. **108** 48.24N 108.15W
Doetinchem Neth. **16** 51.57N 6.17E
Dogai Coring *l.* China **61** 34.30N 89.00E
Doğanbey Turkey **35** 37.37N 27.11E
Dog Creek *town* Canada **100** 51.35N 122.14W
Dogger Bank *f.* North Sea **11** 54.45N 2.00E
Doğubayazit Turkey **65** 39.32N 44.08E
Do'gyaling China **63** 31.58N 88.24E
Doha *see* Ad Dawḩah Qatar **65**
Dohad India **62** 22.50N 74.16E
Doheny Canada **105** 47.04N 72.36W
Dohhi India **63** 24.32N 84.54E
Doilungdêqên China **63** 30.06N 90.32E
Doiran, L. Greece/Macedonia **34** 41.13N 22.44E
Dokkum Neth. **16** 53.20N 6.00E
Dokri Pakistan **62** 27.23N 68.06E
Dolbeau Canada **103** 48.53N 72.14W
Dol-de-Bretagne France **18** 48.33N 1.45W
Dole France **19** 47.06N 5.30E
Dolgellau U.K. **13** 52.44N 3.53W
Dolina Ukraine **37** 49.00N 23.59E
Dolinskaya Ukraine **45** 48.06N 32.46E
Dollard *b.* Germany **38** 53.17N 7.10E
Dolni Dubnik Bulgaria **34** 43.24N 24.26E
Dolni Lom Bulgaria **34** 43.31N 22.47E
Dolny Kubín Slovakia **37** 49.12N 19.17E
Dolomiti *mts.* Italy **30** 46.15N 11.55E
Dolores Argentina **125** 36.19S 57.40W
Dolores Mexico **109** 28.53N 108.27W
Dolores Spain **25** 38.08N 0.46W
Dolores Uruguay **125** 33.33S 58.13W
Dolores U.S.A. **108** 37.28N 108.30W
Dolphin and Union Str. Canada **98** 69.20N 118.00W
Doma Nigeria **77** 8.23N 8.21E
Domadare Somali Rep. **73** 1.48N 41.13E
Domažlice Czech Republic **38** 49.27N 12.56E
Dombås Norway **41** 62.05N 9.08E
Dombe Grande Angola **78** 13.00S 13.06E
Dombes *f.* France **21** 46.00N 5.03E
Dombey, C. Australia **92** 37.12S 139.43E
Dombóvár Hungary **31** 46.23N 18.08E
Domburg Neth. **16** 51.35N 3.31E
Domfront France **18** 48.36N 0.39W
Dominica Windward Is. **117** 15.30N 61.30W
Dominican Republic C. America **117** 18.00N 70.00W
Dominion L. Canada **102** 52.40N 61.42W
Dommel *r.* Neth. **16** 51.44N 5.17E
Domo Ethiopia **71** 7.54N 46.52E
Domodossola Italy **30** 46.07N 8.17E
Dompierre-sur-Besbre France **20** 46.31N 3.41E
Domuyo *mtn.* Argentina **125** 36.37S 70.28W
Domvraína Greece **35** 38.15N 22.59E
Domžale Slovenia **31** 46.08N 14.36E
Don Mexico **109** 26.26N 109.02W
Don *r.* Russian Fed. **45** 47.06N 39.16E
Don *r.* England U.K. **12** 53.41N 0.50W
Don *r.* Scotland U.K. **14** 57.10N 2.05W
Donaghadee U.K. **15** 54.39N 5.33W
Donald Australia **92** 36.25S 143.04E
Donaldsonville U.S.A. **111** 30.06N 90.59W
Donau *r.* Germany *see* Danube *r.* Europe **36**
Donaueschingen Germany **39** 47.57N 8.29E
Donauwörth Germany **39** 48.43N 10.46E
Don Benito Spain **27** 38.53N 5.51W
Doncaster U.K. **12** 53.31N 1.09W
Dondaicha India **62** 21.20N 74.34E
Dondo Angola **78** 9.40S 14.25E
Dondo Mozambique **81** 19.39S 34.39E
Donegal Rep. of Ire. **15** 54.39N 8.06W

Donegal *d.* Rep. of Ire. **15** 54.52N 8.00W
Donegal U.S.A. **114** 40.07N 79.23W
Donegal B. Rep. of Ire. **15** 54.32N 8.18W
Donegal Pt. Rep. of Ire. **15** 52.43N 9.38W
Donetsk Ukraine **45** 48.00N 37.50E
Donga Nigeria **77** 7.45N 10.05E
Donga *r.* Nigeria **77** 8.20N 10.00E
Dongara Australia **89** 29.15S 114.56E
Dongargarh India **63** 21.12N 80.44E
Dongbei Pingyuan *f.* China **54** 42.30N 123.00E
Dongchuan China **52** 26.10N 103.02E
Dongco China **63** 32.07N 84.35E
Dongfang China **55** 19.05N 108.39E
Donggala Indonesia **58** 0.48S 119.45E
Donggou China **54** 39.52N 124.08E
Dongguang China **54** 37.53N 116.32E
Donghai China **54** 34.35N 118.49E
Donghai *i.* China **55** 21.02N 110.25E
Dong Hoi Vietnam **56** 17.32N 106.35E
Dong Jiang *r.* China **55** 23.00N 113.33E
Dongkalang Indonesia **59** 0.12N 120.07E
Dongling China **54** 41.44N 123.32E
Dongtai China **54** 32.42N 120.26E
Dongting Hu *l.* China **55** 29.10N 113.00E
Dongtou *i.* China **55** 27.50N 121.08E
Dong Ujimqin Qi China **54** 45.33N 116.50E
Dongxi China **54** 28.42N 106.40E
Dongxing China **55** 21.33N 107.58E
Donington U.K. **12** 52.55N 0.12W
Donja Stubica Croatia **31** 45.59N 15.58E
Donji Vakuf Bosnia-Herzegovina **31** 44.09N 17.25E
Dönna *i.* Norway **40** 66.05N 12.30E
Donnacona Canada **105** 46.40N 71.47W
Donnybrook Australia **89** 33.34S 115.47E
Donnybrook R.S.A. **80** 29.55S 29.51E
Donora U.S.A. **114** 40.11N 79.52W
Donostia *see* San Sebastián Spain **26**
Doodlakine Australia **89** 31.41S 117.23E
Doolow Somali Rep. **71** 4.13N 42.08E
Doon, Loch U.K. **14** 55.15N 4.23W
Dor Israel **67** 32.37N 34.56E
Dora Baltea *r.* Italy **30** 45.11N 8.05E
Dora, L. Australia **88** 22.05S 122.55E
Doran L. Canada **101** 61.13N 108.06W
Dora Riparia *r.* Italy **30** 45.05N 7.44E
Dorchester U.K. **13** 50.52N 2.28W
Dorchester, C. Canada **99** 65.29N 77.30W
Dordogne *d.* France **20** 45.10N 0.45E
Dordogne *r.* France **20** 45.02N 0.35W
Dordrecht Neth. **16** 51.48N 4.40E
Dordrecht R.S.A. **80** 31.22S 27.02E
Doré L. Canada **101** 54.46N 107.17W
Dore, Mont *mtn.* France **20** 45.35N 2.48E
Dorfen Germany **39** 48.17N 12.08E
Dorgali Italy **32** 40.17N 9.35E
Dori Burkina **76** 14.03N 0.02W
Dorion Canada **105** 45.23N 74.03W
Dorking U.K. **13** 51.14N 0.20W
Dormagen Germany **38** 51.06N 6.50E
Dormans France **19** 49.04N 3.38E
Dornbirn Austria **39** 47.25N 9.44E
Dornie U.K. **14** 57.16N 5.31W
Dornoch U.K. **14** 57.52N 4.02W
Dornoch Firth *est.* U.K. **14** 57.50N 4.04W
Dornogovĭ *d.* Mongolia **54** 44.00N 110.00E
Dornum Germany **38** 53.40N 7.28E
Doro Mali **76** 16.09N 0.51W
Dorohoi Romania **37** 47.57N 26.24E
Dörpen Germany **38** 52.57N 7.20E
Dorre I. Australia **88** 25.08S 113.06E
Dorrigo Australia **93** 30.20S 152.41E
Dorris U.S.A. **108** 41.58N 121.55W
Dorset Canada **104** 45.14N 78.54W
Dorset *d.* U.K. **13** 50.48N 2.25W
Dorset U.S.A. **115** 43.15N 73.06W
Dorset, C. Canada **99** 64.10N 76.40W
Dorset Peak *mtn.* U.S.A. **115** 43.19N 73.02W
Dorsten Germany **38** 51.39N 6.58E
Dortmund Germany **38** 51.31N 7.28E
Dortmund-Ems Kanal Germany **38** 52.00N 7.36E
Dorval Canada **105** 45.27N 73.44W
Dos Bahías, C. Australia **92** 44.55S 65.32W
Dos Hermanas Spain **27** 37.17N 5.55W
Dosquet Canada **105** 46.28N 71.33W
Dosse *r.* Germany **38** 53.13N 12.20E
Dosso Niger **77** 13.03N 3.10E
Dosso *d.* Niger **77** 13.00N 3.15E
Dossor Kazakhstan **45** 47.31N 53.01E
Dothan U.S.A. **113** 31.12N 85.25W
Douai France **19** 50.22N 3.04E
Douako Guinea **76** 9.45N 10.08W
Douala Cameroon **77** 4.05N 9.43E
Douarnenez France **18** 48.06N 4.20W
Double Mer *b.* Canada **103** 54.05N 59.00W
Doubs *d.* France **19** 47.10N 6.25E
Doubs *r.* France **19** 46.54N 5.02E
Doubtless B. New Zealand **86** 35.10S 173.30E
Doudeville France **18** 49.43N 0.48E
Douentza Mali **76** 14.58N 2.48W
Doulaincourt France **19** 48.23N 4.55E
Doulevant-le-Château France **19** 48.23N 4.55E
Doullens France **19** 50.09N 2.21E
Doumé Cameroon **77** 4.13N 13.30E
Douna Mali **76** 12.40N 6.00W

Dourados Brazil **124** 22.09S 54.52W
Dourdan France **19** 48.32N 2.01E
Douro *r.* Portugal **26** 41.08N 8.40W
Douvres France **18** 49.17N 0.23W
Douze *r.* France **20** 43.54N 0.30W
Dove *r.* Derbys. U.K. **12** 52.50N 1.35W
Dover U.K. **13** 51.07N 1.19E
Dover Del. U.S.A. **115** 39.10N 75.32W
Dover N.H. U.S.A. **115** 43.12N 70.56W
Dover N.J. U.S.A. **115** 40.53N 74.34W
Dover Ohio U.S.A. **114** 40.32N 81.29W
Dover Tenn. U.S.A. **113** 36.30N 87.50W
Dover, Pt. Australia **89** 32.32S 125.30E
Dover, Str. of U.K. **13** 51.00N 1.30E
Dovey *r.* U.K. **13** 52.33N 3.56W
Dovrefjell *mts.* Norway **41** 62.06N 9.25E
Dovsk Belarus **37** 53.07N 30.29E
Dowa Malawi **79** 13.40S 33.55E
Dowagiac U.S.A. **112** 41.58N 86.06W
Dowerin Australia **89** 31.15S 117.00E
Dowlat Yār China **89** 34.33N 65.47E
Downey U.S.A. **108** 42.26N 112.07W
Downham Market U.K. **13** 52.36N 0.22E
Downpatrick U.K. **15** 54.21N 5.43W
Downpatrick Head Rep. of Ire. **15** 54.20N 9.22W
Downton, Mt. Canada **100** 52.42N 124.51W
Dowra Rep. of Ire. **15** 54.11N 8.02W
Doylestown U.S.A. **115** 40.19N 75.08W
Dozois, Résr. Canada **105** 47.30N 77.05W
Drâa, Hamada du *f.* Algeria **74** 29.00N 6.00W
Drâa, Oued *wadi* Morocco **74** 28.40N 11.06W
Drac *r.* France **21** 45.13N 5.41E
Drachten Neth. **16** 53.05N 6.06E
Dragaš Yugo. **34** 42.05N 20.35E
Drăgășani Romania **37** 44.40N 24.16E
Dragoman, Pasul *pass* Bulgaria/Yugo. **29** 42.56N 22.52E
Dragonera, Isla *i.* Spain **25** 39.35N 2.19E
Dragon's Mouth *str.* Trinidad **122** 11.00N 61.35W
Dragovishtitsa Bulgaria **34** 42.22N 22.39E
Draguignan France **21** 43.32N 6.28E
Drake Australia **93** 28.55S 152.24E
Drake U.S.A. **110** 47.55N 100.23W
Drakensberg *mts.* R.S.A./Lesotho **80** 30.00S 29.05E
Drake Passage *str.* Atlantic Oc. **127** 59.00S 65.00W
Dráma Greece **34** 41.09N 24.08E
Drammen Norway **42** 59.44N 10.15E
Drås Jammu & Kashmir **62** 34.27N 75.46E
Drau *r.* Austria *see* Drava *r.* Slovenia/Croatia **30**
Drava *r.* Slovenia/Croatia **31** 45.33N 18.55E
Dravinja *r.* Slovenia **31** 46.22N 15.57E
Drayton Valley *town* Canada **100** 53.25N 114.58W
Drenovets Bulgaria **34** 43.42N 22.59E
Drenthe *d.* Neth. **16** 52.52N 6.30E
Dresden Germany **38** 51.03N 13.44E
Dresden U.S.A. **114** 40.07N 82.01W
Dreux France **18** 48.44N 1.22E
Driftwood Canada **102** 49.08N 81.23W
Driftwood U.S.A. **114** 41.20N 78.08W
Drin *r.* Albania **34** 41.37N 20.28E
Drina *r.* Bosnia-Herzegovina **31** 44.53N 19.21E
Drniš Croatia **31** 43.51N 16.09E
Dröbak Norway **42** 59.39N 10.39E
Drocourt Canada **104** 45.47N 80.22W
Drogheda Rep. of Ire. **15** 53.42N 6.23W
Drogobych Ukraine **37** 49.10N 23.30E
Droitwich U.K. **13** 52.16N 2.10W
Drokiya Moldova **37** 48.07N 27.49E
Drôme *d.* France **21** 44.35N 5.10E
Drôme *r.* France **21** 44.46N 4.46E
Dromedary, C. Australia **93** 36.18S 150.15E
Dronero Italy **30** 44.28N 7.22E
Dronfield U.K. **12** 53.18N 1.29W
Dronne *r.* France **20** 45.02N 0.09W
Dronning Denmark **42** 57.09N 10.18E
Dronning Maud Land *f.* Antarctica **128** 74.00S 10.00E
Drumbo Canada **104** 43.14N 80.33W
Drumheller Canada **100** 51.25N 112.40W
Drum Hills Rep. of Ire. **15** 52.03N 7.42W
Drummond U.S.A. **108** 46.02N 83.42W
Drummond I. U.S.A. **104** 46.00N 83.40W
Drummond Range *mts.* Australia **90** 23.30S 147.15E
Drummondville Canada **105** 45.53N 72.29W
Drummore U.K. **14** 54.41N 4.54W
Druskininkai Lithuania **37** 53.48N 23.58E
Drut *r.* Belarus **37** 53.03N 30.42E
Drvar Bosnia-Herzegovina **31** 44.22N 16.24E
Dryanovo Bulgaria **34** 42.58N 25.27E
Dry B. U.S.A. **100** 59.08N 138.25W
Dryden Canada **102** 49.47N 92.50W
Dryden U.S.A. **115** 42.29N 76.18W
Drymen U.K. **14** 56.04N 4.27W
Drysdale *r.* Australia **88** 13.59S 126.51E
Dua *r.* Zaïre **78** 3.12N 20.55E
Du'an China **55** 24.01N 108.06E
Duaringa Australia **90** 23.42S 149.40E
Ḏubā Saudi Arabia **64** 27.21N 35.40E
Dubai *see* Dubayy U.A.E. **65**
Dubawnt *r.* Canada **99** 62.50N 102.00W
Dubawnt L. Canada **101** 63.04N 101.42W
Dubayy U.A.E. **65** 25.13N 55.17E
Dubbo Australia **93** 32.16S 148.41E
Dubica Croatia **31** 45.11N 16.48E
Dublin Rep. of Ire. **15** 53.21N 6.18W
Dublin *d.* Rep. of Ire. **15** 53.20N 6.18W
Dublin U.S.A. **113** 32.31N 82.54W
Dublin B. Rep. of Ire. **15** 53.20N 6.09W
Dubno Ukraine **37** 50.28N 25.40E
Dubois Idaho U.S.A. **108** 44.10N 112.14W
Du Bois Penn. U.S.A. **114** 41.07N 78.46W
Dubovka Russian Fed. **45** 49.04N 44.48E
Dubréka Guinea **76** 9.50N 13.32W
Dubrovitsa Ukraine **37** 51.38N 26.40E
Dubrovnik Croatia **31** 42.38N 18.07E
Dubuque U.S.A. **110** 42.30N 90.41W

Duchesne U.S.A. **108** 40.10N 110.24W
Duchess Australia **90** 21.22S 139.52E
Ducie I. Pacific Oc. **85** 24.40S 124.48W
Du Coüedic, C. Australia **92** 36.00S 136.10E
Duderstadt Germany **38** 51.31N 10.16E
Dudhnai India **63** 25.59N 90.44E
Dudinka Russian Fed. **51** 69.27N 86.13E
Dudley U.K. **13** 52.30N 2.05W
Dudna *r.* India **62** 19.07N 76.54E
Dudweiler Germany **39** 49.17N 7.02E
Duékoué Côte d'Ivoire **76** 6.50N 7.22W
Duerna *r.* Spain **26** 42.19N 5.54W
Duero *r.* Spain *see* Douro *r.* Portugal **26**
Duff Creek *town* Australia **92** 28.28S 135.51E
Dufftown U.K. **14** 57.27N 3.09W
Duga Poljana Yugo. **34** 43.15N 20.14E
Duga Resa Croatia **31** 45.27N 15.30E
Dugi *i.* Croatia **31** 44.00N 15.04E
Du Gué *r.* Canada **103** 57.20N 70.48W
Duifken Pt. Australia **90** 12.33S 141.38E
Duisburg Germany **38** 51.25N 6.46E
Duitama Colombia **122** 5.50N 73.01W
Duiveland *i.* Neth. **16** 51.39N 4.00E
Dujuuma Somali Rep. **79** 1.14N 42.37E
Dukambīya Eritrea **72** 14.42N 37.30E
Dukat Albania **34** 40.16N 19.32E
Duk Fadiat Sudan **73** 7.45N 31.25E
Duk Faiwil Sudan **73** 7.30N 31.29E
Dukhān Qatar **65** 25.24N 50.47E
Dukou China **52** 26.33N 101.44E
Dukye Dzong Bhutan **63** 27.20N 89.30E
Dulce *r.* Argentina **124** 30.40S 62.00W
Duleek Rep. of Ire. **15** 53.39N 6.24W
Dülmen Germany **38** 51.51N 7.16E
Dulovo Bulgaria **37** 43.49N 27.09E
Duluth U.S.A. **110** 46.47N 92.06W
Dümä Syria **66** 33.36N 36.24E
Dumaguete Phil. **59** 9.20N 123.18E
Dumai Indonesia **58** 1.41N 101.27E
Dumaran *i.* Phil. **58** 10.33N 119.50E
Dumaresq *r.* Australia **93** 28.40S 150.28E
Dumaring Indonesia **58** 1.36N 118.12E
Dumas Ark. U.S.A. **111** 33.53N 91.29W
Dumas Tex. U.S.A. **111** 35.52N 101.58W
Dumbarton U.K. **14** 55.57N 4.35W
Dumbleyung Australia **89** 33.18S 117.42E
Dumbrăveni Romania **37** 46.14N 24.35E
Dum-Dum India **63** 22.35N 88.24E
Dumfries U.K. **14** 55.04N 3.37W
Dumfries and Galloway *d.* U.K. **14** 55.05N 3.40W
Dumka India **63** 24.16N 87.15E
Dumoine *r.* Canada **105** 46.13N 77.50W
Dumoine, Lac *l.* Canada **105** 46.53N 77.54W
Dumont, Lac *l.* Canada **105** 46.04N 76.28W
Dumraon India **63** 25.33N 84.09E
Dumyāţ Egypt **66** 31.26N 31.48E
Duna *r.* Hungary *see* Danube *r.* Europe **31**
Dunaföldvár Hungary **31** 46.48N 18.55E
Dunajec *r.* Poland **37** 50.15N 20.44E
Dunajská Streda Slovakia **37** 48.01N 17.35E
Dunany Pt. Rep. of Ire. **15** 53.51N 6.15W
Dunărea *r.* Romania *see* Danube *r.* Europe **37**
Dunării, Delta *f.* Romania **37** 45.05N 29.45E
Dunaújváros Hungary **31** 46.58N 18.57E
Dunav *r.* Yugo. *see* Danube *r.* Europe **37**
Dunav *r.* Bulgaria *see* Danube *r.* Europe **37**
Duna-völgyi-föcsatorno *r.* Hungary **31** 46.12N 18.56E
Dunbar U.K. **14** 56.00N 2.31W
Dunbar U.S.A. **114** 38.22N 81.45W
Dunblane U.K. **14** 56.12N 3.59W
Dunboyne Rep. of Ire. **15** 53.26N 6.30W
Duncan Canada **100** 48.45N 123.40W
Duncan *r.* Canada **100** 50.11N 116.57W
Duncan U.S.A. **111** 34.30N 97.57W
Duncan, C. Canada **102** 52.40N 80.48W
Duncan L. N.W.T. Canada **100** 62.51N 113.58W
Duncan L. Que. Canada **102** 53.35N 77.55W
Duncannon U.S.A. **114** 40.23N 77.02W
Duncansby Head U.K. **14** 58.39N 3.01W
Dundalk Canada **104** 44.10N 80.24W
Dundalk Rep. of Ire. **15** 54.01N 6.25W
Dundalk U.S.A. **115** 39.15N 76.31W
Dundalk B. Rep. of Ire. **15** 53.55N 6.17W
Dundas Canada **104** 43.16N 79.58W
Dundas L. Canada **100** 54.33N 130.50W
Dundas, L. Australia **89** 32.35S 121.50E
Dundas Str. Australia **90** 11.20S 131.35E
Dundee R.S.A. **80** 28.09S 30.14E
Dundee U.K. **14** 56.28N 3.00W
Dundee Mich. U.S.A. **104** 41.57N 83.40W
Dundee N.Y. U.S.A. **114** 42.31N 76.59W
Dundgovĭ *d.* Mongolia **54** 45.00N 106.00E
Dundrum U.K. **15** 54.16N 5.51W
Dundrum B. U.K. **15** 54.12N 5.46W
Dunedin New Zealand **86** 45.52S 170.30E
Dunedin U.S.A. **113** 28.02N 82.47W
Dunedoo Australia **93** 32.00S 149.25E
Dunfermline U.K. **14** 56.04N 3.29W
Dungannon U.K. **15** 54.31N 6.47W
Düngarpur India **62** 23.50N 73.43E
Dungarvan Rep. of Ire. **15** 52.06N 7.39W
Dungeness *c.* U.K. **13** 50.55N 0.58E
Dungiven U.K. **15** 54.56N 6.56W
Dungog Australia **93** 32.24S 151.46E
Dungu Zaïre **79** 3.40N 28.40E
Dunhuang China **52** 40.00N 94.40E
Dunkeld Qld. Australia **91** 26.55S 148.00E
Dunkeld Vic. Australia **92** 37.40S 142.23E
Dunkeld U.K. **14** 56.34N 3.36W
Dunkerque France **19** 51.02N 2.23E
Dunk I. Australia **90** 17.56S 146.10E
Dunkirk *see* Dunkerque France **16**
Dunkirk U.S.A. **114** 42.29N 79.20W
Dunkwa Central Ghana **76** 5.59N 1.45W
Dun Laoghaire Rep. of Ire. **15** 53.17N 6.09W
Dunlap U.S.A. **110** 41.51N 95.36W
Dunleer Rep. of Ire. **15** 53.49N 6.24W

Dun-le-Palestel France 20 46.17N 1.48E
Dunmahon Rep. of Ire. 15 52.09N 7.23W
Dunmarra Australia 90 16.37S 133.22E
Dunmore U.S.A. 115 41.25N 75.38W
Dunnet Head U.K. 14 58.40N 3.23W
Dunning U.S.A. 110 41.50N 100.06W
Dunnville Canada 104 42.54N 79.36W
Dunolly Australia 92 36.50S 143.45E
Dunoon U.K. 14 55.57N 4.57W
Dunqulah Sudan 72 19.10N 30.29E
Dunqunâb Sudan 72 21.06N 37.05E
Duns U.K. 14 55.47N 2.20W
Dunsborough Australia 89 33.37S 115.06E
Dunshaughlin Rep. of Ire. 15 53.30N 6.34W
Dunstable U.K. 13 51.53N 0.32W
Dunstan Mts. New Zealand 86 44.45S 169.45E
Dunster Canada 100 53.08N 119.50W
Dun-sur-Auron France 19 46.53N 2.34E
Dun-sur-Meuse France 19 49.23N 5.11E
Dunyâpur Pakistan 62 29.48N 71.44E
Duolun China 54 42.09N 116.21E
Duong Dong Vietnam 56 10.12N 103.57E
Dupnitsa Bulgaria 34 42.27N 23.09E
Dupont U.S.A. 112 38.53N 85.30W
Duque de Caxias Brazil 126 22.47S 43.18W
Duquesne U.S.A. 114 40.21N 79.51W
Du Quoin U.S.A. 111 38.01N 89.14W
Dūrā Jordan 67 31.30N 35.02E
Duran U.S.A. 109 34.28N 105.24W
Durance r. France 21 43.55N 4.44E
Durand U.S.A. 104 42.55N 83.59W
Durango Mexico 116 24.01N 104.00W
Durango d. Mexico 111 24.30N 104.00W
Durango Spain 26 43.10N 2.37W
Durango U.S.A. 108 37.16N 107.53W
Durant U.S.A. 111 34.00N 96.23W
Duras France 20 44.41N 0.11E
Duraton r. Spain 26 41.37N 4.07W
Durazno Uruguay 125 33.22S 56.31W
Durban R.S.A. 80 29.50S 30.59E
Durbe Latvia 41 56.35N 21.21E
Durbin U.S.A. 114 38.33N 79.50W
Durdevac Croatia 31 46.03N 17.04E
Dureji Pakistan 62 25.53N 67.18E
Düren Germany 38 50.48N 6.28E
Durg India 63 21.11N 81.17E
Durgâpur India 63 23.29N 87.20E
Durham Canada 104 44.10N 80.49W
Durham U.K. 12 54.47N 1.34W
Durham d. U.K. 12 54.42N 1.45W
Durham N.C. U.S.A. 113 36.00N 78.54W
Durham N.H. U.S.A. 115 43.08N 70.56W
Durham Sud Canada 105 45.39N 72.19W
Durlston Head c. U.K. 13 50.35N 1.58W
Durmitor mtn. Yugo. 31 43.08N 19.01E
Durness U.K. 14 58.33N 4.45W
Durrës Albania 34 41.19N 19.26E
Durrow Rep. of Ire. 15 52.51N 7.25W
Dursey Head Rep. of Ire. 15 51.35N 10.15W
Durûz, Jabal ad mtn. Syria 66 32.42N 36.42E
D'Urville I. New Zealand 86 40.45S 173.50E
Dushak Turkmenistan 50 37.13N 60.01E
Dushan China 55 25.50N 107.30E
Dushanbe Tajikistan 52 38.38N 68.51E
Dushore U.S.A. 115 41.31N 76.24W
Duskotna Bulgaria 29 42.52N 27.10E
Düsseldorf Germany 38 51.12N 6.47E
Dutch Creek Canada 100 50.18N 115.58W
Dutlhe Botswana 80 23.55S 23.47E
Dutton Canada 104 42.40N 81.30W
Dutton, L. Australia 92 31.49S 137.08E
Duxbury U.S.A. 115 42.02N 70.40W
Duxun China 55 23.57N 117.37E
Duyun China 55 26.12N 107.29E
Dve Mogili Bulgaria 34 43.36N 25.52E
Dvina r. Europe 9 57.03N 24.00E
Dvinskaya Guba b. Russian Fed. 44 64.40N 39.30E
Dwarda Australia 89 32.45S 116.23E
Dwârka India 62 22.14N 68.58E
Dwellingup Australia 89 32.42S 116.04E
Dwight Canada 104 45.21N 78.58W
Dyatlovichi Belarus 37 52.08N 30.49E
Dyatlovo Belarus 37 53.28N 25.28E
Dyer Bay town Canada 104 45.10N 81.18W
Dyer, C. Canada 99 67.45N 61.45W
Dyérem r. Cameroon 77 6.36N 13.10E
Dyer Plateau Antarctica 128 70.00S 65.00W
Dyersburg U.S.A. 111 36.03N 89.23W
Dyfed d. U.K. 13 52.00N 4.17W
Dykh Tau mtn. Russian Fed. 45 43.04N 43.10E
Dymer Ukraine 37 50.50N 30.20E
Dyulevo Bulgaria 29 42.22N 27.10E
Dyultydag mtn. Russian Fed. 45 41.55N 46.52E
Dzamïn Ūüd Mongolia 54 43.50N 111.53E
Dzerzhinsk Belarus 37 53.40N 27.01E
Dzerzhinsk Russian Fed. 44 56.15N 43.30E
Dzhankoy Ukraine 23 45.42N 34.23E
Dzhardzhan Russian Fed. 51 68.49N 124.08E
Dzhelinde Russian Fed. 51 70.09N 114.00E
Dzhetygara Kazakhstan 50 52.14N 61.10E
Dzhizak Uzbekistan 50 40.06N 67.45E
Dzhugdzhur, Khrebet mts. Russian Fed. 51 57.30N 138.00E
Dzhurin Ukraine 37 48.40N 28.16E
Dzialdowo Poland 37 53.15N 20.10E
Dzierzoniów Poland 36 50.44N 16.39E
Dzodze Ghana 76 6.14N 1.00E

E

Eabamet L. Canada 102 51.30N 88.00W
Eads U.S.A. 110 38.29N 102.47W
Eagle r. Canada 103 53.35N 57.25W
Eagle U.S.A. 110 39.39N 106.50W
Eagle Butte town U.S.A. 110 45.00N 101.14W
Eagle Grove U.S.A. 110 42.40N 93.54W
Eagle L. U.S.A. 112 46.17N 69.20W
Eagle Lake town Canada 104 45.08N 78.29W
Eagle Lake town U.S.A. 112 47.02N 68.36W
Eagle Pass town U.S.A. 111 28.43N 100.30W
Eagle River town U.S.A. 110 45.55N 89.15W
Ealing U.K. 13 51.31N 0.20W
Earlimart U.S.A. 109 35.53N 119.16W
Earlville U.S.A. 115 42.44N 75.33W
Earn r. U.K. 14 56.21N 3.18W
Earn, Loch U.K. 14 56.23N 4.12W
Easingwold U.K. 12 54.08N 1.11W
Easky Rep. of Ire. 15 54.17N 8.58W
Easley U.S.A. 113 34.50N 82.34W
East r. Canada 104 45.20N 79.17W
East Alligator r. Australia 90 12.25S 132.58E
East Anglian Heights hills U.K. 13 52.03N 0.15E
East Angus Canada 105 45.29N 71.40W
East Aurora U.S.A. 114 42.46N 78.37W
East B. U.S.A. 111 29.30N 94.35W
Eastbourne U.K. 13 50.46N 0.18E
East Brady U.S.A. 114 40.59N 79.37W
East Broughton Canada 105 46.14N 71.05W
East C. New Zealand 86 37.45S 178.30E
East Caroline Basin Pacific Oc. 84 3.00N 147.00E
East China Sea Asia 53 29.00N 125.00E
East Dereham U.K. 11 52.40N 0.57E
Easter I. see Pascua, Isla de i. Pacific Oc. 85
Eastern d. Ghana 76 6.20N 0.45W
Eastern d. Kenya 79 0.00 38.00E
Eastern Desert see Sharqîyah, Aş Şahrâ' ash des. Egypt 66
Eastern Ghâts mts. India 61 16.30N 80.30E
Eastern-Indian-Antarctic Basin f. Indian Oc. 49 56.00S 110.00E
Easterville Canada 101 53.06N 99.53W
East Falkland i. Falkland Is. 125 51.45S 58.50W
East Grand Forks U.S.A. 110 47.56N 96.55W
East Grinstead U.K. 13 51.08N 0.01W
Easthampton Mass. U.S.A. 115 42.16N 72.40W
East Hampton N.Y. U.S.A. 115 40.58N 72.11W
East Hartford U.S.A. 115 41.46N 72.39W
East Haven U.S.A. 115 41.17N 72.52W
East Ilsley U.K. 13 51.33N 1.15W
East Kilbride U.K. 14 55.46N 4.09W
East Lansing U.S.A. 104 42.44N 84.29W
Eastleigh U.K. 13 50.58N 1.21W
East Liverpool U.S.A. 114 40.38N 80.35W
East London R.S.A. 80 33.00S 27.54E
Eastmain Canada 102 52.15N 78.30W
Eastmain r. Canada 102 52.15N 78.30W
Eastman Canada 105 45.18N 72.19W
Easton Md. U.S.A. 115 38.46N 76.04W
Easton Penn. U.S.A. 115 40.42N 75.12W
Easton Wash. U.S.A. 108 47.14N 121.11W
East Orange U.S.A. 115 40.46N 74.14W
East Pacific Ridge Pacific Oc. 85 15.00S 112.00W
East Palestine U.S.A. 114 40.50N 80.33W
East Point town U.S.A. 113 33.41N 84.29W
Eastport U.S.A. 115 40.49N 72.44W
East Providence U.S.A. 115 41.49N 71.23W
East Retford U.K. 12 53.19N 0.55W
East Rochester U.S.A. 114 43.07N 77.29W
East Springfield U.S.A. 114 41.57N 80.28W
East St. Louis U.S.A. 110 38.34N 90.04W
East Sussex d. U.K. 13 50.56N 0.12E
East Sydenham r. Canada 104 42.35N 82.23W
East Tawas U.S.A. 104 44.17N 83.29W
Eaton U.S.A. 104 39.44N 84.38W
Eaton Rapids U.S.A. 104 42.30N 104.42W
Eau Claire U.S.A. 110 44.50N 91.30W
Eau-Claire, Lac à l' r. Canada 102 56.10N 74.30W
Eauripik i. Federated States of Micronesia 59 6.42N 143.04E
Eaurpik-N. Guinea Rise Pacific Oc. 84 2.00N 141.00E
Eauze France 20 43.52N 0.06E
Eban Nigeria 77 9.41N 4.54E
Ebbw Vale U.K. 13 51.47N 3.12W
Ebebiyin Equat. Guinea 78 2.09N 11.20E
Ebeltoft Denmark 42 56.12N 10.41E
Ebensburg U.S.A. 114 40.29N 78.44W
Ebensee Austria 39 47.48N 13.46E
Eberbach Germany 39 49.28N 8.59E
Ebermannstadt Germany 38 49.23N 11.13E
Ebern Germany 39 50.05N 10.47E
Eberndorf Austria 31 46.35N 14.38E
Ebersbach Germany 38 51.00N 14.35E
Ebersberg Germany 39 48.04N 11.59E
Eberstein Austria 31 46.48N 14.34E
Eberswalde Germany 38 52.50N 13.49E
Ebingen Germany 39 48.13N 9.01E
Ebinur Hu l. China 52 45.00N 83.00E
Ebola r. Zaïre 73 3.20N 20.57E
Eboli Italy 33 40.37N 15.04E
Ebolowa Cameroon 78 2.56N 11.11E
Ebon i. Pacific Oc. 84 4.38N 168.43E
Ebony Namibia 80 22.05S 15.15E
Ebro r. Spain 25 40.43N 0.54E
Ebro, Delta del f. Spain 25 40.43N 0.54E
Ebro, Embalse del resr. Spain 26 43.00N 4.00W
Ecclefechan U.K. 12 55.03N 3.18W
Eceabat Turkey 34 40.11N 26.21E
Echeng China 55 30.26N 114.00E
Echo Bay town Canada 104 46.29N 84.02W
Echternach Lux. 16 49.49N 6.25E
Echuca Australia 93 36.10S 144.20E
Écija Spain 27 37.32N 5.05W
Eckernförde Germany 38 54.28N 9.50E

Écommoy France 18 47.50N 0.16E
Ecuador S. America 122 1.40S 79.00W
Écueillé France 18 47.05N 1.21E
Êd Eritrea 72 13.52N 41.40E
Ed Sweden 42 58.55N 11.55E
Edam Neth. 16 52.30N 5.02E
Eday i. U.K. 10 59.11N 2.47W
Eddrachillis B. U.K. 14 58.17N 5.15W
Eddystone Pt. Australia 91 40.58S 148.12E
Ede Neth. 16 52.03N 5.40E
Ede Nigeria 77 7.45N 4.26E
Edea Cameroon 78 3.47N 10.15E
Edehon L. Canada 101 60.25N 97.15W
Eden Australia 93 37.04S 149.54E
Eden Canada 104 42.47N 80.46W
Eden r. Cumbria U.K. 12 54.57N 3.02W
Eden U.S.A. 108 42.03N 109.26W
Edenburg R.S.A. 80 29.44S 25.55E
Edendale New Zealand 86 46.19S 168.47E
Edenderry Rep. of Ire. 15 53.21N 7.05W
Edenhope Australia 92 37.04S 141.20E
Edenton U.S.A. 113 36.04N 76.39W
Edeowie Australia 92 31.28S 138.29E
Eder r. Germany 38 51.13N 9.27E
Ederny U.K. 15 54.32N 7.40W
Edgartown U.S.A. 115 41.23N 70.31W
Edgeley U.S.A. 110 46.07N 98.43W
Edgeõya i. Arctic Oc. 128 77.45N 22.30E
Edgeworthstown Rep. of Ire. 15 53.42N 7.38W
Edgington Canada 104 45.23N 79.47W
Édhessa Greece 34 40.48N 22.05E
Ediacara Australia 92 30.18S 137.50E
Edina Liberia 76 6.01N 10.10W
Edinboro U.S.A. 114 41.52N 80.08W
Edinburgh U.K. 14 55.57N 3.13W
Edirne Turkey 34 41.40N 26.34E
Edithburgh Australia 92 35.06S 137.44E
Edjudina Australia 89 29.48S 122.23E
Edmond U.S.A. 111 35.39N 97.29W
Edmonton Canada 100 53.30N 113.30W
Edmundston Canada 103 47.22N 68.20W
Edna U.S.A. 111 28.59N 96.39W
Edo r. Japan 57 35.37N 139.53E
Edo d. Nigeria 77 6.20N 5.55E
Edolo Italy 30 46.11N 10.20E
Edouar r. Germany 38 51.13N 9.27E
Edremit Turkey 29 39.35N 27.02E
Edremit Körfezi b. Turkey 34 39.30N 26.45E
Edsbruk Sweden 43 58.02N 16.28E
Edson Canada 100 53.35N 116.26W
Edward, L. Uganda/Zaïre 79 0.30S 29.30E
Edwards Plateau f. U.S.A. 111 31.20N 101.00W
Eekio Belgium 16 51.11N 3.34E
Eel r. U.S.A. 108 40.40N 124.20W
Efate i. Vanuatu 84 17.40S 168.25E
Eferding Austria 39 48.18N 14.02E
Effingham U.S.A. 112 39.07N 88.33W
Ega r. Spain 25 42.19N 1.55W
Egadi, Isole is. Italy 32 38.00N 12.10E
Egaña Argentina 125 36.57S 59.06W
Eganville Canada 105 45.32N 77.06W
Egbe Nigeria 77 8.13N 5.31E
Egeland U.S.A. 110 48.38N 99.10W
Eger Hungary 37 47.54N 20.23E
Egersund Norway 42 58.27N 6.00E
Egerton, Mt. Australia 88 24.44S 117.40E
Eggenfelden Germany 39 48.25N 12.46E
Egg Harbor U.S.A. 115 39.32N 74.39W
Égletons France 20 45.24N 2.03E
Egmont, Mt. see Taranaki, Mt. New Zealand 86
Eğridir Turkey 64 37.52N 30.51E
Eğridir Gölü l. Turkey 64 38.04N 30.55E
Egtved Denmark 42 55.37N 9.18E
Egypt Africa 72 26.00N 30.00E
Ehingen Germany 39 48.17N 9.43E
Eiao i. Îs. Marquises 85 8.00S 140.40W
Éibar Spain 26 43.11N 2.28W
Eibiswald Austria 31 46.41N 15.15E
Eichstätt Germany 38 48.54N 11.12E
Eidsvåg Norway 40 62.47N 8.03E
Eidsvold Australia 90 25.23S 151.08E
Eidsvoll Norway 42 60.19N 11.14E
Eifel f. Germany 39 50.10N 6.40E
Eigg i. U.K. 14 56.53N 6.09W
Eighty Mile Beach f. Australia 88 19.00S 121.00E
Eildon, L. Australia 93 37.10S 146.00E
Eilenburg Germany 38 51.27N 12.37E
Eil, Loch U.K. 14 56.51N 5.12W
Einasleigh Australia 90 18.31S 144.05E
Einbeck Germany 38 51.49N 9.52E
Eindhoven Neth. 16 51.26N 5.30E
Einsiedeln Switz. 39 47.08N 8.45E
Eirunepé Brazil 122 6.40S 69.52W
Eiseb r. Namibia 80 20.26S 20.05E
Eisenach Germany 38 50.59N 10.19E
Eisenberg Germany 38 50.58N 11.53E
Eisenerz Austria 36 47.33N 14.53E
Eisenhut mtn. Austria 36 47.00N 13.45E
Eisenhüttenstadt Germany 38 52.10N 14.39E
Eisfeld Germany 38 50.26N 10.54E
Eisleben Germany 38 51.31N 11.32E
Eitorf Germany 38 50.46N 7.26E
Ejby Denmark 42 55.26N 9.57E
Ejde Faroe Is. 10 62.03N 7.06W
Ejea de los Caballeros Spain 25 42.08N 1.08W
Ejin Qi China 52 41.50N 100.50E
Ejura Ghana 76 7.24N 1.20W
Ekalaka U.S.A. 108 45.53N 104.33W
Eket Nigeria 77 4.39N 7.56E
Eketahuna New Zealand 86 40.39S 175.44E
Ekhínos Greece 34 41.17N 24.59E
Ekibastuz Kazakhstan 50 51.45N 75.22E
Ekimchan Russian Fed. 51 53.09N 133.00E
Eksjö Sweden 43 57.40N 14.57E
Ekträsk Sweden 40 64.29N 19.50E
Ekuku Zaïre 78 0.42S 21.38E
Ekwan r. Canada 102 53.30N 84.00W

El Aaiún W. Sahara 74 27.09N 13.12W
El Alia Tunisia 32 37.10N 10.03E
Elands r. Trans. R.S.A. 80 24.52S 29.20E
El Arahal Spain 27 37.16N 5.33W
El Arco Mexico 109 28.00N 113.25W
El Arenal Spain 25 39.30N 2.45E
El Asnam Algeria 75 36.10N 1.20E
Elassón Greece 34 39.54N 22.11E
Elat Israel 66 29.33N 34.56E
Elâzığ Turkey 64 38.41N 39.14E
Elba i. Italy 30 42.46N 10.17E
El Barco de Avila Spain 26 40.21N 5.31W
El Barco de Valdeorras Spain 26 42.25N 6.59W
El Barril Mexico 109 28.22N 113.00W
Elbasan Albania 34 41.07N 20.09E
Elbasan Berat d. Albania 34 40.58N 20.00E
El Baúl Venezuela 122 8.59N 68.16W
Elbe r. Germany 38 53.50N 8.14W
Elbe-Havel-Kanal Germany 38 52.23N 12.15E
Elbe-Lübeck-Kanal Germany 38 53.50N 10.36E
El Beni d. Bolivia 124 14.00S 65.30W
Elbert, Mt. U.S.A. 110 39.07N 106.27W
Elberton U.S.A. 113 34.05N 82.54W
Elbeuf France 18 49.17N 1.00E
Elbistan Turkey 64 38.14N 37.11E
Elblâg Poland 37 54.10N 19.25E
El Bonillo Spain 26 38.57N 2.32W
Elbrus mtn. Russian Fed. 45 43.21N 42.29E
Elburg Neth. 16 52.27N 5.50E
El Burgo de Osma Spain 26 41.35N 3.04W
Elburz Mts. see Alborz, Reshteh-ye Kûhhâ- ye Iran 65
El Cajon U.S.A. 109 32.48N 116.58W
El Callao Venezuela 122 7.18N 61.48W
El Campo U.S.A. 111 29.12N 96.16W
El Casco Mexico 111 25.34N 104.35W
El Cenajo, Embalse de resr. Spain 27 38.25N 2.00W
El Centro U.S.A. 109 32.48N 115.34W
Elche Spain 25 38.16N 0.42W
Elche de la Sierra Spain 25 38.27N 2.03W
Elcho U.S.A. 110 45.26N 89.11W
Elcho I. Australia 90 11.55S 135.45E
El Corral Mexico 111 25.09N 97.58W
El Cozón Mexico 109 31.18N 112.29W
El Cuy Argentina 125 39.57S 68.20W
Elda Spain 25 38.29N 0.47W
Elde r. Germany 38 53.17N 12.40E
El Der Ethiopia 71 5.08N 43.08E
Elder, L. Australia 92 30.39S 140.13E
El Desemboque Mexico 109 29.30N 112.27W
Eldon U.S.A. 110 38.21N 93.35W
Eldorado Canada 101 59.35N 108.30W
El Dorado Ark. U.S.A. 111 33.13N 92.40W
El Dorado Kans. U.S.A. 111 37.49N 96.52W
El Dorado Venezuela 122 6.45N 61.37W
Eldoret Kenya 79 0.31N 35.17E
Eldsdro Sweden 43 59.53N 18.33E
Electra U.S.A. 111 34.02N 98.55W
El Eglab f. Algeria 74 26.30N 4.15W
Elei, Wâdî Sudan 72 22.04N 34.27E
Eleja Latvia 41 56.25N 23.42E
Elektrosal Russian Fed. 44 55.46N 38.30E
Elena Bulgaria 34 42.56N 25.53E
Elephant Butte Resr. U.S.A. 109 33.19N 107.10W
Elephant I. Atlantic Oc. 121 61.00S 55.00W
El Eulma Algeria 75 36.09N 5.41E
Eleuthera I. Bahamas 113 25.15N 76.20W
Elevsís Greece 35 38.02N 23.33E
Elevtheroúpolis Greece 34 40.55N 24.16E
El Ferrol Spain 26 43.29N 8.14W
Elgâ Norway 41 62.11N 11.07E
Elgenfield Canada 104 43.10N 81.22W
Elgin l. Ont. Canada 105 44.36N 76.13W
Elgin l. Man. Canada 101 49.26N 100.15W
Elgin U.K. 14 57.39N 3.20W
Elgin Ill. U.S.A. 110 42.03N 88.19W
Elgin Nev. U.S.A. 108 37.21N 114.30W
Elgin Oreg. U.S.A. 108 45.34N 117.55W
Elgin Tex. U.S.A. 111 30.21N 97.22W
El Golea Algeria 75 30.34N 2.53E
Elgon, Mt. Kenya/Uganda 79 1.07N 34.35E
El Grove Spain 26 42.30N 8.52W
El Haouaria Tunisia 32 37.03N 11.02E
Elida U.S.A. 111 33.57N 103.39W
Elim Namibia 80 17.47S 15.30E
Elin Pelin Bulgaria 34 42.40N 23.38E
Elista Russian Fed. 45 46.18N 44.14E
Elizabeth Australia 92 34.45S 138.39E
Elizabeth N.J. U.S.A. 115 40.40N 74.11W
Elizabeth U.S.A. 114 40.16N 79.53W
Elizabeth City U.S.A. 113 36.18N 76.16W
Elizabethton U.S.A. 113 36.21N 82.13W
Elizabethtown Ky. U.S.A. 113 37.41N 85.51W
Elizabethtown N.Y. U.S.A. 115 44.13N 73.36W
Elizabethtown Penn. U.S.A. 115 40.09N 76.36W
El Jadida Morocco 74 33.16N 8.30W
Elk r. Canada 100 49.10N 115.14W
Elk Poland 37 53.50N 22.22E
Elk r. U.S.A. 114 38.21N 81.38W
El Kairouan Tunisia 75 35.41N 10.07E
El Kala Algeria 32 36.50N 8.30E
El Kasserine Tunisia 75 35.11N 8.48E
Elk City U.S.A. 111 35.25N 99.25W
El Kef Tunisia 75 36.11N 8.43E
El-Kelâa-des-Srarhna Morocco 74 32.02N 7.23W
Êl Kerê Ethiopia 73 5.48N 42.10E
Elkhart Ind. U.S.A. 110 41.52N 85.56W
Elkhart Kans. U.S.A. 111 37.00N 101.54W
El Khnâchîch f. Mali 76 21.50N 3.45W
Elkhorn Canada 101 49.58N 101.14W
Elkhorn r. U.S.A. 110 41.07N 96.21W
Elkhovo Bulgaria 34 42.09N 26.36E
Elkins N.Mex. U.S.A. 109 33.41N 104.04W
Elkins W.Va. U.S.A. 114 38.55N 79.51W
Elkland U.S.A. 114 41.59N 77.21W
Elko U.S.A. 108 40.50N 115.46W
Elkton Md. U.S.A. 115 39.36N 75.50W
Elkton Va. U.S.A. 114 38.25N 78.38W
Elleker Australia 89 34.55S 117.40E
Ellenboro U.S.A. 114 39.17N 81.04W

Ellenburg U.S.A. **105** 44.54N 73.51W
Ellendale Australia **88** 17.56S 124.48E
Ellen, Mt. U.S.A. **106** 38.06N 110.50W
Ellensburg U.S.A. **108** 47.00N 120.32W
Ellenville U.S.A. **115** 41.43N 74.24W
Ellesmere I. Canada **99** 78.00N 82.00W
Ellesmere Port U.K. **12** 53.17N 2.55W
Ellicottville U.S.A. **114** 42.17N 78.40W
Elliot R.S.A. **80** 31.19S 27.49E
Elliot Lake *town* Canada **104** 46.23N 82.39W
Elliott Australia **90** 17.33S 133.31E
Elliott U.S.A. **110** 38.56N 99.34W
Elliston Australia **92** 33.39S 134.55E
Ellon U.K. **14** 57.22N 2.05W
Ellora India **62** 20.01N 75.10E
Ellwangen Germany **39** 48.57N 10.07E
Ellwood City U.S.A. **114** 40.50N 80.17W
Elm Switz. **39** 46.55N 9.11E
El Mahdía Tunisia **75** 35.30N 11.04E
Elmali Turkey **64** 36.43N 29.56E
El Maneadero Mexico **109** 31.45N 116.35W
Elmer U.S.A. **115** 39.36N 75.10W
El Metlaoui Tunisia **75** 34.20N 8.24E
Elmhurst U.S.A. **110** 41.54N 87.56W
Elmina Ghana **76** 5.07N 1.21W
Elmira Canada **104** 43.36N 80.33W
Elmira U.S.A. **114** 42.06N 76.49W
El Molinillo Spain **27** 39.28N 4.13W
Elmore Australia **93** 36.30S 144.40E
El Mreiti *well* Mauritania **74** 23.29N 7.52W
El Mreyyé *f.* Mauritania **74** 19.30N 7.00W
Elmshorn Germany **38** 53.45N 9.39E
Elmsta Sweden **43** 59.58N 18.45E
Elmvale Canada **104** 44.35N 79.52W
Elne France **20** 42.36N 2.58E
El Niybo Ethiopia **79** 4.32N 39.59E
El Ouassi *well* Mali **76** 20.23N 0.12E
El Oued Algeria **75** 33.20N 6.53E
Eloy U.S.A. **109** 32.45N 111.33W
El Paso U.S.A. **111** 31.45N 106.29W
El Portal U.S.A. **108** 37.41N 119.47W
El Prat de Llobregat Spain **25** 41.20N 2.06E
El Puente del Arzobispo Spain **27** 39.48N 5.10W
El Quelite Mexico **109** 23.32N 106.28W
El Real Panama **117** 8.06N 77.42W
El Reno U.S.A. **111** 35.32N 97.57W
El Roba Kenya **79** 3.57N 40.01E
Elrose Canada **101** 51.13N 108.01W
El Salto Mexico **109** 23.47N 105.22W
El Salvador C. America **117** 13.30N 89.00W
Elsas Canada **102** 48.32N 82.55W
Elsdorf Germany **16** 50.56N 6.35E
Elsfleth Germany **38** 53.14N 8.28E
Elsinore U.S.A. **108** 38.41N 112.09W
Elspe Germany **38** 51.09N 8.04E
Elsterwerda Germany **38** 51.28N 13.31E
El Sueco Mexico **109** 29.54N 106.24W
El Tabacal Argentina **124** 23.15S 64.14W
El Tarf Algeria **32** 36.45N 8.20E
El Tigre Venezuela **122** 8.44N 64.18W
Eltmann Germany **39** 49.58N 10.40E
Elton, Ozero *l.* Russian Fed. **45** 49.10N 46.34E
El Turbio Argentina **125** 51.41S 72.05W
Elūru India **61** 16.45N 81.10E
Elvas Portugal **27** 38.53N 7.10W
Elvdal Norway **41** 61.38N 11.56E
Elven France **18** 47.44N 2.35W
El Vendrell Spain **25** 41.13N 1.32E
Elverum Norway **41** 60.53N 11.34E
Elvira Argentina **125** 35.15S 59.30W
El Wak Kenya **79** 2.45N 40.52E
Elwood Nebr. U.S.A. **110** 40.36N 99.52W
Elwood N.J. U.S.A. **115** 39.35N 74.43W
Ely U.K. **11** 52.24N 0.16E
Ely Minn. U.S.A. **110** 47.53N 91.52W
Ely Nev. U.S.A. **108** 39.15N 114.53W
Elyria U.S.A. **114** 41.22N 82.06W
Elz *f.* Germany **39** 48.07N 7.45E

Ems-Jade Kanal Germany **38** 53.29N 7.35E
Emyvale Rep. of Ire. **15** 54.20N 6.59W
Enard B. U.K. **14** 58.05N 5.20W
Encarnación Paraguay **126** 27.20S 55.50W
Enchi Ghana **76** 5.53N 2.48W
Encinal U.S.A. **111** 28.02N 99.21W
Encino U.S.A. **109** 34.39N 105.28W
Encontada, Cerro de la *mtn.* Mexico **109** 27.03N 112.31W
Encontrados Venezuela **122** 9.03N 72.14W
Encounter B. Australia **92** 35.35S 138.44E
Endeavour Str. Australia **90** 10.50S 142.15E
Endeh Indonesia **59** 8.51S 121.40E
Enderbury I. Kiribati **84** 3.08S 171.05W
Enderby Canada **100** 50.35N 119.10W
Enderby Land *f.* Antarctica **128** 67.00S 53.00E
Enderlin U.S.A. **110** 46.37N 97.36W
Endicott U.S.A. **115** 42.06N 76.03W
Endicott Arm *f.* U.S.A. **100** 57.38N 133.22W
Endicott Mts. U.S.A. **98** 68.00N 152.00W
Endola Namibia **80** 17.37S 15.50E
Eneabba Australia **89** 29.48S 115.16E
Enewetak *i.* Pacific Oc. **84** 11.30N 162.15E
Enez Turkey **34** 40.44N 26.04E
Enfida Tunisia **75** 36.08N 10.22E
Enfield U.K. **13** 51.40N 0.05W
Enfield U.S.A. **115** 41.58N 72.36W
Engaño, C. Phil. **59** 18.30N 122.20E
Engcobo R.S.A. **80** 31.39S 28.01E
'En Gedi Israel **66** 31.28N 35.23E
Enggano *i.* Indonesia **58** 5.20S 102.15E
Enghershatu *mtn.* Eritrea **72** 16.40N 38.20E
Enghien Belgium **16** 50.42N 4.02E
England U.K. **12** 53.00N 2.00W
Englewood Colo. U.S.A. **108** 39.39N 104.59W
Englewood Fla. U.S.A. **113** 26.58N 82.21W
English Bāzār India **63** 25.00N 88.09E
English Channel U.K. **13** 50.15N 1.00W
English River *town* Canada **102** 49.20N 91.00W
Enguera Spain **25** 38.59N 0.41W
'En Harod Israel **67** 32.33N 35.23E
Enid U.S.A. **111** 36.19N 97.48W
Enkhuizen Neth. **16** 52.42N 5.17E
Enköping Sweden **43** 59.38N 17.04E
Enna Italy **33** 37.34N 14.17E
Ennadai Canada **101** 61.08N 100.53W
Ennadai L. Canada **101** 61.00N 101.00W
Ennedi *f.* Chad **72** 17.15N 22.00E
Enneri Yoo *wadi* Chad **77** 19.24N 16.38E
Enngonia Australia **93** 29.20S 145.53E
Ennis Rep. of Ire. **15** 52.51N 9.00W
Ennis U.S.A. **111** 32.20N 96.38W
Enniscorthy Rep. of Ire. **15** 52.30N 6.35W
Enniskillen U.K. **15** 54.21N 7.40W
Ennistymon Rep. of Ire. **15** 52.56N 9.18W
Enns *r.* Austria **36** 48.14N 14.22E
Enontekiö Finland **40** 68.23N 23.38E
Enosburg Falls U.S.A. **105** 44.55N 72.48W
Enping China **55** 22.11N 112.18E
Ensay Australia **93** 37.24S 147.52E
Enschede Neth. **16** 52.13N 6.54E
Ensenada Argentina **125** 34.51S 57.55W
Ensenada Baja Calif. Norte Mexico **109** 31.52N 116.37W
Ensenada Nuevo León Mexico **111** 25.56N 97.50W
Enshi China **55** 30.18N 109.29E
Enshū-nada *sea* Japan **57** 34.30N 137.30E
Entebbe Uganda **79** 0.08N 32.29E
Enterprise Canada **100** 60.47N 115.45W
Entinas, Punta *c.* Spain **27** 36.41N 2.46W
Entraygues France **20** 44.39N 2.34E
Entrepeñas, Embalse de *resr.* Spain **26** 40.34N 2.42W
Entre Ríos *d.* Argentina **125** 32.10S 59.00W
Entre Rios de Minas Brazil **126** 20.39S 44.06W
Entrocamento Portugal **27** 39.28N 8.28W
Entwistle Canada **100** 53.30N 115.00W
Enugu Nigeria **77** 6.20N 7.29E
Enugu *d.* Nigeria **77** 6.30N 7.30E
Envalira, Port d' *pass* France/Andorra **20** 42.35N 1.45E
Envermeu France **18** 49.54N 1.16E
Envigado Colombia **122** 6.09N 75.35W
Enza *r.* Italy **30** 44.54N 10.31E
Enzan Japan **57** 35.42N 138.44E
Eo *r.* Spain **26** 43.32N 7.03W
Eolie, Isole *is.* Italy **33** 38.50N 15.00E
Epanomi Greece **34** 40.26N 22.56E
Epe Neth. **16** 52.21N 5.59E
Epernay France **19** 49.03N 3.57E
Ephesus *site* Turkey **35** 37.55N 27.17E
Ephraim U.S.A. **108** 39.22N 111.35W
Ephrata Penn. U.S.A. **115** 40.11N 76.10W
Ephrata Wash. U.S.A. **108** 47.19N 119.33W
Epi *i.* Vanuatu **84** 16.43S 168.15E
Épila Spain **25** 41.36N 1.17W
Épinal France **19** 48.11N 6.27E
Epitálion Greece **35** 37.37N 21.30E
Epping U.K. **13** 51.42N 0.07E
Epping U.S.A. **115** 43.02N 71.04W
Epsom U.K. **13** 51.20N 0.16W
Epte *r.* France **19** 49.04N 1.37E
Equateur *d.* Zaïre **78** 0.00 21.00E
Equatorial Guinea Africa **78** 2.00N 10.00E
Equerdreville France **18** 49.40N 1.40W
Eraclea Italy **30** 45.35N 12.40E
Era, Ozero *l.* Russian Fed. **45** 47.38N 45.18E
Erbach Germany **39** 49.40N 8.59E
Erciyas Daği *mtn.* Turkey **64** 38.33N 35.25E
Erdevik Yugo. **31** 45.07N 19.25E
Erding Germany **39** 48.18N 11.54E
Erdre *r.* France **18** 47.11N 1.31W
Erebus, Mt. Antarctica **128** 77.40S 167.20E
Erechim Brazil **126** 27.35S 52.15W
Ereğli Konya Turkey **64** 37.30N 34.02E
Ereğli Zonguldak Turkey **64** 41.17N 31.26E
Erei, Monti *mts.* Italy **33** 37.30N 14.10E
Erenhot China **54** 43.48N 112.00E
Ērer *r.* Ethiopia **71** 7.35N 42.05E
Eresma *r.* Spain **26** 41.26N 4.45W

Eresós Greece **35** 39.11N 25.57E
Erétria Greece **35** 38.23N 23.50E
Erfoud Morocco **74** 31.28N 4.10W
Erft *r.* Germany **16** 51.12N 6.45E
Erfurt Germany **38** 50.58N 11.01E
Ergani Turkey **64** 38.17N 39.44E
Ergel Mongolia **54** 43.08N 109.05E
Ergene *r.* Turkey **29** 41.02N 26.22E
Erges *r. see* Erjas *r.* Spain **27**
Ergig *r.* Chad **77** 11.30N 15.30E
Eria *r.* Spain **26** 42.03N 5.44W
Erice Italy **32** 38.02N 12.36E
Ericeira Portugal **27** 38.59N 9.25W
Erie U.S.A. **114** 42.08N 80.04W
Erie, L. Canada/U.S.A. **114** 42.15N 81.00W
Eriksdale Canada **101** 50.52N 98.06W
Erímanthos *mtn.* Greece **35** 37.59N 21.51E
Erimo misaki *c.* Japan **57** 41.55N 143.13E
Eriskay *i.* U.K. **14** 57.04N 7.17W
Erithraí Greece **35** 38.13N 23.19E
Eritrea *f.* Ethiopia **72** 15.30N 38.00E
Erjas *r.* Portugal **27** 39.47N 7.00W
Erkelenz Germany **16** 51.04N 6.19E
Erldunda Australia **90** 25.14S 133.12E
Erlangen Germany **38** 49.36N 11.01E
Erlano Germany **38** 52.25N 13.45E
Erkner Germany **38** 52.25N 13.45E
Ermelo Neth. **16** 52.19N 5.38E
Ermelo R.S.A. **80** 26.30S 29.59E
Ermidas Portugal **27** 38.00N 8.23W
Ermióni Greece **35** 37.23N 23.15E
Ermoúpolis Greece **35** 37.26N 24.56E
Erne *r.* Rep. of Ire. **11** 54.30N 8.17W
Ernée France **18** 48.18N 0.56W
Ernest U.S.A. **114** 40.41N 79.10W
Erode India **60** 11.21N 77.43E
Eromanga *i.* Vanuatu **84** 18.45S 169.05E
Erota Eritrea **72** 16.13N 37.57E
Er Rachidia Morocco **74** 31.58N 4.25W
Errego Mozambique **79** 16.02S 37.11E
Er Reina Israel **67** 32.43N 35.18E
Errenteria *see* Rentería Spain **26**
Errigal Mtn. Rep. of Ire. **15** 55.02N 8.08W
Erris Head Rep. of Ire. **15** 54.19N 10.00W
Erstein France **19** 48.26N 7.40E
Ertix He *r.* Kazakhstan **52** 48.00N 84.20E
Erudina Australia **92** 31.30S 139.23E
Ervy-le-Châtel France **19** 48.02N 3.55E
Erzgebirge *mts.* Germany **38** 50.34N 13.00E
Erzin Russian Fed. **52** 50.16N 95.14E
Erzincan Turkey **64** 39.44N 39.30E
Erzurum Turkey **64** 39.57N 41.17E
Esbjerg Denmark **42** 55.28N 8.27E
Esbo *see* Espoo Finland **41**
Esca *r.* Spain **25** 42.37N 1.03W
Escalante U.S.A. **108** 37.47N 111.36W
Escalón Mexico **111** 26.45N 104.20W
Escalona Spain **26** 40.10N 4.24W
Escanaba U.S.A. **112** 45.47N 87.04W
Escandón, Puerto de *pass* Spain **25** 40.17N 1.00W
Esch Lux. **16** 49.31N 5.59E
Eschau France **19** 48.29N 7.43E
Eschwege Germany **38** 51.11N 10.04E
Eschweiler Germany **38** 50.49N 6.16E
Escondido *r.* Nicaragua **117** 11.58N 83.45W
Escondido U.S.A. **109** 33.07N 117.05W
Escuinapa Mexico **109** 22.51N 105.48W
Escuintla Guatemala **116** 14.18N 90.47W
Esens Germany **38** 53.39N 7.37E
Ésera *r.* Spain **25** 42.06N 0.15E
Esfahān Iran **65** 32.42N 51.40E
Esgueva *r.* Spain **26** 41.40N 4.43W
Eshbol Israel **67** 31.27N 34.40E
Esher U.K. **13** 51.23N 0.22W
Eshkanān Iran **65** 27.10N 53.38E
Eshowe R.S.A. **80** 28.53S 31.29E
Eshta'ol Israel **67** 31.47N 35.00E
Esk *r.* N. Yorks. U.K. **12** 54.29N 0.37W
Eskifjördhur *town* Iceland **40** 65.05N 14.00W
Eskilstrup Denmark **42** 54.51N 11.54E
Eskilstuna Sweden **43** 59.22N 16.30E
Eskimo Point *town* Canada **101** 61.10N 94.03W
Eskişehir Turkey **64** 39.46N 30.30E
Esla *r.* Spain **26** 41.29N 6.03W
Eslāmābād-e-Gharb Iran **65** 34.08N 46.35E
Eslöv Sweden **43** 55.50N 13.20E
Esmeraldas Ecuador **122** 0.56N 79.40W
Espalion France **20** 44.31N 2.46E
Espanola Canada **104** 46.15N 81.46W
Espanola U.S.A. **109** 36.00N 106.05W
Espe Kazakhstan **50** 43.50N 74.10E
Espejo Spain **27** 37.41N 4.33W
Espelkamp Germany **38** 52.25N 8.36E
Esperance Australia **89** 33.49S 121.52E
Esperance B. Australia **89** 33.51S 121.53E
Esperanza Argentina **125** 31.30S 61.00W
Esperanza Mexico **109** 27.35N 109.56W
Espichel, Cabo *c.* Portugal **27** 38.25N 9.13W
Espinal U.S.A. **109** 26.25N 75.00W
Espinhaço, Serra do *mts.* Brazil **126** 17.15S 43.10W
Espinho Portugal **26** 41.00N 8.38W
Espírito Santo *d.* Brazil **126** 20.00S 40.30W
Espíritu Santo *i.* Vanuatu **84** 15.50S 166.50E
Esposende Portugal **26** 41.32N 8.47W
Espuña, Sierra de *mts.* Spain **25** 37.50N 1.40E
Espungabera Mozambique **80** 20.28S 32.48E
Esquel Argentina **125** 42.55S 71.20W
Esquimalt Canada **100** 48.30N 123.23W
Esquina Argentina **125** 30.00S 59.30W
Essaouira Morocco **74** 31.30N 9.47W
Essen Belgium **16** 51.28N 4.28E
Essen Germany **38** 51.28N 7.01E
Essequibo *r.* Guyana **122** 6.30N 58.40W
Essex Canada **104** 42.10N 82.49W
Essex *d.* U.K. **13** 51.46N 0.30E
Essex U.S.A. **109** 34.45N 115.15W
Essex Junction U.S.A. **105** 44.29N 73.07W

Essexville U.S.A. **104** 43.37N 83.50W
Esslingen Germany **39** 48.45N 9.16E
Essonne *d.* France **19** 48.36N 2.20E
Essoyes France **19** 48.04N 4.32E
Essoyla Russian Fed. **44** 61.47N 33.11E
Es Suki Sudan **73** 13.24N 33.55E
Est *d.* Burkina **76** 12.45N 0.25E
Estaca de Bares, Punta de la *c.* Spain **26** 43.46N 7.42W
Estacado, Llano *f.* U.S.A. **111** 33.30N 102.40W
Estados, Isla de los *i.* Argentina **125** 54.45S 64.00W
Eşţahbānāt Iran **65** 29.05N 54.03E
Estaire Canada **104** 46.21N 80.47W
Estância Brazil **123** 11.15S 37.28W
Estand, Kūh-e *mtn.* Iran **65** 31.18N 60.03E
Estarreja Portugal **26** 40.45N 8.34W
Estats, Pic d' *mtn.* Spain **25** 42.40N 1.23E
Este Italy **30** 45.14N 11.39E
Estelí Nicaragua **97** 13.05N 86.23W
Estella Spain **26** 42.40N 2.02W
Estelline U.S.A. **111** 34.33N 100.26W
Estepa Spain **27** 37.18N 4.54W
Estepona Spain **27** 36.26N 5.08W
Esternay France **19** 48.44N 3.34E
Estevan Canada **101** 49.07N 103.05W
Estevan Is. Canada **100** 53.03N 129.38W
Estevan Pt. Canada **100** 49.23N 126.33W
Estherville U.S.A. **110** 43.24N 94.50W
Estissac France **19** 48.16N 3.49E
Estivane Mozambique **81** 24.07S 32.38E
Eston U.S.A. **12** 54.34N 1.07W
Estonia Europe **44** 59.00N 25.00E
Estoril Portugal **27** 38.42N 9.23W
Est, Pointe de l' *c.* Canada **103** 49.08N 61.41W
Estrela *mtn.* Portugal **26** 40.19N 7.37W
Estrela, Serra da *mts.* Portugal **26** 40.20N 7.40W
Estremoz Portugal **27** 38.51N 7.35W
Esztergom Hungary **37** 47.48N 18.45E
Étables France **18** 48.38N 2.50W
Etadunna Australia **92** 28.43S 138.38E
Etah India **63** 27.38N 78.40E
Étain France **19** 49.13N 5.38E
Etamamiou Canada **103** 50.16N 59.58W
Étampes France **19** 48.26N 2.09E
Étaples France **19** 50.31N 1.39E
Etāwah India **63** 26.46N 79.02E
Ethel Creek *town* Australia **88** 23.05S 120.14E
Ethiopia Africa **73** 9.00N 39.00E
Etive, Loch U.K. **14** 56.27N 5.15W
Etna, Monte *mtn.* Italy **33** 37.46N 15.00E
Etne Norway **42** 59.40N 5.56E
Etolin I. U.S.A. **100** 56.10N 132.30W
Etosha Game Res. Namibia **80** 18.50S 15.40E
Etosha Pan *f.* Namibia **80** 18.50S 16.20E
Etowah U.S.A. **113** 35.20N 84.30W
Étretat France **18** 49.42N 0.12E
Etropole Bulgaria **34** 42.50N 24.00E
Et Taiyiba Israel **67** 32.16N 35.01E
Et Tira Israel **67** 32.14N 34.57E
Ettlingen Germany **39** 48.56N 8.24E
Eu France **18** 50.03N 1.25E
Eua *i.* Tonga **85** 21.23S 174.55W
Euabalong Australia **93** 33.07S 146.28E
Eubank U.S.A. **113** 37.16N 84.40W
Euboea *see* Évvoia *i.* Greece **35**
Eucla Australia **89** 31.40S 128.51E
Euclid U.S.A. **114** 41.34N 81.32W
Eucumbene, L. Australia **93** 36.05S 148.45E
Eudora U.S.A. **113** 33.07N 91.16W
Eudunda Australia **92** 34.09S 139.04E
Eufaula Resr. U.S.A. **107** 35.15N 95.35W
Eugene U.S.A. **108** 44.02N 123.05W
Eugenia, Punta *c.* Mexico **109** 27.50N 115.03W
Eugowra Australia **93** 33.24S 148.25E
Eume *r.* Spain **26** 43.25N 8.08W
Eunice La. U.S.A. **111** 30.30N 92.25W
Eunice N.Mex. U.S.A. **111** 32.26N 103.09W
Eupen Belgium **16** 50.38N 6.04E
Euphrates *r. see* Nahr al Furāt *r.* Asia **65**
Eurdon U.S.A. **111** 33.55N 93.09W
Eure *d.* France **18** 49.10N 1.00E
Eure *r.* France **18** 49.18N 1.12E
Eure-et-Loire *d.* France **18** 48.30N 1.30E
Eureka Calif. U.S.A. **108** 40.47N 124.09W
Eureka Kans. U.S.A. **111** 37.49N 96.17W
Eureka Nev. U.S.A. **108** 39.31N 115.58W
Eureka Utah U.S.A. **108** 39.57N 112.07W
Eurinilla *r.* Australia **92** 30.50S 140.01E
Euriowie Australia **92** 31.22S 141.42E
Euroa Australia **93** 36.46S 145.35E
Europa, Picos de *mts.* Spain **26** 43.10N 4.50W
Europa Pt. Gibraltar **27** 36.10N 5.22W
Europe **8**
Euskirchen Germany **38** 50.39N 6.47E
Euston Australia **92** 34.34S 142.49E
Eutin Germany **38** 54.08N 10.37E
Eutsuk L. Canada **100** 53.20N 126.45W
Evale Angola **78** 16.24S 15.50E
Evans Head *c.* Australia **93** 29.06S 153.25E
Evans, Lac *l.* Canada **102** 50.50N 77.00W
Evanston Ill. U.S.A. **110** 42.02N 87.41W
Evanston Wyo. U.S.A. **108** 41.16N 110.58W
Evansville U.S.A. **112** 38.00N 87.33W
Evelyn Creek *r.* Australia **92** 28.20S 134.50E
Even Yehuda Israel **67** 32.16N 34.53E
Everard, C. Australia **93** 37.50S 149.16E
Everard, L. Australia **92** 31.25S 135.05E
Everard Range *mts.* Australia **91** 27.05S 132.28E
Everest, Mt. China/Nepal **63** 27.59N 86.56E
Everett Penn. U.S.A. **114** 40.01N 78.23W
Everett Wash. U.S.A. **108** 47.59N 122.13W
Everett, Mt. U.S.A. **115** 42.06N 73.25W
Everglades U.S.A. **113** 25.52N 81.23W
Everglades Nat. Park U.S.A. **113** 25.27N 80.53W
Everöd Sweden **43** 55.54N 14.06E
Evesham U.K. **13** 52.06N 1.57W
Évian-les-Bains France **21** 46.23N 6.35E

Evijärvi Finland 40 63.22N 23.29E
Evinayong Equat. Guinea 78 1.27N 10.34E
Evisa France 21 42.15N 8.47E
Evje Norway 42 58.36N 7.51E
Évora Portugal 27 38.34N 7.54W
Évora d. Portugal 27 38.40N 7.55W
Évreux France 18 49.01N 1.09E
'Evron Israel 67 32.59N 35.06E
Évros r. see Meriç r. Greece 34
Evrótas r. Greece 35 36.48N 22.40E
Évry France 19 48.38N 2.27E
Évvoia i. Greece 35 38.40N 24.00E
Ewe, Loch U.K. 14 57.48N 5.38W
Ewing U.S.A. 110 42.16N 98.21W
Ewo Congo 78 0.48S 14.47E
Excelsior Springs town U.S.A. 110 39.20N 94.13W
Exe r. U.K. 13 50.40N 3.28W
Exeter Canada 104 43.21N 81.29W
Exeter U.K. 13 50.43N 3.31W
Exeter Nebr. U.S.A. 110 40.39N 97.27W
Exeter N.H. U.S.A. 115 42.59N 70.57W
Exmoor Forest hills U.K. 13 51.08N 3.45W
Exmore U.S.A. 113 37.32N 75.49W
Exmouth Australia 88 21.54S 114.10E
Exmouth U.K. 13 50.37N 3.24W
Exmouth G. Australia 88 22.00S 114.20E
Expedition Range mts. Australia 90 24.30S 149.05E
Extremadura d. Spain 27 39.25N 6.00W
Exuma Is. Bahamas 117 24.00N 76.00W
Eyasi, L. Tanzania 79 3.40S 35.00E
Eydehavn Norway 42 58.31N 8.53E
Eye U.K. 13 52.19N 1.09E
Eyemouth U.K. 14 55.52N 2.05W
Eygurande France 20 45.40N 2.26E
Eyjafjördhur est. Iceland 40 65.54N 18.15W
Eyl Somali Rep. 71 8.00N 49.51E
Eymet France 20 44.40N 0.24E
Eymoutiers France 20 45.44N 1.44E
Eyrarbakki Iceland 40 63.52N 21.09W
Eyre r. Australia 90 26.40S 139.00E
Eyre, L. Australia 92 28.30S 137.25E
Eyre Pen. Australia 92 34.00S 135.45E
Ezequil Ramos Mexia, Embalse resr. Argentina 125 39.20S 69.00W
Ezine Turkey 34 39.48N 26.12E

F

Faaone Tahiti 85 17.40S 149.18W
Fåberg Norway 41 61.10N 10.22E
Fåborg Denmark 42 55.06N 10.15E
Fabre Canada 104 47.12N 79.23W
Fabriano Italy 30 43.20N 12.54E
Facatativá Colombia 122 4.48N 74.32W
Facundo Argentina 125 45.19S 69.59W
Fada Chad 72 17.14N 21.33E
Fada-N'Gourma Burkina 76 12.03N 0.22E
Fadd Hungary 31 46.28N 18.50E
Faenza Italy 30 44.17N 11.53E
Fafa Mali 76 15.20N 0.43E
Fafe Portugal 26 41.27N 8.10W
Fafen r. Ethiopia 71 6.07N 44.20E
Fagamalo W. Samoa 84 13.24S 172.22W
Făgăraş Romania 37 45.51N 24.58E
Fagernes Norway 41 60.59N 9.17E
Fagersta Sweden 43 60.00N 15.47E
Faguibine, Lac l. Mali 76 16.45N 3.54W
Fagus Egypt 66 30.44N 31.47E
Fā'id Egypt 66 30.19N 32.19E
Fairbanks U.S.A. 98 64.50N 147.50W
Fairborn U.S.A. 112 39.48N 84.03W
Fairbury U.S.A. 110 40.08N 97.11W
Fairfax U.S.A. 111 36.34N 96.42W
Fairfield Ala. U.S.A. 113 33.29N 86.59W
Fairfield Calif. U.S.A. 108 38.15N 122.03W
Fairfield Conn. U.S.A. 115 41.09N 73.15W
Fairfield Ill. U.S.A. 110 38.22N 88.23W
Fairfield Iowa U.S.A. 110 40.56N 91.57W
Fairgrove U.S.A. 104 43.31N 83.33W
Fairhaven Mass. U.S.A. 115 41.39N 70.54W
Fair Haven N.Y. U.S.A. 114 43.19N 76.42W
Fair Haven Vt. U.S.A. 115 43.36N 73.16W
Fair Head U.K. 15 55.13N 6.09W
Fair Isle U.K. 14 59.32N 1.38W
Fairlie New Zealand 86 44.06S 170.50E
Fairmont Minn. U.S.A. 110 43.39N 94.28W
Fairmont W.Va. U.S.A. 114 39.29N 80.09W
Fairport U.S.A. 114 43.06N 77.27W
Fairport Harbor U.S.A. 114 41.45N 81.17W
Fairview Canada 100 56.05N 118.25W
Fairview Mich. U.S.A. 104 44.44N 84.03W
Fairview Mont. U.S.A. 108 47.51N 104.03W
Fairview Okla. U.S.A. 111 36.16N 98.29W
Fairview Penn. U.S.A. 114 42.03N 80.13W
Fairview Utah U.S.A. 108 39.38N 111.26W
Fairweather, Mt. U.S.A. 100 59.00N 137.30W
Faisalābād Pakistan 62 31.25N 73.05E
Faistós site Greece 35 35.01N 24.48E
Faith U.S.A. 110 45.02N 102.02W
Faizābād India 63 26.47N 82.08E
Fajr, Wādī r. Saudi Arabia 64 30.00N 38.25E
Fakaofo Pacific Oc. 84 9.30S 171.15W
Fakenham U.K. 12 52.50N 0.51E
Fakfak Indonesia 59 2.55S 132.17E
Fakse Denmark 43 55.15N 12.08E

Fakse Bugte b. Denmark 43 55.10N 12.15E
Falaise France 18 48.54N 0.12W
Falakrón Óros mts. Greece 34 41.15N 23.58E
Falam Myanmar 56 22.58N 93.45E
Falcarragh Rep. of Ire. 15 55.08N 8.06W
Falconara Marittima Italy 30 43.37N 13.24E
Falconbridge Canada 104 46.35N 80.48W
Falcone, Capo del c. Italy 32 40.57N 8.12E
Falconer U.S.A. 114 42.07N 79.12W
Falcon Resr. U.S.A. 111 26.37N 99.11W
Falealupo W. Samoa 84 13.29S 172.47W
Falémé r. Senegal 76 14.55N 12.00W
Faleshty Moldova 37 47.30N 27.45E
Falfurrias U.S.A. 111 27.14N 98.09W
Falkenberg Germany 38 51.35N 13.14E
Falkenberg Sweden 43 56.54N 12.28E
Falkenhagen Germany 38 53.12N 12.12E
Falkensee Germany 38 52.33N 13.04E
Falkenstein Germany 39 49.06N 12.30E
Falkirk U.K. 14 56.00N 3.48W
Falkland Is. Atlantic Oc. 125 51.45S 59.00W
Falkland Sd. str. Falkland Is. 125 51.45S 59.25W
Falköping Sweden 43 58.10N 13.31E
Fallbrook U.S.A. 109 33.23N 117.15W
Fallon U.S.A. 108 46.50N 105.07W
Fall River town U.S.A. 115 41.43N 71.08W
Falls City U.S.A. 110 40.03N 95.36W
Falmouth U.K. 13 50.09N 5.05W
Falmouth Mass. U.S.A. 115 41.34N 70.38W
Falmouth Va. U.S.A. 114 38.19N 77.28W
False B. R.S.A. 80 34.10S 18.40E
False C. U.S.A. 115 38.29N 74.59W
False Pt. India 63 20.22N 86.52E
Falset Spain 25 41.08N 0.49E
Falster i. Denmark 41 54.48N 11.58E
Falsterbo Sweden 43 55.24N 12.50E
Fălticeni Romania 37 47.28N 26.18E
Falun Sweden 41 60.36N 15.38E
Famagusta see Ammókhostos Cyprus 66
Family L. Canada 101 51.54N 95.30W
Famoso U.S.A. 109 35.36N 119.14W
Fanárion Greece 34 39.50N 21.47E
Fandriana Madagascar 81 20.14S 47.23E
Fangak Sudan 73 9.04N 30.53E
Fangcheng China 54 33.16N 112.59E
Fangdou Shan mts. China 55 30.36N 108.45E
Fang Xian China 55 32.04N 110.47E
Fanjing Shan mtn. China 55 27.57N 108.50E
Fannich, Loch U.K. 14 57.38N 5.00W
Fanning I. see Tabuaeran i. Kiribati 85
Fanø i. Denmark 42 55.25N 8.25E
Fano Italy 30 43.50N 13.00E
Fan Xian China 54 35.59N 115.31E
Faradje Zaïre 79 3.45N 29.43E
Faradofay Madagascar 81 25.02S 47.00E
Farafangana Madagascar 81 22.49S 47.50E
Farāfirah, Wāḩāt al oasis Egypt 64 27.15N 28.10E
Farāh Afghan. 62 32.22N 62.07E
Farāh d. Afghan. 62 33.00N 62.00E
Farāh r. Afghan. 62 31.29N 61.24E
Faranah Guinea 76 10.01N 10.47W
Farasān, Jazā'ir is. Saudi Arabia 72 16.48N 41.54E
Faratsiho Madagascar 81 19.24S 46.57E
Faraulep is. Federated States of Micronesia 59 8.36N 144.33E
Fardes r. Spain 27 37.35N 3.00W
Fareara, Pt. Tahiti 85 17.52S 149.39W
Fareham U.K. 13 50.52N 1.11W
Farewell, C. see Farvel, Kap c. Greenland 99
Farewell, C. New Zealand 86 40.30S 172.35E
Färgelanda Sweden 42 58.34N 11.59E
Fargo U.S.A. 110 46.52N 96.48W
Färi'ah r. Jordan 67 32.06N 35.31E
Faribault U.S.A. 110 44.18N 93.16W
Faridpur Bangla. 63 23.36N 89.50E
Farim Guinea Bissau 76 12.30N 15.09W
Farina Australia 92 30.05S 138.20E
Färjestaden Sweden 43 56.39N 16.27E
Farkwa Tanzania 79 5.26S 35.15E
Farley Canada 105 46.18N 76.00W
Farmerville U.S.A. 111 32.47N 92.24W
Farmington Mo. U.S.A. 111 37.47N 90.25W
Farmington N.H. U.S.A. 115 43.24N 71.04W
Farmington N.Mex. U.S.A. 108 36.44N 108.12W
Farnborough U.K. 13 51.17N 0.46W
Farne Is. U.K. 12 55.38N 1.36W
Farnham Canada 105 45.17N 72.59W
Farnham U.K. 13 51.13N 0.49W
Faro Brazil 123 2.11S 56.44W
Faro Portugal 27 37.01N 7.56W
Faro d. Portugal 27 37.15N 8.10W
Faroe Bank f. Atlantic Oc. 10 61.00N 9.00W
Faroe Is. Europe 10 62.00N 7.00W
Fårön i. Sweden 43 57.56N 19.08E
Fårösund Sweden 43 57.52N 19.03E
Farrell U.S.A. 114 41.13N 80.30W
Farrukhābād India 63 27.24N 79.34E
Fársala Greece 35 39.18N 22.23E
Färsö Denmark 42 56.47N 9.21E
Farson U.S.A. 108 42.06N 109.27W
Farsund Norway 42 58.05N 6.48E
Fartak, Ra's c. Yemen 71 15.38N 52.15E
Farvel, Kap c. Greenland 99 60.00N 44.20W
Farwell U.S.A. 111 34.23N 103.02W
Fasā Iran 65 28.55N 53.38E
Fasano Italy 33 40.50N 17.22E
Fastov Ukraine 37 50.08N 29.59E
Fatehābād India 62 29.31N 75.28E
Fatehjang Pakistan 62 33.34N 72.39E
Fatehpur Rāj. India 62 27.59N 74.57E
Fatehpur Uttar P. India 63 25.56N 80.48E
Fatehpur Pakistan 62 31.10N 71.13E
Fatehpur Sīkri India 63 27.06N 77.40E
Fatick Senegal 76 14.19N 16.27W
Fátima Portugal 27 39.37N 8.39W
Fatu Hiva i. Îs. Marquises 85 10.27S 138.39W
Fatwā India 63 25.31N 85.19E
Faucilles, Monts mts. France 19 48.07N 6.16E

Faulkton U.S.A. 110 45.02N 99.08W
Faulquemont France 19 49.03N 6.36E
Făurei Romania 37 45.04N 27.15E
Fauske Norway 40 67.17N 15.25E
Favara Italy 32 37.19N 13.40E
Faverges France 21 45.45N 6.18E
Favignana i. Italy 32 37.56N 12.19E
Fawcett Canada 100 54.34N 114.06W
Fawcett L. Canada 102 51.20N 91.46W
Fawn r. Canada 102 55.20N 88.20W
Faxaflói b. Iceland 40 64.30N 22.50W
Faxe r. Sweden 40 63.15N 17.15E
Fayence France 21 43.37N 6.41E
Fayette U.S.A. 113 33.42N 87.50W
Fayetteville Ark. U.S.A. 111 36.04N 94.10W
Fayetteville N.C. U.S.A. 113 35.03N 78.53W
Fayetteville N.Y. U.S.A. 115 43.02N 76.00W
Fayetteville Tenn. U.S.A. 113 35.08N 86.33W
Fayl-Billot France 19 47.47N 5.36E
Făzilka India 62 30.24N 74.02E
Fāzilpur Pakistan 62 29.18N 70.27E
Fdérik Mauritania 76 22.30N 12.30W
Feale r. Rep. of Ire. 15 52.28N 9.37W
Fear, C. U.S.A. 113 33.50N 77.58W
Fécamp France 18 49.45N 0.22E
Federación Argentina 125 31.00S 57.55W
Federal Argentina 125 30.55S 58.45W
Federal Capital Territory d. Nigeria 77 8.50N 7.00E
Federated States of Micronesia Pacific Oc. 84 10.00N 155.00E
Fedovo Russian Fed. 44 62.22N 39.21E
Fedulki Russian Fed. 44 65.00N 66.10E
Feeagh, Lough Rep. of Ire. 15 53.56N 9.35W
Feerfeer Somali Rep. 71 5.07N 45.07E
Fehmarn i. Germany 38 54.28N 11.08E
Fehmarn Belt str. Germany 38 54.33N 11.20E
Feia, Lagoa l. Brazil 126 22.00S 41.20W
Feijó Brazil 122 8.09S 70.21W
Feilding New Zealand 86 40.10S 175.25E
Feira Zambia 79 15.30S 30.27E
Feira de Santana Brazil 123 12.17S 38.53W
Felanitx Spain 25 39.28N 3.08E
Feldbach Austria 31 46.57N 15.54E
Feldberg mtn. Germany 39 47.51N 8.02E
Feldkirch Austria 39 47.14N 9.36E
Feldkirchen in Kärnten Austria 39 46.43N 14.05E
Felixstowe U.K. 13 51.58N 1.20E
Fellbach Germany 39 48.48N 9.15E
Felletin France 20 45.53N 2.10E
Feltre Italy 30 46.01N 11.54E
Femunden l. Norway 41 62.12N 11.52E
Femundsenden Norway 41 61.55N 11.55E
Fenelon Falls Canada 104 44.32N 78.45W
Fengcheng Jiangxi China 55 28.10N 115.45E
Fengcheng Liaoning China 54 40.29N 124.00E
Fengfeng China 54 36.35N 114.28E
Fenggang China 55 27.58N 107.47E
Fengjie China 55 31.02N 109.31E
Fengnan China 54 39.30N 117.58E
Fengpin Taiwan 55 23.36N 121.31E
Fengrun China 54 39.50N 118.08E
Fen He r. China 54 35.30N 110.38E
Feni Bangla. 63 23.01N 91.20E
Fenoarivo Madagascar 81 18.26S 46.34E
Fenoarivo Atsinanana Madagascar 81 17.22S 49.25E
Feno, Capo di c. France 21 41.57N 8.36E
Fensfjorden est. Norway 41 60.51N 4.50E
Fenton U.S.A. 112 42.48N 83.42W
Fenwick U.S.A. 114 38.14N 80.35W
Fenyang China 54 37.14N 111.40E
Feodosiya Ukraine 45 45.03N 35.23E
Ferdows Iran 65 34.00N 58.10E
Fère-Champenoise France 19 48.45N 3.59E
Fère-en-Tardenois France 19 49.12N 3.31E
Ferentino Italy 32 41.42N 13.15E
Fergana Uzbekistan 52 40.23N 71.19E
Fergus Canada 104 43.42N 80.22W
Fergus Falls town U.S.A. 110 46.17N 96.04W
Ferguson U.S.A. 110 38.46N 90.19W
Fergusson I. P.N.G. 90 9.30S 150.40E
Ferkéssédougou Côte d'Ivoire 76 9.30N 5.10W
Ferlach Austria 31 46.31N 14.18E
Fermanagh d. U.K. 15 54.21N 7.40W
Fermo Italy 31 43.09N 13.43E
Fermoselle Spain 26 41.19N 6.23W
Fermoy Rep. of Ire. 15 52.08N 8.17W
Fernandina Beach town U.S.A. 113 30.40N 81.26W
Fernando de Noronha i./Atlantic Oc. 127 3.50S 32.25W
Fernán-Núñez Spain 27 37.40N 4.43W
Fernlee Australia 93 28.12S 147.05E
Férrai Greece 34 40.53N 26.10E
Ferrandina Italy 33 40.29N 16.28E
Ferrara Italy 30 44.50N 11.35E
Ferrato, Capo c. Italy 32 39.18N 9.38E
Ferreira do Alentejo Portugal 27 38.03N 8.07W
Ferreñafe Peru 122 6.42S 79.45W
Ferret, Cap c. France 20 44.37N 1.15W
Ferriday U.S.A. 111 31.38N 91.33W
Ferrières France 19 48.05N 2.47E
Fès Morocco 74 34.05N 4.57W
Feshi Zaïre 78 6.08S 18.12E
Festubert Canada 105 47.12N 72.40W
Festus U.S.A. 110 38.13N 90.24W
Feteşti Romania 37 44.23N 27.50E
Fethiye Turkey 64 36.37N 29.06E
Fetlar i. U.K. 14 60.37N 0.52W
Fetsund Norway 42 59.56N 11.10E
Feucht Germany 38 49.22N 11.13E
Feuchtwangen Germany 39 49.10N 10.20E
Feuilles, Rivière aux r. Canada 99 58.47N 70.06W
Feurs France 21 45.45N 4.14E
Fevik Norway 42 58.23N 8.42E
Fevzipaşa Turkey 64 37.07N 36.38E
Fianarantsoa Madagascar 81 21.26S 47.05E
Fichê Ethiopia 73 9.52N 38.46E
Fichtel Gebirge mts. Germany 38 50.00N 11.50E
Fidenza Italy 30 44.52N 10.03E
Field Canada 104 46.32N 80.03W

Fier Albania 34 40.43N 19.33E
Fiesch Switz. 36 46.20N 8.10E
Fife d. U.K. 14 56.10N 3.10W
Fife Ness c. U.K. 14 56.17N 2.36W
Figeac France 20 44.37N 2.02E
Figeholm Sweden 43 57.22N 16.33E
Figueira da Foz Portugal 26 40.09N 8.52W
Figueras Spain 25 42.16N 2.58E
Figueres see Figueras Spain 25
Fihaonana Madagascar 81 18.36S 47.12E
Fiherenana r. Madagascar 81 23.19S 43.37E
Fiji Pacific Oc. 84 18.00S 178.00E
Fik' Ethiopia 71 8.10N 42.18E
Filabres, Sierra de los mts. Spain 27 37.13N 2.20W
Filabusi Zimbabwe 80 20.34S 29.20E
Filadelfia Italy 33 38.48N 16.18E
Fildegrand r. Canada 105 46.18N 77.51W
Filey U.K. 12 54.13N 0.18W
Fili site Greece 35 38.10N 23.40E
Filiaşi Romania 37 44.33N 23.31E
Filiátes Greece 34 39.38N 20.16E
Filiatrá Greece 35 37.09N 21.35E
Filicudi, Isola i. Italy 33 38.35N 14.34E
Filingué Niger 77 14.21N 3.22E
Filippoi site Greece 34 41.00N 24.16E
Filipstad Sweden 43 59.43N 14.10E
Fillmore Canada 101 49.50N 103.25W
Fillmore Calif. U.S.A. 109 34.24N 118.55W
Fillmore Utah U.S.A. 108 38.58N 112.20W
Filtu Ethiopia 73 5.05N 40.42E
Fimi r. Zaïre 78 3.00S 17.00E
Finale Emilia Italy 30 44.50N 11.17E
Finale Ligure Italy 30 44.10N 8.20E
Finarwa Ethiopia 73 13.05N 38.58E
Finch Canada 105 45.11N 75.07W
Findhorn r. U.K. 14 57.38N 3.37W
Findlay U.S.A. 112 41.02N 83.40W
Findlay, Mt. Canada 100 50.04N 116.10W
Finger Lakes U.S.A. 114 42.55N 76.44W
Finistère d. France 18 48.20N 4.00W
Finisterre, Cabo de c. Spain 26 42.53N 9.16W
Finke Australia 90 25.35S 134.34E
Finke r. Australia 91 27.00S 136.10E
Finland Europe 44 64.30N 27.00E
Finland, G. of Finland/Estonia 41 59.30N 24.00E
Finlay r. Canada 100 57.00N 125.05W
Finley Australia 93 35.40S 145.34E
Finmark Canada 102 48.36N 89.44W
Finn r. Rep. of Ire. 15 54.50N 7.30W
Finnmark d. Norway 40 70.10N 26.00E
Finschhafen P.N.G. 59 6.35S 147.51E
Finse Norway 41 60.36N 7.30E
Finspång Sweden 43 58.43N 15.47E
Finsterwalde Germany 38 51.38N 13.42E
Fiora r. Italy 30 42.20N 11.34E
Fiorenzuola d'Arda Italy 30 44.56N 9.55E
Fiq Syria 67 32.47N 35.42E
Firat r. Turkey see Al Furāt r. Asia 64
Firebag r. Canada 101 57.45N 111.20W
Firedrake L. Canada 101 61.25N 104.30W
Firenze Italy 30 43.46N 11.15E
Firenzuola Italy 30 44.07N 11.23E
Firminy France 21 45.23N 4.18E
Firozābād India 63 27.09N 78.25E
Firozpur India 62 30.55N 74.38E
Firozpur Jhirka India 62 27.48N 76.57E
Firth of Clyde est. U.K. 14 55.35N 4.53W
Firth of Forth est. U.K. 14 56.05N 3.00W
Firth of Lorn est. U.K. 14 56.20N 5.40W
Firth of Tay est. U.K. 14 56.24N 3.08W
Firūzābād Iran 65 28.50N 52.35E
Firyuza Turkmenistan 50 37.55N 58.03E
Fish r. Namibia 80 28.07S 17.45E
Fisher U.S.A. 111 35.30N 90.58W
Fishers L. U.S.A. 114 41.16N 72.02W
Fisher Str. Canada 99 63.00N 84.00W
Fishguard U.K. 13 51.59N 4.59W
Fiskárdhon Greece 35 38.27N 20.35E
Fiskebäcksill Sweden 42 58.15N 11.27E
Fiskenaesset Greenland 99 63.05N 50.40W
Fiskivötn l. Iceland 40 64.50N 20.45W
Fismes France 19 49.18N 3.41E
Fitchburg U.S.A. 115 42.35N 71.48W
Fitzgerald U.S.A. 113 31.43N 83.16W
Fitz Roy Argentina 125 47.00S 67.15W
Fitzroy r. Australia 88 17.31S 123.35E
Fitzroy Crossing Australia 88 18.13S 125.33E
Fitzwilliam I. Canada 104 45.30N 81.45W
Fiuggi Italy 32 41.48N 13.13E
Fiumicino Italy 32 41.46N 12.14E
Fivizzano Italy 30 44.14N 10.08E
Fizi Zaïre 79 4.18S 28.56E
Fjällåsen Sweden 40 67.29N 20.10E
Fjällbacka Sweden 42 58.36N 11.17E
Fjällsjo r. Sweden 40 63.27N 17.06E
Fjerritslev Denmark 42 57.05N 9.16E
Fjugesta Sweden 43 59.10N 14.52E
Flå Norway 41 60.25N 9.26E
Flagler U.S.A. 108 39.18N 103.04W
Flagstaff U.S.A. 109 35.12N 111.39W
Flagstaff B. St. Helena 127 15.55S 5.40W
Flåm Norway 41 60.50N 7.07E
Flamborough Head U.K. 12 54.06N 0.05W
Fläming f. Germany 38 52.00N 12.30E
Flaming Gorge Resr. U.S.A. 108 41.15N 109.30W
Flandre f. Belgium 16 51.00N 3.00E
Flannan Is. U.K. 14 58.16N 7.40W
Flåren l. Sweden 43 57.02N 14.06E
Flåsjön l. Sweden 40 64.06N 15.51E
Flat r. Canada 100 61.51N 126.00W
Flathead L. U.S.A. 108 47.52N 114.08W
Flatonia U.S.A. 111 29.47N 97.06W
Flattery, C. Australia 90 14.58S 145.21E
Flattery, C. U.S.A. 106 48.23N 124.43W
Flatts Village Bermuda 127 32.19N 64.44W
Flaxton U.S.A. 110 48.54N 102.24W
Fleetwood U.K. 12 53.55N 3.01W
Flekkefjord town Norway 42 58.17N 6.41E

Flemington U.S.A. **115** 40.31N 74.52W
Flen Sweden **43** 59.04N 16.35E
Flensburg Germany **38** 54.47N 9.26E
Flers France **18** 48.45N 0.34W
Flesherton Canada **104** 44.16N 80.33W
Fletcher Pond *resr.* U.S.A. **104** 44.58N 83.52W
Fleurance France **20** 43.50N 0.40E
Fleur-de-Lys Canada **103** 50.06N 56.08W
Flevoland *d.* Neth. **16** 52.25N 5.30E
Flinders *r.* Australia **90** 17.30S 140.45E
Flinders B. Australia **89** 34.23S 115.19E
Flinders I. S.A. Australia **92** 33.44S 134.30E
Flinders I. Tas. Australia **91** 40.00S 148.00E
Flinders Ranges *mts.* Australia **92** 31.25S 138.45E
Flinders Reefs Australia **90** 17.37S 148.31E
Flin Flon Canada **101** 54.46N 101.53W
Flint U.K. **12** 53.15N 3.07W
Flint U.S.A. **104** 43.01N 83.41W
Flint *r.* Ga. U.S.A. **113** 30.52N 84.38W
Flint *r.* Mich. U.S.A. **104** 43.21N 84.03W
Flint I. Kiribati **85** 11.26S 151.48W
Flinton Australia **91** 27.54S 149.34E
Flisa Norway **41** 60.34N 12.06E
Floby Sweden **43** 58.08N 13.20E
Floda Sweden **43** 57.48N 12.22E
Flora U.S.A. **110** 38.40N 88.30W
Florac France **20** 44.19N 3.36E
Florence *see* Firenze Italy **30**
Florence Ala. U.S.A. **113** 34.48N 87.40W
Florence Ariz. U.S.A. **109** 33.02N 111.23W
Florence Colo. U.S.A. **108** 38.23N 105.08W
Florence Oreg. U.S.A. **108** 43.58N 124.07W
Florence S.C. U.S.A. **113** 34.12N 79.44W
Florence, L. Australia **92** 28.52S 138.08E
Florencia Colombia **122** 1.37N 75.37W
Florennes Belgium **16** 50.14N 4.35E
Florenville Belgium **16** 49.42N 5.19E
Flores *i.* Indonesia **59** 8.40S 121.20E
Floreshty Moldova **37** 47.52N 28.12E
Flores, Laut *sea* Indonesia **59** 7.00S 121.00E
Flores Sea *see* Flores, Laut *sea* Indonesia **59**
Floriano Brazil **123** 6.45S 43.00W
Florianópolis Brazil **126** 27.35S 48.34W
Florida Uruguay **125** 34.06S 56.13W
Florida B. U.S.A. **113** 28.00N 82.00W
Florida B. U.S.A. **113** 25.00N 80.45W
Florida City U.S.A. **113** 25.27N 80.30W
Florida Keys *is.* U.S.A. **113** 24.45N 81.00W
Florida, Str. of U.S.A. **113** 24.00N 81.00W
Floridia Italy **33** 37.04N 15.10E
Florina Australia **92** 32.23S 139.58E
Flórina Greece **34** 40.47N 21.24E
Florø Norway **41** 61.36N 5.00E
Fluessen *l.* Neth. **16** 52.58N 5.23E
Flumen Spain **25** 41.43N 0.09W
Flumendosa *r.* Italy **32** 39.26N 9.38E
Fluminimaggiore Italy **32** 39.26N 8.30E
Fluorite Canada **104** 47.00N 81.50W
Flushing Mich. U.S.A. **104** 43.04N 83.51W
Flushing Ohio U.S.A. **114** 40.09N 81.04W
Fluvia Spain **25** 42.12N 3.07E
Fly *r.* P.N.G. **90** 8.22S 142.23E
Foča Bosnia-Herzegovina **31** 43.31N 18.46E
Focşani Romania **37** 45.40N 27.12E
Foggia Italy **33** 41.27N 15.34E
Foggo Nigeria **77** 11.21N 9.57E
Fogo Canada **103** 49.43N 54.17W
Fogo I. Canada **103** 49.40N 54.13W
Föhr *i.* Germany **38** 54.43N 8.30E
Foia *mtn.* Portugal **27** 37.19N 8.10W
Foins, Lac aux *l.* Canada **104** 47.05N 78.11W
Foix France **20** 42.58N 1.36E
Folda *est.* Nordland Norway **40** 67.36N 14.50E
Folda *est.* N. Trönd. Norway **40** 64.45N 11.20E
Folégandros *i.* Greece **35** 36.38N 24.57E
Foley Botswana **80** 21.34S 27.21E
Foleyet Canada **102** 48.05N 82.26W
Folgares Angola **80** 14.55S 15.03E
Folgefonna *glacier* Norway **41** 60.00N 6.20E
Foligno Italy **30** 42.57N 12.42E
Folkestone U.K. **13** 51.05N 1.11E
Folkston U.S.A. **113** 30.49N 82.02W
Follonica Italy **30** 42.55N 10.45E
Follonica, Golfo di *g.* Italy **30** 42.54N 10.43E
Folsom U.S.A. **108** 38.41N 121.15W
Fominskoye Russian Fed. **44** 59.45N 42.03E
Fond du Lac Canada **101** 59.17N 106.00W
Fond du Lac U.S.A. **110** 43.48N 88.27W
Fondi Italy **32** 41.21N 13.26E
Fonni Italy **32** 40.07N 9.15E
Fonsagrada Spain **26** 43.08N 7.04W
Fonseca, Golfo de *g.* Honduras **117** 13.10N 87.30W
Fontaine France **21** 45.11N 5.40E
Fontainebleau France **19** 48.24N 2.42E
Fonte Boa Brazil **122** 2.33S 65.59W
Fontenay France **18** 46.28N 0.48W
Fonuafo'ou *i.* Tonga **85** 18.47S 173.58W
Fonyód Hungary **31** 46.44N 17.33E
Foochow *see* Fuzhou China **55**
Foothills *town* Canada **100** 53.04N 116.47W
Forbach France **19** 49.11N 6.54E
Forbes Australia **93** 33.24S 148.03E
Forbesganj India **63** 26.18N 87.15E
Forcalquier France **21** 43.58N 5.47E
Forchheim Germany **39** 49.43N 11.04E
Ford City U.S.A. **114** 40.46N 79.32W
Förde Norway **42** 59.36N 5.29E
Ford's Bridge Australia **93** 29.46S 145.25E
Fordyce U.S.A. **111** 33.49N 92.25W
Forécariah Guinea **76** 9.28N 13.06W
Foreland Pt. U.K. **13** 51.15N 3.47W
Forel, Mt. Greenland **99** 67.00N 37.00W
Foremost Canada **101** 49.29N 111.25W
Forest Canada **104** 43.06N 82.00W
Forest City U.S.A. **115** 41.39N 75.28W
Forest of Bowland *hills* U.K. **12** 53.57N 2.30W
Forest of Dean *f.* U.K. **13** 51.48N 2.32W
Forez, Monts du *mts.* France **20** 45.35N 3.48E

Forfar U.K. **14** 56.38N 2.54W
Forked River *town* U.S.A. **115** 39.51N 74.12W
Forksville U.S.A. **115** 41.29N 76.36W
Forlì Italy **30** 44.13N 12.03E
Forman U.S.A. **110** 46.07N 97.38W
Formby Pt. U.K. **12** 53.34N 3.07W
Formentera *i.* Spain **25** 38.42N 1.28E
Formentor, Cabo de *c.* Spain **25** 39.58N 3.12E
Formerie France **19** 49.39N 1.44E
Formia Italy **32** 41.15N 13.37E
Formiga Brazil **126** 20.30S 45.27W
Formosa Argentina **124** 26.06S 58.14W
Formosa *d.* Argentina **124** 25.00S 60.00W
Formosa *see* Taiwan Asia **55**
Formosa Brazil **123** 15.30S 47.22W
Formosa, Serra *mts.* Brazil **123** 12.00S 55.20W
Fornaes *c.* Denmark **42** 56.27N 10.58E
Fornovo di Taro Italy **30** 44.42N 10.06E
Forres U.K. **14** 57.37N 3.38W
Fors Sweden **43** 60.13N 16.18E
Forsayth Australia **90** 18.35S 143.36E
Forserum Sweden **43** 57.42N 14.28E
Forshaga Sweden **43** 59.32N 13.28E
Forssa Finland **41** 60.49N 23.38E
Forst Germany **38** 51.44N 14.39E
Forster Australia **93** 32.12S 152.30E
Forsyth U.S.A. **108** 46.16N 106.41W
Fort Abbâs Pakistan **62** 29.12N 72.52E
Fort Adams U.S.A. **111** 31.05N 91.33W
Fort Albany Canada **102** 52.15N 81.35W
Fortaleza Brazil **123** 3.45S 38.35W
Fort Atkinson U.S.A. **110** 42.56N 88.50W
Fort Augustus U.K. **14** 57.09N 4.41W
Fort Beaufort R.S.A. **80** 32.46S 26.38E
Fort Benning U.S.A. **113** 32.20N 84.58W
Fort Benton U.S.A. **108** 47.49N 110.40W
Fort Carnot Madagascar **81** 21.53S 47.28E
Fort Chimo *see* Kuujjuaq Canada **99**
Fort Chipewyan Canada **101** 58.42N 111.08W
Fort Collins U.S.A. **108** 40.35N 105.05W
Fort Coulonge Canada **105** 45.51N 76.44W
Fort Covington U.S.A. **105** 44.59N 74.30W
Fort-de-France Martinique **117** 14.36N 61.05W
Fort de Possel C.A.R. **77** 5.03N 19.16E
Fort Dodge U.S.A. **110** 42.30N 94.10W
Fort Drum U.S.A. **113** 27.31N 80.49W
Forte dei Marmi Italy **30** 43.57N 10.10E
Fort Erie Canada **104** 42.54N 78.56W
Fortescue *r.* Australia **88** 21.00S 116.06E
Fortezza Italy **30** 46.47N 11.37E
Fort Frances Canada **102** 48.35N 93.25W
Fort Franklin Canada **98** 65.11N 123.45W
Fort Garland U.S.A. **108** 37.26N 105.26W
Fort George *see* Chisasibi Canada **99**
Fort Good Hope Canada **98** 66.16N 128.37W
Fort Grahame Canada **100** 56.30N 124.35W
Forth *r.* U.K. **14** 56.06N 3.48W
Fort Hancock U.S.A. **109** 31.17N 105.53W
Fort Harrison *see* Inukjuak Canada **99**
Fort Hope Canada **102** 51.32N 88.00W
Fortierville Canada **105** 46.29N 72.02W
Fort Klamath U.S.A. **108** 42.42N 122.00W
Fort Lallemand Algeria **75** 31.18N 6.20E
Fort Lauderdale U.S.A. **113** 26.08N 80.08W
Fort Liard Canada **100** 60.15N 123.28W
Fort Lupton U.S.A. **108** 40.05N 104.49W
Fort Mackay Canada **101** 57.12N 111.41W
Fort Macleod Canada **100** 49.45N 113.30W
Fort MacMahon Algeria **75** 29.46N 1.37E
Fort Madison U.S.A. **110** 40.38N 91.27W
Fort Maguire Malaŵi **79** 13.38S 34.59E
Fort McKenzie Canada **103** 56.50N 68.59W
Fort McMurray Canada **101** 56.45N 111.27W
Fort McPherson Canada **98** 67.29N 134.50W
Fort Miribel Algeria **75** 29.26N 3.00E
Fort Morgan U.S.A. **108** 40.15N 103.48W
Fort Myers U.S.A. **113** 26.39N 81.51W
Fort Nelson Canada **100** 58.49N 122.39W
Fort Nelson *r.* Canada **100** 59.30N 124.00W
Fort Norman Canada **98** 64.55N 125.29W
Fort Peck Dam U.S.A. **108** 47.52N 106.38W
Fort Peck Resr. U.S.A. **108** 47.45N 106.50W
Fort Pierce U.S.A. **113** 27.28N 80.20W
Fort Plain U.S.A. **115** 42.56N 74.38W
Fort Portal Uganda **79** 0.40N 30.17E
Fort Providence Canada **100** 61.21N 117.39W
Fort Qu'Appelle Canada **101** 50.45N 103.50W
Fort Randall U.S.A. **98** 55.10N 162.47W
Fort Reliance Canada **101** 63.00N 109.20W
Fort Resolution Canada **100** 61.10N 113.40W
Fortrose New Zealand **86** 46.34S 168.48E
Fortrose U.K. **14** 57.34N 4.09W
Fort Rupert B.C. Canada **100** 50.39N 127.27W
Fort Saint Tunisia **78** 31.59N 9.30E
Fort Sandeman Pakistan **62** 31.20N 69.27E
Fort Saskatchewan Canada **100** 53.40N 113.15W
Fort Scott U.S.A. **111** 37.50N 94.42W
Fort Severn Canada **102** 56.00N 87.40W
Fort Shevchenko Kazakhstan **45** 44.31N 50.15E
Fort Simpson Canada **100** 61.46N 121.15W
Fort Smith Canada **100** 60.00N 111.51W
Fort Smith U.S.A. **111** 35.23N 94.25W
Fort St. John Canada **100** 56.15N 120.51W
Fort Stockton U.S.A. **111** 30.53N 102.53W
Fort Sumner U.S.A. **109** 34.28N 104.15W
Fort Thomas U.S.A. **109** 32.41S 136.00E
Fortuna Calif. U.S.A. **108** 40.36N 124.09W
Fortuna N.Dak. U.S.A. **110** 48.55N 103.47W
Fortune B. Canada **103** 47.25N 55.25W
Fort Valley U.S.A. **113** 32.32N 83.56W
Fort Vermilion Canada **100** 58.24N 116.00W
Fort Wayne U.S.A. **112** 41.05N 85.08W
Fort William U.K. **14** 56.49N 5.07W
Fort Worth U.S.A. **111** 32.45N 97.20W
Fort Yates U.S.A. **110** 46.05N 100.38W
Forty Mile *town* Canada **98** 64.24N 140.31W
Fort Yukon U.S.A. **98** 66.35N 145.20W

Foshan China **55** 23.08N 113.08E
Fossano Italy **30** 44.33N 7.43E
Fossombrone Italy **30** 43.41N 12.48E
Foster Australia **93** 38.39S 146.12E
Fostoria U.S.A. **112** 1.10S 10.31E
Fouesnant France **18** 47.54N 4.01W
Fougamou Gabon **78** 1.10S 10.31E
Fougères France **18** 48.21N 1.12W
Foula *i.* U.K. **14** 60.08N 2.05W
Foulness I. U.K. **13** 51.35N 0.55E
Foulwind, C. New Zealand **86** 41.45S 171.30E
Foumban Cameroon **77** 5.43N 10.50E
Fountain U.S.A. **108** 38.41N 104.42W
Fourmies France **19** 50.00N 4.03E
Foúrnoi *i.* Greece **35** 37.34N 26.30E
Fours France **19** 46.49N 3.43E
Fouta Djalon *f.* Guinea **76** 11.30N 12.30W
Foveaux Str. New Zealand **86** 46.40S 168.00E
Fowey U.K. **13** 50.20N 4.39W
Fowler U.S.A. **108** 38.08N 104.01W
Fowlers B. Australia **91** 31.59S 132.27E
Fowlerton U.S.A. **111** 28.28N 98.48W
Fowlerville U.S.A. **104** 42.40N 84.04W
Fox Creek *town* Canada **100** 54.26N 116.55W
Foxe Basin *b.* Canada **99** 67.30N 79.00W
Foxe Channel Canada **99** 65.00N 80.00W
Foxen *l.* Sweden **42** 59.23N 11.52E
Foxe Pen. Canada **99** 65.00N 76.00W
Fox Glacier *town* New Zealand **86** 43.28S 170.01E
Foxton New Zealand **86** 40.27S 175.18E
Fox Valley *town* Canada **101** 50.29N 109.28W
Foyle *r.* U.K. **15** 55.00N 7.20W
Foyle, Lough U.K. **15** 55.05N 7.10W
Foz do Cunene Angola **78** 17.15S 11.48E
Foz do Iguaçu Brazil **126** 25.33S 54.31W
Foz Giraldo Portugal **27** 40.00N 7.43W
Fraga Spain **25** 41.31N 0.21E
Franca Brazil **126** 20.33S 47.27W
Francavilla Italy **33** 40.31N 17.35E
Francavilla al Mare Italy **31** 42.25N 14.17E
Francavilla Fontana Italy **29** 40.31N 17.35E
France Europe **17** 47.00N 2.00E
Frances Australia **92** 36.41S 140.59E
Frances *r.* Canada **100** 60.16N 129.10W
Frances L. Canada **100** 61.23N 129.30W
Frances Lake *town* Canada **100** 61.15N 129.12W
Francesville U.S.A. **112** 40.59N 86.54W
Franceville Gabon **78** 1.38S 13.31E
Franche-Comté *d.* France **19** 47.10N 6.00E
Francia Uruguay **125** 32.33S 56.37W
Francia, Peña de *mtn.* Spain **26** 40.31N 6.10W
Francistown Botswana **80** 21.12S 27.29E
Francofonte Italy **33** 37.13N 14.53E
François L. Canada **100** 54.00N 125.40W
Franeker Neth. **16** 53.13N 5.31E
Frangy France **21** 46.01N 5.56E
Frankenberg Germany **38** 50.54N 13.01E
Frankenberg-Eder Germany **38** 51.03N 8.48E
Frankenmuth U.S.A. **104** 43.20N 83.46W
Frankford Canada **105** 44.12N 77.36W
Frankfort Kans. U.S.A. **110** 39.42N 96.25W
Frankfort Ky. U.S.A. **112** 38.11N 84.53W
Frankfort N.Y. U.S.A. **115** 43.02N 75.04W
Frankfurt Brandenburg Germany **38** 52.20N 14.33E
Frankfurt Hessen Germany **39** 50.07N 8.40E
Fränkische Rezat *r.* Germany **39** 49.11N 11.01E
Frankland *r.* Australia **89** 34.58S 116.49E
Franklin Ky. U.S.A. **113** 36.42N 86.35W
Franklin La. U.S.A. **111** 29.48N 91.30W
Franklin Mass. U.S.A. **115** 42.05N 71.24W
Franklin N.H. U.S.A. **115** 43.27N 71.39W
Franklin Penn. U.S.A. **114** 41.24N 79.50W
Franklin Tex. U.S.A. **111** 31.02N 96.29W
Franklin W.Va. U.S.A. **114** 38.39N 79.20W
Franklin B. Canada **98** 70.00N 126.30W
Franklin D. Roosevelt L. U.S.A. **108** 48.20N 118.10W
Franklin Harbour Australia **92** 33.42S 136.56E
Franklin I. Antarctica **128** 76.10S 168.30E
Franklinville U.S.A. **114** 42.20N 78.28W
Frankston Australia **91** 38.08S 145.07E
Fransfontein Namibia **80** 20.12S 15.01E
Frantsa Iosifa, Zemlya *is.* Russian Fed. **50** 81.00N 54.00E
Franz Canada **102** 48.28N 84.25W
Franz Josef Land *is. see* Frantsa Iosifa, Zeml ya Russian Fed. **50**
Frascati Italy **32** 41.48N 12.41E
Fraser *r.* B.C. Canada **100** 49.07N 123.11W
Fraser *r.* Nfld. Canada **103** 56.35N 61.55W
Fraserburg R.S.A. **80** 31.55S 21.29E
Fraserburgh U.K. **14** 57.42N 2.00W
Fraser, I. Australia **90** 25.15S 153.10E
Fraser Plateau *f.* Canada **100** 52.52N 124.00W
Frashër Albania **34** 40.23N 20.26E
Fraustro Mexico **111** 25.51N 101.04W
Fray Bentos Uruguay **125** 33.08S 58.18W
Fray Marcos Uruguay **125** 34.11S 55.44W
Frazeysburg U.S.A. **114** 40.07N 82.07W
Frechilla Spain **26** 42.08N 4.50W
Frederica U.S.A. **115** 39.01N 75.28W
Fredericia Denmark **42** 55.35N 9.46E
Frederick Md. U.S.A. **114** 39.23N 77.25W
Frederick Okla. U.S.A. **111** 34.23N 99.01W
Frederick S.Dak. U.S.A. **110** 45.50N 98.30W
Frederick Hills Australia **90** 12.41S 136.00E
Fredericksburg Tex. U.S.A. **111** 30.17N 98.52W
Fredericksburg Va. U.S.A. **114** 38.18N 77.29W
Frederick Sd. U.S.A. **100** 57.00N 133.00W
Fredericktown U.S.A. **114** 40.29N 82.33W
Fredericton Canada **103** 45.58N 66.39W
Frederikshâb Greenland **99** 62.05N 49.30W
Frederikshavn Denmark **42** 57.26N 10.32E
Frederikssund Denmark **43** 55.50N 12.04E
Fredonia Kans. U.S.A. **111** 37.32N 95.49W
Fredonia N.Y. U.S.A. **114** 42.27N 79.20W
Fredrika Sweden **40** 64.05N 18.24E

Fredriksberg Sweden **43** 60.10N 14.22E
Fredrikstad Norway **42** 59.13N 10.57E
Freehold U.S.A. **115** 40.16N 74.17W
Freeland Mich. U.S.A. **104** 43.32N 84.07W
Freeland Penn. U.S.A. **115** 41.01N 75.47W
Freels, C. Canada **103** 49.15N 53.28W
Freelton Canada **104** 43.22N 80.02W
Freeman U.S.A. **110** 43.21N 97.26W
Freeport Bahamas **113** 26.30N 78.45W
Freeport N.S. Canada **103** 44.17N 66.19W
Freeport Ont. Canada **104** 43.80N 80.25W
Freeport Ill. U.S.A. **110** 42.17N 89.38W
Freeport N.Y. U.S.A. **115** 40.39N 73.35W
Freeport Ohio U.S.A. **114** 40.13N 81.16W
Freeport Penn. U.S.A. **114** 40.40N 79.41W
Freeport Tex. U.S.A. **111** 28.58N 95.22W
Freetown Sierra Leone **76** 8.30N 13.17W
Fregenal de la Sierra Spain **26** 38.10N 6.39W
Freiberg Germany **38** 50.54N 13.20E
Freiburg Germany **39** 47.59N 7.51E
Freiburg *see* Fribourg Switz. **39**
Freilingen Germany **16** 50.33N 7.50E
Freising Germany **39** 48.23N 11.44E
Freistadt Austria **36** 48.31N 14.31E
Freital Germany **38** 51.00N 13.39E
Fréjus France **21** 43.26N 6.44E
Fremantle Australia **89** 32.07S 115.44E
Fremont Calif. U.S.A. **108** 37.34N 122.01W
Fremont Nebr. U.S.A. **110** 41.26N 96.30W
Fremont Ohio U.S.A. **112** 41.21N 83.08W
French *r.* Canada **104** 45.56N 80.54W
French Creek *r.* U.S.A. **114** 41.25N 79.50W
Frenchglen U.S.A. **108** 42.48N 118.56W
French I. Australia **93** 38.20S 145.20E
Frenchman Butte *town* Canada **101** 53.35N 109.38W
French River *town* Canada **104** 46.02N 80.35W
Frenda Algeria **75** 35.04N 1.03E
Freren Germany **38** 52.29N 7.32E
Fresco *r.* Brazil **123** 7.10S 52.30W
Freshford Rep. of Ire. **15** 52.44N 7.23W
Fresnes-en-Woëvre France **19** 49.08N 5.39E
Fresne-St. Mamès France **19** 47.33N 5.52E
Fresnillo Mexico **116** 23.10N 102.53W
Fresno U.S.A. **108** 36.45N 119.45W
Fresno, Portillo del *pass* Spain **26** 42.38N 3.46W
Freu, Cabo del *c.* Spain **25** 39.45N 3.27E
Freudenstadt Germany **39** 48.28N 8.25E
Frewena Australia **90** 19.25S 135.25E
Frewsburg U.S.A. **114** 42.03N 79.10W
Fria Guinea **76** 10.27N 13.38W
Fria, C. Namibia **80** 18.25S 12.01E
Frias Argentina **124** 28.40S 65.10W
Fribourg Switz. **39** 46.48N 7.09E
Fribourg *d.* Switz. **39** 46.40N 7.07E
Friedberg Bayern Germany **39** 48.21N 10.58E
Friedberg Hessen Germany **39** 50.20N 8.45E
Friedland Germany **38** 53.40N 13.33E
Friedrichshafen Germany **39** 47.39N 9.28E
Friedrichsort Germany **38** 54.24N 10.10E
Friedrichstadt Germany **38** 54.22N 9.05E
Friendship U.S.A. **114** 42.12N 78.08W
Friesach Austria **31** 46.57N 14.24E
Friesland *d.* Neth. **16** 53.05N 5.45E
Friesoythe Germany **38** 53.01N 7.51E
Frio, Cabo *c.* Brazil **126** 22.59S 42.00W
Frisian Is. Europe **8** 53.30N 6.00E
Fritsla Sweden **43** 57.33N 12.47E
Fritzlar Germany **38** 51.08N 9.16E
Friuli-Venezia Giulia *d.* Italy **30** 46.10N 13.00E
Frobisher B. Canada **99** 63.00N 66.45W
Frobisher Bay *town* Canada **99** 63.45N 68.30W
Frobisher L. Canada **101** 56.25N 108.20W
Frohavet *est.* Norway **40** 63.55N 9.05E
Froid U.S.A. **108** 48.20N 104.30W
Frolovo Russian Fed. **45** 49.45N 43.40E
Frome *r.* Australia **92** 29.49S 138.40E
Frome U.K. **13** 51.16N 2.17W
Frome Downs *town* Australia **92** 31.13S 139.46E
Frome, L. Australia **92** 30.48S 139.48E
Frontera Mexico **116** 18.32N 92.38W
Frontignan France **20** 43.27N 3.45E
Front Royal U.S.A. **114** 38.55N 78.11W
Frosinone Italy **32** 41.38N 13.19E
Frostburg U.S.A. **114** 39.39N 78.56W
Frövi Sweden **43** 59.28N 15.22E
Fröya *i.* Norway **40** 63.45N 8.45E
Fruges France **19** 50.31N 2.08E
Frunzovka Ukraine **37** 47.19N 29.44E
Frutigen Switz. **39** 46.35N 7.39E
Frýdek-Místek Czech Republic **37** 49.41N 18.22E
Fu'an China **55** 27.04N 119.37E
Fuchū Japan **57** 35.40N 139.29E
Fuchuan China **55** 24.50N 111.16E
Fuchun Jiang *r.* China **55** 30.05N 120.00E
Fuding China **55** 27.18N 120.12E
Fuefuki *r.* Japan **57** 35.33N 138.28E
Fuencaliente Spain **26** 38.24N 4.18W
Fuencaliente *mtn.* Spain **26** 38.24N 4.14W
Fuensalida Spain **27** 40.03N 4.12W
Fuensanta, Embalse de la *resr.* Spain **26** 38.23N 2.13W
Fuente de Cantos Spain **26** 38.15N 6.18W
Fuente-obejuna Spain **26** 38.16N 5.25W
Fuentesaúco Spain **26** 41.14N 5.30W
Fuentes de Ebro Spain **25** 41.31N 0.38W
Fuentes de Oñoro Spain **26** 40.33N 6.52W
Fuerte *r.* Mexico **109** 25.50N 109.25W
Fuerteventura *i.* Canary Is. **74** 28.20N 14.10W
Fuga *i.* Phil. **55** 18.53N 121.22E
Fuglö *i.* Faroe Is. **10** 62.22N 6.15W
Fugou China **54** 34.04N 114.23E
Fugu China **54** 39.02N 111.03E
Fuji China **55** 25.09N 138.39E
Fuji *r.* Japan **57** 35.07N 138.38E
Fujian *d.* China **55** 26.00N 118.00E
Fu Jiang *r.* China **55** 30.02N 106.20E
Fujieda Japan **57** 34.52N 138.16E

Fujin China 53 47.15N 131.59E
Fujinomiya Japan 57 35.12N 138.38E
Fuji san mtn. Japan 57 35.22N 138.44E
Fujisawa Japan 57 35.21N 139.29E
Fuji-yoshida Japan 57 35.38N 138.42E
Fukui Japan 57 36.04N 136.12E
Fukuoka Japan 57 33.39N 130.21E
Fukuroi Japan 57 34.45N 137.55E
Fukushima Japan 57 37.44N 140.28E
Fukuyama Japan 57 34.29N 133.21E
Fūlādī, Kūh-e mtn. Afghan. 62 34.38N 67.32E
Fulda Germany 38 50.33N 9.41E
Fulda r. Germany 38 51.25N 9.39E
Fuling China 55 29.40N 107.20E
Fulton Mo. U.S.A. 110 38.52N 91.57W
Fulton N.Y. U.S.A. 115 43.19N 76.25W
Fumay France 19 49.59N 4.42E
Fumel France 20 44.29N 0.57E
Funabashi Japan 57 35.42N 139.59E
Funafuti Tuvalu 84 8.31S 179.13E
Funchal Madeira Is. 127 32.40N 16.55W
Fundão Portugal 27 40.08N 7.30W
Fundy, B. of Canada 103 45.00N 66.00W
Funing China 55 23.37N 105.36E
Funiu Shan mts. China 54 33.40N 112.20E
Funtua Nigeria 77 11.34N 7.18E
Fuping China 54 38.52N 114.12E
Fuqing China 55 25.43N 119.22E
Furakawa Japan 57 38.30N 140.50E
Furancungo Mozambique 79 14.51S 33.38E
Furculeşti Romania 34 43.52N 25.09E
Fürg Iran 65 28.19N 55.10E
Furnas, Reprêsa de resr. Brazil 126 20.45S 46.00W
Furneaux Group is. Australia 91 40.15S 148.15E
Furqlus Syria 66 34.38N 37.08E
Fürstenau Germany 38 52.31N 7.40E
Fürstenberg Germany 38 52.11N 13.10E
Fürstenfeld Austria 31 47.03N 16.05E
Fürstenfeldbruck Germany 39 48.10N 11.15E
Fürstenwalde Germany 38 52.21N 14.04E
Fürth Germany 39 49.28N 10.59E
Furth im Wald Germany 39 49.18N 12.51E
Furu-tone r. Japan 57 35.58N 139.51E
Fusagasugá Colombia 122 4.22N 74.21W
Fushun China 54 41.50N 123.55E
Fusong China 53 42.17N 127.19E
Füssen Germany 38 47.34N 10.42E
Fusui China 55 22.35N 107.57E
Fuwah Egypt 66 31.12N 30.33E
Fu Xian Liaoning China 54 39.35N 122.07E
Fu Xian Shaanxi China 54 36.00N 109.20E
Fuxin China 54 42.08N 121.45E
Fuyang Anhui China 54 32.52N 115.52E
Fuyang Zhejiang China 55 30.03N 119.57E
Fuyang He r. China 54 38.10N 116.08E
Fuyu China 53 45.12N 124.49E
Fuyuan Heilongjiang China 53 48.20N 134.18E
Fuyuan Yunnan China 55 25.40N 104.14E
Fuzhou Fujian China 55 26.09N 119.21E
Fuzhou Jiangxi China 55 28.01N 116.13E
Fyn i. Denmark 42 55.20N 10.30E
Fyne, Loch U.K. 14 55.55N 5.23W
Fyresvatn l. Norway 42 59.06N 8.12E

G

Ga Ghana 76 9.48N 2.28W
Gaalkacyo Somali Rep. 71 6.49N 47.23E
Gabare Bulgaria 34 43.19N 23.55E
Gabas r. France 20 43.46N 0.42W
Gabela Angola 78 10.52S 14.24E
Gabès Tunisia 75 33.53N 10.07E
Gabès, Golfe de g. Tunisia 75 34.00N 10.25E
Gabir Sudan 73 8.35N 24.40E
Gabon Africa 78 0.00 12.00E
Gabon r. Gabon 78 0.15N 10.00E
Gaborone Botswana 80 24.45S 25.55E
Gabras Sudan 73 10.16N 26.14E
Gabriels U.S.A. 105 44.26N 74.13W
Gabriel y Galan, Embalse de resr. Spain 26 40.15N 6.15W
Gabrovo Bulgaria 34 42.52N 25.27E
Gacé France 18 48.48N 0.18E
Gach Sārān Iran 65 30.13N 50.49E
Gacko Bosnia-Herzegovina 31 43.10N 18.32E
Gada Nigeria 77 13.50N 5.40E
Gādarwāra India 63 22.55N 78.47E
Gäddede Sweden 40 64.30N 14.15E
Gádor Spain 27 36.57N 2.29W
Gádor, Sierra de mts. Spain 27 36.54N 2.47W
Gadot Israel 67 33.01N 35.37E
Gadra Pakistan 62 25.40N 70.37E
Gadsden U.S.A. 113 34.00N 86.00W
Gaeta Italy 32 41.12N 13.35E
Gaeta, Golfo di g. Italy 32 41.06N 13.30E
Gaferut i. Federated States of Micronesia 59 9.14N 145.23E
Gaffney U.S.A. 113 35.03N 81.40W
Gafsa Tunisia 75 34.25N 8.48E
Gagarin Russian Fed. 44 55.38N 35.00E
Gagetown U.S.A. 104 43.44N 83.16W
Gagliano del Capo Italy 33 39.50N 18.22E
Gagnoa Côte d'Ivoire 76 6.04N 5.55W

Gagnon Canada 103 51.53N 68.10W
Gagnon, Lac l. Canada 105 46.07N 75.07W
Gaibānda Bangla. 63 25.19N 89.33E
Gaillac France 20 43.54N 1.55E
Gaillon France 18 49.10N 1.20E
Gailtaler Alpen mts. Austria 39 46.42N 13.15E
Gaines U.S.A. 104 42.52N 83.55W
Gainesville Fla. U.S.A. 113 29.37N 82.21W
Gainesville Ga. U.S.A. 113 34.17N 83.50W
Gainesville Mo. U.S.A. 111 36.36N 92.26W
Gainesville Tex. U.S.A. 111 33.37N 97.08W
Gainesville Va. U.S.A. 114 38.48N 77.34W
Gainsborough U.K. 12 53.23N 0.46W
Gairdner r. Australia 89 34.20S 119.30E
Gairdner, L. Australia 92 31.30S 136.00E
Gairloch U.K. 14 57.43N 5.40W
Gaithersburg U.S.A. 114 39.09N 77.12W
Gai Xian China 54 40.25N 122.15E
Gaj Croatia 31 45.29N 17.02E
Galana r. Kenya 79 3.12S 40.09E
Galangue Angola 78 13.40S 16.00E
Galapagos, Islas is. Ecuador 97 0.20S 91.00W
Galaroza Spain 27 37.55N 6.42W
Galashiels U.K. 14 55.37N 2.49W
Galaţi Romania 37 45.27N 27.59E
Galatina Italy 33 40.10N 18.10E
Galaxídhion Greece 35 38.22N 22.23E
Galdhøpiggen mtn. Norway 41 61.37N 8.17E
Galeana Mexico 111 24.50N 100.04W
Galeh Dār Iran 65 27.36N 52.42E
Galena Alas. U.S.A. 98 64.43N 157.00W
Galena Md. U.S.A. 115 39.20N 75.55W
Galesburg U.S.A. 110 40.57N 90.22W
Galeton U.S.A. 114 41.44N 77.39W
Galich Russian Fed. 44 58.20N 42.12E
Galicia d. Spain 26 42.45N 8.00W
Galilee see HaGalil f. Israel 67
Galilee, L. Australia 90 22.21S 145.48E
Galilee, Sea of see Yam Kinneret l. Israel 67
Galion U.S.A. 114 40.44N 82.47W
Galiuro Mts. U.S.A. 109 32.40N 110.20W
Gallarate Italy 30 45.40N 8.47E
Gallatin U.S.A. 113 36.22N 86.28W
Galle Sri Lanka 61 6.01N 80.13E
Gállego r. Spain 25 41.39N 0.51W
Gallegos r. Argentina 125 51.35S 69.00W
Galley Head Rep. of Ire. 15 51.32N 8.57W
Galliate Italy 30 45.29N 8.42E
Gallinas, Punta c. Colombia 122 12.20N 71.30W
Gallipoli Italy 33 40.03N 18.00E
Gallipoli see Gelibolu Turkey 34
Gallipolis U.S.A. 114 38.49N 82.12W
Gällivare Sweden 40 67.07N 20.45E
Gällö Sweden 40 62.56N 15.15E
Gallo, Capo c. Italy 32 38.13N 13.19E
Galloo I. U.S.A. 105 43.54N 76.25W
Galloway f. U.K. 14 55.00N 4.28W
Gallup U.S.A. 109 35.32N 108.44W
Gallur Spain 25 41.52N 1.19W
Gal'on Israel 67 31.38N 34.51E
Galong Australia 93 34.37S 148.34E
Gal, Punta de c. Spain 25 39.10N 1.05E
Galston U.K. 14 55.36N 4.23W
Galty Mts. Rep. of Ire. 15 52.20N 8.10W
Galva U.S.A. 110 41.10N 90.03W
Galveston U.S.A. 111 29.18N 94.48W
Galveston B. U.S.A. 111 29.36N 94.57W
Galvez Argentina 124 32.03S 61.14W
Galway Rep. of Ire. 15 53.17N 9.04W
Galway d. Rep. of Ire. 15 53.25N 9.00W
Galway B. Rep. of Ire. 15 53.12N 9.07W
Gam r. Vietnam 55 18.47N 105.40E
Gamagōri Japan 57 34.50N 137.14E
Gamawa Nigeria 77 12.10N 10.31E
Gamba China 63 28.18N 88.32E
Gambēla Ethiopia 73 8.18N 34.37E
Gambia Africa 76 13.10N 16.00W
Gambia r. Gambia 76 13.28N 15.55W
Gambier I. Australia 92 35.12S 136.32E
Gambier, Îles is. Pacific Oc. 85 23.10S 135.00W
Gambo Canada 103 48.46N 54.14W
Gamboli Pakistan 62 29.50N 68.26E
Gamboma Congo 78 1.50S 15.58E
Gamboula C.A.R. 77 4.05N 15.10E
Gamia Benin 77 10.24N 2.45E
Gamlakarleby see Kokkola Finland 40
Gamleby Sweden 43 57.54N 16.24E
Gamo Gofa d. Ethiopia 73 6.00N 37.00E
Ganado U.S.A. 109 35.43N 109.33W
Gananoque Canada 105 44.20N 76.10W
Ganbashao China 55 26.37N 107.41E
Ganda Angola 78 12.58S 14.38E
Gandajika Zaïre 78 6.46S 23.58E
Gandak r. India 63 25.40N 85.13E
Gāndarbal Jammu & Kashmir 62 34.14N 74.47E
Gandāva Pakistan 62 28.37N 67.29E
Gander Canada 103 48.57N 54.34W
Ganderkesee Germany 38 53.02N 8.32E
Gander L. Canada 103 48.55N 54.40W
Gandesa Spain 25 41.03N 0.26E
Gandevi India 62 20.49N 73.00E
Gāndhi Sāgar resr. India 62 24.18N 75.21E
Gandía Spain 25 38.58N 0.11W
Gandou Congo 78 2.25N 17.25E
Ganga r. India 63 23.22N 90.32E
Gangāpur Rāj. India 62 25.13N 74.16E
Gangāpur Rāj. India 62 26.29N 76.43E
Gangara Niger 77 14.35N 8.40E
Gāngārāmpur India 63 25.24N 88.31E
Gangdhār India 62 23.57N 75.37E
Gangdisê Shan mts. China 63 31.15N 82.00E
Ganges France 20 43.56N 3.42E
Ganges r. see Ganga r. India 63
Gangi Italy 33 37.49N 14.13E
Gangotri India 63 30.56N 79.02E

Gangtok India 63 27.20N 88.37E
Gangu China 54 34.30N 105.30E
Gan Jiang r. China 55 29.10N 116.00E
Ganmain Australia 93 34.47S 147.01E
Gannat France 20 46.06N 3.12E
Gannett Peak mtn. U.S.A. 108 43.11N 109.39W
Ganquan China 54 36.19N 109.19E
Gan Shemu'el Israel 67 32.27N 34.57E
Gansu d. China 52 36.00N 103.00E
Ganta Liberia 76 7.15N 8.59W
Gantheaume, C. Australia 92 36.05S 137.27E
Gan Yavne Israel 67 31.47N 34.43E
Ganye Nigeria 77 8.24N 12.02E
Ganyu China 54 34.50N 119.07E
Ganzhou China 55 25.49N 114.50E
Gao Mali 76 16.19N 0.09W
Gao d. Mali 77 17.20N 1.25E
Gao'an China 55 28.25N 115.22E
Gaohe China 55 22.46N 112.57E
Gaolan China 54 36.23N 103.55E
Gaolou Ling mtn. China 55 24.47N 106.48E
Gaomi China 54 36.23N 119.44E
Gaoping China 54 35.48N 112.55E
Gaotai China 52 39.20N 99.58E
Gaoxiong Taiwan 55 22.40N 120.18E
Gaoyou China 54 32.40N 119.30E
Gaoyou Hu l. China 54 32.50N 119.25E
Gaozhou China 55 21.58N 110.59E
Gap France 21 44.34N 6.05E
Gar China 63 32.11N 79.59E
Garah Australia 93 29.04S 149.38E
Gara, Lough Rep. of Ire. 15 53.57N 8.27W
Garanhuns Brazil 123 8.53S 36.28W
Garba C.A.R. 73 9.12N 20.30E
Gārbosh, Kūh-e mtn. Iran 65 32.36N 50.02E
García de Sola, Embalse de resr. Spain 27 39.15N 5.05W
Gard r. France 21 43.51N 4.37E
Garda Italy 30 45.34N 10.42E
Garda, Lago di l. Italy 30 45.40N 10.41E
Gardelegen Germany 38 52.31N 11.23E
Garden r. Canada 104 46.32N 84.09W
Garden City Ala. U.S.A. 113 34.01N 86.55W
Garden City Kans. U.S.A. 111 37.58N 100.53W
Garden Reach India 63 22.33N 88.17E
Garden River town Canada 104 46.33N 84.09W
Gardermoen Norway 42 60.13N 11.06E
Gardēz Afghan. 62 33.37N 69.07E
Gardiner U.S.A. 105 44.14N 69.46W
Gardiners I. U.S.A. 115 41.05N 72.07W
Gardner U.S.A. 115 42.34N 71.59W
Gardnerville U.S.A. 108 38.56N 119.45W
Gardone Val Trompia Italy 30 45.41N 10.11E
Gardunha, Serra de mts. Portugal 27 40.06N 7.30W
Garešnica Croatia 31 45.35N 16.56E
Garessio Italy 30 44.12N 8.02E
Garet el Djenoun mtn. Algeria 75 25.05N 5.25E
Gargaliánoi Greece 35 37.04N 21.38E
Gargano, Testa del c. Italy 33 41.49N 16.12E
Garhākota India 63 23.46N 79.09E
Garhi Khairo Pakistan 62 28.04N 67.59E
Garibaldi Prov. Park Canada 100 49.50N 122.40W
Garies R.S.A. 80 30.34S 18.00E
Garigliano r. Italy 32 41.13N 13.45E
Gariglione, Monte mtn. Italy 33 39.09N 16.41E
Garissa Kenya 79 0.27S 39.49E
Garko Nigeria 77 11.45N 8.53E
Garland Tex. U.S.A. 111 32.54N 96.39W
Garland Utah U.S.A. 108 41.45N 112.10W
Garlasco Italy 30 45.12N 8.55E
Garlin France 20 43.34N 0.15W
Garm Āb Afghan. 62 32.14N 65.01E
Garmisch Partenkirchen Germany 39 47.29N 11.05E
Garmsār Iran 65 35.15N 52.21E
Garnett U.S.A. 110 38.17N 95.14W
Garo Hills India 63 25.45N 90.30E
Garonne r. France 20 45.02N 0.36W
Garoua Cameroon 77 9.17N 13.22E
Garoua Boulaï Cameroon 77 5.54N 14.33E
Garrel Germany 38 52.57N 8.01E
Garrettsville U.S.A. 114 41.17N 81.06W
Garrison U.S.A. 111 31.49N 94.30W
Garrison Resr. U.S.A. 110 48.00N 102.30W
Garron Pt. U.K. 15 55.03N 5.57W
Garrovillas Spain 27 39.43N 6.33W
Garry L. Canada 99 66.00N 100.00W
Garson Canada 104 46.34N 80.52W
Garub Namibia 80 26.33S 16.00E
Garut Indonesia 59 7.15S 107.55E
Garvão Portugal 26 37.42N 8.21W
Garve U.K. 14 57.37N 4.41W
Garvie Mts. New Zealand 86 45.15S 169.00E
Garwa India 63 24.11N 83.49E
Gary U.S.A. 112 41.34N 87.20W
Garyarsa China 52 31.30N 80.40E
Garzón Colombia 122 2.14N 75.37W
Gas City U.S.A. 112 40.28N 85.37W
Gascogne, Golfe de g. France 17 44.00N 2.40W
Gascony, G. of see Gascogne, Golfe de France 17
Gascoyne r. Australia 88 25.00S 113.40E
Gascoyne Junction Australia 88 25.02S 115.15E
Gash r. Eritrea see Qāsh r. Sudan 72
Gashua Nigeria 77 12.53N 11.02E
Gaspé Canada 103 48.50N 64.30W
Gaspé, Cap de c. Canada 103 48.45N 64.09W
Gaspé, Péninsule de pen. Canada 103 48.30N 65.00W
Gaspésie Prov. Park Canada 103 48.50N 65.45W
Gassaway U.S.A. 114 38.40N 80.47W
Gassol Nigeria 77 8.34N 10.25E
Gasteiz see Vitoria Spain 26
Gastonia U.S.A. 113 35.14N 81.12W
Gastoúni Greece 35 37.51N 21.16E
Gastre Argentina 125 42.17S 69.15W
Gata, Cabo de c. Spain 27 36.44N 2.10W

Gátas, Akrotírion c. Cyprus 66 34.33N 33.03E
Gata, Sierra de mts. Spain 26 40.20N 6.35W
Gatchina Russian Fed. 44 59.32N 30.05E
Gatehouse of Fleet U.K. 14 54.53N 4.12W
Gateshead U.K. 12 54.57N 1.35W
Gatesville U.S.A. 111 31.26N 97.45W
Gatineau Canada 105 45.29N 75.40W
Gatineau r. Canada 105 45.27N 75.40W
Gatineau N.C.C. Park Canada 105 45.30N 75.52W
Gâtine, Hauteurs de hills France 18 46.40N 0.50W
Gattinara Italy 30 45.37N 8.22E
Gatton Australia 91 27.32S 152.18E
Gatun L. Panama 117 9.20N 80.00W
Gauchy France 19 49.49N 3.13E
Gaucín Spain 27 36.31N 5.19W
Gauer L. Canada 101 57.00N 97.50W
Gauhāti India 63 26.11N 91.44E
Gauley r. U.S.A. 114 38.10N 81.12W
Gaurela India 63 22.45N 81.54E
Gauri Sankar mtn. China/Nepal 63 27.57N 86.21E
Gausta mtn. Norway 42 59.50N 8.35E
Gauting Germany 39 48.04N 11.23E
Gavá Spain 25 41.18N 2.00E
Gavāter Iran 65 25.10N 61.31E
Gávdhos i. Greece 35 34.50N 24.06E
Gāv Koshī Iran 65 28.39N 57.13E
Gävle Sweden 41 60.40N 17.10E
Gävleborg d. Sweden 41 61.30N 16.15E
Gavorrano Italy 30 42.55N 10.54E
Gávrion Greece 35 37.52N 24.46E
Gawachab Namibia 80 27.03S 17.50E
Gāwilgarh Hills India 62 21.30N 77.00E
Gawler Australia 92 34.38S 138.44E
Gawler Ranges mts. Australia 92 32.30S 136.00E
Gaya India 63 24.47N 85.00E
Gaya Niger 77 11.53N 3.31E
Gay Head c. U.S.A. 115 41.21N 70.49W
Gaylord U.S.A. 104 45.02N 84.40W
Gayndah Australia 90 25.37S 151.36E
Gayny Russian Fed. 44 60.17N 54.15E
Gaysin Ukraine 37 48.50N 29.29E
Gayvoron Ukraine 37 48.20N 29.52E
Gaza see Ghazzah Egypt 67
Gaza d. Mozambique 81 23.20S 32.35E
Gaza Strip f. Egypt 67 31.20N 34.20E
Gaziantep Turkey 64 37.04N 37.21E
Gbanhui Côte d'Ivoire 76 8.12N 3.02W
Gboko Nigeria 77 7.22N 8.58E
Gcuwa R.S.A. 80 32.20S 28.09E
Gdańsk Poland 37 54.22N 18.38E
Gdansk, G. of Poland 37 54.45N 19.15E
Gdov Russian Fed. 44 58.48N 27.52E
Gdynia Poland 37 54.31N 18.30E
Gebe i. Indonesia 59 0.05S 129.20E
Gebze Turkey 64 40.48N 29.26E
Gech'a Ethiopia 73 7.31N 35.22E
Gedera Israel 67 31.48N 34.46E
Gediz r. Turkey 39 38.37N 26.47E
Gedser Denmark 41 54.35N 11.57E
Geel Belgium 16 51.10N 5.00E
Geelong Australia 92 38.10S 144.26E
Geesthacht Germany 38 53.26N 10.22E
Gê'gyai China 63 32.25N 84.05E
Gehua P.N.G. 90 10.20S 150.25E
Geidam Nigeria 77 12.55N 11.55E
Geikie r. Canada 101 57.45N 103.52W
Geilenkirchen Germany 16 50.58N 6.08E
Geilo Norway 41 60.31N 8.12E
Geisenfeld Germany 39 48.41N 11.37E
Geisenheim Germany 39 49.59N 7.58E
Geislingen Germany 39 48.36N 9.50E
Gejiu China 52 23.25N 103.05E
Gela Italy 33 37.03N 14.15E
Geladī Ethiopia 71 6.58N 44.30E
Gela, Golfo di g. Italy 33 37.00N 14.10E
Gelai mtn. Tanzania 79 2.37S 36.07E
Gelderland d. Neth. 16 52.05N 6.00E
Geldermalsen Neth. 16 51.53N 5.17E
Geldern Germany 38 51.31N 6.20E
Geldrop Neth. 16 51.26N 5.31E
Geleen Neth. 16 50.58N 5.51E
Gélengdeng Chad 77 10.56N 15.32E
Gelibolu Turkey 34 40.24N 26.40E
Gelibolu Yarimadasi c. Turkey 34 40.20N 26.30E
Gélise r. France 20 44.11N 0.17E
Gelligaer U.K. 13 51.40N 3.18W
Gelsenkirchen Germany 38 51.31N 7.07E
Gem Canada 100 50.58N 112.11W
Gemas Malaysia 58 2.35N 102.35E
Gembloux Belgium 16 50.34N 4.42E
Gemena Zaïre 78 3.14N 19.48E
Gemerek Turkey 64 39.13N 36.05E
Gemla Sweden 43 56.52N 14.38E
Gemlik Turkey 64 40.26N 29.10E
Gemona del Friuli Italy 30 46.16N 13.09E
Gemünden Germany 39 50.03N 9.41E
Genalē r. Ethiopia 73 4.15N 42.10E
Genappe Belgium 16 50.37N 4.25E
Gençay France 20 46.23N 0.24E
Gendringen Neth. 16 51.52N 6.26E
General Acha Argentina 125 37.20S 64.35W
General Alvear Buenos Aires Argentina 125 36.00S 60.00W
General Alvear Mendoza Argentina 125 34.59S 67.42W
General Belgrano Argentina 125 35.45S 58.30W
General Campos Argentina 125 31.30S 58.25W
General Conesa Argentina 125 36.30S 57.19W
General Guido Argentina 125 36.40S 57.45W
General Lavalle Argentina 125 36.22S 56.55W
General Madariaga Argentina 125 37.00S 57.05W
General Paz Argentina 125 35.32S 58.18W
General Pico Argentina 125 35.38S 63.46W
General Roca Argentina 125 39.02S 67.33W
General Santos Phil. 59 6.05N 125.15E
Genesee U.S.A. 114 41.59N 77.52W
Genesee r. U.S.A. 114 43.16N 77.36W
Geneseo Ill. U.S.A. 110 41.27N 90.09W

Geneseo N.Y. U.S.A. 114 42.48N 77.49W
Geneva see Genève Switz. 39
Geneva Nebr. U.S.A. 110 40.32N 97.36W
Geneva N.Y. U.S.A. 114 42.52N 77.00W
Geneva Ohio U.S.A. 114 41.48N 80.57W
Geneva, L. see Léman, Lac l. Switz. 39
Genève Switz. 39 46.12N 6.09E
Genève d. Switz. 39 46.15N 6.15E
Genichesk Ukraine 45 46.10N 34.49E
Genil r. Spain 27 37.42N 5.19W
Genk Belgium 16 50.58N 5.34E
Genlis France 19 47.14N 5.13E
Gennargentu, Monti del mts. Italy 32 39.59N 9.19E
Gennep Neth. 16 51.43N 5.58E
Gennes France 18 47.20N 0.14W
Genoa Australia 93 37.29S 149.35E
Genoa see Genova Italy 30
Genoa U.S.A. 110 41.27N 97.44W
Genoa, G. of see Genova, Golfo di g. Italy 30
Genova Italy 30 44.25N 8.57E
Genova, Golfo di g. Italy 30 44.00N 9.00E
Gens de Terre r. Canada 105 46.53N 76.00W
Gent Belgium 16 51.02N 3.42E
Genthin Germany 38 52.24N 12.09E
Gentilly Canada 105 46.24N 72.17W
Gentioux France 20 45.47N 1.59E
Genzano di Roma Italy 32 41.42N 12.41E
Geographe B. Australia 89 33.35S 115.15E
George r. Australia 92 28.24S 136.39E
George r. Canada 99 58.30N 66.00W
George R.S.A. 80 33.57S 22.27E
George B. Canada 103 45.50N 61.45W
George, L. N.S.W. Australia 93 35.07S 149.22E
George, L. S.A. Australia 92 37.26S 140.00E
George, L. Uganda 79 0.00 30.10E
George, L. Fla. U.S.A. 113 29.17N 81.36W
George, L. N.Y. U.S.A. 115 43.35N 73.35W
George's Cove Canada 103 52.40N 55.50W
Georgetown Ascension 127 7.56S 14.25W
Georgetown Qld. Australia 90 18.18S 143.33E
George Town Tas. Australia 90 41.04S 146.48E
Georgetown Canada 103 46.11N 62.32W
Georgetown Cayman Is. 117 19.20N 81.23W
Georgetown Gambia 76 13.31N 14.50W
Georgetown Guyana 122 6.46N 58.10W
George Town Malaysia 58 5.30N 100.16E
Georgetown Del. U.S.A. 115 38.42N 75.23W
Georgetown S.C. U.S.A. 113 33.23N 79.18W
Georgetown Tex. U.S.A. 111 30.38N 97.41W
George V Land f. Antarctica 128 69.00S 145.00E
Georgia Europe 45 42.00N 43.30E
Georgia d. U.S.A. 113 32.50N 83.15W
Georgian B. Canada 104 45.15N 80.50W
Georgia, Str. of Canada 100 49.25N 124.00W
Georgi Dimitrov Bulgaria 34 42.37N 23.04E
Georgina r. Australia 90 23.12S 139.33E
Georgiyevsk Russian Fed. 45 44.10N 43.30E
Gera Germany 38 50.52N 12.04E
Geraardsbergen Belgium 16 50.47N 3.53E
Geral de Goiás, Serra mts. Brazil 123 13.00S 45.40W
Geraldine New Zealand 86 44.05S 171.15E
Geral do Paraná, Serra mts. Brazil 123 14.40S 47.30W
Geraldton Australia 89 28.49S 114.36E
Geraldton Canada 102 49.44N 86.59W
Gerar r. Israel 67 31.24N 34.26E
Gérardmer France 19 48.04N 6.53E
Gerede Turkey 64 40.48N 32.13E
Gereshk Afghan. 62 31.48N 64.34E
Gérgal Spain 27 37.07N 2.33W
Gering U.S.A. 110 41.50N 103.40W
Gerlach U.S.A. 108 40.40N 119.21W
Gerlachovský Štít mtn. Slovakia 37 49.10N 20.05E
Germania U.S.A. 114 41.39N 77.40W
Germany Europe 38 51.05N 9.45E
Germencik Turkey 35 37.51N 27.37E
Germersheim Germany 39 49.13N 8.22E
Germiston R.S.A. 80 26.14S 28.10E
Gerolstein Germany 39 50.13N 6.40E
Gerolzhofen Germany 39 49.54N 10.21E
Gerona Spain 25 41.59N 2.49E
Gerona see Girona Spain 25
Gerona see Girona d. Spain 25
Gerringong Australia 93 34.45S 150.50E
Gers d. France 20 43.40N 0.30E
Gêrzê China 63 32.16N 84.12E
Gescher Germany 38 51.57N 6.59E
Geseke Germany 38 51.38N 8.31E
Getafe Spain 26 40.18N 3.43W
Gete r. Belgium 16 50.58N 5.07E
Gethsémani Canada 103 50.13N 60.40W
Getinge Sweden 43 56.49N 12.44E
Gettysburg Penn. U.S.A. 114 39.50N 77.14W
Gettysburg S.Dak. U.S.A. 110 45.01N 99.57W
Gevän Iran 65 26.03N 57.17E
Gevar'am Israel 67 31.35N 34.37E
Gevelsberg Germany 38 51.19N 7.20E
Gevgelija Macedonia 34 41.09N 22.30E
Gévora r. Spain 27 38.53N 6.57W
Gevulot Israel 67 31.12N 34.28E
Geyikli Turkey 34 39.50N 26.12E
Geysdorp R.S.A. 80 26.31S 25.17E
Geyser U.S.A. 108 47.16N 110.30W
Geyve Turkey 64 40.32N 30.18E
Gezer Israel 67 31.52N 34.55E
Ghabāghib Syria 67 33.10N 36.13E
Ghābat al 'Arab Sudan 73 9.02N 29.29E
Ghadaf, Wādī al r. Jordan 66 31.46N 36.50E
Ghadāmis Libya 75 30.08N 9.30E
Ghaddūwah Libya 75 26.26N 14.18E
Ghāghra r. India 63 25.47N 84.37E
Ghana Africa 76 8.00N 1.00W
Ghanzi Botswana 80 21.42S 21.39E
Ghanzi d. Botswana 80 21.44S 21.38E
Gharb al Istiwā'īyah d. Sudan 73 5.25N 29.00E
Ghardaïa Algeria 75 32.29N 3.40E
Gharghoda India 63 22.10N 83.21E
Ghārib, Jabal mtn. Egypt 66 28.06N 32.54E
Ghārīyat ash Sharqīyah Syria 67 32.40N 36.16E

Gharo Pakistan 62 24.44N 67.35E
Gharyān Libya 75 32.10N 13.01E
Gharyān d. Libya 75 30.35N 12.00E
Ghāt Libya 75 24.58N 10.11E
Ghātsīla India 63 22.36N 86.29E
Ghazāl, Baḥr al r. Sudan 73 9.31N 30.25E
Ghāziābād India 63 28.40N 77.26E
Ghāzipur India 63 25.35N 83.34E
Ghazlūna Pakistan 62 31.24N 67.49E
Ghaznī d. Afghan. 62 32.45N 68.30E
Ghaznī r. Afghan. 62 32.35N 67.58E
Ghazzah Egypt 67 31.30N 34.28E
Ghedi Italy 30 45.24N 10.16E
Gheorgheni Romania 37 46.43N 25.36E
Gherla Romania 37 47.02N 23.55E
Ghisonáccia France 21 42.00N 9.25E
Ghotki Pakistan 62 28.01N 69.19E
Ghowr d. Afghan. 62 34.00N 64.15E
Ghubaysh Sudan 73 12.09N 27.21E
Ghūdāf, Wādī al r. Iraq 64 32.54N 43.33E
Ghūriān Afghan. 62 34.21N 61.30E
Gia Dinh Vietnam 56 10.54N 106.43E
Giarre Italy 33 37.43N 15.11E
Gibb River town Australia 88 16.29S 126.20E
Gibeon Namibia 80 25.09S 17.44E
Gibraleón Spain 27 37.23N 6.58W
Gibraltar Europe 27 36.09N 5.21W
Gibraltar Pt. U.K. 12 53.05N 0.20E
Gibraltar, Str. of Africa/Europe 24 36.00N 5.25W
Gibson Australia 89 33.39S 121.48E
Gibson Desert Australia 88 23.10S 125.35E
Gīda Ethiopia 73 9.40N 35.16E
Giddings U.S.A. 111 30.11N 96.56W
Gien France 19 47.42N 2.38E
Giessen Germany 38 50.35N 8.40E
Gieten Neth. 16 53.01N 6.45E
Gifford r. Canada 99 70.21N 83.05W
Gifford U.S.A. 108 48.20N 118.08W
Gifhorn Germany 38 52.29N 10.33E
Gifu Japan 57 35.25N 136.45E
Gifu d. Japan 57 35.32N 137.15E
Giganta, Sierra de la mts. Mexico 109 25.30N 111.15W
Gigantes, Llanos de los f. Mexico 109 30.00N 105.00W
Gigen Bulgaria 34 43.40N 24.28E
Gigha i. U.K. 14 55.41N 5.44W
Giglio i. Italy 30 42.21N 10.54E
Gijón Spain 26 43.32N 5.40W
Gila r. U.S.A. 109 32.43N 114.33W
Gila Bend U.S.A. 109 32.57N 112.43W
Gila Bend Mts. U.S.A. 109 33.10N 113.10W
Gilardo Dam Canada 105 47.12N 73.48W
Gilat Israel 67 31.19N 34.40E
Gilbert r. Australia 90 16.35S 141.15E
Gilbert Islands Kiribati 84 2.00S 175.00E
Gildford U.S.A. 108 48.34N 110.18W
Gilé Mozambique 79 16.10S 38.17E
Gilgandra Australia 93 31.42S 148.40E
Gil Gil r. Australia 93 29.10S 148.50E
Gilgil Kenya 79 0.29S 36.19E
Gilgit Jammu & Kashmir 60 35.54N 74.20E
Gilgunnia Australia 93 32.25S 146.04E
Giljeva Planina mts. Yugo. 31 43.15N 19.55E
Gilleleje Denmark 43 56.07N 12.19E
Gilles, L. Australia 92 32.50S 136.45E
Gillette U.S.A. 108 44.18N 105.30W
Gillingham Kent U.K. 13 51.24N 0.33E
Gill, Lough Rep. of Ire. 15 54.15N 8.14W
Gill Pt. c. St. Helena 127 15.59S 5.38W
Gilmour Canada 105 44.48N 77.37W
Gīlo r. Ethiopia 73 8.10N 33.15E
Gimli Canada 101 50.39N 97.00W
Gimo Sweden 43 60.11N 18.11E
Gimone r. France 20 44.00N 1.06E
Gimzo Israel 67 31.56N 34.57E
Gingin Australia 89 31.21S 115.42E
Gīnīr Ethiopia 73 7.07N 40.46E
Ginnosar Israel 67 32.51N 35.31E
Ginosa Italy 33 40.34N 16.46E
Ginzo de Limia Spain 26 42.03N 7.43W
Gioia del Colle Italy 33 40.48N 16.56E
Gioia Tauro Italy 33 38.26N 15.54E
Gióna mtn. Greece 35 38.38N 22.14E
Girard Ohio U.S.A. 114 41.10N 80.42W
Girard Penn. U.S.A. 114 42.00N 80.19W
Girardot Colombia 122 4.19N 74.47W
Girdle Ness U.K. 17 57.06N 2.02W
Giresun Turkey 64 40.55N 38.25E
Gīr Hills India 62 21.10N 71.00E
Giri r. Zaïre 78 0.30N 17.58E
Giridih India 63 24.11N 86.18E
Girilambone Australia 93 31.14S 146.55E
Girna r. India 62 21.08N 75.19E
Giromagny France 19 47.45N 6.50E
Girona see Gerona Spain 25
Girona d. Spain 25 42.05N 2.50E
Gironde r. France 20 45.20N 1.00W
Gironde r. France 20 45.35N 1.00W
Girvan U.K. 14 55.15N 4.51W
Girwa r. India 63 27.20N 81.25E
Gisborne New Zealand 86 38.41S 178.02E
Gisborne d. New Zealand 86 38.20S 177.45E
Gislaved Sweden 43 57.18N 13.32E
Gisors France 19 49.17N 1.47E
Gitega Burundi 79 3.25S 29.56E
Giugliano Italy 33 40.56N 14.12E
Giulianova Italy 31 42.45N 13.57E
Giurgiu Romania 34 43.53N 25.57E
Giv'atayim Israel 67 32.04N 34.49E
Giv'at Brenner Israel 67 31.52N 34.48E
Give Denmark 42 55.51N 9.15E
Givet France 17 50.08N 4.49E
Givors France 21 45.35N 4.46E
Givry France 19 46.47N 4.45E
Gīzāb Afghan. 62 33.23N 65.55E
Gizhiga Russian Fed. 51 62.00N 160.34E

Gizhiginskaya Guba g. Russian Fed. 51 61.00N 158.00E
Giżycko Poland 37 54.03N 21.47E
Gjerstad Norway 42 58.54N 9.00E
Gjirokastër Albania 34 40.05N 20.10E
Gjoa Haven town Canada 99 68.39N 96.08W
Gjøvik Norway 41 60.48N 10.42E
Glace Bay town Canada 103 46.12N 59.57W
Glacier Nat. Park U.S.A. 108 48.07N 121.06W
Glacier Peak mtn. U.S.A. 108 48.07N 121.06W
Gladewater U.S.A. 111 32.33N 94.56W
Gladmar Canada 101 49.12N 104.31W
Gladstone Qld. Australia 90 23.52S 151.16E
Gladstone S.A. Australia 92 33.17S 138.22E
Gladstone Mich. U.S.A. 112 45.52N 87.02W
Gladstone N.J. U.S.A. 111 40.43N 74.40W
Gladwin U.S.A. 104 43.59N 84.29W
Glafsfjorden l. Sweden 43 59.34N 12.37E
Glåma r. Norway 42 59.12N 10.57E
Glamoč Bosnia-Herzegovina 31 44.03N 16.51E
Glan r. Germany 16 49.46N 7.43E
Glan l. Sweden 43 58.37N 15.58E
Glanaman U.K. 13 51.49N 3.54W
Glandorf Germany 38 52.05N 7.59E
Glarner Alpen mts. Switz. 39 46.55N 9.00E
Glarus Switz. 39 47.02N 9.04E
Glarus d. Switz. 39 46.59N 9.05E
Glasco Kans. U.S.A. 110 39.22N 97.50W
Glasco N.Y. U.S.A. 115 42.03N 73.57W
Glasgow U.K. 14 55.52N 4.15W
Glasgow Ky. U.S.A. 113 36.59N 85.56W
Glasgow Mont. U.S.A. 108 48.12N 106.38W
Glassboro U.S.A. 115 39.42N 75.07W
Glastonbury U.K. 13 51.09N 2.42W
Glauchau Germany 38 50.49N 12.32E
Glazov Russian Fed. 44 58.09N 52.42E
Gleisdorf Austria 31 47.06N 15.44E
Glen R.S.A. 80 28.57S 26.19E
Glen Affric f. U.K. 14 57.15N 5.03W
Glen Afton Canada 104 46.39N 80.17W
Glénans, Îles de is. France 18 47.43N 3.57W
Glenarm U.K. 15 54.57N 5.58W
Glenburnie Australia 92 37.49S 140.56E
Glen Burnie U.S.A. 115 39.10N 76.37W
Glencoe Australia 92 37.41S 140.05E
Glencoe Canada 104 42.45N 81.43W
Glen Coe f. U.K. 14 56.40N 5.03W
Glencoe U.S.A. 110 44.45N 94.09W
Glen Cove U.S.A. 115 40.52N 73.37W
Glendale Ariz. U.S.A. 109 33.32N 112.11W
Glendale Calif. U.S.A. 109 34.10N 118.17W
Glendale Oreg. U.S.A. 108 42.44N 123.26W
Glen Davis Australia 93 33.07S 150.22E
Glendive U.S.A. 108 47.06N 104.43W
Glenelg r. Australia 92 38.03S 141.00E
Glenfield U.S.A. 115 43.43N 75.24W
Glengarriff Rep. of Ire. 15 51.45N 9.33W
Glen Garry f. Highland U.K. 14 57.03N 5.04W
Glen Head Rep. of Ire. 15 54.44N 8.46W
Glen Helen town Australia 90 23.15S 132.35E
Glen Innes Australia 93 29.42S 151.45E
Glen Lyon U.S.A. 115 41.10N 76.05W
Glen Mòr f. U.K. 14 57.15N 4.30W
Glenmora U.S.A. 111 30.59N 92.35W
Glenmorgan Australia 91 27.19S 149.40E
Glen Moriston f. U.K. 14 57.09N 4.50W
Glennie U.S.A. 104 44.33N 83.44W
Glenns Ferry U.S.A. 108 42.57N 115.18W
Glenrock U.S.A. 108 42.52N 105.52W
Glenrothes U.K. 14 56.12N 3.10W
Glenroy Australia 88 17.23S 126.01E
Glens Falls town U.S.A. 115 43.19N 73.39W
Glenshee f. U.K. 14 56.45N 3.25W
Glen Spean f. U.K. 14 56.53N 4.40W
Glenville U.S.A. 114 38.56N 80.50W
Glenwood Ark. U.S.A. 111 34.20N 93.33W
Glenwood Iowa U.S.A. 110 41.03N 95.45W
Glenwood Oreg. U.S.A. 108 45.39N 123.16W
Glenwood Springs town U.S.A. 108 39.33N 107.19W
Glîfa Greece 35 38.57N 22.58E
Glimåkra Sweden 43 56.18N 14.08E
Glimmingehus Sweden 43 55.30N 14.13E
Glina Croatia 31 45.20N 16.06E
Glina r. Croatia 31 45.20N 16.07E
Glittertind mtn. Norway 41 61.39N 8.33E
Gliwice Poland 37 50.17N 18.40E
Globe U.S.A. 109 33.24N 110.47W
Głogów Poland 36 51.40N 16.06E
Glotovo Russian Fed. 44 63.25N 49.28E
Gloucester Australia 93 31.59S 151.58E
Gloucester U.K. 13 51.52N 2.15W
Gloucester City U.S.A. 115 39.54N 75.07W
Gloucester U.S.A. 115 42.41N 70.39W
Gloucestershire d. U.K. 13 51.45N 2.00W
Glouster U.S.A. 114 39.30N 82.05W
Gloversville U.S.A. 115 43.03N 74.20W
Głubczyce Poland 37 50.13N 17.49E
Glücksburg Germany 38 54.50N 9.33E
Glückstadt Germany 38 53.47N 9.25E
Glusha Belarus 37 53.03N 28.55E
Glyngøre Denmark 42 56.46N 8.52E
Gmünd Austria 38 48.47N 14.59E
Gmunden Austria 39 47.55N 13.48E
Gnadenhutten U.S.A. 114 40.22N 81.26W
Gnarp Sweden 41 62.03N 17.16E
Gnesta Sweden 43 59.03N 17.18E
Gniewkowo Poland 37 52.54N 18.25E
Gniezno Poland 37 52.32N 17.32E
Gnjilane Yugo. 34 42.28N 21.28E
Gnoien Germany 38 53.58N 12.42E
Gnosjö Sweden 43 57.22N 13.44E
Gnowangerup Australia 89 33.57S 117.58E
Gnuca Australia 89 31.08S 117.24E
Goa d. India 60 15.30N 74.00E
Goageb Namibia 80 26.45S 17.18E
Goälpära India 63 26.10N 90.37E
Goat Fell mtn. U.K. 14 55.37N 5.12W
Goba Ethiopia 73 7.02N 40.00E

Goba Mozambique 81 26.11S 32.08E
Gobabis Namibia 80 22.28S 18.58E
Gobi des. Asia 54 45.00N 108.00E
Goch Germany 38 51.41N 6.10E
Gochas Namibia 80 24.50S 18.48E
Godalming U.K. 13 51.11N 0.37W
Godar Pakistan 62 28.10N 63.14E
Godāvari r. India 61 16.40N 82.15E
Godbout Canada 103 49.19N 67.37W
Goderich Canada 104 43.45N 81.43W
Goderville France 18 49.39N 0.22E
Godhavn Greenland 99 69.20N 53.30W
Godhra India 62 22.45N 73.38E
Godoy Cruz Argentina 125 32.55S 68.50W
Gods L. r. Canada 101 56.22N 92.51W
Gods L. Canada 101 54.45N 94.00W
Godthåb Greenland 99 64.10N 51.40W
Goéland, Lac au l. Canada 102 49.47N 76.41W
Goélands, Lac aux l. Canada 103 55.25N 64.20W
Goes Neth. 16 51.30N 3.54E
Goffstown U.S.A. 115 43.01N 71.36W
Gogama Canada 102 47.35N 81.35W
Gogeh Ethiopia 73 3.28N 38.27E
Göggingen Germany 39 48.20N 10.52E
Gogonou Benin 77 10.50N 2.50E
Gogra r. see Ghāghra India 63
Gogrial Sudan 73 8.32N 28.07E
Goha Ethiopia 73 10.25N 34.38E
Gohad India 63 26.26N 78.27E
Goiana Brazil 123 7.30S 35.00W
Goiânia Brazil 123 16.43S 49.18W
Goiás Brazil 123 15.57S 50.07W
Goiás d. Brazil 123 15.00S 48.00W
Goichran India 63 31.04N 78.07E
Góis Portugal 26 40.09N 8.07W
Goito Italy 30 45.15N 10.40E
Gojam d. Ethiopia 73 11.10N 37.00E
Gojō Japan 57 34.21N 135.42E
Gojra Pakistan 62 31.09N 72.41E
Gökçe Turkey 34 40.10N 25.57E
Gökçeada i. Turkey 34 40.10N 26.00E
Göksun Turkey 64 38.03N 36.30E
Gokteik Myanmar 61 22.26N 97.00E
Gokwe Zimbabwe 80 18.14S 28.54E
Gol Norway 41 60.42N 8.57E
Gola Gokaran Nath India 63 28.05N 80.28E
Golan Heights mts. Syria 67 33.55N 35.42E
Golconda U.S.A. 108 40.57N 117.30W
Gold U.S.A. 114 41.52N 77.52W
Gołdap Poland 37 54.19N 22.19E
Gold Beach town U.S.A. 108 42.25N 124.25W
Golden Canada 100 51.20N 117.00W
Golden Rep. of Ire. 15 52.30N 7.59W
Golden U.S.A. 108 39.46N 105.15W
Golden B. New Zealand 86 40.45S 172.50E
Goldendale U.S.A. 108 45.49N 120.50W
Golden Hinde mtn. Canada 100 49.40N 125.44W
Golden L. Canada 105 45.35N 77.20W
Golden Lake town Canada 105 45.35N 77.16W
Golden Ridge town Australia 89 30.51S 121.42E
Golden Vale f. Rep. of Ire. 15 52.30N 8.07W
Goldfield U.S.A. 108 37.42N 117.14W
Goldfields Canada 101 59.28N 108.31W
Goldpines Canada 102 50.45N 93.05W
Goldsand L. Canada 101 56.58N 101.02W
Goldsboro U.S.A. 113 35.23N 78.00W
Goldsworthy Australia 88 20.20S 119.30E
Goleniów Poland 36 53.36N 14.50E
Golets Skalisty mtn. Russian Fed. 51 56.00N 130.40E
Golfito Costa Rica 117 8.42N 83.10W
Golfo degli Aranci town Italy 32 41.00N 9.38E
Goliad U.S.A. 111 28.40N 97.23W
Goljam Perelik mtn. Bulgaria 34 41.36N 24.34E
Golling Austria 39 47.36N 13.10E
Golmud China 52 36.22N 94.55E
Golo r. France 21 42.31N 9.32E
Golovanevsk Ukraine 37 48.25N 30.30E
Golpāyegān Iran 65 33.23N 50.18E
Golspie U.K. 14 57.58N 3.58W
Goma Zaïre 79 1.37S 29.10E
Gomang Co l. China 63 31.10N 89.10E
Gombe Nigeria 77 10.17N 11.20E
Gombe r. Tanzania 79 4.43S 31.30E
Gomel Belarus 37 52.25N 31.00E
Gomera i. Canary Is. 74 28.08N 17.14W
Gómez Palacio Mexico 111 25.34N 103.30W
Gomīshān Iran 65 37.04N 54.06E
Gompa Jammu & Kashmir 62 35.02N 77.20E
Gonaïves Haiti 117 19.29N 72.42W
Gonâve, Golfe de la g. Haiti 117 19.00N 73.00W
Gonâve, Île de la i. Haiti 117 18.50N 73.00W
Gonbad-e Kāvūs Iran 65 37.15N 55.11E
Gonda India 63 27.08N 81.56E
Gondal India 62 21.58N 70.48E
Gonder Ethiopia 73 12.39N 37.29E
Gonder d. Ethiopia 73 12.30N 37.30E
Gondia India 63 21.27N 80.12E
Gondomar Portugal 26 41.09N 8.32W
Gondrecourt-le-Château France 19 48.31N 5.30E
Gonen Israel 67 33.08N 35.39E
Gongbo'gyamda China 63 29.56N 93.23E
Gonggar China 63 29.15N 90.50E
Gongga Shan mtn. China 52 29.30N 101.30E
Gongola r. Nigeria 77 9.30N 12.06E
Gongolgon Australia 93 30.22S 146.56E
Goñi Uruguay 125 33.31S 56.24W
Goniri Nigeria 77 11.30N 12.15E
Gonnesa Italy 32 39.15N 8.28E
Gonzaga Italy 30 44.57N 10.49E
Gonzales U.S.A. 111 29.30N 97.27W
Good Hope, C. of R.S.A. 80 34.21S 18.28E
Good Hope Mtn. Canada 100 51.09N 124.10W
Gooding U.S.A. 108 42.56N 114.43W
Goodland U.S.A. 110 39.21N 101.43W
Goodooga Australia 93 29.08S 147.30E
Goodsprings U.S.A. 109 35.50N 115.26W
Goole U.K. 12 53.42N 0.52W

Goolgowi Australia 93 33.59S 145.42E
Goolma Australia 93 32.21S 149.20E
Gooloogong Australia 93 33.36S 148.27E
Goolwa Australia 92 35.31S 138.45E
Goomalling Australia 89 31.19S 116.49E
Goombalie Australia 93 29.59S 145.24E
Goondiwindi Australia 93 28.30S 150.17E
Goongarrie Australia 89 30.03S 121.09E
Goor Neth. 16 52.16N 6.33E
Goose r. Canada 103 53.18N 60.23W
Goose Bay town Canada 103 53.19N 60.24W
Goose L. U.S.A. 108 41.57N 120.25W
Gopālganj Bangla. 63 23.01N 89.50E
Gopālganj India 63 26.28N 84.26E
Göppingen Germany 39 48.42N 9.40E
Gorakhpur India 63 26.45N 83.22E
Goras India 62 25.32N 76.56E
Goražde Bosnia-Herzegovina 31 43.40N 18.56E
Gordon r. Australia 89 34.12S 117.00E
Gordon U.S.A. 110 42.48N 102.12W
Gordon Downs town Australia 88 18.43S 128.33E
Gordon L. Canada 100 63.05N 113.11W
Gordonvale Australia 90 17.05S 145.47E
Goré Chad 77 7.57N 16.31E
Goré Ethiopia 73 8.08N 35.33E
Gore New Zealand 86 46.06S 168.58E
Gore Bay town Canada 104 45.55N 82.28W
Gore Mtn. U.S.A. 105 44.55N 71.48W
Gorgān Iran 65 36.50N 54.29E
Gorgān r. Iran 65 37.00N 54.00E
Gorgol d. Mauritania 74 15.45N 13.00W
Gori Georgia 65 41.59N 44.05E
Gorinchem Neth. 16 51.50N 4.59E
Gorizia Italy 31 45.57N 13.38E
Gorjani Croatia 31 45.24N 18.21E
Gorki see Nizhniy Novgorod Russian Fed. 44
Gorkovskoye Vodokhranilishche resr. Russian Fed.
 44 56.49N 43.00E
Görlitz Germany 38 51.09N 14.59E
Gorlovka Ukraine 45 48.17N 38.05E
Gorna Oryakhovitsa Bulgaria 34 43.07N 25.40E
Gornja Radogna Slovenia 31 46.41N 16.00E
Gornji Grad Slovenia 31 46.18N 14.49E
Gornji Vakuf Bosnia-Herzegovina 31 43.56N 17.35E
Gorno Altaysk Russian Fed. 50 51.59N 85.56E
Gorno Filinskoye Russian Fed. 50 60.06N 69.58E
Gornyatskiy Russian Fed. 44 67.30N 64.03E
Goroch'an mtn. Ethiopia 73 9.22N 37.04E
Gorodenka Ukraine 37 48.40N 25.30E
Gorodishche Belarus 37 53.18N 26.00E
Gorodishche Belarus 37 53.45N 29.45E
Gorodnitsa Russian Fed. 50 50.50N 27.19E
Gorodnya Ukraine 37 51.54N 31.37E
Gorodok Ukraine 37 49.48N 23.39E
Goroka P.N.G. 59 6.02S 145.22E
Goroke Australia 92 36.43S 141.30E
Gorokhov Ukraine 37 50.30N 24.46E
Gorongosa r. Mozambique 81 20.29S 34.36E
Gorontalo Indonesia 59 0.33N 123.05E
Gort Rep. of Ire. 15 53.04N 8.49W
Goryn Ukraine 37 52.08N 27.17E
Gorzów Wielkopolski Poland 36 52.42N 15.12E
Gosford Australia 93 33.25S 151.18E
Goslar Germany 38 51.54N 10.25E
Gospić Croatia 31 44.33N 15.23E
Gosport U.K. 13 50.48N 1.08W
Gossi Mali 76 15.49N 1.17W
Gossinga Sudan 73 8.39N 25.59E
Gostivar Macedonia 34 41.47N 20.24E
Gostynin Poland 37 52.26N 19.29E
Göta r. Sweden 43 57.42N 11.52E
Göta Kanal Sweden 43 58.45N 14.05E
Göteborg Sweden 43 57.43N 11.58E
Göteborg och Bohus d. Sweden 42 58.30N 11.30E
Gotemba Japan 57 35.18N 138.56E
Götene Sweden 43 58.32N 13.29E
Gotha Germany 38 50.57N 10.41E
Gothem Sweden 43 57.35N 18.43E
Gothenburg see Göteborg Sweden 42
Gothenburg U.S.A. 110 40.56N 100.09W
Gothèye Niger 77 13.51N 1.31E
Gotland d. Sweden 43 57.25N 18.25E
Gotland i. Sweden 43 57.30N 18.33E
Gotse Delchev Bulgaria 34 41.34N 23.44E
Gotska Sandön i. Sweden 43 58.23N 19.16E
Gōtsu Japan 57 35.00N 132.14E
Göttingen Germany 38 51.32N 9.55E
Götzis Austria 39 47.20N 9.38E
Gouarec France 18 48.13N 3.11W
Gouda Neth. 16 52.01N 4.43E
Gough I. Atlantic Oc. 127 40.20S 10.00W
Gouin, Résr. Canada 102 48.38N 74.54W
Goulais River town Canada 104 46.43N 84.18W
Goulburn Australia 93 34.47S 149.43E
Goulburn r. Australia 93 36.08S 144.30E
Goulburn Is. Australia 90 11.33S 133.26E
Gould Canada 105 45.35N 71.24W
Goulimime Morocco 74 28.56N 10.04W
Gouménissa Greece 34 40.56N 22.37E
Goundam Mali 76 17.27N 3.39W
Gourdon France 20 44.44N 1.23E
Gouré Niger 77 13.59N 10.15E
Gourin France 18 48.08N 3.36W
Gourma-Rharous Mali 76 16.58N 1.50W
Gournay France 17 49.29N 1.44E
Gouro Chad 75 19.33N 19.33E
Gouverneur U.S.A. 105 44.20N 75.28W
Governador Valadares Brazil 126 18.51S 42.00W
Govind Balabh Pant Sāgar resr. India 63 24.05N
 82.50E
Govind Sāgar resr. India 62 31.20N 76.45E
Gowanda U.S.A. 114 42.28N 78.56W
Goward Canada 104 47.08N 79.49W
Gowd-e Zereh des. Afghan. 65 30.00N 62.00E
Gower pen. U.K. 13 51.37N 4.10W
Gowmal r. Afghan. see Gumal r. Pakistan 62
Gowmal Kalay Afghan. 62 32.29N 68.55E
Goya Argentina 124 29.10S 59.20W

Goyder r. Australia 90 12.38S 135.11E
Goz Béïda Chad 73 12.13N 21.25E
Gozo i. Malta 28 36.03N 14.16E
Graaff Reinet R.S.A. 80 32.15S 24.31E
Graben Germany 39 49.09N 8.29E
Grabow Germany 38 53.16N 11.34E
Gračac Croatia 31 44.18N 15.51E
Gračanica Bosnia-Herzegovina 31 44.42N 18.19E
Graçay France 19 47.08N 1.51E
Gracefield Canada 105 46.06N 76.03W
Grace, L. Australia 89 33.18S 118.15E
Gracias á Dios, Cabo c. Honduras/Nicaragua 117
 15.00N 83.10W
Gradačac Bosnia-Herzegovina 31 44.53N 18.26E
Grado Italy 30 45.40N 13.23E
Grado Spain 26 43.23N 6.04W
Grafenau Germany 39 48.52N 13.25E
Gräfenhainichen Germany 38 51.44N 12.27E
Grafing Germany 39 48.02N 11.59E
Gråfjell mtn. Norway 42 60.16N 9.29E
Grafton Australia 93 29.40S 152.56E
Grafton Canada 104 44.00N 78.01W
Grafton Mass. U.S.A. 115 42.12N 71.41W
Grafton N.Dak. U.S.A. 110 48.25N 97.25W
Grafton Ohio U.S.A. 114 41.16N 82.04W
Grafton W.Va. U.S.A. 114 39.20N 80.01W
Grafton Wisc. U.S.A. 110 43.20N 87.58W
Graham r. Canada 100 56.31N 122.17W
Graham U.S.A. 111 33.06N 98.35W
Graham I. Canada 100 53.40N 132.30W
Graham Land f. Antarctica 128 67.00S 60.00W
Graham, Mt. U.S.A. 109 32.42N 109.52W
Grahamstown R.S.A. 80 33.18S 26.30E
Graiguenamanagh Rep. of Ire. 15 52.33N 6.57W
Grajaú r. Brazil 123 3.41S 44.48W
Gram Denmark 42 55.17N 9.04E
Gramada Bulgaria 34 43.49N 22.39E
Gramat France 20 44.47N 1.43E
Grammichele Italy 33 37.13N 14.38E
Grámmos, Óros mtn. Greece 34 40.23N 20.45E
Grampian d. U.K. 14 57.22N 2.35W
Grampian Mts. U.K. 14 56.55N 4.00W
Grampians mts. Australia 92 37.12S 142.34E
Gramsh Albania 34 40.52N 20.12E
Granada Nicaragua 117 11.58N 85.59W
Granada Spain 27 37.10N 3.41W
Granada d. Spain 27 37.30N 3.00W
Granby Canada 105 45.24N 72.44W
Gran Canaria i. Canary Is. 74 28.00N 15.30W
Gran Chaco f. S. America 124 22.00S 60.00W
Grand r. Canada 104 42.51N 79.34W
Grand r. Ohio U.S.A. 114 41.46N 81.17W
Grand r. S.Dak. U.S.A. 110 45.40N 100.32W
Grandas Spain 26 43.13N 6.52W
Grandas de Salime, Embalse de resr. Spain 26
 43.10N 6.45W
Grand Bahama I. Bahamas 113 26.40N 78.20W
Grand Ballon mtn. France 19 47.55N 7.08E
Grand Bank town Canada 103 47.06N 55.47W
Grand Bassam Côte d'Ivoire 76 5.14N 3.45W
Grand Bend Canada 104 43.19N 81.45W
Grand Blanc U.S.A. 104 42.56N 83.38W
Grand Canal see Da Yunhe canal China 54
Grand Canyon f. U.S.A. 109 36.10N 112.45W
Grand Canyon town U.S.A. 109 36.03N 112.09W
Grand Canyon Nat. Park U.S.A. 109 36.15N 112.58W
Grand Cayman i. Cayman Is. 117 19.20N 81.30W
Grand Centre Canada 101 54.25N 110.13W
Grand Cess Liberia 76 4.40N 8.12W
Grand Couronne France 18 49.21N 1.00E
Grande r. Bolivia 124 15.10S 64.55W
Grande r. Bahia Brazil 123 11.05S 43.09W
Grande r. Minas Gerais Brazil 124 20.00S 51.00W
Grande r. Spain 25 39.07N 0.44W
Grande, Bahía b. Argentina 125 51.30S 67.30W
Grande Cascapédia Canada 103 48.19N 65.54W
Grande Comore i. Comoros 79 11.35S 43.20E
Grande do Gurupá, Ilha i. Brazil 123 1.00S 51.30W
Grande, Ilha i. Brazil 126 23.07S 44.16W
Grande Prairie Canada 100 55.15N 118.50W
Grand Erg de Bilma des. Niger 77 18.30N 14.00E
Grand Erg Occidental des. Algeria 74 30.10N 0.20E
Grand Erg Oriental des. Algeria 75 30.00N 7.00E
Grande Rivière town Canada 103 48.24N 64.30W
Grandes Bergeronnes Canada 103 48.15N 69.33W
Grande, Sierra mts. Mexico 109 29.35N 104.55W
Grandes, Salinas f. Argentina 124 29.37S 64.56W
Grande Vallée Canada 103 49.14N 65.08W
Grand Falls town N.B. Canada 103 46.55N 67.45W
Grand Falls town Nfld. Canada 103 48.56N 55.40W
Grand Forks Canada 100 49.00N 118.30W
Grand Forks U.S.A. 110 47.55N 97.03W
Grand Fougeray France 18 47.44N 1.44W
Grand Gorge U.S.A. 115 42.22N 74.30W
Grand Hers r. France 20 43.47N 1.20E
Grand Island town U.S.A. 110 40.55N 98.21W
Grand Isle U.S.A. 105 44.44N 72.18W
Grand Junction U.S.A. 108 39.05N 108.33W
Grand L. N.B. Canada 103 45.38N 67.38W
Grand L. Nfld. Canada 103 49.00N 57.25W
Grand L. U.S.A. 112 45.15N 67.50W
Grand Lahou Côte d'Ivoire 76 5.09N 5.01W
Grand Lieu, Lac de l. France 18 47.06N 1.40W
Grand Manan I. Canada 103 44.40N 66.50W
Grand Marais U.S.A. 110 47.45N 90.20W
Grand' Mère Canada 105 46.37N 72.41W
Grandois Canada 103 51.07N 55.46W
Grândola Portugal 27 38.10N 8.34W
Grand Passage N. Cal. 84 18.45S 163.10E
Grand Prairie town U.S.A. 111 32.45N 96.59W
Grand Rapids Canada 101 53.08N 99.20W
Grand Rapids town Mich. U.S.A. 112 42.57N 85.40W
Grand Rapids town Minn. U.S.A. 110 47.14N 93.31W
Grand Récif de Cook reef N. Cal. 84 19.25S 163.50E
Grand Remous Canada 105 46.37N 75.53W
Grandrieu France 20 44.47N 3.38E
Grand St. Bernard, Col du pass Italy/Switz. 30 45.52N
 7.11E

Grand Teton mtn. U.S.A. 108 43.44N 110.48W
Grand Teton Nat. Park U.S.A. 108 43.30N 110.37W
Grand Traverse B. U.S.A. 112 45.02N 85.30W
Grand Valley Canada 104 43.54N 80.19W
Grand Valley town U.S.A. 108 39.27N 108.03W
Grandville U.S.A. 112 42.54N 85.48W
Grañén Spain 25 41.56N 0.22W
Grangärde Sweden 43 60.16N 14.59E
Grangemouth U.K. 14 56.01N 3.44W
Granger U.S.A. 108 41.35N 109.58W
Grängesberg Sweden 43 60.05N 14.59E
Grangeville U.S.A. 108 45.56N 116.07W
Granite City U.S.A. 110 38.43N 90.04W
Granite Falls town U.S.A. 110 44.49N 95.31W
Granite Peak town Australia 88 25.38S 121.21E
Granite Peak mtn. U.S.A. 108 45.10N 109.50W
Granitola, Capo c. Italy 32 37.33N 12.40E
Granity New Zealand 86 41.38S 171.51E
Granja Brazil 123 3.06S 40.50W
Gränna Sweden 43 58.01N 14.28E
Granollers Spain 25 41.37N 2.18E
Granön Sweden 40 64.15N 19.19E
Gran Paradiso mtn. Italy 30 45.32N 7.16E
Gran Sasso d'Italia mts. Italy 31 42.26N 13.35E
Gransee Germany 38 53.00N 13.09E
Grant Mich. U.S.A. 112 43.20N 85.49W
Grant Nebr. U.S.A. 110 40.50N 101.56W
Grant City U.S.A. 110 40.29N 94.25W
Grantham U.K. 12 52.55N 0.39W
Grantown-on-Spey U.K. 14 57.20N 3.38W
Grant Range mts. U.S.A. 108 38.25N 115.30W
Grants U.S.A. 109 35.09N 107.52W
Grants Pass town U.S.A. 108 42.26N 123.19W
Grantsville U.S.A. 108 40.36N 112.28W
Granville France 18 48.50N 1.36W
Granville N.Dak. U.S.A. 110 48.16N 100.47W
Granville N.Y. U.S.A. 115 43.24N 73.16W
Granville L. Canada 101 56.18N 100.30W
Graskop R.S.A. 80 24.55S 30.50E
Gras, Lac de l. Canada 98 64.30N 110.30W
Grassano Italy 33 40.38N 16.18E
Grasse France 21 43.40N 6.55E
Grasset, L. Canada 102 49.55N 78.00W
Grass Lake town U.S.A. 104 42.15N 84.13W
Grass Valley town Calif. U.S.A. 108 39.13N 121.04W
Grass Valley town Oreg. U.S.A. 108 45.22N 120.47W
Gråsten Denmark 42 54.55N 9.36E
Grates Pt. Canada 103 48.09N 52.57W
Graubünden d. Switz. 39 46.42N 9.25E
Grave Neth. 16 51.45N 5.45E
Gravelbourg Canada 101 49.53N 106.34W
Gravenhurst Canada 104 44.55N 79.22W
Grave, Pointe de c. France 20 45.34N 1.04W
Gravesend Australia 93 29.35S 150.20E
Gravesend U.K. 13 51.27N 0.24E
Gravina in Puglia Italy 33 40.49N 16.25E
Gray France 19 47.27N 5.35E
Grayling U.S.A. 104 44.40N 84.43W
Grays U.K. 13 51.29N 0.20E
Graz Austria 31 47.05N 15.27E
Grazalema Spain 27 36.46N 5.22W
Grdelica Yugo. 34 42.54N 22.04E
Great Abaco I. Bahamas 113 26.25N 77.10W
Great Artesian Basin f. Australia 90 26.30S 143.02E
Great Australian Bight Australia 89 33.10S 129.30E
Great B. U.S.A. 115 39.30N 74.23W
Great Bahama Bank f. Bahamas 113 23.15N 78.00W
Great Barrier I. New Zealand 86 36.15S 175.30E
Great Barrier Reef f. Australia 90 16.30S 146.30E
Great Barrington U.S.A. 115 42.12N 73.22W
Great Basin f. U.S.A. 108 40.35N 116.00W
Great Bear L. Canada 98 66.00N 120.00W
Great Bend town U.S.A. 110 38.22N 98.46W
Great Bitter L. see Murrah al Kubrá, Al Buḩayrah al
 Egypt 66
Great Blasket I. Rep. of Ire. 15 52.05N 10.32W
Great Cloche I. Canada 104 46.01N 81.54W
Great Coco i. Myanmar 56 14.06N 93.21E
Great Divide Basin f. U.S.A. 108 42.00N 108.10W
Great Dividing Range mts. Australia 93 29.00S
 152.00E
Great Driffield U.K. 12 54.01N 0.26W
Great Duck I. Canada 104 45.40N 82.58W
Greater Antilles is. C. America 117 17.00N 70.00W
Greater London d. U.K. 13 51.31N 0.06W
Greater Manchester d. U.K. 12 53.30N 2.18W
Great Exuma i. Bahamas 117 23.00N 76.00W
Great Falls town U.S.A. 108 47.30N 111.17W
Great Inagua I. Bahamas 117 21.00N 73.20W
Great Indian Desert see Thar Desert India/Pakistan 62
Great Karoo f. R.S.A. 80 32.40S 22.20E
Great Kei r. R.S.A. 80 32.39S 28.23E
Great L. Australia 91 41.50S 146.43E
Great Malvern U.K. 13 52.07N 2.19W
Great Namaland f. Namibia 80 25.30S 17.20E
Great Nicobar i. India 56 7.00N 93.45E
Great Ouse r. U.K. 12 52.47N 0.23E
Great Pt. U.S.A. 115 41.20N 70.03W
Great Rift Valley f. Africa 70 8.00S 31.30E
Great Ruaha r. Tanzania 79 7.55S 37.52E
Great Sacandaga L. U.S.A. 115 43.08N 74.10W
Great Salt L. U.S.A. 108 41.10N 112.30W
Great Salt Lake Desert U.S.A. 108 40.40N 113.30W
Great Sand Hills Canada 101 50.35N 109.05W
Great Sandy Desert Australia 88 20.30S 123.35E
Great Sandy Desert see An Nafūd des. Saudi Arabia
 64
Great Sea Reef Fiji 84 16.25S 179.20E
Great Slave L. Canada 100 61.23N 115.38W
Great Smoky Mountain Nat. Park U.S.A. 113 35.56N
 82.48W
Great Sound b. Bermuda 127 32.18N 64.60W
Great Victoria Desert Australia 89 29.00S 127.30E
Great Whernside mtn. U.K. 12 54.09N 1.59W
Great Yarmouth U.K. 13 52.40N 1.45E
Great Zimbabwe ruins Zimbabwe 80 20.30S 30.30E
Grebbestad Sweden 42 58.42N 11.15E
Gréboun, Mont mtn. Niger 75 20.01N 8.35E

Gredos, Sierra de mts. Spain 26 40.15N 5.20W
Greece Europe 34 40.00N 23.00E
Greeley U.S.A. 108 40.25N 104.42W
Green r. U.S.A. 108 38.11N 109.53W
Green B. U.S.A. 110 45.00N 87.30W
Green Bay town U.S.A. 110 44.30N 88.01W
Greenbush Mich. U.S.A. 104 44.34N 83.19W
Greenbush Minn. U.S.A. 110 48.42N 96.11W
Greenbushes Australia 89 33.50S 116.00E
Greencastle Ind. U.S.A. 112 39.39N 86.51W
Greencastle Penn. U.S.A. 114 39.47N 77.44W
Greene U.S.A. 115 42.20N 75.46W
Greene I. Canada 104 45.51N 83.08W
Greeneville U.S.A. 113 36.10N 82.50W
Greenfield Ill. U.S.A. 110 39.21N 90.21W
Greenfield Iowa U.S.A. 110 41.18N 94.28W
Greenfield Mass. U.S.A. 115 42.36N 72.36W
Greenfield Mo. U.S.A. 111 37.25N 93.51W
Greenhills Australia 89 31.58S 117.01E
Greening Canada 102 48.08N 74.55W
Greenland N. America 99 68.00N 45.00W
Greenlaw U.K. 14 55.43N 2.28W
Green Mts. U.S.A. 115 43.45N 72.45W
Greenock U.K. 14 55.57N 4.45W
Greenore Pt. Rep. of Ire. 15 52.14N 6.19W
Greenough r. Australia 89 29.22S 114.34E
Greenport U.S.A. 115 41.06N 72.22W
Green River town Utah U.S.A. 108 38.59N 110.10W
Green River town Wyo. U.S.A. 108 41.32N 109.28W
Greensboro N.C. U.S.A. 113 36.04N 79.47W
Greensboro Vt. U.S.A. 105 44.32N 72.17W
Greensburg Ind. U.S.A. 112 39.20N 85.29W
Greensburg Penn. U.S.A. 114 40.18N 79.33W
Greenvale Australia 90 18.57S 144.53E
Greenville Canada 100 55.03N 129.33W
Greenville Liberia 76 5.01N 9.03W
Greenville Ala. U.S.A. 113 31.50N 86.40W
Greenville Maine U.S.A. 111 33.25N 91.05W
Greenville Mich. U.S.A. 112 43.11N 85.13W
Greenville Miss. U.S.A. 111 33.25N 91.05W
Greenville Mo. U.S.A. 111 37.08N 90.27W
Greenville N.C. U.S.A. 113 35.36N 77.23W
Greenville N.H. U.S.A. 115 42.46N 71.49W
Greenville Penn. U.S.A. 114 41.24N 80.23W
Greenville S.C. U.S.A. 113 34.52N 82.25W
Greenville Tex. U.S.A. 111 33.08N 96.07W
Greenwich Conn U.S.A. 115 41.01N 73.38W
Greenwich N.Y. U.S.A. 115 41.05N 73.30W
Greenwich Ohio U.S.A. 114 41.02N 82.31W
Greenwood Miss. U.S.A. 111 33.31N 90.11W
Greenwood N.Y. U.S.A. 114 42.08N 77.39W
Greenwood S.C. U.S.A. 113 34.11N 82.10W
Gregory r. Australia 90 17.53S 139.17E
Gregory U.S.A. 110 43.14N 99.26W
Gregory, L. S.A. Australia 92 28.55S 139.00E
Gregory L. W.A. Australia 88 20.10S 127.20E
Gregory Range mts. Australia 90 19.00S 143.05E
Greifswald Germany 38 54.05N 13.23E
Greifswalder Bodden c. Germany 38 54.15N 13.35E
Greiz Germany 38 50.39N 12.12E
Gremikha Russian Fed. 44 68.03N 39.38E
Grená Denmark 42 56.25N 10.53E
Grenada C. America 117 12.07N 61.40W
Grenade France 20 43.47N 1.10E
Grenchen Switz. 39 47.11N 7.24E
Grenen c. Denmark 42 57.45N 10.40E
Grenfell Australia 93 33.53S 148.11E
Grenoble France 21 45.10N 5.43E
Grenville, C. Australia 90 12.00S 143.13E
Gréoux-les-Bains France 21 43.45N 5.53E
Gresik Indonesia 59 7.12S 112.38E
Gretna U.K. 14 55.00N 3.04W
Gretna U.S.A. 111 29.55N 90.03W
Greven Germany 38 52.05N 7.36E
Grevená Greece 34 40.04N 21.25E
Grevenbroich Germany 16 51.07N 6.33E
Grevesmühlen Germany 38 53.51N 11.10E
Grey r. New Zealand 86 42.28S 171.13E
Greybull U.S.A. 108 44.30N 108.03W
Grey, C. Australia 90 13.00S 136.40E
Grey Is. Canada 103 50.50S 55.37W
Greylock, Mt. U.S.A. 115 42.38N 73.10W
Greymouth New Zealand 86 42.28S 171.12E
Grey Range mts. Australia 91 27.30S 143.59E
Greystones Rep. of Ire. 15 53.09N 6.04W
Greytown R.S.A. 80 29.04S 30.36E
Griesbach Germany 39 48.28N 13.11E
Griesheim Germany 39 49.50N 8.34E
Griffin U.S.A. 107 33.15N 84.17W
Griffith Australia 93 34.18S 146.04E
Griffith Canada 105 45.14N 77.12W
Griffith I. Canada 104 44.51N 80.54W
Griggsville U.S.A. 110 39.42N 90.43W
Grignan France 21 44.25N 4.54E
Grignols France 20 44.23N 0.03W
Grigoriopol Moldova 37 47.08N 29.18E
Grimari C.A.R. 73 5.44N 20.03E
Grim, C. Australia 91 40.45S 144.45E
Grimma Germany 38 51.14N 12.43E
Grimmen Germany 38 54.07N 13.02E
Grimsby Canada 104 43.12N 79.34W
Grimsby U.K. 12 53.35N 0.05W
Grimsel Pass Switz. 39 46.34N 8.21E
Grimstad Norway 42 58.20N 8.36E
Grimsvötn mtn. Iceland 40 64.30N 17.10W
Grindavik Iceland 40 63.50N 22.27W
Grindelwald Switz. 39 46.37N 8.02E
Grindsted Denmark 42 55.45N 8.56E
Grinnell U.S.A. 110 41.45N 92.43W
Grintavec mtn. Slovenia 31 46.21N 14.32E
Griqualand East f. R.S.A. 80 30.40S 29.10E
Griqualand West f. R.S.A. 80 28.50S 23.30E
Gris-Nez, Cap c. France 18 50.52N 1.35E
Grisslehamn Sweden 43 60.06N 18.50E
Griva Russian Fed. 44 60.35N 50.58E
Grmeč mts. Bosnia-Herzegovina 31 44.40N 16.15E
Grobina Latvia 41 56.33N 21.10E
Groblershoop R.S.A. 80 28.55S 20.59E
Grodno Belarus 37 53.40N 23.50E

Grodzisk Poland 36 52.14N 16.22E
Grodzyanka Belarus 37 53.30N 28.41E
Groenlo Neth. 16 52.02N 6.36E
Groix, Île de *i.* France 18 47.38N 3.27W
Gronau Germany 38 52.13N 7.00E
Grong Norway 40 64.27N 12.19E
Groningen Neth. 16 53.13N 6.35E
Groningen *d.* Neth. 16 53.15N 6.45E
Groom U.S.A. 111 35.12N 101.06W
Groot *r.* C.P. r. R.S.A. 80 33.58S 25.03E
Groote Eylandt *i.* Australia 90 14.00S 136.40E
Grootfontein Namibia 80 19.32S 18.07E
Groot Karasberge *mts.* Namibia 80 27.20S 18.50E
Grootlaagte *r.* Botswana 80 20.58S 21.42E
Groot Swartberge *mts.* R.S.A. 80 33.20S 22.00E
Grossenbrode Germany 38 54.22N 11.05E
Grossenhain Germany 38 51.17N 13.31E
Grosser Arber *mtn.* Germany 39 49.07N 13.07E
Grosser Priel *mtn.* Austria 39 47.43N 14.04E
Grosseto Italy 30 42.46N 11.08E
Gross-Gerau Germany 39 49.55N 8.29E
Gross Glockner *mtn.* Austria 30 47.04N 12.42E
Grossräschen Germany 38 51.35N 14.00E
Gross Venediger *mtn.* Austria 30 47.06N 12.21E
Groswater B. Canada 103 54.20N 57.30W
Grote Nete *r.* Belgium 16 51.07N 4.20E
Groton U.S.A. 115 42.35N 76.22W
Grottaglie Italy 33 40.32N 17.26E
Grottaminarda Italy 33 41.04N 15.02E
Grottammare Italy 31 42.59N 13.52E
Groundhog *r.* Canada 102 49.40N 82.06W
Grouse Creek *town* U.S.A. 108 41.22N 113.53W
Grove City U.S.A. 114 41.10N 80.05W
Grover City U.S.A. 108 35.07N 120.37W
Groves U.S.A. 111 29.57N 93.55W
Groveton N.H. U.S.A. 105 44.36N 71.31W
Groveton Tex. U.S.A. 111 31.03N 95.08W
Groznyy Russian Fed. 45 43.21N 45.42E
Grubišno Polje Croatia 31 45.42N 17.10E
Grudziądz Poland 37 53.29N 18.45E
Grumeti *r.* Tanzania 79 2.05S 33.45E
Grumo Appula Italy 33 41.01N 16.43E
Grums Sweden 43 59.21N 13.06E
Grünau Austria 39 47.51N 13.57E
Grünau Namibia 80 27.44S 18.18E
Grundarfjördhur *town* Iceland 40 64.55N 23.20W
Grundy U.S.A. 113 37.13N 82.08W
Grungedal Norway 42 59.44N 7.43E
Grünstadt Germany 39 49.34N 8.10E
Gryazovets Russian Fed. 44 58.52N 40.12E
Gryfice Poland 36 53.56N 15.12E
Grythyttan Sweden 43 59.42N 14.32E
Gstaad Switz. 39 46.28N 7.17E
Guachipas Argentina 124 25.31S 65.31W
Guacuí Brazil 126 20.44S 41.40W
Guadajoz *r.* Spain 27 37.50N 4.51W
Guadalajara Mexico 116 20.30N 103.20W
Guadalajara Spain 26 40.38N 3.10W
Guadalajara *d.* Spain 26 40.50N 2.50W
Guadalamar *r.* Spain 26 38.05N 3.36W
Guadalaviar *r.* Spain 25 40.21N 1.08W
Guadalcanal *i.* Solomon Is. 84 9.32S 160.12E
Guadalcanal Spain 26 38.06N 5.49W
Guadalén Spain 26 38.05N 3.32W
Guadalén, Embalse de *resr.* Spain 26 38.25N 3.15W
Guadalete *r.* Spain 27 36.35N 6.13W
Guadalmena *r.* Spain 26 38.19N 2.56W
Guadalmez *r.* Spain 26 38.46N 5.04W
Guadalope *r.* Spain 25 41.15N 0.03W
Guadalquivir *r.* Spain 27 36.47N 6.22W
Guadalupe Mexico 111 25.41N 100.15W
Guadalupe, Isla de *i.* Mexico 109 29.00N 118.16W
Guadalupe, Sierra de *mts.* Spain 27 39.35N 5.25W
Guadarrama *r.* Spain 27 39.53N 4.10W
Guadarrama, Puerto de *pass* Spain 26 40.43N 4.10W
Guadarrama, Sierra de *mts.* Spain 26 41.00N 3.50W
Guadazaón Spain 25 39.42N 1.36W
Guadeloupe *i.* Leeward Is. 117 16.20N 61.40W
Guadiana *r.* Portugal 27 37.11N 7.24W
Guadiana Menor *r.* Spain 27 37.56N 3.15W
Guadiaro *r.* Spain 27 36.17N 5.17W
Guadix Spain 27 37.18N 3.08W
Guafo, Golfo de *g.* Chile 125 43.35S 74.15W
Guainía *r.* Colombia 122 2.01N 67.07W
Guaíra Brazil 124 24.04S 54.15W
Guajará Mirim Brazil 122 10.48S 65.22W
Guajira, Península de *pen.* Colombia 122 12.00N 72.00W
Gualdo Tadino Italy 30 43.14N 12.47E
Gualeguay Argentina 125 33.10S 59.20W
Gualeguay *r.* Argentina 125 33.18S 59.38W
Gualeguaychu Argentina 125 33.00S 58.30W
Guam *i.* Mariana Is. 84 13.30N 144.40E
Guamal Colombia 122 9.10N 74.15W
Guanajuato Mexico 116 21.00N 101.16W
Guanajuato *d.* Mexico 116 21.00N 101.00W
Guanare Venezuela 122 9.04N 69.45W
Guanarito Venezuela 122 8.43N 69.12W
Guane Cuba 117 22.13N 84.07W
Guang'an China 55 30.30N 106.35E
Guangchang China 55 26.50N 116.16E
Guangdong *d.* China 55 23.00N 113.00E
Guanghan China 55 30.59N 104.15E
Guanghua *see* Laohekou China 54
Guangji China 55 29.42N 115.39E
Guangming Ding *mtn.* China 55 30.09N 118.11E
Guangnan China 55 24.03N 105.03E
Guangrao China 54 37.04N 118.22E
Guangxi Zhuangzu *d.* China 55 23.30N 109.00E
Guangyuan China 54 32.29N 105.55E
Guangze China 55 27.27N 117.23E
Guangzhou China 55 23.08N 113.20E
Guanling China 55 25.57N 105.38E
Guantánamo Cuba 117 20.09N 75.14W
Guan Xian Shandong China 54 36.29N 115.25E
Guan Xian Sichuan China 54 30.59N 103.40E
Guanyun China 54 34.17N 119.15E
Guaporé *r.* Bolivia/Brazil 124 12.00S 65.15W

Guaqui Bolivia 124 16.35S 68.51W
Guarabira Brazil 123 6.46S 35.25W
Guarapuava Brazil 126 25.22S 51.28W
Guara, Sierra de *mts.* Spain 25 42.20N 0.20W
Guaratinguetá Brazil 126 22.49S 45.09W
Guarda Portugal 26 40.32N 7.16W
Guarda *d.* Portugal 26 40.40N 7.15W
Guardavalle Italy 33 38.30N 16.30E
Guardiagrele Italy 31 42.11N 14.13E
Guardo Spain 26 42.47N 4.50W
Guareim *r.* Uruguay *see* Quaraí *r.* Brazil 125
Guareña Spain 27 38.51N 6.06W
Guareña *r.* Spain 26 41.29N 5.23W
Guasave Mexico 109 25.34N 108.27W
Guasipati Venezuela 122 7.28N 61.54W
Guastalla Italy 30 44.55N 10.39E
Guatemala C. America 117 15.40N 90.00W
Guatemala *town* Guatemala 116 14.38N 90.22W
Guatemala Basin Pacific Oc. 85 12.00N 95.00W
Guatemala Trench Pacific Oc. 85 15.00N 93.00W
Guatire Venezuela 122 10.28N 66.32W
Guaviare *r.* Colombia 122 4.00N 67.35W
Guaxupé Brazil 126 21.17S 46.44W
Guayaquil Ecuador 122 2.13S 79.54W
Guayaquil, Golfo de *g.* Ecuador 122 3.00S 80.35W
Guaymallén Argentina 125 32.54S 68.47W
Guaymas Mexico 109 27.56N 110.54W
Guayquiraró *r.* Argentina 125 30.25S 59.36W
Guba Zaïre 78 10.40S 26.26E
Gubakha Russian Fed. 44 58.55N 57.30E
Gubbio Italy 30 43.21N 12.35E
Gubeikou China 54 40.41N 117.09E
Gubin Poland 36 51.59N 14.42E
Gubio Nigeria 77 12.31N 12.44E
Guchab Namibia 80 19.40S 17.47E
Gucheng China 54 37.20N 115.57E
Gúdar, Sierra de *mts.* Spain 25 40.30N 0.40W
Gudbrandsdalen *f.* Norway 41 61.30N 10.00E
Gudhjem Denmark 43 55.13N 14.59E
Gudvangen Norway 41 60.52N 6.50E
Guebwiller France 19 47.55N 7.12E
Guecho Spain 26 43.22N 3.00W
Guékédou Guinea 76 8.35N 10.11W
Guelma Algeria 75 36.28N 7.26E
Guelph Canada 104 43.34N 80.16W
Guelta Zemmur W. Sahara 74 25.15N 12.20W
Guémené-sur-Scorff France 18 48.04N 3.12W
Guera *r.* Chad 77 11.22N 18.00E
Guerande France 18 47.20N 2.26W
Guérard, Lac *l.* Canada 103 56.20N 65.35W
Guéret France 20 46.10N 1.52E
Guernica Spain 26 43.19N 2.40W
Guernsey *i.* Channel Is. Europe 13 49.27N 2.35W
Guerra Mozambique 79 13.05S 35.12E
Guerrero *d.* Mexico 116 18.00N 100.00W
Guiana S. America 123 3.40N 53.00W
Guiana Highlands S. America 122 4.00N 59.00W
Guichen France 18 47.58N 1.48W
Guichón Uruguay 125 32.21S 57.12W
Guidimaka *d.* Mauritania 74 15.20N 12.00W
Guiding China 55 26.32N 107.15E
Guidong China 55 26.12N 114.00E
Guiers, Lac de *l.* Senegal 76 16.12N 15.50W
Gui Jiang *r.* China 55 23.25N 111.20E
Guijuelo Spain 26 40.33N 5.40W
Guildford Australia 89 31.55S 115.55E
Guildford U.K. 13 51.14N 0.35W
Guildhall U.S.A. 105 44.34N 71.34W
Guilin China 55 25.20N 110.10E
Guillaume-Delisle, Lac *l.* Canada 102 56.20N 75.50W
Guillaumes France 21 44.05N 6.51E
Guillestre France 21 44.40N 6.39E
Guilvinec France 18 47.47N 4.17W
Guimarães Brazil 123 2.08S 44.36W
Guimarães Portugal 26 41.27N 8.18W
Guimeng Ding *mtn.* China 54 35.34N 117.50E
Guinan China 54 35.20N 100.50E
Guinea Africa 76 10.30N 11.30W
Guinea Basin *f.* Atlantic Oc. 127 0.00 5.00W
Guinea Bissau Africa 76 11.30N 15.00W
Guinea, G. of Africa 77 3.00N 3.00E
Güines Cuba 117 22.50N 82.02W
Guînes France 19 50.52N 1.52E
Guingamp France 18 48.33N 3.11W
Guinguinéo Senegal 76 14.20N 15.57W
Guiping China 55 23.20N 110.02E
Guipúzcoa *d.* Spain 26 43.00N 2.20W
Guir, Hammada du *f.* Morocco/Algeria 74 31.00N 3.20W
Güiria Venezuela 122 10.37N 62.21W
Guiscard France 19 49.39N 3.03E
Guise France 19 49.54N 3.38E
Guitiriz Spain 26 43.11N 7.54W
Guitres France 20 45.03N 0.11W
Guiuan Phil. 59 11.02N 125.44E
Guixi China 55 28.12N 117.10E
Gui Xian China 55 23.02N 109.40E
Guiyang China 55 26.31N 106.39E
Guizhou *d.* China 55 27.00N 107.00E
Gujarat *d.* India 62 22.20N 70.30E
Gūjar Khān Pakistan 62 33.16N 73.19E
Gujrānwāla Pakistan 62 32.26N 74.33E
Gujrāt Pakistan 62 32.34N 74.05E
Gulang Gansu China 54 37.30N 102.54E
Gulargambone Australia 93 31.21S 148.32E
Gulbarga India 60 17.22N 76.47E
Gulfport U.S.A. 111 30.22N 89.06W
Gulgong Australia 93 32.20S 149.49E
Gulin China 55 28.07N 105.51E
Gulistān Pakistan 62 30.36N 66.35E
Gullholmen Sweden 42 58.11N 11.24E
Gull Lake *town* Canada 101 50.08N 108.27W
Gullspång Sweden 43 58.59N 14.06E
Güllük Turkey 35 37.14N 27.36E
Gulma Nigeria 77 12.41N 4.24E
Gülpinar Turkey 34 39.32N 26.10E
Gulshad Kazakhstan 52 46.37N 74.22E
Gulu Uganda 79 2.46N 32.21E

Guluy Eritrea 72 14.43N 36.45E
Gulwe Tanzania 79 6.27S 36.27E
Gulyantsi Bulgaria 34 43.38N 24.42E
Gumal *r.* Pakistan 62 32.08N 69.50E
Gumel Nigeria 77 12.39N 9.23E
Gumla India 63 23.03N 84.33E
Gummersbach Germany 38 51.02N 7.34E
Gum Spring *town* U.S.A. 113 37.47N 77.54W
Gümüşhane Turkey 64 40.26N 39.26E
Guna India 62 24.39N 77.19E
Gunbar Australia 93 34.04S 145.25E
Gundagai Australia 93 35.07S 148.05E
Gundlupet India 60 11.48N 76.41E
Gungu Zaïre 78 5.43S 19.20E
Gunisao *r.* Canada 101 53.54N 97.58W
Gunisao L. Canada 101 53.33N 96.15W
Gunnebo Sweden 43 57.43N 16.32E
Gunnedah Australia 93 30.59S 150.15E
Gunning Australia 93 34.46S 149.17E
Gunnison Colo. U.S.A. 108 38.33N 106.56W
Gunnison *r.* U.S.A. 108 39.03N 108.35W
Gunnison Utah U.S.A. 108 39.09N 111.49W
Guntersville U.S.A. 113 34.20N 86.18W
Guntersville L. U.S.A. 113 34.45N 86.03W
Guntūr India 61 16.20N 80.27E
Gunungsitoli Indonesia 58 1.17N 97.37E
Gunupur India 61 19.05N 83.49E
Günz *r.* Germany 39 48.27N 10.16E
Günzburg Germany 39 48.27N 10.18E
Gunzenhausen Germany 39 49.07N 10.45E
Guochengyi China 54 36.14N 104.52E
Gurais Jammu & Kashmir 62 34.38N 74.50E
Gura Portiței *f.* Romania 37 44.40N 29.00E
Gurban Obo China 54 43.05N 112.27E
Gurdāspur Jammu & Kashmir 62 32.02N 75.31E
Gurgaon India 62 28.28N 77.02E
Gurgueia *r.* Brazil 123 6.45S 43.35W
Gürha India 62 25.14N 71.45E
Gurk *r.* Austria 31 46.36N 14.31E
Gurskøy *i.* Norway 40 62.16N 5.42E
Gurué Mozambique 81 15.30S 36.58E
Gürün Turkey 64 38.44N 37.15E
Gurupá Brazil 123 1.25S 51.39W
Gurupi *r.* Brazil 123 1.13S 46.06W
Guru Sikhar *mtn.* India 62 24.39N 72.46E
Guruve Zimbabwe 80 16.42S 30.40E
Gusau Nigeria 77 12.12N 6.40E
Gusev Russian Fed. 37 54.32N 22.12E
Gusong China 55 24.38N 105.12E
Guspini Italy 32 39.32N 8.38E
Güssing Austria 31 47.04N 16.20E
Gustav Holm, Kap *c.* Greenland 99 67.00N 34.00W
Güstrow Germany 38 53.48N 12.10E
Gusum Sweden 43 58.16N 16.29E
Gütersloh Germany 38 51.54N 8.23E
Guthrie Ky. U.S.A. 113 36.40N 87.10W
Guthrie Okla. U.S.A. 111 35.53N 97.25W
Guvrin, Nahal *wadi* Israel 67 31.43N 34.42E
Guyana S. America 122 4.40N 59.00W
Guyang China 54 41.03N 110.03E
Guymon U.S.A. 111 36.41N 101.29W
Guyra Australia 93 30.14S 151.40E
Guyuan Hebei China 54 41.40N 115.41E
Guyuan Ningxia Huizu China 54 36.00N 106.25E
Guzhen Anhui China 54 33.19N 117.19E
Guzman, Laguna de *l.* Mexico 109 31.25N 107.25W
Gwa Myanmar 61 17.36N 94.35E
Gwabegar Australia 93 30.34S 149.00E
Gwadabawa Nigeria 77 13.23N 5.15E
Gwādar Pakistan 62 25.07N 62.19E
Gwagwada Nigeria 77 10.15N 7.15E
Gwai Zimbabwe 80 19.15S 27.42E
Gwai *r.* Zimbabwe 80 17.59S 26.55E
Gwalior India 63 26.13N 78.10E
Gwanda Zimbabwe 80 20.59S 29.00E
Gwane Zaïre 79 4.43N 25.50E
Gwasero Nigeria 77 9.30N 8.30E
Gweebarra B. Rep. of Ire. 15 54.52N 8.28W
Gwent *d.* U.K. 13 51.44N 3.00W
Gweru Zimbabwe 80 19.25S 29.50E
Gwydir *r.* Australia 93 29.35S 148.45E
Gwynedd *d.* U.K. 12 53.00N 4.00W
Gy France 19 47.24N 5.49E
Gyaca China 63 29.05N 92.55E
Gyandzha Azerbaijan 45 40.39N 46.20E
Gyangrang China 63 30.47N 85.09E
Gyangzê China 63 28.57N 89.38E
Gyaring Co *l.* China 63 31.05N 88.00E
Gydanskiy Poluostrov *pen.* Russian Fed. 50 70.00N 78.30E
Gyimda China 63 31.03N 97.18E
Gyirong China 63 29.00N 85.13E
Gympie Australia 90 26.11S 152.40E
Gyöda Japan 57 36.08N 139.28E
Gyöngyös Hungary 37 47.47N 19.56E
Györ Hungary 37 47.41N 17.40E
Gypsum Pt. Canada 100 61.53N 114.35W
Gypsumville Canada 101 51.45N 98.35W
Gyueshovo Bulgaria 34 42.14N 22.28E

H

Haag Germany 39 48.10N 12.11E
Haan Germany 16 51.10N 7.02E

Guluy Eritrea 72 14.43N 36.45E
Ha'apai Group *is.* Tonga 85 19.50S 174.30W
Haapajärvi Finland 40 63.45N 25.20E
Haapamäki Finland 40 62.15N 24.28E
Haapavesi Finland 40 64.08N 25.22E
Haapsalu Estonia 41 58.56N 23.33E
Haar Germany 39 48.06N 11.44E
Hä Arava *r.* Israel/Jordan 66 30.30N 35.10E
Haarlem Neth. 16 52.22N 4.38E
Haarlem R.S.A. 80 33.46S 23.28E
Hab *r.* Pakistan 62 24.53N 66.41E
Habahe China 52 47.53N 86.12E
Habarūt Yemen 60 17.18N 52.44E
Habaswein Kenya 79 1.06N 39.26E
Habay-la-Neuve Belgium 16 49.45N 5.38E
Habbān Yemen 71 14.21N 47.05E
Hab Chauki Pakistan 62 25.01N 66.53E
Habiganj Bangla. 63 24.23N 91.25E
Habikino Japan 57 34.33N 135.37E
Habo Sweden 43 57.55N 14.04E
Hachinohe Japan 57 40.30N 141.30E
Hachiōji Japan 57 35.39N 139.20E
Hack, Mt. Australia 92 30.44S 138.45E
Hadāli Pakistan 62 32.18N 72.12E
Hadano Japan 57 35.22N 139.14E
Ḥadāribah, Ra's al *c.* Sudan 72 22.04N 36.54E
Hadarom *d.* Israel 67 31.15N 34.50E
Ḥadbaram Oman 71 17.27N 55.15E
Haddington U.K. 14 55.57N 2.47W
Ḥadd, Ra's al *c.* Oman 65 22.32N 59.49E
Hadejia Nigeria 77 12.30N 10.03E
Hadejia *r.* Nigeria 77 12.47N 10.44E
Hadera Israel 67 32.26N 34.55E
Hadera *r.* Israel 67 32.27N 35.53E
Haderslev Denmark 42 55.15N 9.30E
Hadiboh Yemen 71 12.39N 54.02E
Hadjer Mornou *mtn.* Chad 72 17.12N 23.08E
Hadley N.Y. U.S.A. 115 43.19N 73.51W
Hadley Penn. U.S.A. 114 41.25N 80.14W
Ha Dong Vietnam 55 20.40N 105.58E
Hadsten Denmark 42 56.20N 10.03E
Hadsund Denmark 42 56.43N 10.07E
Haedo, Cuchilla de *mts.* Uruguay 125 31.50S 56.10W
Haegeland Norway 42 58.15N 7.47E
Haeju N. Korea 53 38.04N 125.40E
Haena Hawaiian Is. 85 22.14N 159.34W
Ḥafar al Bāṭin Saudi Arabia 65 28.28N 46.00E
Ḥafirah, Qā'al *l.* Jordan 67 31.06N 36.14E
Hāfizābād Pakistan 62 32.04N 73.41E
Hafnarfjördhur *town* Iceland 40 64.04N 21.58W
Haft Gel Iran 65 31.28N 49.35E
HaGalil *f.* Israel 67 32.54N 35.20E
Hagen Germany 38 51.22N 7.28E
Hagenow Germany 38 53.26N 11.11E
Hagerman U.S.A. 109 33.07N 104.20W
Hagerstown U.S.A. 114 39.39N 77.43W
Hagersville Canada 104 42.58N 80.03W
Hagetmau France 20 43.40N 0.35W
Hagfors Sweden 43 60.02N 13.42E
Hagi Japan 57 34.25N 131.22E
Ha Giang Vietnam 55 22.50N 105.00E
Hagondange France 19 49.15N 6.10E
Hags Head Rep. of Ire. 15 52.56N 9.29W
Hague U.S.A. 115 43.45N 73.31W
Hague, Cap de la *c.* France 18 49.44N 1.56W
Haguenau France 19 48.49N 7.47E
Hahn Germany 38 50.31N 7.53E
Hai'an Shan *mts.* China 55 23.00N 115.30E
Haicheng China 54 40.52N 122.48E
Hai Duong Vietnam 55 20.56N 106.21E
Haifa *see* Hefa Israel 67
Haifa, B. of *see* Mifraz Hefa Israel 67
Haifeng China 55 22.58N 115.20E
Haikang China 55 20.55N 110.04E
Haikou China 55 20.03N 110.27E
Hā'il Saudi Arabia 64 27.31N 41.45E
Hailākāndi India 63 24.41N 92.34E
Hailar China 53 49.15N 119.41E
Haileybury Canada 104 47.27N 79.38W
Hailong China 54 42.39N 125.49E
Hailsham U.K. 13 50.52N 0.17E
Hailun China 53 47.29N 126.58E
Hailuoto *i.* Finland 40 65.02N 24.42E
Haimen China 55 31.52N 121.10E
Haimen China 55 28.41N 121.30E
Hainan *d.* China 55 19.00N 109.30E
Hainaut *d.* Belgium 16 50.30N 3.45E
Haines Oreg. U.S.A. 108 44.55N 117.56W
Haines Alas. U.S.A. 100 59.11N 135.23W
Haines Junction Canada 100 60.45N 137.30W
Haining China 55 30.30N 120.35E
Haiphong Vietnam 55 20.48N 106.40E
Haiti C. America 117 19.00N 73.00W
Haiyang China 54 36.46N 121.09E
Haiyuan China 54 36.35N 105.40E
Ḥajar Banga Sudan 73 11.30N 23.00E
Hajdúböszörmény Hungary 37 47.41N 21.30E
Hajdúszoboszló Hungary 37 47.27N 21.24E
Hajiki saki *c.* Japan 57 38.25N 138.32E
Hājīpur India 63 25.41N 85.13E
Hakkāri Turkey 65 37.36N 43.45E
Hakodate Japan 57 41.46N 140.44E
Hakupu Niue 84 19.07S 169.51W
Hala Pakistan 62 25.49N 68.25E
Halab Syria 64 36.14N 37.10E
Ḥalabjah Iraq 65 35.10N 45.59E
Ḥalā'ib Sudan 72 22.13N 36.38E
Hålaveden *hills* Sweden 43 58.05N 14.45E
Ḥalbā Lebanon 66 34.34N 36.05E
Halberstadt Germany 38 51.54N 11.02E
Halden Norway 42 59.09N 11.23E
Haldensleben Germany 38 52.18N 11.26E
Haldia India 63 22.05N 88.03E
Haldwāni India 63 29.13N 79.31E
Hale U.S.A. 114 44.23N 83.48W
Haleyville U.S.A. 113 34.12N 87.38W
Half Assini Ghana 76 5.04N 2.53W
Halfmoon Bay *town* Canada 100 49.31N 123.54W
Halfmoon Bay *town* New Zealand 86 46.45S 168.08E

169

Ḥalḥūl Jordan 67 31.35N 35.07E
Haliburton Canada 104 45.03N 78.30W
Haliburton Highlands Canada 104 45.16N 78.19W
Halicarnassus site Turkey 35 37.03N 27.28E
Halifax Canada 103 44.39N 63.36W
Halifax U.K. 12 53.43N 1.51W
Halifax U.S.A. 113 36.46N 78.57W
Halīl r. Iran 60 27.35N 58.44E
Halkett, C. U.S.A. 98 71.00N 152.00W
Halkirk U.K. 14 58.30N 3.30W
Halladale r. U.K. 14 58.34N 3.54W
Halland d. Sweden 43 56.48N 12.50E
Halland f. Sweden 43 57.03N 12.45E
Hallands Vāderō i. Sweden 43 56.26N 12.33E
Halle Belgium 16 50.45N 4.14E
Halle Germany 38 51.29N 11.58E
Hällefors Sweden 43 59.47N 14.30E
Hälleforsnäs Sweden 43 59.10N 16.30E
Hallein Austria 39 47.41N 13.06E
Halligen is. Germany 38 54.35N 8.35E
Hallingdal f. Norway 41 60.30N 9.00E
Hall Is. Pacific Oc. 84 8.37N 152.00E
Hall Lake town Canada 99 68.40N 81.30W
Hällnäs Sweden 40 64.19N 19.38E
Hall Pen. Canada 99 63.30N 66.00W
Hallsberg Sweden 43 59.04N 15.07E
Hall's Creek town Australia 88 18.13S 127.39E
Hallstahammar Sweden 43 59.37N 16.13E
Hallstatt Austria 39 47.33N 13.39E
Hallstavik Sweden 43 60.03N 18.36E
Hallstead U.S.A. 115 41.58N 75.45W
Hallton U.S.A. 114 41.26N 78.56W
Halmahera i. Indonesia 59 0.45N 128.00E
Halmstad Sweden 43 56.39N 12.50E
Halsa Norway 40 63.03N 8.14E
Hälsingborg Sweden 43 56.03N 12.42E
Haltern Germany 38 51.46N 7.10E
Haltia Tunturi mtn. Finland 40 69.17N 21.21E
Haltwhistle U.K. 12 54.58N 2.27W
Ham France 19 49.45N 3.04E
Hamada f. see Drâa, Hamada du f. W. Sahara 74
Hamadān Iran 65 34.47N 48.33E
Ḥamādat Marzūq f. Libya 75 26.00N 12.30E
Ḥamaḍ, Wādī al r. Saudi Arabia 64 25.49N 36.37E
Ḥamāh Syria 66 35.09N 36.44E
Hamakita Japan 57 34.48N 137.47E
Hamamatsu Japan 57 34.42N 137.44E
Hamar Norway 41 60.48N 11.06E
Ḥamāṭah, Jabal mtn. Egypt 64 24.11N 35.01E
Hamborn Germany 16 51.29N 6.46E
Hamburg Germany 38 53.33N 9.59E
Hamburg d. Germany 38 53.35N 10.00E
Hamburg R.S.A. 80 33.17S 27.27E
Hamburg N.J. U.S.A. 115 41.09N 74.35W
Hamburg N.Y. U.S.A. 114 42.43N 78.50W
Hamburg Penn. U.S.A. 115 40.34N 75.59W
Hamburgsund Sweden 42 58.33N 11.16E
Hamden U.S.A. 115 41.21N 72.56W
Häme d. Finland 41 61.20N 24.30E
Hämeenlinna Finland 41 61.00N 24.27E
Hamelin B. Australia 89 34.10S 115.00E
Hameln Germany 38 52.06N 9.21E
HaMerkaz d. Israel 67 32.05N 34.55E
Hamer Koke Ethiopia 73 5.12N 36.45E
Hamersley Range mts. Australia 88 22.00S 118.00E
Hamhŭng N. Korea 53 39.54N 127.35E
Hami China 52 42.40N 93.30E
Hamidiye Turkey 34 41.09N 26.40E
Hamilton Australia 92 37.45S 142.04E
Hamilton r. Australia 91 27.12S 135.28E
Hamilton Bermuda 127 32.18N 64.48W
Hamilton Canada 104 43.15N 79.51W
Hamilton New Zealand 86 37.46S 175.18E
Hamilton U.K. 14 55.46N 4.10W
Hamilton Mont. U.S.A. 108 46.15N 114.09W
Hamilton N.Y. U.S.A. 115 42.50N 75.33W
Hamilton Ohio U.S.A. 112 39.23N 84.33W
Hamilton Tex. U.S.A. 111 31.42N 98.07W
Hamley Bridge town Australia 92 34.21S 138.41E
Hamlin Tex. U.S.A. 111 32.53N 100.08W
Hamlin W.Va. U.S.A. 114 38.17N 82.06W
Hamm Germany 38 51.41N 7.49E
Hammamet, Golfe de g. Tunisia 75 36.05N 10.40E
Hammam Lif Tunisia 32 36.44N 10.20E
Hammān, Wādī al Jordan 67 31.38N 36.00E
Ḥammār, Hawr al r. Iraq 65 30.50N 47.00E
Hammel Denmark 42 56.15N 9.52E
Hammelburg Germany 39 50.07N 9.53E
Hammerdal Sweden 40 63.35N 15.20E
Hammerfest Norway 40 70.40N 23.42E
Hammond Australia 92 32.33S 138.20E
Hammond La. U.S.A. 111 30.30N 90.28W
Hammond N.Y. U.S.A. 105 44.27N 75.42W
Hammond B. U.S.A. 104 45.33N 84.00W
Hammondsport U.S.A. 114 42.25N 77.13W
Hammonton U.S.A. 115 39.38N 74.48W
Ham, Mt. Canada 105 45.47N 71.37W
Ham Nord Canada 105 45.54N 71.39W
Hamoir Belgium 16 50.25N 5.32E
Hamoyet, Jabal mtn. Sudan 72 17.33N 38.00E
Hampshire d. U.K. 13 51.03N 1.20W
Hampton N.H. U.S.A. 115 42.56N 70.50W
Hampton S.C. U.S.A. 113 32.52N 81.06W
Hampton Va. U.S.A. 113 37.02N 76.23W
Hampton Bays town U.S.A. 115 40.53N 72.31W
Hamra, Saguia el wadi W. Sahara 74 27.15N 13.21W
Ḥamrīn, Jabal mts. Iraq 65 34.40N 44.10E
Ham Sud Canada 105 45.46N 71.36W
Hāmūn-e Jaz Mūrīān l. Iran 60 27.20N 58.55E
Hana Hawaiian Is. 85 20.45N 155.59W
Hanamaki Japan 57 39.23N 141.07E
Hanang mtn. Tanzania 79 4.30S 35.21E
Hanau Germany 39 50.08N 8.55E
Hancheng China 54 35.29N 110.30E
Hancock Md. U.S.A. 114 39.42N 78.13W
Hancock Mich. U.S.A. 112 47.08N 88.34W
Hancock N.Y. U.S.A. 115 41.57N 75.17W

Handa Japan 57 34.53N 136.56E
Handa Somali Rep. 71 10.39N 51.08E
Handan China 54 36.37N 114.26E
Handen Sweden 43 59.10N 18.08E
Handeni Tanzania 79 5.25S 38.04E
HaNegev des. Israel 66 30.42N 34.55E
Hanford U.S.A. 109 36.20N 119.39W
Hanga Roa i. de Pascua 85 27.09S 109.26W
Hanggin Houqi China 54 40.50N 107.06E
Hanggin Qi China 54 39.56N 108.54E
Hangō Finland 41 59.50N 22.57E
Hangu China 54 39.11N 117.45E
Hangu Pakistan 62 33.32N 71.04E
Hangzhou China 55 30.14N 120.08E
Hangzhou Wan b. China 55 30.25N 121.00E
Hanita Israel 67 33.05N 35.10E
Hanjiang China 55 25.30N 119.14E
Hankey R.S.A. 80 33.50S 24.52E
Hankinson U.S.A. 110 46.04N 96.55W
Hanksville U.S.A. 108 38.21N 110.44W
Hänle Jammu & Kashmir 63 32.48N 79.00E
Hanmer Springs town New Zealand 86 42.31S 172.50E
Hanna Canada 101 51.38N 111.54W
Hannaford U.S.A. 110 47.19N 98.11W
Hannah B. Canada 102 51.20N 80.00W
Hannibal Mo. U.S.A. 107 39.41N 91.25W
Hannibal Ohio U.S.A. 114 39.39N 80.51W
Hann, Mt. Australia 88 15.55S 125.57E
Hannover Germany 38 52.24N 9.44E
Hannut Belgium 16 50.40N 5.05E
Hanöbukten b. Sweden 43 55.47N 15.00E
Hanoi Vietnam 55 21.01N 105.53E
Hanover Canada 104 44.09N 81.02W
Hanover R.S.A. 80 31.04S 24.25E
Hanover Mass. U.S.A. 115 42.07N 70.49W
Hanover N.H. U.S.A. 115 43.42N 72.17W
Hanover Penn. U.S.A. 114 39.48N 76.59W
Hanover, Isla i. Chile 125 50.57S 74.40W
Han Pijesak Bosnia-Herzegovina 31 44.04N 18.59E
Hänsdiha India 63 24.36N 87.05E
Hanshou China 55 28.55N 111.58E
Han Shui r. China 55 30.32N 114.20E
Hänsi Haryana India 62 29.06N 75.58E
Hansi Himachal P. India 63 32.27N 77.50E
Hanson, L. Australia 92 31.02S 136.13E
Hanstholm Denmark 42 57.07N 8.38E
Hantengri Feng mtn. China 52 42.09N 80.12E
Han Ui China 54 45.10N 119.48E
Hanyang China 55 30.32N 114.20E
Hanyin China 54 32.53N 108.37E
Hanzhong China 54 33.08N 107.04E
Haouach, Ouadi wadi Chad 75 16.45N 19.35E
Happy Valley town Canada 103 53.16N 60.14W
Hapsu N. Korea 53 41.12N 128.48E
Hāpur India 63 28.43N 77.47E
Ḥaql Saudi Arabia 66 29.14N 34.56E
Ḥaraḍ Saudi Arabia 65 24.12N 49.08E
Harare Zimbabwe 81 17.49S 31.04E
Har-Ayrag Mongolia 54 45.42N 109.14E
Haraze Chad 73 9.55N 20.48E
Harbin China 53 45.45N 126.41E
Harboör Denmark 42 56.37N 8.12E
Harbor Beach U.S.A. 104 43.51N 82.39W
Harborcreek U.S.A. 114 42.09N 79.57W
Harbour Deep town Canada 103 50.22N 56.27W
Harbour Grace town Canada 103 47.42N 53.13W
Harburg Germany 36 53.27N 9.58E
Hårby Denmark 42 55.13N 10.07E
Harda India 62 22.20N 77.06E
Hardangerfjorden est. Norway 41 60.10N 6.00E
Hardangerjökulen mtn. Norway 41 60.33N 7.26E
Hardanger Vidda f. Norway 42 60.15N 7.20E
Hardeeville U.S.A. 113 32.18N 81.05W
Hardenberg Neth. 16 52.36N 6.40E
Harding R.S.A. 80 30.34S 29.52E
Hardman U.S.A. 108 45.10N 119.40W
Hardoi India 63 27.25N 80.07E
Hardwār India 63 29.58N 78.10E
Hardwick U.S.A. 105 44.30N 72.22W
Hardwicke B. Australia 92 34.52S 137.10E
Hardy U.S.A. 111 36.19N 91.29W
Hare B. Canada 103 51.18N 55.50W
Haren Germany 38 52.47N 7.14E
Härer Ethiopia 73 9.20N 42.10E
Härergé d. Ethiopia 73 8.00N 41.00E
Harfleur France 18 49.30N 0.12E
Hargeysa Somali Rep. 71 9.31N 44.02E
Har Hu l. China 52 38.20N 97.40E
Hari r. Indonesia 58 1.00S 104.15E
Harima nada str. Japan 57 34.30N 134.30E
Harīpur Pakistan 62 33.59N 72.56E
Ḥarīr r. Syria 67 32.45N 35.55E
Harīrūd r. Afghan. 60 35.42N 61.12E
Harlan U.S.A. 110 41.39N 95.19W
Harlech U.K. 12 52.52N 4.08W
Harlem U.S.A. 108 48.32N 108.47W
Harlingen Neth. 16 53.10N 5.25E
Harlingen U.S.A. 111 26.11N 97.42W
Harlow U.K. 13 51.47N 0.08E
Harlowton U.S.A. 108 46.26N 109.50W
Harman U.S.A. 114 38.55N 79.32W
Harnai Pakistan 62 30.06N 67.56E
Harnätän India 63 27.19N 84.01E
Harney Basin f. U.S.A. 108 43.15N 120.40W
Harney L. U.S.A. 108 43.14N 119.07W
Härnösand Sweden 40 62.37N 17.55E
Har Nuur l. Mongolia 52 48.00N 93.25E
Haro Spain 26 42.35N 2.51W
Haroldswick U.K. 10 60.47N 0.50W
Harper Liberia 76 4.25N 7.43W
Harpers Ferry town U.S.A. 114 39.13N 77.45W
Harrai India 63 22.37N 79.13E
Harricana r. Canada 102 51.10N 79.45W
Harrigan, C. Canada 103 55.50N 60.21W
Harrington Australia 93 31.50S 152.43E

Harrington U.S.A. 115 38.56N 75.35W
Harrington Harbour Canada 103 50.31N 59.30W
Harris Canada 101 51.44N 107.35W
Harris i. U.K. 14 57.50N 6.55W
Harrisburg Ill. U.S.A. 111 37.44N 88.33W
Harrisburg Oreg. U.S.A. 108 44.16N 123.10W
Harrisburg Penn. U.S.A. 114 40.16N 76.52W
Harris, L. Australia 92 31.08S 135.14E
Harrismith Australia 89 32.55S 117.50E
Harrismith R.S.A. 80 28.15S 29.07E
Harrison Ark. U.S.A. 111 36.14N 93.07W
Harrison Nebr. U.S.A. 110 42.41N 103.53W
Harrisonburg U.S.A. 114 38.27N 78.54W
Harrison, C. Canada 103 54.55N 57.55W
Harrison L. Canada 100 49.33N 121.50W
Harrisonville U.S.A. 110 38.39N 94.21W
Harris, Sd. of U.K. 14 57.43N 7.05W
Harrisville Mich. U.S.A. 104 44.39N 83.17W
Harrisville N.Y. U.S.A. 105 44.09N 75.19W
Harrisville W.Va. U.S.A. 114 39.13N 81.03W
Harrodsburg U.S.A. 113 37.46N 84.51W
Harrogate U.K. 12 53.59N 1.32W
Harrow Canada 104 42.02N 82.55W
Harrow U.K. 13 51.35N 0.21W
Harrowsmith Canada 105 44.24N 76.40W
Harstad Norway 40 68.48N 16.30E
Harsūd India 62 22.06N 76.44E
Ḥartā Jordan 67 32.48N 36.34E
Hartford U.S.A. 115 41.46N 72.41W
Hart, L. Australia 92 31.08S 136.24E
Hartland Canada 103 46.18N 67.32W
Hartland U.S.A. 104 59.50N 4.29W
Hartland Pt. U.K. 13 51.01N 4.32W
Hartlepool U.K. 12 54.42N 1.11W
Hartley Bay town Canada 100 53.27N 129.18W
Hartola Finland 41 61.35N 26.01E
Hartshorne U.S.A. 111 34.51N 95.33W
Harts Range town Australia 90 23.06S 134.55E
Hartsville U.S.A. 113 34.23N 80.05W
Härünäbäd Pakistan 62 29.37N 73.08E
Har Us Nuur l. Mongolia 52 48.10N 92.10E
Härüt r. Afghan. 62 31.35N 61.18E
Harvey Australia 89 33.06S 115.50E
Harvey Ill. U.S.A. 104 41.37N 87.39W
Harvey N.Dak. U.S.A. 110 47.47N 99.56W
Harwich U.K. 13 51.56N 1.18E
Haryana d. India 62 29.15N 76.30E
Harz mts. Germany 38 51.43N 10.40E
Hasa Oasis see Aḥsā', Wāḥat al oasis Saudi Arabia 65
Ḥasā, Wādī al r. Jordan 67 31.00N 35.29E
Hasdo r. India 63 21.44N 82.44E
Hase r. Germany 38 52.41N 7.18E
Haselünne Germany 38 52.40N 7.29E
Hasenkamp Argentina 125 31.30S 59.50W
Hashābah Sudan 72 14.19N 32.19E
Hashefela f. Israel 67 31.40N 34.55E
Hashimoto Japan 57 34.19N 135.37E
Haskell U.S.A. 111 33.10N 99.44W
Hasle Denmark 43 55.11N 14.43E
Haslemere U.K. 13 51.05N 0.41W
Haslev Denmark 42 55.20N 11.58E
Hasselt Belgium 16 50.56N 5.20E
Hassfurt Germany 39 50.02N 10.31E
Hassi bel Guebbour Algeria 75 28.30N 6.41E
Hassi er Rmel well Algeria 75 32.57N 3.11E
Hassi Messaoud Algeria 75 31.43N 6.03E
Hassi Tagsist well Algeria 74 25.20N 1.35E
Hässleholm Sweden 43 56.09N 13.46E
Hassloch Germany 39 49.22N 8.16E
Hastings Australia 93 38.18S 145.12E
Hastings Canada 105 44.18N 77.57W
Hastings New Zealand 86 39.39S 176.52E
Hastings U.K. 13 50.51N 0.36E
Hastings Nebr. U.S.A. 110 40.35N 98.23W
Hatch U.S.A. 109 32.40N 107.09W
Hatches Creek town Australia 90 20.56S 135.12E
Hatfield Australia 92 33.53S 143.47E
Hatfield U.K. 13 51.46N 0.13W
Hāthras India 63 27.36N 78.03E
Ha Tinh Vietnam 56 18.21N 105.55E
Hatta India 63 24.07N 79.36E
Hattah Australia 92 34.52S 142.23E
Hattem Neth. 16 52.29N 6.06E
Hatteras, C. U.S.A. 113 35.13N 75.32W
Hattiesburg U.S.A. 111 31.19N 89.16W
Hattingen Germany 16 51.24N 7.09E
Hatton U.S.A. 108 46.46N 118.49W
Hatutu i. Îs. Marquises 85 7.56S 140.38W
Hatvan Hungary 37 47.40N 19.41E
Hauge Norway 42 58.18N 6.15E
Haugesund Norway 42 59.25N 5.18E
Haugsdorf Austria 36 48.42N 16.05E
Hauraki G. New Zealand 86 36.30S 175.00E
Hausach Germany 39 48.17N 8.10E
Haut Atlas mts. Morocco 74 31.30N 7.00W
Haute-Corse d. France 21 42.30N 9.20E
Haute Kotto d. C.A.R. 73 7.15N 23.30E
Haute-Loire d. France 20 45.05N 3.50E
Haute-Marne d. France 19 48.05N 5.10E
Haute Maurice Prov. Park Canada 102 48.38N 74.30W
Haute-Normandie d. France 18 49.30N 1.00E
Haute-Pyrénées d. France 20 43.00N 0.10E
Hauterive Canada 103 49.11N 68.16W
Hautes-Alpes d. France 21 44.40N 6.30E
Haute-Saône d. France 19 47.40N 6.10E
Haute-Savoie d. France 21 46.00N 6.20E
Haute-Vienne d. France 20 45.50N 1.15E
Haut Mbomou d. C.A.R. 73 6.25N 26.10E
Hautmont France 19 50.15N 3.56E
Haut-Rhin d. France 19 47.53N 7.13E
Hauts Bassins d. Burkina 76 10.45N 4.30W
Hauts Plateau f. Morocco/Algeria 74 34.00N 0.10W
Haut Zaïre d. Zaïre 79 2.00N 27.00E
Havana see La Habana Cuba 117
Havant U.K. 13 50.51N 0.59W

Havel r. Germany 38 52.53N 11.58E
Havelange Belgium 16 50.23N 5.14E
Havelberg Germany 38 52.50N 12.04E
Havelland f. Germany 38 52.30N 12.35E
Havelock Canada 105 44.26N 77.53W
Havelock New Zealand 86 41.17S 173.46E
Haverfordwest U.K. 13 51.48N 4.59W
Haverhill U.K. 13 52.06N 0.27E
Haverhill U.S.A. 115 42.47N 71.05W
Havlíčkuv Brod Czech Republic 36 49.38N 15.35E
Havre U.S.A. 108 48.33N 109.41W
Havre de Grace U.S.A. 115 39.33N 76.06W
Havre St. Pierre Canada 103 50.15N 63.36W
Hawaii d. U.S.A. 106 21.00N 156.00W
Hawaii i. Hawaii U.S.A. 106 19.30N 155.30W
Hawaiian Is. U.S.A. 106 21.00N 157.00W
Hawdon North, L. Australia 92 37.09S 139.54E
Hawea, L. New Zealand 86 44.30S 169.15E
Hawera New Zealand 86 39.35S 174.19E
Hawick U.K. 14 55.25N 2.47W
Hawke B. New Zealand 86 39.18S 177.15E
Hawker Australia 92 31.53S 138.25E
Hawker Gate Australia 92 29.46S 141.00E
Hawke's Bay d. New Zealand 86 39.00S 176.35E
Hawkesbury Canada 105 45.36N 74.37W
Hawks U.S.A. 104 45.16N 83.53W
Hawley U.S.A. 115 41.28N 75.11W
Hawrān, Wādī r. Iraq 64 33.57N 42.35E
Ḥawsh 'Īsá Egypt 66 30.55N 30.17E
Hawthorne U.S.A. 108 38.32N 118.38W
Hay Australia 93 34.31S 144.31E
Hay r. Australia 90 25.00S 138.00E
Hay r. Canada 100 60.49N 115.52W
Haya r. Japan 57 35.30S 138.00E
Hayange France 19 49.20N 6.03E
Hayban Sudan 71 11.13N 30.31E
Haydān, Wādī al Jordan 67 31.27N 35.36E
Hayden U.S.A. 109 33.00N 110.47W
Hayes r. Canada 101 57.03N 92.09W
Hayes Creek town Australia 88 13.27S 131.25E
Hayesville U.S.A. 110 44.46N 82.16W
Hay-on-Wye U.K. 13 52.04N 3.09W
Hay River town Canada 100 60.51N 115.44W
Hays U.S.A. 110 38.53N 99.20W
Hayward U.S.A. 110 46.02N 91.26W
Haywards Heath f. U.K. 13 51.00N 0.05E
HaZafon d. Israel 67 32.50N 35.20E
Hazārān, Küh-e mtn. Iran 65 29.30N 57.18E
Hazard U.S.A. 113 37.14N 83.11W
Hazāribägh India 63 23.59N 85.21E
Hazel Hurst U.S.A. 114 41.42N 78.35W
Hazelton Canada 100 55.20N 127.42W
Hazelton U.S.A. 110 46.29N 100.17W
Hazen U.S.A. 108 39.34N 119.03W
Hazerim Israel 67 31.14N 34.43E
Hazlehurst Ga. U.S.A. 113 31.53N 82.34W
Hazlehurst Miss. U.S.A. 111 31.52N 90.24W
Hazleton U.S.A. 115 40.58N 75.59W
Hazor Israel 67 32.59N 35.33E
Hazor Ashdod Israel 67 31.46N 34.43E
Head Waters U.S.A. 114 38.20N 79.21W
Healdsburg U.S.A. 108 38.37N 122.52W
Healesville Australia 93 37.40S 145.31E
Healy U.S.A. 98 63.52N 148.58W
Heanor U.K. 12 53.01N 1.20W
Heard I. Indian Oc. 49 53.07S 73.20E
Hearne L. Canada 100 62.20N 113.10W
Hearst Canada 102 49.40N 83.41W
Heathcote Australia 93 36.54S 144.42E
Hebei d. China 54 39.00N 116.00E
Hebel Australia 93 28.55S 147.48E
Heber Springs town U.S.A. 111 35.30N 92.02W
Hebi China 54 35.57N 114.08E
Hebrides is. U.K. 8 57.45N 7.00W
Hebrides, Sea of the U.K. 10 57.00N 7.20W
Hebron Canada 99 58.05N 62.30W
Hebron see Al Khalīl Jordan 67
Hebron N.Dak. U.S.A. 110 46.54N 102.03W
Hebron Nebr. U.S.A. 110 40.10N 97.35W
Heby Sweden 43 59.56N 16.53E
Hecate Str. Canada 100 53.00N 131.00W
Hechi China 55 24.42N 108.02E
Hechingen Germany 39 48.21N 8.58E
Hechtel Belgium 16 51.07N 5.22E
Hechuan China 55 30.05N 106.14E
Hecla U.S.A. 110 45.53N 98.09W
Hede Sweden 41 62.25N 13.30E
Hedemora Sweden 43 60.17N 15.59E
Hedensted Denmark 42 55.46N 9.42E
Hedi Shuiku resr. China 55 21.50N 110.19E
Hedley U.S.A. 111 34.52N 100.39W
Hedmark d. Norway 41 61.20N 11.30E
Heemstede Neth. 16 52.21N 4.38E
Heerde Neth. 16 52.23N 6.02E
Heerenveen Neth. 16 52.57N 5.55E
Heerlen Neth. 16 50.53N 5.59E
Hefa Israel 67 32.49N 34.59E
Hefa d. Israel 67 32.50N 35.00E
Hefei China 55 31.50N 117.16E
Hegang China 53 47.36N 130.30E
Heide Germany 38 54.12N 9.06E
Heide f. Germany 38 52.50N 10.30E
Heidelberg Germany 39 49.25N 8.43E
Heidelberg C.P. R.S.A. 80 34.05S 20.58E
Heidenheim Germany 39 48.40N 10.08E
Heilbronn R.S.A. 80 27.16S 27.57E
Heilbronn Germany 39 49.08N 9.13E
Heiligenblut Austria 39 47.02N 12.50E
Heiligenhafen Germany 38 54.21N 10.58E
Heiligenstadt Germany 38 51.23N 10.09E
Heilongjiang d. China 53 47.15N 128.50E
Heiloo Neth. 16 52.37N 4.43E
Heinola Finland 41 61.13N 26.02E
Heinsberg Germany 38 51.03N 6.05E
Heishan China 54 41.40N 122.03E
Heishui China 54 42.03N 119.21E
Heishuisi China 54 36.01N 108.56E
Hejaz f. see Al Ḥijāz f. Saudi Arabia 64

Hejian China 54 38.26N 116.05E
Hejiang China 55 28.48N 105.47E
Hekinan Japan 57 34.51N 136.58E
Hekla, Mt. Iceland 40 64.00N 19.45W
Hekou China 61 22.39N 103.57E
Hekura jima i. Japan 57 37.52N 136.56E
Helagsfjället mtn. Sweden 40 62.58N 12.25E
Helan China 54 38.35N 106.16E
Helan Shan mts. China 54 38.40N 106.00E
Helbra Germany 38 51.33N 11.29E
Helena U.S.A. 108 46.36N 112.01W
Helen Reef i. Pacific Oc. 59 2.43N 131.46E
Helensburgh U.K. 14 56.01N 4.44W
Helensville New Zealand 86 36.40S 174.27E
Helez Israel 67 31.35N 34.40E
Helgoland i. Germany 38 54.12N 7.53E
Helgoländer Bucht b. Germany 38 54.05N 8.15E
Hellendoorn Neth. 16 52.24N 6.29E
Hellenthal Germany 38 50.29N 6.26E
Hellesylt Norway 41 62.05N 6.54E
Hellevoetsluis Neth. 16 51.49N 4.08E
Hellín Spain 25 38.31N 1.41W
Helmand d. Afghan. 62 31.15N 64.00E
Helmand r. Asia 62 31.12N 61.34E
Helmond Neth. 16 51.28N 5.40E
Helmsdale U.K. 14 58.07N 3.40W
Helmsdale r. U.K. 14 58.05N 3.39W
Helmstedt Germany 38 52.13N 11.00E
Helsingfors see Helsinki Finland 41
Helsingör Denmark 43 56.02N 12.37E
Helsinki Finland 41 60.08N 25.00E
Helston U.K. 13 50.07N 5.17W
Helvecia Argentina 125 31.06S 60.05W
Hemaruka Canada 101 51.48N 111.10W
Hemau Germany 38 49.03N 11.47E
Hemel Hempstead U.K. 13 51.46N 0.28W
Hemingford U.S.A. 110 42.19N 103.04W
Hemmingford Canada 105 45.03N 73.36W
Hempstead N.Y. U.S.A. 115 40.42N 73.37W
Hempstead Tex. U.S.A. 111 30.06N 96.05W
Hemse Sweden 43 57.14N 18.22E
Hemsedal Norway 41 60.52N 8.34E
Henan d. China 54 34.00N 114.00E
Henares r. Spain 26 40.24N 3.30W
Henbury Australia 90 24.35S 133.15E
Hendaye France 20 43.22N 1.46W
Henderson Ky. U.S.A. 113 37.50N 87.35W
Henderson N.C. U.S.A. 113 36.20N 78.26W
Henderson Nev. U.S.A. 109 36.02N 114.59W
Henderson N.Y. U.S.A. 105 43.51N 76.11W
Henderson Tex. U.S.A. 111 32.09N 94.48W
Henderson I. Pacific Oc. 85 24.20S 128.20W
Hendrik Verwoerd Dam R.S.A. 80 30.37S 25.29E
Hendrina R.S.A. 80 26.09S 29.42E
Hengelo Neth. 16 52.16N 6.46E
Hengnan see Hengyang China 55
Hengshan Hunan China 55 27.14N 112.52E
Hengshan Shaanxi China 54 37.57N 109.11E
Hengshui China 54 37.40N 115.48E
Heng Xian China 55 22.35N 109.26E
Hengyang China 55 26.52N 112.35E
Hénin-Beaumont France 19 50.25N 2.56E
Henlopen, C. U.S.A. 115 38.48N 75.05W
Hennebont France 18 47.48N 3.17W
Hennigsdorf Germany 38 52.38N 13.12E
Henniker U.S.A. 115 43.11N 71.49W
Henrietta Maria, C. Canada 102 55.00N 82.15W
Henryetta U.S.A. 111 35.27N 95.59W
Henryville Canada 105 45.08N 73.11W
Hentiesbaai Namibia 80 22.10S 14.19E
Henty Australia 93 35.30S 147.03E
Henzada Myanmar 56 17.36N 95.26E
Heppenheim Germany 39 49.39N 8.38E
Heppner U.S.A. 108 45.21N 119.33W
Hepu China 55 21.31N 109.10E
Hepworth Canada 104 44.37N 81.09W
Heqing China 61 26.34N 100.12E
Herät Afghan. 62 34.20N 62.12E
Herät d. Afghan. 62 34.10N 62.30E
Herault r. France 20 43.17N 3.26E
Herbignac France 18 47.27N 2.19W
Herborn Germany 38 50.40N 8.17E
Herceg-Novi Yugo. 31 42.27N 18.32E
Hereford U.K. 13 52.04N 2.43W
Hereford Md. U.S.A. 115 39.35N 76.40W
Hereford Tex. U.S.A. 111 34.49N 102.24W
Hereford and Worcester d. U.K. 13 52.08N 2.30W
Herencia Spain 27 39.21N 3.22W
Herentals Belgium 16 51.12N 4.42E
Herford Germany 38 52.06N 8.40E
Herington U.S.A. 110 38.40N 96.57W
Herisau Switz. 39 47.23N 9.17E
Herleshausen Germany 38 51.00N 10.09E
Hermagor Austria 39 46.37N 13.22E
Hermannsburg Australia 90 23.56S 132.46E
Hermanus R.S.A. 80 34.24S 19.16E
Hermidale Australia 93 31.33S 146.44E
Hermiston U.S.A. 108 45.51N 119.17W
Hermosillo Mexico 109 29.04N 110.58W
Herndon U.S.A. 114 40.43N 76.50W
Herne Germany 38 51.32N 7.13E
Herne Bay town U.K. 13 51.23N 1.10E
Herning Denmark 42 56.08N 8.59E
Heron Bay town Canada 102 48.40N 86.25W
Herrera del Duque Spain 27 39.10N 5.03W
Herrera de Pisuerga Spain 26 42.36N 4.20W
Herrljunga Sweden 43 58.05N 13.02E
Hershey U.S.A. 115 40.17N 76.39W
Herstal Belgium 16 50.14N 5.38E
Herten Germany 38 51.35N 7.07E
Hertford U.K. 13 51.48N 0.05W
Hertfordshire d. U.K. 13 51.51N 0.05W
Hervás Spain 26 40.16N 5.51W
Hervey B. Australia 90 25.00S 153.00E
Herzberg Brandenburg Germany 38 51.41N 13.14E
Herzberg Nschn. Germany 38 51.39N 10.20E
Herzliyya Israel 67 32.10N 34.50E
Hesbaye f. Belgium 16 50.32N 5.07E

Hesdin France 19 50.22N 2.02E
Hesel Germany 38 53.18N 7.35E
Heshui China 54 35.43N 108.07E
Heshun China 54 37.19N 113.34E
Hesselö i. Denmark 42 56.12N 11.43E
Hessen d. Germany 38 50.44N 9.00E
Hesso Australia 92 32.08S 137.58E
Hetou China 55 21.05N 109.44E
Hettinger U.S.A. 110 46.00N 102.39W
Hettstedt Germany 38 51.38N 11.30E
Hetzerath Germany 39 49.52N 6.49E
Heuvelton U.S.A. 105 44.37N 75.25W
Hevron, Nahal wadi Israel 67 31.15N 34.50E
Hewett, C. Canada 99 70.20N 68.00W
Hexham U.K. 12 54.58N 2.06W
Hexi China 55 24.51N 117.13E
He Xian China 55 24.25N 111.31E
Hexigten Qi China 54 43.17N 117.24E
Heyrieux France 21 45.38N 5.03E
Heysham U.K. 12 54.03N 2.53W
Heyuan China 55 23.42N 114.48E
Heywood Australia 92 38.08S 141.38E
Heywood U.K. 12 53.36N 2.13W
Heze China 54 35.12N 115.15E
Hezhang China 55 27.08N 104.43E
Hiawatha Kans. U.S.A. 110 39.51N 95.32W
Hiawatha Utah U.S.A. 108 39.29N 111.01W
Hibbing U.S.A. 110 47.25N 92.55W
Hickman, Mt. Canada 100 57.11N 131.10W
Hickory U.S.A. 113 35.44N 81.23W
Hicks Bay town New Zealand 86 37.35S 178.18E
Hickson L. Canada 101 56.17N 104.25W
Hicksville U.S.A. 115 40.46N 73.32W
Hidaka Sammyaku mts. Japan 57 42.50N 143.00E
Hidalgo d. Mexico 116 20.50N 98.30W
Hidalgo Nuevo León Mexico 111 25.59N 100.27W
Hidalgo Tamaulipas Mexico 111 24.15N 99.26W
Hidalgo del Parral Mexico 109 26.56N 105.40W
Hieradhsvotn r. Iceland 40 65.45N 18.50W
Hierro i. Canary Is. 74 27.45N 18.00W
Higashimatsuyama Japan 57 36.02N 139.24E
Higashimurayama Japan 57 35.46N 139.29E
Higashiōsaka Japan 57 34.39N 135.35E
Higgins U.S.A. 111 36.07N 100.02W
Higgins L. U.S.A. 104 44.30N 84.45W
Higginsville Australia 89 31.46S 121.43E
Highgate Canada 104 42.30N 81.49W
High Hill r. Canada 101 55.52N 94.42W
High Knob mtn. U.S.A. 114 39.08N 78.26W
Highland d. U.K. 14 57.42N 5.00W
Highland town U.S.A. 115 41.43N 73.58W
Highland Park town U.S.A. 114 42.24N 83.06W
High Level Canada 100 58.31N 117.08W
Highmore U.S.A. 110 44.31N 99.27W
High Peak mtn. U.K. 12 53.22N 1.48W
High Point town U.S.A. 113 35.58N 80.00W
High Prairie Canada 100 55.30N 116.30W
Highrock L. Man. Canada 101 55.45N 100.30W
Highrock L. Sask. Canada 101 57.04N 105.30W
High Willhays mtn. U.K. 13 50.41N 4.00W
High Wycombe U.K. 13 51.38N 0.46W
Hiiumaa i. Estonia 41 58.52N 22.40E
Hijar Spain 25 41.10N 0.27W
Hijāz, Jabal al mts. Saudi Arabia 72 19.45N 41.55E
Hikone Japan 57 35.15N 136.15E
Hikurangi New Zealand 86 35.36S 174.17E
Hikurangi mtn. New Zealand 86 37.50S 178.10E
Hikutavake Niue 84 18.57S 169.53W
Hildburghausen Germany 39 50.25N 10.44E
Hilden Germany 38 51.10N 6.56E
Hildesheim Germany 38 52.09N 9.57E
Hill City Kans. U.S.A. 110 39.22N 99.51W
Hill City Minn. U.S.A. 110 46.59N 93.44W
Hillegom Neth. 16 52.19N 4.35E
Hill End Australia 93 33.01S 149.26E
Hillerød Denmark 43 55.56N 12.19E
Hill Island L. Canada 101 60.30N 109.50W
Hillman U.S.A. 104 45.04N 83.54W
Hillsboro N.H. U.S.A. 115 43.07N 71.54W
Hillsboro Oreg. U.S.A. 108 45.31N 122.59W
Hillsboro Tex. U.S.A. 111 32.01N 97.08W
Hillsdale U.S.A. 112 41.56N 84.37W
Hillsport Canada 102 49.27N 85.34W
Hillston Australia 93 33.30S 145.33E
Hilo Hawaii U.S.A. 106 19.42N 155.04W
Hilton U.S.A. 114 43.17N 77.48W
Hilton Beach Canada 104 46.16N 83.56W
Hilton Head I. U.S.A. 113 32.12N 80.45W
Hiltrup Germany 38 51.54N 7.38E
Hilversum Neth. 16 52.14N 5.12E
Himachal Pradesh d. India 62 32.05N 77.15E
Himalaya mts. Asia 63 29.00N 84.30E
Himanka Finland 40 64.04N 23.39E
Himarë Albania 35 40.08N 19.43E
Himatnagar India 62 23.36N 72.57E
Himeji Japan 57 34.50N 134.40E
Himi Japan 57 36.51N 136.59E
Himmerland f. Denmark 42 56.52N 9.30E
Ḥimş Syria 66 34.44N 36.43E
Hinchinbrook I. Australia 90 18.23S 146.17E
Hinckley U.K. 13 52.33N 1.21W
Hinckley Resr. U.S.A. 115 43.20N 75.05W
Hindaun India 62 26.43N 77.01E
Hindmarsh, L. Australia 92 36.03S 141.53E
Hindubāgh Pakistan 62 30.49N 67.45E
Hindu Kush mts. Asia 60 36.40N 70.00E
Hindupur India 61 13.49N 77.29E
Hines Creek town Canada 100 56.20N 118.40W
Hinganghāt India 63 20.34N 78.50E
Hingol r. Pakistan 62 25.23N 65.28E
Hingoli India 62 19.43N 77.09E
Hinnøy i. Norway 40 68.35N 15.50E
Hinojosa Spain 26 38.30N 5.09W
Hinsdale Mont. U.S.A. 108 48.24N 107.05W
Hinsdale N.H. U.S.A. 115 42.47N 72.29W
Hinterrhein r. Switz. 39 46.49N 9.25E
Hinton Canada 100 53.25N 117.34W
Hipólito Mexico 111 25.41N 101.26W

Hippolytushoef Neth. 16 52.57N 4.58E
Hirakata Japan 57 34.48N 135.38E
Hīrākud India 63 21.31N 83.57E
Hīrākud resr. India 63 21.31N 83.52E
Hīrāpur India 63 24.22N 79.13E
Hiratsuka Japan 57 35.19N 139.21E
Hirmand r. see Helmand r. Iran 62
Hirok Sāmi Pakistan 62 26.02N 63.25E
Hirosaki Japan 57 40.34N 140.28E
Hiroshima Japan 57 34.30N 132.27E
Hirson France 19 49.55N 4.05E
Hîrşova Romania 37 44.41N 27.57E
Hirtshals Denmark 42 57.35N 9.58E
Hisai Japan 57 34.40N 136.28E
Hisār India 62 29.10N 75.43E
Ḥisbān Jordan 67 31.48N 35.48E
Hismá f. Saudi Arabia 66 28.45N 35.56E
Hispaniola i. C. America 117 19.00N 71.00W
Hisua India 63 24.50N 85.25E
Ḥisyah Syria 66 34.24N 36.45E
Hīt Iraq 64 33.38N 42.50E
Hitachi Japan 57 36.35N 140.40E
Hitchin U.K. 13 51.57N 0.16W
Hitra i. Norway 40 63.37N 8.46E
Hiva Oa i. Îs. Marquises 85 9.45S 139.00W
Hixon Canada 100 53.27N 122.36W
Hjälmaren l. Sweden 43 59.15N 15.45E
Hjalmar L. Canada 101 61.33N 109.25W
Hjelmelandsvågen Norway 42 59.14N 6.11E
Hjo Sweden 43 58.18N 14.17E
Hjørring Denmark 42 57.28N 9.59E
Hlotse Lesotho 80 28.52S 28.02E
Ho Ghana 76 6.38N 0.38E
Hòa Bình Vietnam 56 20.49N 105.20E
Hoare B. Canada 99 65.20N 62.30W
Hoarusib r. Namibia 80 19.04S 12.33E
Hobart Australia 91 42.54S 147.18E
Hobart Ind. U.S.A. 112 41.32N 87.14W
Hobart Okla. U.S.A. 111 35.01N 99.06W
Hobbs U.S.A. 111 32.42N 103.08W
Hoboken Belgium 16 51.11N 4.21E
Hoboken U.S.A. 115 40.45N 74.03W
Hobq Shamo des. China 54 40.00N 109.00E
Hobro Denmark 42 56.38N 9.48E
Hoburgen c. Sweden 43 56.55N 18.07E
Hobyo Somali Rep. 71 5.20N 48.30E
Hochgolling mtn. Austria 39 47.16N 13.45E
Ho Chi Minh Vietnam 56 10.46N 106.43E
Höchstadt an der Aisch Germany 39 49.42N 10.44E
Hockenheim Germany 39 49.19N 8.33E
Hocking r. U.S.A. 114 39.12N 81.45W
Hockley U.S.A. 111 30.02N 95.51W
Hodal India 62 27.54N 77.22E
Hodgson Canada 101 51.13N 97.34W
Hod HaSharon Israel 67 32.09N 34.54E
Hodh ech Chargui d. Mauritania 76 19.00N 7.15W
Hodh el Gharbi d. Mauritania 76 16.30N 10.00W
Hodiyya Israel 67 31.41N 34.38E
Hódmezővásárhely Hungary 31 46.25N 20.20E
Hodna, Monts du mts. Algeria 75 35.50N 4.50E
Hoek van Holland Neth. 16 51.59N 4.08E
Hoeryŏng N. Korea 57 42.27N 129.44E
Hof Germany 38 50.18N 11.55E
Hofgeismar Germany 38 51.30N 9.22E
Hofheim Bayern Germany 39 50.08N 10.31E
Hofheim Hessen Germany 39 50.07N 8.26E
Höfn Iceland 40 64.16N 15.10W
Hofors Sweden 41 60.33N 16.17E
Hofsjökull mtn. Iceland 40 64.50N 19.00W
Hofsós Iceland 40 65.53N 19.26W
Höganäs Sweden 43 56.12N 12.33E
Hogansburg U.S.A. 105 44.59N 74.40W
Hogeland U.S.A. 108 48.51N 108.39W
Hogem Ranges f. Canada 100 55.40N 126.00W
Högsby Sweden 43 57.10N 16.02E
Hohe Acht mtn. Germany 39 50.23N 7.00E
Hohenthurn Austria 39 46.33N 13.40E
Hoher Dachstein mtn. Austria 39 47.28N 13.35E
Hohhot China 54 40.42N 111.38E
Hoh Tolgoin Sum China 54 44.27N 112.41E
Hohultslätt Sweden 43 56.58N 15.39E
Hoi An Vietnam 56 15.54N 108.19E
Hoima Uganda 79 1.25N 31.22E
Hojāi India 63 26.00N 92.51E
Höjer Denmark 42 54.58N 8.43E
Hökensås hills Sweden 43 58.11N 14.08E
Hokitika New Zealand 86 42.42S 170.59E
Hokkaidō i. Japan 57 43.00N 143.00E
Hokkaidō d. Japan 57 43.00N 144.00E
Hokksund Norway 42 59.47N 9.59E
Hola Kenya 79 1.29S 40.02E
Holbaek Denmark 42 55.43N 11.43E
Holbrook Australia 93 35.46S 147.20E
Holbrook U.S.A. 109 34.54N 110.10W
Holdrege U.S.A. 110 40.26N 99.22W
Holguín Cuba 117 20.54N 76.15W
Höljes Sweden 41 60.54N 12.36E
Hollabrunn Austria 36 48.34N 16.05E
Holland Mich. U.S.A. 112 42.46N 86.06W
Holland N.Y. U.S.A. 114 42.38N 78.33W
Holland Centre Canada 104 44.24N 80.48W
Hollidaysburg U.S.A. 114 40.26N 78.23W
Holly Kans. U.S.A. 111 38.03N 102.07W
Holly Mich. U.S.A. 104 42.48N 83.38W
Hollywood U.S.A. 113 26.01N 80.09W
Holman Island town Canada 98 70.43N 117.43W
Holmavik Iceland 40 65.43N 21.39W
Holmenkollen Norway 42 59.58N 10.40E
Holmer, Lac l. Canada 103 54.10N 71.44W
Holmestrand Norway 42 59.29N 10.18E
Holmön i. Sweden 40 63.47N 20.53E
Holmsund Sweden 40 63.41N 20.20E
Holon Israel 67 32.01N 34.46E
Holroyd r. Australia 90 14.10S 141.36E
Holstebro Denmark 42 56.21N 8.38E
Holstein Canada 104 44.03N 80.45W
Holsteinsborg Greenland 99 66.55N 53.30W
Holsworthy U.K. 13 50.48N 4.21W

Holt U.K. 12 52.55N 1.04E
Holten Neth. 16 52.18N 6.26E
Holwerd Neth. 16 53.22N 5.54E
Holy Cross U.S.A. 98 62.12N 159.47W
Holyhead U.K. 12 53.18N 4.38W
Holyhead B. U.K. 12 53.22N 4.40W
Holy I. England U.K. 12 55.41N 1.47W
Holy I. Wales U.K. 12 53.15N 4.38W
Holyoke Colo. U.S.A. 110 40.35N 102.18W
Holyoke Mass. U.S.A. 115 42.12N 72.37W
Holýšov Czech Republic 38 49.36N 13.05E
Holywood U.K. 15 54.38N 5.50W
Holzkirchen Germany 39 47.52N 11.42E
Holzminden Germany 38 51.50N 9.27E
Homberg Germany 38 51.02N 9.24E
Hombori Mali 76 15.20N 1.38W
Homburg Germany 39 49.19N 7.20E
Home B. Canada 99 69.00N 66.00W
Home Hill town Australia 90 19.40S 147.25E
Homer Alas. U.S.A. 98 59.40N 151.37W
Homer La. U.S.A. 111 32.48N 93.04W
Homer N.Y. U.S.A. 115 42.38N 76.11W
Homer Tunnel New Zealand 86 44.40S 168.15E
Homestead U.S.A. 113 25.29N 80.29W
Hommersåk Norway 42 58.58N 5.42E
Homoine Mozambique 81 23.45S 35.09E
Homoljske Planina f. Yugo. 37 44.20N 21.45E
Honda Colombia 122 5.15N 74.50W
Hondeklipbaai R.S.A. 80 30.19S 17.12E
Hondo r. Mexico 117 18.33N 88.22W
Hondo U.S.A. 111 29.21N 99.09W
Honduras C. America 117 14.30N 87.00W
Honduras, G. of Carib. Sea 117 16.20N 87.30W
Honefoss France 18 49.25N 0.14E
Höng Denmark 42 55.31N 11.18E
Hong'an China 55 31.18N 114.33E
Hòn Gay Vietnam 55 21.01N 107.02E
Hong Hà r. Vietnam 56 20.15N 106.36E
Honghu China 55 29.42N 113.26E
Hong Hu l. China 55 29.50N 113.15E
Hongjiang China 55 27.08N 109.54E
Hongjian Nur l. China 54 39.09N 109.56E
Hong Kong Asia 55 22.15N 114.15E
Hongor Mongolia 54 45.20N 113.41E
Hongor Mongolia 54 45.45N 112.56E
Hongshui He r. China 55 23.20N 110.04E
Hongtong China 54 36.15N 111.37E
Honguedo, Détroit d' str. Canada 103 49.25N 64.00W
Hongze China 54 33.18N 118.51E
Hongze Hu l. China 54 33.15N 118.40E
Honiton U.K. 13 50.48N 3.13W
Honjō Japan 57 39.23N 140.03E
Honkajoki Finland 41 62.00N 22.15E
Hönö Sweden 42 57.42N 11.39E
Honokaa Hawaiian Is. 85 20.05N 155.28W
Honokahua Hawaiian Is. 85 21.00N 156.39W
Honolulu Hawaii U.S.A. 106 21.19N 157.50W
Honshū i. Japan 57 36.00N 138.00E
Hood, Mt. U.S.A. 108 45.23N 121.41W
Hood Pt. Australia 89 34.23S 119.34E
Hood Range mts. Australia 93 28.35S 144.30E
Hoogeveen Neth. 16 52.44N 6.29E
Hoogezand Neth. 16 53.10N 6.47E
Hooghly r. India 63 21.55N 88.05E
Hoogstade Belgium 16 50.59N 2.42E
Hooker U.S.A. 111 36.52N 101.13W
Hook Head Rep. of Ire. 15 52.07N 6.55W
Hoopa U.S.A. 108 41.03N 123.40W
Hoopeston U.S.A. 110 40.28N 87.41W
Hoopstad R.S.A. 80 27.48S 25.52E
Höör Sweden 43 55.56N 13.32E
Hoorn Neth. 16 52.38N 5.03E
Hoosick Falls town U.S.A. 115 42.54N 73.21W
Hoover Dam U.S.A. 109 36.00N 114.27W
Hope U.S.A. 111 33.40N 93.36W
Hopedale Canada 103 55.50N 60.10W
Hopefield R.S.A. 80 33.04S 18.19E
Hope, L. S.A. Australia 92 28.23S 139.19E
Hope, L. W.A. Australia 89 32.31S 120.25E
Hope, Pt. U.S.A. 96 68.20N 166.49W
Hopetoun Vic. Australia 92 35.43S 142.20E
Hopetoun W.A. Australia 89 33.57S 120.05E
Hopetown R.S.A. 80 29.37S 24.04E
Hopkins r. Australia 92 38.25S 142.00E
Hopkins, L. Australia 88 24.15S 128.50E
Hopkinsville U.S.A. 113 36.50N 87.30W
Hopland U.S.A. 108 38.58N 123.07W
Hoquiam U.S.A. 108 46.59N 123.53W
Horaždovice Czech Republic 38 49.20N 13.43E
Horb Germany 39 48.26N 8.41E
Horbat Qesari site Israel 67 32.30N 34.53E
Hörby Sweden 43 55.51N 13.39E
Hordaland d. Norway 42 60.00N 6.00E
Horde Germany 16 51.29N 7.30E
Horgen Switz. 39 47.15N 8.36E
Hörh Uul mts. Mongolia 54 42.20N 105.30E
Horinger China 54 40.23N 111.53E
Horizonte Mexico 111 25.50N 103.48W
Horlick Mts. Antarctica 128 86.00S 102.00W
Hormuz, Str. of Asia 65 26.35N 56.20E
Horn Austria 36 48.40N 15.40E
Horn r. Canada 100 61.30N 118.01W
Hornavan l. Sweden 40 66.10N 17.30E
Horn, C. see Hornos, Cabo de c. S. America 125
Horncastle U.K. 12 53.13N 0.08W
Horndal Sweden 43 60.18N 16.25E
Hornell U.S.A. 114 42.19N 77.40W
Hornell L. Canada 100 62.20N 119.25W
Hornepayne Canada 102 49.14N 84.48W
Hornindal Norway 41 61.58N 6.31E
Horn Mts. Canada 100 62.15N 119.15W
Hornos, Cabo de c. S. America 125 55.47S 67.00W
Hornsby Australia 93 33.11S 151.06E
Hornsea U.K. 12 53.55N 0.10W
Hornslet Denmark 42 56.19N 10.20E
Hořovice Czech Republic 36 49.50N 13.54E
Horqin Zuoyi Houqi China 54 42.57N 122.21E

Horqin Zuoyi Zhongqi China 54 44.08N 123.18E
Horru China 63 30.30N 91.32E
Horse Creek town U.S.A. 108 41.25N 105.11W
Horseheads U.S.A. 114 42.10N 76.50W
Horsens Denmark 42 55.52N 9.52E
Horsham Australia 92 36.45S 142.15E
Horsham U.K. 13 51.04N 0.20W
Hörsholm Denmark 43 55.53N 12.30E
Horšovský Týn Czech Republic 38 49.32N 12.56E
Horta wadi Chad 72 17.15N 21.52E
Horten Norway 42 59.25N 10.30E
Horton r. Canada 98 70.00N 127.00W
Horton L. Canada 98 67.30N 122.28W
Horvot Mezada site Israel 67 31.19N 35.21E
Hosa'ina Ethiopia 73 7.38N 37.52E
Hösbach Germany 39 50.00N 9.12E
Hose, Pegunungan mts. Malaysia 58 1.30N 114.10E
Hoshāb Pakistan 62 26.01N 63.56E
Hoshangābād India 63 22.45N 77.43E
Hoshiārpur India 62 31.32N 75.54E
Hōsh 'Isa Egypt 66 30.55N 30.17E
Hoskins P.N.G. 87 5.30S 150.27E
Hospital de Orbigo Spain 26 42.28N 5.53W
Hospitalet de Llobregat Spain 25 41.22N 2.08E
Hossegor France 20 43.40N 1.27W
Hoste, Isla i. Chile 125 55.10S 69.00W
Hotan China 52 37.07N 79.57E
Hotazel R.S.A. 80 27.16S 22.57E
Hotham r. Australia 89 32.58S 116.22E
Hotham, Mt. Australia 93 36.58S 147.11E
Hoting Sweden 40 64.07N 16.10E
Hotin Gol China 54 38.58N 104.14E
Hot Springs town Ark. U.S.A. 111 34.30N 93.02W
Hot Springs town S.Dak. U.S.A. 110 43.26N 103.29W
Hottah L. Canada 98 65.04N 118.29W
Houailou N. Cal. 84 21.17S 165.38E
Houdan France 19 48.47N 1.36E
Houeillès France 20 44.12N 0.02E
Houffalize Belgium 16 50.08N 5.50E
Houghton L. U.S.A. 112 44.16N 84.48W
Houghton-le-Spring U.K. 12 54.51N 1.28W
Houlton U.S.A. 112 46.08N 67.51W
Houma China 54 35.36N 111.21E
Houma U.S.A. 111 29.36N 90.43W
Houndé Burkina 76 11.34N 3.31W
Hourn, Loch U.K. 14 57.06N 5.33W
Housatonic r. U.S.A. 115 41.10N 73.07W
Houston Mo. U.S.A. 111 37.22N 91.58W
Houston Tex. U.S.A. 111 29.46N 95.22W
Houtzdale U.S.A. 114 40.49N 78.21W
Hova Sweden 43 58.52N 14.13E
Hovd Mongolia 52 46.40N 90.45E
Hove U.K. 13 50.50N 0.10W
Hövsgöl Mongolia 54 43.36N 109.40E
Hövsgöl Nuur l. Mongolia 52 51.00N 100.30E
Howa, Ouadi see Howar, Wādī Chad 72
Howard L. Canada 101 62.15N 105.57W
Howar, Wādī Sudan 72 17.30N 27.08E
Howe, C. Australia 93 37.30S 149.59E
Howell U.S.A. 104 42.36N 83.55W
Howick Canada 105 45.11N 73.51W
Howitt, Mt. Australia 93 37.15S 146.40E
Howrah India 63 22.35N 88.20E
Howth Head Rep. of Ire. 15 53.22N 6.03W
Höxter Germany 38 51.46N 9.23E
Hoy i. U.K. 14 58.51N 3.17W
Höyanger Norway 41 61.13N 6.05E
Hoyerswerda Germany 38 51.26N 14.14E
Hoyos Spain 27 40.10N 6.43W
Hradec Králové Czech Republic 36 50.13N 15.50E
Hron r. Slovakia 37 47.49N 18.45E
Hrubieszów Poland 37 50.49N 23.55E
Hsenwi Myanmar 56 23.18N 97.58E
Hsipaw Myanmar 56 22.42N 97.21E
Hsuphäng Myanmar 56 20.18N 98.42E
Huab r. Namibia 80 20.55S 13.28E
Huabei Pingyuan f. China 54 35.00N 115.30E
Huachi China 54 36.23N 108.14E
Huacho Peru 122 11.05S 77.36W
Huachuca City U.S.A. 109 31.34N 110.21W
Huade China 54 41.57N 114.04E
Hua Hin Thailand 56 12.34N 99.58E
Huahine i. Is. de la Société 85 16.45S 151.00W
Huai'an Hebei China 54 40.40N 114.18E
Huai'an Jiangsu China 54 33.29N 119.15E
Huaibei China 54 33.58N 116.50E
Huai He r. China 54 32.58N 118.18E
Huaiji China 55 23.58N 112.10E
Huailai China 54 40.25N 115.27E
Huainan China 54 32.39N 117.01E
Huaining China 55 30.21N 116.42E
Huairen China 54 39.50N 113.07E
Huairou China 54 40.20N 116.37E
Huaiyang China 54 33.47N 114.59E
Huaiyuan China 54 32.57N 117.12E
Huajuápan Mexico 116 17.50N 97.48W
Hualian Taiwan 55 24.00N 121.39E
Huallaga r. Peru 122 5.02S 75.30W
Huamanrazo mtn. Peru 122 12.54S 75.04W
Huambo Angola 78 12.47S 15.44E
Huambo d. Angola 78 12.30S 15.45E
Huanan China 53 46.13N 130.31E
Huancané Peru 122 15.10S 69.44W
Huancapi Peru 122 13.35S 74.05W
Huancavelica Peru 122 12.45S 75.03W
Huancayo Peru 122 12.05S 75.12W
Huangchuan China 55 32.07N 115.02E
Huanggang China 55 30.33N 114.59E
Huanggang Shan mtn. China 55 27.50N 117.47E
Huang Hai b. N. Korea 54 39.30N 123.40E
Huang He r. China 54 38.00N 118.40E
Huanghe Kou est. China 54 37.54N 118.48E
Huanghua China 54 38.22N 117.20E
Huangling China 54 35.36N 109.17E
Huangpi China 55 30.52N 114.22E
Huangping China 55 26.54N 107.53E
Huangshan China 55 29.41N 118.22E
Huangshi China 55 30.10N 115.04E

Huang Xian China 54 37.38N 120.30E
Huangyan China 55 28.42N 121.25E
Huan Jiang r. China 54 35.13N 108.00E
Huanren China 54 41.16N 125.21E
Huanta Peru 122 12.54S 74.13W
Huánuco Peru 122 9.55S 76.11W
Huaráz Peru 122 9.33S 77.31W
Huarmey Peru 122 10.05S 78.05W
Huascaran mtn. Peru 122 9.08S 77.36W
Huasco Chile 124 28.28S 71.14W
Huatabampo Mexico 109 26.50N 109.38W
Huatong China 54 40.03N 121.56E
Hua Xian Guangdong China 55 23.22N 113.12E
Hua Xian Shaanxi China 54 34.31N 109.46E
Huayuan China 55 28.37N 109.28E
Hubbard L. U.S.A. 104 44.49N 83.34W
Hubei d. China 55 31.00N 112.00E
Hubli India 60 15.20N 75.14E
Hückelhoven Germany 38 51.03N 6.13E
Hucknall U.K. 12 53.03N 1.12W
Huddersfield U.K. 12 53.38N 1.49W
Huddinge Sweden 43 59.14N 17.59E
Hudiksvall Sweden 41 61.44N 17.07E
Hudson Mich. U.S.A. 104 41.51N 84.21W
Hudson N.Y. U.S.A. 115 42.15N 73.47W
Hudson r. U.S.A. 115 40.42N 74.02W
Hudson Wyo. U.S.A. 108 42.54N 108.35W
Hudson B. Canada 99 58.00N 86.00W
Hudson Bay town Canada 101 52.52N 102.25W
Hudson Falls town U.S.A. 115 43.18N 73.35W
Hudson Highlands U.S.A. 115 41.24N 74.15W
Hudson Hope Canada 100 56.03N 121.59W
Hudson Mts. Antarctica 128 76.00S 99.00W
Hudson Str. Canada 99 62.00N 70.00W
Hue Vietnam 56 16.28N 107.40E
Huebra r. Spain 26 41.02N 6.48W
Huedin Romania 37 46.52N 23.02E
Huehuetenango Guatemala 116 15.19N 91.26W
Huelgoat France 18 48.22N 3.45W
Huelma Spain 27 37.39N 3.27W
Huelva Spain 27 37.16N 6.57W
Huelva d. Spain 27 37.35N 7.10W
Huelva r. Spain 27 37.27N 6.00W
Huércal-Overa Spain 25 37.23N 1.57W
Huerva r. Spain 25 41.39N 0.52W
Huesca Spain 25 42.08N 0.25W
Huesca d. Spain 25 42.20N 0.00
Huéscar Spain 27 37.49N 2.32W
Huete Spain 26 40.08N 2.41W
Ḩufrat an Naḥās Sudan 73 9.45N 24.19E
Hugh r. Australia 90 25.01S 134.01E
Hughenden Australia 90 20.51S 144.12E
Hughes Australia 91 30.40S 129.32E
Hughes U.S.A. 98 66.03N 154.16W
Hugo U.S.A. 111 34.01N 95.31W
Hugoton U.S.A. 111 37.11N 101.21W
Hugou China 54 33.22N 117.07E
Hui'an China 55 25.02N 118.48E
Huiarau Range mts. New Zealand 86 38.20S 177.15E
Huikou China 55 29.49N 116.15E
Huíla d. Angola 78 15.10S 15.30E
Huilai China 55 23.03N 116.17E
Huimin China 54 37.30N 117.29E
Huining China 54 35.42N 105.06E
Huisne r. France 18 47.59N 0.11E
Huixtla Mexico 116 15.09N 92.30W
Huizen Neth. 16 52.18N 5.12E
Huizhou China 55 23.05N 114.29E
Hukuntsi Botswana 80 24.02S 21.48E
Ḩulayfā' Saudi Arabia 64 26.00N 40.47E
Hulda Israel 67 31.50N 34.53E
Hulín Czech Republic 37 49.19N 17.28E
Hull Canada 105 45.26N 75.43W
Hüls Germany 38 51.22N 6.30E
Hulst Neth. 16 51.18N 4.01E
Hultsfred Sweden 43 57.29N 15.50E
Hulun Nur l. China 53 49.00N 117.27E
Ḩulwān Egypt 66 29.51N 31.20E
Humaitá Brazil 122 7.31S 63.02W
Humansdorp R.S.A. 80 34.02S 24.45E
Ḩumaydah Sudan 72 14.22N 22.31E
Humber r. U.K. 12 53.40N 0.12W
Humberside d. U.K. 12 53.48N 0.35W
Humble U.S.A. 111 30.00N 95.16W
Humboldt Canada 101 52.12N 105.07W
Humboldt r. U.S.A. 108 40.02N 118.31W
Humboldt r. U.S.A. 111 35.49N 88.55W
Humboldt r. U.S.A. 108 40.02N 118.31W
Hume, L. Australia 93 36.06S 147.05E
Humenné Slovakia 37 48.56N 21.55E
Humphreys Peak mtn. U.S.A. 109 35.20N 111.40W
Hūn Libya 75 29.07N 15.56E
Húnaflói b. Iceland 40 65.45N 20.50W
Hunan d. China 55 27.30N 111.30E
Hundested Denmark 42 55.58N 11.52E
Hundred U.S.A. 114 39.41N 80.28W
Hundred Mile House town Canada 100 51.38N 121.18W
Hunedoara Romania 37 45.45N 22.54E
Hünfeld Germany 38 50.40N 9.46E
Hungary Europe 37 47.30N 19.00E
Hungerford Australia 92 29.00S 144.26E
Hungerford U.K. 13 51.25N 1.30W
Hungfou Hsü i. Taiwan 55 22.03N 121.33E
Hŭngnam N. Korea 53 39.49N 127.40E
Hung Yen Vietnam 55 20.38N 106.05E
Huningue France 19 47.36N 7.35E
Hunjiang China 54 41.57N 126.36E
Hunnebostrand Sweden 42 58.27N 11.18E
Hunsberge mts. Namibia 80 27.40S 17.12E
Hunse r. Neth. 16 53.20N 6.18E
Hunsrück mts. Germany 39 49.45N 7.00E
Hunstanton U.K. 12 52.57N 0.30E
Hunte r. Germany 38 53.14N 8.18E
Hunter r. Australia 93 32.50S 151.42E
Hunter I. Australia 91 40.30S 144.46E
Hunter I. Canada 100 51.55N 128.00W
Hunter Island Ridge Pacific Oc. 84 21.30S 175.00E
Huntingdon U.K. 13 52.20N 0.11W

Huntingdon U.K. 13 52.20N 0.11W
Huntingdon Penn. U.S.A. 114 40.29N 78.01W
Huntington U.S.A. 112 40.54N 85.30W
Huntington Mass. U.S.A. 115 42.14N 72.53W
Huntington N.Y. U.S.A. 115 40.51N 73.25W
Huntington Oreg. U.S.A. 108 44.21N 117.16W
Huntington Utah U.S.A. 108 39.20N 110.58W
Huntington W.Va. U.S.A. 114 38.25N 82.26W
Huntington Beach town U.S.A. 109 33.39N 118.01W
Huntly New Zealand 86 37.35S 175.10E
Huntly U.K. 14 57.27N 2.47W
Huntsville Canada 104 45.20N 79.14W
Huntsville Ala. U.S.A. 113 34.44N 86.35W
Huntsville Tex. U.S.A. 111 30.43N 95.33W
Hunyani r. Mozambique 81 15.41S 30.38E
Hunyuan China 54 39.45N 113.35E
Huon Pen. P.N.G. 59 6.00S 147.00E
Huonville Australia 91 43.01S 147.01E
Huoshan China 55 31.24N 116.20E
Huqoq Israel 67 32.53N 35.29E
Hurd, C. Canada 104 45.13N 81.44W
Huretin Sum China 54 40.19N 103.02E
Huriel France 20 46.23N 2.29E
Hurlock U.S.A. 115 38.38N 75.52W
Hurmāgai Pakistan 62 28.18N 64.26E
Huron Ohio U.S.A. 114 41.24N 82.33W
Huron r. U.S.A. 104 42.03N 83.14W
Huron S.Dak. U.S.A. 110 44.22N 98.13W
Huron, L. Canada/U.S.A. 114 44.30N 82.15W
Hurso Ethiopia 73 9.38N 41.38E
Hurup Denmark 42 56.45N 8.25E
Húsavík Iceland 40 66.03N 17.21W
Husevig Faroe Is. 10 61.49N 6.41W
Huşi Romania 37 46.40N 28.04E
Huskvarna Sweden 43 57.48N 14.16E
Husum Germany 38 54.28N 9.03E
Hutchinson R.S.A. 80 31.30S 23.10E
Hutchinson U.S.A. 111 38.05N 97.56W
Hüttental Germany 38 50.54N 8.02E
Huttig U.S.A. 111 33.02N 92.11W
Huttonsville U.S.A. 114 38.43N 80.00W
Hutuo He r. China 54 39.10N 117.12E
Hut Yanchi r. China 54 39.24N 105.01E
Ḩuwwārah Jordan 67 32.09N 35.15E
Huy Belgium 16 50.31N 5.14E
Hvar i. Croatia 31 43.09N 16.45E
Hvar town Croatia 31 43.10N 16.27E
Hvarski Kanal str. Croatia 31 43.20N 16.45E
Hvide Sande Denmark 42 55.59N 8.08E
Hvíta r. Iceland 40 64.33N 21.45W
Hvittingfoss Norway 42 59.29N 10.01E
Hwange Zimbabwe 80 18.20S 26.29E
Hwange Nat. Park Zimbabwe 80 19.00S 26.30E
Hwang Ho r. see Huang He r. China 54
Hyannis Mass. U.S.A. 115 41.39N 70.17W
Hyannis Nebr. U.S.A. 110 41.59N 101.44W
Hyargas Nuur l. Mongolia 52 49.30N 93.35E
Hydaburg U.S.A. 100 55.15N 132.50W
Hyde U.K. 12 53.26N 2.04W
Hyden Australia 89 32.27S 118.53E
Hyde Park U.S.A. 104 44.36N 72.37W
Hyde Park Corner town Canada 104 43.00N 81.28W
Hyderābād India 61 17.22N 78.26E
Hyderābād Pakistan 62 25.22N 68.22E
Hydesville U.S.A. 108 40.31N 124.00W
Hydetown U.S.A. 114 41.40N 79.44W
Hyères France 21 43.07N 6.07E
Hyères, Îles d' is. France 21 43.00N 6.20E
Hyland r. Canada 100 59.50N 128.10W
Hyland, Mt. Australia 93 30.09S 152.25E
Hyland Post Canada 100 57.40N 128.10W
Hylestad Norway 42 59.05N 7.32E
Hyllestad Norway 41 61.10N 5.18E
Hyltebruk Sweden 43 57.00N 13.14E
Hyndman U.S.A. 114 39.49N 78.44W
Hyndman Peak U.S.A. 108 43.50N 114.10W
Hysham U.S.A. 108 46.18N 107.14W
Hythe Kent U.K. 13 51.04N 1.05E
Hyvinkää Finland 41 60.38N 24.52E

I

Iakoro Madagascar 81 23.06S 46.40E
Ialomiţa r. Romania 37 44.41N 27.52E
Iar Connacht f. Rep. of Ire. 15 53.21N 9.22W
Iaşi Romania 37 47.09N 27.38E
Íasmos Greece 34 41.07N 25.12E
Iauaretê Brazil 122 0.36N 69.12W
Iaupolo P.N.G. 90 9.34S 150.30E
Ibadan Nigeria 77 7.23N 3.56E
Ibagué Colombia 122 4.25N 75.20W
Ibar r. Yugo. 34 43.15N 20.40E
Ibaraki Japan 57 34.49N 135.34E
Ibarra Ecuador 122 0.23N 78.05W
Ibb Yemen 71 13.58N 44.11E
Ibba Sudan 73 4.48N 29.06E
Ibba wadi Sudan 73 7.09N 28.41E
Ibbenbüren Germany 38 52.16N 7.43E
Iberville Canada 105 45.18N 73.14W
Ibi r. Japan 57 35.03N 136.42E
Ibi Nigeria 77 8.11N 9.44E
Ibiapaba, Serra da mts. Brazil 123 5.30S 41.00W
Ibicaraí Brazil 123 14.52S 39.37W
Ibicuy Argentina 125 33.45S 59.13W

Ibina r. Zaïre 79 1.00N 28.40E
Ibitinga Brazil 126 21.43S 48.47W
Ibiza i. Spain 25 39.00N 1.25E
Ibiza town Spain 25 38.54N 1.26E
Iblei, Monti mts. Italy 33 37.07N 14.40E
Ibor r. Spain 27 39.49N 5.33W
Ibotirama Brazil 123 12.13S 43.12W
Ibrah, Wadi Sudan 73 10.36N 25.05E
'Ibrī Oman 71 23.14N 56.30E
Íbriktepe Turkey 34 41.00N 26.30E
Ibshawāy Egypt 66 29.21N 30.40E
Ibta' Syria 67 32.47N 36.09E
Ibusuki Japan 57 31.16N 130.39E
Içá r. Brazil 122 3.07S 67.58W
Ica Peru 122 14.02S 75.48W
Içana Brazil 122 0.21N 67.19W
Içana r. Brazil 122 0.00 67.10W
Iceland Europe 40 64.45N 18.00W
Ichchāpuram India 63 19.07N 84.42E
Ichihara Japan 57 35.31N 140.05E
Ichikawa Japan 57 35.44N 139.55E
Ichinomiya Japan 57 35.18N 136.48E
Icoraci Brazil 123 1.16S 48.28W
Icy Str. U.S.A. 100 58.20N 135.30W
Idabel U.S.A. 111 33.54N 94.50W
Ida Grove U.S.A. 110 42.21N 95.28W
Idah Nigeria 77 7.05N 6.45E
Idaho d. U.S.A. 108 44.58N 115.56W
Idaho Falls town U.S.A. 108 43.30N 112.02W
Idanha-a-Nova Portugal 27 39.55N 7.14W
Idar India 62 23.50N 73.00E
Idar-Oberstein Germany 39 49.42N 7.19E
Ideles Algeria 75 23.49N 5.55E
Idfū Egypt 64 24.58N 32.52E
Ídhi Óros mtn. Greece 35 35.18N 24.43E
Ídhra i. Greece 35 37.20N 23.32E
Ídhra town Greece 35 37.20N 23.29E
Idiofa Zaïre 78 4.58S 19.38E
Idmū Egypt 66 28.09N 30.41E
Idnah Jordan 67 31.34N 34.59E
Idre Sweden 41 61.52N 12.43E
Idrija Slovenia 31 46.00N 14.01E
Idstein Germany 39 50.13N 8.16E
Ieper Belgium 16 50.51N 2.53E
Ierápetra Greece 35 35.00N 25.44E
Ierissós Greece 34 40.24N 23.52E
Ierzu Italy 32 39.48N 9.32E
Iesi Italy 30 43.31N 13.14E
Iesolo Italy 30 45.32N 12.38E
Ifakara Tanzania 79 8.09S 36.41E
Ifalik is. Federated States of Micronesia 59 7.15N 144.27E
Ifanadiana Madagascar 81 21.19S 47.39E
Ife Oyo Nigeria 77 7.33N 4.34E
Iferouâne Niger 77 19.04N 8.24E
Iga r. Japan 57 34.45N 136.01E
Igatpuri India 62 19.42N 73.33E
Iggesund Sweden 41 61.38N 17.04E
Iglesias Italy 32 39.19N 8.32E
Igli Algeria 74 30.27N 2.18W
Igloolik Island town Canada 99 69.05N 81.25W
Ignace Canada 102 49.30N 91.40W
Iğneada Burnu c. Turkey 29 41.50N 28.05E
Igoumenitsa Greece 34 39.30N 20.16E
Igra Russian Fed. 44 57.31N 53.09E
Iguaçu r. Brazil 126 25.33S 54.35W
Iguaçu, Saltos do f. Brazil/Argentina 126 25.35S 54.22W
Iguala Mexico 116 18.21N 99.31W
Igualada Spain 25 41.35N 1.38E
Iguassu Falls see Iguaçu, Saltos do f. Brazil/Argentina 126
Iguatu Brazil 123 6.22S 39.20W
Iguéla Gabon 78 1.57S 9.22E
Ihiala Nigeria 77 5.51N 6.52E
Ihosy Madagascar 81 22.24S 46.08E
Ihosy r. Madagascar 81 21.58S 43.38E
Ii r. Finland 40 65.19N 25.20E
Iida Japan 57 35.31N 137.50E
Iidaan Somali Rep. 71 6.03N 49.01E
Iide yama mtn. Japan 57 37.50N 139.42E
Iisalmi Finland 40 63.34N 27.11E
Ijebu Ode Nigeria 77 6.47N 3.54E
Ijill, Kediet mtn. Mauritania 74 22.38N 12.33W
IJmuiden Neth. 16 52.28N 4.37E
IJssel r. Zuid Holland Neth. 16 51.54N 4.32E
IJssel r. Overijssel Neth. 16 52.34N 5.50E
IJsselmeer l. Neth. 16 52.45N 5.20E
Ijuí Brazil 126 28.23S 53.55W
Ijzendijke Neth. 16 51.19N 3.37E
Ijzer r. Belgium 16 51.09N 2.44E
Ikaría i. Greece 35 37.41N 26.20E
Ikdū Egypt 66 31.18N 30.18E
Ikela Zaïre 78 1.06S 23.04E
Ikelemba Congo 78 1.15N 16.38E
Ikelemba r. Zaïre 78 0.08N 18.19E
Ikerre Nigeria 77 7.30N 5.14E
Ikhast Denmark 42 56.09N 9.08E
Ikhtiman Bulgaria 34 42.27N 23.48E
Iki shima i. Japan 57 33.47N 129.43E
Ikopa r. Madagascar 81 16.29S 46.43E
Ila Nigeria 77 8.01N 4.55E
Ilagan Phil. 59 17.07N 121.53E
Ilām Iran 65 33.27N 46.27E
Ilām Nepal 63 26.54N 87.56E
Ilan Taiwan 55 24.45N 121.44E
Ilangali Tanzania 79 6.50S 35.06E
Ilanz Switz. 39 46.46N 9.12E
Ilaro Nigeria 77 6.53N 3.03E
Iława Poland 37 53.37N 19.33E
Ilebo Zaïre 78 4.20S 20.35E
Ilek r. Russian Fed. 45 51.30N 54.00E
Ileret Kenya 79 4.22N 36.13E
Ilerh, Oued wadi Algeria 75 20.59N 2.14E
Ilesha Oyo Nigeria 77 7.39N 4.45E
Îles, Lac des l. Canada 105 46.50N 77.10W
Ilford Canada 101 56.04N 95.35W
Ilfracombe Australia 90 23.30S 144.30E

Ilfracombe U.K. **13** 51.13N 4.08W
Ilhabela Brazil **126** 23.47S 45.20W
Ilha Grande, Baía da b. Brazil **126** 23.09S 44.30W
Ilha Grande, Reprêsa resr. Brazil **126** 23.10S 53.40W
Ilhavo Portugal **26** 40.36N 8.40W
Ilhéus Brazil **123** 14.50S 39.06W
Ili r. Kazakhstan **52** 45.00N 74.20E
Ilia Romania **37** 45.56N 22.39E
Iliamna L. U.S.A. **98** 59.30N 155.00W
Ilich Russian Fed. **52** 40.50N 68.29E
Iligan Phil. **59** 8.12N 124.13E
Ilintsy Ukraine **37** 49.08N 29.11E
Ilion U.S.A. **115** 43.01N 75.02W
Ilirska Bistrica Slovenia **31** 45.34N 14.15E
Ilkley U.K. **12** 53.56N 1.49W
Illapel Chile **124** 31.38S 71.10W
Ille-et-Vilaine d. France **18** 48.10N 1.30W
Illéla Niger **77** 14.30N 5.09E
Iller r. Germany **39** 48.23N 9.58E
Illeret Kenya **73** 4.19N 36.13E
Illertissen Germany **39** 48.13N 10.06E
Illescas Spain **26** 40.07N 3.50W
Illiers France **18** 48.18N 1.15E
Illinois d. U.S.A. **110** 40.30N 89.30W
Illinois r. U.S.A. **110** 38.58N 90.27W
Illizi Algeria **75** 26.29N 8.28E
Ilmajoki Finland **40** 62.44N 22.34E
Ilmenau r. Germany **38** 53.23N 10.10E
Ilminster U.K. **13** 50.55N 2.56W
Ilo Peru **124** 17.38S 71.20W
Iloilo Phil. **59** 10.45N 122.33E
Ilorin Nigeria **77** 8.32N 4.34E
Ilovlya Russian Fed. **45** 49.19N 44.01E
Ilubabor d. Ethiopia **73** 7.50N 34.55E
Imabari Japan **57** 34.04N 132.59E
Imala Mozambique **79** 14.39S 39.34E
Imandra Russian Fed. **44** 67.53N 33.30E
Imandra, Ozero l. Russian Fed. **44** 67.30N 32.45E
Imbâbah Egypt **66** 30.05N 31.12E
Imese Zaïre **78** 2.07N 18.06E
Ïmï Ethiopia **73** 6.28N 42.18E
Imlay City U.S.A. **114** 43.02N 83.05W
Immenstadt Germany **38** 47.33N 10.13E
Immingham U.K. **12** 53.37N 0.12W
Immokalee U.S.A. **113** 26.25N 81.26W
Imo d. Nigeria **77** 5.30N 7.20E
Imola Italy **30** 44.21N 11.42E
Imotski Croatia **31** 43.27N 17.13E
Imperatriz Brazil **123** 5.32S 47.28W
Imperia Italy **30** 43.53N 8.03E
Imperial Calif. U.S.A. **109** 32.51N 115.34W
Imperial Nebr. U.S.A. **110** 40.31N 101.39W
Imperial Dam U.S.A. **109** 32.55N 114.30W
Imperial de Aragón, Canal Spain **25** 41.37N 1.00W
Imperial Valley f. U.S.A. **109** 32.50N 115.30W
Impfondo Congo **78** 1.36N 17.58E
Imphäl India **61** 24.47N 93.55E
Imroz i. see Gökçeada i. Turkey **34**
Imst Austria **39** 47.14N 10.44E
Ina Japan **57** 35.50N 137.57E
Ina r. Japan **57** 34.43N 135.28E
In Abbangarit well Niger **77** 17.49N 6.15E
Inaccessible I. Tristan da Cunha **127** 37.19S 12.44W
I-n-Amguel Algeria **75** 23.40N 5.08E
Inangahua Junction New Zealand **86** 41.53S 171.58E
Inanwatan Indonesia **59** 2.08S 132.10E
Inarajan Guam **84** 13.16N 144.45E
Inari l. Finland **40** 69.00N 28.00E
Inari town Finland **40** 68.54N 27.01E
Inazawa Japan **57** 35.15N 136.47E
I-n-Belbel Algeria **74** 27.54N 1.10E
Inca Spain **25** 39.43N 2.54E
Incesu Turkey **64** 38.39N 35.12E
Inchiri d. Mauritania **74** 20.10N 15.00W
Inch'on S. Korea **53** 37.30N 126.38E
Incudine, L' mtn. France **21** 41.51N 9.12E
Indals r. Sweden **40** 62.30N 17.20E
Indaw Myanmar **56** 23.40N 94.46E
Independence Calif. U.S.A. **108** 36.48N 118.12W
Independence Kans. U.S.A. **111** 37.13N 95.42W
Independence Mo. U.S.A. **110** 39.05N 94.24W
Inderborskiy Kazakhstan **45** 48.32N 51.44E
India Asia **61** 23.00N 78.30E
Indian r. Canada **105** 45.16N 76.14W
Indiana d. U.S.A. **112** 40.00N 86.15W
Indiana town U.S.A. **114** 40.37N 79.09W
Indian-Antarctic Ridge f. Indian Oc. **49** 49.00S 125.00E
Indianapolis U.S.A. **112** 39.45N 86.10W
Indian Cabins Canada **100** 59.52N 117.02W
Indian Harbour Canada **103** 54.25N 57.20W
Indian Head Canada **101** 50.32N 103.40W
Indian L. Canada **104** 47.08N 82.08W
Indian L. U.S.A. **115** 43.47N 74.16W
Indian Lake town U.S.A. **105** 43.47N 74.16W
Indian Ocean 49
Indianola U.S.A. **110** 41.22N 93.34W
Indian River town U.S.A. **104** 45.25N 84.37W
Indian River B. U.S.A. **115** 38.36N 75.05W
Indiga Russian Fed. **44** 67.40N 49.00E
Indigirka r. Russian Fed. **51** 71.00N 148.45E
Indija Yugo. **31** 45.03N 20.05E
Indio U.S.A. **109** 33.43N 116.13W
Indonesia Asia **58** 6.00S 118.00E
Indore India **62** 22.43N 75.50E
Indragiri r. Indonesia **58** 0.30S 103.08E
Indramayu Indonesia **58** 6.22S 108.20E
Indrávati r. India **63** 18.44N 80.16E
Indre d. France **19** 46.45N 1.30E
Indre r. France **18** 47.16N 0.19E
Indre-et-Loire d. France **18** 47.15N 0.45E
Indus r. Pakistan **62** 24.20N 67.47E
Inebolu Turkey **64** 41.57N 33.45E
Inegöl Turkey **64** 40.06N 29.31E
I-n-Eker Algeria **75** 24.01N 5.05E
I-n-Ezzane well Algeria **75** 23.29N 11.15E
Infiesto Spain **26** 43.21N 5.22W
I-n-Gall Niger **77** 16.47N 6.56E

Ingatestone U.K. **13** 51.41N 0.22E
Ingelstad Sweden **43** 56.45N 14.55E
Ingende Zaïre **78** 0.17S 18.58E
Ingenika r. Canada **100** 56.43N 125.07W
Ingersoll Canada **104** 43.02N 80.53W
Inggen China **54** 41.35N 104.47E
Ingham Australia **90** 18.35S 146.12E
Ingleborough mtn. U.K. **12** 54.10N 2.23W
Inglewood Qld Australia **93** 28.25S 151.02E
Inglewood Vic. Australia **92** 36.33S 143.53E
Inglewood Canada **104** 43.47N 79.56W
Inglewood New Zealand **86** 39.09S 174.12E
Inglewood U.S.A. **109** 33.58N 118.21W
Ingolstadt Germany **39** 48.46N 11.27E
Ingomar Australia **92** 29.38S 134.48E
Ingraham U.S.A. **105** 44.47N 73.30W
Ingulets Ukraine **45** 47.43N 33.16E
Ingwiller France **19** 48.52N 7.29E
Inhambane Mozambique **81** 23.51S 35.29E
Inhambane d. Mozambique **81** 22.20S 34.00E
Inhaminga Mozambique **81** 18.24S 35.00E
Inharrime Mozambique **81** 24.29S 35.01E
Inhassoro Mozambique **81** 21.32S 35.10E
Inirida r. Colombia **122** 3.59N 67.45W
Inishbofin i. Galway Rep. of Ire. **15** 53.38N 10.14W
Inisheer i. Rep. of Ire. **15** 53.04N 9.32W
Inishmaan i. Rep. of Ire. **15** 53.06N 9.36W
Inishmore i. Rep. of Ire. **15** 53.08N 9.43W
Inishowen Pen. Rep. of Ire. **15** 55.08N 7.20W
Inishturk i. Rep. of Ire. **15** 53.43N 10.08W
Injune Australia **90** 25.51S 148.34E
Inklin Canada **100** 58.56N 133.05W
Inklin r. Canada **100** 58.50N 133.10W
Inkster U.S.A. **104** 42.17N 83.17W
Inn r. Europe **39** 48.35N 13.28E
Innaminka Australia **91** 27.43S 140.46E
Inner Hebrides is. U.K. **14** 56.50N 6.45W
Inner Mongolia d. see Nei Monggol Zizhiqu d. China **54**
Inner Sd. U.K. **14** 57.30N 5.55W
Innisfail Australia **90** 17.32S 146.02E
Innisfail Canada **100** 52.00N 113.57W
Innsbruck Austria **39** 47.16N 11.24E
Inset Norway **40** 68.41N 18.50E
Innviertel f. Austria **39** 48.05N 13.08E
Inongo Zaïre **78** 1.55S 18.20E
Inowrocław Poland **37** 52.49N 18.12E
I-n-Salah Algeria **75** 27.13N 2.28E
Insein Myanmar **56** 16.54N 96.08E
In Tasik well Mali **77** 18.03N 2.00E
Intepe Turkey **34** 40.01N 26.19E
Interlaken Switz. **36** 46.41N 7.51E
International Falls town U.S.A. **110** 48.38N 93.26W
Intracoastal Waterway canal U.S.A. **111** 28.45N 95.40W
Intute Mozambique **79** 14.08S 39.55E
Inubö saki c. Japan **57** 35.41N 140.52E
Inukjuak Canada **99** 58.25N 78.18W
Inuvik Canada **98** 68.16N 133.40W
Inuvik d. Canada **98** 68.00N 130.00W
Inuyama Japan **57** 35.23N 136.56E
Inveraray U.K. **14** 56.24N 5.05W
Inverbervie U.K. **14** 56.51N 2.17W
Invercargill New Zealand **86** 46.26S 168.21E
Inverell Australia **93** 29.46S 151.10E
Invergordon U.K. **14** 57.42N 4.10W
Inverhuron Canada **104** 44.17N 81.34W
Inverness U.K. **14** 57.27N 4.15W
Inverurie U.K. **14** 57.17N 2.23W
Inverway Australia **88** 17.49S 129.40E
Investigator Group is. Australia **92** 33.45S 134.30E
Investigator Str. Australia **92** 35.25S 137.10E
Invinheima r. Brazil **124** 22.52S 53.20W
Inya Russian Fed. **50** 50.24N 86.47E
Inyangani mtn. Zimbabwe **81** 18.18S 32.50E
Inyonga Tanzania **79** 6.43S 32.02E
Inzia r. Zaïre **78** 3.47S 17.57E
Ioánnina Greece **34** 39.39N 20.57E
Iola U.S.A. **111** 37.55N 95.24W
Iona i. U.K. **14** 56.20N 6.25W
Iongo Angola **78** 9.11S 17.45E
Ionia U.S.A. **112** 42.58N 85.06W
Ionian Is. see Iónioi Nísoi is. Greece **35**
Ionian Sea Med. Sea **35** 38.30N 18.45E
Iónioi Nísoi is. Greece **35** 38.40N 20.08E
Íos i. Greece **35** 36.44N 25.16E
Íos town Greece **35** 36.44N 25.16E
Iowa d. U.S.A. **110** 42.00N 93.30W
Iowa r. U.S.A. **110** 41.10N 91.02W
Iowa City U.S.A. **110** 41.40N 91.32W
Iowa Falls town U.S.A. **110** 42.31N 93.16W
Ipati Greece **35** 38.52N 22.14E
Ipatovo Russian Fed. **45** 45.44N 42.56E
Ipeiros f. Greece **34** 39.30N 20.30E
Ipiales Colombia **122** 0.52N 77.38W
Ipiaú Brazil **123** 14.07S 39.43W
Ipixuna Brazil **122** 7.00S 71.30W
Ipoh Malaysia **58** 4.36N 101.02E
Ippa r. Belarus **37** 52.13N 29.08E
Ippy C.A.R. **73** 6.15N 21.12E
Ipsala Turkey **34** 40.55N 26.23E
Ipswich Australia **93** 27.38S 152.40E
Ipswich U.K. **13** 52.04N 1.09E
Ipu Brazil **123** 4.23S 40.44W
Ipuh Indonesia **58** 2.58S 101.28E
Iquique Chile **124** 20.13S 70.10W
Iquitos Peru **122** 3.51S 73.13W
Irago-suidö str. Japan **57** 34.35N 137.00E
Iráklia i. Greece **35** 36.50N 25.28E
Iráklion Greece **35** 35.20N 25.09E
Iran Asia **65** 32.00N 54.30E
Iran, Pegunungan mts. Indonesia/Malaysia **58** 3.20N 115.00E
Ïränshahr Iran **65** 27.14N 60.42E
Irapuato Mexico **116** 20.40N 101.40W
Iraq Asia **64** 33.00N 44.00E
Irauen, Wâdï Libya **75** 26.28N 12.00E
Irayel Russian Fed. **44** 64.23N 55.25E

Irazú mtn. Costa Rica **117** 9.59N 83.52W
Irbid Jordan **67** 32.33N 35.51E
Irbid d. Jordan **67** 32.27N 35.51E
Irbïl Iraq **65** 36.12N 44.01E
Irdning Austria **39** 47.33N 14.01E
Irebu Zaïre **78** 0.37S 17.45E
Iregua r. Spain **26** 42.27N 2.24W
Ireland I. Bermuda **127** 32.19N 64.51W
Irgiz Kazakhstan **9** 48.36N 61.14E
Irgiz r. Kazakhstan **9** 48.00N 62.30E
Irharrhar, Oued wadi Algeria **75** 23.45N 5.55E
Irian Jaya d. Indonesia **59** 4.00S 138.00E
Iriba Chad **72** 15.07N 22.15E
Irié Guinea **76** 8.15N 9.10W
Iringa Tanzania **79** 7.49S 35.39E
Iringa d. Tanzania **79** 8.30S 35.00E
Iriomote jima i. Japan **53** 24.30N 124.00E
Iriri r. Brazil **123** 3.50S 52.40W
Irish Sea U.K./Rep. of Ire. **15** 53.30N 5.40W
Irkutsk Russian Fed. **52** 52.18N 104.15E
Iroise b. France **18** 48.15N 4.55W
Iron Baron Australia **92** 32.59S 137.09E
Iron Bridge town Canada **104** 46.17N 83.14W
Iron Gate f. Romania/Yugo. **37** 44.40N 22.30E
Iron Knob Australia **92** 32.44S 137.08E
Iron Mountain town U.S.A. **112** 45.51N 88.03W
Iron Mts. Rep. of Ire. **15** 54.10N 7.56W
Iron River town U.S.A. **110** 46.05N 88.38W
Irons U.S.A. **112** 44.08N 85.55W
Ironton U.S.A. **114** 38.31N 82.40W
Ironwood U.S.A. **112** 46.25N 90.08W
Iroquois Canada **105** 44.51N 75.19W
Iroquois Falls town Canada **102** 48.40N 80.40W
Irosin Phil. **59** 12.45N 124.02E
Irö-zaki c. Japan **57** 34.36N 138.51E
Irpen Ukraine **37** 50.31N 30.29E
Irrapatana Australia **92** 29.03S 136.28E
Irrawaddy d. Myanmar **56** 17.00N 95.00E
Irrawaddy r. Myanmar **56** 15.50N 95.00E
Irrawaddy Delta Myanmar **56** 16.45N 95.00E
Irsha r. Ukraine **37** 50.45N 29.30E
Irsina Italy **33** 40.45N 16.15E
Irthing r. U.K. **11** 54.55N 2.50W
Irtysh r. Russian Fed. **9** 61.00N 69.00E
Iruma r. Japan **57** 35.57N 139.30E
Irumu Zaïre **79** 1.29N 29.48E
Irún Spain **26** 43.20N 1.48W
Iruñea see Pamplona Spain **25**
Irurzun Spain **25** 42.55N 1.50W
Irvine U.K. **14** 55.37N 4.40W
Irvinestown U.K. **15** 54.29N 7.40W
Irving U.S.A. **111** 32.49N 96.56W
Irvona U.S.A. **114** 40.46N 78.33W
Irwin, Pt. Australia **89** 35.03S 116.20E
Isa Nigeria **77** 13.14N 6.24E
Isaac r. Australia **90** 22.52S 149.20E
Isaba Spain **25** 42.52N 0.55W
Isabelia, Cordillera mts. Nicaragua **117** 13.30N 85.00W
Isábena r. Spain **25** 42.11N 0.21E
Ïsafjördhur town Iceland **40** 66.05N 23.06W
Isaka Tanzania **79** 3.52S 32.54E
Isaka Bandundu Zaïre **78** 2.35S 18.48E
Isaka Equateur Zaïre **78** 1.49S 20.50E
Ïsa Khel Pakistan **62** 32.41N 71.17E
Isakogorka Russian Fed. **44** 64.23N 40.31E
Isangi Zaïre **78** 0.48N 24.03E
Isar r. Germany **39** 48.49N 12.58E
Isbergues France **16** 50.38N 2.24E
Ischia Italy **32** 40.43N 13.57E
Ischia i. Italy **32** 40.43N 13.54E
Ise Japan **57** 34.29N 136.42E
Isefjord b. Denmark **42** 55.52N 11.49E
Iseo, Lago d' l. Italy **30** 45.43N 10.04E
Isère d. France **21** 45.10N 5.50E
Isère r. France **21** 44.59N 4.51E
Iserlohn Germany **38** 51.22N 7.41E
Isernia Italy **33** 41.36N 14.14E
Ise-wan b. Japan **57** 34.45N 136.40E
Iseyin Nigeria **77** 7.59N 3.36E
Isfahan see Esfahän Iran **60**
Ishikari r. Japan **57** 43.15N 141.21E
Ishikari wan b. Japan **57** 43.15N 141.20E
Ishim Russian Fed. **50** 56.10N 69.30E
Ishim r. Russian Fed. **9** 57.50N 71.00E
Ishinomaki Japan **57** 38.25N 141.18E
Ishpeming U.S.A. **112** 46.29N 87.40W
Ishurdi Bangla. **63** 24.09N 89.03E
Isigny France **18** 49.19N 1.06W
Isiolo Kenya **79** 0.20N 37.36E
Isipingo Beach town R.S.A. **80** 30.00S 30.57E
Isiro Zaïre **79** 2.50N 27.40E
Is, Jabal mtn. Sudan **72** 22.03N 35.28E
Iskår r. Bulgaria **34** 43.44N 24.27E
Iskenderun Turkey **64** 36.37N 36.08E
Iskenderun Körfezi g. Turkey **64** 36.40N 35.50E
Iskilip Turkey **64** 40.45N 34.28E
Iskür r. Bulgaria **34** 43.35N 24.20E
Iskür, Yazovir l. Bulgaria **34** 42.27N 23.38E
Isla r. U.K. **14** 56.32N 3.22W
Isla Cristina town Spain **27** 37.12N 7.19W
Islämäbäd Pakistan **62** 33.40N 73.10E
Islämkot Pakistan **62** 24.42N 70.11E
Islämpur Bihar India **63** 25.09N 85.12E
Islämpur W. Bengal India **63** 26.16N 88.12E
Island L. Australia **92** 31.30S 136.40E
Island L. Canada **103** 53.47N 94.25W
Island Magee pen. U.K. **15** 54.48N 5.44W
Islands, B. of Canada **103** 49.10N 58.15W
Islands, B. of New Zealand **86** 35.15S 174.15E
Islay i. U.K. **14** 55.45N 6.20W
Isle r. France **20** 44.55N 0.15W
Isle of Portland f. U.K. **13** 50.32N 2.25W
Isle of Wight d. U.K. **13** 50.40N 1.17W
Isleta U.S.A. **109** 34.55N 106.42W
Ismael Cortinas Uruguay **125** 33.58S 57.06W
Ismay U.S.A. **108** 46.30N 104.48W
Isnä Egypt **64** 25.16N 32.30E

Isny Germany **38** 47.41N 10.02E
Isoka Zambia **79** 10.06S 32.39E
Isola della Scala Italy **32** 45.16N 11.00E
Isola del Liri town Italy **31** 41.41N 13.34E
Isola di Capo Rizzuto town Italy **33** 38.58N 17.06E
Isparta Turkey **64** 37.46N 30.32E
Isperikh Bulgaria **34** 43.43N 26.50E
Ispica Italy **33** 36.46N 14.55E
Ispikän Pakistan **62** 26.14N 62.12E
Israel Asia **67** 32.00N 34.50E
Israelite B. Australia **89** 33.40S 123.55E
Israelite Bay town Australia **89** 33.37S 123.48E
Issia Côte d'Ivoire **76** 6.33N 6.33W
Issigeac France **20** 44.44N 0.36E
Issoire France **20** 45.33N 3.15E
Issoudun France **19** 46.57N 2.00E
Is-sur-Tille France **19** 47.31N 5.06E
Issyk Kul l. Kyrgyzstan **52** 43.30N 77.20E
Istanbul Turkey **29** 41.02N 28.58E
Istanbul Boğazi str. Turkey **34** 41.07N 29.04E
Isthmus of Kra Thailand **56** 10.20N 99.10E
Istiaía Greece **35** 38.57N 23.10E
Istok Yugo. **34** 42.45N 20.24E
Istra pen. Croatia **31** 45.10N 13.55E
Itabaiana Brazil **123** 7.20S 35.20W
Itabira Brazil **126** 19.39S 43.14W
Itabirito Brazil **126** 20.21S 43.45W
Itabuna Brazil **123** 14.48S 39.18W
Itacajuna r. Brazil **123** 5.20S 49.08W
Itacoatiara Brazil **122** 3.06S 58.22W
Itaguí Colombia **122** 6.10N 75.36W
Itaí Brazil **126** 23.23S 49.05W
Itaim r. Brazil **123** 6.43S 42.48W
Itaipu, Reprêsa resr. Brazil/Paraguay **126** 24.30S 54.20W
Itaituba Brazil **123** 4.17S 55.59W
Itajaí Brazil **126** 26.50S 48.39W
Itajubá Brazil **126** 22.24S 45.25W
Itaka Tanzania **79** 8.51S 32.48E
Itálica site Spain **27** 37.30N 6.05W
Italy Europe **28** 43.00N 12.00E
Itami Japan **57** 34.46N 135.25E
Itapecerica Brazil **126** 20.28S 45.09W
Itapecuru Mirim Brazil **123** 3.24S 44.20W
Itaperuna Brazil **126** 21.14S 41.51W
Itapetinga Brazil **123** 15.17S 40.16W
Itapetininga Brazil **126** 23.36S 48.07W
Itapeva Brazil **126** 23.59S 48.59W
Itapicuru r. Brazil **123** 11.50S 37.30W
Itapira Brazil **126** 22.24S 46.56W
Itaqui Brazil **126** 29.07S 56.33W
Itärsi India **63** 22.37N 77.45E
Itatiba Brazil **126** 22.59S 46.51W
Itatinga Brazil **126** 23.06S 48.36W
Itatuba Brazil **122** 5.40S 63.20W
Itaúna Brazil **126** 20.04S 44.14W
Itboyat i. Phil. **55** 20.45N 121.50E
Itéa Greece **35** 38.25N 22.25E
Ithaca U.S.A. **115** 42.27N 76.30W
Ithaki Greece **35** 38.23N 20.42E
Itháki i. Greece **35** 38.24N 20.42E
Itimbiri r. Zaïre **78** 2.02N 22.47E
Itmurinkol, Ozero l. Kazakhstan **45** 49.30N 52.17E
Itö Japan **57** 34.58N 139.05E
Itoko Zaïre **78** 1.00S 21.45E
Iton r. France **18** 49.09N 1.12E
Itsa Egypt **66** 29.14N 30.47E
Ittel, Oued wadi Algeria **75** 34.18N 6.02E
Ittiri Italy **32** 40.36N 8.33E
Itu Brazil **126** 23.17S 47.18W
Ituí r. Brazil **122** 4.38S 70.19W
Itulutaba Brazil **126** 19.00S 49.25W
Ituri r. Zaïre **79** 1.45N 27.06E
Iturup i. Russian Fed. **53** 44.00N 147.30E
Ituverava Brazil **126** 20.22S 47.48W
Ituxi r. Brazil **122** 7.20S 64.50W
Ityäy al Bärüd Egypt **66** 30.53N 30.40E
Itzehoe Germany **38** 53.55N 9.31E
Ivaí r. Brazil **126** 23.20S 53.23W
Ivalo Finland **40** 68.42N 27.30E
Ivalo r. Finland **40** 68.43N 27.36E
Ivanec Croatia **31** 46.13N 16.08E
Ivangrad Yugo. **31** 42.50N 19.52E
Ivanhoe Australia **92** 32.56S 144.22E
Ivanhoe U.S.A. **110** 44.28N 96.12W
Ivanić Grad Croatia **31** 45.42N 16.24E
Ivanjica Yugo. **34** 43.35N 20.14E
Ivano-Frankovsk Ukraine **37** 48.55N 24.42E
Ivanovo Belarus **37** 52.10N 25.13E
Ivanovo Russian Fed. **44** 57.00N 41.00E
Ivdel Russian Fed. **44** 60.45N 60.30E
Ivenets Belarus **37** 53.50N 26.40E
Ivigtût Greenland **99** 61.10N 48.00W
Ivindo Gabon **78** 0.02S 12.13E
Ivittuut see Ivigtût Greenland **99**
Ivíza i. see Ibiza i. Spain **25**
Ivohibe Madagascar **81** 22.29S 45.52E
Ivory Coast see Côte d'Ivoire Africa **76**
Ivösjön l. Sweden **43** 56.06N 14.27E
Ivrea Italy **30** 45.28N 7.52E
Ivujivik Canada **99** 62.24N 77.55W
Ivybridge U.K. **13** 50.24N 3.56W
Ivydale U.S.A. **114** 38.32N 81.03W
Iwaki Japan **57** 36.58N 140.58E
Iwaki r. Japan **57** 41.20N 140.00E
Iwakuni Japan **57** 34.10N 132.09E
Iwata Japan **57** 34.42N 137.48E
Iwo Nigeria **77** 7.38N 4.11E
Ixiamas Bolivia **124** 13.45S 68.09W
Iyo nada str. Japan **57** 33.40N 132.20E
Izabal, Lago de l. Guatemala **117** 15.30N 89.00W
Izberbash Russian Fed. **45** 42.31N 47.52E
Izhevsk Russian Fed. **44** 56.49N 53.11E
Izhma Russian Fed. **44** 65.03N 53.48E
Izhma r. Russian Fed. **44** 65.16N 53.18E
Izmail Ukraine **37** 45.20N 28.50E
Izmir Turkey **29** 38.24N 27.09E
Izmir Körfezi g. Turkey **29** 38.30N 26.45E

173

Izmit Turkey **64** 40.48N 29.55E
Iznajar, Embalse de *resr.* Spain **27** 37.15N 4.20W
Iznalloz Spain **27** 37.23N 3.31W
Izozog, Bañados de *f.* Bolivia **124** 18.30S 62.05W
Izozog Marshes *f. see* Izozog, Bañados de *f.* Bolivia **124**
Izra' Syria **67** 32.51N 36.15E
Izsák Hungary **31** 46.48N 19.22E
Iztochni Rodopi *mts.* Bulgaria **34** 41.44N 25.28E
Izu-hantō *pen.* Japan **57** 34.53N 138.55E
Izuhara Japan **57** 34.12N 129.17E
Izumi Japan **57** 34.29N 135.26E
Izumi-ōtsu Japan **57** 34.30N 135.24E
Izumi-sano Japan **57** 34.25N 135.19E
Izumo Japan **57** 35.33N 132.50E
Izumo *r.* Japan **57** 34.38N 136.33E
Izyaslav Ukraine **37** 50.10N 26.46E
Izyum Ukraine **45** 49.12N 37.19E

J

Jaba Ethiopia **73** 6.17N 35.12E
Jaba' Jordan **67** 32.19N 35.13E
Jabā Syria **67** 33.10N 35.56E
Jabal al Awliyā' Sudan **72** 15.14N 32.30E
Jabal, Baḥr al *r.* Sudan **73** 9.30N 30.30E
Jabal Dūd Sudan **73** 13.22N 33.09E
Jabalón *r.* Spain **26** 38.53N 4.05W
Jabalpur India **63** 23.10N 79.57E
Jabālyah Egypt **67** 31.32N 34.29E
Jabbān, Arḍ al *f.* Jordan **66** 32.08N 36.35E
Jabiru Australia **90** 12.39S 132.55E
Jabjabah, Wādī Egypt **72** 22.37N 33.17E
Jablah Syria **66** 35.22N 35.56E
Jablanac Croatia **31** 44.42N 14.54E
Jablanica Bosnia-Herzegovina **31** 43.39N 17.45E
Jablaničko Jezero *resr.* Bosnia-Herzegovina **31** 43.40N 17.50E
Jablonec nad Nisou Czech Republic **36** 50.44N 15.10E
Jabori Pakistan **62** 34.36N 73.16E
Jaboticabal Brazil **126** 21.15S 48.17W
Jabrat Sa'īd *wells* Sudan **72** 16.06N 31.50E
Jaca Spain **25** 42.34N 0.33W
Jacareí Brazil **126** 23.17S 45.57W
Jackman U.S.A. **112** 45.38N 70.16W
Jackson Ky. U.S.A. **113** 37.32N 83.24W
Jackson Mich. U.S.A. **104** 42.15N 84.24W
Jackson Miss. U.S.A. **111** 32.18N 90.12W
Jackson Mo. U.S.A. **111** 37.23N 89.40W
Jackson Ohio U.S.A. **114** 39.03N 82.39W
Jackson Tenn. U.S.A. **111** 35.37N 88.49W
Jackson Wyo. U.S.A. **108** 43.29N 110.38W
Jackson Bay *town* Canada **100** 50.32N 125.57W
Jacksonville Fla. U.S.A. **113** 30.20N 81.40W
Jacksonville III. U.S.A. **110** 39.44N 90.14W
Jacksonville N.C. U.S.A. **113** 34.45N 77.26W
Jacksonville Tex. U.S.A. **111** 31.58N 95.17W
Jacksonville Beach *town* U.S.A. **113** 30.18N 81.24W
Jacobābād Pakistan **62** 28.17N 68.26E
Jacobina Brazil **123** 11.13S 40.30W
Jacob Lake *town* U.S.A. **109** 36.41N 112.14W
Jacob's Well *see* Bi'r Yaqūb Jordan **67**
Jacques Cartier, Détroit de *str.* Canada **103** 50.00N 63.30W
Jacques Cartier, Mt. Canada **103** 48.59N 65.57W
Jacuí *r.* Brazil **126** 29.56S 51.13W
Jacundá *r.* Brazil **123** 1.57S 50.26W
Jaddi, Rās *c.* Pakistan **62** 25.14N 63.31E
Jade Germany **38** 53.20N 8.14E
Jadebusen *b.* Germany **38** 53.30N 8.10E
Jadraque Spain **26** 40.55N 2.55W
Jādū Libya **75** 31.57N 12.01E
Jaén Peru **122** 5.21S 78.28W
Jaén Spain **27** 37.46N 3.47W
Jaén *d.* Spain **27** 37.55N 3.30W
Jaeren *f.* Norway **42** 58.40N 5.45E
Jāfarābād India **62** 20.52N 71.22E
Jaffa *see* Tel Aviv-Yafo Israel **67**
Jaffa, C. Australia **92** 36.58S 139.39E
Jaffna Sri Lanka **61** 9.38N 80.02E
Jaffrey U.S.A. **115** 42.50N 72.04W
Jagādhri India **62** 30.10N 77.18E
Jāgan Pakistan **62** 28.05N 68.30E
Jagatsingpur India **63** 20.16N 86.10E
Jagdalpur India **63** 19.04N 82.02E
Jaggang China **63** 32.52N 79.45E
Jagodina Yugo. **34** 43.58N 21.16E
Jagst *r.* Germany **39** 49.14N 9.11E
Jagtiāl India **63** 18.48N 78.56E
Jaguarão Brazil **126** 32.30S 53.25W
Jahānābād India **63** 25.13N 84.59E
Jahrom Iran **65** 28.30N 53.30E
Jailolo Indonesia **59** 1.05N 127.29E
Jainti India **63** 26.42N 89.36E
Jaintiāpur Bangla. **63** 25.08N 92.07E
Jaipur India **62** 26.53N 75.50E
Jāis India **63** 26.15N 81.32E
Jaisalmer India **62** 26.55N 70.54E
Jājarkot Nepal **63** 28.42N 82.14E
Jajawijaya Mts. Asia **59** 4.20S 139.10E
Jajce Bosnia-Herzegovina **31** 44.21N 17.16E
Jajjha Pakistan **62** 28.45N 70.34E
Jājpur India **63** 20.51N 86.20E

Jakarta Indonesia **59** 6.08S 106.45E
Jakarta *d.* Indonesia **59** 6.10S 106.48E
Jakhāu India **62** 23.13N 68.43E
Jäkkvik Sweden **40** 66.23N 17.00E
Jakobstad *see* Pietarsaari Finland **40**
Jakupica *mts.* Macedonia **34** 41.45N 21.22E
Jal U.S.A. **111** 32.07N 103.12W
Jalālābād Afghan. **62** 34.26N 70.28E
Jalālah al Baḥrīyah, Jabal *mts.* Egypt **66** 29.20N 32.12E
Jalālat al Qiblīyah, Jabal al *mts.* Egypt **66** 28.42N 32.23E
Jalālpur India **63** 26.19N 82.44E
Jalandhar India **62** 31.20N 75.35E
Jalapa Mexico **116** 19.45N 96.48W
Jālaun India **63** 26.09N 79.21E
Jaldak Afghan. **62** 31.58N 66.44E
Jalesar India **63** 27.29N 78.19E
Jaleswar India **63** 21.49N 87.13E
Jālgaon Mahār. India **62** 21.03N 76.32E
Jālgaon Mahār. India **62** 21.01N 75.34E
Jalingo Nigeria **77** 8.54N 11.21E
Jalisco *d.* Mexico **116** 21.00N 103.00W
Jallas *r.* Spain **26** 42.54N 9.08W
Jālna India **62** 19.50N 75.53E
Jalón *r.* Spain **25** 41.47N 1.04W
Jālor India **62** 25.21N 72.37E
Jalpaiguri India **63** 26.31N 88.44E
Jālū Libya **75** 29.02N 21.33E
Jaluit *i.* Pacific Oc. **84** 6.00N 169.35E
Jalūlā Iraq **65** 34.16N 45.10E
Jamaame Somali Rep. **79** 0.04N 42.46E
Jamaari Nigeria **77** 11.44N 9.53E
Jamaica C. America **117** 18.00N 77.00W
Jamālpur Bangla. **63** 24.55N 89.56E
Jamālpur India **63** 25.18N 86.30E
Jamanxim *r.* Brazil **123** 4.43S 56.18W
Jambes Belgium **16** 50.28N 4.52E
Jambi Indonesia **58** 1.36S 103.39E
Jambi *d.* Indonesia **58** 2.00S 102.30E
Jambusar India **62** 22.03N 72.48E
James *r.* S.Dak. U.S.A. **110** 42.55N 97.28W
James *r.* Va. U.S.A. **113** 36.57N 76.26W
James B. Canada **102** 53.30N 80.00W
James Bay Prov. Park Canada **102** 51.30N 79.00W
Jamestown Australia **92** 33.12S 138.38E
Jamestown St. Helena **127** 15.56S 5.44W
Jamestown N.Dak. U.S.A. **110** 46.54N 98.42W
Jamestown N.Y. U.S.A. **114** 42.06N 79.14W
Jamestown Penn. U.S.A. **114** 41.29N 80.27W
Jamestown Tenn. U.S.A. **113** 36.24N 84.58W
Jamjodhpur India **62** 21.33N 70.02E
Jammerbugt *b.* Denmark **42** 57.20N 9.30E
Jammu Jammu & Kashmir **62** 32.42N 74.52E
Jammu & Kashmir Asia **62** 34.45N 76.00E
Jämnagar India **62** 22.28N 70.04E
Jamnotri India **63** 31.01N 78.27E
Jampang Kulon Indonesia **59** 7.18S 106.33E
Jāmpur Pakistan **62** 28.45N 70.36E
Jamsah Egypt **66** 27.39N 33.35E
Jämsänkoski Finland **41** 61.55N 25.11E
Jamshedpur India **63** 22.48N 86.11E
Jämtland *d.* Sweden **40** 63.00N 14.30E
Jamūī India **63** 24.55N 86.13E
Jamuna *r.* Bangla. **63** 23.51N 89.45E
Jand Pakistan **62** 33.26N 72.01E
Janda, Laguna de la *l.* Spain **27** 36.15N 5.51W
Jandiāla India **62** 31.33N 75.02E
Jándula Spain **26** 38.03N 4.06W
Jándula, Embalse de *resr.* Spain **26** 38.30N 4.00W
Janesville U.S.A. **110** 42.42N 89.02W
Jangamo Mozambique **81** 24.06S 35.21E
Jangipur India **63** 24.28N 88.04E
Janīn Jordan **67** 32.28N 35.18E
Janja Bosnia-Herzegovina **31** 44.40N 19.15E
Janjevo Yugo. **34** 42.35N 21.19E
Janjina Croatia **31** 42.56N 17.26E
Jan Kempdorp R.S.A. **80** 27.55S 24.48E
Jan Mayen *i.* Arctic Oc. **96** 68.00N 8.00W
Jánoshalma Hungary **31** 46.18N 19.20E
Januária Brazil **126** 15.28S 44.23W
Janūb Dārfūr *d.* Sudan **73** 11.45N 25.00E
Janūb Kurdufān *d.* Sudan **73** 11.10N 30.00E
Janzé France **19** 47.58N 1.30W
Jaora India **62** 23.38N 75.08E
Japan Asia **57** 36.00N 138.00E
Japan, Sea of Asia **57** 40.00N 135.00E
Japan Trench Pacific Oc. **84** 33.00N 142.00E
Japla India **63** 24.33N 84.01E
Japurá *r.* Brazil **122** 3.00S 64.50W
Jaraicejo Spain **27** 39.40N 5.49W
Jaraíz de la Vera Spain **27** 40.04N 5.45W
Jarales U.S.A. **109** 34.37N 106.46W
Jarama *r.* Spain **26** 40.02N 3.39W
Jarandilla Spain **27** 40.08N 5.39W
Jaranwāla Pakistan **62** 31.20N 73.26E
Jarash Jordan **67** 32.17N 35.54E
Jardee Australia **89** 34.18S 116.04E
Jardine *r.* Australia **90** 11.07S 142.30E
Jardines de la Reina *is.* Cuba **117** 20.30N 79.00W
Jardinópolis Brazil **126** 20.59S 47.48W
Jargeau France **19** 47.52N 2.07E
Jāria Jhānjail Bangla. **63** 25.02N 90.39E
Jaridih India **63** 23.38N 86.04E
Jarnac France **20** 45.41N 0.10W
Jarocin Poland **37** 51.59N 17.31E
Jarosław Poland **37** 50.02N 22.42E
Jarrāḥī *r.* Iran **65** 30.40N 48.23E
Jartai China **54** 39.45N 105.46E
Jartai Yanchi China **54** 39.43N 105.41E
Jarud Qi China **54** 44.30N 120.35E
Järvenpää Finland **41** 60.28N 25.06E
Jarvis Canada **104** 42.53N 80.06W
Jarvis I. Pacific Oc. **84** 0.23S 160.02W
Jasdan India **62** 22.02N 71.12E
Jäsk Iran **65** 25.40N 57.45E
Jasło Poland **37** 49.45N 21.29E

Jasper Canada **100** 52.55N 118.05W
Jasper Ala. U.S.A. **113** 33.48N 87.18W
Jasper Fla. U.S.A. **113** 30.31N 82.58W
Jasper Tex. U.S.A. **111** 30.55N 94.01W
Jasper Nat. Park Canada **100** 52.50N 118.08W
Jasra India **63** 25.17N 81.48E
Jastrebarsko Croatia **31** 45.40N 15.39E
Jastrowie Poland **36** 53.26N 16.49E
Jászberény Hungary **37** 47.30N 19.55E
Jataí Brazil **126** 17.58S 51.45W
Jāti Pakistan **62** 24.21N 68.16E
Jatibarang Indonesia **59** 6.26S 108.18E
Jatinegara Indonesia **59** 6.12S 106.51E
Játiva Spain **25** 38.59N 0.31W
Jatni India **63** 20.10N 85.42E
Jatt Israel **67** 32.24N 35.02E
Jaú Brazil **126** 22.11S 48.35W
Jauja Peru **122** 11.50S 75.15W
Jaunjelgava Latvia **44** 56.34N 25.02E
Jaunpur India **63** 25.44N 82.41E
Java *i. see* Jawa *i.* Indonesia **59**
Javalambre *r.* Spain **25** 40.06N 1.03W
Javari *r.* Peru **122** 4.30S 71.20W
Java Sea *see* Jawa, Laut *sea* Indonesia **58**
Java Trench *f.* Indonesia **58** 10.00S 110.00E
Jávea Spain **25** 38.47N 0.10E
Jawa *i.* Indonesia **59** 7.25S 110.00E
Jawa Barat *d.* Indonesia **59** 7.10S 107.00E
Jawa, Laut *sea* Indonesia **58** 5.00S 111.00E
Jawa Tengah *d.* Indonesia **59** 7.49S 110.35E
Jawa Timur *d.* Indonesia **59** 8.42S 113.10E
Jayah, Wādī al *see* Hā 'Arava Jordan/Israel **66**
Jayapura Indonesia **59** 2.28S 140.38E
Jaynagar India **63** 26.32N 86.07E
Jay Peak *mtn.* U.S.A. **105** 44.55N 72.32W
Jazīrah Doberai *f.* Indonesia **59** 1.10S 132.30E
Jazzīn Lebanon **66** 33.32N 35.34E
Jean U.S.A. **109** 35.46N 115.20W
Jeanerette U.S.A. **111** 29.55N 91.40W
Jean Marie River *town* Canada **98** 61.32N 120.40W
Jebāl Bārez, Kūh-e *mts.* Iran **65** 28.40N 58.10E
Jebba Nigeria **77** 9.11N 4.49E
Jebri Nigeria **77** 27.18N 65.44E
Jedda *see* Jiddah Saudi Arabia **72**
Jedburgh U.K. **14** 55.29N 2.33W
Jędrzejów Poland **37** 50.39N 20.18E
Jefferson U.S.A. **114** 41.44N 80.46W
Jefferson City U.S.A. **110** 38.34N 92.10W
Jefferson, Mt. Nev. U.S.A. **108** 38.46N 116.55W
Jefferson, Mt. Oreg. U.S.A. **108** 44.40N 121.47W
Jeffersonville U.S.A. **112** 38.16N 85.45W
Jega Nigeria **77** 12.12N 4.23E
Jēkabpils Latvia **44** 56.28N 25.58E
Jelenia Góra Poland **36** 50.55N 15.45E
Jelgava Latvia **41** 56.39N 23.42E
Jelli Sudan **73** 5.22N 31.48E
Jelling Denmark **42** 55.45N 9.26E
Jember Indonesia **59** 8.07S 113.45E
Jena Germany **38** 50.56N 11.35E
Jena U.S.A. **111** 31.41N 92.08W
Jenbach Austria **39** 47.24N 11.47E
Jendouba *d.* Tunisia **32** 36.45N 8.45E
Jennersdorf Austria **31** 46.57N 16.08E
Jenolan Caves *town* Australia **93** 33.53S 150.03E
Jepara Indonesia **59** 6.32S 110.40E
Jeparit Australia **92** 36.09S 141.59E
Jeppo Finland **40** 63.24N 22.37E
Jequié Brazil **123** 13.52S 40.06W
Jequitinhonha *r.* Brazil **126** 16.46S 39.45W
Jerada Morocco **74** 34.17N 2.13W
Jerantut Malaysia **58** 3.56N 102.22E
Jérémie Haiti **117** 18.40N 74.09W
Jerez Spain **27** 38.19N 6.46W
Jerez de la Frontera Spain **27** 36.41N 6.08W
Jerilderie Australia **93** 35.23S 145.41E
Jerome U.S.A. **108** 42.43N 114.31W
Jerramungup Australia **89** 33.57S 118.53E
Jersey *i.* Channel Is. Europe **13** 49.13N 2.08W
Jersey City U.S.A. **115** 40.44N 74.02W
Jersey Shore U.S.A. **114** 41.12N 77.16W
Jerseyville U.S.A. **110** 39.07N 90.20W
Jerusalem *see* Yerushalayim Israel/Jordan **67**
Jervis B. Australia **93** 35.05S 150.44E
Jervis Inlet Canada **100** 49.57N 124.10W
Jesenice Czech Republic **39** 50.04N 13.29E
Jesenice Slovenia **31** 46.27N 14.04E
Jessen Germany **38** 51.47N 12.58E
Jessore Bangla. **63** 23.10N 89.13E
Jesup U.S.A. **113** 31.36N 81.54W
Jesús Carranza Mexico **116** 17.26N 95.02W
Jetmore U.S.A. **111** 38.03N 99.54W
Jetpur India **62** 21.44N 70.37E
Jever Germany **38** 53.34N 7.54E
Jevnaker Norway **42** 60.15N 10.28E
Jewett Ohio U.S.A. **114** 40.22N 81.00W
Jewett Tex. U.S.A. **111** 31.22N 96.09W
Jewett City U.S.A. **115** 41.36N 71.59W
Jeypore India **63** 18.51N 82.35E
Jezerce *mtn.* Albania **34** 42.26N 19.49E
Jeziorak, Jezioro *l.* Poland **37** 53.40N 19.04E
Jhābua India **62** 22.46N 74.36E
Jhajha India **63** 24.46N 86.22E
Jhal Pakistan **62** 28.17N 67.27E
Jhālakāti Bangla. **63** 22.39N 90.12E
Jhālawār India **62** 24.36N 76.09E
Jhal Jhao Pakistan **62** 26.18N 65.35E
Jhālod India **62** 23.06N 74.09E
Jhang Sadar Pakistan **62** 31.16N 72.20E
Jhānsi India **63** 25.26N 78.35E
Jharia India **63** 23.45N 86.24E
Jhārsuguda India **63** 21.51N 84.02E
Jhawāni Nepal **63** 27.35N 84.38E
Jhelum Pakistan **62** 32.56N 73.44E
Jhelum *r.* Pakistan **62** 31.12N 72.08E
Jhinkpāni India **63** 22.25N 85.47E
Jhok Rind Pakistan **62** 31.27N 70.26E
Jhūnjhunu India **62** 28.08N 75.24E
Jiaganj India **63** 24.14N 88.16E

Jialing Jiang *r.* China **55** 29.30N 106.35E
Jiamusi China **53** 46.50N 130.21E
Ji'an China **55** 27.03N 115.00E
Jianchang China **54** 40.50N 119.50E
Jiange China **54** 32.04N 105.26E
Jiangling China **55** 30.20N 112.14E
Jiangmen China **55** 22.31N 113.08E
Jiangshan China **55** 28.43N 118.39E
Jiangsu *d.* China **55** 33.00N 119.30E
Jiangxi *d.* China **55** 27.00N 115.30E
Jiangyou China **55** 31.47N 104.45E
Jianhe China **55** 26.39N 108.35E
Jian'ou China **55** 27.04N 118.17E
Jianping China **54** 41.23N 119.40E
Jianshi China **55** 30.42N 109.20E
Jianyang Fujian China **55** 27.19N 118.01E
Jianyang Sichuan China **55** 30.25N 104.32E
Jiaochangba Sichuan China **54** 32.05N 103.43E
Jiaohe China **53** 43.42N 127.19E
Jiaolai He *r.* China **54** 43.48N 123.00E
Jiaoling China **55** 24.40N 116.10E
Jiaonan China **54** 35.53N 119.58E
Jiao Xian China **54** 36.16N 120.00E
Jiaozou China **54** 35.11N 113.27E
Jiashan China **54** 32.49N 118.01E
Jiawang China **54** 34.27N 117.27E
Jiaxian China **54** 38.02N 110.29E
Jiaxing China **55** 30.52N 120.45E
Jiayi Taiwan **55** 23.30N 120.24E
Jiazi China **55** 22.57N 116.01E
Jiddah Saudi Arabia **72** 21.30N 39.10E
Jiddat al Ḥarāsīs *f.* Oman **71** 19.45N 56.30E
Jiepai China **55** 31.11N 113.42E
Jiexi China **55** 23.26N 115.52E
Jiexiu China **54** 37.00N 111.55E
Jieyang China **55** 23.29N 116.19E
Jifnā Jordan **67** 31.58N 35.13E
Jigawa *d.* Nigeria **77** 12.30N 9.30E
Jihlava Czech Republic **36** 49.24N 15.35E
Jijel Algeria **75** 36.48N 5.46E
Jijiga Ethiopia **71** 9.22N 42.47E
Jijona Spain **25** 38.32N 0.30W
Jilib Somali Rep. **79** 0.28N 42.50E
Jilin China **53** 43.53N 126.35E
Jilin *d.* China **53** 44.50N 125.00E
Jiloca *r.* Spain **25** 41.21N 1.39W
Jilong Taiwan **55** 25.09N 121.45E
Jīma Ethiopia **73** 7.36N 36.50E
Jimbe Angola **78** 10.20S 16.40E
Jimena de la Frontera Spain **27** 36.26N 5.27W
Jiménez Mexico **116** 27.08N 104.55W
Jimeta Nigeria **77** 9.19N 12.25E
Jimo China **54** 36.23N 120.27E
Jinan China **54** 36.41N 117.01E
Jīnd India **62** 29.19N 76.19E
Jindabyne Australia **93** 36.24S 148.37E
Jing'an China **55** 28.52N 115.22E
Jingbian China **54** 37.33N 108.36E
Jingchuan China **54** 35.15N 107.22E
Jingde China **55** 30.19N 118.31E
Jingdezhen China **55** 29.14N 117.14E
Jinggu Gansu China **54** 35.05N 103.41E
Jinggu Yunnan China **61** 23.29N 100.19E
Jinghai China **54** 38.56N 116.31E
Jing He *r.* China **54** 34.26N 109.00E
Jinghong China **52** 21.59N 100.49E
Jingmen China **55** 31.02N 112.06E
Jingning China **54** 35.30N 105.45E
Jingou China **54** 41.37N 120.33E
Jingtai China **54** 37.10N 104.08E
Jingxi China **55** 23.03N 106.36E
Jing Xian China **55** 26.35N 109.41E
Jingyuan Gansu China **54** 36.40N 104.03E
Jingyuan Ningxia Huizu China **54** 35.29N 106.20E
Jinhua China **55** 29.05N 119.40E
Jining Shandong China **54** 35.24N 116.45E
Jining Nei Monggol Zizhiqu China **53** 40.56N 113.00E
Jinja Uganda **79** 0.27N 33.10E
Jinotepe Nicaragua **117** 11.50N 86.10W
Jinsha Jiang *r.* China **61** 26.30N 101.40E
Jinshi China **55** 29.35N 111.56E
Jintang China **55** 30.51N 104.27E
Jinxi Fujian China **55** 26.12N 117.34E
Jinxi Liaoning China **54** 40.48N 120.46E
Jinxian China **55** 28.13N 116.34E
Jin Xian Liaoning China **54** 39.06N 121.49E
Jin Xian Liaoning China **54** 41.10N 121.20E
Jinxiang China **54** 35.08N 116.20E
Jinzhou China **54** 41.06N 121.05E
Jipijapa Ecuador **122** 1.23S 80.35W
Jire Somali Rep. **71** 5.22N 48.05E
Jirjā Egypt **72** 26.20N 31.53E
Jishui China **55** 27.13N 115.07E
Jisr al Ḥusayn Jordan **67** 31.52N 35.32E
Jitarning Australia **89** 32.48S 117.57E
Jiu *r.* Romania **29** 43.44N 23.52E
Jiuding Shan *mtn.* China **55** 31.36N 103.54E
Jiudongshan China **55** 23.44N 117.32E
Jiujiang China **55** 29.39N 116.02E
Jiulian Shan *mts.* China **55** 24.40N 115.00E
Jiuling Shan *mts.* China **55** 28.40N 114.45E
Jiulong Jiang *r.* China **55** 24.30N 117.47E
Jiuzhou Jiang *r.* China **55** 21.25N 109.58E
Jixi China **53** 45.17N 130.59E
Ji Xian Henan China **54** 35.25N 114.05E
Ji Xian Tianjin China **54** 40.03N 117.24E
Jīzān Saudi Arabia **72** 16.54N 42.32E
Jizl, Wādī al *r.* Saudi Arabia **64** 25.37N 38.20E
João Pessoa Brazil **123** 7.06S 34.53W
Jódar Spain **27** 37.50N 3.21W
Jodhpur India **62** 26.17N 73.02E
Jodiya India **62** 22.42N 70.18E
Jodoigne Belgium **16** 50.45N 4.52E
Joensuu Finland **44** 62.35N 29.46E
Joetsu Japan **57** 37.07N 138.15E
Jogdor China **54** 42.30N 115.52E
Johannesburg R.S.A. **80** 26.11S 28.04E

Johannesburg U.S.A. 104 44.59N 84.29W
Johi Pakistan 62 26.41N 67.37E
John Day r. U.S.A. 108 44.25N 118.57W
John Day r. U.S.A. 108 45.44N 120.39W
John I. Canada 104 46.09N 82.32W
John O'Groats U.K. 14 58.39N 3.02W
Johnson U.S.A. 111 37.34N 101.45W
Johnsonburg U.S.A. 114 41.29N 78.41W
Johnson City N.Y. U.S.A. 115 42.07N 75.57W
Johnson City Tenn. U.S.A. 113 36.20N 82.23W
Johnsons Crossing Canada 100 60.29N 133.18W
Johnstone Str. Canada 100 50.28N 126.00W
Johnston I. Pacific Oc. 84 16.45N 169.32W
Johnston, L. Australia 89 32.25S 120.30E
Johnstown N.Y. U.S.A. 115 43.00N 74.22W
Johnstown Ohio U.S.A. 114 40.09N 82.41W
Johnstown Penn. U.S.A. 114 40.20N 78.55W
Johor Baharu Malaysia 58 1.29N 103.40E
Joigny France 19 47.59N 3.24E
Joinville Brazil 126 26.20S 48.49W
Joinville France 19 48.27N 5.08E
Jokkmokk Sweden 40 66.37N 19.50E
Jökulsá á Brú r. Iceland 40 65.33N 14.23W
Jökulsá á Fjöllum r. Iceland 40 66.05N 16.32W
Jolfa Iran 65 32.40N 51.39E
Joliet U.S.A. 111 41.32N 88.05W
Joliette Canada 105 46.01N 73.27W
Joliette Prov. Park Canada 105 46.30N 74.00W
Jolo i. Phil. 59 5.55N 121.20E
Jolo town Phil. 59 6.03N 121.00E
Jombang Indonesia 59 7.30S 112.21E
Jombo r. Angola 78 10.20S 16.37E
Jomda China 61 31.30N 98.16E
Jonava Lithuania 41 55.05N 24.17E
Jonê China 54 34.35N 103.32E
Jonesboro Ark. U.S.A. 111 35.50N 90.42W
Jonesboro La. U.S.A. 111 32.15N 92.43W
Jones Sd. Canada 99 76.00N 85.00W
Jönköping Sweden 43 57.47N 14.11E
Jönköping d. Sweden 43 57.34N 14.40E
Jonzac France 20 45.27N 0.26W
Joplin U.S.A. 111 37.06N 94.31W
Jora India 63 26.20N 77.49E
Jordan Asia 64 31.00N 36.00E
Jordan r. see Al Urdunn r. Asia 67
Jordan Mont. U.S.A. 108 47.19N 106.55W
Jordan N.Y. U.S.A. 105 43.04N 76.29W
Jordan Valley town U.S.A. 108 42.58N 117.03W
Jorhāt India 61 26.45N 94.13E
Jörn Sweden 40 65.04N 20.02E
Jörpeland Norway 42 59.01N 6.03E
Jos Nigeria 77 9.54N 8.53E
José de San Martin Argentina 125 44.04S 70.26W
José Enrique Rodó Uruguay 125 33.41S 57.34W
Joseph Bonaparte G. Australia 88 14.00S 128.30E
Joseph City U.S.A. 109 34.57N 110.20W
Joseph, L. Canada 104 45.14N 79.45W
Joseph, Lac l. Canada 103 52.45N 65.15W
Joshīmath India 63 30.34N 79.34E
Jos Plateau f. Nigeria 77 10.00N 9.00E
Josselin France 18 47.57N 2.33W
Jotunheimen mts. Norway 41 61.38N 8.18E
Joué-lès-Tours France 18 47.21N 0.40E
Joure Neth. 16 52.59N 5.49E
Joverega Botswana 80 19.08S 24.15E
Jowai India 63 25.27N 92.12E
Juan Aldama Mexico 111 24.19N 103.21W
Juan B. Arruabarrena Argentina 30 30.25S 58.15W
Juan de Fuca, Str. of Canada/U.S.A. 100 48.15N 124.00W
Juan de Nova i. Madagascar 81 17.03S 42.45E
Juan Fernández, Islas is. Chile 121 34.20S 80.00W
Juárez Argentina 125 37.40S 59.48W
Juárez Chihuahua Mexico 109 30.20N 108.03W
Juárez Coahuila Mexico 111 27.37N 100.44W
Juárez, Sierra de mts. Mexico 109 32.00N 115.45W
Juàzeiro Brazil 123 9.25S 40.30W
Juàzeiro do Norte Brazil 123 7.10S 39.18W
Jûbâ Sudan 73 4.51N 31.37E
Jūbāl, Maḍīq str. Egypt 66 27.40N 33.55E
Jubal, Str. of see Jūbāl, Maḍīq str. Egypt 66
Jubba r. Somali Rep. 79 0.20S 42.40E
Jubbātā al Khashab Syria 67 33.13N 35.49E
Jubilee Downs town Australia 88 18.22S 125.17E
Juby, Cap c. Morocco 74 27.58N 12.55W
Júcar r. Spain 25 39.09N 0.14W
Juchitán Mexico 116 16.27N 95.05W
Judaea f. Israel/Jordan 67 31.10N 35.00E
Judenburg Austria 36 47.10N 14.40E
Judith Basin f. U.S.A. 108 47.10N 109.58W
Juelsminde Denmark 42 55.43N 10.01E
Jugon France 18 48.25N 2.20W
Juillac France 20 45.19N 1.19E
Juist i. Germany 38 53.40N 7.00E
Juiz de Fora Brazil 126 21.47S 43.23W
Jujuy d. Argentina 124 23.00S 65.30W
Juklegga mtn. Norway 41 61.03N 8.13E
Juliaca Peru 122 15.29S 70.09W
Julia Creek town Australia 90 20.39S 141.45E
Juliana Kanaal canal Neth. 16 51.00N 5.48E
Julian Alps mts. Slovenia 31 46.20N 13.50E
Julianehåb Greenland 99 60.45N 46.00W
Jülich Germany 38 50.55N 6.21E
Jumboo Somali Rep. 79 0.12S 42.38E
Jumet Belgium 16 50.27N 4.27E
Jumilla Spain 25 38.29N 1.17W
Jumla Nepal 63 29.17N 82.13E
Jumna r. see Yamuna India 63
Junāgadh India 62 21.31N 70.28E
Junan China 54 35.11N 118.50E
Junction U.S.A. 111 30.29N 99.46W
Junction B. Australia 90 11.50S 134.15E
Junction City Kans. U.S.A. 110 39.02N 96.50W
Junction City Oreg. U.S.A. 108 44.13N 123.12W
Jundah Australia 90 24.50S 143.02E
Jundiaí Brazil 126 23.10S 46.54W
Juneau U.S.A. 100 58.26N 134.30W

Junee Australia 93 34.51S 147.40E
Jungfrau mtn. Switz. 39 46.32N 7.58E
Junggar Pendi f. Asia 52 44.20N 86.30E
Junglinster Lux. 16 49.41N 6.13E
Jungshāhi Pakistan 62 24.51N 67.46E
Junín Argentina 125 34.35S 60.58W
Junín de los Andes Argentina 125 39.57S 71.05W
Juniville France 19 49.24N 4.23E
Jūniyah Lebanon 66 33.59N 35.38E
Junlian China 55 28.08N 104.29E
Junnah, Jabal mts. Egypt 66 28.52N 34.15E
Junnar India 62 19.12N 73.53E
Junqali d. Sudan 73 7.30N 32.30E
Junsele Sweden 40 63.40N 16.55E
Juntura U.S.A. 108 43.46N 118.05W
Jun Xian China 54 32.40N 111.18E
Jupiter r. Canada 103 49.29N 63.32W
Jupiter U.S.A. 113 26.57N 80.08W
Jur r. Sudan 73 7.45N 28.00E
Jura mts. Europe 39 46.48N 6.30E
Jura d. France 19 46.50N 5.50E
Jura d. Switz. 39 47.20N 7.10E
Jura i. U.K. 14 55.58N 5.55W
Jurado Colombia 122 7.07N 77.46W
Jura Krakowska mts. Poland 37 50.30N 19.30E
Jura, Sd. of U.K. 14 56.00N 5.45W
Jurhen Ul Shan mts. China 63 34.00N 91.00E
Jūrmala Latvia 41 56.58N 23.42E
Juruá r. Brazil 122 2.33S 65.50W
Juruena Brazil 124 12.50S 58.58W
Juruena r. Brazil 123 7.20S 57.30W
Juruti Brazil 123 2.09S 56.04W
Jussey France 19 47.49N 5.54E
Jutaí r. Brazil 122 2.35S 67.00W
Jüterbog Germany 38 51.59N 13.04E
Juticalpa Honduras 117 14.45N 86.12W
Jutland pen. see Jylland pen. Denmark 42
Juye China 54 35.25N 116.06E
Jūyom Iran 65 28.10N 53.52E
Južna r. Iran 65 32.43.40N 21.22E
Juzur al Halaniyat is. Oman 60 17.30N 56.00E
Jwayyā Lebanon 67 33.14N 35.20E
Jyderup Denmark 42 55.40N 11.26E
Jylland pen. Denmark 42 56.12N 9.20E
Jyväskylä Finland 40 62.14N 25.44E

K

K2 mtn. Asia 52 35.53N 76.32E
Ka r. Nigeria 77 11.35N 4.10E
Kaabong Uganda 79 3.28N 34.08E
Kaapstad see Cape Town R.S.A. 80
Kaba Guinea 76 10.08N 11.49W
Kabaena i. Indonesia 59 5.25S 122.00E
Kabala Sierra Leone 76 9.40N 11.36W
Kabale Uganda 79 1.13S 30.00E
Kabalega Falls f. Uganda 79 2.17N 31.46E
Kabalega Falls Nat. Park Uganda 79 2.15N 31.45E
Kabalo Zaïre 78 6.02S 27.00E
Kabambare Zaïre 78 4.40S 27.41E
Kabanga Zambia 80 17.36S 26.45E
Kabba Nigeria 77 7.50N 6.07E
Kabberi Israel 67 33.01N 35.09E
Kabinakagami r. Canada 112 50.20N 84.20W
Kabinda Zaïre 78 6.10S 24.29E
Kabir Kūh mts. Iran 65 33.00N 47.00E
Kabkābīyah Sudan 73 13.39N 24.05E
Kābol Afghan. 62 34.31N 69.12E
Kābol d. Afghan. 62 34.45N 69.15E
Kabompo Zambia 78 13.35S 24.10E
Kabompo r. Zambia 78 14.17S 23.15E
Kabongo Zaïre 78 7.22S 25.34E
Kabonzo Zaïre 79 6.41S 27.49E
Kaboudia, Ra's c. Tunisia 75 35.14N 11.10E
Kabūd Gonbad Iran 65 37.02N 59.46E
Kabul see Kābol Afghan. 62
Kabumbu Zaïre 78 4.07S 26.17E
Kabunda Zaïre 78 12.27S 29.15E
Kabundi Zaïre 79 10.07S 27.13E
Kabwe Zambia 79 14.27S 28.25E
Kačanik Yugo. 34 42.13N 21.12E
Kāchā Kūh mts. Iran 65 29.30N 61.20E
Kachchh, G. of India 62 22.40N 69.30E
Kachin d. Myanmar 56 26.00N 97.30E
Kachiry Kazakhstan 9 53.07N 76.08E
Kachīsī Ethiopia 73 9.39N 37.50E
Kadań Czech Republic 36 50.22N 13.15E
Kadaney r. Afghan. 62 31.20N 65.47E
Kade Ghana 76 6.08N 0.51W
Kadei r. C.A.R. 77 3.28N 16.05E
Kadi India 62 23.18N 72.20E
Kadina Australia 92 33.58S 137.14E
Kadioli Mali 76 10.38N 5.45W
Kadoka U.S.A. 110 43.50N 101.31W
Kadoma Zimbabwe 80 18.23S 29.52E
Kaduna Nigeria 77 10.28N 7.25E
Kaduna d. Nigeria 77 11.00N 7.35E
Kaduna r. Nigeria 77 8.45N 5.45E
Kāduqlī Sudan 73 11.01N 29.43E
Kadusam mtn. China 61 28.30N 96.45E
Kaédi Mauritania 76 16.09N 13.30W
Kaélé Cameroon 77 10.05N 14.28E
Kaesŏng N. Korea 53 37.59N 126.30E
Kafanchan Nigeria 77 9.38N 8.20E

Kaffrine Senegal 76 14.08N 15.34W
Kafia Kingi Sudan 73 9.16N 24.25E
Kafirévs, Ákra c. Greece 35 38.10N 24.35E
Kafr ad Dawwār Egypt 66 31.08N 30.08E
Kafr al Baṭṭīkh Egypt 66 31.24N 31.44E
Kafr ash Shaykh Egypt 66 31.07N 30.56E
Kafr az Zayyāt Egypt 66 30.50N 30.49E
Kafr Kammā Israel 67 32.43N 35.26E
Kafr Kannā Israel 67 32.45N 35.20E
Kafr Mandā Israel 67 32.49N 35.15E
Kafr Naffākh Syria 67 33.04N 35.44E
Kafr Qaddūm Jordan 67 32.13N 35.09E
Kafr Qūd Jordan 67 32.27N 35.14E
Kafr Salīm Egypt 66 31.09N 30.07E
Kafr Yāsīf Israel 67 32.57N 35.10E
Kafu r. Uganda 79 1.40N 32.07E
Kafue Zambia 79 15.40S 28.13E
Kafue r. Zambia 79 15.53S 28.55E
Kafue Dam Zambia 79 15.40S 27.10E
Kafue Nat. Park Zambia 78 15.30S 25.35E
Kafunzo Uganda 79 1.05S 30.26E
Kaga Bandoro C.A.R. 77 7.00N 19.10E
Kāgān Pakistan 62 34.47N 73.32E
Kagan Uzbekistan 50 39.45N 64.32E
Kagarlyk Ukraine 37 49.50N 30.50E
Kagawong Canada 104 45.54N 82.17W
Kagawong L. Canada 104 45.49N 82.18W
Kagaznagar India 63 19.18N 79.50E
Kagera d. Tanzania 79 2.00S 31.20E
Kağizman Turkey 64 40.08N 43.07E
Kagoshima Japan 57 31.37N 130.32E
Kagoshima wan b. Japan 57 31.00N 131.00E
Kagul Moldova 37 45.54N 28.11E
Kahama Tanzania 79 3.48S 32.38E
Kahayan r. Indonesia 58 3.20S 114.04E
Kahemba Zaïre 78 7.20S 19.00E
Kahler Asten mtn. Germany 38 51.11N 8.29E
Kahntah r. Canada 100 58.15N 120.55W
Kahnūj Iran 65 27.55N 57.45E
Kahoolawe i. Hawaiian Is. 85 20.33N 156.37W
Kahraman Maraş Turkey 64 37.34N 36.54E
Kaiama Nigeria 77 9.37N 4.03E
Kaiapoi New Zealand 86 43.23S 172.39E
Kaiedin Sudan 73 9.45N 32.11E
Kaifeng China 54 34.46N 114.22E
Kai, Kepulauan is. Indonesia 59 5.45S 132.55E
Kaikohe New Zealand 86 35.25S 173.49E
Kaikoura New Zealand 86 42.24S 173.41E
Kaikoura Range mts. New Zealand 86 42.00S 173.40E
Kailahun Sierra Leone 76 8.21N 10.21W
Kaili China 55 26.35N 107.55E
Kailu China 54 43.35N 121.12E
Kailua Hawaiian Is. 85 21.24N 157.44W
Kaïmakchalán mtn. Greece 34 40.55N 21.48E
Kaimana Indonesia 59 3.39S 133.44E
Kaimanawa Mts. New Zealand 86 39.10S 176.15E
Kainantu P.N.G. 59 6.16S 145.50E
Kainji Resr. Nigeria 77 10.00N 4.35E
Kaintragarh India 63 20.47N 84.40E
Kaipara Harbour New Zealand 86 36.30S 174.00E
Kaiserslautern Germany 39 49.26N 7.46E
Kaitaia New Zealand 86 35.08S 173.18E
Kaithal India 62 29.48N 76.23E
Kaitum r. Sweden 40 67.30N 21.05E
Kaiwi Channel Hawaiian Is. 85 21.15N 157.30W
Kaiyuan China 54 42.45N 123.50E
Kaizuka Japan 57 34.27N 135.21E
Kajaani Finland 40 64.14N 27.41E
Kajabbi Australia 90 20.02S 140.02E
Kajiado Kenya 79 1.50S 36.48E
Kajo Kaji Sudan 73 3.53N 31.40E
Kajuru Nigeria 77 10.19N 7.40E
Kākā Sudan 73 10.36N 32.11E
Kakamas R.S.A. 80 28.44S 20.35E
Kakamega Kenya 79 0.21N 34.47E
Kakamigahara Japan 57 35.28N 136.48E
Kākdwīp India 63 21.53N 88.11E
Kakegawa Japan 57 34.46N 138.01E
Kakenge Zaïre 78 4.51S 21.55E
Kakhovskoye Vodokhranilishche resr. Ukraine 45 47.33N 34.40E
Kākī Iran 65 28.19N 51.34E
Kākināda India 61 16.55N 82.20E
Kakisa r. Canada 100 61.03N 117.10W
Kakisa L. Canada 100 60.55N 117.40W
Kakonko Tanzania 79 3.19S 30.54E
Kakuma Kenya 79 3.38N 34.48E
Kakuto Uganda 79 0.54S 31.26E
Kala r. Finland 40 64.17N 23.55E
Kalābāgh Pakistan 62 32.58N 71.34E
Kalabahi Indonesia 59 8.13S 124.31E
Kalabáka Greece 34 39.42N 21.43E
Kalabity Australia 92 32.31S 140.18E
Kalabo Zambia 78 14.58S 22.33E
Kalach-na-Donu Russian Fed. 45 48.43N 43.31E
Kaladan r. Myanmar 56 20.09N 92.55E
Kaladar Canada 105 44.39N 77.07W
Kalahari Desert Botswana 80 23.30S 22.00E
Kalahari Gemsbok Nat. Park R.S.A. 80 25.45S 20.25E
Kalajoki Finland 40 64.15N 23.57E
Kalakan Russian Fed. 51 55.10N 116.45E
Kalámai Greece 35 37.04N 22.07E
Kalamariá Greece 34 40.33N 22.55E
Kalamazoo U.S.A. 112 42.17N 85.36W
Kalamb India 62 18.56N 73.55E
Kalamera Tanzania 79 2.07S 33.43E
Kalamurra, L. Australia 91 28.00S 138.00E
Kalandula Angola 78 9.06S 16.11E
Kalanshiyū, Sarīr des. Libya 75 27.00N 21.30E
Kalarash Russian Fed. 37 47.18N 28.16E
Kalavárdha Greece 35 36.19N 27.57E
Kalávrita Greece 35 38.03N 22.08E
Kalbarri Australia 89 27.40S 114.12E
Kalb, Ra's al c. Yemen 71 14.02N 48.41E

Kalchās Pakistan 62 29.21N 69.42E
Kalecik Turkey 64 40.06N 33.22E
Kalehe Zaïre 79 2.05S 28.53E
Kalemie Zaïre 79 5.57S 29.10E
Kalgan r. Australia 89 34.55S 117.58E
Kalgoorlie Australia 89 30.49S 121.29E
Kaliakra, Nos c. Bulgaria 29 43.23N 28.29E
Kalianda Indonesia 58 5.50S 105.45E
Kalima Zaïre 78 2.35S 26.34E
Kalimantan d. Indonesia 58 1.00S 113.00E
Kalimantan f. Indonesia 58 0.05N 112.30E
Kalimantan Barat d. Indonesia 58 0.30N 110.00E
Kalimantan Selatan d. Indonesia 58 2.30S 115.30E
Kalimantan Tengah d. Indonesia 58 2.00S 113.30E
Kalimantan Timur d. Indonesia 58 2.20N 116.30E
Kálimnos Greece 35 36.57N 26.59E
Kálimnos i. Greece 35 37.00N 27.00E
Kālimpong India 63 27.04N 88.29E
Kaliningrad Russian Fed. 41 54.43N 20.30E
Kalinkovichi Belarus 37 52.10N 29.13E
Kalinovik Bosnia-Herzegovina 31 43.31N 18.26E
Kalinovka Ukraine 37 49.29N 28.30E
Kalisat Indonesia 59 8.02S 113.50E
Kāli Sindh r. India 62 25.32N 76.17E
Kalispell U.S.A. 108 48.12N 114.19W
Kalisz Poland 37 51.46N 18.02E
Kaliua Tanzania 79 5.08S 31.50E
Kalix r. Sweden 40 65.50N 23.11E
Kalkar Germany 38 51.44N 6.17E
Kalkfontein Botswana 80 22.08S 20.54E
Kalkrand Namibia 80 24.05S 17.34E
Källandsö i. Sweden 43 58.40N 13.09E
Kallinge Sweden 43 56.14N 15.17E
Kallithea Greece 35 37.05N 23.41E
Kallsjön l. Sweden 40 63.35N 13.00E
Kalmar Sweden 43 56.40N 16.22E
Kalmar d. Sweden 43 57.15N 16.00E
Kalmarsund str. Sweden 43 56.40N 16.25E
Kalmthout Belgium 16 51.23N 4.28E
Kalmykovo Kazakhstan 45 49.02N 51.55E
Kālna India 63 23.13N 88.22E
Kalničko Gorje mts. Croatia 31 46.10N 16.30E
Kalo P.N.G. 90 10.05S 147.45E
Kalocsa Hungary 31 46.32N 18.59E
Kalofer Bulgaria 34 42.37N 24.59E
Kaloko Zaïre 78 6.47S 25.47E
Kālol Gujarat India 62 22.36N 73.27E
Kālol Gujarat India 62 23.15N 72.29E
Kalole Zaïre 79 3.40S 27.22E
Kalomo Zambia 78 16.55S 26.29E
Kalonje Zambia 79 12.21S 31.06E
Kālpi India 63 26.07N 79.44E
Kāl Qal 'eh Afghan. 62 32.38N 62.32E
Kalsö i. Faroe Is. 10 62.18N 6.50W
Kalsūbai mtn. India 62 19.36N 73.43E
Kaltag U.S.A. 98 64.20N 158.44W
Kaluga Russian Fed. 44 54.31N 36.16E
Kālu Khuhar Pakistan 62 25.08N 67.46E
Kalumburu Australia 88 14.14S 126.38E
Kalundborg Denmark 42 55.41N 11.06E
Kalush Ukraine 37 49.02N 24.20E
Kalutara Sri Lanka 61 6.35N 79.58E
Kalyān India 62 19.15N 73.09E
Kama r. Russian Fed. 44 55.30N 52.00E
Kamaishi Japan 57 39.16N 141.53E
Kamakura Japan 57 35.19N 139.33E
Kamālia Pakistan 62 30.44N 72.39E
Kaman Turkey 23 39.22N 33.44E
Kamanashi r. Japan 57 35.33N 138.28E
Kamaniskeg L. Canada 105 45.25N 77.42W
Kamanjab Namibia 80 19.39S 14.50E
Kamarsuk Canada 103 56.18N 61.38W
Kamba Nigeria 77 11.52N 3.42E
Kamba Zaïre 78 4.00S 22.22E
Kambalda Australia 89 31.12S 121.40E
Kambar Pakistan 62 27.36N 68.00E
Kambarka Russian Fed. 44 56.18N 54.13E
Kambia Sierra Leone 76 9.09N 12.53W
Kamchatka, Poluostrov pen. Russian Fed. 51 56.00N 160.00E
Kameda Japan 57 41.48N 140.36E
Kamen mtn. Russian Fed. 51 68.40N 94.20E
Kamenets Podolskiy Ukraine 37 48.40N 26.36E
Kamenka Russian Fed. 44 65.55N 44.02E
Kamenka Russian Fed. 44 53.10N 44.05E
Kamenka Bugskaya Ukraine 37 50.07N 24.30E
Kamen Kashirskiy Ukraine 37 51.32N 24.59E
Kamen-na-Obi Russian Fed. 50 53.46N 81.18E
Kamenskoye Russian Fed. 51 62.31N 165.15E
Kamensk-Shakhtinskiy Russian Fed. 45 48.20N 40.16E
Kamensk-Ural'skiy Russian Fed. 50 56.29N 61.49E
Kamenz Germany 38 51.16N 14.06E
Kāmet mtn. India/China 63 30.54N 79.37E
Kameyama Japan 57 34.51N 136.27E
Kamiah U.S.A. 108 46.14N 116.02W
Kamieskroon R.S.A. 80 30.12S 17.53E
Kamilukuak L. Canada 101 62.22N 101.40W
Kamina Zaïre 78 8.46S 24.58E
Kaminak L. Canada 101 62.10N 95.00W
Kamioka Japan 57 36.25N 137.15E
Kamirós site Greece 35 36.19N 27.57E
Kamloops Canada 100 50.40N 120.24W
Kamloops Plateau f. Canada 100 50.00N 120.20W
Kamnik Slovenia 31 46.13N 14.37E
Kamo r. Japan 57 35.00N 139.52E
Kāmoke Pakistan 62 31.58N 74.13E
Kamp r. Austria 36 48.25N 15.27E
Kamp Germany 39 50.14N 7.37E
Kampa Indonesia 58 1.46S 105.26E
Kampala Uganda 79 0.19N 32.35E
Kampar r. Indonesia 58 0.20N 102.55E
Kampen Neth. 16 52.33N 5.55E
Kampene Zaïre 78 3.36S 26.40E
Kamphaeng Phet Thailand 56 16.28N 99.31E
Kamp-Lintfort Germany 16 51.34N 6.38E
Kamp 'O S. Korea 57 35.48N 129.29E
Kâmpóng Cham Cambodia 56 11.59N 105.26E
Kâmpóng Chhnāng Cambodia 56 12.16N 104.39E
Kâmpóng Saôm see Sihanoukville Cambodia 58

Kâmpóng Thum Cambodia 56 12.42N 104.52E
Kâmpôt Cambodia 56 10.37N 104.11E
Kampti Burkina 76 10.07N 3.22W
Kamsack Canada 101 51.34N 101.54W
Kamskoye Vodokhranilishche resr. Russian Fed. 44 58.55N 56.20E
Kâmthi India 63 21.14N 79.12E
Kamui misaki c. Japan 57 43.30N 140.15E
Kamyshin Russian Fed. 45 50.05N 45.24E
Kana r. Zimbabwe 80 18.30S 26.50E
Kanaaupscow r. Canada 102 53.40N 77.10W
Kanafis Sudan 73 9.48N 25.40E
Kanagawa d. Japan 57 35.25N 139.10E
Kanairiktok r. Canada 103 55.05N 60.20W
Kanâkir Syria 67 33.15N 36.05E
Kanália Greece 34 39.30N 22.53E
Kananga Zaïre 78 5.53S 22.26E
Kanash Russian Fed. 44 55.30N 47.27E
Kanastraíon, Ákra c. Greece 34 39.56N 23.47E
Kanaudi India 63 23.36N 81.23E
Kanawha r. U.S.A. 114 38.50N 82.08W
Kanazawa Japan 57 36.35N 136.40E
Kanchanaburi Thailand 56 14.02N 99.28E
Känchenjunga mtn. Nepal/India 63 27.44N 88.11E
Känchipuram India 61 12.50N 79.44E
Kandähu Pakistan 62 27.33N 69.24E
Kandalaksha Russian Fed. 44 67.09N 32.31E
Kandalakshskaya Guba g. Russian Fed. 44 66.30N 34.00E
Kandangan Indonesia 58 2.50S 115.15E
Kandavu i. Fiji 84 19.05S 178.15E
Kandavu Passage Fiji 84 18.45S 178.00E
Kandel Germany 39 49.05N 8.11E
Kandhkot Pakistan 62 28.14N 69.11E
Kandi Benin 77 11.05N 2.59E
Kändi India 63 23.57N 88.02E
Kandiäro Pakistan 62 27.04N 68.13E
Kandira Turkey 64 41.05N 30.08E
Kandla India 62 23.00N 70.10E
Kandos Australia 93 32.53S 149.59E
Kandräch Pakistan 62 25.29N 65.29E
Kandreho Madagascar 81 17.29S 46.06E
Kandy Sri Lanka 61 7.18N 80.43E
Kane U.S.A. 114 41.40N 78.49W
Kanem d. Chad 77 15.10N 15.30E
Kanevka Russian Fed. 44 67.08N 39.50E
Kang Botswana 80 23.43S 22.51E
Kangaarsussuaq c. see Parry, Kap c. Greenland 99
Kangaba Mali 76 11.56N 8.25W
Kängän Iran 65 27.50N 52.07E
Kangar Malaysia 58 6.28N 100.10E
Kangaroo I. Australia 92 35.50S 137.06E
Kangding China 54 30.05N 102.04E
Kangean, Kepulauan is. Indonesia 59 7.00S 115.30E
Kangerlussuaq see Söndreströmfjord Greenland 99
Kangikajilip Agpalia see Brewster, K. c. Greenland 96
Kangiqsualujjuaq Canada 99 58.35N 65.59W
Kangiqsujuaq Canada 99 61.30N 72.00W
Kangirsuk Canada 99 60.01N 70.01W
Kangle China 54 35.16N 103.39E
Kangmar Xizang China 63 30.45N 85.43E
Kangmar Xizang Zizhiqu China 63 28.30N 89.45E
Kango Gabon 78 0.15N 10.14E
Kangping China 54 42.45N 123.20E
Kangrinboqê Feng Xizang Zizhiqu China 63 31.05N 81.21E
Kangto mtn. China 63 27.54N 92.32E
Kanhar r. India 63 24.28N 83.08E
Kani Côte d'Ivoire 76 8.34N 6.35W
Kaniama Zaïre 78 7.32S 24.11E
Kaningo Kenya 79 0.52S 38.31E
Kanin Nos, Mys c. Russian Fed. 44 68.38N 43.20E
Kanin, Poluostrov pen. Russian Fed. 44 68.00N 45.00E
Kaniva Australia 92 36.33S 141.17E
Kanjiža Yugo. 31 46.04N 20.04E
Kankakee U.S.A. 110 41.08N 87.52W
Kankan Gabon 78 0.03S 12.14E
Kankan Guinea 76 10.22N 9.11W
Känker India 63 20.17N 81.29E
Kankossa Mauritania 74 15.58N 11.31W
Kannack Vietnam 56 14.07N 108.36E
Kannapolis U.S.A. 113 35.30N 80.36W
Kannauj India 63 27.04N 79.55E
Kannod India 62 22.40N 76.44E
Kano r. Japan 57 35.05N 138.52E
Kano Nigeria 77 12.00N 8.31E
Kano d. Nigeria 77 11.45N 8.30E
Kanona Zambia 79 13.03S 30.37E
Kanowna Australia 89 30.36S 121.36E
Kanoya Japan 57 31.22N 130.50E
Känpur India 63 26.28N 80.21E
Kansas d. U.S.A. 110 38.30N 99.00W
Kansas r. U.S.A. 110 39.07N 94.36W
Kansas City Kans. U.S.A. 110 39.07N 94.39W
Kansas City Mo. U.S.A. 110 39.05N 94.35W
Kansenia Zaïre 78 10.19S 26.02E
Kansk Russian Fed. 51 56.11N 95.20E
Kansŏng S. Korea 53 38.20N 128.28E
Kantäbánji India 63 20.29N 82.55E
Kantché Niger 77 13.31N 8.30E
Kantemirovka Russian Fed. 45 49.40N 39.52E
Kantô d. Japan 57 35.35N 139.30E
Kantôheiya f. Japan 57 36.02N 140.10E
Kantô-sanchi mts. Japan 57 36.00N 138.35E
Kanye Botswana 80 24.58S 25.17E
Kanyu Botswana 80 20.05S 24.39E
Kao i. Tonga 85 19.40S 175.01W
Kaohsiung Taiwan 48 22.36N 120.17E
Kaoko Veld f. Namibia 80 18.30S 13.30E
Kaolack Senegal 76 14.09N 16.08W
Kaoma Zambia 78 14.55S 24.48E
Kapaa Hawaiian Is. 85 22.05N 159.19W
Kapadvanj India 62 23.01N 73.04E
Kapanga Zaïre 78 8.22S 22.37E
Kapaonik mts. Yugo. 34 43.10N 21.00E
Kap Arkona c. Germany 38 54.41N 13.26E
Kapchagay Kazakhstan 52 43.51N 77.14E

Kapenguria Kenya 79 1.13N 35.07E
Kapfenberg Austria 36 47.27N 15.18E
Kapiri Mposhi Zambia 79 13.59S 28.40E
Kapiskau Canada 102 52.20N 82.01W
Kapiskau r. Canada 102 52.20N 83.40W
Kapit Malaysia 58 2.01N 112.56E
Kapiti I. New Zealand 86 40.50S 174.50E
Kapoeta Sudan 73 4.47N 33.35E
Kapongolo Zaïre 79 7.51S 28.12E
Kapos r. Hungary 31 46.44N 18.30E
Kaposvár Hungary 31 46.22N 17.47E
Kappar Pakistan 62 25.19N 62.42E
Kappeln Germany 38 54.40N 9.56E
Kappelshamn Sweden 43 57.52N 18.50E
Kapps Namibia 80 22.22S 17.52E
Kapsabet Kenya 79 0.12N 35.05E
Kaptai Bangla. 63 22.21N 92.17E
Kaptol Croatia 31 45.26N 17.44E
Kapuas r. Indonesia 58 0.13S 109.12E
Kapunda Australia 92 34.21S 138.54E
Kapürthala India 62 31.23N 75.23E
Kapuskasing Canada 102 49.25N 82.30W
Kaputar, Mt. Australia 93 30.20S 150.10E
Kapuvár Hungary 37 47.36N 17.02E
Kara Russian Fed. 50 69.12N 65.00E
Kara-Bogaz Gol, Zaliv b. Turkmenistan 65 41.20N 53.40E
Karabük Turkey 64 41.12N 32.36E
Karabutak Kazakhstan 50 49.55N 60.05E
Karáchi Pakistan 62 24.52N 67.03E
Karäd India 60 17.17N 74.12E
Karaganda Kazakhstan 9 49.53N 73.07E
Karaginskiy, Ostrov i. Russian Fed. 51 59.00N 165.00E
Karakas Kazakhstan 52 48.20N 83.30E
Karakelong i. Indonesia 59 4.20N 126.50E
Karakol Kyrgyzstan 52 42.31N 78.22E
Karakoram Pass Asia 61 35.33N 77.51E
Karakoram Range mts. Jammu & Kashmir 60 35.30N 76.30E
Karakoro r. Mauritania 74 14.43N 12.03W
Karaköse see Ağri Turkey 45
Karakumskiy Kanal canal Turkmenistan 65 37.30N 65.48E
Karakumy, Peski f. Turkmenistan 65 37.45N 60.00E
Karakuwisa Namibia 80 18.56S 19.43E
Karaman Turkey 64 37.11N 33.13E
Karamay China 52 45.48N 84.30E
Karamea New Zealand 86 41.15S 172.07E
Karamea Bight b. New Zealand 86 41.15S 171.30E
Karamürsel Turkey 64 40.42N 29.37E
Karand Iran 65 34.16N 46.15E
Käranja India 63 20.29N 77.29E
Karanjia India 63 21.47N 85.58E
Karasburg Namibia 80 28.00S 18.46E
Karasjok Norway 40 69.27N 25.30E
Karasuk Russian Fed. 50 53.45N 78.01E
Karatau, Khrebet mts. Kazakhstan 45 44.15N 52.10E
Karatobe Kazakhstan 45 49.44N 53.30E
Karaton Kazakhstan 45 46.26N 53.32E
Karauli India 62 26.30N 77.01E
Karawa Zaïre 78 3.12N 20.20E
Karawanken mts. Austria 31 46.30N 14.10E
Karazhal Kazakhstan 50 48.00N 70.55E
Karbalä' Iraq 65 32.37N 44.03E
Karcag Hungary 37 47.19N 20.56E
Kardhámaina Greece 35 36.47N 27.09E
Kardhamíla Greece 35 38.34N 26.05E
Kardhítsa Greece 35 39.21N 21.55E
Kärdla Estonia 41 59.00N 22.42E
Kareli India 63 22.55N 79.04E
Karema Tanzania 79 6.50S 30.25E
Karen India 61 12.50N 92.55E
Karepino Russian Fed. 44 61.05N 58.02E
Karesuando Finland 40 68.25N 22.30E
Kargasok Russian Fed. 50 59.07N 80.58E
Kargi Kenya 79 2.31N 37.34E
Kargil Jammu & Kashmir 62 34.34N 76.06E
Kargopol Russian Fed. 44 61.32N 38.59E
Kari Nigeria 77 11.17N 10.35E
Kariaí Greece 34 40.16N 24.15E
Kariba Zimbabwe 80 16.32S 28.50E
Kariba Dam Zimbabwe/Zambia 80 16.15S 28.55E
Kariba, L. Zimbabwe/Zambia 80 16.50S 28.00E
Karibib Namibia 80 21.56S 15.52E
Kärikäl India 61 10.58N 79.50E
Karimama Benin 77 12.02N 3.15E
Karîmganj India 63 24.52N 92.20E
Karin Somali Rep. 71 10.51N 45.45E
Karis Finland 41 60.05N 23.40E
Karisimbi, Mt. Zaïre/Rwanda 79 1.31S 29.25E
Káristos Greece 35 38.01N 24.25E
Kariya Japan 57 34.59N 136.59E
Kariyangwe Zimbabwe 80 17.57S 27.30E
Karkaralinsk Kazakhstan 9 49.21N 75.27E
Karkar I. P.N.G. 59 4.40S 146.00E
Karkas, Küh-e mtn. Iran 65 33.25N 51.40E
Karkheh r. Iran 65 31.45N 47.52E
Karkinitskiy Zaliv g. Ukraine 45 45.50N 32.45E
Karkoo Australia 92 34.02S 135.44E
Karkur Israel 67 32.28N 35.00E
Karlino Poland 36 54.03N 15.51E
Kari-Marx-Stadt see Chemnitz Germany 38
Karlobag Croatia 31 44.32N 15.05E
Karlovac Croatia 31 45.29N 15.34E
Karlovo Bulgaria 34 42.38N 24.48E
Karlovy Vary Czech Republic 39 50.11N 12.52E
Karlsborg Sweden 43 58.32N 14.31E
Karlshamn Sweden 43 56.10N 14.51E
Karlskoga Sweden 43 59.20N 14.31E
Karlskrona Sweden 43 56.10N 15.35E
Karlsruhe Germany 39 49.03N 8.24E
Karlstad Sweden 43 59.22N 13.30E
Karlstad U.S.A. 110 48.35N 96.31W
Karlstadt Germany 39 49.57N 9.45E
Karmah Sudan 72 19.38N 30.25E
Karmel, Har mtn. Israel 67 32.44N 35.02E

Karmi'el Israel 67 32.55N 35.18E
Karmöy i. Norway 42 59.15N 5.15E
Karnafuli Resr. Bangla. 61 22.40N 92.05E
Karnäl India 62 29.41N 76.59E
Karnäli r. Nepal 63 28.45N 81.16E
Karnaphuli Resr. Bangla. 63 22.30N 92.20E
Karnataka d. India 60 14.45N 76.00E
Karnes City U.S.A. 111 28.53N 97.54W
Karnobat Bulgaria 29 42.40N 27.00E
Kärnten d. Austria 39 46.50N 13.30E
Karol Zimbabwe 80 16.51S 29.39E
Karonga Malaŵi 79 9.54S 33.55E
Karonie Australia 89 30.58S 122.32E
Karoonda Australia 92 35.09S 139.54E
Karor Pakistan 62 31.13N 70.57E
Karora Sudan 72 17.42N 38.22E
Káros i. Greece 35 36.54N 25.40E
Karos Dam R.S.A. 80 28.27S 21.39E
Karousádhes Greece 34 39.47N 19.45E
Karpach Moldova 37 48.00N 27.10E
Kárpathos Greece 35 35.40N 27.10E
Kárpathos i. Greece 35 35.40N 27.10E
Karpeníslon Greece 35 38.55N 21.40E
Karpineny Moldova 37 46.46N 28.18E
Karpinsk Russian Fed. 44 59.48N 59.59E
Karpogory Russian Fed. 44 64.01N 44.30E
Karragullen Australia 89 32.05S 116.03E
Karratha Australia 88 20.44S 116.50E
Karridale Australia 89 34.12S 115.04E
Kars Turkey 64 40.35N 43.05E
Karsakpay Kazakhstan 9 47.47N 66.43E
Kärsämaki Finland 40 63.58N 25.46E
Kärsava Russian Fed. 44 56.45N 27.40E
Karskoye More sea Russian Fed. 50 73.00N 65.00E
Karstädt Germany 38 53.09N 11.44E
Kartaly Russian Fed. 50 53.06N 60.37E
Karufa Indonesia 59 3.50S 133.27E
Karumba Australia 90 17.28S 140.50E
Kärün r. Iran 65 30.25N 48.12E
Karunga Kenya 73 1.09S 36.49E
Karungi Sweden 40 66.03N 23.55E
Karungu Kenya 79 0.50S 34.09E
Karup Denmark 42 56.18N 9.10E
Karviná Czech Republic 37 49.50N 18.30E
Kasai r. Zaïre 78 3.10S 16.13E
Kasai Occidental d. Zaïre 78 5.00S 21.30E
Kasaï Oriental d. Zaïre 78 5.00S 24.00E
Kasaji Zaïre 78 10.22S 23.27E
Kasama Zambia 79 10.10S 31.11E
Kasane Botswana 80 17.48S 25.09E
Kasanga Tanzania 79 8.27S 31.10E
Käsaragod India 60 12.30N 75.00E
Kasba India 63 25.51N 87.33E
Kasba L. Canada 101 60.20N 102.10W
Kasba-Tadla Morocco 22 32.34N 6.18W
Kåseberga Sweden 43 55.23N 14.04E
Kasempa Zambia 78 13.28S 25.48E
Kasese Uganda 79 0.07N 30.06E
Käsganj India 63 27.49N 78.39E
Kashi China 52 39.29N 76.02E
Kashin Russian Fed. 44 57.22N 37.39E
Kashipur India 63 29.13N 78.57E
Kashiwa Japan 57 35.52N 139.59E
Käshmar Iran 65 35.12N 58.26E
Kashmor Pakistan 62 28.26N 69.35E
Kasia India 63 26.45N 83.55E
Kasimov Russian Fed. 44 54.55N 41.25E
Kaskaskia r. U.S.A. 111 37.59N 89.56W
Kaskattama r. Canada 101 57.03N 90.07W
Kaskinen Finland 40 62.23N 21.13E
Kaskö see Kaskinen Finland 40
Kaslo Canada 100 49.55N 117.00W
Kasongo Zaïre 78 4.32S 26.33E
Kasongo-Lunda Zaïre 78 6.30S 16.47E
Kásos i. Greece 35 35.22N 26.56E
Kassalä Sudan 72 15.28N 36.24E
Kassalä d. Sudan 72 15.30N 35.00E
Kassándra pen. Greece 34 40.00N 23.30E
Kassel Germany 38 51.19N 9.29E
Kastamonu Turkey 64 41.22N 33.47E
Kastanéaí Greece 34 41.38N 26.28E
Kastl Germany 38 49.22N 11.42E
Kastoria Greece 34 40.30N 21.19E
Kastorías, Límni l. Greece 34 40.30N 21.20E
Kastrávion, Tekhnití Límni l. Greece 35 38.45N 21.20E
Kastrosikiá Greece 35 39.09N 20.36E
Kasugai Japan 57 35.14N 136.58E
Kasukabe Japan 57 35.58N 139.45E
Kasulu Tanzania 79 4.34S 30.06E
Kasumi Japan 57 35.38N 134.38E
Kasungu Malaŵi 79 13.04S 33.29E
Kasür Pakistan 62 31.07N 74.27E
Kataba Zambia 78 16.12S 25.05E
Katako Kombe Zaïre 78 3.27S 24.21E
Katákolon Greece 35 37.38N 21.19E
Katangi India 63 23.27N 79.47E
Katanning Australia 89 33.42S 117.33E
Katanti Zaïre 79 2.19S 27.08E
Katarniän Ghät India 63 28.20N 81.09E
Katchall i. India 61 7.57N 93.22E
Katerini Greece 34 40.16N 22.30E
Katete Zambia 79 14.08S 31.50E
Katha Myanmar 56 24.11N 95.20E
Katherine Australia 90 14.29S 132.20E
Käthgodäm India 63 29.16N 79.32E
Kathia India 62 30.26N 76.47E
Kathmandu Nepal 63 27.42N 85.20E
Kathor India 62 21.18N 72.57E
Kathrabbä Jordan 67 31.08N 35.37E
Kathua Jammu & Kashmir 62 32.22N 75.31E
Kati Mali 76 12.41N 8.04W
Katihär India 63 25.32N 87.35E
Katima Rapids f. Zambia 78 17.15S 24.20E
Katiola Côte d'Ivoire 76 8.10N 5.10W
Kätlang Pakistan 62 34.22N 72.05E

Katlanovo Macedonia 34 41.52N 21.40E
Káto Akhaia Greece 35 38.09N 21.32E
Kätol India 63 21.16N 78.35E
Katonah U.S.A. 115 41.16N 73.41W
Katonga r. Uganda 79 0.03N 30.15E
Katoomba Australia 93 33.42S 150.23E
Katopa Zaïre 78 2.45S 25.06E
Káto Stavrós Greece 34 40.39N 23.43E
Katoúna Greece 35 38.47N 21.07E
Katowice Poland 37 50.15N 18.59E
Kätrïnä, Jabal mtn. Egypt 66 28.30N 33.57E
Katrineholm Sweden 43 59.00N 16.12E
Katrine, Loch U.K. 14 56.15N 4.30W
Katsina Nigeria 77 13.00N 7.32E
Katsina d. Nigeria 77 12.25N 7.55E
Katsina Ala Nigeria 77 7.10N 9.30E
Katsina Ala r. Nigeria 77 7.50N 8.58E
Katsura r. Japan 57 34.53N 135.42E
Katsuura Japan 57 35.08N 140.18E
Kattaviá Greece 35 35.57N 27.46E
Kattegat str. Denmark/Sweden 42 57.25N 11.30E
Katthammarsvik Sweden 43 57.26N 18.50E
Katul, Jabal mtn. Sudan 72 14.16N 29.23E
Katumba Zaïre 78 7.45S 25.18E
Kätwa India 63 23.39N 88.08E
Katwijk aan Zee Neth. 16 52.13N 4.27E
Katzenbuckel mtn. Germany 39 49.28N 9.02E
Katzenfurt Germany 38 50.37N 8.21E
Kauai i. Hawaii U.S.A. 106 22.05N 159.30W
Kaub Germany 39 50.05N 7.46E
Kaufbeuren Germany 39 47.53N 10.37E
Kauhajoki Finland 40 62.26N 22.11E
Kauhava Finland 40 63.06N 23.05E
Kaukauna U.S.A. 110 44.20N 88.16W
Kaukauveld mts. Namibia 80 20.00S 20.15E
Kauliranta Finland 40 66.26N 23.40E
Kaumba Zaïre 78 8.26S 24.40E
Kaunas Lithuania 41 54.54N 23.54E
Kaura Namoda Nigeria 77 12.39N 6.38E
Kautokeino Norway 40 69.00N 23.02E
Kavadarci Macedonia 34 41.26N 22.03E
Kavajë Albania 34 41.11N 19.33E
Kavála Greece 34 40.56N 24.25E
Kävali India 61 14.55N 80.01E
Kavarna Bulgaria 29 43.26N 28.22E
Kavimba Botswana 80 18.05S 24.34E
Kavkaz Russian Fed. 45 45.20N 36.39E
Kävlinge Sweden 43 55.48N 13.06E
Kavungo Angola 78 11.28S 23.01E
Kaw Guiana 123 4.29N 52.02W
Kawachi-nagano Japan 57 34.25N 135.32E
Kawagama L. Canada 104 45.18N 78.45W
Kawagoe Japan 57 35.55N 139.29E
Kawaguchi Japan 57 35.48N 139.43E
Kawambwa Zambia 79 9.47S 29.10E
Kawardha India 63 22.01N 81.15E
Kawartha L. Canada 104 44.40N 78.10W
Kawasaki Japan 57 35.32N 139.43E
Kawerau New Zealand 86 38.05S 176.42E
Kawhia New Zealand 86 38.04S 174.49E
Kawm Sudan 73 13.31N 22.50E
Kawthaung Myanmar 56 10.09N 98.33E
Kaya Burkina 76 13.04N 1.04W
Kayah d. Myanmar 56 19.15N 97.30E
Kayambi Zambia 79 9.26S 32.01E
Kayan r. Indonesia 58 2.47N 117.46E
Kaycee U.S.A. 108 43.43N 106.38W
Kayenta U.S.A. 108 36.44N 110.17W
Kayes Congo 78 4.25S 11.41E
Kayes Mali 76 14.26N 11.28W
Kayes d. Mali 76 14.00N 10.55W
Kayin d. Myanmar 56 17.30N 97.45E
Kayonza Rwanda 73 1.53S 30.31E
Kayseri Turkey 64 38.42N 35.28E
Kaysville U.S.A. 108 41.02N 111.56W
Kazabazua Canada 105 45.56N 76.01W
Kazachye Russian Fed. 51 70.46N 136.15E
Kazakhskiy Zaliv b. Kazakhstan 45 42.43N 52.30E
Kazakhstan Asia 45 48.00N 52.30E
Kazan Russian Fed. 44 55.45N 49.10E
Kazanlük Bulgaria 34 42.38N 25.35E
Kazatin Ukraine 37 49.41N 28.49E
Kazaure Nigeria 77 12.40N 8.25E
Kazbek mtn. Russian Fed. 45 42.42N 44.30E
Käzerün Iran 65 29.35N 51.39E
Kazhim Russian Fed. 44 60.18N 51.34E
Kazima C.A.R. 73 5.16N 26.11E
Kazincbarcika Hungary 37 48.16N 20.37E
Kazo Japan 57 36.07N 139.36E
Kazumba Zaïre 78 6.30S 22.02E
Kbal Dâmrei Cambodia 56 14.03N 105.20E
Kdyně Czech Republic 38 49.23N 13.02E
Kéa Greece 35 37.38N 24.21E
Kéa i. Greece 35 37.34N 24.22E
Kearney U.S.A. 110 40.42N 99.05W
Keban Turkey 64 38.48N 38.45E
Kebbi d. Nigeria 77 11.30N 3.45E
K'ebelë Ethiopia 73 12.52N 40.40E
Kebili Tunisia 75 33.42N 8.58E
Kebnekaise mtn. Sweden 40 67.53N 18.33E
K'ebri Dehar Ethiopia 71 6.47N 44.17E
Kebumen Indonesia 59 7.40S 109.41E
Kecel Hungary 31 46.32N 19.16E
Kech r. Pakistan 62 26.00N 62.44E
Kechika r. Canada 100 59.36N 127.05W
Kecskemét Hungary 37 46.54N 19.42E
Kedada Ethiopia 73 5.20N 36.00E
Kedainiai Lithuania 41 55.17N 24.00E
Kedgwick Canada 103 47.39N 67.21W
Kédhros Greece 35 39.13N 22.03E
Kediri Indonesia 59 7.45S 112.01E
Kédougou Senegal 76 12.35N 12.09W
Keefers Canada 100 50.00N 121.40W
Keele Peak mtn. Canada 98 63.15N 129.50W
Keene Canada 104 44.15N 78.10W
Keene U.S.A. 115 42.56N 72.17W
Keepit, L. Australia 93 30.52S 150.30E
Keer-Weer, C. Australia 90 13.58S 141.30E

Keeseville U.S.A. **105** 44.30N 73.29W
Keetmanshoop Namibia **80** 26.34S 18.07E
Keewatin Canada **102** 49.46N 94.34W
Keewatin d. Canada **99** 65.00N 90.00W
Kefa d. Ethiopia **73** 7.00N 36.30E
Kefallinía i. Greece **35** 38.15N 20.35E
Kefalos Greece **35** 36.45N 27.00E
Kefar 'Eqron Israel **67** 31.51N 34.49E
Kefar Gil'adi Israel **67** 33.15N 35.34E
Kefar Nahum site Israel **67** 32.53N 35.34E
Kefar Sava Israel **67** 32.11N 34.54E
Kefar Szold Israel **67** 33.11N 35.39E
Kefar Tavor Israel **67** 32.41N 35.25E
Kefar Vitkin Israel **67** 32.23N 34.53E
Kefar Yona Israel **67** 32.19N 34.56E
Kefar Zekharya Israel **67** 31.42N 34.57E
Kefar Zetim Israel **67** 32.49N 35.28E
Keffi Nigeria **77** 8.52N 7.53E
Keflavík Iceland **40** 64.01N 22.35W
K'eftya Ethiopia **72** 13.56N 37.13E
Keg River town Canada **100** 57.54N 117.07W
Kehsi Mänsäm Myanmar **56** 21.56N 97.51E
Keighley U.K. **12** 53.52N 1.54W
Keila Estonia **41** 59.18N 24.29E
Keimoes R.S.A. **80** 28.41S 20.58E
Keitele l. Finland **40** 62.55N 26.00E
Keith Australia **92** 36.06S 140.22E
Keith U.K. **14** 57.32N 2.57W
Keith Arm b. Canada **98** 65.20N 122.15W
Kekri India **62** 25.58N 75.09E
Kelang Malaysia **58** 2.57N 101.24E
Kelberg Germany **39** 50.17N 6.55E
Kelem Ethiopia **73** 4.48N 36.06E
Kelheim Germany **39** 48.55N 11.54E
Kelibia Tunisia **32** 36.51N 11.06E
Kelkit r. Turkey **64** 40.46N 36.32E
Kelle Congo **78** 0.05S 14.33E
Keller U.S.A. **108** 48.03N 118.40W
Kellerberrin Australia **89** 31.38S 117.43E
Kellet, C. Canada **98** 71.59N 125.34W
Kelleys I. U.S.A. **114** 41.36N 82.42W
Kelloselkä Finland **44** 66.55N 28.50E
Kells Meath Rep. of Ire. **15** 53.44N 6.53W
Kelme Lithuania **41** 55.38N 22.56E
Kélo Chad **77** 9.21N 15.50E
Kelowna Canada **100** 49.50N 119.25W
Kelso U.K. **14** 55.36N 2.26W
Kelso Calif. U.S.A. **109** 35.01N 115.39W
Kelso Wash. U.S.A. **108** 46.09N 122.54W
Keluang Malaysia **58** 2.01N 103.18E
Kelvedon U.K. **13** 51.50N 0.43E
Kelvington Canada **101** 52.10N 103.30W
Kem Russian Fed. **44** 64.58N 34.39E
Kema Indonesia **59** 1.22N 125.08E
Ke Macina Mali **76** 14.05N 5.20W
Kemah Turkey **64** 39.35N 39.02E
Kemaliye Turkey **64** 39.16N 38.29E
Kemano Canada **100** 53.35N 128.00W
Kembolcha Ethiopia **73** 11.02N 39.43E
Kemerovo Russian Fed. **50** 55.25N 86.10E
Kemi Finland **40** 65.49N 24.32E
Kemi r. Finland **40** 65.47N 24.30E
Kemijärvi Finland **40** 66.36N 27.24E
Kemmerer U.S.A. **108** 41.48N 110.32W
Kemnath Germany **38** 49.52N 11.54E
Kempen l. Belgium **16** 51.05N 5.00E
Kemp Land f. Antarctica **128** 69.00S 57.00E
Kempsey Australia **93** 31.05S 152.50E
Kempten Germany **39** 47.43N 10.19E
Kempt, Lac l. Canada **105** 47.74N 74.22W
Kemptville Canada **105** 45.01N 75.38W
Ken r. India **63** 25.46N 80.31E
Kenai U.S.A. **98** 60.33N 151.15W
Kenai Pen. U.S.A. **96** 64.40N 150.18W
Kenamuke Swamp Sudan **73** 5.55N 33.48E
Kenaston Canada **101** 51.30N 106.18W
Kendal India **63** 22.45N 82.37E
Kendal Indonesia **59** 6.56S 110.14E
Kendal U.K. **12** 54.19N 2.44W
Kendall Australia **93** 31.28S 152.40E
Kendall U.S.A. **114** 43.20N 78.02W
Kendari Indonesia **59** 3.57S 122.36E
Kendenup Australia **89** 34.28S 117.35E
Kendrāpāra India **63** 20.30N 86.25E
Kendrick U.S.A. **108** 46.37N 116.39W
Kenebri Australia **93** 30.45S 149.02E
Kenema Sierra Leone **76** 7.57N 11.11W
Kenge Zaïre **78** 4.56S 17.04E
Kengeja Tanzania **79** 5.24S 39.45E
Keng Tung Myanmar **56** 21.16N 99.39E
Kenhardt R.S.A. **80** 29.21S 21.08E
Kenilworth U.K. **13** 52.22N 1.35W
Kenitra Morocco **74** 34.20N 6.34W
Kenli China **54** 37.35N 118.34E
Kenmare Rep. of Ire. **15** 51.53N 9.36W
Kenmare U.S.A. **110** 48.40N 102.05W
Kenmore U.S.A. **114** 42.58N 78.53W
Kennebec r. U.S.A. **112** 44.00N 69.50W
Kennebunk U.S.A. **115** 43.23N 70.33W
Kenner U.S.A. **113** 29.59N 90.15W
Kennet r. U.K. **13** 51.28N 0.57W
Kennett Square U.S.A. **115** 39.51N 75.43W
Kennewick U.S.A. **108** 46.12N 119.07W
Kenogami r. Canada **102** 50.24N 84.20W
Keno Hill town Canada **98** 63.58N 135.22W
Kenora Canada **102** 49.47N 94.29W
Kenosha U.S.A. **112** 42.35N 87.49W
Kenozero, Ozero l. Russian Fed. **44** 62.20N 37.00E
Kent d. U.K. **13** 51.12N 0.40E
Kent Ohio U.S.A. **114** 41.09N 81.22W
Kent Tex. U.S.A. **109** 31.04N 104.13W
Kent Wash. U.S.A. **108** 47.23N 122.14W
Kentau Kazakhstan **9** 43.28N 68.36E
Kentland U.S.A. **112** 40.46N 87.26W
Kenton U.S.A. **112** 40.38N 83.38W
Kent Pen. Canada **98** 68.30N 107.00W
Kentucky r. U.S.A. **113** 37.30N 85.15W
Kentucky r. U.S.A. **113** 38.40N 85.09W

Kentucky L. U.S.A. **111** 36.25N 88.05W
Kentville Canada **103** 45.05N 64.30W
Kenya Africa **79** 1.00N 38.00E
Kenya, Mt. see Kirinyaga mtn. Kenya **79**
Keokuk U.S.A. **110** 40.24N 91.24W
Keonjhargarh India **63** 21.38N 85.35E
Kepi Indonesia **59** 6.32S 139.19E
Kepno Poland **37** 51.17N 17.59E
Keppel B. Australia **90** 23.21S 150.55E
Kerala d. India **60** 10.30N 76.30E
Kerang Australia **92** 35.42S 143.59E
Keratéa Greece **35** 37.48N 23.59E
Kerch Ukraine **45** 45.22N 36.27E
Kerch Strait str. Ukraine/Russian Fed. **45** 45.15N 36.35E
Kerema P.N.G. **59** 7.59S 145.46E
Kerem Ben Zimra Israel **67** 33.02N 35.28E
Kerem Maharal Israel **67** 32.39N 34.59E
Keren Eritrea **72** 15.46N 38.28E
Kerguelen Basin f. Indian Oc. **49** 35.00S 65.00E
Kerguelen-Gaussberg Ridge f. Indian Oc. **49** 55.00S 75.00E
Kerguelen, Îles de is. Indian Oc. **49** 49.15S 69.10E
Kericho Kenya **79** 0.22S 35.19E
Kerinci, Gunung mtn. Indonesia **58** 1.45S 101.20E
Kerio r. Kenya **79** 3.00N 36.14E
Keríon Greece **35** 37.40N 20.48E
Kerkebet Eritrea **72** 16.13N 37.30E
Kerkenna, Îles is. Tunisia **75** 34.44N 11.12E
Kerki Russian Fed. **44** 63.40N 54.00E
Kerki Turkmenistan **57** 37.53N 65.10E
Kerkinitis, Límni l. Greece **34** 41.10N 23.08E
Kérkira Greece **34** 39.36N 19.56E
Kérkira i. Greece **34** 39.40N 19.42E
Kerkrade Neth. **16** 50.52N 6.02E
Kermadec Is. Pacific Oc. **84** 30.00S 178.30W
Kermadec Trench Pacific Oc. **84** 33.30S 176.00W
Kermän Iran **65** 30.18N 57.05E
Kermänshäh see Bäkhtarän Iran **65**
Kerme Körfezi g. Turkey **35** 36.50N 28.00E
Kermit U.S.A. **111** 31.51N 103.06W
Kerouane Guinea **76** 9.16N 9.00W
Kerpen Germany **16** 50.52N 6.42E
Kerrobert Canada **101** 51.55N 109.08W
Kerrville U.S.A. **111** 30.03N 99.08W
Kerry d. Rep. of Ire. **15** 52.07N 9.35W
Kerry Head Rep. of Ire. **15** 52.24N 9.56W
Kerteminde Denmark **42** 55.27N 10.40E
Kerulen r. Mongolia **53** 48.45N 117.00E
Kesagami L. Canada **102** 50.23N 80.15W
Keşan Turkey **34** 40.51N 26.37E
Keshod India **63** 20.03N 81.34E
Keski-Suomi d. Finland **40** 62.30N 25.30E
Keswick U.K. **12** 54.35N 3.09W
Keszthely Hungary **31** 46.46N 17.15E
Ketapang Jawa Indonesia **59** 6.56S 113.14E
Ketapang Kalimantan Indonesia **58** 1.50S 110.02E
Ketchikan U.S.A. **100** 55.25N 131.40W
Ketchum U.S.A. **108** 43.41N 114.22W
Kete Krachi Ghana **76** 7.50N 0.03W
Keti Bandar Pakistan **62** 24.08N 67.27E
Ketrzyn Poland **37** 54.06N 21.23E
Kettering U.K. **13** 52.24N 0.44W
Kettering U.S.A. **112** 39.41N 84.10W
Kettle r. Canada **101** 56.55N 89.25W
Kettle Falls town U.S.A. **108** 48.36N 118.03W
Kettle Pt. Canada **104** 43.11N 82.01W
Keuka L. U.S.A. **114** 42.27N 77.10W
Keweenaw B. U.S.A. **112** 46.46N 88.26W
Keweenaw Pen. U.S.A. **112** 47.10N 88.30W
Keyala Sudan **73** 4.27N 32.52E
Key Harbour Canada **104** 45.53N 80.44W
Key, Lough Rep. of Ire. **15** 54.00N 8.15W
Keynsham U.K. **13** 51.25N 2.30W
Key West U.S.A. **113** 24.33N 81.48W
Kezhma Russian Fed. **51** 58.58N 101.08E
Kežmarok Slovakia **37** 49.08N 20.25E
Kgalagadi d. Botswana **80** 25.00S 21.30E
Kgatleng d. Botswana **80** 24.20S 26.20E
Khaanziir, Ras c. Somali Rep. **71** 10.55N 45.47E
Khabab Syria **67** 33.01N 36.16E
Khabarovsk Russian Fed. **53** 48.32N 135.08E
Khairāgarh India **63** 21.25N 80.58E
Khairpur Punjab Pakistan **62** 29.35N 72.14E
Khairpur Sind Pakistan **62** 27.32N 68.46E
Khajrāho India **63** 24.50N 79.58E
Khalatse Jammu & Kashmir **62** 34.20N 76.49E
Khalkhāl Iran **65** 37.36N 48.36E
Khálki Greece **34** 39.36N 22.30E
Khálki i. Greece **35** 36.17N 27.35E
Khalkidhikí f. Greece **23** 40.25N 23.27E
Khalkís Greece **35** 38.28N 23.36E
Khalmer Yu Russian Fed. **44** 67.58N 64.48E
Khālsar Jammu & Kashmir **63** 34.31N 77.41E
Khalūf Oman **60** 20.31N 58.04E
Khambhāliya India **62** 22.12N 69.39E
Khambhat, G. of India **62** 20.30N 71.45E
Khāmgaon India **62** 20.41N 76.34E
Khamkeut Laos **58** 18.14N 104.44E
Khānaqin Iraq **65** 34.22N 45.22E
Khān az Zabīb Jordan **67** 31.28N 36.06E
Khandela India **62** 27.36N 75.30E
Khandwa India **62** 21.50N 76.20E
Khäneh Khvodī Iran **65** 36.05N 56.04E
Khānewāl Pakistan **62** 30.18N 71.56E
Khāngarh Punjab Pakistan **62** 29.55N 71.10E
Khāngarh Punjab Pakistan **62** 28.22N 71.43E
Khanh Hung Vietnam **56** 9.36N 105.55E
Khaniá Greece **35** 35.31N 24.02E
Khaníon, Kólpos g. Greece **35** 35.34N 23.48E
Khanka, Ozero l. Russian Fed. **53** 45.00N 132.30E
Khanna India **62** 30.42N 76.14E
Khannā, Qā' f. Jordan **67** 32.04N 36.26E
Khānozai Russian Fed. **62** 30.37N 67.19E
Khānpur Pakistan **62** 28.39N 70.39E
Khanty-Mansiysk Russian Fed. **50** 61.00N 69.00E

Khān Yūnus Egypt **67** 31.21N 34.18E
Khapalu Jammu & Kashmir **62** 35.10N 76.20E
Khapcheranga Russian Fed. **53** 49.46N 112.20E
Kharagpur India **63** 22.20N 87.20E
Khārān r. Iran **65** 27.37N 58.48E
Khārān Pakistan **62** 28.35N 65.25E
Kharbatā Jordan **67** 31.57N 35.04E
Khargon India **62** 21.49N 75.36E
Khāriān Pakistan **62** 32.49N 73.52E
Khariār Road town India **63** 20.54N 82.31E
Khārijah, Al Wāḩāt al oasis Egypt **64** 24.55N 30.35E
Kharkov Ukraine **45** 50.00N 36.15E
Khār Kūh mtn. Iran **65** 31.37N 53.47E
Kharmanli Bulgaria **34** 41.56N 25.54E
Kharovsk Russian Fed. **44** 59.67N 40.07E
Khartoum see Al Kharţūm Sudan **72**
Kharutayuvam Russian Fed. **44** 66.51N 59.31E
Khasavyurt Russian Fed. **45** 43.16N 46.36E
Khāsh Afghan. **62** 31.31N 62.52E
Khāsh r. Afghan. **62** 31.11N 61.50E
Khāsh Iran **65** 28.14N 61.15E
Khāsh, Dasht-e des. Afghan. **62** 31.50N 62.30E
Khashgort Russian Fed. **44** 65.25N 65.40E
Khashm al Qirbah Sudan **72** 14.58N 35.55E
Khaskovo Bulgaria **34** 41.56N 25.33E
Khaskovo d. Bulgaria **34** 41.57N 25.32E
Khatanga Russian Fed. **51** 71.50N 102.31E
Khatangskiy Zaliv g. Russian Fed. **51** 75.00N 112.10E
Khāvda India **62** 23.51N 69.43E
Khawr Barakah r. Sudan **72** 18.13N 37.35E
Khemisset Morocco **74** 33.50N 6.03W
Khemmarat Thailand **56** 16.00N 105.10E
Khenchela Algeria **75** 35.26N 7.08E
Khenifra Morocco **74** 33.00N 5.40W
Khersān r. Iran **65** 31.29N 48.53E
Kherson Ukraine **45** 46.39N 32.38E
Kherwāra India **62** 23.59N 73.35E
Khetia India **62** 21.40N 74.35E
Khewāri Pakistan **62** 26.36N 68.52E
Khiliomódhion Greece **35** 37.48N 22.51E
Khíos Greece **35** 38.22N 26.08E
Khíos i. Greece **35** 38.22N 26.00E
Khipro Pakistan **62** 25.50N 69.22E
Khirbat al Ghazālah Syria **67** 32.44N 36.12E
Khisfin Syria **67** 32.51N 35.47E
Khiva Uzbekistan **65** 41.25N 60.49E
Khmelnik Ukraine **37** 49.36N 27.59E
Khmelnitskiy Ukraine **37** 49.25N 26.49E
Khodorov Ukraine **37** 49.20N 24.19E
Khogali Sudan **73** 6.08N 27.47E
Khok Kloi Thailand **56** 8.19N 98.18E
Kholm Russian Fed. **44** 57.10N 31.11E
Kholmogory Russian Fed. **44** 63.51N 41.46E
Khomas-Hochland mts. Namibia **80** 22.50S 16.25E
Khondmāl Hills India **63** 20.15N 84.00E
Khonu Russian Fed. **51** 66.29N 143.12E
Khoper r. Russian Fed. **45** 49.35N 42.17E
Khorāl India **62** 26.30N 71.14E
Khóra Greece **35** 37.03N 21.42E
Khóra Sfakíon Greece **35** 35.12N 24.09E
Khorixas Namibia **80** 20.24S 14.58E
Khorog Tajikistan **52** 37.32N 71.32E
Khorramābād Iran **65** 33.29N 48.21E
Khorramshahr Iran **65** 30.26N 48.09E
Khotimsk Belarus **37** 53.24N 32.36E
Khotin Ukraine **37** 48.30N 26.31E
Khouribga Morocco **74** 32.54N 6.57W
Khowai India **63** 24.06N 91.38E
Khowrnag, Küh-e mtn. Iran **65** 32.10N 54.38E
Khowst Afghan. **62** 33.22N 69.57E
Khoyniki Belarus **37** 51.54N 30.00E
Khrisoúpolis Greece **34** 40.58N 24.42E
Khudzhand Tajikistan **52** 40.14N 69.40E
Khugiāni Afghan. **62** 31.33N 66.15E
Khūgiāni Šānī Afghan. **62** 31.31N 66.12E
Khūlāla India **62** 27.15N 70.25E
Khuis Botswana **80** 26.37S 21.45E
Khulga r. Russian Fed. **44** 63.33N 61.53E
Khulna Bangla. **63** 22.48N 89.33E
Khumbur Khule Ghar mtn. Afghan. **62** 33.05N 69.00E
Khunti India **63** 23.05N 85.17E
Khurai India **63** 24.03N 78.19E
Khurda India **63** 20.11N 85.37E
Khurja India **62** 28.15N 77.51E
Khurli Pakistan **62** 28.59N 65.52E
Khurra Bārīk r. Iraq **64** 32.00N 44.15E
Khurr, Wādī al r. Iraq **71** 31.02N 42.00E
Khushāb Pakistan **62** 32.18N 72.21E
Khust Ukraine **37** 48.11N 23.19E
Khuwayy Sudan **73** 13.05N 29.14E
Khuzdär Pakistan **62** 27.48N 66.37E
Khvājeh Ra'ūf Afghan. **62** 33.19N 64.43E
Khvor Iran **65** 33.47N 55.06E
Khvormuj Iran **65** 28.40N 51.20E
Khvoy Iran **65** 38.32N 45.02E
Khyber Pass Afghan./Pakistan **62** 34.06N 71.05E
Kiama Australia **93** 34.41S 150.49E
Kiamika Canada **105** 46.33S 151.50E
Kiáton Greece **35** 38.01N 22.45E
Kibaek Denmark **42** 56.02N 8.51E
Kibali r. Zaïre **79** 3.37N 28.38E
Kibamba Zaïre **78** 4.53S 26.33E
Kibar India **63** 32.20N 78.01E
Kibenga Zaïre **78** 7.55S 17.35E
Kibombo Zaïre **78** 3.58S 25.57E
Kibondo Tanzania **79** 3.35S 30.41E
Kibre Mengist Ethiopia **73** 5.52N 39.00E
Kibungu Rwanda **79** 2.10S 30.31E
Kibwesa Tanzania **79** 6.30S 29.57E
Kibwezi Kenya **79** 2.28S 37.57E
Kičevo Macedonia **34** 41.34N 20.59E
Kichiga Russian Fed. **51** 59.50N 163.27E
Kicking Horse Pass Canada **100** 51.27N 116.25W
Kidal Mali **77** 18.27N 1.25E
Kidderminster U.K. **13** 52.24N 2.13W
Kidete Morogoro Tanzania **79** 6.39S 36.42E
Kidsgrove U.K. **12** 53.06N 2.15W
Kiefersfelden Austria **39** 47.37N 12.11E

Kiel Germany **38** 54.20N 10.08E
Kiel Canal see Nord-Ostsee-Kanal Germany **38**
Kielce Poland **37** 50.52N 20.37E
Kielder resr. U.K. **12** 55.12N 2.30W
Kieler Bucht b. Germany **38** 54.35N 10.35E
Kiev see Kiyev Ukraine **37**
Kiffa Mauritania **74** 16.38N 11.28W
Kifisiá Greece **35** 38.04N 23.49E
Kifissós r. Greece **35** 38.30N 23.00E
Kigali Rwanda **79** 1.59S 30.05E
Kiglapatt, C. Canada **103** 57.05N 61.05W
Kigoma Tanzania **79** 4.52S 29.36E
Kigoma d. Tanzania **79** 4.45S 30.00E
Kigosi r. Tanzania **79** 4.37S 31.29E
Kiiminkin r. Finland **40** 65.12N 25.18E
Kii sanchi mts. Japan **57** 34.00N 135.20E
Kii suidō str. Japan **57** 34.00N 135.00E
Kikinda Yugo. **37** 45.51N 20.30E
Kikládhes is. Greece **35** 37.30N 25.00E
Kikongo Zaïre **78** 4.16S 17.11E
Kikori P.N.G. **59** 7.25S 144.13E
Kikori r. P.N.G. **59** 7.10S 144.05E
Kikwissi, L. Canada **104** 47.00N 78.30W
Kikwit Zaïre **78** 5.02S 18.51E
Kil Sweden **43** 59.30N 13.19E
Kilafors Sweden **41** 61.14N 16.34E
Kila Kila P.N.G. **59** 9.31S 147.10E
Kilchu N. Korea **53** 40.55N 129.21E
Kilcoy Australia **91** 26.57S 152.33E
Kilcullen Rep. of Ire. **15** 53.08N 6.46W
Kildare Rep. of Ire. **15** 53.10N 6.55W
Kildare d. Rep. of Ire. **15** 53.10N 6.50W
Kildonan Zimbabwe **80** 17.22S 30.33E
Kilfinan U.K. **14** 55.58N 5.18W
Kilgore U.S.A. **111** 32.23N 94.53W
Kilifi Kenya **79** 3.30S 39.50E
Kilimanjaro d. Tanzania **79** 3.45S 37.40E
Kilimanjaro mtn. Tanzania **79** 3.02S 37.20E
Kilindoni Tanzania **79** 7.55S 39.39E
Kilingi-Nõmme Estonia **41** 58.09N 24.58E
Kilis Turkey **64** 36.43N 37.07E
Kiliya Ukraine **37** 45.30N 29.16E
Kilkee Rep. of Ire. **15** 52.41N 9.40W
Kilkenny Rep. of Ire. **15** 52.39N 7.16W
Kilkenny d. Rep. of Ire. **15** 52.51N 7.15W
Kilkieran B. Rep. of Ire. **15** 53.20N 9.42W
Kilkís Greece **34** 41.00N 22.53E
Killala B. Rep. of Ire. **15** 54.15N 9.10W
Killaloe Canada **105** 45.33N 77.25W
Killard Pt. U.K. **15** 54.19N 5.31W
Killarney Australia **93** 28.18S 152.15E
Killarney Man. Canada **101** 49.12N 99.42W
Killarney Ont. Canada **104** 45.58N 81.31W
Killarney Rep. of Ire. **15** 52.04N 9.32W
Killarney Prov. Park Canada **104** 46.05N 81.30W
Killary Harbour est. Rep. of Ire. **15** 53.38N 9.56W
Killdeer U.S.A. **108** 47.22N 102.45W
Killeen U.S.A. **111** 31.08N 97.44W
Killin U.K. **14** 56.28N 4.19W
Killíni Greece **35** 37.55N 21.09E
Killíni mtn. Greece **35** 37.57N 22.23E
Killorglin Rep. of Ire. **15** 52.07N 9.45W
Killybegs Rep. of Ire. **15** 54.38N 8.27W
Killyleagh U.K. **15** 54.24N 5.39W
Kilmarnock U.K. **14** 55.37N 4.30W
Kilmichael Pt. Rep. of Ire. **15** 52.44N 6.09W
Kilmore Australia **93** 37.18S 144.58E
Kilninver U.K. **14** 56.21N 5.30W
Kilombero r. Tanzania **79** 8.30S 37.28E
Kilosa Tanzania **79** 6.49S 37.00E
Kilronan Rep. of Ire. **15** 53.08N 9.41W
Kilrush Rep. of Ire. **15** 52.39N 9.30W
Kilsyth U.K. **14** 55.59N 4.04W
Kilvo Sweden **40** 66.50N 21.04E
Kilwa Kivinje Tanzania **79** 8.45S 39.21E
Kilwa Masoko Tanzania **79** 8.55S 39.31E
Kimaan Indonesia **59** 7.54S 138.51E
Kimba Australia **92** 33.09S 136.25E
Kimball U.S.A. **110** 41.14N 103.40W
Kimberley Canada **100** 49.40N 115.59W
Kimberley R.S.A. **80** 28.44S 24.44E
Kimberley Plateau Australia **88** 17.20S 127.20E
Kimch'aek N. Korea **57** 40.41N 129.12E
Kími Greece **35** 38.38N 24.06E
Kimito i. Finland **41** 60.10N 22.30E
Kímolos i. Greece **35** 36.47N 24.35E
Kimparana Mali **76** 12.52N 4.59W
Kimry Russian Fed. **44** 56.51N 37.20E
Kimsquit Canada **100** 52.45N 126.57W
Kinabalu mtn. Malaysia **58** 6.10N 116.40E
Kincaid Canada **101** 49.39N 107.00W
Kincardine Canada **104** 44.11N 81.38W
Kindersley Canada **101** 51.27N 109.10W
Kindia Guinea **76** 10.03N 12.49W
Kindu Zaïre **78** 3.00S 25.56E
Kinel Russian Fed. **44** 53.17N 50.42E
Kineshma Russian Fed. **44** 57.28N 42.08E
Kingaroy Australia **90** 26.33S 151.50E
King City U.S.A. **109** 36.13N 121.08W
Kingcome Inlet town Canada **100** 50.58N 125.15W
King Edward r. Australia **88** 14.12S 126.34E
King George Is. Canada **102** 57.20N 78.25W
King George Sd. Australia **89** 35.03S 117.57E
King I. Australia **91** 39.50S 144.00E
King I. Canada **100** 52.10N 127.40W
King Leopold Range mts. Australia **88** 17.00S 125.30E
Kingman Ariz. U.S.A. **109** 35.12N 114.04W
Kingman Kans. U.S.A. **111** 37.39N 98.07W
Kingman Reef Pacific Oc. **84** 6.24N 162.22W
Kingoonya Australia **92** 30.54S 135.18E
Kingri Pakistan **62** 30.27N 69.49E
Kings r. U.S.A. **109** 36.03N 119.49W
Kingsbridge U.K. **13** 50.17N 3.46W
Kings Canyon Australia **90** 24.15S 131.33E
Kings Canyon Nat. Park U.S.A. **108** 36.48N 118.30W
Kingsclere U.K. **13** 51.20N 1.14W
Kingscote Australia **92** 35.40S 137.38E
King Sd. Australia **88** 17.00S 123.30E

Kingsdown Kent U.K. **13** 51.21N 0.17E
Kingsley Dam U.S.A. **106** 41.15N 101.30W
King's Lynn U.K. **12** 52.45N 0.25E
Kingsmill Group *is.* Kiribati **84** 1.00S 175.00E
Kings Peaks *mts.* U.S.A. **108** 40.46N 110.23W
Kingsport U.S.A. **113** 36.33N 82.34W
Kingston Canada **105** 44.14N 76.30W
Kingston Jamaica **117** 17.58N 76.48W
Kingston New Zealand **86** 45.20S 168.43E
Kingston N.H. U.S.A. **115** 42.55N 71.02W
Kingston N.Y. U.S.A. **115** 41.56N 74.00W
Kingston Penn. U.S.A. **115** 41.16N 75.54W
Kingston W.Va. U.S.A. **113** 37.58N 81.19W
Kingston S.E. Australia **92** 36.50S 139.50E
Kingston upon Hull U.K. **12** 53.45N 0.20W
Kingstown St. Vincent **117** 13.12N 61.14W
Kingstree U.S.A. **113** 33.40N 79.50W
Kingsville Canada **104** 42.02N 82.45W
Kingsville U.S.A. **111** 27.31N 97.52W
Kingswood Avon U.K. **13** 51.27N 2.29W
Kings Worthy U.K. **13** 51.06N 1.18W
Kington U.K. **13** 52.12N 3.02W
Kingurutik *r.* Canada **103** 56.49N 62.00W
Kingussie U.K. **14** 57.05N 4.04W
King William I. Canada **99** 69.00N 97.30W
King William's Town R.S.A. **80** 32.52S 27.23E
Kingwood U.S.A. **114** 39.28N 79.41W
Kinki *d.* Japan **57** 35.10N 135.00E
Kinloch Rannoch U.K. **14** 56.42N 4.11W
Kinmount Canada **104** 44.47N 78.39W
Kinna Sweden **43** 57.30N 12.41E
Kinnairds Head U.K. **14** 57.42N 2.00W
Kinnegad Rep. of Ire. **15** 53.28N 7.08W
Kinnekulle *hill* Sweden **43** 58.35N 13.23E
Kinneret Israel **67** 32.44N 35.34E
Kinneret-Negev Conduit *canal* Israel **67** 32.52N
35.32E
Kino *r.* Japan **57** 34.13N 135.09E
Kinross U.K. **14** 56.13N 3.27W
Kinsale Rep. of Ire. **15** 51.42N 8.32W
Kinshasa Zaïre **78** 4.18S 15.18E
Kinsley U.S.A. **111** 37.55N 99.25W
Kintyre *pen.* U.K. **14** 55.35N 5.35W
Kinuso Canada **100** 55.25N 115.25W
Kinvara Rep. of Ire. **15** 53.08N 8.56W
Kinyeti *mtn.* Sudan **73** 3.57N 32.54E
Kinzia Zaïre **78** 3.36S 18.26E
Kiosk Canada **104** 46.06N 78.53W
Kiowa Kans. U.S.A. **111** 37.01N 98.29W
Kiowa Okla. U.S.A. **111** 34.43N 95.54W
Kiparissía Greece **35** 37.15N 21.40E
Kiparissiakós Kólpos *g.* Greece **35** 37.14N 21.40E
Kipawa Canada **104** 46.47N 79.00W
Kipawa, Lac *l.* Canada **104** 46.55N 79.00W
Kipawa Prov. Park Canada **104** 47.15N 78.15W
Kipengere Range *mts.* Tanzania **79** 9.15S 34.15E
Kipili Tanzania **79** 7.30S 30.39E
Kipini Kenya **79** 2.31S 40.32E
Kippure *mtn.* Rep. of Ire. **15** 53.11N 6.20W
Kipungo Angola **78** 14.49S 14.34E
Kipushi Zaïre **79** 11.46S 27.15E
Kirby U.S.A. **108** 43.49N 108.10W
Kirbyville U.S.A. **111** 30.40N 93.54W
Kirchbach in Steiermark Austria **31** 46.54N 15.44E
Kircheimbolanden Germany **39** 49.39N 8.00E
Kirchheim Germany **39** 48.39N 9.27E
Kirchmöser Germany **38** 52.22N 12.25E
Kirensk Russian Fed. **51** 57.45N 108.00E
Kirghizia *see* Kyrgyzstan Asia **52**
Kirgiziya Step *f.* Kazakhstan **45** 50.00N 57.10E
Kirgiz Steppe *see* Kirgiziya Step *f.* Kazakhstan **45**
Kiri Zaïre **78** 1.23S 19.00E
Kiribati Pacific Oc. **84** 6.00S 170.00W
Kirikkale Turkey **64** 39.51N 33.32E
Kirillov Russian Fed. **44** 59.53N 38.21E
Kirínia Cyprus **66** 35.20N 33.20E
Kirinyaga *mtn.* Kenya **79** 0.10S 37.19E
Kiritimati *i.* Kiribati **85** 1.52N 157.20W
Kirkby Lonsdale U.K. **12** 54.13N 2.36W
Kirkby Stephen U.K. **12** 54.27N 2.23W
Kirkcaldy U.K. **14** 56.07N 3.10W
Kirkcudbright U.K. **14** 54.50N 4.03W
Kirkenes Norway **40** 69.40N 30.03E
Kirkfield Canada **104** 44.33N 79.00W
Kirkland Ariz. U.S.A. **109** 34.26N 112.43W
Kirkland Wash. U.S.A. **108** 47.41N 122.12W
Kirkland Lake *town* Canada **102** 48.15N 80.00W
Kirklareli Turkey **29** 41.44N 27.12E
Kirkpatrick, Mt. Antarctica **128** 85.00S 170.00E
Kirksville U.S.A. **110** 40.12N 92.35W
Kirkūk Iraq **65** 35.28N 44.26E
Kirkwall U.K. **14** 58.59N 2.58W
Kirkwood R.S.A. **80** 33.25S 25.24E
Kirkwood U.S.A. **110** 38.35N 90.24W
Kirn Germany **39** 49.47N 7.28E
Kirov Russian Fed. **44** 53.59N 34.20E
Kirovakan Armenia **65** 40.49N 44.30E
Kirovo-Chepetsk Russian Fed. **44** 58.40N 50.02E
Kirovograd Ukraine **45** 48.31N 32.15E
Kirovsk Russian Fed. **44** 67.37N 33.39E
Kirovskiy Russian Fed. **51** 54.25N 155.37E
Kirriemuir Canada **101** 51.56N 110.20W
Kirriemuir U.K. **14** 56.41N 3.01W
Kirs Russian Fed. **44** 59.21N 52.10E
Kirsanov Kazakhstan **45** 51.29N 52.30E
Kirşehir Turkey **64** 39.09N 34.08E
Kirthar Range *mts.* Pakistan **62** 27.15N 67.00E
Kiruna Sweden **40** 67.51N 20.16E
Kiryu Japan **57** 36.26N 139.18E
Kisa Sweden **43** 57.59N 15.37E
Kisaga Tanzania **79** 4.26S 34.26E
Kisangani Zaïre **78** 0.33N 25.14E
Kisantu Zaïre **78** 5.07S 15.05E
Kisaran Indonesia **58** 2.47N 99.29E
Kisarazu Japan **57** 35.23N 139.55E
Kiselevsk Russian Fed. **50** 54.01N 86.41E
Kishanganj India **63** 26.07N 87.56E
Kishangarh Räj. India **62** 26.34N 74.52E

Kishangarh Räj. India **62** 27.52N 70.34E
Kishinev Moldova **37** 47.00N 28.50E
Kishiwada Japan **57** 34.28N 135.22E
Kishorganj Bangla. **63** 24.26N 90.46E
Kishtwār Jammu & Kashmir **62** 33.19N 75.46E
Kisii Kenya **79** 0.40S 34.44E
Kisiju Tanzania **79** 7.23S 39.20E
Kiskitto L. Canada **101** 54.16N 98.34W
Kiskőrös Hungary **31** 46.38N 19.17E
Kiskunfélegyháza Hungary **31** 46.43N 19.52E
Kiskunhalas Hungary **31** 46.26N 19.30E
Kiskunmajsa Hungary **31** 46.30N 19.45E
Kislovodsk Russian Fed. **45** 43.56N 42.44E
Kismaayo Somali Rep. **79** 0.25S 42.31E
Kiso Japan **57** 35.02N 136.45E
Kiso sammyaku *mts.* Japan **57** 35.42N 137.50E
Kissamos Greece **35** 35.20N 23.38E
Kissidougou Guinea **76** 9.48N 10.08W
Kissimmee U.S.A. **113** 28.20N 81.24W
Kississing L. Canada **101** 55.10N 101.20W
Kissū, Jabal *mtn.* Sudan **72** 21.35N 25.09E
Kistanje Croatia **31** 43.59N 15.58E
Kistna *r. see* Krishna *r.* India **60**
Kisumu Kenya **79** 0.07S 34.47E
Kisvárda Hungary **37** 48.13N 22.05E
Kita Mali **76** 13.04N 9.29W
Kitab Uzbekistan **50** 39.08N 66.51E
Kitabu Zaïre **78** 6.31S 26.40E
Kitakyūshū Japan **57** 33.50N 130.50E
Kitale Kenya **79** 1.01N 35.01E
Kit Carson U.S.A. **110** 38.46N 102.48W
Kitchener Australia **89** 31.01S 124.20E
Kitchener Canada **104** 43.27N 80.29W
Kitchigama *r.* Canada **102** 51.12N 78.55W
Kitgum Uganda **79** 3.17N 32.54E
Kíthira Greece **35** 36.09N 23.00E
Kíthira *i.* Greece **35** 36.20N 22.58E
Kíthnos Greece **35** 37.26N 24.26E
Kíthnos *i.* Greece **35** 37.25N 24.28E
Kitikmeot *d.* Canada **98** 80.00N 105.00W
Kitimat Canada **100** 54.05N 128.38W
Kitinen *r.* Finland **40** 67.20N 27.27E
Kítros Greece **34** 40.22N 22.34E
Kitsman Ukraine **37** 48.30N 25.50E
Kittakitaooloo, L. Australia **92** 28.09S 138.09E
Kittanning U.S.A. **114** 40.49N 79.32W
Kittery U.S.A. **115** 43.05N 70.45W
Kittilä Finland **40** 67.40N 24.54E
Kitui Kenya **79** 1.22S 38.01E
Kitunda Tanzania **79** 6.48S 33.17E
Kitwe Zambia **79** 12.50S 28.04E
Kitzbühel Austria **39** 47.27N 12.23E
Kitzingen Germany **39** 49.44N 10.09E
Kiumbi Zaïre **78** 5.31S 26.34E
Kiunga Kenya **79** 1.46S 41.30E
Kivijärvi *l.* Finland **40** 63.10N 25.09E
Kivik Sweden **43** 55.41N 14.15E
Kivotós Greece **34** 40.13N 21.26E
Kivu *d.* Zaïre **79** 3.00S 27.00E
Kivu, L. Rwanda/Zaïre **79** 2.00S 29.10E
Kiyev Ukraine **37** 50.28N 30.29E
Kiyevskoye Vodokhranilishche *resr.* Ukraine **37**
51.00N 30.25E
Kizel Russian Fed. **44** 59.01N 57.42E
Kizema Russian Fed. **44** 61.12N 44.52E
Kizil *r.* Turkey **64** 41.45N 35.57E
Kizlyar Russian Fed. **45** 43.51N 46.43E
Kizlyarskiy Zaliv *b.* Russian Fed. **45** 44.33N 47.00E
Kizu *r.* Japan **57** 34.53N 135.42E
Kizyl-Arvat Turkmenistan **65** 39.00N 56.23E
Kizyl Atrek Turkey **65** 37.37N 54.49E
Kladanj Bosnia-Herzegovina **31** 44.13N 18.41E
Kladno Czech Republic **38** 50.08N 14.05E
Klagenfurt Austria **31** 46.38N 14.18E
Klaipeda Lithuania **41** 55.43N 21.07E
Klakah Indonesia **59** 7.55S 113.12E
Klaksvig Faroe Is. **10** 62.13N 6.34W
Klamath *r.* U.S.A. **108** 41.33N 124.04W
Klamath Falls *town* U.S.A. **108** 42.14N 121.47W
Klamath Mts. U.S.A. **108** 41.40N 123.20W
Klamono Indonesia **59** 1.08S 131.28E
Klar *r.* Sweden **43** 59.23N 13.32E
Klatovy Czech Republic **38** 49.24N 13.18E
Klawer R.S.A. **80** 31.48S 18.34E
Klawock U.S.A. **100** 55.33N 133.06W
Kleena Kleene Canada **100** 51.58N 124.50W
Kleinsee R.S.A. **80** 29.41S 17.04E
Klekovača *mtn.* Bosnia-Herzegovina **31** 44.26N 16.31E
Klerksdorp R.S.A. **80** 26.51S 26.38E
Klevan Ukraine **37** 50.44N 25.50E
Kleve Germany **38** 51.48N 6.09E
Klickitat U.S.A. **108** 45.49N 121.09W
Klimovichi Belarus **37** 53.36N 31.58E
Klimpfjäll Sweden **40** 65.04N 14.52E
Klin Russian Fed. **44** 56.20N 36.45E
Klinaklini *r.* Canada **100** 51.21N 125.40W
Klingenthal Germany **39** 51.21N 12.28E
Klintehamn Sweden **43** 57.24N 18.12E
Klintsy Russian Fed. **37** 52.45N 32.15E
Klipdale R.S.A. **80** 34.18S 19.58E
Klippan Sweden **43** 56.08N 13.06E
Klipplaat R.S.A. **80** 33.03S 24.19E
Klisura Bulgaria **34** 42.40N 24.28E
Klitmöller Denmark **42** 57.02N 8.31E
Klobuck Poland **37** 50.55N 18.57E
Klock Canada **104** 46.18N 78.36W
Kłodzko Poland **36** 50.27N 16.38E
Klöfta Norway **42** 60.04N 11.09E
Klondike Canada **98** 64.02N 139.24W
Klosters Switz. **39** 46.54N 9.53E
Kloten Switz. **39** 47.27N 8.35E
Klötze Germany **38** 52.38N 11.10E
Kluane Nat. Park Canada **100** 60.32N 139.40W
Kluczbork Poland **37** 50.59N 18.13E
Klukwan U.S.A. **100** 59.25N 135.55W
Klungkung Indonesia **59** 8.32S 115.25E
Knäred Sweden **43** 56.32N 13.19E
Knaresborough U.K. **12** 54.01N 1.29W

Knezha Bulgaria **34** 43.30N 23.56E
Knić Yugo. **34** 43.31N 20.43E
Knight Inlet *f.* Canada **100** 50.45N 125.40W
Knighton U.K. **13** 52.21N 3.02W
Knin Croatia **31** 44.02N 16.12E
Knislinge Sweden **43** 56.11N 14.05E
Knivsta Sweden **43** 59.43N 17.48E
Knjaževac Yugo. **34** 43.35N 22.18E
Knobly Mtn. U.S.A. **114** 39.21N 79.32W
Knobs Mtn. U.S.A. **114** 41.12N 78.26W
Knockadoon Head Rep. of Ire. **15** 51.52N 7.52W
Knockalongy *mtn.* Rep. of Ire. **15** 54.12N 8.45W
Knockmealdown Mts. Rep. of Ire. **15** 52.15N 7.55W
Knokke Belgium **16** 51.21N 3.17E
Knolls U.S.A. **108** 40.44N 113.18W
Knossos *site* Greece **35** 35.20N 25.10E
Knox U.S.A. **114** 41.14N 79.32W
Knox, C. Canada **100** 54.11N 133.04W
Knox City U.S.A. **111** 33.25N 99.49W
Knoxville U.S.A. **113** 36.00N 83.57W
Knutsford U.K. **12** 53.18N 2.22W
Knyazhevo Russian Fed. **44** 59.40N 43.51E
Knysna R.S.A. **80** 34.02S 23.03E
Kobarid Slovenia **31** 46.15N 13.35E
Kobar Sink *f.* Ethiopia **72** 14.00N 40.30E
Kōbe Japan **57** 34.41N 135.10E
København Denmark **43** 55.40N 12.35E
Koblenz Germany **39** 50.21N 7.35E
Kobowen Swamp Sudan **73** 5.38N 33.54E
Kobrin Belarus **37** 52.16N 24.22E
Kobroor *i.* Indonesia **59** 6.10S 134.30E
Kočani Macedonia **34** 41.55N 22.25E
Koçarli Turkey **35** 37.45N 27.42E
Kočevje Slovenia **31** 45.38N 14.52E
Kocher *r.* Germany **39** 49.14N 9.12E
Kochi *see* Cochin India **60**
Kōchi Japan **57** 33.33N 133.52E
Kochkoma Russian Fed. **44** 64.03N 34.14E
Kochmes Russian Fed. **44** 66.12N 60.48E
Kodaira Japan **57** 35.44N 139.29E
Kodari Nepal **63** 27.56N 85.56E
Kodarma India **63** 24.28N 85.36E
Kodiak U.S.A. **98** 57.49N 152.30W
Kodiak I. U.S.A. **98** 57.00N 153.50W
Kodima Russian Fed. **44** 62.24N 43.57E
Kodinär India **62** 20.47N 70.42E
Kodok Sudan **73** 9.53N 32.07E
Kodyma Ukraine **37** 48.06N 29.04E
Koekelare Belgium **16** 51.08N 2.59E
Koekenaap R.S.A. **80** 31.30S 18.18E
Koersel Belgium **16** 51.04N 5.19E
Koës Namibia **80** 25.58S 19.07E
Koffiefontein R.S.A. **80** 29.24S 25.00E
Köflach Austria **31** 47.04N 15.05E
Koforidua Ghana **76** 6.01N 0.12W
Kōfu Japan **57** 35.39N 138.35E
Koga Tanzania **79** 6.10S 32.21E
Kogaluk *r.* Canada **103** 56.12N 61.45W
Kōge Denmark **43** 55.27N 12.11E
Kōge Bugt *b.* Denmark **43** 55.30N 12.20E
Kōge Bugt *b.* Greenland **99** 65.00N 40.30W
Kogi *d.* Nigeria **77** 7.15N 7.00E
Kohak Pakistan **62** 25.44N 62.33E
Kohāt Pakistan **62** 33.35N 71.26E
Kohima India **61** 25.40N 94.08E
Kohler Range *mts.* Antarctica **128** 77.00S 110.00W
Kohtla-Järve Estonia **44** 59.28N 27.20E
Koidu Sierra Leone **76** 8.41N 10.55W
Koito *r.* Japan **57** 35.21N 139.52E
Kojonup Australia **89** 33.50S 117.05E
Kokand Uzbekistan **52** 40.33N 70.55E
Kōkar *i.* Finland **43** 59.56N 20.55E
Kokas Indonesia **59** 2.45S 132.26E
Kokemäki Finland **41** 61.15N 22.21E
Kokenau Indonesia **59** 4.42S 136.25E
Kokka Sudan **72** 20.00N 30.35E
Kokkola Finland **40** 63.50N 23.07E
Koko Sokoto Nigeria **77** 11.27N 4.35E
Kokomo U.S.A. **112** 40.30N 86.09W
Kokpekty Kazakhstan **52** 48.45N 82.25E
Kokshetau Kazakhstan **9** 53.18N 69.25E
Koksoak *r.* Canada **99** 58.30N 68.15W
Kokstad R.S.A. **80** 30.32S 29.25E
Kokuora Russian Fed. **51** 71.33N 144.50E
Kolāchi *r.* Pakistan **62** 26.25N 67.50E
Kolahun Liberia **76** 8.24N 10.02W
Kolaka Indonesia **59** 4.04S 121.38E
Kolan Australia **90** 24.42S 152.10E
Kola Pen. *see* Kolskiy Poluostrov *pen.* Russian Fed. **44**
Kolār India **61** 13.10N 78.10E
Kolāras India **63** 25.14N 77.36E
Kolari Finland **40** 67.20N 23.48E
Kolašin Yugo. **31** 42.49N 19.31E
Kolāyat India **62** 27.50N 72.57E
Kolbäck Sweden **43** 59.34N 16.15E
Kolbio Kenya **79** 1.11S 41.10E
Kolbotn Norway **42** 59.49N 10.48E
Kolda Senegal **76** 12.56N 14.55W
Kolding Denmark **42** 55.31N 9.29E
Kole H.Zaïre Zaïre **78** 2.07N 25.26E
Kole K.Oriental Zaïre **78** 3.28S 22.29E
Kolepom *i. see* Yos Sudarsa, Pulau *i.* Indonesia **59**
Kolguyev, Ostrov *i.* Russian Fed. **44** 69.00N 49.00E
Kolhāpur India **60** 16.43N 74.15E
Kolia Côte d'Ivoire **76** 9.46N 6.28W
Kolín Czech Republic **36** 50.02N 15.10E
Kolka Latvia **41** 57.45N 22.35E
Kolki Ukraine **37** 51.09N 25.40E
Kollam *see* Quilon India **60**
Kolmården Sweden **43** 58.41N 16.45E
Köln Germany **38** 50.56N 6.59E
Kolno Poland **37** 53.25N 21.56E
Koło Poland **37** 52.12N 18.37E
Kołobrzeg Poland **36** 54.10N 15.35E
Kolokani Mali **76** 13.35N 7.45W
Kololo Ethiopia **73** 7.29N 41.58E

Kolomna Russian Fed. **44** 55.05N 38.45E
Kolomyya Ukraine **37** 48.31N 25.00E
Kolondiéba Mali **76** 11.05N 6.54W
Kolosib India **63** 24.14N 92.42E
Kolpashevo Russian Fed. **50** 58.21N 82.59E
Kolpino Russian Fed. **44** 59.44N 30.39E
Kolskiy Poluostrov *pen.* Russian Fed. **44** 67.00N
38.00E
Kolsva Sweden **43** 59.36N 15.50E
Kolubara *r.* Yugo. **31** 44.40N 20.15E
Koluszki Poland **37** 51.44N 19.49E
Kolvereid Norway **40** 64.53N 11.35E
Kolwezi Zaïre **78** 10.44S 25.28E
Kolyma *r.* Russian Fed. **51** 68.50N 161.00E
Kolymskiy, Khrebet *mts* Russian Fed. **51** 63.00N
160.00E
Kom *r.* Cameroon **78** 2.20N 10.38E
Kom Kenya **79** 1.06N 38.00E
Koma Ethiopia **73** 8.25N 36.53E
Komadugu Gana *r.* Nigeria **77** 13.06N 12.23E
Komadugu Yobe *r.* Niger/Nigeria **77** 13.43N 13.19E
Komagane Japan **57** 35.43N 137.55E
Komaga-take *mtn.* Japan **57** 35.47N 137.48E
Komaki Japan **57** 35.17N 136.55E
Komandorskiye Ostrova *is.* Russian Fed. **84** 55.00N
167.00E
Komárno Slovakia **37** 47.45N 18.09E
Komarom Hungary **37** 47.44N 18.08E
Komatipoort R.S.A. **81** 25.25S 31.55E
Komatsu Japan **57** 36.24N 136.27E
Komba Zaïre **78** 2.52N 24.03E
Komló Hungary **31** 46.12N 18.16E
Kommunarsk Ukraine **23** 48.30N 38.47E
Kommunizma, Pik *mtn.* Tajikistan **52** 38.39N 72.01E
Komotiní Greece **34** 41.08N 25.25E
Komrat Moldova **37** 46.18N 28.40E
Komsberg *mtn.* R.S.A. **80** 32.40S 20.48E
Komsomolets, Ostrov *i.* Russian Fed. **51** 80.20N
96.00E
Komsomolets, Zaliv *g.* Kazakhstan **45** 45.17N 53.30E
Komsomolsk-na-Amure Russian Fed. **51** 50.32N
136.59E
Kōnan Japan **57** 35.20N 136.53E
Konar *r.* Afghan. **62** 34.26N 70.32E
Konārak India **63** 19.54N 86.07E
Konar-e Khās Afghan. **62** 34.39N 70.54E
Konch India **63** 25.59N 79.09E
Kondagaon India **63** 19.36N 81.40E
Kondakovo Russian Fed. **51** 69.38N 152.00E
Kondinin Australia **89** 32.33S 118.13E
Kondoa Tanzania **79** 4.54S 35.49E
Kondopoga Russian Fed. **44** 62.12N 34.17E
Kondratyevo Russian Fed. **51** 57.22N 98.15E
Kondut Australia **89** 30.44S 117.06E
Koné N. Cal. **84** 21.04S 164.52E
Konevo Russian Fed. **9** 62.09N 39.22E
Kông *r.* Cambodia **56** 13.32N 105.57E
Kong Côte d'Ivoire **76** 8.54N 4.36W
Kong Christian den IX Land *f.* Greenland **99** 68.20N
37.00W
Kong Christian den X Land *f.* Greenland **96** 73.00N
26.00W
Kong Frederik den VIII Land *f.* Greenland **96** 77.30N
25.00W
Kong Frederik den VI Kyst *f.* Greenland **99** 63.00N
44.00W
Kong Haakon VII Hav *sea* Antarctica **128** 65.00S
25.00E
Kongolo Zaïre **79** 5.20S 27.00E
Kongor Sudan **73** 7.10N 31.21E
Kongsberg Norway **42** 59.39N 9.39E
Kongsvinger Norway **43** 60.12N 12.00E
Kongur Shan *mtn.* China **52** 38.40N 75.30E
Kongwa Tanzania **79** 6.13S 36.28E
Königsmoor *f.* Germany **38** 53.15N 9.57E
Königs Wusterhausen Germany **38** 52.18N 13.37E
Konin Poland **37** 52.13N 18.16E
Kónitsa Greece **34** 40.02N 20.45E
Konjic Bosnia-Herzegovina **31** 43.39N 17.57E
Könkämä *r.* Sweden/Finland **40** 68.29N 22.30E
Konkouré *r.* Guinea **76** 9.55N 13.45W
Konongo Ghana **76** 6.38N 1.12W
Konosha Russian Fed. **44** 60.58N 40.08E
Kōnosu Japan **57** 36.03N 139.31E
Konotop Ukraine **45** 51.15N 33.14E
Końskie Poland **37** 51.12N 20.26E
Konstanz Germany **39** 47.40N 9.10E
Kontagora Nigeria **77** 10.24N 5.22E
Kontcha Cameroon **77** 7.59N 12.15E
Kontiomäki Finland **44** 64.21N 28.10E
Kontum Vietnam **56** 14.23N 108.00E
Kontum, Plateau du *f.* Vietnam **56** 14.00N 108.00E
Konya Turkey **64** 37.51N 32.30E
Konz Germany **39** 49.42N 6.34E
Konza Kenya **79** 1.45S 37.07E
Koolkootinnie L. Australia **92** 27.58S 137.47E
Koolyanobbing Australia **89** 30.48S 119.29E
Koondrook Australia **92** 35.39S 144.11E
Koongawa Australia **92** 33.11S 135.52E
Koorawatha Australia **93** 34.02S 148.33E
Koorda Australia **89** 30.50S 117.51E
Kootenay L. Canada **100** 49.45N 117.00W
Kootenay Nat. Park Canada **100** 51.00N 116.00W
Kootjieskolk R.S.A. **80** 31.14S 20.18E
Kopāganj India **63** 26.01N 83.34E
Kopargaon India **62** 19.53N 74.29E
Kópavogur Iceland **40** 64.06N 21.53W
Koper Slovenia **31** 45.33N 13.44E
Kopervik Norway **42** 59.17N 5.18E
Kopet Dag, Khrebet *mts.* Turkmenistan **65** 38.00N
58.00E
Kopeysk Russian Fed. **9** 55.07N 61.37E
Köping Sweden **43** 59.31N 16.00E
Koplik Albania **34** 42.13N 19.26E
Koppány Hungary **31** 46.35N 18.26E
Kopparberg *d.* Sweden **41** 60.50N 15.00E
Koppom Sweden **43** 59.43N 12.09E
Koprivnica Croatia **31** 46.10N 16.50E

Kopychintsy Ukraine 37 49.10N 25.58E
Kor r. Iran 65 29.40N 53.17E
Koralpe mts. Austria 31 46.40N 15.00E
Koraput India 63 18.49N 82.43E
Koratla India 63 18.49N 78.43E
Korba India 63 22.21N 82.41E
Korbach Germany 38 51.16N 8.52E
Korbous Tunisia 32 36.49N 10.35E
Korçë Albania 34 40.37N 20.50E
Korçë d. Albania 34 40.40N 20.50E
Korčula Croatia 31 42.58N 17.08E
Korčula i. Croatia 31 42.57N 16.50E
Korčulanski Kanal str. Croatia 31 43.03N 16.40E
Kord Kūy Iran 65 36.48N 54.07E
Korea Str. S. Korea/Japan 53 35.00N 129.20E
Korem Ethiopia 73 12.30N 39.30E
Korets Ukraine 37 50.39N 27.10E
Korhogo Côte d'Ivoire 76 9.22N 5.31W
Korim Indonesia 59 0.58S 136.10E
Korinthiakós Kólpos g. Greece 35 38.16N 22.30E
Kórinthos Greece 35 37.56N 22.56E
Korinthou, Dhiórix canal Greece 35 37.57N 22.56E
Kōriyama Japan 57 37.23N 140.22E
Korma Belarus 37 53.08N 30.47E
Körmend Hungary 31 47.01N 16.37E
Kornat i. Croatia 31 43.50N 15.16E
Korneshty Moldova 37 47.21N 28.00E
Kornsjö Norway 42 58.57N 11.39E
Koro Côte d'Ivoire 76 8.36N 7.28W
Koro i. Fiji 84 17.22S 179.25E
Koro Mali 76 14.01N 2.58W
Korocha Russian Fed. 45 50.50N 37.13E
Korogwe Tanzania 79 5.10S 38.35E
Koroit Australia 92 38.17S 142.26E
Korong Vale town Australia 92 36.22S 143.45E
Koróni Greece 35 36.48N 21.56E
Koronia, Límni i. Greece 34 40.41N 23.05E
Koropíon Greece 35 37.54N 23.53E
Koror i. Palau 59 7.30N 134.30E
Koro Sea Fiji 84 18.00S 179.00E
Korosten Ukraine 37 51.00N 28.30E
Korostyshev Ukraine 37 50.19N 29.03E
Koro Toro Chad 77 16.05N 18.30E
Korsör Denmark 42 55.20N 11.09E
Korsze Poland 37 54.10N 21.09E
Kortrijk Belgium 16 50.49N 3.17E
Koryakskiy Khrebet mts. Russian Fed. 51 62.20N 171.00E
Koryazhma Russian Fed. 44 61.19N 47.12E
Kos Greece 35 36.53N 27.18E
Kos i. Greece 35 36.50N 27.10E
Kosa Ethiopia 73 7.51N 36.51E
Kościan Poland 36 52.06N 16.38E
Kościerzyna Poland 37 54.08N 18.00E
Kosciusko U.S.A. 111 32.58N 89.35W
Kosciusko, Mt. Australia 93 36.28S 148.17E
Kosha Sudan 72 20.49N 30.32E
Koshikijima rettō is. Japan 57 31.45N 129.49E
Koshk-e Kohneh Afghan. 62 34.52N 62.29E
Košice Slovakia 37 48.44N 21.15E
Koski Finland 41 60.39N 23.09E
Koslan Russian Fed. 44 63.29N 48.59E
Kosovska Mitrovica Yugo. 34 42.54N 20.52E
Kossanto Senegal 76 13.12N 11.56W
Kossovo Belarus 37 52.45N 25.18E
Kosta Sweden 43 56.51N 15.23E
Kostajnica Croatia 31 45.14N 16.33E
Koster R.S.A. 80 25.51S 26.52E
Kostopol Ukraine 37 50.51N 26.22E
Kostroma Russian Fed. 44 57.46N 40.59E
Kostrzyn Poland 36 52.24N 17.11E
Kostyukovichi Belarus 37 53.20N 32.01E
Kosyu Russian Fed. 44 65.36N 59.00E
Koszalin Poland 36 54.12N 16.09E
Kota Madhya P. India 63 22.18N 82.02E
Kota Rāj. India 62 25.11N 75.50E
Kota Baharu Malaysia 58 6.07N 102.15E
Kota Belud Malaysia 58 6.00N 116.00E
Kotabumi Indonesia 58 4.52S 104.59E
Kot Addu Pakistan 62 30.28N 70.58E
Kota Kinabalu Malaysia 58 5.59N 116.04E
Kotari mts. Croatia 31 44.05N 15.17E
Kotelnich Russian Fed. 44 58.20N 48.10E
Kotelnikovo Russian Fed. 45 47.39N 43.08E
Kotel'nyy, Ostrov i. Russian Fed. 51 75.30N 141.00E
Köthen Germany 38 51.45N 11.58E
Kotka Finland 44 60.26N 26.55E
Kot Kapūra India 62 30.35N 74.49E
Kotlas Russian Fed. 44 61.15N 46.28E
Kotli Jammu & Kashmir 62 33.31N 73.55E
Kotlik U.S.A. 98 63.02N 163.33W
Kotor Yugo. 31 42.25N 18.46E
Kotoriba Croatia 31 46.21N 16.49E
Kotor Varoš Bosnia-Herzegovina 31 44.37N 17.23E
Kotovsk Moldova 37 46.50N 28.31E
Kotovsk Ukraine 37 47.42N 29.30E
Kot Pūtli India 62 27.43N 76.12E
Kotra India 62 24.22N 73.10E
Kotri Pakistan 62 25.22N 68.18E
Kotri Allāhrakhio Pakistan 62 24.24N 67.50E
Kötschach Austria 39 46.40N 13.00E
Kottagüdem India 61 17.32N 80.39E
Kotto r. C.A.R. 73 4.14N 22.02E
Kotuy r. Russian Fed. 51 71.40N 103.00E
Kotzebue U.S.A. 98 66.51N 162.40W
Kotzebue Sd. U.S.A. 98 66.20N 163.00W
Kötzting Germany 39 49.11N 12.52E
Kouango C.A.R. 73 4.58N 20.00E
Koudougou Burkina 76 12.15N 2.21W
Kouibli Côte d'Ivoire 76 7.09N 7.16W
Kouki C.A.R. 77 7.09N 17.13E
Koúklia Cyprus 66 34.42N 32.34E
Koula Moutou Gabon 78 1.12S 12.29E
Koulikoro Mali 76 12.55N 7.31W
Koumac N. Cal. 84 20.33S 164.17E
Koumankou Mali 76 11.58N 6.06W
Koumbal C.A.R. 73 9.26N 22.39E
Koumbia Burkina 76 11.18N 3.38W

Koumbia Guinea 76 11.54N 13.40W
Koumbisaleh site Mauritania 74 15.55N 8.05W
Koumongou Togo 76 10.10N 0.29E
Koumra Chad 77 8.56N 17.32E
Koupéla Burkina 76 12.09N 0.22W
Kouroussa Guinea 76 10.40N 9.50W
Kousséri Chad 77 12.05N 14.56E
Koutiala Mali 76 12.20N 5.23W
Kouto Côte d'Ivoire 76 9.53N 6.25W
Kouvola Finland 44 60.54N 26.45E
Kouyou r. Congo 78 0.40S 16.37E
Kovdor Russian Fed. 44 67.33N 30.30E
Kovel Ukraine 37 51.12N 24.48E
Kovpyta Ukraine 37 51.22N 30.51E
Kovrov Russian Fed. 44 56.23N 41.21E
Kovzha r. Russian Fed. 44 61.05N 36.27E
Kowanyama Australia 90 15.29S 141.44E
Kowloon Hong Kong 55 22.19N 114.12E
Kowt-e 'Ashrow Afghan. 62 34.27N 68.48E
Koyukuk r. U.S.A. 98 64.50N 157.30W
Kozan Turkey 64 37.27N 35.47E
Kozáni Greece 34 40.19N 21.47E
Kozara mts. Bosnia-Herzegovina 31 45.05N 16.50E
Kozarac Bosnia-Herzegovina 31 44.58N 16.51E
Kozelets Ukraine 37 50.54N 31.09E
Kozhikode see Calicut India 60
Kozhim Russian Fed. 44 65.45N 59.30E
Kozhposelok Russian Fed. 44 63.10N 38.10E
Kpandu Ghana 76 7.02N 0.17E
Kpessi Togo 77 8.07N 1.17E
Krabi Thailand 56 8.08N 98.52E
Krâchéh Cambodia 56 12.30N 106.00E
Kragan Indonesia 59 6.40S 111.33E
Kragerö Norway 42 58.52N 9.25E
Kragujevac Yugo. 29 44.01N 20.55E
Kraków Poland 37 50.03N 19.55E
Kraljevica Croatia 31 45.16N 14.34E
Kraljevo Yugo. 34 43.43N 20.41E
Kralovice Czech Republic 38 49.59N 13.29E
Kralupy nad Vltavou Czech Republic 38 50.11N 14.18E
Kramatorsk Ukraine 45 48.43N 37.33E
Kramer U.S.A. 110 48.20N 100.42W
Kramfors Sweden 40 62.55N 17.50E
Kranídhion Greece 35 37.22N 23.10E
Kranj Slovenia 31 46.15N 14.21E
Kranskop R.S.A. 80 28.58S 30.52E
Krapina Croatia 31 46.10N 15.52E
Krapkowice Poland 37 50.29N 17.56E
Krasavino Russian Fed. 44 60.58N 46.25E
Krasilov Ukraine 37 49.39N 26.59E
Kraskino Russian Fed. 54 42.42N 130.48E
Kraśnik Poland 37 50.56N 22.13E
Krasnaya Gora Russian Fed. 37 53.00N 31.36E
Krasnodar Russian Fed. 45 45.02N 39.00E
Krasnograd Ukraine 45 49.22N 35.28E
Krasnokamsk Russian Fed. 44 58.05N 55.49E
Krasnoperekopsk Ukraine 45 45.56N 33.47E
Krasnoselkup Russian Fed. 50 65.45N 82.31E
Krasnoturinsk Russian Fed. 44 59.46N 60.10E
Krasnoufimsk Russian Fed. 44 56.40N 57.49E
Krasnouralsk Russian Fed. 50 58.25N 60.00E
Krasnovishersk Russian Fed. 44 60.25N 57.02E
Krasnovodsk Turkmenistan 65 40.01N 53.00E
Krasnovodskiy Poluostrov pen. Turkmenistan 65 40.30N 53.10E
Krasnovodskiy Zaliv g. Turkmenistan 65 39.50N 53.15E
Krasnoyarsk Russian Fed. 51 56.05N 92.46E
Krasnyy Yar Russian Fed. 45 46.32N 48.21E
Kratovo Macedonia 34 42.06N 22.10E
Krawang Indonesia 59 6.15S 107.15E
Krefeld Germany 38 51.20N 6.34E
Kremastón, Tekhnití Límni l. Greece 35 38.52N 21.30E
Kremenchug Ukraine 45 49.03N 33.25E
Kremenchugskoye Vodokhranilishche resr. Ukraine 45 49.20N 32.30E
Kremenets Ukraine 37 50.05N 25.43E
Kremmling U.S.A. 108 40.03N 106.24W
Krems Austria 36 48.25N 15.36E
Krestovka Russian Fed. 44 66.24N 52.31E
Kretinga Lithuania 41 55.53N 21.13E
Kría Vrísi Greece 34 40.41N 22.18E
Kribi Cameroon 77 2.56N 9.56E
Krichev Belarus 37 53.40N 31.44E
Krichim Bulgaria 34 42.08N 24.32E
Kriens Switz. 39 47.02N 8.17E
Krimml Austria 39 47.13N 12.11E
Krionéri Greece 35 38.20N 21.35E
Krishna r. India 61 16.00N 81.00E
Krishnanagar India 63 23.24N 88.30E
Kristdala Sweden 43 57.24N 16.11E
Kristianopel Sweden 43 56.15N 16.02E
Kristiansand Norway 42 58.10N 8.00E
Kristianstad Sweden 43 56.02N 14.08E
Kristianstad d. Sweden 43 56.10N 13.40E
Kristiansund Norway 40 63.07N 7.45E
Kristiinankaupunki Finland 41 62.17N 21.23E
Kristinehamn Sweden 43 59.20N 14.07E
Kristinestad see Kristiinankaupunki Finland 41
Kristinovka Ukraine 37 48.50N 29.58E
Kriti i. Greece 35 35.29N 24.42E
Kritikón Pélagos sea Greece 35 35.46N 23.54E
Kriva r. Macedonia 34 42.12N 22.18E
Krivaja r. Bosnia-Herzegovina 31 44.27N 18.09E
Kriva Palanka Macedonia 34 42.12N 22.20E
Krivodol Bulgaria 34 43.23N 23.29E
Krivoy Rog Ukraine 45 47.55N 33.24E
Križevci Croatia 31 46.02N 16.33E
Krk i. Croatia 31 45.05N 14.36E
Krnov Czech Republic 37 50.05N 17.41E
Kröderen l. Norway 42 60.15N 9.38E
Krokek Sweden 43 58.40N 16.24E
Kroken Norway 40 65.23N 14.15E
Krokom Sweden 40 63.20N 14.30E
Krokowa Poland 43 54.48N 18.11E
Kronach Germany 38 50.14N 11.20E

Krŏng Kaôh Kŏng Cambodia 56 11.37N 102.59E
Kronoberg d. Sweden 43 56.40N 14.35E
Kronprins Olav Kyst f. Antarctica 128 69.00S 42.00E
Kronshtadt Russian Fed. 44 60.00N 29.40E
Kropotkin Russian Fed. 45 45.25N 40.35E
Kropperfjäll hill Sweden 43 58.40N 12.13E
Krosno Poland 37 49.42N 21.46E
Krotoszyn Poland 37 51.42N 17.26E
Kroya Indonesia 59 7.37S 109.13E
Krško Slovenia 31 45.58N 15.29E
Kruger Nat. Park R.S.A. 81 24.10S 31.36E
Krugersdorp R.S.A. 80 26.06S 27.46E
Krujë Albania 34 41.30N 19.48E
Krumbach Germany 39 48.14N 10.22E
Krumovgrad Bulgaria 34 41.29N 25.38E
Krung Thep see Bangkok Thailand 56
Krupki Belarus 37 54.19N 29.05E
Kruševac Yugo. 34 43.35N 21.20E
Kruševo Macedonia 34 41.23N 21.19E
Krušnéhory mts. see Erzgebirge mts. Czech Republic 38
Krylbo Sweden 43 60.08N 16.13E
Krym pen. Ukraine 45 45.30N 34.00E
Krymsk Russian Fed. 45 44.56N 38.00E
Krzyz Poland 36 52.54N 16.01E
Ksar el Boukhari Algeria 75 35.53N 2.45E
Ksar-el-Kebir Morocco 74 35.01N 5.54W
Ksar Rhilane Tunisia 75 33.00N 9.38E
Ksel, Djebel mtn. Algeria 75 33.44N 1.10E
Kuala Dungun Malaysia 58 4.47N 103.26E
Kualakapuas Indonesia 58 3.01S 114.21E
Kuala Lipis Malaysia 58 4.11N 102.00E
Kuala Lumpur Malaysia 58 3.08N 101.42E
Kuala Trengganu Malaysia 58 5.10N 103.10E
Kuancheng China 54 40.36N 118.57E
Kuandang Indonesia 59 0.53N 122.58E
Kuandian China 54 40.47N 124.43E
Kuantan Malaysia 58 3.50N 103.19E
Kuba Azerbaijan 65 41.23N 48.33E
Kuban r. Russian Fed. 45 45.20N 37.17E
Kubbum Sudan 73 11.47N 23.47E
Kubrat Bulgaria 34 43.49N 26.31E
Kuchaiburi India 63 22.16N 86.10E
Kuchāman India 62 27.09N 74.52E
Kuching Malaysia 58 1.32N 110.20E
Kuchinoerabu jima i. Japan 57 30.30N 130.20E
Küchnay Darvīshān Afghan. 62 30.59N 64.11E
Kuçovë Albania 34 40.48N 19.54E
Küçükbakoy Turkey 35 38.33N 26.24E
Kūd Jammu & Kashmir 62 33.05N 75.17E
Kudat Malaysia 58 6.45N 116.47E
Kudus Indonesia 59 6.46S 110.48E
Kufrinjah Jordan 67 32.18N 35.42E
Kufrinjah, Wādī Jordan 67 32.16N 35.33E
Kufsfein Austria 39 47.35N 12.11E
Kühdasht Iran 65 33.32N 47.36E
Kühpāyeh Iran 65 32.42N 52.25E
Kührän, Küh-e mtn. Iran 65 26.46N 58.15E
Kuito Angola 78 12.25S 16.58E
Kuiu I. U.S.A. 100 56.40N 134.00W
Kuivaniemi Finland 44 65.35N 25.11E
Kujū san mtn. Japan 57 33.08N 131.10E
Kuke Botswana 80 23.19S 24.29E
Kukerin Australia 89 33.11S 118.03E
Kukës Albania 34 42.05N 20.20E
Kukshi India 62 22.12N 74.45E
Kül r. Iran 65 28.00N 55.45E
Kula Bulgaria 34 43.52N 22.36E
Kula Turkey 64 38.33N 28.38E
Kula Yugo. 31 45.36N 19.32E
Kulāchi Pakistan 62 31.56N 70.27E
Kulakshi Kazakhstan 45 47.09N 55.22E
Kulal, Mt. Kenya 79 2.44N 36.56E
Kulaura Bangla. 63 24.30N 92.03E
Kuldiga Latvia 41 56.58N 21.59E
Kulen Vakuf Bosnia-Herzegovina 31 44.34N 16.06E
Kulgera Australia 90 25.50S 133.18E
Kulin Australia 89 32.40S 118.10E
Kulja Australia 89 30.28S 117.17E
Kulkyne r. Australia 93 30.16S 144.12E
Kulmbach Germany 38 50.06N 11.27E
Kulpara Australia 92 34.07S 137.59E
Kulsary Kazakhstan 45 46.59N 54.02E
Kulu Turkey 45 39.06N 33.02E
Kulu r. Russian Fed. 51 63.34N 74.87E
Kulunda Russian Fed. 50 52.34N 78.58E
Kulwin Australia 92 35.02S 142.40E
Kulyab Tajikistan 62 37.55N 69.47E
Kuma r. Russian Fed. 45 44.40N 46.55E
Kumagaya Japan 57 36.08N 139.23E
Kumai Indonesia 58 2.45S 111.44E
Kumamoto Japan 57 32.50N 130.42E
Kumanovo Macedonia 34 42.08N 21.43E
Kumara New Zealand 86 42.38S 171.11E
Kumarl Australia 89 32.47S 121.33E
Kumasi Ghana 76 6.45N 1.35W
Kumayri Armenia 45 40.47N 43.49E
Kumba Cameroon 77 4.39N 9.26E
Kumbakonam India 61 10.59N 79.24E
Kum Dag Turkmenistan 65 39.14N 54.33E
Kumdah Saudi Arabia 71 20.23N 45.05E
Kumertau Russian Fed. 44 52.48N 55.46E
Kumi Uganda 79 1.26N 33.54E
Kumla Sweden 43 59.08N 15.08E
Kummerower See l. Germany 38 53.49N 12.52E
Kumon Range mts. Myanmar 56 26.30N 97.15E
Kunashir i. Russian Fed. 53 44.25N 146.00E
Kunchha Nepal 63 28.08N 84.22E
Kundam India 63 23.13N 80.21E
Kundelungu Mts. Zaïre 79 9.30S 27.50E
Kundian Pakistan 62 32.27N 71.28E
Kundip Australia 89 33.44S 120.11E
Kundla India 62 21.20N 71.18E
Kungālv Sweden 42 57.52N 11.58E
Kungsbacka Sweden 43 57.29N 12.04E
Kungshamn Sweden 42 58.22N 11.15E
Kungsör Sweden 43 59.25N 16.05E
Kungu Zaïre 78 2.47N 19.12E

Kungur Russian Fed. 44 57.27N 56.50E
Kuningan Indonesia 59 7.02S 108.30E
Kunkuri India 63 22.45N 83.57E
Kunlong Myanmar 56 23.25N 98.39E
Kunlun Shan mts. China 52 36.40N 88.00E
Kunming China 52 25.04N 102.41E
Kunö i. Faroe Is. 10 62.20N 6.39W
Kunsan S. Korea 53 35.57N 126.42E
Kunshan China 55 31.24N 121.08E
Kunszentmárton Hungary 31 46.51N 20.18E
Kuntair Gambia 76 13.36N 16.20W
Kununoppin Australia 89 31.09S 117.53E
Kununurra Australia 87 15.42S 128.50E
Kunyo Ethiopia 71 6.20N 42.32E
Künzelsau Germany 39 49.16N 9.41E
Kuolayarvi Russian Fed. 40 66.58N 29.12E
Kuopio Finland 44 62.51N 27.30E
Kupa r. Croatia 31 45.28N 16.24E
Küplü Turkey 34 41.07N 26.21E
Kupreanof I. U.S.A. 100 56.50N 133.30W
Kupres Bosnia-Herzegovina 31 44.00N 17.17E
Kupyansk Ukraine 45 49.41N 37.37E
Kuqa China 52 41.43N 82.58E
Kura r. Azerbaijan 65 39.18N 49.22E
Kurashiki Japan 57 34.36N 133.43E
Kuraymah Sudan 72 18.33N 31.51E
Kurayyimah Jordan 67 32.16N 35.36E
Kurchum Kazakhstan 52 48.35N 83.39E
Kürdzhali Bulgaria 34 41.39N 25.22E
Kure Japan 57 34.20N 132.40E
Kuressaare Estonia 41 58.12N 22.30E
Kurgaldzhino Kazakhstan 50 50.35N 70.03E
Kurgan Russian Fed. 9 55.30N 65.20E
Kurigrām Bangla. 63 25.49N 89.39E
Kurikka Finland 40 62.37N 22.25E
Kuril Ridge Pacific Oc. 84 46.10N 152.30E
Kurilskiye Ostrova is. Russian Fed. 53 46.00N 150.30E
Kuril Trench Pacific Oc. 84 46.00N 155.00E
Kuring Kuru Namibia 80 17.36S 18.36E
Kurlovski Russian Fed. 44 55.26N 40.40E
Kurmuk Sudan 73 10.33N 34.17E
Kurnool India 61 15.51N 78.01E
Kurow New Zealand 86 44.45S 170.28E
Kurram Pakistan 62 30.06N 66.31E
Kurri Kurri Australia 93 32.49S 151.29E
Kurseong India 63 26.53N 88.17E
Kursk Russian Fed. 45 51.45N 36.14E
Kuršumlija Yugo. 34 43.09N 21.19E
Kürti Sudan 72 18.07N 31.33E
Kuru Finland 41 61.52N 23.44E
Kuru Sudan 73 7.43N 26.31E
Kuruman R.S.A. 80 27.28S 23.25E
Kuruman r. R.S.A. 80 26.53S 20.38E
Kurume Japan 57 33.20N 130.29E
Kurur, Jabal mtn. Sudan 72 20.31N 31.32E
Kuşadasi Turkey 35 37.51N 27.15E
Kuşadasi Körfezi b. Turkey 35 37.50N 27.08E
Kusatsu Japan 57 35.02N 135.57E
Kusel Germany 39 49.32N 7.24E
Kushälgarh India 62 23.10N 74.27E
Kushchevskaya Russian Fed. 45 46.34N 39.39E
Kushida r. Japan 57 34.36N 136.34E
Kushiro Japan 57 42.58N 144.24E
Kushka Turkmenistan 65 35.14N 62.15E
Kushtia Bangla. 63 23.55N 89.07E
Kusiyāra r. Bangla. 63 24.36N 91.44E
Kuskokwim B. U.S.A. 98 59.45N 162.25W
Kuskokwim Mts. U.S.A. 98 62.50N 156.00W
Kusma Nepal 63 28.13N 83.41E
Kussharo ko l. Japan 57 43.40N 144.20E
Küssnacht Switz. 39 47.05N 8.27E
Kustanay Kazakhstan 50 53.15N 63.40E
Küstenkanal Germany 38 53.08N 8.00E
Kūstī Sudan 73 13.10N 32.40E
Kütahya Turkey 64 39.25N 29.56E
Kutaisi Georgia 45 42.15N 42.44E
Kutina Croatia 31 45.29N 16.46E
Kutiyāna India 62 21.38N 69.59E
Kutná Hora Czech Republic 36 49.57N 15.16E
Kutno Poland 37 52.15N 19.23E
Kutu Zaïre 78 2.42S 18.09E
Kutubdia I. Bangla. 63 21.50N 91.52E
Kutum Sudan 72 14.12N 24.40E
Kutztown U.S.A. 115 40.31N 75.47W
Kuujjuaq Canada 99 58.10N 68.15W
Kuujjuarapik Canada 102 55.25N 77.45W
Kuusamo Finland 44 65.57N 29.15E
Kuvango Angola 78 14.28S 16.25E
Kuwait Asia 65 29.20N 47.40E
Kuwait town see Al Kuwayt Kuwait 65
Kuwana Japan 57 35.04N 136.42E
Kuybyshev see Samara Russian Fed. 44
Kuybyshevskoye Vodokhranilishche resr. Russian Fed. 44 55.00N 49.00E
Kuyeda Russian Fed. 44 56.25N 55.33E
Kuzey Anadolu Dağlari mts. Turkey 64 40.32N 38.00E
Kuznetsk Russian Fed. 44 53.08N 46.36E
Kuzomen Russian Fed. 44 66.18N 36.51E
Kuzreka Russian Fed. 44 66.35N 34.48E
Kvaenangen est. Norway 40 69.50N 21.30E
Kvarner g. Croatia 31 44.45N 14.35E
Kvarnerić str. Croatia 31 44.45N 14.35E
Kvenna r. Norway 42 60.01N 7.56E
Kvina r. Norway 42 58.17N 6.56E
Kwale Kenya 79 4.20S 39.25E
Kwamouth Zaïre 78 3.11S 16.16E
Kwangju S. Korea 53 35.07N 126.52E
Kwango r. Zaïre 78 3.20S 17.23E
Kwara d. Nigeria 77 8.20N 5.35E
Kwatisore Indonesia 59 3.18S 134.50E
Kwa Zulu R.S.A. 80 27.30S 32.00E
Kwekwe Zimbabwe 80 18.59S 29.46E
Kweneng d. Botswana 80 24.30S 25.40E
Kwenge r. Zaïre 78 4.53S 18.47E
Kwethluk U.S.A. 98 60.49N 161.27W
Kwidzyn Poland 37 53.45N 18.56E

179

Kwigillingok U.S.A. **98** 59.51N 163.08W
Kwiguk U.S.A. **98** 62.45N 164.28W
Kwilu *r.* Zaïre **78** 3.18S 17.22E
Kwinana Australia **89** 32.15S 115.48E
Kwoka *mtn.* Indonesia **59** 1.30S 132.30E
Kyabé Chad **77** 9.28N 18.54E
Kyabram Australia **93** 36.18S 145.05E
Kyaiklat Myanmar **56** 16.25N 95.42E
Kyaikto Myanmar **56** 17.16N 97.01E
Kyaka Tanzania **79** 1.16S 31.27E
Kyakhta Russian Fed. **52** 50.22N 106.30E
Kyalite Australia **92** 34.57S 143.31E
Kyancutta Australia **92** 33.08S 135.34E
Kyaukpadaung Myanmar **56** 20.50N 95.08E
Kyaukpyu Myanmar **56** 19.20N 93.33E
Kybybolite Australia **92** 36.54S 140.58E
Kychema Russian Fed. **44** 65.32N 42.42E
Kyle of Lochalsh *town* U.K. **14** 57.17N 5.43W
Kyll *r.* Germany **16** 49.48N 6.42E
Kyllburg Germany **39** 50.02N 6.35E
Kyluchevskaya *mtn.* Russian Fed. **51** 56.00N 160.30E
Kyneton Australia **93** 37.14S 144.28E
Kynnefjäll *hill* Sweden **42** 58.42N 11.41E
Kynuna Australia **90** 21.35S 141.55E
Kyoga, L. Uganda **79** 1.30N 33.00E
Kyogle Australia **93** 28.36S 152.59E
Kyong Myanmar **56** 20.49N 96.40E
Kyonpyaw Myanmar **56** 17.18N 95.12E
Kyotera Uganda **79** 0.40S 31.31E
Kyōto Japan **57** 35.00N 135.45E
Kyōto *d.* Japan **57** 34.55N 135.35E
Kyrgyzstan Asia **52** 41.30N 75.00E
Kyritz Germany **38** 52.56N 12.23E
Kyrkheden Sweden **43** 60.10N 13.29E
Kyrön *r.* Finland **40** 63.14N 21.45E
Kyrta Russian Fed. **44** 64.02N 57.40E
Kyshtym Russian Fed. **9** 55.43N 60.32E
Kyūshū *d.* Japan **57** 32.00N 130.00E
Kyūshū *i.* Japan **57** 32.00N 130.00E
Kyushu Palau Ridge Pacific Oc. **84** 15.00N 135.00E
Kyūshū sanchi *mts.* Japan **57** 32.20N 131.20E
Kyustendil Bulgaria **34** 42.25N 22.41E
Kywong Australia **93** 35.01S 146.45E
Kyyiv *see* Kiyev Ukraine **37**
Kyyjärvi Finland **40** 63.02N 25.04E
Kyzyl Russian Fed. **52** 51.42N 94.28E
Kyzyl Kum, Peski *f.* Uzbekistan **9** 42.00N 64.30E
Kzyl Orda Kazakhstan **9** 44.52N 65.28E

L

La Alagaba Spain **27** 37.28N 6.01W
La Albuera Spain **27** 38.43N 6.49W
La Albufera *l.* Spain **25** 39.20N 0.22W
La Almarcha Spain **27** 39.41N 2.22W
La Almunia de Doña Godina Spain **25** 41.29N 1.22W
Laas Caanood Somali Rep. **71** 8.26N 47.24E
Laas Dawaco Somali Rep. **71** 10.22N 49.03E
Laas Dhaareed Somali Rep. **71** 10.10N 46.01E
Laas Qoray Somali Rep. **71** 11.10N 48.50E
La Asunción Venezuela **122** 11.06N 63.53W
Laâyoune *see* El Aaiún W. Sahara **74**
La Baleine *r.* Canada **99** 58.00N 57.50W
La Banda Argentina **122** 27.44S 64.15W
La Bañeza Spain **26** 42.18N 5.54W
Labao Indonesia **59** 8.12S 122.49E
La Barca Mexico **116** 20.20N 102.33W
La Barge U.S.A. **108** 42.16N 110.12W
La Bassée France **19** 50.32N 2.48E
Labastide-Murat France **20** 44.39N 1.34E
La Baule France **18** 47.17N 2.24W
Labbezanga Mali **76** 14.57N 0.42E
Labe *r.* Czech. *see* Elbe *r.* Germany **38**
Labé Guinea **76** 11.17N 12.11W
Labelle Canada **105** 46.16N 74.44W
La Belle U.S.A. **113** 26.43N 81.27W
Labelle Prov. Park Canada **105** 46.13N 75.19W
Laberge, L. Canada **100** 61.11N 135.12W
Labin Croatia **31** 45.05N 14.07E
Labinsk Russian Fed. **45** 44.39N 40.44E
La Bisbal Spain **25** 41.57N 3.03E
La Blanquilla *i.* Venezuela **117** 11.53N 64.38W
Laboe Germany **38** 54.24N 10.15E
Labouheyre France **20** 44.13N 0.55W
Laboulaye Argentina **125** 34.05S 63.25W
Labrador *f.* Canada **103** 53.00N 62.00W
Labrador Basin *f.* Atlantic Oc. **127** 55.00N 45.00W
Labrador City Canada **103** 52.57N 66.54W
Labrador Sea Canada/Greenland **99** 57.00N 53.00W
Lábrea Brazil **122** 7.16S 64.47W
Labrède France **20** 44.41N 0.31W
Labrit France **20** 44.07N 0.33W
Labuan Indonesia **59** 6.25S 105.49E
Labuan *i.* Malaysia **58** 5.20N 115.15E
Labuha Indonesia **59** 0.37S 127.29E
Labutta Myanmar **56** 16.09N 94.46E
Labyrinth, L. Australia **92** 30.43S 135.07E
Laç Albania **34** 41.38N 19.40E
Lac *d.* Chad **77** 13.30N 14.35E
La Calera Chile **125** 32.47S 71.12W
La Campana Spain **27** 37.34N 5.26W
Lacanau France **20** 44.59N 1.05W
Lacanau, Étang de *b.* France **20** 44.58N 1.07W
La Cañiza Spain **26** 42.13N 8.16W
La Canourgue France **20** 44.26N 3.13E

La Capelle France **19** 49.58N 3.55E
Lacapelle-Marival France **20** 44.44N 1.54E
La Carlota Argentina **125** 33.25S 63.18W
La Carolina Spain **26** 38.15N 3.37W
Lacaune France **20** 43.43N 2.42E
Lacaune, Monts de *mts.* France **20** 43.43N 2.50E
Lac aux Sables *town* Canada **105** 46.52N 72.24W
Lacedonia Italy **33** 41.03N 15.25E
La Ceiba Honduras **117** 15.45N 86.45W
Lacepede B. Australia **92** 36.47S 139.45E
Lac Gatineau *town* Canada **105** 46.34N 75.44W
Lac Giao Vietnam **56** 12.41N 108.02E
La Chaise-Dieu France **20** 45.19N 3.42E
La Chambre France **21** 45.22N 6.18E
Lacha, Ozero *l.* Russian Fed. **44** 61.25N 39.00E
La Charité France **19** 47.11N 3.01E
La Chartre France **18** 47.44N 0.35E
La Châtaigneraie France **18** 46.39N 0.44W
La Châtre France **19** 46.35N 1.59E
La Chaux-de-Fonds Switz. **39** 47.06N 6.50E
Lach Dera *r.* Somali Rep. **79** 0.01S 42.45E
Lachhmangarh India **62** 27.49N 75.02E
Lachine Canada **105** 45.26N 73.40W
Lachine U.S.A. **104** 45.26N 83.40W
Lachlan *r.* Australia **92** 34.21S 143.58E
Lachute Canada **105** 45.38N 74.20W
La Ciotat France **21** 43.10N 5.36E
Lackan Resr. Rep. of Ire. **15** 53.09N 6.31W
Lackawanna U.S.A. **114** 42.49N 78.50W
Läckö Sweden **43** 58.41N 13.13E
Lac la Biche *town* Canada **101** 54.46N 111.58W
Lac la Ronge Prov. Park Canada **101** 55.14N 104.45W
La Clayette France **19** 46.18N 4.19E
La Cocha Argentina **124** 27.45S 65.35W
Lacolle Canada **105** 45.05N 73.22W
Lacombe Canada **100** 52.30N 113.44W
La Concepción Venezuela **122** 10.25N 71.41W
La Concordia Mexico **116** 16.05N 92.38W
Laconia U.S.A. **115** 43.31N 71.29W
La Coruña Spain **26** 43.22N 8.23W
La Coruña *d.* Spain **26** 43.20N 8.30W
La Courtine le-Trucq France **20** 45.42N 2.16E
Lac Rémi *town* Canada **105** 46.01N 74.47W
La Crosse Kans. U.S.A. **110** 38.32N 99.18W
La Crosse Wisc. U.S.A. **110** 43.48N 91.15W
La Cruz Mexico **109** 27.50N 105.11W
La Cruz Uruguay **125** 33.56S 56.15W
Lac St. Paul *town* Canada **105** 46.44N 75.18W
Ladākh Range *mts.* Jammu & Kashmir **63** 34.15N 78.00E
La Demanda, Sierra de *mts.* Spain **24** 42.10N 3.20W
Ládhi Greece **34** 41.28N 26.15E
Ladhón *r.* Greece **35** 37.40N 21.50E
Ladismith R.S.A. **80** 33.29S 21.15E
Ladispoli Italy **32** 41.56N 12.05E
Lädīz Iran **65** 28.57N 61.18E
Lädnun India **62** 27.39N 74.23E
Ladoga *l. see* Ladozhskoye Ozero *l.* Russian Fed. **44**
La Dorada Colombia **122** 5.27N 74.40W
Ladozhskoye Ozero *l.* Russian Fed. **44** 61.00N 32.00E
La Dura Mexico **109** 28.22N 109.33W
Ladushkin Russian Fed. **37** 54.30N 20.05E
Ladva Vetka Russian Fed. **44** 61.16N 34.23E
Ladybrand R.S.A. **80** 29.11S 27.26E
Lady Evelyn L. Canada **104** 47.20N 80.10W
Ladysmith Canada **100** 49.58N 123.49W
Ladysmith R.S.A. **80** 28.32S 29.47E
Ladysmith U.S.A. **114** 45.27N 91.07W
Lae P.N.G. **59** 6.45S 146.30E
Lae Thailand **56** 19.25N 101.40E
Laesö *i.* Denmark **42** 57.16N 11.01E
La Estrada Spain **26** 42.41N 8.29W
La Fayette Ga. U.S.A. **113** 34.42N 85.18W
Lafayette Ind. U.S.A. **112** 40.25N 86.54W
Lafayette La. U.S.A. **111** 30.14N 92.01W
Lafayette, Mt. U.S.A. **105** 44.10N 71.38W
La Fère France **19** 49.40N 3.22E
La Ferté-Bernard France **18** 48.11N 0.40E
La Ferté-Gaucher France **19** 48.47N 3.18E
La Ferté-Macé France **18** 48.36N 0.22W
La Ferté-St. Aubin France **19** 47.43N 1.56E
Lafia Nigeria **77** 8.35N 8.34E
Lafiagi Nigeria **77** 8.50N 5.23E
La Flèche France **18** 47.42N 0.05W
Lafollette U.S.A. **113** 36.23N 84.09W
Laforest Canada **104** 47.02N 81.13W
La Fregeneda Spain **26** 40.59N 6.52W
La Fuente de San Esteban Spain **26** 40.48N 6.15W
La Galite *i.* Tunisia **32** 37.32N 8.56E
La Galite, Canal de *str.* Tunisia **32** 37.20N 9.15E
La Gallega Spain **26** 41.54N 3.16W
Lagan *r.* Sweden **43** 56.33N 12.56E
Lagan *r.* U.K. **15** 54.37N 5.44W
La Garde, Lac *l.* Canada **104** 46.46N 78.14W
Lage Spain **26** 43.13N 9.00W
Lågen *r.* Akershus Norway **41** 60.10N 11.28E
Lågen *r.* Vestfold Norway **42** 59.03N 10.05E
Laghouat Algeria **75** 33.49N 2.55E
Lago Dilolo *town* Angola **78** 11.27S 22.03E
Lagonegro Italy **33** 40.07N 15.46E
Lagos Mexico **116** 21.21N 101.55W
Lagos Nigeria **77** 6.27N 3.28E
Lagos *d.* Nigeria **77** 6.32N 3.30E
Lagos Portugal **27** 37.06N 8.40W
La Goulette Tunisia **32** 36.49N 10.18E
La Granadella Spain **25** 41.21N 0.40E
La Grand'Combe France **20** 44.13N 4.02E
La Grande *r.* Canada **102** 53.20N 79.00W
La Grande U.S.A. **108** 45.20N 118.05W
La Grande Résr. Canada **102** 53.35N 77.10W
La Grande Résr. 3 Canada **102** 53.35N 74.55W
La Grande Résr. 4 Canada **102** 53.50N 73.30W
Lagrange Australia **88** 18.46S 121.49E
La Grange U.S.A. **113** 33.02N 85.02W
La Grave France **21** 45.03N 6.18E
La Guaira Venezuela **122** 10.38N 66.55W
La Guardia Pontevedra Spain **26** 41.54N 8.51W

Laguardia Vascongadas Spain **26** 42.33N 2.35W
La Gudiña Spain **26** 42.04N 7.08W
La Guerche-de-Bretagne France **18** 47.56N 1.14W
La Guerche-sur-l'Aubois France **19** 46.57N 2.57E
Laguiole France **20** 44.41N 2.51E
Laguna Brazil **124** 28.29S 48.47W
Laguna Dam U.S.A. **109** 32.55N 114.25W
Lagunas Chile **124** 20.59S 69.37W
Lagunas Peru **122** 5.10S 75.35W
La Habana Cuba **117** 23.07N 82.25W
Lahad Datu Malaysia **58** 5.05N 118.20E
La Harpe U.S.A. **110** 40.35N 90.57W
Lahat Indonesia **58** 3.46S 103.32E
La Haye-du-Puits France **18** 49.18N 1.33W
Laḥij Yemen **71** 13.04N 44.53E
Lāhījān Iran **65** 37.12N 50.00E
Lahn *r.* Germany **16** 50.18N 7.36E
Lahnstein Germany **39** 50.18N 7.37E
Laholm Sweden **43** 56.31N 13.02E
Laholmsbukten *b.* Sweden **43** 56.35N 12.50E
Lahore Pakistan **62** 31.35N 74.18E
Lahr Germany **39** 48.20N 7.52E
Lahri Pakistan **62** 29.11N 68.13E
Lahti Finland **41** 60.58N 25.40E
Laï Chad **77** 9.22N 16.14E
Laiagam P.N.G. **59** 5.31S 143.39E
Laibin China **55** 23.42N 109.16E
Lai Chau Vietnam **56** 22.04N 103.12E
L'Aigle *r.* Canada **105** 46.28N 76.01W
L'Aigle France **18** 48.45N 0.38E
Laignes France **19** 47.50N 4.22E
Laihia Finland **40** 62.58N 22.01E
Lainá Greece **34** 41.03N 26.19E
Laingsburg R.S.A. **80** 33.11S 20.49E
Laingsburg U.S.A. **104** 42.54N 84.21W
Lainio *r.* Sweden **40** 67.28N 22.50E
Lairg U.K. **14** 58.01N 4.25W
Laisamis Kenya **79** 1.38N 37.47E
Laissac France **20** 44.23N 2.49E
Laitila Finland **41** 60.53N 21.41E
Laiyuan China **54** 39.19N 114.41E
Laizhou Wan *b.* China **54** 37.30N 119.30E
La Jarrie France **20** 46.08N 1.00W
La Javie France **21** 44.10N 6.21E
Lajes Brazil **126** 27.48S 50.20W
La Junta U.S.A. **108** 37.59N 103.33W
Lakaband Pakistan **62** 31.00N 69.30E
Lak Bor *r.* Kenya **73** 1.18N 40.40E
Lak Bor *r.* Somali Rep. **79** 0.32N 42.05E
Lake Biddy *town* Australia **89** 33.01S 118.51E
Lake Boga *town* Australia **92** 35.27S 143.39E
Lake Brown *town* Australia **89** 30.57S 118.19E
Lake Cargelligo *town* Australia **93** 33.19S 146.23E
Lake Charles *town* U.S.A. **111** 30.13N 93.12W
Lake City U.S.A. **113** 30.12N 82.39W
Lake Clear *town* Canada **105** 45.27N 77.17W
Lake District *f.* U.K. **12** 54.30N 3.10W
Lakefield Canada **104** 44.26N 78.16W
Lake George *town* Colo. U.S.A. **108** 38.58N 105.23W
Lake George *town* N.Y. U.S.A. **115** 43.26N 73.43W
Lake Grace *town* Australia **89** 33.06S 118.28E
Lake Harbour *town* Canada **99** 62.50N 69.50W
Lake King *town* Australia **89** 33.05S 119.40E
Lakeland *town* U.S.A. **113** 28.02N 81.59W
Lake Mead Nat. Recreation Area U.S.A. **109** 36.00N 114.30W
Lake Nash *town* Australia **90** 21.00S 137.55E
Lake Orion *town* U.S.A. **114** 42.47N 83.14W
Lakepa Niue **84** 19.01S 169.49W
Lake Placid *town* U.S.A. **112** 44.17N 73.59W
Lake River *town* Canada **102** 54.30N 82.30W
Lakes Entrance *town* Australia **93** 37.53S 147.59E
Lakeshore U.S.A. **108** 37.15N 119.12W
Lakeside Ohio U.S.A. **114** 41.32N 82.45W
Lakeside Utah U.S.A. **108** 41.13N 112.54W
Lake Superior Prov. Park Canada **102** 47.30N 84.50W
Lakeview U.S.A. **108** 42.11N 120.21W
Lake Village *town* U.S.A. **111** 33.20N 91.17W
Lakewood N.J. U.S.A. **115** 40.06N 74.13W
Lakewood N.Mex. U.S.A. **109** 32.39N 104.39W
Lakewood N.Y. U.S.A. **114** 42.06N 79.20W
Lakewood Ohio U.S.A. **114** 41.29N 81.48W
Lākheri India **62** 25.40N 76.10E
Lakhīmpur India **63** 27.57N 80.46E
Lakhish, Nahal *wadi* Israel **67** 31.37N 34.46E
Lakhnādon India **63** 22.36N 79.36E
Lakhpat India **62** 23.49N 68.47E
Lakonikós Kólpos *g.* Greece **35** 36.25N 22.37E
Lakota Côte d'Ivoire **76** 5.50N 5.30W
Lakota U.S.A. **110** 48.02N 98.21W
Laksefjorden *est.* Norway **40** 70.58N 27.00E
Lakselv Norway **40** 70.03N 24.55E
Lakshadweep Is. Indian Oc. **60** 11.00N 72.00E
Lala India **63** 24.25N 92.40E
Lāla Mūsa Pakistan **62** 32.42N 73.58E
Lalaua Mozambique **79** 14.20S 38.30E
Lalbenque France **20** 44.20N 1.33E
Lālehzār, Kūh-e *mtn.* Iran **65** 29.26N 56.48E
Lālganj India **63** 25.52N 85.11E
Lalībela Ethiopia **71** 12.02N 39.02E
La Libertad El Salvador **117** 13.28N 89.20W
Lalín Spain **26** 42.39N 8.07W
Lalinde France **20** 44.51N 0.44E
La Línea Spain **27** 36.10N 5.19W
Lalitpur India **63** 24.41N 78.25E
Lalitpur Nepal **63** 27.41N 85.20E
Lälmanir Hät Bangla. **63** 25.54N 89.27E
La Loche Canada **101** 56.29N 109.27W
La Loche, Lac *l.* Canada **101** 56.25N 109.30W
La Loupe France **18** 48.28N 1.01E
La Louvière Belgium **16** 50.29N 4.11E
Lālpur India **62** 22.12N 69.58E
Lālsot India **62** 26.34N 76.20E
La Maddalena Italy **32** 41.13N 9.24E
Lamar U.S.A. **110** 38.05N 102.37W
Lamarche France **19** 48.04N 5.47E
La Marsa Tunisia **32** 36.53N 10.20E
Lamastre France **21** 44.59N 4.35E

Lamballe France **18** 48.28N 2.31W
Lambaréné Gabon **78** 0.40S 10.15E
Lambasa Fiji **84** 16.25S 179.24E
Lambayeque Peru **122** 6.36S 79.50W
Lambert's Bay *town* R.S.A. **80** 32.06S 18.16E
Lámbia Greece **35** 37.52N 21.53E
Lamé Chad **77** 9.14N 14.33E
Lame Nigeria **77** 9.92N 9.12E
Lamego Portugal **26** 41.06N 7.49W
Lameroo Australia **92** 35.20S 140.33E
La Mesa Calif. U.S.A. **109** 32.46N 117.01W
Lamesa Tex. U.S.A. **111** 32.44N 101.57W
Lamía Greece **35** 38.54N 22.26E
La Minerve Canada **105** 46.15N 74.56W
Lammermuir Hills U.K. **14** 55.51N 2.40W
Lammhult Sweden **43** 57.10N 14.35E
Lamoille *r.* U.S.A. **105** 44.35N 73.10W
Lamongan Indonesia **59** 7.05S 112.26E
Lamont U.S.A. **108** 42.12N 107.28W
La Mothe-Achard France **18** 46.37N 1.40W
Lamotrek *i.* Federated States of Micronesia **59** 7.28N 146.23E
Lamotte-Beuvron France **19** 47.36N 2.01E
La Motte-Chalençon France **21** 44.29N 5.23E
La Motte du-Claire France **21** 44.21N 6.02E
La Moure U.S.A. **110** 46.21N 98.18W
Lampa Peru **122** 15.10S 70.30W
Lampasas U.S.A. **111** 31.04N 98.12W
Lampedusa *i.* Italy **28** 35.30N 12.35E
Lampertheim Germany **39** 49.35N 8.28E
Lampeter U.K. **13** 52.06N 4.06W
Lampinoú Greece **34** 39.22N 23.10E
Lampione *i.* Italy **28** 35.33N 12.18E
Lamu Kenya **79** 2.20S 40.54E
La Mure France **21** 44.54N 5.47E
Lana Italy **30** 46.37N 11.09E
Lanai *i.* Hawaiian Is. **85** 20.50N 156.55W
Lanai City Hawaiian Is. **85** 20.50N 156.55W
La Nao, Cabo de Spain **24** 38.42N 0.15E
Lanark U.K. **14** 55.41N 3.47W
La Nava de Ricomalillo Spain **27** 39.39N 4.59W
Lancashire *d.* U.K. **12** 53.53N 2.30W
Lancaster Canada **105** 45.08N 74.30W
Lancaster Calif. U.S.A. **109** 34.42N 118.08W
Lancaster N.H. U.S.A. **105** 44.29N 71.34W
Lancaster N.Y. U.S.A. **114** 42.54N 78.41W
Lancaster Ohio U.S.A. **114** 39.43N 82.36W
Lancaster Penn. U.S.A. **115** 40.02N 76.19W
Lancaster S.C. U.S.A. **113** 34.43N 80.47W
Lancaster Tex. U.S.A. **111** 32.36N 96.46W
Lancaster Sd. Canada **99** 74.00N 85.00W
Lancelin Australia **89** 31.01S 115.19E
Lanchow *see* Lanzhou China **54**
Lanciano Italy **31** 42.14N 14.23E
Lancun China **54** 36.24N 120.10E
Landau Bayern Germany **39** 48.40N 12.43E
Landau Rhein.-Pfalz. Germany **39** 49.12N 8.07E
Landay Afghan. **62** 30.31N 63.47E
Landeck Austria **39** 47.08N 10.34E
Landen Belgium **16** 50.46N 5.04E
Lander *r.* Australia **90** 20.25S 132.00E
Lander U.S.A. **108** 42.50N 108.44W
Landerneau France **18** 48.27N 4.15W
Landes *d.* France **20** 44.20N 1.00W
Landes *f.* France **20** 44.00N 1.00W
Landete Spain **25** 39.53N 1.25W
Landisville U.S.A. **115** 39.31N 74.55W
Landivisiau France **18** 48.31N 4.04W
Landor Australia **88** 25.06S 116.50E
Landquart Switz. **39** 46.58N 9.33E
Landrecies France **19** 50.08N 3.42E
Landsberg Germany **39** 48.05N 10.55E
Landsbro Sweden **43** 57.22N 14.54E
Lands End *c.* Canada **96** 76.10N 123.00W
Land's End *c.* U.K. **13** 50.03N 5.45W
Landshut Germany **39** 48.33N 12.09E
Landskrona Sweden **43** 55.52N 12.50E
Lanett U.S.A. **113** 32.52N 85.12W
Langå Denmark **42** 56.23N 9.55E
La'nga Co *l.* China **63** 30.45N 81.15E
Langadhás Greece **34** 40.45N 23.04E
Langádhia Greece **35** 37.41N 22.02E
Langanes *c.* Iceland **40** 66.30N 14.30W
Langao China **54** 33.22N 109.04E
Långban Sweden **43** 59.51N 14.15E
Langdon U.S.A. **110** 48.46N 98.22W
Langeac France **20** 45.06N 3.30E
Langeais France **18** 47.20N 0.24E
L'Ange Gardien Canada **105** 46.55N 71.07W
Langeland *i.* Denmark **42** 55.00N 10.50E
Längelmävesi *l.* Finland **41** 61.32N 24.22E
Langen Germany **39** 49.59N 8.41E
Längenfeld Austria **39** 47.04N 10.58E
Langenhagen Germany **38** 52.27N 9.44E
Langenthal Switz. **39** 47.13N 7.47E
Langeoog *i.* Germany **38** 53.46N 7.32E
Langesund Norway **42** 59.00N 9.45E
Langholm U.K. **14** 55.09N 3.00W
Langjökull *ice cap* Iceland **40** 63.43N 20.03W
Langkawi *i.* Malaysia **58** 6.20N 99.30E
Langlade Canada **102** 48.14N 76.00W
Langnau Switz. **39** 46.57N 7.47E
Langogne France **20** 44.43N 3.51E
Langon France **20** 44.33N 0.15W
Langøy *i.* Norway **40** 68.45N 15.00E
Langres France **19** 47.52N 5.20E
Langres, Plateau de *f.* France **19** 47.41N 5.03E
Langsa Indonesia **58** 4.28N 97.59E
Langshan China **54** 41.02N 107.27E
Lang Shan *mts.* China **54** 41.30N 107.10E
Lang Son Vietnam **55** 21.49N 106.45E
Langtry U.S.A. **111** 29.48N 101.34W
Languedoc-Roussillon *d.* France **20** 43.50N 3.30E
Langxi China **55** 31.08N 119.10E

Laniel Canada 104 47.04N 79.18W
Lannemezan France 20 43.08N 0.23E
Lannilis France 18 48.34N 4.31W
Lannion France 18 48.44N 3.28W
L'Annonciation Canada 105 46.25N 74.52W
Lanoraie Canada 105 45.58N 73.13W
Lansdale U.S.A. 115 40.15N 75.17W
Lansdowne India 63 29.50N 78.41E
L'Anse au Loup Canada 103 51.34N 56.48W
Lansing U.S.A. 112 42.44N 84.34W
Lanslebourg France 21 45.17N 6.52E
Lantewa Nigeria 77 12.15N 11.45E
Lanusei Italy 32 39.52N 9.34E
Lanxi China 55 29.17N 119.31E
Lanzarote i. Canary Is. 74 29.00N 13.40W
Lanzhou China 54 36.01N 103.46E
Lanzo Torinese Italy 30 45.16N 7.28E
Laoag Phil. 59 18.14N 120.36E
Lào Cai Vietnam 56 22.30N 104.00E
Laochang China 55 25.12N 104.35E
Laoha He r. China 54 43.30N 120.42E
Laohekou China 54 32.26N 111.41E
Laois d. Rep. of Ire. 15 53.00N 7.20W
Laojun Shan mtn. China 54 33.45N 111.38E
Laon France 19 49.34N 3.40E
Laona U.S.A. 102 45.35N 88.40W
La Orotava Canary Is. 127 28.26N 16.30W
La Oroya Peru 122 11.36S 75.54W
Laos Asia 56 18.30N 104.00E
Lapalisse France 20 46.15N 3.38E
La Palma i. Canary Is. 74 28.50N 18.00W
La Palma Spain 27 37.23N 6.33W
La Pampa d. Argentina 125 37.00S 66.00W
La Paragua Venezuela 122 6.53N 63.22W
La Paz Entre Ríos Argentina 125 30.45S 59.38W
La Paz Mendoza Argentina 125 33.28S 67.34W
La Paz Bolivia 124 16.30S 68.09W
La Paz d. Bolivia 124 16.00S 68.10W
La Paz Mexico 109 24.10N 110.18W
La Paz, Bahía de b. Mexico 109 24.15N 110.30W
La Pedrera Colombia 122 1.18S 69.43W
Lapeer U.S.A. 104 43.03N 83.19W
La Peña, Sierra de mts. Spain 24 42.30N 0.50W
La Perouse Str. Russian Fed. 51 45.50N 142.30E
La Pine U.S.A. 108 43.40N 121.30W
Lapinjärvi Finland 41 60.38N 26.13E
Lapland f. Sweden/Finland 40 68.10N 24.10E
La Plata Argentina 125 34.55S 57.57W
La Plata Md. U.S.A. 114 38.32N 76.59W
La Plata Mo. U.S.A. 110 40.02N 92.29W
La Plata, Río de est. Argentina/Uruguay 125 35.15S 56.45W
Lapointe, Lac l. Canada 103 53.32N 68.56W
Laporte U.S.A. 115 41.25N 76.30W
Lappajärvi l. Finland 40 63.08N 23.40E
Lappeenranta Finland 44 61.04N 28.05E
Lappi d. Finland 40 67.20N 26.00E
Laptevykh, More sea Russian Fed. 51 74.30N 125.00E
Lapua Finland 40 62.57N 23.00E
La Puebla Spain 25 39.46N 3.01E
La Puebla de Cazalla Spain 27 37.14N 5.19W
La Puebla de Montalbán Spain 27 39.52N 4.21W
La Push U.S.A. 108 47.55N 124.38W
La Quiaca Argentina 124 22.05S 65.36W
L'Aquila Italy 30 42.22N 13.22E
Lār Iran 65 27.37N 54.16E
Lara Australia 92 38.01S 144.26E
Laracha Spain 26 43.15N 8.35W
Larache Morocco 74 35.12N 6.10W
Laragne-Montéglin France 21 44.19N 5.49E
La Rambla Spain 27 37.36N 4.44W
Laramie U.S.A. 108 41.19N 105.35W
Laramie Mts. U.S.A. 108 42.00N 105.40W
L'Arbresle France 21 45.50N 4.37E
Lärbro Sweden 43 57.47N 18.47E
Larche, Col de pass France/Italy 21 44.25N 6.53E
Laredo Spain 26 43.24N 3.25W
Laredo U.S.A. 111 27.31N 99.30W
Laredo Sd. Canada 100 52.30N 128.53W
La Réole France 20 44.35N 0.02E
Largeau Chad 77 17.55N 19.07E
L'Argentière-la-Bessée France 21 44.47N 6.33E
Largs U.K. 14 55.48N 4.52W
Lariang Indonesia 58 1.35S 119.25E
Lárimna Greece 35 38.34N 23.17E
Larino Italy 33 41.48N 14.54E
La Rioja Argentina 125 29.25S 66.50W
La Rioja d. Argentina 124 29.00S 66.00W
La Rioja d. Spain 26 42.25N 2.30W
Lárisa Greece 34 39.38N 22.28E
Lark r. U.K. 13 52.26N 0.20E
Lārkāna Pakistan 62 27.33N 68.13E
Larkspur U.S.A. 108 39.13N 104.54W
Larnaca see Lárnax Cyprus 66
Lárnax Cyprus 66 34.54N 33.39E
Larne U.K. 15 54.51N 5.49W
La Robla Spain 26 42.48N 5.37W
La Roca de la Sierra Spain 27 39.07N 6.41W
La Roche Belgium 16 50.11N 5.35E
La Roche-Bernard France 18 47.31N 2.18W
La Rochelle France 20 46.10N 1.10W
La Roche-sur-Yon France 18 46.40N 1.26W
La Roda Spain 27 39.13N 2.09W
La Romana Dom. Rep. 117 18.27N 68.57W
La Ronge Canada 101 55.06N 105.17W
La Ronge, Lac l. Canada 98 55.07N 105.15W
Laroquebrou France 20 44.58N 2.11E
Larrimah Australia 90 15.35S 133.12E
Larvik Norway 42 59.04N 10.00E
La Sagra mtn. Spain 27 37.57N 2.34W
La Salle U.S.A. 110 41.20N 89.06W
Las Animas U.S.A. 108 38.04N 103.13W
La Sarre Canada 102 48.45N 79.15W
Las Cabezas de San Juan Spain 27 36.59N 5.56W
Las Casitas, Cerro mtn. Mexico 109 23.32N 109.59W
L'Ascension Canada 105 46.33N 74.50W
Las Cruces U.S.A. 109 32.23N 106.29W
Las Cuevas Mexico 111 29.38N 101.19W

La Seine, Baie de France 17 49.40N 0.30W
La Serena Chile 124 29.54S 71.16W
La Seu d'Urgell Spain 25 42.22N 1.23E
La Seyne France 21 43.06N 5.53E
Las Flores Argentina 125 36.02S 59.07W
Lâsh-e Joveyn Afghan. 62 31.43N 61.37E
Las Heras Argentina 125 32.50S 68.50W
Lashio Myanmar 56 22.58N 96.51E
Lashkar Gāh Afghan. 62 31.30N 64.21E
Laško Slovenia 31 46.09N 15.14E
Las Lomitas Argentina 124 24.43S 60.35W
Las Marismas f. Spain 27 37.05N 6.20W
La Solana Spain 26 38.56N 3.14W
L'Asomption r. Canada 105 45.43N 73.29W
Las Palmas de Gran Canaria Canary Is. 74 28.08N 15.27W
Las Palomas Mexico 109 31.44N 107.37W
Las Perlas, Archipelago de Panama 117 8.45N 79.30W
La Spezia Italy 30 44.07N 9.50E
Las Piedras Uruguay 125 34.44S 56.13W
Las Plumas Argentina 125 43.40S 67.15W
Lassay France 18 48.26N 0.30W
Lassen Peak mtn. U.S.A. 108 40.29N 121.31W
L'Assomption Canada 105 45.50N 73.25W
Last Chance U.S.A. 108 39.45N 103.36W
Last Mountain L. Canada 101 51.05N 105.10W
Lastoursville Gabon 78 0.50S 12.47E
Lastovo i. Croatia 31 42.45N 16.53E
Lastovski Kanal str. Croatia 31 42.50N 16.59E
Las Tres Vírgenes, Volcán mtn. Mexico 109 27.27N 112.37W
Lastrup Germany 38 52.48N 7.52E
La Suze France 18 47.54N 0.02E
Las Vegas Nev. U.S.A. 109 36.11N 115.08W
Las Vegas N.Mex. U.S.A. 109 35.36N 105.13W
Latacunga Ecuador 122 0.58S 78.36W
La Tagua Colombia 122 0.03S 74.40W
Latakia see Al Lādhiqīyah Syria 66
Latambar Pakistan 62 33.07N 70.52E
Latchford Canada 104 47.20N 79.48W
Lastovo r. Canada 104 47.20N 79.48W
Lātēhar India 63 23.45N 84.30E
La Teste-de-Buch France 20 44.38N 1.09W
Lathen Germany 38 52.52N 7.19E
Lāthi India 62 21.43N 71.23E
Latina Italy 32 41.28N 12.52E
Latisana Italy 30 45.47N 13.00E
La Tortuga i. Venezuela 122 11.00N 65.20W
La Tour-d'Auvergne France 20 45.32N 2.41E
La Tour-du-Pin France 21 45.34N 5.27E
La Tremblade France 20 45.46N 1.08W
La Trimouille France 18 46.28N 1.02E
La Trobe, Mt. Australia 93 39.03S 146.25E
La Truite, Lac à l. Canada 104 47.16N 78.17W
Latrün Jordan 67 31.50N 34.59E
La Tuque Canada 103 47.27N 72.47W
Latvia Europe 44 56.45N 25.00E
Lau Nigeria 77 9.14N 11.15E
Lauchhammer Germany 38 51.30N 13.47E
Lauenburg Germany 38 53.22N 10.33E
Lauf an der Pegnitz Germany 38 49.30N 11.17E
Laughlen, Mt. Australia 90 23.23S 134.23E
Laughlin, Mt. Fiji 84 19.00S 178.30W
Lau Group is. Fiji 84 19.00S 178.30W
Launceston Australia 91 41.25S 147.07E
Launceston U.K. 13 50.38N 4.21W
La Unión Chile 125 40.15S 73.02W
La Unión Spain 25 37.37N 0.52W
Laupheim Germany 39 48.14N 9.52E
Laura Australia 92 33.08S 138.19E
La Urbana Venezuela 122 7.08N 66.56W
Laureana di Borrello Italy 33 38.30N 16.05E
Laurel Del. U.S.A. 115 38.33N 75.34W
Laurel Miss. U.S.A. 111 31.42N 89.08W
Laurel Mont. U.S.A. 108 45.40N 108.46W
Laurel Hill mtn. U.S.A. 114 40.02N 79.17W
Laurel Ridge mtn. U.S.A. 114 39.20N 79.53W
Laureville U.S.A. 114 39.28N 82.44W
Laurencekirk U.K. 14 56.50N 2.29W
Laurens U.S.A. 113 34.29N 82.01W
Laurentians mts. Canada 105 45.43N 75.52W
Laurentides mts. Canada 105 46.25N 73.28W
Laurentides Prov. Park Canada 103 47.30N 71.30W
Lauria Italy 33 40.02N 15.50E
Laurier Canada 105 46.32N 71.38W
Laurière France 20 46.05N 1.28E
Laurieton Australia 93 31.38S 152.46E
Laurinburg U.S.A. 113 34.46N 79.29W
Lauro, Monte mtn. Italy 33 37.08N 14.47E
Lausanne Switz. 39 46.31N 6.38E
Laut i. Indonesia 58 3.45S 116.20E
Lautaro Chile 125 38.31S 72.27W
Lauterbach Germany 38 50.38N 9.24E
Lauterbrunnen Switz. 39 46.36N 7.55E
Lauterecken Germany 39 49.39N 7.35E
Lautoka Fiji 84 17.37S 177.27E
Lauzerte France 20 44.15N 1.08E
Lauzun France 20 44.38N 0.28E
Lavagh More mtn. Rep. of Ire. 15 54.45N 8.07W
Lava Hot Springs town U.S.A. 108 42.37N 112.01W
Laval Canada 105 45.35N 73.45W
Laval France 18 48.04N 0.46W
Lávara Greece 34 41.19N 26.22E
Lavardac France 20 44.11N 0.18E
La Vecilla de Curueño Spain 26 42.51N 5.24W
La Vega Dom. Rep. 117 19.15N 70.33W
La Vela Venezuela 122 11.27N 69.34W
Lavelanet France 20 42.56N 1.51E
Lavello Italy 33 41.03N 15.48E
La Verendrye Prov. Park Canada 105 47.30N 77.30W
Laverlochère Canada 104 47.26N 79.19W
Laverne U.S.A. 111 36.43N 99.54W
Laverton Australia 89 28.49S 122.25E
Lavi Israel 67 32.47N 35.26E
Lavia Finland 41 61.36N 22.36E

Lavielle, L. Canada 104 45.51N 78.14W
Lavigne Canada 104 46.20N 80.05W
Lavik Norway 41 61.06N 5.30E
La Voulte-sur-Rhône France 21 44.48N 4.47E
Lavras Brazil 126 21.15S 44.59W
Lávrion Greece 35 37.44N 24.04E
Lawra Ghana 76 10.40N 2.49W
Lawrence New Zealand 86 45.55S 169.42E
Lawrence Kans. U.S.A. 110 38.58N 95.14W
Lawrence Mass. U.S.A. 115 42.42N 71.09W
Lawrenceburg U.S.A. 113 35.16N 87.20W
Lawrenceville Canada 105 45.25N 72.19W
Lawrenceville Penn. U.S.A. 114 42.00N 77.08W
Lawton Okla. U.S.A. 111 34.37N 98.25W
Lawton Penn. U.S.A. 115 41.46N 76.05W
Lawz, Jabal al mtn. Saudi Arabia 66 28.40N 35.20E
Laxá Sweden 43 58.59N 14.37E
Lay r. France 18 46.20N 1.18W
Laysan i. Hawaiian Is. 84 25.46N 171.44W
Laytonville U.S.A. 108 39.41N 123.29W
Lazio d. Italy 30 42.05N 12.20E
Lead U.S.A. 110 44.21N 103.46W
Leader Canada 101 50.53N 109.31W
Leadhills U.K. 14 55.25N 3.46W
Leamington Canada 104 42.03N 82.36W
Leamington U.S.A. 108 39.31N 112.17W
Learmonth Australia 88 22.13S 114.04E
Leavenworth U.S.A. 110 39.19N 94.55W
Lebak Phil. 59 6.32N 124.03E
Lebane Yugo. 34 42.56N 21.44E
Lebango Congo 78 0.24N 14.44E
Lebanon Asia 66 34.00N 36.00E
Lebanon Ind. U.S.A. 112 40.02N 87.28W
Lebanon Kans. U.S.A. 110 39.49N 98.33W
Lebanon Ky. U.S.A. 113 37.33N 85.15W
Lebanon Mo. U.S.A. 111 37.41N 92.40W
Lebanon N.H. U.S.A. 115 43.38N 72.15W
Lebanon Oreg. U.S.A. 108 44.32N 122.54W
Lebanon Penn. U.S.A. 115 40.20N 76.25W
Lebanon Tenn. U.S.A. 113 36.11N 86.19W
Lebec U.S.A. 109 34.50N 118.52W
Lebesby Norway 40 70.34N 27.00E
Le Blanc France 18 46.38N 1.04E
Łebork Poland 37 54.33N 17.44E
Le Bourg-d'Oisans France 21 45.03N 6.02E
Le Châtelard France 18 45.39N 6.00E
Le Châtelet France 20 46.39N 2.17E
Le Chesne France 19 49.31N 4.46E
Le Cheylard France 21 44.54N 4.25E
Lechiguanas, Islas de las is. Argentina 125 33.26S 59.42W
Lechtaler Alpen mts. Austria 39 47.15N 10.33E
Le Conquet France 18 48.22N 4.46W
L'Écorce, Lac de l. Canada 105 47.05N 76.24W
Le Creusot France 19 46.48N 4.26E
Le Croisic France 18 47.18N 2.31W
Lectoure France 20 43.56N 0.38E
Ledbury U.K. 13 52.03N 2.25W
Ledesma Spain 26 41.05N 6.00W
Le Donjon France 20 46.21N 3.48E
Le Dorat France 20 46.13N 1.05E
Leduc Canada 100 53.20N 113.30W
Lee r. Rep. of Ire. 15 51.53N 8.25W
Lee U.S.A. 115 42.19N 73.15W
Leechburg U.S.A. 114 40.38N 79.36W
Leech L. U.S.A. 110 47.09N 94.23W
Leedey U.S.A. 111 35.52N 99.21W
Leeds Canada 105 46.16N 71.22W
Leeds U.K. 12 53.48N 1.34W
Leeds U.S.A. 113 33.32N 86.31W
Leek U.K. 12 53.07N 2.02W
Leer Germany 38 53.14N 7.26E
Leesburg Fla. U.S.A. 113 28.49N 81.54W
Leesburg Va. U.S.A. 114 39.07N 77.34W
Leeston New Zealand 86 43.46S 172.18E
Leeton Australia 93 34.33S 146.24E
Leeuwarden Neth. 16 53.12N 5.48E
Leeuwin, C. Australia 89 34.22S 115.08E
Leeward Is. C. America 117 18.00N 61.00W
Lefroy, L. Australia 89 31.15S 121.40E
Legazpi Phil. 59 13.10N 123.45E
Legges Tor mtn. Australia 91 41.32S 147.40E
Legget U.S.A. 108 39.52N 123.34W
Leghorn see Livorno Italy 30
Legion Mine Zimbabwe 80 21.23S 28.33E
Legionowo Poland 37 52.25N 20.56E
Legnago Italy 30 45.11N 11.18E
Legnano Italy 30 45.36N 8.54E
Legnica Poland 36 51.12N 16.10E
Le Grand-Lucé France 18 47.52N 0.28E
Le Grand-Quevilly France 18 49.25N 1.02E
Le Grau-du-Roi France 21 43.32N 4.08E
Leh Jammu & Kashmir 63 34.10N 77.35E
Le Havre France 18 49.30N 0.08E
Lehighton U.S.A. 115 40.49N 75.45W
Lehrte Germany 38 52.22N 9.59E
Lehututu Botswana 80 23.54S 21.52E
Leiah Pakistan 62 30.58N 70.56E
Leibnitz Austria 31 46.48N 15.32E
Leicester U.K. 13 52.39N 1.09W
Leicestershire d. U.K. 13 52.29N 1.10W
Leichardt r. Australia 90 17.35S 139.48E
Leiden Neth. 16 52.10N 4.30E
Leie r. Belgium 16 51.03N 3.44E
Leifeng China 55 25.35N 118.17E
Leigh Creek r. Australia 92 29.49S 138.10E
Leigh Creek town Australia 92 30.31S 138.25E
Leighton Buzzard U.K. 13 51.55N 0.39W

Leikanger Norway 41 61.10N 6.52E
Leine r. Germany 38 52.41N 9.36E
Leinster Australia 89 27.59S 120.30E
Leipzig Germany 38 51.19N 12.20E
Leiria Portugal 27 39.45N 8.48W
Leiria d. Portugal 27 39.50N 8.50W
Leirvik Norway 42 59.45N 5.30E
Lei Shui r. China 55 26.57N 112.33E
Leithbridge Canada 100 49.40N 112.45W
Leitrim d. Rep. of Ire. 15 54.08N 8.00W
Leiyang China 55 26.30N 112.42E
Leizhou Bandao pen. China 55 21.00N 110.00E
Lek r. Neth. 16 51.55N 4.29E
Lekhainá Greece 35 37.56N 21.17E
Leksvik Norway 40 63.40N 10.40E
Leland U.S.A. 111 33.24N 90.54W
Leland Lakes Canada 101 60.00N 110.59W
Lelâng l. Sweden 43 59.08N 12.10E
Lelchitsy Belarus 37 51.48N 28.20E
Leleque Argentina 125 42.24S 71.04W
Leling China 54 37.45N 117.13E
Le Lion-d'Angers France 18 47.38N 0.43W
Le Locle Switz. 39 47.03N 6.45E
Le Lude France 18 47.39N 0.09E
Lelystad Neth. 16 52.30N 5.28E
Le Madonie Italy 33 37.55N 14.00E
Léman, Lac l. Switz. 39 46.25N 6.30E
Le Mans France 18 48.00N 0.12E
Le Mars U.S.A. 110 42.47N 96.10W
Le Mayet-de-Montagne France 20 46.05N 3.40E
Leme Brazil 126 22.10S 47.23W
Le Merlerault France 18 48.42N 0.18E
Lemesós Cyprus 66 34.40N 33.03E
Lemgo Germany 38 52.02N 8.54E
Lemhi Range mts. U.S.A. 108 44.30N 113.25W
Lemland i. Finland 43 60.03N 20.10E
Lemmer Neth. 16 52.50N 5.43E
Lemmon U.S.A. 110 45.56N 102.10W
Le Monastier France 20 44.56N 4.00E
Lemoine r. Canada 104 46.25N 3.03E
Lemsid W. Sahara 74 26.32N 13.49W
Lemvig Denmark 42 56.32N 8.18E
Lena r. Russian Fed. 51 72.00N 127.10E
Lena U.S.A. 111 31.47N 92.46W
Lenakel Vanuatu 84 19.32S 169.16E
Lenart Slovenia 31 46.35N 15.50E
Lencloître France 18 46.49N 0.20E
Lendery Russian Fed. 44 63.24N 31.04E
Lendinara Italy 30 45.05N 11.36E
Lengerich Germany 38 52.11N 7.50E
Lengoue r. Congo 78 1.15S 16.42E
Lenhovda Sweden 43 57.00N 15.17E
Lenina, Kanal canal Russian Fed. 45 43.46N 45.00E
Lenina, Pik mtn. Tajikistan 52 40.14N 69.40E
Leningrad see Sankt-Peterburg Russian Fed. 44
Leninogorsk Kazakhstan 50 50.23N 83.32E
Leninsk Russian Fed. 45 48.42N 45.14E
Leninsk Kuznetskiy Russian Fed. 50 54.44N 86.13E
Lenk Switz. 39 46.28N 7.27E
Lenkoran Azerbaijan 65 38.45N 48.50E
Lenmalu Indonesia 59 1.58S 130.00E
Lenne r. Germany 38 51.25N 7.30E
Lennoxville Canada 105 45.22N 71.51W
Lenoir U.S.A. 113 35.56N 81.31W
Lenora Czech Republic 38 48.56N 13.48E
Lenora U.S.A. 110 39.38N 100.03W
Lenore L. Canada 101 52.30N 105.00W
Lenox U.S.A. 115 42.22N 73.17W
Lens France 19 50.26N 2.50E
Lenti Hungary 31 46.37N 16.33E
Lentini Italy 33 37.17N 15.00E
Lenvik Norway 40 69.22N 18.10E
Léo Burkina 76 11.05N 2.06W
Leoben Austria 36 47.23N 15.06E
Leominster U.K. 13 52.15N 2.43W
Leominster U.S.A. 115 42.32N 71.45W
Léon France 20 43.53N 1.18W
León Mexico 116 21.10N 101.42W
León d. Mexico 111 25.00N 100.20W
León Nicaragua 117 12.24N 86.52W
León Spain 26 42.36N 5.34W
Leon U.S.A. 110 40.44N 93.45W
Leonardtown U.S.A. 115 38.17N 76.38W
Leonardville Namibia 80 23.21S 18.47E
Leonárison Cyprus 66 35.28N 34.08E
Leonberg Germany 39 48.48N 9.01E
Leondári Greece 35 39.11N 22.08E
Leonforte Italy 33 37.39N 14.24E
Leongatha Australia 93 38.29S 145.57E
Leonídhion Greece 35 37.10N 22.52E
León, Montes de mts. Spain 26 42.30N 6.15W
Leonora Australia 89 28.54S 121.20E
Leopoldina Brazil 126 21.30S 42.38W
Leopoldsburg Belgium 16 51.08N 5.13E
Leovo Moldova 35 46.29N 28.12E
Le Palais France 18 47.21N 3.09W
Lepe Spain 27 37.15N 7.12W
Lepel Russian Fed. 44 54.48N 28.40E
Le Pellerin France 18 47.12N 1.45W
Leping China 55 28.58N 117.08E
L'Epiphanie Canada 105 45.51N 73.30W
Le Pont-de-Beauvoisin France 21 45.32N 5.40E
Lepontine, Alpi mts. Switz. 39 46.20N 8.37E
Le Puy France 20 45.02N 3.53E
Lequeitio Spain 26 43.22N 2.30W
Le Quesnoy France 19 50.15N 3.38E
Lerbäck Sweden 43 58.58N 15.02E
Lercara Friddi Italy 32 37.45N 13.36E
Léré Chad 77 9.41N 14.17E
Lerici Italy 30 44.04N 9.55E
Lérida Spain 25 41.37N 0.37E
Lérida see Lleida d. Spain 25
Lérida see Lleida d. Spain 25
Lerma Spain 26 42.02N 3.45W
Le Rochefoucauld France 20 45.45N 0.23E
Léros Greece 35 37.10N 26.50E
Leross Canada 101 51.17N 103.53W
Le Roy Kans. U.S.A. 111 38.05N 95.38W

Le Roy Mich. U.S.A. **112** 44.03N 85.29W
Le Roy N.Y. U.S.A. **114** 42.59N 77.59W
Lerwick U.K. **14** 60.09N 1.09W
Les Aix-d'Angillon France **19** 47.12N 2.34E
Les Andelys France **18** 49.15N 1.25E
Les Borges Blanques Spain **25** 41.31N 0.52E
Les Cayes Haiti **117** 18.15N 73.46W
Leschenault, C. Australia **89** 31.50S 115.23E
Les Échelles France **21** 45.26N 5.45E
Les Ecrins mtn. France **21** 44.50N 6.20E
Les Essarts France **18** 46.46N 1.14W
Lesh Albania **34** 41.46N 19.39E
Leshan China **55** 29.30N 103.45E
Les Herbiers France **18** 46.52N 1.01W
Leshukonskoye Russian Fed. **44** 64.55N 45.50E
Lesina, Lago di l. Italy **31** 41.53N 15.26E
Lesjaskog Norway **41** 62.15N 8.22E
Lesjöfors Sweden **43** 59.59N 14.11E
Leskovac Yugo. **34** 42.59N 21.57E
Leslie Ark. U.S.A. **111** 35.50N 92.34W
Leslie Mich. U.S.A. **104** 42.27N 84.26W
Lesotho Africa **80** 29.00S 28.00E
Lesozavodsk Russian Fed. **53** 45.30N 133.29E
Les Pieux France **18** 49.31N 1.48W
Les Riceys France **19** 47.59N 4.22E
Les Sables d'Olonne France **18** 46.30N 1.47W
Lessay France **18** 49.13N 1.32W
Lessebo Sweden **43** 56.45N 15.16E
Lesser Antilles is. C. America **117** 13.00N 65.00W
Lesser Slave L. Canada **100** 55.30N 115.25W
Lesser Sunda Is. see Nusa Tenggara is. Indonesia **58**
Lessines Belgium **16** 50.43N 3.50E
Lesti r. Finland **40** 64.04N 23.38E
Le Sueur U.S.A. **110** 44.27N 93.54W
Les Vans France **21** 44.24N 4.08E
Lésvos i. Greece **35** 39.10N 25.50E
Leszno Poland **36** 51.51N 16.35E
Letchworth U.K. **13** 51.58N 0.13W
Letchworth State Park U.S.A. **114** 42.42N 77.56W
Letenye Hungary **31** 46.26N 16.43E
Lethbridge Canada **100** 49.43N 112.48W
Lethem Guyana **122** 3.18N 59.46W
Le Thillot France **19** 47.53N 6.46E
Letiahau r. Botswana **80** 21.16S 24.00E
Leticia Colombia **122** 4.09S 69.57W
Leti, Kepulauan is. Indonesia **59** 8.20S 128.00E
Leting China **54** 39.26N 118.56E
Letohatchee U.S.A. **113** 32.08N 86.30W
Le Trayas France **21** 43.28N 6.55E
Le Tréport France **18** 50.04N 1.22E
Letterkenny Rep. of Ire. **15** 54.56N 7.45W
Leucate, Étang de b. France **20** 42.51N 3.00E
Leuk Switz. **39** 46.19N 7.38E
Leuser mtn. Indonesia **58** 3.50N 97.10E
Leutkirch Germany **39** 47.49N 10.01E
Leuven Belgium **16** 50.53N 4.45E
Leuze Hainaut Belgium **16** 50.36N 3.37E
Leuze Namur Belgium **16** 50.34N 4.53E
Levack Canada **104** 46.38N 81.23W
Levádhia Greece **35** 38.27N 22.54E
Levanger Norway **40** 63.45N 11.19E
Levanto Italy **30** 44.10N 9.38E
Levanzo, Isola di i. Italy **32** 38.00N 12.20E
Levelland U.S.A. **111** 33.35N 102.23W
Lévêque, C. Australia **88** 16.25S 123.00E
Le Verdon France **20** 45.33N 1.04W
Leverkusen Germany **38** 51.03N 6.59E
Levice Slovakia **37** 48.13N 18.37E
Levier France **19** 46.57N 6.08E
Levin New Zealand **86** 40.37S 175.18E
Lévis Canada **105** 46.48N 71.11W
Levittown U.S.A. **115** 40.41N 73.31W
Lévka Cyprus **35** 35.06N 32.51E
Lévka Óri mtn. Greece **35** 35.18N 24.01E
Levkás Greece **35** 38.48N 20.43E
Levkás i. Greece **35** 38.39N 20.27E
Levkímni Greece **34** 39.25N 20.04E
Levkosía Cyprus **66** 35.11N 33.23E
Levroux France **19** 46.59N 1.37E
Levski Bulgaria **34** 43.21N 25.10E
Lewes U.K. **13** 50.53N 0.02E
Lewes U.S.A. **115** 38.47N 75.08W
Lewis i. U.K. **14** 58.10N 6.40W
Lewisburg U.S.A. **114** 40.58N 76.53W
Lewis Pass f. New Zealand **86** 42.30S 172.15E
Lewisporte Canada **103** 49.15N 55.04W
Lewis Range mts. U.S.A. **108** 48.30N 113.15W
Lewiston Idaho U.S.A. **108** 46.25N 117.01W
Lewiston Maine U.S.A. **112** 44.04N 70.13W
Lewiston Mich. U.S.A. **104** 44.53N 84.18W
Lewistown Mont. U.S.A. **108** 47.04N 109.26W
Lewistown Penn. U.S.A. **114** 40.36N 77.31W
Lexington Ky. U.S.A. **113** 38.03N 84.30W
Lexington Mich. U.S.A. **114** 43.16N 82.32W
Lexington Miss. U.S.A. **111** 33.07N 90.03W
Lexington Nebr. U.S.A. **110** 40.47N 99.45W
Lexington Oreg. U.S.A. **108** 45.27N 119.41W
Leyburn U.K. **12** 54.19N 1.50W
Leydsdorp R.S.A. **80** 23.59S 30.32E
Leyre r. France **20** 44.39N 1.01W
Leyte i. Phil. **59** 10.40N 124.50E
Lezignan France **20** 43.12N 2.46E
Lhari China **63** 30.47N 93.24E
Lhasa China **63** 29.39N 91.06E
Lhasa He r. China **63** 29.21N 90.45E
Lhazê China **63** 29.10N 87.45E
Lhazhong China **63** 32.02N 86.34E
Lhokseumawe Indonesia **58** 5.09N 97.09E
Lhozhag China **63** 28.23N 90.48E
Lhuntsi Dzong Bhutan **63** 27.39N 91.09E
Lhünzê China **63** 28.26N 92.27E
Lhünzhub China **63** 30.00N 91.12E
Li Thailand **56** 17.50N 98.55E
Liancheng China **55** 25.47N 116.48E
Liangcheng China **54** 40.31N 112.29E
Liangdang China **54** 33.59N 106.23E
Lianjiang Fujian China **55** 26.10N 119.33E

Lianjiang Guangdong China **55** 21.33N 110.19E
Lianshan China **55** 24.37N 112.02E
Lianshui China **54** 33.46N 119.18E
Lian Xian China **55** 24.52N 112.27E
Lianyungang China **54** 34.36N 119.10E
Liaocheng China **54** 36.25N 115.58E
Liaodong Bandao pen. China **54** 40.00N 122.20E
Liaodong Wan b. China **54** 40.00N 121.00E
Liao He r. China **54** 40.40N 122.20E
Liaoning d. China **54** 41.40N 121.20E
Liaoyang China **54** 41.17N 123.13E
Liaoyuan China **54** 42.50N 125.08E
Liapádhes Greece **34** 39.40N 19.44E
Liard r. Canada **100** 61.51N 121.18W
Liäri Pakistan **62** 25.41N 66.29E
Liart France **19** 49.46N 4.20E
Libby U.S.A. **108** 48.23N 115.33W
Libenge Zaïre **78** 3.39N 18.39E
Liberal U.S.A. **111** 37.02N 100.55W
Liberdade Brazil **126** 22.01S 44.22W
Liberec Czech Republic **36** 50.48N 15.05E
Liberia Africa **76** 6.30N 9.30W
Liberia Costa Rica **117** 10.39N 85.28W
Liberty N.Y. U.S.A. **115** 41.48N 74.45W
Liberty Tex. U.S.A. **111** 30.03N 94.47W
Lībīyah, Aş Şaḥrā' al des. Africa **64** 24.00N 25.30E
Libo China **55** 25.25N 107.53E
Libourne France **20** 44.55N 0.14W
Libramont Belgium **16** 49.56N 5.22E
Librazhd Albania **34** 41.12N 20.22E
Libreville Gabon **78** 0.25N 9.30E
Libya Africa **75** 26.30N 17.00E
Libyan Desert see Lībīyah, Aş Şaḥrā' al Africa **64**
Libyan Plateau see Aḍ Ḏiffah f. Africa **64**
Licantén Chile **125** 34.59S 72.00W
Licata Italy **32** 37.05N 13.56E
Lich Germany **38** 50.33N 8.50E
Lichfield U.K. **13** 52.40N 1.50W
Lichinga Mozambique **79** 13.09S 35.17E
Lichtenburg R.S.A. **80** 26.08S 26.09E
Lichtenfels Germany **38** 50.09N 11.04E
Lichtenvoorde Neth. **16** 51.59N 6.32E
Lichuan Hubei China **55** 30.18N 108.51E
Lichuan Jiangxi China **55** 27.22N 116.59E
Lickdale U.S.A. **115** 40.28N 76.31W
Lickershamn Sweden **43** 57.50N 18.31E
Licko Polje f. Croatia **31** 44.35N 15.25E
Lida Belarus **37** 53.50N 25.19E
Lida U.S.A. **108** 37.29N 117.29W
Lidan r. Sweden **43** 58.31N 13.09E
Lidhorikion Greece **35** 38.28N 22.12E
Lidingö Sweden **43** 59.22N 18.08E
Lidköping Sweden **43** 58.30N 13.10E
Liechtenstein Europe **39** 47.09N 9.32E
Liège Belgium **16** 50.38N 5.35E
Liège d. Belgium **16** 50.32N 5.35E
Lien-Huong Vietnam **56** 11.13N 108.48E
Lienz Austria **39** 46.51N 12.47E
Liepāja Latvia **41** 56.31N 21.01E
Lier Belgium **16** 51.08N 4.35E
Lierneux Belgium **16** 50.18N 5.50E
Liestal Switz. **39** 47.29N 7.44E
Lieşti Romania **37** 45.38N 27.32E
Lietariegos, Puerto de pass Spain **26** 43.00N 6.25W
Liévin France **19** 50.25N 2.46E
Lièvre, Rivière du r. Canada **105** 45.31N 75.26W
Liffey r. Rep. of Ire. **15** 53.21N 6.14W
Liffré France **18** 48.13N 1.30W
Lifjell mtn. Norway **42** 59.30N 8.52E
Lifou, Île i. N. Cal. **84** 20.53S 167.13E
Lightning Ridge town Australia **93** 29.27S 148.00E
Lignières France **19** 46.45N 2.11E
Ligny-en-Barrois France **19** 48.41N 5.20E
Ligourion Greece **35** 37.37N 23.02E
Ligueil France **18** 47.03N 0.49E
Liguria d. Italy **30** 44.30N 8.50E
Ligurian Sea Med. Sea **30** 43.40N 9.00E
Lihou Reef and Cays Australia **90** 17.25S 151.40E
Lihue Hawaiian Is. **85** 21.59N 159.23W
Lihula Estonia **41** 58.41N 23.50E
Lijiang China **61** 26.50N 100.15E
Lijin China **54** 37.29N 118.16E
Likasi Zaïre **78** 10.58S 26.50E
Likati Zaïre **78** 3.21N 23.53E
Liknes Norway **42** 58.19N 6.59E
Likona r. Congo **78** 0.11N 16.25E
Likouala r. Congo **78** 0.51S 17.17E
Liku Niue **84** 19.03S 169.48W
L'Île Bouchard France **18** 47.07N 0.25E
L'Île Rousse France **21** 42.38N 8.56E
Lilla Edet Sweden **43** 58.08N 12.08E
Lille France **19** 50.38N 3.04E
Lille Baelt str. Denmark **42** 55.20N 9.45E
Lillebonne France **18** 49.31N 0.33E
Lillehammer Norway **41** 61.08N 10.30E
Lillers France **19** 50.34N 2.29E
Lillesand Norway **42** 58.15N 8.24E
Lilleström Norway **42** 59.57N 11.05E
Lillhärdal Sweden **41** 61.51N 14.04E
Lillo Spain **27** 39.43N 3.18W
Lillooet Canada **100** 50.42N 121.56W
Lillooet r. Canada **100** 49.15N 121.57W
Lilongwe Malaŵi **79** 13.58S 33.49E
Liloy Phil. **59** 8.08N 122.40E
Lilydale Australia **92** 32.58S 139.59E
Lim r. Bosnia-Herzegovina **31** 43.45N 19.13E
Lima Peru **122** 12.06S 77.03W
Lima r. Portugal **26** 41.41N 8.50W
Lima Sweden **41** 60.56N 13.26E
Lima Mont. U.S.A. **108** 44.38N 112.36W
Lima Ohio U.S.A. **112** 40.43N 84.06W
Limassol see Lemesós Cyprus **66**
Limavady U.K. **15** 55.03N 6.57W
Limay r. Argentina **125** 39.02S 68.07W
Limbang Malaysia **58** 4.50N 115.00E
Limbara, Monte mtn. Italy **32** 40.51N 9.11E
Limbdi India **62** 22.34N 71.48E
Limbe Cameroon **77** 4.01N 9.12E

Limbourg Belgium **16** 50.36N 5.57E
Limburg d. Belgium **16** 50.36N 5.57E
Limburg d. Neth. **16** 51.15N 5.45E
Limburg an der Lahn Germany **39** 50.23N 8.04E
Limeira Brazil **126** 22.34S 47.25W
Limerick Rep. of Ire. **15** 52.40N 8.37W
Limerick d. Rep. of Ire. **15** 52.40N 8.37W
Limfjorden str. Denmark **42** 56.55N 9.10E
Liminka Finland **40** 64.49N 25.24E
Limmared Sweden **43** 57.32N 13.21E
Limmen Bight Australia **90** 14.45S 135.40E
Límni Greece **35** 38.43N 23.18E
Límnos i. Greece **34** 39.54N 25.21E
Limoges France **20** 45.50N 1.16E
Limogne France **20** 44.24N 1.46E
Limón Costa Rica **117** 10.00N 83.01W
Limon U.S.A. **108** 39.16N 103.41W
Limone Piemonte Italy **30** 44.12N 7.34E
Limousin d. France **20** 45.45N 1.30E
Limousin, Plateaux du f. France **20** 45.30N 1.15E
Limoux France **20** 43.04N 2.14E
Limpopo r. Mozambique **81** 25.14S 33.33E
Linah Saudi Arabia **65** 28.48N 43.45E
Linakhamari Russian Fed. **44** 69.39N 31.21E
Linares Chile **125** 35.51S 71.36W
Linares Mexico **111** 24.52N 99.34W
Linares Spain **26** 38.05N 3.38W
Linariá Greece **35** 38.50N 24.32E
Lincang China **52** 24.00N 100.10E
Lincheng China **54** 37.26N 114.34E
Lincoln Argentina **125** 34.55S 61.30W
Lincoln New Zealand **86** 43.38S 172.29E
Lincoln U.K. **12** 53.14N 0.32W
Lincoln Ill. U.S.A. **110** 40.10N 89.21W
Lincoln Mich. U.S.A. **104** 44.41N 83.25W
Lincoln Nebr. U.S.A. **110** 40.48N 96.42W
Lincoln N.H. U.S.A. **115** 44.03N 71.40W
Lincoln City U.S.A. **108** 44.59N 124.00W
Lincoln Park town U.S.A. **114** 42.14N 83.09W
Lincoln Sea Greenland **128** 82.00N 55.00W
Lincolnshire d. U.K. **12** 53.14N 0.32W
Lincoln Wolds hills U.K. **12** 53.22N 0.08W
Lindau Germany **39** 47.33N 9.41E
Lindeman Group is. Australia **90** 20.28S 149.05E
Linden Ala. U.S.A. **111** 32.18N 87.47W
Linden Penn. U.S.A. **114** 41.15N 77.08W
Lindenhurst U.S.A. **115** 40.41N 73.22W
Linderödsåsen hills Sweden **43** 55.44N 13.06E
Lindesberg Sweden **43** 59.35N 15.14E
Lindesnes c. Norway **42** 58.00N 7.02E
Líndhos Greece **35** 36.06N 28.04E
Líndhos site Greece **35** 36.06N 28.05E
Lindi Tanzania **79** 10.00S 39.41E
Lindi r. Zaïre **78** 0.30N 25.06E
Lindome Sweden **43** 57.34N 12.05E
Lindsay Canada **104** 44.21N 78.44W
Lindsay U.S.A. **109** 36.12N 119.05W
Line Is. Pacific Oc. **85** 3.00S 155.00W
Linesville U.S.A. **114** 41.39N 80.26W
Linfen China **54** 36.07N 111.34E
Lingao China **55** 19.54N 109.40E
Lingayen Phil. **59** 16.02N 120.14E
Lingbo Sweden **41** 61.03N 16.41E
Lingchuan China **55** 25.25N 110.20E
Lingen Germany **38** 52.31N 7.19E
Lingga i. Indonesia **58** 0.20S 104.30E
Lingling China **55** 26.12N 111.30E
Lingshan China **55** 22.17N 109.27E
Lingshui China **55** 18.31N 110.00E
Linguère Senegal **76** 15.22N 15.11W
Linhai China **55** 28.49N 121.08E
Linhe China **54** 40.50N 107.30E
Linköping Sweden **43** 58.25N 15.37E
Linnhe, Loch U.K. **14** 56.35N 5.25W
Linosa i. Italy **28** 35.52N 12.50E
Linquan China **54** 33.09N 115.17E
Linru China **54** 34.12N 112.45E
Lins Brazil **126** 21.40S 49.44W
Linshu China **55** 30.18N 106.55E
Lintan China **54** 34.33N 103.40E
Lintao China **54** 35.20N 104.00E
Linthal Switz. **39** 46.55N 9.00E
Linton Canada **105** 47.16N 72.15W
Linton Ind. U.S.A. **112** 39.01N 87.10W
Linton N.Dak. U.S.A. **110** 46.16N 100.14W
Lintong China **54** 34.24N 109.13E
Lintorf Germany **38** 51.20N 6.49E
Linwood U.S.A. **115** 40.44N 83.59W
Linxe France **20** 43.56N 1.10W
Linxi China **54** 43.30N 118.02E
Linxia China **54** 35.30N 103.10E
Lin Xian China **54** 37.57N 110.57E
Linyi Shandong China **54** 35.08N 118.20E
Linyi Shanxi China **54** 35.12N 110.45E
Linz Germany **38** 50.34N 7.17E
Linz Austria **39** 48.18N 14.18E
Linzigau f. Germany **39** 48.00N 9.20E
Lion, Golfe du g. France **20** 43.00N 4.00E
Lions, G. of see Lion, Golfe du g. France **20**
Lion's Head town Canada **104** 44.59N 81.15W
Liouesso Congo **78** 1.02N 15.43E
Lipari, Isola i. Italy **33** 38.30N 14.57E
Lipéité Congo **78** 3.09N 17.22E
Liphook U.K. **13** 51.05N 0.49W
Liping China **55** 26.16N 109.08E
Lipkany Moldova **37** 48.18N 26.48E
Lipova Romania **37** 46.05N 21.40E
Lipovets Ukraine **37** 49.11N 29.01E
Lippe r. Germany **38** 51.39N 6.38E
Lippstadt Germany **38** 51.40N 8.19E
Lipsoí i. Greece **35** 37.19N 26.50E
Liptovský Mikuláš Slovakia **37** 49.06N 19.37E
Liptrap, C. Australia **93** 38.53S 145.55E
Lipu China **55** 24.28N 110.12E
Lira Uganda **79** 2.15N 32.55E
Liranga Congo **78** 0.43S 17.32E
Liri r. Italy **32** 41.25N 13.52E

Liria Spain **25** 39.38N 0.36W
Liria Sudan **73** 4.38N 32.05E
Lisala Zaïre **78** 2.13N 21.37E
Lisboa Portugal **27** 38.43N 9.08W
Lisboa d. Portugal **27** 39.05N 9.00W
Lisbon see Lisboa Portugal **27**
Lisbon N.Dak. U.S.A. **110** 46.27N 97.41W
Lisbon Ohio U.S.A. **114** 40.47N 80.46W
Lisburn U.K. **15** 54.30N 6.03W
Lisburne, C. U.S.A. **98** 69.00N 165.50W
Liscannor B. Rep. of Ire. **15** 52.55N 9.24W
Liscia r. Italy **32** 41.05N 9.17E
Lishi China **54** 37.30N 111.07E
Lishui China **55** 28.28N 119.59E
Lisianski i. Hawaiian Is. **84** 26.04N 173.58W
Lisichansk Ukraine **45** 48.53N 38.25E
Lisieux France **18** 49.09N 0.14E
Liskeard U.K. **13** 50.27N 4.29W
Liski Russian Fed. **45** 51.00N 39.30E
L'Isle Jourdain H.-Gar. France **20** 43.37N 1.05E
L'Isle Jourdain Poit.-Char. France **18** 46.14N 0.41E
L'Isle-sur-le-Doubs France **19** 47.27N 6.35E
Lismore N.S.W. Australia **93** 28.48S 153.17E
Lismore Vic. Australia **92** 37.58S 143.22E
Lismore Rep. of Ire. **15** 52.08N 7.57W
Liss U.K. **13** 51.03N 0.53W
Lisse Neth. **16** 52.18N 4.33E
Lista f. Norway **42** 58.07N 6.40E
Lištica Bosnia-Herzegovina **31** 43.23N 17.36E
Listowel Canada **104** 43.44N 80.57W
Listowel Rep. of Ire. **15** 52.27N 9.30W
Litang China **55** 23.09N 109.09E
Litang Qu r. China **61** 28.09N 101.30E
Litchfield Conn. U.S.A. **115** 41.45N 73.11W
Litchfield Ill. U.S.A. **110** 39.11N 89.40W
Litchfield Minn. U.S.A. **110** 45.08N 94.31W
Litchfield Nebr. U.S.A. **110** 41.09N 99.09W
Lithgow Australia **93** 33.30S 150.09E
Líthinon, Ákra c. Greece **35** 34.55N 24.44E
Lithuania Europe **44** 55.30N 24.00E
Lititz U.S.A. **115** 40.09N 76.18W
Litókhoron Greece **34** 40.06N 22.30E
Litoměřice Czech Republic **38** 50.35N 14.09E
Little Andaman i. India **56** 10.40N 92.24E
Little Bahama Bank f. Bahamas **113** 26.40N 78.00W
Little Belt Mts. U.S.A. **108** 46.45N 110.35W
Little Cayman i. Cayman Is. **117** 19.40N 80.00W
Little Coco i. Myanmar **56** 13.59N 93.12E
Little Colorado r. U.S.A. **108** 36.11N 111.48W
Little Current r. Canada **102** 50.00N 84.35W
Little Current town Canada **104** 45.58N 81.56W
Little Falls town Minn. U.S.A. **110** 45.59N 94.21W
Little Falls town N.Y. U.S.A. **115** 43.03N 74.52W
Littlefield U.S.A. **111** 33.55N 102.20W
Little Grand Rapids town Canada **101** 52.05N 95.29W
Littlehampton U.K. **13** 50.48N 0.32W
Little Inagua i. Bahamas **117** 21.30N 73.00W
Little Kanawha r. U.S.A. **114** 39.16N 81.34W
Little Karoo f. R.S.A. **80** 33.40S 21.40E
Little Lake town U.S.A. **109** 35.58N 117.53W
Little Mecatina r. Canada **103** 50.28N 59.35W
Little Missouri r. U.S.A. **110** 47.30N 102.25W
Little Nicobar i. India **61** 7.20N 93.40E
Little Ouse r. U.K. **13** 52.34N 0.20E
Little Quill L. Canada **101** 51.55N 104.05W
Little Rann of Kachchh f. India **62** 23.25N 71.30E
Little Rock town U.S.A. **111** 34.44N 92.15W
Little Smoky r. Canada **100** 55.42N 117.38W
Littlestown U.S.A. **114** 39.45N 77.05W
Littleton Colo. U.S.A. **108** 39.37N 105.01W
Littleton N.H. U.S.A. **105** 44.18N 71.46W
Little Topar Australia **92** 31.44S 142.14E
Little Valley town U.S.A. **114** 42.15N 78.48W
Little White r. Canada **104** 46.21N 83.20W
Litvínov Czech Republic **38** 50.37N 13.36E
Liuba China **54** 33.37N 106.55E
Liucheng China **55** 24.39N 109.14E
Liuchong He r. China **55** 26.50N 106.04E
Liuli Tanzania **79** 11.07S 34.34E
Liulin China **54** 37.26N 110.52E
Liuzhou China **55** 24.19N 109.12E
Livadherón Greece **34** 40.02N 21.57E
Livanátai Greece **35** 38.42N 23.03E
Livanjsko Polje f. Bosnia-Herzegovina **31** 44.00N 16.40E
Livarot France **18** 49.01N 0.09E
Lively Canada **104** 46.26N 81.09W
Live Oak U.S.A. **113** 30.19N 82.59W
Livermore, Mt. U.S.A. **109** 30.39N 104.11W
Liverpool Australia **93** 33.57S 150.52E
Liverpool Canada **103** 44.02N 64.43W
Liverpool U.K. **12** 53.25N 3.00W
Liverpool U.S.A. **115** 43.06N 76.13W
Liverpool B. U.K. **12** 53.30N 3.10W
Liverpool, C. Canada **99** 73.38N 78.06W
Liverpool Range mts. Australia **93** 31.45S 150.45E
Livigno Italy **30** 46.32N 10.04E
Livingston U.K. **14** 55.54N 3.31W
Livingston Mont. U.S.A. **108** 45.40N 110.34W
Livingston Tex. U.S.A. **111** 30.43N 94.56W
Livingstone see Maramba Zambia **80**
Livingstonia Malaŵi **79** 10.35S 34.10E
Livno Bosnia-Herzegovina **31** 43.50N 17.01E
Livo r. Finland **40** 65.24N 26.48E
Livonia Mich. U.S.A. **104** 42.25N 83.23W
Livonia N.Y. U.S.A. **114** 42.49N 77.40W
Livorno Italy **30** 43.33N 10.19E
Liwale Tanzania **79** 9.47S 38.00E
Liwan Sudan **73** 4.55N 35.41E
Li Xian Gansu China **54** 34.11N 105.02E
Li Xian Hunan China **55** 29.38N 111.45E
Lixoúrion Greece **35** 38.14N 20.24E
Liyujiang China **55** 25.59N 113.12E
Lizard U.K. **13** 49.58N 5.12W
Lizard Pt. U.K. **13** 49.57N 5.15W
Lizarra see Estella Spain **26**
Lizemores U.S.A. **114** 38.20N 81.12W

Ljan Norway **42** 59.51N 10.48E
Ljubija Bosnia-Herzegovina **31** 44.56N 16.37E
Ljubinje Bosnia-Herzegovina **31** 42.57N 18.05E
Ljubljana Slovenia **31** 46.03N 14.31E
Ljubovija Yugo. **31** 44.11N 19.22E
Ljubŝki Bosnia-Herzegovina **31** 43.12N 17.33E
Ljugarn Sweden **43** 57.19N 18.42E
Ljungan r. Sweden **41** 62.19N 17.23E
Ljungby Sweden **43** 56.50N 13.56E
Ljungbyholm Sweden **43** 56.38N 16.10E
Ljungdalen Sweden **40** 62.54N 12.45E
Ljungsbro Sweden **43** 58.31N 15.30E
Ljusdal Sweden **41** 61.50N 16.05E
Ljusnan r. Sweden **41** 61.12N 17.08E
Ljusne Sweden **41** 61.13N 17.08E
Ljusterö i. Sweden **43** 59.31N 18.37E
Ljutomer Slovenia **31** 46.31N 16.12E
Llança Spain **25** 42.22N 3.09E
Llandeilo U.K. **13** 51.54N 4.00W
Llandovery U.K. **13** 51.59N 3.49W
Llandrindod Wells U.K. **13** 52.15N 3.23W
Llandudno U.K. **12** 53.19N 3.49W
Llanelli U.K. **13** 51.41N 4.11W
Llanes Spain **26** 43.25N 4.45W
Llangadfan U.K. **13** 52.41N 3.28W
Llangollen U.K. **12** 52.58N 3.10W
Llanidloes U.K. **13** 52.28N 3.31W
Llanos f. S. America **122** 7.30N 70.00W
Llanwrtyd Wells U.K. **13** 52.06N 3.39W
Lleida see Lérida Spain **25**
Lleida d. Spain **25** 42.00N 1.10E
Llentrisca, Cabo de c. Spain **25** 38.51N 1.14E
Llerena Spain **26** 38.14N 6.01W
Llobregat r. Spain **25** 41.15N 2.09E
Lloret de Mar Spain **25** 41.42N 2.53E
Lloydminster Canada **101** 53.17N 110.00W
Lluchmayor Spain **25** 39.29N 2.54E
Loange r. Zaïre **78** 4.18S 20.05E
Lobatse Botswana **80** 25.12S 25.39E
Lobaye r. C.A.R. **77** 3.40N 18.35E
Lobería Argentina **125** 38.08S 58.48W
Lobito Angola **78** 12.20S 13.34E
Lobonäs Sweden **41** 61.33N 15.20E
Lobos Argentina **125** 35.10S 59.05W
Locarno Switz. **39** 46.10N 8.48E
Lochboisdale town U.K. **14** 57.09N 7.19W
Lochem Neth. **16** 52.10N 6.25E
Loches France **18** 47.08N 1.00E
Lochgilphead U.K. **14** 56.02N 5.26W
Lochinver U.K. **14** 58.09N 5.15W
Lochmaddy town U.K. **14** 57.36N 7.10W
Lochnagar mtn. U.K. **14** 56.57N 3.15W
Lochranza U.K. **14** 55.42N 5.18W
Loch Raven Resr. U.S.A. **115** 39.27N 76.36W
Lochy, Loch U.K. **14** 56.58N 4.55W
Lock Australia **92** 33.34S 135.46E
Lockeport Canada **103** 43.42N 65.07W
Lockerbie U.K. **14** 55.07N 3.21W
Lockhart Australia **93** 35.16S 146.42E
Lockhart U.S.A. **111** 29.53N 97.41W
Lockhart, L. Australia **89** 33.27S 119.00E
Lockhart River town Australia **90** 12.58S 143.29E
Lock Haven U.S.A. **114** 41.08N 77.27W
Lockport U.S.A. **114** 43.11N 78.42W
Loc Ninh Vietnam **56** 11.51N 106.35E
Locri Italy **33** 38.14N 16.16E
Lod Israel **67** 31.57N 34.54E
Lodalskåpa mtn. Norway **41** 61.47N 7.13E
Loddon r. Australia **92** 35.40S 143.59E
Lodeynoye Pole Russian Fed. **44** 60.43N 33.30E
Lodeve France **20** 43.43N 3.19E
Lodge Grass U.S.A. **108** 45.19N 107.22W
Lodhrän Pakistan **62** 29.32N 71.38E
Lodi Italy **30** 45.19N 9.30E
Lodi Calif. U.S.A. **108** 38.08N 121.16W
Lodi Ohio U.S.A. **114** 41.03N 82.01W
Lodja Zaïre **78** 3.29S 23.33E
Lodosa Spain **25** 42.25N 2.05W
Lodwar Kenya **79** 3.06N 35.38E
Łódź Poland **37** 51.49N 19.28E
Loei Thailand **56** 17.32N 101.34E
Lofer Austria **39** 47.35N 12.41E
Lofoten is. Norway **8** 68.15N 13.50E
Lofoten Vesterålen is. Norway **40** 68.15N 13.50E
Log Russian Fed. **45** 49.28N 43.51E
Loga Niger **77** 13.40N 3.15E
Logan N.Mex. U.S.A. **109** 35.22N 103.25W
Logan Ohio U.S.A. **114** 39.32N 82.25W
Logan Utah U.S.A. **108** 41.44N 111.50W
Logan, Mt. Canada **100** 60.34N 140.24W
Logansport U.S.A. **112** 40.45N 86.25W
Loganton U.S.A. **114** 41.02N 77.18W
Loge r. Angola **78** 7.52S 13.08E
Logone r. Cameroon/Chad **77** 12.10N 15.00E
Logone Occidental d. Chad **77** 8.40N 15.50E
Logone Oriental d. Chad **77** 8.10N 16.00E
Logoysk Belarus **37** 54.08N 27.42E
Logroño Spain **25** 42.28N 2.27W
Logrosán Spain **27** 39.20N 5.29W
Lögstör Denmark **42** 56.58N 9.15E
Løgumkloster Denmark **42** 55.03N 8.57E
Lohärdaga India **63** 23.26N 84.41E
Lohäru India **62** 28.27N 75.49E
Lohja Finland **41** 60.15N 24.05E
Lohjanjärvi l. Finland **41** 60.15N 23.55E
Lohne Germany **38** 52.42N 8.12E
Lohr Germany **39** 50.00N 9.34E
Loikaw Myanmar **56** 19.40N 97.17E
Loimaa Finland **41** 60.51N 23.03E
Loir r. France **18** 47.33N 0.32W
Loire d. France **21** 45.30N 4.00E
Loire r. France **18** 47.16N 2.11W
Loire-Atlantique d. France **18** 47.20N 1.35W
Loiret d. France **18** 47.55N 2.20E
Loir-et-Cher d. France **18** 47.30N 1.30E
Loja Ecuador **122** 3.59S 79.16W

Loja Spain **27** 37.10N 4.09W
Loka Sudan **73** 4.16N 31.01E
Loka Zaïre **78** 0.20N 17.57E
Löken Norway **42** 59.48N 11.29E
Loken tekojärvi resr. Finland **40** 67.55N 27.40E
Lokeren Belgium **16** 51.06N 3.59E
Loket Czech Republic **39** 50.09N 12.43E
Lokichar Kenya **79** 2.23N 35.39E
Lokitaung Kenya **79** 4.15N 35.45E
Lokka Finland **40** 67.49N 27.44E
Lökken Denmark **42** 57.22N 9.43E
Løkken Norway **40** 63.06N 9.43E
Loknya Russian Fed. **44** 56.49N 30.00E
Lokoja Nigeria **77** 7.49N 6.44E
Lokolo r. Zaïre **78** 0.45S 19.36E
Lokoro r. Zaïre **78** 1.40S 18.29E
Lol r. Sudan **73** 9.11N 29.12E
Lolland i. Denmark **41** 54.46N 11.30E
Lom Bulgaria **34** 43.49N 23.14E
Lom Norway **41** 61.50N 8.33E
Loma U.S.A. **108** 47.57N 110.30W
Lomami r. Zaïre **78** 0.45N 24.10E
Lomas de Zamora Argentina **125** 34.46S 58.24W
Lombardia d. Italy **30** 45.45N 9.00E
Lombok i. Indonesia **58** 8.30S 116.20E
Lombok, Selat str. Indonesia **59** 8.38S 115.40E
Lomé Togo **77** 6.10N 1.21E
Lomela Zaïre **78** 2.15S 23.15E
Lomela r. Zaïre **78** 0.14S 20.45E
Lomié Cameroon **77** 3.09N 13.35E
Lomme France **19** 50.39N 2.59E
Lommel Belgium **16** 51.15N 5.18E
Lomond Canada **100** 50.21N 112.39W
Lomond, Loch U.K. **14** 56.07N 4.36W
Lompoc U.S.A. **109** 34.38N 120.27W
Łomża Poland **37** 53.11N 22.04E
Lonaconing U.S.A. **114** 39.34N 78.59W
Londinières France **18** 49.50N 1.24E
London Canada **104** 42.59N 81.14W
London Kiribati **85** 1.58N 157.28W
London U.K. **51** 51.32N 0.06W
Londonderry U.K. **15** 55.00N 7.21W
Londonderry d. U.K. **15** 55.00N 7.00W
Londonderry, C. Australia **88** 13.58S 126.55E
Londonderry, Isla i. Chile **125** 55.03S 70.40W
Londrina Brazil **124** 23.30S 51.13W
Lonely I. Canada **104** 45.34N 81.29W
Lone Pine U.S.A. **109** 36.36N 118.04W
Longa r. Angola **78** 16.15S 19.07E
Longá Greece **35** 36.53N 21.55E
Long'an China **55** 23.11N 107.41E
Longa, Proliv str. Russian Fed. **51** 70.00N 178.00E
Longarone Italy **30** 46.16N 12.18E
Long Beach town Calif. U.S.A. **109** 33.46N 118.11W
Long Beach town N.Y. U.S.A. **115** 40.35N 73.41W
Long Branch U.S.A. **115** 40.18N 74.00W
Longchamps U.S.A. **105** 50.05N 5.42E
Longchang China **55** 29.18N 105.20E
Longchuan China **55** 24.12N 115.25E
Long Creek town U.S.A. **108** 44.43N 119.06W
Long Eaton U.K. **12** 52.54N 1.16W
Longeau France **19** 47.46N 5.18E
Longford Rep. of Ire. **15** 53.44N 7.48W
Longford d. Rep. of Ire. **15** 53.42N 7.45W
Longhua Hebei China **54** 41.17N 117.37E
Long I. Bahamas **117** 23.00N 75.00W
Long I. Canada **102** 54.55N 79.30W
Long I. U.S.A. **115** 40.50N 73.00W
Longido Tanzania **79** 2.43S 36.41E
Longiram Indonesia **58** 0.05S 115.45E
Long Island Sd. U.S.A. **115** 41.05N 72.58W
Long Jiang r. China **55** 24.12N 109.30E
Long, L. Botswana **80** 22.42S 28.11E
Long L. Canada **102** 49.30N 86.50W
Long L. U.S.A. **105** 44.40N 74.20W
Longlac town Canada **102** 49.45N 86.25W
Long Lake town U.S.A. **115** 43.58N 74.25W
Longli China **55** 26.29N 107.59E
Longlin China **55** 24.43N 105.26E
Longmeadow U.S.A. **115** 42.03N 72.34W
Longmont U.S.A. **108** 40.10N 105.06W
Longnan China **55** 24.54N 114.47E
Longnawan Indonesia **58** 1.54N 114.53E
Longniddry U.K. **14** 55.58N 2.53W
Long Point B. Canada **104** 42.40N 80.14W
Long, Pt. Canada **104** 42.33N 80.04W
Longquan China **55** 28.05N 119.07E
Long Range Mts. Nfld. Canada **103** 48.00N 58.30W
Long Range Mts. Nfld. Canada **103** 50.00N 57.00W
Longreach Australia **90** 23.26S 144.15E
Long Sault Canada **105** 45.00N 74.55W
Longsheng China **55** 25.59N 110.01E
Longs Peak U.S.A. **108** 40.15N 105.37W
Longtown U.K. **12** 55.01N 2.58W
Longué France **18** 47.23N 0.06W
Longueuil Canada **105** 45.32N 73.30W
Longuyon France **19** 49.26N 5.36E
Longview Tex. U.S.A. **111** 32.30N 94.44W
Longview Wash. U.S.A. **108** 46.08N 122.57W
Longwood St. Helena **127** 15.57S 5.42W
Longwy France **19** 49.31N 5.46E
Longxi China **54** 34.59N 104.45E
Long Xian China **54** 34.52N 106.50E
Long Xuyen Vietnam **56** 10.23N 105.23E
Longyan China **55** 25.10N 117.02E
Longzhou China **55** 22.24N 106.50E
Lonigo Italy **30** 45.23N 11.23E
Löningen Germany **38** 52.44N 7.46E
Lonja r. Croatia **31** 45.30N 16.40E
Lönsboda Sweden **43** 56.24N 14.19E
Lönsdal Norway **40** 66.46N 15.26E
Lonsdale, L. Australia **92** 37.05S 142.15E
Lons-le-Saunier France **19** 46.40N 5.33E
Looc Phil. **59** 12.20N 122.05E
Looe U.K. **13** 50.51N 4.26W
Lookout, C. U.S.A. **113** 34.35N 76.32W
Loolmalassin mtn. Tanzania **79** 3.00S 35.45E
Loon Lake Mts. U.S.A. **105** 44.35N 74.08W

Loop Head Rep. of Ire. **15** 52.33N 9.56W
Lopari Zaïre **73** 1.15N 19.59E
Lopari r. Zaïre **78** 1.20N 20.22E
Lop Buri Thailand **56** 14.49N 100.37E
Lopez, C. Gabon **78** 0.36S 8.40E
Lopi Congo **78** 2.57N 16.47E
Lop Nur l. China **52** 40.30N 90.30E
Lopphavet est. Norway **40** 70.30N 20.00E
Lopydino Russian Fed. **44** 61.10N 52.02E
Lora Creek r. Australia **92** 28.10S 135.22E
Lora del Río Spain **27** 37.39N 5.32W
Lora, Hämün-i- l. Pakistan **62** 29.20N 64.50E
Lorain U.S.A. **114** 41.28N 82.10W
Loralai Pakistan **62** 30.22N 68.36E
Lorca Spain **25** 37.40N 1.42W
Lord Howe I. Pacific Oc. **84** 31.28S 159.09E
Lord Howe Rise Pacific Oc. **84** 29.00S 162.30E
Lordsburg U.S.A. **109** 32.21N 108.43W
Lorena Brazil **126** 22.44S 45.07W
Lorengau P.N.G. **59** 2.01S 147.15E
Lorenzo Geyres Uruguay **125** 32.05S 57.55W
Loreto Brazil **123** 7.05S 45.09W
Loreto Italy **31** 43.26N 13.36E
Loreto Mexico **109** 26.01N 111.21W
Loretteville Canada **105** 46.51N 71.21W
Lorian Swamp Kenya **79** 0.35N 39.40E
Lorient France **18** 47.45N 3.22W
Loriol France **21** 44.45N 4.49E
Lormes France **19** 47.17N 3.49E
Lorne Australia **92** 38.34S 144.01E
Lörrach Germany **39** 47.37N 7.40E
Lorraine d. France **19** 49.00N 6.00E
Lorrainville Canada **104** 47.20N 79.21W
Lorris France **19** 47.53N 2.31E
Lorsch Germany **39** 49.39N 8.34E
Lorup Germany **38** 52.55N 7.38E
Los Alamos Mexico **111** 28.40N 103.30W
Los Alamos U.S.A. **109** 35.53N 106.19W
Los Andes Chile **125** 32.50S 70.37W
Los Angeles Chile **125** 37.28S 72.21W
Los Angeles U.S.A. **106** 34.00N 118.17W
Los Banos U.S.A. **109** 37.04N 120.51W
Los Bajios Mexico **109** 28.31N 108.25W
Los Blancos Argentina **124** 23.40S 62.35W
Los Blancos Spain **27** 37.38N 0.49W
Los Canarreos, Archipiélago de Cuba **117** 21.40N 82.30W
Los Herreras Mexico **111** 25.55N 99.24W
Lošinj i. Croatia **31** 44.36N 14.24E
Losinovka Ukraine **37** 50.50N 31.57E
Los Llanos de Aridane Canary Is. **127** 28.39N 17.54W
Los Lunas U.S.A. **109** 34.48N 106.44W
Los Mochis Mexico **116** 25.45N 108.57W
Los Navalmorales Spain **27** 39.43N 4.38W
Los Olivos U.S.A. **109** 34.40N 120.06W
Los Palacios y Villafranca Spain **27** 37.10N 5.56W
Los Roques is. Venezuela **122** 12.00N 67.00W
Los Santos de Maimona Spain **27** 38.27N 6.23W
Lossiemouth U.K. **14** 57.43N 3.18W
Lost r. U.S.A. **114** 39.05N 78.36W
Lost Cabin U.S.A. **108** 43.19N 107.36W
Lost City U.S.A. **114** 38.55N 78.51W
Lost River town U.S.A. **114** 38.57N 78.50W
Los Teques Venezuela **122** 10.25N 67.01W
Los Vilos Chile **124** 31.55S 71.31W
Los Yébenes Spain **27** 39.34N 3.53W
Lot d. France **20** 44.35N 1.40E
Lot r. France **20** 44.18N 0.20E
Lota Chile **125** 37.05S 73.10W
Lot-et-Garonne d. France **20** 44.20N 0.20E
Lothian d. U.K. **14** 55.50N 3.00W
Lotoi r. Zaïre **78** 1.30S 18.30E
Lotsani r. Botswana **80** 22.42S 28.11E
Lötschberg Tunnel Switz. **38** 46.25N 7.53E
Lotuke mtn. Sudan **73** 4.07N 33.48E
Louang Namtha Laos **56** 20.57N 101.25E
Louangphrabang Laos **56** 19.53N 102.10E
Loubomo Congo **78** 4.09S 12.40E
Loudéac France **18** 48.10N 2.45W
Loudima Congo **78** 4.06S 13.05E
Loudonville U.S.A. **114** 40.38N 82.14W
Loudun France **18** 47.01N 0.05E
Loué France **18** 48.00N 0.09W
Loue r. France **19** 47.04N 6.10E
Louga Senegal **76** 15.37N 16.13W
Loughborough U.K. **12** 52.47N 1.11W
Loughrea Rep. of Ire. **15** 53.12N 8.35W
Loughros More B. Rep. of Ire. **15** 54.48N 8.32W
Louhans France **19** 46.38N 5.13E
Louisburgh Rep. of Ire. **15** 53.46N 9.49W
Louiseville Canada **105** 46.14N 72.56W
Louisiade Archipelago is. P.N.G. **90** 11.00S 153.00E
Louisiana d. U.S.A. **111** 30.60N 92.30W
Louis Trichardt R.S.A. **80** 23.03S 29.54E
Louisville Ky. U.S.A. **112** 38.13N 85.48W
Louisville Miss. U.S.A. **111** 33.07N 89.03W
Louisville Ohio U.S.A. **114** 40.50N 81.16W
Louis XIV, Pointe c. Canada **102** 54.35N 79.50W
Loukhi Russian Fed. **44** 66.05N 33.04E
Loukouo Congo **78** 3.38S 14.39E
Loulé Portugal **27** 37.08N 8.00W
Loum Cameroon **77** 4.46N 9.45E
Louny Czech Republic **39** 50.19N 13.46E
Lourches France **19** 50.19N 3.21E
Lourdes France **20** 43.06N 0.03W
Loures Portugal **27** 38.50N 9.10W
Lourinhã Portugal **27** 39.14N 9.19W
Lourosa Portugal **26** 40.19N 7.56W
Lousã Portugal **27** 40.07N 8.15W
Louth Australia **93** 30.34S 145.09E
Louth d. Rep. of Ire. **15** 53.55N 6.30W
Louth U.K. **12** 53.23N 0.00
Loutra Greece **35** 37.51N 21.06E
Loutrá Aidhipsoú Greece **35** 38.54N 23.02E
Louviers France **18** 49.13N 1.10E
Louvigné-du-Désert France **18** 48.29N 1.08W
Lövånger Sweden **40** 64.22N 21.18E
Lovat r. Russian Fed. **44** 58.06N 31.37E

Lovech Bulgaria **34** 43.08N 24.43E
Lovech d. Bulgaria **34** 43.10N 25.00E
Loveland U.S.A. **108** 40.24N 105.05W
Lovell U.S.A. **108** 44.50N 108.24W
Lovelock U.S.A. **108** 40.11N 118.28W
Love Point town U.S.A. **115** 39.02N 76.18W
Lovere Italy **30** 45.49N 10.04E
Lovington U.S.A. **111** 32.57N 103.21W
Lovoi r. Zaïre **79** 8.14S 26.40E
Lovosice Czech Republic **38** 50.31N 14.03E
Lovozero Russian Fed. **44** 68.01N 35.08E
Lovrin Romania **37** 45.58N 20.48E
Lovua r. Zaïre **78** 6.08S 20.35E
Low Canada **105** 45.48N 75.57W
Lowa Zaïre **78** 1.24S 25.51E
Lowa r. Kivu Zaïre **78** 1.25S 25.55E
Lowell U.S.A. **115** 42.39N 71.18W
Löwenberg Germany **38** 52.54N 13.08E
Lower Arrow L. Canada **100** 49.40N 118.05W
Lower California pen. see Baja California pen. Mexico **116**
Lower Egypt see Miṣr Baḥrī f. Egypt **66**
Lower Hutt New Zealand **86** 41.13S 174.55E
Lower Lough Erne U.K. **15** 54.28N 7.48W
Lower Pen. f. U.S.A. **104** 44.34N 84.28W
Lower Post Canada **100** 59.55N 128.30W
Lower Red L. U.S.A. **110** 48.00N 94.50W
Lowestoft U.K. **13** 52.29N 1.44E
Lowgar d. Afghan. **62** 34.10N 69.20E
Łowicz Poland **37** 52.06N 19.55E
Lowrah r. Afghan. see Pishīn Lora r. Pakistan **62**
Lowville U.S.A. **105** 43.47N 75.29W
Loxton Australia **92** 34.38S 140.38E
Loyalsock r. U.S.A. **114** 41.14N 76.56W
Loyalty Is. see Loyauté, Îles is. N. Cal. **84**
Loyauté, Îles is. N. Cal. **84** 21.00S 167.00E
Loyoro Uganda **79** 3.22N 34.16E
Lozère d. France **20** 44.30N 3.30E
Loznica Yugo. **31** 44.32N 19.13E
Lozoyuela Spain **26** 40.55N 3.37W
Lua r. Zaïre **78** 2.45N 18.28E
Luabo Mozambique **81** 18.30S 36.10E
Luachimo Angola **78** 7.25S 20.43E
Lualaba r. Zaïre **78** 0.18N 25.32E
Luama r. Zaïre **79** 4.45S 26.55E
Luampa Zambia **78** 15.04S 24.20E
Lu'an China **55** 31.47N 116.30E
Luancheng Guang. Zhuang. China **55** 22.48N 108.55E
Luancheng Hebei China **54** 37.53N 114.39E
Luanda Angola **78** 8.50S 13.20E
Luanda d. Angola **78** 9.00S 13.20E
Luando Game Res. Angola **78** 11.00S 17.45E
Luanginga r. Zambia **78** 15.11S 23.05E
Luangwa r. Central Zambia **79** 15.32S 30.28E
Luan He r. China **54** 39.25N 119.10E
Luanping China **54** 40.55N 117.17E
Luanshya Zambia **79** 13.09S 28.24E
Luan Xian China **54** 39.45N 118.44E
Luapula r. Zambia **9** 9.25S 28.36E
Luarca Spain **26** 43.32N 6.32W
Luau Angola **78** 10.41S 22.09E
Lubalo Angola **78** 9.13S 19.21E
Lubango Angola **78** 14.52S 13.30E
Lubao Zaïre **78** 5.19S 25.43E
Lübben Germany **38** 51.56N 13.53E
Lübbenau Germany **38** 51.52N 13.57E
Lubbock U.S.A. **111** 33.35N 101.51W
Lubeck Australia **92** 36.47S 142.38E
Lübeck Germany **38** 53.52N 10.40E
Lübecker Bucht b. Germany **38** 54.10N 11.20E
Lubefu r. Zaïre **78** 4.05S 23.00E
Lubenka Kazakhstan **45** 50.22N 54.13E
Lubersac France **20** 45.27N 1.24E
Lubia Angola **78** 11.01S 17.06E
Lubika Zaïre **79** 7.50S 29.12E
Lubilash r. Zaïre **78** 4.59S 23.25E
Lubin Poland **36** 51.24N 16.13E
Lublin Poland **37** 51.18N 22.31E
Lubliniec Poland **37** 50.40N 18.41E
Lubny Ukraine **45** 50.01N 33.00E
Lübtheen Germany **38** 53.18N 11.04E
Lubudi r. K.Occidental Zaïre **78** 4.00S 21.23E
Lubudi r. Shaba Zaïre **78** 9.57S 25.59E
Lubudi r. Shaba Zaïre **78** 9.13S 25.40E
Lubumbashi Zaïre **79** 11.44S 27.29E
Lubutu Zaïre **78** 0.48S 26.19E
Lübz Germany **38** 53.27N 12.01E
Lucas González Argentina **125** 32.25S 59.33W
Lucca Italy **30** 43.50N 10.29E
Luce B. U.K. **14** 54.45N 4.47W
Lucena Phil. **59** 13.56N 121.37E
Lucena Spain **27** 37.24N 4.29W
Lucena del Cid Spain **25** 40.08N 0.17W
Lucenay-l'Évêque France **19** 47.05N 4.15E
Luc-en-Diois France **21** 44.37N 5.27E
Lučenec Slovakia **37** 48.20N 19.40E
Lucera Italy **33** 41.30N 15.20E
Lucerne U.S.A. **108** 42.12N 120.38W
Lucero Mexico **109** 30.49N 106.30W
Luchena r. Spain **25** 37.44N 1.50W
Lucin U.S.A. **108** 41.22N 113.55W
Lucindale Australia **92** 36.59S 140.25E
Lucira Angola **78** 13.51S 12.31E
Luckau Germany **38** 51.51N 13.43E
Luckeesarai India **63** 25.11N 86.05E
Luckenwalde Germany **38** 52.05N 13.10E
Lucknow Canada **104** 43.57N 81.31W
Lucknow India **63** 26.51N 80.55E
Luçon France **18** 46.27N 1.10W
Lucy Creek town Australia **90** 22.25S 136.20E
Lüda see Dalian China **54**
Luda Kamchiya r. Bulgaria **34** 42.50N 27.00E
Ludbreg Croatia **31** 46.15N 16.37E
Lüdenscheid Germany **38** 51.13N 7.38E
Lüderitz Namibia **80** 26.37S 15.09E
Ludgate Canada **104** 45.54N 80.32W
Ludhiāna India **62** 30.55N 75.51E

Lüdinghausen Germany 16 51.46N 7.27E
Ludington U.S.A. 112 43.58N 86.27W
Ludlow U.K. 13 52.23N 2.42W
Ludlow Penn. U.S.A. 114 41.44N 78.57W
Ludlow Vt. U.S.A. 115 43.24N 72.42W
Ludogorie mts. Bulgaria 37 43.45N 27.00E
Luduş Romania 37 46.29N 24.05E
Ludvika Sweden 43 60.09N 15.11E
Ludwigsburg Germany 39 48.53N 9.11E
Ludwigsfelde Germany 38 52.17N 13.16E
Ludwigshafen Germany 39 49.29N 8.26E
Ludwigslut Germany 38 53.19N 11.30E
Luebo Zaïre 78 5.16S 21.27E
Luena Angola 78 11.46S 19.55E
Luena r. Angola 78 12.30S 22.37E
Luena Zaïre 78 9.27S 25.47E
Luena Zambia 79 10.40S 30.21E
Luena r. Western Zambia 78 14.47S 23.05E
Luengue r. Angola 78 16.58S 21.15E
Luenha r. Mozambique 81 16.29S 33.40E
Lüeyang China 54 33.20N 106.03E
Lufeng China 55 23.01N 115.35E
Lufira r. Zaïre 78 8.15S 26.30E
Lufkin U.S.A. 107 31.21N 94.47W
Luga Russian Fed. 44 58.42N 29.49E
Lugano Switz. 39 46.01N 8.58E
Lugano, Lago di l. Switz./Italy 39 46.00N 9.00E
Lugansk Ukraine 45 48.35N 39.20E
Luganville Vanuatu 84 15.32S 167.08E
Lugela Mozambique 81 16.25S 36.42E
Lugenda r. Mozambique 79 11.23S 38.30E
Luginy Ukraine 37 51.05N 28.21E
Lugnaquilla Mtn. Rep. of Ire. 15 52.58N 6.28W
Lugo Italy 30 44.25N 11.54E
Lugo Spain 26 43.02N 7.34W
Lugo d. Spain 26 42.55N 7.30W
Lugoj Romania 37 45.42N 21.56E
Luiana Angola 78 17.08S 22.59E
Luiana r. Angola 78 17.28S 23.02E
Luilaka r. Zaïre 78 0.15S 19.00E
Luilu r. Zaïre 78 6.22S 23.53E
Luino Italy 30 46.00N 8.44E
Luiro r. Finland 40 67.18N 27.28E
Luisa Zaïre 78 7.15S 22.27E
Lujiang China 55 31.14N 117.17E
Lukala r. Zaïre 78 5.23S 13.02E
Lukanga Swamp f. Zambia 79 14.15S 27.30E
Lukenie r. Zaïre 78 2.43S 18.12E
Lukka Sudan 72 14.33N 23.42E
Lukovit Bulgaria 34 43.12N 24.10E
Łuków Poland 37 51.56N 22.23E
Lukoyanov Russian Fed. 44 55.03N 44.29E
Lukuga r. Zaïre 79 5.37S 26.58E
Lukula r. Zaïre 78 4.15S 17.59E
Lukulu Zambia 78 14.35S 23.25E
Lukumbule Tanzania 79 11.34S 37.24E
Lule r. Sweden 40 65.35N 22.03E
Luleå Sweden 40 65.34N 22.10E
Lüleburgaz Turkey 29 41.25N 27.23E
Lüliang Shan mts. China 54 37.00N 111.20E
Lulonga r. Zaïre 78 0.42N 18.26E
Lulu r. Zaïre 78 1.18N 23.42E
Lulua r. Zaïre 78 5.03S 21.07E
Lumai Angola 78 13.13S 21.13E
Lumajangdong Co l. China 63 34.02N 81.40E
Lumbala Kaquengue Angola 78 12.37S 22.33E
Lumbala N'guimbo Angola 78 14.02S 21.35E
Lumberton Miss. U.S.A. 111 31.00N 89.27W
Lumberton N.Mex. U.S.A. 108 36.55N 106.56W
Lumbrales Spain 26 40.56N 6.43W
Lumbres France 19 50.42N 2.08E
Lumsden New Zealand 86 45.44S 168.26E
Lūnāvāda India 62 23.08N 73.37E
Lund Sweden 43 55.42N 13.11E
Lund Nev. U.S.A. 108 38.30N 115.00W
Lund Utah U.S.A. 108 38.01N 113.28W
Lunda Norte d. Angola 78 8.30S 19.00E
Lunda Sul d. Angola 78 11.00S 20.00E
Lundazi Zambia 79 12.19S 33.11E
Lundevatn l. Norway 42 58.22N 6.36E
Lundy i. U.K. 13 51.10N 4.41W
Lune r. U.K. 12 54.03N 2.49W
Lüneburg Germany 38 53.15N 10.23E
Lüneburger f. Germany 38 53.06N 10.30E
Lunel France 21 43.41N 4.08E
Lünen Germany 16 51.37N 7.31E
Lunenburg U.S.A. 44 54.28N 71.39W
Lunéville France 19 48.36N 6.30E
Lunga r. Zambia 78 14.28S 26.27E
Lunge Angola 78 12.13S 16.07E
Lunggar China 63 31.10N 84.01E
Lungwebungu r. Zambia 78 14.20S 23.15E
Lūni India 62 26.00N 73.00E
Lūni r. India 62 24.41N 71.15E
Luninets Belarus 37 52.18N 26.50E
Luning U.S.A. 108 38.30N 118.10W
Lūnkaransar India 62 28.32N 73.50E
Luocheng China 55 24.47N 108.54E
Luodian China 55 25.29N 106.39E
Luoding China 55 22.44N 111.32E
Luofo Zaïre 79 0.12S 29.15E
Luogosanto Italy 32 41.04N 9.12E
Luohe China 54 33.30N 114.04E
Luo He r. China 54 34.40N 110.15E
Luonan China 54 34.06N 110.10E
Luoyang China 54 34.48N 112.25E
Lupilichi Mozambique 79 11.45S 35.15E
Luquan China 61 25.35N 102.30E
Luque Spain 27 37.33N 4.16W
Lūrah r. Afghan. 62 31.20N 65.45E
Luray U.S.A. 114 38.40N 78.28W
Lure France 19 47.41N 6.30E
Lurgan U.K. 15 54.28N 6.21W
Lurio Mozambique 79 13.30S 40.30E
Lurio r. Mozambique 79 13.32S 40.31E
Lusaka Zambia 79 15.20S 28.14E
Lusambo Zaïre 78 4.59S 23.26E
Luscar Canada 100 53.05N 117.26W

Lu Shan mtn. China 54 36.18N 118.03E
Lüshi China 54 34.04N 111.02E
Lushnje Albania 34 40.55N 19.41E
Lushoto Tanzania 79 4.48S 38.20E
Lüshun China 54 38.42N 121.15E
Lusignan France 18 46.26N 0.07E
Lusk U.S.A. 108 42.46N 104.27W
Lussac-les-Châteaux France 18 46.24N 0.44E
Luton U.K. 13 51.53N 0.25W
Łutselk'e Canada 101 62.24N 110.44W
Lutsk Ukraine 37 50.42N 25.15E
Lutterworth U.K. 13 52.28N 1.12W
Lützow Germany 38 53.40N 11.11E
Luud r. Somali Rep. 71 10.25N 51.05E
Luuq Somali Rep. 79 3.56N 42.32E
Luverne U.S.A. 110 43.39N 96.13W
Luvua r. Zaïre 79 6.45S 27.00E
Luwegu r. Tanzania 79 8.30S 37.28E
Luwingu Zambia 79 10.13S 30.05E
Luxembourg d. Belgium 16 49.58N 5.30E
Luxembourg Europe 16 49.50N 6.15E
Luxembourg town Lux. 16 49.37N 6.08E
Luxeuil-les-Bains France 19 47.49N 6.23E
Luxi China 55 28.17N 110.10E
Luxor see Al Uqṣur Egypt 64
Luy de Béarn r. France 20 43.36N 0.44W
Luy de France r. France 20 43.38N 0.47W
Luza Russian Fed. 44 60.41N 47.12E
Luza r. Russian Fed. 44 60.45N 46.25E
Luzarches France 19 49.07N 2.25E
Luzern Switz. 39 47.03N 8.18E
Luzern d. Switz. 39 47.12N 8.05E
Luzhai China 55 24.29N 109.29E
Luzhou China 55 28.48N 105.23E
Luziânia Brazil 123 16.18S 47.57W
Luzon i. Phil. 59 17.50N 121.00E
Luzon Str. Pacific Oc. 59 20.20N 122.00E
Luzy France 19 46.48N 3.58E
Lvov Ukraine 37 49.50N 24.00E
Lyantonde Uganda 79 0.26S 31.08E
Lybster U.K. 14 58.18N 3.18W
Lyckeby Sweden 43 56.12N 15.39E
Lycksele Sweden 40 64.36N 18.40E
Lydenburg R.S.A. 80 25.06S 30.27E
Lyell I. Canada 100 52.40N 131.35W
Lygnern l. Sweden 43 57.29N 12.20E
Lykens U.S.A. 114 40.34N 76.43W
Lyme B. U.K. 13 50.40N 2.55W
Lyme Regis U.K. 13 50.44N 2.57W
Lymington U.K. 13 50.46N 1.32W
Łyna r. Poland 37 54.37N 21.14E
Lynchburg U.S.A. 113 37.24N 79.10W
Lynden Canada 104 43.14N 80.09W
Lyndhurst Australia 92 30.19S 138.24E
Lyndonville U.S.A. 114 44.31N 78.23W
Lyngdal Norway 42 58.08N 7.05E
Lyngen Norway 40 69.36N 20.10E
Lyngen est. Norway 40 69.35N 20.20E
Lynn U.S.A. 115 42.28N 70.57W
Lynn Canal U.S.A. 100 58.38N 135.08W
Lynn, L. U.S.A. 114 39.41N 79.55W
Lynn Lake town Canada 101 56.51N 101.03W
Lynton U.K. 13 51.14N 3.50W
Lynx Canada 102 50.08N 85.55W
Lyon France 21 45.45N 4.51E
Lyon Mountain town U.S.A. 105 44.43N 73.55W
Lyonnais, Monts du mts. France 21 45.40N 4.30E
Lyons Australia 92 30.34S 133.50E
Lyons r. Australia 88 25.02S 115.09E
Lyons U.S.A. 114 43.04N 77.00W
Lyons Falls U.S.A. 115 43.37N 75.22W
Lysefjorden est. Norway 42 59.00N 6.14E
Lysekil Sweden 42 58.16N 11.26E
Lyster Canada 105 46.22N 71.38W
Lysva Russian Fed. 44 58.07N 57.49E
Lysyanka Ukraine 37 49.16N 30.49E
Lysyye Gory Russian Fed. 45 51.32N 44.48E
Lytham St. Anne's U.K. 12 53.45N 3.01W
Lyubar Ukraine 37 49.58N 27.41E
Lyubech Ukraine 37 51.42N 30.41E
Lyubertsy Russian Fed. 44 55.38N 37.58E
Lyubeshov Ukraine 37 51.42N 25.32E
Lyubimets Bulgaria 34 41.50N 26.05E
Lyushcha Belarus 37 52.28N 26.41E

M

Ma r. Vietnam 55 19.48N 105.55E
Ma'ād Jordan 67 32.36N 35.37E
Maamakeogh mtn. Rep. of Ire. 15 54.17N 9.29W
Maamturk Mts. Rep. of Ire. 15 53.32N 9.42W
Ma'ān Jordan 66 30.11N 35.43E
Ma'anshan China 55 31.47N 118.33E
Maarianhamina Finland 43 60.06N 19.57E
Maas r. Neth. 16 51.44N 4.42E
Maaseik Belgium 16 51.08N 5.48E
Maassluis Neth. 16 51.58N 4.12E
Maastricht Neth. 16 50.51N 5.42E
Maave Mozambique 81 21.06S 34.48E
Maaza Plateau Egypt 66 27.39N 31.45E
Mabalane Mozambique 81 23.49S 32.36E
Ma'barot Israel 67 32.22N 34.54E
Maberly Canada 105 44.50N 76.30W
Mablethorpe U.K. 12 53.21N 0.14E
Mabrouk Mali 76 19.29N 1.15W

Macá mtn. Chile 125 45.06S 73.12W
Macaé Brazil 126 22.21S 41.48W
Macalister r. Australia 93 37.55S 146.50E
Macão Portugal 27 39.33N 8.00W
Macapá Brazil 123 0.04N 51.04W
Macarthur Australia 92 38.01S 142.01E
Macau Asia 55 22.11N 113.33E
Macau Brazil 123 5.05S 36.37W
Macclesfield U.K. 12 53.16N 2.09W
Macdiarmid Canada 102 49.27N 88.08W
Macdoel U.S.A. 108 41.50N 122.00W
Macdonald, L. Australia 88 23.30S 129.00E
Macdonnell Ranges mts. Australia 90 23.45S 133.20E
Macduff U.K. 14 57.40N 2.29W
Macedo de Cavaleiros Portugal 26 41.32N 6.58W
Macedonia Europe 34 41.53N 21.40E
Macedon, Mt. Australia 93 37.27S 144.34E
Maceió Brazil 123 9.40S 35.44W
Macenta Guinea 76 8.31N 9.32W
Macerata Italy 31 43.18N 13.27E
MacFarlane r. Canada 101 59.12N 107.58W
Macfarlane, L. Australia 92 31.55S 136.42E
Macgillycuddy's Reeks mts. Rep. of Ire. 15 52.00N 9.43W
Machado Brazil 126 21.39S 45.33W
Machala Ecuador 122 3.20S 79.57W
Machattie, L. Australia 90 24.50S 139.48E
Machece Mozambique 81 19.17S 35.33E
Machecoul France 18 47.00N 1.50W
Macheke Zimbabwe 81 18.08S 31.49E
Macheng China 55 31.11N 115.02E
Machevna Russian Fed. 51 60.46N 171.40E
Machias Maine U.S.A. 112 44.43N 67.28W
Machias N.Y. U.S.A. 114 42.25N 78.30W
Machichaco, Cabo c. Spain 26 43.27N 2.45W
Machichi r. Canada 101 57.03N 92.06W
Machida Japan 57 35.32N 139.27E
Machilipatnam India 61 16.13N 81.12E
Machiques Venezuela 122 10.04N 72.37W
Machiya r. Japan 57 35.01N 136.42E
Machrihanish U.K. 14 55.25N 5.44W
Machynlleth U.K. 13 52.35N 3.51W
Maciá Argentina 125 32.11S 59.26W
Macia Mozambique 81 25.03S 33.10E
Macintyre r. Australia 93 28.50S 150.50E
Mackay Australia 90 21.09S 149.11E
MacKay U.S.A. 108 43.55N 113.37W
Mackay, L. Australia 88 22.30S 149.10E
Mackenzie r. Australia 90 22.48S 149.15E
Mackenzie r. Canada 98 69.20N 134.00W
Mackenzie Mts. Canada 98 64.00N 130.00W
Mackenzie King I. Canada 98 77.30N 112.00W
Mackinac I. U.S.A. 104 45.51N 84.38W
Mackinaw City U.S.A. 104 45.47N 84.44W
Mackinnon Road town Kenya 79 3.50S 39.03E
Macklin Canada 101 52.20N 109.56W
Macksville Australia 93 30.43S 152.55E
Maclean Australia 91 29.27S 153.14E
Maclear R.S.A. 80 31.04S 28.21E
Macleay r. Australia 93 30.52S 153.01E
MacLeod, L. Australia 88 24.10S 113.35E
Maçobere Mozambique 81 21.14S 32.50E
Macomer Italy 32 40.16N 8.46E
Mâcon France 21 46.18N 4.50E
Macon Ga. U.S.A. 113 32.49N 83.37W
Macon Mo. U.S.A. 111 39.44N 92.28W
Mâconnais, Monts du mts. France 19 46.18N 4.45E
Macquarie r. Australia 93 30.07S 147.24E
Macquarie-Balleny Ridge Pacific Oc. 84 58.00S 160.00E
Macquarie I. Pacific Oc. 84 54.29S 158.58E
Macquarie, L. Australia 93 33.05S 151.35E
Macquarie Marshes Australia 93 30.50S 147.32E
MacRobertson Land f. Antarctica 128 69.30S 64.00E
Macroom Rep. of Ire. 15 51.54N 8.58W
Mac Tier Canada 104 45.08N 79.47W
Macumba r. Australia 91 27.55S 137.15E
Ma'dabā Jordan 67 31.44N 35.48E
Madagascar Africa 81 17.00S 46.00E
Madan Bulgaria 34 41.30N 24.57E
Madang P.N.G. 59 5.14S 145.45E
Madaoua Niger 77 14.05N 6.27E
Mädärīpur Bangla. 63 23.10N 90.12E
Madawaska Canada 105 45.30N 77.59W
Madawaska r. Canada 105 45.27N 76.21W
Madawaska U.S.A. 112 47.21N 68.20W
Maddalena i. Italy 32 41.13N 9.24E
Maddaloni Italy 33 41.02N 14.23E
Madeira r. Brazil 122 3.20S 59.00W
Madeira i. Madeira Is. 127 32.45N 17.00W
Madeira, Arquipélago da is. Atlantic Oc. 127 32.45N 17.00W
Madeira Is. see Madeira, Arquipélago da is. Atlantic Oc. 127
Mädelegabel mtn. Austria 39 47.18N 10.18E
Madeleine, Îles de la is. Canada 103 47.20N 61.50W
Madera U.S.A. 108 36.57N 120.03W
Madera, Sierra de la mts. Mexico 109 30.20N 109.00W
Madgaon India 60 15.26N 73.50E
Madhubani India 63 26.22N 86.05E
Madhya Pradesh d. India 63 23.30N 78.30E
Madibira Tanzania 79 8.13S 34.47E
Madigan G. Australia 92 28.55S 137.48E
Madill U.S.A. 111 34.06N 96.46W
Madīnat ash Sha'b Yemen 71 12.50N 44.56E
Madingley Rise f. Indian Oc. 49 5.00S 62.00E
Madison Fla. U.S.A. 107 30.29N 83.39W
Madison Ind. U.S.A. 112 38.46N 85.22W
Madison N.J. U.S.A. 115 40.46N 74.25W
Madison Ohio U.S.A. 114 41.47N 81.04W
Madison S.Dak. U.S.A. 110 44.00N 97.07W
Madison Tenn. U.S.A. 113 36.16N 86.44W
Madison Va. U.S.A. 114 38.23N 78.15W
Madison Wisc. U.S.A. 110 43.05N 89.22W
Madison W.Va. U.S.A. 112 38.03N 81.50W
Madison Junction U.S.A. 108 44.39N 110.51W
Madisonville Ky. U.S.A. 113 37.20N 87.30W

Madisonville Tex. U.S.A. 111 30.57N 95.55W
Madiun Indonesia 59 7.37S 111.33E
Madoc Canada 105 44.30N 77.28W
Mado Gashi Kenya 79 0.40N 39.11E
Madoi China 52 34.28N 98.56E
Madonna di Campiglio Italy 30 46.14N 10.49E
Madrakah, Ra's al c. Oman 60 19.00N 57.50E
Madras India 61 13.05N 80.18E
Madras U.S.A. 108 44.38N 121.08W
Madre de Dios r. Bolivia 122 10.24S 65.30W
Madre del Sur, Sierra mts. Mexico 116 17.00N 100.00W
Madre, Laguna b. Mexico 111 25.00N 97.40W
Madre, Laguna b. U.S.A. 111 27.00N 97.35W
Madre Occidental, Sierra mts. Mexico 109 25.00N 105.00W
Madre Oriental, Sierra mts. Mexico 111 28.10N 102.10W
Madre, Sierra mts. Mexico/Guatemala 116 15.20N 92.20W
Madrid Spain 26 40.24N 3.41W
Madrid d. Spain 26 40.15N 3.30W
Madridejos Spain 27 39.28N 3.32W
Madrigalejo Spain 27 39.09N 5.37W
Madrona, Sierra mts. Spain 26 38.30N 3.00W
Madroñera Spain 27 39.26N 5.46W
Madukani Tanzania 79 3.57S 35.49E
Madura i. Indonesia 59 7.02S 113.22E
Madurai India 48 9.55N 78.07E
Maebashi Japan 57 36.30N 139.04E
Mae Klong r. Thailand 56 13.21N 100.00E
Mae Sot Thailand 56 16.40N 98.35E
Maestra, Sierra mts. Cuba 117 20.10N 76.30W
Maestu Spain 26 42.44N 2.27W
Maevatanana Madagascar 81 16.56S 46.49E
Maewo i. Vanuatu 84 15.10S 168.10E
Mafeking Canada 101 52.43N 100.59W
Mafeteng Lesotho 80 29.51S 27.13E
Maffra Australia 93 37.58S 146.59E
Mafia I. Tanzania 79 7.50S 39.50E
Mafikeng R.S.A. 80 25.52S 25.36E
Mafra Portugal 27 38.56N 9.20W
Magadan Russian Fed. 51 59.38N 150.50E
Magadi Kenya 79 1.53S 36.18E
Magallanes, Estrecho de str. Chile 125 53.00S 71.00W
Magallan's Str. see Magallanes, Estrecho de str. Chile 125
Magalluf Spain 25 39.30N 2.30E
Magangué Colombia 122 9.14N 74.46W
Magazine U.S.A. 111 35.10N 93.40W
Magburaka Sierra Leone 76 8.44N 11.57W
Magdalena Argentina 125 35.04S 57.32W
Magdalena Bolivia 124 13.50S 64.08W
Magdalena r. Colombia 122 10.56N 74.58W
Magdalena Mexico 109 30.38N 110.59W
Magdalena, Isla i. Chile 125 44.42S 73.10W
Magdalena, Llano de la f. Mexico 109 24.55N 111.40W
Magdalene mtn. Malaysia 58 4.25N 117.55E
Magdeburg Germany 38 52.08N 11.38E
Magé Brazil 126 22.37S 43.03W
Magee U.S.A. 111 31.52N 89.44W
Magelang Indonesia 59 7.28S 110.11E
Magen Israel 67 31.18N 34.26E
Magenta Italy 30 45.28N 8.53E
Magenta, L. Australia 89 33.26S 119.10E
Magerøya i. Norway 40 71.03N 25.45E
Maggiorasca, Monte mtn. Italy 30 44.33N 9.29E
Maggiore, Lago l. Italy 30 46.00N 8.40E
Maghāghah Egypt 66 28.39N 30.50E
Maghār Israel 67 32.53N 35.24E
Magherafelt U.K. 15 54.45N 6.38W
Magina mtn. Spain 27 37.44N 3.28W
Magione Italy 30 43.08N 12.12E
Maglaj Bosnia-Herzegovina 31 44.33N 18.06E
Magna U.S.A. 108 40.42N 112.06W
Magnetawan Canada 104 45.40N 79.38W
Magnetawan r. Canada 104 45.46N 80.37W
Magnetic I. Australia 90 19.08S 146.50E
Magnitogorsk Russian Fed. 44 53.28N 59.06E
Magnolia Ark. U.S.A. 111 33.16N 93.14W
Magnolia Miss. U.S.A. 111 31.09N 90.28W
Magnolia Tex. U.S.A. 111 30.13N 95.45W
Magny-en-Vexin France 19 49.09N 1.47E
Magog Canada 105 45.16N 72.09W
Magoye Zambia 79 16.00S 27.38E
Magpie r. Canada 103 50.18N 64.28W
Magrath Canada 100 49.25N 112.50W
Magro r. Spain 25 39.11N 0.25W
Magude Mozambique 81 25.01S 32.39E
Magué Mozambique 79 15.46S 31.42E
Maguse River town Canada 101 61.20N 94.25W
Magwe Myanmar 56 20.08N 95.00E
Magwe d. Myanmar 56 23.00N 95.00E
Mahābād Iran 65 36.44N 45.44E
Mahābhārat Range mts. Nepal 63 28.00N 84.30E
Mahabo Madagascar 81 20.23S 44.40E
Mahadday Weyne Somali Rep. 79 2.58N 45.32E
Mahādeo Hills India 62 22.15N 78.30E
Mahaffey U.S.A. 114 40.53N 78.44W
Mahagi Zaïre 79 2.16N 30.59E
Mahajamba r. Madagascar 81 15.33S 47.08E
Mahājan India 62 28.47N 73.50E
Mahajanga Madagascar 81 15.43S 46.19E
Mahajilo r. Madagascar 81 19.42S 45.22E
Mahajjah Syria 67 32.57N 36.14E
Mahalapye Botswana 80 23.04S 26.47E
Mahalás Greece 35 38.41N 21.11E
Mahallāt Iran 65 33.54N 50.28E
Mahānadi India 63 20.19N 86.45E
Mahānadi r. India 61 20.17N 86.43E
Mahanoro Madagascar 81 19.54S 48.48E
Mahanoy City U.S.A. 115 40.49N 76.08W
Mahārājpur India 63 25.01N 79.44E
Mahārāshtra d. India 62 19.40N 76.00E
Mahāsamund India 63 21.06N 82.06E
Maha Sarakham Thailand 56 15.50N 103.47E
Mahavavy r. Madagascar 81 15.57S 45.54E
Mahbés W. Sahara 74 27.13N 9.44W

Mahd adh Dhahab Saudi Arabia **64** 23.30N 40.52E
Mahdia Guyana **122** 5.10N 59.12W
Mahendraganj India **63** 25.20N 89.45E
Mahenge Tanzania **79** 8.46S 36.38E
Mahi r. India **62** 22.30N 72.58E
Mahia Pen. New Zealand **86** 39.10S 177.50E
Mahmūdābād India **63** 27.18N 81.07E
Mahmūd-e 'Erāqī Afghan. **62** 35.01N 69.20E
Mahnomen U.S.A. **110** 47.19N 96.01W
Maho Sri Lanka **61** 7.49N 80.17E
Mahoba India **63** 25.17N 79.52E
Mahón Spain **25** 39.53N 4.15E
Mahone B. Canada **103** 44.30N 64.15W
Mahora Spain **25** 39.13N 1.44W
Mahroni India **63** 24.35N 78.43E
Mahuva India **62** 21.05N 71.48E
Maia Portugal **26** 41.14N 8.37W
Maião i. Ìs. de la Société **85** 17.23S 150.37W
Maïche France **19** 47.15N 6.48E
Maidenhead U.K. **13** 51.32N 0.44W
Maidstone U.K. **13** 51.17N 0.32E
Maiduguri Nigeria **77** 11.53N 13.16E
Maignelay France **19** 49.33N 2.31E
Maihar India **63** 24.16N 80.45E
Maikala Range mts. India **63** 21.45N 81.00E
Maiko r. Zaïre **78** 0.15N 25.35E
Maillezais France **18** 46.22N 0.44W
Main r. Germany **39** 50.00N 8.18E
Mā'īn Jordan **67** 31.41N 35.44E
Mainburg Germany **39** 48.38N 11.47E
Main Camp Kiribati **85** 2.01N 157.25W
Main Centre Canada **101** 50.38N 107.20W
Mai Ndombe l. Zaïre **78** 2.00S 18.20E
Main Duck I. Canada **105** 43.56N 76.37W
Maine d. U.S.A. **112** 45.15N 69.15W
Maine-et-Loire d. France **18** 47.25N 0.30W
Mainhardt Germany **39** 49.04N 9.33E
Mainland i. Orkney Is. U.K. **14** 59.00N 3.10W
Mainoru Australia **90** 14.02S 134.05E
Mainpuri India **63** 27.14N 79.01E
Maintirano Madagascar **81** 18.03S 44.01E
Mainz Germany **39** 50.01N 8.16E
Maípo mtn. Argentina **125** 34.10S 69.50W
Maipú Argentina **125** 36.52S 57.54W
Maiquetía Venezuela **122** 10.03N 66.57W
Maiskhāl I. Bangla. **63** 21.36N 91.56E
Maitland N.S.W. Australia **93** 32.33S 151.33E
Maitland S.A. Australia **92** 34.21S 137.42E
Maitland r. Canada **104** 43.45N 81.43W
Maizhokunggar China **63** 29.50N 91.44E
Maizuru Japan **57** 35.30N 135.20E
Majd el Kurūm Israel **67** 32.55N 35.15E
Majeigha Sudan **73** 11.33N 24.40E
Majene Indonesia **58** 3.33S 118.59E
Majī Ethiopia **73** 6.11N 35.38E
Majiahewan China **54** 37.12N 105.48E
Majiang China **55** 26.30N 107.35E
Majorca i. see Mallorca i. Spain **25**
Majrūr Sudan **72** 14.01N 30.27E
Majuba Hill R.S.A. **80** 27.26S 29.48E
Majuro i. Pacific Oc. **84** 7.09N 171.12E
Makabana Congo **78** 3.25S 12.41E
Makale Indonesia **58** 3.06S 119.53E
Makalu mtn. China/Nepal **63** 27.54N 87.06E
Makarikha Russian Fed. **44** 66.17N 58.28E
Makarska Croatia **31** 43.18N 17.02E
Makaryev Russian Fed. **44** 57.52N 43.40E
Makasar, Selat str. Indonesia **58** 3.00S 118.00E
Makassar Str. see Makasar, Selat str. Indonesia **58**
Makat Kazakhstan **45** 47.38N 53.16E
Makaw Myanmar **56** 26.27N 96.42E
Makaya Zaïre **78** 3.22S 18.02E
Makay, Massif du mts. Madagascar **81** 21.15S 45.15E
Makedonija see Macedonia Europe **34**
Makefu Niue **84** 19.01S 169.55W
Makeni Sierra Leone **76** 8.57N 12.02W
Makere Tanzania **79** 4.15S 30.26E
Makeyevka Ukraine **45** 48.01N 38.00E
Makgadikgadi Salt Pan f. Botswana **80** 20.50S 25.45E
Makhachkala Russian Fed. **45** 42.59N 47.30E
Makham Thailand **56** 12.40N 102.12E
Makhfar al Quwayrah Jordan **66** 29.49N 35.18E
Makhrūq, Wādī al r. Jordan **66** 31.30N 37.10E
Makinsk Kazakhstan **52** 52.37N 70.26E
Makkah Saudi Arabia **72** 21.26N 39.49E
Makkovik Canada **103** 55.00N 59.10W
Makó Hungary **37** 46.13N 20.30E
Mako Senegal **76** 13.00N 12.26W
Makobe L. Canada **104** 47.27N 80.25W
Makokou Gabon **78** 0.38N 12.47E
Makoua Congo **78** 0.01S 15.40E
Makrai India **62** 22.04N 77.06E
Makran f. Asia **65** 26.30N 61.20E
Makrāna India **62** 27.03N 74.43E
Makrān Coast Range mts. Pakistan **62** 25.30N 64.30E
Maksamaa Finland **40** 63.14N 22.05E
Makuliro Tanzania **79** 9.34S 37.26E
Makurdi Nigeria **77** 7.44N 8.35E
Māl India **63** 26.52N 88.44E
Malabo Equat. Guinea **77** 3.45N 8.48E
Malacca see Melaka Malaysia **58**
Malacca, Str. of Indian Oc. **58** 3.00N 100.30E
Malad City U.S.A. **108** 42.12N 112.15W
Málaga Spain **27** 36.43N 4.25W
Málaga d. Spain **27** 36.45N 4.40W
Malaga U.S.A. **109** 32.14N 104.04W
Malagón Spain **27** 39.35N 3.51W
Malagón r. Spain **27** 37.35N 7.29W
Malaimbandy Madagascar **81** 20.20S 45.36E
Malaita Solomon Is. **84** 9.00S 161.00E
Malakāl Sudan **73** 9.31N 31.39E
Mala Kapela mts. Croatia **31** 45.00N 15.20E
Malam Chad **73** 11.27N 20.59E
Malang Indonesia **59** 7.59S 112.45E
Malangwa Nepal **63** 26.52N 85.34E

Malanje Angola **78** 9.36S 16.21E
Malanje d. Angola **78** 8.40S 16.50E
Mälaren l. Sweden **43** 59.30N 17.12E
Malartic Canada **102** 48.09N 78.09W
Malatya Turkey **64** 38.22N 38.18E
Malaucène France **21** 44.10N 5.08E
Malaut India **62** 30.11N 74.30E
Malawi Africa **79** 12.00S 34.00E
Malawi, L. Africa **79** 12.00S 34.30E
Malaya Vishera Russian Fed. **44** 58.53N 32.08E
Maläyer Iran **65** 34.19N 48.51E
Malaysia Asia **58** 5.00N 110.00E
Malazgirt Turkey **64** 39.09N 42.31E
Malbaie r. Canada **103** 47.40N 70.05W
Malbaie, Baie de b. Canada **103** 48.35N 64.16W
Malbooma Australia **92** 30.41S 134.11E
Malbork Poland **37** 54.02N 19.01E
Malchin Germany **38** 53.44N 12.46E
Malchow Germany **38** 53.28N 12.25E
Malcolm Australia **89** 28.56S 121.30E
Malcolm, Pt. Australia **89** 33.47S 123.44E
Malden Mo. U.S.A. **111** 36.34N 89.57W
Malden I. Kiribati **85** 4.03S 154.49W
Maldive Ridge f. Indian Oc. **49** 0.00 73.00E
Maldives Indian Oc. **60** 6.20N 73.00E
Maldon U.K. **13** 51.43N 0.41E
Maldonado Uruguay **126** 34.57S 54.59W
Male Italy **30** 46.21N 10.55E
Maléa, Ákra c. Greece **35** 36.26N 23.12E
Malebo Pool f. Zaïre **78** 4.15S 15.25E
Mälegaon India **62** 20.33N 74.32E
Malek Sudan **73** 6.04N 31.36E
Malek Dīn Afghan. **62** 32.25N 68.04E
Malekula i. Vanuatu **84** 16.15S 167.30E
Malema Mozambique **79** 14.55S 37.09E
Malenga Russian Fed. **44** 65.50N 36.50E
Malente Germany **38** 54.10N 10.33E
Mäler Kotla India **62** 30.32N 75.53E
Malesherbes France **19** 48.18N 2.25E
Malesína Greece **35** 38.37N 23.15E
Malestroit France **18** 47.49N 2.23W
Malgomaj l. Sweden **40** 64.47N 16.12E
Malheur L. U.S.A. **108** 43.20N 118.45W
Mali Africa **76** 17.30N 2.30E
Mali r. Myanmar **56** 25.43N 97.29E
Malik, Wādī al Sudan **72** 18.02N 30.58E
Malili Indonesia **59** 2.38S 121.06E
Málilla Sweden **43** 57.23N 15.48E
Malin Ukraine **37** 50.48N 29.08E
Malinau Indonesia **58** 3.35N 116.38E
Malindi Kenya **79** 3.14S 40.08E
Malingping Indonesia **59** 6.45S 106.01E
Malin Head Rep. of Ire. **15** 55.23N 7.24W
Malin More Rep. of Ire. **15** 54.42N 8.48W
Malipo China **55** 23.11N 104.41E
Maliquit Albania **34** 40.45N 20.48E
Mali Rajinac Croatia **31** 44.48N 15.02E
Mâliya India **62** 23.05N 70.46E
Malkâpur India **62** 20.53N 76.12E
Mallacoota Australia **93** 37.34S 149.43E
Mallacoota Inlet b. Australia **93** 37.34S 149.43E
Mallaig U.K. **14** 57.00N 5.50W
Mallawī Egypt **66** 27.44N 30.50E
Mallersdorf Germany **39** 48.47N 12.16E
Mallnitz Austria **30** 46.59N 13.10E
Mallorca i. Spain **25** 39.30N 3.00E
Mallow Rep. of Ire. **15** 52.08N 8.39W
Malm Norway **40** 64.04N 11.12E
Malmbäck Sweden **43** 57.35N 14.28E
Malmberget Sweden **40** 67.10N 20.40E
Malmédy Belgium **16** 50.25N 6.02E
Malmesbury R.S.A. **80** 33.28S 18.43E
Malmö Sweden **43** 55.36N 13.00E
Malmöhus d. Sweden **43** 55.45N 13.30E
Malmslätt Sweden **43** 58.25N 15.30E
Malmyzh Russian Fed. **44** 56.34N 50.41E
Maloja Switz. **39** 46.24N 9.41E
Malolos Guam **84** 13.18N 144.46E
Malone U.S.A. **105** 44.51N 74.17W
Malonga Zaïre **78** 10.26S 23.10E
Malorita Belarus **37** 51.50N 24.08E
Mâlöy Norway **41** 61.56N 5.07E
Malozemelskaya Tundra f. Russian Fed. **44** 67.40N 50.10E
Malpartida de Plasencia Spain **27** 39.59N 6.02W
Malpas Australia **92** 34.44S 140.43E
Malta Europe **28** 35.55N 14.25E
Malta Mont. U.S.A. **108** 48.21N 107.52W
Malta Ohio U.S.A. **114** 39.39N 81.52W
Malta Channel Med. Sea **28** 36.20N 14.45E
Maltby U.K. **12** 53.25N 1.12W
Malton U.K. **12** 54.09N 0.48W
Maluku d. Indonesia **59** 4.00S 129.00E
Maluku, Laut sea Pacific Oc. **59**
Malumfashi Nigeria **77** 11.48N 7.36E
Malundo Angola **78** 14.51S 22.00E
Malung Sweden **41** 60.40N 13.44E
Malūṭ Sudan **73** 10.26N 32.12E
Malvinas, Islas see Falkland Is. Atlantic Ocean **125**
Mama Russian Fed. **51** 58.20N 112.55E
Mamadysh Russian Fed. **44** 55.43N 51.20E
Mamaia Romania **37** 44.15N 28.37E
Mambasa Zaïre **79** 1.20N 29.05E
Mamberamo r. Indonesia **59** 1.45S 137.25E
Mambéré r. C.A.R. **77** 3.30N 16.08E
Mambilima Falls town Zambia **79** 10.32S 28.45E
Mamers France **18** 48.21N 0.23E
Mamfe Cameroon **77** 5.46N 9.18E
Mamonovo Russian Fed. **37** 54.30N 19.59E
Mamoré r. Bolivia **124** 12.00S 65.15W
Mamou Guinea **76** 10.24N 12.05W
Mampika Congo **78** 2.58S 14.38E
Mampikony Madagascar **81** 16.06S 47.38E
Mampong Ghana **76** 7.06N 1.24W
Mamry, Jezioro l. Poland **37** 54.08N 21.42E
Mamuju Indonesia **58** 2.41S 118.55E
Ma'mūn Sudan **73** 12.15N 22.41E

Man Côte d'Ivoire **76** 7.31N 7.37W
Man Jammu & Kashmir **63** 33.51N 78.32E
Mana r. Guiana **123** 5.35N 53.55W
Mana Hawaiian Is. **85** 22.02N 156.46W
Manacapuru Brazil **122** 3.16S 60.37W
Manacor Spain **25** 39.34N 3.12E
Manado Indonesia **59** 1.30N 124.58E
Managua Nicaragua **117** 12.06N 86.18W
Managua, Lago de l. Nicaragua **117** 12.10N 86.30W
Manahawkin U.S.A. **115** 39.42N 74.16W
Manakara Madagascar **81** 22.08S 48.01E
Manāli India **62** 32.16N 77.10E
Manambao r. Madagascar **81** 17.43S 43.57E
Mananara Madagascar **81** 16.10S 49.46E
Mananara r. Madagascar **81** 23.21S 47.42E
Manangatang Australia **92** 35.02S 142.54E
Mananjary Madagascar **81** 21.13S 48.20E
Manankoro Mali **76** 10.25N 7.26W
Manantenina Madagascar **81** 24.17S 47.19E
Manapouri, L. New Zealand **86** 45.30S 167.00E
Manār r. Iran **65** 34.50N 47.44E
Manāslu mtn. Nepal **63** 28.33N 84.35E
Manasquan U.S.A. **115** 40.07N 74.03W
Manassas U.S.A. **114** 38.45N 77.28W
Manau P.N.G. **59** 8.02S 148.00E
Manaus Brazil **122** 3.06S 60.00W
Manāwar India **62** 22.14N 75.05E
Manawatu-Wanganui d. New Zealand **86** 39.00S 175.25E
Mancelona U.S.A. **112** 44.54N 85.03W
Mancha Real Spain **27** 37.47N 3.37W
Manche d. France **18** 49.00N 1.10W
Mancheräl India **63** 18.52N 79.26E
Manchester U.K. **12** 53.30N 2.15W
Manchester Conn. U.S.A. **115** 41.47N 72.31W
Manchester Mich. U.S.A. **104** 42.09N 84.02W
Manchester N.H. U.S.A. **115** 42.59N 71.28W
Manchester N.Y. U.S.A. **114** 42.58N 77.14W
Manchurian Plain f. see Dongbei Pingyuan f. China **53**
Manciano Italy **30** 42.35N 11.31E
Mand r. Iran **65** 28.09N 51.16E
Manda Iringa Tanzania **79** 10.30S 34.37E
Manda Mbeya Tanzania **79** 7.59S 32.27E
Mandabe Madagascar **81** 21.03S 44.55E
Manda, Jabal mtn. Sudan **73** 8.39N 24.27E
Mandal Norway **42** 58.02N 7.27E
Mandala Peak Indonesia **59** 4.45S 140.15E
Mandalay Myanmar **56** 21.58N 96.04E
Mandalay d. Myanmar **56** 22.00N 96.00E
Mandalgovĭ Mongolia **54** 45.40N 106.10E
Mandals r. Norway **42** 58.20N 7.28E
Mandalya Körfezi b. Turkey **35** 37.12N 27.20E
Mandan U.S.A. **110** 46.50N 100.54W
Mandara Mts. Nigeria/Cameroon **77** 10.30N 13.30E
Mandas Italy **32** 39.39N 9.08E
Mandasor India **62** 24.04N 75.04E
Mandeb, Bâb el str. Asia **73** 13.00N 43.10E
Mandel Afghan. **62** 33.17N 61.52E
Mandera Kenya **79** 3.55N 41.50E
Mandi India **62** 31.42N 76.55E
Mandi Būrewāla Pakistan **62** 30.09N 72.41E
Mandi Dabwāli India **62** 29.58N 74.42E
Mandji Gabon **78** 1.37S 10.53E
Mandla India **63** 22.59N 80.23E
Mandora Australia **88** 19.45S 120.50E
Mandoto Madagascar **81** 19.34S 46.17E
Mandoúdhion Greece **35** 38.48N 23.29E
Mandra Pakistan **62** 33.22N 73.14E
Mandritsara Madagascar **81** 15.50S 48.49E
Mându India **62** 22.22N 75.23E
Mandurah Australia **89** 32.31S 115.41E
Manduria Italy **33** 40.24N 17.38E
Mândvi India **62** 22.50N 69.22E
Mandya India **60** 12.33N 76.54E
Mâne r. Brazil **124** 11.59S 50.25W
Manendragarh India **63** 23.13N 82.13E
Manerbio Italy **32** 45.21N 10.08E
Manevichi Ukraine **37** 51.19N 25.35E
Manfredonia Italy **33** 41.38N 15.55E
Manfredonia, Golfo di g. Italy **33** 41.35N 16.05E
Mangaia I. Cook Is. **85** 21.56S 157.56W
Mangaldai India **63** 26.26N 92.02E
Mangalia Romania **37** 43.50N 28.35E
Mangalore India **60** 12.54N 74.51E
Mangando Angola **78** 8.02S 17.08E
Mangareva i. Pacific Oc. **85** 23.07S 134.57W
Mangawān India **63** 24.41N 81.33E
Mangaweka New Zealand **86** 38.49S 175.48E
Mangeigne Chad **73** 10.31N 21.19E
Mangnai China **52** 37.52N 91.26E
Mango Togo **76** 10.23N 0.30E
Mangochi Malawi **79** 14.29S 35.15E
Mangoky r. Madagascar **81** 21.29S 43.41E
Mangombe Zaïre **79** 1.23S 26.50E
Mangonui New Zealand **86** 35.00S 173.34E
Mangoro r. Madagascar **81** 20.00S 48.45E
Mângrol India **62** 21.07N 70.07E
Manguaíde Portugal **26** 40.36N 7.46W
Mangueira, L. Brazil **126** 33.06S 52.48W
Mangum U.S.A. **111** 34.53N 99.30W
Mangyshlak, Poluostrov pen. Kazakhstan **45** 44.00N 52.30E
Manhattan U.S.A. **110** 39.11N 96.35W
Manhiça Mozambique **81** 25.24S 32.49E
Manhuaçu Brazil **126** 20.16S 42.01W
Manhumirim Brazil **126** 20.22S 41.57W
Mania r. Madagascar **81** 19.42S 45.22E
Maniago Italy **30** 46.10N 12.43E
Manica Mozambique **81** 19.00S 33.00E
Manica d. Mozambique **81** 20.00S 34.00E
Manicoré Brazil **122** 5.49S 61.17W
Manicouagan r. Canada **103** 49.15N 68.20W
Manicouagan, Résr. Canada **103** 51.20N 68.48W
Maniitsoq see Sukkertoppen Greenland **99**
Mānikganj Bangla. **63** 23.19N 87.03E

Mānikpur India **63** 25.04N 81.07E
Manila Phil. **59** 14.36N 120.59E
Manila U.S.A. **108** 40.59N 109.43W
Manildra Australia **93** 33.12S 148.41E
Manilla Australia **93** 30.45S 150.45E
Maningory r. Madagascar **81** 17.13S 49.28E
Manipur d. India **61** 25.00N 93.40E
Manisa Turkey **29** 38.37N 27.28E
Man, Isle of Europe **12** 54.15N 4.30W
Manistee U.S.A. **112** 44.14N 86.20W
Manistee r. U.S.A. **112** 44.14N 86.20W
Manistique U.S.A. **112** 45.58N 86.17W
Manitoba d. Canada **101** 55.00N 96.00W
Manitoba, L. Canada **101** 51.00N 98.45W
Manitou L. Canada **104** 45.48N 82.00W
Manitoulin I. Canada **104** 45.45N 82.30W
Manitowaning Canada **104** 45.45N 81.49W
Manitowoc U.S.A. **112** 44.06N 87.40W
Maniwaki Canada **105** 46.23N 75.58W
Manizales Colombia **122** 5.03N 75.32W
Manjā Jordan **67** 31.45N 35.51E
Manja Madagascar **81** 21.26S 44.20E
Manjakandriana Madagascar **81** 18.55S 47.47E
Mânjhand Pakistan **62** 25.55N 68.14E
Manjīl Iran **65** 36.44N 49.29E
Manjimup Australia **89** 34.14S 116.06E
Mankato U.S.A. **110** 44.10N 94.01W
Mankera Pakistan **62** 31.23N 71.26E
Mankono Côte d'Ivoire **76** 8.01N 6.09W
Manlléu Spain **25** 42.00N 2.17E
Manly Australia **93** 33.47S 151.17E
Manmād India **62** 20.15N 74.27E
Mann r. Australia **90** 12.20S 134.07E
Mann r. N.S.W. Australia **93** 29.38S 152.21E
Manna Indonesia **58** 4.27S 102.55E
Mān Na Myanmar **56** 23.29N 97.14E
Mannahill Australia **92** 32.26S 139.59E
Mannar Sri Lanka **61** 8.59N 79.54E
Mannar, G. of India/Sri Lanka **61** 8.20N 79.00E
Mannessier, Lac l. Canada **103** 55.28N 70.38W
Mannheim Germany **39** 49.29N 8.28E
Mannin B. Rep. of Ire. **15** 53.28N 10.06W
Manning Canada **100** 56.53N 117.39W
Manning U.S.A. **113** 33.42N 80.12W
Mannington U.S.A. **114** 39.32N 80.20W
Manns Choice U.S.A. **114** 40.01N 78.39W
Mannsville U.S.A. **115** 43.43N 76.04W
Mannu r. Sardegna Italy **32** 39.16N 9.00E
Mannu r. Sardegna Italy **32** 40.50N 8.23E
Mannum Australia **92** 34.50S 139.20E
Mano Sierra Leone **76** 8.04N 12.02W
Manoharpur India **63** 22.23N 85.12E
Manokwari Indonesia **59** 0.53S 134.05E
Manolás Greece **35** 38.04N 21.21E
Manombo Madagascar **81** 22.57S 43.28E
Manono Zaïre **79** 7.18S 27.24E
Manorhamilton Rep. of Ire. **15** 54.18N 8.10W
Manosque France **21** 43.50N 5.47E
Manouane Canada **105** 47.14N 74.25W
Manouane r. Canada **103** 49.29N 71.13W
Manouane, Lac l. Canada **103** 50.40N 70.45W
Manouba Tunisia **32** 36.50N 10.06E
Mānpur India **63** 20.22N 80.43E
Manresa Spain **25** 41.44N 1.50E
Mânsa Gujarat India **62** 23.26N 72.40E
Mânsa Punjab India **62** 29.59N 75.23E
Mansa Zambia **79** 11.10S 28.52E
Mânsehra Pakistan **62** 34.20N 73.12E
Mansel I. Canada **99** 62.00N 80.00W
Mansfield U.K. **12** 53.08N 1.12W
Mansfield La. U.S.A. **111** 32.02N 93.43W
Mansfield Mass. U.S.A. **115** 42.02N 71.13W
Mansfield Ohio U.S.A. **114** 40.46N 82.31W
Mansfield Penn. U.S.A. **114** 41.48N 77.05W
Mansfield, Mt. U.S.A. **114** 44.33N 72.49W
Mansle France **20** 45.53N 0.11E
Manso r. Brazil **124** 11.59S 50.25W
Mansôa Guinea Bissau **76** 12.08N 15.18W
Mansūrah Syria **67** 33.08N 35.48E
Manta Ecuador **122** 0.59S 80.44W
Mantaro r. Peru **122** 12.00S 74.00W
Manteca U.S.A. **108** 37.48N 121.13W
Mantes France **19** 48.59N 1.43E
Mantiqueira, Serra da mts. Brazil **126** 22.25S 45.00W
Mantova Italy **30** 45.09N 10.48E
Mänttä Finland **41** 62.02N 24.38E
Mantua U.S.A. **114** 41.17N 81.14W
Manturovo Russian Fed. **44** 58.20N 44.42E
Mäntyluoto Finland **41** 61.35N 21.29E
Manú Peru **122** 12.14S 70.51W
Manua Is. Samoa **84** 14.13S 169.35W
Manuel Benavides Mexico **111** 29.05N 103.55W
Manui i. Indonesia **59** 3.35S 123.08E
Manukau New Zealand **86** 36.59S 174.53E
Manukau Harbour est. New Zealand **86** 37.10S 174.00E
Manunda Creek r. Australia **92** 32.50S 138.58E
Manus i. P.N.G. **59** 2.00S 147.00E
Manville U.S.A. **108** 42.47N 104.37W
Manyane Botswana **80** 23.23S 21.44E
Manyara, L. Tanzania **79** 3.40S 35.50E
Manych r. Russian Fed. **45** 47.14N 40.20E
Manych Gudilo, Ozero l. Russian Fed. **45** 46.20N 42.45E
Manyinga r. Zambia **80** 13.28S 24.25E
Manyoni Tanzania **79** 5.46S 34.50E
Mânzai Pakistan **62** 30.07N 68.52E
Manzanares Spain **27** 39.00N 3.22W
Manzanillo Cuba **117** 20.21N 77.21W
Manzanillo Mexico **97** 19.00N 104.20W
Manzano Mts. U.S.A. **109** 34.48N 106.12W
Manzhouli China **53** 49.36N 117.28E
Manzil Pakistan **62** 29.15N 63.05E
Manzilah, Buḩayrat al l. Egypt **66** 31.20N 32.00E
Manzini Swaziland **80** 26.29S 31.24E
Mao Chad **77** 14.06N 15.11E
Maobitou c. Taiwan **55** 22.00N 120.45E
Maoke, Pegunungan mts. Indonesia **59** 4.00S 137.30E

185

Maokui Shan *mtn.* China 54 33.55N 111.33E
Maoming China 55 21.50N 110.58E
Maoniu Shan *mtn.* China 54 33.00N 103.56E
Ma, Oued el- *wadi* Mauritania 74 24.30N 9.10W
Mapai Mozambique 81 22.51S 32.00E
Mapam Yumco *l.* China 63 30.40N 81.20E
Mapi Indonesia 59 7.06S 139.23E
Mapia, Kepulauan *is.* Indonesia 59 1.00N 134.15E
Mapimí, Bolsóne de *des.* Mexico 111 27.30N 103.15W
Mapinhane Mozambique 81 22.19S 35.03E
Mapire Venezuela 122 7.46N 64.41W
Maple Creek *town* Canada 101 49.55N 109.27W
Maprik P.N.G. 59 3.38S 143.02E
Mapuera *r.* Brazil 123 2.00S 55.40W
Maputo Mozambique 81 25.58S 32.35E
Maputo *d.* Mozambique 81 26.00S 32.30E
Maqnā Saudi Arabia 66 28.26N 34.44E
Maqu China 61 34.05N 102.15E
Maquan He *r.* China 63 29.35N 84.10E
Maqueda Spain 27 40.04N 4.22W
Maquela do Zombo Angola 78 6.06S 15.12E
Maquinchao Argentina 125 41.15S 68.44W
Maquoketa U.S.A. 110 42.04N 90.40W
Mara Tanzania 79 1.30S 34.31E
Mara *d.* Tanzania 79 1.45S 34.30E
Mara *r.* Tanzania 79 1.30S 33.52E
Maraã Brazil 122 1.50S 65.22W
Maraa Tahiti 85 17.46S 149.34W
Marabá Brazil 123 5.23S 49.10W
Marabastad R.S.A. 80 23.58S 29.21E
Maracaibo Venezuela 122 10.44N 71.37W
Maracaibo, Lago de *l.* Venezuela 122 9.50N 71.30W
Maracaju, Serra de *mts.* Brazil 126 21.38S 55.10W
Maracay Venezuela 122 10.20N 67.28W
Marādah Libya 75 29.14N 19.13E
Maradi Niger 77 13.29N 7.10E
Maradi *d.* Niger 77 14.00N 8.10E
Marāgheh Iran 65 37.25N 46.13E
Maragogipe Brazil 123 12.48S 38.59W
Marahuaca, Cerro *mtn.* Venezuela 122 3.37N 65.25W
Marajó, Ilha de *i.* Brazil 123 1.00S 49.40W
Maralal Kenya 79 1.15N 36.48E
Maralinga Australia 89 30.13S 131.32E
Maramba Zambia 78 17.40S 25.50E
Maramsilli Resr. India 63 20.32N 81.41E
Marana U.S.A. 109 32.27N 111.13W
Maranchón Spain 26 41.03N 2.12W
Marand Iran 65 38.25N 45.50E
Maranhão *d.* Brazil 123 6.00S 45.30W
Mārān, Koh-i- *mtn.* Pakistan 62 29.33N 66.53E
Maranoa *r.* Australia 91 27.55S 148.30E
Marañón *r.* Peru 122 4.40S 73.20W
Marans France 20 46.19N 1.00W
Marão Mozambique 81 24.21S 34.07E
Marapi Indonesia 58 0.20S 100.45E
Mărăşeşti Romania 37 45.52N 27.14E
Maratea Italy 33 39.59N 15.43E
Marathón Greece 35 38.09N 23.57E
Marathon N.Y. U.S.A. 115 42.26N 76.02W
Marathon Tex. U.S.A. 111 30.12N 103.15W
Maratua *i.* Indonesia 58 2.10N 118.35E
Marāveh Tappeh Iran 65 37.55N 55.57E
Marav L. Pakistan 62 29.04N 69.18E
Marawi Sudan 72 18.29N 31.49E
Marbella Spain 27 36.31N 4.53W
Marble Bar Australia 88 21.16S 119.45E
Marburg Germany 38 50.49N 8.46E
Marcali Hungary 31 46.35N 17.25E
Marcaria Italy 32 45.07N 10.32E
Marcellus U.S.A. 115 42.59N 76.20W
March U.K. 13 52.33N 0.05E
Marche Belgium 16 50.13N 5.21E
Marche *d.* Italy 30 43.35N 13.00E
Marchena Spain 27 37.20N 5.24W
Mar Chiquita *l.* Argentina 124 30.42S 62.36W
Marcigny France 19 46.17N 4.02E
Marcos Paz Argentina 125 34.49S 58.51W
Marcounda C.A.R. 77 7.37N 16.59E
Marcq-en-Baroeul France 16 50.40N 3.01E
Marcus Hook U.S.A. 115 39.49N 75.25W
Marcus I. Pacific Oc. 84 24.18N 153.58E
Marcy, Mt. U.S.A. 105 44.07N 73.56W
Mardān Pakistan 62 34.12N 72.02E
Mar del Plata Argentina 125 38.00S 57.32W
Marden U.K. 13 51.11N 0.30E
Mardie Australia 88 21.14S 115.57E
Mardin Turkey 64 37.19N 40.43E
Maree, Loch U.K. 14 57.41N 5.28W
Maré, Île *i.* N. Cal. 84 21.30S 168.00E
Marennes France 20 45.50N 1.06W
Marettimo *i.* Italy 32 37.58N 12.04E
Mareuil-sur-Belle France 20 45.28N 0.28E
Marfa U.S.A. 111 30.18N 104.01W
Margai Caka *l.* China 61 35.11N 86.57E
Margaret *r.* Australia 92 29.26S 137.00E
Margaret Bay *town* Canada 100 51.20N 127.20W
Margaret L. Canada 100 58.56N 115.25W
Margaret River *town* W. Aust. Australia 89 33.57S 115.04E
Margaret River *town* W. Aust. Australia 88 18.38S 126.52E
Margarita, Isla de *i.* Venezuela 122 11.00N 64.00W
Margarítion Greece 34 39.22N 20.26E
Margate R.S.A. 80 30.51S 30.22E
Margate U.K. 13 51.23N 1.24E
Margeride, Monts de la *mts.* France 20 44.50N 3.30E
Margherita di Savoia Italy 33 41.23N 16.09E
Mārgow, Dasht-e *des.* Afghan. 62 30.45N 63.10E
Maria Elena Chile 124 22.21S 69.40W
Maria Gail Austria 39 46.36N 13.52E
Mariager Denmark 42 56.39N 10.00E
María Grande Argentina 125 31.40S 59.55W
Maria I. Australia 90 14.52S 135.40E
Mariana Brazil 126 20.23S 43.23W
Marianao Cuba 117 23.03N 82.29W
Mariana Ridge Pacific Oc. 84 17.00N 146.00E
Mariana Trench Pacific Oc. 84 16.00N 148.00E

Marianna Ark. U.S.A. 111 34.46N 90.46W
Marianna Fla. U.S.A. 113 30.45N 85.15W
Mariannelund Sweden 43 57.37N 15.34E
Mariánské Lázně Czech Republic 39 49.59N 12.43E
Marias *r.* U.S.A. 108 47.56N 110.30W
Maribo Denmark 41 54.46N 11.31E
Maribor Slovenia 31 46.33N 15.39E
Marico *r.* R.S.A. 80 24.12S 26.57E
Maricopa U.S.A. 109 35.03N 119.24W
Marīdī Sudan 73 4.55N 29.28E
Marīdī *r.* Sudan 73 6.55N 29.00E
Marié *r.* Brazil 122 0.27S 66.26W
Marieburg Belgium 16 50.07N 4.30E
Mariefred Sweden 43 59.18N 17.15E
Marie-Galante *i.* Guadeloupe 117 15.54N 61.11W
Mariehamn *see* Maarianhamina Finland 43
Mariemberg Neth. 16 52.32N 6.35E
Mariental Namibia 80 24.38S 17.58E
Marienville U.S.A. 114 41.28N 79.07W
Mariestad Sweden 43 58.43N 13.51E
Marietta Ga. U.S.A. 113 33.57N 84.34W
Marietta Ohio U.S.A. 114 39.25N 81.27W
Marieville Canada 105 45.26N 73.10W
Mariga *r.* Nigeria 77 9.37N 5.55E
Marignane France 21 43.25N 5.13E
Marijampolė Lithuania 41 54.33N 23.21E
Marília Brazil 126 22.13S 50.20W
Marín Spain 26 42.23N 8.42W
Marina di Gioiosa Ionica Italy 33 38.18N 16.20E
Marina di Ravenna Italy 30 44.29N 12.17E
Marine City U.S.A. 114 42.43N 82.30W
Marineland U.S.A. 113 29.38N 81.13W
Marinette U.S.A. 110 45.06N 87.38W
Maringá Brazil 126 23.36S 52.02W
Maringa Zaïre 73 1.14N 20.00E
Maringa *r.* Zaïre 78 1.13N 19.50E
Maringue Mozambique 81 17.55S 34.24E
Marinha Grande Portugal 27 39.45N 8.56W
Marion Ga. U.S.A. 113 32.36N 87.20W
Marion Ill. U.S.A. 111 37.44N 88.56W
Marion Ind. U.S.A. 112 40.33N 85.40W
Marion Iowa U.S.A. 110 42.02N 91.36W
Marion Ohio U.S.A. 112 40.35N 83.08W
Marion S.C. U.S.A. 113 34.11N 79.23W
Marion Va. U.S.A. 113 36.51N 81.30W
Marion Bay *town* Australia 92 35.13S 137.00E
Marion, L. U.S.A. 113 33.30N 80.25W
Marion Reef Australia 90 19.10S 152.17E
Mariposa U.S.A. 108 37.29N 119.58W
Mariscal Estigarribia Paraguay 126 22.03S 60.35W
Maritimes, Alpes *mts.* France 21 44.15N 7.10E
Maritsa *r.* Bulgaria 34 42.15N 24.00E
Maritsa *r.* Turkey 29 41.00N 26.15E
Mariupol' Ukraine 45 47.05N 37.34E
Mārkā Jordan 67 31.59N 35.59E
Marka Somali Rep. 79 1.42N 44.47E
Markaryd Sweden 43 56.26N 13.36E
Markdale Canada 104 44.19N 80.39W
Marked Tree U.S.A. 111 35.32N 90.25W
Marken *i.* Neth. 16 52.28N 5.03E
Markerwaard *f.* Neth. 16 52.30N 5.15E
Market Drayton U.K. 12 52.55N 2.30W
Market Harborough U.K. 13 52.29N 0.55W
Market Rasen U.K. 12 53.24N 0.20W
Market Weighton U.K. 12 53.52N 0.04W
Markha *r.* Russian Fed. 51 63.37N 119.00E
Markham Canada 104 43.52N 79.16W
Markham, Mt. Antarctica 128 83.00S 164.00E
Markoupolon Greece 35 37.53N 23.57E
Marks Russian Fed. 45 51.43N 46.45E
Markstay Canada 104 46.29N 80.33W
Marktheidenfeld Germany 39 49.50N 9.36E
Marktoberdorf Germany 39 47.47N 10.37E
Marktredwitz Germany 39 50.00N 12.06E
Marl Germany 38 51.38N 7.05E
Marla Australia 90 27.22S 133.48E
Marlboro U.S.A. 115 42.21N 71.33W
Marlborough Australia 90 22.51S 149.50E
Marlborough U.K. 13 51.26N 1.44W
Marlborough U.S.A. 115 42.21N 71.33W
Marle France 19 49.44N 3.46E
Marlette U.S.A. 114 43.20N 83.05W
Marlin U.S.A. 111 31.18N 96.53W
Marmande France 20 44.30N 0.10E
Marmara *i.* Turkey 29 40.38N 27.37E
Marmara Denizi *sea* Turkey 29 40.45N 28.15E
Marmara, Sea of *see* Marmara Denizi *sea* Turkey 29
Marmaris Turkey 35 36.50N 28.14E
Marmarth U.S.A. 110 46.18N 103.54W
Marmet U.S.A. 114 38.15N 81.04W
Marmion L. Canada 102 48.55N 91.25W
Marmolada *mtn.* Italy 30 46.26N 11.51E
Marmora Canada 105 44.29N 77.41W
Marnay France 19 47.17N 5.46E
Marne *d.* France 19 48.55N 4.10E
Marne *r.* France 19 48.49N 2.24E
Marne Germany 38 53.57N 9.00E
Marne à la Saône, Canal de la France 19 49.44N 4.36E
Marne au Rhin, Canal de la France 19 48.35N 7.47E
Marnoo Australia 92 36.40S 142.55E
Maroantsetra Madagascar 81 15.26S 49.44E
Marobi Pakistan 62 32.36N 69.52E
Marolambo Madagascar 81 20.02S 48.07E
Maromme France 19 49.27N 1.02E
Marondera Zimbabwe 81 18.11S 31.31E
Maroni *r.* Guiana 123 5.30N 54.00W
Maronne *r.* France 20 45.07N 1.57E
Maroochydore Australia 91 26.40S 153.07E
Maros *r.* Hungary 31 46.15N 20.13E
Maroua Cameroon 77 10.35N 14.20E
Marovoay Madagascar 81 16.06S 46.39E
Marquard R.S.A. 80 28.39S 27.25E
Marquesas Is. *see* Marquises, Îles *is.* Pacific Oc. 85
Marquette U.S.A. 112 46.33N 87.23W
Marquina-Jemein Spain 26 43.16N 2.30W
Marquise France 19 50.49N 1.42E
Marquises, Îles *is.* Pacific Oc. 85 9.00S 139.30W

Marra Australia 92 31.11S 144.03E
Marra *r.* Australia 93 30.05S 147.05E
Marracuene Mozambique 81 25.44S 32.41E
Marradi Italy 30 44.04N 11.37E
Marrah, Jabal *mtn.* Sudan 73 13.10N 24.22E
Marrakech Morocco 74 31.49N 8.00W
Marrawah Australia 91 40.55S 144.42E
Marree Australia 92 29.40S 138.04E
Marromeu Mozambique 81 18.20S 35.56E
Marrupa Mozambique 79 13.10S 37.30E
Marsá al Burayqah Libya 72 30.25N 19.35E
Marsabit Kenya 79 2.20N 37.59E
Marsala Italy 32 37.48N 12.26E
Marsá Maţrūḩ Egypt 64 31.21N 27.14E
Marsciano Italy 30 42.54N 12.20E
Marsden Australia 93 33.46S 147.35E
Marseille France 21 43.18N 5.24E
Marseille-en-Beauvaisis France 19 49.35N 1.57E
Mar, Serra do *mts.* Brazil 126 23.00S 44.40W
Marsfjället *mtn.* Sweden 40 65.05N 15.28E
Marshall Liberia 76 6.10N 10.23W
Marshall Ark. U.S.A. 111 35.55N 92.38W
Marshall Minn. U.S.A. 110 44.27N 95.47W
Marshall Mo. U.S.A. 110 39.07N 93.12W
Marshall Tex. U.S.A. 111 32.33N 94.23W
Marshall Va. U.S.A. 114 38.52N 77.52W
Marshall Is. Pacific Oc. 84 10.00N 172.00E
Marshalltown U.S.A. 110 42.03N 92.55W
Marshyhope Creek *r.* U.S.A. 115 38.32N 75.45W
Märsta Sweden 43 59.37N 17.51E
Martaban Myanmar 56 16.32N 97.35E
Martaban, G. of Myanmar 56 15.10N 96.30E
Martapura Indonesia 58 3.22S 114.56E
Marte Nigeria 77 12.23N 13.46E
Martelange Belgium 16 49.50N 5.44E
Marten River *town* Canada 104 46.42N 79.41W
Martés, Sierra *mts.* Spain 25 39.20N 1.10W
Marthaguy Creek *r.* Australia 93 30.16S 147.35E
Martha's Vineyard *i.* U.S.A. 115 41.25N 70.40W
Martigny Switz. 39 46.06N 7.04E
Martigues France 21 43.24N 5.03E
Martin Slovakia 37 49.05N 18.55E
Martín *r.* Spain 25 41.18N 0.19W
Martin U.S.A. 110 43.10N 101.44W
Martina Franca Italy 33 40.42N 17.21E
Martinique *i.* Windward Is. 117 14.40N 61.00W
Martin L. U.S.A. 113 32.50N 85.55W
Martin Pt. U.S.A. 98 70.10N 143.50W
Martinsburg Penn. U.S.A. 114 40.19N 78.20W
Martinsburg W.Va. U.S.A. 114 39.27N 77.58W
Martins Ferry *town* U.S.A. 114 40.06N 80.44W
Martinsville Ind. U.S.A. 112 39.25N 86.25W
Martinsville Va. U.S.A. 113 36.43N 79.53W
Martin Vaz *is.* Atlantic Oc. 127 20.30S 28.51W
Marton New Zealand 86 40.04S 175.25E
Martos Spain 27 37.43N 3.58W
Martre, Lac la *l.* Canada 100 63.15N 116.55W
Martti Finland 40 67.28N 28.28E
Marudi Malaysia 58 4.15N 114.19E
Ma'rūf Afghan. 62 31.34N 67.03E
Marula Zimbabwe 80 20.25S 28.06E
Marum Neth. 16 53.06N 6.16E
Marvejols France 20 44.33N 3.18E
Marvel Loch *town* Australia 89 31.31S 119.30E
Marviken Sweden 43 58.34N 16.51E
Mārwār India 62 25.44N 73.36E
Mary Turkmenistan 50 37.42N 61.54E
Maryborough Qld. Australia 91 25.32S 152.36E
Maryborough Vic. Australia 92 37.05S 143.47E
Marydale R.S.A. 80 29.24S 22.06E
Mary Frances L. Canada 101 63.19N 106.13W
Maryland *d.* U.S.A. 114 39.00N 76.45W
Maryland Beach *town* U.S.A. 115 38.26N 74.59W
Maryport U.K. 12 54.43N 3.30W
Mary's Harbour Canada 103 52.18N 55.51W
Marystown Canada 103 47.11N 55.10W
Marysvale U.S.A. 108 38.27N 112.11W
Marysville Kans. U.S.A. 110 39.51N 96.39W
Marysville Mich. U.S.A. 114 42.54N 82.29W
Marysville Penn. U.S.A. 114 40.20N 76.56W
Maryvale Australia 90 24.41S 134.04E
Maryville Mo. U.S.A. 110 40.21N 94.52W
Maryville Tenn. U.S.A. 113 35.45N 83.59W
Marzūq Libya 75 25.55N 13.55E
Marzūq, Şaḩrā' *des.* Libya 75 24.30N 13.00E
Mas'adah Syria 67 33.14N 35.45E
Masāhim, Kūh-e *mtn.* Iran 65 30.26N 55.08E
Masai Steppe *f.* Tanzania 79 4.30S 37.00E
Masaka Uganda 79 0.20S 31.46E
Masan S. Korea 55 35.10N 128.35E
Masasi Tanzania 79 10.43S 38.48E
Masba Nigeria 77 10.35N 13.01E
Masbate *i.* Phil. 59 12.00N 123.30E
Mascara Algeria 74 35.24N 0.08E
Mascarene Basin *f.* Indian Oc. 49 17.00S 55.00E
Mascarene Is. Indian Oc. 49 21.00S 56.00E
Mascarene Ridge *f.* Indian Oc. 49 10.00S 60.00E
Maseru Lesotho 80 29.18S 27.28E
Mashhad Iran 65 36.16N 59.34E
Mashkai *r.* Pakistan 62 26.02N 65.19E
Māshkel *r.* Pakistan 62 28.02N 63.25E
Māshkel, Hāmūn-i- *l.* Pakistan 62 28.15N 63.00E
Mashki Chāh Pakistan 62 29.01N 62.27E
Mashonaland *f.* Zimbabwe 81 18.20S 32.00E
Mashūray Afghan. 62 32.12N 68.21E
Masi Norway 40 69.26N 23.40E
Masīlah, Wādī al *f.* Yemen 71 15.10N 51.08E
Masi-Manimba Zaïre 78 4.47S 17.54E
Masindi Uganda 79 1.41N 31.45E
Maşīrah *i.* Oman 60 20.30N 58.50E
Maşīrah, Khalīj *b.* Oman 71 20.10N 58.10E
Masjed Soleymān Iran 65 31.59N 49.18E
Maskinongé Canada 105 46.35S 73.26W
Mask, Lough Rep. of Ire. 15 53.38N 9.22W
Mason Mich. U.S.A. 104 42.35N 84.26W
Mason Tex. U.S.A. 111 30.45N 99.14W
Mason W.Va. U.S.A. 114 39.00N 82.02W

Mason City U.S.A. 110 43.09N 93.12W
Masontown U.S.A. 114 39.51N 79.54W
Maspalomas Canary Is. 127 27.42N 15.34W
Masqaţ Oman 65 23.36N 58.37E
Massa Italy 30 44.01N 10.09E
Massachusetts *d.* U.S.A. 115 42.15N 71.50W
Massachusetts B. U.S.A. 115 42.20N 70.50W
Massafra Italy 33 40.35N 17.07E
Massakory Chad 77 13.02N 15.43E
Massa Marittima Italy 30 43.03N 10.53E
Massangena Mozambique 81 21.31S 33.03E
Massangulo Mozambique 81 13.54S 35.24E
Massarosa Italy 30 43.52N 10.20E
Massena U.S.A. 105 44.56N 74.54W
Massenya Chad 77 11.21N 16.09E
Masset Canada 100 54.00N 132.09W
Masseube France 20 43.26N 0.35E
Massey Canada 104 46.12N 82.05W
Massiac France 20 45.15N 3.12E
Massif Central *mts.* France 20 45.00N 3.10E
Massillon U.S.A. 114 40.48N 81.32W
Massinga Mozambique 81 23.20S 35.25E
Massingir Mozambique 81 23.49S 32.04E
Massoukou *see* Franceville Gabon 78
Masterton New Zealand 86 40.57S 175.39E
Mastic Beach *town* U.S.A. 115 40.45N 72.50W
Mastigouche Prov. Park Canada 105 46.39N 73.24W
Mastung Pakistan 62 29.48N 66.51E
Mastūrah Saudi Arabia 64 23.06N 38.50E
Masuda Japan 57 34.40N 131.51E
Masvingo Zimbabwe 80 20.10S 30.49E
Maşyāf Syria 66 35.03N 36.21E
Mat *r.* Albania 34 41.40N 20.00E
Matabeleland *f.* Zimbabwe 80 19.50S 28.15E
Matabuena Spain 26 41.06N 3.48W
Matachel *r.* Spain 26 38.50N 6.17W
Matachewan Canada 102 47.56N 80.39W
Matadi Zaïre 78 5.50S 13.36E
Matagami Canada 102 49.45N 77.34W
Matagami, L. Canada 102 49.50N 77.40W
Matagorda B. U.S.A. 111 28.35N 96.20W
Matakana Australia 93 32.59S 145.53E
Matakana I. New Zealand 86 37.35S 176.15E
Matala Angola 78 14.45S 15.02E
Matam Senegal 74 15.40N 13.15W
Matamata New Zealand 86 37.49S 175.46E
Matameye Niger 77 13.26N 8.28E
Matamoros Coahuila Mexico 111 25.32N 103.15W
Matamoros Tamaulipas Mexico 111 25.53N 97.30W
Ma'ţan Bishrah *well* Libya 72 22.58N 22.39E
Matandu *r.* Tanzania 79 8.44S 39.22E
Matane Canada 103 48.51N 67.32W
Matang China 55 29.30N 113.08E
Matankari Niger 77 13.47N 4.00E
Matanzas Cuba 117 23.04N 81.35W
Mataram Indonesia 59 8.36S 116.07E
Matarani Peru 124 16.58S 72.07W
Mataranka Australia 88 14.56S 133.07E
Mataró Spain 25 41.32N 2.27E
Matarraña *r.* Spain 25 41.14N 0.22E
Matatiele R.S.A. 80 30.19S 28.48E
Matatula, C. Samoa 84 14.15S 170.35W
Mataura *r.* New Zealand 86 46.34S 168.45E
Matautu W. Samoa 84 13.57S 171.56W
Matavera Rarotonga Cook Is. 84 21.13S 159.44W
Matawai New Zealand 86 38.21S 177.32E
Matawin *r.* Canada 105 46.50N 72.45W
Maţāy Egypt 66 28.25N 30.46E
Matehuala Mexico 116 23.40N 100.40W
Mateke Hills Zimbabwe 80 21.48S 31.00E
Matelica Italy 30 43.15N 13.01E
Matera Italy 33 40.40N 16.37E
Matetsi Zimbabwe 80 18.17S 25.57E
Mateur Tunisia 32 37.03N 9.40E
Matfors Sweden 41 62.21N 17.02E
Matha France 20 45.52N 0.19W
Mathews Peak *mtn.* Kenya 79 1.18N 37.20E
Mathis U.S.A. 111 28.06N 97.50W
Mathoura Australia 93 35.49S 144.54E
Mathura India 63 27.30N 77.41E
Mati Phil. 59 6.55N 126.15E
Matias Barbosa Brazil 126 21.52S 43.21W
Matignon France 18 48.36N 2.18W
Matinenda L. Canada 104 46.22N 82.57W
Matipó Brazil 126 20.16S 42.17W
Mātli Pakistan 62 25.02N 68.39E
Matlock U.K. 12 53.09N 1.32W
Matochkin Shar Russian Fed. 50 73.15N 56.35E
Mato Grosso *d.* Brazil 124 13.00S 55.00W
Mato Grosso *town* Brazil 124 15.05S 59.57W
Mato Grosso do Sul *d.* Brazil 124 20.00S 54.30W
Mato Grosso, Planalto do *f.* Brazil 124 16.00S 54.00W
Matope Malawi 79 15.20S 34.57E
Matopo Hills Zimbabwe 80 20.45S 28.30E
Matosinhos Portugal 26 41.11N 8.42W
Maţraḩ Oman 65 23.37N 58.33E
Matrei in Osttirol Austria 39 47.00N 12.32E
Matsena Nigeria 77 13.13N 10.04E
Matsiatra *r.* Madagascar 81 21.25S 45.33E
Matsubara Japan 57 34.34N 135.33E
Matsudo Japan 57 35.47N 139.54E
Matsue Japan 57 35.29N 133.00E
Matsumae Japan 57 41.26N 140.07E
Matsumoto Japan 57 36.18N 137.58E
Matsusaka Japan 57 34.34N 136.32E
Matsuyama Japan 57 33.50N 132.47E
Mattagami *r.* Canada 102 50.43N 81.29W
Mattamuskeet, L. U.S.A. 112 45.31N 68.21W
Mattawa Canada 104 46.19N 78.42W
Mattawamkeag U.S.A. 112 45.31N 68.21W
Mattawin Canada 105 46.55N 72.55W
Matterhorn *mtn.* Switz./Italy 39 45.59N 7.43E
Matterhorn *mtn.* U.S.A. 108 41.49N 115.23W
Matthews Ridge *town* Guyana 122 7.30N 60.10W
Matthew Town Bahamas 117 20.57N 73.40W
Mattice Canada 102 49.39N 83.20W
Mattighofen Austria 39 48.06N 13.09E
Mattmar Sweden 40 63.19N 13.45E
Mattoon U.S.A. 110 39.29N 88.21W

Matua Indonesia 58 2.58S 110.52E
Maturín Venezuela 122 9.45N 63.10W
Maua Mozambique 81 13.53S 37.10E
Mau Aimma India 63 25.42N 81.55E
Maubeuge France 19 50.17N 3.58E
Maudaha India 63 25.41N 80.07E
Maude Australia 92 34.27S 144.21E
Maués Brazil 123 3.24S 57.42W
Mauganj India 63 24.41N 81.53E
Maui i. Hawaii U.S.A. 106 20.45N 156.15W
Mauléon France 18 46.56N 0.45W
Mauléon-Licharre France 20 43.14N 0.54W
Maulvi Bāzār Bangla. 63 24.29N 91.42E
Maumee U.S.A. 112 41.34N 83.41W
Maumee r. U.S.A. 112 41.40N 83.35W
Maumere Indonesia 59 8.35S 122.13E
Maun Botswana 80 19.52S 23.40E
Maunaloa Hawaiian Is. 85 21.08N 157.13W
Mauna Loa mtn. Hawaiian Is. 85 19.29N 155.36W
Maunath Bhanjan India 63 25.57N 83.33E
Mau Rānipur India 63 25.15N 79.08E
Maure-de-Bretagne France 18 47.54N 1.59W
Maures mts. France 21 43.16N 6.23E
Mauriac France 20 45.13N 2.20E
Maurice, L. Australia 90 29.51S 130.58E
Maurice Nat. Park Canada 105 46.42N 73.00W
Mauritania Africa 74 20.00N 10.00W
Mauritius Indian Oc. 49 20.10S 58.00E
Mauritius Basin f. Indian Oc. 49 26.00S 55.00E
Mauron France 18 48.05N 2.18W
Maurs France 20 44.43N 2.11E
Mauston U.S.A. 110 43.48N 90.05W
Mauvezin France 20 43.44N 0.55E
Mavinga Angola 78 15.47S 20.21E
Mavqi'im Israel 67 31.37N 34.35E
Mavuradonha Mts. Zimbabwe 81 16.30S 31.20E
Mawjib, Wādī al Jordan 67 31.28N 35.34E
Mawlaik Myanmar 56 23.50N 94.30E
Mawlamyine see Moulmein Myanmar 56
Maxcanú Mexico 116 20.35N 89.59W
Maxville Canada 105 45.17N 74.51W
Maya Spain 26 43.12N 1.29W
Mayaguana I. Bahamas 117 22.30N 73.00W
Mayagüez Puerto Rico 117 18.13N 67.09W
Mayāmey Iran 65 36.27N 55.40E
Maya Mts. Belize 117 16.30N 89.00W
Maybole U.K. 14 55.21N 4.41W
May, C. U.S.A. 115 38.56N 74.55W
Maych'ew Ethiopia 71 13.02N 39.34E
Maydena Australia 91 42.45S 146.38E
Maydh Somali Rep. 71 10.57N 47.06E
Mayen Germany 39 50.19N 7.13E
Mayenne France 18 48.18N 0.37W
Mayenne d. France 18 48.05N 0.40W
Mayenne r. France 18 47.30N 0.33W
Mayerthorpe Canada 100 53.57N 115.08W
Mayfield U.S.A. 111 36.44N 88.38W
Maykop Russian Fed. 45 44.37N 40.48E
Maymyo Myanmar 56 22.05N 96.28E
Maynooth Canada 105 45.13N 77.57W
Maynooth Rep. of Ire. 15 53.23N 6.37W
Mayo r. Mexico 109 26.45N 109.47W
Mayo d. Rep. of Ire. 15 53.47N 9.07W
Mayo Daga Nigeria 77 6.59N 11.25E
Mayo Landing Canada 98 63.45N 135.45W
Mayo, Plains of f. Rep. of Ire. 15 53.46N 9.05W
Mayor I. New Zealand 86 37.15S 176.15E
May Pen Jamaica 117 17.58N 77.14W
Maysah, Tall al mtn. Jordan 67 31.08N 35.40E
Mays Landing U.S.A. 115 39.27N 74.44W
Maysville U.S.A. 112 38.38N 83.46W
Maythalūn Jordan 67 32.21N 35.16E
Mayumba Gabon 78 3.23S 10.38E
Mayville Mich. U.S.A. 104 43.20N 83.21W
Mayville N.Dak. U.S.A. 110 47.30N 97.19W
Mayville N.Y. U.S.A. 114 42.15N 79.30W
Mazabuka Zambia 79 15.50S 27.47E
Mazagão Brazil 123 0.07S 51.17W
Mazamba Mozambique 81 18.32S 34.50E
Mazamet France 20 43.30N 2.24E
Mazán Peru 122 3.15S 73.00W
Mazara del Vallo Italy 32 37.39N 12.36E
Mazarredo Argentina 125 47.00S 66.45W
Mazarrón Spain 25 37.36N 1.19W
Mazarrón, Golfo de g. Spain 25 37.30N 1.18W
Mazatenango Guatemala 116 14.31N 91.30W
Mazatlán Mexico 109 23.13N 106.25W
Mažeikiai Lithuania 41 56.19N 22.20E
Mazinaw L. Canada 105 44.55N 77.12W
Mazirbe Latvia 41 57.41N 22.21E
Mazowe r. Mozambique 81 16.32S 33.25E
Mazowe Zimbabwe 81 17.30S 30.58E
Mazu Liedao is. China 53 26.12N 120.00E
Mazunga Zimbabwe 80 21.45S 29.52E
Mazurski, Pojezierze lakes Poland 37 53.50N 21.00E
Mbabane Swaziland 80 26.19S 31.08E
Mbagne Mauritania 74 16.06N 14.47W
M'Baïki C.A.R. 77 3.53N 18.01E
Mbala C.A.R. 73 7.48N 20.51E
Mbala Zambia 79 8.50S 31.24E
Mbale Uganda 79 1.04N 34.12E
Mbalmayo Cameroon 77 3.35N 11.31E
Mbamba Bay town Tanzania 79 11.18S 34.50E
Mbandaka Zaïre 78 0.03N 18.21E
Mbanza Congo Angola 78 6.18S 14.16E
Mbarara Uganda 79 0.36S 30.40E
Mbari r. C.A.R. 73 4.34N 22.43E
Mbeya Tanzania 79 8.54S 33.29E
Mbeya d. Tanzania 79 8.30S 32.30E
Mbinda Congo 78 2.11S 12.55E
Mbogo Tanzania 79 7.26S 33.26E
Mbomou d. C.A.R. 73 5.10N 23.00E
Mbomou r. C.A.R. 73 4.08N 22.26E
Mboro Sudan 73 6.18N 28.45E
M'Bour Senegal 76 14.22N 16.54W
Mbout Mauritania 74 16.02N 12.35W
M'bridge r. Angola 78 7.12S 12.55E

Mbua Fiji 84 16.48S 178.37E
Mbuji Mayi Zaïre 78 6.08S 23.39E
Mbulamuti Uganda 79 0.50N 33.05E
Mbura Tanzania 79 11.14S 35.25E
Mbutha Fiji 84 16.39S 179.50E
Mbuzi Zambia 79 12.20S 32.17E
McAlester U.S.A. 111 34.56N 95.46W
McAllen U.S.A. 111 26.12N 98.15W
McArthur r. Australia 90 15.54S 136.40E
McArthur U.S.A. 114 39.15N 82.29W
McArthurs Mills Canada 105 45.06N 77.38W
McBride Canada 100 53.20N 120.10W
McCamey U.S.A. 111 31.08N 102.13W
McClintock Canada 101 57.50N 94.10W
McClintock Channel Canada 99 71.20N 102.00W
McClure U.S.A. 114 40.42N 77.19W
McClure Str. Canada 98 74.30N 116.00W
McComb U.S.A. 111 31.14N 90.27W
McConaughy, L. U.S.A. 110 41.15N 102.00W
McConnel Creek town Canada 100 56.53N 126.30W
McConnelsburg U.S.A. 114 39.57N 78.01W
McConnelsville U.S.A. 114 39.39N 81.51W
McCook U.S.A. 110 40.12N 100.38W
McDermitt U.S.A. 108 41.59N 117.36W
McDouall Peak Australia 92 29.51S 134.55E
McGrath U.S.A. 98 62.58N 155.40W
McGregor U.S.A. 110 46.36N 93.19W
McHenry U.S.A. 110 42.21N 88.16W
Mchinja Tanzania 79 9.44S 39.45E
Mchinji Malaŵi 79 13.48S 32.55E
McIlwraith Range mts. Australia 90 14.00S 143.10E
McKeesport U.S.A. 114 40.21N 79.52W
McKees Rocks town U.S.A. 114 40.28N 80.10W
Mckellar Canada 104 45.30N 79.55W
McKenzie U.S.A. 111 36.08N 88.31W
McKerrow Canada 104 46.18N 81.44W
McKinley, Mt. U.S.A. 98 63.00N 151.00W
McKinney U.S.A. 111 33.12N 96.37W
McKittrick U.S.A. 109 35.18N 119.37W
McLaughlin U.S.A. 110 45.49N 100.49W
McLennan Canada 100 55.42N 116.50W
McLeod r. Canada 100 54.08N 115.42W
McLeod B. Canada 101 62.53N 110.00W
Mcleod Lake town Canada 100 54.58N 123.00W
M'Clintock Canada 100 60.35N 134.25W
McMinnville Oreg. U.S.A. 108 45.13N 123.12W
McMinnville Tenn. U.S.A. 113 35.40N 85.49W
McNary U.S.A. 109 34.04N 109.51W
McPherson U.S.A. 110 38.22N 97.40W
McPherson Range mts. Australia 93 28.15S 153.00E
Mdantsane R.S.A. 80 32.54S 27.24E
Meade U.S.A. 111 37.17N 100.20W
Mead, L. U.S.A. 109 36.05N 114.25W
Meadow Lake town Canada 101 54.07N 108.20W
Meadville U.S.A. 114 41.38N 80.09W
Meaford Canada 104 44.36N 80.35W
Mealhada Portugal 26 40.22N 8.27W
Meander River town Canada 100 59.02N 117.42W
Mearim r. Brazil 123 3.20S 44.20W
Meath d. Rep. of Ire. 15 53.32N 6.40W
Meaux France 19 48.57N 2.52E
Mécatina, Cap c. Canada 103 50.45N 59.01W
Mecca see Makkah Saudi Arabia 72
Mecca U.S.A. 109 33.35N 116.03W
Mechanicsville U.S.A. 114 38.26N 76.44W
Mechanicville U.S.A. 115 42.54N 73.42W
Mechelen Belgium 16 51.01N 4.28E
Mecheria Algeria 74 33.33N 0.17W
Mecidiye Turkey 34 40.38N 26.32E
Mecklenburger Bucht b. Germany 38 54.20N 11.50E
Mecklenburg-Vorpommern d. Germany 38 53.36N 12.45E
Meconta Mozambique 79 15.00S 39.50E
Mecsek mts. Hungary 31 46.15N 18.05E
Mecufi Mozambique 79 13.20S 40.32E
Meda Portugal 26 40.58N 7.16W
Medan Indonesia 58 3.35N 98.39E
Mede Italy 30 45.06N 8.44E
Médéa Algeria 75 36.15N 2.48E
Mededsiz mtn. Turkey 64 37.33N 34.38E
Medegue Gabon 78 0.37N 10.08E
Medellín Colombia 122 6.15N 75.36W
Medemblik Neth. 16 52.48N 5.06E
Médenine Tunisia 75 33.21N 10.30E
Mederdra Mauritania 76 17.02N 15.41W
Medevi Sweden 43 58.40N 14.57E
Medford Mass. U.S.A. 115 42.25N 71.07W
Medford Oreg. U.S.A. 108 42.19N 122.52W
Medford Wisc. U.S.A. 110 45.09N 90.20W
Medgidia Romania 37 44.15N 28.16E
Medi Sudan 73 5.04N 30.44E
Media U.S.A. 115 39.54N 75.23W
Mediaş Romania 37 46.10N 24.21E
Medicina Italy 30 44.28N 11.38E
Medicine Bow Mts. U.S.A. 108 41.10N 106.10W
Medicine Bow Peak mtn. U.S.A. 108 41.21N 106.19W
Medicine Hat Canada 101 50.03N 110.40W
Medicine Lake town U.S.A. 108 48.30N 104.30W
Medicine Lodge U.S.A. 111 37.17N 98.35W
Medina see Al Madinah Saudi Arabia 64
Medina N.Dak. U.S.A. 110 46.54N 99.18W
Medina N.Y. U.S.A. 114 43.13N 78.23W
Medina Ohio U.S.A. 114 41.08N 81.52W
Medinaceli Spain 26 41.10N 2.26W
Medina del Campo Spain 26 41.18N 4.55W
Medina de Ríoseco Spain 26 41.53N 5.02W
Medina-Sidonia Spain 27 36.28N 5.55W
Mediterranean Sea 23 36.00N 16.00E
Medjerda, Monts de la mts. Tunisia 32 36.40N 8.40E
Medjerda, Oued r. Tunisia 32 37.07N 10.13E
Medjez el Bab Tunisia 32 36.39N 9.37E
Medoc d. France 20 45.20N 1.00W
Medstead Canada 101 53.19N 108.02W
Medveda Yugo. 34 42.50N 21.32E
Medveditsa r. Russian Fed. 45 49.35N 42.45E
Medvezh'yegorsk Russian Fed. 44 62.56N 34.28E
Medvin Ukraine 37 49.25N 30.48E

Medway r. U.K. 13 51.24N 0.31E
Medzhibozh Ukraine 37 49.29N 27.28E
Meeberrie Australia 88 26.58S 115.51E
Meekatharra Australia 88 26.35S 118.30E
Meeker U.S.A. 108 40.02N 107.55W
Meer Belgium 16 51.27N 4.46E
Meerane Germany 38 50.51N 12.28E
Meerhusener Moor f. Germany 38 53.35N 7.30E
Meersburg Germany 39 47.41N 9.16E
Meerut India 63 28.59N 77.42E
Mefallesim Israel 67 31.30N 34.34E
Měga Ethiopia 73 4.07N 38.16E
Megalon Khoríon Greece 35 36.27N 27.24E
Megalópolis Greece 35 37.24N 22.08E
Mégara Greece 35 38.00N 23.20E
Megasini mtn. India 63 21.38N 86.21E
Meghalaya d. India 63 25.30N 91.00E
Meghna r. Bangla. 63 22.50N 90.50E
Mégiscane r. Canada 102 48.36N 76.00W
Mehadia Romania 37 44.55N 22.22E
Mehar Pakistan 62 27.11N 67.49E
Mehekar India 62 20.09N 76.34E
Mehidpur India 62 23.49N 75.40E
Mehndāwal India 63 26.59N 83.07E
Mehsāna India 62 23.36N 72.24E
Mehtar Lām Afghan. 62 34.39N 70.10E
Mehun-sur-Yèvre France 19 47.09N 2.13E
Meiktila Myanmar 56 20.53N 95.50E
Meiningen Germany 38 50.34N 10.25E
Meira, Sierra de mts. Spain 26 43.15N 7.15W
Me'ir Shefeya Israel 67 32.35N 34.57E
Meishan China 55 30.02N 103.50E
Meissen Germany 38 51.10N 13.28E
Meixian see Meizhou China 55
Meiyino Sudan 73 6.12N 34.40E
Meizhou China 55 24.20N 116.15E
Mekatina Canada 104 47.05N 84.07W
Mekdela Ethiopia 73 11.28N 39.23E
Mek'elē Ethiopia 73 13.33N 39.30E
Mekerrhane, Sebkha f. Algeria 74 26.22N 1.20E
Mekhtar Pakistan 62 30.28N 69.22E
Mekinac, L. Canada 105 47.05N 73.39W
Meknès Morocco 74 33.53N 5.37W
Mekong r. Asia 56 10.00N 106.40E
Mekong Delta Vietnam 56 10.00N 105.40E
Mekongga mtn. Indonesia 59 3.39S 121.15E
Měkôngk r. Cambodia see Mekong r. Asia 56
Mékrou r. Benin 77 12.20N 2.47E
Melaka Malaysia 58 2.11N 102.16E
Melanesia is. Pacific Oc. 84 5.00N 165.00E
Melbourne Australia 93 37.45S 144.58E
Melbourne U.S.A. 113 28.04N 80.38W
Meldorf Germany 38 54.05N 9.05E
Meldrum Bay town Canada 104 45.56N 83.07W
Mélé C.A.R. 73 9.46N 21.33E
Melegnano Italy 30 45.21N 9.19E
Mélèzes, Rivière aux r. Canada 103 57.40N 69.29W
Melfi Chad 77 11.04N 18.03E
Melfi Italy 33 40.59N 15.40E
Melfort Canada 101 52.52N 104.36W
Melgaço Portugal 26 42.07N 8.16W
Melilla Spain 24 35.17N 2.57W
Melilot Israel 67 31.23N 34.36E
Melipilla Chile 125 33.42S 71.13W
Melito di Porto Salvo Italy 33 37.56N 15.47E
Melitopol Ukraine 45 46.51N 35.22E
Melk Austria 36 48.14N 15.20E
Melle France 18 46.13N 0.09W
Mellen U.S.A. 110 46.20N 90.40W
Mellerud Sweden 43 58.42N 12.28E
Mellid Spain 26 42.55N 8.01W
Mellit Sudan 72 14.08N 25.33E
Melmore Pt. Rep. of Ire. 15 55.15N 7.49W
Mělník Bulgaria 34 41.58N 23.25E
Mělník Czech Republic 36 50.20N 14.29E
Melo Uruguay 126 32.22S 54.10W
Melon Australia 90 12.10S 136.32E
Melrose U.K. 14 55.36N 2.43W
Melrose N.Mex. U.S.A. 109 34.26N 103.38W
Melstone U.S.A. 108 46.36N 107.52W
Melsungen Germany 38 51.08N 9.32E
Meltaus Finland 40 66.54N 25.22E
Melton Australia 93 37.41S 144.36E
Melton Mowbray U.K. 12 52.46N 0.53W
Melun France 19 48.32N 2.40E
Melvich U.K. 14 58.33N 3.55W
Melville B. Australia 90 12.10S 136.32E
Melville, C. Australia 90 14.11S 144.30E
Melville I. Australia 90 11.30S 131.00E
Melville I. Canada 98 75.30N 110.00W
Melville, L. Canada 103 53.45N 59.30W
Melville Hills Canada 98 69.20N 122.00W
Melville Pen. Canada 99 68.00N 84.00W
Melvin U.S.A. of Ire./U.K. 15 54.26N 8.12W
Mélykút Hungary 31 46.13N 19.24E
Melzo Italy 30 45.30N 9.25E
Měmar Co l. China 63 34.10N 82.15E
Memba Mozambique 81 14.16S 40.30E
Memboro Indonesia 58 9.22S 119.32E
Memmingen Germany 39 47.59N 10.11E
Memphis ruins Egypt 66 29.52N 31.12E
Memphis Mich. U.S.A. 114 42.54N 82.46W
Memphis Tenn. U.S.A. 111 35.08N 90.03W
Memphremagog, L. Canada 105 45.05N 72.15W
Mena Ukraine 37 51.30N 32.15E
Mena U.S.A. 111 34.35N 94.15W
Menai Str. U.K. 12 53.17N 4.20W
Ménaka Mali 75 15.55N 2.24E
Mènam Khong r. Laos see Mekong r. Asia 56
Menarandra r. Madagascar 81 25.17S 44.30E
Menard U.S.A. 111 30.55N 99.47W
Menawashei Sudan 73 12.40N 24.59E
Mendawai r. Indonesia 58 3.17S 113.20E
Mende France 20 44.30N 3.30E

Mendebo Mts. Ethiopia 73 7.00N 39.30E
Mendi P.N.G. 59 6.13S 143.39E
Mendip Hills U.K. 13 51.15N 2.40W
Mendocino, C. U.S.A. 108 40.25N 124.25W
Mendooran Australia 93 31.48S 149.08E
Mendoza Argentina 125 32.54S 68.50W
Mendoza d. Argentina 125 34.30S 68.00W
Mendung Indonesia 58 0.31N 103.12E
Ménéac France 18 48.09N 2.28W
Mene Grande Venezuela 122 9.51N 70.57W
Menemen Turkey 64 38.34N 27.03E
Menen Belgium 16 50.48N 3.07E
Menfi Italy 32 37.36N 12.59E
Mengcheng China 54 33.16N 116.33E
Mengzi China 61 23.20N 103.21E
Menihek Lakes Canada 103 54.00N 66.35W
Menindee Australia 92 32.23S 142.30E
Menindee L. Australia 92 32.21S 142.20E
Menominee U.S.A. 110 45.07N 87.37W
Menomonie U.S.A. 110 44.53N 91.55W
Menongue Angola 78 14.40S 17.41E
Menorca i. Spain 25 40.00N 4.00E
Menor, Mar b. Spain 25 37.43N 0.48W
Mens France 21 44.49N 5.45E
Mentawai, Kepulauan is. Indonesia 58 2.50S 99.00E
Mentekab Malaysia 58 3.29N 102.21E
Mentok Indonesia 58 2.04S 105.12E
Menton France 21 43.47N 7.30E
Mentor U.S.A. 114 41.40N 81.20W
Menyapa, Gunung mtn. Indonesia 58 1.00N 116.20E
Menzel Bourguiba Tunisia 32 37.10N 9.48E
Menzel Bou Zelfa Tunisia 32 36.41N 10.36E
Menzel Djemil Tunisia 32 37.14N 9.55E
Menzel Temime Tunisia 32 36.47N 10.59E
Menzies Australia 89 29.41S 121.02E
Menzies, Mt. Antarctica 128 71.50S 61.00E
Me'ona Israel 67 33.01N 35.16E
Meppel Neth. 16 52.42N 6.12E
Meppen Germany 38 52.41N 7.17E
Mer France 18 47.42N 1.30E
Merambéllou, Kólpos g. Greece 35 35.14N 25.47E
Merano Italy 30 46.40N 11.09E
Merauke Indonesia 90 8.30S 140.22E
Merbein Australia 92 34.11S 142.04E
Mercato Saraceno Italy 30 43.57N 12.12E
Merced U.S.A. 108 37.18N 120.29W
Mercedes Buenos Aires Argentina 125 34.40S 59.25W
Mercedes Corrientes Argentina 124 29.15S 58.05W
Mercedes San Luis Argentina 125 33.40S 65.30W
Mercedes Uruguay 125 33.16S 58.01W
Mercer U.S.A. 114 41.14N 80.15W
Mercy, C. Canada 99 65.00N 63.30W
Mere U.K. 13 51.05N 2.16W
Meredith Australia 92 37.50S 144.05E
Meredith, L. U.S.A. 111 35.36N 101.42W
Mereeg Somali Rep. 71 3.47N 47.18E
Merefa Ukraine 45 49.49N 36.05E
Mereke C.A.R. 73 7.34N 23.09E
Mergenevo Kazakhstan 45 49.59N 51.19E
Mergui Myanmar 56 12.26N 98.38E
Mergui Archipelago is. Myanmar 56 11.15N 98.00E
Meribah Australia 92 34.42S 140.53E
Meriç r. Turkey 34 40.52N 26.12E
Mérida Mexico 117 20.59N 89.39W
Mérida Spain 27 38.55N 6.20W
Mérida Venezuela 122 8.24N 71.08W
Mérida, Cordillera de mts. Venezuela 122 8.30N 71.00W
Meriden U.S.A. 115 41.32N 72.48W
Meridian U.S.A. 111 32.22N 88.42W
Mérignac France 20 44.50N 0.42W
Merigur Australia 92 34.21S 141.23E
Merikarvia Finland 41 61.51N 21.30E
Merimbula Australia 93 36.52S 149.55E
Merino Australia 92 37.45S 141.35E
Merir i. Pacific Oc. 59 4.19N 132.18E
Meriruma Brazil 123 1.15N 54.50W
Merizo Guam 84 13.16N 144.40E
Merkendorf Germany 39 49.12N 10.42E
Merksem Belgium 16 51.14N 4.25E
Merlin Canada 104 42.14N 82.14W
Merlo Argentina 125 34.40S 58.45W
Meron, Har mtn. Israel 67 33.00N 35.25E
Merredin Australia 89 31.29S 118.16E
Merrick mtn. U.K. 14 55.08N 4.29W
Merrickville Canada 105 44.55N 75.50W
Merrill Oreg. U.S.A. 108 42.01N 121.36W
Merrill Wisc. U.S.A. 110 45.11N 89.41W
Merriman U.S.A. 110 42.55N 101.42W
Merritt Canada 100 50.10N 120.45W
Merriwa Australia 93 32.08S 150.20E
Mersa Fatma Eritrea 72 14.55N 40.20E
Mersch Lux. 16 49.44N 6.05E
Mersea I. U.K. 13 51.47N 0.58E
Merseburg Germany 38 51.21N 11.59E
Mersey r. U.K. 12 53.22N 2.37W
Merseyside d. U.K. 12 53.28N 3.00W
Mersin Turkey 64 36.47N 34.37E
Mersing Malaysia 58 2.25N 103.50E
Merta India 62 26.39N 74.02E
Merta Road town India 62 26.43N 73.55E
Merthyr Tydfil U.K. 13 51.45N 3.23W
Mértola Portugal 27 37.38N 7.40W
Merton U.K. 13 51.25N 0.12W
Mertzon U.S.A. 111 31.16N 100.49W
Méru France 19 49.14N 2.08E
Meru mtn. Tanzania 79 3.15S 36.44E
Méry France 19 48.30N 3.53E
Merzifon Turkey 64 40.52N 35.28E
Merzig Germany 39 49.27N 6.36E
Mesa r. Spain 25 41.15N 1.48W
Mesa U.S.A. 109 33.25N 111.50W
Mesagne Italy 33 40.33N 17.49E
Mesarás, Kólpos g. Greece 35 34.58N 24.36E
Meschede Germany 38 51.20N 8.17E
Meshoppen U.S.A. 115 41.34N 76.03W
Meslay-du-Maine France 18 47.57N 0.33W
Mesocco Switz. 39 46.23N 9.14E

Mesolóngion Greece 35 38.21N 21.17E
Mesopotamia f. Iraq 65 33.30N 44.30E
Messalo r. Mozambique 79 11.38S 40.27E
Messina Italy 33 38.11N 15.33E
Messina R.S.A. 80 22.20S 30.03E
Messina, Stretto di str. Italy 33 38.10N 15.35E
Messines Canada 105 46.14N 76.01W
Messíni Greece 35 37.03N 22.00E
Messíni site Greece 35 37.11N 21.57E
Messiniakós, Kólpos g. Greece 35 36.58N 22.00E
Messkirch Germany 39 47.59N 9.07E
Mestá Greece 35 38.16N 25.53E
Mesta r. Bulgaria see Néstos r. Greece 34
Mestre Italy 30 45.29N 12.15E
Meta r. Venezuela 122 6.10N 67.30W
Metagama Canada 104 47.05N 81.57W
Metallifere, Colline mts. Italy 30 43.15N 11.00E
Metán Argentina 124 25.30S 65.00W
Metangula Mozambique 79 12.41S 34.51E
Metapontum site Italy 33 40.24N 16.49E
Metéora site Greece 34 39.46N 21.36E
Methóni Greece 35 36.50N 21.43E
Methuen U.S.A. 115 42.44N 71.11W
Metkovets Bulgaria 34 43.37N 23.10E
Metković Croatia 31 43.03N 17.39E
Metlakatla U.S.A. 100 55.09N 131.35W
Metlika Slovenia 31 45.39N 15.19E
Métsovon Greece 34 39.46N 21.11E
Metulla Israel 67 33.16N 35.35E
Metz France 19 49.08N 6.10E
Metzingen Germany 39 48.32N 9.17E
Meu r. France 18 48.02N 1.47W
Meulaboh Indonesia 58 4.10N 96.09E
Meulan France 19 49.01N 1.54E
Meurthe r. France 19 48.47N 6.09E
Meurthe-et-Moselle d. France 19 48.35N 6.10E
Meuse d. France 19 49.00N 5.30E
Meuse r. Belgium see Maas r. Neth. 16
Meuselwitz Germany 38 51.02N 12.17E
Mexia U.S.A. 111 31.41N 96.29W
Mexicali Mexico 100 32.40N 115.29W
Mexico C. America 116 20.00N 100.00W
México d. Mexico 116 19.45N 99.30W
Mexico Mo. U.S.A. 110 39.10N 91.53W
Mexico N.Y. U.S.A. 115 43.28N 76.14W
Mexico B. U.S.A. 113 46.31N 76.17W
Mexico City see Ciudad de México Mexico 116
Mexico, G. of N. America 116 25.00N 90.00W
Meximieux France 21 45.54N 5.12E
Meydän Kalay Afghan. 62 32.25N 66.44E
Meydän Khvolah Afghan. 62 33.36N 69.51E
Meyenburg Germany 38 53.18N 12.14E
Meyersdale U.S.A. 114 39.45N 79.05W
Meymac France 20 45.32N 2.09E
Meymaneh Afghan. 60 35.54N 64.43E
Meyrueis France 20 44.10N 3.26E
Mezdra Bulgaria 34 43.12N 23.35E
Mèze France 20 43.25N 3.36E
Mézel France 21 43.59N 6.12E
Mezen Russian Fed. 44 65.50N 44.20E
Mezen r. Russian Fed. 44 65.50N 44.18E
Mézenc, Mont mtn. France 21 44.55N 4.11E
Mezenskaya Guba g. Russian Fed. 44 66.30N 44.00E
Mezer Israel 67 32.26N 35.03E
Mézières-en-Brenne France 18 46.49N 1.13E
Mézin France 20 44.03N 0.16E
Mezökövesd Hungary 37 47.50N 20.34E
Mezzolombardo Italy 30 46.13N 11.05E
M'goun, Irhil mtn. Morocco 22 31.31N 6.25W
Mhow India 62 22.33N 75.46E
Miahuatlán Mexico 116 16.20N 96.36W
Miajadas Spain 27 39.09N 5.54W
Miäjlar India 62 26.15N 70.23E
Miami Fla. U.S.A. 113 25.45N 80.15W
Miami Okla. U.S.A. 111 36.53N 94.53W
Miami Tex. U.S.A. 111 35.42N 100.38W
Miami Beach town U.S.A. 113 25.47N 80.07W
Miändow Äb Iran 65 36.57N 46.06E
Miandrivazo Madagascar 81 19.31S 45.28E
Miäneh Iran 65 37.23N 47.45E
Miang, Phukao mtn. Thailand 56 16.55N 101.00E
Miäni India 62 21.51N 69.23E
Miäni Hör b. Pakistan 62 25.34N 66.19E
Miänwäli Pakistan 62 32.35N 71.33E
Mianyang Hubei China 55 30.25N 113.30E
Mianyang Sichuan China 55 31.26N 104.45E
Miao'er Shan mtn. China 55 25.50N 110.22E
Miaoli Taiwan 55 24.34N 120.48E
Miarinarivo Madagascar 81 18.57S 46.55E
Miass Russian Fed. 50 55.00N 60.00E
Mibu r. Japan 57 35.49N 137.57E
Mica R.S.A. 80 24.09S 30.49E
Micang Shan mts. China 54 32.40N 107.28E
Michael, L. Canada 103 54.32N 58.15W
Michalovce Slovakia 37 48.45N 21.55E
Michelson, Mt. U.S.A. 98 69.19N 144.17W
Michigan d. U.S.A. 112 44.00N 85.00W
Michigan Center U.S.A. 104 42.14N 84.20W
Michigan City U.S.A. 112 41.43N 86.54W
Michigan, L. U.S.A. 112 44.00N 87.00W
Michipicoten Canada 102 47.59N 84.55W
Michipicoten I. Canada 102 47.40N 85.50W
Michoacán d. Mexico 116 19.20N 101.00W
Michurinsk Russian Fed. 44 52.54N 40.30E
Micronesia is. Pacific Oc. 84 8.00N 160.00E
Midale Canada 101 49.22N 103.27W
Mid Atlantic Ridge f. Atlantic Oc. 127 20.00N 45.00W
Middelburg Neth. 16 51.30N 3.36E
Middelburg C.P. R.S.A. 80 31.29S 25.00E
Middelburg Trans. R.S.A. 80 25.45S 29.27E
Middelfart Denmark 42 55.30N 9.45E
Middelharnis Neth. 16 51.46N 4.09E
Middenmeer Neth. 16 52.51N 4.59E
Middleboro Canada 101 49.01N 95.21W
Middleboro U.S.A. 115 41.49N 70.55W
Middleburg N.Y. U.S.A. 115 42.36N 74.20W
Middleburg Va. U.S.A. 114 38.58N 77.44W
Middlebury U.S.A. 105 44.01N 73.10W

Middlefield U.S.A. 114 41.28N 81.05W
Middle I. Australia 89 34.07S 123.12E
Middle Loup r. U.S.A. 110 41.17N 98.23W
Middleport N.Y. U.S.A. 114 43.13N 78.29W
Middleport Ohio U.S.A. 114 39.00N 82.03W
Middlesboro U.S.A. 113 36.37N 83.43W
Middlesbrough U.K. 12 54.34N 1.13W
Middleton Canada 103 44.57N 65.04W
Middleton Reef Pacific Oc. 84 29.28S 159.06E
Middletown Conn. U.S.A. 115 41.33N 72.39W
Middletown Del. U.S.A. 115 39.25N 75.47W
Middletown Ind. U.S.A. 112 39.31N 84.13W
Middletown N.Y. U.S.A. 115 41.27N 74.25W
Middletown Penn. U.S.A. 114 40.12N 76.44W
Middletown R.I. U.S.A. 115 41.32N 71.17W
Mid Glamorgan d. U.K. 13 51.38N 3.25W
Midi, Canal du France 20 43.26N 1.58E
Midi de Bigorre, Pic du mtn. France 20 42.56N 0.08E
Mid-Indian Basin f. Indian Oc. 49 15.00S 80.00E
Mid-Indian Ridge f. Indian Oc. 49 30.00S 75.00E
Midi-Pyrénées d. France 20 44.10N 2.00E
Midland Canada 104 44.45N 79.53W
Midland Mich. U.S.A. 104 43.37N 84.14W
Midland Tex. U.S.A. 111 32.00N 102.05W
Midland Junction Australia 89 31.54S 115.57E
Midleton Rep. of Ire. 15 51.55N 8.10W
Midnapore India 63 22.26N 87.20E
Midongy-Sud Madagascar 81 23.35S 47.01E
Midou r. France 20 43.54N 0.30W
Midway Is. Hawaiian Is. 84 28.15N 177.25W
Midwest U.S.A. 108 43.25N 106.16W
Midwest City U.S.A. 111 35.27N 97.24W
Midyan f. Saudi Arabia 66 27.50N 35.30E
Midye Turkey 29 41.37N 28.07E
Midzor mtn. Bulgaria/Yugo. 34 43.24N 22.40E
Mie d. Japan 57 34.42N 136.08E
Miechów Poland 37 50.23N 20.01E
Miedzychód Poland 36 52.36N 15.55E
Miélan France 20 43.26N 0.19E
Mielec Poland 37 50.18N 21.25E
Mien l. Sweden 43 56.25N 14.51E
Mienga Angola 78 17.16S 19.50E
Mieres Spain 26 43.15N 5.46W
Miesbach Germany 39 47.47N 11.50E
Mifflin U.S.A. 114 40.34N 77.24W
Mifraz Hefa b. Israel 67 32.52N 35.03E
Migang Shan mtn. China 54 35.32N 106.13E
Migdal Israel 67 32.50N 35.30E
Migdal Ha'Emeq Israel 67 32.41N 35.15E
Miguel Hidalgo, Presa resr. Mexico 109 26.41N 108.19W
Migyaunglaung Myanmar 56 14.40N 98.09E
Mijares r. Spain 25 39.55N 0.01W
Mikhaylov Russian Fed. 44 54.14N 39.00E
Mikhaylovka Russian Fed. 45 50.05N 43.15E
Miki Japan 57 34.48N 134.59E
Mikinai Greece 35 37.43N 22.46E
Mikindani Tanzania 79 10.16S 40.05E
Mikjaylovgrad d. Bulgaria 34 43.25N 23.11E
Mikkeli Finland 44 61.44N 27.15E
Mikkwa r. Canada 100 58.25N 114.46W
Míkonos Greece 35 37.30N 25.25E
Míkonos i. Greece 35 37.29N 25.25E
Mikre Bulgaria 34 43.02N 24.31E
Mikumi Tanzania 79 7.22S 37.00E
Mikun Russian Fed. 44 62.20N 50.01E
Mikuni sammyaku mts. Japan 57 37.00N 139.20E
Milagro Ecuador 122 2.11S 79.36W
Milan see Milano Italy 30
Milan Mich. U.S.A. 104 42.05N 83.40W
Milan Mo. U.S.A. 110 40.12N 93.07W
Milange Mozambique 79 16.09S 35.44E
Milano Italy 30 45.28N 9.12E
Milâs Turkey 35 37.19N 27.47E
Milazzo Italy 33 38.14N 15.15E
Milbank U.S.A. 110 45.14N 96.38W
Milbanke Sd. Canada 100 52.18N 128.33W
Mildenhall U.K. 13 52.20N 0.30E
Mildmay Canada 104 44.03N 81.07W
Mildura Australia 92 34.14S 142.13E
Miléai Greece 35 39.20N 23.09E
Miles Australia 90 26.40S 150.11E
Miles City U.S.A. 108 46.25N 105.51W
Miletto, Monte mtn. Italy 33 41.27N 14.22E
Miletus site Turkey 35 37.30N 27.18E
Milevsko Czech Republic 39 49.27N 14.22E
Milford Conn. U.S.A. 115 41.13N 73.04W
Milford Mass. U.S.A. 115 42.08N 71.32W
Milford Mich. U.S.A. 104 42.35N 83.36W
Milford N.H. U.S.A. 115 42.50N 71.39W
Milford N.Y. U.S.A. 115 42.35N 74.57W
Milford Penn. U.S.A. 115 41.19N 74.48W
Milford Utah U.S.A. 108 38.24N 113.01W
Milford Haven town U.K. 13 51.43N 5.02W
Milford Sound town New Zealand 86 44.41S 167.56E
Miliana Algeria 75 27.21N 2.28E
Miling Australia 89 30.27S 116.20E
Milk r. U.S.A. 108 48.05N 106.15W
Millau France 20 44.06N 3.05E
Millbrook Canada 104 44.09N 78.27W
Millbrook U.S.A. 115 41.47N 73.42W
Mille Lacs L. U.S.A. 110 46.10N 93.45W
Mille Lacs, Lac des l. Canada 102 48.45N 90.35W
Miller r. Australia 92 30.05S 136.07E
Millerovo Russian Fed. 45 48.55N 40.25E
Millers r. U.S.A. 115 42.35N 72.30W
Millersburg Mich. U.S.A. 104 45.20N 84.04W
Millersburg Ohio U.S.A. 114 40.33N 81.55W
Millersburg Penn. U.S.A. 114 40.33N 76.58W
Millerton U.S.A. 115 41.57N 73.31W
Milleur Pt. U.K. 14 55.01N 5.07W
Millicent Australia 92 37.36S 140.22E
Millington U.S.A. 113 35.15N 90.00W
Millinocket U.S.A. 112 45.39N 68.43W
Millmerran Australia 91 27.51S 151.17E
Millom U.K. 12 54.13N 3.16W
Mills L. Canada 100 61.30N 118.10W

Millstatt Austria 31 46.48N 13.35E
Millville U.S.A. 115 39.24N 75.02W
Milne Inlet town Canada 99 72.30N 80.59W
Milnet Canada 104 46.49N 80.59W
Milo r. Guinea 76 11.05N 9.05W
Milos Greece 35 36.45N 24.27E
Milos i. Greece 35 36.41N 24.15E
Milparinka Australia 92 29.45S 141.55E
Milroy U.S.A. 114 40.43N 77.35W
Miltenberg Germany 39 49.42N 9.15E
Milton Australia 93 35.19S 150.24E
Milton Canada 104 43.31N 79.53W
Milton Del. U.S.A. 115 38.47N 75.19W
Milton Mass. U.S.A. 115 42.15N 71.05W
Milton N.H. U.S.A. 115 43.23N 70.59W
Milton Penn. U.S.A. 114 41.01N 76.51W
Milton Vt. U.S.A. 105 44.38N 73.07W
Milton W.Va. U.S.A. 114 38.26N 82.08W
Milton Keynes U.K. 13 52.03N 0.42W
Miltou Chad 77 10.10N 17.30E
Miluo China 55 28.50N 113.05E
Milverton Canada 104 43.34N 80.55W
Milwaukee U.S.A. 112 43.02N 87.55W
Milwaukie U.S.A. 108 45.27N 122.38W
Milyatino Russian Fed. 44 54.30N 34.20E
Mim Ghana 76 6.55N 2.34W
Miminiska L. Canada 102 51.32N 88.33W
Mimizan France 20 44.12N 1.14W
Mina U.S.A. 108 38.24N 118.07W
Mínä 'al Ahmadi Kuwait 60 29.04N 48.08E
Minäb Iran 65 27.07N 57.05E
Miná Baranis Egypt 72 23.55N 35.28E
Minaki Canada 102 50.00N 94.48W
Minamata Japan 57 32.13N 130.24E
Minas Uruguay 125 34.23S 55.14W
Minas Basin b. Canada 103 45.20N 64.00W
Minas Channel str. Canada 103 45.15N 64.45W
Minas de Corrales Uruguay 125 31.35S 55.28W
Minas de Ríotinto Spain 27 37.42N 6.22W
Minas Gerais d. Brazil 126 18.00S 45.00W
Minatitlán Mexico 116 17.59N 94.32W
Minbu Myanmar 56 20.09N 94.52E
Mindanao i. Phil. 59 7.30N 125.00E
Mindanao Sea Phil. 59 9.10N 124.25E
Mindarie Australia 92 34.51S 140.12E
Mindemoya Canada 104 45.44N 82.10W
Minden Canada 104 44.55N 78.43W
Minden Germany 38 52.17N 8.55E
Minden U.S.A. 111 32.37N 93.17W
Minden City U.S.A. 104 43.40N 82.47W
Mindif Cameroon 77 10.25N 14.23E
Mindiptana Indonesia 59 5.45S 140.22E
Mindona L. Australia 92 33.09S 142.09E
Mindoro i. Phil. 59 13.00N 121.00E
Mindoro Str. Pacific Oc. 59 12.30N 120.10E
Mindra mtn. Romania 37 45.20N 23.32E
Minehead U.K. 13 51.12N 3.29W
Mineola U.S.A. 111 32.40N 95.29W
Minerva Australia 90 24.00S 148.05E
Minerva U.S.A. 114 40.44N 81.06W
Minervino Murge Italy 33 41.05N 16.05E
Mingan Canada 103 50.18N 64.02W
Mingary Australia 92 32.09S 140.46E
Mingela Australia 90 19.53S 146.40E
Mingenew Australia 89 29.11S 115.26E
Mingin Myanmar 56 22.52N 94.39E
Mingin Range mts. Myanmar 56 24.00N 95.45E
Minglanilla Spain 25 39.32N 1.36W
Mingorría Spain 26 40.45N 4.40W
Minhe China 54 36.12N 102.59E
Minho r. see Miño r. Portugal 26
Minho r. Portugal 26
Minićevo Yugo. 34 43.42N 22.18E
Minidoka U.S.A. 108 42.46N 113.30W
Minigwal, L. Australia 89 29.35S 123.12E
Min Jiang r. China 55 26.06N 119.15E
Minlaton Australia 92 34.46S 137.37E
Minna Nigeria 77 9.39N 6.32E
Minneapolis Kans. U.S.A. 110 39.08N 97.42W
Minneapolis Minn. U.S.A. 110 44.59N 93.13W
Minnedosa Canada 101 50.14N 99.51W
Minnesota d. U.S.A. 110 46.00N 94.00W
Minnesota r. U.S.A. 110 44.54N 93.10W
Minnesota Lake town U.S.A. 110 43.51N 93.50W
Minnipa Australia 92 32.51S 135.09E
Minnitaki L. Canada 102 50.00N 91.50W
Mino Japan 57 35.34N 136.56E
Miño r. Spain 26 41.52N 8.51W
Minobu-sanchi mts. Japan 57 35.05N 138.15E
Mino-kamo Japan 57 35.26N 137.01E
Mino-mikawa-kögen mts. Japan 57 35.16N 137.10E
Minorca i. see Menorca i. Spain 25
Minot U.S.A. 110 48.16N 101.19W
Minqin China 54 38.42N 103.11E
Minsen Germany 38 53.42N 7.58E
Min Shan mts. China 54 32.40N 104.40E
Minsk Belarus 37 53.51N 27.30E
Minta Cameroon 77 4.37N 12.47E
Minto, Lac l. Canada 102 57.15N 74.50W
Minturno Italy 32 41.15N 13.45E
Minüf Egypt 66 30.28N 30.56E
Min Xian China 54 34.26N 104.02E
Minyä al Qamh Egypt 66 30.31N 31.21E
Minyar Russian Fed. 44 55.06N 57.29E
Mio U.S.A. 104 44.39N 84.08W
Mionica Yugo. 31 44.15N 20.05E
Miquelon i. Canada 102 49.25N 76.32W
Mira Italy 30 45.26N 12.08E
Mira Portugal 26 40.26N 8.44W
Mira r. Portugal 27 37.43N 8.47W
Miräbäd Afghan. 62 30.25N 61.50E
Miracema Brazil 126 21.22S 42.09W
Mirah, Wädi al r. Iraq 64 32.27N 41.21E
Miraj India 60 16.51N 74.42E
Miramas France 21 43.35N 5.00E
Mirambeau France 20 45.23N 0.34W
Miramichi B. Canada 103 47.08N 65.08W
Miram Shäh Pakistan 62 33.01N 70.04E
Miran Pakistan 62 31.24N 70.43E

Miranda de Ebro Spain 26 42.41N 2.57W
Miranda do Douro Portugal 26 41.30N 6.16W
Mirande France 20 43.31N 0.25E
Mirandela Portugal 26 41.29N 7.11W
Mirando City U.S.A. 111 27.26N 99.00W
Mirandola Italy 30 44.53N 11.04E
Miravete, Puerto de pass Spain 27 39.43N 5.43W
Mir Bachcheh Küt Afghan. 62 34.45N 69.08E
Mirbät Oman 60 17.00N 54.45E
Mirebeau-sur-Bèze France 19 47.24N 5.19E
Mirecourt France 19 48.18N 6.08E
Miri Malaysia 58 4.28N 114.00E
Mirim, L. Brazil 126 33.10S 53.30W
Mírina Greece 34 39.52N 25.04E
Mirintu Creek r. Australia 92 28.58S 143.18E
Mironovka Ukraine 37 49.40N 30.59E
Miroşi Romania 37 44.25N 24.58E
Mirow Germany 38 53.16N 12.49E
Mirpur Jammu & Kashmir 62 33.15N 73.55E
Mirpur Batoro Pakistan 62 24.44N 68.16E
Mirpur Khäs Pakistan 60 25.33N 69.05E
Mirpur Sakro Pakistan 62 24.33N 67.37E
Mirtöön Pélagos sea Greece 35 36.51N 23.18E
Miryeny Moldova 37 47.00N 29.06E
Mirzäpur India 63 25.09N 82.35E
Mi saki c. Japan 57 40.09N 141.52E
Misawa Japan 57 40.41N 141.24E
Miscou I. Canada 103 47.57N 64.33W
Mishawaka U.S.A. 112 41.38N 86.10W
Mishima Japan 57 35.07N 138.55E
Mishkino Russian Fed. 44 55.34N 56.00E
Mishmar Ayyalon Israel 67 31.52N 34.57E
Mishmar Ha'Emeq Israel 67 32.36N 35.09E
Mishmar HaNegev Israel 67 31.21N 34.43E
Mishmar Hayarden Israel 67 33.00N 35.36E
Mishomis Canada 105 47.11N 75.40W
Misilmeri Italy 32 38.01N 13.27E
Misima I. P.N.G. 90 10.40S 152.45E
Misiones d. Argentina 124 27.00S 54.40W
Miskī Sudan 72 14.51N 24.13E
Miskolc Hungary 37 48.07N 20.47E
Mismär Sudan 72 18.13N 35.38E
Misool i. Indonesia 59 1.50S 130.10E
Misr al Jadidah Egypt 66 30.06N 31.20E
Misrätah Libya 75 32.23N 15.06E
Misrätah d. Libya 75 30.30N 17.00E
Misr Bahrï f. Egypt 66 30.30N 31.00E
Missinaibi r. Canada 102 50.44N 81.29W
Mission U.S.A. 110 43.18N 100.40W
Mississagi r. Canada 104 46.10N 82.30W
Mississagi Prov. Park Canada 104 46.35N 82.30W
Mississauga Canada 104 43.35N 79.37W
Mississippi r. Canada 105 45.26N 76.16W
Mississippi d. U.S.A. 111 32.40N 90.00W
Mississippi r. U.S.A. 111 29.00N 89.15W
Mississippi Delta U.S.A. 111 29.10N 89.15W
Mississippi L. Canada 105 45.05N 76.12W
Mississippi Sd. U.S.A. 111 30.15N 88.40W
Missoula U.S.A. 108 46.52N 114.01W
Missouri d. U.S.A. 110 38.30N 92.00W
Missouri r. U.S.A. 110 38.50N 90.08W
Missouri Valley town U.S.A. 110 41.33N 95.53W
Mistassini Canada 103 48.54N 72.13W
Mistassini r. Canada 103 48.54N 72.14W
Mistassini, Lac l. Canada 103 51.15N 73.10W
Mistassini Prov. Park Canada 103 51.30N 73.20W
Mistastin Canada 103 55.55N 63.30W
Misterbianco Italy 33 37.31N 15.01E
Mistinibi, L. Canada 103 55.55N 64.10W
Mistretta Italy 33 37.56N 14.22E
Mitchell Australia 90 26.29S 147.58E
Mitchell r. Qld. Australia 90 15.12S 141.35E
Mitchell r. Vic. Australia 93 37.53S 147.41E
Mitchell Canada 104 43.28N 81.12W
Mitchell Oreg. U.S.A. 108 44.34N 120.09W
Mitchell S.Dak. U.S.A. 110 43.40N 98.00W
Mitchell, Mt. U.S.A. 113 35.47N 82.16W
Mitchells Bay town Canada 104 42.28N 82.26W
Mitchelstown Rep. of Ire. 15 52.16N 8.17W
Mît Ghamr Egypt 66 30.43N 31.16E
Mithapur India 62 22.25N 69.00E
Mithi Pakistan 62 24.44N 69.48E
Mitilíni Greece 35 39.00N 26.20E
Mitla, Mamarr pass Egypt 66 30.00N 32.53E
Mitla Pass see Mitla, Mamarr pass Egypt 66
Mito Japan 57 36.30N 140.29E
Mitri Prespa, Límni l. Greece 34 40.55N 21.00E
Mitsinjo Madagascar 81 16.01S 45.52E
Mits'iwa Eritrea 72 15.36N 39.29E
Mits'iwa Channel Ethiopia 72 15.30N 40.00E
Mittagong Australia 93 34.27S 150.25E
Mittelandkanal Germany 38 52.23N 8.00E
Mittenwald Germany 39 47.27N 11.15E
Mittersill Austria 39 47.16N 12.29E
Mittweida Germany 38 50.59N 12.59E
Mitú Colombia 122 1.08N 70.03W
Mitumba, Monts mts. Zaïre 79 3.00S 28.30E
Mitwaba Zaïre 79 8.32S 27.20E
Mitzic Gabon 78 0.48N 11.30E
Miura Japan 57 35.08N 139.37E
Mivtahim Israel 67 31.14N 34.23E
Miya r. Japan 57 34.32N 136.44E
Miyako Japan 57 39.40N 141.59E
Miyako jima i. Japan 53 24.45N 125.25E
Miyakonojö Japan 57 31.43N 131.02E
Miyazaki Japan 57 31.58N 131.50E
Mizdah Libya 75 31.26N 12.59E
Mizen Head Rep. of Ire. 15 51.27N 9.50W
Mizil Romania 37 45.00N 26.26E
Mizoch Ukraine 37 50.30N 25.50E
Mizoram d. India 61 23.40N 92.40E
Mizpa Israel 67 32.47N 35.31E
Mizpe Ramon Israel 67 30.36N 34.48E
Mizra' Israel 67 32.39N 35.17E
Mizukaidö Japan 57 36.01N 139.59E
Mizunami Japan 57 35.22N 137.15E
Mizusawa Japan 57 39.08N 141.08E

Mjölby Sweden 43 58.19N 15.08E
Mjöndalen Norway 42 59.45N 10.01E
Mjörn i. Sweden 43 57.54N 12.25E
Mjösa l. Norway 41 60.40N 11.00E
Mkata Tanga Tanzania 79 5.47S 38.18E
Mkushi Zambia 79 13.40S 29.26E
Mkuze R.S.A. 81 27.10S 32.00E
Mkwaja Tanzania 79 5.46S 38.51E
Mkwiti Tanzania 79 10.27S 39.18E
Mladá Boleslav Czech Republic 36 50.26N 14.55E
Mława Poland 37 53.06N 20.23E
Mljet i. Croatia 29 42.45N 17.30E
Mljet i. Croatia 31 42.45N 17.30E
Mljetski Kanal str. Croatia 31 42.48N 17.35E
Mneni Zimbabwe 80 20.38S 30.03E
Moab U.S.A. 108 38.35N 109.33W
Moa I. Australia 90 10.12S 142.16E
Moama Australia 93 36.05S 144.50E
Moamba Mozambique 81 25.35S 32.13E
Moanda Gabon 78 1.25S 13.18E
Moapa U.S.A. 109 36.40N 114.39W
Moatize Mozambique 81 16.10S 33.40E
Moba Zaïre 79 7.03S 29.42E
Mobara Japan 57 35.25N 140.18E
Mobaye C.A.R. 73 4.19N 21.11E
Moberly U.S.A. 110 39.25N 92.26W
Mobert Canada 102 48.41N 85.40W
Mobile U.S.A. 111 30.42N 88.05W
Mobile B. U.S.A. 111 30.25N 88.00W
Mobridge U.S.A. 110 45.32N 100.26W
Mobutu Sese Seko, L. see Albert, L. Uganda/Zaïre 79
Moçambique town Mozambique 79 15.00S 40.47E
Mocimboa da Praia Mozambique 79 11.19S 40.19E
Mocimboa do Ruvuma Mozambique 79 11.05S 39.15E
Möckeln l. Sweden 43 56.40N 14.10E
Moclips U.S.A. 108 47.14N 124.13W
Mococa Brazil 126 21.28S 47.00W
Moctezuma Mexico 109 30.10N 106.28W
Mocuba Mozambique 79 16.52S 37.02E
Močurica r. Bulgaria 34 42.31N 26.32E
Modane France 21 45.12N 6.40E
Modåsa India 62 23.28N 73.18E
Modder r. R.S.A. 80 29.03S 23.56E
Modena Italy 30 44.40N 10.54E
Modena U.S.A. 108 37.48N 113.57W
Modesto U.S.A. 108 37.39N 121.00W
Modica Italy 33 36.51N 14.47E
Modjamboli Zaïre 78 2.28N 22.06E
Modrica Bosnia-Herzegovina 31 44.57N 18.18E
Moe Australia 93 38.10S 146.15E
Moebase Mozambique 81 17.04S 38.41E
Moelv Norway 41 60.56N 10.42E
Moffat U.K. 14 55.20N 3.27W
Moga India 62 30.48N 75.10E
Mogadishu see Muqdisho Somali Rep. 79
Mogadouro Portugal 26 41.20N 6.39W
Mogaung Myanmar 56 25.15N 96.54E
Mogi das Cruzes Brazil 126 23.33S 46.14W
Mogi-Guaçu Brazil 126 20.55S 48.06W
Mogilev Belarus 37 53.54N 30.20E
Mogilev Podolskiy Ukraine 37 48.29N 27.49E
Mogilno Poland 37 52.40N 17.58E
Mogi-Mirim Brazil 126 22.29S 46.55W
Mogincual Mozambique 79 15.33S 40.29E
Mogliano Veneto Italy 30 45.33N 12.14E
Mogok Myanmar 56 23.00N 96.30E
Mogollon Rim f. U.S.A. 109 32.30N 111.00W
Moguer Spain 27 37.16N 6.50W
Mogumber Australia 89 31.01S 116.02E
Mohács Hungary 31 45.59N 18.42E
Mohammedia Morocco 74 33.44N 7.24W
Mohana India 63 25.54N 77.45E
Mohawk Ariz. U.S.A. 109 32.41N 113.47W
Mohawk N.Y. U.S.A. 115 43.00N 75.00W
Mohawk r. U.S.A. 115 42.47N 73.42W
Moheda Sweden 43 57.00N 14.34E
Mohéli i. Comoros 79 12.22S 43.45E
Mohon France 19 49.45N 4.44E
Mohoro Tanzania 79 8.09S 39.07E
Mohoru Kenya 79 1.01S 34.07E
Moi Norway 42 58.28N 6.32E
Moincêr China 63 31.10N 80.52E
Moindi Gabon 78 3.24S 11.43E
Mointy Kazakhstan 9 47.10N 73.18E
Moira r. Canada 105 44.09N 77.23W
Moira U.S.A. 105 44.50N 74.34W
Mo-i-Rana Norway 40 66.19N 14.10E
Mõisaküla Estonia 41 58.06N 25.11E
Moisdon France 18 47.37N 1.22W
Moisie r. Canada 103 50.13N 66.02W
Moissac France 20 44.06N 1.05E
Moïssala Chad 77 8.20N 17.40E
Moita Portugal 27 38.39N 8.59W
Mojácar Spain 27 37.09N 1.50W
Mojave U.S.A. 109 35.03N 118.10W
Mojave Desert U.S.A. 109 35.00N 117.00W
Mojokerto Indonesia 59 7.25S 112.31E
Mokameh India 63 25.24N 85.55E
Mokau New Zealand 86 38.41S 174.37E
Mokmer Indonesia 59 1.13S 136.13E
Mokpo S. Korea 53 34.50N 126.25E
Mokra Gora mts. Yugo. 34 42.50N 20.30E
Mokren Bulgaria 34 42.45N 26.39E
Mol Belgium 16 51.11N 5.09E
Mola di Bari Italy 33 41.04N 17.05E
Moláoi Greece 35 36.48N 22.52E
Molat i. Croatia 31 44.15N 14.49E
Molchanovo Russian Fed. 50 57.39N 83.45E
Mold U.K. 12 53.10N 3.08W
Moldavia see Moldova Europe 37
Molde Norway 40 62.44N 7.08E
Moldova Europe 37 47.30N 28.30E
Molepolole Botswana 80 24.26S 25.34E
Molfetta Italy 33 41.12N 16.36E
Molihong Shan mtn. China 54 41.44N 124.43E
Molina de Aragón Spain 25 40.51N 1.53W
Molina de Segura Spain 25 38.04N 1.12W
Moline U.S.A. 110 41.30N 90.30W

Molinella Italy 30 44.37N 11.40E
Molino Lacy Mexico 109 30.05N 114.24W
Molins Spain 25 41.25N 2.01E
Moliro Zaïre 79 8.11S 30.29E
Molise d. Italy 33 41.40N 14.30E
Molkom Sweden 43 59.36N 13.43E
Mölle Sweden 43 56.17N 12.29E
Mollendo Peru 124 17.02S 72.01W
Mölln Germany 38 53.37N 10.41E
Mollösund Sweden 42 58.04N 11.28E
Mölndal Sweden 43 57.39N 12.01E
Molodechno Belarus 37 54.16N 26.50E
Molokai i. Hawaii U.S.A. 106 21.20N 157.00W
Molong Australia 93 33.08S 148.53E
Molopo r. R.S.A. 80 28.30S 20.22E
Mólos Greece 35 38.47N 22.37E
Moloundou Cameroon 78 2.55N 12.01E
Molsheim France 19 48.32N 7.29E
Molson L. Canada 101 54.12N 96.45W
Molt U.S.A. 110 46.22N 102.20W
Molteno R.S.A. 80 31.23S 26.21E
Moluccas is. Indonesia 59 4.00S 128.00E
Molucca Sea see Maluku, Laut sea Pacific Oc. 59
Moma Mozambique 79 16.40S 39.10E
Mombasa Kenya 79 4.04S 39.40E
Mombuey Spain 26 42.02N 6.20W
Momchilgrad Bulgaria 34 41.32N 25.25E
Momi Zaïre 79 1.42S 27.03E
Mommark Denmark 36 54.55N 10.03E
Mompós Colombia 122 9.15N 74.29W
Møn i. Denmark 43 55.00N 12.20E
Mon d. Myanmar 56 16.45N 97.25E
Mona i. Puerto Rico 117 18.06N 67.54W
Monaco Europe 21 43.40N 7.25E
Monadhliath Mts. U.K. 14 57.09N 4.08W
Monaghan Rep. of Ire. 15 54.15N 6.58W
Monaghan d. Rep. of Ire. 15 54.10N 7.00W
Monahans U.S.A. 111 31.36N 102.54W
Monarch Mt. Canada 100 51.55N 125.57W
Monastir Tunisia 75 35.35N 10.50E
Moncalieri Italy 30 45.00N 7.40E
Monção Portugal 26 42.05N 8.29W
Moncayo, Sierra del mts. Spain 25 41.48N 1.50W
Monchegorsk Russian Fed. 44 67.55N 33.01E
Mönchen Gladbach Germany 38 51.12N 6.28E
Monchique Portugal 27 37.19N 8.33W
Monclova Mexico 111 26.54N 101.25W
Moncontour France 18 48.21N 2.39W
Moncton Canada 103 46.06N 64.47W
Mondego r. Portugal 26 40.09N 8.52W
Mondego, Cabo c. Portugal 26 40.11N 8.55W
Mondo Tanzania 79 5.00S 35.54E
Mondoñedo Spain 26 43.26N 7.22W
Mondoubleau France 18 47.59N 0.54E
Mondoví Italy 30 44.23N 7.49E
Mondragone Italy 32 41.07N 13.53E
Mondrain I. Australia 89 34.08S 122.15E
Monessen U.S.A. 114 40.09N 79.53W
Monesterio Spain 26 38.05N 6.16W
Monet Canada 102 48.10N 75.40W
Monett U.S.A. 111 36.55N 93.55W
Monfalcone Italy 31 45.48N 13.32E
Monflanquin France 20 44.32N 0.46E
Monforte Portugal 27 39.03N 7.26W
Monforte Spain 26 42.31N 7.33W
Monga Zaïre 73 4.12N 22.49E
Mongala r. Zaïre 78 1.58N 19.56E
Mongalla Sudan 73 5.12N 31.46E
Mong Cai Vietnam 55 21.36N 107.55E
Mongers L. Australia 89 29.15S 117.05E
Monghyr India 63 25.23N 86.28E
Mongo Chad 77 12.14N 18.45E
Mongolia Asia 52 46.30N 104.00E
Mongororo Chad 73 12.01N 22.28E
Mongu Zambia 78 15.10S 23.09E
Monheim Germany 39 48.50N 10.51E
Monifieth U.K. 14 56.29N 2.50W
Monistrol-sur-Loire France 21 45.17N 4.10E
Monitor Range mts. U.S.A. 108 38.45N 116.30W
Monkoto Zaïre 73 1.38S 20.39E
Monmouth U.K. 13 51.48N 2.43W
Monmouth Ill. U.S.A. 110 40.54N 90.39W
Monmouth Oreg. U.S.A. 108 44.51N 123.14W
Monocacy r. U.S.A. 114 39.13N 77.27W
Mono L. U.S.A. 108 38.00N 119.00W
Monomoy Pt. U.S.A. 115 41.33N 70.02W
Monongahela r. U.S.A. 114 40.27N 80.00W
Monopoli Italy 33 40.57N 17.19E
Monor Hungary 37 47.21N 19.27E
Monóvar Spain 25 38.25N 0.47W
Monreal Spain 25 42.42N 1.30W
Monreal del Campo Spain 25 40.47N 1.21W
Monreale Italy 32 38.05N 13.17E
Monroe La. U.S.A. 111 32.33N 92.07W
Monroe Mich. U.S.A. 104 41.55N 83.24W
Monroe N.C. U.S.A. 113 35.00N 80.35W
Monroe N.Y. U.S.A. 115 41.20N 74.11W
Monroe Wisc. U.S.A. 110 42.36N 89.38W
Monroe City U.S.A. 110 39.39N 91.44W
Monroeville U.S.A. 113 31.32N 87.21W
Monrovia Liberia 76 6.20N 10.46W
Mons Belgium 16 50.27N 3.57E
Monselice Italy 30 45.14N 11.45E
Mönsterås Sweden 43 57.02N 16.26E
Montabaur Germany 39 50.26N 7.50E
Montagnana Italy 30 45.14N 11.28E
Montague Canada 103 46.10N 62.39W
Montaigu France 18 46.59N 1.19W
Montaigut-en-Combraille France 20 46.11N 2.38E
Montalbán Spain 25 40.50N 0.48W
Montalbano di Elicona Italy 33 38.02N 15.02E
Montalbano Ionico Italy 33 40.17N 16.34E
Montalcino Italy 30 43.03N 11.29E
Montalegre Portugal 26 41.49N 7.48W
Montalto mtn. Italy 33 38.10N 15.55E
Montalto di Castro Italy 30 42.21N 11.37E
Montalto Uffugo Italy 33 39.25N 16.09E

Montana Bulgaria 34 43.27N 23.16E
Montana Switz. 39 46.18N 7.29E
Montana d. U.S.A. 108 47.14N 109.26W
Montánchez Spain 27 39.13N 6.09W
Montargil Portugal 27 39.05N 8.10W
Montargis France 19 48.00N 2.45E
Montauban France 20 44.01N 1.21E
Montauk U.S.A. 115 41.03N 71.57W
Montbard France 19 47.37N 4.20E
Montbarrey France 19 47.01N 5.39E
Montbéliard France 19 47.31N 6.48E
Montblanch Spain 25 41.22N 1.10E
Montbrison France 21 45.36N 4.03E
Montbron France 20 45.40N 0.30E
Monceau-les-Mines France 19 46.40N 4.22E
Mont Cenis, Col du pass France 21 45.15N 6.54E
Montcerf Canada 105 46.32N 76.02W
Montchannin France 19 46.45N 4.27E
Montcornet France 19 49.41N 4.01E
Mont de Marsan town France 20 43.53N 0.30W
Montdidier France 19 49.39N 2.34E
Monte Alegre town Brazil 123 2.01S 54.04W
Monte Azul town Brazil 126 15.53S 42.53W
Montebello Canada 105 45.39N 74.56W
Montebello Iónico Italy 33 37.59N 15.45E
Monte Carlo Monaco 21 43.44N 7.25E
Monte Caseros Argentina 125 30.15S 57.38W
Montecatini Terme Italy 30 43.53N 10.46E
Montecristi i. Dom. Rep. 117 19.52N 71.39W
Montecristo i. Italy 30 42.20N 10.19E
Montefalco Italy 30 42.54N 12.39E
Montefrío Spain 27 37.19N 4.01W
Montego Bay town Jamaica 117 18.27N 77.56W
Montejicar Spain 27 37.34N 3.30W
Montélimar France 21 44.34N 4.45E
Montellano Spain 27 37.00N 5.34W
Montemor-o-Novo Portugal 27 38.39N 8.13W
Montemor-o-Velho Portugal 26 40.10N 8.41W
Montemura mtn. Portugal 26 40.59N 7.59W
Montendre France 20 45.17N 0.24W
Montenegro see Crna Gora d. Yugo. 31
Montenero di Bisaccia Italy 33 41.57N 14.47E
Montepuez Mozambique 81 13.09S 39.33E
Montepulciano Italy 30 43.05N 11.47E
Montereau France 19 48.23N 2.57E
Monterey Calif. U.S.A. 108 36.37N 121.55W
Monterey Va. U.S.A. 114 38.25N 79.35W
Monterey B. U.S.A. 108 36.45N 121.55W
Montería Colombia 122 8.45N 75.54W
Montero Bolivia 124 17.20S 63.15W
Monteros Argentina 124 27.10S 65.30W
Monterotondo Italy 30 42.03N 12.37E
Monterrey Mexico 111 25.40N 100.19W
Montesano Italy 33 40.16N 15.43E
Monte Sant 'Angelo Italy 33 41.42N 15.59E
Monte Santu, Capo di c. Italy 32 40.05N 9.44E
Montesarchio Italy 33 41.04N 14.38E
Montes Claros Brazil 126 16.45S 43.52W
Montevarchi Italy 30 43.31N 11.34E
Montevideo Uruguay 125 34.53S 56.11W
Montevideo U.S.A. 110 44.57N 95.43W
Montezuma U.S.A. 111 37.36N 100.26W
Montfaucon France 21 45.10N 4.18E
Montfort-sur-Meu France 18 48.08N 1.58W
Montgomery U.K. 13 52.34N 3.09W
Montgomery Ala. U.S.A. 113 32.22N 86.20W
Montgomery Penn. U.S.A. 114 41.10N 76.52W
Montguyon France 20 45.13N 0.11W
Monthey Switz. 39 46.15N 6.57E
Monthois France 19 49.19N 4.43E
Monticello Ark. U.S.A. 111 33.38N 91.47W
Monticello Miss. U.S.A. 111 31.33N 90.07W
Monticello N.Y. U.S.A. 115 41.39N 74.42W
Monticello Utah U.S.A. 108 37.52N 109.21W
Montichiari Italy 30 45.25N 10.23E
Montiel, Campo de f. Spain 26 38.46N 2.45W
Montignac France 20 45.04N 1.10E
Montigny-le-Roi France 19 48.00N 5.30E
Montijo Portugal 27 38.42N 8.58W
Montijo Spain 27 38.55N 6.37W
Montijo Dam Spain 24 38.52N 6.20W
Montilla Spain 27 37.35N 4.38W
Montivilliers France 18 49.33N 0.12E
Mont Joli town Canada 103 48.35N 68.14W
Mont Laurier town Canada 105 46.33N 75.30W
Mont Louis town Canada 103 49.15N 65.46W
Mont-Louis France 20 42.31N 2.07E
Montluçon France 20 46.21N 2.36E
Montmagny Canada 103 46.59N 70.33W
Montmédy France 19 49.31N 5.22E
Montmirail France 19 48.52N 3.32E
Montmoreau St. Cybard France 20 45.24N 0.08E
Montmorillon France 18 46.26N 0.52E
Montmort France 19 48.55N 3.49E
Monto Australia 90 24.52S 151.07E
Montorio al Vomano Italy 31 42.35N 13.38E
Montoro Spain 26 38.01N 4.23W
Montour Falls town U.S.A. 114 42.21N 76.51W
Montoursville U.S.A. 114 41.15N 76.55W
Montpelier Idaho U.S.A. 108 42.20N 111.20W
Montpelier Vt. U.S.A. 105 44.16N 72.35W
Montpellier France 20 43.36N 3.53E
Montpon-sur-l'Isle France 20 45.00N 0.10E
Montreal Canada 105 45.31N 73.34W
Montreal r. Canada 104 47.14N 84.39W
Montreal L. Canada 101 54.20N 105.40W
Montreal Lake town Canada 101 54.03N 105.46W
Montréal-Nord Canada 105 45.36N 73.38W
Montreal River town Canada 104 46.41N 79.50W
Montrejeau France 20 43.05N 0.33E
Montrésor France 18 47.09N 1.12E
Montreuil France 19 50.28N 1.46E
Montreuil-Bellay France 18 47.08N 0.09W
Montreux Switz. 39 46.26N 6.55E
Montrevel France 21 46.20N 5.08E
Montrichard France 18 47.21N 1.11E
Montrose U.K. 14 56.43N 2.29W
Montrose Colo. U.S.A. 108 38.29N 107.53W
Montrose Penn. U.S.A. 115 41.50N 75.56W

Montserrat i. Leeward Is. 117 16.45N 62.14W
Montserrat, Serra de mts. Spain 25 41.15N 0.55E
Mont Tremblant Prov. Park Canada 105 46.42N 74.20W
Montuenga Spain 26 41.03N 4.37W
Montville U.S.A. 115 41.27N 72.08W
Monument Valley f. U.S.A. 108 36.50N 110.20W
Monveda Zaïre 78 2.57N 21.27E
Monywa Myanmar 56 22.05N 95.15E
Monza Italy 30 45.35N 9.16E
Monze Zambia 79 16.16S 27.28E
Monzón Spain 25 41.55N 0.12E
Moolawatana Australia 92 29.55S 139.43E
Mooloogool Australia 88 26.06S 119.05E
Moomba Australia 91 28.08S 140.16E
Moomin Creek r. Australia 93 29.35S 148.45E
Moonbi Range mts. Australia 93 31.00S 151.10E
Moonie Australia 91 27.40S 150.19E
Moonie r. Australia 91 29.30S 148.40E
Moonta Australia 92 34.04S 137.37E
Moora Australia 89 30.40S 116.01E
Moorarie Australia 88 25.56S 117.35E
Moorcroft U.S.A. 108 44.16N 104.57W
Moore r. Australia 89 31.22S 115.29E
Mooréa i. Îs. de la Société 85 17.32S 149.50W
Moorefield U.S.A. 114 39.04N 78.58W
Moorefield r. U.S.A. 114 39.04N 78.58W
Moore, L. Australia 89 29.30S 117.30E
Moorfoot Hills U.K. 14 55.43N 3.03W
Moorhead U.S.A. 110 46.53N 96.45W
Moor Lake town Canada 105 46.09N 77.42W
Moornanyah L. Australia 92 33.02S 143.58E
Mooroopna Australia 93 36.24S 145.22E
Moosburg Germany 39 48.29N 11.57E
Moose Creek town Canada 105 45.15N 74.58W
Moosehead L. U.S.A. 112 45.40N 69.40W
Moose Jaw Canada 101 50.23N 105.32W
Moose Lake town U.S.A. 110 46.26N 92.45W
Moosomin Canada 101 50.07N 101.40W
Moosonee Canada 102 51.17N 80.39W
Mootwingee Australia 92 31.52S 141.14E
Mopanzhang China 54 33.07N 117.22E
Mopêia Velha Mozambique 81 17.58S 35.40E
Mopti Mali 76 14.29N 4.10W
Mopti d. Mali 74 15.30N 3.40W
Moqor Afghan. 62 32.55N 67.40E
Moquegua Peru 124 17.20S 70.55W
Mora Cameroon 77 11.02N 14.07E
Mora Portugal 27 38.56N 8.10W
Mora Spain 27 39.41N 3.46W
Mora Sweden 41 61.00N 14.33E
Mora U.S.A. 110 45.53N 93.18W
Morädäbäd India 63 28.50N 78.47E
Mora de Rubielos Spain 25 40.15N 0.45W
Morafenobe Madagascar 81 17.49S 44.45E
Mórahalom Hungary 31 46.13N 19.54E
Moralana Australia 92 31.42S 138.12E
Moral de Calatrava Spain 26 38.50N 3.35W
Moramanga Madagascar 81 18.56S 48.12E
Moran U.S.A. 104 46.00N 84.50W
Morar, Loch U.K. 14 56.56N 4.00W
Morasverdes Spain 26 40.36N 6.16W
Moratalla Spain 25 38.12N 1.53W
Morava r. Czech Republic 37 48.10N 16.59E
Morava r. Yugo. 37 44.43N 21.02E
Moravia U.S.A. 115 42.43N 76.25W
Moravské Budějovice Czech Republic 36 49.03N 15.49E
Morawhanna Guyana 122 8.17N 59.44W
Moray Firth est. U.K. 14 57.35N 5.15W
Morbach Germany 39 49.48N 7.07E
Morbegno Italy 30 46.08N 9.34E
Morbihan d. France 18 47.55N 2.50W
Mörbylånga Sweden 43 56.31N 16.23E
Morcenx France 20 44.02N 0.55W
Morden Australia 92 30.30S 142.23E
Morden Canada 101 49.11N 98.05W
Mordovo Russian Fed. 45 52.06N 40.45E
Moreau r. U.S.A. 110 45.18N 100.43W
Morecambe U.K. 12 54.03N 2.52W
Morecambe B. U.K. 12 54.05N 3.00W
Moree Australia 93 29.29S 149.53E
Morée France 18 47.54N 1.14E
Morehead U.S.A. 113 38.11N 83.27W
Morehead City U.S.A. 113 34.43N 76.44W
Morelia Mexico 116 19.40N 101.11W
Morella Spain 25 40.37N 0.06W
Morelos d. Mexico 116 18.40N 99.00W
Morena India 63 26.30N 78.09E
Morena, Sierra mts. Spain 27 38.20N 4.25W
Morenci U.S.A. 109 33.05N 109.22W
Moreno Mexico 109 28.29N 110.41W
Möre og Romsdal d. Norway 40 63.00N 9.00E
Moresby I. Canada 100 52.30N 131.40W
Moreton I. Australia 91 27.10S 153.25E
Morez France 19 46.31N 6.02E
Mórfou Cyprus 66 35.12N 33.00E
Mórfou, Kólpos b. Cyprus 66 35.15N 32.50E
Morgan Australia 92 34.02S 139.40E
Morgan U.S.A. 111 32.01N 97.37W
Morgan City U.S.A. 111 29.42N 91.12W
Morganfield U.S.A. 113 37.41N 87.55W
Morgantown U.S.A. 114 39.38N 79.57W
Morghab r. Afghan. 60 36.50N 63.00E
Morgongåva Sweden 43 59.56N 16.57E
Moriki Nigeria 77 12.55N 6.30E
Moringen Germany 38 51.42N 9.52E
Morin Heights Canada 105 45.54N 74.21W
Morioka Japan 57 39.43N 141.10E
Morisset Australia 93 33.06S 151.29E
Moriyama Japan 57 35.04N 135.59E
Morlaix France 18 48.35N 3.50W
Mörlunda Sweden 43 57.19N 15.51E
Mormanno Italy 33 39.53N 16.00E
Mormon Range mts. U.S.A. 108 37.08N 114.20W
Mornington I. Australia 90 16.33S 139.24E
Mornington Mission Australia 90 16.40S 139.10E
Morobe P.N.G. 59 7.45S 147.35E

189

Morocco Africa 74 32.30N 5.00W
Moro G. Phil. 59 6.30N 123.20E
Morogoro Tanzania 79 6.47S 37.40E
Morogoro d. Tanzania 79 8.30S 37.00E
Moroleón Mexico 116 20.08N 101.12W
Morombe Madagascar 81 21.45S 43.22E
Morón Argentina 125 34.39S 58.37W
Morón Cuba 117 22.08N 78.39W
Mörön Mongolia 52 49.36N 100.08E
Morón Spain 27 37.08N 5.27W
Morondava Madagascar 81 20.17S 44.17E
Morón de Almazán Spain 25 41.25N 2.25W
Moroni Comoros 105 11.40S 43.19E
Morotai i. Indonesia 59 2.10N 128.30E
Moroto Uganda 79 2.32N 34.41E
Moroto, Mt. Uganda 79 2.30N 34.46E
Morpeth U.K. 12 55.10N 1.40W
Morrilton U.S.A. 111 35.09N 92.45W
Morrinsville New Zealand 86 37.39S 175.32E
Morris Minn. U.S.A. 110 45.35N 95.55W
Morris Penn. U.S.A. 114 41.36N 77.18W
Morrisburg Canada 105 44.54N 75.11W
Morristown Ariz. U.S.A. 109 33.51N 112.37W
Morristown N.J. U.S.A. 115 40.48N 74.29W
Morristown N.Y. U.S.A. 105 44.35N 75.39W
Morristown S.Dak. U.S.A. 110 45.56N 101.43W
Morristown Tenn. U.S.A. 113 36.13N 83.18W
Morrisville N.Y. U.S.A. 115 42.54N 75.39W
Morrisville Vt. U.S.A. 105 44.34N 72.44W
Mörrum Sweden 43 56.11N 14.45E
Morrumbene Mozambique 81 23.41S 35.25E
Mörrumsån r. Sweden 43 56.09N 14.44E
Mors i. Denmark 42 56.50N 8.45E
Morsbach Germany 38 50.52N 7.43E
Morsi India 63 21.21N 78.00E
Mortagne France 18 48.31N 0.33E
Mortagne r. France 19 48.33N 6.27E
Mortagne-sur-Sèvre France 18 47.00N 0.57W
Mortain France 18 48.39N 0.56W
Mortara Italy 30 45.15N 8.44E
Morteau France 19 47.04N 6.37E
Mortes r. see Manso r. Brazil 124
Mortes r. Brazil 126 21.09S 45.06W
Mortlake town Australia 92 38.05S 142.48E
Morundah Australia 93 34.56S 146.18E
Moruya Australia 93 35.56S 150.06E
Morvan, Monts du mts. France 19 47.05N 4.00E
Morven Australia 90 26.25S 147.05E
Morvern f. U.K. 14 56.37N 5.45W
Morvi India 62 22.49N 70.50E
Morwell Australia 93 38.14S 146.25E
Morzhovets i. Russian Fed. 44 66.45N 42.30E
Mosby Norway 42 58.14N 7.54E
Moscow see Moskva Russian Fed. 44
Moscow U.S.A. 108 46.44N 117.00W
Mosel r. Germany 39 50.22N 7.36E
Moselle d. France 19 49.00N 6.30E
Moselle r. see Mosel r. France 19
Moses Lake town U.S.A. 108 47.08N 119.17W
Mosgiel New Zealand 86 45.53S 170.22E
Moshi Tanzania 79 3.20S 37.21E
Mosjøen Norway 40 65.50N 13.10E
Moskenes Norway 40 67.55N 13.00E
Moskenesøy i. Norway 40 67.55N 13.00E
Moskva Russian Fed. 44 55.45N 37.42E
Moskva r. Russian Fed. 44 55.08N 38.50E
Mosquera Colombia 122 2.30N 78.29W
Mosquero U.S.A. 109 35.47N 103.58W
Mosquitia Plain Honduras 117 15.00N 84.00W
Mosquito Creek Resr. U.S.A. 114 41.10N 80.45W
Mosquitos, Costa de f. Nicaragua 117 13.00N 84.00W
Mosquitos, Golfo de los g. Panama 117 9.00N 81.00W
Moss Norway 42 59.26N 10.42E
Mossaka Congo 78 1.20S 16.44E
Mossburn New Zealand 86 45.41S 168.15E
Mosselbaai R.S.A. 80 34.11S 22.08E
Mossendjo Congo 78 2.52S 12.46E
Mossgiel Australia 93 33.18S 144.05E
Mossman Australia 90 16.28S 145.22E
Mossoró Brazil 123 5.10S 37.18W
Mossuril Mozambique 81 14.58S 40.42E
Moss Vale town Australia 93 34.33S 150.24E
Most Czech Republic 38 50.32N 13.39E
Mostaganem Algeria 74 35.56N 0.05E
Mostar Bosnia-Herzegovina 31 43.20N 17.49E
Mösting, Kap c. Greenland 99 64.00N 41.00W
Mostiska Ukraine 37 49.48N 23.05E
Mosul see Al Mawşil Iraq 64
Mösvatnet l. Norway 42 59.52N 8.05E
Mota del Cuervo Spain 27 39.30N 2.52W
Mota del Marqués Spain 26 41.38N 5.10W
Motagua r. Guatemala 117 15.56N 87.45W
Motala Sweden 43 58.33N 15.03E
Moth India 63 25.43N 78.57E
Motherwell U.K. 14 55.48N 4.00W
Motīhāri India 63 26.39N 84.55E
Motilla del Palancar Spain 25 39.34N 1.53W
Motloutse r. Botswana 80 22.15S 29.00E
Motol Belarus 37 52.25N 25.05E
Motou China 54 32.17N 120.35E
Motril Spain 27 36.45N 3.31W
Mott U.S.A. 108 46.22N 102.20W
Mottola Italy 33 40.38N 17.03E
Motueka New Zealand 86 41.08S 173.01E
Motu Iti i. Îs. de la Société 85 16.15S 151.50W
Mototutapu Niue 84 19.02S 169.52W
Mouali Congo 78 0.10N 15.33E
Mouchalagane r. Canada 103 53.32N 69.00W
Moúdhros Greece 34 39.52N 25.16E
Moudjéria Mauritania 74 17.53N 12.20W
Moudon Switz. 39 46.40N 6.48E
Mouhoun r. Burkina see Black Volta r. Ghana 76
Mouila Gabon 78 1.50S 11.02E
Mouka C.A.R. 73 7.16N 21.52E
Moulamein Australia 92 35.03S 144.05E
Moulhoulé Djibouti 73 12.36N 43.12E

Moulins France 20 46.34N 3.20E
Moulins-la-Marche France 18 48.39N 0.29E
Moulmein Myanmar 56 16.55N 97.49E
Moulouya, Oued r. Morocco 74 35.05N 2.25W
Moultrie U.S.A. 113 31.11N 83.47W
Moultrie, L. U.S.A. 113 33.20N 80.05W
Mound City U.S.A. 110 40.07N 95.14W
Moundou Chad 77 8.36N 16.02E
Moundsville U.S.A. 114 39.55N 80.44W
Moundville U.S.A. 111 32.59N 87.38W
Mountain Ash U.K. 13 51.42N 3.22W
Mountain City U.S.A. 108 41.50N 115.58W
Mountain Grove Canada 105 44.44N 76.51W
Mountain Home Ark. U.S.A. 111 36.20N 92.23W
Mountain Home Idaho U.S.A. 108 43.08N 115.41W
Mountain Nile r. see Jabal, Bahr al r. Sudan 73
Mountain Village U.S.A. 98 62.05N 163.44W
Mount Airy U.S.A. Md. U.S.A. 114 39.23N 77.09W
Mount Airy town N.C. U.S.A. 113 36.31N 80.38W
Mount Barker town S.A. Australia 92 35.06S 138.52E
Mount Barker town W.A. Australia 89 34.36S 117.37E
Mount Beauty town Australia 93 36.43S 147.11E
Mount Bellew town Rep. of Ire. 15 53.28N 8.30W
Mount Brydges town Canada 104 42.54N 81.29W
Mount Carmel town Ill. U.S.A. 110 38.25N 87.46W
Mount Carmel town Penn. U.S.A. 115 40.48N 76.25W
Mount Clemens town U.S.A. 114 42.36N 82.53W
Mount Darwin town Zimbabwe 81 16.46S 31.36E
Mount Drysdale town Australia 93 31.11S 145.51E
Mount Eba town Australia 92 30.12S 135.33E
Mount Fletcher town R.S.A. 80 30.41S 28.30E
Mount Forest town Canada 104 43.59N 80.44W
Mount Gambier town Australia 92 37.51S 140.50E
Mount Gilead town U.S.A. 114 40.33N 82.50W
Mount Hagen town P.N.G. 59 5.54S 144.13E
Mount Holly town U.S.A. 115 39.59N 74.47W
Mount Holly Springs town U.S.A. 114 40.07N 77.11W
Mount Hope town N.S.W. Australia 93 32.49S 145.48E
Mount Hope town S.A. Australia 92 34.07S 135.23E
Mount Hopeless town Australia 92 29.42S 139.41E
Mount Isa town Australia 90 20.50S 139.29E
Mount Lebanon town U.S.A. 114 40.23N 80.03W
Mount Lofty Range mts. Australia 92 34.40S 139.03E
Mount Magnet town Australia 89 28.06S 117.50E
Mount Manara town Australia 92 32.28S 143.59E
Mountmellick Rep. of Ire. 15 53.08N 7.21W
Mount Morgan town Australia 90 23.39S 150.23E
Mount Morris town Mich. U.S.A. 104 43.07N 83.42W
Mount Morris town N.Y. U.S.A. 114 42.44N 77.53W
Mount Morris town Penn. U.S.A. 114 39.44N 80.02W
Mount Murchison town Australia 92 31.23S 143.42E
Mount Pleasant town Canada 104 43.05N 80.19W
Mount Pleasant town Mich. U.S.A. 112 43.36N 84.46W
Mount Pleasant town S.C. U.S.A. 113 32.48N 79.54W
Mount Pleasant town Tex. U.S.A. 111 33.09N 94.58W
Mount Robson town Canada 100 52.56N 119.15W
Mount Savage town U.S.A. 114 39.42N 78.53W
Mount's B. U.K. 13 50.05N 5.25W
Mount Sterling town U.S.A. 113 38.03N 83.56W
Mount Union town U.S.A. 114 40.23N 77.53W
Mount Upton town U.S.A. 115 42.26N 75.23W
Mount Vernon town Australia 88 24.09S 118.10E
Mount Vernon town Ill. U.S.A. 110 38.19N 88.52W
Mount Vernon town N.Y. U.S.A. 115 40.54N 73.50W
Mount Vernon town Ohio U.S.A. 114 40.23N 82.29W
Mount Vernon town Wash. U.S.A. 108 48.25N 122.20W
Mount Walker town Australia 89 27.47S 152.32E
Mount Willoughby Australia 92 27.58S 134.08E
Moura Australia 90 24.33S 149.58E
Moura Brazil 122 1.27S 61.38W
Moura Chad 72 13.47N 21.13E
Moura Portugal 27 38.08N 7.27W
Mourdiah Mali 76 14.35N 7.25W
Mourdi, Dépression de f. Chad 72 18.10N 23.00E
Mourne r. U.K. 11 54.50N 7.29W
Mourne Mts. U.K. 14 54.10N 6.02W
Mouscron Belgium 16 50.46N 3.10E
Moussoro Chad 77 13.41N 16.31E
Mouth of Seneca U.S.A. 114 38.52N 79.21W
Moutier Switz. 39 47.17N 7.23E
Moûtiers France 21 45.29N 6.32E
Mouzáklon Greece 34 39.26N 21.40E
Moxico Angola 78 11.50S 20.05E
Moxico d. Angola 78 13.00S 21.00E
Moy r. Rep. of Ire. 15 54.10N 9.09W
Moyale Kenya 79 3.31N 39.04E
Moyamba Sierra Leone 76 8.04N 12.03W
Moyen Atlas mts. Morocco 74 33.30N 5.00W
Moyen-Chari d. Chad 77 9.20N 17.35E
Moyeni Lesotho 80 30.24S 27.41E
Moyeuvre-Grande France 19 49.15N 6.02E
Moyie Canada 100 49.17N 115.50W
Moyobamba Peru 122 6.04S 76.56W
Moyowosi r. Tanzania 79 4.59S 30.58E
Moza Israel 67 31.47N 35.09E
Mozambique Africa 81 17.30S 35.45E
Mozambique Channel Indian Oc. 81 16.00S 42.30E
Mozdok Russian Fed. 45 43.45N 44.43E
Mozyr Belarus 37 52.02N 29.10E
Mpala Zaïre 79 6.45S 29.31E
M'Pama r. Congo 78 0.59S 15.40E
Mpanda Tanzania 79 6.21S 31.01E
Mpésoba Mali 76 12.31N 5.39W
Mphoengs Zimbabwe 80 21.10S 27.51E
Mpika Zambia 79 11.52S 31.30E
Mponela Malaŵi 79 13.32S 33.43E
Mporokoso Zambia 79 9.22S 30.06E
M'Pouya Congo 78 2.38S 16.08E
Mpunde mtn. Tanzania 79 6.12S 33.48E
Mpwapwa Tanzania 79 6.23S 36.38E
M'qoun, Irhil mtn. Morocco 74 31.31N 6.25W
Mrhila, Djebel mtn. Tunisia 75 35.25N 9.14E
Mrkonjić Grad Bosnia-Herzegovina 31 44.25N 17.05E
Mrkopalj Croatia 31 45.19N 14.51E
Msaken Tunisia 22 35.42N 10.33E
Mseleni R.S.A. 81 27.21S 32.33E
Msingu Tanzania 79 4.52S 39.08E

Msta r. Russian Fed. 44 58.28N 31.20E
Mtakuja Tanzania 79 7.21S 30.37E
Mtama Tanzania 79 10.20S 39.19E
Mtito Andei Kenya 79 2.32S 38.10E
Mtsensk Russian Fed. 44 53.18N 36.35E
Mtwara Tanzania 79 10.17S 40.11E
Mtwara d. Tanzania 79 10.00S 38.30E
Mu r. Japan 57 42.30N 142.20E
Muaná Brazil 123 1.32S 49.13W
Muangangla Angola 78 13.33S 18.04E
Muang Chiang Rai Thailand 56 19.56N 99.51E
Muang Khammouan Laos 56 17.22N 104.50E
Muang Khon Kaen Thailand 56 16.25N 102.52E
Muang Lampang Thailand 56 18.16N 99.30E
Muang Lamphun Thailand 56 18.36N 99.02E
Muang Nakhon Phanom Thailand 56 17.22N 104.45E
Muang Nakhon Sawan Thailand 56 15.42N 100.04E
Muang Nan Thailand 56 18.47N 100.50E
Muang Ngoy Laos 56 20.43N 102.41E
Muang Pak Lay Laos 56 18.12N 101.25E
Muang Phaya Thailand 56 19.10N 99.55E
Muang Phetchabun Thailand 56 16.25N 101.08E
Muang Phichit Thailand 56 16.29N 100.21E
Muang Phitsanulok Thailand 56 16.45N 100.18E
Muang Phrae Thailand 56 18.07N 100.09E
Muang Sakon Nakhon Thailand 56 17.10N 104.08E
Muang Sing Laos 56 21.11N 101.09E
Muang Soum Laos 56 18.46N 102.36E
Muang Ubon Thailand 56 15.15N 104.50E
Muar Malaysia 58 2.01N 102.35E
Muara Brunei 58 5.01N 115.01E
Muara Indonesia 58 0.32S 101.20E
Muarakaman Indonesia 58 0.02S 116.45E
Muaratewe Indonesia 58 0.57S 114.53E
Muāri, Rās c. Pakistan 62 24.49N 66.40E
Mubende Uganda 79 0.30N 31.24E
Mubi Nigeria 77 10.16N 13.17E
Mucanona Angola 78 8.13S 16.39E
Muchea Australia 89 31.36S 115.57E
Mücheln Germany 38 51.18N 11.48E
Muchinga Mts. Zambia 79 12.15S 31.00E
Muck i. U.K. 14 56.50N 6.14W
Mucojo Mozambique 79 12.05S 40.26E
Muconda Angola 78 10.31S 21.20E
Mudanjiang China 54 44.36N 129.42E
Mudaysīsāt, Jabal al mtn. Jordan 67 31.39N 36.14E
Mudgee Australia 93 32.37S 149.36E
Mudon Myanmar 56 16.15N 97.44E
Mudyuga Russian Fed. 44 63.45N 39.29E
Mueda Mozambique 79 11.40S 39.31E
Muene Quibau Angola 78 11.27S 19.14E
Mufulira Zambia 79 12.33S 28.12E
Mufu Shan mts. China 55 29.30N 114.45E
Muganskaya Ravnina f. Azerbaijan 65 39.40N 48.30E
Mughr Syria 67 33.05N 35.43E
Mughshin, Wādī Oman 71 19.44N 55.15E
Mugi Japan 57 33.40N 134.25E
Muğía Spain 26 43.06N 9.10W
Muğla Turkey 29 37.12N 28.22E
Muhamdi India 63 27.57N 80.13E
Muhammad, Ra's c. Egypt 66 27.42N 34.13E
Mühlacker Germany 39 48.57N 8.50E
Mühldorf Germany 39 48.15N 12.32E
Mühlhausen Germany 38 51.12N 10.27E
Mühlig Hofmann fjella mts. Antarctica 128 72.30S 5.00E
Muhola Finland 40 63.20N 25.05E
Muhos Finland 40 64.48N 26.00E
Muhu i. Estonia 41 58.32N 23.20E
Muhuru Kenya 79 1.05S 34.07E
Muhu Väin str. Estonia 41 58.45N 23.30E
Mui Ca Mau c. Vietnam 56 8.30N 104.35E
Muine Bheag town Rep. of Ire. 15 52.42N 6.58W
Muir, L. Australia 89 34.30S 116.30E
Mukachevo Ukraine 37 48.26N 22.45E
Mukah Malaysia 58 2.56N 112.02E
Mukallik, Wādī al Jordan 67 31.46N 35.29E
Mukandwara India 62 24.49N 75.59E
Mukawa P.N.G. 90 9.48S 150.00E
Mukāwir site Jordan 67 31.34N 35.38E
Mukerian India 62 31.57N 75.37E
Mukinbudin Australia 89 30.52S 118.08E
Muko r. Japan 57 34.41N 135.23E
Mukoba Zaïre 78 6.32S 23.30E
Mukongo Zaïre 78 6.32S 23.30E
Muktsar India 62 30.28N 74.31E
Mukwela Zambia 78 17.00S 26.40E
Mūl India 63 20.04N 79.40E
Mula r. India 62 19.35N 74.50E
Mūla r. Pakistan 62 27.57N 67.37E
Mula Spain 25 38.03N 1.30W
Mulanje Mts. Malaŵi 79 15.57S 35.33E
Mulchén Chile 125 37.43S 72.14W
Mulde r. Germany 38 51.10N 12.48E
Mulgathing Australia 92 30.15S 134.00E
Mulgrave Canada 103 45.37N 61.23W
Mulhacén mtn. Spain 27 37.03N 3.19W
Mülheim N.-Westfalen Germany 38 51.24N 6.54E
Mülheim N.-Westfalen Germany 38 50.58N 7.00E
Mulhouse France 19 47.45N 7.20E
Mull i. U.K. 14 56.28N 5.56W
Mullaghanattin mtn. Rep. of Ire. 15 51.56N 9.51W
Mullaghareirk Mts. Rep. of Ire. 15 52.19N 9.06W
Mullaghmore mtn. Rep. of Ire. 15 54.14N 6.51W
Mullaley Australia 93 31.06S 149.55E
Mullen U.S.A. 110 42.03N 101.01W
Mullengudgery Australia 93 31.40S 147.23E
Mullens U.S.A. 113 37.35N 81.25W
Mullet Pen. Rep. of Ire. 15 54.12N 10.04W
Mullett L. U.S.A. 104 45.30N 84.30W
Mullewa Australia 89 28.33S 115.31E
Müllheim Germany 39 47.48N 7.38E
Mullingar Rep. of Ire. 15 53.31N 7.21W
Mull of Galloway c. U.K. 14 54.39N 4.52W
Mull of Kintyre c. U.K. 14 55.17N 5.45W
Mullovka Russian Fed. 44 54.12N 49.26E
Mull, Sd. of str. U.K. 14 56.32N 5.55W
Mullsjö Sweden 43 57.55N 13.53E

Mullumbimby Australia 93 28.32S 153.30E
Mulobezi Zambia 80 16.49S 25.09E
Muloorina Australia 92 29.10S 137.51E
Multai India 63 21.46N 78.15E
Multān Pakistan 62 30.11N 71.29E
Multyfarnham Rep. of Ire. 15 53.37N 7.25W
Mulyungarie Australia 92 31.30S 140.45E
Mumbai see Bombay India 62
Mumbwa Zambia 79 14.57S 27.01E
Mumcular Turkey 35 37.05N 27.40E
Mun r. Thailand 56 15.15N 104.50E
Muna i. Indonesia 59 5.00S 122.30E
Munābão India 62 25.45N 70.17E
Munan Pass China/Vietnam 55 22.06N 106.46E
Münchberg Germany 38 50.11N 11.47E
München Germany 39 48.08N 11.34E
Muncho Lake town Canada 100 59.00N 125.50W
Muncie U.S.A. 112 40.11N 85.23W
Mundaring Weir Australia 89 31.59S 116.13E
Münden Germany 38 51.25N 9.39E
Mundiwindi Australia 88 23.50S 120.07E
Mundo r. Spain 25 38.19N 1.40W
Mundra India 62 22.51N 69.44E
Munera Spain 27 39.02N 2.28W
Mungari Mozambique 81 17.12S 33.31E
Mungbere Zaïre 79 2.40N 28.25E
Mungeli India 63 22.04N 81.41E
Mungeranie Australia 92 28.00S 138.36E
Mungindi Australia 93 28.58S 148.56E
Munhango Angola 78 12.10S 18.36E
Munich see München Germany 39
Muniesa Spain 25 41.02N 0.48W
Muniz Freire Brazil 126 20.25S 41.23W
Mun, Jabal mtn. Sudan 72 14.08N 22.42E
Munkedal Sweden 42 58.29N 11.41E
Munkfors Sweden 43 59.50N 13.32E
Munning r. Australia 93 31.50S 152.30E
Münsingen Germany 39 48.25N 9.29E
Münsingen Switz. 39 46.53N 7.34E
Munster France 19 48.03N 7.08E
Munster Nschn. Germany 38 52.59N 10.05E
Münster N.-Westfalen Germany 38 51.57N 7.37E
Muntadgin Australia 89 31.45S 118.32E
Munuscong L. U.S.A. 104 46.10N 84.08W
Munyati r. Zimbabwe 80 17.32S 29.23E
Muong Hinh Vietnam 55 19.49N 105.03E
Muonio Finland 40 67.57N 23.42E
Muonio r. Finland/Sweden 40 67.10N 23.40E
Mupa Angola 80 16.07S 15.45E
Mupa r. Mozambique 81 19.07S 35.50E
Muping China 54 37.23N 121.35E
Muqaddam, Wādī Sudan 72 18.04N 31.30E
Muqdisho Somali Rep. 79 2.02N 45.21E
Mur r. Austria see Mura r. Croatia 31
Mura r. Croatia 31 46.18N 16.53E
Muralión mtn. Argentina/Chile 125 49.48S 73.25W
Muranga Kenya 79 0.43S 37.10E
Murashi Russian Fed. 44 59.20N 48.59E
Murat France 20 45.07N 2.52E
Muravera Italy 32 39.25N 9.35E
Murau Austria 39 47.07N 14.10E
Murça Portugal 26 41.24N 7.27W
Murchison Australia 93 36.36S 145.14E
Murchison r. Australia 88 27.30S 114.10E
Murchison New Zealand 86 41.48S 172.20E
Murcia Spain 25 37.59N 1.07W
Murcia d. Spain 25 37.55N 1.40W
Mur-de-Barrez France 20 44.51N 2.39E
Murdo U.S.A. 110 43.53N 100.43W
Mureş r. Romania 37 46.16N 20.10E
Muret France 20 43.28N 1.21E
Murewa Zimbabwe 81 17.40S 31.47E
Murfreesboro U.S.A. 113 35.50N 86.25W
Murg r. Germany 39 48.55N 8.10E
Murgha Faqīrzai Pakistan 62 31.03N 67.48E
Murgha Kibzai Pakistan 62 30.44N 69.25E
Murgon Australia 90 26.15S 151.57E
Murguía Spain 26 42.57N 2.49W
Muri Cook Is. 84 21.14S 159.43W
Muriaé Brazil 126 21.08S 42.33W
Muria, Gunung mtn. Indonesia 59 6.39S 110.51E
Müritzsee l. Germany 38 53.25N 12.43E
Murjek Sweden 40 66.29N 20.50E
Murliganj India 63 25.54N 86.59E
Murmansk Russian Fed. 44 68.59N 33.08E
Murnau Germany 39 47.40N 11.12E
Murnei Sudan 73 12.57N 22.52E
Muro, Capo di c. France 21 41.44N 8.40E
Muro Lucano Italy 30 40.45N 15.30E
Murom Russian Fed. 44 55.04N 42.04E
Muroran Japan 57 42.21N 140.59E
Muros Spain 26 42.47N 9.02W
Muros y Noya, Ría de est. Spain 26 42.45N 9.00W
Murrah al Kubrá, Al Buhayrah al l. Egypt 66 30.20N 32.20E
Murra Murra Australia 93 28.18S 146.48E
Murray r.S.A. Australia 92 35.23S 139.20E
Murray r.W.A. Australia 89 32.35S 115.46E
Murray r. Canada 100 56.11N 120.45E
Murray Ky. U.S.A. 111 36.37N 88.19W
Murray Utah U.S.A. 108 40.40N 111.53W
Murray Bridge town Australia 92 35.10S 139.17E
Murray, L. P.N.G. 59 7.00S 141.30E
Murray, L. U.S.A. 113 34.04N 81.23W
Murrayville Australia 92 35.16S 141.14E
Murree Pakistan 62 33.54N 73.24E
Murrhardt Germany 39 48.59N 9.34E
Murringo Australia 93 34.19S 148.36E
Murrumbidgee r. Australia 92 34.38S 143.10E
Murrumburrah Australia 93 34.33S 148.21E
Murrurundi Australia 93 31.47S 150.51E
Murshidābād India 63 24.11N 88.16E
Murska Sobota Slovenia 31 46.40N 16.10E
Murten Switz. 39 46.56N 7.07E
Murtoa Australia 92 36.40S 142.31E
Murtosa Portugal 26 40.44N 8.38W
Murud mtn. Malaysia 58 3.45N 115.30E

Murwāra India 63 23.51N 80.24E
Murwillumbah Australia 93 28.20S 153.24E
Muş Turkey 64 38.45N 41.30E
Musadi Zaïre 78 2.31S 22.50E
Mūsá, Jabal mtn. Egypt 66 28.31N 33.59E
Mūsa Khel Pakistan 62 32.38N 71.44E
Mūsa Khel Bāzār Pakistan 62 30.52N 69.49E
Musala mtn. Bulgaria 34 42.13N 23.37E
Musan N. Korea 57 42.14N 129.13E
Mūsā Qal 'eh Afghan. 62 32.05N 64.51E
Mūsā Qal 'eh r. Afghan. 62 32.22N 64.46E
Musay'īd Qatar 65 24.47N 51.36E
Mūsāzai Pakistan 62 30.23N 66.32E
Muscat see Masqaţ Oman 65
Muscatine U.S.A. 110 41.25N 91.03W
Müsgebi Turkey 35 37.02N 27.21E
Musgrave Australia 90 14.47S 143.30E
Musgrave Ranges mts. Australia 88 26.10S 131.50E
Mushāsh, Wādī al Jordan 67 31.35N 35.22E
Mushie Zaïre 78 2.59S 16.55E
Mushima Zambia 80 14.13S 25.05E
Mushin Nigeria 77 6.33N 3.22E
Musi r. Indonesia 58 2.20S 104.57E
Muskegon U.S.A. 112 43.13N 86.15W
Muskegon r. U.S.A. 112 43.13N 86.16W
Muskegon Heights town U.S.A. 112 43.03N 86.16W
Muskingum r. U.S.A. 114 40.03N 81.59W
Muskö i. Sweden 43 59.00N 18.06E
Muskogee U.S.A. 111 35.45N 95.22W
Muskoka, L. Canada 104 45.00N 79.25W
Muskwa r. Alta. Canada 100 56.16N 114.06W
Muskwa r. B.C. Canada 100 58.47N 122.48W
Musoma Tanzania 79 1.31S 33.48E
Mussari Angola 80 13.07S 17.56E
Musselburgh U.K. 14 55.57N 3.04W
Musselkanaal Neth. 16 52.57N 7.01E
Musselshell r. U.S.A. 108 47.21N 107.58W
Mussende Angola 78 10.33S 16.02E
Musserra Angola 78 7.31S 13.02E
Mussidan France 20 45.02N 0.22E
Mussomeli Italy 32 37.35N 13.46E
Mustahil Ethiopia 73 5.12N 44.17E
Mustäng Nepal 63 29.11N 83.57E
Mustjala Estonia 41 58.28N 22.14E
Muswellbrook Australia 93 32.17S 150.55E
Müţ Egypt 72 25.29N 28.59E
Mut Turkey 64 36.38N 33.27E
Mutala Mozambique 81 15.54S 37.51E
Mutalau Niue 84 18.58S 169.50W
Mutanda Zambia 78 12.23S 26.16E
Mutare Zimbabwe 81 18.59S 32.40E
Mutbīn Syria 67 33.09N 36.15E
Mutoko Zimbabwe 81 17.23S 32.13E
Mutooroo Australia 92 32.30S 140.58E
Mutoray Russian Fed. 51 61.20N 100.32E
Mutshatsha Zaïre 78 10.39S 24.27E
Mutsu Japan 57 41.17N 141.10E
Mutsu wan b. Japan 57 41.10N 141.05E
Mutton Bay town Canada 103 50.47N 59.02W
Muwale Tanzania 79 6.22S 33.46E
Muxima Angola 78 9.33S 13.58E
Muya Russian Fed. 51 56.28N 115.50E
Muyinga Burundi 79 2.48S 30.21E
Muzaffarābād Jammu & Kashmir 62 34.22N 73.28E
Muzaffargarh Pakistan 62 30.04N 71.12E
Muzaffarnagar India 63 29.28N 77.41E
Muzaffarpur India 63 26.07N 85.24E
Muzhi Russian Fed. 44 65.25N 64.40E
Muzillac France 18 47.33N 2.29W
Muzoka Zambia 80 16.43S 27.18E
Muztag mtn. China 52 36.25N 87.25E
Mvadhi Gabon 78 1.13N 13.10E
Mvolo Sudan 73 6.03N 29.56E
Mvomero Tanzania 79 6.18S 37.26E
Mvuma Zimbabwe 80 19.16S 30.30E
Mvurwi Range mts. Zimbabwe 80 17.10S 30.45E
Mwali see Mohéli i. Comoros 79
Mwanza Tanzania 79 2.30S 32.54E
Mwanza d. Tanzania 79 3.00S 32.30E
Mwanza Zaïre 78 7.51S 26.43E
Mwaya Mbeya Tanzania 79 9.33S 33.56E
Mweka Zaïre 78 4.51S 21.34E
Mwene Ditu Zaïre 78 7.04S 23.27E
Mwenezi r. Mozambique 81 22.42S 31.45E
Mwenezi Zimbabwe 80 21.22S 30.45E
Mweru, L. Zaïre/Zambia 79 9.00S 28.40E
Mwingi Kenya 79 1.00S 38.04E
Mwinilunga Zambia 78 11.44S 24.24E
Myanaung Myanmar 61 18.25N 95.10E
Myanmar Asia 56 21.45N 97.00E
Mya, Oued wadi Algeria 75 31.40N 5.15E
Myaungmya Myanmar 56 16.33N 94.55E
Myingyan Myanmar 56 21.26N 95.28E
Myinkyado Myanmar 56 20.56N 96.42E
Myinmu Myanmar 56 21.58N 95.24E
Myitkyinā Myanmar 56 25.24N 97.25E
Mymensingh Bangla. 63 24.45N 90.24E
Myrdal Norway 41 60.44N 7.08E
Myrdalsjökull ice cap Iceland 40 63.40N 19.06W
Myrtle Beach town U.S.A. 113 33.42N 78.54W
Myrtle Creek town U.S.A. 108 43.01N 123.17W
Myrtleford Australia 93 36.35S 146.44E
Myrtle Point town U.S.A. 108 43.04N 124.08W
Mysen Norway 42 59.33N 11.20E
Myślenice Poland 37 49.51N 19.56E
Mysore India 60 12.18N 76.37E
Mystic U.S.A. 115 41.21N 71.58W
My Tho Vietnam 56 10.21N 106.21E
Mytishchi Russian Fed. 44 55.54N 37.47E
Mziha Tanzania 79 5.53S 37.48E
Mzimba Malawi 79 12.00S 33.39E

N

Naab r. Germany 39 49.01N 12.02E
Naalehu Hawaiian Is. 85 19.04N 155.35W
Na'ām r. Sudan 73 6.48N 29.57E
Na'an Israel 67 31.53N 34.51E
Naantali Finland 41 60.27N 22.02E
Naas Rep. of Ire. 15 53.13N 6.41W
Näätamö r. Norway 40 69.40N 29.30E
Nababeep R.S.A. 80 29.36S 17.44E
Nabadwīp India 63 23.25N 88.22E
Nabā, Jabal mtn. Jordan 67 31.46N 35.45E
Nabari r. Japan 57 34.45N 136.01E
Naberezhnyye Chelny Russian Fed. 44 55.42N 52.20E
Nabeul Tunisia 75 36.28N 10.44E
Nabeul d. Tunisia 32 36.45N 10.45E
Nābha India 62 30.22N 76.09E
Nabingora Uganda 79 0.31N 31.11E
Nabī Shu'ayb, Jabal an mtn. Yemen 71 15.17N 43.59E
Naboomspruit R.S.A. 80 24.31S 28.24E
Nabq Egypt 66 28.04N 34.26E
Nābulus Jordan 67 32.13N 35.16E
Nābulus d. Jordan 67 32.15N 35.17E
Nacala Mozambique 81 14.34S 40.41E
Nacchio Ethiopia 73 7.30N 40.15E
Nachikapau L. Canada 103 56.44N 68.00W
Nachingwea Tanzania 79 10.21S 38.46E
Nāchna India 62 27.30N 71.43E
Nacka Sweden 43 59.18N 18.10E
Naco Mexico 109 31.20N 109.56W
Nacogdoches U.S.A. 111 31.36N 94.39W
Nadela Spain 26 42.58N 7.30W
Nadiād India 62 22.42N 72.52E
Nador Morocco 74 35.12N 2.55W
Nadūshan Iran 65 32.03N 53.33E
Nadvoitsy Russian Fed. 44 63.56N 34.20E
Nadvornaya Ukraine 37 48.37N 24.30E
Nadym Russian Fed. 50 65.25N 72.40E
Naenwa India 62 25.46N 75.51E
Naerbö Norway 42 58.40N 5.39E
Naeröy Norway 40 64.48N 11.17E
Naestved Denmark 42 55.14N 11.46E
Nafada Nigeria 77 11.08N 11.20E
Nafishah Egypt 66 30.34N 32.15E
Naft-e Safid Iran 65 31.38N 49.20E
Nāg Pakistan 62 27.24N 65.08E
Naga Phil. 59 13.36N 123.12E
Nāgāland d. India 61 26.10N 94.30E
Nagambie Australia 93 36.48S 145.12E
Nagano Japan 57 36.39N 138.10E
Nagano d. Japan 57 35.33N 137.50E
Nagaoka Japan 57 37.30N 138.50E
Nagaon Assam India 63 26.21N 92.40E
Nāgappattinam India 61 10.45N 79.50E
Nagara r. Japan 57 35.01N 136.43E
Nagar Pārkar Pakistan 62 24.22N 70.45E
Nagarzê China 63 28.58N 90.24E
Nagasaki Japan 57 32.45N 129.52E
Nāgaur India 62 27.12N 73.44E
Nāgāvali r. India 63 18.13N 83.56E
Nāgda India 62 23.42S 75.25E
Nāgercoil India 60 8.11N 77.30E
Nagichot Sudan 73 4.16N 33.34E
Nagīna India 63 29.27N 78.27E
Nagles Mts. Rep. of Ire. 15 52.06N 8.26W
Nagold Germany 39 48.33N 8.43E
Nagorskoye Russian Fed. 44 58.18N 50.50E
Nagoya Japan 57 35.10N 136.55E
Nāgpur India 63 21.09N 79.06E
Naggên China 63 31.32N 96.13E
Nagqu China 63 31.30N 92.00E
Nagyatád Hungary 31 46.14N 17.22E
Nagybajom Hungary 31 46.23N 17.31E
Nagykanizsa Hungary 31 46.27N 16.59E
Naha Japan 53 26.10N 127.40E
Nahalal Israel 67 32.41N 35.12E
Nāhan India 63 30.33N 77.18E
Nahanni Butte town Canada 98 61.03N 123.31W
Nahariyya Israel 67 33.01N 35.05E
Nahāvand Iran 65 34.13N 48.23E
Nahe r. Germany 49 49.58N 7.57E
Nahf Israel 67 32.56N 35.19E
Nahr al Furāt r. Asia 65 31.00N 47.27E
Nahunta U.S.A. 113 31.12N 82.00W
Nai Ga Myanmar 56 27.48N 97.30E
Naila Germany 38 50.19N 11.42E
Naiman Qi China 54 42.53N 120.40E
Nain Canada 103 57.00N 61.40W
Nā'īn Iran 65 32.52N 53.05E
Naini Tāl India 63 29.23N 79.27E
Nainpur India 63 22.26N 80.07E
Nairn Canada 104 46.21N 81.36W
Nairn U.K. 14 57.35N 3.52W
Nairobi Kenya 79 1.17S 36.50E
Naita mtn. Ethiopia 73 5.31N 35.18E
Naivasha Kenya 79 0.44S 36.26E
Najac France 20 44.17N 2.00E
Najd f. Saudi Arabia 64 25.00N 45.00E
Nájera Spain 26 42.25N 2.44W
Naj 'Hammādī Egypt 64 26.04N 32.13E
Najrān see Abā as Su'ūd Saudi Arabia 71
Nāka Khārari Pakistan 62 25.15N 66.44E
Nakambe r. Burkina see White Volta r. Ghana 76
Nakaminato Japan 57 36.21N 140.36E
Nakano shima i. Japan 57 29.55N 129.55E
Nakape Sudan 73 4.10N 33.10E
Nakatsu Japan 57 33.37N 131.11E
Nakatsugawa Japan 57 35.29N 137.30E
Nak'fa Eritrea 72 16.43N 38.32E
Nakhichevan Azerbaijan 65 39.12N 45.24E
Nakhodka Russian Fed. 53 42.53N 132.54E
Nakhola India 63 26.07N 92.11E
Nakhon Pathom Thailand 56 13.50N 100.01E

Nakhon Ratchasima Thailand 56 14.58N 102.06E
Nakhon Si Thammarat Thailand 56 8.24N 99.58E
Nakhtarana India 62 23.20N 69.15E
Nakina Canada 102 50.10N 86.40W
Nakło Poland 37 53.08N 17.35E
Naknek U.S.A. 98 58.45N 157.00W
Nakskov Denmark 41 54.50N 11.09E
Nakten l. Sweden 40 65.50N 14.35E
Nakuru Kenya 79 0.16S 36.04E
Nāl r. Pakistan 62 26.02N 65.19E
Nalbāri India 63 26.26N 91.30E
Nalchik Russian Fed. 45 43.31N 43.38E
Nalón r. Spain 26 43.32N 6.04W
Nālūt Libya 75 31.52N 10.59E
Namacurra Mozambique 79 17.35S 37.00E
Namakī r. Iran 65 31.02N 55.20E
Namanga Kenya 79 2.33S 36.48E
Namangan Uzbekistan 52 40.59N 71.41E
Namanyere Tanzania 79 7.34S 31.00E
Namapa Mozambique 81 13.48S 39.44E
Namaponda Mozambique 81 15.51S 39.52E
Namari Senegal 74 15.05N 13.39W
Namarroi Mozambique 81 15.58S 36.55E
Namatele Tanzania 79 10.01S 38.26E
Namba Angola 78 11.32S 15.33E
Nambala Zambia 80 15.07S 27.02E
Nambour Australia 91 26.36S 152.59E
Nambucca Heads town Australia 93 30.38S 152.59E
Namco China 63 30.53N 91.06E
Nam Co l. China 63 30.45N 90.30E
Nam Dinh Vietnam 55 20.21N 106.09E
Namecala Mozambique 81 12.50S 39.38E
Nametil Mozambique 81 15.41S 39.30E
Namib Desert Namibia 80 23.00S 15.20E
Namibe Angola 78 15.10S 12.10E
Namibe d. Angola 80 15.30S 12.30E
Namibia Africa 80 21.30S 16.45E
Namīn Iran 65 38.25N 48.30E
Namlea Indonesia 59 3.15S 127.07E
Namling China 63 29.40N 89.03E
Namoi r. Australia 93 30.14S 148.28E
Namonuito i. Pacific Oc. 84 8.46N 150.02E
Namous, Oued wadi Algeria 74 30.28N 0.14W
Nampa Canada 100 56.02N 117.07W
Nampa U.S.A. 108 43.44N 116.34W
Nam Phan f. Vietnam 56 10.40N 106.00E
Nam Phong Thailand 56 16.45N 102.52E
Namp'o N. Korea 53 38.40N 125.30E
Nampula Mozambique 81 15.09S 39.14E
Nampula d. Mozambique 81 15.00S 39.00E
Namsen r. Norway 40 64.27N 12.19E
Namtu Myanmar 56 23.04N 97.26E
Namu Canada 100 51.52N 127.41W
Namuchabawashan mtn. China 61 29.30N 95.10E
Namungua Mozambique 79 13.11S 40.30E
Namur Belgium 16 50.28N 4.52E
Namur d. Belgium 16 50.20N 4.45E
Namur Canada 105 45.54N 74.56W
Namutoni Namibia 80 18.48S 16.58E
Namwala Zambia 78 15.44S 26.25E
Nanaimo Canada 100 49.10N 124.00W
Nanam N. Korea 57 41.43N 129.41E
Nanango Australia 91 26.42S 151.58E
Nanao Japan 57 37.03N 136.58E
Nanchang China 55 28.37N 115.57E
Nancheng China 55 27.35N 116.32E
Nanchong China 55 30.53N 106.05E
Nanchuan China 55 29.12N 107.30E
Nancy France 19 48.41N 6.12E
Nanda Devi mtn. India 63 30.23N 79.59E
Nandan China 55 24.59N 107.32E
Nānded India 62 19.09N 77.20E
Nandewar Range mts. Australia 93 30.20S 150.45E
Nāndgaon India 62 20.19N 74.39E
Nandi Fiji 84 17.48S 177.25E
Nandu Jiang r. China 55 20.04N 110.20E
Nandurbār India 62 21.22N 74.15E
Nandyāl India 61 15.29N 78.29E
Nanfeng China 55 27.10N 116.24E
Nanga Eboko Cameroon 77 4.41N 12.21E
Nānga Parbat mtn. Jammu & Kashmir 60 35.10N 74.35E
Nangapinoh Indonesia 58 0.20S 111.44E
Nangola Mali 76 12.41N 6.35W
Nangqên China 52 32.15N 96.13E
Nangrül Pīr India 62 20.19N 77.21E
Nang Xian China 55 29.03N 93.12E
Nanhui China 55 31.03N 121.46E
Nanjiang China 55 32.21N 106.50E
Nanjing China 55 32.02N 118.52E
Nanking see Nanjing China 55
Nanling China 55 30.56N 118.19E
Nan Ling mts. China 55 25.10N 110.00E
Nannine Australia 89 26.53S 118.20E
Nanning China 55 22.48N 108.18E
Nannup Australia 89 33.57S 115.42E
Nanortalik Greenland 99 60.09N 45.15W
Nānpāra India 63 27.52N 81.30E
Nanpi China 54 38.02N 116.42E
Nanping Fujian China 55 26.38N 118.10E
Nanpu Xi r. China 55 26.38N 118.10E
Nanri i. China 55 25.13N 119.30E
Nansa r. Spain 26 43.22N 4.29W
Nansei shotō is. Japan 53 26.30N 125.00E
Nansei-Shotō Trench Pacific Oc. 84 25.00N 129.00E
Nanshan is. S. China Sea 58 10.30N 116.00E
Nant France 20 44.01N 3.18E
Nantes France 18 47.13N 1.33W
Nanteuil-le-Haudouin France 19 49.08N 2.48E
Nanticoke U.S.A. 115 41.12N 76.00W
Nanton Canada 100 50.21N 113.46W
Nantong China 55 32.02N 120.55E
Nantou Taiwan 55 23.54N 120.41E
Nantucket U.S.A. 115 41.17N 70.06W
Nantucket I. U.S.A. 115 41.16N 70.03W

Nantucket Sd. U.S.A. 115 41.30N 70.15W
Nantwich U.K. 12 53.05N 2.31W
Nanumea i. Tuvalu 84 5.40S 176.10E
Nanwan Shuiku resr. China 55 32.05N 113.55E
Nanxi China 55 28.52N 104.59E
Nan Xian China 55 29.22N 112.25E
Nanxiong China 55 25.10N 114.16E
Nanyang China 55 33.07N 112.30E
Nanyō Japan 57 38.03N 140.10E
Nanzhang China 55 31.47N 111.42E
Nao, Cabo de la c. Spain 25 38.44N 0.14E
Naococane, Lac l. Canada 103 52.50N 70.40W
Naogaon Bangla. 63 24.47N 88.56E
Naokot Pakistan 62 24.51N 69.27E
Náousa Greece 34 40.37N 22.05E
Napa U.S.A. 108 38.18N 122.17W
Napadogan Canada 103 46.24N 67.01W
Napanee Canada 105 44.15N 76.57W
Napę Laos 56 18.18N 105.07E
Napier New Zealand 86 39.29S 176.58E
Napierville Canada 105 45.11N 73.25W
Naples see Napoli Italy 33
Naples Fla. U.S.A. 113 26.09N 81.48W
Naples N.Y. U.S.A. 114 42.37N 77.25W
Napo China 55 23.23N 105.48E
Napo r. Peru 122 3.30S 73.10W
Napoleon U.S.A. 112 41.24N 84.09W
Napoli Italy 33 40.51N 14.17E
Napoli, Golfo di g. Italy 33 40.45N 14.15E
Naqb Ishtar Jordan 66 30.00N 35.30E
Nara Japan 57 34.41N 135.50E
Nara d. Japan 57 34.27N 135.55E
Nara Mali 74 15.13N 7.20W
Nāra Pakistan 62 24.07N 69.07E
Naracoorte Australia 92 36.58S 140.46E
Naradhan Australia 93 33.39S 146.20E
Naraini India 63 25.11N 80.29E
Narathiwat Thailand 56 6.25N 101.48E
Nara Visa U.S.A. 111 35.37N 103.06W
Nārāyanganj Bangla. 63 23.37N 90.30E
Narbada r. see Narmada r. India 62
Narbonne France 20 43.11N 3.00E
Narcea Spain 26 43.28N 6.06W
Nardò Italy 33 40.11N 18.02E
Narembeen Australia 89 32.04S 118.23E
Nares Str. Canada 99 78.30N 75.00W
Naretha Australia 89 31.01S 124.50E
Nāri r. Pakistan 62 29.10N 67.50E
Naria Bangla. 63 23.18N 90.25E
Narita Japan 57 35.47N 140.19E
Närke f. Sweden 43 59.03N 14.55E
Narmada r. India 62 21.40N 73.00E
Närnaul India 62 28.03N 76.06E
Narni Italy 30 42.31N 12.31E
Naro Italy 32 37.17N 13.48E
Narodichi Ukraine 37 51.11N 29.01E
Narodnaya mtn. Russian Fed. 44 65.00N 61.00E
Narok Kenya 79 1.04S 35.54E
Nāro, Koh-i- mtn. Pakistan 62 29.15N 63.30E
Narón Spain 26 43.32N 8.10W
Narooma Australia 93 36.15S 150.06E
Narrabri Australia 93 30.20S 149.49E
Narrabri West Australia 93 30.22S 149.47E
Narran r. Australia 93 29.45S 147.20E
Narrandera Australia 93 34.36S 146.34E
Narran L. Australia 93 29.40S 147.25E
Narrogin Australia 89 32.58S 117.10E
Narromine Australia 93 32.17S 148.20E
Narsimhapur India 63 22.57N 79.12E
Narsingdi Bangla. 63 23.55N 90.43E
Narsinghgarh India 62 23.42N 77.06E
Narubis Namibia 80 26.56S 18.36E
Narva Russian Fed. 44 59.22N 28.17E
Narvik Norway 40 68.26N 17.25E
Nār, Wādī an Jordan 67 31.40N 35.27E
Narwana India 62 29.37N 76.07E
Naryan Mar Russian Fed. 44 67.37N 53.02E
Naryilco Australia 92 28.41S 141.50E
Naryn Kyrgyzstan 52 41.24N 76.00E
Nasa mtn. Norway 40 66.29N 15.23E
Nasarawa Nigeria 77 8.35N 7.44E
Nasbinals France 20 44.40N 3.03E
Naseby New Zealand 86 45.01S 170.09E
Nashua Iowa U.S.A. 110 42.57N 92.32W
Nashua Mont. U.S.A. 108 48.08N 106.22W
Nashua N.H. U.S.A. 115 42.46N 71.27W
Nashville U.S.A. 113 36.10N 86.50W
Naşīb Syria 67 32.33N 36.11E
Našice Croatia 35 45.29N 18.06E
Näsijärvi l. Finland 41 61.37N 23.42E
Nāsik India 62 19.59N 73.48E
Nāşir Sudan 73 8.36N 33.04E
Nasīrābād India 62 26.18N 74.44E
Nasīrābād Pakistan 62 28.23N 68.24E
Nāşir, Buḩayrat l. Egypt 72 22.40N 32.00E
Naskaupi r. Canada 103 53.45N 60.50W
Naşr Egypt 66 30.36N 30.23E
Nass r. Canada 100 55.00N 129.50W
Nassau Bahamas 113 25.05N 77.21W
Nassau I. Cook Is. 84 11.33S 165.25W
Nassereith Austria 39 47.19N 10.50E
Nasser, L. see Nāşir, Buḩayrat l. Egypt 72
Nassian Côte d'Ivoire 76 8.33N 3.18W
Nässjö Sweden 43 57.39N 14.41E
Nastapoca r. Canada 102 56.55N 76.33W
Nastapoka Is. Canada 102 57.00N 77.00W
Nata Botswana 80 20.12S 26.12E
Natal Brazil 123 5.46S 35.15W
Natal Indonesia 58 0.35N 99.07E
Natal Basin f. Indian Oc. 49 35.00S 39.00E
Natanes Plateau f. U.S.A. 109 33.35N 110.15W
Naţanz Iran 65 33.30N 51.57E
Natashquan Canada 103 50.11N 61.49W
Natashquan r. Canada 103 50.06N 61.49W
Natchez U.S.A. 111 31.34N 91.23W
Natchitoches U.S.A. 111 31.46N 93.05W
Nathalia Australia 93 36.02S 145.14E
Nāthdwāra India 62 24.56N 73.49E

National City U.S.A. 109 32.40N 117.06W
Natitingou Benin 77 10.17N 1.19E
Natl Jordan 67 31.39N 35.52E
Natoma U.S.A. 110 39.11N 99.01W
Natron, L. Tanzania 79 2.18S 36.05E
Naṭrūn, Wādī an f. Egypt 66 30.25N 30.18E
Natuna Besar i. Indonesia 58 4.00N 108.20E
Naturaliste, C. Australia 89 33.32S 115.01E
Naubinway U.S.A. 112 46.05N 85.27W
Naucelle France 20 44.12N 2.20E
Nauders Austria 39 46.53N 10.30E
Nauen Germany 38 52.36N 12.52E
Naugatuck U.S.A. 115 41.30N 73.04W
Naumburg Germany 38 51.09N 11.48E
Nāʿūr Jordan 67 31.53N 35.50E
Nauroz Kalāt Pakistan 62 28.47N 65.38E
Nauru Pacific Oc. 84 0.32S 166.55E
Naushahro Fīroz Pakistan 62 26.50N 68.07E
Naustdal Norway 41 61.31N 5.43E
Nauta Peru 122 4.30S 73.40W
Nautanwa India 63 27.26N 83.25E
Nautla Mexico 116 20.13N 96.47W
Nava Mexico 111 28.25N 100.46W
Nava r. Zaïre 79 1.45N 27.06E
Nava del Rey Spain 26 41.20N 5.05W
Navahermosa Spain 27 39.38N 4.28W
Navalcarnero Spain 26 40.18N 4.00W
Navalmoral de la Mata Spain 27 39.54N 5.32W
Navalvillar de Pela Spain 27 39.06N 5.28W
Navan Rep. of Ire. 15 53.39N 6.42W
Navāpur India 62 21.15N 73.55E
Navarra d. Spain 25 42.45N 1.30W
Navarre Australia 92 36.54S 143.09E
Navarre U.S.A. 114 40.43N 81.32W
Navarro Argentina 125 35.00S 59.10W
Navasota U.S.A. 111 30.23N 96.05W
Naver r. U.K. 14 58.32N 4.14W
Navia Spain 26 43.32N 6.43W
Navia r. Spain 26 43.33N 6.44W
Navlya Russian Fed. 44 52.51N 34.30E
Navoi Uzbekistan 9 40.04N 65.20E
Navojoa Mexico 109 27.06N 109.26W
Návpaktos Greece 35 38.23N 21.50E
Návplion Greece 35 37.34N 22.48E
Navrongo Ghana 76 10.51N 1.03W
Navsāri India 62 20.57N 72.59E
Nawá Syria 67 32.53N 36.03E
Nawābganj Bangla. 63 24.36N 88.17E
Nawābganj India 63 26.56N 81.13E
Nawābshāh Pakistan 62 26.15N 68.25E
Nawāda India 63 24.53N 85.32E
Nāwah Afghan. 62 32.19N 67.53E
Nawākot Nepal 63 27.55N 85.10E
Nawa Kot Pakistan 62 28.20N 71.22E
Nawalgarh India 62 27.51N 75.16E
Nawāpāra India 63 20.58N 81.51E
Naxi China 55 28.44N 105.27E
Náxos Greece 35 37.06N 25.23E
Náxos i. Greece 35 37.02N 25.35E
Nayāgarh India 63 20.08N 85.06E
Nayak Afghan. 62 34.44N 66.57E
Nayarit d. Mexico 116 22.00N 104.00W
Nāy Band Iran 65 32.20N 57.34E
Nāy Band Iran 65 27.23N 52.38E
Nāy Band, Kūh-e mtn. Iran 65 32.25N 57.30E
Nayoro Japan 57 44.21N 142.28E
Nazaré Brazil 123 13.00S 39.00W
Nazaré Portugal 27 39.36N 9.04W
Nazareth see Nazerat Israel 67
Nazareth Trough f. Indian Oc. 49 15.00S 64.00E
Nazarovka Russian Fed. 44 54.19N 41.20E
Nazas r. Mexico 116 25.34N 103.25W
Nazca Peru 122 14.53S 74.54W
Nazerat Israel 67 32.41N 35.16E
Nazilli Turkey 64 37.55N 28.20E
Nazinon r. Burkina see Red Volta r. Ghana 76
Nāzir Hāt Bangla. 63 22.38N 91.47E
Nazrēt Ethiopia 73 8.32N 39.22E
Nazuo China 55 24.06N 105.19E
Nchanga Zambia 79 12.30S 27.55E
Ncheu Malaŵi 79 14.50S 34.45E
N'dalatando Angola 78 9.12S 14.54E
Ndali Benin 77 9.53N 2.45E
Ndasegera mtn. Tanzania 79 1.58S 35.41E
Ndélé C.A.R. 73 8.24N 20.39E
Ndélélé Cameroon 77 4.03N 14.55E
N'Dendé Gabon 78 2.20S 11.23E
Ndikiniméki Cameroon 77 4.46N 10.49E
N'Djamena Chad 77 12.10N 14.59E
Ndjolé Gabon 78 0.07S 10.45E
Ndola Zambia 80 12.58S 28.39E
Ndoro Gabon 78 0.24S 12.34E
Ndrhamcha, Sebkha de f. Mauritania 74 18.45N 15.48W
Ndungu Tanzania 79 4.25S 38.04E
Nea r. Norway 40 63.15N 11.00E
Neagh, Lough U.K. 15 54.36N 6.25W
Néa Kallikrátia Greece 34 40.21N 23.01E
Neale, L. Australia 90 24.21S 130.04E
Néa Páfos Cyprus 66 34.45N 32.25E
Neápolis Greece 34 40.20N 21.24E
Neápolis Greece 35 36.31N 23.03E
Neápolis Kríti Greece 35 35.15N 25.37E
Neath U.K. 13 51.39N 3.49W
Nebit-Dag Turkmenistan 65 39.31N 54.24E
Nebraska d. U.S.A. 110 41.50N 100.06W
Nebraska City U.S.A. 110 40.41N 95.52W
Nebrodi, Monti mts. Italy 33 37.55N 14.35E
Nechako r. Canada 100 53.30N 122.44W
Neches r. U.S.A. 111 29.55N 93.50W
Neckar r. Germany 39 49.31N 8.26E
Neckarsulm Germany 39 49.12N 9.13E
Necochea Argentina 125 38.31S 58.46W
Necuto Angola 78 4.55S 12.38E
Nèdong China 63 29.14N 91.48E
Nedroma Algeria 74 35.00N 1.44W
Nedstrand Norway 42 59.21N 5.51E
Needles U.S.A. 109 34.51N 114.37W

Neepawa Canada 101 50.13N 99.29W
Neerpelt Belgium 16 51.13N 5.28E
Nefta Tunisia 75 33.52N 7.33E
Neftegorsk Russian Fed. 45 44.21N 39.44E
Nefyn U.K. 12 52.55N 4.31W
Negara Indonesia 59 8.21S 114.35E
Negaunee U.S.A. 112 46.31N 87.37W
Negba Israel 67 31.40N 34.41E
Negele Ethiopia 73 5.20N 39.36E
Negev des. see HaNegev des. Israel 66
Negoiu mtn. Romania 37 45.36N 24.32E
Negomano Mozambique 79 11.26S 38.30E
Negombo Sri Lanka 61 7.13N 79.50E
Negotin Yugo. 37 44.14N 22.33E
Negrais, C. Myanmar 56 16.00N 94.12E
Negra, Punta c. Peru 120 6.06S 81.09W
Negreira Spain 26 42.54N 8.44W
Negritos Peru 122 4.42S 81.18W
Negro r. Argentina 125 40.50S 63.00W
Negro r. Brazil 122 3.00S 59.55W
Negro r. Uruguay 125 33.27S 58.20W
Negro, Baia del b. Somali Rep. 71 7.52N 49.50E
Negros i. Phil. 59 10.00N 123.00E
Negru-Vodă Romania 37 43.50N 28.12E
Neheim-Hüsten Germany 38 51.27N 7.57E
Neijiang China 55 29.29N 105.03E
Nei Monggol Zizhiqu d. China 54 41.50N 112.30E
Neisse r. Germany 38 52.04N 14.46E
Neiva Colombia 122 2.58N 75.15W
Nejanilini L. Canada 101 59.33N 97.48W
Nejdek Czech Republic 39 50.17N 12.42E
Nejo Ethiopia 73 9.30N 35.30E
Nek'emtē Ethiopia 73 9.02N 36.31E
Neksō Denmark 43 55.04N 15.09E
Nelidovo Russian Fed. 44 56.13N 32.46E
Neligh U.S.A. 110 42.08N 98.02W
Nelkan Russian Fed. 51 57.40N 136.04E
Nelligen Australia 93 35.39S 150.06E
Nellore India 61 14.29N 80.00E
Nelson Australia 92 38.04S 141.05E
Nelson Canada 100 49.30N 117.20W
Nelson r. Canada 101 57.04N 92.30W
Nelson New Zealand 86 41.18S 173.17E
Nelson U.K. 12 53.50N 2.14W
Nelson U.S.A. 109 35.30N 113.16W
Nelson Bay town Australia 93 32.43S 152.08E
Nelson, C. Australia 92 38.27S 141.35E
Nelson, Estrecho str. Chile 125 51.33S 74.40W
Nelson Forks Canada 100 59.30N 124.00W
Nelson-Marlborough d. New Zealand 86 41.40S 173.40E
Nelsonville U.S.A. 114 39.27N 82.14W
Nelspoort R.S.A. 80 32.07S 23.00E
Nelspruit R.S.A. 80 25.27S 30.58E
Néma Mauritania 74 16.40N 7.15W
Nembe Nigeria 77 4.32N 6.25E
Neméa Greece 35 37.49N 22.40E
Nemours France 19 48.16N 2.42E
Nemunas r. Lithuania 41 55.18N 21.23E
Nemuro Japan 57 43.22N 145.36E
Nemuro kaikyō str. Japan 57 44.00N 145.50E
Nenagh Rep. of Ire. 15 52.52N 8.13W
Nenana U.S.A. 98 64.35N 149.20W
Nene r. U.K. 12 52.49N 0.12E
Nenjiang China 53 49.10N 125.15E
Neodesha U.S.A. 111 37.25N 95.41W
Néon Karlovásion Greece 35 37.47N 26.40E
Néon Petrítsi Greece 34 41.16N 23.15E
Neosho U.S.A. 111 36.52N 94.22W
Neosho r. U.S.A. 110 35.48N 95.18W
Nepal Asia 63 28.00N 84.00E
Nepālganj Nepal 63 28.03N 81.38E
Nepa Nagar India 62 21.28N 76.23E
Nephi U.S.A. 108 39.43N 111.50W
Nephin mtn. Rep. of Ire. 15 54.02N 9.38W
Nephin Beg Range mts. Rep. of Ire. 15 54.00N 9.37W
Nepomuk Czech Republic 38 49.29N 13.36E
Nera r. Italy 30 42.26N 12.24E
Nera r. Italy 28 42.33N 12.43E
Nérac France 20 44.08N 0.20E
Nerekhta Russian Fed. 44 57.30N 40.40E
Néret, Lac l. Canada 103 54.45N 70.50W
Neretva r. Bosnia-Herzegovina 31 43.01N 17.27E
Neriquinha Angola 80 15.50S 21.40E
Nerja Spain 27 36.44N 3.52W
Néronde France 17 45.50N 4.14E
Nérondes France 19 47.00N 2.49E
Nerva France 20 37.42N 6.32W
Nes Neth. 16 53.27N 5.46E
Nesbyen Norway 41 60.34N 9.09E
Nesher Israel 67 32.46N 35.03E
Nesle France 19 49.46N 2.55E
Nesna Norway 40 66.13N 13.04E
Nesöy i. Norway 40 66.35N 12.40E
Nesselwang Germany 38 47.37N 10.30E
Ness, Loch U.K. 14 57.16N 4.30W
Nestaocano r. Canada 103 48.40N 73.25W
Nestórion Greece 34 40.24N 21.02E
Néstos r. Greece 34 40.41N 24.44E
Nesttun Norway 42 60.19N 5.23E
Nesvizh Belarus 37 53.16N 26.40E
Nes Ziyyona Israel 67 31.55N 34.48E
Netanya Israel 67 32.20N 34.51E
Netcong U.S.A. 115 40.54N 74.42W
Netherlands Europe 16 52.00N 5.30E
Netherlands Antilles S. America 117 12.30N 69.00W
Neto r. Italy 33 39.13N 17.08E
Netolice Czech Republic 39 49.03N 14.12E
Netrakona Bangla. 63 24.53N 90.43E
Nettilling L. Canada 99 66.30N 70.40W
Nettuno Italy 32 41.27N 12.39E
Neubrandenburg Germany 38 53.33N 13.15E
Neuburg an der Donau Germany 39 48.44N 11.11E
Neuchâtel Switz. 39 47.00N 6.56E
Neuchâtel d. Switz. 39 47.02N 6.50E
Neuchâtel, Lac de l. Switz. 39 46.52N 6.50E

Neuenhagen Germany 38 52.32N 13.41E
Neuenhaus Germany 38 52.30N 6.59E
Neuf-Brisach France 19 48.01N 7.32E
Neufchâteau Belgium 16 49.51N 5.26E
Neufchâteau France 19 48.21N 5.42E
Neufchâtel France 18 49.44N 1.27E
Neuhausen Switz. 39 47.41N 8.37E
Neuillé-Pont-Pierre France 18 47.33N 0.33E
Neu-Isenberg Germany 39 50.03N 8.41E
Neumarkt Austria 39 48.16N 13.45E
Neumarkt Germany 39 49.16N 11.28E
Neumarkt in Steiermark Austria 31 47.05N 14.26E
Neumarkt-Sankt-Veit Germany 39 48.22N 12.30E
Neumünster Germany 38 54.04N 9.59E
Neunkirchen Germany 39 49.30N 7.29E
Neuquén Argentina 125 39.00S 68.05W
Neuquén d. Argentina 125 38.30S 70.00W
Neuquén r. Argentina 125 39.02S 68.07W
Neuruppin Germany 38 52.55N 12.48E
Neuse r. U.S.A. 113 35.06N 76.30W
Neusiedler See l. Austria 36 47.52N 16.45E
Neuss Germany 38 51.12N 6.41E
Neustadt Bayern Germany 39 49.34N 10.37E
Neustadt Bayern Germany 39 49.44N 12.11E
Neustadt B.-Würt. Germany 39 47.54N 8.13E
Neustadt Sch.-Hol. Germany 38 54.06N 10.48E
Neustadt Thüringen Germany 38 50.44N 11.44E
Neustadt an der Weinstrasse Germany 39 49.21N 8.08E
Neustadt bei Coburg Thüingen Germany 38 50.19N 11.07E
Neustrelitz Germany 38 53.21N 13.04E
Neu-Ulm Germany 39 48.23N 10.01E
Neuvic France 20 45.23N 2.16E
Neuville-de-Poitou France 18 46.41N 0.15E
Neuville-sur-Saône France 21 45.52N 4.51E
Neuwied Germany 39 50.25N 7.27E
Nevada U.S.A. 111 37.51N 94.22W
Nevada d. U.S.A. 108 39.00N 116.10W
Nevada, Sierra mts. Spain 27 37.05N 3.10W
Nevada, Sierra mts. U.S.A. 106 37.30N 119.00W
Nevanka Russian Fed. 51 56.31N 98.57E
Nevatim Israel 67 31.13N 34.54E
Nevel Russian Fed. 44 56.00N 29.59E
Nevers France 19 47.00N 3.09E
Nevertire Australia 93 31.52S 147.47E
Nevesinje Bosnia-Herzegovina 31 43.15N 18.07E
Nevinnomyssk Russian Fed. 45 44.38N 41.59E
Nevlunghamn Norway 42 58.58N 9.52E
Nevşehir Turkey 64 38.38N 34.43E
Newala Tanzania 79 10.56S 39.15E
New Albany Ind. U.S.A. 112 38.17N 85.50W
New Albany Miss. U.S.A. 111 34.29N 89.00W
New Amsterdam Guyana 123 6.18N 57.30W
New Angledool Australia 93 29.06S 147.57E
Newark Del. U.S.A. 115 39.41N 75.45W
Newark N.J. U.S.A. 115 40.44N 74.10W
Newark N.Y. U.S.A. 114 43.03N 77.06W
Newark Ohio U.S.A. 114 40.04N 82.24W
Newark-on-Trent U.K. 12 53.06N 0.48E
Newark Valley town U.S.A. 115 42.14N 76.11W
New Athens U.S.A. 110 38.19N 89.53W
New Bedford U.S.A. 115 41.38N 70.56W
Newberg U.S.A. 108 45.18N 122.58W
New Berlin U.S.A. 115 42.38N 75.20W
New Bern U.S.A. 113 35.05N 77.04W
Newberry Mich. U.S.A. 112 46.22N 85.30W
Newberry S.C. U.S.A. 113 34.17N 81.39W
New Bethlehem U.S.A. 114 41.00N 79.20W
Newbiggin-by-the-Sea U.K. 12 55.11N 1.30W
New Bloomfield U.S.A. 114 40.25N 77.11W
Newboro Canada 105 44.39N 76.19W
Newboro L. Canada 105 44.38N 76.20W
New Boston U.S.A. 105 43.47N 75.45W
New Braunfels U.S.A. 111 29.42N 98.08W
New Britain i. P.N.G. 87 6.00S 150.00E
New Britain U.S.A. 115 41.40N 72.47W
New Brunswick d. Canada 103 46.50N 66.00W
New Brunswick U.S.A. 115 40.29N 74.27W
Newburgh U.S.A. 115 41.30N 74.01W
Newbury U.K. 13 51.24N 1.19W
Newburyport U.S.A. 115 42.49N 70.53W
New Bussa Nigeria 77 9.53N 4.29E
New Caledonia is. see Nouvelle Calédonie is. Pacific Oc. 84
Newcastle Australia 93 32.55S 151.46E
Newcastle N.B. Canada 103 47.00N 65.34W
Newcastle Ont. Canada 104 43.55N 78.35W
Newcastle R.S.A. 80 27.44S 29.55E
Newcastle U.K. 15 54.13N 5.53W
New Castle Penn. U.S.A. 114 41.00N 80.20W
Newcastle Wyo. U.S.A. 108 43.50N 104.11W
Newcastle B. Australia 90 10.50S 142.37E
Newcastle Emlyn U.K. 13 52.02N 4.29W
Newcastle-under-Lyme U.K. 12 53.02N 2.15W
Newcastle upon Tyne U.K. 12 54.58N 1.36W
Newcastle Waters town Australia 90 17.24S 133.24E
Newcastle West Rep. of Ire. 15 52.26N 9.04W
New City U.S.A. 115 41.09N 73.59W
Newcomerstown U.S.A. 114 40.16N 81.36W
New Concord U.S.A. 114 40.00N 81.44W
New Cumberland U.S.A. 114 40.30N 80.36W
Newdegate Australia 89 33.06S 119.01E
New Delhi India 62 28.36N 77.12E
New Denver Canada 100 50.00N 117.25W
New England U.S.A. 110 46.32N 102.52W
New England Range mts. Australia 93 30.30S 151.50E
Newenham, C. U.S.A. 98 58.37N 162.12W
Newent U.K. 13 51.56N 2.24W
Newfane U.S.A. 114 43.17N 78.43W
New Forest f. U.K. 13 50.50N 1.35W
Newfoundland d. Canada 103 54.00N 60.10W
Newfoundland i. Canada 103 48.30N 56.00W
New Freedom U.S.A. 114 39.44N 76.42W
New Galloway U.K. 14 55.05N 4.09W
Newgate Canada 100 49.01N 115.08W
New Glasgow Canada 103 45.35N 62.39W
New Guinea i. Austa. 59 5.00S 140.00E

New Hamburg Canada 104 43.23N 80.42W
New Hampshire d. U.S.A. 112 43.35N 71.40W
New Hanover i. Pacific Oc. 87 2.00S 150.00E
Newhaven U.K. 13 50.47N 0.04E
New Haven U.S.A. 115 41.18N 72.56W
New Hebrides Basin Pacific Oc. 84 16.00S 162.00E
New Holland U.S.A. 114 40.06N 76.05W
New Iberia U.S.A. 111 30.00N 91.49W
New Ireland i. P.N.G. 87 2.30S 151.30E
New Jersey d. U.S.A. 115 40.15N 74.30W
New Kensington U.S.A. 114 40.34N 79.46W
New Lexington U.S.A. 114 39.43N 82.31W
New Liskeard Canada 102 47.31N 79.41W
New London Conn. U.S.A. 115 41.21N 72.07W
New London Minn. U.S.A. 110 45.18N 94.56W
New London Ohio U.S.A. 114 41.05N 82.24W
Newman Australia 88 23.22S 119.43E
Newman U.S.A. 109 31.55N 106.20W
Newman, Mt. Australia 88 23.15S 119.33E
Newmarket Canada 104 44.03N 79.28W
Newmarket Rep. of Ire. 15 52.13N 9.00W
Newmarket U.K. 13 52.15N 0.23E
Newmarket U.S.A. 115 43.05N 70.56W
Newmarket on Fergus Rep. of Ire. 15 52.46N 8.55W
New Marshfield U.S.A. 114 39.20N 82.15W
New Martinsville U.S.A. 114 39.39N 80.52W
New Matamoras U.S.A. 114 39.31N 81.06W
New Meadows U.S.A. 108 44.58N 116.32W
New Mexico d. U.S.A. 108 33.30N 106.00W
New Milford Conn. U.S.A. 115 41.35N 73.25W
New Milford Penn. U.S.A. 115 41.52N 75.44W
Newnan U.S.A. 113 33.23N 84.48W
New Norcia Australia 89 30.58S 116.15E
New Norfolk Australia 91 42.46S 147.02E
New Orleans U.S.A. 111 29.58N 90.07W
New Oxford U.S.A. 114 39.52N 77.04W
New Philadelphia U.S.A. 114 40.30N 81.27W
New Plymouth New Zealand 86 39.03S 174.04E
Newport Mayo Rep. of Ire. 15 53.53N 9.34W
Newport Tipperary Rep. of Ire. 15 52.42N 8.25W
Newport Dyfed U.K. 13 52.01N 4.51W
Newport Essex U.K. 13 51.58N 0.13E
Newport Gwent U.K. 13 51.34N 2.59W
Newport Hants. U.K. 13 50.43N 1.18W
Newport Ark. U.S.A. 111 35.35N 91.16W
Newport Maine U.S.A. 112 44.50N 69.17W
Newport N.H. U.S.A. 115 43.21N 72.09W
Newport N.Y. U.S.A. 115 43.11N 75.01W
Newport Oreg. U.S.A. 108 44.38N 124.03W
Newport Penn. U.S.A. 114 40.29N 77.08W
Newport R.I. U.S.A. 115 41.13N 71.18W
Newport Vt. U.S.A. 105 44.57N 72.12W
Newport News U.S.A. 113 36.59N 76.26W
New Providence I. Bahamas 113 25.25N 78.35W
Newquay U.K. 13 50.24N 5.06W
New Quay U.K. 13 52.13N 4.22W
New Radnor U.K. 13 52.15N 3.10W
New Rochelle U.S.A. 115 40.55N 73.47W
New Rockford U.S.A. 110 47.41N 99.15W
New Romney U.K. 13 50.59N 0.58E
New Ross Rep. of Ire. 15 52.24N 6.57W
Newry U.K. 15 54.11N 6.21W
New Scone U.K. 14 56.25N 3.25W
New Smyrna Beach town U.S.A. 113 29.01N 80.56W
New South Wales d. Australia 93 32.40S 147.40E
Newton Ill. U.S.A. 110 38.59N 88.10W
Newton Iowa U.S.A. 110 41.42N 93.03W
Newton Kans. U.S.A. 111 38.03N 97.21W
Newton Mass. U.S.A. 115 42.21N 71.11W
Newton N.J. U.S.A. 115 41.03N 74.45W
Newton Abbot U.K. 13 50.32N 3.37W
Newton Aycliffe U.K. 12 54.36N 1.34W
Newton Falls town N.Y. U.S.A. 105 44.13N 74.59W
Newton Falls town Ohio U.S.A. 114 41.11N 80.59W
Newtonmore U.K. 14 57.04N 4.08W
Newton Stewart U.K. 14 54.57N 4.29W
Newtown U.K. 13 52.31N 3.19W
Newtownabbey U.K. 15 54.39N 5.57W
Newtownards U.K. 15 54.35N 5.41W
Newtown Butler U.K. 15 54.12N 7.22W
Newtown St. Boswells U.K. 14 55.35N 2.40W
Newtownstewart U.K. 15 54.43N 7.25W
New Washington U.S.A. 114 40.58N 82.51W
New Waterford Canada 103 46.15N 60.05W
New Westminster Canada 100 49.10N 122.52W
New York U.S.A. 115 40.43N 74.01W
New York d. U.S.A. 115 40.43N 74.01W
New York State Barge Canal U.S.A. 114 43.05N 78.43W
New Zealand Austa. 86 41.00S 175.00E
New Zealand Plateau Pacific Oc. 84 50.00S 170.00E
Nexon France 20 45.41N 1.11E
Neya Russian Fed. 44 58.18N 43.40E
Neyagawa Japan 57 34.46N 135.38E
Neyriz Iran 65 29.14N 54.19E
Neyshābūr Iran 65 36.13N 58.49E
Nezhin Ukraine 37 51.03N 31.54E
Ngala Nigeria 77 12.21N 14.10E
Ngambwe Rapids f. Zambia 78 17.08S 24.10E
Ngami, L. Botswana 80 20.32S 22.38E
Ngamiland d. Botswana 80 19.40S 22.00E
Ngamiland f. Botswana 80 20.00S 22.30E
Ngamring China 63 29.14N 87.10E
Ngangla Ringco l. China 63 31.40N 83.00E
Nganglong Kangri mtn. China 63 32.40N 81.00E
Nganglong Kangri mts. China 63 32.50N 82.00E
Ngangzê Co l. China 63 31.00N 87.00E
Nganjuk Indonesia 59 7.36S 111.56E
N'Gao Congo 78 2.28S 15.40E
Ngaoundéré Cameroon 77 7.20N 13.35E
Ngara-Binsam Congo 78 1.36N 13.30E
Ngardlam C.A.R. 73 9.00N 20.58E
Ngaruawahia New Zealand 86 37.40S 175.09E
Ngaruroro r. New Zealand 86 39.34S 176.54E
Ngatangiia Rarotonga Cook Is. 84 21.14S 159.44W
Ngau i. Fiji 84 18.02S 179.18E
Ngauruhoe mtn. New Zealand 86 39.10S 175.35E

Ngawi Indonesia **59** 7.23S 111.22E
Ngaya *mtn.* C.A.R. **73** 9.18N 23.28E
Ng'iro, Mt. Kenya **79** 2.06N 36.44E
N'Giva Angola **80** 17.03S 15.47E
Ngoc Linh *mtn.* Vietnam **56** 15.04N 107.59E
Ngoma Zambia **78** 16.04S 26.06E
Ngomba Tanzania **79** 8.16S 32.51E
Ngomeni Kenya **79** 3.00S 40.11E
Ngong Kenya **79** 1.22S 36.40E
Ngonye Falls *f.* Zambia **78** 16.35S 23.39E
Ngorongoro Crater *f.* Tanzania **79** 3.13S 35.32E
Ngouo, Mont *mtn.* C.A.R. **73** 7.55N 24.38E
Ngozi Burundi **79** 2.52S 29.50E
Nguigmi Niger **77** 14.00N 13.11E
Nguru Nigeria **77** 12.53N 10.30E
Nguruka Tanzania **79** 5.08S 30.58E
Ngwaketse *d.* Botswana **80** 25.10S 25.00E
Ngwerere Zambia **79** 15.18S 28.20E
Nhaccongo Mozambique **81** 24.18S 35.14E
Nhachengue Mozambique **81** 22.52S 35.10E
Nhandugue *r.* Mozambique **81** 18.47S 34.30E
Nha Trang Vietnam **56** 12.15N 109.10E
Nhill Australia **92** 36.20S 141.40E
Nhulunbuy Australia **90** 12.11S 136.46E
Nhungo Angola **80** 13.17S 20.06E
Niafounké Mali **74** 15.56N 4.00W
Niagara Canada **104** 43.05N 79.20W
Niagara Escarpment *f.* Canada **104** 44.25N 80.30W
Niagara Falls *town* Canada **104** 43.06N 79.04W
Niagara Falls *town* U.S.A. **114** 43.06N 79.02W
Niah Malaysia **58** 3.52N 113.44E
Niamey Niger **77** 13.32N 2.05E
Niamey *d.* Niger **77** 14.00N 1.40E
Nianforando Guinea **76** 9.37N 10.36W
Niangara Zaïre **79** 3.47N 27.54E
Nia-Nia Zaïre **79** 1.30N 27.41E
Niapa, Gunung *mtn.* Indonesia **58** 1.45N 117.30E
Nias *i.* Indonesia **58** 1.05N 97.30E
Niassa *d.* Mozambique **79** 13.00S 36.30E
Nibe Denmark **42** 56.59N 9.38E
Nicaragua C. America **117** 13.00N 85.00W
Nicaragua, Lago de *l.* Nicaragua **117** 11.30N 85.30W
Nicastro Italy **33** 38.59N 16.20E
Nice France **21** 43.42N 7.16E
Nichelino Italy **30** 44.59N 7.38E
Nicholson Australia **88** 18.02S 128.54E
Nicholson *r.* Australia **90** 17.31S 139.36E
Nicholson U.S.A. **115** 41.38N 75.47W
Nicholson L. Canada **101** 62.40N 102.35W
Nicobar Is. India **56** 8.00N 93.30E
Nicolet Canada **105** 46.13N 72.37W
Nicolet *r.* Canada **105** 46.14N 72.39W
Nicolls Town Bahamas **117** 25.08N 78.00W
Nicosia *see* Levkosía Cyprus **66**
Nicosia Italy **33** 37.45N 14.24E
Nicotera Italy **33** 38.34N 15.57E
Nicoya, Golfo de *g.* Costa Rica **117** 9.30N 85.00W
Nicoya, Península de *pen.* Costa Rica **117** 10.30N 85.30W
Nid *r.* Norway **42** 58.24N 8.48E
Nida *r.* Poland **37** 50.18N 20.52E
Nido, Sierra de *mts.* Mexico **109** 29.30N 107.00W
Nidzica Poland **37** 53.22N 20.26E
Niebüll Germany **38** 54.48N 8.50E
Niederbronn-les-Bains France **19** 48.57N 7.38E
Niederösterreich *d.* Austria **36** 48.20N 15.50E
Niedersachsen *d.* Germany **38** 52.53N 9.30E
Niekerkshoop R.S.A. **80** 29.19S 22.48E
Niellé Côte d'Ivoire **76** 10.05N 5.28W
Nienburg Germany **38** 52.38N 9.13E
Niéré Chad **72** 14.30N 21.09E
Niers *r.* Neth. **16** 51.43N 5.56E
Niesky Germany **38** 51.17N 14.49E
Nieuw Nickerie Surinam **123** 5.57N 56.59W
Nieuwpoort Belgium **16** 51.08N 2.45E
Nièvre *d.* France **19** 47.05N 3.30E
Nifi Ya'qūb Jordan **67** 31.30N 35.14E
Niğde Turkey **64** 37.58N 34.42E
Niger Africa **70** 17.00N 10.00E
Niger *d.* Nigeria **77** 9.50N 6.00E
Niger *r.* Nigeria **77** 4.15N 6.05E
Niger Delta Nigeria **77** 4.00N 6.10E
Nigeria Africa **77** 9.00N 9.00E
Nightcaps New Zealand **86** 45.58S 168.02E
Nightingale I. Tristan da Cunha **127** 37.28S 12.32W
Nigrita Greece **34** 40.55N 23.30E
Nihing *r.* Pakistan **62** 26.00N 62.44E
Nihoa *i.* Hawaiian Is. **84** 23.03N 161.55W
Niigata Japan **57** 37.58N 139.02E
Niihama Japan **57** 33.57N 133.15E
Niihau *i.* Hawaiian Is. **85** 21.55N 160.10W
Niiza Japan **57** 35.48N 139.34E
Níjar Spain **27** 36.58N 2.11W
Nijmegen Neth. **16** 51.50N 5.52E
Nikel Russian Fed. **40** 69.20N 30.00E
Nikiniki Indonesia **89** 9.49S 124.29E
Nikki Benin **77** 9.55N 3.18E
Nikolayev Ukraine **45** 46.57N 32.00E
Nikolayevskiy Russian Fed. **45** 50.05N 45.32E
Nikolayevsk-na-Amure Russian Fed. **51** 53.20N 140.44E
Nikolsk Russian Fed. **44** 59.33N 45.30E
Nikopol Bulgaria **34** 43.43N 24.54E
Nikopol Ukraine **45** 47.34N 34.25E
Niksar Turkey **64** 40.35N 36.59E
Nikshahr Iran **65** 26.14N 60.15E
Nikšić Yugo. **34** 42.46N 18.56E
Nikumaroro *i.* Kiribati **84** 4.40S 174.32W
Nila *i.* Indonesia **59** 6.45S 129.30E
Nil, An *r.* Egypt **66** 31.30N 30.25E
Nile *r. see* Nîl, An *r.* Egypt **66**
Nile Delta Egypt **66** 31.00N 31.00E
Niles Mich. U.S.A. **112** 41.51N 86.15W
Niles Ohio U.S.A. **114** 41.11N 80.45W
Nilgaut, Lac *l.* Canada **105** 46.36N 77.15W
Nilgiri India **63** 21.28N 86.46E
Nilgiri Hills India **60** 11.30N 77.30E
Nīmach India **62** 24.28N 74.52E

Nimai *r.* Myanmar **56** 25.44N 97.30E
Nimba, Mt. Guinea **76** 7.35N 8.28W
Nimbin Australia **93** 28.35S 153.12E
Nîmes France **21** 43.50N 4.21E
Nimfaíon, Ákra *c.* Greece **34** 40.05N 24.20E
Nīm Ka Thāna India **62** 27.44N 75.48E
Nīmrūz *d.* Afghan. **62** 30.40N 62.15E
Nimule Sudan **73** 3.36N 32.03E
Nindigully Australia **93** 28.20S 148.47E
Ninety-East Ridge *f.* Indian Oc. **49** 21.00S 89.00E
Ninety Mile Beach *f.* Australia **93** 38.07S 147.30E
Ninety Mile Beach *f.* New Zealand **86** 34.45S 173.00E
Nineveh *ruins* Iraq **64** 36.24N 43.08E
Ningbo China **55** 29.56N 121.32E
Ningde China **55** 26.41N 119.32E
Ningdu China **55** 26.29N 115.46E
Ninggang China **55** 26.45N 113.58E
Ningguo China **55** 30.38N 118.58E
Ningming China **55** 22.04N 107.02E
Ningnan China **52** 27.03N 102.46E
Ningwu China **54** 38.59N 112.12E
Ningxia Huizu *d.* China **54** 37.00N 105.00E
Ning Xian China **54** 35.27N 107.50E
Ningxiang China **55** 28.15N 112.33E
Ninh Binh Vietnam **56** 20.14N 106.00E
Ninove Belgium **16** 50.50N 4.02E
Niobrara U.S.A. **110** 42.45N 98.02W
Niobrara *r.* U.S.A. **110** 42.45N 98.00W
Nioki Zaïre **78** 2.43S 17.41E
Nioro Mali **74** 15.12N 9.35W
Nioro du Rip Senegal **76** 13.40N 15.50W
Niort France **18** 46.19N 0.27W
Niout *well* Mauritania **74** 16.48N 8.17W
Nipigon Canada **102** 49.50N 88.17W
Nipigon B. Canada **102** 48.55N 88.00W
Nipigon, L. Canada **102** 49.50N 88.30W
Nipissing Canada **104** 46.06N 79.30W
Nipissing *r.* Canada **104** 46.00N 78.30W
Nipissing, L. Canada **104** 46.17N 80.00W
Niquelândia Brazil **126** 14.27S 48.27W
Nirasaki Japan **57** 35.42N 138.27E
Nirim Israel **67** 31.20N 34.24E
Nirmal India **63** 19.06N 78.21E
Nirmali India **63** 26.19N 86.35E
Nirwāno Pakistan **62** 26.22N 62.43E
Nir Yisra'el Israel **67** 31.41N 34.38E
Niš Yugo. **34** 43.19N 21.58E
Nisa Portugal **27** 39.31N 7.39W
Nisava *r.* Yugo. **34** 43.20N 22.10E
Niscemi Italy **33** 37.08N 14.24E
Nishi China **55** 29.54N 110.38E
Nishinomiya Japan **57** 34.43N 135.20E
Nísiros *i.* Greece **35** 36.35N 27.10E
Niška Banja Yugo. **34** 43.17N 22.02E
Niskibi *r.* Canada **102** 56.28N 88.10W
Nisko Poland **37** 50.35N 22.07E
Nissan *r.* Sweden **43** 56.40N 12.51E
Nissedal Norway **42** 59.15N 8.30E
Nisser *l.* Norway **42** 59.10N 8.30E
Nissum Bredning *b.* Denmark **42** 56.38N 8.22E
Nissum Fjord *est.* Denmark **42** 56.21N 8.14E
Niţā' Saudi Arabia **65** 27.13N 48.25E
Nitchequon Canada **103** 53.12N 70.47W
Niterói Brazil **126** 22.54S 43.06W
Nith *r.* Canada **104** 43.12N 80.22W
Nith *r.* U.K. **14** 55.00N 3.35W
Nitra Slovakia **37** 48.20N 18.05E
Nitro *r.* Germany **38** 53.42N 7.10E
Nitro U.S.A. **114** 38.25N 81.50W
Nittedal Norway **42** 60.04N 10.53E
Niue *i.* Cook Is. **84** 19.02S 169.52W
Niut, Gunung *mtn.* Indonesia **58** 1.00N 110.00E
Nivala Finland **40** 63.55N 24.58E
Nivelles Belgium **16** 50.36N 4.20E
Nixon U.S.A. **114** 29.16N 97.46W
Nizāmābād India **61** 18.40N 78.05E
Nīzgān *r.* Afghan. **62** 33.05N 63.20E
Nizhneangarsk Russian Fed. **51** 55.48N 109.35E
Nizhnekamskoye Vodokhranilishche Russian Fed. **44** 55.45N 53.50E
Nizhne Kolymsk Russian Fed. **51** 68.34N 160.58E
Nizhneudinsk Russian Fed. **51** 54.55N 99.00E
Nizhnevartovsk Russian Fed. **50** 60.57N 76.40E
Nizhniy Novgorod Russian Fed. **44** 56.20N 44.00E
Nizhniy Tagil Russian Fed. **44** 58.00N 60.00E
Nizhnyaya Tunguska *r.* Russian Fed. **51** 65.50N 88.00E
Nizhnyaya Tura Russian Fed. **44** 58.40N 59.48E
Nizke Tatry *mts.* Slovakia **37** 48.54N 19.40E
Nizza Monferrato Italy **30** 44.46N 8.21E
Nizzanim Israel **67** 31.43N 34.38E
Njazídja *see* Grande Comore *i.* Comoros **79**
Njombe Tanzania **79** 9.20S 34.47E
Njombe *r.* Tanzania **79** 7.02S 35.55E
Njoro Tanzania **79** 5.16S 36.30E
Nkalagu Nigeria **77** 6.28N 7.46E
Nkawkaw Ghana **76** 6.35N 0.47W
Nkayi Zimbabwe **80** 19.00S 28.54E
Nkhata Bay *town* Malawi **79** 11.37S 34.20E
Nkhotakota Malawi **79** 12.55S 34.19E
Nkongsamba Cameroon **77** 4.59N 9.53E
Nkungwe Mt. Tanzania **79** 6.15S 29.54E
Noakhāli Bangla. **63** 22.51N 91.06E
Noatak U.S.A. **98** 67.34N 162.59W
Nobel Canada **104** 45.25N 80.06W
Nobeoka Japan **57** 32.36N 131.40E
Noboribetsu Japan **57** 42.21N 141.11E
Noce *r.* Italy **30** 46.09N 11.04E
Nocera Italy **30** 43.44N 14.39E
Noci Italy **33** 40.48N 17.08E
Noelville Canada **104** 46.09N 80.26W
Nogales Mexico **109** 31.20N 110.56W
Nogara Italy **32** 45.11N 11.04E
Nogaro France **20** 43.46N 0.02W
Nogayskiye Step *f.* Russian Fed. **45** 44.25N 45.30E
Nogent-le-Rotrou France **18** 48.19N 0.50E

Nogent-sur-Seine France **19** 48.29N 3.30E
Nogoyá Argentina **125** 32.22S 59.49W
Noguera Pallaresa *r.* Spain **25** 42.15N 0.54E
Noguera Ribagorçana *r.* Spain **25** 41.40N 0.43E
Nohar India **62** 29.11N 74.46E
Nohta India **63** 23.40N 79.34E
Noire *r.* Que. Canada **105** 45.55N 76.56W
Noire *r.* Que. Canada **105** 45.33N 72.58W
Noire, Montagne *f.* France **18** 48.11N 3.40W
Noire, Montagne *mts.* France **20** 43.26N 2.12E
Noirétable France **20** 45.49N 3.46E
Noirmoutier France **18** 47.00N 2.14W
Noirmoutier, Île de *i.* France **18** 47.00N 2.15W
Nojima-zaki *c.* Japan **57** 34.56N 139.53E
Nokha India **62** 27.35N 73.29E
Nokia Finland **41** 61.28N 23.30E
Nok Kundi Pakistan **62** 28.46N 62.46E
Nokomis Canada **101** 51.30N 105.00W
Nokou Chad **77** 14.35N 14.47E
Nola C.A.R. **77** 3.28N 16.08E
Nola Italy **33** 40.55N 14.33E
Nolinsk Russian Fed. **44** 57.38N 49.52E
Noman L. Canada **101** 62.15N 108.55W
Noma Omuramba *r.* Botswana **80** 19.14S 22.15E
Nombre de Dios Mexico **109** 28.41N 106.05W
Nome U.S.A. **98** 64.30N 165.30W
Nomgon Mongolia **54** 42.50N 105.10E
Nominingue Canada **105** 46.24N 75.02W
Nomuka Group *is.* Tonga **85** 20.15S 174.46W
Nonancourt France **18** 48.46N 1.12E
Nonburg Russian Fed. **44** 65.32N 50.37E
Nong Khai Thailand **56** 17.50N 102.46E
Nongoma R.S.A. **81** 27.58S 31.35E
Nongpoh India **63** 25.54N 91.53E
Nongstoin India **63** 25.31N 91.16E
Nonning Australia **92** 32.30S 136.30E
Nonthaburi Thailand **56** 13.48N 100.11E
Nontron France **20** 45.32N 0.40E
Noojee Australia **93** 37.57S 146.00E
Noonamah Australia **88** 12.35S 131.03E
Noonan U.S.A. **110** 48.54N 103.01W
Noongaar Australia **89** 31.21S 118.55E
Noonkanbah Australia **88** 18.30S 124.50E
Noonthorangee Range *mts.* Australia **92** 31.00S 142.20E
Noorama Creek *r.* Australia **93** 28.05S 145.55E
Noord Beveland *f.* Neth. **16** 51.35S 3.45E
Noord Brabant *d.* Neth. **16** 51.37N 5.00E
Noord Holland *d.* Neth. **16** 52.37N 4.50E
Noordoost-Polder *f.* Neth. **16** 52.45N 5.45E
Noordwijk Neth. **16** 52.16N 4.29E
Noorvik U.S.A. **98** 66.50N 161.14W
Noosa Heads *town* Australia **90** 26.23S 153.07E
Nootka I. Canada **100** 49.32N 126.42W
Noqui Angola **78** 5.51S 13.25E
Nora Sweden **43** 59.31N 15.02E
Noranda Canada **102** 48.20N 79.00W
Norberg Sweden **43** 60.04N 15.56E
Norcia Italy **30** 42.48N 13.05E
Nord *d.* Burkina **76** 13.50N 2.20W
Nord *d.* France **19** 50.20N 3.40E
Nordaustlandet *i.* Arctic Oc. **128** 79.55N 23.00E
Nordborg Denmark **42** 55.03N 9.45E
Norddeich Germany **38** 53.37N 7.10E
Nordegg Canada **101** 52.30N 116.05W
Norden Germany **38** 53.36N 7.12E
Nordenham Germany **38** 53.29N 8.28E
Norderney Germany **38** 53.42N 7.08E
Norderney *i.* Germany **38** 53.42N 7.10E
Norderstedt Germany **38** 53.43N 9.59E
Nordfjord *est.* Norway **41** 61.54N 5.12E
Nordfjordeid Norway **41** 61.54N 6.00E
Nordfold Norway **40** 67.48N 15.20E
Nordfriesische Inseln *is.* Germany **38** 54.35N 8.30E
Nordhausen Germany **38** 51.30N 10.47E
Nordhorn Germany **38** 52.27N 7.05E
Nordkapp *c.* Norway **40** 71.11N 25.48E
Nordkinnhalvøya *pen.* Norway **40** 70.55N 27.45E
Nordland *d.* Norway **40** 66.50N 14.50E
Nördlingen Germany **39** 48.51N 10.30E
Nord-Ostsee-Kanal Germany **38** 54.10N 9.25E
Nordrhein-Westfalen *d.* Germany **38** 52.04N 7.20E
Nordstrand *i.* Germany **38** 54.30N 8.53E
Nord Tröndelag *d.* Norway **40** 64.20N 12.00E
Nordvik Russian Fed. **51** 73.40N 110.50E
Nore Norway **42** 60.10N 9.01E
Nore *r.* Rep. of Ire. **15** 52.25N 6.58W
Norfolk *d.* U.K. **13** 52.39N 1.00E
Norfolk Conn. U.S.A. **115** 41.59N 73.12W
Norfolk Nebr. U.S.A. **110** 42.02N 97.25W
Norfolk Va. U.S.A. **113** 36.54N 76.18W
Norfolk Broads *f.* U.K. **12** 52.43N 1.35E
Norfolk I. Pacific Oc. **84** 29.02S 167.57E
Norfolk Island Ridge Pacific Oc. **84** 29.00S 167.00E
Norheimsund Norway **41** 60.22N 6.08E
Norilsk Russian Fed. **51** 69.21N 88.02E
Norland Canada **104** 44.43N 78.49W
Normal U.S.A. **110** 40.31N 89.00W
Norman *r.* Australia **90** 17.28S 140.49E
Norman U.S.A. **111** 35.13N 97.26W
Normanby *r.* Australia **90** 14.25S 144.08E
Normanby New Zealand **86** 39.32S 174.16E
Normanby I. P.N.G. **90** 10.05S 151.05E
Normandie, Collines de *hills* France **18** 48.55N 0.45W
Normanton Australia **90** 17.40S 141.05E
Norman Wells Canada **98** 65.19N 126.46W
Nornalup Australia **89** 34.58S 116.49E
Ñorquinco Argentina **125** 41.50S 70.55W
Norrahammar Sweden **43** 57.42N 14.06E
Norra Kvarken *str.* Sweden/Finland **40** 63.36N 20.43E
Norra Storfjället *mtn.* Sweden **40** 65.52N 15.18E
Norrbotten *d.* Sweden **40** 67.00N 19.50E
Nörresundby Denmark **42** 57.04N 9.55E
Norris L. U.S.A. **113** 36.18N 83.58W
Norristown U.S.A. **115** 40.07N 75.21W
Norrköping Sweden **43** 58.36N 16.11E

Norrsundet Sweden **41** 60.56N 17.08E
Norrtälje Sweden **43** 59.46N 18.42E
Norseman Australia **89** 32.15S 121.47E
Norsjå *l.* Norway **42** 59.18N 9.20E
Norsk Russian Fed. **51** 52.22N 129.57E
Norte *d.* W. Sahara **74** 26.50N 11.15W
Norte, C. Brazil **123** 1.40N 49.55W
Norte, Cabo *c.* I. de Pascua **85** 27.03S 109.24W
Norte Interior *d.* Portugal **26** 41.30N 7.00W
Norte Litoral *d.* Portugal **26** 41.00N 8.25W
Norte, Punta *c.* Argentina **125** 36.17S 56.46W
North Adams U.S.A. **115** 42.42N 73.07W
Northallerton U.K. **12** 54.20N 1.26W
Northam Australia **89** 31.41S 116.40E
North America **96**
Northampton Australia **89** 28.21S 114.37E
Northampton U.K. **13** 52.14N 0.54W
Northampton Mass. U.S.A. **115** 42.19N 72.38W
Northampton Penn. U.S.A. **115** 40.41N 75.30W
Northamptonshire *d.* U.K. **13** 52.18N 0.55W
North Augusta Canada **105** 44.44N 75.45W
North Battleford Canada **101** 52.47N 108.17W
North Bay *town* Canada **104** 46.19N 79.28W
North Bend Penn. U.S.A. **114** 41.21N 77.42W
North Berwick U.K. **14** 56.04N 2.43W
North Bourke Australia **93** 30.01S 145.59E
North Bradley U.S.A. **104** 43.44N 84.31W
North C. Antarctica **128** 71.00S 166.00E
North, C. Canada **103** 47.01N 60.28W
North, C. New Zealand **86** 34.28S 173.00E
North Canadian *r.* U.S.A. **111** 35.17N 95.31W
North Caribou L. Canada **102** 52.50N 90.50W
North Carolina *d.* U.S.A. **113** 35.30N 80.00W
North Channel Canada **104** 46.02N 82.50W
North Channel *str.* Canada **104** 46.02N 82.50W
North Channel U.K. **15** 55.15N 5.52W
North Chicago U.S.A. **112** 42.20N 87.51W
North China Plain *f. see* Huabei Pingyuan *f.* China **54**
Northcliffe Australia **89** 34.36S 116.04E
North Creek *town* U.S.A. **115** 43.42N 73.59W
North Dakota *d.* U.S.A. **110** 47.00N 100.00W
North Dorset Downs *hills* U.K. **13** 50.46N 2.25W
North Downs *hills* U.K. **13** 51.18N 0.40E
North East *d.* Botswana **80** 20.45S 27.05E
North East U.S.A. **114** 42.13N 79.50W
North Eastern *d.* Kenya **79** 1.00N 40.00E
North Eastern Atlantic Basin *f.* Atlantic Oc. **127** 45.00N 17.00W
North East Pt. Kiribati **85** 1.57N 157.16W
Northeim Germany **38** 51.42N 10.00E
Northern *d.* Ghana **76** 9.00N 1.30W
Northern Indian L. Canada **101** 57.20N 97.20W
Northern Ireland *d.* U.K. **15** 54.40N 6.45W
Northern Mariana Islands Pacific Oc. **84** 15.00N 145.00E
Northern Territory *d.* Australia **90** 20.00S 133.00E
North Esk *r.* U.K. **14** 56.45N 2.25W
Northfield U.S.A. **105** 44.09N 72.40W
North Fiji Basin Pacific Oc. **84** 17.00S 173.00E
North Foreland *c.* U.K. **13** 51.23N 1.26E
North French *r.* Canada **102** 51.04N 80.46W
North Frisian Is. *see* Nordfriesische Inseln *is.* Germany **36**
North Gower Canada **105** 45.08N 75.43W
North Head *c.* Canada **103** 53.42N 56.24W
North Henik L. Canada **101** 61.45N 97.40W
North Horr Kenya **79** 3.19N 37.00E
North I. Kenya **73** 4.04N 36.03E
North I. New Zealand **86** 39.00S 175.00E
Northiam U.K. **13** 50.59N 0.39E
North Knife *r.* Canada **101** 58.53N 94.45W
North Korea Asia **53** 40.00N 128.00E
Northland *d.* New Zealand **86** 35.25S 174.00E
North Las Vegas U.S.A. **109** 36.12N 115.07W
North Little Rock U.S.A. **111** 34.46N 92.14W
North Loup *r.* U.S.A. **110** 41.17N 98.23W
North Mankato U.S.A. **110** 44.15N 94.06W
North Nahanni *r.* Canada **100** 62.15N 123.20W
North Ogden U.S.A. **108** 41.18N 112.00W
North Olmsted U.S.A. **114** 41.25N 81.56W
Northome U.S.A. **110** 47.52N 94.17W
North Platte U.S.A. **110** 41.08N 100.46W
North Platte *r.* U.S.A. **110** 41.15N 100.45W
Northport U.S.A. **113** 33.14N 87.33W
North Powder U.S.A. **108** 45.03N 117.55W
North Pt. Canada **103** 47.05N 64.00W
North Pt. U.S.A. **104** 45.02N 83.16W
North Rona *i.* U.K. **10** 59.09N 5.43W
North Ronaldsay *i.* U.K. **14** 59.23N 2.26W
North Saskatchewan *r.* Canada **101** 53.15N 105.06W
North Sea Europe **36** 54.00N 4.00E
North Seal *r.* Canada **101** 58.50N 98.10W
North Sporades *see* Voríai Sporádhes *is.* Greece **35**
North Stratford U.S.A. **105** 44.46N 71.36W
North Sydney Canada **103** 46.13N 60.15W
North Syracuse U.S.A. **115** 43.08N 76.08W
North Taranaki Bight *b.* New Zealand **86** 38.45S 174.15E
North Tawton U.K. **13** 50.48N 3.55W
North Thames *r.* Canada **104** 42.59N 81.16W
North Thompson *r.* Canada **100** 50.40N 120.20W
North Tonawanda U.S.A. **114** 43.02N 78.53W
North Troy U.S.A. **105** 45.00N 72.24W
North Twin I. Canada **102** 53.20N 80.00W
North Uist *i.* U.K. **14** 57.35N 7.20W
Northumberland *d.* U.K. **12** 55.12N 2.00W
Northumberland *d.* U.S.A. **114** 40.49N 76.39W
Northumberland, C. Australia **92** 38.04S 140.40E
Northumberland Is. Australia **90** 21.40S 150.00E
Northumberland Str. Canada **103** 46.00N 63.30W
Northville U.S.A. **115** 43.13N 74.11W
North Walsham U.K. **12** 52.49N 1.22E
Northway U.S.A. **98** 62.58N 142.00W
North West C. Australia **88** 21.48S 114.10E
North West *d.* Zambia **80** 13.00S 25.00E
North Western Atlantic Basin *f.* Atlantic Oc. **127** 33.00N 55.00W

Northwest Frontier d. Pakistan 62 33.45N 71.00E
North West Highlands U.K. 14 57.30N 5.15W
Northwest Providence Channel Bahamas 113 26.10N 78.20W
North West Pt. Kiribati 85 2.02N 157.29W
North West River town Canada 103 53.32N 60.09W
Northwest Territories d. Canada 99 66.00N 95.00W
Northwich U.K. 12 53.16N 2.30W
Northwood Iowa U.S.A. 110 43.27N 93.13W
Northwood N.Dak. U.S.A. 110 47.44N 97.34W
North Woodstock U.S.A. 105 44.02N 71.41W
North York Moors hills U.K. 12 54.21N 0.50W
North Yorkshire d. U.K. 12 54.14N 1.14W
Norton Kans. U.S.A. 110 39.50N 99.53W
Norton W.Va. U.S.A. 114 38.58N 79.55W
Norton Sound b. U.S.A. 98 63.50N 164.00W
Nortorf Germany 38 54.10N 9.50E
Nort-sur-Erdre France 18 47.26N 1.30W
Norwalk Conn. U.S.A. 115 41.07N 73.27W
Norwalk Ohio U.S.A. 114 41.15N 82.37W
Norway Europe 40 65.00N 13.00E
Norway House town Canada 101 53.59N 97.50W
Norwegian Dependency Antarctica 128 77.00S 10.00E
Norwegian Sea Europe 128 65.00N 5.00E
Norwich Canada 104 42.59N 80.36W
Norwich U.K. 13 52.38N 1.17E
Norwich Conn. U.S.A. 115 41.32N 72.05W
Norwich N.Y. U.S.A. 115 42.32N 75.31W
Norwood Canada 105 44.23N 77.59W
Norwood Mass. U.S.A. 115 42.11N 71.12W
Norwood N.Y. U.S.A. 105 44.45N 75.00W
Norwood Ohio U.S.A. 112 39.12N 84.21W
Nosbonsing, L. Canada 104 46.12N 79.13W
Noshiro Japan 57 40.12N 140.02E
Noshul Russian Fed. 44 60.04N 49.30E
Nosovka Ukraine 37 50.55N 31.37E
Noşratābād Iran 65 29.54N 59.58E
Nossebro Sweden 43 58.11N 12.43E
Noss Head U.K. 14 58.28N 3.03W
Nosy Be i. Madagascar 81 13.20S 48.15E
Nosy Boraha i. Madagascar 81 16.50S 49.55E
Nosy Varika Madagascar 81 20.35S 48.32E
Noteć r. Poland 36 52.44N 16.26E
Notera Israel 67 33.06N 35.38E
Noto Italy 33 36.53N 15.05E
Notodden Norway 42 59.34N 9.17E
Noto, Golfo di g. Italy 33 36.50N 15.15E
Notre Dame B. Canada 103 49.45N 55.15W
Notre Dame de la Salette Canada 105 45.46N 75.35W
Notre Dame du Lac town Canada 104 46.19N 80.10W
Notre Dame du Laus Canada 105 46.05N 75.37W
Notre Dame, Monts mts. Canada 103 48.00N 69.00W
Nottawasaga r. Canada 104 44.32N 80.01W
Nottawasaga B. Canada 104 44.40N 80.30W
Nottaway r. Canada 102 51.25N 78.50W
Nottingham U.K. 12 52.57N 1.10W
Nottinghamshire d. U.K. 12 53.10N 1.00W
Notwani r. Botswana 80 23.46S 26.57E
Nouadhibou Mauritania 74 20.54N 17.01W
Nouakchott Mauritania 74 18.09N 15.58W
Nouméa N.Cal. 84 22.16S 166.27E
Nouna Burkina 76 12.44N 3.54W
Noupoort R.S.A. 80 31.11S 24.56E
Nouvelle Anvers Zaïre 78 1.38N 19.10E
Nouvelle Calédonie is. Pacific Oc. 84 21.30S 165.30E
Nouzonville France 19 49.49N 4.45E
Nova Caipemba Angola 78 7.25S 14.36E
Novafeltria Bagnoli Romagna Italy 30 43.53N 12.17E
Nova Friburgo Brazil 126 22.16S 42.32W
Nova Gradiška Croatia 31 45.16N 17.23E
Nova Iguaçu Brazil 126 22.45S 43.27W
Nova Lamego Guinea Bissau 76 12.19N 14.11W
Nova Lima Brazil 126 19.59S 43.51W
Novara Italy 30 45.28N 8.38E
Nova Scotia d. Canada 103 45.00N 63.30W
Nova Sofala Mozambique 81 20.09S 34.24E
Novato U.S.A. 108 38.06N 122.34W
Nova Varoš Yugo. 31 43.28N 19.48E
Novaya Ladoga Russian Fed. 44 60.09N 32.15E
Novaya Lyalya Russian Fed. 50 59.02N 60.38E
Novaya Sibir, Ostrov i. Russian Fed. 51 75.20N 148.00E
Novaya Ushitsa Ukraine 37 48.50N 27.12E
Novaya Zemlya i. Russian Fed. 44 74.00N 56.00E
Nova Zagora Bulgaria 34 42.29N 26.01E
Novelda Spain 25 38.23N 0.46W
Nové Zámky Slovakia 37 47.59N 18.11E
Novgorod Russian Fed. 44 58.30N 31.20E
Novgorod Severskiy Belarus 44 52.00N 33.15E
Novi Bečej Yugo. 31 45.36N 20.08E
Novi di Modena Italy 30 44.54N 10.54E
Novigrad Croatia 31 45.19N 13.34E
Novi Ligure Italy 30 44.46N 8.47E
Novi Pazar Yugo. 34 43.08N 20.31E
Novi Sad Yugo. 31 45.15N 19.50E
Novi Vinodolski Croatia 31 45.08N 14.48E
Novoalekseyevka Ukraine 45 46.14N 34.36E
Novoanninskiy Russian Fed. 45 50.32N 42.42E
Novo Arkhangel'sk Ukraine 37 48.34N 30.50E
Novocherkassk Russian Fed. 45 47.25N 40.05E
Novofedorovka Ukraine 45 47.04N 35.18E
Novograd Volynskiy Ukraine 37 50.34N 27.32E
Novogrudok Belarus 37 53.35N 25.50E
Novo Hamburgo Brazil 126 29.37S 51.07W
Novokazalinsk Kazakhstan 9 45.48N 62.06E
Novokuznetsk Russian Fed. 50 53.45N 87.12E
Novo Mesto Slovenia 31 45.48N 15.10E
Novomoskovsk Russian Fed. 44 54.06N 38.15E
Novomoskovsk Ukraine 45 48.38N 35.15E
Novorossiysk Russian Fed. 45 44.44N 37.46E
Novoshakhtinsk Russian Fed. 45 47.46N 39.55E
Novosibirsk Russian Fed. 9 55.04N 83.05E
Novosibirskiye Ostrova is. Russian Fed. 51 76.00N 144.00E
Novouzensk Russian Fed. 45 50.29N 48.08E
Novo-Vyatsk Russian Fed. 44 58.30N 49.40E
Novozybkov Russian Fed. 37 52.31N 31.58E
Novska Croatia 31 45.21N 16.59E

Nový Bor Czech Republic 38 50.40N 14.33E
Nový Jičín Czech Republic 37 49.36N 18.00E
Novyy Bykhov Belarus 37 53.20N 30.21E
Novyy Port Russian Fed. 50 67.38N 72.33E
Nowa Ruda Poland 36 50.34N 16.30E
Nowa Sól Poland 36 51.49N 15.41E
Nowendoc Australia 93 31.35S 151.45E
Nowgong Madhya P. India 63 25.04N 79.27E
Nowingi Australia 92 34.36S 142.15E
Nowra Australia 93 35.54S 150.36E
Nowrangapur India 63 19.14N 82.33E
Nowshera Pakistan 62 34.01N 71.59E
Nowy Dwór Mazowiecki Poland 37 52.26N 20.43E
Nowy Korczyn Poland 37 50.19N 20.48E
Nowy Sącz Poland 37 49.39N 20.40E
Nowy Targ Poland 37 49.29N 20.02E
Nowy Tomýśl Poland 36 52.20N 16.07E
Now Zād Afghan. 62 32.24N 64.28E
Noxon U.S.A. 108 48.01N 115.47W
Noya Spain 26 42.47N 8.53W
Noya r. Spain 25 41.28N 1.56E
Noyant France 18 47.31N 0.08E
Noyes I. U.S.A. 100 55.30N 133.40W
Noyon France 19 49.35N 3.00E
Nozay France 18 47.34N 1.38W
Nsanje Malaŵi 79 16.55S 35.12E
Nsawam Ghana 76 5.49N 0.20W
Nsok Equat. Guinea 78 1.10N 11.19E
Nsombo Zambia 79 10.50S 29.56E
Nsukka Nigeria 77 6.51N 7.29E
Nuatja Togo 77 6.59N 1.11E
Nubian Desert Sudan 72 20.30N 34.00E
Nueces r. U.S.A. 111 27.50N 97.30W
Nueces Plains f. U.S.A. 111 28.30N 99.15W
Nueltin L. Canada 101 60.30N 99.30W
Nueva Casas Grandes Mexico 109 30.25N 107.55W
Nueva Gerona Cuba 117 21.53N 82.49W
Nueva Helvecia Uruguay 125 34.19S 57.13W
Nueva Palmira Uruguay 125 33.53S 58.25W
Nueva Rosita Mexico 111 27.57N 101.13W
Nueve de Julio Argentina 125 35.30S 60.50W
Nuevitas Cuba 117 21.34N 77.18W
Nuevo d. Mexico 111 26.00N 100.00W
Nuevo Berlín Uruguay 125 32.59S 58.03W
Nuevo, Golfo g. Argentina 125 42.42S 64.35W
Nuevo Laredo Mexico 111 27.30N 99.31W
Nuevo León d. Mexico 116 26.00N 99.00W
Nuevo Rocafuerte Ecuador 122 0.56S 75.24W
Nũh, Rãs c. Pakistan 62 25.05N 62.24E
Nui i. Tuvalu 84 7.12S 177.10E
Nuits-St. Georges France 19 47.08N 4.57E
Nu Jiang r. China see Salween r. Myanmar 61
Nukha Azerbaijan 65 41.12N 47.10E
Nukhaylah Sudan 72 19.03N 26.19E
Nuku'alofa Tonga 85 21.07S 175.12W
Nuku Hiva i. Ís. Marquises 85 8.56S 140.00W
Nukunonu Pacific Oc. 84 9.10S 171.55W
Nulato U.S.A. 98 64.43N 158.06W
Nules Spain 25 39.51N 0.09W
Nullagine Australia 88 21.56S 120.06E
Nullarbor Australia 89 31.26S 130.55E
Nullarbor Plain f. Australia 89 31.30S 128.00E
Numalla, L. Australia 92 28.45S 144.21E
Numan Nigeria 77 9.30N 12.01E
Numazu Japan 57 35.06N 138.52E
Numedal f. Norway 42 60.06N 9.06E
Numurkah Australia 93 36.05S 145.26E
Nunavik c. Greenland 99 71.55N 55.00W
Nunda U.S.A. 114 42.35N 77.57W
Nundle Australia 93 31.28S 151.08E
Nungo Mozambique 81 13.25S 37.45E
Nunivak I. U.S.A. 98 60.00N 166.30W
Nunkun mtn. Jammu & Kashmir 62 33.59N 76.01E
Nuoro Italy 32 40.19N 9.20E
Nuqüb Yemen 71 14.59N 45.48E
Nurallao Italy 32 39.46N 9.05E
Nürburg Germany 39 50.21N 6.57E
Nure r. Italy 30 45.03N 9.49E
Nuriootpa Australia 92 34.27S 139.02E
Nürnberg Germany 39 49.27N 11.04E
Nurri Italy 32 39.42N 9.14E
Nurri, Mt. Australia 93 31.44S 146.04E
Nürtingen Germany 39 48.38N 9.20E
Nusa Tenggara is. Indonesia 58 8.30S 118.00E
Nusa Tenggara Barat d. Indonesia 58 8.50S 117.30E
Nusa Tenggara Timur d. Indonesia 59 9.30S 122.00E
Nusaybin Turkey 64 37.05N 41.11E
Nushki Pakistan 62 29.33N 66.01E
Nutak Canada 103 57.30N 61.50W
Nutter Fort U.S.A. 114 39.20N 80.19W
Nuuk see Godthåb Greenland 99
Nuwäkot Nepal 63 28.08N 83.53E
Nuwaybi'al Muzayyinah Egypt 66 28.58N 34.38E
Nuweveldberge mts. R.S.A. 80 32.15S 21.50E
Nuyts Archipelago is. Australia 91 32.35S 133.17E
Nuyts, Pt. Australia 89 35.05S 116.32E
Nxaunxau Botswana 80 18.19S 21.04E
Nyaake Liberia 76 4.52N 7.37W
Nyabing Australia 89 33.32S 118.09E
Nyahua Tanzania 79 5.25S 33.16E
Nyahururu Falls town Kenya 79 0.04N 36.22E
Nyah West Australia 92 35.11S 143.21E
Nyainqêntanglha Feng mtn. China 63 30.27N 90.33E
Nyainqêntanglha Shan mts. China 63 30.00N 90.00E
Nyainrong China 63 32.02N 92.15E
Nyakanazi Tanzania 79 3.05S 31.16E
Nyaksimvol Russian Fed. 44 62.30N 60.52E
Nyala Sudan 73 12.03N 24.53E
Nyalam China 63 28.10N 85.59E
Nyamandhlovu Zimbabwe 80 19.50S 28.15E
Nyamapanda Zimbabwe 81 16.59S 32.50E
Nyamlell Sudan 73 9.07N 26.58E
Nyamtukusa Tanzania 79 3.03S 32.44E
Nyandoma Russian Fed. 44 61.30N 40.05E
Nyanga r. Gabon 78 3.00S 10.17E
Nyang Qu r. China 63 29.19N 88.52E

Nyanza d. Kenya 79 0.30S 34.30E
Nyanza Rwanda 79 2.20S 29.42E
Nyashabozh Russian Fed. 44 65.28N 53.42E
Nyaunglebin Myanmar 56 17.57N 96.44E
Nyaungu Myanmar 56 21.12N 94.55E
Nyborg Denmark 42 55.19N 10.48E
Nybro Sweden 43 56.45N 15.54E
Nyda Russian Fed. 50 66.35N 72.58E
Nyêmo China 63 29.25N 90.15E
Nyeri Kenya 79 0.22S 36.56E
Nyerol Sudan 73 8.41N 32.02E
Nyhammar Sweden 43 60.17N 14.58E
Nyika Plateau f. Malaŵi 79 10.25S 33.50E
Nyima China 63 31.50N 87.48E
Nyimba Zambia 79 14.33S 30.49E
Nyíregyháza Hungary 37 47.59N 21.43E
Nykøbing Falster Denmark 41 54.46N 11.53E
Nykøbing Jylland Denmark 42 56.48N 8.52E
Nykøbing Sjaelland Denmark 42 55.55N 11.41E
Nyköping Sweden 43 58.45N 17.00E
Nykroppa Sweden 43 59.38N 14.18E
Nylstroom R.S.A. 80 24.42S 28.24E
Nymagee Australia 93 32.05S 146.20E
Nymboida Australia 93 29.57S 152.32E
Nymboida r. Australia 93 29.39S 152.30E
Nymburk Czech Republic 36 50.11N 15.03E
Nynäshamn Sweden 43 58.54N 17.57E
Nyngan Australia 93 31.34S 147.14E
Nyngynderry Australia 92 32.16S 143.22E
Nyoma Jammu & Kashmir 63 33.11N 78.38E
Nyon Switz. 39 46.23N 6.14E
Nyong r. Cameroon 77 3.15N 9.55E
Nyons France 21 44.22N 5.08E
Nýřany Czech Republic 38 49.43N 13.13E
Nýrsko Czech Republic 38 49.18N 13.09E
Nysa Poland 37 50.29N 17.20E
Nysa Kłodzka r. Poland 37 50.49N 17.50E
Nyssa U.S.A. 108 43.53N 117.00W
Nyuksenitsa Russian Fed. 44 60.24N 44.08E
Nyunzu Zaïre 79 5.55S 28.00E
Nyurba Russian Fed. 51 63.18N 118.28E
Nyuri India 63 27.42N 92.13E
Nzega Tanzania 79 4.13S 33.09E
N'zérékoré Guinea 76 7.49N 8.48W
N'zeto Angola 78 7.13S 12.56E
Nzwani see Anjouan i. Comoros 79 12.12S 44.28E

O

Oahe Resr. U.S.A. 110 45.30N 100.25W
Oahu i. Hawaiian Is. 85 21.30N 158.00W
Oakbank Australia 92 33.07S 140.33E
Oakdale U.S.A. 111 30.49N 92.40W
Oakesdale U.S.A. 108 47.08N 117.15W
Oakey Australia 91 27.26S 151.43E
Oak Harbour U.S.A. 108 48.18N 122.39W
Oak Hill town Fla. U.S.A. 113 28.52N 80.52W
Oak Hill town Ohio U.S.A. 114 38.54N 82.34W
Oakland Calif. U.S.A. 108 37.47N 122.13W
Oakland Md. U.S.A. 114 39.25N 79.24W
Oakland Oreg. U.S.A. 108 43.25N 123.18W
Oaklands Australia 93 35.33S 146.15E
Oakley U.S.A. 108 42.15N 113.53W
Oakover r. Australia 88 20.49S 120.40E
Oak Ridge f. Canada 104 44.01N 79.19W
Oakridge U.S.A. 108 43.45N 122.28W
Oak Ridge town U.S.A. 113 36.02N 84.12W
Oakvale Australia 92 33.01S 140.41E
Oakville Canada 104 43.27N 79.41W
Oamaru New Zealand 86 45.07S 170.58E
Oates Land f. Antarctica 128 70.00S 155.00E
Oaxaca Mexico 116 17.05N 96.41W
Oaxaca d. Mexico 116 17.30N 97.00W
Ob r. Russian Fed. 44 66.50N 69.00E
Oba Canada 102 49.04N 84.07W
Oba i. Vanuatu 84 15.25S 167.50E
Oban U.K. 14 56.26N 5.28W
Oberá Argentina 124 27.30S 55.07W
Oberammergau Germany 39 47.35N 11.04E
Oberdrauburg Austria 39 46.45N 12.58E
Obergurgl Austria 39 46.52N 11.01E
Oberhausen Germany 38 51.28N 6.50E
Oberkirch Germany 39 48.31N 8.05E
Oberlin Kans. U.S.A. 110 39.49N 100.32W
Oberlin Ohio U.S.A. 114 41.18N 82.13W
Obernai France 19 48.28N 7.29E
Oberon Australia 93 33.41S 149.52E
Oberösterreich d. Austria 39 48.05N 13.40E
Oberpfälzer Wald mts. Germany 39 49.35N 12.15E
Oberursel Germany 39 50.11N 8.35E
Obervellach Austria 39 46.56N 13.12E
Obi i. Indonesia 59 1.45S 127.30E
Óbidos Brazil 123 1.55S 55.31W
Obihiro Japan 57 42.55N 143.00E
Obing Germany 39 48.00N 12.24E
Obitsu r. Japan 57 35.24N 139.54E
Obo C.A.R. 73 5.24N 26.30E
Obock Djibouti 73 11.59N 43.16E
Obodovka Ukraine 37 48.28N 29.10E
Oboyan Russian Fed. 45 51.13N 36.17E
Obozerskiy Russian Fed. 44 63.28N 40.29E
Obregón, Presa resr. Mexico 109 28.00N 109.50W
Obrenovac Yugo. 31 44.39N 20.12E
Obrovac Croatia 31 44.12N 15.41E

Obruk Platosu f. Turkey 64 38.00N 33.30E
Obskaya Guba g. Russian Fed. 50 68.30N 74.00E
Ōbu Japan 57 35.00N 136.58E
Obuasi Ghana 76 6.15N 1.36W
Obudu Nigeria 77 6.42N 9.07E
Ocala U.S.A. 113 29.11N 82.09W
Ocaña Colombia 122 8.16N 73.21W
Ocaña Spain 27 39.56N 3.31W
Occidental, Cordillera mts. Colombia 122 5.00N 76.15W
Occidental, Cordillera mts. S. America 124 17.00S 69.00W
Ocean City Md. U.S.A. 115 38.20N 75.05W
Ocean City N.J. U.S.A. 115 39.16N 74.36W
Ocean Falls town Canada 100 52.25N 127.40W
Ocean I. see Banaba i. Kiribati 84
Oceanside Calif. U.S.A. 109 33.12N 117.23W
Oceanside N.Y. U.S.A. 115 40.38N 73.38W
Ochamchire Georgia 45 42.44N 41.30E
Ochil Hills U.K. 14 56.16N 3.25W
Ochsenfurt Germany 39 49.40N 10.03E
Ockelbo Sweden 41 60.53N 16.43E
Öckerö Sweden 42 57.43N 11.39E
Ocmulgee r. U.S.A. 113 31.58N 82.32W
Oconee r. U.S.A. 113 31.58N 82.32W
Oconto U.S.A. 110 44.55N 87.52W
Ocotal Nicaragua 117 13.37N 86.30W
Ocotlán Mexico 116 20.21N 102.42W
Ocreza, Ribeira da r. Portugal 27 39.32N 7.50W
Octeville France 18 49.37N 1.39W
Ocua Mozambique 81 13.40S 39.46E
Oda Ghana 76 5.55N 0.56W
Odádhahraun mts. Iceland 40 65.00N 17.30W
Oda, Jabal mtn. Sudan 72 20.21N 36.39E
Ōdate Japan 57 40.16N 140.34E
Odawara Japan 57 35.15N 139.10E
Odda Norway 42 60.04N 6.33E
Odder Denmark 42 55.58N 10.10E
Ödeborg Sweden 43 58.30N 12.01E
Odeleite r. Portugal 27 37.21N 7.27W
Odemira Portugal 27 37.36N 8.38W
Ödemiş Turkey 29 38.12N 28.00E
Odense Denmark 42 55.24N 10.23E
Odenwald mts. Germany 39 49.35N 9.05E
Oder r. Germany see Odra r. Poland 36
Oderberg Germany 38 52.52N 14.02E
Oderhaff b. Germany 38 53.46N 14.14E
Oder-Havel-Kanal Germany 38 52.51N 13.30E
Oder-Spree-Kanal Germany 38 52.16N 14.30E
Oderzo Italy 30 45.47N 12.29E
Ödeshög Sweden 43 58.14N 14.39E
Odessa Ukraine 37 46.30N 30.46E
Odessa N.Y. U.S.A. 114 42.20N 76.48W
Odessa Tex. U.S.A. 111 31.51N 102.22W
Odiel r. Spain 27 37.10N 6.55W
Odienné Côte d'Ivoire 76 9.36N 7.32W
Odorhei Romania 37 46.18N 25.18E
Odra r. Poland 36 53.30N 14.36E
Odžaci Yugo. 31 45.30N 19.16E
Odžak Bosnia-Herzegovina 31 45.03N 18.18E
Odzi r. Zimbabwe 81 19.46S 32.22E
Oebisfelde Germany 38 52.25N 10.59E
Oegstgeest Neth. 16 52.12N 4.31E
Oeiras Brazil 123 7.00S 42.07W
Oelde Germany 38 51.59N 8.08E
Oelrichs U.S.A. 110 43.10N 103.13W
Oelwein U.S.A. 110 42.41N 91.55W
Oeno I. Pacific Oc. 85 23.55S 130.45W
Oettingen in Bayern Germany 39 48.57N 10.36E
Oetz Austria 39 47.12N 10.54E
Ofanto r. Italy 33 41.22N 16.13E
Ofaqim Israel 67 31.19N 34.37E
Offa Nigeria 77 8.09N 4.44E
Offaly d. Rep. of Ire. 15 53.15N 7.30W
Offenbach Germany 39 50.08N 8.47E
Offenburg Germany 39 48.28N 7.57E
Offerdal Sweden 40 63.28N 14.03E
Offida Italy 31 42.56N 13.41E
Offranville France 18 49.52N 1.03E
Ofir Portugal 26 41.31N 8.47W
Ofotfjorden est. Norway 40 68.25N 17.00E
Ofu i. Samoa 84 14.11S 169.40W
Ōfunato Japan 57 39.04N 141.43E
Oga Japan 57 39.53N 139.51E
Ogadēn f. Ethiopia 71 7.50N 45.40E
Ōgaki Japan 57 35.21N 136.37E
Ogallala U.S.A. 110 41.08N 101.43W
Ogbomosho Nigeria 77 8.05N 4.11E
Ogden Iowa U.S.A. 110 42.02N 94.02W
Ogden Utah U.S.A. 108 41.14N 111.58W
Ogdensburg U.S.A. 105 44.42N 75.29W
Ogeechee r. U.S.A. 113 31.51N 81.06W
Ogilvie Mts. Canada 98 65.00N 139.30W
Oginskiy, Kanal canal Belarus 37 52.25N 25.55E
Oglio r. Italy 30 45.02N 10.39E
Ognon r. France 19 47.20N 5.29E
Ogoja Nigeria 77 6.40N 8.45E
Ogoki Canada 102 51.35N 86.00W
Ogoki r. Canada 102 51.35N 86.00W
Ogoki Resr. Canada 102 51.00N 88.15W
Ogooué r. Gabon 78 1.00S 9.05E
Ogosta r. Bulgaria 34 43.35N 23.35E
Ogr Sudan 73 12.02N 27.06E
Ogražden mts. Bulgaria/Macedonia 34 41.30N 22.50E
Ogulin Croatia 31 45.16N 15.14E
Ogun d. Nigeria 77 6.50N 3.20E
Ogunquit U.S.A. 115 43.15N 70.36W
Ohai New Zealand 86 45.56S 167.57E
Ohanet Algeria 75 28.40N 8.50E
Ohey Belgium 16 50.26N 5.06E
O'Higgins, Cabo c. I. de Pascua 85 27.05S 109.15W
O'Higgins, L. Chile 125 48.03S 73.10W
Ohio d. U.S.A. 112 40.15N 82.45W
Ohio r. U.S.A. 112 36.59N 89.08W
Ōhito Japan 57 34.00N 138.56E
Ohne Germany 38 52.42N 8.12E
Ohře r. Czech Republic 39 50.32N 14.08E

Ohrid Macedonia 34 41.07N 20.47E
Ohrid, L. Albania/Macedonia 34 41.08N 20.52E
Öhringen Germany 39 49.12N 9.29E
Ōi r. Japan 57 34.45N 138.18E
Oil City U.S.A. 114 41.26N 79.42W
Oise d. France 19 49.30N 2.30E
Oise r. France 19 49.00N 2.04E
Oisterwijk Neth. 16 51.34N 5.10E
Oita Japan 57 33.15N 131.40E
Ojai U.S.A. 109 34.27N 119.15W
Ojika zan pen. Japan 57 38.20N 141.32E
Ojocaliente Mexico 116 22.35N 102.18W
Ojo de Agua Argentina 124 29.30S 63.44W
Ojos del Salado mtn. Argentina/Chile 124 27.05S 68.05W
Oka Canada 105 45.29N 74.06W
Oka Nigeria 77 7.28N 5.48E
Oka r. Russian Fed. 44 56.09N 43.00E
Okaba Indonesia 59 8.06S 139.46E
Okahandja Namibia 80 21.58S 16.44E
Okanagan L. Canada 100 50.00N 119.30W
Okanogan U.S.A. 108 48.39N 120.41W
Okanogan r. U.S.A. 108 48.22N 119.35W
Okaputa Namibia 80 20.08S 16.58E
Okāra Pakistan 62 30.49N 73.27E
Okarito New Zealand 86 43.14S 170.07E
Okaukuejo Namibia 80 19.12S 15.56E
Okavango r. Botswana 80 18.30S 22.04E
Okavango Basin f. Botswana 80 19.30S 22.30E
Okayama Japan 57 34.40N 133.54E
Okeechobee U.S.A. 113 27.14N 80.50W
Okeechobee, L. U.S.A. 113 26.55N 80.45W
Okefenokee Swamp f. U.S.A. 113 30.42N 82.20W
Okehampton U.K. 13 50.44N 4.01W
Okere r. Uganda 79 1.37N 33.53E
Okha Russian Fed. 51 53.35N 142.50E
Okhaldhunga Nepal 63 27.19N 86.31E
Okhansk Russian Fed. 44 57.42N 55.20E
Okhotsk Russian Fed. 51 59.20N 143.15E
Okhotskiy Perevoz Russian Fed. 51 61.55N 135.40E
Okhotsk, Sea of Russian Fed. 51 55.00N 150.00E
Okiep R.S.A. 80 29.36S 17.49E
Oki guntō is. Japan 57 36.10N 133.10E
Okinawa jima i. Japan 53 26.30N 128.00E
Okipoko r. Namibia 80 18.40S 16.03E
Okitipupa Nigeria 77 6.31N 4.50E
Oklahoma d. U.S.A. 111 35.20N 98.00W
Oklahoma City U.S.A. 111 35.28N 97.32W
Okmulgee U.S.A. 111 35.37N 95.58W
Oknitsa Moldova 37 48.22N 27.30E
Okola Cameroon 77 4.03N 11.23E
Okolona U.S.A. 111 34.00N 88.45W
Okondja Gabon 78 0.03S 13.45E
Oko, Wâdî Sudan 72 21.15N 35.56E
Okoyo Congo 78 1.28S 15.00E
Oksbøl Denmark 42 55.38N 8.17E
Oksskolten mtn. Norway 40 65.59N 14.15E
Oktyabr'sk Kazakhstan 45 49.30N 57.22E
Oktyabrskiy Belarus 37 52.35N 28.45E
Oktyabr'skoy Revolyutsii, Ostrov i. Russian Fed. 51 79.30N 96.00E
Okučani Croatia 31 45.16N 17.12E
Okuru New Zealand 86 43.56S 168.55E
Okushiri tō i. Japan 57 42.00N 139.50E
Okuta Nigeria 77 9.13N 3.12E
Ola U.S.A. 111 35.02N 93.13W
Ólafsvík Iceland 40 64.53N 23.44W
Olancha U.S.A. 109 36.17N 118.01W
Öland i. Sweden 43 56.45N 16.38E
Olary Australia 92 32.18S 140.19E
Olascoaga Argentina 125 35.14S 60.37W
Olavarría Argentina 125 36.51S 60.20W
Oława Poland 37 50.57N 17.17E
Olbia Italy 32 40.55N 9.29E
Old Bar Australia 93 31.59S 152.35E
Old Crow Canada 98 67.34N 139.43W
Oldenburg f. Germany 38 53.06N 8.25E
Oldenburg Nschn. Germany 38 53.08N 8.13E
Oldenburg Sch.-Hol. Germany 38 54.17N 10.52E
Oldenzaal Neth. 16 52.19N 6.55E
Old Forge N.Y. U.S.A. 115 43.43N 74.58W
Old Forge Penn. U.S.A. 115 41.22N 75.44W
Old Fort r. Canada 101 58.30N 110.30W
Old Gumbiro Tanzania 79 10.00S 35.24E
Oldham U.K. 12 53.33N 2.08W
Old Head of Kinsale c. Rep. of Ire. 15 51.37N 8.33W
Oldman r. Canada 101 49.56N 111.42W
Old Moolawatana Australia 92 30.04S 140.02E
Olds Canada 100 51.50N 114.10W
Old Saybrook U.S.A. 115 41.18N 72.23W
Old Town U.S.A. 112 44.56N 68.39W
Olean U.S.A. 114 42.05N 78.26W
Olecko Poland 37 54.03N 22.30E
Olekma r. Russian Fed. 51 60.20N 120.30E
Olekminsk Russian Fed. 51 60.25N 120.00E
Olema Russian Fed. 44 64.25N 40.15E
Ölen Norway 42 59.36N 5.48E
Oleněk Russian Fed. 51 68.38N 112.15E
Oleněk r. Russian Fed. 51 73.00N 120.00E
Oleněkskiy Zaliv g. Russian Fed. 51 74.00N 120.00E
Oléron, Île d' France 20 45.56N 1.15W
Oleśnica Poland 37 51.13N 17.23E
Olevsk Ukraine 37 51.12N 27.35E
Olga Russian Fed. 53 43.46N 135.17E
Olga L. Canada 102 49.44N 77.18W
Olga, Mt. Australia 90 25.18S 130.44E
Ölgiy Mongolia 52 48.54N 90.00E
Ölgod Denmark 42 55.49N 8.37E
Olgopol Ukraine 37 48.10N 29.30E
Olhão Portugal 27 37.02N 8.50W
Olib i. Croatia 31 44.22N 14.48E
Oliena Italy 32 40.16N 9.24E
Olifants r. Namibia 80 25.28S 19.23E
Olifants r. C.P. R.S.A. 80 31.42S 18.10E
Olifants r. Trans. R.S.A. 80 24.08S 32.39E
Olimbía site Greece 35 37.38N 21.41E
Ólimbos mtn. Cyprus 66 34.55N 32.52E
Ólimbos Greece 35 35.44N 27.11E

Ólimbos mtn. Greece 34 40.05N 22.21E
Olinda Brazil 123 8.00S 34.51W
Olite Spain 25 42.29N 1.39W
Oliva Argentina 124 32.05S 63.35W
Oliva Spain 25 38.55N 0.07W
Oliva de la Frontera Spain 27 38.16N 6.55W
Olivares Spain 23 39.46N 2.20W
Oliveira Brazil 126 20.39S 44.47W
Olivenza Spain 27 38.41N 7.06W
Olmedillo de Roa Spain 26 41.47N 3.56W
Olmedo Spain 26 41.23N 4.41W
Olney U.K. 13 52.09N 0.42W
Olney U.S.A. 110 38.45N 88.05W
Olofström Sweden 43 56.16N 14.30E
Olomouc Czech Republic 37 49.36N 17.16E
Olonets Russian Fed. 44 61.00N 32.59E
Oloron France 20 43.12N 0.36W
Oloron, Gave d' r. France 20 43.33N 1.05W
Olosega i. Samoa 84 14.12S 169.38W
Olot Spain 25 42.11N 2.29E
Olovyannaya Russian Fed. 53 50.58N 115.35E
Olshammar Sweden 43 58.45N 14.48E
Olsztyn Poland 37 53.48N 20.29E
Olsztynek Poland 37 53.36N 20.17E
Olt r. Romania 34 43.43N 24.51E
Olten Switz. 39 47.21N 7.54E
Olteniţa Romania 34 44.05N 26.31E
Olteţ r. Romania 37 44.13N 24.28E
Olvera Spain 27 36.56N 5.16W
Olympia U.S.A. 108 47.03N 122.53W
Olympic Mts. U.S.A. 108 47.50N 123.45W
Olympic Nat. Park U.S.A. 108 47.48N 123.30W
Olympus mtn. see Ólimbos mtn. Greece 34
Olympus, Mt. U.S.A. 108 47.48N 123.43W
Oma China 63 32.30N 83.14E
Omae-zaki c. Japan 57 34.36N 138.14E
Omagh U.K. 15 54.36N 7.20W
Omaha U.S.A. 110 41.16N 95.57W
Oman Asia 60 22.30N 57.30E
Oman, G. of Asia 65 25.00N 58.00E
Omaramara New Zealand 86 44.29S 169.58E
Omaruru Namibia 80 21.25S 15.57E
Omate Peru 124 16.40S 70.58W
Omberg hill Sweden 43 58.20N 14.39E
Omboué Gabon 78 1.38S 9.20E
Ombrone r. Italy 30 42.39N 11.00E
Ombu China 63 31.20N 86.34E
Omdurman see Umm Durmān Sudan 72
Omegna Italy 30 45.53N 8.24E
Omeo Australia 93 37.05S 147.37E
'Omer Israel 67 31.17N 34.51E
Omer U.S.A. 104 44.03N 83.50W
Ometepec Mexico 116 16.41N 98.25W
Om Hâjer Ethiopia 72 14.24N 36.46E
Ōmi-hachiman Japan 57 35.08N 136.06E
Omineca r. Canada 100 56.05N 124.30W
Omišalj Croatia 31 45.13N 14.34E
Ōmiya Japan 57 35.54N 139.38E
Ommen Neth. 16 52.32N 6.25E
Ömnögovĭ d. Mongolia 54 43.00N 105.00E
Omo r. Ethiopia 73 4.51N 36.55E
Omolon r. Russian Fed. 51 68.50N 158.30E
Omomee Canada 104 44.19N 78.31W
Omono r. Japan 57 39.44N 140.05E
Ompah Canada 105 45.00N 76.49W
Omulew r. Poland 37 53.05N 21.32E
Omuramba Omatako r. Namibia 80 18.19S 19.52E
Omurtag Bulgaria 34 43.08N 26.26E
Ōmuta Japan 57 33.02N 130.26E
Oña Spain 26 42.43N 3.25W
Onaga U.S.A. 110 39.29N 96.10W
Onai Angola 80 16.43S 17.33E
Onancock U.S.A. 113 37.43N 75.46W
Onaping L. Canada 104 46.57N 81.30W
Onaway U.S.A. 104 45.21N 84.14W
Oncócua Angola 80 16.40S 13.25E
Onda Spain 25 39.58N 0.15W
Ondangua Namibia 80 17.59S 16.02E
Ondo d. Nigeria 77 7.10N 5.20E
Onega Russian Fed. 44 63.57N 38.11E
Onega r. Russian Fed. 44 63.59N 38.11E
Oneida U.S.A. 115 43.06N 75.39W
Oneida L. U.S.A. 115 43.13N 76.00W
O'Neill U.S.A. 110 42.27N 98.39W
Oneonta U.S.A. 115 42.27N 75.04W
Oneşti Romania 37 46.14N 26.44E
Onezhskaya Guba b. Russian Fed. 44 63.55N 37.30E
Onezhskoye Ozero l. Russian Fed. 44 62.00N 35.30E
Ongerup Australia 89 33.58S 118.29E
Ongiyn Gol r. Mongolia 54 43.40N 103.45E
Ongniud Qi China 54 43.00N 118.43E
Ongole India 61 15.31N 80.04E
Onilahy r. Madagascar 81 23.34S 43.45E
Onitsha Nigeria 77 6.10N 6.47E
Ons, Isla de i. Spain 26 42.23N 8.56W
Onslow Australia 88 21.41S 115.12E
Onslow B. U.S.A. 113 34.20N 77.20W
Onstwedde Neth. 16 53.04N 7.02E
Ontario d. Canada 102 51.00N 88.00W
Ontario Calif. U.S.A. 109 34.04N 117.39W
Ontario Oreg. U.S.A. 108 44.02N 116.58W
Ontario, L. Canada/U.S.A. 114 43.45N 78.00W
Onteniente Spain 25 38.49N 0.37W
Ontonagon U.S.A. 112 46.52N 89.18W
Oodnadatta Australia 91 27.30S 135.27E
Ooldea Australia 90 30.21S 131.50E
Oostelijk-Flevoland f. Neth. 16 52.30N 5.40E
Oostende Belgium 16 51.13N 2.55E
Oosterhout Neth. 16 51.38N 4.50E
Oosterschelde est. Neth. 16 51.35N 3.57E
Oosthuizen Neth. 16 52.33N 5.00E
Oostmalle Belgium 16 51.18N 4.45E
Oost Vlaanderen d. Belgium 16 51.00N 3.45E
Oost Vlieland Neth. 16 53.18N 5.04E
Ootsa L. Canada 100 53.50N 126.20W

Opaka Bulgaria 34 43.28N 26.10E
Opal Mexico 111 24.18N 102.22W
Opala Russian Fed. 51 51.58N 156.30E
Opala Zaïre 78 0.42S 24.15E
Oparino Russian Fed. 44 59.53N 48.10E
Opasatika Canada 102 49.30N 82.50W
Opasatika r. Canada 102 50.24N 82.26W
Opasquia Canada 102 53.16N 93.34W
Opatija Croatia 31 45.21N 14.19E
Opava Czech Republic 37 49.56N 17.54E
Opelousas U.S.A. 111 30.32N 92.05W
Opeongo L. Canada 104 45.42N 78.23W
Opheim U.S.A. 108 48.51N 106.24W
Opinaca r. Canada 102 52.20N 78.00W
Opinnagau r. Canada 102 54.12N 82.21W
Opiscotéo, Lac l. Canada 103 53.10N 68.10W
Opochka Russian Fed. 44 56.41N 28.42E
Opole Poland 37 50.40N 17.56E
Oporto see Porto Portugal 26
Opotiki New Zealand 86 38.00S 177.18E
Opp U.S.A. 113 31.16N 86.18W
Oppdal Norway 40 62.36N 9.41E
Oppida Mamertina Italy 33 38.16N 16.00E
Oppland d. Norway 41 61.30N 9.00E
Opportunity U.S.A. 108 47.39N 117.15W
Opunake New Zealand 86 39.27S 173.51E
Ora Italy 30 46.21N 11.18E
Ora Banda Australia 89 30.27S 121.04E
Oradea Romania 37 47.03N 21.55E
Öraefajökull mtn. Iceland 40 64.02N 16.39W
Orahovica Croatia 31 45.31N 17.53E
Orai India 63 25.59N 79.28E
Oran Algeria 74 35.42N 0.38W
Orán Argentina 124 23.07S 64.16W
Orange Australia 93 33.19S 149.10E
Orange France 21 44.08N 4.48E
Orange r. R.S.A. 80 28.38S 16.38E
Orange Mass. U.S.A. 115 42.35N 72.19W
Orange N.J. U.S.A. 115 40.46N 74.14W
Orange Tex. U.S.A. 111 30.01N 93.44W
Orangeburg U.S.A. 113 33.28N 80.53W
Orange, C. Brazil 123 4.25N 51.32W
Orangevale U.S.A. 108 38.41N 121.13W
Orangeville Canada 104 43.55N 80.06W
Oranienburg Germany 38 52.45N 13.14E
Oranjefontein R.S.A. 80 23.27S 27.40E
Oranjemund Namibia 80 28.35S 16.26E
Orange, C. Brazil 123 4.25N 51.32W
Or 'Aqiva Israel 67 32.30N 34.55E
Orarak Sudan 73 6.15N 32.23E
Oras Phil. 59 12.10N 125.22E
Orbe Switz. 39 46.43N 6.32E
Orbetello Italy 30 42.27N 11.13E
Orbieu r. France 20 43.14N 2.54E
Orbigo r. Spain 26 41.58N 5.40W
Orbisonia U.S.A. 114 40.15N 77.54W
Orbost Australia 93 37.42S 148.30E
Örbyhus Sweden 41 60.14N 17.42E
Orcera Spain 26 38.19N 2.39W
Orchies France 19 50.28N 3.14E
Orchila i. Venezuela 117 11.52N 66.10W
Orco r. Italy 30 45.10N 7.52E
Ord r. Australia 88 15.30S 128.30E
Ordenes Spain 26 43.04N 8.24W
Ordu Turkey 64 41.00N 37.52E
Orduña Spain 26 42.58N 2.58W
Örebro Sweden 43 59.17N 15.13E
Örebro d. Sweden 43 59.30N 15.00E
Oregon d. U.S.A. 108 43.49N 120.36W
Oregon City U.S.A. 108 45.21N 122.36W
Öregrund Sweden 41 60.20N 18.26E
Orekhovo-Zuyevo Russian Fed. 44 55.47N 39.00E
Orel Russian Fed. 44 52.58N 36.04E
Orellana, Embalse de resr. Spain 27 39.00N 5.25W
Orem U.S.A. 108 40.19N 111.42W
Orenburg Russian Fed. 44 51.50N 55.00E
Orense Spain 26 42.20N 7.51W
Orense d. Spain 26 42.15N 7.40W
Oressa r. Belarus 37 52.33N 28.45E
Orestiás Greece 34 41.30N 26.31E
Orfanoú, Kólpos g. Greece 34 40.33N 24.00E
Orford U.S.A. 105 43.54N 72.10W
Orford, Mt. Canada 105 45.18N 72.08W
Orford Ness c. Australia 90 11.22S 142.50E
Orford Ness c. U.K. 13 52.05N 1.36E
Orgaz Spain 27 39.39N 3.54W
Orgelet France 19 46.31N 5.37E
Orgeyev Moldova 37 47.24N 28.50E
Orgün Afghan. 62 32.55N 69.10E
Orick U.S.A. 108 41.17N 124.04W
Oriental, Cordillera mts. Bolivia 124 17.00S 65.00W
Oriental, Cordillera mts. Colombia 122 5.00N 74.30W
Origny France 19 49.54N 3.30E
Orihuela Spain 25 38.05N 0.57W
Orillia Canada 104 44.37N 79.25W
Orimattila Finland 41 60.48N 25.45E
Orinduik Guyana 122 4.42N 60.01W
Orinoco r. Venezuela 122 9.00N 61.30W
Orinoco, Delta del r. Venezuela 122 9.00N 61.00W
Orissa d. India 63 20.20N 84.00E
Oristano Italy 32 39.54N 8.35E
Oristano, Golfo di g. Italy 32 39.50N 8.30E
Orizaba Mexico 116 18.51N 97.08W
Örje Norway 42 59.29N 11.39E
Orjen mtn. Yugo. 31 42.30N 18.38E
Orjiva Spain 27 36.53N 3.24W
Orkanger Norway 40 63.17N 9.52E
Orkney Is. U.K. 14 59.00N 3.00W
Orlândia Brazil 126 20.55S 47.54W
Orlando U.S.A. 113 31.47N 81.06W
Orléans Canada 105 45.28N 75.31W
Orléans France 19 47.55N 1.54E
Orleans Mass. U.S.A. 115 41.47N 70.00W
Orleans N.H. U.S.A. 105 44.49N 72.12W
Orléans, Canal d' France 19 47.54N 1.55E
Orlov Russian Fed. 44 58.38N 48.50E
Ormāra Pakistan 62 25.12N 64.38E
Ormāra, Rās c. Pakistan 62 25.09N 64.35E
Ormilia Greece 34 40.16N 23.33E

Ormoc Phil. 59 11.00N 124.37E
Ormond New Zealand 86 38.35S 177.58E
Ormond Beach town U.S.A. 113 29.26N 81.03W
Ormož Slovenia 31 46.25N 16.09E
Ormskirk U.K. 12 53.35N 2.53W
Ormstown Canada 105 45.08N 74.00W
Ornans France 19 47.06N 6.09E
Orne d. France 18 48.60N 0.05E
Orne r. France 18 49.17N 0.11W
Ornö i. Sweden 43 59.04N 18.24E
Örnsköldsvik Sweden 40 63.17N 18.50E
Orobie, Alpi mts. Italy 30 46.03N 10.00E
Orocué Colombia 122 4.48N 71.20W
Orodara Burkina 76 11.00N 4.54W
Orogrande U.S.A. 109 32.23N 106.28W
Orohena mtn. Tahiti 85 17.37S 149.28W
Oromocto Canada 103 45.51N 66.29W
Oron Israel 66 30.55N 35.01E
Oron Nigeria 77 4.49N 8.15E
Orona i. Kiribati 84 4.29S 172.10W
Orono Canada 104 43.59N 78.37W
Orono U.S.A. 112 44.53N 68.40W
Orosei Italy 32 40.23N 9.42E
Orosei, Golfo di g. Italy 32 40.10N 9.50E
Orosháza Hungary 37 46.34N 20.40E
Orote Pen. Guam 84 13.26N 144.38E
Orotukan Russian Fed. 51 62.16N 151.43E
Oroville Calif. U.S.A. 108 39.31N 121.33W
Oroville Wash. U.S.A. 108 48.56N 119.26W
Orrefors Sweden 43 56.50N 15.45E
Orroroo Australia 92 32.46S 138.39E
Orrville U.S.A. 114 40.50N 81.46W
Orsa Sweden 43 56.50N 15.45E
Orsha Belarus 44 54.30N 30.23E
Orsières Switz. 39 46.02N 7.09E
Orsk Russian Fed. 44 51.13N 58.35E
Orşova Romania 37 44.42N 22.22E
Ortaklar Turkey 35 37.53N 27.30E
Orta Nova Italy 33 41.19N 15.42E
Ortegal, Cabo c. Spain 26 43.45N 7.53W
Orthez France 20 43.29N 0.46W
Ortigueira Spain 26 43.41N 7.51W
Ortigueira, Ría de est. Spain 26 43.45N 7.50W
Ortisei Italy 30 46.34N 11.40E
Ortona Italy 32 42.21N 14.24E
Ortonville U.S.A. 110 45.18N 96.28W
Orūmīyeh Iran 65 37.32N 45.02E
Oruro Bolivia 124 17.59S 67.09W
Oruro d. Bolivia 124 18.00S 72.30W
Orust i. Sweden 42 58.10N 11.38E
Orūzgān Afghan. 62 32.56N 66.38E
Orūzgān d. Afghan. 62 33.40N 66.00E
Orvieto Italy 30 42.43N 12.07E
Orwell U.S.A. 114 41.32N 80.52W
Oryakhovo Bulgaria 34 43.40N 23.57E
Or Yehuda Israel 67 32.01N 34.51E
Orzinuovi Italy 30 45.24N 9.55E
Os Norway 40 62.31N 11.11E
Osage Iowa U.S.A. 110 43.17N 92.49W
Osage r. U.S.A. 107 38.35N 91.57W
Osage Wyo. U.S.A. 108 43.59N 104.25W
Ōsaka Japan 57 34.40N 135.30E
Ōsaka d. Japan 57 34.24N 135.25E
Ōsaka-wan b. Japan 57 34.30N 135.18E
Osa, Península de pen. Costa Rica 117 8.20N 83.30W
Osborne U.S.A. 110 39.26N 98.42W
Osby Sweden 43 56.22N 13.59E
Osceola Iowa U.S.A. 111 41.02N 93.46W
Osceola Mo. U.S.A. 111 38.03N 93.42W
Osceola Mills U.S.A. 114 40.51N 78.16W
Oschatz Germany 38 51.18N 13.07E
Oschersleben Germany 38 52.01N 11.13E
Oscoda U.S.A. 104 44.26N 83.20W
Osečina Yugo. 31 44.23N 19.36E
Osen Norway 40 64.18N 10.32E
Osh Kyrgyzstan 50 40.37N 72.49E
Oshawa Canada 104 43.53N 78.51W
Ō shima i. Hokkaido Japan 57 41.40N 139.40E
Ō shima i. Tosan Japan 57 34.43N 139.24E
Oshkosh Nebr. U.S.A. 110 41.24N 102.21W
Oshmyany Belarus 37 54.22N 25.52E
Oshnovīyeh Iran 65 37.03N 45.05E
Oshogbo Nigeria 77 7.50N 4.35E
Oshtorān, Kūh mtn. Iran 65 33.18N 49.15E
Oshvor Russian Fed. 44 66.59N 62.59E
Oshwe Zaïre 78 3.27S 19.32E
Osiān India 62 26.43N 72.55E
Osijek Croatia 31 45.33N 18.41E
Osilo Italy 32 40.44N 8.39E
Osimo Italy 31 43.29N 13.29E
Osipovichi Belarus 37 53.19N 28.36E
Oskaloosa U.S.A. 110 41.18N 92.39W
Oskarshamn Sweden 43 57.16N 16.26E
Oskarström Sweden 43 56.48N 12.58E
Oskol r. Ukraine 45 49.08N 37.10E
Oslo Norway 42 59.55N 10.45E
Oslofjorden est. Norway 42 59.20N 10.35E
Osmancik Turkey 64 40.58N 34.50E
Osmaniye Turkey 64 37.04N 36.15E
Ösmo Sweden 43 58.59N 17.54E
Osnabrück Germany 38 52.16N 8.02E
Osogovska Planina mts. Macedonia 34 42.08N 22.18E
Osorno Chile 125 40.35S 73.14W
Osorno Spain 26 42.24N 4.22W
Osøyra Norway 42 60.11N 5.28E
Osprey Reef Australia 90 13.55S 146.38E
Oss Neth. 16 51.46N 5.31E
Ossa mtn. Greece 34 39.47N 22.42E
Ossabaw I. U.S.A. 113 31.47N 81.06W
Ossa, Mt. Australia 91 41.52S 146.04E
Osse r. France 20 44.07N 0.17E
Osse r. Nigeria 77 5.55N 5.15E
Ossineke U.S.A. 104 44.54N 83.27W
Ossining U.S.A. 115 41.10N 73.52W
Ossokmanuan L. Canada 103 53.25N 65.00W
Ostaboningue, L. Canada 104 47.09N 78.53W
Ostashkov Russian Fed. 44 57.09N 33.10E
Oste r. Germany 38 53.33N 9.10E

Ostend see Oostende Belgium 16
Oster Ukraine 37 50.55N 30.53E
Oster r. Ukraine 37 53.47N 31.46E
Osterburg Germany 38 52.47N 11.44E
Österbybruk Sweden 43 60.12N 17.54E
Österbymo Sweden 43 57.50N 15.16E
Österdal r. Sweden 41 61.03N 14.30E
Österdalen f. Norway 41 61.15N 11.10E
Östergötland d. Sweden 43 58.20N 16.00E
Östergötland f. Sweden 43 58.17N 15.40E
Osterholz-Scharmbeck Germany 38 53.14N 8.47E
Österö i. Faroe Is. 10 62.16N 6.54W
Osterode Germany 38 51.43N 10.14E
Osterøy i. Norway 41 60.33N 5.35E
Östersund Sweden 40 63.10N 14.40E
Östervåla Sweden 43 60.11N 17.11E
Osterwieck Germany 38 51.58N 10.42E
Östfold d. Norway 42 59.20N 11.25E
Ostfriesische Inseln is. Germany 38 53.44N 7.25E
Östhammar Sweden 43 60.16N 18.22E
Ostia Italy 32 41.44N 12.14E
Östmark Sweden 43 60.17N 12.45E
Ostrava Czech Republic 37 49.50N 18.15E
Ostróda Poland 37 53.43N 19.59E
Ostrog Ukraine 37 50.20N 26.29E
Ostrołeka Poland 37 53.06N 21.34E
Ostrov Czech Republic 39 50.17N 12.57E
Ostrov Russian Fed. 44 57.22N 28.22E
Ostrowiec-Świetokrzyski Poland 37 50.57N 21.23E
Ostrów Mazowiecka Poland 37 52.50N 21.51E
Ostrów Wielkopolski Poland 37 51.39N 17.49E
Ostuni Italy 33 40.44N 17.35E
Osum r. Albania 34 40.40N 20.10E
Osŭm r. Bulgaria 29 43.41N 24.51E
Ōsumi kaikyō str. Japan 57 31.30N 131.00E
Ōsumi shotō is. Japan 53 30.30N 131.00E
Osun d. Nigeria 77 7.15N 4.30E
Osuna Spain 27 37.14N 5.07W
Oswego U.S.A. 115 43.27N 76.31W
Oswestry U.K. 12 52.52N 3.03W
Otago d. New Zealand 86 45.10S 169.20E
Otago Pen. New Zealand 86 45.48S 170.45E
Otaki New Zealand 86 40.45S 175.08E
Otaru Japan 57 43.14N 140.59E
Otavalo Ecuador 122 0.14N 78.16W
Otavi Namibia 80 19.37S 17.21E
Ōtawara Japan 57 36.52N 140.02E
Otelec Romania 37 45.36N 20.50E
Otematata New Zealand 86 44.37S 170.11E
Othonoí i. Greece 33 39.04N 19.26E
Óthris, Óros mtn. Greece 35 39.04N 22.42E
Oti r. Ghana 76 8.43N 0.10E
Otira New Zealand 86 42.51S 171.33E
Otish, Monts mts. Canada 103 52.22N 70.30W
Otisville U.S.A. 115 41.28N 74.32W
Otiwarongo Namibia 80 20.30S 16.39E
Otjiwero Namibia 80 17.59S 13.22E
Otju Namibia 80 18.15S 13.18E
Otočac Croatia 31 44.52N 15.14E
Otog Qi China 54 39.05N 107.59E
Otosquen Canada 101 53.17N 102.01W
Otra r. Norway 42 58.09N 8.00E
Otradnyy Russian Fed. 44 53.26N 51.30E
Otranto Italy 33 40.09N 18.30E
Otranto, Str. of Med. Sea 33 40.00N 19.00E
Otrokovice Czech Republic 37 49.13N 17.31E
Otsego U.S.A. 112 42.26N 85.42W
Otsego L. U.S.A. 115 42.45N 74.52W
Otsego Lake town U.S.A. 104 44.55N 84.41W
Ōtsu Japan 57 35.02N 135.50E
Ōtsuki Japan 57 35.36N 138.57E
Otta Norway 41 61.46N 9.32E
Ottawa Canada 105 45.25N 75.42W
Ottawa r. Canada 105 45.20N 73.58W
Ottawa Ill. U.S.A. 110 41.21N 88.51W
Ottawa Kans. U.S.A. 110 38.37N 95.16W
Ottawa Is. Canada 99 59.50N 80.00W
Ottenby Sweden 43 56.14N 16.25E
Otter r. U.K. 13 50.38N 3.19W
Otterbäcken Sweden 43 58.57N 14.02E
Otterburn U.K. 12 55.14N 2.10W
Otter Creek r. U.S.A. 115 44.13N 73.17W
Otter L. Canada 101 55.35N 104.39W
Otter Lake town Canada 105 45.51N 76.26W
Otterndorf Germany 38 53.48N 8.53E
Otterøy i. Norway 40 62.45N 6.50E
Otterup Denmark 42 55.31N 10.24E
Ottosdal R.S.A. 80 26.48S 26.00E
Ottumwa U.S.A. 110 41.01N 92.25W
Oturkpo Nigeria 77 7.13N 8.10E
Otway, C. Australia 92 38.51S 143.34E
Ötztaler Alpen mts. Austria/Italy 30 46.52N 10.50E
Ou r. Laos 56 20.03N 102.19E
Ouachita r. U.S.A. 111 31.38N 91.49W
Ouachita, L. U.S.A. 111 34.40N 93.25W
Ouachita Mts. U.S.A. 111 34.40N 94.25W
Ouada, Djebel mtn. C.A.R. 73 8.56N 23.26E
Ouadane Mauritania 74 20.56N 11.37W
Ouadda C.A.R. 73 8.04N 22.24E
Ouaddaï d. Chad 73 13.00N 21.00E
Ouagadougou Burkina 76 12.20N 1.40W
Ouahigouya Burkina 76 13.31N 2.21W
Ouaka d. C.A.R. 73 6.00N 21.00E
Oualâta Mauritania 74 17.18N 7.02W
Ouallam Niger 77 14.23N 2.09E
Ouallene Algeria 74 24.35N 1.17E
Ouanda Djallé C.A.R. 73 8.54N 22.48E
Ouarane f. Mauritania 74 21.00N 9.30W
Ouararda, Passe de pass Mauritania 74 21.01N 13.03W
Ouareau r. Canada 105 45.56N 73.25W
Ouargla Algeria 75 31.57N 5.20E
Ouarra r. C.A.R. 73 5.05N 24.26E
Ouarzazate Morocco 74 30.57N 6.50W
Ouassous well Mali 74 16.01N 1.26E
Ouche r. France 19 47.06N 5.16E
Ouddorp Neth. 16 51.49N 3.57E
Oudenaarde Belgium 16 50.50N 3.37E

Oudenbosch Neth. 16 51.35N 4.30E
Oude Rijn r. Neth. 16 52.14N 4.26E
Oudon r. France 18 47.47N 1.02W
Oudtshoorn R.S.A. 80 33.35S 22.11E
Oued Zarga Tunisia 32 36.40N 9.25E
Oued-Zem Morocco 74 32.55N 6.30W
Ouellé Côte d'Ivoire 76 7.26N 4.01W
Ouenza Algeria 75 35.57N 8.07E
Ouessant, Île d' i. France 18 48.28N 5.05W
Ouesso Congo 78 1.38N 16.03E
Ouezzane Morocco 74 34.52N 5.35W
Oughter, Lough Rep. of Ire. 15 54.01N 7.28W
Ouham r. Chad 77 9.15N 18.13E
Ouimet Canada 102 48.43N 88.35W
Ouistreham France 18 49.17N 0.15W
Oujda Morocco 74 34.41N 1.45W
Oujeft Mauritania 74 20.02N 13.04W
Oulins r. Finland 40 64.20N 27.15E
Oum Chalouba Chad 75 15.48N 20.46E
Oumé Côte d'Ivoire 76 6.25N 5.23W
Oum er Rbia, Oued r. Morocco 74 33.19N 8.21W
Oumm ed Droûs Guebli, Sebkhet f. Mauritania 74 24.03N 11.45W
Oumm ed Droûs Telli, Sebkhet f. Mauritania 74 24.20N 11.30W
Ounas r. Finland 40 66.30N 25.45E
Oundle U.K. 13 52.28N 0.28W
Ounianga Kébir Chad 75 19.04N 20.29E
Our r. Lux. 16 49.53N 6.16E
Ouray U.S.A. 108 40.06N 109.40W
Ourcq r. France 19 49.01N 3.01E
Ourense see Orense Spain 26
Ouri Chad 75 21.34N 19.13E
Ourinhos Brazil 126 23.00S 49.54W
Ourique Portugal 26 37.39N 8.13W
Ouro Fino Brazil 126 22.16S 46.25W
Ouro Prêto Brazil 126 20.54S 43.30W
Ourthe r. Belgium 16 50.38N 5.36E
Ouse r. Humber. U.K. 12 53.41N 0.42W
Oust r. France 18 47.39N 2.06W
Outardes, Rivière aux r. Canada 103 49.04N 68.25W
Outer Hebrides is. U.K. 14 57.40N 7.35W
Outjo Namibia 80 20.07S 16.10E
Outlook U.S.A. 108 48.53N 104.47W
Ouvèze r. France 21 43.59N 4.51E
Ouyen Australia 92 35.06S 142.22E
Ouzouer-le-Marché France 19 47.55N 1.32E
Ouzzal, Oued i-n- wadi Algeria 75 20.54N 2.28E
Ovalle Chile 124 30.36S 71.12W
Ovamboland f. Namibia 80 17.45S 16.00E
Ovar Portugal 26 40.52N 8.38W
Ovens r. Australia 93 36.20S 146.18E
Overath Germany 16 50.56N 7.18E
Overflakkee i. Neth. 16 51.45N 4.08E
Overijssel d. Neth. 16 52.25N 6.30E
Överkalix Sweden 40 66.21N 22.56E
Overland Park town U.S.A. 110 38.59N 94.40W
Overton U.S.A. 109 36.33N 114.27W
Övertorneå Sweden 40 66.23N 23.40E
Överum Sweden 43 57.59N 16.19E
Ovid Mich. U.S.A. 114 43.01N 84.22W
Ovid N.Y. U.S.A. 114 42.41N 76.49W
Ovidiopol Ukraine 37 46.18N 30.28E
Oviedo Spain 26 43.21N 5.50W
Ovinishche Russian Fed. 44 58.20N 37.00E
Övörhangay d. Mongolia 54 45.00N 103.00E
Ovruch Ukraine 37 51.20N 28.50E
Owaka New Zealand 86 46.27S 169.40E
Owando Congo 78 0.30S 15.48E
Owase Japan 57 34.04N 136.12E
Owatonna U.S.A. 110 44.06N 93.10W
Owbeh Afghan. 62 34.22N 63.10E
Owego U.S.A. 115 42.06N 76.16W
Owel, Lough Rep. of Ire. 15 53.34N 7.24W
Owen Channel Canada 104 45.31N 81.48W
Owendo Gabon 78 0.17N 9.30E
Owen Falls Dam Uganda 79 0.30N 33.07E
Owensboro U.S.A. 113 37.46N 87.07W
Owen Sd. b. Canada 104 44.40N 80.55W
Owens L. U.S.A. 109 36.25N 117.56W
Owen Sound town Canada 104 44.34N 80.56W
Owen Stanley Range mts. P.N.G. 90 9.30S 148.00E
Owerri Nigeria 77 5.29N 7.02E
Owl r. Canada 101 57.51N 92.44W
Owo Nigeria 77 7.10N 5.39E
Owosso U.S.A. 104 43.00N 84.10W
Owyhee r. U.S.A. 108 43.46N 117.02W
Oxelösund Sweden 43 58.40N 17.06E
Oxford U.K. 13 51.45N 1.15W
Oxford Md. U.S.A. 115 38.42N 76.10W
Oxford Mich. U.S.A. 104 42.49N 83.16W
Oxford Penn. U.S.A. 115 39.47N 75.59W
Oxfordshire d. U.K. 13 51.46N 1.10W
Oxley Australia 92 34.13S 144.10E
Oxnard U.S.A. 109 34.12N 119.11W
Oxtongue Lake town Canada 104 45.22N 78.55W
Oyapock r. Guiana 123 4.10N 51.40W
Oyem Gabon 78 1.34N 11.31E
Oyen Canada 101 51.22N 110.28W
Öyeren l. Norway 41 61.12N 10.22E
Öyeren l. Norway 42 59.48N 11.14E
Oykel r. U.K. 14 57.53N 4.21W
Oymyakon Russian Fed. 51 63.30N 142.44E
Oyo Nigeria 77 7.50N 3.55E
Oyo d. Nigeria 77 8.10N 3.40E
Oyonnax France 21 46.15N 5.40E
Ozamiz Phil. 59 8.09N 123.59E
Ozarichi Belarus 37 52.28N 29.12E
Ozark Ala. U.S.A. 113 31.27N 85.40W
Ozark Ark. U.S.A. 111 35.29N 93.50W
Ozark Mo. U.S.A. 111 37.01N 93.12W
Ozark Plateau U.S.A. 111 37.00N 93.00W
Ózd Hungary 37 48.14N 20.18E
Ozernoye Russian Fed. 44 51.45N 51.29E
Ozersk Russian Fed. 37 54.26N 22.00E
Ozieri Italy 32 40.35N 9.00E
Ozinki Russian Fed. 45 51.11N 49.43E

Ozona U.S.A. 111 30.43N 101.12W

P

Paamiut see Frederikshåb Greenland 99
Pa-an Myanmar 56 16.51N 97.37E
Paarl R.S.A. 80 33.44S 18.58E
Pabianice Poland 37 51.40N 19.22E
Pābna Bangla. 63 24.00N 89.15E
Pacaraima, Sierra mts. Venezuela 122 4.00N 62.30W
Pacasmayo Peru 122 7.27S 79.33W
Pachino Italy 33 36.42N 15.06E
Pachmarhi India 63 22.28N 78.26E
Pāchora India 62 20.40N 75.21E
Pachuca Mexico 116 20.10N 98.44W
Pacific-Antarctic Basin Pacific Oc. 85 58.00S 98.00W
Pacific-Antarctic Ridge Pacific Oc. 85 57.00S 145.00W
Pacific Ocean 85
Pacitan Indonesia 59 8.12S 111.05E
Packsaddle Australia 92 30.28S 141.28E
Packwood U.S.A. 108 46.36N 121.40W
Pacy-sur-Eure France 18 49.01N 1.23E
Padam Jammu & Kashmir 62 33.28N 76.53E
Padampur India 63 20.59N 83.04E
Padang Indonesia 58 0.55S 100.21E
Padangpanjang Indonesia 58 0.30S 100.26E
Padangsidempuan Indonesia 58 1.20N 99.11E
Padany Russian Fed. 44 63.12N 33.20E
Padauari r. Brazil 122 0.15S 64.05W
Paden City U.S.A. 114 39.36N 80.56W
Paderborn Germany 38 51.43N 8.45E
Padilla Bolivia 124 19.19S 64.20W
Padlei Canada 101 62.10N 97.05W
Padloping Island town Canada 99 67.00N 62.50W
Padova Italy 32 45.25N 11.53E
Pādra India 62 22.14N 73.06E
Padrauna India 63 26.55N 83.59E
Padre I. U.S.A. 111 27.00N 97.15W
Padrón Spain 26 42.44N 8.40W
Padstow U.K. 13 50.33N 4.57W
Padthaway Australia 92 36.37S 140.28E
Padua see Padova Italy 32
Paducah U.S.A. 111 34.01N 100.18W
Paducah U.S.A. 113 37.05N 88.36W
Paeroa New Zealand 86 37.23S 175.41E
Paestum site Italy 33 40.25N 15.00E
Pafúri Mozambique 81 22.27S 31.21E
Pag Croatia 31 44.27N 15.04E
Pag i. Croatia 31 44.30N 15.00E
Pagadian Phil. 59 7.50N 123.30E
Pagai Selatan i. Indonesia 58 3.00S 100.18E
Pagai Utara i. Indonesia 58 2.42S 100.05E
Pagan Myanmar 56 21.07N 94.53E
Pagasitikós Kólpos b. Greece 35 39.15N 23.12E
Page U.S.A. 108 36.57N 111.27W
Pager r. Uganda 79 3.05N 32.28E
Paget Canada 104 46.18N 80.48W
Paghmān Afghan. 62 34.36N 68.57E
Pago Pago Samoa 84 14.16S 170.42W
Pagosa Springs town U.S.A. 108 37.16N 107.01W
Pagri China 63 27.45N 89.10E
Paguchi L. Canada 102 49.38N 91.40W
Pagwa River town Canada 102 50.02N 85.14W
Pahala Hawaii U.S.A. 106 19.12N 155.28W
Pahiatua New Zealand 86 40.26S 175.49E
Paible U.K. 14 57.35N 7.27W
Paihia New Zealand 86 35.16S 174.05E
Päijänne l. Finland 41 61.35N 25.30E
Paikū Co l. China 63 28.48N 85.36E
Paimboeuf France 18 47.17N 2.02W
Paimpol France 18 48.46N 3.03W
Painan Indonesia 58 1.21S 100.34E
Painesville U.S.A. 114 41.43N 81.15W
Pains Brazil 126 20.23S 45.38W
Paintsville U.S.A. 113 37.49N 82.48W
Paisley Canada 104 44.18N 81.16W
Paisley U.K. 14 55.50N 4.26W
País Vasco d. Spain 26 43.00N 2.25W
Paiton Indonesia 59 7.42S 113.30E
Pajala Sweden 40 67.11N 23.22E
Pajares, Puerto de pass Spain 26 43.00N 5.46W
Pajule Uganda 79 2.58N 32.53E
Pakaraima Mts. Guyana 122 5.00N 60.00W
Pakaur India 63 24.38N 87.51E
Pakenham Canada 105 45.20N 76.17W
Paki Nigeria 77 11.33N 8.08E
Pakokku Myanmar 56 21.20N 95.10E
Pākpattan Pakistan 62 30.21N 73.24E
Paks Hungary 31 46.39N 18.53E
Paktiā d. Afghan. 62 33.25N 69.30E
Pakwach Uganda 79 2.27N 31.18E
Pakxé Laos 56 15.07N 105.47E
Pala Chad 77 9.25N 15.05E
Palagonia Italy 33 37.19N 14.45E
Palaiá Epídhavros Greece 35 37.38N 23.09E
Palaiá Kórinthos site Greece 35 37.54N 22.56E
Palaiá Psará Greece 35 38.46N 25.36E
Palaiokhóra Greece 35 35.14N 23.41E
Pálairos Greece 35 38.45N 20.51E
Palaiseau France 19 48.43N 2.15E
Palamás Greece 35 39.26N 22.04E
Palamós Spain 25 41.51N 3.08E
Palana Russian Fed. 51 59.05N 159.59E

Palangkaraya Indonesia 58 2.16S 113.56E
Palanguinos Spain 24 42.27N 5.31W
Pālanpur India 62 24.10N 72.26E
Palanquinos Spain 26 42.27N 5.30W
Palapye Botswana 80 22.33S 27.07E
Palas del Rey Spain 26 42.52N 7.52W
Palatka U.S.A. 113 29.38N 81.40W
Palau is. Pacific Oc. 59 7.00N 134.25E
Palaw Myanmar 56 12.58N 98.39E
Palawan i. Phil. 58 9.30N 118.30E
Palazzolo Acreide Italy 33 37.03N 14.54E
Palazzo San Gervasio Italy 33 40.56N 16.00E
Paldiski Estonia 41 59.20N 24.06E
Paleleh Indonesia 59 1.04N 121.57E
Palembang Indonesia 58 2.59S 104.50E
Palena Italy 33 41.59N 14.08E
Palencia Spain 26 42.01N 4.32W
Palencia d. Spain 26 42.30N 4.40W
Palenque Mexico 116 17.32N 91.59W
Palermo Italy 32 38.07N 13.21E
Palermo, Golfo di g. Italy 32 38.10N 13.30E
Palestine U.S.A. 111 31.46N 95.38W
Palestrina Italy 32 41.50N 12.53E
Paletwa Myanmar 56 21.25N 92.49E
Pāli India 62 25.46N 73.20E
Palimé Togo 76 6.55N 0.38E
Palinges France 19 46.35N 4.13E
Palisades Resr. U.S.A. 108 43.15N 111.05W
Pālitāna India 62 21.31N 71.50E
Palizada Mexico 116 18.15N 92.05W
Palk Str. India/Sri Lanka 61 10.00N 79.40E
Pallès, Bishti i c. Albania 34 41.24N 19.24E
Pallinup r. Australia 89 34.29S 118.54E
Palliser, C. New Zealand 86 41.35S 175.15E
Pallu India 62 28.56N 74.13E
Palma Mozambique 79 10.48S 40.25E
Palma Spain 25 39.34N 2.39E
Palma, Bahía de b. Spain 25 39.27N 2.35E
Palma del Río Spain 27 37.42N 5.17W
Palma di Montechiaro Italy 32 37.11N 13.46E
Palmahim Israel 67 31.56N 34.42E
Palmanova Italy 30 45.54N 13.19E
Palmares Brazil 123 8.41S 35.36W
Palmas, C. Liberia 76 4.30N 7.55W
Palmas, Golfo di g. Italy 32 39.00N 8.30E
Palm Beach town U.S.A. 113 26.41N 80.02W
Palmeira dos Índios Brazil 123 9.25S 36.38W
Palmeirinhas, Punta das Angola 78 9.09S 12.58E
Palmer r. Australia 88 24.46S 133.25E
Palmer U.S.A. 98 61.36N 149.07W
Palmer Land Antarctica 128 74.00S 61.00W
Palmerston Canada 104 43.50N 80.51W
Palmerston New Zealand 86 45.29S 170.43E
Palmerston Atoll Cook Is. 84 18.04S 163.10W
Palmerston, C. Australia 90 21.32S 149.29E
Palmerston North New Zealand 86 40.20S 175.39E
Palmerton U.S.A. 115 40.48N 75.37W
Palmetto U.S.A. 113 27.31N 82.32W
Palmi Italy 33 38.21N 15.51E
Palmira Colombia 122 3.33N 76.17W
Palm Is. Australia 90 18.48S 146.37E
Palms U.S.A. 114 43.37N 82.46W
Palm Springs town U.S.A. 109 33.50N 116.33W
Palmyra i. Pacific Oc. 84 5.52N 162.05W
Palmyras Pt. India 63 20.46N 87.02E
Paloh Indonesia 58 1.46N 109.17E
Paloich Sudan 73 10.28N 32.32E
Palojoensuu Finland 40 68.17N 23.05E
Palomani mtn. Bolivia 124 14.38S 69.14W
Palopo Indonesia 59 3.01S 120.12E
Palos, Cabo de c. Spain 25 37.38N 0.41W
Pålsboda Sweden 43 59.04N 15.20E
Palu Turkey 64 38.43N 39.56E
Palu Indonesia 59 0.54S 119.52E
Palwal India 62 28.09N 77.20E
Pama Burkina 76 11.15N 0.44E
Pamanukan Indonesia 59 6.16S 107.46E
Pamekasan Indonesia 59 7.11S 113.30E
Pameungpeuk Indonesia 59 7.39S 107.40E
Pamiers France 20 43.07N 1.36E
Pamir mts. Tajikistan 52 37.50N 73.30E
Pamlico Sd. U.S.A. 113 35.20N 75.55W
Pampa U.S.A. 111 35.32N 100.58W
Pampas f. Argentina 125 34.00S 64.00W
Pamplona Colombia 122 7.24N 72.38W
Pamplona Spain 25 42.49N 1.38W
Pana U.S.A. 110 39.23N 89.05W
Panaca U.S.A. 108 37.47N 114.23W
Panache, L. Canada 104 46.15N 81.20W
Panagyurishte Bulgaria 34 42.39N 24.15E
Panaji India 60 15.29N 73.50E
Panama C. America 117 9.00N 80.00W
Panamá town Panama 117 8.57N 79.30W
Panama Sri Lanka 61 6.46N 81.47E
Panama City U.S.A. 113 30.10N 85.41W
Panamá, Golfo de g. Panama 117 8.30N 79.00W
Panamint Range mts. U.S.A. 109 36.30N 117.20W
Panarea, Isola i. Italy 33 38.38N 15.05E
Panaro r. Italy 32 44.55N 11.25E
Panay i. Phil. 59 11.10N 122.30E
Panayía Greece 34 39.56N 25.20E
Pandan Phil. 59 11.45N 122.10E
Pandaria India 63 22.14N 81.25E
Pandeglang Indonesia 59 6.19S 106.05E
Pāndharkawada India 63 20.01N 78.32E
Pāndhurna India 63 21.36N 78.31E
Pando d. Bolivia 124 11.20S 67.40W
Pando Uruguay 125 34.43S 55.57W
Panevežys Lithuania 41 55.44N 24.21E
Panga Zaïre 78 1.51N 26.25E
Pangaíon Óros mts. Greece 34 40.50N 24.00E
Pangandaran Indonesia 59 7.41S 108.40E
Pangani Tanga Tanzania 79 5.21S 39.00E
Pangi Zaïre 78 3.10S 26.38E
Pangkalpinang Indonesia 58 2.05S 106.09E
Pang Long Myanmar 61 23.11N 98.45E
Pangnirtung Canada 99 66.05N 65.45W
Panipāt India 62 29.23N 76.58E
Panjāb Afghan. 62 34.22N 67.01E

Panjgūr Pakistan **62** 26.58N 64.06E
Panjpāi Pakistan **62** 29.55N 66.30E
Pankshin Nigeria **77** 9.22N 9.25E
Panna India **63** 24.43N 80.12E
Pannawonica Australia **88** 21.42S 116.22E
Páno Lévkara Cyprus **66** 34.55N 33.10E
Páno Plátres Cyprus **66** 34.53N 32.52E
Pánormos Greece **35** 37.38N 25.02E
Panshan China **54** 41.10N 122.01E
Pantano del Esla *l.* Spain **24** 41.40N 5.50W
Pantelleria Italy **32** 36.49N 11.57E
Pantelleria *i.* Italy **32** 36.47N 12.00E
Panton *r.* Australia **88** 17.05S 128.46E
Pánuco Mexico **116** 22.03N 98.10W
Panvel India **62** 18.59N 73.06E
Pan Xian China **55** 25.46N 104.39E
Panyu China **55** 23.00N 113.30E
Paola Italy **33** 39.22N 16.03E
Paola U.S.A. **110** 38.35N 94.53W
Paoua C.A.R. **77** 7.09N 16.20E
Paôy Pêt Thailand **56** 13.41N 102.34E
Papa Hawaiian Is. **85** 19.12N 155.53W
Pápa Hungary **37** 47.19N 17.28E
Papa Stour *i.* U.K. **10** 60.20N 1.42W
Papa Westray *i.* U.K. **10** 59.22N 2.54W
Papeete Tahiti **85** 17.32S 149.34W
Papenburg Germany **38** 53.05N 7.23E
Papenoo Tahiti **85** 17.30S 149.25W
Papetoai Ìs. de la Société **85** 17.29S 149.52W
Paphos *see* Néa Páfos Cyprus **66**
Papigochic *r.* Mexico **109** 29.09N 109.40W
Papillion U.S.A. **110** 41.09N 96.04W
Papineau, Lac *l.* Canada **105** 45.48N 74.46W
Papineau Prov. Park Canada **105** 45.55N 75.20W
Papineauville Canada **105** 45.37N 75.01W
Papua, G. of P.N.G. **90** 8.30S 145.00E
Papua New Guinea Austa. **87** 6.00S 144.00E
Papun Myanmar **56** 18.05N 97.26E
Papunya Australia **90** 23.15S 131.53E
Para *d.* Brazil **123** 4.00S 53.00W
Paraburdoo Australia **88** 23.12S 117.40E
Paracatu Brazil **126** 17.14S 46.52W
Paracatu *r.* Brazil **126** 16.30S 45.10W
Paracel Is. S. China Sea **58** 16.20N 112.00E
Parachilna Australia **92** 31.09S 138.24E
Pārachinār Pakistan **62** 33.54N 70.06E
Paraćin Yugo. **34** 43.52N 21.24E
Pará de Minas Brazil **126** 19.53S 44.35W
Paradip India **63** 20.15N 86.35E
Paradise *r.* Canada **103** 53.23N 57.18W
Paradise Calif. U.S.A. **108** 39.46N 121.37W
Paradise Nev. U.S.A. **109** 36.09N 115.10W
Paragonah U.S.A. **108** 37.53N 112.46W
Paragould U.S.A. **111** 36.03N 90.29W
Paragua *r.* Venezuela **122** 6.55N 62.55W
Paraguaçu *r.* Brazil **123** 12.35S 38.59W
Paraguaná, Península de *pen.* Venezuela **122** 11.50N 69.50W
Paraguarí Paraguay **126** 25.36S 57.06W
Paraguay *r.* Argentina **126** 27.30S 58.50W
Paraguay S. America **126** 23.00S 57.00W
Paraíba *d.* Brazil **123** 7.30S 36.30W
Paraíba *r.* Brazil **126** 21.45S 41.10W
Paraibuna Brazil **126** 23.24S 45.32W
Paraisópolis Brazil **126** 22.33S 45.48W
Parakou Benin **77** 9.23N 2.40E
Parálion Astrous Greece **35** 37.25N 22.45E
Paramagudi India **61** 9.33N 78.36E
Paramaribo Surinam **123** 5.52N 55.14W
Paramithiá Greece **34** 39.30N 20.35E
Paramonga Peru **122** 10.42S 77.50W
Paraná Argentina **125** 31.45S 60.30W
Paraná *r.* Argentina **125** 34.00S 58.30W
Paraná Brazil **123** 12.33S 47.48W
Paraná *d.* Brazil **126** 24.30S 52.00W
Paraná *r.* Brazil **123** 12.30S 48.10W
Paranaguá Brazil **126** 25.32S 48.36W
Paranaíba Brazil **126** 19.53S 51.00W
Paranaíba *r.* Brazil **126** 20.00S 51.00W
Paranapanema *r.* Brazil **123** 22.30S 53.03W
Paranapiacaba, Serra *mts.* Brazil **126** 24.30S 49.15W
Paranavaí Brazil **126** 23.02S 52.36W
Paranéstion Greece **34** 41.16N 24.32E
Parangaba Brazil **123** 3.45S 38.33W
Paraparaumu New Zealand **86** 40.55S 175.00E
Paratoo Australia **92** 32.46S 139.40E
Paray-le-Monial France **19** 46.27N 4.07E
Pārbati *r.* India **62** 25.51N 76.36E
Pārbatipur Bangla. **63** 25.39N 88.55E
Parbhani India **62** 19.16N 76.47E
Parchim Germany **38** 53.25N 11.51E
Parczew Poland **37** 51.39N 22.54E
Pardes Hanna Israel **67** 32.28N 34.58E
Pārdi India **62** 20.31N 72.57E
Pardo *r.* Bahia Brazil **126** 15.40S 39.38W
Pardo *r.* Mato Grosso Brazil **126** 21.56S 52.07W
Pardo *r.* São Paulo Brazil **126** 20.10S 48.36W
Pardubice Czech Republic **36** 50.03N 15.45E
Parecis, Serra dos *mts.* Brazil **122** 13.30S 58.30W
Paredes de Nava Spain **26** 42.09N 4.41W
Pareloup, Lac de *l.* France **20** 44.15N 2.45E
Parent Canada **102** 47.55N 74.35W
Parentis-en-Born France **20** 44.21N 1.05W
Parent, Lac *l.* Canada **102** 48.40N 77.03W
Parepare Indonesia **58** 4.03S 119.40E
Párga Greece **35** 39.17N 20.23E
Pargas Finland **41** 60.18N 22.18E
Paria, Golfo de *g.* Venezuela **122** 10.30S 62.00W
Pariaguán Venezuela **122** 8.51N 64.43W
Pariaman Indonesia **58** 0.36S 100.09E
Paria, Península de *pen.* Venezuela **122** 10.45N 62.30W
Parichi Belarus **37** 52.48N 29.25E
Parigi Indonesia **59** 0.49S 120.10E
Parika Guyana **122** 6.51N 58.25W
Parima, Sierra *mts.* Venezuela **122** 2.30N 64.00W
Parinari Peru **122** 4.35S 74.25W
Paringa Australia **92** 34.10S 140.49E

Parintins Brazil **123** 2.36S 56.44W
Paris Canada **104** 43.12N 80.23W
Paris France **19** 48.52N 2.20E
Paris Kiribati **85** 1.56N 157.29W
Paris Ill. U.S.A. **110** 39.35N 87.41W
Paris Ky. U.S.A. **112** 38.13N 84.15W
Paris Tenn. U.S.A. **111** 36.19N 88.20W
Paris Tex. U.S.A. **111** 33.40N 95.33W
Parish U.S.A. **115** 43.24N 76.08W
Parisienne *d.* France **19** 48.30N 2.30E
Parisienne, Île *i.* Canada **104** 46.40N 84.44W
Parkano Finland **41** 62.01N 23.01E
Parkbeg Canada **101** 50.28N 106.18W
Parker Ariz. U.S.A. **109** 34.09N 114.17W
Parker Penn. U.S.A. **114** 41.06N 79.41W
Parker, C. Canada **99** 75.04N 79.40W
Parker Dam U.S.A. **109** 34.18N 114.10W
Parkersburg U.S.A. **114** 39.17N 81.32W
Parkes Australia **93** 33.10S 148.13E
Park Falls *town* U.S.A. **110** 45.56N 90.32W
Park Forest *town* U.S.A. **110** 41.35N 87.41W
Parkhill Canada **104** 43.09N 81.41W
Parkland U.S.A. **108** 47.09N 122.26W
Park Range *mts.* U.S.A. **108** 40.00N 106.30W
Parkton U.S.A. **115** 39.38N 76.40W
Parlākimidi India **63** 18.46N 84.05E
Parma Italy **30** 44.48N 10.20E
Parma *r.* Italy **30** 44.56N 10.26E
Parma U.S.A. **114** 41.22N 81.43W
Parnaguá Brazil **123** 10.17S 44.39W
Parnaíba Brazil **123** 2.58S 41.46W
Parnaíba *r.* Brazil **123** 2.58S 41.47W
Parnassós *mtn.* Greece **35** 38.17N 21.30E
Parndana Australia **92** 35.44S 137.14E
Párnis *mtn.* Greece **35** 38.11N 23.42E
Párnon Óros *mts.* Greece **35** 37.18N 22.35E
Pärnu Estonia **41** 58.24N 24.32E
Pärnu *r.* Estonia **41** 58.23N 24.29E
Pārola India **62** 20.53N 75.07E
Paroo *r.* Australia **92** 31.30S 143.34E
Páros Greece **35** 37.04N 25.08E
Páros *i.* Greece **35** 37.08N 25.12E
Parrakie Australia **92** 35.18S 140.12E
Parral Chile **125** 36.09S 71.50W
Parramatta Australia **93** 33.50S 150.57E
Parras Mexico **111** 25.30N 102.11W
Parras, Sierra de *mts.* Mexico **111** 25.20N 102.10W
Parrett *r.* U.K. **13** 51.10N 3.00W
Parry Canada **101** 49.47N 104.41W
Parry I. Canada **104** 45.18N 80.10W
Parry Is. Canada **99** 76.00N 102.00W
Parry, Kap *c.* Greenland **99** 76.50N 71.00W
Parry Sound Canada **104** 45.21N 80.02W
Parsad India **62** 24.11N 73.42E
Parsęta *r.* Poland **36** 54.12N 15.33E
Parsnip *r.* Canada **100** 55.10N 123.02W
Parsons Kans. U.S.A. **111** 37.20N 95.16W
Parsons W.Va. U.S.A. **114** 39.06N 79.41W
Partanna Italy **32** 37.43N 12.53E
Parthenay France **18** 46.39N 0.15W
Partille Sweden **43** 57.44N 12.07E
Partinico Italy **32** 38.03N 13.07E
Partry Mts. Rep. of Ire. **15** 53.40N 9.30W
Paru *r.* Brazil **123** 1.33S 52.38W
Pärvatīpuram India **63** 18.47N 83.26E
Paryang China **63** 30.04N 83.28E
Parys R.S.A. **80** 26.54S 27.26E
Pasadena Calif. U.S.A. **109** 34.09N 118.09W
Pasadena Tex. U.S.A. **111** 29.42N 95.13W
Pasaje Ecuador **122** 3.23S 79.50W
Pasawng Myanmar **56** 18.52N 97.18E
Pascagoula U.S.A. **111** 30.23N 88.31W
Pașcani Romania **37** 47.15N 26.44E
Pasco U.S.A. **108** 46.14N 119.06W
Pascoag U.S.A. **115** 41.57N 71.42W
Pascua, Isla de *i.* Pacific Oc. **85** 27.08S 109.23W
Pas-de-Calais *d.* France **19** 50.30N 2.20E
Pasewalk Germany **38** 53.30N 14.00E
Pasfield L. Canada **101** 58.25N 105.20W
Pasinler Turkey **64** 39.59N 41.41E
Pasir Puteh Malaysia **58** 5.50N 102.24E
Påskallavik Sweden **43** 57.10N 16.27E
Pasley, C. Australia **89** 33.55S 123.30E
Pašman *i.* Croatia **31** 43.58N 15.21E
Pasmore *r.* Australia **92** 31.07S 139.48E
Pasni Pakistan **62** 25.16N 63.28E
Paso de Bermejo *f.* Argentina **121** 32.50S 70.00W
Paso de los Libres *town* Argentina **125** 29.45S 57.05W
Paso de los Toros *town* Uruguay **125** 32.49S 56.31W
Paso Robles U.S.A. **109** 35.38N 120.41W
Paso Socompa *f.* Chile **121** 24.27S 68.18W
Paspébiac Canada **103** 48.01N 65.20W
Pasquia Hills Canada **101** 53.13N 102.37W
Pasrūr Pakistan **62** 32.16N 74.40E
Passaic U.S.A. **115** 40.51N 74.08W
Passau Germany **39** 48.35N 13.28E
Passero, Capo *c.* Italy **33** 36.40N 15.09E
Passo Fundo Brazil **126** 28.16S 52.20W
Passos Brazil **126** 20.45S 46.38W
Pastaza *r.* Peru **122** 4.50S 76.25W
Pasto Colombia **122** 1.12N 77.17W
Pastrana Spain **26** 40.25N 2.55W
Pasuquin Phil. **55** 18.25N 120.37E
Pasuruan Indonesia **59** 7.38S 112.54E
Pātan India **62** 23.50N 72.07E
Patchewollock Australia **92** 35.25S 142.14E
Patchogue U.S.A. **115** 40.46N 73.00W
Patea New Zealand **86** 39.46S 174.29E
Pategi Nigeria **77** 8.44N 5.47E
Pate I. Kenya **79** 2.08S 41.02E
Paternion Austria **39** 46.43N 13.38E
Paternò Italy **33** 37.34N 14.54E
Paterson U.S.A. **115** 40.55N 74.10W
Pathānkot India **62** 32.17N 75.39E
Pathein *see* Bassein Myanmar **56**

Pathfinder Resr. U.S.A. **108** 42.30N 106.50W
Pathiong Sudan **73** 6.46N 30.54E
Pati Indonesia **59** 6.45S 111.00E
Patía *r.* Colombia **122** 1.54N 78.30W
Patiäla India **62** 30.19N 76.23E
Pati Pt. Guam **84** 13.36N 144.57E
Patkai Hills Myanmar **56** 26.30N 95.30E
Pátmos *i.* Greece **35** 37.20N 26.33E
Patna India **63** 25.36N 85.07E
Patnāgarh India **63** 20.43N 83.09E
Patos Brazil **123** 6.55S 37.15W
Patos de Minas Brazil **126** 18.35S 46.32W
Patos, Lagoa dos *l.* Brazil **126** 31.00S 51.10W
Patquía Argentina **124** 30.02S 66.55W
Pátrai Greece **35** 38.15N 21.44E
Patraïkós Kólpos *g.* Greece **35** 38.14N 21.15E
Patrasuy Russian Fed. **44** 63.35N 61.50E
Patrickswell Rep. of Ire. **15** 52.36N 8.43W
Pattada Italy **32** 40.35N 9.07E
Pattani Thailand **56** 6.51N 101.16E
Pattaya Thailand **56** 12.57N 100.53E
Patterson Creek *r.* U.S.A. **114** 39.34N 78.23W
Patti Italy **33** 38.09N 14.58E
Patti, Golfo di *g.* Italy **33** 38.12N 15.05E
Pattoki Pakistan **62** 31.01N 73.51E
Patton U.S.A. **114** 40.38N 78.39W
Patuākhāli Bangla. **63** 22.21N 90.21E
Patuca *r.* Honduras **117** 15.50N 84.18W
Pātūr India **62** 20.27N 76.56E
Patuxent *r.* U.S.A. **115** 38.18N 76.25W
Pau France **20** 43.18N 0.22W
Pau, Gave de *r.* France **20** 43.33N 1.12W
Pauillac France **20** 45.12N 0.44W
Paúl do Mar Madeira Is. **127** 32.45N 17.14W
Paulhan France **20** 43.32N 3.27E
Paulina U.S.A. **108** 44.09N 119.58W
Paulistana Brazil **123** 8.09S 41.09W
Paulo Afonso Brazil **123** 9.25S 38.15W
Paulsboro U.S.A. **115** 39.50N 75.15W
Pauls Valley *town* U.S.A. **111** 34.44N 97.13W
Paungde Myanmar **56** 18.30N 95.30E
Pauni India **63** 20.47N 79.38E
Pauri Uttar P. India **63** 30.09N 78.47E
Pavia Italy **30** 45.10N 9.10E
Pavilly France **18** 49.34N 0.58E
Pavlikeni Bulgaria **34** 43.14N 25.20E
Pavlodar Kazakhstan **52** 52.21N 76.59E
Pavlograd Ukraine **45** 48.34N 35.50E
Pavlovo Russian Fed. **44** 55.58N 43.05E
Pavlovsk Russian Fed. **45** 50.28N 40.07E
Pavullo nel Frignano Italy **30** 44.20N 10.50E
Pawnee U.S.A. **111** 36.20N 96.48W
Pawtucket U.S.A. **115** 41.53N 71.23W
Paxoí *i.* Greece **35** 39.14N 20.12E
Paxton U.S.A. **110** 41.07N 101.21W
Payerne Switz. **39** 46.49N 6.56E
Payette U.S.A. **108** 44.05N 116.56W
Payne, L. Canada **99** 59.25N 74.00W
Paynes Find Australia **89** 29.15S 117.41E
Paysandú Uruguay **125** 32.19S 58.05W
Pays de Caux *f.* France **18** 49.40N 0.40E
Pays de la Loire *d.* France **18** 47.30N 1.00W
Pazardzhik Bulgaria **34** 42.12N 24.20E
Pazin Croatia **31** 45.14N 13.56E
Pčinja *r.* Yugo. **34** 42.00N 21.45E
Peace *r.* Canada **100** 59.00N 111.25W
Peace River *town* Canada **100** 56.15N 117.18W
Peach Springs *town* U.S.A. **109** 35.32N 113.25W
Peacock Hills Canada **98** 66.05N 110.45W
Peak Creek *r.* Australia **92** 28.05S 136.07E
Peak Hill *town* N.S.W. Australia **93** 32.47S 148.13E
Peak Range *mts.* Australia **90** 23.18S 148.30E
Peak, The *mtn.* Ascension **127** 7.57S 14.21W
Peale, Mt. U.S.A. **108** 38.26N 109.14W
Pearl *r.* U.S.A. **111** 30.11N 89.32W
Pearland U.S.A. **111** 29.34N 95.17W
Pearsall U.S.A. **111** 28.53N 99.06W
Peary Land *f.* Greenland **96** 83.00N 35.00W
Pebane Mozambique **81** 17.14S 38.10E
Pebas Peru **122** 3.17S 71.55W
Peć Yugo. **34** 42.40N 20.17E
Pechenga Russian Fed. **40** 69.28N 31.04E
Pechora Russian Fed. **44** 65.14N 57.18E
Pechora *r.* Russian Fed. **44** 68.10N 54.00E
Pechorskaya Guba *g.* Russian Fed. **44** 69.00N 56.00E
Pechorskoye More *sea* Russian Fed. **44** 69.00N 55.00E
Pecoraro, Monte *mtn.* Italy **33** 38.32N 16.20E
Pecos U.S.A. **111** 31.25N 103.30W
Pecos *r.* U.S.A. **111** 29.42N 101.22W
Pécs Hungary **31** 46.05N 18.13E
Pécs *d.* Hungary **31** 46.05N 18.10E
Peddie R.S.A. **80** 33.12S 27.07E
Pedras Salgadas Portugal **26** 41.32N 7.36W
Pedregulho Brazil **126** 20.15S 47.29W
Pedreiras Brazil **123** 4.32S 44.40W
Pedrinhas Brazil **123** 11.12S 37.41W
Pedro Afonso Brazil **123** 8.59S 48.11W
Pedro de Valdivia Chile **124** 22.36S 69.40W
Pedrógão Grande Portugal **27** 39.55N 8.09W
Pedro Juan Caballero Paraguay **126** 22.30S 55.44W
Pedro Muñoz Spain **27** 39.24N 2.58W
Peduyim Israel **67** 31.20N 34.37E
Peebinga Australia **92** 34.55S 140.57E
Peebles U.K. **14** 55.39N 3.12W
Peebles U.S.A. **112** 38.57N 83.14W
Peekskill U.S.A. **115** 41.17N 73.55W
Peel *r.* Canada **98** 68.13N 135.00W
Peel I.o.M. Europe **12** 54.14N 4.42W
Peel Inlet Australia **89** 32.35S 115.44E
Peel Pt. Canada **98** 73.22N 114.35W
Peene *r.* Germany **38** 54.09N 13.46E
Peera Peera Poolanna L. Australia **90** 26.43S 137.42E
Peerless L. Canada **100** 56.37N 114.35W
Pegasus B. New Zealand **86** 43.15S 173.00E
Pegin Albania **34** 41.04N 19.44E

Pegnitz Germany **38** 49.45N 11.33E
Pegnitz *r.* Germany **38** 49.29N 11.00E
Pego Spain **25** 38.51N 0.07W
Pegu Myanmar **56** 17.20N 96.36E
Pegu *d.* Myanmar **56** 17.30N 96.30E
Pegunungan Van Rees *mts.* Indonesia **59** 2.35S 138.15E
Pegu Yoma *mts.* Myanmar **56** 18.30N 96.00E
Pehčevo Macedonia **34** 41.41N 23.03E
Pehuajó Argentina **125** 35.50S 61.50W
Peikang Taiwan **55** 23.35N 120.19E
Peine Germany **38** 52.19N 10.13E
Peipus, L. Estonia/Russian Fed. **44** 58.30N 27.30E
Peissenberg Germany **39** 47.48N 11.04E
Peixe Brazil **123** 12.03S 48.32W
Pei Xian China **54** 34.44N 116.55E
Pekalongan Indonesia **59** 6.54S 109.37E
Pekanbaru Indonesia **58** 0.33N 101.20E
Pekin U.S.A. **110** 40.34N 89.40W
Peking *see* Beijing China **54**
Pelabuanratu Indonesia **59** 7.00S 106.32E
Pelat, Mont *mtn.* France **21** 44.16N 6.42E
Peleaga *mtn.* Romania **37** 45.22N 22.54E
Pelee I. Canada **114** 41.46N 82.39W
Pelee, Mt. Canada **114** 41.54N 82.30W
Peleng *i.* Indonesia **59** 1.30S 123.10E
Peleniya Moldova **37** 47.58N 27.48E
Pelican U.S.A. **100** 57.55N 136.10W
Pelister *mtn.* Macedonia **34** 41.00N 21.12E
Pelješac, Poluotok *pen.* Croatia **31** 42.58N 17.20E
Pelkum Germany **38** 51.39N 7.45E
Pélla *site* Greece **34** 40.45N 22.33E
Pelleg i Drinit *b.* Albania **34** 41.45N 19.28E
Pellegrino, Cozzo *mtn.* Italy **33** 39.45N 16.03E
Pello Finland **40** 66.47N 24.00E
Pellston U.S.A. **104** 45.33N 84.47W
Pellworm *i.* Germany **38** 54.31N 8.38E
Pelly *r.* Canada **98** 62.50N 137.35W
Pelly Bay *town* Canada **98** 68.38N 89.45W
Pelly L. Canada **99** 65.59N 101.12W
Peloncillo Mts. U.S.A. **109** 32.16N 109.00W
Peloponnisos *f.* Greece **35** 37.30N 22.00E
Peloritani, Monti *mts.* Italy **33** 38.00N 15.25E
Pelotas Brazil **126** 31.45S 52.20W
Pelvoux, Massif du *f.* France **21** 44.55N 6.20E
Pemalang Indonesia **59** 6.53S 109.21E
Pematangsiantar Indonesia **58** 2.59N 99.01E
Pemba Mozambique **81** 13.02S 40.30E
Pemba Zambia **79** 16.33S 27.20E
Pemba I. Tanzania **79** 5.10S 39.45E
Pemberton Australia **89** 34.28S 116.01E
Pemberton Canada **100** 50.20N 122.48W
Pembina *r.* Canada **100** 54.45N 114.15W
Pembina Canada **105** 45.49N 77.07W
Pembroke U.K. **13** 51.41N 4.57W
Pembroke Canada **105** 45.49N 77.07W
Pembroke U.S.A. **113** 32.09N 81.39W
Penacook U.S.A. **115** 43.17N 71.37W
Penafiel Portugal **26** 41.12N 8.17W
Peñafiel Spain **26** 41.36N 4.07W
Peñagolosa *mtn.* Spain **25** 40.13N 0.21W
Peñalara *mtn.* Spain **26** 40.51N 3.57W
Penang *see* Pinang, Pulau *i.* Malaysia **58**
Peñaranda de Bracamonte Spain **26** 40.54N 5.12W
Pen Argyl U.S.A. **115** 40.52N 75.16W
Peñarroya *mtn.* Spain **25** 40.24N 0.40W
Peñarroya-Pueblonuevo Spain **26** 38.18N 5.16W
Penarth U.K. **13** 51.26N 3.11W
Peñas, Cabo de *c.* Spain **26** 43.39N 5.51W
Penas, Golfo de *g.* Chile **125** 47.20S 75.00W
Peña, Sierra de la *mts.* Spain **25** 42.30N 0.50W
Pendálofon Greece **34** 40.14N 21.12E
Pende *r.* Chad **77** 7.30N 16.20E
Pendembu Eastern Sierra Leone **76** 8.09N 10.42W
Pendine U.K. **13** 51.44N 4.33W
Pendleton U.S.A. **108** 45.40N 118.47W
Penedo Brazil **123** 10.16S 36.33W
Penedono Portugal **26** 40.59N 7.24W
Penela Portugal **27** 40.02N 8.23W
Penetanguishene Canada **104** 44.47N 79.55W
Penfield U.S.A. **114** 41.13N 78.34W
Penganga *r.* India **63** 19.53N 79.09E
Penge Zaïre **78** 5.31S 24.37E
Penghu Liedao *is.* Taiwan **55** 23.35N 119.32E
Pengshui China **55** 29.17N 108.13E
Peniche Portugal **27** 39.21N 9.23W
Penicuik U.K. **14** 55.49N 3.13W
Peninsular Malaysia *d.* Malaysia **58** 5.00N 102.00E
Peñíscola Spain **25** 40.21N 0.25E
Penmarc'h, Pointe de *c.* France **18** 47.48N 4.22W
Penne Italy **31** 42.27N 13.55E
Penne-d'Agenais France **20** 44.23N 0.49E
Penneshaw Australia **92** 35.42S 137.55E
Pennsauken U.S.A. **115** 39.58N 75.04W
Pennsboro U.S.A. **114** 39.17N 80.58W
Penns Grove U.S.A. **115** 39.43N 75.28W
Pennsylvania *d.* U.S.A. **114** 40.45N 77.30W
Penn Yan U.S.A. **114** 42.40N 77.03W
Penny Highland *mtn.* Canada **99** 67.10N 66.50W
Penobscot *r.* U.S.A. **112** 44.30N 68.50W
Penola Australia **92** 37.23S 140.21E
Penong Australia **89** 31.55S 133.01E
Penonomé Panama **117** 8.30N 80.20W
Penrhyn Atoll Cook Is. **85** 9.00S 158.00W
Penrith Australia **93** 33.47S 150.44E
Penrith U.K. **12** 54.40N 2.45W
Penryn U.K. **13** 50.10N 5.07W
Pensacola U.S.A. **113** 30.26N 87.12W
Pensacola Mts. Antarctica **128** 84.00S 45.00W
Penshurst Australia **92** 37.52S 142.20E
Pentecost I. Vanuatu **84** 15.42S 168.10E
Penticton Canada **100** 49.30N 119.30W
Pentland Australia **90** 20.32S 145.24E
Pentland Firth *str.* U.K. **14** 58.40N 3.00W
Pentland Hills U.K. **14** 55.50N 3.20W
Penylan L. Canada **101** 61.50N 106.20W
Penza Russian Fed. **44** 53.11N 45.00E
Penzance U.K. **13** 50.07N 5.32W

Penzberg Germany **39** 47.45N 11.23E

Penzhinskaya Guba g. Russian Fed. 51 61.00N 163.00E
Peoria Ariz. U.S.A. 109 33.35N 112.14W
Peoria Ill. U.S.A. 110 40.43N 89.38W
Pepacton Resr. U.S.A. 115 42.06N 74.54W
Peper Sudan 73 7.04N 33.00E
Pepperell U.S.A. 115 42.40N 71.35W
Perabumulih Indonesia 58 3.29S 104.14E
Perales de Alfambra Spain 25 40.38N 1.00W
Perche, Collines du hills France 18 48.25N 0.40E
Percival Lakes Australia 88 21.25S 125.00E
Perdido, Monte mtn. Spain 25 42.40N 0.05E
Pereira Colombia 122 4.47N 75.46W
Perekop Ukraine 45 46.10N 33.42E
Perené r. Peru 124 11.02S 74.19W
Perevolotskiy Russian Fed. 44 51.10N 54.15E
Pereyaslav-Khmelnitskiy Ukraine 37 50.05N 31.28E
Pergamino Argentina 125 33.53S 60.35W
Pergine Valsugana Italy 30 46.04N 11.14E
Pergola Italy 30 43.34N 12.50E
Perham U.S.A. 110 46.36N 95.34W
Péribonca r. Canada 103 48.45N 72.05W
Pericos Mexico 109 25.03N 107.42W
Périers France 18 49.11N 1.25W
Périgueux France 20 45.11N 0.43E
Perija, Sierra de mts. Venezuela 122 10.30N 72.30W
Peri L. Australia 92 30.44S 143.34E
Perleberg Germany 38 53.04N 11.51E
Perm Russian Fed. 44 58.01N 56.10E
Përmet Albania 34 40.15N 20.21E
Pernambuco d. Brazil 123 8.00S 39.00W
Pernatty L. Australia 92 31.31S 137.14E
Pernik Bulgaria 34 42.36N 23.02E
Perniö Finland 41 60.12N 23.08E
Péronne France 19 49.56N 2.56E
Perosa Argentina Italy 30 44.58N 7.10E
Pérouse, Bahía la b. i. de Pascua 85 27.04S 109.20W
Perpendicular, Pt. Australia 93 35.03S 150.50E
Perpignan France 20 42.41N 2.53E
Perranporth U.K. 13 50.21N 5.09W
Perro, Punta del c. Spain 27 36.45N 6.26W
Perros-Guirec France 18 48.49N 3.27W
Perry Fla. U.S.A. 113 30.08N 83.36W
Perry Iowa U.S.A. 110 41.50N 94.06W
Perry Mich. U.S.A. 104 42.50N 84.13W
Perry Okla. U.S.A. 111 36.17N 97.17W
Perryton U.S.A. 111 36.24N 100.48W
Perryville U.S.A. 111 37.43N 89.52W
Persberg Sweden 43 59.45N 14.15E
Persepolis ruins Iran 65 29.55N 53.00E
Perth Australia 89 31.58S 115.49E
Perth Canada 105 44.54N 76.15W
Perth U.K. 14 56.24N 3.28W
Perth Amboy U.S.A. 115 40.31N 74.16W
Pertuis France 21 43.41N 5.30E
Peru S. America 122 10.00S 75.00W
Peru Ill. U.S.A. 110 41.19N 89.11W
Peru Basin Pacific Oc. 85 19.00S 96.00W
Peru-Chile Trench Pacific Oc. 121 23.00S 71.30W
Perugia Italy 30 43.08N 12.22E
Perušić Croatia 31 44.39N 15.23E
Péruwelz Belgium 16 50.32N 3.36E
Pervomaysk Ukraine 37 48.03N 30.50E
Pervouralsk Russian Fed. 44 56.59N 59.58E
Pesaro Italy 30 43.54N 12.55E
Pescara Italy 31 42.28N 14.13E
Pescara r. Italy 31 42.28N 14.13E
Pescia Italy 30 43.54N 10.41E
Peshāwar Pakistan 62 34.01N 71.33E
Peshīn Jān Afghan. 62 33.25N 61.28E
Peshkopi Albania 34 41.41N 20.25E
Peshtera Bulgaria 34 42.02N 24.18E
Pesmes France 19 47.17N 5.34E
Peso da Régua Portugal 26 41.10N 7.47W
Pesqueira Brazil 123 8.24S 36.38W
Pesquería r. Mexico 111 25.55N 99.28W
Pessac France 20 44.48N 0.38W
Pesteana Jiu Romania 37 44.50N 23.15E
Pestovo Russian Fed. 44 58.32N 35.42E
Petah Tiqwa Israel 67 32.05N 34.53E
Petalídhion Greece 35 36.57N 21.55E
Petalión, Kólpos g. Greece 35 37.59N 24.02E
Petaluma U.S.A. 108 38.14N 122.39W
Pétange Lux. 16 49.32N 5.56E
Petare Venezuela 122 10.31N 66.50W
Petatlán Mexico 116 17.31N 101.16W
Petauke Zambia 79 14.16S 31.21E
Petawawa Canada 105 45.54N 77.17W
Petawawa r. Canada 105 45.55N 77.15W
Peterborough S.A. Australia 92 33.00S 138.51E
Peterborough Vic. Australia 92 38.36S 142.55E
Peterborough Canada 104 44.18N 78.19W
Peterborough U.K. 13 52.35N 0.14W
Peterborough U.S.A. 115 42.53N 71.57W
Peterhead U.K. 14 57.30N 1.46W
Peterlee U.K. 12 54.45N 1.18W
Petermann Ranges mts. Australia 88 25.00S 129.46E
Peter Pond L. Canada 101 55.55N 108.44W
Petersburg Alas. U.S.A. 100 56.49N 132.58W
Petersburg Va. U.S.A. 113 37.14N 77.24W
Petersburg W.Va. U.S.A. 114 39.00N 79.09W
Petersfield U.K. 13 51.00N 0.56W
Petilia Policastro Italy 33 39.07N 16.47E
Petitot r. Canada 100 60.14N 123.29W
Petitsikapau L. Canada 103 54.45N 66.25W
Petit St. Bernard, Col du pass France/Italy 30 45.40N 6.53E
Petläd India 62 22.30N 72.45E
Petoskey U.S.A. 112 45.22N 84.59W
Petra ruins Jordan 66 30.19N 35.26E
Petre, Pt. Canada 105 43.50N 77.09W
Petrich Bulgaria 34 41.24N 23.13E
Petrikov Belarus 37 52.09N 28.30E
Petrodvorets Russian Fed. 44 59.50N 29.57E
Petrolia Canada 104 42.52N 82.09W
Petrolina Brazil 123 9.22S 40.30W
Petropavlovsk Kazakhstan 9 54.53N 69.13E

Petropavlovsk Kamchatskiy Russian Fed. 51 53.03N 158.43E
Petrópolis Brazil 126 22.30S 43.06W
Petroşani Romania 37 45.25N 23.22E
Petrovaradin Yugo. 31 45.16N 19.55E
Petrovsk Russian Fed. 44 52.20N 45.24E
Petrovsk Zabaykal'skiy Russian Fed. 51 51.20N 108.55E
Petrozavodsk Russian Fed. 44 61.46N 34.19E
Petrus Steyn R.S.A. 80 27.38S 28.08E
Peuerbach Austria 39 48.21N 13.56E
Peureulak Indonesia 58 4.48N 97.45E
Pevek Russian Fed. 51 69.41N 170.19E
Peyruis France 21 44.02N 5.56E
Pézenas France 20 43.27N 3.25E
Pezinok Slovakia 37 48.18N 17.17E
Pezmog Russian Fed. 44 61.50N 51.45E
Pezu Pakistan 62 32.19N 70.44E
Pfaffenhofen Germany 39 48.31N 11.30E
Pfalzel Germany 39 49.47N 6.41E
Pfarrkirchen Germany 39 48.27N 12.56E
Pforzheim Germany 39 48.54N 8.42E
Pfronten Germany 39 47.34N 10.33E
Pfunds Austria 39 46.58N 10.33E
Pfungstadt Germany 39 49.48N 8.36E
Phagwāra India 62 31.13N 75.47E
Phalodi India 62 27.08N 72.22E
Phalsbourg France 19 48.46N 7.16E
Phangan, Ko i. Thailand 58 9.50N 100.00E
Phangnga Thailand 56 8.29N 98.31E
Phan Rang Vietnam 56 11.34N 109.00E
Phan Thiet Vietnam 56 11.00N 108.06E
Pharenda India 63 27.06N 83.17E
Phariāro Pakistan 62 27.12N 68.59E
Phat Diem Vietnam 55 20.06N 106.07E
Phatthalung Thailand 56 7.38N 100.04E
Phelps U.S.A. 114 42.57N 77.03W
Phelps L. Canada 101 59.15N 103.15W
Phenix City U.S.A. 113 32.28N 85.01W
Phet Buri Thailand 56 13.00N 99.58E
Philadelphia Miss. U.S.A. 111 32.46N 89.07W
Philadelphia N.Y. U.S.A. 105 44.09N 75.43W
Philadelphia Penn. U.S.A. 115 39.57N 75.07W
Philippeville Belgium 16 50.12N 4.32E
Philippi U.S.A. 114 39.09N 80.02W
Philippines Asia 59 13.00N 123.00E
Philippine Sea Pacific Oc. 84 18.00N 135.00E
Philippine Trench Pacific Oc. 59 8.45N 127.20E
Philipsburg Canada 105 45.02N 73.05W
Philipsburg U.S.A. 114 40.45N 78.14W
Philip Smith Mts. U.S.A. 98 68.30N 147.00W
Philipstown R.S.A. 80 30.25S 24.26E
Phillip U.S.A. 110 44.02N 101.40W
Phillip Edward I. Canada 104 45.58N 81.17W
Phillip I. Australia 93 38.29S 145.14E
Phillips r. Australia 89 33.55S 120.01E
Phillips Maine U.S.A. 112 44.49N 70.21W
Phillips Wisc. U.S.A. 110 45.41N 90.24W
Phillipsburg Kans. U.S.A. 110 39.45N 99.19W
Phillipsburg N.J. U.S.A. 115 40.42N 75.12W
Phillipson, L. Australia 92 29.28S 134.28E
Philo U.S.A. 114 39.52N 81.55W
Phnom Penh Cambodia 56 11.35N 104.55E
Phoenicia U.S.A. 115 42.05N 74.19W
Phoenix Ariz. U.S.A. 109 33.27N 112.05W
Phoenix N.Y. U.S.A. 115 43.14N 76.18W
Phoenix Is. Kiribati 84 4.00S 172.00W
Phoenixville Conn. U.S.A. 115 41.51N 72.03W
Phoenixville Penn. U.S.A. 115 40.08N 75.31W
Phon Thailand 56 15.50N 102.35E
Phôngsali Laos 56 21.40N 102.11E
Phou Loi mtn. Laos 56 20.16N 103.18E
Phu Huu Vietnam 55 19.00N 105.35E
Phukao Miang mtn. Thailand 61 16.50N 101.00E
Phuket Thailand 56 7.55N 98.23E
Phuket, Ko i. Thailand 56 8.10N 98.20E
Phu Ly Vietnam 55 20.30N 105.58E
Phumĭ Chuuk Vietnam 56 10.50N 104.28E
Phumĭ Sâmraŏng Cambodia 56 14.12N 103.31E
Phu Quoc i. Cambodia 56 10.20N 104.00E
Phu Tho Vietnam 56 21.23N 105.13E
Phu Vinh Vietnam 56 9.57N 106.20E
Piacá Brazil 123 7.42S 47.18W
Piacenza Italy 30 45.01N 9.40E
Pialba Australia 90 25.13S 152.55E
Pian r. Australia 93 30.03S 148.18E
Piana France 21 42.14N 8.38E
Pianella Italy 31 42.24N 14.02E
Piangil Australia 91 35.04S 143.20E
Pianoro Italy 30 44.22N 11.20E
Pianosa i. Italy 30 42.36N 10.04E
Piatra-Neamţ Romania 37 46.56N 26.22E
Piauí d. Brazil 123 7.45S 42.30W
Piauí r. Brazil 123 6.14S 42.51W
Piave r. Italy 30 45.32N 12.44E
Piawaning Australia 89 30.51S 116.22E
Piazza Armerina Italy 33 37.23N 14.22E
Pibor r. Sudan 73 8.26N 33.13E
Pibor Post Sudan 73 6.48N 33.08E
Pic r. Canada 102 48.38N 86.25W
Picardie d. France 19 49.42N 2.40E
Pickens U.S.A. 114 38.39N 80.13W
Pickerel r. Canada 104 45.55N 80.50W
Pickerel River town Canada 104 46.01N 80.45W
Pickering U.K. 12 54.15N 0.46W
Pickford U.S.A. 104 46.10N 84.22W
Pickle Crow Canada 102 51.30N 90.04W
Pickwick L. resr. U.S.A. 111 34.55N 88.10W
Picos Brazil 123 7.05S 41.28W
Picos Ancares, Sierra de mts. Spain 26 42.51N 6.52W
Picquigny France 19 49.57N 2.09E
Picton Australia 93 34.12S 150.35E
Picton Canada 105 44.00N 77.08W
Picton New Zealand 86 41.17S 174.02E
Picún Leufú Argentina 125 39.30S 69.15W
Pidálion, Akrotírion c. Cyprus 66 34.56N 34.05E
Pidark Pakistan 62 25.51N 63.14E
Piedecuesta Colombia 122 6.59N 73.03W

Piedicroce France 21 42.23N 9.23E
Piedimonte Matese Italy 33 41.21N 14.22E
Piedmont U.S.A. 113 33.55N 85.39W
Piedrabuena Spain 27 39.02N 4.10W
Piedrafita, Puerto de pass Spain 26 42.40N 7.01W
Piedrahita Spain 26 40.28N 5.19W
Piedras r. Peru 122 12.30S 69.10W
Piedras Negras Mexico 111 28.40N 100.32W
Piedra Sola Uruguay 125 32.04S 56.21W
Piedras, Punta c. Argentina 125 35.25S 57.07W
Pielavesi Finland 40 63.14N 26.45E
Pielinen l. Finland 44 63.20N 29.50E
Piemonte d. Italy 30 44.55N 8.00E
Pienza Italy 30 43.04N 11.41E
Pierce U.S.A. 108 46.29N 115.48W
Pierr-Buffière France 20 45.42N 1.21E
Pierre U.S.A. 110 44.22N 100.21W
Pierreville Canada 105 46.04N 72.49W
Piesseville Australia 89 33.11S 117.12E
Pietarsaari Finland 40 63.40N 22.42E
Pietermaritzburg R.S.A. 80 29.36S 30.23E
Pietersburg R.S.A. 80 23.54S 29.27E
Pietrasanta Italy 30 43.57N 10.14E
Piet Retief R.S.A. 80 27.00S 30.49E
Pietrosu mtn. Romania 37 47.36N 24.38E
Pietrosul mtn. Romania 37 47.08N 25.11E
Pieve di Cadore Italy 30 46.26N 12.22E
Pigailoe i. Federated States of Micronesia 59 8.08N 146.40E
Pigeon U.S.A. 104 43.50N 83.16W
Pigeon L. Canada 104 44.30N 78.30W
Pigna Italy 30 43.56N 7.40E
Pigón, Limni Greece 34 39.45N 21.15E
Pihtipudas Finland 40 63.23N 25.34E
Pikangikum Canada 101 51.49N 94.00W
Pikes Peak mtn. U.S.A. 108 38.51N 105.03W
Pikesville U.S.A. 114 39.25N 77.25W
Piketberg R.S.A. 80 32.54S 18.43E
Piketon U.S.A. 112 39.03N 83.01W
Pikeville U.S.A. 113 37.29N 82.33W
Pila Argentina 125 36.00S 58.10W
Piła Poland 36 53.09N 16.44E
Pilar Paraguay 126 26.52S 58.23W
Pilar do Sul Brazil 126 23.48S 47.45W
Pilcomayo r. Argentina/Paraguay 124 25.15S 57.43W
Pilibhit India 63 28.38N 79.48E
Pilica r. Poland 37 51.52N 21.17E
Pilliga Australia 93 30.23S 148.55E
Pílos Greece 35 36.55N 21.43E
Pilot Point town U.S.A. 111 33.24N 96.58W
Pilsum Germany 38 53.29N 7.04E
Pimba Australia 92 31.18S 136.47E
Pimenta Bueno Brazil 122 11.40S 61.14W
Pina Spain 25 41.29N 0.32W
Pinang, Pulau i. Malaysia 58 5.30N 100.10E
Pinar Turkey 35 37.20N 27.57E
Pinarbaşi Turkey 64 38.43N 36.23E
Pinar del Rio Cuba 117 22.24N 83.42W
Pincher Creek town Canada 100 49.30N 113.57W
Pinconning U.S.A. 104 43.51N 83.58W
Píndhos Óros mts. Greece 34 39.49N 21.14E
Pindiga Nigeria 77 9.58N 10.53E
Pindi Gheb Pakistan 62 33.14N 72.16E
Pindus Mts. see Píndhos Óros mts. Greece 34
Pindwāra India 62 24.48N 73.04E
Pine r. Canada 100 56.08N 120.41W
Pine r. U.S.A. 104 43.33N 84.08W
Pine Bluff town U.S.A. 111 34.13N 92.01W
Pine Bluffs town U.S.A. 108 41.11N 104.04W
Pine, C. Canada 103 46.37N 53.30W
Pine City U.S.A. 110 45.50N 92.59W
Pine Creek town Australia 88 13.51S 131.50E
Pine Creek r. U.S.A. 114 41.10N 77.16W
Pinega Russian Fed. 44 64.42N 43.28E
Pinega r. Russian Fed. 44 63.51N 41.48E
Pine Grove U.S.A. 115 40.33N 76.23W
Pinehouse L. Canada 101 55.32N 106.35W
Pine Is. U.S.A. 113 26.35N 82.06W
Pine Point town Canada 100 60.50N 114.28W
Pine River town Canada 101 51.45N 100.40W
Pine River town U.S.A. 110 46.43N 94.24W
Pinerolo Italy 30 44.53N 7.21E
Pinetown R.S.A. 80 29.49S 30.52E
Pineville U.S.A. 111 31.19N 92.26W
Piney France 19 48.22N 4.20E
Ping r. Thailand 56 15.47N 100.05E
Pingaring Australia 89 34.45S 118.34E
Pingba China 55 26.25N 106.15E
Pingdingshan Henan China 54 33.38N 113.30E
Pingdingshan Liaoning China 54 41.28N 124.45E
Pingdong Taiwan 55 22.44N 120.30E
Pingelap i. Pacific Oc. 84 6.15N 160.40E
Pingelly Australia 89 32.34S 117.04E
Pingle China 55 24.38N 110.38E
Pingliang China 54 35.21N 107.12E
Pingluo China 54 38.56N 106.34E
Pingnan China 55 23.33N 110.23E
Pingrup Australia 89 33.33S 118.30E
Pingtan China 55 25.36N 119.48E
Pingwu China 54 32.25N 104.36E
Pingxiang Guang. Zhuang. China 55 22.07N 106.42E
Pingxiang Jiangxi China 55 27.36N 113.48E
Pingyang China 55 27.40N 120.33E
Pingyao China 54 37.12N 112.08E
Pingyi China 54 35.30N 117.36E
Pingyuan China 54 24.34N 115.54E
Pinhal Brazil 126 22.10S 46.46W
Pinhal Novo Portugal 27 38.38N 8.55W
Pinhel Portugal 26 40.46N 7.04W
Pini i. Indonesia 58 0.10N 98.30E
Piniós r. Greece 34 39.54N 22.45E
Pinjarra Australia 89 32.37S 115.53E
Pinnaroo Australia 92 35.18S 140.54E
Pinneberg Germany 38 53.40N 9.47E
Pinos, Isla de i. Cuba 117 21.40N 82.40W
Pinos-Puente Spain 27 37.15N 3.45W

Pinrang Indonesia 58 3.48S 119.41E
Pins, Île des i. N. Cal. 84 22.37S 167.30E
Pinsk Belarus 37 52.08N 26.01E
Pins, Pointe aux c. Canada 104 42.15N 81.51W
Pinto Argentina 124 29.09S 62.38W
Pinto Butte mtn. Canada 101 49.22N 107.25W
Pinyug Russian Fed. 44 60.10N 47.43E
Pinzgau f. Austria 39 47.09N 12.30E
Piombino Italy 30 42.55N 10.32E
Piorini, L. Brazil 122 3.34S 63.15W
Piotrków Trybunalski Poland 37 51.25N 19.42E
Piove di Sacco Italy 30 45.18N 12.02E
Pīpār India 62 26.23N 73.32E
Piparia India 63 22.45N 78.21E
Pipestone r. Ont. Canada 102 52.48N 89.35W
Pipestone r. Sask. Canada 101 58.40N 105.45W
Pipestone U.S.A. 110 43.58N 96.10W
Pipinas Argentina 125 35.30S 57.19W
Piplán Pakistan 62 32.17N 71.21E
Pipmouacane, Résr. Canada 103 49.35N 70.30W
Piqua U.S.A. 112 40.08N 84.14W
Piracicaba Brazil 126 22.45S 47.40W
Piracicaba r. Brazil 126 22.35S 48.14W
Piracuruca Brazil 123 3.56S 41.42W
Piraeus see Piraiévs Greece 35
Piraiévs Greece 35 37.57N 23.38E
Piram I. India 62 21.36N 72.41E
Piran Slovenia 31 45.32N 13.34E
Pirassununga Brazil 126 21.59S 47.25W
Pirdop Bulgaria 34 42.42N 24.11E
Pírgos Greece 35 37.41N 21.28E
Pírgos Greece 35 36.38N 22.22E
Pirin Planina mts. Bulgaria 34 41.40N 23.30E
Pirmasens Germany 39 49.12N 7.36E
Pirna Germany 38 50.58N 13.56E
Pirojpur Bangla. 63 22.34N 89.59E
Pirón r. Spain 26 41.23N 4.31W
Pirot Yugo. 34 43.09N 22.39E
Pir Panjāl Range mts. Jammu & Kashmir 62 33.50N 74.30E
Piryatin Ukraine 45 50.14N 32.31E
Pisa Italy 30 43.43N 10.23E
Pisco Peru 122 13.46S 76.12W
Piseco L. U.S.A. 115 43.24N 74.33W
Písek Czech Republic 39 49.19N 14.10E
Pishan China 52 37.30N 78.20E
Pishīn Pakistan 62 30.35N 67.00E
Pishīn Lora r. Pakistan 62 29.09N 64.55E
Pissos France 20 44.19N 0.47W
Pisticci Italy 33 40.23N 16.34E
Pistoia Italy 30 43.55N 10.54E
Pisuerga r. Spain 26 41.33N 4.52W
Pisz Poland 37 53.38N 21.49E
Pita Guinea 76 11.05N 12.15W
Pitalito Colombia 122 1.51N 76.01W
Pitarpunga, L. Australia 92 34.23S 143.32E
Pitcairn I. Pacific Oc. 85 25.04S 130.06W
Pite r. Sweden 40 65.14N 21.32E
Piteå Sweden 40 65.20N 21.30E
Piteşti Romania 37 44.52N 24.51E
Pithápuram India 61 17.07N 82.16E
Pithion Greece 34 41.24N 26.40E
Pithiviers France 19 48.10N 2.15E
Pithoragarh India 63 29.35N 80.13E
Piti Guam 84 13.28N 144.41E
Pitigliano Italy 30 42.38N 11.40E
Pitlochry U.K. 14 56.43N 3.45W
Pitomača Croatia 31 45.59N 17.14E
Pitt I. Canada 100 53.35N 129.45W
Pittsburg Kans. U.S.A. 111 37.25N 94.42W
Pittsburg N.H. U.S.A. 105 45.03N 71.21W
Pittsburg Tex. U.S.A. 111 32.60N 94.58W
Pittsburgh U.S.A. 114 40.26N 80.00W
Pittsfield U.S.A. 115 42.27N 73.15W
Pittston U.S.A. 115 41.19N 75.47W
Pittsville U.S.A. 115 38.24N 75.52W
Pittville U.S.A. 108 41.03N 121.20W
Piūí Brazil 126 20.28S 45.58W
Piura Peru 122 5.15S 80.38W
Piuthān Nepal 63 28.06N 82.54E
Piva r. Yugo. 31 43.21N 18.51E
Pizzo Italy 33 38.44N 16.10E
Placentia Canada 103 47.15N 53.58W
Placentia B. Canada 103 47.15N 54.30W
Plačkovica mts. Macedonia 34 41.45N 22.30E
Plain Dealing U.S.A. 111 32.54N 93.42W
Plainfield Conn. U.S.A. 115 41.41N 71.55W
Plainfield N.J. U.S.A. 115 40.37N 74.26W
Plains U.S.A. 108 47.27N 114.53W
Plainview U.S.A. 111 34.11N 101.43W
Plakenska Planina mts. Macedonia 34 41.10N 21.10E
Plampang Indonesia 58 8.48S 117.48E
Planá Czech Republic 39 49.52N 12.44E
Plana Cays is. Bahamas 117 22.31N 72.14W
Plana, Isla i. Spain 25 38.10N 0.28W
Plantagenet Canada 105 45.32N 75.00W
Plasencia Spain 27 40.02N 6.05W
Plaški Croatia 31 45.05N 15.22E
Plaster Rock town Canada 103 46.54N 67.24W
Plasy Czech Republic 39 49.56N 13.24E
Platani r. Italy 32 37.23N 13.16E
Plateau d. Nigeria 77 8.50N 9.00E
Plate, R. est. see La Plata, Río de Argentina/Uruguay 125
Platí Greece 34 40.38N 22.31E
Platí, Ákra c. Greece 34 40.27N 24.00E
Platikambos Greece 34 39.37N 22.32E
Platinum U.S.A. 98 59.00N 161.50W
Plato Colombia 122 9.54N 74.46W
Platte r. U.S.A. 110 41.04N 95.53W
Platteville U.S.A. 110 42.44N 90.29W
Plattling Germany 39 48.47N 12.54E
Plattsburgh U.S.A. 105 44.42N 73.28W
Plau Germany 38 53.27N 12.16E
Plauen Germany 38 50.30N 12.08E
Plauer See l. Germany 38 53.30N 12.20E

Plav Yugo. 34 42.38N 19.57E
Plavsk Russian Fed. 44 53.40N 37.20E
Playa de Castilla *f.* Spain 27 37.05N 6.35W
Pleasant City U.S.A. 114 39.54N 81.34W
Pleasantville U.S.A. 115 39.23N 74.32W
Pleasonton U.S.A. 111 28.58N 98.29W
Pléaux France 20 45.08N 2.14E
Pleiku Vietnam 56 13.57N 108.01E
Pleisse *r.* Germany 38 51.20N 12.22E
Pléneuf France 18 48.36N 2.33W
Plenty, B. of New Zealand 86 37.40S 176.50E
Plentywood U.S.A. 108 48.47N 104.34W
Plesetsk Russian Fed. 44 62.42N 40.21E
Pleshchenitsy Belarus 37 54.24N 27.52E
Plessisville Canada 105 46.14N 71.47W
Pleszew Poland 37 51.54N 17.48E
Pleternica Croatia 31 45.17N 17.48E
Plétipi, Lac *l.* Canada 103 51.44N 70.06W
Pleven Bulgaria 34 43.25N 24.37E
Plješevica *mts.* Croatia 31 44.30N 15.45E
Pljevlja Yugo. 34 43.21N 19.21E
Ploče Croatia 31 43.04N 17.26E
Płock Poland 37 52.33N 19.43E
Plöckenpass Austria/Italy 30 46.36N 12.58E
Plocno *mtn.* Bosnia-Herzegovina 31 43.35N 17.34E
Ploërmel France 18 47.56N 2.24W
Ploieşti Romania 37 44.57N 26.02E
Plomárion Greece 35 38.59N 26.22E
Plomb du Cantal *mtn.* France 20 45.03N 2.46E
Plombières France 19 47.58N 6.29E
Plön Germany 38 54.09N 10.25E
Plonge, Lac la *l.* Canada 101 55.05N 107.15W
Płońsk Poland 37 52.38N 20.23E
Plouay France 18 47.55N 3.20W
Ploudalmézeau France 18 48.32N 4.39W
Plouescat France 18 48.40N 4.10W
Plouguenast France 18 48.17N 2.43W
Plouha France 18 48.41N 2.56W
Plovdiv Bulgaria 34 42.09N 24.45E
Plovdiv *d.* Bulgaria 34 41.58N 25.10E
Plum I. U.S.A. 115 41.11N 72.12W
Plumtree Zimbabwe 80 20.30S 27.50E
Plunkett Canada 101 51.56N 105.29W
Plymouth U.K. 13 50.23N 4.09W
Plymouth Ind. U.S.A. 114 41.20N 86.19W
Plymouth Mass. U.S.A. 115 41.58N 70.41W
Plymouth N.H. U.S.A. 105 43.45N 71.41W
Plymouth Ohio U.S.A. 114 41.00N 82.40W
Plymouth Penn. U.S.A. 115 41.14N 75.58W
Plymouth Vt. U.S.A. 115 43.32N 72.45W
Plymouth Wisc. U.S.A. 110 43.44N 87.58W
Plzeň Czech Republic 36 49.45N 13.23E
Pô Burkina 76 11.11N 1.10W
Po *r.* Italy 30 44.57N 12.04E
Pobé Benin 77 7.00N 2.56E
Pobeda, Gora *mtn.* Russian Fed. 51 65.20N 145.50E
Pobla de Segur Spain 25 42.15N 0.58E
Pocahontas Canada 100 53.15N 118.00W
Pocahontas Ark. U.S.A. 111 36.16N 90.58W
Pocahontas Iowa U.S.A. 110 42.44N 94.40W
Pocatello U.S.A. 108 42.52N 112.27W
Pocklington U.K. 12 53.56N 0.48W
Pocono Mts. U.S.A. 115 41.10N 75.20W
Poços de Caldas Brazil 126 21.48S 46.33W
Poděbrady Czech Republic 36 50.08N 15.07E
Podensac France 20 44.39N 0.22W
Podgaytsy Ukraine 37 49.19N 25.10E
Podgorica Yugo. 31 42.26N 19.14E
Podkamennaya Tunguska Russian Fed. 51 61.45N 90.13E
Podkamennaya Tunguska *r.* Russian Fed. 51 61.40N 90.00E
Podolsk Russian Fed. 44 55.23N 37.32E
Podor Senegal 76 16.35N 15.02W
Podporozhye Russian Fed. 44 60.55N 34.02E
Podravska Slatina Croatia 31 45.42N 17.42E
Podujevó Yugo. 34 42.54N 21.10E
Poel *i.* Germany 38 54.00N 11.26E
Pofadder R.S.A. 80 29.08S 19.22E
Poggibonsi Italy 30 43.28N 11.09E
Pogoniani Greece 34 40.00N 20.25E
Pogradec Albania 34 40.57N 20.48E
Pogrebishche Ukraine 37 49.30N 29.15E
Poh Indonesia 59 1.00S 122.52E
P'ohang S. Korea 53 36.00N 129.26E
Pohorje *mts.* Slovenia 31 46.30N 15.20E
Poiana Mare Romania 34 43.57N 23.05E
Poinsett, C. Antarctica 128 65.35S 113.00E
Point Arena *t.* U.S.A. 108 38.55N 123.41W
Pointe-à-Pitre Guadeloupe 117 16.14N 61.32W
Pointe-au-Baril *town* Canada 104 45.35N 80.30W
Pointe-au-Baril Station *town* Canada 104 45.36N 80.23W
Pointe aux Anglais *town* Canada 103 49.34N 67.10W
Pointe-aux-Trembles *town* Canada 105 45.39N 73.30W
Pointe-Claire Canada 105 45.26N 73.50W
Point Edward *town* Canada 104 43.00N 82.24W
Pointe Noire *town* Congo 78 4.46S 11.53E
Point Hope *town* U.S.A. 98 68.21N 166.41W
Point Lookout *town* Australia 93 30.33S 152.20E
Point Marion *town* U.S.A. 114 39.44N 79.53W
Point of Rocks *town* U.S.A. 114 39.17N 77.32W
Point Pelee Nat. Park Canada 104 41.57N 82.30W
Point Pleasant *town* U.S.A. 115 40.05N 74.04W
Point Pleasant *town* W.Va. U.S.A. 114 38.52N 82.08W
Point Samson *town* Australia 88 20.46S 117.10E
Poisson Blanc, Lac *l.* Canada 105 46.00N 75.45W
Poissy France 19 48.56N 2.03E
Poitiers France 18 46.35N 0.20E
Poitou-Charentes *d.* France 20 46.00N 0.00
Poix France 19 49.47N 1.59E
Poix-Terron France 19 49.39N 4.39E
Pokaran India 62 26.55N 71.55E
Pokhara Nepal 63 28.12N 83.59E
Poko Zaïre 78 3.08N 26.51E
Pokoinu Rarotonga Cook Is. 84 21.12S 159.50W
Pokrovsk Russian Fed. 45 51.30N 46.07E

Polacca U.S.A. 109 35.50N 110.23W
Pola de Laviana Spain 26 43.15N 5.34W
Pola de Lena Spain 26 43.10N 5.49W
Pola de Siero Spain 26 43.23N 5.40W
Polän Iran 65 25.29N 61.15E
Poland Europe 37 52.30N 19.00E
Polatlı Turkey 64 39.34N 32.08E
Polch Germany 39 50.18N 7.18E
Polda Australia 92 33.30S 135.10E
Pole Zaïre 78 2.51S 23.12E
Polesye *f.* Belarus 37 52.15N 28.00E
Poli Cameroon 77 8.30N 13.15E
Políaigos *i.* Greece 35 36.45N 24.38E
Policastro, Golfo di *g.* Italy 33 40.00N 15.30E
Poligny France 19 46.50N 5.43E
Polikastron Greece 34 41.00N 22.34E
Políkhnitos Greece 35 39.04N 26.10E
Pólis Cyprus 66 35.02N 32.26E
Polistena Italy 33 38.25N 16.05E
Políyiros Greece 34 40.23N 23.27E
Polk U.S.A. 114 41.22N 79.56W
Polla Italy 33 40.30N 15.30E
Pollino, Monte *mtn.* Italy 33 39.55N 16.11E
Pollock Reef Australia 89 34.28S 123.40E
Polnovat Russian Fed. 50 63.47N 65.54E
Polonnoye Ukraine 37 50.10N 27.30E
Polotsk Russian Fed. 44 55.30N 28.43E
Polperro U.K. 13 50.19N 4.31W
Polski Trümbesh Bulgaria 34 43.20N 25.38E
Polson U.S.A. 108 47.41N 114.09W
Poltava Ukraine 45 49.35N 34.35E
Polunochnoye Russian Fed. 44 60.52N 60.28E
Polyarnyy Russian Fed. 44 69.14N 33.30E
Polynesia *is.* Pacific Oc. 84 4.00S 165.00W
Pomarkku Finland 41 61.42N 22.00E
Pombal Brazil 126 6.45S 37.45W
Pombal Portugal 27 39.55N 8.38W
Pomene Mozambique 81 22.53S 35.33E
Pomeranian Bay Germany 38 54.06N 14.25E
Pomeroy Ohio U.S.A. 114 39.02N 82.02W
Pomeroy Wash. U.S.A. 108 46.28N 117.36W
Pomona Namibia 80 27.09S 15.18E
Pomona U.S.A. 109 34.04N 117.45W
Pompano Beach *town* U.S.A. 113 26.14N 80.07W
Pompei *site* Italy 33 40.45N 14.30E
Pompey's Pillar *town* U.S.A. 108 45.59N 107.56W
Ponape *i.* Pacific Oc. 84 6.55N 158.15E
Ponca City U.S.A. 111 36.42N 97.05W
Ponce Puerto Rico 117 18.00N 66.40W
Pondicherry India 61 11.59N 79.50E
Pond Inlet *str.* Canada 99 72.30N 75.00W
Ponds, I. of Canada 103 53.24N 55.55W
Ponferrada Spain 26 42.33N 6.35W
Pongani P.N.G. 90 9.05S 148.35E
Pongo *r.* Sudan 73 8.52N 27.40E
Pongola *r.* Mozambique 81 26.13S 32.38E
Ponnäni India 60 10.46N 75.54E
Ponnyadaung Range *mts.* Myanmar 56 22.30N 94.20E
Ponoka Canada 100 52.42N 113.40W
Ponorogo Indonesia 59 7.51S 111.30E
Ponoy Russian Fed. 44 67.02N 41.03E
Ponoy *r.* Russian Fed. 44 67.00N 41.10E
Pons France 20 45.35N 0.33W
Ponsul *r.* Portugal 27 39.40N 7.31W
Ponta Grossa Brazil 126 25.00S 50.09W
Pont-à-Mousson France 19 48.54N 6.04E
Pontão Portugal 27 39.55N 8.22W
Ponta Porã Brazil 126 22.27S 55.39W
Pontarlier France 19 46.54N 6.22E
Pontassieve Italy 30 43.46N 11.26E
Pont-Audemer France 18 49.21N 0.31E
Pontaumur France 20 45.52N 2.40E
Pont-Aven France 18 47.51N 3.45W
Pontax *r.* Canada 102 51.30N 78.48W
Pont Canavese Italy 30 45.25N 7.36E
Pontchartrain, L. U.S.A. 111 30.10N 90.10W
Pontchâteau France 18 47.26N 2.05W
Pont-Croix France 18 48.02N 4.29W
Pont d'Ain France 21 46.03N 5.20E
Pont-de-Salars France 20 44.17N 2.44E
Pont-de-Vaux France 21 46.26N 4.56E
Pontecorvo Italy 32 41.27N 13.40E
Ponte da Barca Portugal 26 41.48N 8.25W
Pontedera Italy 30 43.40N 10.38E
Ponte de Sor Portugal 27 39.15N 8.01W
Ponte do Lima Portugal 26 41.46N 8.35W
Pontefract U.K. 12 53.42N 1.19W
Ponteix Canada 101 49.49N 107.30W
Ponte Nova Brazil 126 20.25S 42.54W
Pontevedra Spain 26 42.26N 8.38W
Pontevedra *d.* Spain 26 42.35N 8.35W
Pontevedra, Ría de *est.* Spain 26 42.22N 8.45W
Pontgibaud France 20 45.50N 2.51E
Pontiac Ill. U.S.A. 110 40.54N 88.36W
Pontiac Mich. U.S.A. 104 42.37N 83.18W
Pontiac Prov. Park Canada 105 46.36N 76.32W
Pontianak Indonesia 58 0.05S 109.16E
Pontivy France 18 48.04N 2.59W
Pont-l'Abbé France 18 47.52N 4.13W
Pont l'Évêque France 18 49.18N 0.11E
Pontoise France 19 49.03N 2.06E
Pontorson France 18 48.33N 1.31W
Pontremoli Italy 30 44.22N 9.53E
Pontresina Switz. 36 46.28N 9.53E
Pontrilas U.K. 13 51.56N 2.53W
Pont Rouge Canada 105 46.45N 71.42W
Ponts Spain 25 41.55N 1.12E
Pont-sur-Yonne France 19 48.17N 3.12E
Pontypool U.K. 13 51.42N 3.01W
Pontypridd U.K. 13 51.36N 3.21W
Ponziane, Isole *is.* Italy 32 40.55N 12.57E
Poochera Australia 92 32.42S 134.52E
Poole U.K. 13 50.42N 2.02W
Poonacarie Australia 92 33.23S 142.34E
Poopelloe L. Australia 92 31.39S 144.00E
Poopó, Lago de *l.* Bolivia 124 19.00S 67.00W

Popayán Colombia 122 2.27N 76.32W
Poperinge Belgium 16 50.51N 2.44E
Popes Creek *town* U.S.A. 114 38.09N 76.58W
Popilta L. Australia 92 33.09S 141.45E
Popintsi Bulgaria 34 42.25N 24.17E
Poplar *r.* Canada 101 53.00N 97.18W
Poplar U.S.A. 108 48.07N 105.12W
Poplar Bluff *town* U.S.A. 111 36.45N 90.24W
Poplarville U.S.A. 111 30.51N 89.32W
Popocatépetl *mtn.* Mexico 116 19.02N 98.38W
Popokabaka Zaïre 78 5.41S 16.40E
Popoli Italy 31 42.10N 13.50E
Popondetta P.N.G. 90 8.45S 148.15E
Popovo Bulgaria 34 43.21N 26.18E
Poppi Italy 30 43.43N 11.46E
Poprad Slovakia 37 49.03N 20.18E
Popricani Romania 37 47.18N 27.31E
Porâli *r.* Pakistan 62 25.30N 66.25E
Porbandar India 62 21.38N 69.36E
Por Chaman Afghan. 62 33.08N 63.51E
Porcher I. Canada 100 54.00N 130.30W
Porcuna Spain 27 37.52N 4.11W
Porcupine *r.* U.S.A. 98 66.25N 145.20W
Porcupine Hills Canada 101 52.30N 101.45W
Pordenone Italy 32 45.57N 12.39E
Pordim Bulgaria 34 43.23N 24.51E
Poreč Croatia 31 45.13N 13.37E
Pori Finland 41 61.29N 21.47E
Porirua New Zealand 85 41.08S 174.50E
Porjus Sweden 40 66.57N 19.50E
Porkhov Russian Fed. 44 57.43N 29.31E
Porkkala Finland 41 59.59N 24.26E
Porlamar Venezuela 122 11.01N 63.54W
Porma *r.* Spain 26 42.29N 5.28W
Pornic France 18 47.07N 2.06W
Porog Russian Fed. 44 63.50N 38.32E
Poronaysk Russian Fed. 51 49.13N 142.55E
Póros Greece 35 37.30N 23.30E
Porosozero Russian Fed. 44 62.45N 32.48E
Porrentruy Switz. 39 47.25N 7.05E
Porretta Terme Italy 30 44.09N 10.59E
Porsangen *est.* Norway 40 70.58N 25.30E
Porsangerhalvöya *pen.* Norway 40 70.50N 25.00E
Porsgrunn Norway 42 59.09N 9.40E
Porsuk *r.* Turkey 64 39.41N 31.56E
Portachuela Bolivia 124 17.21S 63.24W
Portadown U.K. 15 54.25N 6.27W
Portaferry U.K. 15 54.23N 5.33W
Portage Penn. U.S.A. 114 40.23N 78.41W
Portage Wisc. U.S.A. 110 43.33N 89.28W
Portage du Fort Canada 105 45.36N 76.38W
Portage la Prairie *town* Canada 101 49.57N 98.25W
Port Alberni Canada 100 49.14N 124.48W
Port Albert Australia 93 38.09S 146.40E
Portalegre Portugal 27 39.17N 7.26W
Portalegre *d.* Portugal 27 39.10N 7.40W
Portales U.S.A. 110 34.11N 103.20W
Port Alfred R.S.A. 80 33.36S 26.52E
Port Alice Canada 100 50.25N 127.25W
Port Allegany U.S.A. 114 41.49N 78.17W
Port Angeles U.S.A. 108 48.07N 123.27W
Port Antonio Jamaica 117 18.10N 76.27W
Port Arthur Australia 91 43.08S 147.50E
Port Arthur U.S.A. 111 29.55N 93.55W
Port Augusta Australia 92 32.30S 137.46E
Port au Port Canada 103 48.33N 58.45W
Port-au-Prince Haiti 117 18.33N 72.20W
Port Austin U.S.A. 104 44.03N 83.01W
Port Bergé Madagascar 81 15.33S 47.40E
Port Blair India 56 11.40N 92.40E
Port Bolster Canada 104 44.20N 79.10W
Portbou Spain 25 42.25N 3.09E
Port Bouet Côte d'Ivoire 76 5.14N 3.58W
Port Bradshaw *b.* Australia 90 12.30S 136.42E
Port Broughton Australia 92 33.38S 137.56E
Port Burwell Canada 104 42.39N 80.49W
Port Campbell Australia 92 38.37S 143.04E
Port Canning India 63 22.18N 88.40E
Port Carling Canada 104 45.07N 79.35W
Port Cartier Canada 103 50.01N 66.53W
Port Chalmers New Zealand 85 45.49S 170.37E
Port Chester U.S.A. 115 41.00N 73.40W
Port Clinton U.S.A. 114 41.31N 82.56W
Port Colborne Canada 104 42.53N 79.14W
Port Coquitlam Canada 100 49.20N 122.45W
Port Credit Canada 104 43.33N 79.35W
Port Curtis Australia 90 23.50S 151.13E
Port Dalhousie Canada 104 43.12N 79.16W
Port-de-Paix Haiti 117 19.57N 72.50W
Port Dover Canada 104 42.47N 80.12W
Port Edward R.S.A. 80 31.03S 30.13E
Portel Portugal 27 38.18N 7.42W
Portela Brazil 126 21.38S 41.59W
Port Elgin Canada 104 44.26N 81.24W
Port Elizabeth R.S.A. 80 33.57S 25.34E
Port Ellen U.K. 14 55.38N 6.12W
Port-en-Bessin France 18 49.21N 0.45W
Port Erin I.o.M. Europe 12 54.05N 4.45W
Porter Landing Canada 100 58.46N 130.05W
Porterville R.S.A. 80 33.01S 19.00E
Porterville U.S.A. 109 36.04N 119.01W
Porte-Vecchio France 22 41.35N 9.16E
Port Fairy Australia 92 38.23S 142.17E
Port Gentil Gabon 78 0.40S 8.46E
Port Germein Australia 92 33.01S 138.00E
Port Gibson U.S.A. 111 31.58N 90.58W
Port Glenone U.K. 15 54.52N 6.30W
Port Harcourt Nigeria 77 4.43N 7.05E
Port Harrison *see* Inoucdjouac Canada 99
Port Hawkesbury Canada 103 45.37N 61.21W
Porthcawl U.K. 13 51.28N 3.42W
Port Hedland Australia 88 20.24S 118.36E
Port Henry U.S.A. 105 44.03N 73.28W
Porthill U.S.A. 108 49.00N 116.30W
Porthmadog U.K. 12 52.55N 4.08W
Port Hope Canada 104 43.57N 78.18W
Port Hope U.S.A. 104 43.57N 82.43W
Port Huron U.S.A. 114 42.58N 82.27W

Portimão Portugal 27 37.08N 8.32W
Port Isaac B. U.K. 13 50.36N 4.50W
Portiţei, Gura *f.* Romania 29 44.40N 29.00E
Port Jefferson U.S.A. 115 40.57N 73.04W
Port Jervis U.S.A. 115 41.22N 74.41W
Port Keats Australia 88 14.15S 129.35E
Port Kembla Australia 93 34.28S 150.54E
Port Kenny Australia 92 33.09S 134.42E
Portland N.S.W. Australia 93 33.20S 150.00E
Portland Vic. Australia 92 38.21S 141.38E
Portland Canada 105 44.41N 76.13W
Portland Maine U.S.A. 112 43.39N 70.17W
Portland Oreg. U.S.A. 108 45.33N 122.36W
Portland Tex. U.S.A. 111 27.53N 97.20W
Portland Pt. Ascension 127 7.58S 14.26W
Port-La-Nouvelle France 20 43.01N 3.03E
Port Laoise Rep. of Ire. 15 53.03N 7.20W
Port Lavaca U.S.A. 111 28.37N 96.38W
Port Lincoln Australia 92 34.43S 135.49E
Port Loko Sierra Leone 76 8.50N 12.50W
Port Loring Canada 104 45.56N 79.58W
Port Louis France 18 47.43N 3.21W
Port Luck Canada 104 46.20N 83.52W
Port MacDonnell Australia 92 38.03S 140.46E
Port Macquarie Australia 93 31.28S 152.25E
Port Maitland N.S. Canada 103 43.59N 66.09W
Port Maitland Ont. Canada 104 42.52N 79.34W
Portmarnock Rep. of Ire. 15 53.25N 6.09W
Port Menier Canada 103 49.49N 64.20W
Port Moresby P.N.G. 90 9.30S 147.07E
Port Musgrave *b.* Australia 90 11.59S 142.00E
Portnaguiran U.K. 14 58.15N 6.10W
Port Neill Australia 92 34.07S 136.20E
Port Nelson Canada 101 57.03N 92.36W
Portneuf Canada 105 46.42N 71.53W
Portneuf Prov. Park Canada 105 47.12N 72.05W
Port Nolloth R.S.A. 80 29.16S 16.54E
Port Norris U.S.A. 115 39.15N 75.02W
Porto Portugal 26 41.11N 8.36W
Porto *d.* Portugal 26 41.15N 8.15W
Pôrto Alegre Brazil 126 30.03S 51.10W
Porto Amboim Angola 78 10.45S 13.43E
Pôrto de Mós Portugal 27 39.36N 8.39W
Pôrto de Moz Brazil 123 1.45S 52.13W
Porto Empedocle Italy 32 37.17N 13.32E
Porto Esperança Brazil 126 19.36S 57.24W
Porto Farina Tunisia 32 37.10N 10.12E
Pôrto Feliz Brazil 123 23.11S 47.32W
Portoferraio Italy 30 42.49N 10.19E
Port of Ness U.K. 14 58.30N 6.13W
Pôrto Franco Brazil 123 6.21S 47.25W
Port of Spain Trinidad 117 10.38N 61.31W
Porto Grande Brazil 123 0.42N 51.24W
Portogruaro Italy 30 45.47N 12.50E
Pórto Lágo Greece 34 41.01N 25.06E
Pörtom Finland 40 62.42N 21.37E
Portomaggiore Italy 30 44.42N 11.48E
Porto Moniz Madeira Is. 127 32.52N 17.12W
Pôrto Murtinho Brazil 126 21.42S 57.52W
Porton U.K. 13 51.08N 1.44W
Pôrto Nacional Brazil 123 10.42S 48.25W
Porto-Novo Benin 77 6.30N 2.47E
Port Ontario U.S.A. 115 43.32N 76.11W
Pôrto Primavera, Reprêsa *resr.* Brazil 126 21.50S 52.00W
Porto Recanati Italy 31 43.26N 13.40E
Porto San Giorgio Italy 31 43.11N 13.48E
Porto Santo *i.* Madeira Is. 74 33.04N 16.20W
Porto Santo Stefano Italy 30 42.26N 11.07E
Porto Tolle Italy 30 44.56N 12.22E
Porto Torres Italy 32 40.50N 8.23E
Pôrto Valter Brazil 122 8.15S 72.45W
Porto-Vecchio France 21 41.35N 9.16E
Pôrto Velho Brazil 122 8.45S 63.54W
Portoviejo Ecuador 122 1.07S 80.28W
Portpatrick U.K. 14 54.51N 5.07W
Port Perry Canada 104 44.06N 78.57W
Port Phillip B. Australia 93 38.05S 144.50E
Port Pirie Australia 92 33.11S 138.01E
Port Radium Canada 103 50.01N 118.02W
Portree U.K. 14 57.24N 6.12W
Port Renfrew Canada 100 48.30N 124.20W
Port Rowan Canada 104 42.37N 80.28W
Port Rupert *see* Waskaganish Canada 102
Portrush U.K. 15 55.12N 6.40W
Port Said *see* Bûr Sa'îd Egypt 66
Port-Sainte-Marie France 20 44.15N 0.24E
Port Sanilac U.S.A. 114 43.26N 82.33W
Port Saunders Canada 103 50.39N 57.18W
Portsea Australia 93 38.19S 144.43E
Port Severn Canada 104 44.47N 79.42W
Port Shepstone R.S.A. 80 30.44S 30.27E
Port Simpson Canada 100 54.32N 130.25W
Portsmouth U.K. 13 50.48N 1.06W
Portsmouth N.H. U.S.A. 115 43.04N 70.46W
Portsmouth Ohio U.S.A. 114 38.45N 82.59W
Portsmouth Va. U.S.A. 113 36.50N 76.20W
Portsoy U.K. 14 57.41N 2.41W
Port Stanley Canada 104 42.40N 81.13W
Portstewart U.K. 15 55.11N 6.43W
Port St. Joe U.S.A. 113 29.49N 85.19W
Port St. Louis France 21 43.23N 4.48E
Port Sudan *see* Bûr Sûdân Sudan 72
Port Talbot U.K. 13 51.35N 3.48W
Porttipahdan tekojärvi *resr.* Finland 40 68.08N 26.40E
Port Townsend U.S.A. 108 48.07N 122.46W
Portugal Europe 24 39.30N 8.05W
Portugalete Spain 26 43.19N 3.01W
Portumna Rep. of Ire. 11 53.06N 8.14W
Port Vendres France 20 42.31N 3.07E
Port Victoria Australia 92 34.30S 137.30E
Portville U.S.A. 114 42.02N 78.20W
Port Wakefield Australia 92 34.12S 138.11E
Port Warrender Australia 88 14.30S 125.50E
Porvenir Chile 125 53.18S 70.22W
Porz Germany 38 50.53N 7.03E
Porzuna Spain 27 39.09N 4.09W
Posada Italy 32 40.38N 9.43E

Posada r. Italy 32 40.39N 9.45E
Posadas Argentina 124 27.25S 55.48W
Posavina f. Croatia 31 45.20N 17.00E
Poschiavo Switz. 39 46.18N 10.04E
Posen U.S.A. 104 45.16N 83.42W
Posets, Pico de mtn. Spain 25 42.39N 0.25E
Posht r. Iran 65 29.09N 58.09E
Positano Italy 33 40.38N 14.29E
Poso Indonesia 59 1.23S 120.45E
Posse Brazil 126 14.05S 46.22W
Possidhonia site Greece 35 37.40N 24.00E
Pössneck Germany 38 50.42N 11.37E
Post U.S.A. 111 33.12N 101.23W
Postavy Lithuania 44 55.07N 26.50E
Poste Maurice Cortier Algeria 74 22.18N 1.05E
Poste Weygand Algeria 74 24.29N 0.40E
Postmasburg R.S.A. 80 28.19S 23.03E
Postojna Slovenia 31 45.47N 14.13E
Postoli Belarus 37 52.30N 28.00E
Potamós Greece 35 36.38N 22.59E
Potchefstroom R.S.A. 80 26.42S 27.05E
Poteau U.S.A. 111 35.03N 94.37W
Potelu, Lacul l. Romania 34 43.44N 24.20E
Potenza Italy 33 40.38N 15.49E
Potes Spain 26 43.09N 4.37W
Potgietersrus R.S.A. 80 24.11S 29.00E
Poti r. Brazil 123 5.01S 42.48W
Poti Georgia 45 42.11N 41.41E
Potiskum Nigeria 77 11.40N 11.03E
Potomac r. U.S.A. 114 38.00N 76.18W
Potomac, North Branch r. U.S.A. 114 39.15N 79.21W
Potomac, South Branch r. U.S.A. 114 39.04N 78.59W
Potosí Bolivia 124 19.35S 65.45W
Potosí d. Bolivia 124 21.00S 67.00W
Potosi Cerro mtn. Mexico 111 24.50N 100.15W
Pototan Phil. 59 10.54N 122.38E
Potsdam Germany 38 52.24N 13.04E
Potsdam U.S.A. 105 44.40N 74.59W
Pottstown U.S.A. 115 40.15N 75.38W
Pottsville U.S.A. 115 40.41N 76.12W
Pouancé France 18 47.44N 1.11W
Poughkeepsie U.S.A. 115 41.42N 73.56W
Poultney U.S.A. 115 43.31N 73.14W
Pournári, Tekhníti Límni l. Greece 35 39.15N 21.00E
Pouso Alegre Brazil 126 22.13S 45.49W
Pouté Senegal 74 15.42N 14.10W
Poŭthĭsăt Cambodia 56 12.27N 103.50E
Pouzauges France 18 46.47N 0.50W
Povenets Russian Fed. 44 62.52N 34.05E
Póvoa de Varzim Portugal 26 41.23N 8.46W
Povorino Russian Fed. 45 51.12N 42.15E
Powassan Canada 104 46.05N 79.22W
Powder r. U.S.A. 108 46.44N 105.26W
Powder River town U.S.A. 108 43.03N 106.58W
Powell U.S.A. 108 44.45N 108.46W
Powell, L. U.S.A. 108 37.25N 110.45W
Powell River town Canada 100 49.22N 124.31W
Powers U.S.A. 102 45.42N 87.31W
Powers Lake town U.S.A. 110 48.34N 102.39W
Powhatan Point town U.S.A. 114 39.52N 80.49W
Pownal U.S.A. 115 42.46N 73.14W
Powys d. U.K. 13 52.26N 3.26W
Poyang Hu l. China 55 29.10N 116.20E
Požarevac Yugo. 37 44.38N 21.12E
Poza Rica de Hidalgo Mexico 116 20.34N 97.26W
Požega Yugo. 34 43.50N 20.02E
Poznań Poland 36 52.25N 16.53E
Pozo Alcón Spain 27 37.42N 2.56W
Pozoblanco Spain 26 38.22N 4.51W
Pozo-Cañada Spain 25 38.48N 1.45W
Pozuela de Alarcón Spain 26 40.26N 3.49W
Pozzallo Italy 33 36.43N 14.52E
Pozzuoli Italy 33 40.49N 14.07E
Prachatice Czech Republic 38 49.01N 14.00E
Prachin Buri Thailand 56 14.02N 101.23E
Prachuap Khiri Khan Thailand 56 11.50N 99.49E
Pradera Colombia 122 3.23N 76.11W
Prades France 20 42.38N 2.25E
Praestø Denmark 43 55.07N 12.03E
Prague see Praha Czech Republic 39
Praha Czech Republic 38 50.05N 14.26E
Praha d. Czech Republic 39 50.05N 14.25E
Praha mtn. Czech Republic 39 49.40N 13.49E
Prainha Amazonas Brazil 122 7.16S 60.23W
Prainha Para Brazil 123 1.48S 53.29W
Prairie City U.S.A. 108 44.28N 118.43W
Prairie du Chien town U.S.A. 110 43.03N 91.09W
Prairie Village U.S.A. 110 39.01N 94.38W
Pramánda Greece 34 39.32N 21.08E
Prang Ghana 76 8.02N 0.58W
Prasónisi, Ákra c. Greece 35 35.42N 27.46E
Pratāpgarh India 62 24.02N 74.47E
Prato Italy 30 43.53N 11.06E
Pratt U.S.A. 111 37.39N 98.44W
Pravia Spain 26 43.29N 6.07W
Predazzo Italy 30 46.19N 11.36E
Predejane Yugo. 34 42.51N 22.09E
Predlitz Austria 39 47.04N 13.55E
Pré-en-Pail France 18 48.27N 0.12W
Preesall U.K. 12 53.55N 2.58W
Preetz Germany 38 54.14N 10.16E
Pregel r. Russian Fed. 37 54.41N 20.22E
Preko Croatia 31 44.05N 15.11E
Premer Australia 93 31.26S 149.54E
Premier Canada 100 56.04N 129.56W
Premnitz Germany 38 52.32N 12.19E
Premuda i Croatia 31 44.20N 14.37E
Prenjas Albania 34 41.06N 20.32E
Prentice U.S.A. 110 45.33N 90.17W
Prenzlau Germany 38 53.19N 13.52E
Preparis i. Myanmar 56 14.51N 93.38E
Přerov Czech Republic 37 49.27N 17.27E
Prescott Canada 105 44.43N 75.31W
Prescott Ariz. U.S.A. 109 34.33N 112.28W
Prescott Ark. U.S.A. 111 33.48N 93.23W
Preševo Yugo. 34 42.19N 21.39E
Presho U.S.A. 110 43.54N 100.04W

Presidencia Roque Sáenz Peña Argentina 124 26.50S 60.30W
Presidente Epitácio Brazil 126 21.56S 52.07W
Presidente Hermes Brazil 124 11.17S 61.55W
Presidente Prudente Brazil 126 22.09S 51.24W
Presidio U.S.A. 111 29.33N 104.23W
Prešov Slovakia 37 49.00N 21.15E
Prespa, L. Macedonia/Greece 34 40.45N 21.00E
Presque Isle town Maine U.S.A. 112 46.41N 68.01W
Presque Isle town Mich. U.S.A. 104 45.16N 83.29W
Prestea Ghana 76 5.26N 2.07W
Presteigne U.K. 13 52.17N 3.00W
Přeštice Czech Republic 38 49.34N 13.20E
Preston Canada 104 43.23N 80.21W
Preston U.K. 12 53.46N 2.42W
Preston Idaho U.S.A. 108 42.06N 111.53W
Preston Minn. U.S.A. 110 43.40N 92.04W
Prestonpans U.K. 14 55.57N 3.00W
Prestwick U.K. 14 55.30N 4.36W
Prêto r. Brazil 126 22.00S 43.21W
Pretoria R.S.A. 80 25.43S 28.11E
Préveza Greece 35 38.57N 20.44E
Prey Vêng Cambodia 56 11.29N 105.19E
Priboj Yugo. 31 43.35N 19.31E
Příbram Czech Republic 38 49.42N 14.01E
Price Md. U.S.A. 115 39.06N 75.58W
Price Utah U.S.A. 108 39.36N 110.48W
Prichard U.S.A. 111 30.44N 88.07W
Priego Spain 26 40.27N 2.18W
Priego de Córdoba Spain 27 37.26N 4.11W
Prien Germany 39 47.51N 12.20E
Prieska R.S.A. 80 29.40S 22.43E
Prieta, Peña mtn. Spain 26 43.01N 4.44W
Prijedor Bosnia-Herzegovina 31 44.59N 16.43E
Prijepolje Yugo. 31 43.23N 19.39E
Prikaspiyskaya Nizmennost see Caspian Depression Russian Fed./Kazakhstan 45
Prilep Macedonia 34 41.20N 21.33E
Priluki Russian Fed. 44 63.05N 42.05E
Priluki Ukraine 45 50.35N 32.24E
Primorsk Russian Fed. 44 60.18N 28.35E
Primorsk Russian Fed. 43 54.44N 20.01E
Primorskiy Russian Fed. 57 43.10N 131.40E
Primor'ye Russian Fed. 43 54.57N 20.02E
Primrose L. Canada 101 54.55N 109.45W
Primstal Germany 39 49.32N 6.58E
Prince Albert Canada 101 53.12N 105.46W
Prince Albert R.S.A. 80 33.14S 22.02E
Prince Albert Nat. Park Canada 101 54.00N 106.25W
Prince Albert Sd. Canada 98 70.25N 115.00W
Prince Alfred C. Canada 98 74.30N 125.00W
Prince Charles I. Canada 99 67.50N 76.00W
Prince Edward B. Canada 105 43.57N 76.57W
Prince Edward-Crozet Ridge f. Indian Oc. 49 45.00S 42.00E
Prince Edward I. Canada 96 46.15N 63.00W
Prince Edward Is. Indian Oc. 49 46.35S 37.56E
Prince Edward Island d. Canada 103 46.45N 63.00W
Prince Frederick U.S.A. 115 38.33N 76.35W
Prince George Canada 100 53.50N 122.50W
Prince of Wales, C. U.S.A. 98 66.00N 168.30W
Prince of Wales I. Australia 90 10.40S 142.10E
Prince of Wales I. Canada 99 73.00N 99.00W
Prince of Wales I. U.S.A. 100 55.00N 132.30W
Prince Patrick I. Canada 98 77.00N 120.00W
Prince Regent Inlet str. Canada 99 73.00N 90.30W
Prince Rupert Canada 100 54.09N 130.20W
Princess Charlotte B. Australia 90 14.25S 144.00E
Princess Royal I. Canada 100 53.00N 128.40W
Princeton U.S.A. 112 38.21N 87.33W
Princeton Ky. U.S.A. 113 37.06N 87.55W
Princeton Mo. U.S.A. 110 40.24N 93.35W
Princeton N.J. U.S.A. 115 40.21N 74.40W
Príncipe i. São Tomé & Príncipe 77 1.37N 7.27E
Príncipe da Beira Brazil 122 12.23S 64.28W
Prinzapolca Nicaragua 117 13.19N 83.35W
Prior, Cabo c. Spain 26 43.34N 8.19W
Priozersk Russian Fed. 44 61.01N 50.08E
Pripet r. Europe 37 51.08N 30.30E
Pripet Marshes see Polesye f. Belarus 37
Pripyat r. Belarus see Pripet r. Europe 37
Priština Yugo. 34 42.40N 21.13E
Pritzwalk Germany 38 53.09N 12.10E
Privas France 21 44.44N 4.36E
Priverno Italy 32 41.28N 13.11E
Privolzhskaya Vozvyshennost f. Russian Fed. 44 53.15N 45.45E
Prizren Yugo. 34 42.13N 20.45E
Prizzi Italy 32 37.43N 13.26E
Prnjavor Bosnia-Herzegovina 31 44.52N 17.40E
Probolinggo Indonesia 59 7.45S 113.09E
Probstzella Germany 38 50.32N 11.22E
Proctor U.S.A. 115 43.40N 73.02W
Proddatūr India 61 14.44N 78.33E
Proença-a-Nova Portugal 27 39.45N 7.55W
Progreso Mexico 117 21.20N 89.40W
Prokletije mts. Albania 34 42.30N 19.45E
Prokop'yevsk Russian Fed. 50 53.55N 86.45E
Prokuplje Yugo. 34 43.16N 21.36E
Prome see Pyè Myanmar 56
Prophet r. Canada 100 58.48N 122.40W
Propriá Brazil 123 10.15S 36.51W
Propriano France 21 41.40N 8.55E
Proserpine Australia 90 20.24S 148.34E
Prosotsáni Greece 34 41.10N 23.59E
Prostějov Czech Republic 37 49.29N 17.07E
Protection U.S.A. 111 37.12N 99.29W
Protville Tunisia 32 36.54N 10.01E
Provence-Côte d'Azur d. France 21 43.45N 6.00E
Providence U.S.A. 115 41.50N 71.25W
Providence Bay town Canada 104 45.41N 82.16W
Providence Mts. U.S.A. 109 34.55N 115.35W
Providencia, Isla de i. Colombia 117 13.21N 81.22W
Provincetown U.S.A. 115 42.03N 70.11W
Provins France 19 48.33N 3.18E
Provo U.S.A. 108 40.14N 111.39W
Prozor Bosnia-Herzegovina 31 43.49N 17.37E
Prudhoe Bay town U.S.A. 98 70.20N 148.25W

Prüm Germany 39 50.12N 6.25E
Prüm r. Germany 16 49.50N 6.29E
Pruszcz Gdański Poland 37 54.17N 18.40E
Pruszków Poland 37 52.11N 20.48E
Prut r. Romania/Ukraine 37 45.29N 28.14E
Prutz Austria 39 47.05N 10.40E
Pruzhany Belarus 37 52.33N 24.28E
Prydz B. Antarctica 128 68.30S 74.00E
Pryor U.S.A. 111 36.19N 95.19W
Przemyśl Poland 37 49.48N 22.48E
Przeworsk Poland 37 50.05N 22.29E
Psakhná Greece 35 38.34N 23.35E
Psará i. Greece 35 38.35N 25.37E
Psárion Greece 35 37.20N 21.51E
Psel r. Ukraine 45 49.00N 33.30E
Pskov Russian Fed. 44 57.48N 28.00E
Pskov, Lake l. Russian Fed. 44 58.00N 27.55E
Pteleón Greece 35 39.03N 22.57E
Ptich Belarus 37 52.15N 28.49E
Ptich r. Belarus 37 52.09N 28.52E
Ptolemaís Greece 34 40.30N 21.43E
Ptuj Slovenia 31 46.25N 15.52E
Puán Argentina 125 37.30S 62.45W
Pu'an China 55 25.47N 104.57E
Puapua W. Samoa 84 13.34S 172.12W
Pucallpa Peru 122 8.21S 74.33W
Pucarani Bolivia 124 16.23S 68.30W
Pucheng China 55 27.56N 118.32E
Pučišća Croatia 31 43.21N 16.44E
Pudasjärvi Finland 40 65.25N 26.50E
Pūdeh Tal r. Afghan. 62 31.00N 61.50E
Pudozh Russian Fed. 44 61.50N 36.32E
Pudozhgora Russian Fed. 44 62.18N 35.54E
Puebla d. Mexico 116 19.03N 98.10W
Puebla d. Mexico 116 18.30N 98.00W
Puebla de Alcocer Spain 26 38.59N 5.15W
Puebla de Don Fadrique Spain 27 37.58N 2.26W
Puebla de Don Rodrigo Spain 27 39.05N 4.37W
Puebla de Sanabria Spain 26 42.03N 6.38W
Puebla de Trives Spain 26 42.20N 7.15W
Pueblo U.S.A. 108 38.16N 104.37W
Pueblo Hundido Chile 124 26.23S 70.03W
Puelches Argentina 125 38.09S 65.58W
Puelén Argentina 125 37.32S 67.38W
Puente Alta Chile 125 33.37S 70.35W
Puenteareas Spain 26 42.11N 8.30W
Puente-Caldelas Spain 26 42.23N 8.30W
Puentedeume Spain 26 43.24N 8.10W
Puente-Genil Spain 27 37.23N 4.47W
Puente la Reina Spain 25 42.40N 1.49W
Puerto Aisén Chile 125 45.27S 72.58W
Puerto Ángel Mexico 116 15.40N 96.29W
Puerto Armuelles Panama 117 8.19N 82.15W
Puerto Ayacucho Venezuela 122 5.39N 67.32W
Puerto Barrios Guatemala 117 15.41N 88.32W
Puerto Bermúdez Peru 122 10.20S 75.00W
Puerto Berrío Colombia 122 6.28N 74.28W
Puerto Cabello Venezuela 122 10.29N 68.02W
Puerto Cabezas Nicaragua 117 14.02N 83.24W
Puerto Carreño Colombia 122 6.08N 67.27W
Puerto Casado Paraguay 124 22.20S 57.55W
Puerto Coig Argentina 125 50.54S 69.15W
Puerto Cortés Costa Rica 117 8.58N 83.32W
Puerto Cortés Honduras 117 15.50N 87.55W
Puerto de Nutrias Venezuela 122 8.07N 69.18W
Puerto de Pollensa Spain 25 39.55N 3.05E
Puerto de Santa María Spain 27 36.36N 6.13W
Puerto Heath Bolivia 122 12.30S 68.40W
Puerto Juárez Mexico 117 21.26N 86.51W
Puerto La Cruz Venezuela 122 10.14N 64.40W
Puerto Leguízamo Colombia 122 0.12S 74.46W
Puertollano Spain 26 38.41N 4.07W
Puerto Lobos Argentina 125 42.01S 65.04W
Puerto Madryn Argentina 125 42.46S 65.02W
Puerto Maldonado Peru 122 12.37S 69.11W
Puerto Melendez Peru 122 4.30S 77.30W
Puerto Montt Chile 125 41.28S 73.00W
Puerto Natales Chile 125 51.44S 72.31W
Puerto Páez Venezuela 122 6.13N 67.28W
Puerto Peñasco Mexico 109 31.20N 113.33W
Puerto Pinasco Paraguay 126 22.36S 57.53W
Puerto Plata Dom. Rep. 117 19.48N 70.41W
Puerto Princesa Phil. 58 9.46N 118.45E
Puerto Quepos Costa Rica 117 9.28N 84.10W
Puerto Real Spain 27 36.32N 6.11W
Puerto Rey Colombia 122 8.48N 76.34W
Puerto Rico C. America 117 18.20N 66.30W
Puerto Rico Trench Atlantic Oc. 117 19.50N 66.00W
Puerto Saavedra Chile 125 38.47S 73.24W
Puerto Santa Cruz Argentina 125 50.03S 68.35W
Puerto Sastre Paraguay 126 22.02S 58.00W
Puerto Siles Bolivia 124 12.48S 65.05W
Puerto Suspiro del Moro Spain 27 37.03N 3.43W
Puerto Tejado Colombia 122 3.16N 76.22W
Puerto Vallarta Mexico 116
Puerto Varas Chile 125 41.20S 73.00W
Pugachev Russian Fed. 44 52.02N 48.49E
Puget-Théniers France 21 43.57N 6.54E
Puglia d. Italy 33 41.00N 16.40E
Puig Major mtn. Spain 25 39.48N 2.48E
Puigmal mtn. Spain 25 42.23N 2.07E
Puisaye, Collines de la hills France 19 47.34N 3.28E
Pujehun Sierra Leone 76 7.23N 11.44W
Pukaki, L. New Zealand 86 44.00S 170.10E
Pukatawagan Canada 101 55.45N 101.20W
Pukë Albania 34 42.03N 19.54E
Pukekohe New Zealand 86 37.12S 174.56E
Pukeuri New Zealand 86 45.02S 171.02E
Pukhovichi Belarus 37 53.28N 28.18E
Pula Croatia 31 44.52N 13.50E
Pulacayo Bolivia 124 20.25S 66.41W
Pulaski N.Y. U.S.A. 115 43.34N 76.08W
Pulaski Tenn. U.S.A. 113 35.11N 87.02W
Pulaski Va. U.S.A. 113 37.03N 80.47W
Puławy Poland 37 51.25N 21.57E
Pulgaon India 63 20.44N 78.20E
Pulkkila Finland 40 64.16N 25.52E
Pullman U.S.A. 108 46.44N 117.10W

Pulog mtn. Phil. 59 16.50N 120.50E
Pulozero Russian Fed. 44 68.22N 33.15E
Pulpito, Punta c. Mexico 109 26.31N 111.28W
Pulsano Italy 33 40.23N 17.22E
Pułtusk Poland 37 52.42N 21.02E
Puma Tanzania 79 5.02S 34.46E
Puma Yumco l. China 63 28.35N 90.20E
Punakha Bhutan 63 27.37N 89.52E
Puncak Jaya mtn. Indonesia 59 4.00S 137.15E
Pünch Jammu & Kashmir 62 33.46N 74.06E
Pune India 60 18.34N 73.58E
Punjab d. India 62 30.45N 75.30E
Punjab d. Pakistan 62 30.25N 72.30E
Puno Peru 122 15.53S 70.03W
Punta Alta town Argentina 125 38.50S 62.00W
Punta Arenas town Chile 125 53.10S 70.56W
Puntable Australia 92 32.15S 134.13E
Punta Delgada town Argentina 125 42.43S 63.38W
Punta Gorda town Belize 117 16.10N 88.45W
Punta Gorda town U.S.A. 113 26.56N 82.01W
Puntarenas Costa Rica 117 10.00N 84.50W
Punto Fijo Venezuela 122 11.50N 70.16W
Punxsutawney U.S.A. 114 40.57N 78.59W
Puolanka Finland 40 64.52N 27.40E
Puqi China 55 29.40N 113.52E
Puquio Peru 122 14.44S 74.07W
Pur r. Russian Fed. 50 67.30N 75.30E
Pūranpur India 63 28.31N 80.09E
Purari r. P.N.G. 59 7.49S 145.10E
Purcell U.S.A. 111 35.01N 97.22W
Purchena Spain 27 37.21N 2.22W
Purgatoire r. U.S.A. 108 38.04N 103.10W
Puri India 63 19.48N 85.51E
Purisima, Sierra de la mts. Mexico 111 26.28N 101.45W
Purli India 62 18.51N 76.32E
Pûrna r. India 62 19.07N 77.02E
Purnea India 63 25.47N 87.31E
Purros Namibia 80 18.38S 12.59E
Purūlia India 63 23.20N 86.22E
Purus r. Brazil 122 3.58S 61.25W
Pŭrvomay Bulgaria 34 42.08N 25.17E
Purwakarta Indonesia 59 6.30S 107.25E
Purwodadi Indonesia 59 7.05S 110.53E
Purwokerto Indonesia 59 7.28S 109.09E
Purworejo Indonesia 59 7.45S 110.04E
Pusad India 63 19.54N 77.35E
Pusan S. Korea 53 35.05N 129.02E
Pushkar India 62 26.30N 74.33E
Pushkin Russian Fed. 44 59.43N 30.22E
Pushkino Russian Fed. 45 51.16N 47.09E
Pūspökladány Hungary 37 47.19N 21.07E
Pustoshka Russian Fed. 44 56.20N 29.20E
Putao Myanmar 56 27.22N 97.27E
Putaruru New Zealand 86 38.03S 175.47E
Putian China 55 25.29N 119.04E
Puting, Tanjung c. Indonesia 58 3.35S 111.52E
Putney U.S.A. 115 42.59N 72.31W
Putorana, Gory mts. Russian Fed. 51 68.30N 96.00E
Putsonderwater R.S.A. 80 29.14S 21.50E
Puttalam Sri Lanka 61 8.02N 79.50E
Puttgarden Germany 38 54.30N 11.13E
Putumayo r. Brazil 122 3.05S 68.10W
Puulavesi l. Finland 41 61.50N 26.42E
Puyallup U.S.A. 108 47.11N 122.18W
Puyang China 54 35.40N 115.02E
Puy-de-Dôme d. France 20 45.45N 3.05E
Puy de Dôme mtn. France 20 45.47N 2.58E
Puy de Sancy mtn. France 20 45.32N 2.49E
Puylaurens France 20 43.34N 2.01E
Puy L'Évêque France 20 44.30N 1.08E
Puymorens, Col de pass France 20 42.30N 1.50E
Puysegur Pt. New Zealand 86 46.10S 166.35E
Pūzak, Jehil-e l. Afghan. 62 31.30N 61.45E
Pwani d. Tanzania 79 7.00S 39.00E
Pweto Zaïre 79 8.27S 28.52E
Pwllheli U.K. 12 52.53N 4.25W
Pyaozero, Ozero l. Russian Fed. 44 66.00N 31.00E
Pyapon Myanmar 56 16.15N 95.40E
Pyasina r. Russian Fed. 51 73.10N 84.55E
Pyatigorsk Russian Fed. 45 44.04N 43.06E
Pyè Myanmar 56 18.50N 95.14E
Pyhä r. Finland 40 64.28N 24.13E
Pyhäjärvi l. Oulu Finland 40 63.35N 25.57E
Pyhäjärvi l. Turku-Pori Finland 41 61.00N 22.20E
Pyhäjoki Finland 40 64.28N 24.14E
Pyinmana Myanmar 56 19.45N 96.12E
Pymatuning Resr. U.S.A. 114 41.37N 80.30W
Pyŏngyang N. Korea 53 39.00N 125.47E
Pyramid U.S.A. 108 40.05N 119.43W
Pyramid Hill town Australia 92 36.03S 144.24E
Pyramid Hills Canada 103 57.35N 65.00W
Pyramid L. U.S.A. 108 40.00N 119.35W
Pyramids Egypt 72 29.52N 31.00E
Pyrénées mts. France/Spain 25 42.40N 0.00
Pyrénées-Atlantiques d. France 20 43.15N 1.00W
Pyrénées Orientales d. France 20 42.30N 2.20E
Pyrzyce Poland 36 53.10N 14.55E
Pythonga, Lac l. Canada 105 46.23N 76.26W
Pytteggja mtn. Norway 41 62.13N 7.42E
Pyu Myanmar 56 18.29N 96.26E

Q

Qaanaaq see Thule Greenland 99
Qabalān Jordan 67 32.06N 35.17E
Qabātiyah Jordan 67 32.25N 35.17E
Qā'emshahr Iran 65 36.28N 52.53E
Qagan Nur l. China 54 43.30N 114.35E
Qagbasērag China 63 30.51N 92.42E
Qagcaka China 63 32.32N 81.52E
Qahā Egypt 66 30.17N 31.12E
Qalāt Afghan. 62 32.07N 66.54E
Qal'at Bīshah Saudi Arabia 72 19.50N 42.36E
Qal 'eh Kāh Afghan. 62 32.18N 61.31E
Qal'eh-ye Now Afghan. 65 34.58N 63.04E
Qal'eh-ye Sāber Afghan. 62 34.02N 69.01E
Qallābāt Sudan 73 12.58N 36.09E
Qalqīlyah Jordan 67 32.11N 34.58E
Qalyūb Egypt 66 30.11N 31.12E
Qam Jordan 67 32.35N 35.44E
Qamar, Ghubbat al b. Yemen 71 16.00N 52.30E
Qamdo China 52 31.11N 97.18E
Qamīnis Libya 75 31.40N 20.01E
Qamr-ud-dīn Kārez Pakistan 62 31.39N 68.25E
Qānā Lebanon 67 33.13N 35.18E
Qan'abah Syria 67 33.08N 35.40E
Qanāṭir Muhammad 'Alī Egypt 66 30.12N 31.08E
Qanayah Syria 67 33.01N 36.11E
Qandahār Afghan. 62 31.32N 65.30E
Qandahār d. Afghan. 62 31.00N 65.30E
Qandala Somali Rep. 71 11.23N 49.53E
Qaqortoq see Julianehåb Greenland 99
Qārah Egypt 64 27.37N 26.30E
Qarā, Jabal al mts. Oman 71 17.15N 54.15E
Qārat Khazzī Iran 62 21.26N 24.30E
Qardho Somali Rep. 71 9.30N 49.03E
Qareh Sū Iran 65 34.52N 51.25E
Qareh Sū r. Iran 65 35.58N 56.25E
Qarqan He r. China 52 40.56N 86.27E
Qārūn, Birkat l. Egypt 66 29.30N 30.40E
Qaryat al Qaddāḥīyah Libya 75 31.22N 15.14E
Qāsh r. Sudan 72 16.48N 35.51E
Qasigiannguit see Christianshåb Greenland 99
Qāsim Syria 67 32.59N 36.05E
Qaṣr al Farāfirah Egypt 64 27.15N 28.10E
Qaṣr al Mushāsh ruin Jordan 67 31.49N 36.19E
Qaṣr al Mushattá site Jordan 67 31.44N 36.01E
Qaṣr al Qarābūllī Libya 75 32.45N 13.43E
Qaṣr-e Qand Iran 65 26.15N 60.37E
Qa'ṭabah Yemen 71 13.51N 44.42E
Qatanā Syria 67 33.27N 36.04E
Qatar Asia 65 25.20N 51.10E
Qaṭrānī, Jabal mts. Egypt 66 29.40N 30.36E
Qattara Depression see Qaṭṭārah, Munkhafaḍ al f.
  Egypt 64
Qaṭṭārah, Munkhafaḍ al f. Egypt 64 29.40N 27.30E
Qawz Rajab Sudan 72 16.04N 35.34E
Qāyen Iran 65 33.44N 59.07E
Qaysān Sudan 73 10.45N 34.48E
Qāzigund Jammu & Kashmir 62 33.38N 75.09E
Qazvīn Iran 65 36.16N 50.00E
Qeqertarsuaq see Godhavn Greenland 99
Qeqertarsuatsiaat see Fiskenaesset Greenland 99
Qeshm Iran 65 26.58N 57.17E
Qeshm i. Iran 65 26.48N 55.48E
Qezel Owzan r. Iran 65 36.44N 49.27E
Qezi'ot Israel 67 30.52N 34.28E
Qian'an China 54 45.00N 124.00E
Qianjiang China 55 29.28N 108.43E
Qianxi China 54 40.10N 118.19E
Qianyang China 55 27.22N 110.14E
Qiaotou China 54 42.58N 118.54E
Qibyā Jordan 67 31.59N 35.01E
Qidong Hunan China 55 26.47N 112.07E
Qidong Jiangsu China 55 31.49N 121.40E
Qiemo China 52 38.08N 85.33E
Qijiang China 55 29.00N 106.40E
Qila Abdullāh Pakistan 62 30.43N 66.38E
Qila Lādgasht Pakistan 62 27.54N 62.57E
Qila Saifullāh Pakistan 62 30.43N 68.21E
Qilian Shan mts. China 54 38.30N 99.20E
Qimantag mts. China 52 37.45N 89.40E
Qimen China 55 29.50N 117.38E
Qinā Egypt 64 26.10N 32.43E
Qinā, Wādī r. Egypt 64 26.07N 32.42E
Qingdao China 54 36.02N 120.25E
Qinghai d. China 63 34.20N 91.00E
Qinghai Hu l. China 52 36.40N 100.00E
Qingjian China 54 37.02N 110.06E
Qingjiang China 55 28.01N 115.30E
Qing Jiang Shuiku resr. China 55 30.00N 112.12E
Qinglong Guizhou China 55 25.47N 105.12E
Qinglong Hebei China 54 40.24N 118.53E
Qingshui Jiang r. China 55 28.08N 110.06E
Qing Xian China 54 38.35N 116.48E
Qingxu China 54 37.36N 112.21E
Qingyang China 54 36.03N 107.52E
Qingyuan Guangdong China 55 23.42N 113.00E
Qingyuan Jilin China 54 42.05N 125.01E
Qingyuan Zhejiang China 55 27.37N 119.03E
Qing Zang Gaoyuan f. China 52 33.40N 86.00E
Qinhuangdao China 54 39.52N 119.42E
Qin Ling mts. China 54 33.30N 109.00E
Qin Xian China 54 36.45N 112.41E
Qinyang China 54 35.06N 112.57E
Qinzhou China 55 21.58N 108.34E
Qionghai China 55 19.12N 110.31E
Qiongshan China 55 19.59N 110.30E
Qiongzhou Haixia str. China 55 20.09N 110.20E
Qipanshan China 54 42.05N 117.37E
Qiqihar China 53 47.23N 124.00E
Qira China 52 37.02N 80.53E
Qiryat Ata Israel 67 32.48N 35.06E
Qiryat Bialik Israel 67 32.50N 35.05E
Qiryat Gat Israel 67 31.37N 34.47E

Qiryat Motzkin Israel 67 32.50N 35.04E
Qiryat Shemona Israel 67 33.13N 35.35E
Qiryat Tiv'on Israel 67 32.43N 35.08E
Qiryat Yam Israel 67 32.51N 35.04E
Qishn Yemen 60 15.25N 51.40E
Qishon r. Israel 67 32.49N 35.02E
Qiuxizhen China 55 29.54N 104.40E
Qi Xian Henan China 54 35.35N 114.08E
Qi Xian Henan China 54 34.30N 114.50E
Qom Iran 65 34.40N 50.57E
Qonggyai China 63 29.03N 91.41E
Qornet'es Sauda mtn. Lebanon 66 34.17N 36.04E
Qoṭūr Iran 65 38.28N 44.25E
Quabbin Resr. U.S.A. 115 42.22N 72.18W
Quadeville Canada 105 45.18N 77.24W
Quairading Australia 89 32.00S 117.22E
Quakenbrück Germany 38 52.40N 7.57E
Quakertown U.S.A. 115 40.26N 75.21W
Qu'alī China 55 29.46N 117.15E
Quambatook Australia 92 35.52S 143.36E
Quambone Australia 93 30.54S 147.55E
Quang Ngai Vietnam 56 15.09N 108.50E
Quang Tri Vietnam 56 16.44N 107.10E
Quang Yen Vietnam 56 20.56N 106.49E
Quan Long Vietnam 56 9.11N 105.09E
Quannan China 55 24.45N 114.32E
Quantico U.S.A. 114 38.31N 77.17W
Quanzhou Fujian China 55 24.57N 118.36E
Quanzhou Guang. Zhuang. China 55 26.00N 111.00E
Qu'Appelle r. Canada 101 50.33N 101.20W
Quaqtaq Canada 99 61.05N 69.36W
Quaraí Brazil 125 30.23S 56.27W
Quaraí r. Brazil 125 30.12S 57.36W
Quarryville U.S.A. 115 39.54N 76.10W
Quartu Sant'Elena Italy 32 39.14N 9.11E
Quartzsite U.S.A. 109 33.40N 114.13W
Quatsino Sd. Canada 100 50.42N 127.58W
Qūchān Iran 65 37.04N 58.29E
Queanbeyan Australia 93 35.24S 149.17E
Québec Canada 105 46.50N 71.20W
Québec d. Canada 103 51.20N 68.45W
Quebracho Uruguay 125 31.57S 57.53W
Quedlinburg Germany 38 51.48N 11.09E
Queen Anne U.S.A. 115 38.55N 75.57W
Queen Charlotte Canada 100 53.18N 132.04W
Queen Charlotte Is. Canada 100 53.00N 132.00W
Queen Charlotte Sd. Canada 100 51.30N 129.30W
Queen Charlotte Str. Canada 100 51.00N 128.00W
Queen Elizabeth Is. Canada 99 78.30N 99.00W
Queen Maud G. Canada 98 68.30N 99.00W
Queen Maud Range mts. Antarctica 128 86.20S
  165.00W
Queens Channel Australia 88 14.46S 129.24E
Queenscliff Australia 93 38.17S 144.42E
Queensland d. Australia 90 23.30S 144.00E
Queenstown Australia 91 42.07S 145.33E
Queenstown New Zealand 86 45.03S 168.41E
Queenstown R.S.A. 80 31.52S 26.51E
Queenstown U.S.A. 115 38.59N 76.09W
Queguay Grande r. Uruguay 125 32.09S 58.09W
Queimadas Brazil 123 10.58S 39.38W
Quela Angola 78 9.18S 17.05E
Quelimane Mozambique 79 17.53S 36.57E
Quemado U.S.A. 109 34.20N 108.30W
Quemoy i. China 55 24.30N 118.20E
Quentico Prov. Park Canada 102 48.20N 91.30W
Quequén Argentina 125 38.34S 58.42W
Querétaro Mexico 116 20.38N 100.23W
Querétaro d. Mexico 116 21.03N 100.00W
Querobabi Mexico 109 30.03N 111.01W
Quesada Spain 27 37.51N 3.04W
Queshan China 54 32.48N 114.01E
Quesnel Canada 100 53.05N 122.30W
Quesnel r. Canada 100 52.58N 122.29W
Questembert France 18 47.40N 2.27W
Quetta Pakistan 62 30.12N 67.00E
Quettehou France 18 49.36N 1.18W
Quevedo Ecuador 122 0.59S 79.27W
Quezaltenango Guatemala 116 14.50N 91.30W
Quezon City Phil. 59 14.39N 121.01E
Quibala Angola 78 10.48S 14.56E
Quibaxi Angola 78 8.34S 14.37E
Quibdó Colombia 122 5.40N 76.38W
Quiberon France 18 47.29N 3.07W
Quibocolo Angola 78 6.20S 15.05E
Quicama Nat. Park Angola 78 9.40S 13.30E
Quiet L. Canada 100 61.05N 133.05W
Quilán, C. Chile 125 43.16S 74.27W
Quilengues Angola 78 14.09S 14.04E
Quillabamba Peru 122 12.50S 72.50W
Quillacollo Bolivia 124 17.26S 66.17W
Quillan France 20 42.52N 2.11E
Quillota Chile 125 32.53S 71.16W
Quilon India 60 8.53N 76.38E
Quilpie Australia 90 26.37S 144.15E
Quilpué Chile 125 33.03S 71.27W
Quimbele Angola 78 6.29S 16.25E
Quimilí Argentina 124 27.35S 62.25W
Quimper France 18 48.00N 4.06W
Quimperlé France 18 47.52N 3.33W
Quincy Ill. U.S.A. 110 39.56N 91.23W
Quincy Mass. U.S.A. 115 42.15N 71.01W
Quincy Wash. U.S.A. 108 47.14N 119.51W
Qui Nhon Vietnam 56 13.47N 109.11E
Quintanar de la Orden Spain 27 39.34N 3.03W
Quintana Roo d. Mexico 117 19.00N 88.00W
Quinte, B. of Canada 105 44.07N 77.15W
Quinter U.S.A. 110 39.04N 100.14W
Quintin France 18 48.24N 2.55W
Quinto Spain 25 41.25N 0.29W
Quinzau Angola 78 6.51S 12.46E
Quionga Mozambique 79 10.37S 40.31E
Quipar r. Spain 25 38.14N 1.36W
Quirigua ruins Guatemala 116 15.20N 89.25W
Quirindi Australia 93 31.30S 150.42E
Quiroga Spain 26 42.29N 7.16W
Quiros, C. Vanuatu 84 14.55S 167.01E

Quissanga Mozambique 79 12.24S 40.33E
Quissico Mozambique 81 24.42S 34.44E
Quitapa Angola 78 10.10S 18.16E
Quiterajo Mozambique 79 11.46S 40.25E
Quito Ecuador 122 0.14S 78.30W
Qu Jiang r. China 55 30.02N 106.20E
Qumigxung China 63 30.53N 86.38E
Qumrān site Jordan 67 31.44N 35.27E
Quorn Australia 92 32.20S 138.02E
Qurayyah, Wādī r. Egypt 66 30.26N 34.01E
Qurdud Sudan 73 10.17N 29.56E
Qurlurtuuq see Coppermine Canada 98
Quṣrah Jordan 67 32.05N 35.20E
Qū' Wishām f. Oman 71 18.55N 55.55E
Quxian China 55 30.50N 106.54E
Qu Xian China 55 28.59N 118.56E
Quyon Canada 105 45.31N 76.14W
Qūzū China 63 29.21N 90.39E

R

Raab r. see Rába r. Austria 31
Raahe Finland 40 64.41N 24.29E
Raalte Neth. 16 52.22N 6.17E
Ra'ananna Israel 67 32.11N 34.53E
Raasay i. U.K. 14 57.25N 6.05W
Raas Caseyr c. Somali Rep. 71 11.48N 51.22E
Rab Croatia 31 44.46N 14.46E
Rab i. Croatia 31 44.45N 14.45E
Rába r. Hungary 31 47.42N 17.38E
Raba Indonesia 58 8.27S 118.45E
Rabaçal r. Portugal 26 41.30N 7.12W
Rábade Spain 26 43.07N 7.37W
Rabak Sudan 73 13.09N 32.44E
Rabang China 63 33.03N 80.29E
Rabat Morocco 74 34.02N 6.51W
Rabbit Flat town Australia 88 20.10S 129.53E
Rabbit L. Canada 104 47.00N 79.37W
Rabbitskin r. Canada 100 61.47N 120.42W
Rābor Iran 65 29.18N 56.56E
Rabyānah Libya 73 24.14N 21.59E
Rabyānah, Ṣaḥrā' f. Libya 75 24.30N 21.00E
Racconigi Italy 30 44.46N 7.46E
Raccoon Creek r. U.S.A. 114 40.02N 82.24W
Race, C. Canada 103 46.40N 53.10W
Race Pt. U.S.A. 115 42.04N 70.14W
Rach Gia Vietnam 56 10.02N 105.05E
Racibórz Poland 37 50.06N 18.13E
Racine U.S.A. 110 42.42N 87.50W
Raco U.S.A. 104 46.24N 84.31W
Rādāuṭi Romania 37 47.51N 25.55E
Råde Norway 42 59.21N 10.51E
Radeberg Germany 38 51.13N 13.43E
Radebeul Germany 38 51.06N 13.40E
Radeče Slovenia 31 46.04N 15.11E
Radekhov Ukraine 37 50.18N 24.35E
Radford U.S.A. 113 37.07N 80.34W
Rādhanpur India 62 23.50N 71.36E
Radium Hill town Australia 92 32.30S 140.32E
Radium Hot Springs town Canada 100 50.48N
  116.12W
Radnevo Bulgaria 34 42.18N 25.56E
Radnice Czech Republic 38 49.51N 13.37E
Radom Poland 37 51.26N 21.10E
Radomir Bulgaria 34 42.37N 23.04E
Radomsko Poland 37 51.05N 19.25E
Radomyshl Ukraine 37 50.30N 29.14E
Radotín Czech Republic 38 50.00N 14.22E
Radoviš Macedonia 34 41.38N 22.28E
Radovljica Slovenia 31 46.21N 14.11E
Radøy i. Norway 41 60.40N 5.05E
Radstadt Austria 39 47.23N 13.27E
Radstock U.K. 13 51.17N 2.25W
Radstock, C. Australia 92 33.11S 134.21E
Radville Canada 101 49.27N 104.17W
Raḍwā, Jabal mtn. Saudi Arabia 64 24.36N 38.18E
Rae Canada 100 62.50N 116.03W
Rāe Bareli India 63 26.13N 81.14E
Raeren Germany 38 50.41N 6.07E
Raeside, L. Australia 89 29.30S 122.00E
Rafaela Argentina 124 31.16S 61.44W
Rafah Egypt 67 31.18N 34.15E
Rafaï C.A.R. 73 4.58N 23.56E
Raffadali Italy 32 37.24N 13.33E
Raffili Mission Sudan 73 6.53N 27.58E
Rafḥā Saudi Arabia 64 29.38N 43.30E
Rafsanjān Iran 65 30.24N 56.00E
Raga Sudan 73 8.28N 25.41E
Ragged, Mt. Australia 89 33.27S 123.27E
Ragunda Sweden 40 63.06N 16.23E
Ragusa Italy 33 36.55N 14.44E
Raha Indonesia 59 4.50S 122.43E
Rahad r. Sudan 72 14.28N 33.31E
Rahad al Bardī Sudan 73 11.18N 23.53E
Raḥā, Ḥarrat ar f. Saudi Arabia 66 28.00N 36.35E
Rahīm Ki Bāzār Pakistan 62 24.19N 69.09E
Rahīmyār Khān Pakistan 62 28.25N 70.18E
Raiatea i. Îs. de la Société 85 16.50S 151.25W
Rāichūr India 60 16.15N 77.20E
Raiganj India 63 25.37N 88.07E
Raigarh India 63 21.54N 83.24E
Rainbow Australia 92 35.56S 142.01E
Rainelle U.S.A. 113 37.58N 80.46W
Rainier, Mt. U.S.A. 108 46.52N 121.46W
Rainy L. Canada/U.S.A. 102 48.42N 93.10W

Rainy River town Canada 102 48.43N 94.29W
Raipur India 63 21.14N 81.38E
Raipur Uplands mts. India 63 20.45N 82.30E
Rairākhol India 63 21.03N 84.23E
Ra'īs Saudi Arabia 64 23.35N 38.36E
Raisen India 63 23.20N 77.48E
Raisin r. U.S.A. 104 41.53N 83.20W
Raivavae i. Pacific Oc. 85 23.52S 147.40W
Rājahmundry India 61 17.01N 81.52E
Rajāj Sudan 73 10.55N 24.43E
Rajang r. Malaysia 58 2.10N 112.45E
Rājanpur Pakistan 62 29.06N 70.19E
Rājapālaiyam India 60 9.26N 77.36E
Rājasthān d. India 62 26.15N 74.00E
Rājasthān Canal India 62 31.10N 75.00E
Rājbāri Bangla. 63 23.46N 89.39E
Rāj Gāngpur India 63 22.11N 84.36E
Rājgarh Madhya P. India 62 23.56N 76.58E
Rājgarh Rāj. India 62 27.14N 76.38E
Rājgarh Rāj. India 62 28.38N 75.23E
Rājkot India 62 22.18N 70.47E
Rāj-Nāndgaon India 63 21.06N 81.02E
Rājpīpla India 62 21.47N 73.34E
Rājpur India 62 21.56N 75.08E
Rājshāhi Bangla. 63 24.22N 88.36E
Rājula India 62 21.01N 71.34E
Rakahanga Atoll Cook Is. 84 10.03S 161.06W
Rakaia New Zealand 86 43.45S 172.01E
Rakaia r. New Zealand 86 43.52S 172.13E
Raka Zangbo r. China 63 29.24N 87.58E
Rakhni Pakistan 62 30.03N 69.55E
Rakhov Ukraine 37 48.02N 24.10E
Rakhshān r. Pakistan 62 27.10N 63.25E
Rākīn Jordan 67 31.14N 35.42E
Rakitnoye Ukraine 37 51.18N 27.10E
Rakkestad Norway 42 59.26N 11.21E
Rakops Botswana 80 21.00S 24.32E
Rakov Belarus 37 53.58N 26.59E
Rakovník Czech Republic 39 50.05N 13.43E
Rakovski Bulgaria 34 42.18N 24.58E
Rakulka Russian Fed. 44 62.19N 46.52E
Rākvåg Norway 40 63.47N 10.10E
Rakvere Estonia 46 59.22N 26.28E
Raleigh U.S.A. 113 35.46N 78.39W
Raleigh B. U.S.A. 113 34.47N 76.09W
Ralik Chain is. Pacific Oc. 84 8.00N 168.00E
Ram r. Canada 100 62.01N 123.41W
Rama Israel 67 32.56N 35.22E
Rama Nicaragua 117 12.09N 84.15W
Ramacca Italy 33 37.23N 14.42E
Rāmah Saudi Arabia 65 25.33N 47.08E
Ramales de la Victoria Spain 26 43.15N 3.27W
Rām Allāh Jordan 67 31.55N 35.12E
Ramallo Argentina 125 33.28S 60.02W
Rāmānuj Ganj India 63 23.48N 83.42E
Ramat Dawid Israel 67 32.40N 35.12E
Ramat Gan Israel 67 32.05N 34.48E
Ramat HaSharon Israel 67 32.09N 34.50E
Ramat HaShofet Israel 67 32.37N 35.06E
Ramat Yishay Israel 67 32.42N 35.10E
Ramat Yohanan Israel 67 32.47N 35.07E
Rambau, Lac l. Canada 103 53.40N 70.10W
Rambervillers France 19 48.21N 6.38E
Rambla del Judío r. Spain 25 38.15N 1.27W
Rambouillet France 19 48.39N 1.50E
Rām Dās India 62 31.58N 74.55E
Rame Head Australia 93 37.50S 149.25E
Rame Head U.K. 13 50.18N 4.13W
Ramelton Rep. of Ire. 15 55.02N 7.40W
Rāmgarh Bangla. 63 22.59N 91.43E
Rāmgarh Bihār India 63 23.38N 85.31E
Rāmgarh Rāj. India 62 27.22N 70.30E
Rāmgarh Rāj. India 62 27.15N 75.11E
Rāmhormoz Iran 65 31.14N 49.37E
Ramillies Belgium 16 50.39N 4.56E
Ramingstein Austria 39 47.04N 13.50E
Ramīs r. Ethiopia 73 7.59N 41.34E
Ramla Israel 67 31.56N 34.52E
Ramlu mtn. Eritrea 73 13.20N 41.45E
Rämnagar India 63 29.24N 79.07E
Ramnäs Sweden 43 59.46N 16.12E
Ramo Ethiopia 73 6.50N 41.15E
Ramona Calif. U.S.A. 109 33.08N 116.52W
Ramona Okla. U.S.A. 111 36.32N 95.55W
Ramore Canada 102 48.30N 80.25W
Ramos Arizpe Mexico 111 25.33N 100.58W
Ramot Naftali Israel 67 33.06N 35.33E
Rāmpur Himachal P. India 63 31.27N 77.38E
Rāmpur Uttar P. India 63 28.49N 79.02E
Rampura India 62 24.28N 75.26E
Ramree I. Myanmar 56 19.06N 93.48E
Ramsey I.o.M. Europe 12 54.19N 4.23W
Ramsey England U.K. 13 52.27N 0.06W
Ramsey L. Canada 104 47.15N 82.16W
Ramsgate U.K. 13 51.20N 1.25E
Rāmshīr Iran 65 30.54N 49.24E
Ramsjö Sweden 41 62.11N 15.39E
Rämtek India 63 21.24N 79.20E
Ramu r. P.N.G. 59 4.00S 144.40E
Ramusio, Lac l. Canada 103 51.35N 64.10W
Ranau Malaysia 58 5.58N 116.41E
Rancagua Chile 125 34.10S 70.45W
Rance r. France 18 48.31N 1.59W
Rancheria r. Canada 100 60.13N 129.07W
Rānchi India 63 23.21N 85.20E
Rand Australia 93 35.34S 146.35E
Randalstown U.K. 15 54.45N 6.20W
Randan France 20 46.01N 3.21E
Randazzo Italy 33 37.53N 14.57E
Randburg R.S.A. 80 26.07S 28.02E
Rånder India 62 21.14N 72.47E
Randers Denmark 42 56.28N 10.03E
Randolph Kans. U.S.A. 110 39.27N 96.44W
Randolph N.Y. U.S.A. 114 42.10N 78.59W
Randolph Vt. U.S.A. 105 43.55N 72.40W
Randsburg U.S.A. 109 35.22N 117.39W
Randsfjorden l. Norway 41 60.25N 10.24E
Råne r. Sweden 40 65.52N 22.19E

Råneå to Riobamba

Råneå Sweden 40 65.52N 22.18E
Räner India 62 28.53N 73.17E
Ranfurly New Zealand 86 45.08S 170.08E
Rangdong China 54 32.51N 112.18E
Rangely U.S.A. 108 40.05N 108.48W
Ranger U.S.A. 113 38.07N 82.10W
Ranger L. Canada 104 46.54N 83.35W
Ranger Lake town Canada 104 46.52N 83.36W
Rangia India 63 26.28N 91.38E
Rangiora New Zealand 86 43.18S 172.38E
Rangiroa i. Pacific Oc. 85 15.00S 147.40W
Rangitaiki r. New Zealand 86 37.55S 176.50E
Rangkasbitung Indonesia 59 6.21S 106.12E
Rangoon see Yangon Myanmar 56
Rangpur Bangla. 63 25.45N 89.15E
Rānīganj India 63 23.37N 87.08E
Rānīkhet India 63 29.39N 79.25E
Rānīwāra India 62 24.45N 72.13E
Rankin Inlet town Canada 99 62.52N 92.00W
Rankins Springs Australia 93 33.52S 146.18E
Rannoch, Loch U.K. 14 56.41N 4.20W
Rann of Kachchh f. India 62 23.50N 69.50E
Ranohira Madagascar 81 22.29S 45.24E
Rano Kao mtn. I. de Pascua 85 27.11S 109.27W
Ranong Thailand 56 9.59N 98.40E
Ransäter Sweden 43 59.46N 13.26E
Rantauprapat Indonesia 58 2.05N 99.46E
Rantekombola mtn. Indonesia 58 3.30S 119.58E
Råö Sweden 42 57.24N 11.56E
Rao Co mtn. Laos 56 18.10N 105.25E
Raoping China 55 23.45N 117.05E
Raoul i. Pacific Oc. 84 29.15S 177.55W
Rapa i. Pacific Oc. 85 27.35S 144.20W
Rapallo Italy 30 44.21N 9.14E
Rāpar India 62 23.34N 70.38E
Rapidan r. U.S.A. 114 38.22N 77.37W
Rapid Bay town Australia 92 35.33S 138.09E
Rapid City U.S.A. 110 44.05N 103.14W
Rapides des Joachims town Canada 105 46.13N 77.43W
Rappahannock r. U.S.A. 114 37.34N 76.18W
Rapperswil Switz. 39 47.14N 8.50E
Rapsáni Greece 34 39.54N 22.33E
Raquette r. U.S.A. 105 45.00N 74.42W
Raquette L. U.S.A. 105 43.52N 74.38W
Raquette Lake town U.S.A. 105 43.49N 74.41W
Rarotonga i. Cook Is. 84 21.14S 159.46W
Ra's al Ḥadd c. Oman 60 22.32N 59.49E
Ra's al Khaymah U.A.E. 65 25.48N 55.56E
Ra's al Unūf Libya 75 30.31N 18.34E
Ra's an Nabq town Egypt 66 29.36N 34.51E
Ra's an Naqb town Jordan 66 30.30N 35.29E
Ras Dashen mtn. Ethiopia 73 13.20N 38.10E
Ras Djebel Tunisia 32 37.13N 10.09E
Râs Ghârib Egypt 66 28.22N 33.04E
Rashâd Sudan 73 11.51N 31.04E
Rashîd Egypt 66 31.25N 30.25E
Rashîd Qal 'eh Afghan. 62 31.31N 67.31E
Rasht Iran 65 37.18N 49.38E
Rasina r. Yugo. 34 43.38N 21.21E
Raška Yugo. 34 43.17N 20.37E
Rās Koh mtn. Pakistan 62 28.50N 65.12E
Rason L. Australia 89 28.46S 124.20E
Rasra India 63 25.51N 83.51E
Rastatt Germany 39 48.51N 8.12E
Rastede Germany 38 53.15N 8.11E
Rasu, Monte mtn. Italy 32 40.25N 9.00E
Ratak Chain is. Pacific Oc. 84 8.00N 172.00E
Ratangarh India 62 28.05N 74.36E
Rat Buri Thailand 56 13.30N 99.50E
Ratcatchers L. Australia 92 32.40S 143.12E
Rāth India 63 25.35N 79.34E
Rathcormack Rep. of Ire. 15 52.05N 8.18W
Rathdrum Rep. of Ire. 15 52.56N 6.15W
Rathenow Germany 38 52.36N 12.20E
Rathlin I. U.K. 15 55.17N 6.15W
Rath Luirc Rep. of Ire. 15 52.21N 8.41W
Rathmullen Rep. of Ire. 15 55.06N 7.32W
Ratlām India 62 23.19N 75.04E
Ratnāgiri India 60 16.59N 73.18E
Ratno Ukraine 37 51.40N 24.32E
Ratodero Pakistan 62 27.48N 68.18E
Raton U.S.A. 108 36.54N 104.24W
Rats, Rivière aux r. Canada 105 47.12N 72.52W
Rattlesnake Range mts. U.S.A. 108 42.45N 107.10W
Rattray Head U.K. 14 57.37N 1.50W
Rättvik Sweden 41 60.53N 15.06E
Ratzeburg Germany 38 53.42N 10.46E
Ratzeburger See l. Germany 38 53.45N 10.47E
Rauch Argentina 125 36.47S 59.05W
Raufoss Norway 41 60.43N 10.37E
Raul Soares Brazil 126 20.04S 42.27W
Rauma Finland 41 61.08N 21.30E
Rauma r. Norway 40 62.32N 7.43E
Raung, Gunung mtn. Indonesia 59 8.07S 114.03E
Raurkela India 63 22.13N 84.53E
Rautas Sweden 40 68.00N 19.55E
Ravalgaon India 62 20.38N 74.25E
Ravanusa Italy 32 37.16N 13.58E
Rāvar Iran 65 31.14N 56.51E
Rava-Russkaya Ukraine 37 50.15N 23.36E
Ravena U.S.A. 115 42.29N 73.49W
Ravenna Italy 30 44.25N 12.12E
Ravenna U.S.A. 114 41.09N 81.15W
Ravensburg Germany 39 47.47N 9.37E
Ravenshoe Australia 90 17.37S 145.29E
Ravensthorpe Australia 89 33.35S 120.02E
Ravenswood U.S.A. 114 38.57N 81.46W
Räver India 62 21.15N 76.05E
Ravī r. Pakistan 60 30.30N 72.13E
Ravna Gora Croatia 31 45.23N 14.57E
Rawaki i. Kiribati 84 3.43S 170.43W
Rāwalpindi Pakistan 62 33.36N 73.04E
Rawāndūz Iraq 65 36.38N 44.32E
Rawdon Canada 105 46.03N 73.44W
Rawene New Zealand 86 35.24S 173.30E
Rawicz Poland 36 51.37N 16.52E
Rawlinna Australia 89 31.00S 125.21E

Rawlins U.S.A. 108 41.47N 107.14W
Rawson Argentina 125 34.40S 60.02W
Raxaul India 63 26.59N 84.51E
Ray U.S.A. 110 48.21N 103.10W
Raya mtn. Indonesia 58 0.45S 112.45E
Rāyagada India 63 19.10N 83.25E
Ray, C. Canada 103 47.40N 59.18W
Rāyen Iran 65 29.34N 57.26E
Raymond Canada 100 49.30N 112.35W
Raymond U.S.A. 108 46.41N 123.44W
Raymond Terrace Australia 93 32.47S 151.45E
Raymondville U.S.A. 111 26.29N 97.47W
Rayong Thailand 56 12.43N 101.20E
Razan Iran 65 35.22N 49.02E
Razanj Yugo. 34 43.40N 21.31E
Razdelnaya Ukraine 37 46.50N 30.02E
Razgrad Bulgaria 34 43.33N 26.34E
Razgrad d. Bulgaria 34 43.32N 26.10E
Razlog Bulgaria 34 41.53N 23.28E
Raz, Pointe du c. France 18 48.02N 4.44W
Reading U.K. 13 51.27N 0.57W
Reading U.S.A. 115 40.20N 75.56W
Readsboro U.S.A. 115 42.46N 72.57W
Realicó Argentina 125 35.02S 64.14W
Réalmont France 20 43.47N 2.12E
Reay Forest f. U.K. 14 58.17N 4.48W
Rebecca, L. Australia 89 30.07S 122.32E
Rebi Indonesia 59 6.24S 134.07E
Rebiana Sand Sea see Rabyānah, Şaḥrā' f. Libya 75
Reboly Russian Fed. 44 63.50N 32.10E
Rebun jima i. Japan 57 45.25N 141.04E
Recalde Argentina 125 36.39S 61.05W
Recanati Italy 31 43.24N 13.32E
Rechāh Lām Afghan. 62 34.58N 70.51E
Recherche, Archipelago of the is. Australia 89 34.05S 122.45E
Rechitsa Belarus 37 52.21N 30.24E
Recife Brazil 123 8.06S 34.53W
Recklinghausen Germany 38 51.36N 7.13E
Recknitz r. Germany 38 54.14N 12.28E
Reconquista Argentina 124 29.08S 59.38W
Recreo Argentina 124 29.20S 65.04W
Red r. Canada 101 50.20N 96.50W
Red r. U.S.A. 111 31.00N 91.40W
Red r. see Hong Hà r. Vietnam 56
Red Bank U.S.A. 115 40.21N 74.03W
Red Basin f. see Sichuan Pendi f. China 55
Red Bay town Canada 103 51.44N 56.45W
Red Bluff U.S.A. 108 40.11N 122.15W
Redcar U.K. 12 54.37N 1.04W
Red Cliffs town Australia 92 34.22S 142.13E
Red Cloud U.S.A. 110 40.04N 98.31W
Red Deer Canada 100 52.15N 113.50W
Red Deer r. Canada 101 50.56N 109.54W
Redding U.S.A. 108 40.35N 122.24W
Redditch U.K. 13 52.18N 1.57W
Rede r. U.K. 12 55.08N 2.13W
Redfield U.S.A. 110 44.53N 98.31W
Redhill town Australia 92 33.34S 138.12E
Red Hook U.S.A. 115 41.55N 73.53W
Red Indian L. Canada 103 48.40N 56.50W
Red L. U.S.A. 107 48.00N 95.00W
Red Lake town Canada 102 51.03N 93.49W
Redlands U.S.A. 109 34.03N 117.11W
Red Lion U.S.A. 115 39.54N 76.36W
Red Lodge U.S.A. 108 45.11N 109.15W
Redmond U.S.A. 108 44.17N 121.11W
Rednitz r. Germany 38 49.28N 10.59E
Red Oak U.S.A. 110 41.01N 95.14W
Redon France 18 47.39N 2.05W
Redondela Spain 26 42.17N 8.36W
Redondo Portugal 27 38.39N 7.33W
Redondo Beach town U.S.A. 109 33.51N 118.23W
Red Rock Canada 100 53.39N 122.41W
Redrock U.S.A. 109 32.35N 111.19W
Redruth U.K. 13 50.14N 5.14W
Red Sea Africa/Asia 71 20.00N 39.00E
Redstone Canada 100 52.13N 123.50W
Red Sucker L. Canada 101 54.09N 93.40W
Red Volta r. Ghana 76 10.32N 0.31W
Redwater Alta. Canada 100 53.55N 113.06W
Redwater Ont. Canada 104 46.54N 79.34W
Red Wing U.S.A. 110 44.33N 92.31W
Redwood City U.S.A. 108 37.29N 122.13W
Reed City U.S.A. 112 43.54N 85.31W
Reeder U.S.A. 110 46.06N 102.57W
Reedsport U.S.A. 108 43.42N 124.06W
Reedy U.S.A. 114 38.54N 81.26W
Reefton New Zealand 86 42.07S 171.52E
Ree, Lough Rep. of Ire. 15 53.31N 7.58W
Reese r. U.S.A. 108 40.39N 116.54W
Reftele Sweden 43 57.11N 13.35E
Refuge Cove town Canada 100 50.07N 124.50W
Refugio U.S.A. 111 28.18N 97.17W
Rega r. Poland 36 54.10N 15.18E
Regavim Israel 67 32.32N 35.02E
Regen Germany 39 48.59N 13.07E
Regen r. Germany 39 49.01N 12.06E
Regensburg Germany 39 49.01N 12.06E
Reggane Algeria 74 26.42N 0.10E
Reggello Italy 30 43.41N 11.32E
Reggio Calabria Italy 33 38.07N 15.39E
Reggio Emilia-Romagna Italy 30 44.43N 10.36E
Reghin Romania 37 46.47N 24.42E
Regina Canada 101 50.25N 104.39W
Regiwar Pakistan 62 25.57N 65.44E
Regnéville Rep. of Ire. 15 49.01N 1.33W
Reguengos de Monsaraz Portugal 27 38.25N 7.32W
Rehau Germany 39 50.15N 12.02E
Rehoboth Namibia 80 23.19S 17.10E
Rehoboth B. U.S.A. 115 38.40N 75.06W
Rehoboth Beach town U.S.A. 115 38.43N 75.05W
Rehovot Israel 67 31.54N 34.46E
Reichenbach Germany 38 50.37N 12.18E
Reidsville U.S.A. 113 36.21N 79.40W
Reigate U.K. 13 51.14N 0.13W
Ré, Île de i. France 20 46.10N 1.26W
Reims France 19 49.15N 4.02E

Reinach Switz. 39 47.30N 7.35E
Reindeer L. Canada 101 57.15N 102.40W
Reinosa Spain 26 43.00N 4.08W
Reisterstown U.S.A. 114 39.28N 76.50W
Rejmyra Sweden 43 58.50N 15.55E
Rekarne Sweden 43 59.14N 15.58E
Rekovac Yugo. 34 43.51N 21.03E
Relizane Algeria 75 35.45N 0.33E
Remanso Brazil 123 9.41S 42.04W
Remarkable, Mt. Australia 92 32.48S 138.10E
Rembang Indonesia 59 6.45S 111.22E
Remeshk Iran 65 26.52N 58.46E
Remich Lux. 16 49.34N 6.23E
Remington U.S.A. 114 38.32N 77.49W
Remiremont France 19 48.01N 6.35E
Remoulins France 21 43.56N 4.34E
Remscheid Germany 38 51.11N 7.11E
Remsen U.S.A. 115 43.19N 75.11W
Rena Norway 41 61.08N 11.22E
Rende Italy 33 39.19N 16.11E
Rendina Greece 35 39.04N 21.58E
Rendsburg Germany 38 54.18N 9.40E
Renfrew Canada 105 45.28N 76.41W
Rengat Indonesia 58 0.26S 102.35E
Rengo Chile 125 34.25S 70.52W
Renheji China 55 31.56N 115.07E
Reni India 62 28.41N 75.02E
Reni Ukraine 37 45.28N 28.17E
Renkum Neth. 16 51.59N 5.46E
Renmark Australia 92 34.10S 140.45E
Rennell Sd. Canada 100 53.23N 132.35W
Renner Springs town Australia 90 18.20S 133.48E
Rennes France 18 48.05N 1.41W
Reno r. Italy 30 44.37N 12.17E
Reno U.S.A. 108 39.31N 119.48W
Renovo U.S.A. 114 41.20N 77.38W
Rensselaer U.S.A. 115 42.39N 73.44W
Rentería Spain 26 43.19N 1.54W
Renton U.S.A. 108 47.30N 122.11W
Ren Xian China 54 37.07N 114.41E
Réo Burkina 76 12.20N 2.27W
Repki Ukraine 37 51.47N 31.06E
Republic Penn. U.S.A. 114 39.56N 79.55W
Republic Wash. U.S.A. 108 48.39N 118.44W
Republican r. U.S.A. 110 39.03N 96.48W
Republic of Ireland Europe 15 53.00N 8.00W
Republic of South Africa Africa 80 28.30S 24.50E
Repulse B. Australia 90 20.36S 148.43E
Repulse Bay town Canada 99 66.35N 86.20W
Requa U.S.A. 108 41.34N 124.05W
Requena Peru 122 5.05S 73.52W
Requena Spain 25 39.29N 1.06W
Réquista France 20 44.02N 2.31E
Resadiye Karimadasi pen. Turkey 35 36.45N 27.40E
Reschenpass Italy/Austria 39 46.50N 10.30E
Resen Macedonia 34 41.05N 21.00E
Reserve Canada 101 52.28N 102.39W
Resistencia Argentina 124 27.28S 59.00W
Reşiţa Romania 37 45.17N 21.53E
Resolute Canada 99 74.40N 95.00W
Resolution I. Canada 99 61.30N 65.00W
Resolution I. New Zealand 86 45.40S 166.30E
Restigouche r. Canada 103 48.04N 66.20W
Restoule Canada 104 46.03N 79.47W
Rethel France 19 49.31N 4.22E
Réthimnon Greece 35 35.22N 24.29E
Réunion i. Indian Oc. 49 22.00S 55.00E
Reus Spain 25 41.09N 1.07E
Reusel Neth. 16 51.21N 5.09E
Reuterstadt Stavenhagen Germany 38 53.40N 12.54E
Reutlingen Germany 39 48.29N 9.11E
Reutte Austria 39 47.29N 10.43E
Revda Russian Fed. 44 56.49N 59.58E
Revelstoke Canada 100 51.00N 118.00W
Revigny-sur-Ornain France 19 48.50N 4.59E
Revilla del Campo Spain 26 42.13N 3.32W
Revillagigedo I. U.S.A. 100 55.50N 131.20W
Revilla Gigedo, Islas de is. Mexico 116 19.00N 111.00W
Revin France 19 49.56N 4.38E
Revue r. Mozambique 81 19.58S 34.40E
Rewa India 63 24.32N 81.18E
Rewāri India 62 28.11N 76.37E
Rexburg U.S.A. 108 43.49N 111.47W
Rexford U.S.A. 108 48.53N 115.13W
Rey Iran 65 35.35N 51.27E
Reykjavík Iceland 40 64.09N 21.58W
Reynoldsville U.S.A. 114 41.06N 78.53W
Rezé France 18 47.12N 1.34W
Rēzekne Latvia 44 56.30N 27.22E
Rhaetian Alps mts. Switz. 39 46.45N 9.55E
Rhayader U.K. 13 52.19N 3.30W
Rheda-Wiedenbrück Schloss Germany 38 51.51N 8.17E
Rheden Neth. 16 52.01N 6.02E
Rhein r. Europe 16 51.53N 6.03E
Rheinbach Germany 38 50.37N 6.57E
Rheine Germany 38 52.17N 7.26E
Rheinfelden Germany 39 47.33N 7.47E
Rheinland-Pfalz d. Germany 39 49.50N 7.30E
Rheinsberg Germany 38 53.06N 12.53E
Rhenen Neth. 16 51.58N 5.34E
Rhine see Rhein r. Europe 16
Rhinebeck U.S.A. 115 41.56N 73.55W
Rhinelander U.S.A. 110 45.39N 89.23W
Rhino Camp town Uganda 79 2.58N 31.20E
Rhir, Cap c. Morocco 74 30.38N 9.55W
Rho Italy 30 45.32N 9.02E
Rhode Island d. U.S.A. 115 41.40N 71.30W
Rhode Island Sd. U.S.A. 115 41.25N 71.15W
Rhodes i. see Ródhos i. Greece 35
Rhodope Mts. see Rhodopi Planina mts. Bulgaria 34
Rhodopi Planina mts. Bulgaria 34 41.40N 24.20E
Rhondda U.K. 13 51.39N 3.30W
Rhône d. France 21 45.54N 4.35E
Rhône r. France 21 43.20N 4.50E
Rhône-Alpes d. France 21 45.20N 5.45E

Rhône au Rhin, Canal du France 19 47.06N 5.19E
Rhosneigr U.K. 12 53.14N 4.31W
Rhue r. France 20 45.23N 2.29E
Rhyl U.K. 12 53.19N 3.29W
Riachão Brazil 123 7.22S 46.37W
Riāng India 63 27.32N 92.56E
Riánsares r. Spain 27 39.32N 3.18W
Riāsi Jammu & Kashmir 62 33.05N 74.50E
Riau d. Indonesia 58 0.00 102.35E
Riau, Kepulauan is. Indonesia 58 0.50N 104.00E
Riaza Spain 26 41.17N 3.28W
Riaza r. Spain 26 41.42N 3.55W
Ribadeo Spain 26 43.33N 7.02W
Ribadesella Spain 26 43.28N 5.04W
Ribarroja, Embalse de resr. Spain 25 41.12N 0.20E
Ribauè Mozambique 79 14.57S 38.27E
Ribble r. U.K. 12 53.45N 2.44W
Ribe Denmark 42 55.21N 8.46E
Ribeauvillé France 19 48.12N 7.19E
Ribécourt France 19 49.31N 2.55E
Ribeirão Prêto Brazil 126 21.09S 47.48W
Ribera Italy 32 37.30N 13.16E
Ribérac France 20 45.14N 0.22E
Riberalta Bolivia 124 10.59S 66.06W
Ribnica Slovenia 31 45.44N 14.44E
Ribnitz-Damgarten Germany 38 54.15N 12.28E
Ribstone Creek r. Canada 101 52.51N 110.05W
Riccia Italy 33 41.29N 14.50E
Riccione Italy 30 43.59N 12.39E
Rice U.S.A. 109 34.06N 114.50W
Rice L. Canada 104 44.08N 78.13W
Rice Lake town U.S.A. 110 45.30N 91.43W
Richard's Bay town R.S.A. 81 28.47S 32.06E
Richardson r. Canada 101 58.30N 111.30W
Richardson U.S.A. 111 32.57N 96.44W
Rich, C. Canada 104 44.43N 80.38W
Richelieu r. Canada 105 46.03N 73.07W
Richelieu France 18 47.01N 0.19E
Richfield Idaho U.S.A. 108 43.03N 114.09W
Richfield Utah U.S.A. 108 38.46N 112.05W
Richfield Springs U.S.A. 115 42.51N 74.59W
Richford U.S.A. 105 45.00N 72.40W
Rich Hill town U.S.A. 111 38.06N 94.22W
Richibucto Canada 103 46.41N 64.52W
Richland U.S.A. 108 46.17N 119.18W
Richmond Qld. Australia 90 20.45S 143.08E
Richmond Ont. Canada 105 45.11N 75.50W
Richmond Que. Canada 105 45.40N 72.09W
Richmond New Zealand 86 41.20S 173.10E
Richmond C.P. R.S.A. 80 31.24S 23.56E
Richmond U.K. 12 54.24N 1.43W
Richmond Ind. U.S.A. 112 39.50N 84.51W
Richmond Utah U.S.A. 108 41.55N 111.48W
Richmond Va. U.S.A. 113 37.34N 77.27W
Richmond Dale U.S.A. 114 39.13N 82.54W
Richmond Hill Canada 104 43.52N 79.27W
Richmond Range mts. Australia 93 29.00S 152.48E
Richwood U.S.A. 114 38.14N 80.32W
Ricobayo, Embalse de resr. Spain 26 41.30N 5.55W
Ridderkerk Neth. 16 51.53N 4.39E
Rideau r. Canada 105 45.27N 75.42W
Rideau Hills Canada 105 44.37N 77.00W
Rideau Lakes Canada 105 44.45N 76.17W
Ridgetown Canada 104 42.26N 81.54W
Ridgway U.S.A. 114 41.26N 78.44W
Riding Mtn. Canada 101 50.37N 99.50W
Riding Mtn. Nat. Park Canada 101 50.55N 100.25W
Ried Austria 39 48.13N 13.30E
Riemst Belgium 16 50.49N 5.38E
Riesa Germany 38 51.18N 13.17E
Riesi Italy 33 37.17N 14.05E
Rieti Italy 30 42.24N 12.51E
Rifle U.S.A. 108 39.32N 107.47W
Rift Valley d. Kenya 79 1.00N 36.00E
Riga Latvia 41 56.53N 24.08E
Riga, G. of Latvia/Estonia 41 57.30N 23.35E
Rīgān Iran 65 28.40N 58.58E
Rīgas Jūras Līcis see Riga, G. of g. Latvia 41
Rīgestān f. Afghan. 62 30.35N 65.00E
Riggins U.S.A. 108 45.25N 116.19W
Rig Matī Iran 65 27.40N 58.11E
Rigo P.N.G. 90 9.50S 147.35E
Rigolet Canada 103 54.20N 58.35W
Riia Laht g. see Riga, G. of Estonia 41
Riihimäki Finland 41 60.45N 24.46E
Riiser-Larsenhalvøya pen. Antarctica 128 68.00S 35.00E
Riječki Zaljev b. Croatia 31 45.15N 14.25E
Rijeka Croatia 31 45.20N 14.27E
Rijssen Neth. 16 52.19N 6.31E
Rijswijk Neth. 16 52.03N 4.22E
Rila Planina mts. Bulgaria 34 42.10N 23.30E
Riley U.S.A. 108 43.31N 119.28W
Rimah, Wādī ar r. Saudi Arabia 64 26.10N 44.00E
Rimavská Sobota Slovakia 37 48.23N 20.02E
Rimbo Sweden 43 59.45N 18.22E
Rimersburg U.S.A. 114 41.02N 79.30W
Rimforsa Sweden 43 58.08N 15.40E
Rimini Italy 30 44.04N 12.34E
Rîmnicu-Sărat Romania 37 45.24N 27.06E
Rîmnicu-Vîlcea Romania 37 45.06N 24.22E
Rimouski Canada 103 48.27N 68.32W
Rinbung China 63 29.16N 89.54E
Rinconada Argentina 124 22.26S 66.10W
Rindal Norway 40 63.04N 9.13E
Ringe Denmark 42 55.14N 10.29E
Ringebu Norway 41 61.31N 10.10E
Ringerike Norway 42 60.10N 10.18E
Ringim Nigeria 77 12.09N 9.08E
Ringkøbing Denmark 42 56.05N 8.15E
Ringkøbing Fjord est. Denmark 42 56.00N 8.15E
Ringling U.S.A. 108 46.16N 110.49W
Ringsted Denmark 42 55.27N 11.49E
Ringus India 62 27.21N 75.34E
Ringvassöy i. Norway 40 69.55N 19.10E
Ringwood U.S.A. 13 50.50N 1.48W
Rintein Germany 38 52.11N 9.04E
Riobamba Ecuador 122 1.44S 78.40W

Rio Branco Brazil 122 9.59S 67.49W
Rio Bueno Chile 125 40.20S 72.55W
Rio Casca Brazil 126 20.13S 42.38W
Rio Claro Brazil 126 22.19S 47.35W
Río Cuarto Argentina 125 33.08S 64.20W
Rio de Janeiro Brazil 126 22.53S 43.17W
Rio de Janeiro d. Brazil 126 22.00S 42.30W
Río Gallegos Argentina 125 51.37S 69.10W
Rio Grande town Argentina 125 53.50S 67.40W
Rio Grande town Brazil 126 32.03S 52.08W
Río Grande r. Mexico/U.S.A. 111 25.57N 97.09W
Río Grande r. Nicaragua 117 12.48N 83.30W
Rio Grande City U.S.A. 111 26.23N 98.49W
Rio Grande do Norte d. Brazil 123 6.00S 36.30W
Rio Grande do Sul d. Brazil 126 30.15S 53.30W
Ríohacha Colombia 122 11.34N 72.58W
Riom France 20 45.54N 3.07E
Río Negro d. Argentina 125 40.00S 67.00W
Rio Negro Brazil 126 26.06S 49.48W
Río Negro, Embalse del resr. Uruguay 125 32.45S 56.00W
Rionero in Vulture Italy 33 40.56N 15.41E
Rio Novo Brazil 126 21.15S 43.09W
Ríópar Spain 26 38.30N 2.27W
Rio Piracicaba Brazil 126 19.54S 43.10W
Rio Pomba Brazil 126 21.15S 43.12W
Rio Prêto Brazil 126 22.06S 43.52W
Ríosucio Colombia 122 7.27N 77.07W
Rio Tercero Argentina 124 32.10S 64.05W
Rio Verde town Brazil 124 17.50S 50.55W
Rioz France 19 47.25N 6.04E
Ripatransone Italy 31 43.00N 13.46E
Ripley Canada 104 44.04N 81.34W
Ripley N.Y. U.S.A. 114 42.16N 79.43W
Ripley W.Va. U.S.A. 114 38.49N 81.43W
Ripoll Spain 25 42.12N 2.12E
Ripon Canada 105 45.47N 75.06W
Ripon U.K. 12 54.08N 1.31W
Riposto Italy 33 37.45N 15.12E
Rirapora Brazil 126 17.20S 45.02W
Risbäck Sweden 40 64.42N 15.32E
Riscle France 20 43.40N 0.05W
Rishã, Wâdï ar r. Saudi Arabia 65 25.40N 44.08E
Rishïkesh India 63 30.07N 78.42E
Rishiri tö i. Japan 57 45.11N 141.15E
Rishon LeZiyyon Israel 67 31.57N 34.48E
Rishpon Israel 67 32.12N 34.49E
Risle r. France 18 49.26N 0.23E
Risnjak mtn. Croatia 31 45.26N 14.37E
Rison U.S.A. 111 33.58N 92.11W
Risör Norway 42 58.43N 9.14E
Rissani Morocco 74 31.23N 4.09W
Riti Nigeria 77 7.57N 9.41E
Ritidian Pt. Guam 84 13.39N 144.51E
Rittman U.S.A. 114 40.58N 81.47W
Ritzville U.S.A. 108 47.08N 118.23W
Riva Italy 30 45.53N 10.50E
Rivadavia Argentina 124 24.11S 62.53W
Rivarolo Canavese Italy 30 45.19N 7.43E
Rivas Nicaragua 117 11.26N 85.50W
Rive-de-Gier France 21 45.32N 4.37E
Rivera Uruguay 125 30.54S 55.31W
River Cess town Liberia 76 5.28N 9.32W
Rivergaro Italy 30 44.55N 9.36E
Riverhead U.S.A. 115 40.55N 72.40W
Riverina f. Australia 93 34.30S 145.20E
Rivers Canada 101 50.02N 100.12W
Rivers d. Nigeria 77 4.45N 6.35E
Riversdale R.S.A. 80 34.05S 21.15E
Riverside U.S.A. 109 33.59N 117.22W
Rivers Inlet town Canada 100 51.40N 127.20W
Riverton Australia 92 34.21S 138.24E
Riverton Canada 101 50.59N 96.59W
Riverton New Zealand 86 46.21S 168.01E
Riverton U.S.A. 108 43.02N 108.23W
River Valley town Canada 104 46.35N 80.10W
Rivesaltes France 20 42.46N 2.52E
Rivesville U.S.A. 114 39.32N 80.07W
Riviera di Levante f. Italy 30 44.00N 9.40E
Riviera di Ponente f. Italy 30 43.40N 8.00E
Rivière à Pierre town Canada 105 46.59N 72.11W
Rivière aux Rats town Canada 105 47.13N 72.54W
Rivière-du-Loup town Canada 103 47.50N 69.32W
Rivière Pentecôte town Canada 103 49.47N 67.10W
Rivoli Italy 30 45.04N 7.31E
Riyadh see Ar Riyâd Saudi Arabia 65
Rize Turkey 64 41.03N 40.31E
Rizhao China 54 35.26N 119.27E
Rizokárpason Cyprus 66 35.35N 34.24E
Rizzuto, Capo c. Italy 33 38.54N 17.06E
Rjukan Norway 42 59.52N 8.34E
Roa Norway 42 60.17N 10.37E
Roa Spain 26 41.42N 3.55W
Roag, Loch U.K. 14 58.14N 6.50W
Roanne France 21 46.02N 4.04E
Roanoke Ala. U.S.A. 113 33.09N 85.24W
Roanoke r. U.S.A. 113 35.56N 76.43W
Roanoke Va. U.S.A. 113 37.15N 79.58W
Roanoke Rapids town U.S.A. 113 36.28N 77.40W
Roaring Branch U.S.A. 114 41.34N 76.57W
Roaring Spring U.S.A. 114 40.20N 78.24W
Roaring Springs U.S.A. 111 33.54N 100.52W
Robât Iran 65 30.04N 54.49E
Robe Australia 92 37.11S 139.45E
Röbel Germany 38 53.23N 12.35E
Robe, Mt. Australia 92 31.39S 141.16E
Robertsdale U.S.A. 114 40.11N 78.07W
Robertsganj India 63 24.42N 83.04E
Robertson R.S.A. 80 33.48S 19.52E
Robertsport Liberia 76 6.45N 11.22W
Robertstown Australia 92 33.59S 139.03E
Roberval Canada 103 48.31N 72.13W
Robin Hood's Bay U.K. 12 54.26N 0.31W
Robinson r. Australia 90 16.03S 137.16E
Robinson Range mts. Australia 88 25.45S 119.00E
Robinvale Australia 92 34.37S 142.50E
Robleda Spain 26 40.23N 6.36W

Robledo Spain 26 38.46N 2.26W
Roblin Man. Canada 101 51.17N 101.28W
Roblin Ont. Canada 105 44.21N 77.01W
Roboré Bolivia 124 18.20S 59.45W
Robson, Mt. Canada 100 53.10N 119.10W
Rocas i. Atlantic Oc. 127 3.50S 33.50W
Roccadaspide Italy 33 40.26N 15.12E
Roccastrada Italy 30 43.00N 11.10E
Roccella Italy 29 38.19N 16.24E
Rocciamelone mtn. Italy 30 45.12N 7.05E
Rocella Italy 33 38.20N 16.24E
Rocha Uruguay 126 34.30S 54.22W
Rocha da Gale, Barragem resr. Portugal 27 38.20N 7.25W
Rochdale U.K. 12 53.36N 2.10W
Rochechouart France 20 45.50N 0.50E
Rochefort Belgium 16 50.10N 5.13E
Rochefort France 20 45.57N 0.58W
Rochefort-Montagne France 20 45.41N 2.48E
Rochelle U.S.A. 110 41.55N 89.05W
Rocher River town Canada 100 61.23N 112.44W
Rochester Australia 93 36.22S 144.42E
Rochester Kent U.K. 13 51.22N 0.30E
Rochester Minn. U.S.A. 110 44.01N 92.27W
Rochester N.H. U.S.A. 115 43.18N 70.59W
Rochester N.Y. U.S.A. 114 43.10N 77.36W
Rochester Penn. U.S.A. 114 40.43N 80.17W
Rochfort Bridge Rep. of Ire. 15 53.25N 7.19W
Rochlitz Germany 38 51.03N 12.47E
Rock r. Canada 100 60.07N 127.07W
Rock L. U.S.A. 112 46.03N 87.10W
Rockall i. U.K. 10 57.39N 13.44W
Rock Creek town U.S.A. 114 41.40N 80.52W
Rockdale U.S.A. 114 39.21N 76.46W
Rockefeller Plateau Antarctica 128 80.00S 140.00W
Rockford U.S.A. 110 42.17N 89.06W
Rock Hall U.S.A. 115 39.08N 76.14W
Rockhampton Australia 90 23.22S 150.32E
Rock Hill town U.S.A. 113 34.55N 81.01W
Rockingham Australia 89 32.16S 115.21E
Rockingham U.S.A. 113 34.56N 79.47W
Rock Island town Canada 105 45.01N 72.06W
Rock Island U.S.A. 110 41.30N 90.34W
Rockland Canada 105 45.32N 75.19W
Rockland Idaho U.S.A. 108 42.34N 112.53W
Rockland Maine U.S.A. 112 44.06N 69.06W
Rockland Mich. U.S.A. 112 46.44N 89.12W
Rocklands Resr. Australia 92 37.13S 141.52E
Rockport Canada 105 44.22N 75.58W
Rockport U.S.A. 108 39.45N 123.47W
Rock Rapids town U.S.A. 110 43.26N 96.10W
Rock Sound town Bahamas 117 24.54N 76.11W
Rocksprings Tex. U.S.A. 111 30.01N 100.13W
Rock Springs Wyo. U.S.A. 108 41.35N 109.13W
Rockville U.S.A. 114 39.05N 77.09W
Rockwood Mich. U.S.A. 114 42.04N 83.15W
Rockwood Penn. U.S.A. 114 39.54N 79.09W
Rockwood Tenn. U.S.A. 113 35.52N 84.40W
Rocky Ford U.S.A. 106 38.03N 103.44W
Rocky Gully town Australia 89 34.31S 117.01E
Rocky Island L. Canada 104 46.56N 83.04W
Rocky Mount town U.S.A. 113 35.56N 77.48W
Rocky Mountain Foothills f. Canada 100 57.17N 123.21W
Rocky Mountain Nat. Park U.S.A. 108 40.19N 105.42W
Rocky Mountain Trench f. Canada 100 56.45N 124.47W
Rocky Mts. N. America 108 43.21N 109.50W
Rocky Pt. Namibia 80 19.00S 12.29E
Rocky River town U.S.A. 114 41.30N 81.40W
Rocroi France 19 49.55N 4.31E
Rod Pakistan 62 28.06N 63.12E
Rodalben Germany 39 49.14N 7.38E
Rodalquilar Spain 27 37.40N 2.08W
Rödberg Norway 42 60.16N 8.58E
Rödby Denmark 41 54.42N 11.24E
Roddickton Canada 103 50.52N 56.08W
Rödekro Denmark 42 55.04N 9.21E
Rodel U.K. 14 57.44N 6.58W
Rodeo Mexico 111 25.11N 104.34W
Rodewisch Germany 39 50.32N 12.24E
Rodez France 20 44.21N 2.35E
Ródhos i. Greece 35 36.10N 28.00E
Ródhos town Greece 35 36.26N 28.13E
Rodi Garganico Italy 31 41.55N 15.53E
Roding Germany 39 49.12N 12.32E
Rodney Canada 104 42.34N 81.41W
Rodney, Cape U.S.A. 98 64.44N 4.00W
Rodniki Russian Fed. 44 57.05N 41.44E
Rodó Portugal ... (not listed)
Rodrigues i. Indian Oc. 49 19.42S 63.25E
Roebourne Australia 88 20.45S 117.08E
Roebuck B. Australia 88 18.04S 122.17E
Roe, L. Australia 89 30.40S 122.10E
Roermond Neth. 16 51.12N 6.00E
Roeselare Belgium 16 50.57N 3.06E
Rogachev Belarus 37 53.05N 30.02E
Rogaland d. Norway 42 59.10N 6.25E
Rogaška Slatina Slovenia 31 46.14N 15.38E
Rogatica Bosnia-Herzegovina 31 43.48N 19.00E
Rogers City U.S.A. 104 45.25N 83.49W
Rogers, Mt. U.S.A. 113 36.35N 81.32W
Rogerson U.S.A. 108 42.14N 114.47W
Roggan r. Canada 102 54.24N 78.05W
Roggan L. Canada 102 54.10N 77.58W
Roggan River town Canada 102 54.24N 78.05W
Roggeveen, Cabo c. I. de Pascua 85 27.06S 109.16W
Roggiano Gravina Italy 33 39.37N 16.09E
Rogliano France 21 42.57N 9.25E
Rogliano Italy 33 39.11N 16.20E
Rogue r. U.S.A. 108 42.25N 124.25W
Rohri Pakistan 62 27.41N 68.54E
Rohtak India 62 28.54N 76.34E
Rojas Argentina 125 34.15S 60.44W
Rokan r. Indonesia 58 2.00N 101.00E
Rokel r. Sierra Leone 76 8.36N 12.55W
Rokycany Czech Republic 38 49.45N 13.36E
Rola Co l. China 61 35.26N 88.24E

Röldal Norway 42 59.49N 6.48E
Roldskov f. Denmark 42 56.46N 9.50E
Rolette U.S.A. 110 48.40N 99.51W
Rolla Mo. U.S.A. 111 37.57N 91.46W
Rolla N.Dak. U.S.A. 110 48.52N 99.37W
Rolle Switz. 39 46.28N 6.20E
Rolleston Australia 90 24.25S 148.35E
Rolleville Bahamas 117 23.41N 76.00W
Rolvsöya i. Norway 40 70.58N 24.00E
Roma Australia 90 26.35S 148.47E
Roma Italy 32 41.54N 12.29E
Roma Sweden 43 57.32N 18.28E
Romain, C. U.S.A. 113 33.00N 79.22W
Romaine r. Canada 103 50.18N 63.47W
Roman Romania 37 46.55N 26.56E
Romanche r. France 21 45.05N 5.43E
Romang i. Indonesia 59 7.45S 127.20E
Romania Europe 37 46.30N 24.00E
Romano, C. U.S.A. 113 25.50N 81.41W
Romans France 21 45.03N 5.03E
Romanshorn Switz. 39 47.34N 9.22E
Rome see Roma Italy 32
Rome Ga. U.S.A. 113 34.01N 85.02W
Rome N.Y. U.S.A. 115 43.13N 75.27W
Romeleåsen f. Sweden 43 55.34N 13.33E
Romeo U.S.A. 114 42.48N 83.01W
Romilly France 19 48.31N 3.43E
Romney Marsh f. U.K. 13 51.03N 0.55E
Römö i. Denmark 42 55.08N 8.31E
Romont Switz. 39 46.42N 6.55E
Romorantin France 19 47.22N 1.45E
Rona i. U.K. 14 57.33N 5.58W
Ronan U.S.A. 108 47.32N 114.06W
Ronas Hill U.K. 10 60.32N 1.26W
Roncesvalles Spain 25 43.01N 1.19W
Ronchamp France 21 47.42N 6.39E
Ronda Spain 27 36.44N 5.10W
Ronda, Serranía de mts. Spain 27 36.44N 5.05W
Rondane mtn. Norway 41 61.55N 9.45E
Rondônia d. Brazil 122 12.10S 62.30W
Rondonópolis Brazil 123 16.29S 54.37W
Rondout Resr. U.S.A. 115 41.54N 74.29W
Ronehamn Sweden 43 57.10N 18.29E
Rongcheng China 54 37.09N 122.23E
Ronge, Lac la l. Canada 101 55.07N 104.45W
Rongjiang China 55 25.56N 108.31E
Rongxar China 61 28.34N 87.44E
Rong Xian China 55 29.28N 104.32E
Roniu mtn. Tahiti 84 17.49S 149.12W
Rönne Denmark 43 55.06N 14.42E
Ronneby Sweden 43 56.12N 15.18E
Ronse Belgium 16 50.45N 3.36E
Ronuro r. Brazil 123 11.56S 53.33W
Roof Butte mtn. U.S.A. 109 36.28N 109.05W
Roorkee India 63 29.52N 77.53E
Roosendaal Neth. 16 51.32N 4.28E
Roosevelt r. Brazil 122 7.35S 60.20W
Roosevelt U.S.A. 108 40.18N 109.59W
Roosevelt I. Antarctica 128 79.00S 161.00W
Root r. Canada 100 61.55N 125.10W
Ropcha Russian Fed. 44 62.50N 51.55E
Roper r. Australia 90 14.40S 135.30E
Roquefort France 20 44.02N 0.19W
Roquemaure France 21 44.03N 4.47E
Roque Pérez Argentina 125 35.23S 59.22W
Roraima d. Brazil 122 2.00N 62.00W
Roraima, Mt. Guyana 122 5.14N 60.44W
Rörholtfjorden l. Norway 42 59.01N 9.15E
Rorketon Canada 101 51.26N 99.32W
Röros Norway 40 62.35N 11.23E
Rorschach Switz. 39 47.29N 9.30E
Rosa, Cap c. Algeria 32 36.58N 8.15E
Rosamond U.S.A. 109 34.52N 118.10W
Rosa, Monte mtn. Italy/Switz. 39 45.57N 7.53E
Rosans France 21 44.23N 5.28E
Rosario Argentina 125 32.57S 60.40W
Rosário Brazil 123 3.00S 44.15W
Rosario Mexico 109 23.00N 105.52W
Rosario Uruguay 125 34.19S 57.21W
Rosario de la Frontera Argentina 124 25.50S 64.55W
Rosario del Tala Argentina 125 32.20S 59.10W
Rosário do Sul Brazil 126 30.15S 54.55W
Rosarito Mexico 109 28.38N 114.04W
Rosarito, Embalse de resr. Spain 27 40.05N 5.15W
Rosarno Italy 33 38.29N 15.59E
Roscoe N.Y. U.S.A. 115 41.56N 74.55W
Roscoe S.Dak. U.S.A. 110 45.27N 99.20W
Roscoff France 18 48.44N 4.00W
Roscommon Rep. of Ire. 15 53.38N 8.13W
Roscommon d. Rep. of Ire. 15 53.38N 8.11W
Roscommon U.S.A. 104 44.30N 84.35W
Roscrea Rep. of Ire. 15 52.57N 7.49W
Roseau r. Canada 101 49.10N 97.20W
Roseau Dominica 117 15.18N 61.23W
Roseau U.S.A. 110 48.51N 95.46W
Rose Blanche Canada 103 47.37N 58.43W
Rosebud Australia 93 38.21S 144.54E
Rosebud r. Canada 100 51.25N 112.37W
Roseburg U.S.A. 108 43.13N 123.20W
Rose City U.S.A. 104 44.25N 84.07W
Rose Harbour Canada 100 52.15S 131.10W
Rosenberg U.S.A. 111 29.33N 95.48W
Rosendal Norway 42 59.59N 6.01E
Rosenheim Germany 39 47.51N 12.07E
Roses Spain 25 42.19N 3.10E
Roses, Golf de g. Spain 25 42.10N 3.15E
Roseto degli Abruzzi Italy 31 42.41N 14.00E
Rosetown Canada 101 51.33N 108.00W
Rosetta R.S.A. 80 29.18S 29.58E
Roseville Calif. U.S.A. 108 38.45N 121.17W
Roseville Mich. U.S.A. 114 42.30N 82.56W
Roshage c. Denmark 42 57.08N 8.37E
Rosh Ha'Ayin Israel 67 32.06N 34.57E
Rosh Pinna Israel 67 32.58N 35.32E
Rosières France 19 49.49N 2.43E
Rosignano Marittimo Italy 30 43.24N 10.28E
Roşiori-de-Vede Romania 37 44.07N 25.00E

Rositsa Bulgaria 37 43.57N 27.57E
Roska r. Ukraine 37 49.27N 29.45E
Roskilde Denmark 43 55.39N 12.05E
Roslagen f. Sweden 43 59.40N 18.30E
Roslags-Näsby Sweden 43 59.26N 18.04E
Roslavl Russian Fed. 44 53.55N 32.53E
Roslev Denmark 42 56.42N 8.59E
Ross New Zealand 86 42.54S 170.49E
Rossano Italy 33 39.35N 16.39E
Ross Dependency Antarctica 128 75.00S 170.00W
Rosseau, L. Canada 104 45.10N 79.35W
Rossignol, L. Canada 103 44.10N 65.10W
Rossing Namibia 80 22.31S 14.52E
Rossiter U.S.A. 114 40.53N 78.56W
Rosslare Rep. of Ire. 15 52.17N 6.23W
Rosslau Germany 38 51.53N 12.14E
Rossmore Canada 105 44.06N 77.23W
Rosso Mauritania 74 16.30N 15.49W
Rosso, Cap c. France 21 42.14N 8.33E
Ross-on-Wye U.K. 13 51.55N 2.36W
Rossosh Russian Fed. 45 50.12N 39.35E
Ross River town Canada 100 62.30N 131.30W
Rössvatnet l. Norway 40 65.45N 14.00E
Rosta Norway 40 69.58N 19.40E
Rosthern Canada 101 52.40N 106.17W
Rostock Germany 38 54.05N 12.07E
Rostov Russian Fed. 45 47.15N 39.45E
Rostov Russian Fed. 44 57.11N 39.23E
Roswell U.S.A. 113 34.02N 84.21W
Roswell N.Mex. U.S.A. 109 33.24N 104.32W
Rota Spain 27 36.37N 6.21W
Rotem Belgium 16 51.04N 5.44E
Rotenburg Hessen Germany 38 51.00N 9.45E
Rotenburg Nschn. Germany 38 53.06N 9.24E
Roth Germany 38 49.14N 11.04E
Rothaargebirge mts. Germany 38 51.05N 8.15E
Rothbury U.K. 12 55.19N 1.54W
Rothenburg ob der Tober Germany 39 49.23N 10.10E
Rother r. U.K. 13 50.56N 0.46E
Rotherham U.K. 12 53.26N 1.21W
Rothes U.K. 14 57.31N 3.13W
Rothesay Canada 103 45.23N 66.00W
Rothesay U.K. 14 55.50N 5.03W
Roti i. Indonesia 88 10.30S 123.10E
Roto Australia 93 33.04S 145.27E
Rotondella Italy 33 40.10N 16.32E
Rotondo, Monte mtn. France 21 42.13N 9.03E
Rotorua New Zealand 86 38.07S 176.17E
Rotorua, L. New Zealand 86 38.00S 176.00E
Rottenburg Germany 39 48.28N 8.56E
Rottenburg an der Laaber Germany 39 48.42N 12.02E
Rotterdam Neth. 16 51.55N 4.29E
Rottnest I. Australia 89 32.01S 115.28E
Rottweil Germany 39 48.10N 8.37E
Roubaix France 16 50.42N 3.10E
Roudnice Czech Republic 38 50.22N 14.16E
Rouen France 18 49.26N 1.05E
Rouge r. Canada 105 45.39N 74.41W
Rougé France 18 47.47N 1.27W
Rougemont France 21 47.29N 6.21E
Rouillac France 20 45.47N 0.04W
Rouku P.N.G. 90 8.40S 141.35E
Round I. U.S.A. 104 45.51N 84.37W
Round L. Canada 105 45.38N 77.32W
Round Mt. Australia 93 30.26S 152.15E
Round Pond l. Canada 103 48.10N 56.00W
Roundup U.S.A. 108 46.27N 108.33W
Rousay i. U.K. 14 59.10N 3.02W
Roussillon f. France 20 42.30N 2.30E
Rouyn Canada 102 48.20N 79.00W
Rovaniemi Finland 40 66.30N 25.40E
Rovato Italy 30 45.34N 10.00E
Rovereto Italy 30 45.53N 11.02E
Roverud Norway 43 60.15N 12.03E
Rovigo Italy 32 45.04N 11.47E
Rovinj Croatia 31 45.05N 13.38E
Rovno Ukraine 37 50.39N 26.10E
Rowanton Canada 105 46.24N 77.46W
Rowena Australia 93 29.49S 148.54E
Rowlesburg U.S.A. 114 39.21N 79.40W
Rowley Shoals f. Australia 88 17.30S 119.00E
Roxboro U.S.A. 113 36.24N 79.00W
Roxburgh New Zealand 86 45.33S 169.19E
Roxby Downs town Australia 92 30.42S 136.46E
Roxen l. Sweden 43 58.30N 15.41E
Roxo, Barragem do resr. Portugal 27 38.00N 8.10W
Roxton Canada 105 45.29N 72.36W
Roy U.S.A. 109 35.57N 104.12W
Royale, Isle i. U.S.A. 104 48.00N 89.00W
Royal L. Canada 101 56.00N 103.15W
Royal Leamington Spa U.K. 13 52.18N 1.32W
Royal Oak U.S.A. 104 42.30N 83.08W
Royal Tunbridge Wells U.K. 13 51.07N 0.16E
Royan France 20 45.37N 1.01W
Roye France 19 49.42N 2.48E
Royston U.K. 13 52.03N 0.01W
Rožaj Yugo. 34 42.50N 20.10E
Rozhishche Ukraine 37 50.58N 25.15E
Rožňava Slovakia 37 48.40N 20.32E
Roztoky Czech Republic 38 50.09N 14.22E
Rrëshen Albania 34 41.47N 19.54E
Rrogozhinë Albania 34 41.04N 19.19E
Rtishchevo Russian Fed. 44 52.16N 43.45E
Ruahine Range mts. New Zealand 86 40.00S 176.00E
Ruapehu mtn. New Zealand 86 39.20S 175.30E
Ruapuke I. New Zealand 86 46.45S 168.30E
Rub 'al Khali des. see Ar Rub 'al Khālī des. Saudi Arabia 60
Rubbestadneset Norway 42 59.49N 5.17E
Rubi r. Zaïre 78 2.50N 24.06E
Rubino Côte d'Ivoire 76 6.04N 4.18W
Rubio Colombia 122 7.42N 72.23W
Rubryn Belarus 37 51.52N 27.30E
Rubtsovsk Russian Fed. 50 51.29N 81.10E
Ruby Mts. U.S.A. 108 40.25N 115.35W

Rūdān r. Iran 65 27.02N 56.53E
Rudauli India 63 26.45N 81.45E
Rūdbār Afghan. 62 30.09N 62.36E
Rüdersdorf Germany 38 52.29N 13.47E
Rudewa Tanzania 79 6.40S 37.08E
Rudki Ukraine 37 49.40N 23.28E
Rudköbing Denmark 42 54.56N 10.43E
Rudnaya Pristan Russian Fed. 53 44.18N 135.51E
Rudnichnyy Russian Fed. 44 59.10N 52.28E
Rudnik Poland 37 50.28N 22.15E
Rudnyy Kazakhstan 52 53.00N 63.05E
Rudo Bosnia-Herzegovina 31 43.37N 19.22E
Rudolstadt Germany 38 50.43N 11.20E
Rudozem Bulgaria 34 41.29N 24.51E
Rudrón r. Spain 26 42.44N 3.25W
Rudyard U.S.A. 104 46.14N 84.36W
Rue France 19 50.16N 1.40E
Ruel Canada 104 47.16N 81.29W
Ruen mtn. Bulgaria/Macedonia 34 42.10N 22.31E
Rufā'ah Sudan 72 14.46N 33.22E
Ruffec France 20 46.02N 0.42E
Ruffieux France 21 45.51N 5.50E
Rufiji r. Tanzania 79 8.02S 39.19E
Rufino Argentina 125 34.16S 62.45W
Rufisque Senegal 76 14.43N 17.16W
Rufunsa Zambia 79 15.02S 29.35E
Rugao China 54 32.25N 120.40E
Rugby U.K. 13 52.23N 1.16W
Rugby U.S.A. 110 48.22N 100.00W
Rügen i. Germany 38 54.25N 13.24E
Ruhpolding Germany 39 47.45N 12.38E
Ruhr f. Germany 38 51.21N 7.26E
Ruhr r. Germany 38 51.27N 6.44E
Rui'an China 55 26.50N 120.40E
Ruijin China 55 25.49N 116.00E
Ruinen Neth. 16 52.47N 6.21E
Rukwa d. Tanzania 79 7.05S 31.25E
Rukwa, L. Tanzania 79 8.00S 32.20E
Rum i. U.K. 14 57.00N 6.20W
Ruma Yugo. 31 45.00N 19.49E
Rumaysh Lebanon 67 33.05N 35.22E
Rumbek Sudan 73 6.48N 29.41E
Rum Cay i. Bahamas 117 23.41N 74.53W
Rumford U.S.A. 112 44.33N 70.33W
Rummāna Israel 67 32.47N 35.18E
Rummānah Egypt 66 31.01N 32.40E
Rumney U.S.A. 105 43.58N 71.49W
Rumoi Japan 57 43.56N 141.39E
Runcorn U.K. 12 53.20N 2.44W
Runde r. Zimbabwe 81 21.20S 32.23E
Rundvik Sweden 40 63.30N 19.24E
Rungāni Pakistan 62 26.38N 65.43E
Rungwa r. Tanzania 79 7.38S 31.55E
Rungwa Singida Tanzania 79 6.57S 33.35E
Rungwe Mt. Tanzania 79 9.10S 33.40E
Runka Nigeria 77 12.28N 7.20E
Ruoqiang China 52 39.00N 88.00E
Ruo Shui r. China 52 42.15N 101.03E
Rūpar India 62 30.58N 76.32E
Rupert r. Canada 102 51.30N 78.45W
Rupununi r. Guyana 122 4.00N 58.30W
Ruqqad r. Syria 67 32.44N 35.46E
Rur r. Neth. 16 51.12N 5.58E
Rurutu i. Pacific Oc. 85 22.25S 151.20W
Rusape Zimbabwe 81 18.30S 32.08E
Ruşayriş, Khazzān ar resr. Sudan 73 11.40N 34.20E
Ruse Bulgaria 34 43.48N 25.59E
Rusera India 63 25.45N 86.02E
Rushan China 54 36.54N 121.30E
Rushden U.K. 13 52.17N 0.37W
Rush Springs U.S.A. 111 34.47N 97.58W
Rusken i. Sweden 43 57.17N 14.20E
Russell Canada 105 45.17N 75.17W
Russell U.S.A. 105 44.26N 75.11W
Russellkonda India 63 19.56N 84.35E
Russell L. Man. Canada 101 56.15N 101.30W
Russell L. N.W.T. Canada 100 63.05N 115.44W
Russell Pt. Canada 98 73.30N 115.00W
Russell Range mts. Australia 89 33.15S 123.30E
Russellville U.S.A. 111 35.17N 93.08W
Rüsselsheim Germany 39 50.00N 8.25E
Russian Federation Europe/Asia 50 62.00N 80.00E
Russkaya Polyana Russian Fed. 50 53.48N 73.54E
Rustavi Georgia 45 41.34N 45.03E
Rustenburg R.S.A. 80 25.39S 27.13E
Ruston U.S.A. 111 32.32N 92.38W
Rutana Burundi 79 3.58S 30.00E
Rutanzige, L. see Edward, L. Uganda/Zaïre 79
Rütenbrock Germany 38 52.50N 7.10E
Ruteng Indonesia 59 8.35S 120.28E
Rutenga Zimbabwe 80 21.15S 30.46E
Ruth U.S.A. 108 39.17N 114.59W
Rutherglen Canada 104 46.16N 79.04W
Ruthin U.K. 12 53.07N 3.18W
Rutland U.S.A. 111 34.47N 76.59W
Rutledge r. Canada 101 61.04N 112.00W
Rutledge L. Canada 101 61.33N 110.47W
Rutog China 63 33.27N 79.43E
Rutshuru Zaïre 79 1.10S 29.26E
Rutter Canada 104 46.06N 80.40W
Ruvu Coast Tanzania 79 6.50S 38.42E
Ruvuma r. Mozambique/Tanzania 79 10.30S 40.30E
Ruvuma d. Tanzania 79 10.45S 36.15E
Ruwaybah wells Sudan 72 15.39N 28.45E
Ruwayfi, Jabal ar mtn. Jordan 67 31.12N 36.00E
Ruwenzori Range mts. Uganda/Zaïre 79 0.30N 30.00E
Ruyigi Burundi 79 3.26S 30.14E
Ruzayevka Russian Fed. 44 54.04N 44.55E
Ruzitgort Russian Fed. 44 62.51N 64.52E
Ružomberok Slovakia 37 49.06N 19.18E
Rwanda Africa 79 2.00S 30.00E
Ryan, Loch U.K. 14 54.56N 5.02W
Ryasna Belarus 37 54.00N 31.14E
Ryazan Russian Fed. 44 54.37N 39.43E
Ryazhsk Russian Fed. 44 53.40N 40.07E
Rybachiy, Poluostrov pen. Russian Fed. 44 69.45N
   32.30E

Rybachye Kazakhstan 52 46.27N 81.30E
Rybinsk Russian Fed. 44 58.01N 38.52E
Rybinskoye Vodokhranilishche resr. Russian Fed. 44
   58.30N 38.25E
Rybnik Poland 37 50.06N 18.32E
Rybnitsa Moldova 37 47.42N 29.00E
Ryd Sweden 43 56.28N 14.41E
Rydaholm Sweden 43 56.59N 14.16E
Rye U.K. 13 50.57N 0.46E
Rye r. U.K. 12 54.10N 0.44W
Ryfylke f. Norway 42 59.30N 5.30E
Rygnestad r. Norway 42 59.16N 7.29E
Ryki Poland 37 51.39N 21.56E
Rylstone Australia 93 32.48S 149.58E
Ryōtsu Japan 57 38.05N 138.26E
Ryūgasaki Japan 57 35.54N 140.11E
Ryukyu Is. see Nansei shotō is. Japan 53
Rzeszów Poland 37 50.04N 22.00E
Rzhev Russian Fed. 44 56.15N 34.18E

S

Saa Cameroon 77 4.24N 11.25E
Sa'ad Israel 67 31.28N 34.32E
Saale r. Germany 38 51.57N 11.55E
Saales France 19 48.21N 7.07E
Saalfeld Germany 38 50.39N 11.22E
Saanich Canada 100 48.28N 123.22W
Saar r. Germany 39 49.42N 6.34E
Saarbrücken Germany 39 49.14N 6.59E
Saarburg Germany 39 49.36N 6.33E
Saaremaa i. Estonia 41 58.25N 22.30E
Saarijärvi Finland 40 62.43N 25.16E
Saariselkä mts. Finland 40 68.15N 28.30E
Saarland d. Germany 39 49.25N 6.45E
Saarlouis Germany 39 49.21N 6.45E
Saba i. Leeward Is. 117 17.42N 63.26W
Šabac Yugo. 31 44.45N 19.42E
Sabadell Spain 25 41.33N 2.06E
Sabah d. Malaysia 58 5.30N 117.00E
Sabalān, Kūhhā-ye mts. Iran 65 38.15N 47.50E
Sabana, Archipiélago de Cuba 117 23.30N 80.00W
Sabanalarga Colombia 122 10.38N 75.00W
Sabasţīyah Jordan 67 32.17N 35.12E
Sab'atayn, Ramlat as f. Yemen 71 15.30N 46.10E
Sabatini, Monti mts. Italy 30 42.10N 12.15E
Sabaudia Italy 32 41.18N 13.01E
Sabbioneta Italy 32 45.00N 10.39E
Sabhā Libya 75 27.02N 14.26E
Sabhā d. Libya 75 27.02N 15.30E
Sabiñánigo Spain 25 42.31N 0.22W
Sabinas Mexico 111 27.51N 101.07W
Sabinas Hidalgo Mexico 111 26.30N 100.10W
Sabine r. U.S.A. 111 30.00N 93.45W
Sabine L. U.S.A. 111 29.50N 93.50W
Sabini, Monti mts. Italy 30 42.13N 12.50E
Sabkhat al Bardawīl i. Egypt 66 31.10N 33.15E
Sablayan Phil. 59 12.50N 120.50E
Sable, C. Canada 103 43.25N 65.35W
Sable, C. U.S.A. 113 25.05N 65.50W
Sable I. Canada 103 43.55N 59.50W
Sablé-sur-Sarthe France 19 47.50N 0.20W
Sabon Birni Nigeria 77 13.37N 6.15E
Sabongidda Nigeria 77 6.54N 5.56E
Sabor r. Portugal 26 41.10N 7.07W
Sabres France 20 44.09N 0.44W
Sabrina Coast f. Antarctica 128 67.00S 120.00E
Sabugal Portugal 26 40.21N 7.05W
Şabyā Saudi Arabia 72 17.09N 42.37E
Sabzevār Iran 65 36.13N 57.38E
Sacaca Bolivia 124 18.05S 66.25W
Sacajawea mtn. U.S.A. 108 45.15N 117.17W
Sacandica Angola 78 5.58S 15.56E
Sac City U.S.A. 110 42.25N 95.00W
Sacedón Spain 26 40.29N 2.43W
Sachigo r. Canada 102 55.20N 89.00W
Sachigo L. Canada 102 53.50N 92.00W
Sachsen d. Germany 38 50.59N 13.15E
Sachsen f. Germany 38 52.20N 11.20E
Sachsen-Anhalt d. Germany 38 51.58N 11.30E
Sachsenburg Austria 39 46.50N 13.21E
Sackets Harbor U.S.A. 105 43.57N 76.07W
Säckingen Germany 39 47.43N 7.56E
Sackville Canada 103 45.54N 64.22W
Saco U.S.A. 115 43.29N 70.28W
Sacramento Brazil 126 19.51S 26.47W
Sacramento U.S.A. 108 38.35N 121.30W
Sacramento r. U.S.A. 108 38.03N 121.56W
Sacramento Mts. U.S.A. 109 33.10N 105.50W
Sacramento Valley f. U.S.A. 108 39.15N 122.00W
Sada Spain 26 43.21N 8.15W
Sádaba Spain 25 42.17N 1.16W
Sadani Tanzania 79 6.00S 38.40E
Sadda Pakistan 62 33.42N 70.20E
Sa Dec Vietnam 56 10.19N 105.45E
Sādiqābād Pakistan 62 28.18N 70.08E
Sadiya India 61 27.49N 95.38E
Sado i. Japan 57 38.00N 138.20E
Sado r. Portugal 27 38.29N 8.55W
Sādri India 62 25.11N 73.26E
Sadulgarh India 62 29.35N 74.19E
Saeby Denmark 42 57.20N 10.32E
Saegertown U.S.A. 114 41.43N 80.09W
Safāfah des. Saudi Arabia 64 26.30N 39.30E
Şafānīyah Egypt 66 28.49N 30.48E

Şafarābād Iran 65 38.59N 47.25E
Säffle Sweden 43 59.08N 12.56E
Saffron Walden U.K. 13 52.02N 0.15E
Safi Morocco 74 32.20N 9.17W
Safīd r. Iran 65 37.23N 50.11E
Safonovo Russian Fed. 44 65.40N 48.10E
Safonovo Russian Fed. 44 55.08N 33.16E
Saga China 63 29.30N 85.09E
Saga Japan 57 33.08N 130.30E
Sagaing Myanmar 56 22.00N 96.00E
Sagaing d. Myanmar 56 24.00N 95.00E
Sagala Mali 76 14.09N 6.38W
Sagami r. Japan 57 35.14N 139.23E
Sagamihara Japan 57 35.32N 139.23E
Sagami-nada b. Japan 57 34.55N 139.30E
Sagamore Mass. U.S.A. 115 41.45N 70.33W
Sagamore Penn. U.S.A. 114 40.47N 79.14W
Sāgar India 63 23.50N 78.43E
Sagara Japan 57 34.41N 138.12E
Sage U.S.A. 108 41.49N 110.59W
Sag Harbor U.S.A. 115 41.00N 72.18W
Saginaw U.S.A. 104 43.25N 83.58W
Saginaw r. U.S.A. 104 43.39N 83.51W
Saginaw B. U.S.A. 104 43.50N 83.40W
Sagiz Kazakhstan 45 47.31N 54.55E
Sagres Portugal 27 37.00N 8.56W
Saguache U.S.A. 108 38.05N 106.08W
Sagua la Grande Cuba 117 22.55N 80.05W
Saguenay r. Canada 103 48.10N 69.43W
Sagunto Spain 25 39.41N 0.16W
Sāgwāra India 62 23.41N 74.01E
Sa'gya China 63 28.55N 88.03E
Saḩāb Jordan 67 31.53N 36.00E
Sahaba Sudan 72 18.55N 30.28E
Sahagún Spain 26 42.22N 5.02W
Saḩam Jordan 67 32.42N 35.47E
Saḩam al Jawlān Syria 67 32.46N 35.56E
Sahara des. Africa 75 22.30N 3.00E
Sahāranpur India 63 29.58N 77.33E
Saharsa India 63 25.53N 86.36E
Sahaswān India 63 28.05N 78.45E
Sahbā, Wādī as r. Saudi Arabia 65 23.48N 49.50E
Sahel d. Burkina 76 14.00N 0.50W
Sāhibganj India 63 25.15N 87.39E
Sāhiwāl Punjab Pakistan 62 31.58N 72.20E
Sāhiwāl Punjab Pakistan 62 30.40N 73.06E
Sahtaneh r. Canada 100 59.02N 122.28W
Sahuarita U.S.A. 109 31.57N 110.58W
Sahwat al Qamḩ Syria 67 32.36N 36.23E
Saibai i. Australia 90 9.24S 142.40E
Sa'idābād Iran 65 29.28N 55.43E
Saidpur Bangla. 63 25.48N 88.54E
Saidu Pakistan 62 34.45N 72.21E
Saigon see Ho Chi Minh Vietnam 56
Saillans France 21 44.42N 5.11E
Saimaa i. Finland 44 61.20N 28.00E
Saimbeyli Turkey 64 38.07N 36.08E
Saindak Pakistan 62 29.17N 61.34E
St. Abb's Head U.K. 14 55.54N 2.07W
St. Afrique France 20 43.57N 2.53E
St. Agapit Canada 105 46.34N 71.27W
St. Agathe des Monts Canada 105 46.03N 74.17W
St. Agrève France 21 45.01N 4.24E
St. Alban's Canada 103 47.52N 55.51W
St. Albans U.K. 13 51.46N 0.21W
St. Albans Vt. U.S.A. 105 44.49N 73.05W
St. Albans W.Va. U.S.A. 114 38.23N 81.49W
St. Albert Canada 100 53.37N 113.40W
St. Alexis des Monts Canada 105 46.28N 73.08W
St. Amand France 19 50.26N 3.26E
St. Amand-Mont-Rond France 19 46.44N 2.30E
St. Ambroix France 21 44.15N 4.11E
St. Amour France 19 46.26N 5.21E
St. André-les-Alpes France 21 43.58N 6.30E
St. Andrews U.K. 14 56.20N 2.48W
St. Andries Belgium 16 51.12N 3.10E
St. Anicet Canada 105 45.07N 74.22W
St. Ann's Bay town Jamaica 117 18.26N 77.12W
St. Anthony Canada 103 51.22N 55.35W
St. Anthony U.S.A. 106 43.59N 111.40W
St. Antoine Canada 105 46.39N 71.34W
St. Antonin France 20 44.09N 1.45E
St. Astier France 20 45.09N 0.32E
St. Auban France 21 43.51N 6.44E
St. Augustin r. Canada 103 51.14N 58.41W
St. Augustine U.S.A. 113 29.54N 81.19W
St. Augustin Saguenay Canada 103 51.14N 58.39W
St. Aulaye France 20 45.12N 0.08E
St. Austell U.K. 13 50.20N 4.48W
St. Avold France 19 49.06N 6.42E
St. Barthélemy Canada 105 46.12N 73.08W
St. Barthélemy i. Leeward Is. 117 17.55N 62.50W
St. Basile de Portneuf Canada 105 46.45N 71.49W
St. Béat France 20 42.55N 0.42E
St. Bees Head U.K. 12 54.31N 3.39W
St. Benoît-du-Sault France 18 46.27N 1.23E
St. Boniface Canada 101 49.55N 97.06W
St. Bonnet-de-Joux France 19 46.29N 4.27E
St. Brides B. U.K. 13 51.48N 5.03W
St. Brieuc France 18 48.31N 2.47W
St. Bruno de Guigues Canada 104 47.27N 79.26W
St. Calais France 18 47.55N 0.45E
St. Casimir Canada 105 46.40N 72.08W
St. Catharines Canada 104 43.10N 79.15W
St. Catherine's Pt. U.K. 13 50.34N 1.18W
St. Céré France 20 44.52N 1.53E
St. Chamond France 21 45.28N 4.30E
St. Charles Mich. U.S.A. 104 43.18N 84.09W
St. Charles Mo. U.S.A. 110 38.47N 90.29W
St. Chély d'Apcher France 20 44.48N 3.17E
St. Ciers-sur-Gironde France 20 45.18N 0.37W
St. Clair U.S.A. 114 42.49N 82.30W
St. Clair r. Canada 104 42.25N 82.41W
St. Clair Shores town U.S.A. 114 42.30N 82.54W
St. Clairsville U.S.A. 114 40.05N 80.54W

St. Claud France 20 45.53N 0.23E
St. Claude Canada 105 45.40N 72.00W
St. Claude France 19 46.23N 5.52E
St. Cloud U.S.A. 110 45.33N 94.10W
St. Croix i. U.S.V.Is. 117 17.45N 64.35W
St. Cyprien France 20 44.52N 1.02E
St. Cyrille de Wendover Canada 105 45.56N 72.26W
St. David's U.K. 13 51.54N 5.16W
St. David's I. Bermuda 127 32.23N 64.42W
St. Denis France 19 48.56N 2.22E
St. Dié France 19 48.17N 6.57E
St. Dizier France 19 48.38N 4.57E
St. Donat Canada 105 46.19N 74.13W
Sainte-Agathe-des-Monts Canada 102 46.03N 74.17W
Sainte Anne de Beaupré Canada 105 47.02N 70.56W
Sainte Anne de la Pérade Canada 105 46.35N 72.12W
Sainte-Anne-des-Monts Canada 103 49.07N 66.29W
Sainte Anne du Lac Canada 105 46.52N 75.21W
Sainte Anne, Rivière r. Canada 105 46.52N 71.49W
Sainte Croix Canada 105 46.38N 71.44W
Sainte-Croix Switz. 39 46.49N 6.31E
Sainte Emelie Canada 105 46.19N 73.39W
Sainte Famille d'Aumond Canada 105 46.27N 75.52W
Sainte Foy la Grande France 20 44.50N 0.13E
Sainte Hermine France 18 46.33N 1.04W
St. Elias, Mt. U.S.A. 100 60.18N 140.55W
St. Elias Mts. Canada 100 60.30N 139.30W
St. Éloi Canada 103 48.02N 69.13W
Sainte-Lucia France 21 41.42N 9.22E
Sainte Lucie France 18 46.07N 74.13W
Sainte Marguerite Canada 105 46.03N 74.05W
Sainte Marguerite r. Canada 103 50.10N 66.40W
Sainte-Marie-aux-Mines France 19 48.15N 7.11E
Sainte-Mathieu, Pointe de c. France 18 48.20N 4.46W
Sainte Maure de Touraine France 18 47.07N 0.37E
Sainte-Maxime France 21 43.18N 6.38E
Sainte Menehould France 19 49.05N 4.54E
Sainte Mère-Église France 18 49.24N 1.19W
St. Enimie France 20 44.22N 3.26E
Saintes France 20 45.44N 0.38W
Saintes-Maries-de-la-Mer France 21 43.27N 4.26E
St. Espirit Canada 105 45.56N 73.40W
Sainte Thècle Canada 105 46.49N 72.31W
Sainte-Thérèse-de-Blainville Canada 105 45.38N
   73.51W
St. Étienne France 21 45.26N 4.24E
St. Fargeau France 19 47.38N 3.04E
St. Faustin Canada 105 46.07N 74.30W
St. Félix Canada 105 46.10N 73.26W
Saintfield U.K. 15 54.28N 5.50W
St. Fintan's Canada 103 48.10N 58.50W
St. Florent France 21 42.41N 9.18E
St. Florent France 19 48.00N 3.44E
St. Florent-sur-Cher France 19 46.59N 2.15E
St. Flour France 20 45.02N 3.05E
St. Francis U.S.A. 110 39.47N 101.47W
St. Francisville U.S.A. 111 30.47N 91.23W
St. Francois r. Canada 105 46.07N 72.55W
St. François, Lac l. Canada 105 45.55N 71.10W
St. Gabriel Canada 105 46.17N 73.23W
St. Gallen Switz. 39 47.25N 9.23E
St. Gallen d. Switz. 39 47.00N 9.15E
St. Gaudens France 20 43.07N 0.44E
St. Gaultier France 18 46.38N 1.25E
St. Genis-de-Saintonge France 20 45.29N 0.34W
St. George Australia 91 28.03S 148.30E
St. George Bermuda 127 32.24N 64.42W
St. George N.B. Canada 103 45.11N 66.57W
St. George Ont. Canada 104 43.15N 80.15W
St. George U.S.A. 108 37.06N 113.35W
St. George, C. U.S.A. 113 29.35N 85.04W
St. Georges Belgium 16 50.37N 5.20E
St. Georges Canada 105 46.37N 72.40W
St. George's Grenada 117 12.04N 61.44W
St. Georges Guiana 123 3.54N 51.48W
St. George's B. Canada 103 48.20N 59.00W
St. George's Channel Rep. of Ire./U.K. 15 51.30N
   6.20W
St. George's I. Bermuda 127 32.24N 64.42W
St. Germain France 19 48.54N 2.05E
St. Germain de Grantham Canada 105 45.50N 72.34W
St. Germain-du-Bois France 19 46.45N 5.15E
St. Germain-Lembron France 20 45.28N 3.14E
St. Germain-l'Herm France 20 45.28N 3.33E
St. Gervais d'Auvergne France 20 46.02N 2.49E
St. Géry France 20 44.29N 1.35E
St. Gheorghe's Mouth est. Romania 29 44.51N 29.37E
St. Gilles-Croix-de-Vie France 18 46.42N 1.57W
St. Girons France 20 42.59N 1.09E
St. Gotthard Pass Switz. 17 46.30N 8.55E
St. Govan's Head U.K. 13 51.36N 4.55W
St. Grégoire Canada 105 46.16N 72.30W
St. Guénolé France 18 47.49N 4.20W
St. Guillaume d'Upton Canada 105 45.53N 72.46W
St. Helena i. Atlantic Oc. 127 15.58S 5.43W
St. Helena B. R.S.A. 80 32.35S 18.05E
St. Helens U.K. 12 53.28N 2.43W
St. Helens U.S.A. 108 45.52N 122.48W
St. Helens, Mt. U.S.A. 108 46.12N 122.11W
St. Helier Channel Is. Europe 13 49.12N 2.07W
St. Hilaire-du-Harcouët France 18 48.35N 1.06W
St. Hippolyte France 19 47.19N 6.49E
St. Hubert Belgium 16 50.02N 5.22E
St. Hyacinthe Canada 105 45.37N 72.57W
St. Ignace U.S.A. 104 45.52N 84.43W
St. Ignace du Lac Canada 105 46.43N 73.49W
St. Ives U.K. 13 50.13N 5.29W
St. Jacobs Canada 104 43.32N 80.33W
St. Jacques Canada 105 45.57N 73.34W
St. Jean Canada 105 45.19N 73.16W
St. Jean r. Canada 103 50.17N 64.20W
St. Jean Canada 105 45.19N 73.16W
St. Jean-d'Angély France 20 45.57N 0.31W
St. Jean-de-Bournay France 21 45.29N 5.08E
St. Jean-de-Losne France 19 47.06N 5.15E
St. Jean-de-Luz France 20 43.23N 1.40W
St. Jean de Matha Canada 105 46.14N 73.33W
St. Jean-de-Monts France 18 46.48N 2.03W

St. Jean-du-Gard France 20 44.06N 3.53E
St. Jean, Lac *l.* Canada 103 48.35N 72.00W
St. Jean Pied-de-Port France 20 43.10N 1.14W
St. Jérôme Canada 105 45.47N 74.00W
St. John Canada 103 45.16N 66.03W
St. John *r.* Canada 103 45.16N 66.04W
St. John U.S.A. 111 38.00N 98.46W
St. John B. Canada 103 50.40N 57.08W
St. John, C. Canada 103 50.00N 55.32W
St. John's Antigua 117 17.07N 61.51W
St. John's Canada 103 47.34N 52.43W
St. Johns U.S.A. 109 34.30N 109.22W
St. Johns *r.* U.S.A. 113 30.24N 81.24W
St. Johnsbury U.S.A. 105 44.25N 72.01W
St. John's Pt. U.K. 15 54.14N 5.39W
St. Jordi, Golf de *g.* Spain 25 40.53N 1.00E
St. Joseph La. U.S.A. 111 31.55N 91.14W
St. Joseph Mich. U.S.A. 112 42.05N 86.30W
St. Joseph Mo. U.S.A. 110 39.46N 94.51W
St. Joseph I. Canada 104 46.13N 83.57W
St. Joseph, L. Canada 102 51.05N 90.35W
St. Jovite Canada 105 46.07N 74.36W
St. Jude Canada 105 45.46N 72.59W
St. Julien-en-Born France 20 44.04N 1.14W
St. Julien-en-Genevois France 21 46.08N 6.05E
St. Junien France 20 45.53N 0.54E
St. Just-en-Chaussée France 19 49.30N 2.26E
St. Just-en-Chevalet France 20 45.55N 3.50E
Kilda *i.* U.K. 10 57.55N 8.20W
St. Kitts-Nevis Leeward Is. 117 17.20N 62.45W
St. Lambert Canada 105 45.30N 73.30W
St. Laurent Man. Canada 101 50.24N 97.56W
St. Laurent Que. Canada 105 45.30N 73.40W
St. Laurent du Maroni Guiana 123 5.30N 54.02W
St. Laurent-et-Benon France 20 45.09N 0.49W
St. Lawrence *r.* Canada 105 44.15N 76.10W
St. Lawrence, G. of Canada 103 48.00N 62.00W
St. Lawrence I. U.S.A. 98 63.00N 170.00W
St. Léonard d'Astarac Canada 105 46.06N 72.22W
St. Lewis Sd. Canada 103 52.20N 55.40W
St. Lin Canada 105 45.51N 73.45W
St. Lô France 18 49.07N 1.05W
St. Louis Senegal 76 16.01N 16.30W
St. Louis U.S.A. 110 38.38N 90.11W
St. Louis Park town U.S.A. 110 44.56N 93.22W
St. Loup-sur-Semouse France 19 47.53N 6.16E
St. Lucia Windward Is. 117 14.05N 61.00W
St. Lucia, L. R.S.A. 81 28.05S 32.26E
St. Magnus B. U.K. 10 60.25N 1.35W
St. Maixent France 18 46.25N 0.12W
St. Malo Canada 105 45.12N 71.30W
St. Malo France 18 48.39N 2.01W
St. Malo, Golfe de *g.* France 18 48.45N 2.00W
St. Mamert France 21 43.53N 4.12E
St.-Marc Haiti 117 19.08N 72.41W
St. Marc des Carrières Canada 105 46.41N 72.03W
St. Marcellin France 21 45.09N 5.19E
St. Margaret's Hope U.K. 14 58.49N 2.57W
St. Maries U.S.A. 108 47.19N 116.35W
St. Martin Channel Is. Europe 13 49.27N 2.34W
St. Martin *i.* Leeward Is. 117 18.05N 63.05W
St. Martin B. Canada 104 45.57N 84.35W
St. Martin-de-Londres France 20 43.47N 3.44E
St. Martin d'Hères France 21 45.10N 5.46E
St. Martin, L. Canada 101 51.37N 98.29W
St. Martin's *i.* U.K. 13 49.59N 6.16W
St. Mary Channel Is. Europe 13 49.14N 2.10W
St. Mary *r.* U.S.A. 104 46.30N 84.36W
St. Mary Peak Australia 92 31.30S 138.35E
St. Marys Australia 91 41.33S 148.12E
St. Mary's Canada 104 43.14N 81.08W
St. Mary's *r.* Canada 103 45.02N 61.54W
St. Mary's *i.* U.K. 13 49.55N 6.16W
St. Marys Penn. U.S.A. 114 41.26N 78.34W
St. Marys W.Va. U.S.A. 114 39.23N 81.12W
St. Mary's B. Canada 103 46.50N 53.47W
St. Mary's, C. Canada 103 46.49N 54.12W
St. Mathieu France 20 45.42N 0.46E
St. Matthew I. U.S.A. 98 60.30N 172.45W
St. Maur France 19 48.48N 2.30E
St. Maurice *r.* Canada 105 46.21N 72.31W
St. Maurice Prov. Park Canada 105 46.52N 73.10W
St. Méen-le-Grand France 18 48.11N 2.12W
St. Michel des Saints Canada 105 46.41N 73.55W
St. Mihiel France 19 48.54N 5.33E
St. Moritz Switz. 39 46.30N 9.50E
St. Nazaire France 18 47.17N 2.12W
St. Neots U.K. 13 52.14N 0.16W
St. Niklaas Belgium 16 51.10N 4.09E
St. Omer France 19 50.45N 2.15E
St. Pacôme Canada 103 47.24N 69.57W
St. Pascal Canada 103 47.32N 69.48W
St. Patrick, Lac *l.* Canada 105 46.21N 77.18W
St. Paul *r.* Canada 103 51.26N 57.40W
St. Paul A.H.Prov. France 21 44.31N 6.45E
St. Paul Pyr. Or. France 20 42.49N 2.29E
St. Paul Ark. U.S.A. 111 35.50N 93.48W
St. Paul Minn. U.S.A. 110 45.00N 93.10W
St. Paul Nebr. U.S.A. 110 41.13N 98.27W
St. Paul de Chester Canada 105 45.57N 71.49W
St. Paul du Nord Canada 103 48.27N 69.15W
St. Paulien France 20 45.08N 3.49E
St. Paul, Île *i.* Indian Oc. 49 38.43S 77.29E
St. Paulin Canada 105 46.25N 73.01W
St. Paul Rocks *is.* Atlantic Oc. 127 1.00N 29.23W
St. Peter U.S.A. 110 44.17N 93.57W
St. Peter Port Channel Is. Europe 13 49.27N 2.32W
St. Petersburg U.S.A. 113 27.45N 82.40W
St. Pierre Char. Mar. France 20 45.59N 1.14W
St. Pierre S.Mar. France 19 49.48N 0.29E
St. Pierre and Miquelon *is.* N. America 103 46.55N 56.10W
St. Pierre-Église France 18 49.40N 1.24W
St. Pierre, Lac *l.* Canada 105 46.12N 72.52W
St. Pierre le Moûtier France 19 46.48N 3.07E
St. Pierreville France 21 44.49N 4.29E
St. Pol-de-Léon France 18 48.41N 3.59W
St. Pol-sur-Ternoise France 19 50.23N 2.20E

St. Pölten Austria 36 48.13N 15.37E
St. Polycarpe Canada 105 45.18N 74.18W
St. Pons France 20 43.29N 2.46E
St. Pourçain France 20 46.19N 3.17E
St. Priest France 21 45.42N 4.57E
St. Quentin France 19 49.51N 3.17E
St. Raphaël France 21 43.25N 6.46E
St. Raymond Canada 105 46.54N 71.50W
St. Regis Falls U.S.A. 105 44.40N 74.33W
St. Rémy France 21 43.47N 4.50E
St. Renan France 18 48.26N 4.37W
St. Roch de Mekinac Canada 105 46.48N 72.44W
St. Savin France 18 46.34N 0.52E
St. Savinien France 20 45.53N 0.50W
St. Seine-l'Abbaye France 19 47.26N 4.47E
St. Siméon Canada 103 47.55N 69.58W
St. Stephen Canada 103 45.12N 67.17W
St. Sulpice les Feuilles France 20 46.19N 1.22E
St. Symphorien France 20 44.26N 0.30W
St. Thomas Canada 104 42.47N 81.12W
St. Thomas *i.* U.S.V.Is. 117 18.22N 64.57W
St. Tite Canada 105 46.44N 72.34W
St. Tropez France 21 43.16N 6.38E
St. Truiden Belgium 16 50.49N 5.11E
St. Ubald Canada 105 46.45N 72.16W
St. Valéry France 18 49.52N 0.44E
St. Valéry-sur-Somme France 19 50.11N 1.38E
St. Vallier France 21 45.10N 4.49E
St. Vallier-de-Thiey France 21 43.42N 6.51E
St. Varent France 18 46.53N 0.14W
St. Vincent and the Grenadines Windward Is. 117 13.00N 61.15W
St. Vincent-de-Tyrosse France 20 43.40N 1.18W
St. Vincent, G. Australia 92 35.00S 138.05E
St. Vith Belgium 16 50.15N 6.08E
St. Vivien-de-Médoc France 20 45.26N 1.02W
St. Wendel Germany 39 49.28N 7.10E
St. Yrieix France 20 45.31N 1.12E
St. Zénon Canada 105 46.33N 73.49W
Sairs, L. Canada 104 46.51N 78.12W
Saitama *d.* Japan 57 38.55N 139.51E
Sajama *mtn.* Bolivia 124 18.06S 69.00W
Saka Kenya 79 0.09S 39.18E
Sakai Japan 57 34.35N 135.28E
Sakākah Saudi Arabia 64 29.59N 40.12E
Sakakawea, L. *see* Garrison Resr. U.S.A. 110
Sakami *r.* Canada 102 53.40N 76.40W
Sakami, Lac *l.* Canada 102 53.10N 77.00W
Sâkâne, Erg i-n *f.* Mali 74 21.00N 1.00W
Sakania Zaïre 79 12.44S 28.34E
Sakarya *r.* Turkey 64 41.08N 30.36E
Sakata Japan 57 38.55N 139.51E
Sakété Benin 77 6.45N 2.45E
Sakhalin *i.* Russian Fed. 53 50.00N 143.00E
Sākhar Afghan. 62 32.57N 65.32E
Sakhi Sarwar Pakistan 62 29.59N 70.18E
Sakhnīn Israel 67 32.52N 35.17E
Sakht-Sar Iran 65 36.54N 50.41E
Sākib Jordan 67 32.17N 35.49E
Sākoli India 63 21.05N 79.59E
Sakrand Pakistan 62 26.08N 68.16E
Sakri India 62 21.02N 74.40E
Sakti India 63 22.02N 82.58E
Sakuma Japan 57 35.05N 137.48E
Sal *r.* Russian Fed. 45 47.33N 40.40E
Sala Eritrea 72 16.58N 37.27E
Sala Sweden 43 59.55N 16.36E
Salaca *r.* Latvia 41 57.45N 24.21E
Salacgrīva Latvia 41 57.45N 24.21E
Sala Consilina Italy 33 40.24N 15.36E
Salado *r.* Buenos Aires Argentina 125 35.44S 57.22W
Salado *r.* Santa Fé Argentina 125 31.40S 60.41W
Salado *r.* La Pampa Argentina 125 36.15S 66.55W
Salado *r.* Mexico 111 26.50N 99.17W
Salaga Ghana 76 8.36N 0.32W
Salailua W. Samoa 84 13.42S 172.35W
Salālah Oman 60 17.00N 54.04E
Salālah Sudan 72 21.19N 36.13E
Salamanca Spain 26 40.58N 5.40W
Salamanca *d.* Spain 26 40.45N 6.00W
Salamanca U.S.A. 114 42.10N 78.43W
Salamat *d.* Chad 73 11.00N 20.40E
Salāmbek Pakistan 62 28.18N 65.09E
Salamina Colombia 122 5.24N 75.31W
Salamís *i.* Greece 35 37.54N 23.26E
Salamís town Greece 35 37.59N 23.28E
Salām Khān Afghan. 62 31.47N 66.45E
Salani W. Samoa 84 14.02S 171.35W
Salar de Uyuni *f.* Bolivia 121 20.30S 67.45W
Salas de los Infantes Spain 26 42.01N 3.17W
Salatiga Indonesia 59 7.15S 110.34E
Salāya India 62 22.19N 69.35E
Sala y Gomez *i.* Pacific Oc. 85 26.28S 105.28W
Salbris France 19 47.26N 2.03E
Salcia Romania 34 43.57N 24.56E
Salcombe U.K. 13 50.14N 3.47W
Saldaña Spain 26 42.31N 4.44W
Saldus Latvia 41 56.40N 22.30E
Sale Australia 93 38.06S 147.06E
Salé Morocco 74 34.04N 6.50W
Salekhard Russian Fed. 44 66.33N 66.35E
Salelologa W. Samoa 84 13.43S 172.13W
Salem Ind. U.S.A. 112 38.38N 86.06W
Salem Mass. U.S.A. 115 42.31N 70.55W
Salem Mo. U.S.A. 111 37.39N 91.32W
Salem N.H. U.S.A. 115 42.47N 71.12W
Salem N.J. U.S.A. 115 39.34N 75.28W
Salem N.Y. U.S.A. 115 43.10N 73.20W
Salem Ohio U.S.A. 114 40.54N 80.52W
Salem Oreg. U.S.A. 108 44.57N 123.01W
Salem Va. U.S.A. 113 37.17N 80.04W
Salem W.Va. U.S.A. 114 39.17N 80.34W
Salemi Italy 32 37.49N 12.49E
Sälen Sweden 41 61.10N 13.16E

Salerno Italy 33 40.41N 14.47E
Salerno, Golfo di *g.* Italy 33 40.32N 14.42E
Salers France 20 45.08N 2.30E
Salfit Jordan 67 32.05N 35.11E
Salford U.K. 12 53.30N 2.17W
Salgótarján Hungary 37 48.07N 19.48E
Salgueiro Brazil 123 8.04S 39.05W
Sali Croatia 31 43.56N 15.10E
Salies-de-Béarn France 20 43.29N 0.55W
Salignac Eyvignes France 20 44.59N 1.19E
Salima Malaŵi 79 13.45S 34.29E
Salim's Tanzania 79 10.37S 36.33E
Salina U.S.A. 110 38.50N 97.37W
Salina Cruz Mexico 116 16.11N 95.12W
Salina, Isola *i.* Italy 33 38.34N 14.51E
Salinas Ecuador 122 2.13S 80.58W
Salinas U.S.A. 108 36.40N 121.38W
Salinas *r.* U.S.A. 106 36.45N 121.48W
Salinas, Cabo de *c.* Spain 25 39.16N 3.03E
Saline U.S.A. 104 42.10N 83.47W
Saline *r.* U.S.A. 110 38.51N 97.30W
Salineville U.S.A. 114 40.37N 80.51W
Salinópolis Brazil 123 0.37S 47.20W
Salins France 19 46.57N 5.53E
Salisbury U.K. 13 51.04N 1.48W
Salisbury Md. U.S.A. 115 38.22N 75.36W
Salisbury N.C. U.S.A. 113 35.20N 80.30W
Salisbury Plain *f.* U.K. 13 51.15N 1.55W
Salisbury Sd. U.S.A. 100 57.30N 135.56W
Şalkhad Syria 66 32.29N 36.42E
Sallanches France 21 45.56N 6.38E
Salles-Curan France 20 44.11N 2.47E
Salling *f.* Denmark 42 56.40N 9.00E
Sallisaw U.S.A. 111 35.28N 94.47W
Salluit Canada 99 62.10N 75.40W
Sallyāna Nepal 63 28.22N 82.12E
Salmās Iran 65 38.13N 44.50E
Salmi Russian Fed. 44 61.19N 31.46E
Salmon *r.* Canada 100 54.03N 122.40W
Salmon U.S.A. 108 45.11N 113.55W
Salmon *r.* U.S.A. 108 45.51N 116.46W
Salmon Gums Australia 89 32.59S 121.39E
Salmon River Mts. U.S.A. 108 44.45N 115.30W
Salo Finland 41 60.23N 23.08E
Salò Italy 30 45.36N 10.31E
Salobreña Spain 27 36.44N 3.35W
Salome U.S.A. 109 33.47N 113.37W
Salon France 21 43.38N 5.06E
Salonga *r.* Zaïre 78 0.09S 19.52E
Salonika *see* Thessaloníki Greece 34
Salonta Romania 37 46.48N 21.40E
Salor *r.* Spain 27 39.39N 7.03W
Salsk Russian Fed. 45 46.30N 41.33E
Salso *r.* Italy 32 37.05N 13.57E
Salsomaggiore Terme Italy 30 44.49N 9.59E
Salt *r.* U.S.A. 109 33.23N 112.18W
Salta Argentina 124 24.47S 65.24W
Salta *d.* Argentina 124 25.00S 65.00W
Saltdal Norway 40 67.06N 15.25E
Saltee Is. Rep. of Ire. 15 52.08N 6.36W
Saltfjorden *est.* Norway 40 67.15N 14.10E
Saltfleet U.K. 12 53.25N 0.11E
Salt Fork *r.* U.S.A. 107 36.41N 97.05W
Saltillo Mexico 111 25.25N 101.00W
Salt Lake City U.S.A. 108 40.46N 111.53W
Salto Argentina 125 34.17S 60.15W
Salto Brazil 126 23.10S 47.16W
Salto *r.* Italy 30 42.23N 12.54E
Salto Uruguay 125 31.23S 57.58W
Salto da Divisa Brazil 123 16.04S 40.00W
Salto Grande, Embalse de resr. Argentina/Uruguay 125 31.00S 57.50W
Salton Sea *l.* U.S.A. 109 33.19N 115.50W
Salūmbar India 62 24.08N 74.03E
Saluzzo Italy 30 44.39N 7.29E
Salvador Brazil 123 12.58S 38.29W
Salvador Canada 101 52.12N 109.32W
Salvaterra de Magos Portugal 27 39.01N 8.48W
Salversville U.S.A. 113 37.43N 83.06W
Salviac France 20 44.41N 1.16E
Salween *r.* Myanmar 56 16.32N 97.35E
Salyany Azerbaijan 65 39.36N 48.59E
Salzach *r.* Austria 39 48.12N 12.56E
Salzbrunn Namibia 80 24.23S 18.00E
Salzburg Austria 39 47.48N 13.02E
Salzburg *d.* Austria 39 47.15N 13.00E
Salzgitter Germany 38 52.02N 10.22E
Salzkammergut *f.* Austria 39 47.38N 13.30E
Salzwedel Germany 38 52.51N 11.09E
Sam India 62 26.50N 70.31E
Sama Spain 26 43.18N 5.41W
Samalambo Angola 78 14.16S 17.53E
Samālūt Egypt 66 28.18N 30.43E
Samaná Dom. Rep. 117 19.14N 69.20W
Samana Cay *i.* Bahamas 117 23.05N 73.45W
Samanga Tanzania 79 8.24S 39.18E
Samannūd Egypt 66 30.58N 31.14E
Samar *i.* Phil. 59 11.45N 125.15E
Samara Russian Fed. 44 53.10N 50.15E
Samara *r.* Russian Fed. 44 53.17N 50.42E
Samarai P.N.G. 90 10.37S 150.40E
Samaria *see* As Sāmirah *f.* Jordan 67
Samarinda Indonesia 58 0.30S 117.09E
Samarkand Uzbekistan 9 39.40N 66.57E
Sāmarrā Iraq 65 34.13N 43.52E
Samāstipur India 63 25.51N 85.47E
Samawāri Pakistan 62 28.34N 66.46E
Samba Zaïre 78 4.38N 26.22E
Sambalpur India 63 21.27N 83.58E
Sambao *r.* Madagascar 81 16.45S 44.26E
Sambava Madagascar 81 14.16S 50.10E
Sambāza Pakistan 62 31.46N 69.20E
Sambhal India 63 28.35N 78.33E
Sāmbhar India 62 26.55N 75.12E
Sāmbhar L. India 62 26.58N 75.05E
Sambor Ukraine 37 49.31N 23.10E

Samborombón, Bahía *b.* Argentina 125 36.00S 57.00W
Sambre *r.* Belgium 16 50.29N 4.52E
Samburu Kenya 79 3.46S 39.17E
Samch'ŏk S. Korea 53 37.30N 129.10E
Samdari India 62 25.49N 72.35E
Same Tanzania 79 4.10S 37.43E
Samnū Libya 75 27.16N 14.54E
Samoa *is.* Pacific Oc. 84 14.20S 170.00W
Samoa Is. Pacific Oc. 84 14.00S 171.00W
Samobor Slovenia 36 45.48N 15.43E
Samokov Bulgaria 34 42.20N 23.33E
Samorogouan Burkina 76 11.21N 4.57W
Sámos *i.* Greece 35 37.45N 26.50E
Sámos town Greece 35 37.45N 27.00E
Samothráki *i.* Greece 34 40.30N 25.32E
Samothráki town Greece 34 40.28N 25.31E
Sampang Indonesia 59 7.13S 113.15E
Sampit Indonesia 58 2.34S 112.59E
Sampson U.S.A. 114 42.44N 76.54W
Sam Rayburn Resr. U.S.A. 111 31.27N 94.37W
Samsang China 63 30.22N 82.57E
Samsö Denmark 42 55.52N 10.37E
Sam Son Vietnam 55 19.44N 105.53E
Samsun Turkey 64 41.17N 36.22E
Samtredia Georgia 45 42.10N 42.22E
Samui, Ko *i.* Thailand 56 9.30N 100.00E
Samur *r.* Russian Fed. 45 42.00N 48.20E
Samut Prakan Thailand 56 13.32N 100.35E
Samut Sakhon Thailand 56 13.31N 100.13E
San *r.* Cambodia 56 13.32N 105.57E
San Mali 76 13.21N 4.57W
San *r.* Poland 37 50.25N 22.20E
Sana *r.* Bosnia-Herzegovina 31 45.03N 16.23E
Şan'ā' Yemen 71 15.23N 44.14E
Sana *see* Şan'ā' Yemen 71
Sanaba Burkina 76 12.25N 3.47W
Sanaga *r.* Cameroon 77 3.35N 9.40E
San Ambrosio *i.* Chile 121 26.28S 79.53W
Sānand India 62 22.59N 72.23E
Sanandaj Iran 65 35.18N 47.01E
San Andreas U.S.A. 108 38.12N 120.41W
San Andrés, Isla de *i.* Colombia 117 12.33N 81.42W
San Andrés Tuxtla Mexico 116 18.27N 95.13W
San Angelo U.S.A. 111 31.28N 100.26W
San Antonio Chile 125 33.35S 71.38W
San Antonio N.Mex. U.S.A. 109 33.55N 106.52W
San Antonio Tex. U.S.A. 111 29.28N 98.31W
San Antonio Abad Spain 25 38.59N 1.18E
San Antonio, C. Cuba 117 21.50N 84.57W
San Antonio, Cabo *c.* Argentina 125 36.40S 56.42W
San Antonio de Areco Argentina 125 34.15S 59.30W
San Antonio Oeste Argentina 125 40.44S 64.57W
San Antonio, Punta *c.* Mexico 109 29.45N 115.41W
San Antonio, Sierra de *mts.* Mexico 109 30.00N 110.10W
San Augustine U.S.A. 111 31.32N 94.07W
Sanāwad India 62 22.11N 76.04E
San Bartolomeo Italy 33 41.24N 15.01E
San Benedetto Italy 31 42.57N 13.53E
San Benedetto Po Italy 30 45.02N 10.55E
San Benito Guatemala 117 16.55N 89.54W
San Benito U.S.A. 111 26.08N 97.38W
San Bernardino U.S.A. 109 34.06N 117.17W
San Bernardo Chile 125 33.36S 70.43W
San Blas, C. U.S.A. 113 29.40N 85.22W
San Bonifacio Italy 30 45.24N 11.16E
Sanbornville U.S.A. 115 43.30N 70.57W
San Candido Italy 30 46.44N 12.17E
San Carlos Chile 125 36.25S 71.58W
San Carlos Mexico 111 29.01N 100.51W
San Carlos Nicaragua 117 11.07N 84.47W
San Carlos Phil. 59 15.59N 120.22E
San Carlos Venezuela 122 1.55N 67.04W
San Carlos Venezuela 122 9.39N 68.35W
San Carlos de Bariloche Argentina 125 41.08S 71.15W
San Carlos del Zulia Venezuela 122 9.01N 71.55W
San Cataldo Italy 32 37.29N 14.00E
Sancergues France 19 47.09N 2.55E
Sancerre France 19 47.20N 2.51E
Sancerrois, Collines du hills France 19 47.25N 2.45E
Sancha He *r.* China 55 26.50N 106.04E
San Clemente Spain 27 39.24N 2.26W
San Clemente U.S.A. 109 33.26N 117.37W
San Clemente I. U.S.A. 109 32.54N 118.29W
Sancoins France 19 46.50N 2.55E
San Cristóbal Argentina 124 30.20S 61.41W
San Cristóbal Dom. Rep. 117 18.27N 70.07W
San Cristóbal Venezuela 122 7.46N 72.15W
Sancti Spíritus Cuba 117 21.55N 79.28W
Sand Norway 42 59.29N 6.15E
Sanda *i.* U.K. 14 55.17N 5.34W
Sandakan Malaysia 58 5.52N 118.04E
Sandanski Bulgaria 34 41.34N 23.17E
Sandaré Mali 76 14.40N 10.15W
Sandared Sweden 43 57.43N 12.47E
Sanday *i.* U.K. 14 59.15N 2.33W
Sandbach U.K. 12 53.09N 2.23W
Sandefjord Norway 42 59.08N 10.14E
Sanders U.S.A. 109 35.13N 109.20W
Sanderson U.S.A. 111 30.09N 102.24W
Sandersville U.S.A. 113 32.59N 82.49W
Sandgate Australia 93 27.18S 153.00E
Sandhammaren *c.* Denmark 43 55.23N 14.12E
Sandhornöy *i.* Norway 40 67.05N 14.10E
Sāndi India 63 27.18N 79.57E
Sandia Peru 122 14.14S 69.25W
San Diego U.S.A. 109 32.43N 117.09W
San Diego, C. Argentina 125 54.38S 65.05W
Sandīla India 63 27.05N 80.31E
Sand Lake town Canada 102 47.45N 84.30W
Sandnes Norway 42 58.51N 5.44E
Sandness U.K. 10 60.18N 1.38W
Sandö *i.* Faroe Is. 10 61.50N 6.45W
Sandoa Zaïre 78 9.41S 22.56E
Sandomierz Poland 37 50.41N 21.45E
San Donà di Piave Italy 30 45.38N 12.34E

Sandover r. Australia 90 21.43S 136.32E
Sandoway Myanmar 56 18.28N 94.20E
Sandown U.K. 13 50.39N 1.09W
Sandpoint town U.S.A. 108 48.17N 116.34W
Sandringham U.K. 12 52.50N 0.30E
Sandstone Australia 89 27.59S 119.17E
Sandu Shuizu Zizhixian China 55 25.59N 107.52E
Sandusky Mich. U.S.A. 114 43.25N 82.50W
Sandusky Ohio U.S.A. 114 41.27N 82.42W
Sandveld r. Namibia 80 21.25S 20.00E
Sandvika Norway 42 59.54N 10.31E
Sandviken Sweden 41 60.37N 16.46E
Sandwich B. Canada 103 53.35N 57.15W
Sandwip I. Bangla. 63 22.29N 91.26E
Sandy U.S.A. 108 40.35N 111.53W
Sandy B. St. Helena 127 16.02S 5.42W
Sandy Bight b. Australia 89 33.53S 123.25E
Sandy C. Australia 90 24.42S 153.17E
Sandy Creek town U.S.A. 115 43.39N 76.05W
Sandy Desert Pakistan 62 28.00N 65.00E
Sandy Hook f. U.S.A. 115 40.27N 74.00W
Sandy L. Nfld. Canada 103 49.16N 57.00W
Sandy L. Ont. Canada 102 53.00N 93.00W
Sandy Lake town Ont. Canada 102 53.00N 93.00W
Sandy Lake town Sask. Canada 101 57.00N 107.15W
San Enrique Argentina 125 35.47S 60.22W
San Esteban de Gormaz Spain 26 41.35N 3.12W
San Esteban, Isla i. Mexico 109 28.41N 112.35W
San Felipe Chile 125 32.45S 70.44W
San Felipe Colombia 122 1.55N 67.06W
San Felipe Mexico 109 31.00N 114.52W
San Felipe Venezuela 122 10.25N 68.40W
San Félix i. Chile 121 26.23S 80.05W
San Fernando Argentina 125 34.26S 58.34W
San Fernando Chile 125 34.35S 71.00W
San Fernando r. Mexico 111 24.55N 97.40W
San Fernando Phil. 59 16.39N 120.19E
San Fernando Spain 27 36.28N 6.12W
San Fernando Trinidad 122 10.16N 61.28W
San Fernando de Apure Venezuela 122 7.35N 67.15W
San Fernando de Atabapo Venezuela 122 4.03N 67.45W
Sanford r. Australia 88 27.22S 115.53E
Sanford Fla. U.S.A. 113 28.49N 81.17W
Sanford Maine U.S.A. 115 43.26N 70.46W
Sanford N.C. U.S.A. 113 35.29N 79.10W
San Francisco Argentina 124 31.29S 62.06W
San Francisco Mexico 109 30.50N 112.40W
San Francisco U.S.A. 108 37.48N 122.24W
San Francisco r. U.S.A. 109 32.59N 109.22W
San Francisco, C. Ecuador 122 0.50N 80.05W
San Francisco del Oro Mexico 109 26.52N 105.51W
San Francisco de Macorís Dom. Rep. 117 19.19N 70.15W
San Fratelo Italy 33 38.01N 14.36E
Sanga Angola 78 11.09S 15.21E
Sanga-Tolon Russian Fed. 51 61.44N 149.30E
San Gavino Monreale Italy 32 39.33N 8.48E
Sang-e Mäsheh Afghan. 62 33.08N 67.27E
Sangerhausen Germany 38 51.28N 11.17E
Sanggan He r. China 54 40.23N 115.18E
Sangha r. Congo 78 1.10S 16.47E
Sanghar Pakistan 62 26.02N 68.57E
Sangihe i. Indonesia 59 3.30N 125.30E
Sangihe, Kepulauan is. Indonesia 59 2.45N 125.20E
San Gil Colombia 122 6.35N 73.08W
San Gimignano Italy 30 43.28N 11.02E
San Giovanni in Fiore Italy 33 39.16N 16.42E
San Giovanni in Persiceto Italy 30 44.38N 11.11E
San Giovanni Rotondo Italy 31 41.42N 15.44E
San Giovanni Valdarno Italy 30 43.34N 11.32E
Sangkulirang Indonesia 58 1.00N 117.58E
Sängli India 60 16.55N 74.37E
Sangmélima Cameroon 77 2.55N 12.01E
Sangonera r. Spain 25 37.59N 1.04W
San Gottardo, Passo del pass Switz. 39 46.33N 8.34E
Sangre de Cristo Mts. U.S.A. 108 37.30N 105.15W
San Gregorio Uruguay 125 32.37S 55.40W
Sangri China 63 29.18N 92.05E
Sangro r. Italy 31 42.14N 14.32E
Sangrür India 62 30.14N 75.51E
Sangsues, Lac aux l. Canada 105 46.29N 77.57W
Sangüesa Spain 25 42.35N 1.17W
Sangzhi China 55 29.24N 110.09E
Sanhala Côte d'Ivoire 76 10.01N 6.48W
San Ignacio Bolivia 124 16.23S 60.59W
San Ignacio Mexico 109 27.27N 112.51W
San Ignacio Paraguay 124 26.52S 57.03W
San Ignacio, Laguna l. Mexico 109 26.50N 113.11W
San Ildefonso o La Granja Spain 26 40.54N 4.00W
San Isidro Argentina 125 34.29S 58.31W
Sanïyah, Hawr as l. Iraq 65 31.52N 46.50E
San Javier Argentina 125 30.40S 59.55W
San Javier Bolivia 124 16.22S 62.38W
San Javier Chile 125 35.35S 71.45W
Sanjäwi Pakistan 62 30.17N 68.21E
Sanjö Japan 57 37.37N 138.57E
San Joaquin r. U.S.A. 108 38.03N 121.50W
San Jorge, Bahía de b. Mexico 109 31.08N 113.15W
San Jorge, Golfo g. Argentina 125 46.00S 66.00W
San José Costa Rica 117 9.59N 84.04W
San José Guatemala 116 13.58N 90.50W
San José U.S.A. 109 27.32N 110.09W
San Jose U.S.A. 108 37.20N 121.53W
San José de Chiquitos Bolivia 124 17.53S 60.45W
San José de Feliciano Argentina 125 30.25S 58.45W
San José de Guanipa Venezuela 122 8.54N 64.09W
San José del Cabo town Mexico 109 23.03N 109.41W
San José del Guaviare Colombia 122 2.35N 72.38W
San José de Mayo Uruguay 125 34.20S 56.42W
San José de Ocuné Colombia 122 4.15N 70.20W
San José, Isla i. Mexico 109 25.00N 110.38W
San Juan Argentina 124 31.30S 68.30W
San Juan d. Argentina 124 31.00S 69.00W
San Juan r. Costa Rica 117 10.50N 83.40W
San Juan Dom. Rep. 117 18.40N 71.05W
San Juan Peru 122 15.20S 75.09W
San Juan Phil. 59 8.25N 126.22E

San Juan Puerto Rico 117 18.29N 66.08W
San Juan r. U.S.A. 108 37.18N 110.28W
San Juan Bautista Spain 25 39.05N 1.30E
San Juan, C. Argentina 125 54.45S 63.50W
San Juan de Guadalupe Mexico 111 24.38N 102.44W
San Juan del Norte Nicaragua 117 10.58N 83.40W
San Juan de los Morros Venezuela 122 9.53N 67.23W
San Juan del Río Durango Mexico 111 24.47N 104.27W
San Juan del Río Querétaro Mexico 116 20.23N 100.00W
San Juan, Embalse de resr. Spain 26 40.25N 4.25W
San Juan Mts. U.S.A. 108 37.35N 107.10W
San Julián Argentina 121 49.19S 67.40W
San Justo Argentina 125 30.47S 60.35W
Sankh r. India 63 22.15N 84.48E
Sankheda India 62 22.10N 73.35E
Sänkra India 63 20.18N 82.03E
Sankt Anton Austria 39 47.08N 10.16E
Sankt Gilgen Austria 39 47.46N 13.22E
Sankt Ingbert Germany 39 49.17N 7.06E
Sankt Johann im Pongau Austria 39 47.21N 13.12E
Sankt Johann in Tirol Austria 39 47.31N 12.26E
Sankt Niklaus Switz. 39 46.11N 7.48E
Sankt Paul Austria 31 46.42N 14.52E
Sankt Peter Germany 38 54.18N 8.38E
Sankt-Peterburg Russian Fed. 44 59.55N 30.25E
Sankt Veit an der Glan Austria 31 46.46N 14.21E
Sankt Wolfgang Austria 39 47.44N 13.27E
Sankuru r. Zaïre 78 4.20S 20.27E
San Lázaro, Cabo c. Mexico 109 24.50N 112.18W
San Lázaro, Sierra de mts. Mexico 109 23.20N 110.00W
San Leonardo Spain 26 41.51N 3.05W
San Leonardo in Passiria Italy 30 46.49N 11.15E
Sanliurfa Turkey 64 37.08N 38.45E
San Lorenzo Argentina 125 32.45S 60.44W
San Lorenzo mtn. Chile 125 47.37S 72.19W
San Lorenzo Ecuador 122 1.17N 78.50W
San Lorenzo r. Mexico 109 24.15N 107.25W
San Lorenzo de El Escorial Spain 26 40.35N 4.09W
San Lorenzo de la Parrilla Spain 27 39.51N 2.22W
Sanlúcar de Barrameda Spain 27 36.47N 6.21W
Sanlúcar la Mayor Spain 27 37.23N 6.12W
San Lucas Bolivia 124 20.06S 65.07W
San Lucas, Cabo c. Mexico 109 22.50N 109.55W
San Luis Argentina 125 33.20S 66.20W
San Luis d. Argentina 125 34.00S 66.00W
San Luis Cuba 117 20.13N 75.50W
San Luis Obispo U.S.A. 109 35.17N 120.40W
San Luis Potosí Mexico 116 22.10N 101.00W
San Luis Potosí d. Mexico 116 23.00N 100.00W
San Luis Río Colorado Mexico 109 32.29N 114.48W
San Luis Valley f. U.S.A. 108 37.25N 106.00W
Sanluri Italy 32 39.33N 8.54E
San Marco Spain 26 43.13N 8.17W
San Marcos U.S.A. 111 29.53N 97.57W
San Marino Europe 30 43.56N 12.25E
San Marino town San Marino 30 43.55N 12.28E
San Martin r. Bolivia 124 12.25S 64.25W
San Martin de Valdeiglesias Spain 26 40.21N 4.24W
San Mateo Spain 25 40.28N 0.11E
San Mateo U.S.A. 108 37.35N 122.19W
San Matías Bolivia 124 16.22S 58.24W
San Matías, Golfo g. Argentina 125 41.30S 64.00W
Sanmenxia China 54 34.45N 111.10E
Sanmenxia Shuiku resr. China 54 34.38N 111.05E
San Miguel r. Bolivia 124 12.25S 64.25W
San Miguel El Salvador 117 13.28N 88.10W
San Miguel del Monte Argentina 125 35.25S 58.49W
San Miguel de Tucumán Argentina 124 26.49S 65.13W
San Miguelito Panama 117 9.02N 79.30W
Sanming China 55 26.25N 117.35E
San Miniato Italy 30 43.41N 10.51E
Sannär Sudan 73 13.33N 33.38E
Sannicandro Italy 31 41.50N 15.34E
San Nicolas Argentina 125 33.20S 60.13W
Sanniquellie Liberia 76 7.24N 8.45W
Sanok Poland 37 49.35N 22.10E
San Pablo Phil. 59 13.58N 121.10E
San Pedro Buenos Aires Argentina 125 33.40S 59.41W
San Pedro Jujuy Argentina 124 24.14S 64.50W
San Pedro Côte d'Ivoire 76 4.45N 6.37W
San Pedro Dom. Rep. 117 18.30N 69.18W
San Pedro Sonora Mexico 109 27.00N 109.53W
San Pedro Paraguay 124 24.08S 57.08W
San Pedro de las Colonais Mexico 111 25.45N 102.59W
San Pedro Mártir, Sierra mts. Mexico 109 30.45N 115.30W
San Pedro, Punta c. Costa Rica 117 8.38N 83.45W
San Pedro, Sierra de mts. Spain 27 39.20N 6.40W
San Pedro Sula Honduras 117 15.26N 88.01W
San Pellegrino Terme Italy 30 45.50N 9.40E
San Pietro i. Italy 28 39.09N 8.16E
Sanquhar U.K. 14 55.22N 3.56W
San Quintín Mexico 109 30.28N 115.58W
San Rafael U.S.A. 108 37.59N 122.31W
San Raphael Argentina 125 34.40S 68.21W
San Remo Italy 30 43.49N 7.46E
San Roque Spain 27 36.13N 5.24W
San Salvador Argentina 125 31.37S 58.30W
San Salvador i. Bahamas 117 24.00N 74.32W
San Salvador El Salvador 117 13.40N 89.10W
San Salvador de Jujuy Argentina 124 24.10S 65.20W
Sansebastián Argentina 125 53.15S 68.30W
San Sebastián Spain 26 43.19N 1.59W
Sansepolcro Italy 30 43.34N 12.08E
San Severino Marche Italy 30 43.13N 13.10E
San Severo Italy 31 41.41N 15.23E
Sanshui China 55 23.09N 112.52E
San Simon U.S.A. 109 32.16N 109.14W
Sanski Most Bosnia-Herzegovina 31 44.46N 16.40E
Santa r. Peru 122 9.00S 78.35W
Santa Amalia Spain 26 39.01N 6.01W
Santa Ana Argentina 124 27.20S 65.35W
Santa Ana Bolivia 124 13.45S 65.35W

Santa Ana El Salvador 117 14.00N 89.31W
Santa Ana Mexico 109 30.33N 111.07W
Santa Ana U.S.A. 109 33.44N 117.54W
Santa Bárbara Mexico 109 26.48N 105.49W
Santa Barbara U.S.A. 109 34.25N 119.42W
Santa Catalina de Armara Spain 26 43.02N 8.49W
Santa Catarina d. Brazil 126 27.00S 52.00W
Santa Catarina Mexico 111 25.41N 100.28W
Santa Cesarea Terme Italy 33 40.02N 18.29E
Santa Clara Cuba 117 22.25N 79.58W
Santa Clara Calif. U.S.A. 108 37.21N 121.57W
Santa Clara Utah U.S.A. 108 37.08N 113.39W
Santa Clotilde Peru 122 2.25S 73.35W
Santa Coloma de Farners Spain 25 41.52N 2.40E
Santa Comba Dão Portugal 26 40.24N 8.08W
Santa Cruz d. Argentina 125 48.00S 69.30W
Santa Cruz r. Argentina 125 50.03S 68.35W
Santa Cruz d. Bolivia 124 17.45S 62.00W
Santa Cruz Madeira Is. 127 17.45S 63.14W
Santa Cruz U.S.A. 108 36.58N 122.08W
Santa Cruz i. U.S.A. 109 34.01N 119.45W
Santa Cruz de la Zarza Spain 27 39.58N 3.10W
Santa Cruz de Mudela Spain 26 38.38N 3.28W
Santa Cruz de Tenerife Canary Is. 74 28.28N 16.15W
Santa Cruz Is. Solomon Is. 84 10.30S 166.00E
Santa Domingo Mexico 109 25.32N 112.02W
Santa Elena Argentina 125 31.00S 59.50W
Santa Elena I.S.A.1 211.26.46N 98.30W
Santa Elena, C. Costa Rica 117 10.54N 85.56W
Santa Eufemia Spain 26 38.36N 4.52W
Santa Eugenia Spain 26 42.33N 9.00W
Santa Eulalia Spain 25 40.34N 1.19W
Santa Eulalia del Río Spain 25 38.59N 1.31E
Santa Fé Argentina 125 31.40S 60.40W
Santa Fé d. Argentina 124 30.00S 61.00W
Santa Fe Spain 27 37.11N 3.43W
Santa Fe U.S.A. 109 35.42N 106.57W
Santa Filomena Brazil 123 9.07S 45.56W
Sant'Agata di Militello Italy 33 38.04N 14.38E
Santai China 55 31.10N 105.02E
Santa Inés, Isla i. Chile 125 53.40S 73.00W
Santa Isabel Argentina 125 36.15S 66.55W
Santa Isabel do Morro Brazil 123 11.36S 50.37W
Säntalpur India 62 23.45N 71.10E
Santa Lucía Uruguay 125 34.27S 56.24W
Santa Lucía r. Uruguay 125 34.48S 56.22W
Santa Lucia Range mts. U.S.A. 108 36.00N 121.20W
Santa Luzia Portugal 26 37.44N 8.24W
Santa Margarita, Isla de i. Mexico 109 24.25N 111.50W
Santa Margarita, Sierra de mts. Mexico 109 30.00N 110.00W
Santa Margherita Ligure Italy 30 44.20N 9.12E
Santa María Brazil 126 29.40S 53.47W
Santa María U.S.A. 109 34.57N 120.26W
Santa Maria, Cabo de c. Portugal 27 36.58N 7.54W
Santa Maria di Leuca, Capo c. Italy 33 39.47N 18.22E
Santa Maria, Laguna de l. Mexico 109 31.07N 107.17W
Santa María la Real de Nieva Spain 26 41.04N 4.24W
Santa María Madalena Brazil 126 21.58S 42.02W
Santa-Maria-Siché France 30 41.52N 8.59E
Santa Marinella Italy 30 42.02N 11.51E
Santa Marta Colombia 122 11.18N 74.10W
Santa Marta, Sierra Nevada de mts. Colombia 122 11.20N 73.00W
Santa Monica U.S.A. 109 34.01N 118.30W
Santana Madeira Is. 127 32.48N 16.54W
Santana do Livramento Brazil 125 30.53S 55.31W
Santander Colombia 122 3.00N 76.25W
Santander Spain 26 43.28N 3.48W
Sant'Angelo dei Lombardi Italy 33 40.56N 15.11E
Santanoni Pk. U.S.A. 115 44.08N 74.11W
Sant'Antioco Italy 32 39.02N 8.30E
Sant'Antioco, Isola di i. Italy 32 39.00N 8.25E
Santañy Spain 25 39.22N 3.07E
Santa Pola, Cabo de c. Spain 25 38.12N 0.31W
Sant'Arcangelo Italy 30 43.15N 16.17E
Santarém Brazil 123 2.26S 54.41W
Santarém Portugal 27 39.14N 8.41W
Santarém d. Portugal 27 39.10N 8.40W
Santa Rosa Argentina 125 36.00S 64.40W
Santa Rosa Bolivia 122 10.36S 67.25W
Santa Rosa Brazil 126 27.52S 54.29W
Santa Rosa Honduras 117 14.47N 88.46W
Santa Rosa Calif. U.S.A. 108 38.26N 122.34W
Santa Rosa i. U.S.A. 109 33.58N 120.06W
Santa Rosa N.Mex. U.S.A. 109 34.57N 104.41W
Santa Rosa de Cabal Colombia 122 4.52N 75.37W
Santa Rosalía Mexico 109 27.19N 112.17W
Santa Rosa, Mt. Guam 84 13.32N 144.55E
Santa Rosa Range mts. U.S.A. 108 41.00N 117.40W
Santa Teresa Mexico 111 25.19N 97.50W
Santa Teresa, Embalse de resr. Spain 26 40.40N 5.37W
Santa Teresa Gallura Italy 32 41.15N 9.12E
Santa Vitória do Palmar Brazil 126 33.31S 53.21W
Sant Boi de Llobregat Spain 25 41.21N 2.03E
Sant Carles de la Rápita Spain 25 40.37N 0.36E
San Telmo Mexico 109 31.00N 116.06W
Sant'Eufemia, Golfo di g. Italy 33 38.50N 16.00E
Sant Feliu de Guíxols Spain 25 41.47N 3.02E
Santhià Italy 30 45.22N 8.10E
Santiago Chile 125 33.27S 70.40W
Santiago Dom. Rep. 117 19.30N 70.42W
Santiago Panama 117 8.08N 80.59W
Santiago r. Peru 122 4.30S 77.48W
Santiago de Compostela Spain 26 42.53N 8.33W
Santiago de Cuba Cuba 117 20.00N 75.49W
Santiago del Estero Argentina 124 27.50S 64.15W
Santiago del Estero d. Argentina 124 27.40S 63.30W
Santiago do Cacém Portugal 27 38.01N 8.42W
Santiago Vázquez Uruguay 125 34.48S 56.21W
Säntipur India 63 23.15N 88.26E
Säntis mtn. Switz. 39 47.15N 9.21E
Santisteban del Puerto Spain 26 38.15N 3.12W

Santo Amaro Brazil 123 12.35S 38.41W
Santo André Brazil 126 23.39S 46.29W
Santo Angelo Brazil 126 28.18S 54.16W
Santo Antônio do Içá Brazil 122 3.05S 67.57W
Santo Domingo Dom. Rep. 117 18.30N 69.57W
Santo Domingo de la Calzada Spain 26 42.26N 2.57W
Santo Domingo Pueblo U.S.A. 109 35.31N 106.22W
Santolea, Embalse de resr. Spain 25 40.47N 0.19W
Santoña Spain 26 43.27N 3.27W
Santos Brazil 126 23.56S 46.22W
Santos Dumont Brazil 126 21.30S 43.34W
Santo Tirso Portugal 26 41.21N 8.28W
Santo Tomás Peru 122 14.34S 72.30W
Santo Tomé Argentina 124 28.31S 56.03W
Santpoort Neth. 16 52.27N 4.38E
Şānūr Jordan 67 32.21N 35.15E
San Valentin, Cerro mtn. Chile 125 46.40S 73.25W
San Vicente El Salvador 117 13.38N 88.42W
San Vicente de Alcántara Spain 27 39.21N 7.08W
San Vicente de la Barquera Spain 26 43.23N 4.24W
San Vincenzo Italy 30 43.06N 10.32E
San Vito Italy 32 39.27N 9.32E
San Vito al Tagliamento Italy 30 45.54N 12.52E
San Vito, Capo c. Italy 32 38.11N 12.43E
San Vito del Normanni Italy 33 40.39N 17.42E
Sanya China 55 18.19N 109.32E
Sanyuan China 54 34.30N 108.54E
Sanza Pombo Angola 78 7.20S 16.12E
São Borja Brazil 126 28.35S 56.01W
São Bras de Alportel Portugal 27 37.08N 7.58W
São Caetano do Sul Brazil 126 23.36S 46.34W
São Carlos Brazil 126 22.01S 47.54W
São Domingos Guinea Bissau 76 12.22N 16.08W
São Francisco r. Brazil 123 10.20S 36.20W
São Francisco do Sol Brazil 126 26.17S 48.39W
São Gabriel Brazil 126 30.20S 54.19W
São Gonçalo do Sapucaí Brazil 126 21.54S 45.35W
Sao Hill town Tanzania 79 8.21S 35.10E
São João da Boa Vista Brazil 126 21.59S 46.45W
São João da Madeira Portugal 26 40.54N 8.30W
São João del Rei Brazil 126 21.08S 44.15W
São João do Piauí Brazil 123 8.21S 42.15W
São Joaquim da Barra Brazil 126 20.36S 47.51W
São José do Calçado Brazil 126 21.01S 41.37W
São José do Rio Prêto Brazil 126 20.50S 49.20W
São José dos Campos Brazil 126 23.07S 45.52W
São Leopoldo Brazil 126 29.46S 51.09W
São Lourenço Brazil 126 22.08S 45.05W
São Luís Brazil 123 2.34S 44.16W
São Manuel Brazil 126 22.00S 48.35W
São Manuel r. see Teles Pires r. Brazil 123
São Miguel d'Oeste Brazil 126 26.45S 53.34W
Saona i. Dom. Rep. 117 18.09N 68.42W
Saône r. France 21 45.44N 4.50E
Saône-et-Loire d. France 19 46.42N 4.45E
Saoner India 63 21.23N 78.54E
São Paulo Brazil 126 23.33S 46.39W
São Paulo d. Brazil 126 22.05S 48.00W
São Paulo de Olivença Brazil 122 3.34S 68.55W
São Pedro do Sul Portugal 26 40.45N 8.04W
São Roque Brazil 126 23.31S 47.09W
São Roque, Cabo de c. Brazil 121 5.00S 35.00W
São Sebastião Brazil 126 23.48S 45.26W
São Sebastião do Paraíso Brazil 126 20.54S 46.59W
São Sebastião, Ilha de i. Brazil 126 23.53S 45.17W
São Tiago Brazil 126 20.54S 44.30W
São Tomé & Príncipe Africa 70 0.19N 6.05E
Saoura, Oued wadi Algeria 74 28.48N 0.50W
São Vicente Brazil 126 23.57S 46.23W
São Vicente, Cabo de c. Portugal 27 37.01N 8.59W
São Vicente de Minas Brazil 126 21.40S 44.26W
Sápai Greece 34 41.02N 25.41E
Sapé Brazil 123 7.06S 35.13W
Sapele Nigeria 77 5.53N 5.41E
Sapelo I. U.S.A. 113 31.28N 81.15W
Sapporo Japan 57 43.05N 141.21E
Sapri Italy 33 40.04N 15.38E
Sapt Kosi r. Nepal 63 26.30N 86.55E
Sapu Angola 78 12.28S 19.26E
Sapulpa U.S.A. 111 36.00N 96.06W
Saqin Sum China 54 42.06N 111.03E
Saqqärah Egypt 66 29.51N 31.13E
Saqqez Iran 65 36.14N 46.15E
Saräb Iran 65 37.56N 47.35E
Saräbïyüm Egypt 66 30.23N 32.17E
Sara Buri Thailand 56 14.30N 100.59E
Saragossa see Zaragoza Spain 25
Saräi Naurang Pakistan 62 32.50N 70.47E
Sarajevo Bosnia-Herzegovina 31 43.52N 18.26E
Saranac L. U.S.A. 105 44.20N 74.10W
Saranac Lake town U.S.A. 105 44.20N 74.08W
Sarandë Albania 34 39.52N 20.00E
Sarandí del Yi Uruguay 125 33.21S 55.38W
Sarandí Grande Uruguay 125 33.44S 56.20W
Särangarh India 63 21.36N 83.05E
Särangpur India 62 23.34N 76.28E
Saranley Somali Rep. 73 2.28N 42.08E
Saranpaul Russian Fed. 44 64.16N 60.58E
Saransk Russian Fed. 44 54.12N 45.10E
Sarapul Russian Fed. 44 56.30N 53.49E
Sarar Plain Somali Rep. 71 9.35N 46.15E
Sarasota U.S.A. 113 27.20N 82.32W
Sarata Ukraine 37 46.00N 29.40E
Saratoga U.S.A. 108 37.16N 122.02W
Saratoga Springs U.S.A. 115 43.05N 73.47W
Saratov Russian Fed. 45 51.30N 45.55E
Saravan Laos 56 15.43N 106.24E
Sarawak d. Malaysia 58 2.00N 113.00E
Sarayakpinar Turkey 34 41.46N 26.29E
Saraychik Kazakhstan 45 47.29N 51.42E
Sarbäz Iran 65 26.39N 61.20E
Sárbogárd Hungary 31 46.53N 18.38E
Sarcelles France 19 49.00N 2.23E
Sardär Chäh Pakistan 62 27.58N 64.50E
Sardärpur India 62 22.39N 74.59E
Sardärshahr India 62 28.26N 74.29E
Sardegna d. Italy 32 40.15N 9.00E
Sardegna i. Italy 32 40.00N 9.00E

Sardinia *i. see* Sardegna *i.* Italy **32**
Sarek *mtn.* Sweden **40** 67.25N 17.46E
Sareks Nat. Park Sweden **40** 67.15N 17.30E
Sargasso Sea Atlantic Oc. **127** 28.00N 60.00W
Sargodha Pakistan **60** 32.01N 72.40E
Sarh Chad **77** 9.08N 18.22E
Sarhro, Jbel *mts.* Morocco **74** 31.00N 5.55W
Sarī Iran **65** 36.33N 53.06E
Saría *i.* Greece **35** 35.50N 27.15E
Sarikamiş Turkey **64** 40.19N 42.35E
Sarikei Malaysia **58** 2.07N 111.31E
Sarina Australia **90** 21.26S 149.13E
Sariñena Spain **25** 41.48N 0.10W
Sarita U.S.A. **111** 37.13N 97.47W
Sark *i.* Channel Is. Europe **13** 49.26N 2.22W
Sarlat France **20** 44.53N 1.13E
Sărmaşu Romania **37** 46.46N 24.11E
Sármellék Hungary **31** 46.44N 17.10E
Sarmi Indonesia **59** 1.51S 138.45E
Sarmiento Argentina **125** 45.35S 69.05W
Särna Sweden **41** 61.41N 13.08E
Sarnen Switz. **39** 46.54N 8.15E
Sarnia Canada **104** 42.58N 82.23W
Sarno Italy **33** 40.49N 14.37E
Sarny Ukraine **37** 51.21N 26.31E
Saronikós Kólpos *g.* Greece **35** 37.54N 23.12E
Saronno Italy **30** 45.38N 9.02E
Saros Körfezi *g.* Turkey **34** 40.30N 26.20E
Sárospatak Hungary **37** 48.19N 21.34E
Šar Planina *mts.* Macedonia/Yugo. **34** 42.10N 21.00E
Sarpsborg Norway **42** 59.17N 11.07E
Sarralbe France **19** 49.00N 7.01E
Sarre *r. see* Saar *r.* France **19**
Sarrebourg France **19** 48.44N 7.03E
Sarreguemines France **19** 49.06N 7.03E
Sarre-Union France **19** 48.56N 7.05E
Sarria Spain **26** 42.47N 7.24W
Sarro Mali **76** 13.40N 5.05W
Sartène France **21** 41.36N 8.59E
Sarthe *d.* France **18** 48.00N 0.05E
Sarthe *r.* France **18** 47.30N 0.32W
Sartilly France **18** 48.45N 1.27W
Sartynya Russian Fed. **50** 63.22N 63.11E
Sárvár Hungary **36** 47.15N 16.57E
Sárvíz *r.* Hungary **31** 46.24N 18.41E
Saryshagan Kazakhstan **52** 46.08N 73.32E
Sarzana Italy **30** 44.07N 9.58E
Sarzeau France **18** 47.32N 2.46W
Sasa Israel **67** 33.02N 35.24E
Sasabeneh Ethiopia **71** 7.55N 43.39E
Sasarām India **63** 24.57N 84.02E
Sasebo Japan **57** 33.10N 129.42E
Saseginaga, L. Canada **104** 47.06N 78.35W
Saser *mtn.* Jammu & Kashmir **63** 34.50N 77.50E
Saskatchewan *d.* Canada **101** 55.00N 106.00W
Saskatchewan *r.* Canada **101** 53.12N 99.16W
Saskatoon Canada **101** 52.07N 106.38W
Sasovo Russian Fed. **44** 54.21N 41.58E
Sassandra Côte d'Ivoire **76** 4.58N 6.08W
Sassandra *r.* Côte d'Ivoire **76** 5.00N 6.04W
Sassari Italy **32** 40.44N 8.33E
Sassnitz Germany **38** 54.31N 13.38E
Sassoferrato Italy **30** 43.26N 12.51E
Sasso Marconi Italy **30** 44.24N 11.15E
Sassuolo Italy **30** 44.33N 10.47E
Sastown Liberia **76** 4.44N 8.01W
Sasyk, Ozero *l.* Ukraine **37** 45.38N 29.38E
Satadougou Mali **76** 12.30N 11.30W
Satäna India **62** 20.36N 74.12E
Satanta U.S.A. **111** 37.26N 100.59W
Sátão Portugal **26** 40.44N 7.44W
Sätära India **60** 17.43N 74.05E
Satīt *r.* Sudan **72** 14.20N 35.50E
Satkänia Bangla. **63** 22.04N 92.03E
Satna India **63** 24.35N 80.50E
Sátoraljaújhely Hungary **37** 48.24N 21.39E
Sätpura Range *mts.* India **62** 21.30N 76.00E
Satu Mare Romania **37** 47.48N 22.52E
Satun Thailand **56** 6.38N 100.05E
Sauce Argentina **125** 30.05S 58.45W
Sauda Norway **42** 59.39N 6.20E
Saudi Arabia Asia **64** 26.00N 44.00E
Sauerland *f.* Germany **38** 51.23N 8.00E
Saugeen *r.* Canada **104** 44.30N 81.22W
Saujon France **20** 45.40N 0.56W
Sauk Centre U.S.A. **110** 45.44N 94.57W
Saulgau Germany **39** 48.01N 9.30E
Saulieu France **19** 47.16N 4.14E
Sault-de-Vaucluse France **21** 44.05N 5.25E
Sault Sainte Marie Canada **104** 46.31N 84.20W
Sault Sainte Marie U.S.A. **104** 46.30N 84.21W
Saumarez Reef Australia **90** 21.50S 153.40E
Saumur France **18** 47.16N 0.05W
Saurimo Angola **78** 9.38S 20.20E
Sausar India **63** 21.42N 78.52E
Sauveterre-de-Béarn France **20** 43.29N 0.56W
Sauveterre-en-Guyenne France **20** 44.42N 0.05W
Sava *r.* Europe **31** 44.50N 20.26E
Sava Italy **33** 40.24N 17.34E
Savage U.S.A. **108** 47.27N 104.21W
Savai'i *i.* W. Samoa **84** 13.36S 172.27W
Savalou Benin **77** 7.55N 1.59E
Savanna U.S.A. **110** 42.06N 90.07W
Savannah Ga. U.S.A. **113** 32.04N 81.05W
Savannah *r.* U.S.A. **113** 32.02N 80.53W
Savannah Tenn. U.S.A. **111** 35.14N 88.14W
Savannakhét Laos **56** 16.34N 104.48E
Savant L. Canada **102** 50.48N 90.20W
Savant Lake Canada **102** 50.20N 90.40W
Savé Benin **77** 8.04N 2.37E
Save *r.* France **20** 43.47N 1.17E
Save *r.* Mozambique **81** 20.59S 35.02E
Save *r.* Zimbabwe **81** 21.16S 32.20E
Säveh Iran **65** 35.00N 50.25E
Savelugu Ghana **76** 9.39N 0.48W
Savenay France **18** 47.22N 1.57W

Saverdun France **20** 43.14N 1.35E
Saverne France **19** 48.44N 7.22E
Savigliano Italy **30** 44.38N 7.40E
Savigny-sur-Braye France **18** 47.53N 0.49E
Savoie *d.* France **21** 45.30N 6.25E
Savona Italy **30** 44.17N 8.30E
Savonlinna Finland **44** 61.52N 28.51E
Savoonga U.S.A. **98** 63.42N 170.27W
Sawai Mädhopur India **62** 25.59N 76.22E
Sawäkin Sudan **72** 19.07N 37.20E
Sawatch Range *mts.* U.S.A. **110** 39.10N 106.25W
Sawbridgeworth U.K. **13** 51.50N 0.09W
Sawdã', Jabal as *hills* Libya **75** 28.40N 15.00E
Sawdä', Qurnat as *mtn.* Lebanon **66** 34.17N 36.04E
Sawdirī Sudan **72** 14.25N 29.05E
Sawfajjīn, Wādī Libya **75** 31.54N 15.07E
Sawhāj Egypt **64** 26.33N 31.42E
Sawqirah, Ghubbat *b.* Oman **71** 18.35N 57.00E
Sawston U.K. **13** 52.07N 0.11E
Sawtell Australia **93** 30.21S 153.05E
Sawtooth Mts. U.S.A. **110** 48.10N 114.35W
Sawu *i.* Indonesia **59** 10.30S 121.50E
Sawu, Laut *sea* Pacific Oc. **59** 9.30S 122.30E
Saxmundham U.K. **13** 52.13N 1.29E
Saxon Switz. **39** 46.09N 7.11E
Saxton U.S.A. **114** 40.13N 78.15W
Say Mali **76** 13.50N 4.57W
Say Niger **77** 13.08N 2.22E
Sayama Japan **57** 35.51N 139.24E
Şaydā Lebanon **66** 33.32N 35.22E
Sayers Lake Australia **92** 32.46S 143.20E
Saylün *site* Jordan **67** 32.03N 35.17E
Saynshand Mongolia **54** 44.58N 110.12E
Saynshand Mongolia **54** 43.33N 102.13E
Sayre U.S.A. **115** 41.59N 76.32W
Sayula Mexico **116** 19.52N 103.36W
Sayville U.S.A. **115** 40.44N 73.05W
Sázava *r.* Czech Republic **36** 49.53N 14.21E
Sazliyka *r.* Bulgaria **34** 42.15N 25.50E
Sbaa Algeria **74** 28.13N 0.10W
Scaër France **18** 48.02N 3.42W
Scafell Pike *mtn.* U.K. **12** 54.27N 3.12W
Scalea Italy **33** 39.49N 15.48E
Scalloway U.K. **14** 60.08N 1.17W
Scammon Bay *town* U.S.A. **98** 61.50N 165.35W
Scansano Italy **30** 42.41N 11.20E
Scapa Flow *str.* U.K. **14** 58.53N 3.05W
Scarborough Canada **104** 43.44N 79.16W
Scarborough Tobago **122** 11.11N 60.45W
Scarborough U.K. **12** 54.17N 0.24W
Scenic U.S.A. **108** 43.46N 102.32W
Schaalsee *l.* Germany **38** 53.35N 10.57E
Schaerbeek Belgium **16** 50.54N 4.20E
Schaffhausen Switz. **39** 47.42N 8.38E
Schaffhausen *d.* Switz. **39** 47.40N 8.36E
Schagen Neth. **16** 52.47N 4.47E
Schärding Austria **39** 48.27N 13.26E
Schefferville Canada **99** 54.50N 67.00W
Scheinfeld Germany **39** 49.40N 10.27E
Schelde *r.* Belgium **16** 51.13N 4.25E
Schell Creek Range *mts.* U.S.A. **108** 39.10N 114.40W
Schenectady U.S.A. **115** 42.47N 73.53W
Schesslitz Germany **39** 49.59N 11.01E
Scheveningen Neth. **16** 52.07N 4.16E
Schiedam Neth. **16** 51.55N 4.25E
Schiermonnikoog *i.* Neth. **16** 53.28N 6.15E
Schiltigheim France **19** 48.36N 7.45E
Schio Italy **30** 45.43N 11.21E
Schkeuditz Germany **38** 51.24N 12.13E
Schladming Austria **39** 47.23N 13.41E
Schleiden Germany **38** 50.31N 6.28E
Schleswig Germany **38** 54.31N 9.33E
Schleswig-Holstein *d.* Germany **38** 54.39N 9.30E
Schleusingen Germany **39** 50.31N 10.45E
Schlitz Germany **38** 50.40N 9.33E
Schlüchtern Germany **39** 50.20N 9.31E
Schmalkalden Germany **38** 50.43N 10.26E
Schmidmühlen Germany **39** 49.16N 11.56E
Schmölln Germany **38** 50.53N 12.20E
Schmutter *r.* Germany **39** 48.43N 10.47E
Schneeberg Germany **38** 50.03N 11.51E
Schneverdingen Germany **38** 53.07N 9.47E
Schoharie U.S.A. **115** 42.40N 74.19W
Schoharie Creek *r.* U.S.A. **115** 42.57N 74.18W
Schönebeck Germany **38** 52.01N 11.45E
Schongau Germany **39** 47.49N 10.54E
Schopfheim Germany **39** 47.39N 7.49E
Schorndorf Germany **39** 48.48N 9.31E
Schouten, Kepulauan *is.* Indonesia **59** 0.45S 135.50E
Schouwen *i.* Neth. **16** 51.42N 3.45E
Schramberg Germany **39** 48.13N 8.23E
Schreiber Canada **102** 48.45N 87.20W
Schroon Lake *town* U.S.A. **105** 43.47N 73.46W
Schuler Canada **101** 50.22N 110.05W
Schuylkill *r.* U.S.A. **115** 39.53N 75.12W
Schuylerville U.S.A. **115** 43.06N 73.35W
Schuylkill Haven U.S.A. **115** 40.38N 76.12W
Schwabach Germany **39** 49.20N 11.01E
Schwaben *f.* Germany **39** 48.10N 10.50E
Schwäbische Alb *mts.* Germany **39** 48.30N 9.38E
Schwäbisch Gmünd Germany **39** 48.48N 9.47E
Schwäbisch Hall Germany **39** 49.07N 9.44E
Schwabmünchen Germany **39** 48.11N 10.45E
Schwandorf Germany **39** 49.20N 12.08E
Schwaner, Pegunungan *mts.* Indonesia **58** 0.45S 113.20E
Schwarze Elster *r.* Germany **38** 51.49N 12.51E
Schwarzenburg Switz. **39** 46.49N 7.21E
Schwarzrand *mts.* Namibia **80** 25.40S 16.53E
Schwarzwald *f.* Germany **36** 48.00N 7.45E
Schwaz Austria **39** 47.20N 11.42E
Schwedt Germany **38** 53.03N 14.17E
Schweich Germany **39** 49.49N 6.45E
Schweinfurt Germany **39** 50.03N 10.14E

Schweitzingen Germany **39** 49.23N 8.34E
Schwelm Germany **38** 51.17N 7.17E
Schwenningen Germany **39** 48.04N 8.32E
Schwerin Germany **38** 53.38N 11.25E
Schweriner See *l.* Germany **38** 53.45N 11.28E
Schwyz Switz. **39** 47.02N 8.40E
Schwyz *d.* Switz. **39** 47.00N 8.45E
Schyan Canada **105** 46.10N 77.00W
Sciacca Italy **32** 37.30N 13.06E
Scicli Italy **33** 36.47N 14.43E
Scilla Italy **33** 38.15N 15.44E
Scilly, Isles of U.K. **13** 49.55N 6.20W
Ščit *mtn.* Bosnia-Herzegovina **31** 44.02N 17.47E
Scituate U.S.A. **115** 42.12N 70.44W
Scobey U.S.A. **108** 48.47N 105.25W
Scone Australia **93** 32.01S 150.53E
Scordia Italy **33** 37.18N 14.51E
Scorno, Punta di *c.* Italy **32** 41.07N 8.19E
Scotia Calif. U.S.A. **108** 40.26N 123.31W
Scotia N.Y. U.S.A. **115** 42.47N 73.59W
Scotia Ridge *f.* Atlantic Oc. **127** 60.00S 35.00W
Scotia Sea Atlantic Oc. **127** 57.00S 45.00W
Scotland U.K. **14** 55.30N 4.00W
Scotsbluff U.S.A. **110** 41.52N 103.40W
Scotstown Canada **105** 45.32N 71.17W
Scott Canada **105** 46.30N 71.04W
Scottburgh R.S.A. **80** 30.17S 30.45E
Scott City U.S.A. **110** 38.29N 100.54W
Scottdale U.S.A. **114** 40.06N 79.35W
Scott Is. Canada **100** 50.48N 128.40W
Scott L. Canada **101** 59.55N 106.18W
Scott Reef Australia **88** 14.00S 121.50E
Scottsbluff U.S.A. **108** 41.52N 103.40W
Scottsboro U.S.A. **111** 34.40N 86.02W
Scottsdale Australia **91** 41.09S 147.31E
Scottsdale U.S.A. **109** 33.30N 111.56W
Scottsville U.S.A. **111** 36.45N 86.11W
Scranton U.S.A. **115** 41.24N 75.40W
Scugog, L. Canada **104** 44.10N 78.51W
Scunthorpe U.K. **12** 53.35N 0.38W
Scuol Switz. **39** 46.48N 10.18E
Scutari, L. Yugo./Albania **34** 42.17N 19.17E
Seabrook, L. Australia **89** 30.56S 119.40E
Seaford U.S.A. **115** 38.39N 75.37W
Seaforth Canada **104** 43.33N 81.24W
Seagroves U.S.A. **111** 32.57N 102.34W
Seahouses U.K. **12** 55.35N 1.38W
Sea Isle City U.S.A. **115** 39.09N 74.42W
Seal *r.* Canada **101** 59.04N 94.48W
Sea Lake *town* Australia **92** 35.31S 142.54E
Seal Bight Canada **103** 52.27N 55.40W
Searchlight U.S.A. **109** 35.28N 114.55W
Seascale U.K. **12** 54.24N 3.29W
Seaside Calif. U.S.A. **108** 36.37N 121.50W
Seaside Oreg. U.S.A. **108** 46.02N 123.55W
Seaton U.K. **13** 50.43N 3.05W
Seattle U.S.A. **108** 47.36N 122.20W
Seaview Range *mts.* Australia **90** 18.56S 146.00E
Sebastian U.S.A. **113** 27.50N 80.29W
Sebastián Vizcaíno, Bahía *b.* Mexico **109** 28.00N 114.30W
Sebba Burkina **76** 13.27N 0.33E
Sebeş Romania **37** 45.58N 23.34E
Sebewaing U.S.A. **104** 43.44N 83.27W
Sebidiro P.N.G. **59** 9.00S 142.15E
Sebinkarahisar Turkey **64** 40.19N 38.25E
Sebnitz Germany **38** 50.58N 14.16E
Sebou, Oued *r.* Morocco **74** 34.15N 6.40W
Sebring U.S.A. **113** 27.30N 81.28W
Sechura, Desierto de *des.* Peru **122** 6.00S 80.30W
Seclin France **16** 50.34N 3.01E
Sêda *r.* Portugal **27** 38.55N 8.01W
Sedalia U.S.A. **110** 38.42N 93.14W
Sedan France **19** 49.42N 4.57E
Sedan U.S.A. **111** 37.08N 96.11W
Sedano Spain **26** 42.43N 3.45W
Seddon New Zealand **85** 41.40S 174.04E
Séderon France **21** 44.12N 5.32E
Sederot Israel **67** 31.31N 34.35E
Sedgewick Canada **101** 52.46N 111.41W
Sédhiou Senegal **76** 12.44N 15.30W
Sedini Italy **32** 40.50N 8.49E
Sedom Israel **66** 31.04N 35.23E
Sedot Yam Israel **67** 32.29N 34.53E
Seefeld Austria **39** 47.20N 11.11E
Seehausen Germany **38** 52.53N 11.45E
Seeheim Namibia **80** 26.50S 17.45E
Seeleys Bay *town* Canada **105** 44.29N 76.14W
Seelow Germany **38** 52.32N 14.23E
Sées France **18** 48.36N 0.10E
Seesen Germany **38** 51.53N 10.10E
Seevetal Germany **38** 53.26N 9.58E
Sefrou Morocco **74** 33.50N 4.50W
Segbwema Sierra Leone **76** 8.00N 11.00W
Segesta *site* Italy **33** 37.56N 12.50E
Seggueur, Oued es *wadi* Algeria **75** 31.44N 2.18E
Segni Italy **30** 41.41N 13.01E
Ségou Mali **76** 13.28N 6.18W
Ségou *d.* Mali **76** 13.55N 6.20W
Segovia U.S.A. **109** 40.57N 4.07W
Segovia *d.* Spain **26** 41.10N 4.00W
Segozero, Ozero *l.* Russian Fed. **44** 63.15N 33.40E
Segré France **18** 47.41N 0.53W
Segre *r.* Spain **25** 40.48N 0.43E
Séguédine Niger **77** 20.12N 12.59E
Séguéla Côte d'Ivoire **76** 7.58N 6.44W
Seguin U.S.A. **111** 29.34N 97.58W
Segura Portugal **27** 39.50N 6.59W
Segura *r.* Spain **25** 38.06N 0.38W
Segura, Sierra de *mts.* Spain **27** 38.15N 2.30W
Sehore India **62** 23.12N 77.05E
Sehwän Pakistan **62** 26.26N 67.52E
Seia Portugal **26** 40.25N 7.42W
Seiches-sur-le-Loir France **18** 47.35N 0.22W
Seiland *i.* Norway **40** 70.25N 23.10E
Seilhac France **20** 45.22N 1.42E
Seille *r.* France **19** 49.07N 6.11E
Seinäjoki Finland **40** 62.47N 22.50E

Seine *r.* France **18** 49.26N 0.26E
Seine, Baie de la *b.* France **18** 49.25N 0.15E
Seine-et-Marne *d.* France **19** 48.30N 3.00E
Seine-Maritime *d.* France **19** 49.45N 1.00E
Seixal Portugal **27** 38.38N 9.06W
Sejerö *i.* Denmark **42** 55.53N 11.09E
Sekayu Indonesia **58** 2.58S 103.58E
Seki Japan **57** 35.29N 136.55E
Sekoma Botswana **80** 24.41S 23.50E
Sekondi-Takoradi Ghana **76** 4.57N 1.44W
Sek'ot'a Ethiopia **71** 12.38N 39.03E
Seküheh Iran **65** 30.45N 61.29E
Selaru *i.* Indonesia **90** 8.09S 131.00E
Selatan Natuna, Kepulauan *is.* Indonesia **58** 3.00N 108.50E
Selatan, Tanjung *c.* Indonesia **58** 4.20S 114.45E
Selayar *i.* Indonesia **59** 6.07S 120.28E
Selb Germany **39** 50.10N 12.08E
Selbu Norway **40** 63.14N 11.03E
Selby U.K. **12** 53.47N 1.05W
Selbyville U.S.A. **115** 38.28N 75.13W
Seldovia U.S.A. **98** 59.27N 151.43W
Sele *r.* Italy **33** 40.27N 14.58E
Selenga *r.* Russian Fed. **52** 52.20N 106.20E
Selenge Mörön *r. see* Selenga Mongolia **52**
Selenicë Albania **34** 40.33N 19.39E
Sélestat France **19** 48.16N 7.27E
Seligman U.S.A. **109** 35.20N 112.53W
Selimiye Turkey **35** 37.24N 27.40E
Sélingue, Lac de *l.* Mali **76** 11.25N 8.15W
Selinoús Greece **35** 37.35N 21.37E
Selinsgrove U.S.A. **114** 40.48N 76.52W
Selinunte *site* Italy **32** 37.35N 12.50E
Seljord Norway **42** 59.29N 8.37E
Selkirk Man. Canada **101** 50.09N 96.52W
Selkirk Ont. Canada **104** 42.49N 79.56W
Selkirk U.K. **14** 55.33N 2.51W
Selkirk Mts. Canada **100** 50.02N 116.20W
Selles-sur-Cher France **19** 47.16N 1.33E
Sells U.S.A. **109** 31.55N 111.53W
Selma Ala. U.S.A. **111** 32.25N 87.01W
Selma Calif. U.S.A. **108** 36.34N 119.37W
Selmer U.S.A. **111** 35.11N 88.36W
Selseleh ye Safid Küh *mts.* Afghan **65** 34.30N 63.30E
Selsey Bill *c.* U.K. **13** 50.44N 0.47W
Selty Russian Fed. **44** 57.19N 52.12E
Sélune *r.* France **18** 48.35N 1.15W
Selva Argentina **126** 29.50S 62.02W
Selvas *f.* Brazil **122** 6.00S 65.00W
Selwyn L. Canada **101** 60.00N 104.30W
Selwyn Mts. Canada **98** 63.00N 130.00W
Selwyn Range *mts.* Australia **90** 21.35S 140.35E
Seman *r.* Albania **34** 40.45N 19.50E
Semara W. Sahara **74** 26.44N 14.41W
Semarang Indonesia **59** 6.58S 110.29E
Sembabule Uganda **79** 0.08S 31.27E
Semeru, Gunung *mtn.* Indonesia **59** 8.04S 112.53E
Seminoe Resr. U.S.A. **108** 42.00N 106.50W
Seminole U.S.A. **111** 32.43N 102.39W
Semiozernoye Kazakhstan **50** 52.22N 64.06E
Semīrom Iran **65** 31.31N 52.10E
Semipalatinsk Kazakhstan **9** 50.26N 80.16E
Semiyarka Kazakhstan **50** 50.52N 78.23E
Semliki *r.* Zaïre **79** 1.12N 30.27E
Semmering Pass Austria **36** 47.40N 16.00E
Semnän Iran **65** 35.31N 53.24E
Semois *r.* France **16** 49.53N 4.45E
Semporna Malaysia **58** 4.27N 118.36E
Semu *r.* Tanzania **79** 3.57S 34.20E
Semur-en-Auxois France **19** 47.29N 4.20E
Sena Mozambique **79** 17.36S 35.00E
Senador Pompeu Brazil **123** 5.30S 39.25W
Sena Madureira Brazil **122** 9.04S 68.40W
Senanga Zambia **78** 15.52S 23.19E
Senatobia U.S.A. **111** 34.39N 89.58W
Sendai Kyushu Japan **57** 31.49N 130.18E
Sendai Tofuku Japan **57** 38.20N 140.50E
Sendenhorst Germany **38** 51.50N 7.49E
Sendhwa India **62** 21.41N 75.06E
Sendurjana India **63** 21.32N 78.17E
Seneca Oreg. U.S.A. **108** 44.08N 118.58W
Seneca S.C. U.S.A. **113** 34.41N 82.59W
Seneca Falls *town* U.S.A. **114** 42.55N 76.48W
Seneca L. U.S.A. **114** 42.40N 76.57W
Senegal Africa **76** 14.30N 14.30W
Sénégal *r.* Senegal/Mauritania **76** 16.00N 16.28W
Senekal R.S.A. **80** 28.18S 27.37E
Senetosa, Punta di *c.* France **21** 41.33N 8.47E
Senftenberg Germany **38** 51.31N 14.00E
Senhor do Bonfim Brazil **123** 10.28S 40.11W
Senica Slovakia **37** 48.41N 17.22E
Senigallia Italy **30** 43.43N 13.13E
Senise Italy **33** 40.09N 16.18E
Senj Croatia **31** 44.59N 14.54E
Senja *i.* Norway **40** 69.15N 17.20E
Senlis France **19** 49.12N 2.35E
Senmonoron Vietnam **56** 12.27N 107.12E
Sennan Japan **57** 34.22N 135.17E
Sennen U.K. **13** 50.04N 5.42W
Sennestadt Germany **38** 51.57N 8.31E
Senneterre Canada **102** 48.25N 77.15W
Sennori Italy **32** 40.48N 8.34E
Sens France **19** 48.12N 3.17E
Senta Yugo. **31** 45.56N 20.04E
Sentinel U.S.A. **109** 32.53N 113.12W
Šentjur Slovenia **31** 46.13N 15.24E
Seonäth *r.* India **63** 21.44N 82.28E
Seoni India **63** 22.05N 79.32E
Seoni Mälwa India **63** 22.27N 77.28E
Seorīnäräyan India **63** 21.44N 82.35E
Seoul *see* Sŏul S. Korea **53**
Sepik *r.* P.N.G. **59** 3.54S 144.30E
Sepopa Botswana **80** 18.45S 22.11E
Sept Îles *town* Canada **103** 50.13N 66.23W
Sepúlveda Spain **26** 41.18N 3.45W
Sequeros Spain **26** 40.31N 6.01W

Seraing Belgium 16 50.37N 5.33E
Seram i. Indonesia 59 3.10S 129.30E
Seram, Laut sea Pacific Oc. 59 2.50S 128.00E
Serang Indonesia 59 6.07S 106.09E
Serbia d. see Srbija d. Yugo. 31
Serdo Ethiopia 73 11.59N 41.30E
Seremban Malaysia 58 2.42N 101.54E
Serengeti Nat. Park Tanzania 79 2.30S 35.00E
Serengeti Plain f. Tanzania 79 3.00S 35.00E
Serenje Zambia 79 13.12S 30.50E
Sergach Russian Fed. 44 55.32N 45.27E
Sergipe d. Brazil 123 11.00S 37.00W
Sergiyev Posad Russian Fed. 44 56.20N 38.10E
Sergiyevsk Russian Fed. 44 53.56N 50.01E
Seria Brunei 58 4.39N 114.23E
Serian Malaysia 58 1.10N 110.35E
Sericho Kenya 73 1.05N 39.05E
Sérifos Greece 35 37.09N 24.31E
Sérifos i. Greece 35 37.11N 24.31E
Sérigny r. Canada 103 55.59N 68.43W
Serkout, Djebel mtn. Algeria 75 23.40N 6.48E
Serle, Mt Australia 92 30.34S 138.55E
Sermata i. Indonesia 59 8.30S 129.00E
Serodino Argentina 125 32.37S 60.57W
Serov Russian Fed. 44 59.42N 60.32E
Serowe Botswana 80 22.22S 26.42E
Serpa Portugal 27 37.56N 7.36W
Serpeddì, Punta mtn. Italy 32 39.22N 9.18E
Serpentine r. Australia 89 32.33S 115.46E
Serpent's Mouth str. Venezuela 122 9.50N 61.00W
Serpis r. Spain 25 38.59N 0.09W
Serpukhov Russian Fed. 44 54.53N 37.25E
Serra do Navio Brazil 123 0.59N 52.03W
Sérrai Greece 34 41.05N 23.32E
Serramanna Italy 32 39.25N 8.54E
Serra San Bruno Italy 33 38.35N 16.20E
Serra Talhada Brazil 123 8.01S 38.17W
Serrat, Cap c. Tunisia 32 37.14N 9.13E
Serravalle Scrivia Italy 30 44.43N 8.51E
Serre r. France 16 49.40N 3.22E
Serres France 21 44.26N 5.43E
Serri Italy 32 39.41N 9.09E
Serrières France 21 45.19N 4.45E
Serrinha Brazil 123 11.38S 38.56W
Sersale Italy 33 39.01N 16.44E
Sertã Portugal 27 39.48N 8.06W
Sêru Ethiopia 73 7.50N 40.28E
Serui Indonesia 59 1.53S 136.15E
Serule Botswana 80 21.54S 27.17E
Sérvia Greece 34 40.09N 21.58E
Serviceton Australia 92 36.22S 141.02E
Seseganaga L. Canada 102 50.00N 90.10W
Sese Is. Uganda 79 0.20S 32.30E
Sesepe Indonesia 59 1.30S 127.59E
Sesheke Zambia 78 17.14S 24.22E
Sesia r. Italy 30 45.05N 8.37E
Sesimbra Portugal 24 38.26N 9.06W
Şeş, Munţii mts. Romania 37 47.05N 22.30E
Sessa Aurunca Italy 32 41.14N 13.56E
Sestao Spain 26 43.18N 3.00W
Sestri Levante Italy 30 44.16N 9.24E
Setana Japan 57 42.26N 139.51E
Sète France 20 43.24N 3.41E
Sete Lagoas Brazil 126 19.29S 44.15W
Setesdal f. Norway 42 59.25N 7.25E
Sétif Algeria 32 36.10N 5.26E
Seto Japan 57 35.14N 137.06E
Settat Morocco 74 33.04N 7.37W
Setté Cama Gabon 78 2.32S 9.46E
Settimo Torinese Italy 30 45.09N 7.46E
Settle U.K. 12 54.05N 2.18W
Settlement of Edinburgh Tristan da Cunha 127 37.03S 12.18W
Setúbal Portugal 27 38.32N 8.54W
Setúbal d. Portugal 27 38.15N 8.35W
Setúbal, Baía de b. Portugal 27 38.20N 9.00W
Seugne r. France 20 45.41N 0.34W
Seui Italy 32 39.50N 9.20E
Seul, Lac l. Canada 102 50.20N 92.30W
Seurre France 19 47.00N 5.09E
Sevagram India 63 20.45N 78.30E
Sevan, Ozero l. Armenia 45 40.22N 45.20E
Sevastopol' Ukraine 45 44.36N 33.31E
Sevenoaks U.K. 13 51.16N 0.12E
Seven Sisters Peaks mts. Canada 100 54.56N 128.10W
Sévérac France 20 44.19N 3.04E
Severn r. Australia 93 29.08S 150.50E
Severn r. Canada 102 56.00N 87.38W
Severn r. U.K. 13 51.50N 2.21W
Severnaya Zemlya is. Russian Fed. 51 80.00N 96.00E
Severn Falls Canada 104 44.51N 79.38W
Severnyy Russian Fed. 44 69.55N 49.01E
Severnyy Donets r. Ukraine 45 49.08N 37.28E
Severnyy Dvina r. Russian Fed. 44 57.03N 24.00E
Severočeský d. Czech Republic 39 50.26N 13.45E
Severodvinsk Russian Fed. 44 64.35N 39.50E
Severomorsk Russian Fed. 44 69.05N 33.30E
Severskiy Donets r. Russian Fed./Ukraine 23 47.35N 40.55E
Sevier r. U.S.A. 108 39.04N 113.06W
Sevier L. U.S.A. 108 38.55N 113.09W
Sevilla Spain 27 37.23N 5.59W
Sevilla d. Spain 27 37.35N 6.00W
Sevlievo Bulgaria 34 43.01N 25.06E
Sèvre-Nantaise r. France 18 47.08N 1.26W
Sèvre Niortaise r. France 20 46.20N 1.09W
Sewa r. Sierra Leone 76 7.15N 12.08W
Seward Alas. U.S.A. 98 60.05N 149.34W
Seward Nebr. U.S.A. 110 40.55N 97.06W
Seward Penn. U.S.A. 114 40.25N 79.01W
Seward Pen. U.S.A. 98 65.00N 164.10W
Seychelles Indian Oc. 49 5.00S 55.00E
Seydhisfjördhur town Iceland 40 65.16N 14.02W
Seyïac Somali Rep. 71 11.21N 43.30E
Seym r. Ukraine 45 51.30N 32.30E
Seymour Australia 93 37.01S 145.10E
Seymour U.S.A. 111 33.35N 99.16W

Seyne France 21 44.21N 6.21E
Seyssel France 21 45.57N 5.49E
Sežana Slovenia 31 45.42N 13.52E
Sézanne France 19 48.43N 3.43E
Sezimbra Portugal 27 38.26N 9.06W
Sezze Italy 32 41.30N 13.03E
Sfax Tunisia 22 34.45N 10.43E
Sfîntu-Gheorghe Romania 37 45.52N 25.50E
Sforströmmen str. Denmark 42 54.58N 11.55E
'sGravenhage Neth. 16 52.05N 4.16E
Shaanxi d. China 54 35.00N 108.30E
Shaba d. Zaïre 79 8.00S 27.00E
Shabeelle r. Somali Rep. 79 0.30N 43.10E
Shabunda Zaïre 79 2.42S 27.20E
Shache China 52 38.27N 77.16E
Shafter U.S.A. 109 35.30N 119.16W
Shaftesbury U.K. 13 51.00N 2.12W
Shagamu r. Canada 102 55.50N 86.48W
Shāhābād India 63 27.39N 79.57E
Shāhāda India 62 21.28N 74.18E
Shahbā' Syria 66 32.51N 36.37E
Shāhbandar Pakistan 62 24.10N 67.54E
Shāhbāz Kalāt Pakistan 62 26.42N 63.58E
Shahdād Iran 65 30.27N 57.44E
Shāhdādkot Pakistan 62 27.51N 67.54E
Shāhdādpur Pakistan 62 25.56N 68.37E
Shahdol India 63 23.17N 81.21E
Shāhganj India 63 26.03N 82.41E
Shāhgarh India 62 27.07N 69.54E
Shaḥḥāt Libya 72 32.50N 21.52E
Shāh Jahān, Kūh-e mts. Iran 65 37.00N 58.00E
Shāhjahānpur India 63 27.53N 79.55E
Shāh Jūy Afghan. 62 32.31N 67.25E
Shāh Kot Pakistan 62 31.34N 73.29E
Shāh Kūh mtn. Iran 65 31.38N 59.16E
Shāhpur Pakistan 62 28.43N 68.25E
Shāhpura India 62 25.35N 75.00E
Shāhpur Chākar Pakistan 62 26.09N 68.39E
Shahrak Afghan. 62 34.06N 64.18E
Shahr-e Bābak Iran 65 30.08N 55.04E
Shahrestān Afghan. 62 34.22N 66.47E
Shahrezā Iran 65 32.00N 51.52E
Shahr Kord Iran 65 32.40N 50.52E
Sha'ib Abā al Qūr wadi Saudi Arabia 64 31.02N 42.00E
Shaikhpura India 63 25.09N 85.51E
Shājāpur India 62 23.26N 76.16E
Shakawe Botswana 80 18.22S 21.50E
Shaker Heights town U.S.A. 114 41.29N 81.36W
Shakhty Russian Fed. 23 47.43N 40.16E
Shakhunya Russian Fed. 44 57.41N 46.46E
Shaki Nigeria 77 8.41N 3.24E
Shakshūk Egypt 66 29.28N 30.42E
Shala Häyk' l. Ethiopia 73 7.25N 38.30E
Shalingzi China 54 40.42N 114.55E
Shallotte U.S.A. 113 33.58N 78.25W
Shalwa Israel 67 31.34N 34.46E
Shamāl Dārfūr d. Sudan 72 17.15N 25.30E
Shamāl Kurdufān d. Sudan 72 14.00N 29.00E
Shāmat al Akbād des. Saudi Arabia 64 28.15N 43.05E
Shamir Israel 67 33.10N 35.39E
Shām, Jabal ash mtn. Oman 65 23.14N 57.17E
Shāmli India 62 29.27N 77.19E
Shamokin U.S.A. 115 40.47N 76.34W
Shamrock U.S.A. 111 35.13N 100.15W
Shamva Zimbabwe 79 17.20S 31.38E
Shan d. Myanmar 56 22.00N 98.00E
Shandī Sudan 72 16.42N 33.26E
Shandong d. China 54 36.00N 119.00E
Shandong Bandao pen. China 54 37.00N 121.30E
Shangcheng China 55 31.48N 115.24E
Shangdu China 54 41.33N 113.31E
Shanggao China 55 28.15N 114.55E
Shanghai China 55 31.18N 121.50E
Shanghai d. China 55 31.00N 121.30E
Shanglin China 55 23.26N 120.46E
Shangqiu China 54 34.21N 115.40E
Shangrao China 55 28.24N 117.56E
Shangshui China 54 33.31N 114.39E
Shangxian see Shangzhou China 54
Shangyi China 54 41.06N 114.00E
Shangyou Shuiku resr. China 55 25.52N 114.21E
Shangyu China 55 30.01N 120.52E
Shangzhou China 54 33.49N 109.56E
Shanhaiguan China 54 39.58N 119.45E
Shannon r. Rep. of Ire. 15 52.39N 8.43W
Shannon, Mouth of the est. Rep. of Ire. 15 52.29N 9.57W
Shan Plateau Myanmar 56 18.50N 98.00E
Shanshan China 52 42.52N 90.10E
Shantarskiy Ostrova is. Russian Fed. 51 55.00N 138.00E
Shantou China 55 23.22N 116.39E
Shanwa Tanzania 79 3.09S 33.48E
Shanxi d. China 54 37.00N 112.00E
Shanyin China 54 39.30N 112.50E
Shaoguan China 55 24.53N 113.31E
Shaoxing China 55 30.01N 120.40E
Shaoyang China 55 27.10N 111.14E
Shap U.K. 12 54.32N 2.40W
Shapinsay i. U.K. 14 59.03N 2.51W
Shapur ruins Iran 65 29.42N 51.30E
Shaqrā Lebanon 67 33.12N 35.28E
Shaqrā' Saudi Arabia 65 25.17N 45.14E
Shaqrā' Syria 67 32.54N 36.46E
Shaqrā' Yemen 71 13.21N 45.42E
Sharan Jogīzai Pakistan 62 31.02N 68.33E
Sharbot Lake town Canada 105 44.46N 76.41W
Shark B. Australia 88 25.30S 113.30E
Sharlyk Russian Fed. 44 52.58N 54.46E
Sharm ash Shaykh Egypt 66 27.51N 34.16E
Sharon U.S.A. 114 41.14N 80.31W
Sharon Springs town U.S.A. 110 38.54N 101.45W
Sharq al Istīwā'īyah d. Sudan 73 5.00N 33.00E
Sharqī, Al Jabal ash mts. Lebanon 66 34.00N 36.25E
Sharqīyah, Aṣ Ṣaḥrā' ash des. Egypt 66 27.40N 32.00E
Sharya Russian Fed. 44 58.22N 45.50E
Shashi r. Botswana/Zimbabwe 80 22.10S 29.15E

Shashi China 55 30.18N 112.20E
Shasta, Mt. U.S.A. 108 41.20N 122.20W
Shatt al Arab r. Iraq 65 30.00N 48.30E
Shaunavon Canada 101 49.40N 108.25W
Shawanaga Canada 104 45.32N 80.24W
Shawangunk Mts. U.S.A. 115 41.35N 74.30W
Shawano U.S.A. 102 44.46N 88.38W
Shawbridge Canada 105 45.52N 74.05W
Shaw I. Australia 90 20.29S 149.05E
Shawinigan Canada 105 46.33N 72.45W
Shawinigan Sud Canada 105 46.30N 72.45W
Shawnee Ohio U.S.A. 114 39.36N 82.13W
Shawnee Okla. U.S.A. 111 35.20N 96.55W
Shawville Canada 105 45.36N 76.29W
Sha Xi r. China 55 26.38N 118.10E
Sha Xian China 55 26.27N 117.42E
Shayang China 55 30.42N 112.29E
Shay Gap town Australia 88 20.28S 120.05E
Shaykh, Jabal ash mtn. Lebanon 66 33.24N 35.52E
Shaykh 'Uthmān Yemen 71 12.52N 44.59E
Shchara r. Belarus 37 53.27N 24.45E
Shchelyayur Russian Fed. 44 65.16N 53.17E
Shchors Ukraine 37 51.50N 31.59E
Sheboygan U.S.A. 110 43.46N 87.36W
Shebshi Mts. Nigeria 77 8.30N 11.45E
Shediac Canada 103 46.13N 64.32W
Sheeffry Hills Rep. of Ire. 15 53.41N 9.42W
Sheelin, Lough Rep. of Ire. 15 53.48N 7.20W
Sheep Range mts. U.S.A. 109 36.45N 115.05W
Sheet Harbour Canada 103 44.55N 62.32W
Shefar'am Israel 67 32.48N 35.10E
Sheffield U.K. 12 53.23N 1.28W
Sheffield Ala. U.S.A. 113 34.46N 87.40W
Sheffield Penn. U.S.A. 114 41.42N 79.02W
Sheffield Tex. U.S.A. 111 30.41N 101.49W
Shefford U.K. 13 52.02N 0.20W
Shegaon India 62 20.47N 76.41E
Sheguiandah Canada 104 45.53N 81.57W
Shekatika Bay town Canada 103 51.17N 58.20W
Shēkhābād Afghan. 62 34.05N 68.45E
Shek Hasan Ethiopia 73 12.09N 35.54E
Shekhūpura Pakistan 62 31.42N 73.59E
Sheki Azerbaijan 45 41.12N 47.10E
Sheksna r. Russian Fed. 44 60.00N 37.49E
Shelburne N.S. Canada 103 43.46N 65.19W
Shelburne Ont. Canada 104 44.04N 80.12W
Shelburne U.S.A. 105 44.22N 73.15W
Shelburne B. Australia 90 11.49S 143.00E
Shelby Mich. U.S.A. 112 43.36N 86.22W
Shelby Mont. U.S.A. 108 48.30N 111.51W
Shelby Ohio U.S.A. 114 40.53N 82.40W
Shelbyville Ill. U.S.A. 112 39.31N 85.46W
Shelbyville Ind. U.S.A. 114 39.40N 85.47W
Shelbyville Tenn. U.S.A. 113 35.29N 86.30W
Sheldon Iowa U.S.A. 110 43.11N 95.51W
Sheldon N.Dak. U.S.A. 110 46.35N 97.30W
Sheldrake Canada 103 50.20N 64.51W
Shelikof Str. U.S.A. 98 58.00N 153.45W
Shelley U.S.A. 108 43.23N 112.07W
Shellharbour Australia 93 34.35S 150.52E
Shell Lake town Canada 101 53.18N 107.07W
Shelton U.S.A. 108 47.13N 123.06W
Shenandoah Iowa U.S.A. 110 40.46N 95.22W
Shenandoah Penn. U.S.A. 115 40.49N 76.12W
Shenandoah r. U.S.A. 114 38.56N 78.12W
Shenandoah Va. U.S.A. 114 38.29N 78.37W
Shenandoah Mts. U.S.A. 114 38.55N 78.56W
Shenandoah Nat. Park U.S.A. 114 38.48N 78.12W
Shenandoah, North Fork r. U.S.A. 114 38.57N 78.12W
Shenandoah, South Fork r. U.S.A. 114 38.57N 78.12W
Shenandoah Tower mtn. U.S.A. 114 38.30N 79.09W
Shenandoah Valley f. U.S.A. 114 38.42N 78.48W
Shenchi China 54 39.08N 112.10E
Shēngjin Albania 34 41.50N 19.35E
Shengze China 55 30.53N 120.40E
Shenkursk Russian Fed. 44 62.05N 42.58E
Shenmu China 54 38.54N 110.24E
Shennongjia China 55 31.44N 110.44E
Shen Xian China 54 36.15N 115.40E
Shenyang China 54 41.48N 123.27E
Shenzhen China 55 22.32N 114.08E
Sheo India 62 26.11N 71.15E
Sheoganj India 62 25.09N 73.04E
Sheopur India 62 25.40N 76.42E
Shepetovka Ukraine 37 50.12N 27.01E
Shepherd Is. Vanuatu 84 16.55S 168.36E
Shepparton Australia 93 36.25S 145.26E
Sheppey, Isle of U.K. 13 51.24N 0.50E
Sherada Ethiopia 73 7.21N 36.32E
Sherborne U.K. 13 50.56N 2.31W
Sherbro I. Sierra Leone 76 7.30N 12.50W
Sherbrooke Canada 105 45.24N 71.54W
Sherburne U.S.A. 115 42.41N 75.30W
Sheridan U.S.A. 108 44.48N 106.58W
Sheringa Australia 92 33.51S 135.15E
Sheringham U.K. 12 52.56N 1.11E
Sherkin I. Rep. of Ire. 15 51.28N 9.25W
Sherman N.Y. U.S.A. 114 42.10N 79.36W
Sherman Tex. U.S.A. 111 33.38N 96.36W
Sherman Mills U.S.A. 114 45.52N 68.23W
Sherridon Canada 101 55.07N 101.05W
'sHertogenbosch Neth. 16 51.42N 5.19E
Shesh Gäv Afghan. 62 33.45N 68.33E
Shetland Is. d. U.K. 14 60.20N 1.15W
Shetpe Kazakhstan 45 44.09N 52.06E
Shetrunji r. India 62 21.20N 72.05E
Shevchenko see Aktau Kazakhstan 45
Shewa d. Ethiopia 73 8.40N 38.00E
Shewa Gimīra Ethiopia 73 7.00N 35.50E
Sheyang China 54 33.47N 120.19E
Sheyenne r. U.S.A. 110 47.05N 96.50W
Shiawassee r. U.S.A. 104 43.06N 84.10W
Shibām Yemen 71 15.56N 48.38E
Shibecha Japan 57 43.17N 144.36E
Shibīn al Kawm Egypt 66 30.33N 31.00E
Shibīn al Qanāţir Egypt 66 30.19N 31.19E
Shibogama L. Canada 102 53.35N 88.10W
Shickshinny U.S.A. 115 41.09N 76.09W

Shidao China 54 36.52N 122.26E
Shiel, Loch U.K. 14 56.48N 5.33W
Shiga d. Japan 57 34.55N 136.00E
Shigaib Sudan 72 15.01N 23.36E
Shihpao Shan mts. China 55 30.00N 112.00E
Shijak Albania 34 41.21N 19.33E
Shijiazhuang China 54 38.03N 114.26E
Shijiu Hu l. China 55 31.20N 118.48E
Shikārpur Pakistan 62 27.57N 68.38E
Shikohābād India 63 27.06N 78.36E
Shikoku d. Japan 57 33.30N 133.00E
Shikoku i. Japan 57 33.30N 133.00E
Shikoku sanchi mts. Japan 57 34.00N 134.00E
Shikotsu ko l. Japan 57 43.50N 141.26E
Shilabo Ethiopia 71 6.05N 44.48E
Shilka Russian Fed. 53 51.55N 116.01E
Shilka r. Russian Fed. 53 53.20N 121.10E
Shillington U.S.A. 115 40.18N 75.58W
Shillong India 63 25.34N 91.53E
Shiloh see Saylūn Jordan 67
Shilong China 55 23.02N 113.50E
Shima Japan 57 34.13N 136.51E
Shimada Japan 57 34.49N 138.11E
Shima-hantō pen. Japan 57 34.25N 136.45E
Shimizu Japan 57 35.01N 138.29E
Shimla India 62 31.06N 77.09E
Shimoda Japan 57 34.40N 138.57E
Shimoga India 60 13.56N 75.31E
Shimo jima i. Japan 57 32.10N 130.30E
Shimo Koshiki jima i. Japan 57 31.50N 130.00E
Shimonoseki Japan 57 34.02N 130.58E
Shimpek Kazakhstan 52 44.50N 74.10E
Shinano r. Japan 57 37.58N 139.02E
Shindand Afghan. 62 33.18N 62.08E
Shinglehouse U.S.A. 114 41.58N 78.12W
Shingleton U.S.A. 112 46.21N 86.28W
Shingū Japan 57 33.44N 135.59E
Shinkay Afghan. 62 31.57N 67.26E
Shin, Loch U.K. 14 58.06N 4.32W
Shin Naray Afghan. 62 31.19N 66.43E
Shinnston U.S.A. 114 39.24N 80.18W
Shinshār Syria 66 34.36N 36.45E
Shinshiro Japan 57 34.54N 137.30E
Shinyanga Tanzania 79 3.40S 33.20E
Shinyanga d. Tanzania 79 3.30S 33.00E
Shiono zaki c. Japan 57 33.28N 135.47E
Ship Bottom U.S.A. 115 39.39N 74.11W
Shipka Pass Bulgaria 34 42.46N 25.33E
Shippegan Canada 103 47.45N 64.42W
Shippensburg U.S.A. 114 40.03N 77.31W
Shiprock U.S.A. 108 36.47N 108.41W
Shipston on Stour U.K. 13 52.04N 1.38W
Shiqian China 55 27.20N 108.10E
Shiqiao China 55 22.22N 113.21E
Shiqizhen China 55 22.22N 113.21E
Shiqma r. Israel 67 31.36N 34.30E
Shiquan China 54 33.03N 108.17E
Shiquan He r. China 52 32.30N 79.40E
Shirakawa Japan 57 37.10N 140.15E
Shirakskaya Step f. Georgia 65 41.40N 46.20E
Shirane san mtn. Japan 57 35.40N 138.15E
Shīrāz Iran 65 29.36N 52.33E
Shirbīn Egypt 66 31.13N 31.31E
Shire r. Mozambique 79 17.46S 35.20E
Shiriya saki c. Japan 57 41.24N 141.30E
Shīr Kūh mtn. Iran 65 31.38N 54.07E
Shiroishi Japan 57 38.00N 140.37E
Shirpur India 62 21.21N 74.53E
Shīrvān Iran 65 37.24N 57.55E
Shivpuri India 63 25.26N 77.39E
Shiwan Dashan mts. China 55 21.48N 107.50E
Shiyan Hubei China 55 32.38N 110.47E
Shizuishan China 54 39.14N 106.47E
Shizuoka Japan 57 34.58N 138.23E
Shizuoka d. Japan 57 35.00N 138.00E
Shklov Belarus 37 54.10N 30.18E
Shkodër Albania 34 42.05N 19.30E
Shkodër d. Albania 34 42.10N 19.40E
Shkumbin r. Albania 34 41.01N 19.26E
Shoal C. Australia 89 33.51S 121.10E
Shoalhaven r. Australia 93 34.51S 150.40E
Sholāpur India 60 17.43N 75.56E
Shomera Israel 67 33.05N 35.17E
Shonai r. Japan 57 35.04N 136.50E
Shoshone Calif. U.S.A. 109 35.58N 116.17W
Shoshone Idaho U.S.A. 108 42.57N 114.25W
Shoshone Mts. U.S.A. 108 39.25N 117.15W
Shoshoni U.S.A. 108 43.14N 108.07W
Shostka Belarus 44 51.53N 33.30E
Shou Xian China 54 32.30N 116.35E
Shouyang China 54 37.55N 113.10E
Show Low U.S.A. 109 34.15N 110.02W
Shpola Ukraine 37 49.00N 31.25E
Shreve U.S.A. 114 40.41N 82.01W
Shreveport U.S.A. 111 32.30N 93.45W
Shrewsbury U.K. 13 52.42N 2.45W
Shropshire d. U.K. 13 52.35N 2.40W
Shuangliao China 54 43.28N 123.27E
Shuangyashan China 53 46.37N 131.22E
Shu'ayb, Wādī Jordan 67 31.54N 35.38E
Shubenacadie Canada 103 45.05N 63.25W
Shuicheng China 55 26.36N 104.51E
Shujāābād Pakistan 62 29.53N 71.18E
Shujālpur India 62 23.24N 76.43E
Shuksan U.S.A. 108 48.55N 121.43W
Shule China 52 39.25N 76.06E
Shumagin Is. U.S.A. 98 55.00N 160.00W
Shumerlya Russian Fed. 44 55.30N 46.25E
Shumikha Russian Fed. 50 55.15N 63.14E
Shumyachi Russian Fed. 37 53.52N 32.25E
Shūnat Nimrīn Jordan 67 31.54N 35.37E
Shunayn, Sabkhat f. Libya 72 30.10N 21.00E
Shunchang China 55 26.48N 117.47E
Shunde China 55 22.40N 113.20E
Shuo Xian China 54 39.19N 112.25E
Shūr r. Khorāsān Iran 65 34.11N 60.07E

Shūr *r.* Kermān Iran **65** 30.45N 57.55E
Shūr *r.* Kermān Iran **65** 31.14N 55.29E
Shūrāb Iran **65** 28.09N 60.18E
Shūrāb *r.* Iran **65** 31.30N 55.18E
Shurugwi Zimbabwe **80** 19.40S 30.00E
Shūshtar Iran **65** 32.04N 48.53E
Shuswap L. Canada **100** 50.55N 119.03W
Shuwak Sudan **72** 14.23N 35.52E
Shuya Russian Fed. **44** 56.49N 41.23E
Shwebo Myanmar **56** 22.35N 95.42E
Shymkent Kazakhstan **52** 42.16N 69.05E
Shyok Jammu & Kashmir **63** 34.11N 78.08E
Siāhān Range *mts.* Pakistan **62** 27.30N 64.30E
Siālkot Pakistan **62** 32.30N 74.31E
Sian *see* Xi'an China **54**
Siargao *i.* Phil. **59** 9.55N 126.05E
Siari Jammu & Kashmir **62** 34.56N 76.44E
Siasconset U.S.A. **115** 41.16N 69.58W
Siátista Greece **34** 40.15N 21.33E
Siau *i.* Indonesia **59** 2.42N 125.24E
Siauliai Lithuania **41** 55.56N 23.19E
Sibasa R.S.A. **80** 22.56S 30.28E
Šibenik Croatia **31** 43.44N 15.54E
Siberut *i.* Indonesia **58** 1.30S 99.00E
Sibi Pakistan **62** 29.33N 67.53E
Sibiti Congo **78** 3.40S 13.24E
Sibiti *r.* Tanzania **79** 3.47S 34.45E
Sibiu Romania **29** 45.47N 24.09E
Sibley U.S.A. **110** 43.25N 95.43W
Sibolga Indonesia **58** 1.42N 98.48E
Sibu Malaysia **58** 2.18N 111.49E
Sibut C.A.R. **77** 5.46N 19.06E
Sicasica Bolivia **124** 17.22S 67.45W
Siccus *r.* Australia **92** 31.26S 139.30E
Sichuan *d.* China **52** 30.30N 103.00E
Sichuan Pendi *f.* China **55** 31.00N 106.00E
Sicié, Cap *c.* France **21** 43.03N 5.51E
Sicilia *d.* Italy **33** 37.45N 14.00E
Sicilia *i.* Italy **33** 37.30N 14.00E
Sicily *i. see* Sicilia *i.* Italy **33**
Sicuani Peru **122** 14.21S 71.13W
Šid Yugo. **31** 45.08N 19.13E
Sidamo *d.* Ethiopia **73** 4.30N 39.00E
Sidaouet Niger **77** 18.34N 8.03E
Siderno Italy **33** 38.16N 16.18E
Sídheros, Ákra *c.* Greece **35** 35.19N 26.19E
Sidhi India **63** 24.25N 81.53E
Sidhirókastron Greece **34** 41.14N 23.22E
Sidhpur India **62** 23.55N 72.23E
Sidi Barrāni Egypt **64** 31.38N 25.58E
Sidi bel Abbès Algeria **74** 35.12N 0.38W
Sidi Daoud Tunisia **32** 37.01N 10.55E
Sidi Ifni Morocco **74** 29.24N 10.12W
Sidi-Kacem Morocco **74** 34.15N 5.39W
Sidi Sālim Egypt **66** 31.16N 30.47E
Sidi Smaïl Morocco **74** 32.49N 8.30W
Sidlaw Hills U.K. **14** 56.31N 3.10W
Sidley, Mt. Antarctica **128** 77.30S 125.00W
Sidmouth U.K. **13** 50.40N 3.13W
Sidney Canada **100** 48.39N 123.24W
Sidney Mont. U.S.A. **108** 47.43N 104.09W
Sidney Nebr. U.S.A. **110** 41.09N 102.59W
Sidney N.Y. U.S.A. **115** 42.19N 75.24W
Sidney Ohio U.S.A. **112** 40.16N 84.10W
Sidon *see* Şaydā Lebanon **66**
Sidra, G. of *see* Surt, Khalīj *g.* Libya **75**
Siedlce Poland **37** 52.10N 22.18E
Sieg *r.* Germany **16** 50.49N 7.11E
Siegburg Germany **38** 50.47N 7.12E
Siegen Germany **38** 50.52N 8.02E
Siemiatycze Poland **37** 52.26N 22.53E
Siĕmréab Cambodia **58** 13.21N 103.50E
Siena Italy **30** 43.19N 11.21E
Sieradz Poland **37** 51.36N 18.45E
Sierck-les-Bains France **19** 49.26N 6.21E
Sierpc Poland **37** 52.52N 19.41E
Sierra Blanca *town* U.S.A. **109** 31.11N 105.12W
Sierra Colorada Argentina **125** 40.35S 67.50W
Sierra de Outes *town* Spain **26** 42.51N 8.54W
Sierra Leone Africa **76** 9.00N 12.00W
Sierra Mojada *town* Mexico **111** 27.17N 103.42W
Sierra Nevada *mts.* U.S.A. **108** 37.45N 119.30W
Sierre Switz. **39** 46.18N 7.32E
Sifení Ethiopia **73** 12.20N 40.24E
Sífnos *i.* Greece **35** 36.59N 24.40E
Sig Algeria **74** 35.32N 0.11W
Sig Russian Fed. **44** 65.31N 34.16E
Sigean France **20** 43.02N 2.59E
Sighetul Marmaţiei Romania **37** 47.56N 23.54E
Sighişoara Romania **37** 46.13N 24.49E
Sigli Indonesia **58** 5.23N 95.57E
Siglufjördhur Iceland **40** 66.12N 18.55W
Sigmaringen Germany **38** 48.05N 9.13E
Signy France **19** 49.42N 4.25E
Sigtuna Sweden **43** 59.37N 17.43E
Sigüenza Spain **26** 41.04N 2.38W
Sigües Spain **25** 42.38N 1.00W
Siguiri Guinea **76** 11.28N 9.07W
Sihanoukville Cambodia **58** 10.38N 103.30E
Sihor India **62** 21.42N 71.58E
Sihorã India **63** 23.29N 80.07E
Siika *r.* Finland **40** 64.50N 24.44E
Si'ir Jordan **67** 31.35N 35.09E
Siirt Turkey **64** 37.56N 41.56E
Sikanni Chief *r.* Canada **100** 58.20N 121.50W
Sīkar India **62** 27.37N 75.09E
Sikasso Mali **76** 11.18N 5.38W
Sikasso *d.* Mali **76** 11.20N 6.05W
Sikeston U.S.A. **111** 36.53N 89.35W
Sikhote Alin *mts.* Russian Fed. **53** 44.00N 135.00E
Sikiá Greece **34** 40.02N 23.56E
Síkinos *i.* Greece **35** 36.39N 25.06E
Sikión *site* Greece **34** 37.59N 22.44E
Sikkim *d.* India **63** 27.30N 88.30E
Sil *r.* Spain **26** 42.27N 7.43W
Silandro Italy **30** 46.38N 10.46E
Silba Croatia **31** 44.23N 14.42E
Silba *i.* Croatia **31** 44.23N 14.42E

Silchar India **61** 24.49N 92.47E
Silcox Canada **101** 57.12N 94.10W
Silet Algeria **75** 22.39N 4.35E
Silgarhi-Doti Nepal **63** 29.16N 80.58E
Silghāt India **63** 26.37N 92.56E
Silifke Turkey **64** 36.22N 33.57E
Siliguri India **63** 26.42N 88.26E
Silīil Somali Rep. **71** 10.59N 43.31E
Siling Co *l.* China **63** 31.45N 88.50E
Silistra Bulgaria **29** 44.07N 27.17E
Šiljak *mtn.* Yugo. **34** 43.45N 21.50E
Siljan *l.* Sweden **41** 60.50N 14.45E
Silkeborg Denmark **42** 56.10N 9.34E
Sillé-le-Guillaume France **18** 48.12N 0.08W
Sillian Austria **39** 46.45N 12.25E
Sillian Italy **30** 46.45N 12.25E
Sillon de Talbert *c.* France **18** 48.53N 3.05W
Silloth U.K. **12** 54.53N 3.25W
Silogui Indonesia **58** 1.10S 98.46E
Silsbee U.S.A. **111** 30.21N 94.11W
Silvassa India **62** 20.17N 73.00E
Silver Bow U.S.A. **108** 46.00N 112.40W
Silver City U.S.A. **109** 32.46N 108.17W
Silver Creek *town* U.S.A. **114** 42.33N 79.10W
Silverdalen Sweden **43** 57.32N 15.44E
Silver Lake *town* U.S.A. **108** 43.08N 120.56W
Silver Spring *town* U.S.A. **114** 39.02N 77.03W
Silverstone U.K. **13** 52.05N 1.03W
Silverthrone Mtn. Canada **100** 51.31N 126.06W
Silverton Australia **92** 31.53S 141.13E
Silverton U.S.A. **108** 45.01N 122.47W
Silves Portugal **27** 37.11N 8.26W
Silvi Italy **31** 42.34N 14.05E
Simanggang Malaysia **58** 1.10N 111.32E
Simârd, Lac *l.* Canada **102** 47.40N 78.40W
Simav *r.* Turkey **29** 40.24N 28.31E
Simba Kenya **79** 2.10S 37.37E
Simba Zaïre **78** 0.36N 22.55E
Simbach Germany **39** 48.34N 12.45E
Simbirsk Russian Fed. **44** 54.19N 48.22E
Simcoe Canada **104** 42.50N 80.18W
Simcoe, L. Canada **104** 44.20N 79.20W
Simdega India **63** 22.37N 84.31E
Simenga Russian Fed. **51** 62.42N 108.25E
Simeonovgrad Bulgaria **34** 42.02N 25.50E
Simeria Romania **29** 45.51N 23.01E
Simeto *r.* Italy **33** 37.24N 15.06E
Simeulue *i.* Indonesia **58** 2.30N 96.00E
Simferopol' Ukraine **45** 44.57N 34.05E
Sími Greece **35** 36.35N 27.50E
Sími *i.* Greece **35** 36.35N 27.50E
Simikot Nepal **63** 29.58N 81.51E
Simitli Bulgaria **34** 41.52N 23.07E
Simiyu *r.* Tanzania **79** 2.32S 33.25E
Simleul Silvaniei Romania **37** 47.14N 22.48E
Simmern Germany **39** 49.59N 7.31E
Simo *r.* Finland **40** 65.37N 25.03E
Simojärvi *l.* Finland **40** 66.06N 27.03E
Simon, Lac *l.* Canada **105** 45.58N 75.05W
Simon's Town R.S.A. **80** 34.12S 18.26E
Simoom Sound *town* Canada **98** 50.45N 126.45W
Simplon Pass Switz. **39** 46.15N 8.02E
Simplon Tunnel Switz. **39** 46.15N 8.10E
Simpson Desert Australia **90** 25.00S 136.50E
Simrishamn Sweden **43** 55.33N 14.20E
Simuco Mozambique **79** 14.00S 40.35E
Sinadhago Somali Rep. **71** 5.22N 46.22E
Sinai *see* Sīnā', Shibh Jazīrat *pen.* Egypt **66**
Sinaloa *d.* Mexico **109** 25.00N 107.30W
Sinaloa *r.* Mexico **109** 25.18N 108.30W
Sinalunga Italy **30** 43.12N 11.44E
Sinan China **55** 27.51N 108.24E
Sīnā', Shibh Jazīrat *pen.* Egypt **66** 29.00N 34.00E
Sināwin Libya **75** 31.02N 10.36E
Sincelejo Colombia **122** 9.17N 75.23W
Sinclair U.S.A. **108** 41.47N 107.07W
Sinclair Mills Canada **100** 54.05N 121.40W
Sind *r.* India **63** 26.26N 79.13E
Sindal Denmark **42** 57.27N 10.10E
Sindara Gabon **78** 1.07S 10.41E
Sindelfingen Germany **39** 48.42N 9.00E
Sindh *d.* Pakistan **62** 26.45N 69.00E
Sindhūli Garhi Nepal **63** 27.16N 85.58E
Sindri India **63** 23.45N 86.42E
Sines Portugal **26** 37.57N 8.52W
Sines, Cabo de *c.* Portugal **26** 37.57N 8.53W
Sinfâis Portugal **26** 41.04N 8.05W
Sinfra Côte d'Ivoire **76** 6.35N 5.56W
Singãlila *mtn.* India **63** 27.13N 88.01E
Singapore Asia **58** 1.20N 103.45E
Singapore *town* Singapore **58** 1.20N 103.45E
Singaraja Indonesia **59** 8.06S 115.07E
Singatoka Fiji **84** 18.08S 177.30E
Sing Buri Thailand **56** 14.56N 100.21E
Singida Tanzania **79** 4.45S 34.42E
Singida *d.* Tanzania **79** 6.00S 34.30E
Singing India **61** 28.53N 94.47E
Singitikós Kólpos *g.* Greece **34** 40.06N 24.00E
Singkaling Hkämti Myanmar **61** 26.00N 95.42E
Singkang Indonesia **59** 4.09S 120.02E
Singkawang Indonesia **58** 0.57N 108.57E
Singkep *i.* Indonesia **58** 0.30S 104.20E
Singleton Australia **93** 32.33S 151.11E
Singoli India **62** 25.00N 75.25E
Singosan N. Korea **53** 38.50N 127.27E
Siniscola Italy **32** 40.34N 9.41E
Sinj Croatia **31** 43.42N 16.38E
Sinjah Sudan **73** 13.09N 33.56E
Sinjajevina *mts.* Yugo. **31** 43.00N 19.15E
Sinjil Jordan **67** 32.02N 35.16E
Sinkät Sudan **72** 18.50N 36.50E
Sinkiang *d. see* Xinjiang Uygur Zizhiqu *d.* China **52**
Sinnai Italy **32** 39.18N 9.12E
Sinnar India **62** 19.51N 74.00E
Sinnemahoning U.S.A. **114** 41.19N 78.06W
Sinnes Norway **42** 58.56N 6.50E
Sinni *r.* Italy **33** 40.09N 16.42E

Sînnicolau Mare Romania **29** 46.05N 20.38E
Sinnūris Egypt **66** 29.25N 30.52E
Sinop Turkey **64** 42.02N 35.09E
Sinsheim Germany **39** 49.16N 8.53E
Sintang Indonesia **58** 0.03N 111.31E
Sint Eustatius *i.* Leeward Is. **117** 17.33N 63.00W
Sint Maarten *i. see* St. Martin *i.* Leeward Is. **117**
Sinton U.S.A. **111** 29.41N 95.58W
Sintra Portugal **27** 38.48N 9.23W
Sinŭiju N. Korea **53** 40.04N 124.25E
Sinyavka Belarus **37** 52.58N 26.30E
Sinyukha *r.* Ukraine **37** 48.03N 30.51E
Sió *r.* Hungary **31** 46.24N 18.55E
Siocon Phil. **59** 7.42N 122.08E
Siófok Hungary **31** 46.54N 18.04E
Sion Switz. **39** 46.14N 7.21E
Sioux City U.S.A. **110** 42.30N 96.23W
Sioux Falls *town* U.S.A. **110** 43.32N 96.44W
Sioux Lookout *town* Canada **102** 50.06N 91.55W
Siphaqeni R.S.A. **80** 31.05S 29.29E
Siping Hubei China **55** 31.58N 111.10E
Siping Jilin China **54** 43.10N 124.24E
Sipiwesk L. Canada **101** 55.05N 97.35W
Sipura *i.* Indonesia **58** 2.10S 99.40E
Sira Norway **42** 58.25N 6.38E
Sira *r.* Norway **42** 58.17N 6.24E
Siracusa Italy **33** 37.04N 15.17E
Sirãjganj Bangla. **63** 24.27N 89.43E
Sirakoro Mali **76** 12.41N 9.14W
Sirasso Côte d'Ivoire **76** 9.16N 6.06W
Sirdalsvatn *l.* Norway **42** 58.33N 6.41E
Sirē Ethiopia **73** 9.00N 36.55E
Sir Edward Pellew Group *is.* Australia **90** 15.40S 136.48E
Siret *r.* Romania **29** 45.28N 27.56E
Sirevåg Norway **42** 58.30N 5.47E
Sirha Nepal **63** 26.39N 86.12E
Sirhān, Wādī as *f.* Saudi Arabia **64** 31.00N 37.30E
Sir James MacBrien, Mt. Canada **100** 62.07N 127.41W
Sir Joseph Banks Group *is.* Australia **92** 34.35S 136.12E
Sirohi India **62** 24.53N 72.52E
Sironj India **63** 24.06N 77.42E
Síros *i.* Greece **35** 37.26N 24.54E
Sirrah, Wādī as *r.* Saudi Arabia **65** 23.10N 44.22E
Sirsa India **62** 29.32N 75.02E
Sir Wilfrid, Mt. Canada **105** 46.41N 75.35W
Sisak Croatia **31** 45.29N 16.23E
Sisaket Thailand **56** 15.08N 104.18E
Sishen R.S.A. **80** 27.46S 22.59E
Sisimiut *see* Holsteinsborg Greenland **99**
Sisipuk L. Canada **101** 55.45N 101.50W
Sisŏphŏn Cambodia **56** 13.37N 102.58E
Sissach Switz. **39** 47.28N 7.49E
Sisseton U.S.A. **110** 45.40N 97.03W
Sissonne France **19** 49.34N 3.54E
Sistema Central *mts.* Spain **26** 41.00N 3.30W
Sistema Ibérico *mts.* Spain **26** 41.00N 2.25W
Sistemas Béticos *mts.* Spain **27** 37.20N 3.00W
Sisteron France **21** 44.12N 5.56E
Sītāmarhi India **63** 26.36N 85.29E
Sītāpur India **63** 27.34N 80.41E
Sithonia *pen.* Greece **34** 40.00N 23.45E
Sitía Greece **35** 35.13N 26.06E
Sitka U.S.A. **100** 57.05N 135.20W
Sitnica *r.* Yugo. **34** 42.45N 21.01E
Sittang *r.* Myanmar **56** 17.25N 96.50E
Sittard Neth. **16** 51.00N 5.52E
Sittensen Germany **38** 53.17N 9.30E
Sittwe Myanmar **56** 20.09N 92.50E
Situbondo Indonesia **59** 7.40S 114.01E
Siuruan *r.* Finland **40** 65.20N 25.55E
Sivan *r.* Iran **65** 29.50N 52.47E
Sivas Turkey **64** 39.44N 37.01E
Sivomaskinskiy Russian Fed. **44** 66.45N 62.44E
Sivrihisar Turkey **64** 39.29N 31.32E
Sīwah Egypt **64** 29.12N 25.31E
Sīwah, Wāḥat *oasis* Egypt **64** 29.10N 25.40E
Siwalik Range *mts.* India **63** 31.15N 77.45E
Siwān India **63** 26.13N 84.22E
Siwa Oasis *see* Sīwah, Wāḥat *oasis* Egypt **64**
Sixmilecross U.K. **15** 54.34N 7.08W
Siya Russian Fed. **44** 63.38N 41.40E
Sizun France **18** 48.24N 4.05W
Sjaelland *i.* Denmark **42** 55.30N 11.45E
Sjaellands Odde *c.* Denmark **42** 55.58N 11.22E
Sjenica Yugo. **34** 43.16N 20.00E
Sjeništa *mtn.* Bosnia-Herzegovina **31** 43.42N 18.37E
Sjöbo Sweden **43** 55.38N 13.42E
Sjötorp Sweden **43** 58.50N 13.59E
Skaelskör Denmark **42** 55.15N 11.19E
Skaerbaek Denmark **42** 55.09N 8.46E
Skagafjördhur *est.* Iceland **40** 65.55N 19.35W
Skagen Denmark **42** 57.44N 10.36E
Skagern *l.* Sweden **43** 58.59N 14.17E
Skagerrak *str.* Norway/Denmark **42** 58.00N 9.30E
Skagway U.S.A. **100** 59.23N 135.20W
Skaill U.K. **16** 58.55N 2.43W
Skala Greece **35** 36.51N 22.40E
Skála Oropoú Greece **35** 38.20N 23.46E
Skala Podolskaya Ukraine **37** 48.51N 26.11E
Skalat Ukraine **37** 49.20N 25.59E
Skalderviken *b.* Sweden **43** 56.18N 12.38E
Skanderborg Denmark **42** 56.02N 9.56E
Skåne *f.* Sweden **43** 55.59N 13.30E
Skaneateles U.S.A. **115** 42.57N 76.26W
Skånevik Norway **42** 59.44N 5.59E
Skanör Sweden **43** 55.25N 12.52E
Skara Sweden **43** 58.23N 13.25E
Skärhamn Sweden **43** 57.59N 11.33E
Skarnes Norway **42** 60.15N 11.41E
Skarżysko-Kamienna Poland **37** 51.08N 20.53E
Skead Canada **104** 46.40N 80.45W
Skeena *r.* Canada **100** 54.09N 130.02W
Skeena Mts. Canada **100** 57.00N 128.30W
Skegness U.K. **12** 53.09N 0.20E
Skeleton L. Canada **104** 45.15N 79.27W

Skellefte *r.* Sweden **40** 64.42N 21.06E
Skellefteå Sweden **40** 64.46N 20.57E
Skelleftehamn Sweden **40** 64.41N 21.14E
Skelmersdale U.K. **12** 53.34N 2.49W
Skene Sweden **43** 57.29N 12.38E
Skerries Rep. of Ire. **15** 53.35N 6.07W
Skhíza *i.* Greece **35** 36.43N 21.46E
Ski Norway **42** 59.43N 10.50E
Skíathos Greece **35** 39.10N 23.29E
Skíathos *i.* Greece **35** 39.12N 23.30E
Skiddaw *mtn.* U.K. **12** 54.40N 3.09W
Skidel Belarus **37** 53.37N 24.19E
Skien Norway **42** 59.12N 9.36E
Skierniewice Poland **37** 51.58N 20.08E
Skikda Algeria **75** 36.53N 6.54E
Skillingaryd Sweden **43** 57.26N 14.05E
Skinners Eddy U.S.A. **115** 41.37N 76.08W
Skinnskatteberg Sweden **43** 59.50N 15.41E
Skipness U.K. **14** 56.45N 5.22W
Skipton U.K. **12** 53.57N 2.01W
Skíros Greece **35** 38.55N 24.34E
Skíros *i.* Greece **35** 38.53N 24.32E
Skive Denmark **42** 56.34N 9.02E
Skjálfanda Fljót *r.* Iceland **40** 65.55N 17.30W
Skjálfandi *est.* Iceland **40** 66.08N 17.38W
Skjern Denmark **42** 55.57N 8.30E
Skjönsta Norway **40** 67.12N 15.45E
Škofja Loka Slovenia **31** 46.10N 14.18E
Skoghall Sweden **43** 59.19N 13.26E
Skópelos Greece **35** 39.09N 26.47E
Skópelos Greece **35** 39.07N 23.43E
Skópelos *i.* Greece **35** 39.10N 23.40E
Skopje Macedonia **34** 42.01N 21.32E
Skörping Denmark **42** 56.50N 9.53E
Skotfoss Norway **42** 59.12N 9.30E
Skotterud Norway **43** 59.59N 12.07E
Skövde Sweden **43** 58.24N 13.50E
Skovorodino Russian Fed. **51** 54.00N 123.53E
Skradin Croatia **31** 43.49N 15.56E
Skreia Norway **41** 60.39N 10.56E
Skruv Sweden **43** 56.41N 15.22E
Skudeneshavn Norway **42** 59.09N 5.17E
Skull Rep. of Ire. **15** 51.32N 9.33W
Skultorp Sweden **43** 58.21N 13.49E
Skultuna Sweden **43** 59.43N 16.25E
Skuodas Lithuania **41** 56.16N 21.32E
Skurup Sweden **43** 55.28N 13.30E
Skutskär Sweden **41** 60.38N 17.25E
Skvira Ukraine **37** 49.42N 29.40E
Skye *i.* U.K. **14** 57.20N 6.15W
Slagelse Denmark **42** 55.24N 11.22E
Stalowa Wola Poland **37** 50.40N 22.05E
Slamet *mtn.* Indonesia **59** 7.14S 109.10E
Slaney *r.* Rep. of Ire. **15** 52.21N 6.30W
Slano Croatia **31** 42.47N 17.54E
Slantsy Russian Fed. **44** 59.09N 28.09E
Slaný Czech Republic **38** 50.11N 14.04E
Slatina Romania **29** 44.26N 24.23E
Slatina Yugo. **34** 43.04N 20.58E
Slaton U.S.A. **111** 33.26N 101.39W
Slave *r.* Canada **100** 61.18N 113.39W
Slavgorod Belarus **37** 53.25N 31.00E
Slavgorod Russian Fed. **9** 53.01N 78.37E
Slavonsko Požega Croatia **31** 45.20N 17.41E
Slavuta Ukraine **37** 50.20N 26.58E
Slavyansk Ukraine **45** 48.51N 37.36E
Sławno Poland **36** 54.22N 16.40E
Sleaford U.K. **12** 53.00N 0.22W
Sleaford B. Australia **92** 35.00S 136.50E
Sleat, Sd. of *str.* U.K. **14** 57.05N 5.48W
Sledge U.S.A. **111** 34.26N 90.13W
Sledmere U.K. **12** 54.04N 0.35W
Sleeper Is. Canada **102** 56.50N 80.30W
Sleetmute U.S.A. **98** 61.40N 157.11W
Slide Mtn. U.S.A. **115** 42.00N 74.23W
Sliedrecht Neth. **16** 51.48N 4.46E
Slieve Aughty Mts. Rep. of Ire. **15** 53.05N 8.31W
Slieve Bloom Mts. Rep. of Ire. **15** 53.03N 7.35W
Slieve Callan *mtn.* Rep. of Ire. **15** 52.51N 9.18W
Slieve Donard *mtn.* U.K. **15** 54.11N 5.56W
Slieve Gamph *mts.* Rep. of Ire. **15** 54.06N 8.52W
Slievekimalta *mtn.* Rep. of Ire. **15** 52.45N 8.17W
Slieve Mish *mts.* Rep. of Ire. **15** 52.48N 9.48W
Slieve Miskish *mts.* Rep. of Ire. **15** 51.41N 9.56W
Slievenamon *mtn.* Rep. of Ire. **15** 52.25N 7.34W
Slieve Snaght *mtn.* Donegal Rep. of Ire. **15** 55.12N 7.20W
Sligo Rep. of Ire. **15** 54.17N 8.28W
Sligo *d.* Rep. of Ire. **15** 54.10N 8.35W
Sligo U.S.A. **114** 41.07N 79.29W
Sligo B. Rep. of Ire. **15** 54.18N 8.40W
Slippery Rock *town* U.S.A. **114** 41.04N 80.03W
Slite Sweden **43** 57.43N 18.48E
Sliven Bulgaria **34** 42.42N 26.19E
Slivnitsa Bulgaria **34** 42.50N 23.00E
Sloan U.S.A. **110** 42.14N 96.14W
Slobodka Ukraine **37** 47.56N 29.18E
Slobodskoy Russian Fed. **44** 58.42N 50.10E
Slobozia Romania **34** 44.34N 27.23E
Slonim Belarus **37** 53.05N 25.21E
Slough U.K. **13** 51.30N 0.35W
Slovakia Europe **37** 48.25N 19.20E
Slovechna *r.* Belarus **37** 51.41N 29.41E
Slovechno Ukraine **37** 51.23N 28.20E
Slovenia Europe **31** 46.00N 15.00E
Slovenjgradec Slovenia **31** 46.31N 15.05E
Slovenska Bistrica Slovenia **31** 46.23N 15.34E
Słubice Poland **36** 52.20N 14.32E
Sluch *r.* Belarus **37** 52.08N 27.31E
Sluis Neth. **16** 51.18N 3.23E
Slunj Croatia **31** 45.07N 15.35E
Słupsk Poland **36** 54.28N 17.01E
Slurry R.S.A. **80** 25.48S 25.49E
Slyne Head Rep. of Ire. **15** 53.25N 10.12W
Slyudyanka Russian Fed. **52** 51.40N 103.40E
Småland *f.* Sweden **43** 57.20N 15.00E

Smålandsfarvandet str. Denmark 42 55.05N 11.20E
Smålandsstenar Sweden 43 57.10N 13.24E
Smallwood Resr. Canada 103 54.00N 64.00W
Smeaton Canada 101 53.30N 104.49W
Smederevo Yugo. 29 44.40N 20.56E
Smela Ukraine 45 49.15N 31.54E
Smethport U.S.A. 114 41.49N 78.27W
Smilde Neth. 16 52.58N 6.28E
Smilovichi Belarus 37 53.45N 28.00E
Smith Canada 100 55.10N 114.00W
Smith Arm b. Canada 98 66.15N 124.00W
Smithers Canada 100 54.45N 127.10W
Smithfield R.S.A. 80 30.11S 26.31E
Smiths Falls town Canada 105 44.54N 76.01W
Smithton Australia 91 40.52S 145.07E
Smithtown Australia 93 31.03S 152.53E
Smithville U.S.A. 114 39.04N 81.06W
Smoke Hole U.S.A. 114 38.52N 79.18W
Smoky r. Canada 100 56.10N 117.21W
Smoky Bay town Australia 92 32.22S 133.56E
Smoky C. Australia 93 30.55S 153.05E
Smoky Hill r. U.S.A. 110 39.03N 96.48W
Smøla i. Norway 40 63.20N 8.00E
Smolensk Russian Fed. 44 54.49N 32.04E
Smolevichi Belarus 37 54.00N 28.01E
Smólikas mtn. Greece 34 40.06N 20.52E
Smolyan Bulgaria 34 41.36N 24.38E
Smorgon Belarus 37 54.28N 26.20E
Smygehuk c. Sweden 43 55.21N 13.23E
Smyrna U.S.A. 115 39.18N 75.36W
Snaefell mtn. I.o.M. Europe 12 54.16N 4.28W
Snaefell mtn. Iceland 40 64.48N 15.34W
Snake r. Idaho U.S.A. 106 43.50N 117.05W
Snake r. Wash. U.S.A. 108 46.12N 119.02W
Snake Range mts. U.S.A. 108 39.00N 114.15W
Snake River town U.S.A. 108 44.10N 110.40W
Snake River Plain f. U.S.A. 108 43.00N 113.00W
Snåsa Norway 40 64.15N 12.23E
Snåsavatn l. Norway 40 64.05N 12.00E
Snedsted Denmark 42 56.54N 8.32E
Sneek Neth. 16 53.03N 5.40E
Sneem Rep. of Ire. 15 51.50N 9.54W
Sneeuwberg mts. R.S.A. 80 32.30S 19.09E
Snežnik mtn. Slovenia 31 45.35N 14.27E
Śniardwy, Jezioro l. Poland 37 53.46N 21.44E
Snina Slovakia 37 48.59N 22.07E
Snizort, Loch U.K. 14 57.35N 6.30W
Snøhetta mtn. Norway 41 62.20N 9.17E
Snov r. Ukraine 37 51.45N 31.45E
Snowbird L. Canada 101 60.45N 103.00W
Snowdon mtn. U.K. 12 53.05N 4.05W
Snowdrift see Łutselk'e Canada 101
Snowdrift r. Canada 101 62.24N 110.44W
Snowflake U.S.A. 109 34.30N 110.05W
Snow Hill town U.S.A. 113 38.11N 75.23W
Snowtown Australia 92 33.47S 138.13E
Snowy r. Australia 93 37.48S 148.30E
Snowy Mts. Australia 93 36.30S 148.20E
Snyatyn Ukraine 37 48.30N 25.50E
Snyder U.S.A. 111 32.44N 100.05W
Soacha Colombia 122 4.35N 74.13W
Soalala Madagascar 81 16.06S 45.20E
Soanierana-Ivongo Madagascar 81 16.55S 49.35E
Soasiu Indonesia 59 0.40N 127.25E
Soavinandriana Madagascar 81 19.09S 46.45E
Sob r. Ukraine 37 48.42N 29.17E
Sobat r. Sudan 73 9.30N 31.30E
Sobernheim Germany 39 49.47N 7.38E
Soboko C.A.R. 73 6.49N 24.50E
Sobradinho, Reprêsa de resr. Brazil 123 10.00S 42.30W
Sobrado Portugal 26 41.02N 8.16W
Sobral Brazil 123 3.45S 40.20W
Sochi Russian Fed. 45 43.35N 39.46E
Société, Îles de la is. Pacific Oc. 85 17.00S 150.00W
Society Is. see Société, Îles de la is. Pacific Oc. 85
Socorro Colombia 122 6.30N 73.16W
Socorro U.S.A. 109 34.04N 106.54W
Socorro, Isla i. Mexico 116 18.45N 110.58W
Socotra i. see Suquṭrá i. Yemen 71
Socuéllamos Spain 27 39.17N 2.48W
Sodankylä Finland 40 67.29N 26.32E
Söderhamn Sweden 41 61.18N 17.03E
Söderköping Sweden 43 58.29N 16.18E
Södermanland d. Sweden 43 59.12N 16.49E
Södermanland f. Sweden 43 58.56N 16.50E
Södertälje Sweden 43 59.12N 17.37E
Sodium R.S.A. 80 30.10S 23.08E
Sodo Ethiopia 73 6.52N 37.47E
Södra Vi Sweden 43 57.45N 15.48E
Sodražica Slovenia 31 45.46N 14.38E
Sodus U.S.A. 114 43.14N 77.04W
Sodus Point town U.S.A. 114 43.16N 76.59W
Soest Germany 38 51.34N 8.07E
Sofádhes Greece 35 39.20N 22.06E
Sofala Australia 93 33.05S 149.42E
Sofala d. Mozambique 81 19.00S 34.39E
Sofia see Sofiya Bulgaria 34
Sofia r. Madagascar 81 15.27S 47.23E
Sofikón Greece 35 37.47N 23.03E
Sofiya Bulgaria 34 42.41N 23.19E
Sofiya d. Bulgaria 34 42.02N 23.05E
Sofiysk Russian Fed. 51 52.19N 133.55E
Sofporog Russian Fed. 44 65.47N 31.30E
Sogamoso Colombia 122 5.43N 72.56W
Sögel Germany 38 52.50N 7.31E
Sögne Norway 42 58.05N 7.49E
Sognefjorden est. Norway 41 61.06N 5.10E
Sogn og Fjordane d. Norway 41 61.30N 6.50E
Söğüt Turkey 64 40.02N 30.10E
Sog Xian China 63 31.51N 93.40E
Sohâgpur India 63 22.42N 78.12E
Soignies Belgium 16 50.35N 4.04E
Soissons France 19 49.22N 3.20E
Sojat India 62 25.55N 73.40E
Sokal Ukraine 37 50.30N 24.10E
Söke Turkey 35 37.45N 27.24E
Sokhós Greece 34 40.48N 23.22E

Sokna Norway 42 60.14N 9.54E
Soko Banja Yugo. 34 43.40N 21.51E
Sokodé Togo 77 8.59N 1.11E
Sokol Russian Fed. 44 59.28N 40.04E
Sokółka Poland 37 53.25N 23.31E
Sokolo Mali 76 14.53N 6.11W
Sokolov Czech Republic 39 50.09N 12.40E
Sokoto Nigeria 77 13.02N 5.15E
Sokoto d. Nigeria 77 11.50N 5.05E
Sokoto r. Nigeria 77 13.05N 5.13E
Sola Norway 42 58.53N 5.36E
Solbad Hall Austria 39 47.17N 11.31E
Solec Kujawski Poland 37 53.06N 18.14E
Soledad Venezuela 122 8.10N 63.34W
Solesmes France 19 50.11N 3.30E
Solginskiy Russian Fed. 44 61.07N 41.30E
Solheim Norway 41 60.53N 5.27E
Soligalich Russian Fed. 44 59.02N 42.15E
Solihull U.K. 11 52.26N 1.47W
Solikamsk Russian Fed. 44 59.40N 56.45E
Sol-Iletsk Russian Fed. 44 51.09N 55.00E
Soliman Tunisia 32 36.42N 10.30E
Solingen Germany 38 51.10N 7.05E
Solleftea Sweden 40 63.12N 17.20E
Sollentuna Sweden 43 59.28N 17.54E
Sóller Spain 25 39.46N 2.42E
Sollia Norway 41 61.47N 10.24E
Solling mts. Germany 38 51.45N 9.35E
Solna Sweden 43 59.22N 18.01E
Solola Somali Rep. 73 0.08N 41.30E
Solomon Is. Pacific Oc. 84 8.00S 160.00E
Solomons U.S.A. 115 38.21N 76.29W
Solomon Sea Pacific Oc. 87 7.00S 150.00E
Solomon's Pool see Birak Sulaymān site Jordan 67
Solon U.S.A. 112 44.57N 69.52W
Solon Springs U.S.A. 112 46.22N 91.48W
Solopaca Italy 33 41.11N 14.33E
Solothurn Switz. 39 47.13N 7.32E
Solothurn d. Switz. 39 47.20N 7.45E
Solovetskiye, Ostrova is. Russian Fed. 44 65.05N 35.30E
Solsona Spain 25 41.59N 1.31E
Solt Hungary 31 46.48N 19.00E
Šolta i. Croatia 31 43.23N 16.15E
Soltānābād Iran 65 36.25N 58.02E
Soltau Germany 38 52.59N 9.49E
Sölvesborg Sweden 43 56.03N 14.33E
Solway Firth est. U.K. 12 54.50N 3.30W
Solwezi Zambia 78 12.11S 26.23E
Solzach r. Austria 48 48.35N 13.30E
Soma Turkey 29 39.11N 27.36E
Somabhula Zimbabwe 80 19.40S 29.38E
Somali Basin f. Indian Oc. 49 0.00 55.00E
Somali Republic Africa 71 5.30N 47.00E
Sombor Yugo. 31 45.46N 19.07E
Sombrerete Mexico 116 23.38N 103.39W
Somerset d. U.K. 13 51.09N 3.00W
Somerset Ky. U.S.A. 113 37.05N 84.38W
Somerset Ohio U.S.A. 114 39.48N 82.18W
Somerset Penn. U.S.A. 114 40.01N 79.05W
Somerset East R.S.A. 80 32.43S 25.33E
Somerset I. Bermuda 127 32.18N 64.53W
Somerset I. Canada 99 73.00N 93.30W
Somerset Resr. U.S.A. 115 43.00N 72.56W
Somers Point town U.S.A. 115 39.20N 74.36W
Somersworth U.S.A. 115 43.16N 70.52W
Somerville Mass. U.S.A. 115 42.23N 71.06W
Somerville N.J. U.S.A. 115 40.34N 74.37W
Somes r. Hungary 37 48.40N 22.30E
Somme d. France 19 49.55N 2.30E
Somme r. France 19 50.11N 1.39E
Sommen l. Sweden 43 58.01N 15.15E
Sömmerda Germany 38 51.10N 11.07E
Somogy d. Hungary 31 46.30N 17.40E
Somosierra, Puerto de pass Spain 26 41.09N 3.35W
Sompeta India 63 18.56N 84.36E
Somport, Puerto de pass Spain 25 42.48N 0.31W
Sompuis France 19 48.41N 4.23E
Son r. India 63 25.42N 84.52E
Sonāmarg Jammu & Kashmir 62 34.18N 75.18E
Sonāmura India 63 23.29N 91.17E
Sönbong N. Korea 53 42.19N 130.24E
Sönderborg Denmark 42 54.55N 9.47E
Sönder Omme Denmark 42 55.50N 8.54E
Sondershausen Germany 38 51.22N 10.52E
Söndreströmfjord Greenland 99 66.30N 50.52W
Sondrio Italy 30 46.10N 9.52E
Sonepur India 63 20.50N 83.55E
Songa r. Norway 42 59.47N 7.41E
Song-Cau Vietnam 56 13.27N 109.13E
Songe Norway 42 58.41N 9.00E
Songea Tanzania 79 10.42S 35.39E
Songhua Jiang r. China 53 47.46N 132.30E
Songjiang China 53 31.01N 121.20E
Songkhla Thailand 56 7.12N 100.35E
Songololo Zaïre 78 5.40S 14.05E
Songpan China 54 32.36N 103.36E
Songtao Miaozu Zizhixian China 55 28.12N 109.12E
Song Xian China 54 34.02N 111.48E
Sonid Youqi China 54 42.44N 112.40E
Sonid Zuoqi China 54 43.58N 113.59E
Sonīpat India 62 28.59N 77.01E
Son La Vietnam 56 21.20N 103.55E
Sonmiāni Pakistan 62 25.26N 66.36E
Sonmiāni B. Pakistan 62 25.15N 66.30E
Sonneberg Germany 39 50.22N 11.10E
Sonoita Mexico 109 31.51N 112.50W
Sonora d. Mexico 109 29.30N 110.40W
Sonora r. Mexico 109 28.50N 111.33W
Sonora U.S.A. 111 30.34N 100.39W
Sonseca Spain 27 39.41N 3.57W
Sonsorol i. Pacific Oc. 59 5.20N 132.13E
Son Tay Vietnam 55 21.15N 105.17E
Sonthofen Germany 38 47.31N 10.17E
Sopi Indonesia 59 2.40N 128.28E
Sopo r. Sudan 73 8.51N 26.11E
Sopot Poland 37 54.28N 18.34E
Sopotskin Belarus 37 53.49N 23.42E

Soppero Sweden 40 68.07N 21.40E
Sopron Hungary 36 47.41N 16.36E
Sop's Arm town Canada 103 49.46N 56.56W
Sopur Jammu & Kashmir 62 34.18N 74.28E
Sora Italy 31 41.43N 13.37E
Sorada India 63 19.45N 84.26E
Sorbas Spain 27 37.06N 2.07W
Sore France 20 44.20N 0.35W
Sorel Canada 105 46.02N 73.07W
Soreq r. Israel 67 31.56N 34.42E
Sörfjorden Norway 40 66.29N 13.20E
Sörfold Norway 40 67.30N 15.30E
Sorgono Italy 32 40.01N 9.06E
Sorgues France 21 44.00N 4.52E
Soria Spain 26 41.46N 2.28W
Soria d. Spain 26 41.40N 2.45W
Soriano Uruguay 125 33.24S 58.19W
Sör Kvalöy i. Norway 40 69.40N 18.30E
Sörli Norway 40 64.15N 13.50E
Sor Mertvyy Kultuk f. Kazakhstan 45 45.30N 54.00E
Sorø Denmark 42 55.26N 11.34E
Soro India 63 21.17N 86.40E
Sorocaba Brazil 126 23.29S 47.27W
Sorochinsk Russian Fed. 44 52.29N 53.15E
Soroki Moldova 37 48.08N 28.12E
Sorol i. Federated States of Micronesia 59 8.09N 140.25E
Soron India 63 27.53N 78.45E
Sorong Indonesia 59 0.50S 131.17E
Soroti Uganda 79 1.40N 33.37E
Söröya i. Norway 40 70.35N 22.30E
Sorraia r. Portugal 24 39.00N 8.51W
Sorrento Italy 33 40.37N 14.22E
Sor, Ribeira de r. Portugal 27 39.00N 8.17W
Sör-Rondane mts. Antarctica 128 72.30S 22.00E
Sorsele Sweden 40 65.30N 17.30E
Sort Spain 25 42.24N 1.08E
Sortavala Russian Fed. 44 61.40N 30.40E
Sortland Norway 40 68.44N 15.25E
Sör Tröndelag d. Norway 40 63.00N 10.20E
Sorūbī Afghan. 62 34.36N 69.43E
Sos del Rey Católico Spain 25 42.30N 1.13W
Sosnogorsk Russian Fed. 44 63.32N 53.55E
Sosnovo Russian Fed. 44 60.33N 30.11E
Sosnovyy Russian Fed. 44 66.01N 32.40E
Sosnowiec Poland 37 50.18N 19.08E
Šoštanj Slovenia 31 46.23N 15.03E
Sosva Russian Fed. 44 59.10N 61.50E
Sosyka Russian Fed. 45 46.11N 38.49E
Sotik Kenya 79 0.40S 35.08E
Sotonera, Embalse de la resr. Spain 25 42.05N 0.48W
Sotra i. Norway 42 60.18N 5.05E
Sotteville France 18 49.25N 1.06E
Soubré Côte d'Ivoire 76 5.50N 6.35W
Souderton U.S.A. 115 40.19N 75.19W
Soufflay Congo 78 2.00N 14.54E
Souflión Greece 34 41.12N 26.18E
Souillac France 20 44.54N 1.29E
Souilly France 19 49.01N 5.17E
Souk Ahras Algeria 75 36.17N 7.57E
Souk-el-Arba-du-Rharb Morocco 74 34.43N 6.01W
Sŏul S. Korea 53 37.30N 127.00E
Soulac-sur-Mer France 20 45.31N 1.07W
Soúnion, Ákra c. Greece 35 37.37N 24.01E
Sources, Mont-aux- mtn. Lesotho 80 28.44S 28.52E
Soure Portugal 27 40.03N 8.38W
Souris Man. Canada 101 49.38N 100.15W
Souris P.E.I. Canada 105 46.21N 62.15W
Souris r. Canada 101 49.39N 99.34W
Soúrpi Greece 35 39.06N 22.54E
Sousa Brazil 123 6.41S 38.14W
Sousel Portugal 27 38.57N 7.40W
Sous le Vent, Îles is. Îs. de la Société 85 16.30S 151.30W
Sous, Oued wadi Morocco 74 30.27N 9.31W
Sousse Tunisia 75 35.48N 10.38E
Soustons France 20 43.45N 1.19W
South Alligator r. Australia 90 12.53S 132.29E
South America 120
Southampton Canada 104 44.29N 81.23W
Southampton U.K. 13 50.54N 1.23W
Southampton U.S.A. 115 40.53N 72.24W
Southampton I. Canada 99 64.30N 84.00W
South Atlantic Ocean 121
South Aulatsivik I. Canada 103 56.45N 61.30W
South Australia d. Australia 92 30.00S 137.00E
South Australian Basin f. Indian Oc. 49 40.00S 130.00E
South Baymouth Canada 104 45.33N 82.01W
South Bend Ind. U.S.A. 112 41.40N 86.15W
South Bend Wash. U.S.A. 108 46.40N 123.48W
South Boston U.S.A. 113 36.42N 78.58W
South Branch U.S.A. 104 44.27N 83.53W
Southbridge U.S.A. 115 42.05N 72.02W
South Carolina d. U.S.A. 113 34.00N 81.00W
South Charleston U.S.A. 114 38.22N 81.44W
South China Sea Asia 58 12.30N 115.00E
South Dakota d. U.S.A. 110 45.00N 100.00W
South Dorset Downs hills U.K. 13 50.40N 2.25W
South Downs hills U.K. 13 50.04N 0.34W
South East d. Botswana 80 25.00S 25.61E
South East C. Australia 91 43.38S 146.48E
South Eastern Atlantic Basin f. Atlantic Oc. 127 20.00S 0.00
South East Head c. Ascension 127 7.58S 14.18W
South East Indian Basin f. Indian Oc. 49 35.00S 105.00E
South-East Indian Ridge f. Indian Oc. 49 32.00S 96.00E
South East Is. Australia 89 34.23S 123.30E
South East Pt. Kiribati 85 1.40N 157.10W
Southend-on-Sea U.K. 13 51.32N 0.43E
Southern d. Zambia 80 16.30S 26.40E
Southern Alps mts. New Zealand 86 43.20S 170.45E
Southern Cross Australia 89 31.14S 119.16E
Southern Indian L. Canada 101 57.10N 98.40W
Southern Lueti r. Zambia 80 16.15S 23.12E

Southern Ocean Pacific Oc. 84 44.00S 130.00E
Southern Pines U.S.A. 113 35.12N 79.23W
Southern Uplands hills U.K. 14 55.30N 3.30W
South Esk r. U.K. 14 56.43N 2.32W
South Esk Tablelands f. Australia 88 20.50S 126.40E
Southey Canada 101 50.56N 104.30W
South Fiji Basin Pacific Oc. 84 27.00S 176.00E
South Georgia i. Atlantic Oc. 121 54.00S 37.00W
South Glamorgan d. U.K. 13 51.27N 3.22W
South-haa U.K. 14 60.34N 1.17W
South Hâtia I. Bangla. 63 22.19N 91.07E
South Haven U.S.A. 112 42.25N 86.16W
South Henik L. Canada 101 61.30N 97.30W
South Honshu Ridge Pacific Oc. 84 22.00N 141.00E
South Horr Kenya 79 2.10N 36.45E
South I. Kenya 79 2.36N 36.38E
South I. New Zealand 86 43.00S 171.00E
South Knife r. Canada 101 58.55N 94.37W
South Korea Asia 53 36.00N 128.00E
South Lake Tahoe U.S.A. 108 38.57N 119.57W
Southland d. New Zealand 86 45.40S 168.00E
South Loup r. U.S.A. 110 41.04N 98.40W
South Lyon U.S.A. 104 42.28N 83.39W
South Molton U.K. 13 51.01N 3.50W
South Nahanni r. Canada 100 61.03N 123.21W
South Nation r. Canada 105 45.35N 75.06W
South Orkney Is. Atlantic Oc. 121 60.50S 45.00W
South Platte r. U.S.A. 110 41.07N 100.42W
Southport Qld. Australia 92 27.58S 153.20E
Southport Tas. Australia 91 43.25S 146.59E
Southport U.K. 12 53.38N 3.01W
Southport U.S.A. 113 33.55N 78.00W
South River town Canada 104 45.45N 79.25W
South River town U.S.A. 115 40.27N 74.23W
South Ronaldsay i. U.K. 14 58.47N 2.56W
South Sandwich Is. Atlantic Oc. 121 58.00S 27.00W
South Sandwich Trench f. Atlantic Oc. 121 57.00S 25.00W
South Saskatchewan r. Canada 101 53.15N 105.05W
South Seal r. Canada 101 58.48N 98.08W
South Shields U.K. 12 55.00N 1.24W
South Sioux City U.S.A. 110 42.28N 96.24W
South Tasmania Ridge f. Pac. Oc./Ind. Oc. 84 46.00S 147.00E
South Thompson r. Canada 100 50.40N 120.20W
South Tucson U.S.A. 109 32.12N 110.58W
South Twin I. Canada 102 53.00N 79.50W
South Tyne r. U.K. 14 54.59N 2.08W
South Uist i. U.K. 14 57.15N 7.20W
South Wabasca L. Canada 100 55.54N 113.45W
South West Australian Ridge f. Indian Oc. 49 38.00S 112.00E
Southwest C. New Zealand 86 47.15S 167.30E
South Western Pacific Basin Pacific Oc. 85 39.00S 148.00W
South-West Indian Ridge f. Indian Oc. 49 33.00S 56.00E
South West Peru Ridge Pacific Oc. 85 20.00S 82.00W
Southwest Pt. c. Kiribati 85 1.52N 157.33W
South West Pt. c. St. Helena 127 16.00S 5.48W
South Windham U.S.A. 112 43.44N 70.26W
Southwold U.K. 13 52.19N 1.41E
South Yorkshire d. U.K. 12 53.28N 1.25W
Soutpansberg mts. R.S.A. 80 22.58S 29.50E
Souvigny France 20 46.32N 3.11E
Soverato Italy 33 38.41N 16.33E
Sovetsk Lithuania 41 55.05N 21.53E
Sovetsk Russian Fed. 44 57.39N 48.59E
Sovetskaya Gavan Russian Fed. 51 48.57N 140.16E
Soweto R.S.A. 80 26.16S 27.51E
Soyo Angola 78 6.12S 12.25E
Soyopa Mexico 109 28.47N 109.39W
Sozh r. Belarus 37 51.57N 30.48E
Spa Belgium 16 50.29N 5.52E
Spain Europe 24 40.00N 4.00W
Spalding Australia 92 33.29S 138.40E
Spalding U.K. 12 52.47N 0.09W
Spalding U.S.A. 110 41.41N 98.22W
Spandau Germany 38 52.32N 13.12E
Spanish Canada 104 46.12N 82.21W
Spanish r. Canada 104 46.21N 81.52W
Spanish Fork U.S.A. 108 40.07N 111.39W
Sparks U.S.A. 108 39.32N 119.45W
Sparreholm Sweden 43 59.04N 16.49E
Sparrows Point town U.S.A. 115 39.13N 76.29W
Sparta Ga. U.S.A. 113 33.17N 82.58W
Sparta N.J. U.S.A. 115 41.02N 74.38W
Sparta Wisc. U.S.A. 110 43.57N 90.47W
Spartanburg U.S.A. 113 34.56N 81.57W
Spárti Greece 35 37.05N 22.27E
Spartivento, Capo c. Calabria Italy 33 37.56N 16.04E
Spartivento, Capo c. Sardegna Italy 32 38.53N 8.50E
Spátha, Ákra c. Greece 35 35.42N 23.44E
Spatsizi Plateau Wilderness Prov. Park Canada 100 57.13N 127.53W
Spearman U.S.A. 111 36.12N 101.12W
Speculator U.S.A. 115 43.30N 74.23W
Speke G. Tanzania 79 2.20S 33.30E
Spello Italy 30 43.00N 12.40E
Spence Canada 104 45.34N 79.40W
Spencer Idaho U.S.A. 108 44.21N 112.11W
Spencer Iowa U.S.A. 110 43.09N 95.09W
Spencer Mass. U.S.A. 115 42.15N 71.59W
Spencer S.Dak. U.S.A. 110 43.44N 97.36W
Spencer W.Va. U.S.A. 114 38.48N 81.21W
Spencer, C. Australia 92 35.18S 136.53E
Spencer G. Australia 92 34.00S 137.00E
Spencerville Canada 105 44.51N 75.33W
Spences Bridge town Canada 100 50.25N 121.20W
Sperkhíos r. Greece 35 38.57N 22.03E
Sperrin Mts. U.K. 15 54.49N 7.06W
Sperryville U.S.A. 114 38.39N 78.14W
Spétsai i. Greece 35 37.16N 23.09E
Spey r. U.K. 14 57.40N 3.06W
Speyer Germany 39 49.19N 8.26E
Spezzano Albanese Italy 33 39.40N 16.19E
Spiekeroog i. Germany 38 53.46N 7.42E

Spiez Switz. 39 46.41N 7.39E
Spilimbergo Italy 30 46.07N 12.54E
Spilsby U.K. 12 53.10N 0.06E
Spina ruins Italy 30 44.42N 12.08E
Spinazzola Italy 33 40.58N 16.06E
Spīn Būldak Afghan. 62 31.01N 66.24E
Spincourt France 19 49.20N 5.40E
Spirit River town Canada 100 55.45N 118.50W
Spišská Nova Ves Slovakia 37 48.57N 20.34E
Spithead str. U.K. 13 50.45N 1.05W
Spitsbergen is. Europe 48 78.00N 17.00E
Spittal an der Drau Austria 39 46.48N 13.30E
Split Croatia 31 43.31N 16.27E
Split L. Canada 101 56.08N 96.15W
Splügen Switz. 39 46.33N 9.20E
Spofford U.S.A. 111 29.11N 100.25W
Spokane U.S.A. 108 47.40N 117.23W
Spokane r. U.S.A. 108 47.44N 118.20W
Spoleto Italy 30 42.44N 12.44E
Spooner U.S.A. 110 45.50N 91.53W
Spragge Canada 104 46.13N 82.40W
Spratly i. S. China Sea 58 8.45N 111.54E
Spray U.S.A. 108 44.50N 119.48W
Spreča r. Bosnia-Herzegovina 31 44.45N 18.06E
Spree r. Germany 36 52.32N 13.15E
Spremberg Germany 38 51.34N 14.22E
Springbok R.S.A. 80 29.40S 17.50E
Springdale Canada 103 49.30N 56.04W
Springe Germany 38 52.12N 9.32E
Springer U.S.A. 108 36.22N 104.36W
Springerville U.S.A. 109 34.08N 109.17W
Springfield New Zealand 86 43.20S 171.56E
Springfield Colo. U.S.A. 111 37.24N 102.37W
Springfield Ill. U.S.A. 111 39.46N 89.39W
Springfield Mass. U.S.A. 115 42.07N 72.36W
Springfield Miss. U.S.A. 111 37.11N 93.19W
Springfield Mo. U.S.A. 111 37.14N 93.17W
Springfield Ohio U.S.A. 112 39.55N 83.48W
Springfield Oreg. U.S.A. 108 44.03N 123.01W
Springfield Tenn. U.S.A. 111 36.30N 86.54W
Springfield Vt. U.S.A. 115 43.18N 72.29W
Springfield W.Va. U.S.A. 114 39.26N 78.48W
Springfontein R.S.A. 80 30.15S 25.41E
Spring Grove U.S.A. 114 39.52N 76.52W
Springhill Canada 103 45.39N 64.03W
Springs town R.S.A. 80 26.16S 28.27E
Springsure Australia 90 24.07S 148.05E
Springvale U.S.A. 115 43.28N 70.48W
Spring Valley town U.S.A. 110 43.41N 92.23W
Springville N.Y. U.S.A. 114 42.31N 78.40W
Springville Utah U.S.A. 108 40.10N 111.37W
Spruce Knob mtn. U.S.A. 114 38.42N 79.32W
Spruce Knob-Seneca Rocks Nat. Recreation Area
 U.S.A. 114 38.50N 79.20W
Spry U.S.A. 108 37.55N 112.28W
Spulico, Capo c. Italy 33 39.58N 16.39E
Spurn Head U.K. 12 53.35N 0.08E
Spuzzum Canada 100 49.37N 121.23W
Squamish Canada 100 49.45N 123.10W
Squaw Rapids town Canada 101 53.41N 103.20W
Squillace Italy 33 38.46N 16.31E
Squillace, Golfo di g. Italy 33 38.50N 16.50E
Squinzano Italy 33 40.26N 18.03E
Sragen Indonesia 59 7.24S 111.00E
Srbija d. Yugo. 31 44.30N 19.30E
Srbobran Yugo. 31 45.33N 19.48E
Sredna Gora mts. Bulgaria 34 42.40N 25.00E
Srednekolymsk Russian Fed. 51 67.27N 153.35E
Sredne Russkaya Vozvyshennost f. Russian Fed. 44
 53.00N 37.00E
Sredne Sibirskoye Ploskogor'ye f. Russian Fed. 51
 66.00N 108.00E
Sredni Rodopi mts. Bulgaria 34 41.40N 24.45E
Srê Moat Cambodia 56 13.15N 107.10E
Sremska Mitrovica Yugo. 31 44.59N 19.37E
Srêpôk r. Cambodia 56 13.33N 106.16E
Sretensk Russian Fed. 53 52.15N 117.52E
Sri Dūngargarh India 62 28.05N 74.00E
Sri Gangānagar India 62 29.55N 73.52E
Srīkākulam India 61 18.18N 83.54E
Sri Lanka Asia 61 7.30N 80.50E
Sri Mohangarh India 62 27.17N 71.14E
Srīnagar Jammu & Kashmir 62 34.05N 74.49E
Srīpur Bangla. 63 24.12N 90.29E
Srirampur India 62 19.30N 74.32E
Srnetica Bosnia-Herzegovina 31 44.26N 16.40E
Staaten r. Australia 90 16.24S 141.17E
Stade Germany 38 53.36N 9.28E
Stadskanaal Neth. 16 53.02N 6.55E
Stadt Allendorf Germany 38 50.50N 9.01E
Stadthagen Germany 38 52.19N 9.13E
Stadtkyll Germany 39 50.21N 6.32E
Stadtlohn Germany 38 51.59N 6.55E
Stadtoldendorf Germany 38 51.53N 9.37E
Staffa i. U.K. 14 56.26N 6.21W
Staffelstein Germany 38 50.06N 11.00E
Stafford U.K. 12 52.49N 2.09W
Stafford U.S.A. 114 38.09N 76.51W
Staffordshire d. U.K. 12 52.40N 1.57W
Staines U.K. 13 51.26N 0.31W
Stainforth U.K. 12 53.37N 1.01W
Stainz Austria 31 46.54N 15.16E
Stakhanov Ukraine 45 48.34N 38.40E
Stalina Kanal canal Russian Fed. 44 64.33N 34.48E
Stålldalen Sweden 43 59.56N 14.56E
Stamford U.K. 13 52.39N 0.28W
Stamford Conn. U.S.A. 115 41.03N 73.32W
Stamford N.Y. U.S.A. 115 42.25N 74.37W
Stamford Tex. U.S.A. 111 44.59N 99.48W
Stanardsville U.S.A. 114 38.18N 78.26W
Stanberry U.S.A. 110 40.13N 94.34W
Standerton R.S.A. 80 26.57S 29.14E
Standish U.S.A. 104 43.59N 83.57W
Stanger R.S.A. 80 29.20S 31.17E
Stanley Canada 98 55.45N 104.55W
Stanley Falkland Is. 125 51.42S 57.51W

Stanley U.K. 12 54.53N 1.42W
Stanley Idaho U.S.A. 108 44.13N 114.35W
Stanley Wisc. U.S.A. 110 44.58N 90.56W
Stanley Mission Canada 101 55.27N 104.33W
Stanovoy Khrebet mts. Russian Fed. 51 56.00N
 125.40E
Stanthorpe Australia 93 28.37S 151.52E
Stanton U.S.A. 111 32.08N 101.48W
Stapleton U.S.A. 110 41.29N 100.31W
Starachowice Poland 37 51.03N 21.04E
Stara Dorogi Belarus 37 53.02N 28.18E
Stara Pazova Yugo. 31 44.59N 20.10E
Stara Planina mts. Bulgaria 34 43.15N 25.00E
Staraya Russa Russian Fed. 44 58.00N 31.22E
Staraya Sinyava Ukraine 37 49.38N 27.39E
Stara Zagora Bulgaria 34 42.26N 25.39E
Starbuck I. Kiribati 85 5.37S 155.55W
Stargard Szczeciński Poland 36 53.21N 15.01E
Stari Bar Yugo. 31 42.06N 19.08E
Stari Grad Croatia 31 43.11N 16.36E
Staritsa Russian Fed. 44 56.29N 34.59E
Starke U.S.A. 113 29.55N 82.06W
Starkville U.S.A. 111 33.28N 88.48W
Starnberg Germany 39 48.00N 11.20E
Starnberger See l. Germany 39 47.55N 11.18E
Starobin Belarus 37 52.40N 27.29E
Starogard Gdański Poland 37 53.59N 18.33E
Starokonstantinov Ukraine 37 49.48N 27.10E
Start Pt. U.K. 13 50.13N 3.38W
Staryy Oskol Russian Fed. 45 51.20N 37.50E
Stassfurt Germany 38 51.51N 11.34E
State College U.S.A. 114 40.48N 77.52W
Staten I. see Estados, Isla de los i. Argentina 125
Statesville U.S.A. 113 35.46N 80.54W
Staunton U.S.A. 113 38.09N 79.04W
Stavanger Norway 42 58.58N 5.45E
Stavelot Belgium 16 50.23N 5.54E
Staveren Neth. 16 52.53N 5.21E
Stavern Norway 42 59.00N 10.02E
Stavropol' Russian Fed. 45 45.03N 41.59E
Stavropolskaya Vozvyshennost mts. Russian Fed. 45
 45.00N 42.30E
Stavrós Greece 34 39.18N 22.15E
Stavroúpolis Greece 34 41.12N 24.45E
Stawell Australia 92 37.06S 142.52E
Stawiski Poland 37 53.23N 22.09E
Stayner Canada 104 44.25N 80.05W
Stayton U.S.A. 108 44.48N 122.48W
Steamboat Springs town U.S.A. 108 40.29N 106.50W
Steele U.S.A. 110 46.51N 99.55W
Steelpoort R.S.A. 80 24.44S 30.13E
Steelton U.S.A. 114 40.14N 76.49W
Steenbergen Neth. 16 51.36N 4.19E
Steenvoorde France 19 50.48N 2.35E
Steenwijk Neth. 16 52.47N 6.07E
Steep Rock Lake town Canada 102 48.50N 91.38W
Stege Denmark 43 54.59N 12.18E
Stegeborg Sweden 43 58.26N 16.35E
Steiermark d. Austria 36 47.10N 15.10E
Steilloopbrug R.S.A. 80 23.26S 28.37E
Steinach Austria 39 47.05N 11.28E
Steinbach Canada 101 49.32N 96.41W
Steinhuder Meer l. Germany 38 52.28N 9.19E
Steinkjer Norway 40 64.00N 11.30E
Steinkopf R.S.A. 80 29.16S 17.41E
Stella R.S.A. 80 26.32S 24.51E
Stellarton Canada 103 45.34N 62.40W
Stellenbosch R.S.A. 80 33.56S 18.51E
Stelvio, Passo dello pass Italy 30 46.32N 10.27E
Stenay France 19 49.29N 5.11E
Stendal Germany 38 52.36N 11.51E
Stenstorp Sweden 43 58.16N 13.43E
Stenstrup Denmark 42 56.59N 9.52E
Stenträsk Sweden 40 66.20N 19.50E
Stepan Ukraine 37 51.09N 26.18E
Stephens City U.S.A. 114 39.05N 78.13W
Stephenville Canada 103 48.33N 58.35W
Stephenville U.S.A. 111 32.13N 98.12W
Stepnyak Kazakhstan 50 52.52N 70.49E
Steps Pt. c. Samoa 84 14.22S 170.45W
Sterkstroom R.S.A. 80 31.32S 26.31E
Sterling Colo. U.S.A. 108 40.37N 103.13W
Sterling Ill. U.S.A. 110 41.48N 89.43W
Sterling Mich. U.S.A. 104 44.02N 84.02W
Sterling Run U.S.A. 114 41.25N 78.12W
Sterlitamak Russian Fed. 44 53.40N 55.59E
Šternberk Czech Republic 37 49.44N 17.18E
Stettler Canada 100 52.19N 112.40W
Steuben U.S.A. 112 46.12N 86.27W
Steubenville U.S.A. 114 40.22N 80.37W
Stevenage U.K. 13 51.54N 0.11W
Stevenson L. Canada 101 53.56N 96.09W
Stevens Point U.S.A. 110 44.32N 89.33W
Stevenson U.K. 14 55.39N 4.45W
Stewart Canada 100 55.56N 130.01W
Stewart I. New Zealand 86 47.00S 168.00E
Stewart River town Canada 98 63.19N 139.26W
Stewartstown U.S.A. 105 45.01N 71.30W
Steynsburg R.S.A. 80 31.17S 25.48E
Steyr Austria 36 48.04N 14.25E
Stigliano Italy 33 40.24N 16.14E
Stigtomta Sweden 43 58.48N 16.47E
Stikine r. Canada/U.S.A. 100 56.40N 132.30W
Stikine Mts. Canada 98 59.00N 129.00W
Stikine Plateau f. Canada 100 58.45N 130.00W
Stiklestad Norway 40 63.48N 11.22E
Stilbaai R.S.A. 80 34.22S 21.22E
Stilís Greece 35 38.55N 22.36E
Stillwater U.S.A. 111 36.07N 97.04W
Stillwater Range mts. U.S.A. 108 39.50N 118.15W
Stillwater Resr. U.S.A. 115 43.57N 74.58W
Stilo, Punta c. Italy 33 38.28N 16.36E
Stilton U.K. 13 52.29N 0.17W
Stimson Canada 102 48.58N 80.36W
Stinchar r. U.K. 14 55.06N 5.00W
Stînisoara, Munţii mts. Romania 37 47.10N 26.00E

Štip Macedonia 34 41.42N 22.10E
Stira Greece 35 38.09N 24.14E
Stirling Canada 105 44.18N 77.33W
Stirling U.K. 14 56.07N 3.57W
Stirling Range mts. Australia 89 34.23S 117.50E
Stjernøya i. Norway 40 70.17N 22.40E
Stjördalshalsen Norway 40 63.29N 10.51E
Stobi site Macedonia 34 41.34N 21.58E
Stockach Germany 39 47.51N 9.00E
Stockaryd Sweden 43 57.18N 14.35E
Stockbridge U.K. 13 51.07N 1.30W
Stockbridge U.S.A. 104 42.27N 84.11W
Stockdale U.S.A. 111 29.14N 97.58W
Stockerau Austria 36 48.23N 16.13E
Stockett U.S.A. 47.21N 111.10W
Stockholm Sweden 43 59.20N 18.03E
Stockholm d. Sweden 43 59.20N 18.03E
Stockinbingal Australia 93 34.03S 147.53E
Stockport U.K. 12 53.25N 2.11W
Stocksbridge U.K. 12 53.30N 1.36W
Stockton Calif. U.S.A. 108 37.57N 121.17W
Stockton Kans. U.S.A. 110 39.26N 99.16W
Stockton-on-Tees U.K. 12 54.34N 1.20W
Stoeng Tréng Cambodia 56 13.31N 105.59E
Stoffberg R.S.A. 80 25.25S 29.49E
Stogovo mts. Macedonia 34 41.31N 20.38E
Stoke-on-Trent U.K. 12 53.01N 2.11W
Stokes Bay town Canada 104 45.00N 81.23W
Stokhod r. Ukraine 37 51.52N 25.38E
Stokksund Norway 40 64.03N 10.05E
Stolac Bosnia-Herzegovina 31 43.05N 17.58E
Stolberg Germany 38 50.46N 6.13E
Stolbtsy Belarus 37 53.30N 26.44E
Stolin Belarus 37 51.52N 26.51E
Ston Croatia 31 42.50N 17.42E
Stone U.K. 12 52.55N 2.10W
Stoneboro U.S.A. 114 41.20N 80.07W
Stonecliffe Canada 105 46.12N 77.54W
Stone Harbor U.S.A. 115 39.03N 74.45W
Stonehaven U.K. 14 56.58N 2.13W
Stony I. Canada 103 53.00N 55.48W
Stony Pt. c. Canada 104 44.33N 78.05W
Stony Rapids town Canada 101 59.16N 105.50W
Stooping r. Canada 102 52.08N 82.00W
Storå r. Denmark 42 56.19N 8.19E
Stora Gla l. Sweden 43 59.30N 12.30E
Stora Le l. Sweden 42 59.05N 11.53E
Stora Lulevatten l. Sweden 40 67.10N 19.16E
Stora Möja Sweden 43 59.26N 18.55E
Stora Sjöfallets Nat. Park Sweden 40 67.44N 18.16E
Storavan l. Sweden 40 65.40N 18.15E
Storby Finland 41 60.13N 19.34E
Stord i. Norway 42 59.50N 5.11E
Store Baelt str. Denmark 42 55.30N 11.00E
Store Heddinge Denmark 43 55.19N 12.25E
Stor Elvdal Norway 41 61.32N 11.02E
Støren Norway 40 63.03N 10.18E
Storfors Sweden 43 59.32N 14.16E
Storlien Sweden 40 63.20N 12.05E
Storm Lake town U.S.A. 110 42.39N 95.10W
Stornoway U.K. 14 58.12N 6.23W
Storozhevsk Russian Fed. 44 62.00N 52.20E
Storozhinets Ukraine 37 48.11N 25.40E
Storsjön l. Sweden 40 63.10N 14.20E
Storuman Sweden 40 65.06N 17.06E
Storuman l. Sweden 40 65.10N 16.40E
Storvreta Sweden 43 59.58N 17.42E
Stouffville Canada 104 43.59N 79.15W
Stoughton U.S.A. 110 42.55N 89.13W
Stour r. Dorset U.K. 13 50.43N 1.47W
Stour r. Kent U.K. 13 51.19N 1.22E
Stour r. Suffolk U.K. 13 51.56N 1.03E
Stourport-on-Severn U.K. 13 52.21N 2.16W
Stowmarket U.K. 13 52.11N 1.00E
Stow on the Wold U.K. 13 51.55N 1.42W
Strabane U.K. 15 54.50N 7.30W
Stradbally Laois Rep. of Ire. 15 53.01N 7.09W
Stradbroke I. Australia 91 27.38S 153.45E
Stradella Italy 30 45.05N 9.18E
Straelen Germany 38 51.27N 6.16E
Strahan Australia 91 42.08S 145.21E
Strakonice Czech Republic 38 49.16N 13.55E
Stralsund Germany 38 54.19N 13.05E
Strand R.S.A. 80 34.07S 18.50E
Stranda Norway 40 62.19N 6.58E
Strandfjord Lough U.K. 15 54.28N 5.35W
Strangways town Australia 92 29.08S 136.35E
Stranraer U.K. 14 54.54N 5.02W
Strasbourg France 19 48.35N 7.45E
Strasburg Germany 38 53.30N 13.44E
Strasburg N.Dak. U.S.A. 110 46.08N 100.10W
Strasburg Ohio U.S.A. 114 40.36N 81.32W
Strasburg Va. U.S.A. 114 38.59N 78.22W
Strasswalchen Austria 39 47.59N 13.15E
Stratford Australia 93 37.57S 147.05E
Stratford Canada 104 43.22N 80.57W
Stratford New Zealand 86 39.20S 174.18E
Stratford Conn. U.S.A. 115 41.14N 73.07W
Stratford N.H. U.S.A. 105 44.40N 71.34W
Stratford Tex. U.S.A. 111 36.20N 102.04W
Stratford-upon-Avon U.K. 13 52.12N 1.42W
Strathalbyn Australia 92 35.16S 138.54E
Strathclyde d. U.K. 14 55.45N 4.45W
Strathcona Prov. Park Canada 100 49.38N 125.40W
Strathmore r. Tayside U.K. 14 56.44N 2.45W
Strathroy Canada 104 42.57N 81.38W
Strathspey f. U.K. 14 57.25N 3.25W
Stratton U.S.A. 110 39.18N 102.36W
Stratton Mtn. U.S.A. 115 43.05N 72.56W
Straubing Germany 39 48.53N 12.34E
Straumnes c. Iceland 40 66.30N 23.05W
Strausberg Germany 38 52.35N 13.53E
Strawn U.S.A. 111 32.33N 98.30W
Streaky B. Australia 92 32.36S 134.08E
Streaky Bay town Australia 92 32.48S 134.13E
Streator U.S.A. 110 41.07N 88.53W
Street U.K. 13 51.07N 2.43W

Streeter U.S.A. 110 46.39N 99.21W
Streetsville Canada 104 43.35N 79.42W
Stresa Italy 30 45.53N 8.32E
Stretton Australia 89 32.30S 117.42E
Strimon r. Greece 34 40.47N 23.51E
Stromboli i. Italy 33 38.48N 15.13E
Stromeferry U.K. 14 57.21N 5.34W
Stromness U.K. 14 58.57N 3.18W
Strömö i. Faroe Is. 10 62.08N 7.00W
Strömsbruk Sweden 41 61.53N 17.19E
Strömstad Sweden 42 58.56N 11.10E
Strömsund Sweden 40 63.51N 15.35E
Strömsvattudal f. Sweden 40 64.15N 15.00E
Strongfield Canada 101 51.20N 106.36W
Strongoli Italy 33 39.15N 17.03E
Stronsay i. U.K. 14 59.07N 2.36W
Stroud Australia 93 32.25S 151.58E
Stroud U.K. 13 51.44N 2.12W
Stroudsburg U.S.A. 115 40.59N 75.12W
Struan Australia 92 37.08S 140.49E
Struer Denmark 42 56.29N 8.28E
Struga Macedonia 34 41.11N 20.40E
Struma r. Bulgaria see Strimon r. Greece 34
Strumica Macedonia 34 41.28N 22.41E
Struthers U.S.A. 114 41.04N 80.38W
Stryama r. Bulgaria 34 42.40N 24.28E
Strydenburg R.S.A. 80 29.56S 23.39E
Stryker U.S.A. 108 48.40N 114.44W
Stryy Ukraine 37 49.16N 23.51E
Strzelecki Creek r. Australia 92 29.37S 139.59E
Strzelno Poland 37 52.38N 18.11E
Stuart Fla. U.S.A. 113 27.12N 80.16W
Stuart Nebr. U.S.A. 110 42.36N 99.08W
Stuart Creek town Australia 92 29.43S 137.01E
Stuart L. Canada 100 54.30N 124.30W
Stuart Range mts. Australia 92 29.10S 134.56E
Stuart Town Australia 93 32.51S 149.08E
Stubbeköbing Denmark 43 54.53N 12.03E
Studenica Yugo. 34 43.21N 20.35E
Studen Kladenets, Yazovir l. Bulgaria 34 41.37N
 25.29E
Studsvik Sweden 43 58.46N 17.23E
Stupart r. Canada 101 56.00N 93.22W
Sturgeon r. Canada 104 46.19N 79.58W
Sturgeon Bay town U.S.A. 110 44.50N 87.23W
Sturgeon Falls town Canada 104 46.22N 79.55W
Sturgeon L. Ont. Canada 102 50.00N 90.40W
Sturgeon L. Ont. Canada 104 44.28N 78.42W
Sturgis U.S.A. 110 44.25N 103.31W
Sturminster Newton U.K. 13 50.56N 2.18W
Sturt B. Australia 92 35.24S 137.08E
Sturt Creek r. Australia 88 20.08S 127.24E
Sturt Desert Australia 92 28.30S 141.12E
Sturt Plain f. Australia 90 17.00S 132.48E
Stutterheim R.S.A. 80 32.32S 27.25E
Stuttgart Germany 39 48.46N 9.11E
Stviga r. Belarus 37 52.04N 27.54E
Stykkishólmur Iceland 40 65.06N 22.48W
Styr r. Belarus 37 52.07N 26.35E
Suao Taiwan 55 24.36N 121.51E
Subarnarekha r. India 63 21.34N 87.24E
Subay', 'Urūq f. Saudi Arabia 72 22.15N 43.05E
Subei Guangai Zongqu canal China 54 34.06N
 120.19E
Subiaco Italy 30 41.55N 13.06E
Subotica Yugo. 31 46.06N 19.39E
Suceava Romania 37 47.39N 26.19E
Suchan Russian Fed. 57 43.03N 133.05E
Suck r. Rep. of Ire. 15 53.16N 8.04W
Suckling, Mt. P.N.G. 90 9.45S 148.55E
Sucre Bolivia 124 19.02S 65.17W
Sucuriu r. Brazil 126 20.44S 51.40W
Sudalsvatnet l. Norway 42 59.35N 6.45E
Sudan Africa 72 14.30N 29.00E
Sudan U.S.A. 111 34.04N 102.32W
Sudbury Canada 104 46.30N 81.00W
Sudbury U.K. 13 52.03N 0.45E
Sude r. Germany 38 53.22N 10.45E
Sudety mts. Czech Republic/Poland 36 50.30N 16.30E
Sud Ouest d. Burkina 76 10.45N 3.10W
Sudzukhe Russian Fed. 57 42.50N 133.43E
Sueca Spain 25 39.12N 0.19W
Suez see As Suways Egypt 66
Suez Canal see Suways, Qanāt as canal Egypt 66
Suez, G. of see Suways, Khalīj as g. Egypt 66
Sūf Jordan 67 32.19N 35.50E
Şufaynah Saudi Arabia 64 23.09N 40.32E
Suffolk d. U.K. 13 52.16N 1.00E
Suffolk U.S.A. 113 36.44N 76.37W
Sugargrove U.S.A. 114 41.59N 79.21W
Sugar I. U.S.A. 104 46.25N 84.12W
Suhaia, Lacul l. Romania 34 43.45N 25.15E
Şuḩār Oman 65 24.23N 56.43E
Sühbaatar d. Mongolia 54 45.30N 114.00E
Suhl Germany 38 50.37N 10.41E
Suhopolje Croatia 31 45.48N 17.30E
Suĭ Pakistan 62 28.37N 69.19E
Suibin China 53 47.19N 131.49E
Suichang China 55 28.36N 119.16E
Suichuan China 55 26.24N 114.31E
Suide China 54 37.35N 110.08E
Suihua China 53 46.39N 126.59E
Suileng China 53 47.15N 127.05E
Suining Jiangsu China 54 33.54N 117.56E
Suining Sichuan China 55 30.31N 105.32E
Suipacha Argentina 125 34.47S 59.40W
Suippes France 19 49.08N 4.32E
Suir r. Rep. of Ire. 15 52.17N 7.00W
Suita Japan 57 34.45N 135.32E
Sui Xian Henan China 54 34.25N 115.04E
Sui Xian Hubei China 55 31.45N 113.30E
Suiyang Guizhou China 55 27.57N 107.11E
Suizhong China 54 40.25N 120.25E
Suj China 54 42.02N 107.58E
Sūjāngarh India 62 27.42N 74.28E

211

Sujāwal Pakistan 62 24.36N 68.05E
Sukabumi Indonesia 59 6.55S 106.50E
Sukadana Indonesia 58 1.15S 110.00E
Sukaraja Indonesia 58 2.23S 110.35E
Sukhinichi Russian Fed. 44 54.07N 35.21E
Sukhona r. Russian Fed. 44 61.30N 46.28E
Sukhumi Georgia 45 43.01N 41.01E
Sukkertoppen Greenland 99 65.40N 53.00W
Sukkur Pakistan 62 27.42N 68.52E
Sukoharjo Indonesia 59 7.40S 110.50E
Sukumo Japan 57 32.56N 132.44E
Sul d. Portugal 27 38.50N 8.05W
Sula i. Norway 41 61.08N 4.55E
Sulaimān Range mts. Pakistan 62 30.00N 69.50E
Sulak r. Russian Fed. 45 43.18N 47.35E
Sula, Kepulauan is. Indonesia 59 1.50S 125.10E
Sulawesi i. Indonesia 59 2.00S 120.30E
Sulawesi Selatan d. Indonesia 59 3.45S 120.30E
Sulawesi Utara d. Indonesia 59 1.45S 120.30E
Sulechów Poland 36 52.06N 15.37E
Sulejów Poland 37 51.22N 19.53E
Sulina Romania 29 45.08N 29.40E
Sulingen Germany 38 52.41N 8.47E
Sulitjelma Norway 40 67.10N 16.05E
Sullana Peru 122 4.52S 80.39W
Sullivan U.S.A. 110 38.13N 91.10W
Sully France 19 47.46N 2.22E
Sulmona Italy 31 42.03N 13.55E
Sulphur U.S.A. 111 34.31N 96.58W
Sultan Canada 102 47.36N 82.47W
Sultan Hamud Kenya 79 2.02S 37.20E
Sultānpur India 63 26.16N 82.04E
Sulu Archipelago Phil. 59 5.30N 121.00E
Sulūq Libya 75 31.40N 20.15E
Sulu Sea Pacific Oc. 59 8.00N 120.00E
Sulzbach-Rosenburg Germany 38 49.30N 11.45E
Sumatera i. Indonesia 58 2.00S 102.00E
Sumatera Barat d. Indonesia 58 1.00S 100.00E
Sumatera Selatan d. Indonesia 58 3.00S 104.00E
Sumatera Utara d. Indonesia 58 2.00N 99.00E
Sumatra see Sumatera i. Indonesia 58
Sumatra U.S.A. 108 46.38N 107.31W
Sumba i. Indonesia 58 9.30S 119.55E
Sumbar r. Turkmenistan 65 38.00N 55.20E
Sumbawa i. Indonesia 58 8.45S 117.50E
Sumbawanga Tanzania 79 7.58S 31.36E
Sumbe Angola 78 11.11S 13.52E
Sumbilla Spain 25 43.10N 1.40W
Sumburgh Head U.K. 14 59.51N 1.16W
Sumedang Indonesia 59 6.54S 107.55E
Sümeg Hungary 31 46.59N 17.17E
Šumen Bulgaria 29 43.15N 26.55E
Sumenep Indonesia 59 7.01S 113.51E
Sumgait Azerbaijan 65 40.35N 49.38E
Summerland Canada 100 49.32N 119.41W
Summerside Canada 103 46.24N 63.47W
Summersville U.S.A. 114 38.17N 80.51W
Summerville Ga. U.S.A. 113 34.29N 85.21W
Summerville S.C. U.S.A. 113 33.02N 80.11W
Šumperk Czech Republic 36 49.58N 16.58E
Sumprabum Myanmar 56 26.33N 97.34E
Sumusţā al Waqf Egypt 66 28.55N 30.51E
Sumy Ukraine 45 50.55N 34.49E
Sunagawa Japan 57 43.30N 141.55E
Sunām India 62 30.08N 75.48E
Sunāmganj Bangla. 63 25.04N 91.24E
Sunart, Loch U.K. 14 56.43N 5.45W
Sunburst U.S.A. 108 48.53N 111.55W
Sunbury Australia 93 37.36S 144.45E
Sunbury Ohio U.S.A. 114 40.14N 82.52W
Sunbury Penn. U.S.A. 114 40.52N 76.47W
Sundance U.S.A. 108 44.24N 104.23W
Sundarbans f. India/Bangla. 63 21.45N 89.00E
Sundargarh India 63 22.07N 84.02E
Sunda, Selat str. Indonesia 58 6.00S 105.50E
Sundays r. R.S.A. 80 33.43S 25.50E
Sundbyberg Sweden 43 59.22N 17.58E
Sunde Norway 42 59.50N 5.43E
Sunderland Canada 104 44.16N 79.04W
Sunderland U.K. 12 54.55N 1.22W
Sundridge Canada 104 45.46N 79.24W
Sundsvall Sweden 41 62.23N 17.18E
Sungai Kolok Thailand 56 6.02N 101.58E
Sungaipakning Indonesia 58 1.19N 102.00E
Sungaipenuh Indonesia 58 2.00S 101.28E
Sungguminasa Indonesia 58 5.14S 119.27E
Sungurlu Turkey 64 40.10N 34.23E
Sunjikāy Sudan 73 12.20N 29.46E
Sunne Sweden 43 59.50N 13.09E
Sunnersta Sweden 43 59.48N 17.39E
Sunnyside U.S.A. 108 46.20N 120.00W
Suntar Russian Fed. 51 62.10N 117.35E
Suntsar Pakistan 62 25.31N 62.00E
Sun Valley town U.S.A. 106 43.42N 114.21W
Sunwu China 53 49.40N 127.10E
Sunyani Ghana 76 7.22N 2.18W
Suō nada str. Japan 57 33.45N 131.30E
Suoyarvi Russian Fed. 44 62.02N 32.20E
Supaul India 63 26.07N 86.36E
Superior Mont. U.S.A. 108 47.12N 114.53W
Superior Wisc. U.S.A. 110 46.42N 92.05W
Superior Wyo. U.S.A. 108 41.46N 108.58W
Superior, L. Canada/U.S.A. 112 48.00N 88.00W
Supetar Croatia 31 43.23N 16.33E
Suphan Buri Thailand 56 14.14N 100.07E
Suphan Buri r. Thailand 56 13.34N 100.15E
Süphan Dagi mtn. Turkey 45 38.55N 42.55E
Suqian China 54 33.59N 118.25E
Suquţrá i. Yemen 71 12.30N 54.00E
Şūr Lebanon 67 33.16N 35.12E
Şūr Oman 65 22.23N 59.32E
Sur d. W. Sahara 74 23.40N 14.15W
Sura Russian Fed. 44 53.52N 45.45E
Sūrāb Pakistan 62 28.29N 66.16E
Surabaya Indonesia 59 7.14S 112.45E
Surakarta Indonesia 59 7.32S 110.50E
Şūrān Syria 66 35.18N 36.44E
Surany Slovakia 37 48.06N 18.14E

Surat Australia 91 27.09S 149.05E
Surat India 62 21.12N 72.50E
Sūratgarh India 62 29.18N 73.54E
Surat Thani Thailand 56 9.09N 99.23E
Surazh Russian Fed. 37 53.00N 32.22E
Sur, Cabo c. I. de Pascua 85 27.12S 109.26W
Surdulica Yugo. 34 42.41N 22.10E
Sûre r. Lux. 16 49.43N 6.31E
Sureau, Lac l. Canada 103 53.10N 70.50W
Surendranagar India 62 22.42N 71.41E
Surfer's Paradise Australia 93 27.58S 153.26E
Surgères France 20 46.07N 0.45W
Surgut Russian Fed. 9 61.13N 73.20E
Sūri India 63 23.55N 87.32E
Surigao Phil. 59 9.47N 125.29E
Surin Thailand 56 14.58N 103.33E
Surinam S. America 123 4.00N 56.00W
Suriname r. Surinam 123 5.52N 55.14W
Sur, Punta c. Argentina 125 36.53S 56.41W
Surrey d. U.K. 13 51.16N 0.30W
Sursee Switz. 39 47.10N 8.06E
Surt Libya 75 31.13N 16.35E
Surtanāhu Pakistan 62 26.22N 70.00E
Surte Sweden 43 57.49N 12.01E
Surt, Khalīj g. Libya 75 31.45N 17.50E
Surtsey i. Iceland 40 63.18N 20.30W
Surud Ad mtn. Somali Rep. 71 10.41N 47.18E
Suruga-wan b. Japan 57 34.45N 138.30E
Susa Italy 30 45.08N 7.03E
Susak i. Croatia 31 44.31N 14.18E
Susanino Russian Fed. 51 52.46N 140.09E
Susanville U.S.A. 108 40.25N 120.39W
Sušice Czech Republic 38 49.14N 13.32E
Susquehanna U.S.A. 115 41.57N 75.36W
Susquehanna r. U.S.A. 115 39.33N 76.05W
Susquehanna, West Branch r. U.S.A. 114 40.53N 76.47W
Sussex N.J. U.S.A. 115 41.13N 74.36W
Sussex Wyo. U.S.A. 108 43.42N 106.19W
Sutak Jammu & Kashmir 63 33.12N 77.28E
Sutherland Australia 93 34.02S 151.04E
Sutherland R.S.A. 80 32.23S 20.38E
Sutherlin U.S.A. 108 43.25N 123.19W
Sutlej r. Pakistan 62 29.23N 71.02E
Sutton Canada 104 44.18N 79.22W
Sutton r. Canada 102 55.22N 83.48W
Sutton England U.K. 13 51.22N 0.12W
Sutton Nebr. U.S.A. 110 40.36N 97.52W
Sutton W. Va. U.S.A. 114 38.40N 80.43W
Sutton in Ashfield U.K. 12 53.08N 1.16W
Suva Fiji 84 18.08S 178.25E
Suva Planina mts. Yugo. 34 43.10N 22.05E
Suva Reka Yugo. 34 42.21N 20.50E
Suwa Eritrea 72 14.16N 41.10E
Suwałki Poland 37 54.07N 22.56E
Suwanee r. U.S.A. 113 29.18N 83.09W
Suwaymah Jordan 67 31.47N 35.36E
Suways, Khalīj as g. Egypt 66 28.48N 33.00E
Suways, Qanāt as canal Egypt 66 30.40N 32.20E
Suwon S. Korea 53 37.16N 126.59E
Suzhou China 55 31.22N 120.45E
Suzu Japan 57 37.25N 137.17E
Suzuka Japan 57 34.54N 136.39E
Suzuka-sammyaku mts. Japan 57 35.00N 136.20E
Suzu misaki c. Japan 57 37.30N 137.21E
Suzzara Italy 30 45.00N 10.45E
Svalyava Ukraine 37 48.33N 23.00E
Svaneke Denmark 43 55.08N 15.09E
Svanskog Sweden 43 59.11N 12.33E
Svanvik Norway 40 69.25N 30.00E
Svappavaara Sweden 40 67.39N 21.04E
Svarhofthalvöya Norway 40 70.35N 26.00E
Svartå Sweden 43 59.08N 14.31E
Svartån r. Sweden 43 59.37N 16.33E
Svartisen mtn. Norway 40 66.40N 13.56E
Svatovo Ukraine 45 49.24N 38.11E
Svay Riêng Cambodia 56 11.05N 105.48E
Svedala Sweden 43 55.30N 13.14E
Sveg Sweden 41 62.02N 14.21E
Svelgen Norway 41 61.47N 5.15E
Svelvik Norway 42 59.37N 10.24E
Svendborg Denmark 42 55.03N 10.37E
Svenljunga Sweden 43 57.30N 13.07E
Svenstrup Denmark 42 56.59N 9.52E
Sverdlovsk see Yekaterinburg Russian Fed. 44
Sveti Nikole Macedonia 34 41.51N 21.56E
Svetlograd Russian Fed. 45 45.25N 42.58E
Svetogorsk Russian Fed. 44 61.07N 28.50E
Svilengrad Bulgaria 34 41.49N 26.12E
Svindal Norway 42 58.30N 7.28E
Svinesund Sweden 42 59.06N 11.16E
Svinninge Denmark 42 55.43N 11.28E
Svinö i. Faroe Is. 10 62.17N 6.18W
Svir r. Russian Fed. 44 60.09N 32.15E
Svishtov Bulgaria 34 43.36N 25.23E
Svisloch Belarus 37 53.28N 29.00E
Svitavy Czech Republic 36 49.45N 16.27E
Svobodnyy Russian Fed. 53 51.24N 128.05E
Svoge Bulgaria 34 42.58N 23.21E
Svolvaer Norway 40 68.15N 14.40E
Swaffham U.K. 13 52.38N 0.42E
Swain Reefs Australia 90 21.40S 152.15E
Swains I. Samoa 84 11.03S 171.06W
Swakop r. Namibia 80 22.38S 14.32E
Swakopmund Namibia 80 22.40S 14.34E
Swale r. U.K. 12 54.05N 1.40W
Swan r. Australia 89 32.03S 115.45E
Swanage U.K. 13 50.36N 1.59W
Swan Hill town Australia 92 35.23S 143.37E
Swan Hills Canada 100 54.42N 115.24W
Swan L. Canada 101 52.30N 100.45W
Swan River town Canada 101 52.10N 101.17W
Swansea Australia 91 42.08S 148.00E
Swansea U.K. 13 51.37N 3.57W
Swanton U.S.A. 105 44.55N 73.07W

Swastika Canada 102 48.07N 80.06W
Swatow see Shantou China 55
Swaziland Africa 80 26.30S 32.00E
Sweden Europe 40 63.00N 16.00E
Swedru Ghana 76 5.31N 0.42W
Sweetwater U.S.A. 111 32.28N 100.25W
Swidnica Poland 36 50.51N 16.29E
Swiebodzin Poland 36 52.15N 15.32E
Swietokrzyskie, Góry mts. Poland 37 51.00N 20.30E
Swift Current town Canada 101 50.17N 107.50W
Swilly, Lough Rep. of Ire. 15 55.10N 7.32W
Swindon U.K. 13 51.33N 1.47W
Swinoujście Poland 36 53.55N 14.18E
Switzerland Europe 39 46.45N 8.30E
Swords Rep. of Ire. 11 53.27N 6.15W
Syderö i. Faroe Is. 10 61.30N 6.50W
Sydney Australia 93 33.55S 151.10E
Sydney Canada 103 46.09N 60.11W
Sydney Mines town Canada 103 46.14N 60.14W
Sydpröven Greenland 99 60.30N 45.35W
Syke Germany 38 52.54N 8.49E
Syktyvkar Russian Fed. 44 61.42N 50.45E
Sylacauga U.S.A. 113 33.10N 86.15W
Sylhet Bangla. 63 24.54N 91.52E
Sylt i. Germany 38 54.54N 8.20E
Sylte Norway 40 62.31N 7.07E
Sylvan Lake town Canada 100 52.20N 114.10W
Syracuse see Siracusa Italy 33
Syracuse Kans. U.S.A. 111 37.59N 101.45W
Syracuse N.Y. U.S.A. 115 43.03N 76.09W
Syr Darya r. Kazakhstan 9 46.00N 61.21E
Syria Asia 64 35.00N 38.00E
Syriam Myanmar 58 16.45N 96.17E
Syrian Desert see Bādiyat ash Shām des. Asia 64
Syzran Russian Fed. 44 53.10N 48.29E
Szarvas Hungary 37 46.52N 20.34E
Szczecin Poland 36 53.25N 14.32E
Szczecinek Poland 36 53.42N 16.41E
Szczytno Poland 37 53.34N 21.00E
Szécsény Hungary 37 48.06N 19.31E
Szeged Hungary 31 46.15N 20.09E
Székesfehérvár Hungary 37 47.12N 18.25E
Szekszárd Hungary 31 46.21N 18.42E
Szentes Hungary 31 46.39N 20.16E
Szentgotthárd Hungary 31 46.57N 16.18E
Szolnok Hungary 37 47.10N 20.12E
Szombathely Hungary 36 47.12N 16.38E
Sztutowo Poland 37 54.20N 19.15E

T

Tabagne Côte d'Ivoire 76 7.59N 3.04W
Ţābah Saudi Arabia 64 27.02N 42.10E
Tábara Spain 26 41.49N 5.57W
Tabarka Tunisia 32 36.57N 8.45E
Tabas Khorāsān Iran 65 32.48N 60.14E
Ţabas Khorāsān Iran 65 33.36N 56.55E
Tabasco d. Mexico 116 18.30N 93.00W
Tābask, Kūh-e mtn. Iran 65 29.51N 51.52E
Tabelbala Algeria 74 29.24N 3.15W
Taber Canada 100 49.47N 112.08W
Tabernes de Valldigna Spain 25 39.04N 0.16W
Tabili Zaïre 79 0.04N 28.01E
Table B. R.S.A. 80 33.52S 18.26E
Tábor Czech Republic 36 49.25N 14.41E
Tabora Tanzania 79 5.02S 32.50E
Tabora d. Tanzania 79 5.30S 32.50E
Tabou Côte d'Ivoire 76 4.28N 7.20W
Tabrīz Iran 65 38.05N 46.18E
Tabuaço Portugal 26 41.07N 7.34W
Tabuaeran i. Kiribati 83 3.52N 159.20W
Tabūk Saudi Arabia 66 28.23N 36.36E
Tabulam Australia 93 28.50S 152.35E
Ţabūt Yemen 71 15.55N 52.09E
Tachia Taiwan 55 24.21N 120.37E
Tachikawa Japan 57 35.42N 139.25E
Tachov Czech Republic 38 49.48N 12.38E
Tacloban Phil. 59 11.15N 124.59E
Tacna Peru 124 18.01S 70.15W
Tacoma U.S.A. 108 47.15N 122.27W
Taconic Mts. U.S.A. 115 42.36N 73.14W
Taconic State Park U.S.A. 115 42.05N 73.34W
Tacora mtn. Chile 124 17.40S 69.45W
Tacuarembó Uruguay 125 31.44S 55.59W
Tademaït, Plateau du f. Algeria 75 28.30N 2.15E
Tadjetaret, Oued Algeria 75 21.00N 7.30E
Tadjmout Algeria 75 25.30N 3.42E
Tadjoura, Golfe de g. Djibouti 71 11.42N 43.00E
Tadmor New Zealand 86 41.26S 172.47E
Tadmur Syria 64 34.36N 38.15E
Tadoule L. Canada 101 58.36N 98.20W
Tadoussac Canada 103 48.09N 69.43W
Taegu S. Korea 53 35.52N 128.36E
Taejin S. Korea 53 36.34N 129.24E
Taejön S. Korea 53 36.20N 127.26E
Tafalla Spain 25 42.31N 1.40W
Ţafas Syria 67 32.44N 36.04E
Tafassasset, Oued wadi Niger 75 22.00N 9.55E
Tafassasset, Ténéré du des. Niger 77 21.00N 11.00E
Taffanel, Lac l. Canada 103 53.22N 70.56W
Tafí Viejo Argentina 124 26.45S 65.15W
Tafraout Morocco 74 29.40N 8.58W
Taftān, Kūh-e mtn. Iran 65 28.38N 61.08E
Taga W. Samoa 84 13.47S 172.30W
Taganrog Russian Fed. 45 47.14N 38.55E

Taganrog, Gulf of g. Ukraine/Russian Fed. 45 47.00N 38.30E
Tagant d. Mauritania 74 18.30N 10.30W
Tagant f. Mauritania 74 18.20N 11.00W
Tagaytay City Phil. 59 14.07N 120.58E
Tagbilaran Phil. 59 9.38N 123.53E
Tagish Canada 100 60.19N 134.16W
Tagliacozzo Italy 30 42.04N 13.14E
Tagliamento r. Italy 30 45.38N 13.06E
Taglio di Po Italy 30 45.00N 12.12E
Tagounit Morocco 74 29.58N 5.36W
Tagula I. P.N.G. 90 11.30S 153.30E
Tagum Phil. 59 7.33N 125.53E
Tagus r. Portugal/Spain see Tejo r. Portugal 27
Tahaa i. Îs. de la Société 85 16.38S 151.30W
Tahara Japan 57 34.40N 137.16E
Tahat mtn. Algeria 75 23.18N 5.32E
Tahe China 53 52.35N 124.48E
Tahiti i. Îs. de la Société 85 17.37S 149.27W
Tahiti, Archipel de is. Îs. de la Société 85 17.00S 149.35W
Tahlequah U.S.A. 111 35.55N 94.58W
Tahoe, L. U.S.A. 108 39.07N 120.03W
Tahoua Niger 77 14.57N 5.16E
Tahoua d. Niger 77 15.38N 4.50E
Ţahţā Egypt 64 26.46N 31.30E
Tahuna Indonesia 59 3.37N 125.29E
Taï Côte d'Ivoire 76 5.52N 7.28W
Tai'an China 54 36.16N 117.13E
Taiarapu, Presqu'île de pen. Tahiti 85 17.47S 149.14W
Taibai China 54 36.08N 108.41E
Taibai Shan mtn. China 54 33.55N 107.45E
Taibus Qi China 54 41.55N 115.23E
Taidong Taiwan 55 22.49N 121.10E
Taigu China 54 37.23N 112.34E
Taihang Shan mts. China 54 36.00N 113.35E
Taihape New Zealand 86 39.40S 175.48E
Taihe Anhui China 54 33.10N 115.36E
Taihe Jiangxi China 55 26.48N 114.56E
Tai Hu l. China 55 31.15N 120.10E
Tailai China 53 46.23N 123.24E
Tailem Bend town Australia 92 35.14S 139.29E
Tain U.K. 14 57.48N 4.04W
Tainan Taiwan 55 23.01N 120.12E
Taínaron, Ákra c. Greece 35 36.22N 22.30E
Tai-o-haé Îs. Marquises 85 8.55S 140.04W
Taipei Taiwan 55 25.05N 121.30E
Taiping Anhui China 55 30.18N 118.06E
Taiping Malaysia 58 4.54N 100.42E
Taishan China 55 22.10N 112.57E
Taito, Península de pen. Chile 125 46.30S 74.25W
Taitze He r. China 54 41.07N 122.43E
Taivalkoski Finland 40 65.34N 28.15E
Taiwan Asia 55 24.00N 121.00E
Taiwan Str. China/Taiwan 55 24.30N 119.30E
Taiyetos Óros mts. Greece 35 37.16N 22.12E
Taiyuan China 54 38.00N 112.33E
Taiyue Shan mts. China 54 36.40N 112.00E
Taizhong Taiwan 55 24.11N 120.40E
Taizhou China 54 32.22N 119.58E
Ta'izz Yemen 71 13.35N 44.02E
Tajarhī Libya 75 24.21N 14.28E
Tajikistan Asia 52 39.00N 70.30E
Tajimi Japan 57 35.19N 137.08E
Tajitos Mexico 109 30.58N 112.18W
Tajo r. Spain see Tejo r. Portugal 27
Tajrīsh Iran 65 35.48N 51.20E
Tajuna r. Spain 24 40.10N 3.35W
Tak Thailand 56 16.51N 99.08E
Takaka New Zealand 86 40.51S 172.48E
Takalar Indonesia 58 5.29S 119.26E
Takamatsu Japan 57 34.28N 134.05E
Takaoka Japan 57 36.47N 137.00E
Takapuna New Zealand 86 36.48S 174.47E
Takarazuka Japan 57 34.49N 135.21E
Takasaki Japan 57 36.20N 139.00E
Takatsuki Japan 57 34.51N 135.37E
Takayama Japan 57 36.08N 137.15E
Takêv Cambodia 56 11.00N 104.46E
Takhādīd well Iraq 65 29.59N 44.30E
Takhtamukayskiy Russian Fed. 44 54.30N 53.30E
Takla L. Canada 100 55.15N 125.45W
Taklimakan Shamo des. China 52 38.10N 82.00E
Taku r. Canada/U.S.A. 100 58.30N 133.50W
Talā Egypt 66 30.41N 30.56E
Tala Uruguay 125 34.21S 55.46W
Talagang Pakistan 62 32.55N 72.25E
Talagante Chile 125 33.40S 70.56W
Talāja India 62 21.21N 72.03E
Tālāla India 62 21.02N 70.32E
Talangbetutu Indonesia 58 2.48S 104.42E
Talara Peru 122 4.38S 81.18W
Talarrubias Spain 27 39.02N 5.14W
Talasskiy Alatau mts. Kyrgyzstan 52 42.20N 73.20E
Talata Mafara Nigeria 77 12.37N 6.05E
Talaud, Kepulauan is. Indonesia 59 4.20N 126.50E
Talavera de la Reina Spain 27 39.57N 4.50W
Talawdi Sudan 73 10.38N 30.23E
Talbragar r. Australia 93 32.12S 148.37E
Talca Chile 125 35.26S 71.40W
Talcahuano Chile 125 36.43S 73.07W
Tālcher India 63 20.57N 85.13E
Taldom Russian Fed. 44 56.49N 37.30E
Taldykorgan Kazakhstan 52 45.02N 78.23E
Taleex well Somali Rep. 71 9.12N 48.23E
Talia Australia 92 33.16S 134.53E
Taliabu i. Indonesia 59 1.50S 124.55E
Tali Post Sudan 73 5.54N 30.47E
Talkeetna U.S.A. 98 62.20N 150.09W
Ţalkhā Egypt 66 31.04N 31.22E
Tallahassee U.S.A. 113 30.26N 84.19W
Tallangatta Australia 93 36.13S 147.19E
Tallard France 21 44.28N 6.03E
Tallinn Estonia 41 59.22N 24.48E
Tall Kūshik Syria 64 36.48N 42.04E

Tall Salḩab Syria 66 35.15N 36.22E
Tallulah U.S.A. 111 32.25N 91.11W
Ṭallūzā Jordan 67 32.16N 35.18E
Talmont France 18 46.28N 1.37W
Talnoye Ukraine 37 48.55N 30.40E
Taloda India 62 21.34N 74.13E
Talofofo Guam 84 13.21N 144.45E
Taloyoak Canada 99 69.30N 93.20W
Talsi Latvia 41 57.15N 22.36E
Taltal Chile 124 25.24S 70.29W
Talvik Norway 40 70.05N 22.52E
Talwood Australia 93 28.29S 149.25E
Talyawalka r. Australia 93 31.49S 143.25E
Tama r. Japan 57 35.32N 139.47E
Tamala Australia 88 26.42S 113.47E
Tamale Ghana 76 9.26N 0.49W
Tamanar Morocco 74 31.00N 9.35W
Tamanrasset Algeria 75 22.47N 5.31E
Tamanrasset, Oued wadi Algeria 74 21.24N 1.00E
Tamanthi Myanmar 56 25.19N 95.18E
Tamaqua U.S.A. 115 40.48N 75.58W
Tamar r. U.K. 13 50.28N 4.13W
Tamarite de Litera Spain 25 41.52N 0.26E
Tamási Hungary 31 46.38N 18.18E
Tamaské Niger 77 14.55N 5.55E
Tamaulipas d. Mexico 111 24.30N 98.50W
Tamazunchale Mexico 116 21.16N 98.47W
Tambacounda Senegal 76 13.45N 13.40W
Tambara Mozambique 79 16.42S 34.17E
Tambar Springs town Australia 93 31.20S 149.50E
Tambellup Australia 89 34.03S 117.36E
Tambo Australia 90 24.53S 146.15E
Tambo r. Australia 93 37.51S 147.48E
Tambohorano Madagascar 81 17.30S 43.58E
Tambor Mexico 109 25.08N 105.27W
Tambov Russian Fed. 44 52.44N 41.28E
Tambre r. Spain 26 42.49N 8.53W
Tambura Sudan 73 5.36N 27.28E
Tamchaket Mauritania 74 17.25N 10.40W
Tâmega r. Portugal 26 41.05N 8.21W
Tamil Nadu d. India 61 11.15N 79.00E
Tamkuhi India 63 26.41N 84.11E
Tam Ky Vietnam 56 15.34N 108.29E
Tammisaari Finland 41 59.58N 23.26E
Ţammūn Jordan 67 32.17N 35.23E
Tämnaren l. Sweden 43 60.10N 17.20E
Tampa U.S.A. 113 27.58N 82.38W
Tampa B. U.S.A. 113 27.45N 82.35W
Tampere Finland 41 61.30N 23.45E
Tampico Mexico 116 22.18N 97.52W
Tamra Hazafon Israel 67 32.51N 35.24E
Tamra Hazafon Israel 67 32.51N 35.12E
Tamri Morocco 74 30.43N 9.43W
Tamsagbulag Mongolia 53 47.10N 117.21E
Tamworth Australia 93 31.07S 150.57E
Tamworth Canada 105 44.29N 77.00W
Tamworth U.K. 13 52.38N 1.42W
Tana r. Kenya 79 2.32S 40.32E
Tana r. Norway 40 70.26N 28.14E
Tana r. Norway 40 69.45N 28.15E
Tana i. Vanuatu 84 19.30S 169.20E
Tanacross U.S.A. 98 63.12N 143.30W
Tanafjorden Norway 40 70.54N 28.40E
T'ana Häyk' l. Ethiopia 73 12.00N 37.20E
Tanahgrogot Indonesia 58 1.55S 116.12E
Tanahmerah Indonesia 59 6.08S 140.18E
Tanakpur India 63 29.05N 80.07E
Tanami Desert Australia 88 19.50S 130.50E
Tanana U.S.A. 98 65.11N 152.10W
Tanana r. U.S.A. 98 65.09N 151.55W
Tananarive see Antananarivo Madagascar 81
Tanaro r. Italy 30 45.01N 8.47E
Tanch 'Ǒn N. Korea 57 40.27N 128.54E
Tanda Côte d'Ivoire 76 7.48N 3.10W
Tānda India 63 26.33N 82.39E
Tandalti Sudan 73 13.01N 31.50E
Tăndărei Romania 37 44.38N 27.40E
Tandil Argentina 125 37.18S 59.10W
Tandjilé d. Chad 77 9.45N 16.28E
Tando Ādam Pakistan 62 25.46N 68.40E
Tando Allāhyār Pakistan 62 25.28N 68.43E
Tando Bāgo Pakistan 62 24.47N 68.58E
Tando Muhammad Khan Pakistan 62 25.08N 68.32E
Tandou L. Australia 92 32.38S 142.05E
Tanega shima i. Japan 57 30.32N 131.00E
Taneytown U.S.A. 114 39.40N 77.10W
Tanezrouft des. Algeria 74 22.25N 0.30E
Tanga Tanzania 79 5.07S 39.05E
Tanga d. Tanzania 79 5.20S 38.30E
Tangalla Sri Lanka 61 6.02N 80.47E
Tanganyika, L. Africa 79 6.00S 29.30E
Tanger Morocco 74 35.48N 5.45W
Tangerhütte Germany 38 52.26N 11.48E
Tangermünde Germany 38 52.32N 11.58E
Tanggo China 63 31.37N 93.18E
Tanggu China 54 39.01N 117.43E
Tanggula Shan mts. China 63 33.00N 90.00E
Tanggula Shankou pass China 63 32.45N 92.24E
Tanggulashanqu China 63 34.10N 92.23E
Tanghe China 54 32.41N 112.49E
Tāngi India 63 19.57N 85.30E
Tangi Pakistan 62 34.18N 71.40E
Tangier see Tanger Morocco 74
Tangmarg Jammu & Kashmir 62 34.02N 74.26E
Tangra Yumco l. China 63 31.00N 86.15E
Tangshan China 54 39.32N 118.08E
Tangtse Jammu & Kashmir 63 34.02N 78.11E
Tanguiéta Benin 77 10.37N 1.18E
Tanimbar, Kepulauan is. Indonesia 59 7.50S 131.30E
Tanishpa mtn. Pakistan 62 31.10N 68.24E
Tanjay Phil. 59 9.31N 123.10E
Tanjona Ankaboa c. Madagascar 81 21.57S 43.16E
Tanjona Bobaomby c. Madagascar 81 11.57S 49.17E
Tanjona Masoala c. Madagascar 81 15.59S 50.13E

Tanjona Vilanandro c. Madagascar 81 16.11S 44.27E
Tanjona Vohimena c. Madagascar 81 25.36S 45.08E
Tanjung Indonesia 58 2.10S 115.25E
Tanjungbalai Indonesia 58 2.59N 99.46E
Tanjungkarang Indonesia 58 5.28S 105.16E
Tanjungpandan Indonesia 58 2.44S 107.36E
Tanjungredeb Indonesia 58 2.09N 117.29E
Tānk Pakistan 62 32.13N 70.23E
Tankapirtti Finland 40 68.16N 27.20E
Tannersville U.S.A. 115 42.12N 74.08W
Tannin Canada 102 49.40N 91.00W
Tannis Bugt b. Denmark 42 57.40N 10.15E
Tannu Ola mts. Russian Fed. 51 51.00N 93.30E
Tannūrah, Ra's c. Saudi Arabia 71 26.39N 50.10E
Tano r. Ghana 76 5.07N 2.54W
Tanout Niger 77 14.55N 8.49E
Ţanţā Egypt 66 30.48N 31.00E
Tanumshede Sweden 42 58.44N 11.19E
Tanzania Africa 79 5.00S 35.00E
Tao'an China 54 45.20N 122.48E
Taole China 54 38.50N 106.40E
Taormina Italy 33 37.52N 15.17E
Taoudenni Mali 76 22.45N 4.00W
Tapachula Mexico 116 14.54N 92.15W
Tapajós r. Brazil 123 2.25S 54.40W
Tapaktuan Indonesia 58 3.30N 97.10E
Tapalqué Argentina 125 36.20S 60.02W
Tapanahoni r. Surinam 123 4.20N 54.25W
Tapanlieh Taiwan 55 21.58N 120.47E
Tapanui New Zealand 86 45.57S 169.16E
Tapauá r. Brazil 122 5.40S 64.20W
Tapeta Liberia 76 6.25N 8.47W
Tapirapecó, Serra mts. Venezuela/Brazil 122 1.00N 64.30W
Tāplejung Nepal 63 27.21N 87.40E
Tapolca Hungary 31 46.53N 17.27E
Tāpti r. India 62 21.05N 72.40E
Tapurucuara Brazil 122 0.24S 65.02W
Taquari r. Brazil 126 19.00S 57.27W
Taquaritinga Brazil 126 21.23S 48.33W
Tar r. U.S.A. 113 35.33N 77.05W
Tara Canada 104 44.28N 81.09W
Tara Russian Fed. 9 56.55N 74.24E
Tara r. Russian Fed. 50 56.30N 74.40E
Tara r. Yugo. 31 43.21N 18.51E
Taraba d. Nigeria 77 8.15N 11.00E
Tarabine, Oued Ti-n- wadi Algeria 75 21.16N 7.24E
Tarabuco Bolivia 124 19.10S 64.57W
Ṭarābulus Lebanon 66 34.27N 35.50E
Ṭarābulus f. Libya 75 32.40N 13.15E
Ṭarābulus f. Libya 75 31.00N 13.30E
Ṭarābulus town Libya 75 32.58N 13.12E
Tarago Australia 93 35.05S 149.10E
Tarakan Indonesia 58 3.20N 117.38E
Taranaki d. New Zealand 86 39.00S 174.30E
Taranaki, Mt. New Zealand 86 39.20S 174.05E
Tarancón Spain 27 40.01N 3.01W
Taranto Italy 33 40.28N 17.15E
Taranto, Golfo di g. Italy 33 40.00N 17.10E
Tarapacá Colombia 122 2.52S 69.44W
Tarapoto Peru 122 6.31S 76.23W
Tarare France 21 45.54N 4.26E
Tarascon Ariège France 20 42.51N 1.36E
Tarascon Vaucluse France 21 43.48N 4.40E
Tarashcha Ukraine 37 49.35N 30.20E
Tarasovo Russian Fed. 44 66.14N 46.43E
Tarauacá Brazil 122 8.06S 70.46W
Tarauacá r. Brazil 122 6.42S 69.48W
Taravao, Isthme de Tahiti 85 17.43S 149.19W
Taravo r. France 21 41.42N 8.49E
Tarawa i. Kiribati 84 1.25N 173.00E
Tarawera New Zealand 86 39.02S 176.36E
Tarazona Spain 25 41.54N 1.44W
Tarazona de la Mancha Spain 25 39.15N 1.55W
Tarbagatay, Khrebet mts. Kazakhstan 52 47.00N 83.00E
Tarbat Ness c. U.K. 14 57.52N 3.46W
Tarbert Rep. of Ire. 15 52.34N 9.24W
Tarbert Strath. U.K. 14 55.51N 5.25W
Tarbert W. Isles U.K. 14 57.54N 6.49W
Tarbes France 20 43.14N 0.05E
Tarcento Italy 30 46.13N 13.13E
Tarcoola S.A. Australia 92 30.41S 134.33E
Tarcoon Australia 93 30.19S 146.43E
Tarcutta Australia 93 35.17S 147.45E
Tardajos Spain 26 42.21N 3.49W
Taree Australia 93 31.54S 152.26E
Tarella Australia 92 30.55S 143.06E
Tärendö Sweden 40 67.10N 22.38E
Tarentum U.S.A. 114 40.36N 79.45W
Ṭarfā, Wādī aṭ r. Egypt 66 28.36N 30.50E
Tarfaya Morocco 74 27.58N 12.55W
Targon France 20 44.44N 0.16W
Tarhjicht Morocco 74 29.05N 9.24W
Tarifa Spain 27 36.01N 5.36W
Tarifa, Punta de c. Spain 27 36.00N 5.37W
Tarija Bolivia 124 21.31S 64.45W
Tarija d. Bolivia 124 21.40S 64.20W
Tarim Yemen 71 16.03N 49.00E
Tarim He r. China 52 41.00N 83.30E
Tarīn Kowt Afghan. 62 32.52N 65.38E
Taritatu r. Indonesia 59 2.54S 138.27E
Tarkwa Ghana 76 5.16N 1.59W
Tarm Denmark 42 55.55N 8.32E
Tarma Peru 122 11.28S 75.41W
Tarn d. France 20 43.50N 2.00E
Tarn r. France 20 44.05N 1.06E
Tärnaby Sweden 40 65.43N 15.16E
Tarnak r. Afghan. 62 31.26N 65.31E
Tarn-et-Garonne d. France 20 44.05N 1.20E
Tarnica mtn. Poland 37 49.05N 22.44E
Tarnobrzeg Poland 37 50.35N 21.41E
Tarnów Poland 37 50.01N 20.59E
Tärnsjö Sweden 43 60.09N 16.56E
Taro r. Italy 30 45.00N 10.15E

Taroom Australia 90 25.39S 149.49E
Tarouca Portugal 26 41.00N 7.40W
Taroudannt Morocco 74 30.31N 8.55W
Tarpon Springs town U.S.A. 113 28.08N 82.45W
Tarquinia Italy 30 42.15N 11.45E
Tarqūmiyah Jordan 67 31.35N 35.01E
Tarragona Spain 25 41.07N 1.15E
Tarragona d. Spain 25 41.10N 0.40E
Tarran Hills Australia 93 32.27S 146.27E
Tarrasa Spain 25 41.34N 2.01E
Tárrega Spain 25 41.39N 1.09E
Tarrytown U.S.A. 115 41.05N 73.52W
Tarso Ahon mtn. Chad 77 20.23N 18.18E
Tarso Ouri mtn. Chad 77 21.25N 18.56E
Tarsus Turkey 64 36.52N 34.52E
Tartagal Argentina 124 22.32S 63.50W
Tartas France 20 43.50N 0.48W
Tartu Estonia 44 58.20N 26.44E
Ṭarṭūs Syria 66 34.55N 35.52E
Tarutino Ukraine 37 46.09N 29.04E
Tarutung Indonesia 58 2.01N 98.54E
Tarvisio Italy 31 46.30N 13.35E
Tashan China 54 40.51N 120.56E
Tashauz Uzbekistan 9 41.49N 59.58E
Tashi Gang Dzong Bhutan 63 27.19N 91.34E
Tashkent Uzbekistan 9 41.16N 69.13E
Tasiilaq see Ammassalik Greenland 99
Tasikmalaya Indonesia 59 7.20S 108.16E
Tasīl Syria 67 32.50N 35.58E
Tåsinge i. Denmark 42 55.00N 10.36E
Tåsjön Sweden 40 64.15N 15.47E
Tasman B. New Zealand 86 41.00S 173.15E
Tasmania d. Australia 91 42.00S 147.00E
Tasman Mts. New Zealand 86 41.00S 172.40E
Tasman Pen. Australia 91 43.08S 147.51E
Tasman Sea Pacific Oc. 84 38.00S 162.00E
Tassili-n-Ajjer f. Algeria 75 26.05N 7.00E
Tassili oua-n-Ahaggar f. Algeria 75 20.30N 5.00E
Tataa, Pt. Tahiti 85 17.33S 149.36W
Tatabánya Hungary 37 47.34N 18.26E
Tatarsk Russian Fed. 50 55.14N 76.00E
Tatarskiy Proliv g. Russian Fed. 51 47.40N 141.00E
Tateyama Japan 57 34.59N 139.52E
Tathlina L. Canada 100 60.32N 117.32W
Tathra Australia 93 36.44S 149.58E
Tatinnai L. Canada 101 60.55N 97.40W
Tatnam, C. Canada 101 57.16N 91.00W
Tatong Australia 93 36.46S 146.03E
Tatta Pakistan 62 24.45N 67.55E
Tatvan Turkey 64 38.42N 42.15E
Tau Norway 42 59.04N 5.54E
Tau i. Samoa 84 14.15S 169.30W
Taubaté Brazil 126 23.00S 45.36W
Tauber r. Germany 39 49.46N 9.31E
Tauberbischofsheim Germany 39 49.37N 9.40E
Taulihawa Nepal 63 27.32N 83.05E
Taumarunui New Zealand 86 38.53S 175.16E
Taumaturgo Brazil 122 8.57S 72.48W
Taung R.S.A. 80 27.32S 24.46E
Taungdwingyi Myanmar 56 20.00N 95.30E
Taung-gyi Myanmar 56 20.49N 97.01E
Taungup Myanmar 56 18.51N 94.14E
Taunoa Tahiti 85 17.45S 149.21W
Taunsa Pakistan 62 30.42N 70.39E
Taunton U.K. 13 51.01N 3.07W
Taunton U.S.A. 115 41.54N 71.06W
Taunus mts. Germany 36 50.07N 7.48E
Taupo New Zealand 86 38.42S 176.06E
Taupo, L. New Zealand 86 38.45S 175.30E
Taurage Lithuania 41 55.15N 22.17E
Tauranga New Zealand 86 37.42S 176.11E
Taureau, Résr. Canada 105 46.46N 73.50W
Taurianova Italy 33 38.21N 16.01E
Taurus Mts. see Toros Dağları mts. Turkey 64
Tauste Spain 25 41.55N 1.15W
Tautira Tahiti 85 17.45S 149.10W
Tavani Canada 101 62.10N 93.30W
Tavda Russian Fed. 50 58.04N 65.12E
Tavda r. Russian Fed. 50 57.40N 67.00E
Taveta Kenya 79 3.23S 37.42E
Taveuni i. Fiji 84 16.56S 179.58W
Tavira Portugal 27 37.07N 7.39W
Tavistock Canada 104 43.19N 80.50W
Tavistock U.K. 13 50.33N 4.09W
Távora r. Portugal 26 41.08N 7.35W
Tavor, Har mtn. Israel 67 32.41N 35.23E
Tavoy Myanmar 56 14.02N 98.12E
Tavropoú, Tekhnití Límni l. Greece 35 39.20N 21.45E
Taw r. U.K. 13 51.05N 4.05W
Tawas City U.S.A. 104 44.16N 83.31W
Tawau Malaysia 58 4.16N 117.54E
Tawitawi i. Phil. 59 5.10N 120.05E
Ţawkar Sudan 72 18.26N 37.44E
Tawu Taiwan 55 22.22N 120.54E
Tāwurghā', Sabkhat f. Libya 22 31.10N 15.15E
Tay r. U.K. 14 56.21N 3.18W
Tayabamba Peru 122 8.15S 77.15W
Tayan Indonesia 58 0.02S 110.05E
Tayeegle Somali Rep. 71 4.02N 44.36E
Tay, L. Australia 89 33.00S 120.52E
Tay, Loch U.K. 14 56.32N 4.08W
Taylor Tex. U.S.A. 111 30.34N 97.25W
Taylor, Mt. U.S.A. 109 35.14N 107.37W
Taylors Island town U.S.A. 115 38.28N 76.18W
Taymā' Saudi Arabia 64 27.37N 38.30E
Taymyr, Ozero l. Russian Fed. 51 74.20N 101.00E
Taymyr, Poluostrov pen. Russian Fed. 51 75.30N 99.00E
Tay Ninh Vietnam 56 11.21N 106.02E
Tayport U.K. 14 56.27N 2.53W
Tayshet Russian Fed. 51 55.56N 98.01E
Tayside d. U.K. 14 56.35N 3.28W
Taytay Phil. 58 10.47N 119.32E
Taz r. Russian Fed. 50 67.30N 78.50E
Taza Morocco 74 34.16N 4.01W
Tazawa ko l. Japan 57 39.43N 140.40E
Tazenakht Morocco 74 30.35N 7.12W
Tazin L. Canada 101 59.40N 109.00W

Tāzirbū Libya 72 25.45N 21.00E
Tazovskiy Russian Fed. 50 67.28N 78.43E
Tbilisi Georgia 65 41.43N 44.48E
Tchad, Lac see Chad, L. Africa 77
Tchamba Togo 77 9.05N 1.27E
Tchibanga Gabon 78 2.52S 11.07E
Tchien Liberia 76 6.00N 8.10W
Tchigaï, Plateau du f. Niger/Chad 77 21.30N 14.50E
Tcholliré Cameroon 77 8.25N 14.10E
Tczew Poland 37 54.06N 18.47E
Te Anau New Zealand 86 45.25S 167.43E
Te Anau, L. New Zealand 86 45.10S 167.15E
Teaneck U.S.A. 115 40.53N 74.01W
Teano Italy 33 41.15N 14.04E
Teapa Mexico 116 17.33N 92.57W
Te Araroa New Zealand 86 37.38S 178.25E
Teba Spain 27 36.58N 4.56W
Tébessa Algeria 75 35.22N 8.08E
Tebingtinggi Sumatera Selatan Indonesia 58 3.37S 103.09E
Tebingtinggi Sumatera Utara Indonesia 58 3.20N 99.08E
Tébourba Tunisia 32 36.49N 9.51E
Teboursouk, Monts de mts. Tunisia 32 36.45N 9.20E
Tebulos Mta mtn. Georgia 45 42.34N 45.17E
Tech r. France 20 42.36N 3.03E
Techiman Ghana 76 7.36N 1.55W
Tecuci Romania 37 45.49N 27.27E
Tecumseh U.S.A. 104 42.00N 83.57W
Tedesa Ethiopia 73 5.07N 37.45E
Tees r. U.K. 12 54.35N 1.11W
Tefé Brazil 122 3.24S 64.45W
Tefé r. Brazil 122 3.35S 64.47W
Tegal Indonesia 59 6.52S 109.07E
Tegelen Neth. 16 51.20N 6.08E
Tegernsee Germany 39 47.43N 11.45E
Tegina Nigeria 77 10.06N 6.11E
Tego Australia 93 28.48S 146.47E
Tegouma well Niger 77 15.33N 9.19E
Tegucigalpa Honduras 117 14.05N 87.14W
Teguidda i-n-Tessoum Niger 77 17.21N 6.32E
Tehamiyam Sudan 72 18.20N 36.32E
Tehata Bangla. 63 23.43N 88.32E
Téhini Côte d'Ivoire 76 9.39N 3.32W
Tehkummah Canada 104 45.39N 81.59W
Tehrān Iran 65 35.40N 51.26E
Tehri India 63 30.23N 78.29E
Tehuacán Mexico 116 18.30N 97.26W
Tehuantepec Mexico 116 16.21N 95.13W
Tehuantepec, Golfo de g. Mexico 116 16.00N 95.00W
Tehuantepec, Istmo de f. Mexico 116 17.00N 94.30W
Teifi r. U.K. 13 52.05N 4.41W
Teignmouth U.K. 13 50.33N 3.30W
Teixeiras Brazil 126 20.37S 42.52W
Tejakula Indonesia 59 8.09S 115.19E
Tejo r. Portugal 27 38.40N 9.24W
Te Kaha New Zealand 86 37.44S 177.52E
Tekamah U.S.A. 110 41.47N 96.13W
Tekapo, L. New Zealand 86 43.35S 170.30E
Tekax Mexico 117 20.12N 89.17W
Teke Burnu c. Turkey 34 40.02N 26.10E
Tekezē r. Ethiopia see Satīt r. Sudan 72
Tekirdağ Turkey 29 40.59N 27.30E
Tekkali India 63 18.37N 84.14E
Tekouiat, Oued wadi Algeria 75 22.20N 2.30E
Tekro well Chad 72 19.30N 20.58E
Te Kuiti New Zealand 86 38.20S 175.10E
Tel r. India 63 20.50N 83.54E
Tela Honduras 117 15.56N 87.25W
Tel 'Adashim Israel 67 32.39N 35.18E
Tel Arshaf site Israel 67 32.12N 34.48E
Tel Ashqelon site Israel 67 31.39N 34.32E
Telavåg Norway 42 60.16N 4.49E
Telavi Georgia 65 41.56N 45.30E
Tel Aviv d. Israel 67 32.05N 34.48E
Tel Aviv-Yafo Israel 67 32.05N 34.46E
Tele r. Zaïre 72 2.48N 24.00E
Telegraph Creek town Canada 100 57.55N 131.10W
Telemark d. Norway 42 59.40N 8.45E
Teleneshty Moldova 37 47.35N 28.17E
Teles Pires r. Brazil 123 7.20S 57.30W
Telfer Australia 88 21.42S 122.13E
Telford U.K. 13 52.42N 2.30W
Telfs Austria 39 47.18N 11.04E
Telgte Germany 38 51.59N 7.47E
Tel Hazor site Israel 67 33.01N 35.34E
Télimélé Guinea 76 10.54N 13.02W
Tel Lakhish site Israel 67 31.34N 34.51E
Tell Atlas mts. Algeria 75 36.00N 1.00E
Tell City U.S.A. 113 37.56N 86.46W
Teller U.S.A. 98 65.16N 166.22W
Tel Megiddo site Israel 67 32.35N 35.11E
Tel Mond Israel 67 32.15N 34.56E
Telpos-Iz mtn. Russian Fed. 44 63.56N 59.02E
Telsen Argentina 125 42.25S 67.00W
Telšiai Lithuania 41 55.59N 22.15E
Telti Italy 32 40.52N 9.21E
Teltow Germany 38 52.23N 13.16E
Telukbetung Indonesia 58 5.28S 105.16E
Teluk Intan Malaysia 58 4.00N 101.00E
Tema Ghana 76 5.41N 0.01W
Temagami, L. Canada 104 47.00N 80.05W
Te Manga mtn. Rarotonga Cook Is. 84 21.13S 159.45W
Temaverachi, Sierra mts. Mexico 109 29.30N 109.30W
Tembleque Spain 27 39.42N 3.30W
Tembo Aluma Angola 78 7.42S 17.15E
Teme r. U.K. 13 52.10N 2.13W
Temerin Yugo. 31 45.24N 19.53E
Temir Kazakhstan 45 49.09N 57.06E
Temirtau Kazakhstan 9 50.05N 72.55E
Témiscaming Canada 104 46.43N 79.06W
Temora Australia 93 34.27S 147.35E
Tempe U.S.A. 109 33.25N 111.56W
Tempino Indonesia 58 1.55S 103.23E
Tempio Italy 32 40.54N 9.07E
Temple U.S.A. 111 31.06N 97.21W
Temple B. Australia 90 12.10S 143.04E
Templemore Rep. of Ire. 15 52.48N 7.51W

Templin Germany **38** 53.07N 13.30E
Temuco Chile **125** 38.44S 72.36W
Tenabo Mexico **116** 20.03N 90.14W
Tenaha U.S.A. **111** 31.57N 94.15W
Tenasserim Myanmar **56** 12.05N 99.00E
Tenasserim d. Myanmar **56** 13.00N 99.00E
Tenby U.K. **13** 51.40N 4.42W
Tenby Bay town Canada **104** 46.06N 83.56W
Tendaho Ethiopia **73** 11.48N 40.52E
Tende France **21** 44.05N 7.36E
Tende, Col de pass France/Italy **30** 44.09N 7.34E
Ten Degree Channel Indian Oc. **56** 10.00N 93.00E
Tendrara Morocco **74** 33.04N 1.59W
Tenenkou Mali **76** 14.25N 4.58W
Ténès Algeria **75** 36.31N 1.18E
Teng r. Myanmar **56** 19.50N 97.40E
Tengchong China **61** 25.02N 98.28E
Tengger Shamo des. China **54** 39.00N 104.10E
Tengiz, Ozero l. Kazakhstan **9** 50.30N 69.00E
Teng Xian China **54** 35.08N 117.20E
Tenke Zaïre **78** 10.34S 26.07E
Tenkodogo Burkina **76** 11.47N 0.19W
Tenna r. Italy **31** 43.14N 13.47E
Tennant Creek town Australia **90** 19.31S 134.15E
Tennessee d. U.S.A. **113** 35.50N 85.30W
Tennessee r. U.S.A. **113** 37.04N 88.33W
Tenosique Mexico **116** 17.29N 91.26W
Tenryū Japan **57** 34.52N 137.49E
Tenryū r. Japan **57** 34.35N 137.47E
Tensift, Oued r. Morocco **74** 32.02N 9.22W
Tenterfield Australia **93** 29.01S 152.04E
Teófilo Otoni Brazil **126** 17.52S 41.31W
Tepa Indonesia **59** 7.52S 129.31E
Tepa Pt. Niue **84** 19.07S 169.56W
Tepelenë Albania **34** 40.18N 20.01E
Tepic Mexico **116** 21.30N 104.51W
Teplice Czech Republic **38** 50.39N 13.48E
Ter r. Spain **25** 42.01N 3.12E
Téra Niger **76** 14.01N 0.45E
Tera r. Portugal **27** 38.55N 8.04W
Tera r. Spain **26** 41.54N 5.44W
Teramo Italy **31** 42.39N 13.42E
Terang Australia **92** 38.13S 142.56E
Tercan Turkey **64** 39.47N 40.23E
Terebovlya Ukraine **37** 49.18N 25.44E
Terekhova Belarus **37** 52.13N 31.28E
Teresina Brazil **123** 5.09S 42.46W
Teresópolis Brazil **126** 22.26S 42.59W
Terevaka mtn. I. de Pascua **85** 27.05S 109.23W
Tergnier France **19** 49.39N 3.18E
Terhazza Mali **76** 23.45N 4.59W
Termez Uzbekistan **52** 37.15N 67.15E
Termination I. Australia **89** 34.25S 121.53E
Termini Italy **28** 37.59N 13.42E
Termini Imerese Italy **32** 37.59N 13.42E
Termini Imerese, Golfo di g. Italy **32** 38.05N 13.50E
Términos, Laguna de b. Mexico **116** 18.30N 91.30W
Termoli Italy **33** 41.58N 14.59E
Ternate Indonesia **59** 0.48N 127.23E
Terneuzen Neth. **16** 51.20N 3.50E
Terni Italy **30** 42.34N 12.37E
Ternopol Ukraine **37** 49.35N 25.39E
Terra Alta U.S.A. **114** 39.25N 79.35W
Terra Bella U.S.A. **109** 35.58N 119.03W
Terrace Canada **100** 54.31N 128.35W
Terracina Italy **32** 41.17N 13.15E
Terralba Italy **32** 39.43N 8.38E
Terrassa see Tarrasa Spain **25**
Terrasson-la-Villedieu France **20** 45.08N 1.18E
Terre Adélie f. Antarctica **128** 80.00S 140.00E
Terrebonne Canada **105** 45.42N 73.38W
Terre Haute U.S.A. **112** 39.27N 87.24W
Terrenceville Canada **103** 47.42N 54.43W
Terry U.S.A. **108** 46.47N 105.19W
Terschelling i. Neth. **16** 53.25N 5.25E
Teruel Spain **25** 40.21N 1.06W
Teruel d. Spain **25** 40.40N 1.00W
Tervola Finland **40** 66.05N 24.48E
Tešanj Bosnia-Herzegovina **31** 44.37N 18.00E
Tesaret, Oued wadi Algeria **75** 25.32N 2.52E
Teshio Japan **57** 44.53N 141.44E
Teshio r. Japan **57** 44.53N 141.44E
Teslić Bosnia-Herzegovina **31** 44.37N 17.51E
Teslin Canada **100** 60.10N 132.43W
Teslin r. Canada **100** 61.34N 134.54W
Teslin L. Canada **100** 60.15N 132.57W
Tessalit Mali **76** 20.12N 1.00E
Tessaoua Niger **77** 13.46N 7.55E
Tessy-sur-Vire France **18** 48.58N 1.04W
Test r. U.K. **13** 50.55N 1.29W
Testa, Capo c. Italy **32** 41.14N 9.09E
Têt r. France **20** 42.44N 3.02E
Tetachuck L. Canada **100** 53.18N 125.55W
Tete Mozambique **81** 16.10S 33.30E
Tete d. Mozambique **79** 15.30S 33.00E
Teterev r. Ukraine **37** 51.03N 30.30E
Teterow Germany **38** 53.46N 12.34E
Tethul r. Canada **100** 60.35N 112.12W
Tetiaora i. Îs. de la Société **85** 17.05S 149.32W
Tetiyev Ukraine **37** 49.22N 29.40E
Tétouan Morocco **74** 35.34N 5.23W
Tetovo Macedonia **34** 42.01N 21.02E
Tetuan see Tétouan Morocco **74**
Tetyukhe Pristan Russian Fed. **57** 44.31N 135.31E
Teulada Italy **32** 38.58N 8.46E
Teulada, Capo c. Italy **32** 38.52N 8.39E
Teun i. Indonesia **59** 6.59S 129.08E
Teutoburger Wald Germany **38** 52.10N 8.15E
Teuva Finland **40** 62.29N 21.44E
Tevere r. Italy **30** 41.44N 12.14E
Teverya Israel **67** 32.48N 35.32E
Teviot r. U.K. **14** 55.36N 2.27W
Teviotdale U.K. **12** 55.26N 2.46W
Teviothead U.K. **14** 55.20N 2.56W
Tewkesbury U.K. **13** 51.59N 2.09W

Tewksburg U.S.A. **115** 42.37N 71.14W
Texarkana Ark. U.S.A. **111** 33.26N 94.02W
Texarkana Tex. U.S.A. **111** 33.26N 94.03W
Texarkana, L. U.S.A. **111** 33.16N 94.14W
Texas Australia **93** 28.50S 151.09E
Texas d. U.S.A. **111** 31.30N 100.00W
Texas town U.S.A. **115** 43.30N 76.16W
Texas City U.S.A. **111** 29.23N 94.54W
Texel i. Neth. **16** 53.05N 4.47E
Texoma, L. U.S.A. **111** 33.55N 96.37W
Texon U.S.A. **111** 31.13N 101.43W
Teyea site Greece **35** 37.29N 22.24E
Teyvareh Afghan. **62** 33.21N 64.25E
Tezpur India **63** 26.38N 92.48E
Tha-anne r. Canada **101** 60.31N 94.37W
Thabana Ntlenyana mtn. Lesotho **80** 29.28S 29.17E
Thabazimbi R.S.A. **80** 24.36S 27.23E
Thādiq Saudi Arabia **65** 25.18N 45.52E
Thai Binh Vietnam **55** 20.30N 106.26E
Thailand Asia **56** 17.00N 101.30E
Thailand, G. of Asia **56** 11.00N 101.00E
Thai Nguyen Vietnam **55** 21.46N 105.52E
Thak Pakistan **62** 30.32N 70.13E
Thal Pakistan **62** 33.22N 70.33E
Thal Desert Pakistan **62** 31.30N 71.40E
Thale Luang l. Thailand **56** 7.40N 100.20E
Thallon Australia **93** 28.39S 148.49E
Thalwil Switz. **39** 47.17N 8.34E
Thamarīt Oman **60** 17.39N 54.02E
Thames r. Canada **104** 42.19N 82.28W
Thames New Zealand **86** 37.08S 175.35E
Thames r. U.K. **13** 51.30N 0.05E
Thamesford Canada **104** 43.04N 81.00W
Thamesville Canada **104** 42.33N 81.59W
Thāna India **62** 19.12N 72.58E
Thāna Pakistan **62** 28.55N 63.45E
Thanh Hóa Vietnam **55** 19.47N 105.49E
Thanjāvūr India **61** 10.46N 79.09E
Thann France **19** 47.49N 7.05E
Thāno Bula Khān Pakistan **62** 25.22N 67.50E
Tharād India **62** 24.24N 71.38E
Thar Desert Pakistan/India **62** 28.00N 72.00E
Thargomindah Australia **91** 27.59S 143.45E
Tharrawaddy Myanmar **56** 17.37N 95.48E
Tharthār, Wādī ath r. Iraq **64** 34.18N 43.07E
Thásos Greece **34** 40.47N 24.42E
Thásos i. Greece **34** 40.41N 24.47E
Thatcher U.S.A. **109** 32.51N 109.56W
Thaton Myanmar **56** 16.50N 97.21E
Thau, Bassin de b. France **20** 43.23N 3.36E
Thaungdut Myanmar **56** 24.26N 94.45E
Thayer U.S.A. **111** 36.31N 91.33W
Thayetmyo Myanmar **56** 19.20N 95.10E
Thazi Myanmar **56** 20.51N 96.05E
Theano Pt. Canada **104** 47.17N 84.43W
Thebes ruins Egypt **64** 25.41N 32.40E
The Bight town Bahamas **117** 24.19N 75.24W
The Cherokees, L. O' U.S.A. **111** 36.45N 94.50W
The Cheviot mtn. U.K. **12** 55.29N 2.10W
The Cheviot Hills U.K. **12** 55.22N 2.24W
The Coorong g. Australia **92** 36.00S 139.30E
The Dalles town U.S.A. **108** 45.36N 121.10W
Thedford Canada **104** 43.09N 81.51W
Thedford U.S.A. **110** 41.59N 100.35W
The Everglades f. U.S.A. **113** 26.00N 80.40W
The Fens f. U.K. **13** 52.30N 4.13W
The Gulf Asia **65** 27.00N 50.00E
The Hague see 'sGravenhage Neth. **16**
Thekulthili L. Canada **101** 61.03N 110.00W
The Little Minch str. U.K. **14** 57.40N 6.45W
Thelon r. Canada **99** 64.23N 96.15W
The Machers f. U.K. **14** 54.45N 4.28W
The Minch str. U.K. **14** 58.10N 5.50W
The Needles c. U.K. **13** 50.39N 1.35W
Thénezay France **18** 46.43N 0.02W
Theodore Australia **90** 24.57S 150.05E
Theodore Roosevelt L. U.S.A. **109** 33.30N 110.57W
Theog India **62** 31.07N 77.21E
Theológos Greece **34** 40.39N 24.41E
The Pas Canada **101** 53.50N 101.15W
The Pennines hills U.K. **12** 55.40N 2.20W
Thérain r. France **19** 49.15N 2.27E
Theresa U.S.A. **105** 44.13N 75.48W
The Rhinns f. U.K. **14** 54.50N 5.02W
Thermaïkós Kólpos g. Greece **34** 40.23N 22.47E
Thermopolis U.S.A. **108** 43.39N 108.13W
Thermopylae Pass Greece **35** 38.48N 22.33E
The Rock town Australia **93** 35.16S 147.07E
The Salt L. Australia **92** 30.05S 142.10E
The Snares is. New Zealand **84** 48.00S 166.30E
The Solent str. U.K. **13** 50.45N 1.20W
The Sound str. Denmark/Sweden **43** 55.30N 12.40E
Thesprotikón Greece **35** 39.15N 20.47E
Thessalía f. Greece **34** 39.30N 22.00E
Thessalon Canada **104** 46.15N 83.34W
Thessaloníki Greece **34** 40.38N 22.56E
Thetford U.K. **13** 52.25N 0.44E
Thetford Mines town Canada **105** 46.05N 71.18W
The Twins town Australia **92** 30.00S 135.16E
The Wash b. U.K. **12** 52.55N 0.15E
The Weald f. U.K. **13** 51.05N 0.20E
Thibodaux U.S.A. **111** 29.48N 90.49W
Thicket Portage Canada **101** 55.19N 97.42W
Thief River Falls town U.S.A. **110** 48.07N 96.10W
Thiene Italy **30** 45.42N 11.29E
Thiers France **20** 45.51N 3.34E
Thiès Senegal **76** 14.50N 16.55W
Thiesi Italy **32** 40.31N 8.43E
Thika Kenya **79** 1.04S 37.04E
Thimbu Bhutan **63** 27.28N 89.39E
Thingvallavatn l. Iceland **40** 64.10N 21.10W
Thionville France **19** 49.22N 6.10E
Thíra i. Greece **35** 36.24N 25.29E
Thíra town Greece **35** 36.24N 25.27E
Thirsk U.K. **12** 54.15N 1.20W
Thiruvananthapuram see Trivandrum India **60**
Thisted Denmark **42** 56.57N 8.42E
Thistilfjördhur b. Iceland **40** 66.11N 15.20W

Thistle I. Australia **92** 35.00S 136.09E
Thívai Greece **35** 38.21N 23.19E
Thiviers France **20** 45.25N 0.56E
Thjórsá r. Iceland **40** 63.53N 20.38W
Thoa r. Canada **101** 60.31N 109.47W
Thoen Thailand **56** 17.41N 99.14E
Tholen i. Neth. **16** 51.34N 4.07E
Thomas U.S.A. **114** 39.09N 79.30W
Thomaston U.S.A. **113** 32.55N 84.20W
Thomasville Ala. U.S.A. **111** 31.55N 87.51W
Thomasville Fla. U.S.A. **113** 30.50N 83.59W
Thompson Canada **101** 55.45N 97.52W
Thompson Utah U.S.A. **108** 38.58N 109.43W
Thompson Landing Canada **101** 62.56N 110.40W
Thompsonville U.S.A. **112** 44.32N 85.57W
Thomson r. Australia **90** 25.11S 142.53E
Thonburi Thailand **56** 13.43N 100.27E
Thonon-les-Bains France **21** 46.22N 6.29E
Thórisvatn l. Iceland **40** 64.15N 18.50W
Thornbury Canada **104** 44.34N 80.26W
Thornton U.S.A. **114** 39.22N 79.56W
Thorshavn Faroe Is. **10** 62.02N 6.47W
Thorshöfn Iceland **40** 66.12N 15.17W
Thouars France **18** 46.59N 0.13W
Thousand Is. Canada **105** 44.15N 76.12W
Thowa r. Kenya **73** 1.33S 40.03E
Thrace f. Greece **34** 41.10N 25.30E
Thrakikón Pélagos f. Greece **34** 40.15N 24.28E
Thrapston U.K. **13** 52.24N 0.32W
Three Forks town U.S.A. **108** 45.54N 111.33W
Three Hills town Canada **100** 51.43N 113.15W
Three Kings Is. New Zealand **84** 34.09S 172.09E
Three Rivers town Australia **88** 25.07S 119.09E
Three Rivers town U.S.A. **111** 28.28N 98.11W
Three Sisters Mt. U.S.A. **108** 44.10N 121.46W
Thueyts France **21** 44.41N 4.13E
Thuin Belgium **16** 50.21N 4.20E
Thul Pakistan **62** 28.14N 68.46E
Thule Greenland **99** 77.30N 69.29W
Thun Switz. **39** 46.45N 7.37E
Thunder B. U.S.A. **104** 44.58N 83.24W
Thunder Bay town Canada **102** 48.25N 89.14W
Thunder Bay r. U.S.A. **104** 45.04N 83.25W
Thunder Hills Canada **101** 54.30N 106.00W
Thunersee l. Switz. **39** 46.40N 7.45E
Thung Song Thailand **56** 8.10N 99.41E
Thunkar Bhutan **63** 27.55N 91.00E
Thurgau d. Switz. **39** 47.30N 9.10E
Thuringen d. Germany **38** 50.50N 10.35E
Thüringen f. Germany **38** 50.57N 11.30E
Thüringer Wald mts. Germany **38** 50.40N 10.52E
Thurles Rep. of Ire. **15** 52.41N 7.50W
Thurloo Downs town Australia **92** 29.18S 143.30E
Thurmont U.S.A. **114** 39.37N 77.25W
Thursday I. Australia **84** 10.35S 142.13E
Thursday Island town Australia **90** 10.34S 142.14E
Thurso U.K. **14** 58.35N 3.32W
Thurso r. U.K. **10** 58.35N 3.32W
Thury-Harcourt France **18** 48.59N 0.29W
Thusis Switz. **39** 46.42N 9.26E
Thy f. Denmark **42** 57.00N 8.30E
Thyborön Denmark **42** 56.42N 8.13E
Thysville Zaïre **78** 5.15S 14.52E
Tiandong China **55** 23.36N 107.08E
Tian'e China **55** 25.00N 107.10E
Tian Head Canada **100** 53.47N 133.06W
Tianjin China **54** 39.07N 117.08E
Tianjin d. China **54** 39.30N 117.20E
Tianjun China **52** 37.16N 98.52E
Tianlin China **54** 24.18N 106.13E
Tianmen China **55** 30.39N 113.25E
Tian Shan mts. Asia **52** 42.00N 80.30E
Tianshui China **54** 34.25N 105.58E
Tiantai China **55** 29.09N 121.02E
Tianyang China **55** 23.45N 106.54E
Tiarei Tahiti **85** 17.32S 149.20W
Tiaret Algeria **75** 35.28N 1.21E
Tiavea W. Samoa **84** 13.57S 171.28W
Tibasti, Sarīr des. Libya **75** 24.00N 17.00E
Tibati Cameroon **77** 6.25N 12.33E
Tiber r. see Tevere r. Italy **30**
Tiberias see Teverya Israel **67**
Tiberias, L. see Yam Kinneret l. Israel **67**
Tibesti mts. Chad **77** 21.00N 17.30E
Tibet d. see Xizang d. China **52**
Tibetan Plateau see Qing Zang Gaoyuan f. China **52**
Tibooburra Australia **92** 29.28S 142.04E
Tibro Sweden **43** 58.26N 14.10E
Tiburón, Isla Mexico **109** 29.00N 112.20W
Tichborne Canada **105** 44.40N 76.41W
Tichît Mauritania **74** 18.28N 9.30W
Tichla W. Sahara **74** 21.35N 14.58W
Ticino r. Italy **30** 45.09N 9.14E
Ticino d. Switz. **30** 46.20N 8.45E
Ticonderoga U.S.A. **105** 43.51N 73.26W
Tidaholm Sweden **43** 58.11N 13.57E
Tidikelt f. Algeria **75** 27.00N 1.30E
Tidioute U.S.A. **114** 41.41N 79.24W
Tidirhine, Jbel mtn. Morocco **74** 34.50N 4.30W
Tidjikdja Mauritania **74** 18.29N 11.31W
Tiel Neth. **16** 51.53N 5.26E
Tieling China **54** 42.13N 123.48E
Tielt Belgium **16** 51.00N 3.20E
Tienen Belgium **16** 50.49N 4.56E
Tiénigbé Côte d'Ivoire **76** 8.11N 5.43W
Tientsin see Tianjin China **54**
Tierga Spain **25** 41.37N 1.36W
Tierp Sweden **41** 60.20N 17.30E
Tierra Amarilla U.S.A. **109** 36.42N 106.33W
Tierra Blanca Mexico **116** 18.28N 96.12W
Tierra del Fuego d. Argentina **125** 54.30S 67.00W
Tierra del Fuego i. Argentina/Chile **125** 54.00S 69.00W
Tietar r. Spain **27** 39.50N 6.01W
Tietê Brazil **126** 23.04S 47.41W
Tifrah Israel **67** 31.20N 34.40E
Tifton U.S.A. **113** 31.27N 83.31W
Tiger U.S.A. **108** 48.42N 117.24W
Tiger Hills Canada **101** 49.25N 99.30W

Tigil Russian Fed. **51** 57.49N 158.40E
Tiglit Morocco **74** 28.31N 10.15W
Tignère Cameroon **77** 7.23N 12.37E
Tignish Canada **103** 46.57N 64.02W
Tigray d. Ethiopia **72** 14.10N 39.35E
Tigre r. Venezuela **122** 9.20N 62.30W
Tigris r. see Dijlah r. Asia **65**
Tihāmah f. Saudi Arabia **72** 19.00N 41.00E
Tīh, Jabal at f. Egypt **66** 28.50N 34.00E
Tijesno Croatia **31** 43.48N 15.39E
Tijuana Mexico **109** 32.32N 117.01W
Tikamgarh India **63** 24.44N 78.50E
Tikaré Burkina **76** 13.16N 1.44W
Tikhoretsk Russian Fed. **45** 45.52N 40.07E
Tikhvin Russian Fed. **44** 59.35N 33.29E
Tikitiki New Zealand **86** 37.47S 178.25E
Tiksha Russian Fed. **44** 64.04N 32.35E
Tiksi Russian Fed. **51** 71.40N 128.45E
Tilburg Neth. **16** 51.34N 5.05E
Tilbury Canada **104** 42.16N 82.26W
Tilbury U.K. **13** 51.28N 0.23E
Tilemsi, Vallée du f. Mali **76** 16.15N 0.02E
Tilghman U.S.A. **115** 38.42N 76.20W
Tilhar India **63** 27.59N 79.44E
Till r. Northum. U.K. **12** 55.41N 2.12W
Tillabéri Niger **77** 14.28N 1.27E
Tillamook U.S.A. **108** 45.27N 123.51W
Tillsonburg Canada **104** 42.51N 80.44W
Tílos i. Greece **35** 36.25N 27.25E
Tilpa Australia **92** 30.57S 144.24E
Tilton U.S.A. **115** 43.27N 71.35W
Timagami Canada **104** 47.05N 79.50W
Timanskiy Kryazh mts. Russian Fed. **44** 66.00N 49.00E
Timaru New Zealand **86** 44.23S 171.41E
Timashevsk Russian Fed. **45** 45.38N 38.56E
Timbákion Greece **35** 35.04N 24.45E
Timbédra Mauritania **74** 16.17N 8.16W
Timber Creek town Australia **88** 15.38S 130.28E
Timboon Australia **92** 38.32S 143.02E
Timbuktu see Tombouctou Mali **76**
Timfi Óros mtn. Greece **34** 39.59N 20.45E
Timimoun Algeria **74** 29.15N 0.15E
Timimoun, Sebkha de f. Algeria **74** 29.10N 0.05E
Timiris, Cap c. Mauritania **76** 19.23N 16.32W
Timiş r. Yugo./Romania **37** 44.49N 20.28E
Timiskaming, L. Canada **104** 47.35N 79.35W
Timişoara Romania **37** 45.47N 21.15E
Timmernabben Sweden **43** 56.58N 16.26E
Timmins Canada **102** 48.28N 81.25W
Timok r. Yugo. **34** 44.10N 22.40E
Timor i. Indonesia **88** 9.30S 125.00E
Timor Sea Austa. **88** 11.00S 127.00E
Timor Timur Indonesia **59** 9.00S 125.00E
Timpahute Range mts. U.S.A. **109** 37.38N 115.34W
Tinahely Rep. of Ire. **15** 52.48N 6.19W
Tindouf Algeria **74** 27.42N 8.09W
Tindouf, Sebkha de f. Algeria **74** 27.45N 7.30W
Tineo Spain **26** 43.20N 6.25W
Tingha Australia **93** 29.58S 151.16E
Tingley Denmark **42** 54.56N 9.15E
Tingo María Peru **122** 9.09S 75.56W
Tingping China **55** 26.10N 110.17E
Tingréla Côte d'Ivoire **76** 10.26N 6.20W
Tingri China **63** 28.30N 86.34E
Tingsryd Sweden **43** 56.32N 14.59E
Tingstäde Sweden **43** 57.44N 18.36E
Tinguipaya Bolivia **124** 19.11S 65.51W
Tinkisso r. Guinea **76** 11.25N 9.05W
Tinnenburra Australia **93** 28.40S 145.30E
Tinnoset Norway **42** 59.58N 9.02E
Tínos i. Greece **35** 37.38N 25.10E
Tínos town Greece **35** 37.32N 25.10E
Tinsukia India **61** 27.30N 95.22E
Tintinara Australia **92** 35.52S 140.04E
Tinto r. Spain **27** 37.10N 6.54W
Tioga U.S.A. **114** 41.55N 77.08W
Tioman, Pulau i. Malaysia **58** 2.45N 104.10E
Tionaga Canada **102** 48.05N 82.00W
Tione di Trento Italy **30** 46.02N 10.43E
Tionesta U.S.A. **114** 41.30N 79.27W
Tionesta Creek r. U.S.A. **114** 41.28N 79.22W
Tioughnioga r. U.S.A. **115** 42.14N 75.51W
Tipperary Rep. of Ire. **15** 52.29N 8.10W
Tipperary d. Rep. of Ire. **15** 52.37N 7.55W
Tiranë Albania **34** 41.20N 19.50E
Tiranë Durrës d. Albania **34** 41.19N 19.26E
Tirān, Jazīrat Saudi Arabia **66** 27.56N 34.34E
Tirano Italy **30** 46.13N 10.11E
Tiraspol Moldova **37** 46.50N 29.38E
Tirat Karmel Israel **67** 32.46N 34.58E
Tirat Yehuda Israel **67** 32.01N 34.57E
Tirat Zevi Israel **67** 32.25N 35.32E
Tirebolu Turkey **64** 41.02N 38.49E
Tiree i. U.K. **14** 56.30N 6.50W
Tîrgovişte Romania **37** 44.56N 25.27E
Tîrgu-Jiu Romania **37** 45.03N 23.17E
Tîrgu-Lăpuş Romania **37** 47.27N 23.52E
Tîrgu Mureş Romania **37** 46.33N 24.34E
Tîrgu-Neamţ Romania **37** 47.12N 26.22E
Tîrgu-Ocna Romania **37** 46.15N 26.37E
Tîrgu-Secuiesc Romania **37** 46.00N 26.08E
Tirins site Greece **35** 37.36N 22.48E
Tiris Zemmour d. Mauritania **74** 24.00N 9.00W
Tírnavos Greece **34** 39.45N 22.17E
Tirodi India **63** 21.41N 79.42E
Tirol d. Austria **39** 47.10N 11.00E
Tirón r. Spain **26** 42.33N 4.31W
Tirso r. Italy **32** 39.52N 8.33E
Tiruchchirāppalli India **61** 10.50N 78.43E
Tirunelveli India **60** 8.45N 77.43E
Tirupati India **61** 13.39N 79.25E
Tiruppur India **60** 11.05N 77.20E
Tisa r. Yugo. **31** 45.09N 20.16E
Tis'ah Egypt **66** 30.02N 32.35E

Tisdale Canada 101 52.51N 104.04W
Tisnaren *l.* Sweden 43 58.57N 15.57E
Tisza *r.* Hungary *see* Tisa *r.* Yugo. 31
Tit Algeria 75 22.58N 5.11E
Titicaca, L. Bolivia/Peru 124 16.00S 69.00W
Titikaveka Rarotonga Cook Is. 84 21.16S 159.45W
Titiwa Nigeria 77 12.14N 12.53E
Titlagarh India 63 20.18N 83.09E
Titova Korenica Croatia 31 44.45N 15.43E
Titov Veles Macedonia 34 41.46N 21.47E
Titov Vrh *mtn.* Macedonia 34 42.00N 20.51E
Titran Norway 40 63.42N 8.22E
Ti Tree Australia 90 22.06S 133.17E
Tittabawassee *r.* U.S.A. 104 43.23N 83.59W
Tittmoning Germany 39 48.04N 12.46E
Titule Zaïre 78 3.17N 25.32E
Titusville Fla. U.S.A. 113 28.37N 80.50W
Titusville Penn. U.S.A. 114 41.38N 79.41W
Tiuni India 63 30.57N 77.51E
Tivaouane Senegal 76 14.57N 16.49W
Tiveden *hills* Sweden 43 58.45N 14.40E
Tiverton U.K. 13 50.54N 3.30W
Tiverton U.S.A. 115 41.38N 71.12W
Tivoli Italy 32 41.58N 12.48E
Tizimín Mexico 117 21.10N 88.09W
Tizi Ouzou Algeria 75 36.44N 4.05E
Tiznit Morocco 74 29.43N 9.44W
Tjeuke Meer *l.* Neth. 16 52.55N 5.51E
Tjöme *i.* Norway 42 59.07N 10.24E
Tjörn *i.* Sweden 42 58.00N 11.38E
Tlaxcala *d.* Mexico 116 19.45N 98.20W
Tlemcen Algeria 74 34.52N 1.19W
Tmassah Libya 75 26.22N 15.48E
Tni Haïa *well* Algeria 74 24.15N 2.45W
Toab U.K. 14 59.53N 1.16W
Toamasina Madagascar 81 18.10S 49.23E
Toano Italy 30 44.23N 10.34E
Toanoano Tahiti 85 17.52S 149.12W
Toba Japan 57 34.29N 136.51E
Toba, Danau *l.* Indonesia 58 2.45N 98.50E
Toba Kàkar Range *mts.* Pakistan 62 31.15N 68.00E
Tobar U.S.A. 108 40.53N 114.54W
Tobarra Spain 25 38.35N 1.41W
Toba Tek Singh Pakistan 62 30.58N 72.29E
Tobelo Indonesia 59 1.45N 127.59E
Tobermory Canada 104 45.15N 81.39W
Tobermory U.K. 14 56.37N 6.04W
Tobi *i.* Pacific Oc. 59 3.01N 131.10E
Tobin L. Canada 101 53.40N 103.35W
Tobi shima *i.* Japan 57 39.12N 139.32E
Toboali Indonesia 58 3.00S 106.30E
Tobol *r.* Russian Fed. 9 58.15N 68.12E
Tobolsk Russian Fed. 9 58.15N 68.12E
Tobruk *see* Ṭubruq Libya 72
Tobseda Russian Fed. 44 68.34N 52.16E
Tocantinópolis Brazil 123 6.20S 47.25W
Tocantins *d.* Brazil 123 10.15S 48.30W
Tocantins *r.* Brazil 123 1.50S 49.15W
Toccoa U.S.A. 113 34.34N 83.21W
Töcksfors Sweden 42 59.30N 11.50E
Tocopilla Chile 124 22.05S 70.12W
Tocorpuri *mtn.* Bolivia/Chile 124 22.26S 67.53W
Tocumwal Australia 93 35.51S 145.34E
Tocuyo *r.* Venezuela 122 11.03N 68.23W
Todenyang Kenya 79 4.34N 35.52E
Todi Italy 30 42.47N 12.24E
Todos Santos Mexico 109 23.27N 110.13W
Todtnau Germany 38 47.50N 7.56E
Tofte Norway 42 59.33N 10.34E
Tofua *i.* Tonga 85 19.45S 175.05W
Togian, Kepulauan *is.* Indonesia 59 0.20S 122.00E
Togo Africa 76 8.00N 1.00E
Tōhuku *d.* Japan 57 35.00N 137.00E
Toi Niue 84 18.58S 169.52W
Toijala Finland 41 61.10N 23.52E
Toili Indonesia 59 1.25S 122.23E
Tojg Afghan. 62 32.04N 61.48E
Tokaj Hungary 37 48.08N 21.27E
Tokala *mtn.* Indonesia 59 1.36S 121.41E
Tokara kaikyō *str.* Japan 57 30.10N 130.10E
Tokat Turkey 64 40.20N 36.35E
Tokelau Is. Pacific Oc. 84 9.00S 171.45W
Toki Japan 57 35.21N 137.11E
Toki *r.* Japan 57 35.12N 136.52E
Tokmak Kyrgyzstan 52 42.49N 75.15E
Tokoname Japan 57 34.53N 136.51E
Tokoroa New Zealand 86 38.13S 175.53E
Tokuno shima *i.* Japan 53 27.40N 129.00E
Tokushima Japan 57 34.03N 134.34E
Tokuyama Japan 57 34.04N 131.48E
Tōkyō Japan 57 35.40N 139.40E
Tōkyō-wan *b.* Japan 57 35.25N 139.45E
Tolaga Bay *town* New Zealand 86 38.22S 178.18E
Toledo Spain 27 39.52N 4.01W
Toledo *d.* Spain 27 39.45N 4.10W
Toledo U.S.A. 112 41.40N 83.35W
Toledo Bend Resr. U.S.A. 111 31.46N 93.25W
Toledo, Montes de *mts.* Spain 27 39.33N 4.20W
Tolentino Italy 30 43.12N 13.17E
Toliara Madagascar 81 23.21S 43.40E
Tolland U.S.A. 115 41.52N 72.22W
Tollense *r.* Germany 38 53.54N 13.02E
Tollarp Sweden 43 55.56N 13.59E
Tolmezzo Italy 30 46.24N 13.01E
Tolmin Slovenia 30 46.11N 13.44E
Tolna Hungary 31 46.26N 18.46E
Tolna *d.* Hungary 31 46.35N 18.30E
Tolosa Spain 26 43.08N 2.04W
Tolo, Teluk *g.* Indonesia 59 2.00S 122.30E
Tolstyy-Les Ukraine 37 51.24N 29.48E
Tolti Jammu & Kashmir 62 35.02N 76.06E
Toluca Mexico 116 19.20N 99.40W
Toluca *mtn.* Mexico 116 19.10N 99.40W
Tol'yatti Russian Fed. 44 53.32N 49.24E
Tomah U.S.A. 110 43.59N 90.30W
Tomakomai Japan 57 42.39N 141.33E
Tomar Portugal 27 39.36N 8.25W
Tomás Gomensoro Uruguay 125 30.26S 57.26W

Tomaszów Lubelski Poland 37 50.28N 23.25E
Tomaszów Mazowiecki Poland 37 51.32N 20.01E
Tombe Sudan 73 5.49N 31.41E
Tombigbee *r.* U.S.A. 111 31.04N 87.58W
Tombos Brazil 126 20.53S 42.03W
Tombouctou Mali 76 16.49N 2.59W
Tombouctou *d.* Mali 76 19.35N 3.20W
Tombua Angola 78 15.55S 11.51E
Tomé Chile 125 36.37S 72.57W
Tomelilla Sweden 43 55.33N 13.57E
Tomelloso Spain 27 39.10N 3.01W
Tomiko Canada 104 46.32N 79.49W
Tomingley Australia 93 32.06S 148.15E
Tomini Indonesia 59 0.31N 120.30E
Tomini, Teluk *g.* Indonesia 59 0.30S 120.45E
Tomintoul U.K. 14 57.15N 3.24W
Tomislavgrad Bosnia-Herzegovina 31 43.43N 17.14E
Tomkinson Ranges *mts.* Australia 88 26.11S 129.05E
Tom Price Australia 88 22.49S 117.51E
Tomra China 63 30.52N 87.30E
Tomra Norway 40 62.34N 6.55E
Tomsk Russian Fed. 50 56.30N 85.05E
Toms River *town* U.S.A. 115 39.57N 74.07W
Tomtabacken *hill* Sweden 43 57.30N 14.28E
Tonalá Mexico 116 16.08N 93.41W
Tonalea U.S.A. 109 36.20N 110.58W
Tonanda U.S.A. 114 43.01N 78.53W
Tonasket U.S.A. 108 48.42N 119.26W
Tonawanda U.S.A. 114 43.01N 78.53W
Tonbridge U.K. 13 51.12N 0.16E
Tondano Indonesia 59 1.19N 124.56E
Tönder Denmark 43 54.56N 8.54E
Tondibi Mali 76 16.39N 0.14W
Tondoro Namibia 80 17.45S 18.50E
Tone *r.* Japan 57 35.44N 140.51E
Tonga Pacific Oc. 85 20.00S 175.00W
Tonga Sudan 73 9.28N 31.03E
Tongaat R.S.A. 80 29.34S 31.07E
Tong'an China 55 24.44N 118.09E
Tongatapu *i.* Tonga 85 21.10S 175.10W
Tongatapu Group *is.* Tonga 85 21.10S 175.10W
Tonga Trench *f.* Pacific Oc. 84 20.00S 173.00W
Tongchuan China 54 35.05N 109.10E
Tongeren Belgium 16 50.47N 5.28E
Tongguan Hunan China 55 28.27N 112.48E
Tongguan Shaanxi China 54 34.32N 110.26E
Tonghai China 61 24.07N 102.45E
Tonghua China 53 41.40N 125.54E
Tongking, G. of China/Vietnam 56 20.00N 108.00E
Tongliao China 54 43.40N 122.20E
Tongling China 55 30.55N 117.42E
Tonglu China 55 29.49N 119.40E
Tongnae S. Korea 57 35.12N 129.05E
Tongo Australia 92 30.30S 143.47E
Tongoa *i.* Vanuatu 84 16.54S 168.34E
Tongobory Madagascar 81 23.32S 44.20E
Tongoy Chile 124 30.15S 71.30W
Tongren China 55 27.41N 109.08E
Tongsa Dzong Bhutan 63 27.31N 90.30E
Tongtianheyan China 63 33.50N 92.19E
Tongue U.K. 14 58.28N 4.25W
Tongue *r.* U.S.A. 108 46.24N 105.25W
Tongwei China 54 35.18N 105.10E
Tong Xian China 54 39.52N 116.45E
Tongxin China 54 36.59N 105.50E
Tongyu China 54 44.48N 123.06E
Tongzi China 55 28.08N 106.49E
Tonj Sudan 73 7.17N 28.45E
Tonk India 62 26.10N 75.47E
Tonkābon Iran 65 36.49N 50.54E
Tônlé Sap *l.* Cambodia 56 12.50N 104.15E
Tonnay-Boutonne France 20 45.58N 0.42W
Tonneins France 20 44.23N 0.19E
Tonnerre France 19 47.51N 3.58E
Tönning Germany 38 54.19N 8.56E
Tonopah U.S.A. 108 38.04N 117.14W
Tonota Botswana 80 21.28S 27.24E
Tons *r.* India 63 25.17N 82.04E
Tönsberg Norway 42 59.17N 10.25E
Tonstad Norway 42 58.40N 6.43E
Tonto Basin *town* U.S.A. 109 33.55N 111.18W
Toobeah Australia 93 28.22S 149.50E
Toodyay Australia 89 31.35S 116.26E
Tooele U.S.A. 108 40.32N 112.18W
Toolondo Australia 92 36.55S 142.00E
Toowoomba Australia 91 27.35S 151.54E
Topeka U.S.A. 110 39.03N 95.41W
Topki *mtn.* Russian Fed. 51 57.20N 138.10E
Topley Canada 100 54.32N 126.05W
Toplica *r.* Yugo. 34 43.15N 21.30E
Topliţa Romania 37 46.55N 25.21E
Topock U.S.A. 109 34.44N 114.27W
Topolovgrad Bulgaria 34 42.05N 26.20E
Topozero, Ozero *l.* Russian Fed. 44 65.45N 32.00E
Toppenish U.S.A. 108 46.23N 120.19W
Tor Ethiopia 73 7.53N 33.40E
Tora-Khem Russian Fed. 51 52.31N 96.13E
Torbat-e Ḥeydarīyeh Iran 65 35.16N 59.13E
Torbat-e Jām Iran 65 35.15N 60.37E
Tördal Norway 42 59.16N 8.49E
Tordera *r.* Spain 25 41.39N 2.47E
Tordesillas Spain 26 41.30N 5.00W
Tordino Italy 31 42.44N 13.59E
Töre Sweden 40 65.54N 22.39E
Töreboda Sweden 43 58.43N 14.08E
Torekov Sweden 43 56.26N 12.37E
Toreno Spain 26 42.42N 6.30W
Torgau Germany 38 51.34N 13.00E
Torhamn Sweden 43 56.05N 15.50E
Torhout Belgium 16 51.04N 3.06E
Toride Japan 57 35.53N 140.04E
Torino Italy 30 45.03N 7.40E
Torio *r.* Spain 26 42.35N 5.34W
Torit Sudan 73 4.24N 32.34E
Tormes *r.* Spain 26 41.18N 6.29W
Torne *r.* Sweden *see* Tornio *r.* Finland 40
Torneträsk Sweden 40 68.15N 19.30E
Torneträsk *l.* Sweden 40 68.20N 19.10E

Tornio Finland 40 65.52N 24.10E
Tornio *r.* Finland 40 65.53N 24.07E
Tornquist Argentina 125 38.06S 62.14W
Toro Spain 26 41.31N 5.24W
Toronaíos Kólpos *g.* Greece 34 40.05N 23.30E
Toronto Canada 104 43.39N 79.23W
Toropets Russian Fed. 44 56.30N 31.40E
Tororo Uganda 79 0.42N 34.13E
Toros Dağları *mts.* Turkey 64 37.15N 34.15E
Torquay Australia 92 38.20S 144.20E
Torquay U.K. 13 50.27N 3.31W
Torquemada Spain 26 42.02N 4.19W
Torrance U.S.A. 109 33.50N 118.19W
Torrão Portugal 27 38.18N 8.13W
Torre Annunziata Italy 33 40.45N 14.27E
Torre Baja Spain 25 40.07N 1.15W
Torreblanca Spain 25 40.13N 0.12E
Torrecilla *mtn.* Spain 27 36.41N 4.59W
Torrecilla en Cameros Spain 26 42.16N 2.37W
Torre del Campo Spain 27 37.46N 3.53W
Torre de Moncorvo Portugal 26 41.10N 7.03W
Torredonjimeno Spain 27 37.46N 3.57W
Torrejoncillo Spain 27 39.54N 6.28W
Torrejón de Ardoz Spain 26 40.27N 3.29W
Torrejón, Embalse de *resr.* Spain 27 39.50N 5.50W
Torrelaguna Spain 26 40.50N 3.32W
Torrelavega Spain 26 43.21N 4.03W
Torremaggiore Italy 33 41.41N 15.17E
Torremolinos Spain 27 36.37N 4.30W
Torrens Creek *r.* Australia 90 22.22S 145.09E
Torrens Creek *town* Australia 90 20.50S 145.00E
Torrens, L. Australia 92 31.00S 137.50E
Torrente Spain 25 39.26N 0.28W
Torreón Mexico 111 25.33N 103.26W
Torre Pellice Italy 30 44.49N 7.13E
Torreperogil Spain 26 38.02N 3.17W
Torres Novas Portugal 27 39.29N 8.32W
Torres Str. Australia 90 10.00S 142.20E
Torres Vedras Portugal 27 39.06N 9.16W
Torrevieja Spain 25 37.59N 0.41W
Torrey U.S.A. 108 38.18N 111.25W
Torridge *r.* U.K. 13 51.01N 4.12W
Torridon U.K. 14 57.23N 5.31W
Torridon, Loch U.K. 14 57.35N 5.45W
Torriglia Italy 30 44.31N 9.10E
Torrijos Spain 27 39.59N 4.17W
Torrington Conn. U.S.A. 115 41.48N 73.08W
Torrington Wyo. U.S.A. 108 42.04N 104.11W
Torrox Spain 27 36.46N 3.58W
Torsås Sweden 43 56.24N 16.00E
Torsby Sweden 43 60.08N 13.00E
Torsö *i.* Sweden 43 58.48N 13.30E
Tortola *i.* B.V.Is. 117 18.28N 64.40W
Tortoli Italy 32 39.55N 9.39E
Tortona Italy 30 44.54N 8.52E
Tortorici Italy 33 38.02N 14.39E
Tortosa Spain 25 40.49N 0.31E
Tortosa, Cabo de *c.* Spain 25 40.43N 0.55E
Tortue, Île de la *i.* Cuba 117 20.05N 72.57W
Toruń Poland 37 53.01N 18.35E
Torup Sweden 43 56.58N 13.05E
Tory Hill *town* Canada 104 44.58N 78.18W
Tory I. Rep. of Ire. 15 55.16N 8.13W
Tory Sd. Rep. of Ire. 15 55.14N 8.15W
Torzhok Russian Fed. 44 57.02N 34.51E
Tosas, Puerto de *pass* Spain 25 42.19N 2.01E
Tosa wan *b.* Japan 57 33.10N 133.40E
Toscana *d.* Italy 30 43.35N 11.00E
Tosen Norway 40 65.16N 12.50E
Toshkent *see* Tashkent Uzbekistan 9
Tosno Russian Fed. 44 59.38N 30.46E
Tostado Argentina 124 29.15S 61.45W
Totak *l.* Norway 42 59.42N 7.57E
Totana Spain 25 37.46N 1.30W
Tôtes France 18 49.41N 1.03E
Totma Russian Fed. 44 59.59N 42.44E
Totora Bolivia 124 17.42S 65.09W
Tottenham Australia 93 32.14S 147.24E
Tottenham Canada 104 44.01N 79.49W
Tottori Japan 57 35.32N 134.12E
Touba Côte d'Ivoire 76 8.22N 7.42W
Toubkal *mtn.* Morocco 74 31.03N 7.57W
Toucy France 19 47.44N 3.18E
Tougan Burkina 76 13.05N 3.04W
Touggourt Algeria 75 33.06N 6.04E
Tougué Guinea 76 11.25N 11.50W
Toul France 19 48.41N 5.54E
Toulnustouc *r.* Canada 103 49.35N 68.25W
Toulon France 21 43.07N 5.56E
Toulon-sur-Arroux France 19 46.42N 4.08E
Toulouse France 20 43.36N 1.26E
Toummo Niger 75 22.45N 14.08E
Tounassine, Hamada *des.* Algeria 74 28.36N 5.00W
Toungoo Myanmar 56 18.57N 96.26E
Touques *r.* France 18 49.22N 0.06E
Tourassine *well* Mauritania 74 24.40N 11.20W
Tourcoing France 19 50.43N 3.09E
Tourinan, Cabo *c.* Spain 26 43.03N 9.18W
Tournai Belgium 16 50.36N 3.23E
Tournon France 21 45.04N 4.50E
Tournus France 19 46.34N 4.54E
Tours France 18 47.23N 0.41E
Toury France 19 48.12N 1.56E
Toustain Algeria 32 36.40N 8.15E
Touwsrivier *town* R.S.A. 80 33.20S 20.02E
Toužim Czech Republic 39 50.04N 13.00E
Tovdals *r.* Norway 42 58.13N 8.08E
Towada ko *l.* Japan 57 40.28N 140.55E
Towanda U.S.A. 115 41.46N 76.27W
Towcester U.K. 13 52.07N 0.56W
Tower U.S.A. 110 47.47N 92.19W
Towner U.S.A. 110 48.21N 100.25W
Townsend, Mt. Australia 93 36.24S 148.15E
Townshend I. Australia 90 22.15S 150.30E
Townsville Australia 90 19.13S 146.48E
Towrzi Afghan. 62 30.11N 65.59E
Towson U.S.A. 115 39.24N 76.36W
Towyn U.K. 13 52.37N 4.08W

Toyah U.S.A. 111 31.19N 103.47W
Toyama Japan 57 36.42N 137.14E
Toyama wan *b.* Japan 57 36.50N 137.10E
Toyo *r.* Japan 57 34.47N 137.20E
Toyohashi Japan 57 34.46N 137.23E
Toyokawa Japan 57 34.49N 137.24E
Toyota Japan 57 35.05N 137.09E
Tozeur Tunisia 75 33.55N 8.08E
Traben-Trarbach Germany 39 49.57N 7.06E
Trabzon Turkey 64 41.00N 39.43E
Tracadie Canada 103 47.31N 64.54W
Tracy Canada 105 46.01N 73.09W
Tracy U.S.A. 110 44.14N 95.37W
Trade Town Liberia 76 5.43N 9.56W
Trafalgar, Cabo *c.* Spain 27 36.11N 6.02W
Tragacete Spain 25 40.21N 1.51W
Traid Spain 25 40.40N 1.49W
Traiguén Chile 125 38.15S 72.41W
Trail Canada 100 49.05N 117.40W
Trajanova Vrata *pass* Bulgaria 34 42.18N 23.58E
Trakt Russian Fed. 44 62.40N 51.26E
Tralee Rep. of Ire. 15 52.16N 9.42W
Tralee B. Rep. of Ire. 15 52.18N 9.55W
Tranås Sweden 43 58.03N 14.59E
Tranco, Embalse del *resr.* Spain 26 38.10N 2.45W
Trancoso Portugal 26 40.47N 7.21W
Tranebjerg Denmark 42 50.50N 10.36E
Trang Thailand 56 7.35N 99.35E
Trangan *i.* Indonesia 59 6.30S 134.15E
Trangie Australia 93 32.03S 148.01E
Trani Italy 33 41.17N 16.26E
Tranoroa Madagascar 81 24.42S 45.04E
Tranqueras Uruguay 125 31.12S 55.45W
Transkei Africa 80 31.30S 29.00E
Transkei *f.* R.S.A. 80 32.12S 28.20E
Transylvanian Alps *see* Carpaţii Meridionali *mts.* Romania 29
Trapani Italy 32 38.01N 12.31E
Traralgon Australia 93 38.12S 146.32E
Traryd Sweden 43 56.35N 13.45E
Trarza *d.* Mauritania 74 18.00N 14.50W
Trarza *f.* Mauritania 74 18.00N 15.00W
Trasacco Italy 31 41.57N 13.32E
Trasimeno, Lago *l.* Italy 30 43.08N 12.06E
Träslövsläge Sweden 43 57.04N 12.16E
Trat Thailand 56 12.14N 102.33E
Traun Austria 39 48.13N 14.14E
Traunsee *l.* Austria 39 47.51N 13.48E
Traunstein Germany 39 47.52N 12.38E
Trave *r.* Germany 38 53.54N 10.50E
Travellers L. Australia 92 33.18S 142.00E
Traverse City U.S.A. 112 44.46N 85.38W
Travers, Mt. New Zealand 86 42.05S 172.45E
Travnik Bosnia-Herzegovina 31 44.14N 17.40E
Trayning Australia 89 31.09S 117.46E
Trbovlje Slovenia 31 46.10N 15.03E
Trebbia *r.* Italy 30 45.04N 9.41E
Trebel *r.* Germany 38 53.55N 13.01E
Třebíč Czech Republic 36 49.13N 15.55E
Trebinje Bosnia-Herzegovina 31 42.43N 18.20E
Trebisacce Italy 33 39.52N 16.32E
Trebišov Slovakia 37 48.40N 21.47E
Třeboň Czech Republic 36 49.01N 14.50E
Trecate Italy 30 45.26N 8.44E
Tredegar U.K. 13 51.47N 3.16W
Treene *r.* Germany 38 54.22N 9.05E
Tregaron U.K. 13 52.14N 3.56W
Tregosse Islets and Reefs Australia 90 17.41S 150.43E
Tréguier France 18 48.47N 3.14W
Treinta-y-Tres Uruguay 126 33.16S 54.17W
Treis Germany 39 50.10N 7.17E
Trélazé France 18 47.27N 0.28W
Trelew Argentina 125 43.15S 65.20W
Trelleborg Sweden 43 55.22N 13.10E
Trélon France 19 50.04N 4.06E
Tremadog B. U.K. 12 52.52N 4.14W
Tremblant, Mont *mtn.* Canada 105 46.16N 74.35W
Tremont U.S.A. 115 40.38N 76.23W
Tremp Spain 25 42.10N 0.54E
Trena Ethiopia 73 10.45N 40.38E
Trenčín Slovakia 37 48.54N 18.04E
Trenggalek Indonesia 59 8.01S 111.38E
Trenque Lauquen Argentina 125 35.56S 62.43W
Trent *r.* Canada 105 44.06N 77.34W
Trent *r.* U.K. 12 53.41N 0.41W
Trente-un Milles, Lac des *l.* Canada 105 46.12N 75.49W
Trentino-Alto Adige *d.* Italy 30 46.35N 11.20E
Trento Italy 30 46.04N 11.08E
Trenton Canada 105 44.06N 77.35W
Trenton Mich. U.S.A. 104 42.09N 83.11W
Trenton Mo. U.S.A. 110 40.05N 93.37W
Trenton Nebr. U.S.A. 110 40.11N 101.01W
Trenton N.J. U.S.A. 115 40.13N 74.45W
Trepassey Canada 103 46.44N 53.22W
Tres Árboles Uruguay 125 32.24S 56.43W
Tres Arroyos Argentina 125 38.26S 60.17W
Três Corações Brazil 126 21.44S 45.15W
Três Lagoas Brazil 126 20.46S 51.43W
Três Marias, Reprêsa *resr.* Brazil 126 18.15S 45.15W
Três Pontas Brazil 126 21.23S 45.29W
Três Rios Brazil 126 22.07S 43.12W
Treuchtlingen Germany 39 48.57N 10.54E
Treuenbrietzen Germany 38 52.06N 12.52E
Treviglio Italy 30 45.31N 9.35E
Treviño Spain 26 42.44N 2.45W
Treviso Italy 30 45.40N 12.15E
Trévoux France 21 45.56N 4.46E
Trgovište Yugo. 34 42.21N 22.05E
Triánda Greece 35 36.25N 28.10E
Triberg Germany 39 48.08N 8.13E
Tribsees Germany 38 54.05N 12.45E
Tribulation, C. Australia 90 16.03S 145.30E
Tribune Canada 101 49.16N 104.05W
Tricarico Italy 33 40.37N 16.09E
Tricase Italy 33 39.56N 18.22E

Trida Australia 93 33.00S 145.01E
Trier Germany 39 49.45N 6.38E
Trieste Italy 31 45.40N 13.46E
Trieux r. France 18 48.47N 3.07W
Triglav mtn. Slovenia 31 46.23N 13.50E
Trigno r. Italy 33 42.04N 14.48E
Trigueros Spain 27 37.23N 6.50W
Trikala Greece 34 39.34N 21.46E
Trikhonís, Limni l. Greece 35 38.34N 21.28E
Tríkomon Cyprus 66 35.17N 33.53E
Triman Pakistan 62 29.38N 69.05E
Trincomalee Sri Lanka 61 8.34N 81.13E
Trinidad Bolivia 124 14.47S 64.47W
Trinidad Colombia 122 5.25N 71.40W
Trinidad Cuba 117 21.48N 80.00W
Trinidad Uruguay 125 33.32S 56.54W
Trinidad U.S.A. 108 37.10N 104.31W
Trinidad & Tobago S. America 117 10.30N 61.20W
Trinity r. U.S.A. 111 29.55N 94.45W
Trinity B. Australia 90 16.26S 145.26E
Trinity B. Canada 103 48.00N 53.40W
Trinity Range mts. U.S.A. 108 40.13N 119.12W
Trinkitat Sudan 72 18.41N 37.43E
Trino Italy 30 45.12N 8.18E
Tripoli see Ţarābulus Lebanon 66
Tripoli see Ţarābulus Libya 75
Trípolis Greece 35 37.31N 22.21E
Tripolitania f. see Ţarābulus f. Libya 75
Tripp U.S.A. 110 43.13N 97.58W
Tripura d. India 63 23.50N 92.00E
Tristan da Cunha i. Atlantic Oc. 127 37.50S 12.30W
Triste Spain 25 42.23N 0.43W
Trivandrum India 60 8.41N 76.57E
Trivento Italy 33 41.47N 14.33E
Trnava Slovakia 37 48.23N 17.35E
Troarn France 18 49.11N 0.11W
Trobriand Is. P.N.G. 90 8.35S 151.05E
Trogir Croatia 31 43.31N 16.15E
Troglav mtn. Croatia 31 43.57N 16.36E
Troia Italy 33 41.22N 15.18E
Troina Italy 33 37.47N 14.37E
Troisdorf Germany 38 50.49N 7.08E
Trois-Rivières town Canada 105 46.21N 72.33W
Troitsk Russian Fed. 9 54.08N 61.33E
Troitsko-Pechorsk Russian Fed. 44 62.40N 56.08E
Troitskoye Russian Fed. 44 52.18N 56.26E
Troitskoye Ukraine 37 47.38N 30.19E
Trölladyngja mtn. Iceland 46 64.54N 17.16W
Trollheimen mts. Norway 40 62.50N 9.15E
Tromelin i. Indian Oc. 49 15.52S 54.25E
Troms d. Norway 40 69.30E
Tromsø Norway 40 69.42N 19.00E
Trondheim Norway 40 63.36N 10.23E
Trondheimsfjorden est. Norway 40 63.40N 10.30E
Troödos mts. Cyprus 66 34.57N 32.50E
Troon U.K. 14 55.33N 4.40W
Tropea Italy 33 38.41N 15.54E
Tropic U.S.A. 108 37.37N 112.05W
Tropoja Albania 34 42.23N 20.10E
Trosa Sweden 43 58.54N 17.33E
Trosh Russian Fed. 44 66.24N 56.08E
Trostan mtn. U.K. 15 55.03N 6.10W
Trostyanets Ukraine 37 48.35N 29.10E
Trout r. Canada 100 61.19N 119.51W
Trout Creek town Canada 104 45.59N 79.22W
Trout L. N.W.T. Canada 100 60.35N 121.10W
Trout L. Ont. Canada 102 51.13N 93.20W
Trout River town Canada 103 49.29N 58.08W
Trout Run U.S.A. 114 41.23N 77.03W
Trouville France 18 49.22N 0.05E
Trowbridge U.K. 13 51.18N 2.12W
Troy site Turkey 34 39.57N 26.15E
Troy Ala. U.S.A. 113 31.49N 86.00W
Troy Mo. U.S.A. 110 38.59N 90.59W
Troy Mont. U.S.A. 108 48.28N 115.53W
Troy N.H. U.S.A. 115 42.50N 72.11W
Troy N.Y. U.S.A. 115 42.43N 73.40W
Troy Ohio U.S.A. 112 40.02N 84.12W
Troy Penn. U.S.A. 114 41.47N 76.47W
Troyan Bulgaria 34 42.51N 24.43E
Troyes France 19 48.18N 4.05E
Troy Peak mtn. U.S.A. 108 38.19N 115.30W
Trpanj Croatia 31 43.00N 17.17E
Trstenik Yugo. 34 43.37N 21.00E
Truchas Peak mtn. U.S.A. 109 35.58N 105.39W
Truckee U.S.A. 108 39.20N 120.11W
Trujillo Honduras 117 15.55N 86.00W
Trujillo Peru 122 8.06S 79.00W
Trujillo Spain 27 39.28N 5.53W
Trujillo Venezuela 122 9.20N 70.37W
Trumansburg U.S.A. 115 42.33N 76.40W
Trûn Bulgaria 34 42.51N 22.38E
Trundle Australia 93 32.54S 147.35E
Trung-Luong Vietnam 56 13.55N 109.15E
Trunmore B. Canada 103 53.48N 57.10W
Truro Australia 92 34.23S 199.09E
Truro Canada 103 45.22N 63.16W
Truro U.K. 13 50.17N 5.02W
Trûstenik Bulgaria 34 43.31N 24.28E
Trustrup Denmark 42 56.21N 10.47E
Truth or Consequences U.S.A. 109 33.08N 107.15W
Truyère r. France 20 44.39N 2.34E
Tryavna Bulgaria 34 42.54N 25.25E
Trysil Norway 41 61.19N 10.40E
Trysil r. Norway 41 61.03N 12.30E
Trzemeszno Poland 37 52.35N 17.50E
Tržič Slovenia 31 46.22N 14.19E
Ťsamandás Greece 35 39.46N 20.21E
Tsaratanana Madagascar 81 16.47S 47.39E
Tsaratanana, Massif de mts. Madagascar 81 14.00S 49.00E
Tsarevo Bulgaria 29 42.09N 27.51E
Tsaritsáni Greece 34 39.53N 22.14E
Tsau Botswana 80 20.10S 22.29E
Tsavo Nat. Park Kenya 79 2.45S 38.45E
Tsenova Bulgaria 34 43.32N 25.39E
Tses Namibia 80 25.58S 18.08E

Tsévié Togo 77 6.28N 1.15E
Tshabong Botswana 80 26.03S 22.25E
Tshane Botswana 80 24.02S 21.54E
Tshela Zaïre 78 4.57S 12.57E
Tshesebe Botswana 80 20.45S 27.31E
Tshikapa Zaïre 78 6.28S 20.48E
Tshofa Zaïre 78 5.13S 25.20E
Tshopo r. Zaïre 78 0.30N 25.07E
Tshuapa r. Zaïre 78 0.14S 20.45E
Tsihombé Madagascar 81 25.18S 45.29E
Tsimlyansk Russian Fed. 45 47.40N 42.06E
Tsimlyanskoye Vodokhranilishche resr. Russian Fed. 45 48.00N 43.00E
Tsinan see Jinan China 54
Tsínga mtn. Greece 34 41.23N 24.44E
Tsingtao see Qingdao China 54
Tsiribihina Madagascar 81 19.42S 44.31E
Tsiroanomandidy Madagascar 81 18.46S 46.02E
Tsivilsk Russian Fed. 44 55.50N 47.28E
Tsivory Madagascar 81 24.04S 46.05E
Tskhinvali Georgia 45 42.14N 43.58E
Tsna Belarus 37 52.10N 27.03E
Tsna r. Russian Fed. 44 54.45N 41.54E
Tsobis Namibia 80 19.27S 17.30E
Tso Morīri l. Jammu & Kashmir 63 32.54N 78.20E
Tsu Japan 57 34.43N 136.31E
Tsuchiura Japan 57 36.05N 140.12E
Tsudakhar Russian Fed. 45 42.20N 47.11E
Tsugaru kaikyō str. Japan 57 41.30N 140.50E
Tsumeb Namibia 80 19.12S 17.43E
Tsuru Japan 57 35.30N 138.56E
Tsuruga Japan 57 35.40N 136.05E
Tsuruoka Japan 57 38.44N 139.50E
Tsushima Japan 57 35.10N 136.43E
Tsushima i. Japan 57 34.30N 129.20E
Tsuyama Japan 57 35.04N 134.01E
Tua r. Portugal 26 41.13N 7.26W
Tuam Rep. of Ire. 15 53.32N 8.52W
Tuamotu, Îles is. Pacific Oc. 85 17.00S 142.00W
Tuapa Niue 84 18.59S 169.54W
Tuapse Russian Fed. 45 44.06N 39.05E
Tuatapere New Zealand 86 46.08S 167.41E
Tubac U.S.A. 109 31.37N 111.03W
Tuba City U.S.A. 109 36.08N 111.14W
Tuban Indonesia 59 6.55S 112.01E
Tubarão Brazil 126 28.30S 49.01W
Ţubās Jordan 67 32.19N 35.22E
Ţubayq, Jabal aţ mts. Saudi Arabia 66 29.30N 37.15E
Tubbercurry Rep. of Ire. 15 54.03N 8.45W
Tübingen Germany 39 48.31N 9.02E
Ţubjah, Wādī r. Saudi Arabia 64 25.35N 38.22E
Ţubruq Libya 72 32.06N 23.58E
Tubuai i. Pacific Oc. 85 23.23S 149.27W
Tubuai Is. Pacific Oc. 85 23.00S 150.00W
Tucacas Venezuela 122 10.48N 68.19W
Tuchola Poland 37 53.35N 17.50E
Tuckerton U.S.A. 115 39.36N 74.20W
Tucson U.S.A. 109 32.13N 110.58W
Tucumán d. Argentina 124 26.30S 65.20W
Tucumcari U.S.A. 109 35.10N 103.44W
Tucupita Venezuela 122 9.02N 62.04W
Tucuruí Brazil 123 3.42S 49.44W
Tucuruí, Reprêsa de resr. Brazil 123 4.35S 49.33W
Tudela Spain 26 42.05N 1.36W
Tudela de Duero Spain 26 41.35N 4.35W
Tuela r. Portugal 26 41.30N 7.12W
Tufi P.N.G. 90 9.05S 149.20E
Tugela R.S.A. 80 29.10S 31.25E
Tug Hill mtn. U.S.A. 115 43.45N 75.39W
Tuguegarao Phil. 59 17.36N 121.44E
Tugur Russian Fed. 51 53.44N 136.45E
Tuineje Canary Is. 127 28.18N 14.03W
Tukangbesi, Kepulauan is. Indonesia 59 5.30S 124.00E
Tukayyid well Iraq 65 29.47N 45.36E
Ţūkh Egypt 66 30.21N 31.12E
Ţūkrah Libya 75 32.32N 20.34E
Tuktoyaktuk Canada 98 69.27N 133.00W
Tukums Latvia 41 57.00N 23.10E
Tukuyu Tanzania 79 9.20S 33.37E
Tula Mexico 116 23.00N 99.43W
Tula Russian Fed. 44 54.11N 37.38E
Tülak Afghan. 62 33.58N 63.44E
Tulare U.S.A. 109 36.13N 119.21W
Tulare L. resr. U.S.A. 109 36.03N 119.49W
Tularosa U.S.A. 109 33.04N 106.01W
Tulcan Ecuador 122 0.50N 77.48W
Tulcea Romania 29 45.10N 28.50E
Tulchin Ukraine 37 48.40N 28.49E
Tulemalu L. Canada 101 62.58N 99.25W
Tuli Zimbabwe 80 21.50S 29.15E
Tuli r. Zimbabwe 80 21.49S 29.00E
Tulia U.S.A. 111 34.32N 101.46W
Ţūlkarm Jordan 67 32.19N 35.02E
Tullahoma U.S.A. 113 35.21N 86.12W
Tullamore Australia 93 32.39S 147.39E
Tullamore Rep. of Ire. 15 53.17N 7.31W
Tulle France 20 45.16N 1.46E
Tullins France 21 45.18N 5.29E
Tullow Rep. of Ire. 15 52.49N 6.45W
Tully Australia 90 17.55S 145.59E
Tully U.S.A. 115 42.48N 76.07W
Tuloma r. Russian Fed. 44 68.56N 33.00E
Tulsa U.S.A. 111 36.09N 95.58W
Tulsequah Canada 100 58.39N 133.35W
Tuluá Colombia 122 4.05N 76.12W
Tulumbasy Russian Fed. 44 57.27N 57.40E
Tulun Russian Fed. 51 54.32N 100.35E
Tulungagung Indonesia 59 8.03S 111.54E
Tulu Welel mtn. Ethiopia 73 8.53N 34.47E
Tum Indonesia 59 3.28S 130.21E
Tumaco Colombia 122 1.51N 78.46W
Tumba Sweden 43 59.12N 17.49E
Tumba, L. Zaïre 78 0.45S 18.00E
Tumbarumba Australia 93 35.49S 148.01E
Tumbes Peru 122 3.37S 80.27W
Tumbler Ridge Canada 100 55.20N 120.49W
Tumby Bay town Australia 92 34.20S 136.05E

Tumd Youqi China 54 40.33N 110.30E
Tumd Zuoqi China 54 40.42N 111.08E
Tumeremo Venezuela 122 7.18N 61.30W
Tummel, Loch U.K. 14 56.43N 3.55W
Tump Pakistan 62 26.07N 62.22E
Tumsar India 63 21.23N 79.44E
Tumuc Humac Mts. S. America 123 2.20N 54.50W
Tumut Australia 93 35.20S 148.14E
Tunari mtn. Bolivia 124 17.18S 66.22W
Tünat al Jabal Egypt 66 27.46N 30.44E
Tunceli Turkey 64 39.07N 39.34E
Tuncurry Australia 93 32.17S 152.29E
Tundubai well Sudan 72 18.31N 28.33E
Tunduma Tanzania 79 9.19S 32.47E
Tunduru Tanzania 79 11.08S 37.21E
Tundzha r. Bulgaria 34 42.00N 26.35E
Tungabhadra r. India 60 16.00N 78.15E
Tungaru Sudan 73 10.14N 30.42E
Tungchiang Taiwan 55 22.28N 120.26E
Tungsten Canada 100 62.00N 128.15W
Tungsten U.S.A. 108 40.48N 118.08W
Tunica U.S.A. 111 34.41N 90.23W
Tunis Tunisia 32 36.48N 10.11E
Tunis, Golfe de g. Tunisia 32 37.00N 10.30E
Tunisia Africa 75 34.00N 9.00E
Tunja Colombia 122 5.33N 73.23W
Tunkhannock U.S.A. 115 41.32N 75.57W
Tunnsjøen l. Norway 40 64.45N 13.25E
Tunungayualok I. Canada 103 56.05N 61.05W
Tunuyán r. Argentina 125 33.33S 67.30W
Tunxi see Huangshan China 55
Tuoy-Khaya Russian Fed. 51 62.33N 111.25E
Tupã Brazil 126 21.57S 50.28W
Tupelo U.S.A. 111 34.16N 88.43W
Tupinambaranas, Ilha f. Brazil 123 3.00S 58.00W
Tupiza Bolivia 124 21.27S 65.43W
Tupper Lake town U.S.A. 105 44.13N 74.29W
Tuquan China 54 45.22N 121.41E
Túquerres Colombia 122 1.06N 77.37W
Tura India 63 25.31N 90.13E
Tura Russian Fed. 51 64.05N 100.00E
Tura Tanzania 79 5.30S 33.50E
Turabah Saudi Arabia 72 21.13N 41.39E
Turangi New Zealand 86 38.59S 175.48E
Turano r. Italy 30 42.26N 12.47E
Turbaco Colombia 122 10.20N 75.25W
Turbat Pakistan 62 25.59N 63.04E
Turbine Canada 104 46.22N 81.31W
Turbo Colombia 122 8.06N 76.44W
Turda Romania 37 46.34N 23.47E
Turek Poland 37 52.02N 18.30E
Turgay Kazakhstan 9 49.38N 63.25E
Turgeon r. Canada 102 50.00N 78.54W
Tŭrgovishte Bulgaria 34 43.17N 26.38E
Turgutlu Turkey 29 38.30N 27.43E
Turhal Turkey 64 40.23N 36.05E
Tūri Estonia 41 58.48N 25.26E
Turia r. Spain 25 39.27N 0.19W
Turiaçu Brazil 123 1.41S 45.21W
Turiaçu r. Brazil 123 1.36S 45.19W
Turin Canada 100 49.59N 112.35W
Turin see Torino Italy 30
Turka Ukraine 37 49.10N 23.02E
Turkana, L. Kenya 79 4.00N 36.00E
Turkestan Kazakhstan 52 43.17N 68.16E
Turkey Asia 64 39.00N 35.00E
Turkey U.S.A. 111 34.23N 100.54W
Turkey Creek town Australia 88 17.04S 128.15E
Turkmenistan Asia 9 40.00N 60.00E
Turks Is. Turks & Caicos Is. 117 21.30N 71.10W
Turku Finland 41 60.27N 22.17E
Turku-Pori d. Finland 41 61.00N 22.35E
Turkwel r. Kenya 79 3.08N 35.39E
Turnagain r. Canada 100 59.06N 127.35W
Turnberry Canada 101 53.25N 101.45W
Turneffe Is. Belize 117 17.30N 87.45W
Turner U.S.A. 108 48.51N 108.24W
Turnhout Belgium 16 51.19N 4.57E
Turnu Măgurele Romania 34 43.45N 24.53E
Turnu Roşu, Pasul pass Romania 29 45.37N 24.17E
Turnu-Severin Romania 29 44.37N 22.39E
Turon r. Australia 93 33.03S 149.33E
Turon U.S.A. 111 37.48N 98.26W
Turopolje f. Croatia 31 45.40N 16.00E
Turov Belarus 37 52.04N 27.40E
Turpan China 52 42.55N 89.06E
Turpan Pendi f. China 52 43.40N 89.00E
Turquino mtn. Cuba 117 20.05N 76.50W
Turriff U.K. 14 57.32N 2.28W
Turtkul Uzbekistan 65 41.30N 61.00E
Turtle Lake town N.Dak. U.S.A. 110 47.31N 100.53W
Turtle Lake town Wisc. U.S.A. 110 45.23N 92.09W
Turtle Mtn. Canada/U.S.A. 101 49.05N 99.45W
Turukhansk Russian Fed. 51 65.21N 88.05E
Turya r. Ukraine 37 51.48N 24.52E
Tuscaloosa U.S.A. 113 33.12N 87.33W
Tuscany see Toscana d. Italy 30
Tuscarawas r. U.S.A. 114 40.17N 81.52W
Tuscarora U.S.A. 108 41.19N 116.14W
Tuscarora Mts. U.S.A. 114 40.10N 77.45W
Tuscola Ill. U.S.A. 110 39.48N 88.17W
Tuscola Tex. U.S.A. 111 32.12N 99.48W
Tutera see Tudela Spain 25
Tuticorin India 61 8.48N 78.10E
Tutin Yugo. 34 43.00N 20.20E
Tutóia Brazil 123 2.45S 42.16W
Tutrakan Bulgaria 29 44.02N 26.40E
Tuttle U.S.A. 110 47.09N 100.00W
Tuttlingen Germany 39 47.59N 8.49E
Tutuala Indonesia 59 8.24S 127.15E
Tutubu Tanzania 79 5.28S 32.43E
Tutuila i. Samoa 84 14.18S 170.42W
Tuţūn Egypt 66 29.15N 30.46E
Tutzing Germany 39 47.54N 11.17E
Tuul Gol r. Mongolia 52 48.53N 104.35E
Tuvalu Pacific Oc. 84 8.00S 178.00E
Tuwayq, Jabal mts. Saudi Arabia 71 23.30N 46.20E

Tuxpan Mexico 116 21.00N 97.23W
Tuxtla Gutiérrez Mexico 116 16.45N 93.09W
Túy Spain 26 42.03N 8.38W
Tuyen Quang Vietnam 55 21.48N 105.21E
Tuz Gölü l. Turkey 64 38.45N 33.24E
Ţūz Khurmātū Iraq 65 34.53N 44.38E
Tuzla Bosnia-Herzegovina 31 44.32N 18.41E
Tvaerå Faroe Is. 10 61.34N 6.48W
Tvedestrand Norway 42 58.37N 8.55E
Tveitsund Norway 42 59.01N 8.32E
Tver' Russian Fed. 44 56.47N 35.57E
Tvürditsa Bulgaria 34 42.42N 25.52E
Tweed Canada 105 44.29N 77.19W
Tweed r. U.K. 15 55.46N 2.00W
Tweed Heads town Australia 93 28.13S 153.33E
Tweedsmuir Prov. Park Canada 100 52.55N 126.20W
Twentynine Palms U.S.A. 109 34.08N 116.03W
Twin Bridges town U.S.A. 108 45.33N 112.20W
Twin Falls town U.S.A. 108 42.34N 114.28W
Twining U.S.A. 104 44.07N 83.48W
Twins Creek r. Australia 92 29.10S 139.27E
Twin Valley town U.S.A. 110 47.16N 96.16W
Twizel New Zealand 86 44.15S 170.06E
Twofold B. Australia 93 37.06S 149.55E
Two Harbors town U.S.A. 110 47.02N 91.40W
Twyford U.K. 13 51.01N 1.19W
Tygart r. U.S.A. 114 38.30N 80.03W
Tyler Minn. U.S.A. 110 44.17N 96.08W
Tyler Tex. U.S.A. 111 32.21N 95.18W
Tylösand Sweden 43 56.39N 12.44E
Tylöskog hills Sweden 43 58.45N 15.20E
Tyndinskiy Russian Fed. 51 55.11N 124.34E
Tyne r. U.K. 12 55.00N 1.25W
Tyne and Wear d. U.K. 12 54.57N 1.35W
Tynemouth U.K. 12 55.01N 1.24W
Tynset Norway 41 62.17N 10.47E
Tyre see Şūr Lebanon 67
Tyrifjorden l. Norway 42 60.02N 10.08E
Tyringe Sweden 43 56.10N 13.35E
Tyron U.S.A. 113 35.13N 82.14W
Tyrone d. U.K. 15 54.35N 7.15W
Tyrone U.S.A. 114 40.40N 78.14W
Tyrrel Canada 101 54.35N 99.10W
Tyrrell r. Australia 92 35.28S 142.55E
Tyrrell, L. Australia 92 35.22S 142.50E
Tyrrhenian Sea Med. Sea 32 40.00N 12.00E
Tysnesøy i. Norway 42 60.00N 5.35E
Tyssedal Norway 42 60.07N 6.34E
Tyumen Russian Fed. 9 57.11N 65.29E
Tywi r. U.K. 13 51.46N 4.22W
Tzaneen R.S.A. 80 23.49S 30.10E

U

Ua Huka i. Îs. Marquises 85 8.55S 139.32W
Ua Pu i. Îs. Marquises 85 9.25S 140.00W
Uatumã r. Brazil 123 2.30S 57.40W
Uaupés Brazil 122 0.07S 67.05W
Uaupés r. Brazil 122 0.00S 67.10W
Ubá Brazil 126 21.08S 42.59W
Ubangi r. Congo/Zaïre 78 0.25S 17.40E
Ubatuba Brazil 126 23.26S 45.05W
Ubauro Pakistan 62 28.10N 69.44E
Ubayyiḑ, Wādī al r. Iraq 64 32.04N 42.17E
Ube Japan 57 34.00N 131.16E
Ubeda Spain 26 38.01N 3.22W
Uberaba Brazil 126 19.47S 47.57W
Uberlândia Brazil 126 18.57S 48.17W
Überlingen Germany 39 47.46N 9.10E
Ubombo R.S.A. 81 27.35S 32.05E
Ubort r. Belarus 37 52.06N 28.28E
Ubrique Spain 27 36.41N 5.27W
Ubundu Zaïre 78 0.24S 25.28E
Ucayali r. Peru 122 4.40S 73.20W
Uch Pakistan 62 29.14N 71.03E
Uchiura wan b. Japan 57 42.20N 140.40E
Uckermark f. Germany 38 52.11N 13.50E
Udaipur India 62 24.35N 73.41E
Udalguri India 63 26.46N 92.08E
Udaquiola Argentina 125 36.35S 58.30W
Udaypur Nepal 63 26.54N 86.32E
Udbina Croatia 31 44.32N 15.46E
Uddeholm Sweden 43 60.01N 13.37E
Uddevalla Sweden 42 58.21N 11.55E
Uddjaur l. Sweden 40 65.55N 17.49E
Udhampur Jammu & Kashmir 62 32.56N 75.08E
Udine Italy 30 46.03N 13.14E
Udipi India 60 13.21N 74.45E
údolní nádrž Lipno l. Czech Republic 39 48.43N 14.04E
Udon Thani Thailand 56 17.25N 102.45E
Ueckermünde Germany 38 53.44N 14.03E
Uele r. Zaïre 73 4.09N 22.26E
Uelzen Germany 38 52.58N 10.33E
Ueno Japan 57 34.45N 136.08E
Uere r. Zaïre 73 3.42N 25.24E
Uetersen Germany 38 53.41N 9.39E
Ufa Russian Fed. 44 54.45N 55.58E
Ufa r. Russian Fed. 44 54.45N 56.00E
Uffculme U.K. 13 50.45N 3.19W
Uffenheim Germany 39 49.32N 10.14E
Ugab r. Namibia 80 21.12S 13.37E
Ugalla r. Tanzania 79 5.43S 31.10E
Uganda Africa 79 2.00N 33.00E
Ugep Nigeria 77 5.48N 8.05E

Ughelli Nigeria **77** 5.33N 6.00E
Ugijar Spain **27** 36.57N 3.03W
Ugine France **21** 45.45N 6.25E
Uglegorsk Russian Fed. **51** 49.01N 142.04E
Ugljan *i.* Croatia **31** 44.05N 15.10E
Uglovka Russian Fed. **51** 58.13N 33.30E
Ugoma *mtn.* Zaïre **79** 4.00S 28.45E
Ugra *r.* Russian Fed. **44** 54.30N 36.10E
Ugürchin Bulgaria **34** 43.06N 24.26E
Uherské Hradiště Czech Republic **37** 49.05N 17.28E
Uhrichsville U.S.A. **114** 40.24N 81.20W
Uig U.K. **14** 57.35N 6.22W
Uíge Angola **78** 7.40S 15.09E
Uíge *d.* Angola **78** 7.00S 15.30E
Uil Kazakhstan **45** 49.08N 54.43E
Uil *r.* Kazakhstan **45** 48.33N 52.25E
Uinta Mts. U.S.A. **108** 40.45N 110.05W
Uitenhage R.S.A. **80** 33.46S 25.23E
Uithuizen Neth. **16** 53.24N 6.41E
Uivileq *see* Nanortalik Greenland **99**
Ujhäni India **63** 28.01N 79.01E
Uji *r.* Japan **57** 34.53N 135.48E
Ujiji Tanzania **79** 4.55S 29.39E
Ujjain India **62** 23.11N 75.46E
Ujpest Hungary **37** 47.33N 19.05E
Ujście Poland **36** 53.04N 16.43E
Ujung Pandang Indonesia **58** 5.09S 119.28E
Uka Russian Fed. **51** 57.50N 162.02E
Ukerewe I. Tanzania **79** 2.00S 33.00E
Ukhta Russian Fed. **44** 63.33N 53.44E
Ukiah U.S.A. **108** 39.09N 123.13W
Ukmerge Lithuania **44** 55.14N 24.49E
Ukraine Europe **37** 49.45N 27.00E
Ukrina *r.* Bosnia-Herzegovina **31** 45.05N 17.56E
Uku Angola **78** 11.24S 14.15E
Ukwi Botswana **80** 23.22S 20.30E
Ulaanbaatar Mongolia **52** 47.54N 106.52E
Ulaangom Mongolia **52** 49.59N 92.00E
Ulamba Zaïre **78** 9.07S 23.40E
Ulan Bator *see* Ulaanbaatar Mongolia **52**
Ulansuhai Nur *l.* China **54** 40.56N 108.49E
Ulan-Ude Russian Fed. **52** 51.55N 107.40E
Ulan Ul Hu *l.* China **61** 34.45N 90.25E
Ulcinj Yugo. **31** 41.55N 19.11E
Ulefoss Norway **42** 59.17N 9.16E
Ulenia, L. Australia **92** 29.57S 142.24E
Ulfborg Denmark **42** 56.16N 8.20E
Ulhāsnagar India **62** 19.13N 73.07E
Uliastay Mongolia **52** 47.42N 96.52E
Ulindi *r.* Zaïre **78** 1.41S 25.55E
Ulla *r.* Spain **26** 42.40N 8.43W
Ulladulla Australia **93** 35.21S 150.25E
Ullånger Sweden **40** 62.58N 18.16E
Ullapool U.K. **14** 57.54N 5.10W
Ullswater *l.* U.K. **12** 54.34N 2.52W
Ulm Germany **39** 48.24N 10.00E
Ulongwé Mozambique **79** 14.34S 34.21E
Ulsan S. Korea **57** 35.34N 129.19E
Ulsberg Norway **40** 62.45N 9.59E
Ulster U.S.A. **115** 41.51N 76.30W
Ultima Australia **92** 35.30S 143.20E
Ulúa *r.* Honduras **117** 15.50N 87.38W
Uluguru Mts. Tanzania **79** 7.05S 37.40E
Uluru *mtn.* Australia **90** 25.20S 131.01E
Ulverston U.K. **12** 54.13N 3.07W
Ulverstone Australia **91** 41.09S 146.10E
Ulysses U.S.A. **111** 37.35N 101.22W
Ulzë Albania **34** 41.41N 19.54E
Umag Croatia **31** 45.25N 13.32E
Umaisha Nigeria **77** 8.01N 7.12E
Umala Bolivia **124** 17.21S 68.00W
Uman Ukraine **37** 48.45N 30.10E
Umaria India **63** 23.32N 80.50E
Umarkot Pakistan **62** 25.22N 69.44E
Umbertide Italy **30** 43.18N 12.20E
Umbria *d.* Italy **30** 43.05N 12.30E
Ume *r.* Sweden **40** 63.47N 20.16E
Ume *r.* Zimbabwe **80** 17.00S 28.22E
Umeå Sweden **40** 63.45N 20.20E
Umfors Sweden **40** 65.56N 15.00E
Umfuli *r.* Zimbabwe **80** 17.32S 29.23E
Umiat U.S.A. **98** 69.25N 152.20W
Umm-al-Qaywayn U.A.E. **65** 25.32N 55.34E
Umm Badr Sudan **72** 14.14N 27.57E
Umm Bel Sudan **73** 13.32N 28.04E
Umm Durmān Sudan **72** 15.37N 32.59E
Umm el Faḥm Israel **67** 32.31N 35.09E
Umm Kuwaykah Sudan **73** 12.49N 31.52E
Umm Lajj Saudi Arabia **64** 25.03N 37.17E
Umm Qays Jordan **67** 32.39N 35.41E
Umm Qurayn Sudan **73** 9.58N 25.83E
Umm Ruwābah Sudan **73** 12.54N 31.13E
Umm Shalil Sudan **73** 10.51N 23.42E
Umm Shanqah Sudan **73** 13.14N 27.14E
Umniati Zimbabwe **80** 18.41S 29.45E
Umrer India **63** 20.51N 79.20E
Umreth India **62** 22.42N 73.07E
Umtata R.S.A. **80** 31.35S 28.47E
Umuahia Nigeria **77** 5.31N 7.26E
Umzimkulu R.S.A. **80** 30.15S 29.56E
Umzimvubu R.S.A. **80** 31.37S 29.32E
Una *r.* Bosnia-Herzegovina **31** 45.16N 16.55E
Una India **62** 20.49N 71.02E
Unac *r.* Bosnia-Herzegovina **31** 44.30N 16.09E
Unadilla *r.* U.S.A. **115** 42.14S 44.33W
Unalakleet U.S.A. **98** 63.53N 160.47W
'Unayzah Jordan **66** 30.29N 35.48E
'Unayzah Saudi Arabia **65** 26.05N 43.57E
'Unayzah, Jabal *mtn.* Iraq **64** 32.15N 39.19E
Uncia Bolivia **124** 18.27S 66.37W
Uncompahgre Peak U.S.A. **108** 38.04N 107.28W
Uncompahgre Plateau *f.* U.S.A. **108** 38.30N 108.25W
Unden *l.* Sweden **43** 58.47N 14.26E
Underberg R.S.A. **80** 29.46S 29.26E
Underbool Australia **92** 35.10S 141.50E
Undu, C. Fiji **84** 16.08S 179.57W

Unecha Russian Fed. **37** 52.52N 32.42E
Ungarie Australia **93** 33.38S 147.00E
Ungava B. Canada **99** 59.00N 67.30W
Ungava, Péninsule d' *pen.* Canada **99** 60.00N 74.00W
União Brazil **123** 4.35S 42.52W
União da Vitória Brazil **126** 26.13S 51.05W
Unije *i.* Croatia **31** 44.38N 14.15E
Unimak I. U.S.A. **98** 54.50N 164.00W
Unini Peru **122** 10.41S 73.59W
Union Miss U.S.A. **111** 32.34N 89.14W
Union S.C. U.S.A. **113** 34.42N 81.37W
Union City Penn. U.S.A. **114** 41.54N 79.51W
Union City Tenn. U.S.A. **111** 36.26N 89.03W
Uniondale R.S.A. **80** 33.39S 23.07E
Union Gap U.S.A. **108** 46.34N 120.34W
Union Springs *town* U.S.A. **113** 32.08N 85.44W
Uniontown U.S.A. **114** 39.54N 79.44W
Unionville U.S.A. **110** 40.29N 93.01W
United Arab Emirates Asia **65** 24.00N 54.00E
United Kingdom Europe **11** 55.00N 2.00W
United States of America N. America **106** 39.00N 100.00W
Unity Canada **101** 52.27N 109.10W
Universales, Montes *mts.* Spain **25** 40.20N 1.30W
University Park Texas U.S.A. **109** 32.17N 106.45W
Unjha India **62** 23.48N 72.24E
Unna Germany **38** 51.32N 7.41E
Unnão India **63** 26.32N 80.30E
Unst *i.* U.K. **14** 60.45N 0.55W
Unstrut *r.* Germany **38** 51.10N 11.48E
Unterwalden *d.* Switz. **39** 46.55N 8.17E
Ünye Turkey **64** 41.09N 37.15E
Upata Venezuela **122** 8.02N 62.25W
Upemba, L. Zaïre **78** 8.35S 26.28E
Upemba Nat. Park Zaïre **78** 9.00S 26.30E
Upernavik Greenland **99** 72.50N 56.00W
Upington R.S.A. **80** 28.26S 21.12E
Upleta India **62** 21.44N 70.17E
Upolu *i.* W. Samoa **84** 13.55S 171.45W
Upolu Pt. Hawaiian Is. **85** 20.16N 155.51W
Upper Arrow L. Canada **100** 50.30N 117.50W
Upper East *d.* Ghana **76** 10.40N 0.20W
Upper Egypt *f.* Egypt *see* Aş Şa'īd *f.* Egypt **64**
Upper Hutt New Zealand **86** 41.07S 175.04E
Upper Klamath L. U.S.A. **108** 42.23N 122.55W
Upper Laberge Canada **100** 60.54N 135.12W
Upper Lough Erne U.K. **15** 54.13N 7.32W
Upper Pen. *f.* U.S.A. **104** 46.12N 84.32W
Upper Red L. U.S.A. **110** 48.05N 94.50W
Upper Tean U.K. **12** 52.57N 1.59W
Upper Volta *see* Burkina Africa **76**
Upper West *d.* Ghana **76** 10.25N 2.00W
Upper Yarra Resr. Australia **93** 37.43S 145.56E
Uppland *f.* Sweden **43** 59.59N 17.48E
Upplands-Väsby Sweden **43** 59.31N 17.54E
Uppsala Sweden **43** 59.52N 17.38E
Uppsala *d.* Sweden **41** 60.10N 17.50E
Upshi Jammu & Kashmir **63** 33.50N 77.49E
Upton Canada **105** 45.39N 72.41W
Upton U.S.A. **108** 44.06N 104.38W
Uqlat aş Şuqūr Saudi Arabia **64** 25.50N 42.12E
Ur *ruins* Iraq **65** 30.55N 46.07E
Uracoa Venezuela **122** 9.03N 62.27W
Uraga-suido *str.* Japan **57** 35.10N 139.42E
Urahoro Japan **57** 42.48N 143.39E
Urakawa Japan **57** 42.09N 142.47E
Ural *r.* Kazakhstan **45** 47.00N 52.00E
Uralla Australia **93** 30.40S 151.31E
Ural Mts. *see* Ural'skiye Gory *mts.* Russian Fed. **44**
Ural'sk Kazakhstan **45** 51.19N 51.20E
Ural'skiye Gory *mts.* Russian Fed. **44** 60.00N 59.00E
Urana Australia **93** 35.21S 146.19E
Urana, L. Australia **93** 35.21S 146.19E
Urandangi Australia **90** 21.36S 138.18E
Uranium City Canada **101** 59.28N 108.40W
Urapunga Australia **90** 14.41S 134.34E
Uraricoera *r.* Brazil **122** 3.10N 60.30W
Urawa Japan **57** 35.51N 139.39E
Uray Russian Fed. **50** 60.11N 65.00E
Urbana U.S.A. **114** 40.07N 88.12W
Urbania Italy **30** 43.40N 12.31E
Urbino Italy **30** 43.43N 12.38E
Urcos Peru **122** 13.40S 71.38W
Urda Kazakhstan **45** 48.44N 47.30E
Urdzhar Kazakhstan **50** 47.06N 81.33E
Ure *r.* U.K. **12** 54.05N 1.20W
Urechye Belarus **37** 52.59N 27.50E
Uren Russian Fed. **44** 57.30N 45.50E
Urengoy Russian Fed. **50** 65.59N 78.30E
Ures Mexico **116** 29.26N 110.24W
Ürgüp Turkey **64** 38.39N 34.55E
Uri *d.* Switz. **39** 46.45N 8.35E
Uribia Colombia **122** 11.43N 72.16W
Urim Israel **67** 31.18N 34.31E
Urisino Australia **92** 29.44S 143.49E
Urjala Finland **41** 61.05N 23.32E
Urk Neth. **16** 52.40N 5.36E
Urlingford Rep. of Ire. **15** 52.44N 7.35W
Urmia, L. *see* Daryācheh-ye Orūmīyeh *l.* Iran **65**
Uroševac Yugo. **34** 42.22N 21.09E
Ursus Poland **37** 52.12N 20.53E
Uruaçu Brazil **123** 14.30S 49.10W
Uruapan Mexico **116** 19.26N 102.04W
Urubamba Peru **122** 13.20S 72.07W
Urubamba *r.* Peru **122** 10.43S 73.55W
Urucará Brazil **123** 2.32S 57.45W
Uruçuí Brazil **123** 7.14S 44.33W
Uruguaiana Brazil **125** 29.45S 57.05W
Uruguay *r.* Argentina/Uruguay **125** 34.00S 58.30W
Uruguay S. America **126** 33.15S 56.00W
Ürümqi China **52** 43.43N 87.38E
Urun P.N.G. **90** 8.36S 147.15E
Urunga Australia **93** 30.30S 152.28E
Urup *r.* Russian Fed. **45** 44.59N 41.12E
Uryu ko *l.* Japan **57** 44.22N 142.15E
Urzhum Russian Fed. **44** 57.08N 50.00E
Urziceni Romania **29** 44.43N 26.38E
Usa *r.* Russian Fed. **44** 65.58N 56.35E

Uşak Turkey **64** 38.42N 29.25E
Usakos Namibia **80** 22.02S 15.35E
Usambara Mts. Tanzania **79** 4.45S 38.25E
Ušće Yugo. **34** 43.28N 20.37E
Usedom *i.* Germany **38** 54.00N 14.00E
Ushant *i.* *see* Ouessant, Île d' *i.* France **18**
Ush-Tobe Kazakhstan **52** 45.15N 77.59E
Ushuaia Argentina **125** 54.47S 68.20W
Ushumun Russian Fed. **51** 52.48N 126.27E
Usisya Malawi **79** 11.10S 34.12E
Usk *r.* U.K. **13** 51.34N 2.59W
Uskedal Norway **42** 59.56N 5.52E
Üsküdar Turkey **29** 41.00N 29.03E
Uslar Germany **38** 51.39N 9.38E
Usman Russian Fed. **45** 52.02N 39.43E
Usovo Ukraine **37** 51.20N 28.01E
Uspenskiy Kazakhstan **50** 48.41N 72.43E
Ussel France **20** 45.33N 2.18E
Ussuriysk Russian Fed. **53** 43.48N 131.59E
Ustaoset Norway **41** 60.30N 8.04E
Ustaritz France **20** 43.24N 1.27W
Ustica *i.* Italy **32** 38.42N 13.10E
Ust'-Ilga Russian Fed. **51** 54.59N 105.00E
Ústí nad Labem Czech Republic **38** 50.40N 14.02E
Ust Ishim Russian Fed. **50** 57.45N 71.05E
Ustka Poland **36** 54.35N 16.50E
Ust'kamchatsk Russian Fed. **51** 56.14N 162.28E
Ust-Kamenogorsk Kazakhstan **50** 50.00N 82.40E
Ust Kulom Russian Fed. **44** 61.34N 53.40E
Ust Kut Russian Fed. **51** 56.40N 105.50E
Ust Lyzha Russian Fed. **44** 65.45N 56.38E
Ust'Maya Russian Fed. **51** 60.25N 134.28E
Ust Nem Russian Fed. **44** 61.38N 54.50E
Ust Olenëk Russian Fed. **51** 72.59N 120.00E
Ust-Omchug Russian Fed. **51** 61.08N 149.38E
Ust Port Russian Fed. **50** 69.44N 84.23E
Ust Tapsuy Russian Fed. **44** 62.25N 61.42E
Ust'Tsilma Russian Fed. **44** 65.28N 53.09E
Ust-Tungir Russian Fed. **51** 55.25N 120.15E
Ust Ura Russian Fed. **44** 63.06N 44.41E
Ust Vaga Russian Fed. **44** 62.42N 42.45E
Ust Vym Russian Fed. **44** 62.15N 50.25E
Ustyurt, Plateau *f.* Kazakhstan **45** 43.30N 55.00E
Usu China **52** 44.27N 84.37E
Usumacinta *r.* Mexico **116** 18.22N 92.40W
U.S. Virgin Is. C. America **117** 18.30N 65.00W
Ut Belarus **37** 52.18N 31.10E
Utah *d.* U.S.A. **108** 39.37N 112.28W
Utah L. U.S.A. **108** 40.13N 111.49W
'Uta Vava'u Tonga **85** 18.35S 174.00W
Utembo *r.* Angola **78** 17.03S 22.00E
Utengule Tanzania **79** 8.55S 35.43E
Utersum Germany **38** 54.43N 8.24E
Utete Tanzania **79** 8.00S 38.49E
Uthal Pakistan **62** 25.48N 66.37E
Utiariti Brazil **122** 13.02S 58.17W
Utica Kans. U.S.A. **110** 38.39N 100.10W
Utica Mich. U.S.A. **114** 42.38N 83.02W
Utica N.Y. U.S.A. **115** 43.05N 75.14W
Utica Ohio U.S.A. **114** 40.14N 82.27W
Utiel Spain **25** 39.34N 1.12W
Utikuma L. Canada **100** 55.50N 115.30W
Utique Tunisia **32** 37.03N 10.03E
Utö *i.* Sweden **43** 58.56N 18.16E
Utopia Australia **90** 22.14S 134.33E
Utraula India **63** 27.19N 82.25E
Utrecht Neth. **16** 52.04N 5.07E
Utrecht *d.* Neth. **16** 52.04N 5.10E
Utrecht R.S.A. **80** 27.38S 30.20E
Utrera Spain **27** 37.11N 5.47W
Utsira Norway **42** 59.18N 4.54E
Utsjoki Finland **40** 69.53N 27.00E
Utsunomiya Japan **57** 36.40N 139.52E
Utta Russian Fed. **45** 46.24N 46.01E
Uttaradit Thailand **56** 17.38N 100.05E
Uttarkāshi India **63** 30.44N 78.27E
Uttar Pradesh *d.* India **63** 26.30N 81.30E
Utterson Canada **104** 45.13N 79.20W
Uturoà Is. de la Société **85** 16.44S 151.25W
Uummannarsuaq *see* Farvel, K. *c.* Greenland **99**
Uusikaupunki Finland **41** 60.48N 21.25E
Uusimaa *d.* Finland **41** 60.30N 25.00E
Uvalde U.S.A. **111** 29.13N 99.47W
Uvarovichi Belarus **37** 52.35N 30.44E
Uvat Russian Fed. **50** 59.10N 68.49E
Uvdal Norway **42** 60.16N 8.44E
Uvéa, Île *i.* N. Cal. **84** 20.30S 166.35E
Uvinza Tanzania **79** 5.08S 30.23E
Uvira Zaïre **79** 3.22S 29.06E
Uvs Nuur *l.* Mongolia **52** 50.30N 92.30E
Uwajima Japan **57** 33.13N 132.32E
Uwayl Sudan **73** 8.46N 27.24E
'Uwaynāt, Jabal al *mtn.* Libya/Sudan **72** 21.54N 24.58E
Uxbridge Canada **104** 44.06N 79.07W
Uxin Qi China **54** 38.30N 108.53E
Uyo Nigeria **77** 5.01N 7.56E
Uyuni Bolivia **124** 20.28S 66.50W
Uyuni, Salar de *f.* Bolivia **124** 20.20S 67.42W
Uzbekistan Asia **50** 42.00N 63.00E
Uzda Belarus **37** 53.28N 27.11E
Uzerche France **20** 45.26N 1.34E
Uzès France **21** 44.01N 4.25E
Uzh *r.* Ukraine **37** 51.15N 30.12E
Uzhgorod Ukraine **37** 48.38N 22.15E
Užice Yugo. **31** 43.51N 19.51E
Uzunköpru Turkey **34** 41.16N 26.41E

Vä Sweden **43** 55.59N 14.05E
Vaagö *i.* Faroe Is. **10** 62.03N 7.14W
Vaal *r.* R.S.A. **80** 29.04S 23.37E
Vaala Finland **40** 64.26N 26.48E
Vaal Dam R.S.A. **80** 26.51S 28.08E
Vaasa Finland **40** 63.06N 21.36E
Vaasa *d.* Finland **40** 62.50N 22.50E
Vác Hungary **37** 47.49N 19.10E
Vaccarès, Étang de *b.* France **21** 43.32N 4.34E
Vadodara India **60** 22.19N 73.14E
Vado Ligure Italy **30** 44.17N 8.27E
Vadsö Norway **40** 70.05N 29.46E
Vadstena Sweden **43** 58.27N 14.54E
Vaduz Liech. **39** 47.09N 9.31E
Vaerøy *i.* Norway **40** 67.40N 12.40E
Vaga *r.* Russian Fed. **44** 62.45N 42.48E
Vågåmo Norway **41** 61.53N 9.06E
Vaganski Vrh *mtn.* Croatia **31** 44.22N 15.31E
Vaggeryd Sweden **43** 57.30N 14.07E
Váh *r.* Slovakia **37** 47.40N 17.50E
Vahsel B. Antarctica **128** 77.00S 38.00W
Vaiea Niue **84** 19.08S 169.53W
Vaihu *l.* de Pascua **85** 27.10S 109.22W
Vaijāpur India **62** 19.55N 74.44E
Vailly-sur-Aisne France **19** 49.25N 3.31E
Vairao Tahiti **85** 17.48S 149.17W
Vaison-la-Romaine France **21** 44.14N 5.04E
Vaitupu *i.* Tuvalu **84** 7.28S 178.41E
Vakaga C.A.R. **73** 9.50N 22.30E
Vakarai Sri Lanka **61** 8.08N 81.26E
Váládalen Sweden **40** 63.09N 13.00E
Valais *d.* Switz. **39** 46.00N 7.20E
Valandovo Macedonia **34** 41.19N 22.34E
Valatie U.S.A. **115** 42.25N 73.41W
Valavsk Belarus **37** 51.21N 28.38E
Val Barrette Canada **105** 46.31N 75.22W
Välberg Sweden **43** 59.24N 13.12E
Valcartier Canada **105** 46.56N 71.27W
Valcheta Argentina **125** 40.40S 66.10W
Valdagno Italy **30** 45.39N 11.18E
Valdavia *r.* Spain **26** 42.24N 4.16W
Valday Russian Fed. **44** 57.59N 33.10E
Valdayskaya Vozvyshennost *mts.* Russian Fed. **44** 57.10N 33.00E
Valdecañas, Embalse de *resr.* Spain **27** 39.45N 5.30W
Valdemárpils Latvia **44** 57.23N 22.00E
Valdemarsvik Sweden **43** 58.12N 16.36E
Valdepeñas Spain **26** 38.46N 3.23W
Valderaduey *r.* Spain **26** 41.31N 5.42W
Valderas Spain **26** 42.05N 5.27W
Valderrobres Spain **25** 40.53N 0.09E
Val des Bois Canada **105** 45.54N 75.35W
Valdés, Pen. Argentina **125** 42.30S 64.00W
Valdez U.S.A. **98** 61.07N 146.17W
Val di Mazara *f.* Italy **32** 37.50N 13.00E
Val di Noto *f.* Italy **33** 36.54N 14.45E
Val d'Isère France **21** 45.27N 6.59E
Valdivia Chile **125** 39.46S 73.15W
Val d'Oise *d.* France **19** 49.10N 2.10E
Val d'Or *town* Canada **102** 48.07N 77.47W
Valdosta U.S.A. **113** 30.51N 83.51W
Valdoviño Spain **26** 43.36N 8.08W
Valença Bahia Brazil **123** 13.22S 39.06W
Valença R. de Janeiro Brazil **126** 22.14S 43.45W
Valença Portugal **26** 42.02N 8.38W
Valençay France **19** 47.09N 1.34E
Valence France **21** 44.56N 4.54E
Valencia Spain **25** 39.28N 0.22W
Valencia *d.* Spain **25** 39.20N 0.45W
Valencia Venezuela **122** 10.14N 67.59W
Valencia de Alcántara Spain **27** 39.25N 7.14W
Valencia de Don Juan Spain **26** 42.18N 5.31W
Valencia, Golfo de *g.* Spain **25** 39.30N 0.20W
Valenciennes France **19** 50.21N 3.32E
Valentín Russian Fed. **57** 43.09N 134.15E
Valentine U.S.A. **110** 42.52N 100.30W
Valentine N.Mex. U.S.A. **109** 30.34N 104.29W
Vale of Evesham *f.* U.K. **13** 52.05N 1.55W
Vale of Pewsey *f.* U.K. **13** 51.21N 1.45W
Vale of York *f.* U.K. **12** 54.12N 1.25W
Valera Venezuela **122** 9.21N 70.38W
Valga Estonia **44** 57.44N 26.00E
Valguarnera Caropepe Italy **33** 37.30N 14.24E
Valinco, Golfe de *g.* France **21** 41.40N 8.50E
Valjevo Yugo. **34** 44.16N 19.53E
Valkeakoski Finland **41** 61.16N 24.02E
Valkenswaard Neth. **16** 51.21N 5.27E
Valladolid Mexico **117** 20.41N 88.12W
Valladolid Spain **26** 41.39N 4.43W
Valladolid *d.* Spain **26** 41.45N 4.50W
Vall de Uxó Spain **25** 39.49N 0.14W
Valle Norway **42** 59.12N 7.33E
Valle d'Aosta *d.* Italy **30** 45.50N 7.25E
Valle de Cabuérniga Spain **26** 43.14N 4.18W
Valle de la Pascua Venezuela **122** 9.15N 66.00W
Valledupar Colombia **122** 10.31N 73.16W
Valle Edén Uruguay **125** 31.50S 56.09W
Vallegrande Bolivia **124** 18.29S 64.06W
Valle Hermoso Mexico **111** 25.39N 97.52W
Vallenar Chile **124** 28.35S 70.46W
Vallentuna Sweden **43** 59.32N 18.05E
Vallet France **18** 47.10N 1.16W
Valletta Malta **28** 35.53N 14.31E
Valley City U.S.A. **110** 46.57N 97.58W
Valley Falls *town* U.S.A. **108** 42.29N 120.16W
Valleyfield Canada **105** 45.15N 74.08W
Valley Head *town* U.S.A. **114** 38.33N 80.02W
Valley Stream *town* U.S.A. **115** 40.40N 73.42W
Valleyview Canada **100** 55.04N 117.17W
Vallgrund *i.* Finland **40** 63.12N 21.14E
Vallo della Lucania Italy **33** 40.14N 15.17E
Vallon France **21** 44.24N 4.24E

Vallorbe Switz. 19 46.43N 6.22E
Valls Spain 25 41.17N 1.15E
Val Marie Canada 101 49.14N 107.44W
Valmiera Latvia 44 57.32N 25.29E
Valnera mtn. Spain 26 43.09N 3.40W
Valognes France 18 49.31N 1.28W
Valongo Portugal 26 41.11N 8.30W
Valoria la Buena Spain 26 41.48N 4.32W
Valparaíso Chile 125 33.02S 71.38W
Valparaíso Mexico 116 22.46N 103.34W
Valparaiso U.S.A. 110 30.30N 86.31W
Valpovo Croatia 31 45.39N 18.25E
Valréas France 21 44.23N 4.59E
Vals, Tanjung c. Indonesia 59 8.30S 137.30E
Valverde Dom. Rep. 117 19.37N 71.04W
Valverde del Camino Spain 27 37.34N 6.45W
Vammala Finland 41 61.20N 22.54E
Vamsadhāra r. India 63 18.21N 84.08E
Van Turkey 64 38.28N 43.20E
Van Blommestein Meer, W.J. resr. Surinam 123 4.45N 55.05W
Van Buren Ark. U.S.A. 111 35.26N 94.21W
Van Buren Mo. U.S.A. 111 37.00N 91.01W
Vancouver Canada 100 49.20N 123.10W
Vancouver U.S.A. 108 45.39N 122.40W
Vancouver I. Canada 100 49.45N 126.00W
Vandalia Ill. U.S.A. 110 38.58N 89.06W
Vandalia Mo. U.S.A. 110 39.19N 91.29W
Vanderbilt U.S.A. 104 45.09N 84.40W
Vandergrift U.S.A. 114 40.36N 79.34W
Vanderlin I. Australia 90 15.44S 137.02E
Van Diemen, C. Australia 90 16.31S 139.41E
Van Diemen G. Australia 90 11.50S 132.00E
Vandry Canada 103 47.50N 73.34W
Vänern l. Sweden 43 58.55N 13.30E
Vang Norway 41 61.10N 8.40E
Vanga Kenya 79 4.37S 39.13E
Vangaindrano Madagascar 81 23.21S 47.36E
Van Gölü l. Turkey 64 38.35N 42.52E
Vanier Canada 105 45.26N 75.40W
Vanimo P.N.G. 59 2.40S 141.17E
Vankarem Russian Fed. 51 67.50N 175.51E
Vankleek Hill town Canada 105 45.31N 74.39W
Vanna i. Norway 40 70.10N 19.40E
Vännäs Sweden 40 63.58N 19.48E
Vannes France 18 47.39N 2.46W
Vanoise, Massif de la mts. France 21 45.20N 6.40E
Vanrhynsdorp R.S.A. 80 31.37S 18.42E
Vansbro Sweden 41 60.31N 14.13E
Vantaa Finland 41 60.13N 25.01E
Van Tassell U.S.A. 108 42.40N 104.02W
Vanthali India 62 21.29N 70.20E
Vanua Levu i. Fiji 84 16.33S 179.15E
Vanua Mbalavu i. Fiji 84 17.40S 178.57W
Vanuatu Pacific Oc. 84 16.00S 167.00E
Van Wert U.S.A. 112 40.53N 84.36W
Vanzylsrus R.S.A. 80 26.51S 22.03E
Vapnyarka Ukraine 37 48.31N 28.44E
Var d. France 21 43.30N 6.20E
Var r. France 21 43.39N 7.11E
Vara Sweden 43 58.16N 12.57E
Varades France 18 47.23N 1.02W
Varallo Italy 30 45.49N 8.15E
Varämīn Iran 65 35.20N 51.39E
Vārānasi India 63 25.20N 83.00E
Varangerfjorden est. Norway 40 70.00N 30.00E
Varangerhalvöya pen. Norway 40 70.25N 29.30E
Varano, Lago di l. Italy 33 41.53N 15.45E
Varaždin Croatia 31 46.19N 16.20E
Varazze Italy 30 44.22N 8.34E
Varberg Sweden 43 57.06N 12.15E
Vardak d. Afghan. 62 34.15N 68.30E
Vardar r. Macedonia see Axiós r. Greece 34
Varde Denmark 42 55.38N 8.29E
Vardhoúsia Óri mts. Greece 35 38.44N 22.07E
Varel Germany 38 53.24N 8.08E
Varennes Canada 105 45.41N 73.26W
Varennes France 20 46.19N 3.24E
Vareš Bosnia-Herzegovina 31 44.09N 18.19E
Varese Italy 30 45.48N 8.48E
Varese Ligure Italy 30 44.22N 9.37E
Vårgårda Sweden 43 58.02N 12.48E
Varginha Brazil 126 21.33S 45.25W
Vargön Sweden 43 58.22N 12.22E
Varkhän r. Afghan. 62 32.55N 65.30E
Varley Australia 89 32.48S 119.31E
Värmeln l. Sweden 43 59.32N 12.54E
Värmland d. Sweden 43 59.45N 13.15E
Värmland f. Sweden 43 60.05N 13.25E
Värmlandsnäs c. Sweden 43 59.00N 13.10E
Varna Bulgaria 37 43.13N 27.57E
Värnamo Sweden 43 57.11N 14.02E
Varnsdorf Germany 36 50.52N 14.40E
Värö Sweden 43 57.16N 12.11E
Várpalota Hungary 37 47.12N 18.09E
Vartofta Sweden 43 58.06N 13.40E
Varvarin Yugo. 34 43.43N 21.19E
Varzo Italy 30 46.12N 8.15E
Varzy France 19 47.22N 3.23E
Vasa see Vaasa Finland 40
Vasai India 62 19.21N 72.48E
Vascão r. Portugal 27 37.31N 7.31W
Vashka r. Russian Fed. 44 64.55N 45.50E
Vasilika Greece 34 40.28N 23.08E
Vasilkov Ukraine 37 50.12N 30.15E
Vaslui Romania 37 46.38N 27.44E
Väsman l. Sweden 43 60.11N 15.04E
Vassar U.S.A. 104 43.22N 83.35W
Västerås Sweden 43 59.37N 16.33E
Västerbotten d. Sweden 40 64.50N 18.10E
Västerdal r. Sweden 41 60.33N 15.08E
Västergötland Sweden 43 58.01N 13.03E
Västerhaninge Sweden 43 59.07N 18.06E
Västernorrland d. Sweden 40 63.20N 17.30E
Västervik Sweden 43 57.45N 16.38E
Västmanland d. Sweden 43 59.53N 16.20E
Västmanland f. Sweden 43 59.47N 15.45E

Vasto Italy 33 42.07N 14.42E
Vasvár Hungary 31 47.03N 16.49E
Vatan France 19 47.05N 1.48E
Váthia Greece 35 36.29N 22.29E
Vatican City Europe 32 41.54N 12.27E
Vaticano, Capo c. Italy 33 38.38N 15.50E
Vatnajökull mts. Iceland 40 64.20N 17.00W
Vatneyri Iceland 40 65.36N 23.59W
Vatomandry Madagascar 81 19.20S 48.59E
Vatra Dornei Romania 37 47.21N 25.21E
Vättern l. Sweden 43 58.24N 14.36E
Vaucluse d. France 21 44.00N 5.20E
Vaucouleurs France 19 48.36N 5.40E
Vaud d. Switz. 39 46.38N 6.30E
Vaughan Canada 104 43.50N 79.32W
Vaughn Mont. U.S.A. 108 47.35N 111.34W
Vaughn N.Mex. U.S.A. 109 34.36N 105.13W
Vaupés r. Colombia 122 0.20N 69.00W
Vauvert France 21 43.42N 4.17E
Vava'u Group is. Tonga 85 18.40S 174.00W
Vavuniya Sri Lanka 61 8.45N 80.30E
Växjö Sweden 43 56.52N 14.49E
Vaygach Russian Fed. 50 70.28N 58.59E
Vaygach, Ostrov i. Russian Fed. 44 70.00N 59.00E
Vecht r. Neth. 16 52.39N 6.01E
Vechta Germany 38 52.43N 8.16E
Vecsés Hungary 37 47.26N 19.19E
Veddige Sweden 43 57.16N 12.19E
Vedea r. Romania 34 44.00N 25.20E
Veendam Neth. 16 53.08N 6.52E
Veenendaal Neth. 16 52.03N 5.32E
Vega i. Norway 40 65.39N 11.50E
Vega U.S.A. 111 35.15N 102.26W
Vegarsvatn l. Norway 42 58.50N 8.50E
Veghel Neth. 16 51.37N 5.35E
Vegreville Canada 100 53.30N 112.05W
Veinticinco de Mayo Argentina 125 35.25S 60.11W
Vejen Denmark 42 55.29N 9.09E
Vejer Spain 27 36.15N 5.58W
Vejle Denmark 42 55.42N 9.32E
Vela Luka Croatia 31 42.58N 16.43E
Velddrif R.S.A. 80 32.47S 18.09E
Velebit Planina mts. Croatia 31 44.35N 15.00E
Velebitski Kanal str. Croatia 31 44.40N 14.55E
Velenje Slovenia 31 46.21N 15.06E
Velestínon Greece 35 39.23N 22.45E
Vélez-Málaga Spain 27 36.47N 4.06W
Vélez Rubio Spain 25 37.39N 2.04W
Velhas r. Brazil 126 17.20S 44.55W
Velika Gorica Croatia 31 45.43N 16.05E
Velika Kapela mts. Croatia 31 45.20N 15.00E
Velike Lašče Slovenia 31 45.50N 14.38E
Veliki Canal Yugo. 31 45.45N 19.07E
Veliki Preslav Bulgaria 34 43.10N 26.52E
Veliki Vitorog mtn. Bosnia-Herzegovina 31 44.07N 17.03E
Velikiye-Luki Russian Fed. 44 56.19N 30.31E
Velikiy Ustyug Russian Fed. 44 60.48N 45.15E
Veliko Tŭrnovo Bulgaria 34 43.05N 25.41E
Veli Lošinj Croatia 31 44.31N 14.30E
Velletri Italy 30 41.41N 12.47E
Vellinge Sweden 43 55.28N 13.01E
Vellore India 61 12.56N 79.09E
Velsen Neth. 16 52.28N 4.39E
Velsk Russian Fed. 44 61.05N 42.06E
Velten Germany 38 52.41N 13.10E
Veluwe f. Neth. 16 52.17N 5.45E
Velvendós Greece 34 40.15N 22.06E
Vemdalen Sweden 40 62.29N 13.55E
Ven i. Sweden 43 55.54N 12.41E
Venado Tuerto Argentina 125 33.45S 61.56W
Venafro Italy 33 41.29N 14.02E
Venaria Italy 30 45.08N 7.38E
Vence France 21 43.43N 7.07E
Venda Africa 80 22.40S 30.40E
Venda Nova Portugal 26 41.40N 7.58W
Vendas Novas Portugal 27 38.41N 8.28W
Vendée d. France 18 46.40N 1.20W
Vendée r. France 18 46.40N 1.10W
Vendée r. France 18 46.30N 0.45W
Vendeuvre-sur-Barse France 19 48.14N 4.28E
Vendôme France 18 47.48N 1.04E
Vendsyssel f. Denmark 42 57.20N 10.00E
Veneto d. Italy 30 45.50N 12.00E
Venev Russian Fed. 44 54.22N 38.15E
Venezia Italy 30 45.26N 12.20E
Venezuela S. America 122 7.00N 65.20W
Venezuela, Golfo de g. Venezuela 122 11.30N 71.00W
Venezuelan Basin f. Carib. Sea. 127 14.30N 68.00W
Vengurla India 61 15.55N 73.38E
Veniaminof Mtn. U.S.A. 98 56.05N 159.20W
Venice see Venezia Italy 30
Venice U.S.A. 113 27.05N 82.26W
Venice, G. of Med. Sea 30 45.20N 13.00E
Vénissieux France 21 45.41N 4.53E
Venlo Neth. 16 51.22N 6.10E
Vennesla Norway 42 58.17N 7.59E
Venosa Italy 33 40.57N 15.49E
Venraij Neth. 16 51.32N 5.58E
Vent Austria 30 46.52N 10.56E
Venta r. Latvia 42 57.24N 21.33E
Ventersdorp R.S.A. 80 26.19S 26.48E
Vent, Îles du is. Îs. de la Société 85 17.30S 149.30W
Ventimiglia Italy 30 43.47N 7.36E
Ventnor U.K. 13 50.35N 1.12W
Ventspils Latvia 41 57.24N 21.36E
Ventuari r. Venezuela 122 4.00N 67.35W
Venus B. Australia 93 38.40S 145.43E
Vera Argentina 126 29.31S 60.30W
Vera Spain 27 37.15N 1.51W
Veracruz Mexico 116 19.11N 96.10W
Veracruz d. Mexico 116 18.00N 95.00W
Veräval India 62 20.54N 70.22E
Verbania Italy 30 45.56N 8.33E

Vercel France 19 47.11N 6.23E
Vercelli Italy 30 45.19N 8.25E
Vercors d. France 21 44.57N 5.25E
Verde r. Argentina 125 42.10S 65.03W
Verde r. Brazil 124 19.11S 50.44W
Verden Germany 38 52.55N 9.13E
Verdhikoúsa Greece 34 39.47N 21.59E
Verdon r. France 21 43.43N 5.46E
Verdun Canada 105 45.27N 73.34W
Verdun Meuse France 19 49.10N 5.23E
Verdun T.G. France 20 43.52N 1.14E
Verdun-sur-le-Doubs France 19 46.54N 5.01E
Vereeniging R.S.A. 80 26.40S 27.55E
Vergara Spain 26 43.07N 2.25W
Vergelee R.S.A. 80 25.46S 24.09E
Vergennes U.S.A. 105 44.10N 73.15W
Vergoritis, Límni l. Greece 34 40.45N 21.49E
Vergt France 20 45.02N 0.43E
Verín Spain 26 41.56N 7.26W
Verkhniy Baskunchak Russian Fed. 45 48.14N 46.44E
Verkhniy Lyulyukary Russian Fed. 44 65.45N 64.28E
Verkhniy Shar Russian Fed. 44 68.21N 50.45E
Verkhniy Ufaley Russian Fed. 44 56.05N 60.14E
Verkhnyaya Taymyra r. Russian Fed. 51 74.10N 99.50E
Verkhnyaya Tura Russian Fed. 44 58.22N 59.50E
Verkhovye Russian Fed. 44 52.49N 37.14E
Verkhoyansk Russian Fed. 51 67.25N 133.25E
Verkhoyanskiy Khrebet mts. Russian Fed. 51 66.00N 130.00E
Vermenton France 19 47.40N 3.44E
Vermilion Canada 101 53.22N 110.51W
Vermilion r. Canada 104 46.16N 81.41W
Vermilion U.S.A. 114 41.25N 82.22W
Vermilion Bay town Canada 102 49.51N 93.24W
Vermilion Chutes Canada 100 58.22N 114.51W
Vermillion U.S.A. 110 42.48N 96.55W
Vermont d. U.S.A. 105 43.50N 72.45W
Vernal U.S.A. 108 40.27N 109.32W
Verner Canada 104 46.25N 80.07W
Verneuil France 18 48.44N 0.56E
Vernon Canada 100 50.20N 119.15W
Vernon France 18 49.05N 1.29E
Vernon U.S.A. 111 34.09N 99.17W
Verny France 19 49.01N 6.12E
Vero r. Spain 25 42.00N 0.10E
Vero Beach town U.S.A. 113 27.39N 80.24W
Véroia Greece 34 40.31N 22.12E
Verona Italy 30 45.27N 11.00E
Verónica Argentina 125 35.24S 57.22W
Verrès Italy 30 45.40N 7.42E
Versailles France 19 48.48N 2.08E
Versailles U.S.A. 113 38.02N 84.45W
Vert, Cap c. Senegal 76 14.45N 17.25W
Verteillac France 20 45.21N 0.22E
Vertou France 18 47.10N 1.29W
Vertus France 19 48.54N 4.00E
Vervey Switz. 39 46.28N 6.51E
Verviers Belgium 16 50.36N 5.52E
Vervins France 19 49.50N 3.54E
Vesanto Finland 40 62.56N 26.25E
Vescovato France 21 42.30N 9.26E
Veselí nad Lužnicí Czech Republic 36 49.11N 14.43E
Vesle r. France 19 49.23N 3.38E
Vesoul France 19 47.38N 6.10E
Vest-Agder d. Norway 42 58.45N 7.00E
Vestbygd Norway 42 58.06N 6.35E
Vesterö Havn Denmark 42 57.18N 10.56E
Vestfjorden est. Norway 40 68.10N 15.00E
Vestfold d. Norway 42 59.20N 10.10E
Vestmanhavn Faroe Is. 10 62.09N 7.11W
Vestmannaeyjar is. Iceland 40 63.30N 20.20W
Vestvågöy i. Norway 40 68.10N 13.50E
Vesuvio mtn. Italy 33 40.49N 14.26E
Vesyegonsk Russian Fed. 44 58.38N 37.19E
Veszprém Hungary 37 47.06N 17.55E
Vésztő Hungary 37 46.55N 21.16E
Vetka Belarus 37 52.35N 31.13E
Vetlanda Sweden 43 57.26N 15.04E
Vetluga Russian Fed. 44 57.50N 45.42E
Vetluga r. Russian Fed. 44 56.18N 46.19E
Vetovo Bulgaria 34 43.42N 26.16E
Vetralla Italy 30 42.19N 12.03E
Vetren Bulgaria 34 42.15N 24.03E
Vetschau Germany 38 51.47N 14.04E
Vettore, Monte mtn. Italy 30 42.49N 13.16E
Veurne Belgium 16 51.04N 2.40E
Vevelstad Norway 40 65.43N 12.30E
Vevey Switz. 39 46.28N 6.51E
Vévi Greece 34 40.47N 21.38E
Veynes France 21 44.32N 5.49E
Vézelise France 19 48.29N 6.05E
Vézère r. France 20 44.53N 0.53E
Vezhen mtn. Bulgaria 34 42.50N 24.20E
Viacha Bolivia 122 16.40S 68.17W
Viadana Italy 30 44.56N 10.31E
Viana Brazil 123 3.13S 45.00W
Viana Portugal 27 38.20N 8.00W
Viana del Bollo Spain 26 42.11N 7.06W
Viana do Castelo Portugal 26 41.42N 8.50W
Viana do Castelo d. Portugal 26 41.55N 8.30W
Viangchan see Vientiane Laos 56
Viar r. Spain 27 37.36N 5.50W
Viareggio Italy 30 43.52N 10.14E
Viaur r. France 20 44.08N 2.23E
Viborg Denmark 42 56.26N 9.24E
Vibo Valentia Italy 33 38.40N 16.06E
Vibraye France 18 48.03N 0.44E
Vic see Vich Spain 25
Vic-en-Bigorre France 20 43.06N 0.05E
Vicente López Argentina 125 34.32S 58.29W
Vicenza Italy 30 45.33N 11.33E
Vich Spain 25 41.56N 2.15E
Vichada r. Colombia 122 4.58N 67.35W
Vichuga Russian Fed. 44 57.12N 41.50E
Vichy France 20 46.08N 3.26E
Vicksburg U.S.A. 111 32.14N 90.56W
Vico France 21 42.10N 8.48E

Viçosa Alagoas Brazil 123 9.22S 36.10W
Viçosa Minas Gerais Brazil 126 20.45S 42.53W
Vic-sur-Cère France 20 44.59N 2.37E
Victor U.S.A. 114 42.59N 77.24W
Victor Harbor Australia 92 35.36S 138.35E
Victoria Argentina 125 32.40S 60.10W
Victoria d. Australia 93 37.20S 145.00E
Victoria r. Australia 88 15.12S 129.43E
Victoria Canada 100 48.30N 123.25W
Victoria Chile 125 38.13S 72.20W
Victoria Guinea 76 10.50N 14.32W
Victoria U.S.A. 111 28.48N 97.00W
Victoria Beach town Canada 101 50.43N 96.33W
Victoria de las Tunas Cuba 117 20.58N 76.59W
Victoria Falls f. Zimbabwe/Zambia 80 17.58S 25.45E
Victoria Harbour Canada 104 44.45N 79.46W
Victoria I. Canada 98 71.00N 110.00W
Victoria, L. Africa 79 1.00S 33.00E
Victoria, L. Australia 92 34.00S 141.15E
Victoria L. Australia 92 32.29S 143.22E
Victoria, Mt. Myanmar 56 21.12N 93.55E
Victoria, Mt. P.N.G. 90 8.55S 147.35E
Victoria Nile r. Uganda 79 2.14N 31.20E
Victoria River town Australia 88 15.36S 131.06E
Victoria River Downs town Australia 90 16.24S 131.00E
Victoriaville Canada 105 46.03N 71.57W
Victoria West R.S.A. 80 31.24S 23.07E
Victorica Argentina 125 36.15S 65.25W
Vidalia U.S.A. 113 32.14N 82.24W
Vidauban France 21 43.26N 6.26E
Videbaek Denmark 42 56.05N 8.38E
Videle Romania 37 44.16N 25.31E
Viderö i. Faroe Is. 10 62.21N 6.30W
Vidigueira Portugal 27 38.13N 7.48W
Vidin Bulgaria 34 43.59N 22.52E
Vidisha India 63 23.32N 77.49E
Vidöstern l. Sweden 43 57.04N 14.01E
Viechtach Germany 39 49.05N 12.53E
Viedma Argentina 125 40.50S 63.00W
Viedma, L. Argentina 125 49.40S 72.30W
Vieira do Minho Portugal 26 41.39N 8.09W
Viella Spain 25 42.42N 0.48E
Vienna see Wien Austria 36
Vienna Md. U.S.A. 115 38.29N 75.49W
Vienna S.Dak. U.S.A. 110 44.42N 97.30W
Vienna Va. U.S.A. 114 38.54N 77.16W
Vienne d. France 18 46.35N 0.30E
Vienne r. France 18 47.13N 0.05E
Vientiane Laos 56 17.59N 102.38E
Vieques i. Puerto Rico 117 18.08N 65.30W
Viernheim Germany 39 49.33N 8.39E
Viersen Germany 38 51.15N 6.23E
Vierwaldstätter See l. Switz. 39 47.00N 8.28E
Vierzon France 19 47.13N 2.05E
Vieste Italy 31 41.53N 16.10E
Vietnam Asia 56 15.00N 108.30E
Viet Tri Vietnam 55 21.20N 105.26E
Vieux-Condé France 16 50.29N 3.31E
Vif France 21 45.03N 5.40E
Vigan France 20 43.59N 3.35E
Vigan Phil. 59 17.35N 120.23E
Vigeland Norway 42 58.05N 7.18E
Vigevano Italy 30 45.19N 8.51E
Vignemale, Pic de mtn. France 20 42.46N 0.08W
Vigneulles-lès-Hattonchâtel France 19 48.59N 5.43E
Vigo Spain 26 42.14N 8.43W
Vigo, Ría de est. Spain 26 42.15N 8.45W
Vigrestad Norway 42 58.34N 5.42E
Vihāri Pakistan 62 30.02N 72.21E
Vihiers France 18 47.09N 0.32W
Vihowa Pakistan 62 31.08N 70.30E
Vijāpur India 62 23.35N 72.45E
Vijayawāda India 61 16.34N 80.40E
Vik Norway 40 65.19N 12.10E
Vikajärvi Finland 40 66.37N 26.12E
Vikeke Indonesia 59 8.42S 126.30E
Viken Sweden 43 56.09N 12.34E
Viken l. Sweden 43 58.39N 14.20E
Vikersund Norway 42 59.59N 10.02E
Vikmanshyttan Sweden 43 60.17N 15.49E
Vikna i. Norway 40 64.52N 10.57E
Vikulovo Russian Fed. 50 56.51N 70.30E
Vila Vanuatu 84 17.44S 168.19E
Vila da Maganja Mozambique 79 17.25S 37.32E
Vila de Rei Portugal 27 39.40N 8.09W
Vila do Bispo Portugal 27 37.05N 8.55W
Vila do Conde Portugal 26 41.21N 8.45W
Vila Flor Portugal 26 41.18N 7.09W
Vila Franca Portugal 27 38.57N 8.59W
Vilafranca del Penedès Spain 25 41.21N 1.42E
Vilaine r. France 18 47.30N 2.27W
Vilanculos Mozambique 81 21.59S 35.16E
Vila Nova de Famalicão Portugal 26 41.25N 8.32W
Vila Nova de Fozcoa Portugal 26 41.05N 7.12W
Vila Nova de Gaia Portugal 26 41.45N 8.34W
Vila Nova de Ourém Portugal 27 39.39N 8.35W
Vilanova i La Geltrú see Villanueva y Geltrú Spain 25
Vila Real Portugal 26 41.18N 7.45W
Vila Real d. Portugal 26 41.35N 7.35W
Vila Real de Santo António Portugal 27 37.12N 7.25W
Vilar Formoso Portugal 26 40.35N 6.53W
Vila Velha Brazil 126 20.20S 40.17W
Vila Velha de Ródão Portugal 27 39.38N 7.40W
Vila Verde Portugal 26 41.39N 8.26W
Vila Veríssimo Sarmento Angola 78 8.08S 20.38E
Vila Viçosa Portugal 27 38.47N 7.25W
Vildbjerg Denmark 42 56.12N 8.46E
Vileyka Belarus 37 54.30N 26.50E
Vilhelmina Sweden 40 64.37N 16.39E
Vilhena Brazil 122 12.40S 60.08W
Viliga Kushka Russian Fed. 51 61.35N 156.55E
Viljandi Estonia 44 58.22N 25.30E
Vilkaviškis Lithuania 37 54.39N 23.02E
Vil'kitskogo, Proliv str. Russian Fed. 51 77.57N 102.30E
Vilkovo Ukraine 37 45.28N 29.32E
Villa Adriana site Italy 30 41.56N 12.45E

Villa Angela Argentina 124 27.34S 60.45W
Villa Bella Bolivia 124 10.23S 65.24W
Villablino Spain 26 42.56N 6.19W
Villacañas Spain 27 39.38N 3.20W
Villacarriedo Spain 26 43.14N 3.48W
Villacarrillo Spain 26 38.07N 3.05W
Villacastín Spain 26 40.47N 4.25W
Villach Austria 31 46.36N 13.50E
Villa Clara Argentina 125 31.46S 58.50W
Villa Constitución Argentina 125 33.14S 60.21W
Villada Spain 26 42.15N 4.59W
Villa del Río Spain 27 37.59N 4.17W
Villa de Santiago Mexico 111 25.26N 100.09W
Villadiego Spain 26 42.31N 4.00W
Villa Dolores Argentina 124 31.58S 65.12W
Villafranca del Bierzo Spain 26 42.36N 6.48W
Villafranca de los Barros Spain 27 38.34N 6.20W
Villafranca di Verona Italy 30 45.21N 10.50E
Villagarcía Spain 26 42.36N 8.45W
Villaguay Argentina 125 31.55S 59.00W
Villahermosa Mexico 116 18.00N 92.53W
Villa Hernandarias Argentina 125 31.15S 59.58W
Villa Huidobro Argentina 125 34.50S 64.34W
Villaines-la-Juhel France 18 48.21N 0.17W
Villajoyosa Spain 25 38.30N 0.14W
Villalba Spain 26 43.18N 7.41W
Villalón de Campos Spain 26 42.06N 5.02W
Villalpando Spain 26 41.52N 5.24W
Villa María Argentina 124 32.25S 63.15W
Villamartín Spain 27 36.52N 5.38W
Villa Montes Bolivia 124 21.15S 63.30W
Villandraut France 20 44.28N 0.23W
Villa Nova Monteleone Italy 32 40.30N 8.28E
Villanueva y Geltrú Spain 25 41.14N 1.44E
Villanueva de Córdoba Spain 26 38.20N 4.37W
Villanueva de la Serena Spain 26 38.58N 5.48W
Villanueva de los Infantes Spain 27 38.45N 3.01W
Villanueva del Río y Minas Spain 27 37.39N 5.42W
Villaputzu Italy 32 39.28N 9.33E
Villarcayo Spain 26 42.56N 3.34W
Villard-de-Lans France 21 45.04N 5.33E
Villardefrades Spain 26 41.43N 5.15W
Villar del Arzobispo Spain 25 39.44N 0.49W
Villarobledo Spain 27 39.16N 2.36W
Villarreal Spain 25 39.56N 0.06W
Villarrica Chile 125 39.15S 72.15W
Villarrica Paraguay 126 25.45S 56.28W
Villarrobledo Spain 24 39.16N 2.36W
Villarrubia de los Ojos Spain 27 39.13N 3.36W
Villa San Giovanni Italy 33 38.13N 15.39E
Villa San José Argentina 125 32.12S 58.15W
Villasayas Spain 26 41.21N 2.37W
Villasimus Italy 32 39.09N 9.31E
Villasor Italy 32 39.22N 8.57E
Villavicencio Colombia 122 4.09N 73.38W
Villaviciosa Spain 26 43.29N 5.26W
Villaviciosa de Córdoba Spain 26 38.05N 5.01W
Villazón Bolivia 124 22.06S 65.36W
Villé France 19 48.20N 7.18E
Villedieu France 18 48.50N 1.13W
Villefort France 20 44.26N 3.56E
Villefranche France 21 45.59N 4.43E
Villefranche-de-Rouergue France 20 44.21N 2.02E
Ville Marie Canada 104 47.19N 79.26W
Villena Spain 25 38.38N 0.51W
Villenauxe-la-Grande France 19 48.35N 3.33E
Villeneuve France 20 44.25N 0.42E
Villeneuve-d'Ascq France 19 50.37N 3.10E
Villeneuve-d'Aveyron France 20 44.26N 2.02E
Villeneuve-de-Berg France 21 44.33N 4.30E
Villeneuve-St. Georges France 19 48.44N 2.27E
Villeneuve-sur-Yonne France 19 48.05N 3.18E
Villeroy Canada 105 46.23N 71.53W
Villers Bocage France 18 49.05N 0.39W
Villers-Cotterêts France 19 49.15N 3.05E
Villersexel France 19 47.33N 6.26E
Villers sur Mer France 18 49.21N 0.02W
Villeurbanne France 21 45.46N 4.53E
Villingen Germany 39 48.03N 8.27E
Vilnius Lithuania 37 54.40N 25.19E
Vils r. Germany 39 48.39N 13.11E
Vilsbiburg Germany 39 48.27N 12.12E
Vilshofen Germany 39 48.39N 13.12E
Vilvoorde Belgium 16 50.56N 4.25E
Vilyuy r. Russian Fed. 51 64.20N 126.55E
Vilyuysk Russian Fed. 51 63.46N 121.35E
Vimianzo Spain 26 43.07N 9.02W
Vimmerby Sweden 43 57.40N 15.51E
Vimoutiers France 18 48.55N 0.12E
Vimperk Czech Republic 38 49.03N 13.47E
Vina r. Chad 77 7.43N 15.30E
Viña del Mar Chile 125 33.02S 71.34W
Vinaroz Spain 25 40.28N 0.29E
Vincennes France 19 48.51N 2.26E
Vincennes U.S.A. 110 38.41N 87.32W
Vincent U.S.A. 114 39.23N 81.40W
Vindel r. Sweden 40 63.54N 19.52E
Vindeln Sweden 40 64.12N 19.44E
Vinderup Denmark 42 56.29N 8.47E
Vindhya Range mts. India 62 22.45N 75.30E
Vineland U.S.A. 115 39.29N 75.02W
Vineyard Haven U.S.A. 115 41.27N 70.36W
Vineyard Sd. U.S.A. 115 41.25N 70.46W
Vingåker Sweden 43 59.02N 15.52E
Vinh Vietnam 56 18.42N 105.41E
Vinhais Portugal 26 41.50N 7.00W
Vinh Long Vietnam 56 10.15N 105.59E
Vinica Slovenia 31 45.28N 15.15E
Vinita U.S.A. 111 36.39N 95.09W
Vinju Mare Romania 37 44.26N 22.52E
Vinkovci Croatia 31 45.17N 18.49E
Vinnitsa Ukraine 37 49.11N 28.30E
Vinson Massif Antarctica 128 78.00S 85.00W
Vintar Phil. 55 18.16N 120.40E
Vinton U.S.A. 110 42.10N 92.01W
Viooolsdrif R.S.A. 80 28.45S 17.33E
Vipava Slovenia 31 45.51N 13.58E
Vipiteno Italy 30 46.54N 11.26E

Vir i. Croatia 31 44.18N 15.04E
Virac Phil. 59 13.35N 124.15E
Viramgām India 62 23.07N 72.02E
Viranşehir Turkey 64 37.13N 39.45E
Virden Canada 101 49.51N 100.55W
Vire France 18 48.50N 0.53W
Vire r. France 18 49.20N 1.07W
Vírgenes, C. Argentina 125 52.00S 68.50W
Virgin Gorda i. B.V.Is. 117 18.30N 64.26W
Virginia U.S.A. 110 47.31N 92.32W
Virginia d. U.S.A. 113 37.30N 78.45W
Virginia Beach town U.S.A. 113 36.51N 75.59W
Virginia City Mont. U.S.A. 108 45.18N 111.56W
Virginia City Nev. U.S.A. 108 39.19N 119.39W
Virieu-le-Grand France 21 45.51N 5.39E
Virje Croatia 31 46.04N 16.59E
Virovitica Croatia 31 45.50N 17.23E
Virpazar Yugo. 31 42.15N 19.05E
Virrat Finland 40 62.14N 23.47E
Virserum Sweden 43 57.19N 15.35E
Virton Belgium 16 49.35N 5.32E
Virtsu Estonia 41 58.34N 23.31E
Virunga Nat. Park Zaïre 79 0.30S 29.15E
Vis Croatia 31 43.03N 16.12E
Vis i. Croatia 31 43.02N 16.11E
Visalia U.S.A. 109 36.20N 119.18W
Visayan Sea Phil. 59 11.35N 123.51E
Visby Sweden 43 57.38N 18.18E
Visconde do Rio Branco Brazil 126 21.00S 42.51W
Viscount Melville Sd. Canada 98 74.30N 104.00W
Visé Belgium 16 50.44N 5.42E
Višegrad Bosnia-Herzegovina 31 43.47N 19.17E
Viserum Sweden 43 57.21N 15.34E
Viseu Brazil 123 1.12S 46.07W
Viseu Portugal 26 40.39N 7.55W
Viseu d. Portugal 26 40.50N 7.55W
Viseu de Sus Romania 37 47.44N 24.22E
Vishākhapatnam India 61 17.42N 83.24E
Viskafors Sweden 43 57.38N 12.50E
Viskan r. Sweden 43 57.14N 12.12E
Visnagar India 62 23.42N 72.33E
Visoko Bosnia-Herzegovina 31 43.59N 18.11E
Viso, Monte mtn. Italy 30 44.40N 7.07E
Visp Switz. 39 46.18N 7.53E
Vissefjärda Sweden 43 56.32N 15.35E
Visselhövede Germany 38 52.59N 9.35E
Vista U.S.A. 109 33.12N 117.15W
Vistula r. see Wisła r. Poland 37
Vit r. Bulgaria 34 43.30N 24.30E
Vitanje Slovenia 31 46.23N 15.18E
Vitarte Peru 122 12.03S 76.51W
Vitebsk Belarus 45 55.10N 30.14E
Viterbo Italy 30 42.25N 12.06E
Vitigudino Spain 26 41.00N 6.26W
Viti Levu i. Fiji 84 18.00S 178.00E
Vitim Russian Fed. 51 59.28N 112.35E
Vitim r. Russian Fed. 51 59.30N 112.36E
Vitoria Spain 26 42.51N 2.40W
Vitória Espírito Santo Brazil 126 20.19S 40.21W
Vitré France 18 48.08N 1.12W
Vitry-le-François France 19 48.44N 4.35E
Vitteaux France 19 47.24N 4.32E
Vittel France 19 48.12N 5.57E
Vittoria Italy 33 36.57N 14.32E
Vittorio Veneto Italy 32 45.59N 12.18E
Vittsjö Sweden 43 56.20N 13.40E
Viveiro see Vivero Spain 26
Viver Spain 25 39.55N 0.36W
Vivero Spain 26 43.38N 7.35W
Viviers France 21 44.29N 4.41E
Vivonne France 18 46.26N 0.16E
Vivonne Bay town Australia 92 35.58S 137.10E
Vizcaíno, Desierto de des. Mexico 109 27.40N 114.40W
Vizcaíno, Sierra mts. Mexico 109 27.20N 114.30W
Vizcaya d. Spain 26 43.25N 2.45W
Vizianagaram India 61 18.07N 83.30E
Vizille France 21 45.05N 5.46E
Vižinada Croatia 31 45.20N 13.46E
Vizinga Russian Fed. 44 61.06N 50.05E
Vizzini Italy 33 37.09N 14.46E
Vjosë r. Albania 34 40.37N 19.20E
Vlaardingen Neth. 16 51.55N 4.20E
Vladičin Han Yugo. 34 42.42N 22.04E
Vladikavkaz Russian Fed. 45 43.02N 44.43E
Vladimir Russian Fed. 44 56.08N 40.25E
Vladimirets Ukraine 37 51.28N 26.03E
Vladimir Volynskiy Ukraine 37 50.51N 24.19E
Vladivostok Russian Fed. 53 43.09N 131.53E
Vlasenica Bosnia-Herzegovina 31 44.11N 18.56E
Vlieland i. Neth. 16 53.15N 5.00E
Vlissingen Neth. 16 51.27N 3.35E
Vlorë Albania 34 40.27N 19.30E
Vlorë d. Albania 34 40.29N 19.29E
Vltava r. Czech Republic 39 50.21N 14.30E
Vočin Croatia 31 45.37N 17.32E
Vöcklabruck Austria 39 48.01N 13.39E
Vodňany Czech Republic 39 49.09N 14.11E
Vodnjan Croatia 31 44.57N 13.51E
Voerde Germany 16 51.37N 6.39E
Vogelkop f. see Jazirah Doberai f. Indonesia 59
Vogelsberg mts. Germany 38 50.30N 9.15E
Voghera Italy 30 44.59N 9.01E
Voh N. Cal. 84 20.58S 164.42E
Vohibinany Madagascar 81 18.49S 49.04E
Vohimarina Madagascar 81 13.21S 50.02E
Vohipeno Madagascar 81 22.22S 47.51E
Voi Kenya 79 3.23S 38.35E
Void France 19 48.41N 5.37E
Voiron France 21 45.22N 5.35E
Voitsberg Austria 31 47.03N 15.10E
Vojens Denmark 42 55.15N 9.19E
Vojnić Croatia 31 45.19N 15.43E
Volary Czech Republic 38 48.55N 13.54E
Volborg U.S.A. 108 45.50N 105.40W
Volcano Is. Japan 84 25.00N 141.00E
Volda Norway 41 62.09N 6.06E
Volga r. Russian Fed. 45 45.45N 47.50E

Volgograd Russian Fed. 45 48.45N 44.30E
Volgogradskoye Vodokhranilishche resr. Russian Fed. 45 51.00N 46.05E
Volissós Greece 35 38.29N 25.58E
Volkach Germany 39 49.52N 10.13E
Volkhov Russian Fed. 44 59.54N 32.47E
Volkhov r. Russian Fed. 44 60.15N 32.15E
Völklingen Germany 39 49.15N 6.50E
Volkovysk Belarus 37 53.10N 24.28E
Vollenhove Neth. 16 52.41N 5.59E
Volnovakha Ukraine 45 47.36N 37.32E
Volochanka Russian Fed. 51 70.59N 94.18E
Volochisk Ukraine 37 49.34N 26.10E
Volodarsk Russian Fed. 44 56.14N 43.10E
Vologda Russian Fed. 44 59.10N 39.55E
Volokolamsk Russian Fed. 44 56.02N 35.56E
Volonne France 21 44.07N 6.01E
Vólos Greece 35 39.21N 22.56E
Volovets Ukraine 37 48.44N 23.14E
Volsk Russian Fed. 44 52.04N 47.22E
Volta d. Ghana 76 7.30N 0.25E
Volta r. Ghana 76 5.50N 0.41E
Volta, L. Ghana 76 7.00N 0.00
Volta-Noire d. Burkina 76 12.30N 3.25W
Volta Redonda Brazil 126 22.31S 44.05W
Volterra Italy 30 43.24N 10.51E
Voltri Italy 30 44.26N 8.45E
Volturno r. Italy 33 41.01N 13.55E
Volvi, Límni l. Greece 34 40.41N 23.23E
Volyně Czech Republic 38 49.10N 13.53E
Volzhskiy Russian Fed. 45 48.48N 44.45E
Vondrozo Madagascar 81 22.49S 47.20E
Vónitsa Greece 35 38.53N 20.58E
Voorburg Neth. 16 52.04N 4.22E
Vopnafjördhur est. Iceland 40 65.50N 14.30W
Vopnafjördhur town Iceland 40 65.46N 14.50W
Vorarlberg d. Austria 39 47.13N 9.55E
Vóras Óros mts. Greece 34 40.57N 21.45E
Vorderrhein r. Switz. 39 46.49N 9.25E
Vordingborg Denmark 42 55.01N 11.55E
Voríai Sporádhes is. Greece 35 39.17N 23.23E
Vórios-Evvoïkós Kólpos b. Greece 35 38.45N 23.15E
Vorkuta Russian Fed. 44 67.27N 64.00E
Vorma r. Norway 42 60.09N 11.27E
Vormsi i. Estonia 41 59.00N 23.20E
Voronezh Russian Fed. 45 51.40N 39.13E
Voronovo Belarus 37 54.09N 25.19E
Vosges d. France 19 48.10N 6.20E
Vosges mts. France 19 48.30N 7.10E
Voss Norway 41 60.39N 6.26E
Vostochno Sibirskoye More sea Russian Fed. 51 73.00N 160.00E
Vostochnyy Sayan mts. Russian Fed. 52 51.30N 102.00E
Vostok I. Kiribati 85 10.05S 152.23W
Votkinsk Russian Fed. 44 57.02N 53.59E
Votkinskoye Vodokhranilishche resr. Russian Fed. 44 57.00N 55.00E
Votuporanga Brazil 124 20.26S 49.53W
Vouga r. Portugal 26 40.41N 8.40W
Vouillé France 18 46.39N 0.10E
Voulou C.A.R. 73 8.33N 22.36E
Vouziers France 19 49.24N 4.42E
Voves France 19 48.16N 1.38E
Voxna Sweden 41 61.20N 15.30E
Voxna r. Sweden 41 61.17N 16.26E
Voyvozh Russian Fed. 44 64.19N 55.12E
Vozhega Russian Fed. 44 60.29N 40.11E
Voznesensk Ukraine 23 47.34N 31.21E
Vrå Denmark 42 57.21N 9.57E
Vrådal Norway 42 59.20N 8.25E
Vrakhnéika Greece 35 38.10N 21.40E
Vrangelya, Ostrov i. Russian Fed. 51 71.00N 180.00
Vranje Yugo. 34 42.34N 21.54E
Vratsa Bulgaria 34 43.13N 23.30E
Vrbas r. Bosnia-Herzegovina 31 45.06N 17.31E
Vrbas Yugo. 31 45.35N 19.39E
Vrbovec Croatia 31 45.53N 16.25E
Vrbovsko Croatia 31 45.23N 15.05E
Vrede R.S.A. 80 27.24S 29.09E
Vredendal R.S.A. 80 31.40S 18.28E
Vrena Sweden 43 58.52N 16.41E
Vresse Belgium 16 49.53N 4.57E
Vrgnmost Croatia 31 45.21N 15.52E
Vrhnika Slovenia 31 45.58N 14.18E
Vries Neth. 16 53.06N 6.35E
Vrigstad Sweden 43 57.21N 14.28E
Vrindâvan India 63 27.35N 77.42E
Vrlika Croatia 31 43.55N 16.24E
Vrnograč Bosnia-Herzegovina 31 45.10N 15.57E
Vrondádhes Greece 35 38.25N 26.08E
Vršac Yugo. 37 45.08N 21.18E
Vryburg R.S.A. 80 26.57S 24.42E
Vught Neth. 16 51.39N 5.18E
Vukovar Croatia 31 45.21N 19.00E
Vulcano, Isola i. Italy 33 38.27N 14.58E
Vülchedruma Bulgaria 34 43.42N 23.16E
Vung Tau Vietnam 56 10.21N 107.04E
Vurshets Bulgaria 34 43.12N 23.17E
Vyāra India 62 21.07N 73.24E
Vyatka Russian Fed. 44 58.38N 49.38E
Vyatka r. Russian Fed. 50 55.40N 51.40E
Vyatskiye Polyany Russian Fed. 44 56.14N 51.08E
Vyazma Russian Fed. 44 55.12N 34.17E
Vyazniki Russian Fed. 44 56.14N 42.08E
Vyborg Russian Fed. 44 60.45N 28.41E
Vychegda r. Russian Fed. 44 61.15N 46.28E
Vychodné Beskydy mts. Europe 37 49.30N 22.00E
Vygozero, Ozero l. Russian Fed. 44 63.30N 34.30E
Vyrnwy, L. U.K. 12 52.46N 3.30W
Vyshka Turkmenistan 65 39.19N 54.10E
Vyshniy-Volochek Russian Fed. 44 57.34N 34.23E
Vyšší Brod Czech Republic 39 48.37N 14.19E
Vytegra Russian Fed. 44 61.04N 36.27E

W

Wa Ghana 76 10.07N 2.28W
Waal r. Neth. 16 51.45N 4.40E
Waalwijk Neth. 16 51.42N 5.04E
Wabag P.N.G. 59 5.28S 143.40E
Wabasca r. Canada 100 58.22N 115.20W
Wabash U.S.A. 110 40.47N 85.48W
Wabash r. U.S.A. 110 37.46N 88.02W
Wabē Mena r. Ethiopia 73 6.20N 40.41E
Wabeno U.S.A. 110 45.27N 88.38W
Wabera Ethiopia 73 6.25N 40.45E
Wabē Shebelē r. Ethiopia see Shabeelle r. Somali Rep. 71
Wabrzeźno Poland 37 53.17N 18.57E
Wabush City Canada 103 52.53N 66.50W
Waco U.S.A. 111 31.55N 97.08W
Wacouno r. Canada 103 50.50N 65.58W
Wad Pakistan 62 27.21N 66.22E
Wad Bandah Sudan 73 13.06N 27.57E
Waddān Libya 75 29.10N 16.08E
Waddeneilanden is. Neth. 16 53.20N 5.00E
Waddenzee b. Neth. 16 53.15N 5.05E
Waddikee Australia 92 33.18S 136.12E
Waddington U.S.A. 105 44.52N 75.12W
Waddington, Mt. Canada 100 51.23N 125.15W
Wadena U.S.A. 110 46.26N 95.08W
Wädenswil Switz. 39 47.14N 8.40E
Wad Ḥāmid Sudan 72 16.30N 32.48E
Wadhurst U.K. 13 51.03N 0.21E
Wādī as Sir town Jordan 67 31.57N 35.49E
Wādī Ḥalfa' Sudan 64 21.56N 31.20E
Wādī Mūsā town Jordan 66 30.19N 35.29E
Wad Madanī Sudan 72 14.24N 33.32E
Wad Nimr Sudan 72 14.32N 32.08E
Wadsworth U.S.A. 114 41.02N 81.44W
Wafrah Kuwait 65 28.39N 47.56E
Wageningen Neth. 16 51.58N 5.39E
Wager B. Canada 99 65.26N 88.40W
Wager Bay town Canada 99 65.55N 90.40W
Wagga Wagga Australia 93 35.07S 147.24E
Wagin Australia 89 33.18S 117.21E
Wagon Mound town U.S.A. 109 36.01N 104.42W
Wagrien f. Germany 38 54.15N 10.45E
Wahai Indonesia 59 2.48S 129.30E
Wāhat Salīmah Sudan 72 21.22N 29.19E
Wahiawa Hawaiian Is. 85 21.30N 158.01W
Wahiba Sands des. Oman 60 21.56N 58.55E
Wahpeton U.S.A. 110 46.16N 96.36W
Waiau New Zealand 86 42.39S 173.03E
Waiblingen Germany 39 48.50N 9.19E
Waidhān India 63 24.04N 82.20E
Waidhofen Austria 36 47.58N 14.47E
Waigeo i. Indonesia 59 0.05S 130.30E
Waihi New Zealand 86 37.24S 175.50E
Waikato d. New Zealand 86 38.15S 175.10E
Waikato r. New Zealand 86 37.19S 174.50E
Waikerie Australia 92 34.11S 139.59E
Waikokopu New Zealand 86 39.05S 177.50E
Waikouaiti New Zealand 86 45.36S 170.41E
Wailuku Hawaiian Is. 85 20.53N 156.30W
Waimakariri r. New Zealand 86 43.23S 172.40E
Waimate New Zealand 86 44.45S 171.03E
Waimea Hawaiian Is. 85 20.01N 155.41W
Wainganga r. India 63 18.50N 79.55E
Waingapu Indonesia 59 9.30S 120.10E
Wainwright Canada 101 52.49N 110.52W
Wainwright U.S.A. 98 70.39N 160.00W
Waiouru New Zealand 86 39.29S 175.40E
Waipara New Zealand 86 43.03S 172.45E
Waipawa New Zealand 86 39.56S 176.35E
Waipiro New Zealand 86 38.02S 178.21E
Waipu New Zealand 86 35.59S 174.26E
Waipukurau New Zealand 86 40.00S 176.33E
Wairau r. New Zealand 86 41.32S 174.08E
Wairoa New Zealand 86 39.03S 177.25E
Waitaki r. New Zealand 86 44.56S 171.10E
Waitara New Zealand 86 38.59S 174.13E
Waiuku New Zealand 86 37.15S 174.44E
Wajima Japan 57 37.24N 136.54E
Wajir Kenya 79 1.46N 40.05E
Waka Ethiopia 73 7.07N 37.26E
Waka Zaïre 78 0.48S 20.10E
Wakasa wan b. Japan 57 35.50N 135.40E
Wakatipu, L. New Zealand 86 45.10S 168.30E
Wakayama Japan 57 34.13N 135.11E
Wakefield Canada 105 45.38N 75.56W
Wakefield U.K. 12 53.41N 1.31W
Wakefield U.S.A. 115 41.26N 71.30W
Wake I. Pacific Oc. 84 19.17N 166.36E
Wakema Myanmar 56 16.36N 95.11E
Wakkanai Japan 57 45.26N 141.43E
Wakonassin r. Canada 104 46.28N 81.51W
Wakre Indonesia 59 0.30S 131.05E
Wakuach, L. Canada 103 55.40N 67.40W
Walamba Zambia 79 13.27S 28.44E
Wałbrzych Poland 36 50.48N 16.19E
Walcha Australia 93 31.00S 151.36E
Walcheren f. Neth. 16 51.32N 3.35E
Wałcz Poland 36 53.17N 16.28E
Waldbröl Germany 16 50.52N 7.34E
Waldeck Germany 38 51.12N 9.04E
Walden U.S.A. 108 40.34N 106.11W
Waldkirch Germany 39 48.05N 7.57E
Waldorf U.S.A. 114 38.37N 76.54W
Waldport U.S.A. 108 44.26N 124.04W
Waldron U.S.A. 111 34.54N 94.05W
Waldshut Germany 39 47.37N 8.13E
Wales d. U.K. 13 52.30N 3.45W
Wales U.S.A. 110 47.13N 91.41W
Walgett Australia 93 30.03S 148.10E
Walhonding r. U.S.A. 114 40.18N 81.53W
Walikale Zaïre 79 1.29S 28.05E

Walker U.S.A. 110 47.06N 94.35W
Walker L. U.S.A. 108 38.44N 118.43W
Walkerton Canada 104 44.07N 81.09W
Wall U.S.A. 108 43.59N 102.14W
Wallace Canada 104 45.23N 78.05W
Wallace Idaho U.S.A. 108 47.28N 115.55W
Wallace Nebr. U.S.A. 110 40.50N 101.10W
Wallaceburg Canada 104 42.36N 82.23W
Wallachia f. Romania 37 44.35N 25.00E
Wallambin, L. Australia 89 30.58S 117.30E
Wallangarra Australia 93 28.51S 151.52E
Wallaroo Australia 92 33.57S 137.36E
Walla Walla Australia 93 35.48S 146.52E
Walla Walla U.S.A. 108 46.08N 118.20W
Wallenpaupack, L. U.S.A. 115 41.25N 75.12W
Wallingford U.S.A. 115 41.27N 72.50W
Wallis, Îles is. Pacific Oc. 84 13.16S 176.15W
Wallkill r. U.S.A. 115 41.51N 74.03W
Wallowa U.S.A. 108 45.34N 117.32W
Wallowa Mts. U.S.A. 108 45.10N 117.30W
Wallsend Australia 93 32.55S 151.40E
Walpole Australia 89 34.57S 116.44E
Walsall U.K. 13 52.36N 1.59W
Walsenburg U.S.A. 108 37.37N 104.47W
Walsrode Germany 38 52.52N 9.35E
Walterboro U.S.A. 113 32.54N 80.21W
Waltershausen Germany 38 50.53N 10.33E
Waltham Canada 105 45.55N 76.57W
Walton N.Y. U.S.A. 115 42.10N 75.08W
Walton W.Va. U.S.A. 114 38.40N 81.26W
Walton on the Naze U.K. 13 51.52N 1.17E
Walton on the Wolds U.K. 12 52.49N 0.49W
Walvis Bay Namibia 80 22.56S 14.35E
Walvis Ridge f. Atlantic Oc. 127 28.00S 4.00E
Wamanfo Ghana 76 7.16N 2.44W
Wamba Kenya 79 0.58N 37.19E
Wamba Nigeria 77 8.57N 8.42E
Wamba Zaïre 79 2.10N 27.59E
Wamba r. Zaïre 78 4.35S 17.15E
Wami r. Tanzania 79 6.10S 38.50E
Wampsville U.S.A. 115 43.05N 75.42W
Wamsasi Indonesia 59 3.30S 126.07E
Wan Indonesia 90 8.23S 137.55E
Wāna Pakistan 62 32.17N 69.35E
Wanaaring Australia 92 29.42S 144.14E
Wanaka New Zealand 86 44.42S 169.08E
Wanaka, L. New Zealand 86 44.30S 169.10E
Wan'an China 55 26.27N 114.46E
Wanapiri Indonesia 59 4.30S 135.50E
Wanapitei r. Canada 104 46.02N 80.51W
Wanapitei L. Canada 104 46.45N 80.45W
Wanbi Australia 92 34.46S 140.19E
Wandana Australia 92 32.04S 133.45E
Wandoan Australia 90 26.09S 149.51E
Wanganella Australia 93 35.13S 144.53E
Wanganui New Zealand 86 39.56S 175.00E
Wangaratta Australia 93 36.22S 146.20E
Wangary Australia 92 34.30S 135.26E
Wangdu China 54 38.43N 115.09E
Wangdu Phodrang Bhutan 63 27.29N 89.54E
Wangen Germany 39 47.42N 9.50E
Wangerooge i. Germany 38 53.46N 7.55E
Wanghai Shan mtn. China 54 41.40N 121.43E
Wangianna Australia 92 29.42S 137.32E
Wangjiang China 55 30.07N 116.41E
Wangpan Yang b. China 55 30.30N 121.30E
Wangqing China 57 43.20N 129.48E
Wangyuanqiao China 54 38.24N 106.16E
Wani India 63 20.04N 78.57E
Wänkäner India 62 22.37N 70.56E
Wanle Weyne Somali Rep. 71 2.38N 44.55E
Wannian China 55 28.42N 117.03E
Wanning China 55 18.48N 110.22E
Wānow Afghan. 62 32.38N 65.54E
Wantage U.K. 13 51.35N 1.25W
Wanup Canada 104 46.24N 80.49W
Wanxian China 55 30.52N 108.20E
Wanyang Shan mts. China 55 26.01N 113.48E
Wanyuan China 54 32.04N 108.02E
Wanzai China 55 28.06N 114.27E
Wanzleben Germany 38 52.03N 11.26E
Wāpi India 62 20.22N 72.54E
Wapiti r. Canada 100 55.05N 118.18W
Wappingers Falls U.S.A. 115 41.36N 73.55W
Waqqâs Jordan 67 32.33N 35.36E
Wārah Pakistan 62 27.27N 67.48E
Warangal India 61 18.00N 79.35E
Waranga Resr. Australia 93 36.32S 145.04E
Wārāseoni India 63 21.45N 80.02E
Waratah B. Australia 91 38.55S 146.04E
Warburg Germany 38 51.29N 9.08E
Warburton r. Australia 91 27.55S 137.15E
Warburton Range mts. S.A. Australia 92 30.30S 134.32E
Warburton Range mts. W.A. Australia 88 26.09S 126.38E
Ward Rep. of Ire. 15 53.26N 6.20W
Warden R.S.A. 80 27.49S 28.57E
Wardenburg Germany 38 53.04N 8.11E
Wardha India 63 20.45N 78.37E
Wardha r. India 63 19.38N 79.48E
Ward Hill U.K. 10 58.54N 3.20W
Wardlow Canada 101 50.54N 111.33W
Ware U.S.A. 115 42.16N 72.15W
Wareham U.S.A. 115 41.46N 70.43W
Waren Germany 38 53.31N 12.40E
Warendorf Germany 38 51.57N 7.59E
Warfordsburg U.S.A. 114 39.44N 78.15W
Warialda Australia 93 29.33S 150.36E
Wark Forest hills U.K. 12 55.06N 2.24W
Warkopi Indonesia 59 1.12S 134.09E
Warkworth New Zealand 86 36.24S 174.40E
Warley U.K. 13 52.29N 2.02W
Warmbad Namibia 80 28.26S 18.41E
Warminster U.K. 13 51.12N 2.11W
Warm Springs town U.S.A. 108 39.39N 114.49W
Warnemünde Germany 38 54.10N 12.04E

Warner U.S.A. 115 43.17N 71.49W
Warner Robins U.S.A. 113 32.35N 83.37W
Warnow r. Germany 38 54.06N 12.09E
Waroona Australia 89 32.51S 115.50E
Warracknabeal Australia 92 36.15S 142.28E
Warragul Australia 93 38.11S 145.55E
Warrakalanna, L. Australia 92 28.13S 139.23E
Warrambool r. Australia 93 30.04S 147.38E
Warrego r. Australia 93 30.25S 145.18E
Warrego Range mts. Australia 90 24.55S 146.20E
Warren Australia 93 31.44S 147.53E
Warren Ont. Canada 104 46.27N 80.20W
Warren Ark. U.S.A. 111 33.37N 92.04W
Warren Mich. U.S.A. 114 42.28N 83.01W
Warren Minn. U.S.A. 110 48.12N 96.46W
Warren N.H. U.S.A. 105 43.56N 71.54W
Warren Ohio U.S.A. 114 41.14N 80.52W
Warren Penn. U.S.A. 114 41.51N 79.08W
Warren R.I. U.S.A. 115 41.43N 71.17W
Warren Vt. U.S.A. 105 44.06N 72.52W
Warrenpoint U.K. 15 54.06N 6.15W
Warrensburg Mo. U.S.A. 110 38.46N 93.44W
Warrensburg N.Y. U.S.A. 115 43.30N 73.46W
Warrenton R.S.A. 80 28.07S 24.49E
Warrenton U.S.A. 114 38.43N 77.48W
Warri Nigeria 77 5.36N 5.46E
Warrina Australia 92 28.10S 135.49E
Warriner Creek r. Australia 92 29.15S 137.03E
Warrington U.K. 12 53.25N 2.38W
Warrington U.S.A. 111 30.23N 87.16W
Warrnambool Australia 92 38.23S 142.03E
Warroad U.S.A. 110 48.54N 95.19W
Warrumbungle Range mts. Australia 93 31.20S 149.00E
Warsaw see Warszawa Poland 37
Warsaw Ind. U.S.A. 112 41.13N 85.52W
Warsaw N.Y. U.S.A. 114 42.44N 78.08W
Warsaw Ohio U.S.A. 114 40.20N 82.00W
Warshiikh Somali Rep. 71 2.19N 45.50E
Warszawa Poland 37 52.15N 21.00E
Warta r. Poland 36 52.45N 15.09E
Warud India 63 21.28N 78.16E
Warwick Australia 93 28.12S 152.00E
Warwick Canada 105 45.56N 71.59W
Warwick U.K. 13 52.17N 1.36W
Warwick N.Y. U.S.A. 115 41.16N 74.22W
Warwick R.I. U.S.A. 115 41.43N 71.28W
Warwickshire d. U.K. 13 52.13N 1.30W
Wasaga Beach Canada 104 44.31N 80.01W
Wasatch Plateau f. U.S.A. 108 39.20N 111.30W
Wasco Calif. U.S.A. 109 35.36N 119.20W
Wasco Oreg. U.S.A. 108 45.35N 120.42W
Washago Canada 104 44.45N 79.20W
Washburn N.Dak. U.S.A. 110 47.17N 101.02W
Washburn Wisc. U.S.A. 110 46.41N 90.52W
Washburn L. Canada 98 70.03N 106.50W
Wāshim India 62 20.06N 77.09E
Washington U.K. 12 54.55N 1.30W
Washington d. U.S.A. 108 47.43N 120.00W
Washington D.C. U.S.A. 114 38.55N 77.00W
Washington Ga. U.S.A. 113 33.43N 82.46W
Washington Ind. U.S.A. 112 38.40N 87.10W
Washington Iowa U.S.A. 110 41.18N 91.42W
Washington N.C. U.S.A. 113 35.33N 77.04W
Washington Penn. U.S.A. 114 40.10N 80.15W
Washington Utah U.S.A. 108 37.08N 113.30W
Washington Va. U.S.A. 114 38.43N 78.10W
Washington Crossing U.S.A. 115 40.18N 74.52W
Wāshuk Pakistan 62 27.44N 64.48E
Wasian Indonesia 59 1.51S 133.21E
Wasior Indonesia 59 2.38S 134.27E
Wasiri Indonesia 59 7.30S 126.30E
Waskaganish Canada 102 51.29N 78.45W
Waskesiu L. Canada 101 53.56N 106.10W
Waskigomog L. Canada 104 46.00N 78.59W
Wassen Switz. 39 46.42N 8.36E
Wassenaar Neth. 16 52.10N 4.26E
Wasseralfingen Germany 39 48.52N 10.06E
Wasserburg Germany 39 48.04N 12.13E
Wasserkuppe mtn. Germany 38 50.30N 9.56E
Wassy France 19 48.30N 4.57E
Waswanipi Lac l. Canada 102 49.35N 76.40W
Watampone Indonesia 59 4.33S 120.20E
Watchet U.K. 13 51.10N 3.20W
Waterbury U.S.A. 115 41.33N 73.02W
Waterbury L. Canada 101 58.16N 105.00W
Waterford Canada 104 42.56N 80.17W
Waterford U.S.A. 114 41.57N 79.59W
Waterford Rep. of Ire. 15 52.16N 7.08W
Waterford d. Rep. of Ire. 15 52.10N 7.40W
Waterford Harbour est. Rep. of Ire. 15 52.12N 6.56W
Waterloo Belgium 16 50.44N 4.24E
Waterloo Ont. Canada 104 43.28N 80.31W
Waterloo Que. Canada 105 45.21N 72.31W
Waterloo Iowa U.S.A. 110 42.30N 92.20W
Waterloo N.Y. U.S.A. 114 42.54N 76.52W
Waterton Glacier International Peace Park U.S.A./Canada 108 48.47N 113.45W
Watertown N.Y. U.S.A. 105 43.59N 75.55W
Watertown S.Dak. U.S.A. 110 44.54N 97.07W
Watervale Australia 92 33.58S 138.39E
Water Valley town U.S.A. 111 34.09N 89.38W
Waterville Canada 105 45.16N 71.54W
Waterville Rep. of Ire. 15 51.50N 10.11W
Waterville Maine U.S.A. 112 44.33N 69.38W
Waterville N.Y. U.S.A. 115 42.56N 75.23W
Waterville Wash. U.S.A. 108 47.39N 120.04W
Watervliet U.S.A. 115 42.44N 73.42W
Watford Canada 104 42.57N 81.53W
Watford U.K. 13 51.40N 0.25W
Watford City U.S.A. 110 47.48N 103.17W
Wa'th Sudan 73 7.24N 28.58E
Wathaman L. Canada 101 56.55N 103.43W
Watkins Glen U.S.A. 114 42.23N 76.52W
Watonga U.S.A. 111 35.51N 98.25W
Watrous Canada 101 51.40N 105.28W
Watsa Zaïre 79 3.03N 29.29E
Watson Canada 101 52.07N 104.31W

Watson Lake town Canada 100 60.06N 128.49W
Watsontown U.S.A. 114 41.05N 76.52W
Watsonville U.S.A. 108 36.55N 121.45W
Wattiwarriganna Creek r. Australia 92 28.57S 136.10E
Wattwil Switz. 39 47.18N 9.06E
Watzmann mtn. Germany 39 47.33N 12.55E
Wau P.N.G. 59 7.22S 146.40E
Wauchope N.S.W. Australia 93 31.27S 152.43E
Wauchope N.T. Australia 90 20.39S 134.13E
Waukaringa Australia 92 32.18S 139.27E
Waukegan U.S.A. 110 42.22N 87.50W
Waukesha U.S.A. 110 43.01N 88.14W
Waukon U.S.A. 110 43.16N 91.29W
Wauneta U.S.A. 110 40.25N 101.23W
Waurika U.S.A. 111 34.10N 98.00W
Wausau U.S.A. 110 44.58N 89.40W
Wautoma U.S.A. 110 44.05N 89.17W
Wauwatosa U.S.A. 110 43.04N 88.02W
Wave Hill town Australia 88 17.29S 130.57E
Waveney r. U.K. 13 52.29N 1.46E
Waverly Ill. U.S.A. 110 39.36N 89.57W
Waverly Iowa U.S.A. 110 42.44N 92.29W
Waverly N.Y. U.S.A. 114 42.00N 76.32W
Wavre Belgium 16 50.43N 4.37E
Wâw Sudan 73 7.42N 28.00E
Wāw al Kabīr Libya 75 25.20N 16.43E
Waxahachie U.S.A. 111 32.24N 96.51W
Waxweiler Germany 39 50.05N 6.22E
Waycross U.S.A. 113 31.12N 82.22W
Way, L. Australia 88 26.47S 120.21E
Wayland U.S.A. 114 42.34N 77.35W
Wayne N.J. U.S.A. 115 40.03N 75.23W
Wayne W.Va. U.S.A. 114 38.13N 82.27W
Waynesboro Ga. U.S.A. 113 33.04N 82.01W
Waynesboro Penn. U.S.A. 114 39.45N 77.35W
Waynesboro Va. U.S.A. 113 38.04N 78.53W
Waynesburg Ohio U.S.A. 114 40.40N 81.16W
Waynesburg Penn. U.S.A. 114 39.54N 80.11W
Waynesville U.S.A. 113 35.30N 82.58W
Waynoka U.S.A. 111 36.35N 98.53W
Wazay Afghan. 63 33.04N 69.26E
Waziers France 17 50.23N 3.07E
Wazīrābād Pakistan 62 32.27N 74.07E
Wear r. U.K. 12 54.55N 1.21W
Weatherford Okla. U.S.A. 111 35.32N 98.42W
Weatherford Tex. U.S.A. 111 32.46N 97.48W
Webbwood Canada 104 46.16N 81.53W
Webster Mass. U.S.A. 115 42.03N 71.53W
Webster N.Y. U.S.A. 114 43.13N 77.26W
Webster Wisc. U.S.A. 110 45.53N 92.22W
Webster City U.S.A. 110 42.28N 93.49W
Webster Groves U.S.A. 110 38.35N 90.21W
Webster Springs town U.S.A. 114 38.29N 80.25W
Weda Indonesia 59 0.30N 127.52E
Weddell Sea Antarctica 128 70.00S 40.00W
Wedderburn Australia 92 36.26S 143.39E
Wedgeport Canada 103 43.44N 65.59W
Wedmore U.K. 13 51.14N 2.50W
Wedza Zimbabwe 81 18.37S 31.33E
Weedon Canada 105 45.42N 71.28W
Weedsport U.S.A. 115 43.03N 76.34W
Weeho r. Canada 100 63.20N 115.10W
Weelde Belgium 16 51.25N 5.00E
Weemelah Australia 93 29.02S 149.15E
Weert Neth. 16 51.14N 5.40E
Wee Waa Australia 93 30.34S 149.27E
Wegorzyno Poland 36 53.32N 15.33E
Wegrów Poland 37 52.25N 22.01E
Wegscheid Germany 39 48.36N 13.48E
Weichang China 54 41.56N 117.34E
Weida Germany 38 50.45N 12.04E
Weiden in der Oberpfalz Germany 39 49.41N 12.10E
Weifang China 54 36.40N 119.10E
Weihai China 54 37.28N 122.05E
Wei He r. Shaanxi China 54 34.27N 109.30E
Wei He r. Shandong China 54 36.47N 115.42E
Weilburg Germany 38 50.29N 8.15E
Weilheim Germany 39 47.50N 11.08E
Weilmoringle Australia 93 29.16S 146.55E
Weimar Germany 38 50.59N 11.19E
Weinan China 54 34.25N 109.30E
Weinheim Germany 39 49.32N 8.39E
Weipa Australia 90 12.41S 141.52E
Weir r. Australia 93 29.10S 149.06E
Weirton U.S.A. 114 40.25N 80.35W
Weiser U.S.A. 108 44.37N 116.58W
Weishan Hu l. China 54 34.40N 117.25E
Weishi China 54 34.24N 114.14E
Weisse Elster r. Germany 38 51.26N 11.57E
Weissenburg in Bayern Germany 38 49.01N 10.58E
Weissenfels Germany 38 51.12N 11.58E
Weisswasser Germany 38 51.30N 14.38E
Wei Xian China 54 36.21N 114.56E
Weixin China 55 27.48N 105.05E
Weiya China 52 41.50N 94.24E
Weizhou i. China 55 21.01N 109.03E
Wejherowo Poland 37 54.37N 18.15E
Wekusko Canada 101 54.45N 99.45W
Weldiya Ethiopia 73 11.50N 39.36E
Weldon U.S.A. 109 35.40N 118.20W
Welega d. Ethiopia 73 9.40N 35.50E
Welkom R.S.A. 80 27.59S 26.42E
Welland Canada 104 42.59N 79.14W
Welland r. U.K. 12 52.53N 0.00
Wellesley Is. Australia 90 16.42S 139.30E
Wellfleet U.S.A. 115 41.56N 70.02W
Wellin Belgium 16 50.05N 5.07E
Wellingborough U.K. 13 52.18N 0.41W
Wellington N.S.W. Australia 93 32.33S 148.59E
Wellington S.A. Australia 92 35.21S 139.23E
Wellington Canada 105 43.57N 77.21W
Wellington New Zealand 86 41.17S 174.47E
Wellington d. New Zealand 86 40.00S 175.30E
Wellington Shrops. U.K. 13 52.42N 2.31W
Wellington Somerset U.K. 13 50.58N 3.13W
Wellington Kans. U.S.A. 111 37.16N 97.24W
Wellington Nev. U.S.A. 108 38.45N 119.22W
Wellington Ohio U.S.A. 114 41.10N 82.13W

Wellington, Isla i. Chile 125 49.30S 75.00W
Wells U.K. 13 51.12N 2.39W
Wells Maine U.S.A. 115 43.20N 70.35W
Wells Nev. U.S.A. 108 41.07N 114.58W
Wells N.Y. U.S.A. 115 43.24N 74.17W
Wellsboro U.S.A. 114 41.45N 77.18W
Wellsburg U.S.A. 114 40.16N 80.37W
Wells Gray Prov. Park Canada 100 52.30N 120.15W
Wells L. Canada 101 57.55N 101.00W
Wells-next-the-Sea U.K. 12 52.57N 0.51E
Wells River town U.S.A. 105 44.09N 72.06W
Wellston U.S.A. 114 39.07N 82.32W
Wellsville Mo. U.S.A. 110 39.04N 91.34W
Wellsville N.Y. U.S.A. 114 42.07N 77.57W
Wellton U.S.A. 109 32.40N 114.08W
Welmel r. Ethiopia 73 6.00N 40.20E
Welo d. Ethiopia 73 11.30N 40.00E
Wels Austria 39 48.10N 14.02E
Welshpool U.K. 13 52.40N 3.09W
Welwyn Garden City U.K. 13 51.48N 0.13W
Wem U.K. 12 52.52N 2.45W
Wembere r. Tanzania 79 4.07S 34.15E
Wemindji Canada 102 53.02N 78.55W
Wenatchee U.S.A. 108 47.25N 120.19W
Wenchang China 55 19.37N 110.43E
Wenchi Ghana 76 7.40N 2.06W
Wendel U.S.A. 108 40.20N 120.14W
Wendo Ethiopia 73 6.40N 38.27E
Wendover U.S.A. 108 40.44N 114.02W
Wenebegon L. Canada 102 47.25N 83.05W
Wengfengzhen China 54 34.56N 104.38E
Wenlock r. Australia 90 12.02S 141.55E
Wenquan China 63 33.13N 91.50E
Wenshan China 55 23.20N 104.11E
Wensleydale f. U.K. 12 54.19N 2.04W
Wentworth Australia 92 34.06S 141.56E
Wen Xian China 54 32.52N 104.40E
Wenzhou China 55 28.02N 120.40E
Weott U.S.A. 108 40.19N 123.54W
Wepener R.S.A. 80 29.43S 27.01E
Werda Botswana 80 25.15S 23.16E
Werdau Germany 38 50.44N 12.22E
Werdër well Ethiopia 71 6.58N 45.21E
Werder Germany 38 52.23N 12.56E
Werdohl Germany 38 51.15N 7.45E
Were Īlu Ethiopia 73 10.37N 39.28E
Werl Indonesia 59 3.10S 132.30E
Werne Germany 16 51.39N 7.36E
Wernigerode Germany 38 51.50N 10.47E
Werra r. Germany 38 51.26N 9.39E
Werribee Australia 93 37.54S 144.40E
Werris Creek town Australia 93 31.20S 150.41E
Wertheim Germany 39 49.46N 9.31E
Wertingen Germany 39 48.34N 10.41E
Wesel Germany 38 51.40N 6.38E
Weser r. Germany 38 53.15N 8.34E
Weslaco U.S.A. 111 26.09N 97.59W
Weslemkoon L. Canada 105 45.02N 77.25W
Wesleyville Canada 103 49.09N 53.34W
Wesleyville U.S.A. 114 42.08N 80.01W
Wessel, C. Australia 90 10.59S 136.46E
Wessel Is. Australia 90 11.30S 136.25E
Wessington U.S.A. 110 44.27N 98.42W
Wessington Springs town U.S.A. 110 44.05N 98.34W
West U.S.A. 111 31.48N 97.06W
West r. U.S.A. 115 42.52N 72.33W
West Australian Basin f. Indian Oc. 49 15.00S 100.00E
West B. U.S.A. 111 29.15N 94.57W
West Bank Jordan 67 32.00N 35.15E
West Bend U.S.A. 110 43.25N 88.11W
West Bengal d. India 63 23.00N 88.00E
West Branch U.S.A. 104 44.17N 84.14W
West Bromwich U.K. 13 52.32N 2.01W
Westbrook U.S.A. 112 43.41N 70.21W
West Burke U.S.A. 105 44.38N 71.59W
West Burra i. U.K. 10 60.05N 1.21W
West Canada Creek r. U.S.A. 115 43.01N 74.58W
West Caroline Basin Pacific Oc. 84 5.00N 139.00E
West Chester U.S.A. 115 39.58N 75.36W
West Coast d. New Zealand 86 43.15S 170.10E
West Des Moines U.S.A. 110 41.35N 93.43W
Westende Belgium 16 51.10N 2.46E
Westerland Germany 38 54.54N 8.18E
Westerly U.S.A. 115 41.22N 71.50W
Western d. Ghana 76 6.00N 2.40W
Western d. Kenya 79 0.30N 34.30E
Western d. Zambia 80 16.00S 23.45E
Western Australia d. Australia 88 24.20S 122.30E
Western Duck I. Canada 104 45.45N 83.00W
Western Ghāts mts. India 60 15.30N 74.30E
Western Isles d. U.K. 14 57.40N 7.10W
Westernport U.S.A. 114 39.29N 79.03W
Western Sahara Africa 74 25.00N 13.30W
Western Samoa Pacific Oc. 84 13.55S 172.00W
Westerschelde est. Neth. 16 51.25N 3.40E
Westerstede Germany 38 53.15N 7.55E
Westerville U.S.A. 114 40.08N 82.56W
Westerwald f. Germany 38 50.40N 7.45E
West Falkland i. Falkland Is. 125 51.40S 60.00W
West Felton U.K. 12 52.49N 2.58W
Westfield Mass. U.S.A. 115 42.08N 72.45W
Westfield N.J. U.S.A. 115 40.39N 74.21W
Westfield N.Y. U.S.A. 114 42.19N 79.35W
Westfield Penn. U.S.A. 114 41.55N 77.32W
Westfield r. U.S.A. 115 42.05N 72.35W
West Fork r. U.S.A. 114 39.28N 80.09W
West Frankfort U.S.A. 111 37.54N 88.55W
West Frisian Is. see Waddeneilanden Neth. 36
West Glamorgan d. U.K. 13 51.42N 3.47W
Westhampton U.S.A. 115 40.49N 72.39W
West Haven U.S.A. 115 41.16N 72.57W
Westhope U.S.A. 110 48.55N 101.01W
West Indies is. C. America 127 21.00N 74.00W
West Lafayette U.S.A. 112 40.26N 86.56W
West Leyden U.S.A. 115 43.28N 75.28W
West Linton U.K. 14 55.45N 3.21W
Westlock Canada 100 54.09N 113.55W

West Lorne Canada 104 42.36N 81.36W
Westmeath Canada 105 45.49N 76.54W
Westmeath d. Rep. of Ire. 15 53.30N 7.30W
West Memphis U.S.A. 111 35.08N 90.11W
West Middlesex U.S.A. 114 41.10N 80.27W
West Midlands d. U.K. 13 52.28N 1.50W
Westminster U.S.A. 114 39.35N 77.00W
Westmoreland Australia 90 17.18S 138.12E
Westmoreland U.S.A. 115 42.59N 72.25W
West Nicholson Zimbabwe 80 21.06S 29.25E
Weston Malaysia 58 5.14N 115.35E
Weston U.S.A. 114 39.02N 80.28W
Weston-Super-Mare U.K. 13 51.20N 2.59W
West Palm Beach town U.S.A. 113 26.42N 80.05W
West Plains town U.S.A. 111 36.44N 91.51W
West Point town U.S.A. 111 33.36N 88.39W
Westport Canada 105 44.41N 76.26W
Westport New Zealand 86 41.46S 171.38E
Westport Rep. of Ire. 15 53.48N 9.32W
Westport Conn. U.S.A. 115 41.09N 73.22W
Westport N.Y. U.S.A. 105 44.13N 73.39W
Westport Wash. U.S.A. 106 46.53N 124.06W
Westray Canada 101 53.36N 101.24W
Westray i. U.K. 14 59.18N 2.58W
Westree Canada 104 47.26N 81.34W
West Road r. Canada 100 53.18N 122.53W
West Siberian Plain f. see Zapadno-Sibirskaya Ravnina Russian Fed. 9
West Springfield U.S.A. 115 42.06N 72.38W
West Sussex d. U.K. 13 50.58N 0.30W
West Terschelling Neth. 16 53.22N 5.13E
West Union U.S.A. 114 39.18N 80.47W
West Virginia d. U.S.A. 114 38.45N 80.30W
West Vlaanderen d. Belgium 16 51.00N 3.00E
West Wyalong Australia 93 33.54S 147.12E
West Yellowstone U.S.A. 108 44.30N 111.05W
West York U.S.A. 114 39.57N 76.46W
West Yorkshire d. U.K. 12 53.45N 1.40W
Wetar i. Indonesia 59 7.45S 126.00E
Wetaskiwin Canada 100 52.55N 113.24W
Wetteren Belgium 16 51.00N 3.51E
Wetzlar Germany 38 50.33N 8.29E
Wewak P.N.G. 59 3.35S 143.35E
Wewoka U.S.A. 111 35.09N 96.30W
Wexford Rep. of Ire. 15 52.20N 6.28W
Wexford d. Rep. of Ire. 15 52.20N 6.25W
Wexford B. Rep. of Ire. 15 52.27N 6.18W
Weyburn Canada 101 49.41N 103.52W
Weyib r. Ethiopia 73 4.11N 42.09E
Weymouth U.K. 13 50.36N 2.28W
Weymouth, C. Australia 90 12.32S 143.36E
Whakatane New Zealand 86 37.58S 177.00E
Whalan r. Australia 93 29.10S 148.42E
Whale Cove town Canada 101 62.11N 92.36W
Whalsay i. U.K. 14 60.22N 0.59W
Whangarei New Zealand 86 35.43S 174.20E
Wharfe r. U.K. 12 53.50N 1.07W
Wharfedale f. U.K. 12 54.00N 1.55W
Wharton U.S.A. 111 29.19N 96.06W
Whataroa New Zealand 86 43.16S 170.22E
Wheatland U.S.A. 108 42.03N 104.57W
Wheatley Canada 104 42.06N 82.27W
Wheaton Md. U.S.A. 114 39.03N 77.03W
Wheaton Minn. U.S.A. 110 45.48N 96.30W
Wheeler r. Que. Canada 103 58.05N 67.12W
Wheeler r. Sask. Canada 101 57.25N 105.30W
Wheeler Peak mtn. Nev. U.S.A. 108 38.59N 114.19W
Wheeler Peak mtn. N.Mex. U.S.A. 108 36.34N 105.25W
Wheeler Ridge town U.S.A. 109 35.06N 119.01W
Wheeler Springs town U.S.A. 109 34.30N 119.18W
Wheeling U.S.A. 114 40.05N 80.42W
Whernside mtn. U.K. 12 54.14N 2.25W
Whidbey Is. Australia 92 34.50S 135.00E
Whiskey Gap town Canada 100 49.00N 113.03W
Whitby Canada 104 43.52N 78.56W
Whitby U.K. 12 54.29N 0.37W
Whitchurch Shrops. U.K. 12 52.58N 2.42W
White r. Ark. U.S.A. 111 33.53N 91.10W
White r. Ind. U.S.A. 112 38.29N 87.45W
White r. S.Dak. U.S.A. 110 43.42N 99.22W
White r. Utah U.S.A. 106 40.04N 109.41W
White r. Vt. U.S.A. 105 43.37N 72.20W
White B. Canada 103 50.00N 56.30W
White Cliffs town Australia 92 30.51S 143.05E
Whiteface, Mt. U.S.A. 105 44.22N 73.54W
Whitefield U.S.A. 105 44.22N 71.36W
Whitefish Canada 104 46.23N 81.20W
Whitefish U.S.A. 108 48.25N 114.20W
Whitefish B. U.S.A. 104 46.40N 84.50W
Whitefish Falls town Canada 104 46.07N 81.44W
Whitefish L. Canada 101 62.41N 106.48W
Whitefish Point town U.S.A. 104 46.45N 84.59W
Whitefish Pt. U.S.A. 104 46.45N 85.00W
Whitehall Mont. U.S.A. 108 45.52N 112.06W
Whitehall N.Y. U.S.A. 115 43.33N 73.25W
Whitehall Ohio U.S.A. 114 39.58N 82.54W
Whitehall Wisc. U.S.A. 110 44.22N 91.19W
Whitehaven U.K. 12 54.33N 3.35W
White Haven U.S.A. 115 41.04N 75.47W
Whitehorse Canada 100 60.43N 135.03W
White, L. Australia 88 21.05S 129.00E
White, L. Canada 105 45.18N 76.31W
White, L. U.S.A. 111 29.45N 92.30W
Whitemark Australia 91 40.07S 148.00E
White Mountain Peak U.S.A. 108 37.38N 118.15W
White Mts. Calif. U.S.A. 108 37.30N 118.15W
White Mts. N.H. U.S.A. 105 44.10N 71.35W
Whitemud r. Canada 100 56.41N 117.15W
White Nile r. see Abyaḑ, Al Baḥr al r. Sudan 72
White Otter L. Canada 102 49.09N 91.50W
White Plains Liberia 76 6.28N 10.40W
White Plains town U.S.A. 115 41.02N 73.46W
Whitesand r. Canada 101 51.34N 101.55W
Whitesboro U.S.A. 115 43.07N 75.18W
White Sea see Beloye More sea Russian Fed. 44
Whiteshell Prov. Park. Canada 101 50.00N 95.25W

Whitetail U.S.A. 108 48.54N 105.10W
White Volta r. Ghana 76 9.13N 1.15W
Whitewater Baldy mtn. U.S.A. 109 33.20N 108.39W
Whitfield Australia 93 36.49S 146.22E
Whithorn U.K. 14 54.44N 4.25W
Whitianga New Zealand 86 36.50S 175.42E
Whiting U.S.A. 115 39.57N 74.23W
Whitley Bay town U.K. 12 55.03N 1.25W
Whitney Canada 104 45.30N 78.14W
Whitney, Mt. U.S.A. 109 36.35N 118.18W
Whitney Point town U.S.A. 115 42.20N 75.58W
Whitstable U.K. 13 51.21N 1.02E
Whitsunday I. Australia 90 20.17S 148.59E
Whittemore U.S.A. 104 44.14N 83.48W
Whittier U.S.A. 98 60.46N 148.41W
Whittlesea Australia 93 37.31S 145.08E
Whitton U.K. 12 53.42N 0.39W
Wholdaia L. Canada 101 60.43N 104.20W
Whyalla Australia 92 33.02S 137.35E
Wiarton Canada 104 44.45N 81.09W
Wichita U.S.A. 111 37.41N 97.20W
Wichita Falls town U.S.A. 111 33.54N 98.30W
Wick U.K. 14 58.26N 3.06W
Wickenburg U.S.A. 109 33.58N 112.44W
Wickepin Australia 89 32.45S 117.31E
Wickliffe U.S.A. 114 41.36N 81.28W
Wicklow Rep. of Ire. 15 52.59N 6.03W
Wicklow d. Rep. of Ire. 15 52.59N 6.25W
Wicklow Head Rep. of Ire. 15 52.58N 6.00W
Wicklow Mts. Rep. of Ire. 15 53.06N 6.20W
Widdifield Canada 104 46.25N 79.20W
Widen U.S.A. 114 38.28N 80.52W
Widgiemooltha Australia 89 31.30S 121.34E
Widnes U.K. 12 53.22N 2.44W
Wiehl Germany 38 50.57N 7.31E
Wiek Germany 38 54.37N 13.17E
Wieluń Poland 37 51.14N 18.34E
Wien Austria 36 48.13N 16.22E
Wiener Neustadt Austria 36 47.49N 16.15E
Wieprz r. Poland 37 51.34N 21.49E
Wiesbaden Germany 39 50.05N 8.14E
Wiesloch Germany 39 49.17N 8.42E
Wietze Germany 38 52.39N 9.50E
Wigan U.K. 12 53.33N 2.38W
Wight, Isle of U.K. 13 50.40N 1.17W
Wigton U.K. 12 54.50N 3.09W
Wigtown U.K. 14 54.47N 4.26W
Wigtown B. U.K. 14 54.47N 4.15W
Wikwemikong Canada 104 45.48N 81.44W
Wil Switz. 39 47.27N 9.03E
Wilber U.S.A. 110 40.29N 96.58W
Wilberforce Canada 105 45.03N 78.15W
Wilcannia Australia 92 31.33S 143.24E
Wilcox U.S.A. 114 41.35N 78.41W
Wilderness U.S.A. 114 38.19N 77.48W
Wildhorn mtn. Switz. 38 46.22N 7.22E
Wildon Austria 31 46.53N 15.31E
Wildrose U.S.A. 110 48.38N 103.11W
Wildspitze mtn. Austria 39 46.53N 10.52E
Wildwood U.S.A. 115 38.59N 74.49W
Wilgena Australia 92 30.46S 134.44E
Wilhelm II Land Antarctica 128 68.00S 89.00E
Wilhelm, Mt. P.N.G. 59 6.00S 144.55E
Wilhelm-Pieck-Stadt Guben Germany 38 51.57N 14.43E
Wilhelmshaven Germany 38 53.31N 8.08E
Wilkes-Barre U.S.A. 115 41.14N 75.53W
Wilkesboro U.S.A. 113 36.08N 81.09W
Wilkes Land f. Antarctica 128 69.00S 120.00E
Wilkie Canada 101 52.25N 108.43W
Wilkinsburg U.S.A. 114 40.27N 79.53W
Wilkinson Lakes Australia 91 29.40S 132.39E
Willandra Billabong r. Australia 92 33.08S 144.06E
Willard N.Mex. U.S.A. 109 34.36N 106.02W
Willard Ohio U.S.A. 114 41.03N 82.44W
Willemstad Neth. Antilles 122 12.12N 68.56W
Willeroo Australia 88 15.17S 131.35E
William Creek town Australia 92 28.52S 136.18E
William, Mt. Australia 92 37.20S 142.41E
Williams Australia 89 33.01S 116.45E
Williams r. Australia 92 32.59S 116.24E
Williamsburg U.S.A. 113 37.17N 76.43W
Williams Lake town Canada 100 52.08N 122.10W
Williamson U.S.A. 113 37.42N 82.16W
Williamsport Md. U.S.A. 114 39.32N 77.50W
Williamsport Penn. U.S.A. 114 41.14N 77.00W
Williamston U.S.A. 113 35.53N 77.05W
Williamstown N.J. U.S.A. 115 39.41N 75.00W
Williamstown N.Y. U.S.A. 115 43.26N 75.55W
Williamstown W.Va. U.S.A. 114 39.24N 81.27W
Willimantic U.S.A. 115 41.43N 72.12W
Willis Group is. Australia 90 16.18S 150.00E
Williston R.S.A. 80 31.21S 20.53E
Williston U.S.A. 110 48.09N 103.37W
Williston L. Canada 100 55.40N 123.40W
Willits U.S.A. 108 39.25N 123.21W
Willmar U.S.A. 110 45.07N 95.03W
Willmore Wilderness Park Canada 100 53.45N 119.00W
Willochra Australia 92 32.12S 138.10E
Willochra r. Australia 92 31.57S 137.52E
Willoughby U.S.A. 114 41.38N 81.25W
Willow r. U.S.A. 98 61.42N 150.08W
Willow Grove U.S.A. 115 40.08N 75.06W
Willow Hill town U.S.A. 114 40.06N 77.48W
Willow L. Canada 100 62.10N 119.08W
Willowmore R.S.A. 80 33.18S 23.12E
Willow Ranch U.S.A. 108 41.55N 120.21W
Willow River town Canada 100 54.06N 122.28W
Willsboro U.S.A. 105 44.22N 73.26W
Willunga Australia 92 35.18S 138.33E
Wilmette U.S.A. 110 42.04N 87.43W
Wilmington Del. U.S.A. 115 39.44N 75.33W
Wilmington N.C. U.S.A. 113 34.14N 77.55W
Wilmington Vt. U.S.A. 115 42.52N 72.52W
Wilmslow U.K. 12 53.19N 2.14W
Wilpena r. Australia 92 31.13S 139.25E
Wilson N.C. U.S.A. 113 35.43N 77.56W

Wilson N.Y. U.S.A. 114 43.19N 78.50W
Wilson's Promontory c. Australia 93 39.06S 146.23E
Wilton r. Australia 90 14.45S 134.33E
Wilton U.K. 13 51.05N 1.52W
Wilton N.Dak. U.S.A. 110 47.10N 100.47W
Wilton N.H. U.S.A. 115 42.51N 71.44W
Wiltshire d. U.K. 13 51.20N 0.34W
Wiltz Lux. 16 49.59N 5.53E
Wiluna Australia 88 26.36S 120.13E
Wimmera r. Australia 92 36.05S 141.56E
Winam b. Kenya 79 0.15S 34.30E
Wincanton U.K. 13 51.03N 2.24W
Winchendon U.S.A. 115 42.41N 72.03W
Winchester Canada 105 45.06N 75.21W
Winchester U.K. 13 51.04N 1.19W
Winchester Ky. U.S.A. 113 38.00N 84.10W
Winchester N.H. U.S.A. 115 42.46N 72.23W
Winchester Va. U.S.A. 114 39.11N 78.10W
Winchester Wyo. U.S.A. 108 43.51N 108.10W
Windber U.S.A. 114 40.14N 78.50W
Windermere l. U.K. 12 54.20N 2.56W
Windfall Canada 100 54.12N 116.13W
Windham U.S.A. 114 41.14N 81.03W
Windhoek Namibia 80 22.34S 17.06E
Windom U.S.A. 110 43.52N 95.07W
Windorah Australia 90 25.26S 142.39E
Wind River Range mts. U.S.A. 108 43.05N 109.25W
Windsor Australia 93 33.38S 150.47E
Windsor Nfld. Canada 103 48.58N 55.40W
Windsor N.S. Canada 103 44.59N 64.08W
Windsor Ont. Canada 104 42.18N 83.01W
Windsor Que. Canada 105 45.34N 72.00W
Windsor U.K. 13 51.29N 0.38W
Windsor Conn. U.S.A. 115 41.51N 72.39W
Windsor N.Y. U.S.A. 115 42.05N 75.39W
Windsor Vt. U.S.A. 115 43.29N 72.23W
Windsor Locks U.S.A. 115 41.56N 72.38W
Windward Is. C. America 117 13.00N 60.00W
Windward Passage str. Carib. Sea 117 20.00N 74.00W
Winfield Kans. U.S.A. 111 37.15N 96.59W
Winfield W.Va. U.S.A. 114 38.32N 81.53W
Wingen Australia 93 31.43S 150.54E
Wingham Australia 93 31.50S 152.20E
Wingham Canada 104 43.53N 81.19W
Winifred U.S.A. 108 47.34N 109.23W
Winisk Canada 102 55.20N 85.15W
Winisk r. Canada 102 55.00N 85.20W
Winisk L. Canada 102 53.00N 88.00W
Winkler Canada 101 49.11N 97.56W
Winklern Austria 39 46.52N 12.52E
Winneba Ghana 76 5.22N 0.38W
Winnebago, L. U.S.A. 110 44.00N 88.25W
Winnemucca U.S.A. 106 40.58N 117.45W
Winnemucca L. U.S.A. 108 40.09N 119.20W
Winner U.S.A. 110 43.22N 99.51W
Winnfield U.S.A. 111 31.55N 92.38W
Winnipeg Canada 101 49.53N 97.09W
Winnipeg r. Canada 101 50.38N 96.19W
Winnipeg, L. Canada 101 52.00N 97.00W
Winnipegosis, L. Canada 101 52.30N 100.00W
Winnipesaukee, L. U.S.A. 115 43.35N 71.20W
Winnsboro La. U.S.A. 111 32.10N 91.43W
Winnsboro S.C. U.S.A. 113 34.22N 81.05W
Winona Kans. U.S.A. 110 39.04N 101.15W
Winona Minn. U.S.A. 110 44.03N 91.39W
Winona Miss. U.S.A. 111 33.29N 89.44W
Winooski U.S.A. 105 44.29N 73.11W
Winooski r. U.S.A. 105 44.30N 73.15W
Winschoten Neth. 16 53.07N 7.02E
Winsen Germany 38 53.22N 10.12E
Winsford U.K. 12 53.12N 2.31W
Winslow Ariz. U.S.A. 109 35.01N 110.42W
Winslow Maine U.S.A. 112 44.32N 69.38W
Winsted U.S.A. 115 41.55N 73.04W
Winston U.S.A. 108 46.28N 111.38W
Winston-Salem U.S.A. 113 36.05N 80.18W
Winsum Neth. 16 53.20N 6.31E
Winter Haven U.S.A. 113 28.02N 81.46W
Winterset U.S.A. 110 41.20N 94.01W
Winterswijk Neth. 16 51.58N 6.44E
Winterthur Switz. 39 47.30N 8.43E
Winthrop Minn. U.S.A. 110 44.32N 94.22W
Winthrop Wash. U.S.A. 108 48.29N 120.11W
Winton Australia 90 22.22S 143.00E
Winton New Zealand 86 46.10S 168.20E
Winton U.S.A. 108 41.45N 109.10W
Wipper r. Germany 38 51.47N 11.42E
Wirrabara Australia 92 33.03S 138.18E
Wirraminna Australia 92 31.11S 136.04E
Wirrappa Australia 92 31.28S 137.00E
Wirrega Australia 92 36.11S 140.37E
Wirrida, L. Australia 92 29.45S 134.39E
Wirrulla Australia 92 32.24S 134.33E
Wisbech U.K. 13 52.39N 0.10E
Wisconsin d. U.S.A. 110 44.30N 90.00W
Wisconsin r. U.S.A. 110 43.00N 91.15W
Wisconsin Dells U.S.A. 110 43.38N 89.46W
Wisconsin Rapids town U.S.A. 110 44.24N 89.50W
Wisdom U.S.A. 108 45.37N 113.27W
Wisła r. Poland 37 54.23N 18.52E
Wismar Germany 38 53.53N 11.28E
Wisner U.S.A. 110 41.59N 96.55W
Wissembourg France 19 49.02N 7.57E
Wissen Germany 38 50.47N 7.43E
Wissmar Germany 38 50.38N 8.41E
Wisznice Poland 37 51.48N 23.12E
Witchekan L. Canada 101 53.25N 107.35W
Witham r. U.K. 12 52.56N 0.04E
Witherbee U.S.A. 105 44.05N 73.32W
Withernsea U.K. 12 53.43N 0.02E
Witkowo Poland 37 52.27N 17.47E
Witney U.K. 13 51.47N 1.29W
Witsand R.S.A. 80 34.23S 20.49E
Witten Germany 16 51.26N 7.19E
Wittenberg Germany 38 51.53N 12.39E
Wittenberge Germany 38 53.00N 11.44E
Wittenburg Germany 38 53.31N 11.04E

Wittenoom Australia 88 22.19S 118.21E
Wittingen Germany 38 52.43N 10.44E
Wittlich Germany 39 49.59N 6.53E
Wittstock Germany 38 53.10N 12.29E
Witu Kenya 79 2.22S 40.20E
Witvlei Namibia 80 22.25S 18.29E
Witzenhausen Germany 38 51.20N 9.51E
Wiveliscombe U.K. 13 51.02N 3.20W
Wkra r. Poland 37 52.27N 20.44E
Władysławowo Poland 37 54.49N 18.25E
Włocławek Poland 37 52.39N 19.01E
Włodawa Poland 37 51.33N 23.31E
Wodonga Australia 93 36.08S 146.09E
Woerden Neth. 16 52.07N 4.55E
Wohutun China 54 43.40N 123.30E
Wokam i. Indonesia 59 5.45S 134.30E
Woking Canada 100 55.35N 118.50W
Woking U.K. 13 51.20N 0.34W
Wolcott U.S.A. 114 43.13N 76.49W
Woleai i. Pacific Oc. 84 7.21N 143.52E
Wolf r. U.S.A. 110 44.07N 88.43W
Wolfach Germany 39 48.17N 8.13E
Wolfboro U.S.A. 115 43.35N 71.12W
Wolf Creek town U.S.A. 108 46.50N 112.20W
Wolfe Island town Canada 105 44.12N 76.26W
Wolfen Germany 38 51.40N 12.16E
Wolfenbüttel Germany 38 52.10N 10.32E
Wolfhagen Germany 38 51.19N 9.10E
Wolf Point town U.S.A. 108 48.05N 105.39W
Wolfratshausen Germany 39 47.54N 11.25E
Wolfsberg Austria 31 46.51N 14.51E
Wolfsburg Germany 38 52.25N 10.47E
Wolgast Germany 38 54.03N 13.46E
Wolin Poland 36 53.51N 14.38E
Wollaston L. Canada 101 58.15N 103.20W
Wollaston Pen. Canada 98 70.00N 115.00W
Wollongong Australia 93 34.25S 150.52E
Wolmaransstad R.S.A. 80 27.11S 25.58E
Wołomin Poland 37 52.21N 21.14E
Wolseley Australia 92 36.21S 140.55E
Wolseley Bay town Canada 104 46.07N 80.22W
Wolverhampton U.K. 13 52.35N 2.06W
Wolverine U.S.A. 104 45.16N 84.36W
Womelsdorf U.S.A. 115 40.22N 76.11W
Wondai Australia 90 26.19S 151.52E
Wongan Hills town Australia 89 30.55S 116.41E
Wonogiri Indonesia 59 7.48S 110.52E
Wonosari Indonesia 59 7.55S 110.39E
Wonosobo Indonesia 59 7.21S 109.56E
Wŏnsan N. Korea 53 39.07N 127.26E
Wonthaggi Australia 93 38.38S 145.37E
Woocalla Australia 92 31.44S 137.10E
Woodbine U.S.A. 115 39.14N 74.49W
Woodbridge U.K. 13 52.06N 1.19E
Woodbridge U.S.A. 114 38.39N 77.15W
Wood Buffalo Nat. Park Canada 100 59.00N 113.41W
Woodburn Australia 93 29.04S 153.21E
Woodbury U.S.A. 115 39.50N 75.10W
Wooded Bluff f. Australia 93 29.22S 153.22E
Woodenbong Australia 93 28.28S 152.35E
Woodgate U.S.A. 115 43.32N 75.12W
Woodland U.S.A. 108 38.41N 121.46W
Woodlark I. P.N.G. 90 9.05S 152.50E
Wood Mts. Canada 101 49.14N 106.20W
Woodroffe, Mt. Australia 90 26.20S 131.45E
Woodsfield U.S.A. 114 39.46N 81.07W
Woods Hole U.S.A. 115 41.31N 70.40W
Woodside Australia 93 38.31S 146.52E
Woods, L. Australia 90 17.50S 133.30E
Woods L. Canada 103 54.40N 64.21W
Woods, L. of the Canada/U.S.A. 102 49.15N 94.45W
Woodstock Canada 104 43.08N 80.45W
Woodstock U.K. 13 51.51N 1.20W
Woodstock U.S.A. 115 43.37N 72.31W
Woodstown U.S.A. 115 39.39N 75.20W
Woodsville U.S.A. 105 44.09N 72.02W
Woodville New Zealand 86 40.20S 175.52E
Woodward U.S.A. 111 36.26N 99.24W
Wooler U.K. 12 55.33N 2.01W
Woolgoolga Australia 93 30.07S 153.12E
Wooltana Australia 92 30.28S 139.26E
Woomera Australia 92 31.11S 136.54E
Woonsocket U.S.A. 115 42.00N 71.31W
Wooramel Australia 88 25.42S 114.20E
Wooramel r. Australia 88 25.47S 114.10E
Woorong, L. Australia 92 29.24S 134.06E
Wooster U.S.A. 114 40.48N 81.56W
Worb Switz. 19 46.56N 7.34E
Worcester R.S.A. 80 33.39S 19.25E
Worcester U.K. 13 52.12N 2.12W
Worcester U.S.A. 115 42.16N 71.48W
Wörgl Austria 39 47.29N 12.04E
Workington U.K. 12 54.39N 3.34W
Worksop U.K. 12 53.19N 1.09W
Workum Neth. 16 53.00N 5.26E
Worland U.S.A. 108 44.01N 107.57W
Worms Germany 39 49.38N 8.22E
Wörnitz r. Germany 39 48.42N 10.45E
Wörrstadt Germany 39 49.50N 8.07E
Wörther See l. Austria 31 46.37N 14.10E
Worthing U.K. 13 50.49N 0.21W
Worthington Minn. U.S.A. 110 43.37N 95.36W
Worthington Ohio U.S.A. 112 40.03N 83.03W
Worthville U.S.A. 112 38.38N 85.05W
Wosi Indonesia 59 0.15S 128.00E
Wour Chad 77 21.21N 15.57E
Woutchaba Cameroon 77 5.13N 13.05E
Wowoni i. Indonesia 59 4.10S 123.10E
Wragby U.K. 12 53.17N 0.18E
Wrangel I. see Vrangelya, Ostrov i. Russian Fed. 51
Wrangell U.S.A. 100 56.28N 132.23W
Wrangell Mts. U.S.A. 98 62.00N 143.00W
Wrangle U.K. 12 53.03N 0.09E
Wrath, C. U.K. 14 58.37N 5.01W
Wray U.S.A. 110 40.05N 102.13W
Wrecks, B. of Kiribati 85 1.52N 157.17W
Wrexham U.K. 12 53.05N 3.00W

221

Wrigley Canada **98** 63.16N 123.39W
Wrocław Poland **37** 51.05N 17.00E
Wronki Poland **36** 52.43N 16.23E
Wroxeter Canada **104** 43.50N 81.07W
Września Poland **37** 52.20N 17.34E
Wubin Australia **89** 30.06S 116.38E
Wuchang China **55** 30.21N 114.19E
Wucheng China **54** 37.12N 116.04E
Wuchuan Guangdong China **55** 21.21N 110.40E
Wuchuan Nei Monggol Zizhiqu China **54** 41.08N 111.24E
Wuda China **54** 39.40N 106.40E
Wuday'ah Saudi Arabia **71** 16.05N 47.05E
Wudham 'Alwā Oman **65** 23.48N 57.33E
Wudinna Australia **92** 33.03S 135.28E
Wudu China **54** 33.24N 104.50E
Wufeng China **55** 30.12N 110.36E
Wugang China **55** 26.42N 110.31E
Wugong Shan *mts.* China **55** 27.15N 114.00E
Wuhai China **54** 39.50N 106.40E
Wuhan China **55** 30.37N 114.19E
Wuhu China **55** 31.25N 118.25E
Wūjiang China **63** 33.38N 79.55E
Wu Jiang *r.* China **55** 29.41N 107.24E
Wukari Nigeria **77** 7.57N 9.42E
Wulian China **54** 35.45N 119.12E
Wuliang Shan *mts.* China **52** 24.27N 100.43E
Wum Cameroon **77** 6.25N 10.03E
Wumbulgal Australia **93** 34.25S 146.16E
Wuming China **55** 23.10N 108.16E
Wuning China **55** 29.17N 115.06E
Wunnummin L. Canada **102** 52.50N 89.20W
Wun Rog Sudan **73** 9.00N 28.21E
Wunstorf Germany **38** 52.25N 9.26E
Wuppertal Germany **38** 51.16N 7.11E
Wuppertal R.S.A. **80** 32.16S 19.12E
Wuqi China **54** 37.03N 108.14E
Wuqiao China **54** 37.38N 116.22E
Wuqing China **54** 39.19N 117.05E
Wurno Nigeria **77** 13.20N 5.28E
Wurtsboro U.S.A. **115** 41.35N 74.29W
Würzburg Germany **39** 49.48N 9.56E
Wurzen Germany **38** 51.22N 12.44E
Wusong China **55** 31.20N 121.30E
Wutach *r.* Germany **39** 47.37N 8.15E
Wutongqiao China **55** 29.20N 103.48E
Wuwei China **54** 38.00N 102.59E
Wuxi Jiangsu China **55** 31.34N 120.20E
Wuxi Sichuan China **55** 31.28N 109.36E
Wuxing China **55** 30.59N 120.04E
Wuyi Shan *mts.* China **55** 27.00N 117.00E
Wuyuan China **54** 41.06N 108.16E
Wuzhan China **53** 50.14N 125.18E
Wuzhi Shan *mts.* China **55** 18.50N 109.30E
Wuzhou China **55** 23.28N 111.21E
Wyalkatchem Australia **89** 31.21S 117.22E
Wyalong Australia **93** 33.55S 147.17E
Wyandotte U.S.A. **114** 42.12N 83.10W
Wyandra Australia **91** 27.15S 146.00E
Wyangala Resr. Australia **93** 33.58S 148.55E
Wyara, L. Australia **92** 28.42S 144.16E
Wycheproof Australia **92** 36.04S 143.14E
Wye U.K. **13** 51.11N 0.56E
Wye *r.* U.K. **13** 51.37N 2.40W
Wyk Germany **38** 54.42N 8.34E
Wymondham U.K. **13** 52.34N 1.07E
Wynbring Australia **91** 30.33S 133.32E
Wyndham Australia **88** 15.29S 128.05E
Wynne U.S.A. **111** 35.14N 90.47W
Wyoming Canada **104** 42.57N 82.07W
Wyoming *d.* U.S.A. **108** 43.10N 107.36W
Wyong Australia **93** 33.17S 151.25E
Wyszków Poland **37** 52.36N 21.28E
Wytheville U.S.A. **113** 36.57N 81.07W

X

Xa Cassau Angola **78** 9.02S 20.17E
Xagquka China **63** 31.50N 92.46E
Xainza China **63** 30.56N 88.40E
Xaitongmoin China **63** 29.22N 88.15E
Xai-Xai Mozambique **81** 25.05S 33.38E
Xalin *well* Somali Rep. **71** 9.08N 48.47E
Xam Nua Laos **56** 20.25N 104.10E
Xangdoring China **63** 32.06N 82.02E
Xangongo Angola **78** 16.31S 15.00E
Xanten Germany **38** 51.39N 6.26E
Xánthi Greece **34** 41.08N 24.53E
Xarardheere Somali Rep. **71** 4.32N 47.53E
Xar Hudag China **54** 45.07N 114.28E
Xar Moron He *r.* China **54** 43.30N 120.42E
Xarrama *r.* Portugal **27** 38.14N 8.20W
Xassengue Angola **78** 10.26S 18.32E
Xau, L. Botswana **80** 21.15S 24.50E
Xebert China **54** 44.02N 122.00E
Xenia U.S.A. **112** 39.41N 83.56W
Xequessa Angola **78** 16.47S 19.05E
Xertigny France **19** 48.03N 6.24E
Xhora R.S.A. **80** 31.58S 28.40E
Xiachuan *i.* China **55** 21.40N 112.37E
Xiaguan *see* Dali China **52**
Xiamen China **54** 24.30N 118.08E
Xi'an China **54** 34.11N 108.55E
Xianfeng China **55** 29.41N 109.02E
Xiangcheng China **54** 33.50N 113.29E

Xiangfan China **55** 32.04N 112.05E
Xiangfen China **54** 35.52N 111.24E
Xiang Jiang *r.* China **55** 28.49N 112.30E
Xiangkhoang Laos **56** 19.21N 103.23E
Xiangquan He *r.* China **63** 31.45N 78.40E
Xiangshan China **55** 29.29N 121.51E
Xiangtan China **55** 27.50N 112.49E
Xiangtang China **55** 28.26N 115.58E
Xiangyin China **55** 28.40N 112.53E
Xiangyuan China **54** 36.32N 113.02E
Xiangzhou China **55** 23.58N 109.41E
Xianju China **55** 28.51N 120.44E
Xianning China **55** 29.53N 114.13E
Xian Xian China **54** 38.12N 116.07E
Xianyang China **54** 34.20N 108.40E
Xianyou China **55** 25.28N 118.50E
Xiao Hinggan Ling *mts.* China **53** 48.40N 128.30E
Xiaojiang China **55** 27.34N 120.27E
Xiaojiao China **54** 38.24N 113.42E
Xiaowutai Shan *mtn.* China **54** 39.57N 114.59E
Xiapu China **55** 26.58N 119.57E
Xiayang China **55** 26.45N 117.58E
Xichang China **52** 27.53N 102.18E
Xichou China **55** 23.27N 104.40E
Xichuan China **54** 33.15N 111.27E
Xifeng China **55** 27.06N 106.44E
Xigazê China **52** 29.18N 88.50E
Xiheying China **54** 39.53N 114.42E
Xiji China **54** 35.52N 105.35E
Xi Jiang *r.* China **55** 22.23N 113.20E
Xiliao He *r.* China **54** 43.48N 123.00E
Xilin China **55** 24.30N 105.03E
Xilókastron Greece **35** 38.04N 22.43E
Ximeng China **61** 22.45N 99.29E
Xin'anjiang China **55** 29.27N 119.14E
Xin'anjiang Shuiku *resr.* China **55** 29.32N 119.00E
Xincheng Guang. Zhuang. China **55** 24.04N 108.40E
Xincheng Ningxia Huizu China **54** 38.33N 106.10E
Xincheng Shanxi China **54** 37.57N 112.35E
Xindu China **55** 30.50N 104.12E
Xinfeng Guangdong China **55** 24.04N 114.12E
Xinfeng Jiangxi China **55** 25.27N 114.58E
Xing'an China **55** 25.35N 110.32E
Xingcheng China **54** 40.37N 120.43E
Xinghua China **54** 32.51N 119.50E
Xingkai Hu *l. see* Khanka, Ozero Russian Fed./China **53**
Xingren China **55** 25.26N 105.14E
Xingshan China **55** 31.10N 110.51E
Xingtai China **54** 37.04N 114.26E
Xingu *r.* Brazil **123** 1.40S 52.15W
Xing Xian China **54** 38.31N 111.04E
Xingyi China **55** 25.00N 104.59E
Xinhe Hebei China **54** 37.22N 115.14E
Xinhe Xin. Uygur Zizhiqu China **52** 41.34N 82.38E
Xinhua China **55** 27.45N 111.18E
Xining China **52** 36.35N 101.55E
Xinji China **54** 35.17N 115.35E
Xinjiang Uygur Zizhiqu *d.* China **52** 41.15N 87.00E
Xinjie China **54** 39.15N 109.36E
Xinjin Liaoning China **54** 39.27N 121.48E
Xinjin Sichuan China **55** 30.30N 103.47E
Xinle China **54** 38.15N 114.40E
Xinlitun China **54** 42.00N 122.09E
Xinmin China **54** 42.01N 122.48E
Xinning China **55** 26.31N 110.48E
Xinshao China **55** 27.20N 111.26E
Xin Xian China **54** 38.24N 112.47E
Xinxiang China **54** 35.12N 113.57E
Xinyang China **54** 32.08N 114.04E
Xinyi Guangdong China **55** 22.21N 110.57E
Xinyi Jiangsu China **54** 34.20N 118.30E
Xinyu China **55** 27.50N 114.55E
Xinzheng China **54** 34.25N 113.46E
Xinzhu Taiwan **55** 24.50N 120.58E
Xiping Henan China **54** 33.23N 114.02E
Xiping Zhejiang China **55** 28.27N 119.29E
Xique Xique Brazil **123** 10.47S 42.44W
Xi Ujimqin Qi China **54** 44.32N 117.40E
Xiuning China **55** 29.48N 118.20E
Xiushan China **55** 28.27N 108.59E
Xiushui China **55** 29.01N 114.37E
Xixabangma Feng *mtn.* China **63** 28.21N 85.47E
Xixia China **54** 33.30N 111.30E
Xizang Zizhiqu *d.* China **63** 31.45N 87.00E
Xorkol China **52** 39.04N 91.05E
Xuancheng China **55** 30.59N 118.40E
Xuang *r.* Laos **56** 19.59N 102.20E
Xuanhan China **55** 31.25N 107.38E
Xuanhua China **54** 40.30N 115.00E
Xuanwei China **55** 26.16N 104.01E
Xuchang China **54** 34.02N 113.50E
Xuddur Somali Rep. **71** 4.10N 43.53E
Xuefeng Shan *mts.* China **55** 27.30N 111.00E
Xueshuiwen China **53** 49.15N 129.39E
Xugou China **54** 34.40N 119.26E
Xunyang China **54** 32.48N 109.27E
Xupu China **55** 27.54N 110.35E
Xushui China **54** 39.01N 115.39E
Xuwen China **55** 20.25N 110.20E
Xuyong China **55** 28.17N 105.21E
Xuzhou China **54** 34.14N 117.20E

Y

Ya Gabon **78** 1.17S 14.14E
Ya'an China **61** 30.00N 102.59E
Yaapeet Australia **92** 35.48S 142.07E
Ya'bad Jordan **67** 32.27N 35.10E
Yabassi Cameroon **77** 4.30N 9.55E
Yabēlo Ethiopia **73** 4.54N 38.05E
Yābis, Wādī al Jordan **67** 32.24N 35.35E
Yablonovyy Khrebet *mts.* Russian Fed. **51** 53.20N 115.00E
Yabrai Shan *mts.* China **54** 39.50N 103.30E
Yabrai Yanchang China **54** 39.24N 102.43E
Yabrūd Syria **66** 33.58N 36.40E
Yacheng China **55** 18.35N 109.13E
Yacuiba Bolivia **124** 22.00S 63.25W
Yādgīr India **60** 16.46N 77.08E
Yadong China **63** 27.29N 88.54E
Yagaba Ghana **76** 10.13N 1.14W
Yagoua Cameroon **77** 10.23N 15.13E
Yagra China **63** 31.32N 82.27E
Yagur Israel **67** 32.44N 35.04E
Yahagi *r.* Japan **57** 34.50N 136.59E
Yahisuli Zaïre **78** 0.08S 24.04E
Yahuma Zaïre **78** 1.06N 23.10E
Yaizu Japan **57** 34.52N 138.20E
Yajua Nigeria **77** 11.27N 12.49E
Yakchāl Afghan. **62** 31.47N 64.41E
Yakima U.S.A. **108** 46.36N 120.31W
Yakmach Pakistan **62** 28.45N 63.51E
Yaksha Russian Fed. **44** 61.51N 56.59E
Yaku shima *i.* Japan **57** 30.20N 130.40E
Yakutat U.S.A. **100** 59.29N 139.49W
Yakutat B. U.S.A. **100** 59.29N 139.49W
Yakutsk Russian Fed. **51** 62.10N 129.20E
Yala Thailand **56** 6.32N 101.19E
Yale U.S.A. **114** 43.08N 82.48W
Yalgoo Australia **89** 28.20S 116.41E
Yalinga C.A.R. **73** 6.31N 23.15E
Yallourn Australia **93** 38.09S 146.22E
Yalong Jiang *r.* China **52** 26.35N 101.44E
Yalta Ukraine **45** 44.30N 34.09E
Yalu Jiang *r.* China **54** 40.10N 124.25E
Yalutorovsk Russian Fed. **50** 56.41N 66.12E
Yamagata Japan **57** 38.16N 140.19E
Yamaguchi Japan **57** 34.10N 131.28E
Yamal, Poluostrov *pen.* Russian Fed. **50** 70.20N 70.00E
Yamanashi Japan **57** 35.40N 138.40E
Yamanashi *d.* Japan **57** 35.30N 138.35E
Yamandjo Zaïre **78** 1.38N 23.27E
Yamaska Canada **105** 46.01N 72.55W
Yamaska *r.* Canada **105** 46.06N 72.56W
Yamato Japan **57** 35.29N 139.29E
Yamato-takada Japan **57** 34.31N 135.45E
Yamba N.S.W. Australia **93** 29.26S 153.22E
Yamba S.A. Australia **92** 34.15S 140.54E
Yambéring Guinea **76** 11.49N 12.18W
Yambio Sudan **73** 4.34N 28.23E
Yambol Bulgaria **34** 42.30N 26.30E
Yamdena *i.* Indonesia **59** 7.30S 131.00E
Yamenyingzi China **54** 42.23N 121.03E
Yamethin Myanmar **56** 20.24N 96.08E
Yam HaMelah *see* Dead Sea Jordan **67**
Yam Kinneret *l.* Israel **67** 32.49N 35.36E
Yamma Yamma, L. Australia **90** 26.20S 141.25E
Yamoussoukro Côte d'Ivoire **76** 6.51N 5.18W
Yampi Sound Australia **88** 16.11S 123.30E
Yampol Ukraine **37** 48.13N 28.12E
Yamuna *r.* India **63** 25.25N 81.50E
Yamzho Yumco *l.* China **63** 29.00N 90.40E
Yan Nigeria **77** 10.05N 12.11E
Yana *r.* Russian Fed. **51** 71.30N 135.00E
Yanac Australia **92** 36.09S 141.29E
Yan'an China **54** 36.45N 109.22E
Yanbu'al Baḥr Saudi Arabia **64** 24.07N 38.04E
Yancannia Australia **92** 30.16S 142.50E
Yancheng China **54** 33.22N 120.05E
Yanchep Australia **89** 31.32S 115.33E
Yanchi China **54** 37.47N 107.24E
Yanchuan China **54** 36.51N 110.05E
Yanco Australia **93** 34.36S 146.25E
Yanco Glen *town* Australia **92** 31.43S 141.39E
Yanda *r.* Australia **93** 30.22S 145.38E
Yandong China **55** 24.02N 107.09E
Yandoon Myanmar **56** 17.02N 95.39E
Yanfolila Mali **76** 11.11N 8.09W
Yangarey Russian Fed. **44** 68.46N 61.29E
Yangchun China **55** 22.03N 111.46E
Yangcun China **55** 23.26N 114.30E
Yangjiang China **55** 21.50N 111.54E
Yangmingshan Taiwan **55** 25.18N 121.35E
Yangon Myanmar **56** 16.47N 96.10E
Yangon *see* Rangoon Myanmar **56**
Yangqu China **54** 38.03N 112.36E
Yangquan China **54** 37.49N 113.28E
Yangshan Guangdong China **55** 24.29N 112.38E
Yangshan Liaoning China **54** 41.15N 120.18E
Yangshuo China **55** 24.47N 110.30E
Yangtze *r. see* Chang Jiang *r.* China **55**
Yang Xian China **54** 33.10N 107.35E
Yangxin China **55** 29.50N 115.10E
Yangze China **55** 26.59N 118.19E
Yangzhou China **54** 32.22N 119.26E
Yanhuqu China **63** 32.32N 82.44E
Yanji China **53** 42.45N 129.25E
Yanko Creek *r.* Australia **93** 35.25S 145.27E
Yankton U.S.A. **110** 42.53N 97.23W
Yanqi China **52** 42.00N 86.30E
Yanshan China **61** 23.36N 104.20E
Yanshiping China **63** 33.35N 92.04E
Yanskiy Zaliv *g.* Russian Fed. **51** 72.00N 136.10E
Yantabulla Australia **93** 29.13S 145.01E
Yantai China **54** 37.27N 121.26E

Yantra *r.* Bulgaria **34** 43.35N 25.37E
Yanxi China **55** 28.11N 110.58E
Yanzhou China **54** 35.35N 116.52E
Yao Chad **77** 12.52N 17.34E
Yao Japan **57** 34.37N 135.36E
Yaopu China **55** 26.05N 105.42E
Yaoundé Cameroon **77** 3.51N 11.31E
Yao Xian China **54** 34.52N 109.01E
Yap *i.* Federated States of Micronesia **59** 9.30N 138.09E
Yapehe Zaïre **78** 0.10S 24.20E
Yapen *i.* Indonesia **59** 1.45S 136.10E
Yaqui *r.* Mexico **109** 27.37N 110.39W
Yar Russian Fed. **44** 58.13N 52.08E
Yaraka Australia **90** 24.53S 144.04E
Yaransk Russian Fed. **44** 57.22N 47.49E
Yardea Australia **92** 32.23S 135.32E
Yare *r.* U.K. **13** 52.34N 1.45E
Yaremcha Ukraine **37** 48.26N 24.29E
Yarensk Russian Fed. **44** 62.10N 49.07E
Yargora Moldova **37** 46.25N 28.20E
Yariga take *mtn.* Japan **57** 36.21N 137.39E
Yārīn Lebanon **67** 33.06N 35.14E
Yaritagua Venezuela **122** 10.05N 69.07W
Yarkant He *r.* China **52** 40.30N 80.55E
Yarker Canada **105** 44.22N 76.46W
Yarlung Zangbo Jiang *r.* China *see* Brahmaputra *r.* Asia **63**
Yarmouth Canada **103** 43.50N 66.07W
Yarmūk *r.* Jordan/Syria **67** 32.38N 35.34E
Yaroslavl Russian Fed. **44** 57.34N 39.52E
Yarqon *r.* Israel **67** 32.06N 34.47E
Yarra *r.* Australia **93** 37.51S 144.54E
Yarram Australia **93** 38.30S 146.41E
Yarrawonga Australia **93** 36.02S 145.59E
Yarrow *r.* U.K. **14** 55.32N 2.51W
Yar Sale Russian Fed. **50** 66.50N 70.48E
Yartsevo Russian Fed. **51** 60.17N 90.02E
Yartsevo Russian Fed. **44** 55.06N 32.43E
Yarumal Colombia **122** 6.59N 75.25W
Yasanyama Zaïre **73** 4.18N 21.11E
Yaselda *r.* Belarus **37** 52.07N 26.28E
Yasen Belarus **37** 53.10N 28.55E
Yashi Nigeria **77** 12.23N 7.54E
Yashkul Russian Fed. **45** 46.10N 45.20E
Yasinya Ukraine **37** 48.12N 24.20E
Yasothon Thailand **56** 15.46N 104.12E
Yass Australia **93** 34.51S 148.55E
Yas'ur Israel **67** 32.54N 35.10E
Yatakala Niger **76** 14.52N 0.22E
Yaté N. Cal. **84** 22.09S 166.57E
Yates Center U.S.A. **111** 37.53N 95.44W
Yathkyed L. Canada **101** 62.40N 98.00W
Yatsuo Japan **57** 36.35N 137.10E
Yatsushiro Japan **57** 32.32N 130.35E
Yaṭṭah Jordan **67** 31.27N 35.05E
Yāval India **62** 21.10N 75.42E
Yavatmāl India **63** 20.24N 78.08E
Yaví, Cerro *mtn.* Venezuela **122** 5.32N 65.59W
Yavne Israel **67** 31.53N 34.45E
Yavne'el Israel **67** 32.42N 35.30E
Yavorov Ukraine **37** 49.59N 23.20E
Yawng-hwe Myanmar **56** 20.35N 96.58E
Yaxi China **55** 27.35N 106.40E
Ya Xian *see* Sanya China **55**
Yazd Iran **65** 31.54N 54.22E
Yazmān Pakistan **62** 29.08N 71.45E
Yazoo *r.* U.S.A. **111** 32.22N 91.00W
Yazoo City U.S.A. **111** 32.51N 90.28W
Ybbs Austria **36** 48.11N 15.05E
Yding Skovhöj *hill* Denmark **42** 56.00N 9.48E
Ydstebøhavn Norway **42** 59.08N 5.15E
Ye Myanmar **56** 15.15N 97.50E
Yea Australia **93** 37.12S 145.25E
Yecla Spain **25** 38.37N 1.07W
Yedintsy Moldova **45** 48.09N 27.18E
Yeeda Australia **88** 17.36S 123.39E
Yefremov Russian Fed. **44** 53.08N 38.08E
Yegorlyk *r.* Russian Fed. **45** 46.30N 41.52E
Yegoryevsk Russian Fed. **44** 55.21N 39.01E
Yegros Paraguay **126** 26.24S 56.25W
Yei Sudan **73** 4.05N 30.40E
Yei *r.* Sudan **73** 7.20N 30.39E
Yeji China **55** 31.51N 115.01E
Yekaterinburg Russian Fed. **44** 56.52N 60.35E
Yelets Russian Fed. **44** 52.36N 38.30E
Yeletskiy Russian Fed. **44** 67.04N 64.00E
Yélimané Mali **76** 15.08N 10.34W
Yell *i.* U.K. **14** 60.35N 1.05W
Yellowdine Australia **89** 31.19S 119.36E
Yellowhead Pass Canada **100** 52.53N 118.25W
Yellowknife Canada **100** 62.27N 114.21W
Yellowknife *r.* Australia **93** 32.19S 146.50E
Yellow Mt. Australia **93** 32.19S 146.50E
Yellow Sea Asia **53** 35.00N 123.00E
Yellowstone *r.* U.S.A. **106** 47.55N 103.45W
Yellowstone L. U.S.A. **108** 44.25N 110.38W
Yellowstone Nat. Park U.S.A. **108** 44.30N 110.35W
Yell Sd. U.K. **14** 60.30N 1.11W
Yelma Australia **88** 26.30S 121.40E
Yelsk Belarus **37** 51.50N 29.10E
Yelwa Nigeria **77** 10.48N 4.42E
Yemen Asia **71** 14.00N 47.00E
Yemilchino Ukraine **37** 50.58N 27.40E
Yenagoa Nigeria **77** 4.59N 6.15E
Yenangyaung Myanmar **56** 20.28N 94.54E
Yen Bai Vietnam **56** 21.43N 104.44E
Yenda Australia **93** 34.15S 146.13E
Yendi Ghana **76** 9.29N 0.01W
Yengan Myanmar **56** 21.06N 96.30E
Yenisey *r.* Russian Fed. **51** 69.00N 86.00E
Yeniseysk Russian Fed. **51** 58.27N 92.13E
Yeniseyskiy Zaliv *g.* Russian Fed. **50** 73.00N 79.00E
Yenshui Taiwan **55** 23.20N 120.16E
Yenyuka Russian Fed. **51** 57.57N 121.15E
Yeo I. Canada **104** 45.24N 81.49W
Yeo L. Australia **89** 28.04S 124.23E
Yeola India **62** 20.02N 74.29E

Yeoval Australia 93 32.44S 148.39E
Yeovil U.K. 13 50.57N 2.38W
Yepáchic U.S.A. 109 28.27N 108.25W
Yeppoon Australia 90 23.08S 150.45E
Yeráki Greece 35 37.00N 22.42E
Yerbent Turkmenistan 65 39.23N 58.35E
Yercha Russian Fed. 51 69.34N 147.30E
Yerda Australia 92 31.05S 135.04E
Yerepol Russian Fed. 51 65.15N 168.43E
Yerevan Armenia 65 40.10N 44.31E
Yerington U.S.A. 108 38.59N 119.10W
Yermitsa Russian Fed. 44 66.56N 52.20E
Yermo Mexico 111 26.23N 104.01W
Yermo U.S.A. 109 34.54N 116.50W
Yerolimín Greece 35 36.28N 22.24E
Yershov Russian Fed. 45 51.22N 48.16E
Yertom Russian Fed. 44 63.31N 47.51E
Yerushalayim d. Israel 67 31.45N 35.00E
Yerushalayim Israel/Jordan 67 31.47N 35.13E
Yesa, Embalse de resr. Spain 25 42.36N 1.09W
Yeşil r. Turkey 64 41.22N 36.37E
Yeso U.S.A. 109 34.26N 104.37W
Yessey Russian Fed. 51 68.29N 102.15E
Yeste Spain 26 38.22N 2.18W
Yetman Australia 93 28.55S 150.49E
Yeu Myanmar 56 22.49N 95.26E
Yeu, Île d' i. France 18 46.42N 2.20W
Yevpatoriya Ukraine 45 45.12N 33.20E
Yevstratovskiy Russian Fed. 45 50.07N 39.45E
Yew Mtn. U.S.A. 114 38.05N 80.16W
Yeysk Russian Fed. 45 46.43N 38.17E
Yi r. Uruguay 125 33.17S 58.08W
Yiannitsá Greece 34 40.46N 22.24E
Yíaros i. Greece 35 37.36N 24.40E
Yibin China 55 28.42N 104.34E
Yibug Caka l. China 63 33.50N 87.00E
Yichang China 55 30.21N 111.21E
Yichuan China 54 34.25N 112.26E
Yidu China 54 36.45N 118.24E
Yifag Ethiopia 73 12.02N 37.44E
Yiftah Israel 67 33.07N 35.33E
Yijun China 54 35.23N 109.07E
Yilan China 53 46.22N 129.31E
Yilehuli Shan mts. China 53 51.20N 124.20E
Yilliminning Australia 89 32.54S 117.22E
Yilong China 55 31.34N 106.24E
Yimen China 54 34.21N 107.07E
Yinan China 54 35.33N 118.27E
Yinchuan China 54 38.27N 106.18E
Yindarlgooda, L. Australia 89 30.45S 121.55E
Yingcheng China 55 30.57N 113.33E
Yingde China 55 24.07N 113.20E
Yinggehai China 55 18.31N 108.40E
Yingkou China 54 40.39N 122.18E
Yingshan China 55 31.06N 106.35E
Yingshang China 54 32.42N 116.20E
Yingtan China 55 28.11N 116.55E
Yinkanie Australia 92 34.21S 140.20E
Yinning China 52 43.57N 81.23E
Yin Shan mts. China 54 41.30N 109.00E
Yirga' Alem Ethiopia 73 6.52N 38.22E
Yirol Sudan 73 6.33N 30.30E
Yirwa Sudan 73 7.47N 27.15E
Yishan China 55 24.37N 108.32E
Yithion Greece 35 36.45N 22.34E
Yiwu China 55 29.18N 120.04E
Yi Xian China 54 41.30N 121.14E
Yiyang Henan China 54 34.30N 112.10E
Yiyang Hunan China 55 28.20N 112.30E
Yiyuan China 54 36.12N 118.08E
Yizhang China 55 25.24N 112.57E
Yizre'el Israel 67 32.33N 35.20E
Ylitornio Finland 40 66.19N 23.40E
Ylivieska Finland 40 64.05N 24.33E
Yngaren l. Sweden 43 58.52N 16.35E
Yoakum U.S.A. 111 29.17N 97.09W
Yobe d. Nigeria 77 12.30N 11.45E
Yodo r. Japan 57 34.41N 135.25E
Yogyakarta Indonesia 59 7.48S 110.24E
Yogyakarta d. Indonesia 59 7.48S 110.22E
Yokadouma Cameroon 77 3.26N 15.06E
Yokkaichi Japan 57 34.58N 136.37E
Yoko Cameroon 77 5.29N 12.19E
Yokohama Japan 57 35.27N 139.39E
Yokosuka Japan 57 35.18N 139.40E
Yola Nigeria 77 9.14N 12.32E
Yom r. Thailand 56 15.47N 100.05E
Yona Guam 84 13.25N 144.47E
Yonago Japan 57 35.27N 133.20E
Yŏndŏk S. Korea 57 36.26N 129.23E
Yongcheng China 54 33.56N 116.22E
Yongchuan China 55 29.19N 105.55E
Yongchun China 55 25.19N 118.17E
Yongdeng China 54 36.44N 103.24E
Yonghe China 54 36.44N 110.39E
Yongnian China 54 36.47N 114.30E
Yongring China 55 22.45N 108.29E
Yongshou China 54 34.40N 108.04E
Yongxiu China 55 28.58N 115.43E
Yonkers U.S.A. 115 40.56N 73.52W
Yonne d. France 19 47.55N 3.45E
Yonne r. France 19 48.23N 2.58E
York Australia 89 31.55S 116.45E
York Canada 104 43.41N 79.29W
York U.K. 12 53.58N 1.07W
York Nebr. U.S.A. 110 40.52N 97.36W
York Penn. U.S.A. 114 39.58N 76.44W
York r. U.S.A. 113 37.15N 76.23W
York, C. Australia 90 10.42S 142.31E
Yorke Pen. Australia 92 35.00S 137.30E
Yorketown Australia 92 35.02S 137.36E
York Factory town Canada 101 57.00N 92.18W
York Haven U.S.A. 114 40.07N 76.43W
Yorkshire Wolds hills U.K. 12 54.00N 0.39W
Yorkton Canada 101 51.13N 102.28W
York Village U.S.A. 115 43.08N 70.38W

Yoro Honduras 117 15.09N 87.07W
Yŏrŏ Japan 57 35.32N 140.04E
Yosemite Nat. Park U.S.A. 108 37.45N 119.35W
Yoshino r. Japan 57 34.22N 135.40E
Yoshkar Ola Russian Fed. 44 56.38N 47.52E
Yos Sudarsa, Pulau i. Indonesia 59 8.00S 138.30E
Yŏsu S. Korea 53 34.46N 127.45E
Youghal Rep. of Ire. 15 51.58N 7.51W
You Jiang r. Guang. Zhuang. China 55 23.28N 111.18E
Youkou Côte d'Ivoire 76 5.16N 7.16W
Youkounkoun Guinea 76 12.35N 13.11W
Young Australia 93 34.19S 148.20E
Young r. Australia 89 33.45S 121.12E
Young Uruguay 125 32.41S 57.38W
Young U.S.A. 109 34.06N 110.57W
Younghusband, L. Australia 92 30.51S 136.05E
Younghusband Pen. Australia 92 36.00S 139.15E
Youngstown Canada 101 51.32N 111.13W
Youngstown U.S.A. 114 41.06N 80.39W
Youngsville U.S.A. 114 41.48N 74.54W
You Xian China 55 26.59N 113.12E
Youyang China 55 28.50N 108.45E
Youyu China 54 39.59N 112.27E
Yoxford U.K. 13 52.16N 1.30E
Yozgat Turkey 64 39.50N 34.48E
Ypsilanti U.S.A. 104 42.15N 83.36W
Yreka U.S.A. 108 41.44N 122.38W
Yssingeaux France 21 45.08N 4.07E
Ystad Sweden 43 55.25N 13.49E
Ythan r. U.K. 14 57.21N 2.01W
Ytterhogdal Sweden 41 62.12N 14.51E
Yu'alliq, Jabal mtn. Egypt 66 30.21N 33.31E
Yuanbaoshan China 54 42.15N 119.14E
Yuan Jiang r. Hunan China 55 29.00N 111.55E
Yuan Jiang r. Yunnan China see Hong Hà r. Vietnam 52
Yuanling China 55 28.28N 110.15E
Yuanping China 54 38.42N 112.46E
Yuba City U.S.A. 108 39.08N 121.27W
Yūbari Japan 57 43.04N 141.59E
Yubdo Ethiopia 73 9.00N 35.22E
Yucatán d. Mexico 117 19.30N 89.00W
Yucatan Channel Carib. Sea 117 21.30N 86.00W
Yucatan Pen. Mexico 116 19.00N 90.00W
Yucca U.S.A. 109 34.52N 114.09W
Yuci China 54 37.37N 112.47E
Yudino Russian Fed. 50 55.05N 67.55E
Yudu China 55 25.57N 115.16E
Yuendumu Australia 90 22.14S 131.47E
Yueqing China 55 28.08N 120.57E
Yuexi China 52 28.36N 102.35E
Yueyang China 55 29.22N 113.10E
Yugan China 55 28.41N 116.41E
Yugorskiy Poluostrov pen. Russian Fed. 44 69.00N 62.30E
Yugoslavia Europe 29 44.00N 20.00E
Yuhang China 55 30.25N 120.18E
Yuhebu China 54 37.59N 109.51E
Yukon r. U.S.A. 98 62.35N 164.20W
Yukon Territory d. Canada 98 65.00N 135.00W
Yulara Australia 90 25.14S 131.02E
Yule r. Australia 88 20.19S 118.08E
Yuleba Australia 90 26.37S 149.20E
Yulin Guang. Zhuang. China 55 22.38N 110.10E
Yulin Shaanxi China 54 38.14N 109.33E
Yuma Ariz. U.S.A. 109 32.43N 114.37W
Yuma Colo. U.S.A. 108 40.08N 102.43W
Yumen China 52 40.19N 97.12E
Yunan China 55 23.14N 111.35E
Yuncheng China 54 35.02N 111.00E
Yungas f. Bolivia 124 16.20S 65.00W
Yungera Australia 92 34.48S 143.10E
Yungxiao China 55 23.59N 117.27E
Yunkai Dashan mts. China 55 22.30N 111.05E
Yunnan d. China 52 24.30N 101.30E
Yunta Australia 92 32.37S 139.34E
Yunxi China 54 33.00N 110.22E
Yun Xian China 54 32.48N 110.50E
Yunyang China 55 30.55N 108.56E
Yuqing China 55 27.12N 107.56E
Yuribey Russian Fed. 50 71.02N 77.02E
Yurimaguas Peru 122 5.54S 76.07W
Yuryuzan Russian Fed. 44 54.51N 58.25E
Yu Shan mtn. Taiwan 55 23.20N 121.03E
Yushu China 52 33.06N 96.48E
Yūtō Japan 57 34.42N 137.38E
Yu Xian China 54 34.10N 113.28E
Yuxikou China 55 31.29N 118.16E
Yuyao China 55 30.03N 120.11E
Yuzhno Sakhalinsk Russian Fed. 53 46.58N 142.45E
Yuzhnyy Bug r. Ukraine 37 46.55N 31.59E
Yuzhong China 54 35.52N 104.02E
Yvelines d. France 19 48.50N 1.50E
Yverdon Switz. 39 46.47N 6.39E
Yvetot France 18 49.37N 0.46E

Z

Zaandam Neth. 16 52.27N 4.49E
Zabïd Yemen 72 14.12N 43.19E
Žabljak Yugo. 31 43.09N 19.07E
Zābol d. Afghan. 62 32.00N 67.00E
Zābol Iran 65 31.00N 61.32E
Zābolī Iran 65 27.08N 61.36E

Zabqung China 63 31.38N 87.20E
Zabrze Poland 37 50.18N 18.47E
Zacapa Guatemala 117 15.00N 89.30W
Zacatecas Mexico 116 22.48N 102.33W
Zacatecas d. Mexico 116 24.00N 103.00W
Zadar Croatia 31 44.07N 15.14E
Zafra Spain 27 38.25N 6.25W
Zafriyya Israel 67 32.00N 34.51E
Zaglivérion Greece 34 40.36N 23.15E
Zagorá Greece 34 39.27N 23.06E
Zagreb Croatia 31 45.48N 15.58E
Zāgros, Kūhhā-ye mts. Iran 65 32.00N 51.00E
Zagros Mts. see Zāgros, Kūhhā-ye mts. Iran 65
Zāhedān Iran 65 29.32N 60.54E
Zaḥlah Lebanon 67 33.50N 35.55E
Zahrān Saudi Arabia 71 17.40N 43.30E
Zaindeh r. Iran 65 32.40N 52.50E
Zaïre Africa 78 2.00S 22.00E
Zaïre d. Angola 78 6.30S 13.30E
Zaïre r. Zaïre 78 6.00S 12.30E
Zaječar Yugo. 34 43.53N 22.18E
Zákas Greece 34 40.02N 21.16E
Zákinthos i. Greece 35 37.52N 20.44E
Zákinthos town Greece 35 37.47N 20.54E
Zakinthou, Porthmós str. Greece 35 37.50N 21.00E
Zakopane Poland 37 49.19N 19.57E
Zala d. Hungary 31 46.35N 16.40E
Zalaegerszeg Hungary 31 46.51N 16.51E
Zalalövö Hungary 31 46.51N 16.35E
Zalamea de la Serena Spain 26 38.39N 5.39W
Zalaszentgrót Hungary 31 46.59N 17.02E
Zalău Romania 37 47.11N 23.03E
Žalec Slovenia 31 46.15N 15.10E
Zaleshchiki Ukraine 37 48.39N 25.50E
Zalīm Saudi Arabia 66 22.43N 42.11E
Zalingei Sudan 73 12.54N 23.29E
Zambezi r. Mozambique/Zambia 81 18.15S 35.55E
Zambezi Zambia 78 13.30S 23.12E
Zambezia d. Mozambique 81 16.30S 37.30E
Zambia Africa 79 14.00S 28.00E
Zamboanga Phil. 59 6.55N 122.05E
Zambrów Poland 37 53.00N 22.15E
Zambue Mozambique 80 15.09S 30.47E
Zamfara r. Nigeria 77 12.04N 4.00E
Zamora Mexico 116 20.00N 102.18W
Zamora Spain 26 41.30N 5.45W
Zamora d. Spain 26 41.45N 6.00W
Zamość Poland 37 50.43N 23.15E
Zamtang China 61 32.26N 101.06E
Zaña Peru 122 7.00S 79.30W
Záncara r. Spain 26 38.39N 3.18W
Zanda China 63 31.29N 79.50E
Zanesville U.S.A. 114 39.56N 82.01W
Zangoza see Sangüesa Spain 25
Zanjān Iran 65 36.40N 48.30E
Zanthus Australia 89 31.02S 123.34E
Zanzibar Tanzania 79 6.10S 39.16E
Zanzibar i. Tanzania 79 6.00S 39.20E
Zaouatallaz Algeria 75 24.52N 8.26E
Zaouiet Azmour Tunisia 32 36.55N 11.01E
Zaouiet el Mgaïz Tunisia 32 36.56N 10.50E
Zaozhuang China 54 34.48N 117.50E
Zapadna Morava r. Yugo. 34 43.50N 20.15E
Zapadni Rodopi mts. Bulgaria 34 41.49N 23.58E
Zapadno-Sibirskaya Ravnina f. Russian Fed. 9 60.00N 75.00E
Zapadnyy Sayan mts. Russian Fed. 51 53.00N 92.00E
Západočeský d. Czech Republic 38 49.40N 13.00E
Zapala Argentina 125 38.55S 70.05W
Zapardiel r. Spain 26 41.29N 5.02W
Zapata U.S.A. 111 26.52N 99.19W
Zaporozhye Ukraine 45 47.50N 35.10E
Zapug China 63 33.17N 80.50E
Zara Turkey 64 39.55N 37.44E
Zaragoza Spain 25 41.38N 0.53W
Zaragoza d. Spain 25 41.40N 1.10W
Zarand Iran 65 30.50N 56.35E
Zaranj Afghan. 62 31.06N 61.53E
Zárate Argentina 125 34.05S 59.02W
Zarauz Spain 26 43.17N 2.10W
Zaraza Venezuela 122 9.23N 65.20W
Zard Kūh mtn. Iran 65 32.21N 50.04E
Zarembo I. U.S.A. 100 56.20N 132.50W
Zarghūn Shahr Afghan. 60 32.51N 68.25E
Zari Nigeria 77 13.03N 12.46E
Zaria Nigeria 77 11.01N 7.44E
Zárkon Greece 34 39.37N 22.07E
Zaruma Ecuador 122 3.40S 79.30W
Zarzal Colombia 122 4.24N 76.01W
Zāskār r. Jammu & Kashmir 62 34.10N 77.20E
Zāskār Mts. Jammu & Kashmir 63 33.15N 78.00E
Zaslavl Belarus 37 54.00N 27.15E
Za'tarï, Wādī az Jordan 67 32.09N 36.15E
Žatec Czech Republic 39 50.18N 13.32E
Zatishye Ukraine 37 47.20N 29.58E
Zave Zimbabwe 80 17.14S 30.02E
Zavet Bulgaria 34 43.46N 26.40E
Zavidovići Bosnia-Herzegovina 31 44.27N 18.09E
Zavitinsk Russian Fed. 53 50.08N 129.24E
Zāwa Pakistan 62 28.04N 66.23E
Zawilah Libya 75 26.10N 15.07E
Zāwiyat al Amwāt Egypt 66 28.04N 30.50E
Zāwiyat al Mukhaylá Libya 72 32.10N 22.17E
Zāyandeh r. Iran 65 32.40N 52.50E
Zaydābād Afghan. 62 34.17N 69.07E
Zaydī, Wādī az Syria 67 32.45N 35.50E
Zaysan Kazakhstan 52 47.30N 84.57E
Zaysan, Ozero l. Kazakhstan 52 48.00N 83.30E
Zayzūn Syria 67 32.24N 35.56E
Zbarazh Ukraine 37 49.40N 25.49E
Zborov Ukraine 37 49.40N 25.09E
Zbraslav Czech Republic 38 49.59N 14.24E
Zdolbunov Ukraine 37 50.30N 26.10E
Zduńska Wola Poland 37 51.36N 18.57E
Zeballos Canada 100 49.59N 126.50W
Zebediela R.S.A. 80 24.19S 29.17E

Zeebrugge Belgium 16 51.20N 3.13E
Zeehan Australia 91 41.55S 145.21E
Zeeland d. Neth. 16 51.30N 3.45E
Ze'elim Israel 67 31.12N 34.32E
Zeerust R.S.A. 80 25.32S 26.04E
Zefa' Israel 67 31.07N 35.12E
Zefat Israel 67 32.57N 35.27E
Zehdenick Germany 38 52.59N 13.20E
Zeist Neth. 16 52.03N 5.16E
Zeitz Germany 38 51.03N 12.08E
Zelechów Poland 37 51.49N 21.54E
Zelengora mts. Bosnia-Herzegovina 31 43.20N 18.30E
Zelenodolsk Russian Fed. 44 55.50N 48.30E
Zelenogorsk Russian Fed. 44 60.15N 29.31E
Zelenokumsk Russian Fed. 45 44.25N 43.54E
Zelentsovo Russian Fed. 44 59.51N 44.59E
Zelina Croatia 31 45.58N 16.15E
Zell Germany 39 50.01N 7.10E
Zella-Mehlis Germany 38 50.39N 10.39E
Zell am Ziller Austria 39 47.14N 11.53E
Zelts Ukraine 37 46.38N 30.00E
Zelzate Belgium 16 51.12N 3.49E
Zembra, Île i. Tunisia 32 37.08N 10.48E
Zemio C.A.R. 73 5.02N 25.08E
Zemoul, Oued wadi Morocco 74 29.12N 7.52W
Zemun Yugo. 29 44.51N 20.23E
Zendeh Jān Afghan. 62 34.21N 61.45E
Zenica Bosnia-Herzegovina 31 44.12N 17.55E
Zenn r. Germany 39 49.30N 10.58E
Zenne r. Belgium 16 51.04N 4.25E
Zerbst Germany 38 51.58N 12.04E
Zereh, Gowd-e l. Afghan. 62 29.45N 61.50E
Zergan Albania 34 41.30N 20.21E
Zetel Germany 38 53.25N 7.58E
Zeulenroda Germany 38 50.39N 11.58E
Zeven Germany 38 53.18N 9.16E
Zevenaar Neth. 16 51.57N 6.04E
Zevenbergen Neth. 16 51.41N 4.42E
Zeya Russian Fed. 51 53.48N 127.14E
Zeya r. Russian Fed. 51 50.20N 127.30E
Zêzere r. Portugal 27 39.28N 8.20W
Zgierz Poland 37 51.52N 19.25E
Zgorzelec Poland 36 51.12N 15.01E
Zhailma Kazakhstan 50 51.37N 61.33E
Zhambyl Kazakhstan 52 42.54N 71.25E
Zhanatas Kazakhstan 52 43.11N 69.35E
Zhangbei China 54 41.08N 114.44E
Zhanghua Taiwan 55 24.05N 120.30E
Zhangjiakou China 54 40.47N 114.56E
Zhangping China 55 25.25N 117.28E
Zhangpu China 55 24.06N 117.37E
Zhangwu China 54 42.22N 122.31E
Zhang Xian China 54 34.48N 104.27E
Zhangye China 52 38.56N 100.27E
Zhangzhou China 54 24.57N 118.32E
Zhanjiang China 55 21.08N 110.22E
Zhanyu China 54 44.31N 122.40E
Zhao'an China 55 23.45N 117.14E
Zhaoping China 55 24.06N 110.48E
Zhaoqing China 55 23.02N 112.29E
Zhari Namco l. China 63 31.00N 85.30E
Zharkent Kazakhstan 52 44.10N 80.01E
Zhashkov Ukraine 37 49.12N 30.05E
Zhashui China 54 33.41N 109.06E
Zhaxi Co l. China 52 32.10N 85.00E
Zhaxigang China 63 32.31N 79.33E
Zhejiang d. China 55 29.00N 120.00E
Zheleznodorozhnyy Russian Fed. 44 67.59N 64.47E
Zheleznodorozhnyy Russian Fed. 44 62.39N 50.59E
Zhen'an China 54 32.34N 107.58E
Zhenba China 54 32.34N 107.58E
Zheng'an China 55 28.30N 107.32E
Zhenghe China 55 27.23N 118.51E
Zhengyang China 54 32.36N 114.23E
Zhengzhou China 54 34.40N 113.38E
Zhenhai China 55 29.58N 121.45E
Zhenjiang China 54 32.09N 119.30E
Zhenning China 54 25.58N 105.45E
Zhenxiong China 55 27.27N 104.50E
Zhenyuan China 54 35.42N 106.58E
Zherdnoye Belarus 37 51.40N 30.11E
Zherong China 55 27.13N 119.52E
Zhezkazgan Kazakhstan 50 47.48N 67.24E
Zhidachov Ukraine 37 49.20N 24.22E
Zhigansk Russian Fed. 51 66.48N 123.27E
Zhijiang China 55 27.27N 109.41E
Zhitkovichi Belarus 37 52.12N 27.49E
Zhitomir Ukraine 37 50.18N 28.40E
Zhlobin Belarus 37 52.50N 30.00E
Zhmerinka Ukraine 37 49.00N 28.02E
Zhob r. Pakistan 62 32.04N 69.50E
Zhongba China 63 29.40N 84.07E
Zhongdian China 61 28.00N 99.30E
Zhongli Taiwan 55 24.54N 121.09E
Zhongning China 54 37.28N 105.41E
Zhongshan Guangdong China 55 22.31N 113.22E
Zhongtiao Shan mts. China 54 36.00N 113.30E
Zhongwei China 54 37.30N 105.15E
Zhoucun China 54 36.49N 117.49E
Zhoushan i. China 55 30.05N 122.15E
Zhouzhi China 54 34.08N 108.14E
Zhuanghe China 54 39.41N 123.02E
Zhucheng China 54 36.00N 119.24E
Zhugqu China 54 33.46N 104.18E
Zhuji China 55 29.43N 120.14E
Zhumadian China 54 32.58N 114.02E
Zhuo Xian China 54 39.29N 115.55E
Zhuozhou China 54 39.29N 115.55E
Zhupanovo Russian Fed. 51 53.40N 159.52E
Zhuxi China 54 32.19N 109.52E
Zhuzhou China 55 27.42N 113.05E
Ziārat Pakistan 62 30.23N 67.43E
Ziārat-e Shāh Maqsūd Afghan. 62 31.59N 65.30E
Žiar nad Hronom Slovakia 37 48.36N 18.52E
Zibo China 54 36.50N 118.00E
Zicavo France 21 41.54N 9.08E
Ziegenhain Germany 38 50.50N 9.07E
Ziel, Mt. Australia 88 23.24S 132.23E

Zielona Góra to Zywiec

Zielona Góra Poland 36 51.57N 15.30E
Ziesar Germany 38 52.16N 12.17E
Ziftâ Egypt 66 30.43N 31.14E
Zigey Chad 77 14.43N 15.47E
Zigong China 55 29.18N 104.45E
Zigui China 55 31.01N 110.35E
Ziguinchor Senegal 76 12.35N 16.20W
Zikhron Ya'aqov Israel 67 32.34N 34.57E
Zile Turkey 64 40.18N 35.52E
Žilina Slovakia 37 49.14N 18.46E
Zillah Libya 75 28.33N 17.35E
Zillertaler Alpen mts. Austria/Italy 30 47.00N 11.55E
Zima Russian Fed. 51 53.58N 102.02E
Zimatlán Mexico 116 16.52N 96.45W
Zimba Zambia 78 17.20S 26.25E
Zimbabwe Africa 80 18.55S 30.00E
Zimbor Romania 37 47.00N 23.16E
Zimi Sierra Leone 76 7.22N 11.21W
Zimnicea Romania 34 43.39N 25.21E
Zimniy Bereg f. Russian Fed. 44 65.50N 41.30E
Zinder Niger 77 13.46N 8.58E
Zinder d. Niger 77 14.20N 9.30E
Zinga Mtwara Tanzania 79 9.01S 38.47E
Ziniaré Burkina 76 12.34N 1.12W
Zinkgruvan Sweden 43 58.49N 15.05E
Zinnowitz Germany 38 54.04N 13.55E
Zion Grove U.S.A. 115 40.54N 76.13W
Zippori Israel 67 32.45N 35.17E
Žirje i. Croatia 31 43.40N 15.39E

Ziro India 61 27.38N 93.42E
Zi Shui r. China 55 28.38N 112.30E
Zitong China 55 31.38N 105.11E
Zítsa Greece 34 39.47N 20.40E
Zittau Germany 38 50.54N 14.47E
Zitundo Mozambique 81 26.45S 32.49E
Ziway Häyk' l. Ethiopia 73 8.00N 38.50E
Zixi China 55 27.42N 117.05E
Ziyang China 55 30.02N 104.42E
Zizhong China 55 29.48N 104.51E
Zlarin Croatia 31 43.42N 15.50E
Zlatar Croatia 31 46.06N 16.05E
Zlatograd Bulgaria 34 41.22N 25.07E
Zlatoust Russian Fed. 44 55.10N 59.38E
Zletovo Macedonia 34 41.59N 22.17E
Zlín Czech Republic 37 49.13N 17.41E
Zlițan Libya 75 32.28N 14.34E
Złoczew Poland 37 51.25N 18.36E
Złotów Poland 37 53.22N 17.02E
Žlutice Czech Republic 39 50.03N 13.10E
Zlynka Russian Fed. 37 52.24N 31.45E
Zmeinogorsk Russian Fed. 50 51.11N 82.14E
Žminj Croatia 31 45.09N 13.55E
Zmiyevka Russian Fed. 44 52.40N 36.22E
Znamenka Ukraine 45 48.42N 32.40E
Znin Poland 37 52.52N 17.43E
Znojmo Czech Republic 36 48.52N 16.05E
Zobia Zaïre 78 2.58N 25.56E
Zobue Mozambique 81 15.35S 34.26E

Zoétélé Cameroon 77 3.17N 11.54E
Zogno Italy 30 45.48N 9.40E
Zohreh r. Iran 65 30.04N 49.32E
Zolochev Ukraine 37 49.48N 24.51E
Zolotonosha Ukraine 45 49.39N 32.05E
Zomba Malaŵi 79 15.22S 35.22E
Zonguldak Turkey 64 41.26N 31.47E
Zong Xian China 55 30.16N 108.01E
Zorita Spain 27 39.17N 5.42W
Zorzor Liberia 76 7.46N 9.28W
Zouar Chad 77 20.27N 16.32E
Zouîrât Mauritania 74 22.35N 12.20W
Zoutkamp Neth. 16 53.21N 6.18E
Zrenjanin Yugo. 29 45.22N 20.23E
Zrmanja r. Croatia 31 44.15N 15.32E
Zuckerhütl mtn. Austria 30 46.58N 11.09E
Zuénoula Côte d'Ivoire 76 7.34N 6.03W
Zuera Spain 25 41.52N 0.47W
Zug Switz. 39 47.10N 8.31E
Zug d. Switz. 39 47.10N 8.40E
Zugspitze mtn. Germany 39 47.25N 10.59E
Zuid Beveland f. Neth. 16 51.30N 3.50E
Zuidelijk-Flevoland f. Neth. 16 52.22N 5.22E
Zuid Holland d. Neth. 16 52.00N 4.30E
Zuidhorn Neth. 16 53.16N 6.25E
Zújar r. Spain 26 39.01N 5.47W
Zújar, Embalse del resr. Spain 26 38.50N 5.20W
Zülpich Germany 38 50.41N 6.39E
Zululand see Kwa Zulu f. R.S.A. 80

Zumbo Mozambique 80 15.36S 30.24E
Zungeru Nigeria 77 9.48N 6.03E
Zunyi China 55 27.39N 106.48E
Županja Croatia 31 45.04N 18.42E
Zurich Neth. 16 53.08N 5.25E
Zürich Switz. 39 47.23N 8.32E
Zürich d. Switz. 39 47.25N 8.45E
Zürichsee l. Switz. 39 47.13N 8.45E
Zuru Nigeria 77 11.26N 5.16E
Zushi Japan 57 35.18N 139.35E
Žut i. Croatia 31 43.52N 15.19E
Zutphen Neth. 16 52.08N 6.12E
Zuwârah Libya 75 32.56N 12.06E
Zuwayzā Jordan 67 31.42N 35.55E
Žužemberk Slovenia 31 45.50N 14.56E
Zvenigorodka Ukraine 37 49.05N 30.58E
Zverinogolovskoye Kazakhstan 50 54.23N 64.47E
Zvishavane Zimbabwe 80 20.20S 30.05E
Zvolen Slovakia 37 48.35N 19.08E
Zweibrücken Germany 39 49.15N 7.21E
Zweisimmen Switz. 39 46.33N 7.22E
Zwettl Austria 36 48.37N 15.10E
Zwickau Germany 38 50.44N 12.29E
Zwiesel Germany 39 49.01N 13.14E
Zwischenahn Germany 38 53.12N 8.00E
Zwoleń Poland 37 51.22N 21.35E
Zwolle Neth. 16 52.31N 6.06E
Zyryanovsk Kazakhstan 50 49.45N 84.16E
Zywiec Poland 37 49.41N 19.12E